ENCYCLOPEDIA OF LATIN AMERICAN AND CARIBBEAN LITERATURE 1900–2003

ENCYCLOPEDIA OF LATIN AMERICAN AND CARIBBEAN LITERATURE 1900–2003

Edited by Daniel Balderston and Mike Gonzalez

Routledge
Taylor & Francis Group
LONDON AND NEW YORK

First published 2004
by Routledge
11 New Fetter Lane, London EC4P 4EE

Simultaneously published in the USA and Canada
by Routledge
29 West 35th Street, New York, NY 10001

Routledge is an imprint of the Taylor & Francis Group

Typeset in Baskerville and Optima by Taylor & Francis Books Ltd

Printed and bound in Great Britain by
TJ International Ltd, Padstow, Cornwall

British Library Cataloguing in Publication Data
A catalogue record for this book is available from the British Library

Library of Congress Cataloging in Publication Data
Encyclopedia of Latin American and Caribbean literature, 1900–2003 /
edited by Daniel Balderston and Mike Gonzalez.
p.cm.
Includes bibliographical references and index.
1. Latin American literature–Encyclopedias. 2. Caribbean literature–Encyclopedias.
I. Balderston, Daniel, 1952– II. Gonzalez, Mike.

PQ7081.A1E558 2003 2003058528

ISBN 0–415–30686–8 (hbk)
ISBN 0–415–30687–6 (pbk)

Contents

Contributors

Roseanne Adderley
Tulane University, USA

Gonzalo Aguilar
Universidad de Buenos Aires, Argentina

Funso Aiyejina
Trinidad

Pablo Alabarces
Universidad de Buenos Aires, Argentina

Jill E. Albada-Jelgersma
USA

Alfredo Alonso Estenoz
University of Iowa, USA

Daniel Altamiranda
Argentina

Adriana Amante
Universidad de Buenos Aires, Argentina

Danny J. Anderson
University of Kansas, USA

Raul Antelo
Universidade Federal de Santa Catarina, Brazil

Charles Arthur
UK

Jon Askeland
University of Bergen, Norway

Daniel Balderston
University of Iowa, USA

Maria José Somerlate Barbosa
University of Iowa, USA

Efraín Barradas
University of Florida, USA

Isabel Bastos
University of Maryland, USA

Diego Bentivegna
Universidad de Buenos Aires, Argentina

Alvaro Bernal
University of Iowa, USA

Leopoldo M. Bernucci
University of Texas, USA

Esperanza Bielsa
University of Glasgow, UK

César Braga-Pinto
Rutgers University, USA

Luis Britto Garcia
Universidad Central de Venezuela

Aart G. Broek
Curaçao

James Buckwalter-Arias
Hanover College, USA

Erik Camayd-Freixas
Florida International University, USA

Wilfredo Cancio Isla
Nuevo Herald, USA

Luis E. Cárcamo-Huechante
Harvard University, USA

Miguel A. Cardinale
Frostburg State University, USA

Rafael Castillo Zapata
Universidad Central de Venezuela

Sara Castro-Klaren
Johns Hopkins University, USA

Silvia Chaves
USA

Sergio Chejfec
Nueva Sociedad, Venezuela

Santiago Colás
University of Michigan, USA

Eduardo Contreras Soto
CENIDIM, Mexico

Scott A. Cooper
Hanover College, USA

Sandra Courtman
UK

Linda J. Craft
North Park University, USA

Leslie H. Damasceno
Duke University, USA

María Julia Daroqui
Spain

J. Michael Dash
New York University, USA

Silvana Daszuk
Argentina

Sergio de la Mora
University of California at Davis, USA

J. M. de la Vega Rodríguez
Bolivia

Catherine Den Tandt
University of Montreal, Canada

Mark Dinneen
University of Southampton, UK

Christopher Dunn
Tulane University, USA

Pat Dunn
University of the West Indies, Jamaica

Thomas Edsall
University of the Holy Cross, USA

Juan Armando Epple
University of Oregon, USA

José Antonio Evora
Nuevo Herald, USA

Héctor D. Fernández L'Hoeste
Georgia State University, USA

Alvaro Fernández-Bravo
Universidad de San Andrés, Argentina

Cristina Ferreira-Pinto
Southwest Texas State University, USA

Nuala Finnegan
National University of Ireland, Cork

Evelyn Fishburn
University of North London, UK

Enrique Foffani
University of La Plata, Argentina

Jacinto Fombona
Fordham University, USA

María Irene Fornés
USA

Merlin H. Forster
Brigham Young University, USA

David William Foster
Arizona State University, USA

Jean Franco
Columbia University, USA

Víctor Galarraga Oropeza
University of Iowa, USA

Juan Carlos Gamboa
USA

Sandra Garabano
University of Texas at El Paso, USA

Magdalena García Pinto
University of Missouri, USA

Florencia Garramuño
Universidad de Buenos Aires, Argentina

Sandra Gasparini
Universidad de Buenos Aires, Argentina

Gabriel Giorgi
University of Southern California, USA

Norah Giraldi Dei Cas
Université de Lille, France

Margo Glantz
UNAM, Mexico

John Gledson
University of Liverpool, UK

Florinda F. Goldberg
Hebrew University of Jerusalem, Israel

Brian Gollnick
University of Iowa, USA

Mike Gonzalez
University of Glasgow, UK

Andrew Graham-Yooll
Argentina

Mihai Grünfeld
Vassar College, USA

Lucía Guerra
University of California at Irvine, USA

Eduardo Guízar-Alvarez
Northwestern University, USA

Laura G. Gutiérrez
University of Iowa, USA

Cristina Guzzo
Arizona State University, USA

Regina Harrison
University of Maryland, USA

Milton Hatoum
Universidade Nacional de Amazonas, Brazil

Ben A. Heller
Notre Dame University, USA

James Higgins
University of Liverpool, UK

Norman S. Holland
Hampshire College, USA

Cristina Iglesia
Universidad de Buenos Aires, Argentina

Veronica Jaffé
Venezuela

Jesús Jambrina
University of Iowa, USA

Louis James
University of Kent at Canterbury, UK

Keith Jardim
Trinidad

Randal Johnson
University of California at Los Angeles, USA

Bridget Jones
UK

Amy Kaminsky
University of Minnesota, USA

Gwen Kirkpatrick
Georgetown University, USA

John Kraniauskas
Birkbeck College, University of London, UK

Pablo Kreimer
Universidad de Quilmes, Argentina

Alejandra Laera
Universidad de Buenos Aires, Argentina

Lorraine Leu
King's College London, UK

Lázaro Lima
Bryn Mawr College, USA

Daniel Link
Universidad de Buenos Aires, Argentina

Sita Dickson Littlewood
UK

Ana M. López
Tulane University, USA

W. George Lovell
Queen's University, Canada

Marco Maggi
USA

Anne Malena
University of Alberta, Canada

Monica Mansóur
Mexico

Celina Manzoni
Universidad de Buenos Aires, Argentina

José J. Maristany
Universidad Nacionale de La Pampa, Argentina

Gerald Martin
University of Pittsburgh, USA

Stella Martini
Argentina

Judith Maxwell
Tulane University, USA

Nora Mazziotti
Universidad de Buenos Aires, Argentina

José Antonio Mazzotti
Harvard University, USA

Ximena Medinaceli
Bolivia

Teresa Méndez-Faith
Saint Anselm College, USA

Graciela Montaldo
Universidad Simón Bolívar, Venezuela

Winston Moore
Bolivia

Pamela Mordecai
Canada

Graciela Musachi
Argentina

Edith Negrín
Colegio de México, Mexico

Eugenia Neves
Universidad de Chile

Rafael Olea Franco
Colegio de México, Mexico

Juan Carlos Orihuela
Bolivia

Eliana Ortega
The Grange, Chile

Roberto Carlos Ortiz
Tulane University, USA

Carola Oyarzún
Pontificia Universidad Católica de Chile

Jussi Pakkasvirta
University of Helsinki, Finland

John H. Patton
Tulane University, USA

Rodrigo Peiretti
Argentina

Marta Peixoto
New York University, USA

Juan Pellicer
University of Oslo, Norway

Amalia Pereira
St Mary's College, USA

César Pérez
University of Iowa, USA

John D. Perivolaris
University of Manchester, UK

Charles A. Perrone
University of Florida, USA

Derek Petrey
Ohio State University, USA

Marina Pianca
University of California at Riverside, USA

Julio Premat
Université de Paris-St. Denis, France

Antonio Prieto-Stambaugh
El Colegio de Michoacán, Mexico

Shalini Puri
University of Pittsburgh, USA

Susan Canty Quinlan
University of Georgia, USA

Juan Carlos Quintero Herencia
University of Maryland, USA

José Quiroga
Emory University, USA

Fernando Rabossi
Argentina

Marcie D. Rinka
Tulane University, USA

Alicia Ríos
Universidad Simón Bolívar, Venezuela

Humberto E. Robles
Northwestern University, USA

Mercedes M. Robles
Loyola University of Chicago, USA

Ileana Rodríguez
Tufts University, USA

María Cristina Rodríguez
University of Puerto Rico

Jorge Romero León
Universidad Central de Venezuela

Fernando J. Rosenberg
Yale University, USA

Victoria Ruétalo
University of Alberta, Canada

César Salas
Arizona State University, USA

Josefa Salmón
Loyola University of New Orleans, USA

Eduardo Santa Cruz
Hanover College, USA

Vivaldo A. Santos
Georgetown University, USA

Oscar D. Sarmiento
State University of New York at Potsdam, USA

Elaine Savory
USA

Jorge Schwartz
Universidade de São Paulo, Brazil

Marcy E. Schwartz
Rutgers University, USA

Nicolau Sevcenko
Universidade de São Paulo, Brazil

Peggy Sharpe
University of Mississippi, USA

Amelia Simpson
University of Florida, USA

Elzbieta Sklodowska
Washington University, USA

Saúl Sosnowski
University of Maryland, USA

Cynthia Steele
University of Washington, USA

Maarten Steenmeijer
University of Nijmegen, The Netherlands

Camilla Stevens
Rutgers University, USA

Claudia Torre
Universidad de Buenos Aires, Argentina

Víctor F. Torres
Universidad de Puerto Rico

Oscar Alberto Torres Duque
University of Iowa, USA

Mary Jane Treacy
Simmons College, USA

David Treece
King's College London, UK

Liliana Trevizán
State University of New York at Potsdam, USA

Vicky Unruh
University of Kansas, USA

Nicasio Urbina
Tulane University, USA

Fernando Valerio-Holguín
Colorado State University, USA

Raúl Vallejo
Universidad Andina Simón Bolívar, Ecuador

Tito Vasconcelos
UNAM, Mexico

Antonio Carlos Vaz
USA

Adam Versényi
University of North Carolina, USA

María Dora Villa Gómez
Bolivia

Berta Waldman
Universidade Estadual de Campinas, Brazil

Carol J. Wallace
Central College, USA

Liliana Weinberg
UNAM, Mexico

Gay Wilentz
East Carolina University, USA

Raymond L. Williams
University of California at Riverside, USA

Eileen Willingham
University of Iowa, USA

Juan Zevallos Aguilar
Temple University, USA

Marc Zimmerman
University of Houston, USA

Liliana Zuccotti
Universidad de Buenos Aires, Argentina

Fernanda A. Zullo
Hanover College, USA

Introduction

The literary map of Latin America and the Caribbean is peppered with imaginary places, from the Seven Cities of Cibola to Onetti's Santa María and the now universally recognized city of Macondo. But alongside these imaginary places sit Buenos Aires, Mexico City, Rio, the Venezuelan llano, the Brazilian *sertão*, the rainforest, the wind-swept wastes of Patagonia, the many islands of the Caribbean. All of these are contained within frontiers – political, linguistic and cultural – which are as subject to change or re-imagining as the borders of Macondo or Santa María. It is often a treacherous business to seek precise correspondence between the literary and the geographical atlases: they sometimes mirror one another, and at other times they are in a relation of mutual denial. That relationship can be a central theme, for example, as writers grapple with political issues, historical responsibilities, the consequences of economic organization, ethnic, social and gender divides, and rapid change in rural and urban life. But it is equally possible that literary expression will not take as its theme the materials of actual experience. Does that make it any less representative of the region? Do literary texts that explicitly refer to social realities necessarily express the deep configurations of lived experience? This distinction may be false in any event, since we are dealing with constructions of the imagined.

At the same time, the century that concerns us in this volume is certainly one in which the question of the relations between literature and the real world have been profoundly contested, nowhere more intensely than in Latin America and the Caribbean. This is a feature of the period that begins at the end of the nineteenth century, when Latin American and Caribbean literature began to seek forms of literary expression which, while acknowledging their debt to Europe, are nonetheless original and new. Perhaps the emphasis on novelty or originality was at first a statement of aesthetic independence from the old colonial centres (often expressed with new force during the centenary celebrations of national independence in Spanish America and Brazil, in the period between 1910 and 1922). The implications of this disengagement from the European reality, however, often produced – or demanded – a new kind of engagement with the real.

Modernismo, the Avant Garde and Regionalism

> Yo persigo una forma que no encuentra mi estilo
> botón de pensamiento que busca ser la rosa
>
> Rubén Darío

There is no doubt that the towering figure in the movement known as *modernismo* in Spanish America (the Brazilian movement would begin later) is the Nicaraguan poet Rubén Darío. His *Prosas profanas* (1896) contains a preface which to all intents and purposes is a manifesto for the modernista movement. An expression of the aesthetic aspirations of cosmopolitan intellectuals in peripheral countries ('mi mujer es de mi patria, mi novia es de París'), it drew on some of the formal developments in the French literature of the time and on notions of 'art for art's sake' (Wilde, Whistler, etc.) with their implications of what could be described as an aristocracy of the spirit. The same idea is expressed in the most famous long essay of the period, José Enrique Rodó's *Ariel* (1900), which exhorts the youth of Latin America to follow a higher spiritual calling (associated with 'Latin' culture, presumably as much French as Spanish) against the utilitarian culture Rodó associates with the Anglo-Saxon world, particularly the United States. That key opposition echoes an earlier essay by the Cuban José Martí, who in 1891, in his essay 'Nuestra América' similarly contrasted the spiritual and the utilitarian, this time in a rousing call to cultural and political independence both from Europe and from the colossus of the north. To underline the fact that this was a general preoccupation across the continent, one could mention the growth of a modernista movement in Mexico reflected in key journals such as the *Revista azul* and *Revista moderna*. In Brazil, Joaquim Maria Machado de Assis had expressed in his 'Instinto da nacionalidade' (1873) similar ideas about the distance that Brazilian literature had acquired relative to Portuguese literature (and to European literature more generally), which he (like Borges some decades later) considered something of an advantage, since it allowed for irreverence and innovation.

Darío's later work *Cantos de vida y esperanza* (1905) includes a number of significant political poems such as 'Canto a Roosevelt' and 'Cuauhtémoc' which are similarly concerned with the forging of a Latin American cultural identity founded on national projects informed by intellectual and spiritual ideals. Curiously these are not the most familiar poems of Darío's today, since his earlier 'art for art's sake' poems (a good example is the famous 'Sonatina') seemed to capture best the cultural aspirations of the *fin de siècle*. In contrast, Rodó's essay spawned a whole series of so-called 'arielista' texts, which later influenced the tradition of the essay of national identity (Alcides Arguedas, Antonio S. Pedreira, Octavio Paz, Ezequiel Martínez Estrada).

One result of these cultural interventions in the debates about political independence was in a sense to compromise the isolationism (what Darío called the 'reino interior', studied by Roberto González Echevarría in an important essay on Rodó and the supposed autonomy of art). Perhaps that was the significance of Enrique González Martínez's call in a sonnet of 1914 to 'twist the swan's neck', a call taken up later in a very different kind of poetry by the younger poets of the avant-garde.

The poets and writers who contributed to the new experimental literature assembled under the concept of the avant-garde shared common attitudes to language and form. Beyond that their views and attitudes differed greatly. In some senses, this new phase in Latin American writing challenged – or to use a current rather than a contemporary term, *deconstructed* – language and broke through the certainties that form enshrined. If the modernistas in some sense appropriated the symbolic universes of the *fin de siècle*, the Latin American avant-garde addressed and circumvented the idea of totality. Modernity as they were experiencing it was fragmentary and incomplete; it was utopia and dystopia at once. Perhaps that was in its way a function of a new communication between Europe and Latin America, an exchange of ideas and experiences that took many artists to Europe – César Vallejo, Oliverio Girondo, Vicente Huidobro, José Juan Tablada, Jorge Luis Borges – but drew European artists and writers to Latin America in search of a different cultural history. André Breton travelled repeatedly to Mexico, for example, while Le Corbusier, the key figure in architecture of that period, found his most enthusiastic following in Brazil.

While the avant-garde is a complex movement, it would be wholly wrong to see it as a mere imitation of Europe. The highly significant Modern Art Week in São Paulo in 1922 evolved into the Antropofagia movement led by Oswald de Andrade which insisted that Brazil must absorb, or cannibalize, Europe. César Vallejo dismembered the language of all the historic certainties that Europe had bequeathed to Latin America. Vicente Huidobro embarked on his extraordinary poem *Altazor* in 1919 and completed it with a kind of verbal cataclysm in 1931. The speed and cacophony of the modern city found echoes in the work of Girondo, the Estridentista group in Mexico, and in the writings of the group around Graça Aranha in Brazil. And the impact of the mass communications media, the beginning of cinema, the proliferation of radio, all emphasized the new possibilities and the gap between the different locations of the national experience.

In a sense, the impulse to revolutionize and transform was present throughout the avant-garde – a function of the sense of the collapse of an old order in the 1920s and onwards. Yet there was no agreement as to how that transformation might be achieved materially, nor on the relationship between the imagined new world and its political expression. Thus many writers felt their vanguardism a political obligation, broadly interpreted. The Boedo group in Argentina took its social obligations very seriously, while those who wrote for the avant-garde journals such as *Martín Fierro* tended towards a social conservatism in uneasy co-existence with aesthetic experimentation. For Nicolás Guillén in Cuba or the Puerto Rican poet Luis Palés Matos, the new direction was a return to the language of black or mulatto music and speech, a new encounter with orality and the invisible cultures of oppressed minorities. The *indigenista* writers were at least in part moved by the same concerns, yet their work was often aesthetically conservative, at least until the generation of José María Arguedas and Manuel Scorza in Peru drew on the innovative aesthetics of the avant-garde.

The 1920s and 1930s are witness to literary and cultural movements which at first sight appear to move in quite contrary directions. On the one hand, there was the regionalism that considered the issues of cultural creation through a developmentalist lens. Here the issue was to reproduce in some senses the European experience of progress and enlightenment, two functions of a single process. This is expressed particularly in the iconic novels of the era, Rivera's *La vorágine* (1924) and Gallegos's *Doña Bárbara* (1929), as well as the early *indigenista* writing. The essays and autobiographies of José Vasconcelos in Mexico may be seen in the same framework; he was engaged in the active construction of a new national culture in Mexico, where the Revolution of 1910–17 had inaugurated a new 'revolutionary' state. And the writings and activism of José Carlos Mariátegui in Peru may both be seen as explorations of the encounter between politics and culture in the context of a struggle to define national culture. In a different sense, Claude McKay's *Banana Bottom* (1933) may be set in the same framework, exploring as it does the historical experience of plantation life that informs and distorts the historical present.

In this regard, it was of particular concern to these writers that substantial sectors of the national population (peasants, blacks, Indians) remained apart from the state projects; these writers found themselves writing 'about' and yet 'for' a community which had not yet been forged, a community that had been imagined but did not exist. This leads to a literature that is plagued by good intentions: Jorge Icaza's *Huasipungo* (1934), for instance, while denouncing the condition of Ecuadoran Indians, reads today as a racist text, and the same could be said of a number of other products of the *indigenista* and *negrista* currents. Mariátegui stated with considerable prescience that *indigenismo* writes about the Indian, but that a true indigenous literature would only be written when there were Indian writers to produce it.

A new world, then, was emerging and projects for change and cultural transformation found their expression in every area of Latin American culture through the 1920s and early 1930s. But by then the impact of the Great Depression served both to radicalize the national project and bring home the material obstacles in the way of its realization. That contradiction was explored in many ways – in pastiche and parody, in a denunciatory social realism and a passionate utopianism, and increasingly in an ironic distancing. All of these features may be found, for example, in the emblematic work of the period, Aimé Césaire's *Cahier d'un retour au pays natal* (1939) which still carried the revolutionary impulse of an earlier modernism. Especially in the wake of the Spanish Civil War, whose effects were perhaps more immediately palpable in Latin America than the World War of 1939–45, disillusionment and withdrawal permeate a range of literary expression – from Vallejo and Huidobro to the sceptical fictions of Borges.

The beginning of the recognition of the failure of the avant-garde yields the space to a different project, often involved with a nation-building literature (sometimes closely associated with state projects). What is at stake in these cultural nationalist projects is the uncertainty about how a national culture can be forged, particularly in a culturally and economically peripheral nation and in a period of deepening crisis. It is clearly not enough for the cultural disposition to exist: there is an inescapable relationship between that disposition and the material circumstances which are a limiting condition. That is a core preoccupation, for example, of the poets and writers who gathered around Caribbean literary journals such as *Bim* and

Kyk-over-al through the 1940s in a common search for a renewed language and a validation of the experience of the colonized. Some, such as George Lamming in *In the Castle of My Skin* (1953), turned to Africa; others, many of them in an exile enforced by the lack of cultural and economic opportunities in the region, recreated a Caribbean of the imagination in the language of the metropolis.

For many writers, the focus of their attention in this period of national consolidation turns towards the modern sector, and to the growing cities in which this sector is located. The hope of a leap forward into industrialization and modernity would be fulfilled in the growing urban environment – and the struggles in the countryside come to occupy a diminishing proportion of cultural attention, at least as the source of cultural renewal. The *Antología de la literatura fantástica* (1940), compiled by Borges, Adolfo Bioy Casares and Silvina Ocampo, was the signal for writers to return to imagined worlds, although whether those imaginary places were the product of the individual imagination or the collective unconscious would continue to be debated. For Alejo Carpentier, for example, writing in the preface to his 1949 novel *El reino de este mundo*, the marvellous was a facet of a Latin American reality as multi-layered and contradictory as an excited André Breton, the founder of surrealism, had hoped it would be. Julio Cortázar, José Donoso and Juan Rulfo each moved between the real and the symbolic. Juan Carlos Onetti and Ernesto Sábato moved in urban settings. The shaping development, however, was the growth of national-populist projects such as those of Juan Domingo Perón in Argentina and Getúlio Vargas in Brazil in which cosmopolitanism would often be seen as a mode of withdrawal from the construction of the state. Yet the overwhelming tenor of the times was a descriptive narrative of alternative histories, of ethnography, and of a debate on national identity expressed and developed in every area of culture, from music and architecture to narrative and theatre. Mário de Andrade, Octavio Paz, Germán Arciniegas, Gilberto Freyre, Fernando Ortiz, Augusto Salazar Bondy and many others contributed to the discussion.

In the 1950s the limits of the industrialization that occurred in Latin America were reached. On the one hand, state control over the economic process had not led to independence from the market. By the middle of the decade it was clear that while growth and urbanization had occurred, these had not served to level, let alone eliminate, the internal inequities within Latin America, or within each country. Carlos Fuentes's novel *La región más transparente* (1958), set in a burgeoning Mexico City, provided a vast mural of the contradictory dynamics of the capital. Juan Rulfo's iconic *Pedro Páramo* (1955) and Onetti's *El astillero* (1961) might, in their different ways, be read as allegories of the failure of a project.

Yet Fuentes, together with Mario Vargas Llosa and Gabriel García Márquez, would within the decade become Latin America's most successful cultural exports with the commercial impact of the 'Boom' in the Latin American novel. Fuentes's first major contribution to the phenomenon, his novel *La muerte de Artemio Cruz*, in 1962, was completed three years after, and against the background of, the Cuban Revolution. This was not a coincidence.

The Cuban Revolution, the Cold War and the Boom

The Cuban Revolution of 1959 was in the first instance an event in the terrain of politics. The fall of the dictatorship of Batista, a loyal defender of US interests in the region, and the triumphant entry into Havana of the revolutionaries of the 26th of July movement, resonated around the continent. The hegemony of the United States throughout Latin America – its ability to use its ideological influence and economic power to control events – had been successfully challenged. What followed, in Washington, was what John Gerassi called the 'great fear' that such a challenge might be mounted elsewhere. In Latin America itself, the overthrow of Batista privileged the Cuban experience in all subsequent political debate. Its methods became the model, and its project for national independence the road to follow.

The rejection of US hegemony was at once political and cultural; the new Cuban government under Castro returned to the question of national culture and its role in nation-building that had been such a central preoccupation for earlier cultural movements. Its first formulation – though not necessarily a very clear one – came in 1961, when Castro delivered his 'Words to the intellectuals' at a conference in April of that year. The phrase that crystallized his injunction became something of a formula – albeit one whose imprecision allowed endless re-interpretations – 'Within the revolution everything, outside the revolution nothing'. The suggestion of open debate and flexibility was a little disingenuous, especially when a number of Cuba's pre-revolutionary intellectuals found themselves under mounting pressure to write *for* the revolution, as opposed to simply within it. Increasingly, as the decade wore on, loyalty to the revolution and loyalty to the Cuban government were deemed to be one and the same thing. In Cuba itself, this produced a number of debates among Latin American writers who had initially supported the revolution, for example, Mario Vargas Llosa and Carlos Fuentes. Julio Cortázar, the Argentine writer who was an enthusiastic supporter, took part in a three-sided debate with Vargas Llosa and Oscar Collazos (published in 1971) around issues of creative freedom for the writer and the imposition of 'acceptable' styles and models of writing. And the whole issue came to a dramatic crisis in 1968, with the announcement of the result of the Casa de las Américas prize for that year.

Casa de las Américas was a project the purpose of which was to bring together Latin American writers and artists who supported the Cuban Revolution and shared its aspiration to create a new Latin American culture. The assumption was that these two kinds of commitment were interchangeable. Yet while the innovative work of Cuban filmmakers and musicians was opening new creative avenues, the situation of writers became less clear, especially if they expressed an unwillingness to 'place their writing at the service of the revolution'. Thus, when the results of the prestigious Casa prize competitions were announced, they included the poet Heberto Padilla and the playwright Antón Arrufat among the victors. Yet when their work was published, both were prefaced by critical official statements that denounced their questioning of the revolutionary project in their respective works. A year later, Padilla was detained by the Cuban authorities and released only after he had made a humiliating confession of his errors.

For many Latin American intellectuals, this represented a parting of the ways. A new generation of young poets and writers of fiction – as well as some more seasoned – held to the limits set down by the cultural policies of the Castro government, producing forms of expression that in some way or another adhered to notions of social responsibility and public testimony. And just as it did in the economic and military realm, the United States responded with a sustained cultural challenge enshrined in an ill-fated journal – *Mundo Nuevo* – edited in Paris by Emir Rodríguez Monegal (and later continued in Buenos Aires by others), which drew together both critics of the Cuban regime and those who in a more nebulous way defended intellectual freedom and creative individualism.

Yet the debate about literature and its social function was not easily reduced to political positions. For just as the idea of a revolutionary poetry found echoes in the young guerrilla poets of the 1960s, writing (and dying) in Peru, Guatemala, Colombia and Nicaragua, so the argument about imaginative freedom was explored through a rediscovery of the discussions about myth and reality embedded in the concept of 'lo real maravilloso'. Wilson Harris's polyphonic novel *The Palace of the Peacock* (1960) in some senses marked the track. In its new manifestation, that of magical realism, the Latin American novel invaded the expanding world publishing market. Carlos Fuentes's *La muerte de Artemio Cruz* (1962), Mario Vargas Llosa's *La ciudad y los perros* (1962), Julio Cortázar's *Rayuela* (1963) and, most dramatically of all, Gabriel García Márquez's *Cien años de soledad* (1967) marked the peaks of what became known as the Boom. The term defined the group only in terms of its commercial success. A number of critics followed who set out to define its aesthetics or, in the case of Donoso, its social origins. No consensual explanation emerged, but the phenomenon of what Fuentes called 'la nueva novela latinoamericana' can tentatively be situated historically and in terms of literary histories and developments. It is not a coincidence, for example, that the new novel coincided with the economic re-integration of Latin America into the world market after the failure of a model of import substitution (and its attendant cultural projects) to open the way to forms of autonomous development. From the perspective of Europe and North America, by contrast, a new generation was turning its gaze towards a third world seen as enshrining in some sense an unmistakable reality of oppression and resistance. If magical realism drew into a single narrative the conflicting perspectives of the official and the unofficial histories, the written and the spoken, the historical and the mythic, then that could and did respond to a political and ideological vision centred on the inescapable conflicts – class, national, sexual and ethnic – which characterized a global capitalist system.

In poetry, too, these conflicts are enacted as challenges to language and within language – in Ernesto Cardenal, Nicanor Parra, Brazil's mimeograph poets; in theatre, performance as an extension of public debate and a means of personal transformation, is an idea developed in and through the work of Augusto Boal and his followers and, in a different sense, through the theatre movement in Colombia that has Enrique Buenaventura at its heart. In the same sense the poets of 'nation-language' and the spoken and performed word brought the subversive impact of orality into the very heart of an Anglophone literary world in the 1960s and 1970s. In prose fiction, Kamau Brathwaite echoed that new direction.

Yet the 1970s are, in some sense, a time of reflux, a reassessment of the revolutionary possibilities in the light of the repressive military regimes now established in Chile, Uruguay, Argentina, Brazil and Guatemala. The critical impulse so characteristic of the previous decade has made culture an enemy of tyrannies. The earliest decrees of the Pinochet regime in Chile, for example, identified and banned a series of cultural expressions. Exile became an identifying shared experience for many Latin American writers and artists and as a result the creation of imaginary countries or a withdrawal into the past in a search for explanations – or perhaps even solace. Augusto Roa Bastos's *Yo el Supremo* (1974) and Carpentier's *El recurso del método* (also 1974) may stand as examples. For those who remained within the repressive national milieus, the critical voice became often oblique and obscure, allusive and challenging as much by the collapse of reason as by an alternative rationality – Diamela Eltit and Raúl Zurita in Chile, or Ricardo Piglia in Argentina, for example.

At the same time the work of Manuel Puig in Argentina and Luis Rafael Sánchez in Puerto Rico, or the new *crónica* form developed particularly in Mexico by Carlos Monsiváis found resistance and distance in the vocabulary of mass culture – a new rhetoric, or anti-rhetoric, at once pastiche and critique. Its development was theorised in its turn by Néstor García Canclini and Roberto Schwarz.

It is one of the curiosities of the Boom that while it was extraordinarily influential and widely disseminated outside Latin America, it produced very few younger adherents on the continent itself. It may be that the engagement with history, whether from a conservative or a progressive point of view, that was at the heart of the movement, seemed less possible in the real conditions of the 1970s; it may be that historical optimism encountered its limiting experience in the overthrow of the Allende government in Chile. Whatever the reason, the literature of the late 1980s did not return to the ample visions of the decade of the 1960s, despite the 'transition to democracy' which largely replaced military by civilian governments across the continent. The revolutionary voices of Nicaragua, in the wake of the 1979 Revolution, were increasingly compromised by the tenuous hold of the Sandinistas on power and by what appeared to be at best the stalemate, at worst the defeat of the resistance elsewhere in Central America. It seemed that by and large writers now jealously preserved a degree of distance from their subjects, preferring instead to explore psychological and subjective landscapes.

It was that very process which produced a major debate around the issue of authenticity and self-expression. If the voice of the oppressed had not echoed with sufficient strength in the works of magical realists, 'how then could the subaltern speak', to use Gayatri Chakravorty Spivak's now famous phrase? One answer was the 'literatura de testimonio', the direct narrative in which the 'author' was solely a facilitator, exemplified by the autobiographical accounts of Rigoberta Menchú and Domitila Barrios among others. The difficulty, it soon emerged, was that the agent – the scribe – could not be and never was neutral, but instead in translating orality into the realm of the written embedded it precisely within the dominant culture itself. Worse still, that echoed back on to the speaker, according to David Stoll, so that the authentic voice became a conscious participant in a narrative genre.

The contemporary scene

It is hard to define the contours of the contemporary writing scene in Latin America and the Caribbean because many phenomena are taking place and are difficult to place in perspective. A few observations are possible, however. One is the solid place in contemporary writing of voices that might once have been considered to come 'from the margin', though that very formulation seems offensive now. Derek Walcott's *Omeros* (1990) shifts the heartland of cultural enquiry to an unmistakable Caribbean milieu – from the centre to the margins. Women's writing is central everywhere, and women are an important share of the reading public: the public success around the world of Isabel Allende was more a symptom than a catalyst, with important voices such as Elena Poniatowska and Carmen Boullosa in Mexico, Zee Edgell and Zoila Ellis in Belize, Ana María Del Río in Chile, Ana Lydia Vega and Mayra Santos Febres in Puerto Rico. Another central fact of literary production today is the importance of gay and lesbian writing, with central figures such as Juan Pablo Sutherland and Pedro Lemebel in Chile, Mario Bellatín in Mexico, Sylvia Molloy in Argentina, and Norge Espinosa and Pedro de Jesús Pez Acosta in Cuba. Indigenous and mestizo writers, including Elicura Chihuailaf in Chile, Humberto Ak'abal in Guatemala, and a whole array of Paraguayan poets who write in Guarani, are bringing to fruition Mariátegui's predictions about the emergence of an indigenous literature, and are exploring the literary possibilities of indigenous languages (some of which did not have written traditions in the past) and of bilingual writing. Writing by African-Latin Americans and African-Caribbeans – including such important voices as Nancy Morejón in Cuba and Mayra Santos Febres in Puerto Rico – are central to the literary scenes in their countries.

If today's world is increasingly fluid and dislocated, then the displacement of writers has also become a central part of this story. While some writers have long written from the metropolitan centres – V.S. Naipaul in England is perhaps the pre-eminent example – recent displacements have affected writers of the most diverse class, ethnic and racial backgrounds, and have often resulted in linguistic displacement as well. Julia Alvarez of the Dominican Republic, Edwidge Danticat of Haiti, Cristina García and Achy Obejas of Cuba, all of whom live in the US, have written their literary work in English. The 'border arts' performance movement, associated especially with the name of Guillermo Gómez Peña, has made aggressive use of Spanglish and of a sharp questioning of fixed identities. Some artists are working across not just languages but media, as is the case of the Chilean Catalina Parra. And the growth of new expressions, like the urban 'crónicas', suggest that the local may have found ways to subvert the global culture market in literary acts at once transient and as dynamic as the constantly changing speech of the Latin American street. Thus the curiously eclectic writings of the Zapatista leader Subcomandante Marcos suggest just such a will to speak from the margins to the discontented heartlands of the megacities of the new millennium. The relation in some has reversed, and the brutal realism of the inner city, or the slums, ironically has come to fascinate and terrify the global audience for film and the new harsh fictions of inner-city alienation. It may be a peculiarly appropriate sign of the times that the golden lands that brought the colonizers to Latin America's shores over 500 years ago should now have become Paulo Lins's 'Cidade de Deus' and Patricia Melo's *Inferno* (1999), from which the excluded watch knowingly the explosive growth of Rio de Janeiro and São Paulo and await the reckoning so subtly suggested in the apocalyptic fables of Mario Bellatín, Fernando Vallejo or Diamela Eltit.

Acknowledgements

We are grateful for the help of several University of Iowa students: Kathleen Costello, Alvaro Bernal, Megan Paul, Nicolas Lucero and Brandi Miller, who worked on bringing the entries up to date and filling in bibliographical details.

Daniel Balderston and Mike Gonzalez

Chronology

1898	
Cuba achieves independence from Spain US takes possession of Puerto Rico	Mario Vargas Vila, *Flor de fango* Amado Nervo founds *Revista moderna* in Mexico
1899	
US administration in Cuba	Machado de Assis, *Dom Casmurro* José Enrique Rodó, *Rubén Darío*
1900	
	Rodó, *Ariel*
1901	
Platt Amendment: US on right to intervene in Cuba	Horacio Quiroga, *Los arrecifes de coral* Manuel Díaz Rodríguez, *Idolos rotos*
1902	
Beginning of Cuban Republic	Euclides da Cunha, *Os sertões* Graça Aranha, *Canãa* Augusto D'Halmar, *Juana Lucero*
1903	
Panama declares independence from Gran Colombia and is immediately recognized by the US government	Federico Gamboa, *Santa* Florencio Sánchez, *Canillita, M'hijo el Dotor*
1904	
Roosevelt Corollary to the Monroe Doctrine	Florencio Sánchez, *La gringa* Roberto J. Payró, *Sobre las ruinas* José Herrera y Reissig, *Los éxtasis en la montaña* Alberto Blest Gana, *Los trasplantados*
1905	
	Rubén Darío, *Cantos de vida y esperanza* Leopoldo Lugones, *Los crepúsculos del jardín*

1906

First concessions in Guatemala to the United Fruit Company	José Santos Chocano, *Alma América*

1907

Divorce law approved in Uruguay	Delmira Agustini, *El libro blanco*

1908

Beginning of dictatorship of Juan Vicente Gómez in Venezuela	Enrique Larreta, *La gloria de Don Ramiro* Manuel González Prada, *Horas de lucha* Evaristo Carriego, *Misas herejes* Machado de Assis, *Memorial de Ayres*

1909

US occupation of Nicaragua	Lugones, *Lunario sentimental* René Maran, *La maison du bonheur* Rodó, *Motivos de Proteo* Alcides Arguedas, *Pueblo enfermo*

1910

Madero launches Mexican Revolution	Agustini, *Cantos de la mañana* Lugones, *Odas seculares* Alberto Gerchunoff, *Los gauchos judíos* Rafael Barrett, *Lo que son los yerbales* Zorrilla de San Martín, *La epopeya de Artigas*

1911

Emiliano Zapata publishes his manifesto in Mexico, the Plan de Ayala	Barrett, *El dolor paraguayo* José María Eguren, *Simbólicas*

1912

US intervention in Nicaragua and Honduras	Pedro Prado, *La casa abandonada*

1913

Madero overthrown by the counter-revolution led by Victoriano Huerta in Mexico	Agustini, *Los cálices vacíos* José Martí, *Versos libres*, published posthumously

1914

Opening of Panama Canal Beginning of First World War US occupies the Dominican Republic	Manuel Gálvez, *La maestra normal* Gabriela Mistral, *Sonetos a la muerte* Vicente Huidobro's first manifesto, 'Non serviam'

1915

Carranza overthrows Huerta in Mexico and assumes the Presidency	Afonso Henriques de Lima Barreto, *Triste fim de Policarpo Quaresma* Enrique González Martínez, 'Tuércele el cuello al cisne' César Fernández Moreno, *Las iniciales del misal*

1916	
Hipólito Yrigoyen elected to the Argentine Presidency on behalf of the Radical Party	Mariano Azuela, *Los de abajo* Huidobro, *El espejo del agua* Enrique López Velarde, *La sangre devota* Eguren, *La canción de las figuras* Lugones, *El payador*
1917	
Russian Revolution New Mexican Constitution agreed to and signed at Querétaro Earthquake destroys Guatemala City	Alfonso Reyes, *Visión de Anáhuac* Quiroga, *Cuentos de amor, de locura y de muerte* Gálvez, *El mal metafísico*
1918	
La Reforma Universitaria begins in Córdoba, Argentina	César Vallejo, *Los heraldos negros* Huidobro, *Poemas árticos*
1919	
La Semana Trágica in Buenos Aires, when police shot and killed demonstrators Emiliano Zapata killed at the Chinameca hacienda	Gálvez, *Nacha Regules* Ramón López Velarde, *Zozobra* Manuel Bandeira, *Carnaval* Alcides Arguedas, *Raza de bronce*
1920	
Alvaro Obregón elected to the Mexican Presidency Overthrow of Guatemalan dictator Manuel Estrada Cabrera	Nervo, *La amada inmóvil* published posthumously Pedro Prado, *Alsino* José Juan Tablada, *Li Po y otros poemas ideográficos* Jorge Edwards Bello, *El roto* Quiroga, *El salvaje*
1921	
Mexican Mural project begins under patronage of José Vasconcelos	López Velarde, *Suave patria* Reyes, *Simpatías y diferencias*
1922	
Tenentes revolt in Brazil Massacre of 2,000 strikers at Guayaquil, Ecuador	Semana de Arte Moderna in São Paulo launches Brazilian modernism Mário de Andrade, *Paulicéia desvairada* Mistral, *Desolación* Eduardo Barrios, *El hermano asno* César Vallejo, *Trilce* Manuel Zeno Gandia, *Redentores*
1923	
Pancho Villa assassinated near his ranch in Chihuahua, Mexico	Pablo Neruda, *Crepusculario* Jorge Luis Borges, *Fervor de Buenos Aires*

1924	
Prestes Column begins its march across Brazil Haya de la Torre founds APRA in Peru	Neruda, *Veinte poemas de amor y una canción desesperada* José Eustasio Rivera, *La vorágine* Mistral, *Ternura* Teresa de la Parra, *Ifigenia*
1925	
End of US military occupation in Nicaragua	José Vasconcelos, *La raza cósmica* Alfonsina Storni, *Ocre* Borges, *Inquisiciones*
1926	
Beginning of Sandino's insurgency in Nicaragua Beginning of Cristero revolt in Mexico	José Carlos Mariátegui launches the journal, *Amauta* Roberto Arlt, *El juguete rabioso* Ricardo Güiraldes, *Don Segundo Sombra*
1927	
Augusto César Sandino launches his guerrilla war against US occupation of Nicaragua	Lugones, *Poemas solariegos* Ricardo Molinari, *El imaginero*
1928	
Strike in Colombian banana plantations against United Fruit Company	Mariátegui, *Siete ensayos* ... Mário de Andrade, *Macunaíma* Martín Luis Guzmán, *El águila y la serpiente*
1929	
Collapse of the US stock market	Rómulo Gallegos, *Doña Bárbara* Teresa de la Parra, *Memorias de Mamá Blanca* Guzmán, *La sombra del caudillo*
1930	
Establishment of the New Republic in Brazil Military *coup* in Argentina ends fifty years of constitutional rule	Miguel Angel Asturias, *Leyendas de Guatemala* Bandeira, *Libertinagem* Raquel de Queiroz, *O quinze* Victoria Ocampo founds the journal, *Sur*
1931	
Beginning of Ubico dictatorship in Guatemala	Nicolás Guillén, *Sóngoro cosongo* Huidobro, *Altazor* Arturo Uslar Pietri, *Las lanzas coloradas* César Vallejo, *El tungsteno* and *Rusia en 1931*
1932	
Rising in El Salvador suppressed, leaving 30,000 dead The Chaco War between Bolivia and Paraguay begins	Oliverio Girondo, *Espantapájaros* Pablo Palacio, *Vida del ahorcado* José Lins do Rego, *Menino de engenho*

1933	
Roosevelt announces his 'Good Neighbour Policy' towards Latin America	Ezequiel Martínez Estrada, *Radiografía de la pampa* Neruda, first part of *Residencia en la tierra* Xavier Villaurrutia, *Nocturnos*
1934	
Election of Lázaro Cárdenas to Mexican presidency Sandino murdered in Nicaragua	Jorge Icaza, *Huasipungo* Gallegos, *Cantaclaro* Graciliano Ramos, *São Bernardo* Emilio Ballagas, *Cuaderno de poesía negra* Guillén, *West Indies, Ltd.*
1935	
End of Chaco War Death of Juan Vicente Gómez in Venezuela after twenty-seven years in power	María Luisa Bombal, *La última niebla* Pablo Neruda, *Residencia en la Tierra*, vol. II Ballagas, *Antología de la poesía negra hispanoamericana* Borges, *Historia universal de la infamia* José María Arguedas, *Agua* Jorge Amado, *Cacau*
1936	
Spanish Civil War begins Anastasio Somoza takes power in Nicaragua	Bandeira, *Estrela de Manhã* Raúl González Tuñón, *La rosa blindada*
1937	
Vargas declares the Estado Novo in Brazil Congress of Culture meets in Madrid	Luis Palés Matos, *Tuntún de pasa y grifería* José Lezama Lima, *Muerte de Narciso* Neruda, *España en el corazón* Léon Damas, *Pigments*
1938	
Mexico nationalizes foreign oil companies	Bombal, *La amortajada* Lugones, *Romances de Río Seco* Mistral, *Tala* José Rubén Romero, *La vida inútil de Pito Pérez* Villaurrutia, *Nostalgia de la muerte* César Vallejo, *Poemas humanos* Rodolfo Usigli, *El gesticulador*
1939	
Outbreak of Second World War	César Vallejo, *España, aparta de mí este cáliz*, published posthumously Juan Carlos Onetti, *El pozo* Aimé Césaire *Cahier d'un retour au pays natal* José Gorostiza, *Muerte sin fin*
1940	
Assassination of Leon Trotsky in Mexico City Death of Paraguayan president Estigarribia in a plane accident	Adolfo Bioy Casares, *La invencón de Morel* Samuel Eichelbaum, *Pájaro de barro* Carlos Drummond de Andrade, *Sentimento do mundo*

Borges, Silvina Ocampo and Bioy Casares, *Antología de la literatura fantástica*

1941

TIAR (Interamerican Treaty of Reciprocal Assistance) signed in Rio de Janeiro
US enters Second World War after attack on Pearl Harbour

Ciro Alegría, *El mundo es ancho y ajeno*
Onetti, *Tierra de nadie*
José María Arguedas, *Yawar fiesta*
Carlos Luis Fallas, *Mamita Yunai*
Enrique Amorim, *El caballo y su sombra*
José Bianco, *Sombras suele vestir*
José Revueltas, *Los muros de agua*

1942

Founding of Movimiento Nacionalista Revolucionario in Bolivia

Reyes, *Ultimo Tule*
Cecilia Meireles, *Vaga música*
Felisberto Hernández, *Por los tiempos de Clemente Colling*
Reyes, *La experiencia literaria*
Mário de Andrade, *O movimento modernista*
Founding of journal, *Bim*

1943

'GOU' (military group led by Juan Domingo Perón) leads overthrow of Ramón Castillo in Argentina and installs General Rawson in his place; beginning of rise of Perón

Amado, *Terras do sem fim*
Rego, *Fogo morto*
Neruda, *Nuevo canto de amor a Stalingrado*
Bianco, *Las ratas*
Oswald de Andrade, *Marco Zero*, vol. I

1944

Juan José Arévalo to power in Guatemala

Borges, *Ficciones*
Arthur Seymour, *Over Guiana*
Clarice Lispector, *Perto do coração selvagem*

1945

Vargas regime overthrown in Brazil
Second World War ends – in Europe in May, in Japan in August

Gabriela Mistral awarded the Nobel Prize for Literature
João Cabral do Melo Neto, *O engenheiro*
Carlos Drummond de Andrade, *A roso do povo*
Meireles, *Mar absoluto e outros poemas*
Seminal BBC programme *Caribbean Voices* begins
Founding of journal, *Kyk-Over-Al*

1946

Juan Domingo Perón becomes President of Argentina

Asturias, *El Señor Presidente*
Augusto Céspedes, *El metal del diablo*
Joño Guimarães, Rosa, *Sagarana*
Oliverio Girondo, *Campo nuestro*

1947	
Civil war in Paraguay Women get right to vote in Argentina Rómulo Gallegos elected President of Venezuela	Guillén, *El son entero* Jorge de Lima, *Poemas negros* Agustín Yáñez, *Al filo del agua*
1948	
OAS (Organization of American States) charter signed in Bogotá 'La Violencia' begins in Colombia with the murder of Liberal Presidential candidate Eliecer Gaitán in Bogotá	Leopoldo Marechal, *Adán Buenosayres* Ernesto Sábato, *El túnel* Bioy Casares, *La trama celeste*
1949	
Coup in Paraguay New Peronist constitution in Argentina	Asturias, *Hombres de maíz* Alejo Carpentier, *El reino de este mundo* Lezama Lima, *La fijeza* Borges, *El aleph* Erico Veríssimo, *O tempo e o vento* Octavio Paz, *Libertad bajo palabra*
1950	
New constitution and Nationalist revolt in Puerto Rico Return to power of Getúlio Vargas in Brazil	Onetti, *La vida breve* Paz, *El laberinto de la soledad* Neruda, *Canto general* Joseph Zobel, *La rue cases-nègres*
1951	
Granting of autonomy for Aruba, Curaçao and Bonaire	Manuel Rojas, *Hijo de ladrón* Julio Cortázar, *Bestiario* Paz, *¿Aguila o sol?* René Marqués, *La carreta*
1952	
Death of Eva Perón Revolution in Bolivia	Frantz Fanon, *Peau noire, masques blancs*
1953	
Fidel Castro leads assault on Moncada Barracks in Santiago de Cuba	Carpentier, *Los pasos perdidos* Juan Rulfo, *El llano en llamas* Juan Antonio Corretjer, *Alabanza de la torre de Ciales*
1954	
Vargas, President of Brazil, commits suicide President Jacobo Arbenz of Guatemala overthrown by a military *coup* supported by the USA Alfredo Stroessner becomes President of Paraguay	Nicanor Parra, *Poemas y antipoemas* Juan José Arreola, *La hora de todos* Bioy Casares, *El sueño de los héroes* Neruda, *Odas elementales* Nelson Estupiñán Bass, *Cuando los guayacanes florecían*

1955

Perón overthrown by military *coup*	Marco Denevi, *Rosaura a las diez* Gabriel García Márquez, *La hojarasca* Rulfo, *Pedro Páramo* Jaime Torres Bodet, *Tiempo de arena*

1956

Landing of yacht Granma in Cuba Assassination of Anastasio Somoza in Nicaragua; power passes to his son Luis Somoza Debayle Beginning of Kubitschek Presidency in Brazil	Melo Neto, *Morte e vida severina* João Guimarães Rosa, *Grande sertão: Veredas* Paz, *El arco y la lira* Mario Benedetti, *Poemas de la oficina* José Donoso, *Coronación*

1957

Founding of People's National Congress in Guyana	Rosario Castellanos, *Balún Canán* Paz, *Piedra de sol* Marqués, *La muerte no entrará en palacio* Ariano Suassuna, *Auto da compadecida*

1958

Overthrow of Venezuelan dictator Marcos Pérez Jiménez	Amado, *Gabriela, cravo e canela* José María Arguedas, *Los ríos profundos* Carlos Fuentes, *La región más transparente* Lima, *Invencao de Orfeu*

1959

Cuban Revolution Election of Rómulo Betancourt as President of Venezuela	Pablo Antonio Cuadra, *El jaguar y la luna* V.S. Naipaul, *Miguel Street* Benedetti, *Montevideanos*

1960

US embargo on Cuba made official Cuba withdraws from the OAS Brasília inaugurated	Ernesto Cardenal, *Hora Cero* Augusto Roa Bastos, *Hijo de hombre* Benedetti, *La tregua* Lispector, *Laços de família* Salarrué, *La espada y otras narraciones* Guillermo Cabrera Infante, *Así en la paz como en la guerra* Carlos Droguett, *Eloy* Wilson Harris, *Palace of the Peacock*

1961

Failed CIA-backed Bay of Pigs (Playa Girón) invasion of Cuba Rafael Trujillo, military dictator of the Dominican republic, is killed Cuban Revolution declared socialist Alliance for Progress formed	Javier Heraud, *El viaje* V.S. Naipaul, *A House for Mr Biswas* García Márquez, *El coronel no tiene quien le escriba* Onetti, *El astillero* Sábato, *Sobre héroes y tumbas* Fidel Castro's 'Palabras a los intelectuales'

1962

Cuban Missile Crisis Jamaica wins independence Independence of Trinidad and Tobago Election of Juan Bosch to the Presidency of the Dominican Republic	Arreola, *Confabulario total* Carpentier, *El siglo de las luces* Castellanos, *Oficio de tinieblas* Fuentes, *La muerte de Artemio Cruz* García Márquez, *Los funerales de la Mamá Grande* Nicanor Parra, *Versos de salón* Cortázar, *Historia de cronopios y famas* Vargas Llosa, *La ciudad y los perros*

1963

Bosch overthown in the Dominican Republic Argentine Congress reopened Eighty-day general strike in British Guiana (later Guyana)	Cortázar, *Rayuela* Egon Wolff, *Los invasores* Enrique Lihn, *La pieza oscura* Severo Sarduy, *Gestos*

1964

Military *coup* in Brazil against government of João Goulart In Haiti, François Duvalier has himself declared President for life.	Onetti, *Juntacadáveres* Guillén, *Tengo* Revueltas, *Los errores* Neruda, *Memorial de Isla Negra* Gonzalo Rojas, *Contra la muerte* José María Arguedas, *Todas las sangres* Sebastián Salazar Bondy, *Lima la horrible* Journal *Zona Franca* founded Angel Rama's 'Diez problemas para el novelista latinoamericano' published in Cuban journal, *Casa de las Américas*

1965

US Marines invade Dominican Republic Tupamaros formed in Uruguay	Alejandra Pizarnik, *Los trabajos y los noches* Ernesto Cardenal, *Oración por Marilyn Monroe y otros poemas* Ernesto Desnoes, *Memorias del subdesarrollo* Julieta Campos, *Muerte por agua* Antonio Candido, *Literatura e sociedade* Haroldo de Campos and Decio Pignatari, *Teoria da poesía concreta* J.R. Ribeyro, *Los geniecillos dominicales* José Triana, *La noche de los asesinos* Ernesto Che Guevara, 'El hombre y el socialismo en Cuba' Marechal, *El banquete de Severo Arcángelo*

1966

New military *coup* in Argentina Tricontinental Conference in Havana Massacre of San Juan, Llallagua mine, Bolivia Independence of Barbados and Guyana	José Donoso, *El lugar sin límites* and, *Este domingo* Lezama Lima, *Paradiso* Vargas Llosa, *La casa verde* Martín Adán, *La piedra absoluta*

Lihn, *Poesía de paso*
Cortázar, *Todos los fuegos el fuego*
Miguel Barnet, *Biografía de un cimarrón*
Louise Bennett, *Jamaica Labrish*
Luis Harss, *Los nuestros*
Jean Rhys, *Wide Sargasso Sea*
Amado, *Dona Flor e seus dois maridos*
First publication of *Mafalda*

1967

Death of Che Guevara in Bolivia
Autonomy of Dominica, Granada and St Lucia

García Márquez, *Cien años de soledad*
Cabrera Infante, *Tres tristes tigres*
Nicanor Parra, *Canciones rusas*
Cortázar, *La vuelta al día en ochenta mundos*
Fuentes, *Cambio de piel*
Sarduy, *De donde son los cantantes*
Néstor Sánchez, *Siberia Blues*
Paz, *Corriente alterna*
E.K. Brathwaite, *Rights of Passage*
Harris, *Tradition, the Writer and Society*
Founding of Caribbean Artists Movement (CAM)
Asturias wins Nobel Prize for Literature

1968

Student movement in Mexico culminates in the massacre of Tlatelolco Square
Octavio Paz resigns as Mexican ambassador to India
Military *coup* in Panama brings Omar Torrijos to power
In Peru, Juan Velasco Alvarado comes to power after a military *coup*
Brazilian Congress closed down
Guyana wins independence

Manuel Puig, *La traición de Rita Hayworth*
Antonio Cisneros, *Canto ceremonial contra un oso hormiguero*
Francisco Urondo, *Adolecer*
Enrique Buenaventura, *Los papeles del infierno* (4 plays)
Heberto Padilla, *Fuera del juego*
Antón Arrufat, *Los siete contra Tebas*
After winning the Casa de las Américas jury prize for poetry and drama respectively, Padilla and Arrufat are denounced by the Cuban Writers Union (UNEAC) for counter-revolutionary tendencies

1969

Barrientos, President of Bolivia, dies in an air crash
Popular rising in Córdoba, Argentina, known as the Cordobazo
Agitation and mutinies in Curaçao

Reinaldo Arenas, *El mundo alucinante*
Vargas Llosa, *Conversación en la Catedral*
José Emilio Pacheco, *No me preguntes cómo pasa el tiempo*
Puig, *Boquitas pintadas*
Fuentes, *La nueva novela latinoamericana*
Juan José Saer, *Cicatrices*
Amado, *A tenda dos milagres*

1970

Salvador Allende elected to the Presidency of Chile
Luis Echeverría becomes President of Mexico

Donoso, *El obsceno pájaro de la noche*
Borges, *El informe de Brodie*

Juan José Torres sworn in as President of Bolivia Black Power riots in Trinidad	José María Arguedas, *El zorro de arriba y el zorro de abajo*, published posthumously Vargas Llosa, Cortázar and Oscar Collazos, *Literatura en la revolución y revolución en la literatura*
1971	
Strikes and demonstrations in Córdoba and Rosario, Argentina Ex-President Aramburu murdered in Argentina Torres government in Bolivia overthrown by military *coup* 'March of the Empty Pots' mobilized by the Right in Chile to coincide with visit of Fidel Castro Death of Papa Doc Duvalier, dictator of Haiti; he is succeeded by his son Baby Doc	Neruda wins Nobel Prize for Literature Pizarnik, *Los pequeños cantos* and, *El infierno musical* Haroldo Conti, *En vida*
1972	
Earthquake devastates Managua 'State of Internal War' declared in Uruguay after Bordaberry takes over government	Luisa Valenzuela, *El gato eficaz* Jorge Díaz, *El lugar donde mueren los mamíferos* Castellanos, *Poesía no eres tú* Manuel Scorza, *Historia de Garabombo el invisible* Derek Walcott, *Another Life*
1973	
Military *coup* in Chile overthrows the government of Allende Juan Domingo Perón returns to Argentina	Lygia Fagundes Telles, *As meninas* Vargas Llosa, *Pantaleón y las visitadoras*
1974	
Death of Perón Sandinistas take National Palace in Managua and hold hostages until their manifesto is published and the guerrillas given safe passage	Carpentier, *Concierto barroco* Roa Bastos, *Yo el Supremo* Carpentier, *El recurso del método*
1975	
Velasco overthrown in Peru by an internal army *coup*; he is replaced by Morales Bermúdez Suriname wins full independence	Fuentes, *Terra nostra* García Márquez, *El otoño del patriarca* Brathwaite, *Other Exiles* Borges, *El libro de arena* Castellanos, *El eterno femenino*, published posthumously
1976	
New military *coup* in Argentina and the beginning of the 'Dirty War'	Puig, *El beso de la mujer araña* Piglia, *Nombre falso*
1977	
US and Panama sign treaty on the Panama Canal State of Siege declared in El Salvador	Luis Valenzuela, *Como en la guerra* Vargas Llosa, *La tía Julia y el escribidor* Nicanor Parra, *Sermones y prédicas del Cristo de Elqui*

Lezama Lima, *Oppiano Licario*, published posthumously
Luis Rafael Sánchez, *La guaracha del macho Camacho*
Lispector, *A hora da estrela*
Monsiváis, *Amor perdido*

1978

Major strikes in the ABC metallurgical plants in Brazil

Donoso, *Casa de campo*
Jorge Edwards, *Los convidados de piedra*
Sarduy, *Maitreya*
Osvaldo Soriano, *No habrá más penas ni olvido*

1979

Nicaraguan Revolution overthrows the Somoza dictatorship and brings the Sandinistas to power

Darcy Ribeiro, *Maíra*
Griselda Gambaro, *Dios no nos quiere contentos*
Cabrera Infante, *La Habana para un infante difunto*
V.S. Naipaul, *A Bend in the River*
Luis Zapata, *El vampiro de la Colonia Roma*

1980

January rising in El Salvador
Mariel boatlift of refugees from Cuba, including Reinaldo Arenas

Piglia, *Respiración artificial*
Rosario Ferré, *Sitio a Eros*
Saer, *Nadie nada nunca*
Luis Britto García, *Abrapalabra*
Carlos Monsiváis, *A ustedes les consta* (anthology of *crónicas*)
Rulfo, *Inframundo*
Mayra Jiménez (ed.), *Poesía campesina de Solentiname*
Manlio Argueta, *Un día en la vida*

1981

Crisis in El Salvador; arrival of US military advisers

Vargas Llosa, *La guerra del fin del mundo*
García Márquez, *Crónica de una muerte anunciada*
José Emilio Pacheco, *Las batallas en el desierto*
Sylvia Molloy, *En breve cárcel*
Roque Dalton, *Miguel Mármol*
Margo Glantz, *Las genealogías*

1982

Malvinas/Falklands War
Crisis in Peru due to Sendero Luminoso

Benedetti, *Primavera con esquina rota*
Isabel Allende, *La casa de los espíritus*
Paz, *Sor Juana Inés de la Cruz o las trampas de la fe*
Elena Poniatowska, *El último guajolote*
John Agard, *Man to Pan*
Saer, *El entenado*
Ferré, *Fábulas de la garza desangrada*

1983

US invasion of Grenada

Rubem Fonseca, *A grande arte*

Debt crisis Contadora Group seeks peace in Central America Elections in Argentina after seven years of military dictatorship	Cristina Peri Rossi, *El museo de los esfuerzos inútiles* *Me llamo Rigoberta Menchú . . .* M. Zapata Olivella, *Changó el gran putas*
1984	
Elections in Uruguay after ten years of military dictatorship	Vargas Llosa, *Historia de Mayta* Allende, *De amor y de sombra* Rama, *La ciudad letrada*
1985	
Transition to democracy in Brazil	Tomás Eloy Martínez, *La novela de Perón* Olive Senior, *Talking of Trees* Silviano Santiago, *Stella Manhattan* Angeles Mastretta, *Arráncame la vida*
1986	
Soviet bloc changes its relationship with Cuba with introduction of *perestroika*	Luis Cardoza y Aragón, *El río* Saer, *Glosa* P. Burnett (ed.), *Penguin Book of Caribbean Verse in English* S. Brown (ed.), *Caribbean Poetry Now*
1987	
Arias Peace Plan in Central America	Abel Posse, *Los perros del paraíso* V.S. Naipaul, *The Enigma of Arrival* Sarduy, *El Cristo de la rue Jacob* Fuentes, *Cristóbal nonato*
1988	
Pinochet calls referendum in Chile; beginning of transition to democracy Murder of Chico Mendes, leader of the rubber tappers, in Brazil	Sergio Ramírez, *Castigo divino* Nélida Piñón, *A doce canção de Caeyra* Puig, *Cae la noche tropical* Diamela Eltit, *El cuarto mundo* Coelho, *O alquimista* Peri Rossi, *Solitario de amor*
1989	
Democratic election in Chile Cuba introduces ‘Special Period in Time of Peace’ as Soviet bloc collapses US invasion of Panama	Cardenal, *Cántico cósmico* García Márquez, *El general en su laberinto* Laura Esquivel, *Como agua para chocolate* João Gilberto Noll, *Hotel Atlântico* Moacyr Scliar, *O olho enigmático* Néstor García Canclini, *Culturas híbridas* Napoleón Baccino Ponce de León, *Maluco* Roa Bastos returns to Paraguay after forty-two years in exile

1990	
Rettig Report in Chile In Nicaragua the Sandinistas are defeated in elections and replaced by a right-wing coalition led by Violeta Chamorro Assassination of Carlos Pizarro, presidential candidate of the M-19 in Colombia	Walcott, *Omeros* Edwards, *Adiós, Poeta...* (biography of Neruda) Allende, *Los cuentos de Eva Luna*
1991	
Cholera epidemic spreads from Peru	Humberto Ak'abal, *El animalero* Chico Buarque, *Estorvo* Senel Paz, *El lobo, el bosque y el hombre nuevo*
1992	
Columbian quincentenary, indigenous marches and organizing in Ecuador and elsewhere	Rigoberta Menchú awarded Nobel Peace Prize Piglia, *La ciudad ausente* Arenas, *Antes que anochezca*, published posthumously Sepúlveda, *Un viejo que leía novelas de amor* Poniatowska, *Tinísima* Walcott wins Nobel Prize for Literature
1993	
Brazilian President Fernando Collor impeached for financial irregularities	Sabina Berman, *Entre Villa y una mujer desnuda* Raúl Zurita, *La vida nueva*
1994	
NAFTA founded Zapatista rebellion in Chiapas coincides with founding of NAFTA Collor acquitted	García Márquez, *Del amor y otros demonios* Jaime Bayly, *No se lo digas a nadie* Fernando Vallejo, *La virgen de los sicarios* Eltit and Paz Errázuriz, *El infarto del alma*
1995	
Inauguration of Fernando Henrique Cardoso as Brazilian president Sandinista Front in Nicaragua splits	Buarque, *Benjamim* Ramírez, *Un baile de máscaras* José Emilio Pacheco, *El silencio de la luna*
1996	
Helms-Burton Act passed by US Congress strengthens economic embargo against Cuba Hostage crisis in Peru as Japanese embassy in Lima seized by Tupac Amaru Revolutionary Front Government and rebels sign peace agreement in Guatemala	Pedro Lemebel, *Loco afán: Crónicas del sidario* Rodrigo Rey Rosa, *El cojo bueno* García Márquez, *Noticia de un secuestro*
1997	
Peruvian hostage crisis ends in April as troops storm the embassy Acteal massacre in Chiapas	Piglia, *Plata quemada* Cabrera Infante, *Mea Cuba* Patricia Melo, *O matador*

1998

Pinochet named Senator for Life
Pinochet arrested in London with warrant for extradition issued by Spanish judge Baltasar Garzón

Ramírez, *Margarita está linda la mar*

1999

Elián González case begins in Miami

Bayly, *Yo amo a mi mamá*
Mario Bellatín, *Salón de belleza*
Benedetti, *Buzón de tiempo*
Cabrera Infante, *Cuentos casi completos*
Fuentes, *Los años con Laura Díaz*
Piñón, *La república de los sueños*
Melo, *Elogio da mentira*
Sepúlveda, *La última película de El Gordo y El Flaco*

2000

Mass strikes and indigenous rebellion against 'dollarization' of the economy brings down the government of Ecuador
Panama Canal handed over by US government
Mass movement in Bolivia
Fujimori re-elected to Peruvian Presidency; he later stands down

Vargas Llosa, *La fiesta del chivo*

2001

Aristide elected for second presidential term in Haiti
MAS-Pueblo formed in Bolivia
ALCA (FTAA-Free Trade of the Americas) founded at Quebec summit
December, the Argentinazo, a mass movement of protest at economic crisis, brings down three governments in quick succession

Fuentes, *Instinto de Inez*
Coelho, *O demonio e a Srta Pym*
Naipaul wins Nobel Prize for Literature

2002

Lula elected to Brazilian Presidency
Cocalero rising in Bolivia
Attempted coup in Venezuela

Mauricio Rosencof, *Las cartas que no llegaron*
Alfredo Bryce Echenique, *El huerto de mi amada*
Molloy, *El común olvido*
Antonio José Ponte, *Contrabando de sombras*
Bayly, *La mujer de mi hermano*
Martínez, *El vuelo de la reina*
Garcia Márquez, *Vivir para contarla*

2003

Kirchner elected to Argentine presidency
Bolivian crisis

Lemebel, *El Zanjón de la Aguada*
Vargas Llosa, *El Paraíso en la otra Esquina*
Bellessi, *La edad dorada*

A

Abreu, Caio Fernando

b. 1948, Santiago, Rio Grande do Sul, Brazil; d. 1996, Menino, Porto Alegre, Brazil

Short story writer and novelist

An urban writer, Abreu speaks for the generation that lived through the turmoil of the 1960s, the drug and sexual revolutions, and, in Brazil, through the political repression of the military regime. His fiction displays a poignant lyricism combined with elements of pop culture, and his characters typically deal with social and psychological alienation. In several of his stories, Abreu focuses on homosexuality and society's violent reaction to it. In *Onde andará Dulce Veiga?* (Where is Dulce Veiga?) (1989), a novel in which the fast, parodic, self-mocking style reflects the chaos of contemporary urban life, Abreu discusses AIDS, which he later described as a metaphor for the contemporary human condition. Already a widely acclaimed author, Abreu was the focus of national attention in 1995, when he publicly acknowledged having AIDS. In an interview with *Istoé* he brought this taboo subject to light, fostering public awareness and debate on the issues.

Further reading

Abreu, Caio Fernando (1977) *Pedras de Calcutá: Contos*, São Paulo: Editora Alfa-Omega.

—— (1983) *Triângulo das águas: Noturnos*, Rio de Janeiro: Editora Nova Fronteira.

—— (1997) *Teatro completo*, Porto Alegre: Editora Sulina: Instituto Estadual do Livro.

—— (2000) *Whatever happened to Dulce Veiga?: A B-novel*, Austin: University of Texas Press.

Arenas, F. (1999) 'Writing After Paradise and Before a Possible Dream: Brazil's Caio Fernando Abreu', *Luso-Brazilian Review* 36: 13–21.

—— (2002) 'Small Epiphanies in the Night of the World: The Writing of Caio Fernando Abreu', in F. Arenas and S.C. Quinlan (ed.), *Lusosex*, Minneapolis: University of Minnesota Press, 235–57.

CRISTINA FERREIRA-PINTO

Achugar, Hugo

b. 1943, Montevideo, Uruguay

Writer and critic

An accomplished poet, Achugar has received important awards for several of his books. He is also an influential critical voice, writing on a range of Latin American literature and cultural topics. A disciple of Angel **Rama**, his investigations aim at interpreting literary works in their historical context. He has made an important contribution to modernism (see **Spanish American modernism**), focusing on Uruguay in *Poesía y sociedad: Uruguay 1880–1911* (Poetry and Society. Uruguay 1880–1911) (1985). Since the 1980s, he has made Uruguayan society and culture the centre of his reflections as he examines the impact of the millennium.

Further reading

Achugar, Hugo (1985) *Poesía y sociedad: Uruguay, 1880–1911*, Montevideo: Arca.
—— (1996) *Narrativa vanguardista hispanoamericana*, Mexico City: Coordinación de Difusión Cultural, Dirección de Literatura and UNAM.
—— (2000) *Uruguay: Imaginarios culturales*, Pittsburgh: IILI.

MAGDALENA GARCÍA PINTO

Acosta, Agustín

b. 1886, Matanzas, Cuba; d. 1979, Miami, Florida, USA

Poet

Acosta was a precursor of the 1920s current of social poetry in Cuba, characterized by its nationalism in the face of US domination. A graduate in law, he was a political prisoner throughout the Machado regime. His volume *La Zafra* (The Harvest) (1926) included his best-known and most popular poems, 'Las carretas en la noche' (Carts in the Night) and 'Mediodía en el campo' (Midday in the Country). His later volumes include *Las islas desoladas* (The Desolate Islands) (1943) and *Caminos de hierro* (Iron Roads) (1963). He left Cuba in 1973.

Further reading

Acosta, Agustín (1936) *Los camellos distantes*, Habana: Molina.

WILFREDO CANCIO ISLA

Acosta, Delfina

b. 1956, Asunción, Paraguay

Writer

A pharmacist by profession, Acosta has been devoted to literature since she was young. Her first poems appeared in 1984 in *Poesía itinerante* (Itinerant Poetry), a collective publication. Subsequently she published two books of poetry: *Todas las voces, mujer . . .* (All the Voices, Woman . . .) (1986) and *La cruz del colibrí* (Hummingbird's Cross) (1993). Several of her works have received literary awards, including *Pilares de Asunción* (Pillars of Asunción) (1987) and the short story 'La fiesta en la mar' (The Party at Sea). *El viaje* (The Trip) (1995) is a collection of prize-winning short stories.

Further information

www.cervantesvirtual.com

TERESA MÉNDEZ-FAITH

Acosta, Oscar

b. 1933, Tegucigalpa, Honduras

Writer

Primarily a short story writer, Acosta has also published highly praised poems and essays and edited several anthologies. His *El arca* (The Chest) (1956) renovated the short story in Honduras, following new narrative themes and techniques introduced by **Borges**. His stories of the quotidian and intimate have a clear, sober and unaffected style. His poetry is intensely lyrical and flows naturally; rhythms are neither forced nor excessively free. Active in Honduras's cultural life and the winner of various prizes, Acosta has served as president of the Honduran PEN Club and the Press Association.

Further reading

Acosta, Oscar (1968) *Antología del cuento hondureño*, Tegucigalpa: Departamento de Extensión Universitaria.
—— (1971) *Exaltación de Honduras; antología*, Tegucigalpa: Universidad Nacional Autónoma de Honduras Dirección de Extensión Universitaria.
—— (1994) *Poesía menor*, Tegucigalpa: Editorial Universitaria.

LINDA J. CRAFT

Adán, Martín

b. 1907, Lima, Peru; d. 1985, Lima

Poet and novelist

Martín Adán was the pen name of Rafael de la Fuente Benavides. He published his first poems in ***Amauta***, the influential cultural and literary magazine founded by José Carlos **Mariátegui**, who remarked on the innovative format of Adán's modern sonnets as 'anti-sonnets'. Adán's *Itinerario de primavera* (Springtime Itinerary) (1928) is endowed with an anti-traditional tone that signals his affinity with the generation of writers who claimed that poets could aspire to the divine power of creation by the alchemy of the word.

Equally innovative in prose, his *Casa de cartón* (Cardboard Shack) (1928) is a vanguardist novel much admired for the linguistic experimentation that foregrounded the centrality of language. With a thin plot and undetermined characterization, it is a dynamic stylistic adventure of the first order. His major work is *Travesía de extramares* (Voyage beyond the Seas) (1950), where the poet is the explorer of the other side of life. It is a voyage into the unknown nourished by the yearning to break down boundaries, a quest powerfully reflected in its expressive system of lexical and syntactic experimentation, alluded to in the title of the collection. The volume consists of sonnets, and his strict adherence to traditional versification allows him to confine the maximum of emotion within the most prestigious of classical forms. The nautical metaphor of the title is one of the central images of the book. Adán shared with other poets, for example César **Moro**, the idea that poetry's reality is elsewhere, unreachable even for the poet him- or herself. He skilfully constructed a poetic system based on the Romantic music of Frédéric Chopin and the language of French symbolist poetry, hence its subtitle *Sonetos a Chopin* (Sonnets to Chopin). His other two important works are *La mano desasida: Canto a Macchu Picchu* (The Unclutched Hand: A Song to Macchu Picchu) (1964) and *Diario de un poeta* (Diary of a Poet) (1975).

Further reading

Adán, M. (1980) *Obra poética*, ed. R. Silva Santisteban, Lima: Edubanco.

—— (1982) *Obra en prosa*, ed. R. Silva Santisteban, Lima: Edubanco.

Bendezú, E. (1969) *La poética de Martín Adán*, Lima: Villanueva.

Higgins, J. (1982) *The Poet in Peru: Alienation and the Quest for a Super-Reality*, Liverpool: Francis Cairns.

Kinsella, J.M. (1997) 'Martín Adán', in V. Smith (ed.), *Encyclopedia of Latin American Literature*, London: Fitzroy Dearborn, 3–4.

Lauer, M. (1983) *Los exilios interiores: Una introducción a Martín Adán*, Lima: Hueso Húmero.

MAGDALENA GARCÍA PINTO

Adoum, Jorge Enrique

b. 1923, Ambato, Ecuador

Writer

An influential writer, Adoum's work constitutes an itinerary of the Ecuadorean experience, from colonial times to the present. A denunciation of the poverty and social problems of his native country are constants, as are the sense of alienation and the search for identity. He frequently experiments with language and the form and nature of poetry and narrative. His writings include *Los cuadernos de la tierra* (Notebooks of the Land) (1963), *No son todos los que están* (Not All Are Here) (1979), *Entre Marx y una mujer desnuda* (Between Marx and a Naked Woman) (1976), which was made into a film by Camilo Luzuriaga in 1996, and *Ciudad sin ángel* (City without Angel) (1995).

Further reading

Adoum, Jorge Enrique (1957) *Poesía del siglo XX: Valery, Rilke, Claudel, Lubicz-Milosz, Hughes, Eliot, Nicolás Guillén*, Quito: Editorial Casa de la Cultura Ecuatoriana.

—— (1997) *Los amores fugaces: Memorias imaginarias*, Quito: Seix Barral.

—— (1998) *Antología poética: 1949–1998*, Madrid: Visor.
—— (1999) *... ní están todos los que son: poesía*, Quito: Eskeletra.
Martínez, P.A. (1997) 'Jorge Enrique Adoum', in V. Smith (ed.), *Encyclopedia of Latin American Literature*, London: Fitzroy Dearborn, 5–8.

HUMBERTO E. ROBLES

Agard, John

b. 1949, British Guiana

Actor and writer

Author of several books for children in Guyanese vernacular, Agard started acting and writing during his teens, eventually touring the Caribbean with the All Ah We performance group. In 1977 he went to England, where he worked for the Commonwealth Institute. His poetry includes *Shoot Me with Flowers* (1973), *Quetzy de Saviour* (1976; a story in verse) and *Man to Pan*, winner of the **Casa de las Américas** prize (1982). In recognition of the oral sources of Caribbean poetry and story-telling, he coined the term 'poetsonian'.

Further reading

Agard, John (1982) *Man to Pan*, Ciudad de La Habana, Cuba: Casa de las Américas.
—— (1985) *Mangoes & Bullets: Selected and New Poems, 1972–84*, London: Pluto Press.
—— (1994) *From the Devil's Pulpit*, Cambridge, MA: Candlewick Press.
—— (2000) *Weblines*, Newcastle upon Tyne, England: Bloodaxe Books.

KEITH JARDIM

Aguilar, Rosario

b. 1938, León, Nicaragua

Novelist

Aguilar's novel *Aquel mar sin fondo ni playa* (That Sea without Depth or Beach) (1970) was the first published by a Nicaraguan woman. A member of one of León's most respected families, her father was a university chancellor and mentor to a generation of intellectuals. In her own writing Aguilar is concerned with feminine ontology, yet does not declare herself a feminist; although politically progressive, she never openly supported the Sandinistas. Her intimate, subjective narrative concentrates on the world of women, on their psychological obsessions and doubts. Her early novels were raw and unfinished, but her later work shows a greater sense of her craft.

Further reading

Aguilar, Rosario (1992) *La niña blanca y los pájaros sin pies*, Managua: Editorial Nueva Nicaragua.
—— (1998) *The Lost Chronicles of Terra Firma*, Fredonia, NY : White Pine Press.

SILVIA CHAVES AND ILEANA RODRÍGUEZ

Aguilera Malta, Demetrio

b. 1909, Guayaquil, Ecuador; d. 1982, Mexico City

Writer

A member of the **Guayaquil Group**, which also included Joaquín **Gallegos Lara** and Enrique **Gil Gilbert**, Aguilera Malta was co-author of ***Los que se van*** (Those Who Leave) (1930), which crystallized the nativist orientation of social protest literature that shaped writers of his generation. His later work *Don Goyo* (1933), *La isla virgen* (Solitary Island) (1942) and his masterpiece *Siete lunas y siete serpientes* (Seven Moons and Seven Serpents) (1970), explored legends, myth and superstitions. He also wrote historical novels and drama, which evolved from an early realism to expressionism. In 1979 he was named Ecuadorian ambassador to Mexico.

Further reading

Aguilera Malta, D. (1979) *Seven Serpents & Seven Moons*, trans. G. Rabassa, Austin: University of Texas Press.

—— (1980) *Don Goyo*, trans. J. and C. Brushwood, Clifton, NJ: Humana Press.
Waag, C.M. (1997) 'Demetrio Aguilera Malta', in V. Smith (ed.), *Encyclopedia of Latin American Literature*, London: Fitzroy Dearborn, 14–16.

MERCEDES M. ROBLES

Aguinis, Marcos

b. 1935, Río Cuarto, Córdoba, Argentina

Writer

A neurosurgeon and psychiatrist, Aguinis reflects in his writings a fascination with human drives and motivations. His fiction reflects his wide-ranging interests, including national politics (he was Secretary of Culture in the Alfonsín government), international affairs (notably concerning Israel and the Palestinians) and music. His works span subjects from the medieval Jewish philosopher Maimonides to probing analyses of authoritarianism and re-democratization. From *La cruz invertida* (The Inverted Cross) (1970), his writing gained a growing readership; *La gesta del marrano* (The Converso's Story) (1993), a novel based on the sixteenth-century trial of Francisco Maldonado da Silva, was a best-seller.

Further reading

Aguinis, Marcos (1989) *Profanación del amor*, Buenos Aires: Planeta.
—— (1993) *Un país de novela: Viaje hacia la mentalidad de los argentinos*, Buenos Aires: Planeta.
—— (1996) *Diálogos sobre la Argentina y el fin del milenio*, Buenos Aires: Editorial Sudamericana.
—— (2000) *Los iluminados*, Buenos Aires and Mexico City: Editorial Atlántida.

SAÚL SOSNOWSKI

Agustín, José

b. 1944, Acapulco, Mexico

Novelist

José Agustín was the Mexican literary scene's *enfant terrible* of the late 1960s and the leading novelist of 'La **Onda**', a literary and counter-cultural movement characterized by an extensive use of urban middle-class slang and an irreverent attitude towards Mexican ideology, institutions and authority. His recent works draw heavily on Jungian theory to explore the crisis in Mexican politics. His major novels include *De perfil* (In Profile) (1966), *Se está haciendo tarde (final en laguna)* (It's Getting Late (Ending in the Lake)) (1973); *Ciudades desiertas* (Deserted Cities) (1982), a satirical novel about the International Writing Program of the University of Iowa; and *Cerca del fuego* (Near the Fire) (1986).

Further reading

Agustín, J. (1978) *Literature and Censorship in Latin America Today: Dream within a Dream*, Denver: Dept of Foreign Languages and Literatures, University of Denver.
Carter, J.C.D. and D.L. Schmidt (eds) (1986) *Onda and Beyond*, Columbia: University of Missouri Press.
Schaffer, S. (1986) 'The Drug Experience in José Agustín's Fiction, *Mosaic* 19(4).
Serna, J.A. (1997) 'José Agustín', in V. Smith (ed.), *Encyclopedia of Latin American Literature*, London: Fitzroy Dearborn, 16–18.

CYNTHIA STEELE

Agustini, Delmira

b. 1886, Montevideo, Uruguay; d. 1914, Montevideo

Poet

Agustini's violent death age 28 at the hands of her former husband, Enrique Job Reyes, in 1914 continues to serve as a lens through which we read her poetry. Eduardo Galeano's brief entry in *El siglo del viento* (1914 Montevideo: Delmira) is succinct in its dramatic recapitulation of the juxtaposition of her murder with the legacy of her erotic poetry. Such a link appears inevitable, and not just because of the sensationalist nature of the photographs taken at the crime scene. The body, especially the female body, is everywhere present in Agustini's poetry. Sometimes fragmented, sometimes ecstatic with erotic desire and sometimes in pain, this body asserts itself above and beyond any symbolic representation.

Consternation, expansion, breaking and surprise are descriptions of Agustini's first entrance into public life with the publication of her poems as an adolescent. The strict limitations of her prosperous bourgeois milieu of early twentieth-century Uruguay, and her formation within the masculine-dominated trend of poetic *modernismo*, did not predict that her poetry would show such overt eroticism nor that she would, as her friend and fellow writer Manuel **Ugarte** noted, serve as the foundational figure of a new tradition of **women's writing** in Latin America. Although her poetry constantly refers to the search for transcendence, this movement towards fulfilment takes place in an extremely corporal universe, often a sexualized one. In Agustini's poetic universe there is a disorder of physicality, fragments and multiplications, and a resistance to viewing the body as a harmonious whole in a functional system. Her first book publication was *El libro blanco* (Frágil) (1907), followed by *Cantos de la mañana* (1910), and a third compilation (including the second book) *Los cálices vacíos* in 1913. Posthumously (1924) two more volumes were published, *Los astros del abismo* and *El rosario de Eros*.

Although Agustini has been read as both a mystic and as an 'unbridled erotic', more thoughtful readings of her poetry show us that her language about the body, and about the physical world in general, in its excess and repetition, and insistent fragmentation, does not even pretend to present a portrait of the exterior world of early twentieth-century Uruguay. There is no overt representation of the important processes of modernization of her epoch. The universe represented in her poetry is as distanced from contemporary events, as is the idealized 'reino interior' designed by **Rodó** in *Ariel* (see ***Ariel* and *arielismo***). Yet the integration of spirit, body and purpose proposed by Rodó is exploded by Agustini in a dynamic whirl of dislocations.

Further reading

Agustini, D. (1993) *Poesías completas*, ed. M. García-Pinto, Madrid: Cátedra.

—— (1999) *Poesías completas*, ed. A. Caceres, Montevideo: Ediciones de la Plaza.

Alvar, M. (1989) 'Delmira Agustini', in C.A. Solé and M.I. Abreu (eds), *Latin American Writers*, New York: Scribners, 2, 649–54.

Escaja, T. (ed.) (2000) *Delmira Agustini y el Modernismo: Nuevas propuestas de género*, Rosario: Beatriz Viterbo.

—— (2001) *Salomé decapitada. Delmira Agustini y la estética finisecular de la fragmentación*. Amsterdam and New York: Rodopi.

Molloy, S. (1985) 'Dos lecturas del cisne: Rubén Darío y Delmira Agustini', in Patricia González and E. Ortega (eds), *La sartén por el mango*, Río Piedras, PR: Ediciones Huracán.

Scott, R. (1997) 'Delmira Agustini', in V. Smith (ed.), *Encyclopedia of Latin American Literature*, London: Fitzroy Dearborn, 18–20.

Silva, C. (1972) *Pasión y gloria de Delmira Agustini*, Buenos Aires: Editorial Losada.

GWEN KIRKPATRICK

Aínsa, Fernando

b. 1937, Palma de Mallorca, Spain

Writer

Aínsa's fiction includes short stories and two novels – *El testigo* (The Witness) (1964) and *Con cierto asombro* (With Some Surprise) (1968). His essays address literary criticism, the analysis of cultural movements – in *La narración y el teatro en los años 20* (Narrative and Theatre of the Twenties) (1968) and *Nuevas fronteras de la narrativa uruguaya (1960–1993)* (New Frontiers of Uruguayan Narrative) (1993) – and seminal reflections on Latin American culture in volumes such as *Identidad cultural de Iberoamérica en su narrativa* (Cultural Identity of Iberoamerica in its Narrative) (1986). Ainsía is a regular contributor to journals and newspapers in Uruguay and works for UNESCO in Paris.

Further reading

Aínsa, Fernando (1977) *Los buscadores de la Utopía: La significación novelesca del espacio latinoamericano*, Caracas: Monte Avila.
—— (1986) *Identidad cultural de Iberoamérica en su narrativa*, Madrid: Gredos.
—— (1999) *La reconstrucción de la utopía*, Buenos Aires: Ediciones del Sol.

CELINA MANZONI

Aira, César

b. 1949, Coronel Pringles, Argentina

Writer

A friend and disciple of Osvaldo **Lamborghini**, Aira has published more than twenty books, among them *Ema, la cautiva* (Emma, the Captive) (1981), a parody of nineteenth-century frontier literature. Concerned in general with recurrent themes such as perception, childhood and the nature of 'the Argentine', his novels always display a subtle humour as well as rich and explosive descriptions. His novel *La abeja* (The Bee) (1996) is a satire of the terrors felt by the Argentine middle classes.

Further reading

Aira, César (1981) *Ema, la cautiva*, Buenos Aires: Editorial de Belgrano.
—— (1997) *La serpiente*, Rosario, Argentina: Beatriz Viterbo Editora.
—— (1998) *The Hare*, London and New York: Serpent's Tail.
—— (2001) *Un sueño realizado*, Buenos Aires: Alfaguara.

DANIEL LINK

Ak'abal, Humberto

b. 1952, Totonicapán, Guatemala

Writer

Ak'abal, whose name means 'Dawn' in his native Quiché, is a prime late twentieth-century example of the re-emergence of Mayan literature in Guatemala. The grandson of Mayan religious leaders, he grew up poor and without formal Spanish-language schooling. His first collection of poems, *El animalero* (1991), met with immediate success. Ak'abal writes in Quiché and then translates his work into an inflected Spanish. His poems are imbued with Mayan images and lore. Often they are humorous presentations of life in the country, but at times they become oppositional and political.

Further reading

Ak'abal, Humberto (1995) *El animalero*, Guatemala: Editorial Cholsamaj.

MARC ZIMMERMAN

Alberto, Eliseo

b. 1951, Arroyo Naranjo, Cuba

Writer and screenwriter

A member of one of the most important literary families of Cuba, Alberto was the son of poet Eliseo **Diego**. His aunt and uncle are also important writers. He is 'an all round literary man': he has written poetry, essays, memoirs and screenplays, but he enjoys international success for his novels. In 1998 *Caracol Beach* received the first Alfaguara International Prize, shared with Tomas Borge. Since 1997, when he published *Informe contra mí mismo* (Report Against Myself), he has demonstrated his critical views of the Cuban regime. Although he has resided in Mexico for more than ten years, Cuban reality, transfigured by his poetic and realist prose, is always the obsessive theme of his writing. He has taught at the International School of Cinema in San Antonio de los Baños, and at the Sundance Institute. Other works include *La eternidad por fin comienza un lunes* (Finally, Eternity Begins One Monday) (1992) *and La fábula de José* (Jose's Fable) (2000). His screenplays include *El elefante y la bicicleta* (The Elephant and the Bicycle) (1995) and *Guantanamera* (1995).

Further reading

Alberto, Eliseo (1997) *Informe contra mí mismo*, Madrid: Alfaguara.

—— (1998) *Caracol Beach*, Buenos Aires: Alfaguara.

—— (2000) *La fábula de José*, Mexico City: Alfaguara.

CÉSAR PÉREZ

Alcántara Almánzar, José

b. 1946, Santo Domingo, Dominican Republic

Writer and critic

Sociologist and critic, Alcántara Almánzar is a prolific short story writer with several published short story collections, among them *Callejón sin salida* (Blind Alley) (1975) and *La carne estremecida* (Quivering Flesh) (1989). Two of his books have received awards at the Premio Anual de Cuento (Annual Short Story Prize). As a critic, he has published articles and reviews in magazines and newspapers since the early 1970s; he is also the editor of an anthology of Dominican literature and has taught at several universities in the Dominican Republic.

Further reading

Alcántara Almánzar, José (1972) *Antología de la literatura dominicana*, Santo Domingo: ECD (Editorial Cultural Dominicana).

—— (1979) *Estudios de poesía dominicana*, Santo Domingo: Editora Alfa y Omega.

—— (1990) *Los escritores dominicanos y la cultura*, Santo Domingo: Instituto Tecnológico de Santo Domingo.

FERNANDO VALERIO-HOLGUÍN

Alegría, Ciro

b. 1909, Sartimbanba, Huamachuco, Peru; d. 1967, Trujillo, Peru

Writer

A key figure in ***indigenismo***, Ciro Alegría's 1941 novel *El mundo es ancho y ajeno* (Broad and Alien is the World) marked a turning point from the brutal social realism of earlier representations of the Indian in works such as Jorge **Icaza**'s *Huasipungo* (1934) and Alegría's own *Los perros hambrientos* (The Hungry Dogs) (1938). *El mundo* …, by contrast, portrays a complex Indian community which first resists then unsuccessfully seeks integration into a wider Peruvian society. The book's vision reflected Alegría's lifelong involvement with APRA, whose central idea was a notion of 'community' rooted in an Indian past as represented, somewhat idealistically, by Alegría.

Further reading

Alegría, Ciro (1945) *Novelas completas*, Madrid: Aguilar.

Bünte, Hans (1961) *Ciro Alegría y su obra, dentro de la evolución literaria Hispanoamericana*, Lima: J. Mejía Baca.

Rodríguez Luis, J. (1980) *Hermenéutica y praxis del indigenismo: La novela indigenista de Clorinda Matto a José María Arguedas*, Mexico City: Fondo de Cultura Económica, 111–21.

Urrello, A. (1989) 'Ciro Alegría', in C.A. Solé and M.I. Abreu (eds), *Latin American Writers*, New York: Scribners, 3, 1099–1103.

MIKE GONZALEZ

Alegría, Claribel

b. 1924, Managua, Nicaragua

Writer

One of the most important Central American writers of the second half of the twentieth century, Alegría is an outstanding poet and narrator, with more than twenty-five titles to her name and translations into a dozen languages. Her first publication was *Anillo de silencio* (Ring of Silence) (1948), but it was *Cenizas de Izalco* (1966) (Ashes of Izalco; 1989) that gained her international renown. Written in collaboration with her husband Darwin J. Flakoll (the translation is his), *Cenizas de Izalco* describes the 1932 genocide of the Izalco Indians. It is important because of its testimonial nature and because of its female narrator, who eventually confesses her love for a visitor from the USA, exposing the repression and unhappiness of life with her husband. In this respect, *Cenizas de Izalco* is a revolutionary narrative, contesting Latin American political, social and aesthetic paradigms.

Alegría's poetry reflects both her literary skill and her social preoccupations. From *Vía única* (Only Way) (1965), to *Y este poema río* (And This Poem-River) (1988), we see the relentless search for a simple poetic language which probes the limits of the establishment. Her poems are tender and beautiful, but always subvert somehow the tradition and canons that sustain them. *Luisa en el país de la realidad* (Luisa in Realityland) (1987) is an excellent collection of poems that presents life in a Salvadoran town through the eyes of a little girl. In this intelligent reversal of Lewis Carroll's famous work, childhood innocence clearly formulates and denounces the atrocities and cruelty of Salvadoran society.

Alegría has contributed important texts to the history of the Central American people's struggles for freedom and democracy. *No me agarran viva: La mujer salvadoreña en lucha* (They Won't Take Me Alive: Salvadoran Women in Struggle for National Liberation) (1987) is an impressive and painful ***testimonio*** of women's involvement in that civil war. On the other hand, there are books such as *Pueblo de Dios y de Mandinga* (Family Album) (1985), about an artists' community in Sitges, on the Mediterranean coast of Spain. To these accomplishments Alegría adds a dozen and a half English translations, many in collaboration with Flakoll, which provide wider access to new and high-quality young Latin American poets and narrators. She is currently living in Nicaragua, although she continues to travel widely; she holds Salvadoran citizenship.

Further reading

Alegría, Claribel (1982) *Nicaragua, la revolución sandinista: Una crónica política, 1855–1979*, Mexico City: Ediciones Era.

—— (1987) *They Won't Take Me Alive: Salvadorean Women in Struggle for National Liberation*, London: Women's Press.

Finnegan, N. (1997) 'Claribel Alegría', in V. Smith (ed.), *Encyclopedia of Latin American Literature*, London: Fitzroy Dearborn, 20–3.

NICASIO URBINA

Alegría, Fernando

b. 1918, Santiago, Chile

Writer

In his first novel *Recabarren* (1938), Alegría rescues the marginalized figure of a leftist leader, modifying the traditional repertoire of national icons. His subsequent novels reveal a dissident position concerning the authorized versions of history and official memory. While *El paso de los gansos* (The Goosestep) (1980) and *Coral de guerra* (War Chorale) (1979) present military dictatorship in Chile through fragmentation and a plurality of voices, *La rebelión de los placeres* (The Pleasure Rebellion) (1990) is an ironic postmodern re-elaboration of history. Alegría is also the author of critical studies on Chilean and Latin American literature, and is Professor Emeritus at Stanford University.

Further reading

Alegría, Fenando (1980) *The Chilean Spring*, Pittsburgh: Latin American Literary Review Press.

Donahue, Moraima de Semprún (1981) *Figuras y contrafiguras en la poesía de Fernando Alegría*, Pittsburgh: Latin American Literary Review Press.

LUCÍA GUERRA

Alexis, Jacques Stephen

b. 1922, Gonaives, Haiti; d. 1961, place unknown

Novelist and essayist

One of Haiti's major novelists, Alexis's life was tragically cut short in a political murder. Born during the US Occupation, he was the son of the Haitian diplomat and novelist Stephen Alexis. He was influenced at an early age by the Marxist politics of Jacques **Roumain** and later by

surrealism thanks to André Breton's visit to Haiti and Alejo **Carpentier**'s theory of *lo* ***real maravilloso*** (marvellous realism). He rose to prominence as one of the leaders of the student movement La Ruche, which played a leading role in the overthrow of the government in 1946. After studying neurology in Paris, he returned home where he wrote his major works, lyrical and dense novels about the Haitian masses. Like Alejo Carpentier, Alexis used history as a source of narrative. His 1955 novel, ***Compère Général Soleil*** (Comrade General Sun), dealt with the massacre of Haitian cane-cutters in the Dominican Republic by General Trujillo's troops. *Les arbres musiciens* (The Musical Trees) (1957) documented the effects of the Catholic Church's anti-superstition campaign to get rid of the Vodun religion. His later work tended to be less conventionally historical, taking greater liberties with the **novel** form. An interest in the marvellous is ever present in Alexis's fiction and his 1959 novel *L'espace d'un cillement* (In the Twinkling of an Eye), less constrained by recorded history, is a symbolic narrative in which a Dominican prostitute and a Cuban mechanic encounter each other in a Haitian brothel. His last published work was a book of folktales, which most fully elaborated his concept of the marvellous in the popular imagination. *Romancero aux étoiles* (Songbook to the Stars) (1960) recounts a number of tales both traditional and invented which evoke the Haitian people's creative response to their history of privation and dislocation.

Like his predecessor, Jacques Roumain, Alexis remained a dedicated Marxist for his entire life and while in Paris as a student he became a member of the French Communist Party. On his return to Haiti, he founded the Party of Popular Accord and in 1959 published his *Manifesto for Haiti's Second Independence*, a continuation of the Marxist analysis of Haitian society begun by Roumain in 1934. Alexis is best known for his 1956 paper on the 'Marvellous Realism of the Haitians', presented at the First Congress of Black Writers in Paris. Because of his opposition to the Duvalier regime, he went into exile and travelled to the Soviet Union, China and Cuba. His life came to a tragic end in 1961 at the hands of the Tontons Macoutes after landing clandestinely in Haiti.

Further reading

Antoine, Y. (1993) *Semiologie et personnages romanesques chez Jacques Stephen Alexis*, Montreal: Ed. Balzac.

Dash, J.M. (1975) *Jacques Stephen Alexis*, Toronto: Black Images.

Hoffman, L.F. (1997) 'Jacques-Stéphen Alexis', in V. Smith (ed.), *Encyclopedia of Latin American Literature*, London: Fitzroy Dearborn, 25–27.

J. MICHAEL DASH

Allende, Isabel

b. 1942, Lima, Peru

Writer

Isabel Allende worked as a journalist in Santiago, Chile until the 1973 military *coup d'état* that ousted and assassinated President Salvador Allende, her uncle. She then went into exile in Venezuela, and began writing fiction in 1981 when she was unable to find work as a journalist. After the publication of her third novel in English, she moved to the USA, where she currently resides.

Permanent exile and the constant changing of countries and cultures has marked many twentieth-century Latin American writers and **intellectuals**. Allende is one of these writers in exile. In her first two books, *La casa de los espíritus* (The House of the Spirits) (1982) and *De amor y sombras* (Of Love and Shadows) (1984), the context of the stories is Chile, although never mentioned in the former, but clearly suggested by historical figures. As her work brought her international acclaim and best-seller status (see **best-sellers**), her fictional settings became less anchored in a Latin American context, as is clear in her novel *Eva Luna* (1987). The collection of short stories entitled *Los cuentos de Eva Luna* (The Stories of Eva Luna) (1990), offer the fictional stories of the protagonist Eva Luna, alluded to but not included in the 1987 work. Allende uses repetition and allusion to former characters as well as the theme of writing about writing a story as recurrent elements in her work. She has remarked that both Eva Luna books marked the emergence of a new woman that had learned to appreciate womanhood as a force rather than a handicap in life. Since then, she has increasingly shaped her view of the world from a feminist viewpoint, a stance that she was hesitant to take at the beginning of her literary career. Her fifth novel, *El plan infinito* (The Infinite Plan) (1991), takes place in California. Her novels, *La hija de la fortuna* (Daughter of Fortune) and *Retrato en sepia* (Portrait in Sepia), were both published in 1999. Her most recent work, *Ciudad de las bestias* (City of Beasts) (2002), was followed in 2003 by a book of memoirs of her native country *Mi país imaginario* (My Imaginary Country).

Another recent best-seller, *Paula* (1994), is named after her daughter, who suffered a long illness and died at the age of 28. She wrote the book during the several months she spent in a hospital and in her hotel room in Madrid. Coincidentally, these are also the time markers that indicate the division of the book into two parts. Her vigil over her daughter's illness provided the context for reflecting on her own life trajectory, which she records in great detail. She harks back to her life in Chile, giving a colourful recollection of picturesque relatives with whom she grew up, her youth and romance with her first husband, the military *coup* against her uncle, President Salvador Allende, her difficulties under General Augusto Pinochet's regime, her leaving Chile, settling in Caracas, Venezuela, and her immediate success as a world-acclaimed writer of stories whose romantic component has had an extraordinary appeal worldwide. Allende is the first Latin American woman of letters to succeed in the international literary scene on such a grand scale (see **women's writing**). She has acquired celebrity status, simultaneously providing new possibilities for other women in the literary field and bringing attention to women's literary production. Her novels have been translated into many languages.

Further reading

Cortínez, V. (2002) 'Isabel Allende', in C. Solé and K. Müller-Bergh (eds), *Latin American Writers: Supplement I*, New York: Scribners, 1–14.

García Pinto, M. (1991) 'Isabel Allende', in *Women Writers of Latin America. Intimate Histories*, trans. Trudy Balch and M. García Pinto, Austin: University of Texas Press, 23–42.

Guerra Cunningham, L. (ed.) (1990) *Splintering Darkness: Latin American Women Writers in Search for themselves*, Pittsburgh: Latin American Literary Review Press.

Hart, P. (1989) *Narrative Magic in the Fiction of Isabel Allende*, Cranbury, NJ: Associated University Presses.

Shaw, D. (1997) 'Isabel Allende', in V. Smith (ed.), *Encyclopedia of Latin American Literature*, London: Fitzroy Dearborn, 115–17.

MAGDALENA GARCÍA PINTO

Allfrey, Phyllis Shand

b. 1908, Dominica, West Indies; d. 1986, Dominica

Writer and politician

A poet and journalist as well as a leading political figure in Dominica, Allfrey settled in England in the 1930s, becoming an active member of the Labour Party. In 1953 she published *The Orchid House*, a multi-generational novel about a white creole family on a Caribbean island moving towards independence, after which she returned to Dominica. She was a founder member of the Dominica Labour Party in 1954, and later served as Minister of Labour for the Federation of the West Indies. She edited the Dominican *Star* (1965–82) and published several volumes of poetry.

Further reading

Allfrey, Phyllis Shand (1982) *The Orchid House*, London: Virago.

LOUIS JAMES

Allsopp, Richard

b. 1923, British Guiana

Lexicographer and writer

In 1996, Oxford University Press published Allsopp's *Dictionary of Caribbean English Usage*, a monumental work involving research in eighteen Caribbean territories from Guyana through the Bahamas and Belize. It was the culmination of a long and distinguished career in Caribbean lexicography. Allsopp earned his PhD at the University of London in 1962, and lectured for many years at the University of the West Indies' Barbados campus. His many awards and academic posts include the Crane Gold Medal for Education, British Guiana 1958 and a Visiting Lectureship at Howard University. He has contributed over sixty essays on Caribbean English usage and remains one of the most eminent scholars in his field.

KEITH JARDIM

Alone

b. 1891, Santiago, Chile; d. 1979, Santiago

Writer

For half a century, Alone (Hernán Díaz Arrieta) was a polemical figure in Chilean letters. His book reviews in *El Diario Ilustrado* and *El Mercurio* could determine the commercial success of a book. Although he advocated subjectivity and impressionism in literary criticism, his books offer a well-organized overview of the Chilean literary canon. *Memorialistas chilenos* (Chilean Memoir Writers) (1960) is a comprehensive study of autobiographical texts; Alone's own memoirs, entitled *Pretérito imperfecto* (Past Imperfect) (1976), and his *Historia personal de la literatura chilena* (Personal History of Chilean Culture) (1954), offer important insights into Chilean history and culture. His film criticism has been collected as *Alone y la crítica de cine* (Alone and Cinema Criticism) (1993).

Further reading

Díaz Arrieta, Hernán (1962) *Los cuatro grandes de la literatura chilena durante el siglo XX*, Santiago de Chile: Zig Zag.

—— (1997) *Alone, 50 años de crónica literaria: El vicio impune*, ed. A. Calderón, Santiago: Ediciones RiL.

—— (2001) *Diario íntimo, 1917–1947*, Santiago de Chile: Empresa Editora Zig Zag.

LUCÍA GUERRA

Altazor

Vicente **Huidobro**'s *Altazor* (1919–31), a meditation upon language and the subject, is one of the most radical experiments in Latin American poetry. In the preface, the poet's doppelgänger – Altazor – nostalgically recreates a fable of his own beginnings, plunging the reader into seven cantos enacting the character's supposed fall from grace. After the third canto, the hero disappears in a sea of words that perversely try to create a linguistic universe without a subject. In *Altazor*, words are troped upon themselves by means of visual games. The last canto is a random collection of vowels hurling through space, opaque remnants from the debris of words: sounds crystallized, the skin and the cloth of Altazor's broken parachute.

Further reading

Huidobro, Vicente (1988) *Altazor, or, A voyage in a parachute (1919): A poem in VII Cantos*, St Paul, MN: Graywolf Press.

JOSÉ QUIROGA

Alturas de Macchu Picchu

Written after a visit to the abandoned city of Machu Picchu in 1945, the poem 'Alturas de Macchu Picchu' (Heights of Machu Picchu) is included in Pablo **Neruda**'s ***Canto general*** (1950). Its twelve metaphorically charged sections stage a mystical encounter between the poetic subject and the monumental Inca city of Machu Picchu. The first five parts describe a cosmological quest for truth; the fifth signals the ascent of the poet to a city which resonates with ancestral history. The final sections delve into the human and American past concealed beneath the ruins.

Neruda's text appeals to a dead 'brother' who embodies the ancestors of the indigenous South America as well as the oppressed people of the present and future.

Further reading

Felstiner, John (1980) *Translating Neruda: The Way to Macchu Picchu*, Stanford: Stanford University Press.

Neruda, Pablo (1986) *The Heights of Macchu Picchu*, Bandon, OR: Songs Before Zero Press.

LUIS E. CÁRCAMO-HUECHANTE

Alvarez Benítez, Mario Rubén

b. 1954, Potrero Yvaté, Paraguay

Writer

A poet and professor of Guarani, Alvarez Benítez was twice awarded first prize by the Instituto de Cultura Hispánica del Paraguay (1977, 1979) for his poetry. His poems have appeared in collective volumes: *... Y ahora la palabra* (... And Now the Word) (1979), *Poesía-taller* (Poetry Workshop) (1982) and *Poesía itinerante* (Itinerant Poetry) (1984). In 1992 he published *La sangre insurrecta* (The Insurgent Blood), and later translated into Guarani *Ecos de monte y de arena* (Echoes of Woodland and Sand) (1994), a book of ecological short stories by Luisa Moreno de Gabaglio, under the title *Kapi'yva*. He has also worked as a radio journalist.

TERESA MÉNDEZ-FAITH

Alvarez Gardeazábal, Gustavo

b. 1945, Tuluá, Colombia

Writer and polititian

Alvarez Gardeazábal was one of Colombia's most productive and irreverent novelists. His early works, *La tara del papa* (The Pope's Idiocy) (1971), ***Cóndores no entierran todos los días*** (They Don't Bury Condors Every Day) (1972), about La Violencia, *Dabeiba* (1973) and *El bazar de los idiotas* (The Idiots' Bazaar) (1974), were strong social critiques set in Tuluá, a small town in Western Colombia near Cali. His most virulent satire of the local oligarchy was *Los mios* (My People) (1981). He is also a journalist, and in the 1990s was actively involved in politics. After serving as mayor of Tuluá and as governor of Cauca department, he spent several years in prison for alleged involvement with drug traffickers, although an international campaign cast these accusations in doubt; he was released in 2002.

Further reading

Alvarez Gardeazábal, Gustavo (1991) *Bazaar of the Idiots*, Pittsburgh: Latin American Literary Review Press.

—— (2000) *La novela colombiana, entre la verdad y la mentira*, Bogotá: Plaza & Janés.

Williams, R.L. (ed.) (1977) *Aproximaciones a Gustavo Alvarez Gardeazábal*, Bogotá: Plaza y Janés.

RAYMOND L. WILLIAMS

Amado, Jorge

b. 1912, Itabuna, Bahia, Brazil, d. 2002, Salvador, Bahia

Novelist

The social conflicts, customs and rich popular culture of Amado's native Bahia provided most of the raw material for his writing which, during a literary career of over sixty years, passed through several distinct phases. He established himself as one of Brazil's major social realist novelists in the 1930s with works such as *Suor* (Sweat) (1934), *Mar morto* (Sea of Death) (1936) and *Capitães de areia* (Captains of the Sands) (1937). These works focus on the struggle of the Bahian working classes, attempting to show how their acquisition of political consciousness and development of solidarity opens the way for social change.

The communist sympathies underlying his works resulted in Amado's arrest on several occasions during the Estado Novo dictatorship, and in the public burning of copies of his novels in 1937. For many critics, the high point of his documentary realism was reached with the publication in 1943 of

Terras do sem fim (translated as The Violent Land). Amado's parents had been involved in *cacao* planting, and the violence of the land disputes that accompanied the expansion of *cacao* production in Southern Bahia provided the theme for that highly acclaimed work. By the mid-1940s Amado was fully active in the Brazilian Communist Party, which was legalized again following the collapse of the Estado Novo in 1945. That same year he was elected Federal Deputy for the Party, representing the state of São Paulo. He served until 1947 when the party was outlawed once more, and he went into exile.

Amado's writing during this period was shaped by the dictates of **socialist realism**, as proposed by the Communist Party, and culminated with the publication in 1954 of *Os subterraneos da liberdade* (The Freedom Underground), a trilogy which focused on the struggle of the Brazilian Communist Party during the dictatorship. The anti-Stalin revelations of the mid-1950s and the Soviet invasion of Hungary finally led Amado to leave the Communist Party in 1956 and to reject socialist realism. A new phase of his writing career was launched in 1958 with the publication of *Gabriela, cravo e canela* (Gabriela, Clove and Cinnamon), a highly popular novel of comedy and social satire, far removed from the overtly political works of previous years. This set the pattern for the narratives that followed, such as *Os pastores da noite* (Shepherds of the Night) (1964) and, in 1966, *Dona Flor e seus dois maridos* (Dona Flor and her Two Husbands). These works, relying considerably on humour, irony and regional colour, confirmed Amado as Brazil's best-selling novelist.

Always keenly interested in Bahian popular culture, Amado gave Candomblé and ***literatura de cordel*** a central role in his novels. The Afro-Brazilian deities central to Candomblé ritual intervene directly in the plot of his novel *A tenda dos milagres* (Tent of Miracles) (1969), which Amado declared to be his most important work, since it focuses on what he believed to be one of the most vital and yet frequently neglected issues in Brazilian society: that of racial prejudice and the role of black culture. *Tereza Batista cansada de guerra* (Tereza Batista, Home from the Wars) (1972) not only includes popular religion but also draws on the traditions of *literatura de cordel* as the basis for its themes, tone and structure. For Amado, popular culture provides the means for examining the continual resistance of the poor, although what results at times is exoticism.

Amado was a prolific writer who also produced biographies, short stories, children's books and, to mark his eightieth birthday in 1992, a book of memoirs, but it is his novels, now translated into nearly forty languages, that made him Brazil's best-known twentieth-century writer. The popularity of his work has undoubtedly been increased through the many adaptations that have been made of his novels for television soap operas and for the cinema, with wide acclaim given to such films as *Dona Flor e seus dois maridos* by Bruno Barreto, *A tenda dos milagres* by Nelson Pereira dos Santos and *Gabriela, cravo e canela* by Luiz Carlos Barreto and Bruno Barreto. Amado's work has thus reached new audiences in Brazil and abroad, well beyond the novel-reading public. He became a national celebrity, and in 1986 a government decree founded the Casa de Jorge Amado Foundation in Salvador to further promote his work. However, he also generated more controversy than any other contemporary Brazilian writer. Some argue that his writing became increasingly dependent on the market, which compromised both its political commitment and its quality. In his defence, others claim that his long-lasting popularity testified to his considerable skills as a narrator, and that he never abandoned social protest but simply found more sophisticated techniques through which to express it.

Further reading

Chamberlain, B. (1990) *Jorge Amado*, New York: Twayne.

Dinneen, M. (1997) 'Jorge Amado', in V. Smith (ed.), *Encyclopedia of Latin American Literature*, London: Fitzroy Dearborn, 31–3.

Vieira, N.H. (2002) 'Jorge Amado', in C. Solé and K. Müller-Bergh (eds), *Latin American Writers: Supplement I*, New York: Scribners, 15–30.

Vincent, J.S. (1989) 'Jorge Amado', in C.A. Solé and M.I. Abreu (eds), *Latin American Writers*, New York: Scribners, 3, 1153–62.

MARK DINNEEN

Amauta

A cultural magazine edited monthly by José Carlos **Mariátegui** in Lima between 1926 and 1930, *Amauta* (the title comes from the Quechua name given to the philosophers of the Inca State) was the leading channel of Mariátegui's socialist, anti-imperialist and indigenist ideas as well as a continentally distributed cultural magazine. In his first editorials, Mariátegui described the magazine as the starting point of a new era, during which Peruvian problems would be studied scientifically and from a socialist perspective.

Mariátegui began publishing *Amauta* during Augusto B. Leguía's dictatorship, and the magazine was repeatedly closed down for political reasons. Contributions to the magazine came from all over Latin America as well as from leading European left-wing intellectuals. *Amauta* also reproduced and translated articles, for example Leon Trotsky's article on Lenin and Sigmund Freud's introduction to psychoanalysis.

Amauta's most distinctive aspect, however, was Mariátegui's new interpretation of the role of indigenous people, which rejected the previous idealized or paternalistic attitudes of Latin American intellectuals. That is why *Amauta* included many articles on the indigenous cultures. The magazine was striking, illustrated with *indigenista* graphics inspired by pre-Columbian art.

Amauta ceased to appear shortly after Mariátegui died in 1930. However, the magazine still maintains its symbolic continental importance, not least because its role was later glorified as a crucial part of Mariátegui's life work by the Peruvian Editorial Amauta and by Latin American leftist **intellectuals**.

See also: *indigenismo*

Further reading

Amauta (1982) *Edición facsímil*, Lima: Empresa Editora Amauta S.A.

Tauro, A. (1974) *Amauta y su influencia*, Lima: Empresa Editora Amauta.

JUSSI PAKKASVIRTA

Amorim, Enrique

b. 1900, Salto, Uruguay; d. 1960, Salto

Writer

Amorim wrote in various genres but is remembered for his novels with rural settings and his questioning of the romantic myth of the gaucho. His novels included *La carreta* (The Cart) (1929) and *El paisano Aguilar* (Aguilar the Countryman) (1934). In 1947 he joined the Communist Party, and in 1950 left Argentina, where he had been living, for political reasons. Amorim also wrote two crime novels, *El asesino desvelado* (The Murderer Revealed) (1945), published by **Borges** and **Bioy Casares** in the *Séptimo círculo* (Seventh Circle) series, and *Feria de farsantes* (Rogues' Fair) (1952).

Further reading

Amorim, Enrique (1943) *The Horse and its Shadow*, trans. R.L. O'Connell and J. Graham Luján, New York: Scribners.

—— (1962) *La trampa del pajonal, cuentos y novelas*, Montevideo: Ediciones Del Rio de la Plata.

Ruffinelli, J. (1997) 'Enrique Amorim', in V. Smith (ed.), *Encyclopedia of Latin American Literature*, London: Fitzroy Dearborn, 36–7.

GONZALO AGUILAR

Ampuero, Roberto

b. 1953, Valparaíso, Chile

Novelist

Ampuero is the most important practitioner of **crime fiction** in Chile today. He is known for a series of detective novels featuring the exiled Cuban detective Cayetano Brulé, including *¿Quien mato a Cristián Kustermann?* (Who Killed Christian Kustermann?) (1993), *Boleros en La Habana* (Boleros in Havana) (1994), *El alemán de Atacama* (The German in Atacama) (1996) and *Cita en el azul profundo* (A Date in the Deep Blue) (2001). His novel *Nuestros años verde olivo* (Our Years in Olive Green) (2000) concerns the situation of exiled Chileans in Cuba in the 1970s, based in part on Ampuero's own experience there. (After his exile from Chile in 1973 Ampuero lived for a time in Cuba and East Germany before moving to West Germany, Sweden and now thc USA.) His other writings include the short-story collection *El hombre golondrina* (The Swallow Man) (1998) and the children's novel *La guerra de los duraznos* (The War of the Peaches) (1999). His novels have been translated into Italian, French, Portuguese and German. He writes a weekly column in the Sunday edition of the Santiago newspaper *La tercera*.

Further reading

Moody, M. (1999) 'Roberto Ampuero y la novela negra, una entrevista', *Confluencia* 15(1): 127–41.

DANIEL BALDERSTON

Anderson Imbert, Enrique

b. 1910, Córdoba, Argentina, d. 2000, Buenos Aires, Argentina

Writer

Imbert's diversity is evidenced by his contributions to the socialist newspaper *La Vanguardia* from 1931 to 1937, the novel *Vigilia* (Vigil) (1934), the collection of essays *La flecha en el aire* (The Arrow in the Air) (1937) and the fantastic (see **fantastic literature**) short stories of *El grimorio* (The Other Side of the Mirror) in 1961. He began teaching in 1940. In his canonical yet problematic *Historia de la literatura hispanoamericana* (Spanish-American Literature: A History) (1954) he categorized literature by generation and offered only impressionistic views of female writers.

Further reading

Anderson Imbert, E. (1954) *Historia de la literatura hispanoamericana*, Mexico City: Fondo de Cultura Económica.

—— (1961) *El grimorio*, Buenos Aires: Editorial Losada.

—— (1984) *La crítica literaria, sus métodos y problemas*, Madrid: Alianza Editorial.

—— (1997) *Modernidad y postmodernidad: Ensayos*, Buenos Aires: Torres Agüero Editor.

—— (1998) *La prosa: modalidades y usos*, Barcelona: Editorial Ariel.

Giacoman, H. (ed.) (1974) *Homenaje a Enrique Anderson Imbert*, New York: Las Americas Publishing.

Rosenberg, F. (1989) 'Enrique Anderson Imbert', in C.A. Solé and M.I. Abreu (eds), *Latin American Writers*, New York: Scribners, 3: 1105–10.

FERNANDA A. ZULLO

Andrade, Carlos Drummond de

b. 1902, Itabira do Mato Dentro, Minas Gerais, Brazil; d. 1987, Rio de Janeiro, Brazil

Poet and journalist

Born in a small agricultural and iron-mining town some 300 miles inland from Rio de Janeiro, Drummond was the youngest son of a land-owning family. After a surprise expulsion from a Jesuit boarding school age 17 ('I lost the faith: I lost time'), he moved with his family to Belo Horizonte, capital of Minas Gerais. There, he became the unofficial leader of the group of poets who adhered to the modernist movement (see **Brazilian modernism**) led by Mário de **Andrade** and others from São Paulo. In 1930 he published his first collection, *Alguma poesia* (Some Poetry). The poems are short and prosaic, with an offhand humour. Some of them have achieved considerable fame (or notoriety), including 'In the Middle of the Road', in which this phrase, with the addition of 'there was a stone' is repeated some six times, making up almost the whole poem. As Drummond said, for years this poem served to divide Brazilians into two categories (roughly, those who had some notion of what modern life was about and those who did not). He is regarded as the greatest Brazilian poet of the twentieth century, and continued to produce good poetry until almost the moment of his death. The variety of his work offers something for everyone. Underlying it, there is an honesty and ability to question his own motives ('Set fire to everything, including myself') which put him on a level with his reader in experience, if not in finding the words to express it.

Drummond married in 1925, and had one daughter. In 1934 he moved to Rio as secretary to the Minister of Education in the Vargas government, Gustavo Capanema. He kept this job until 1944, in spite of the dictatorial nature of the regime: this was more a matter of personal loyalty to Capanema than of political conviction. His poetry, especially the three collections published during the 1940s – *Sentimento do mundo* (The Feeling of the World) (1940), *José* and *A rosa do povo* (The People's Rose) (1945) – shows that he was moving to the Left during this period, and in 1945 he all but joined the Communist Party. There is, however, little that is directly political about his poetry, which is concerned above all with the place of the alienated individual in mass urban society ('I have only two hands/and the feeling of the world'). Within this alienation, the poet has the duty to bring new life to words and so allow people to communicate, with themselves, with each other and with society at large. This central period ends on a high note of optimism, with the long, six-page 'Song to the man of the people Charlie Chaplin'. Chaplin as a silent filmmaker emerges from the blackness of the cinema to make us laugh and vicariously kick the backsides of the rich and powerful. Yet at the end, he can also give a verbal message for the whole of humanity (as Chaplin had done in his film *The Great Dictator*), which transcends political rhetoric.

This moment did not last. In the collections of the 1950s, beginning with *Claro enigma* (Clear Enigma) (1951), there is a new sense of disgust and disenchantment with the public world, and a turn to formalism and traditional 'poetic' topics: love, or nostalgia for his provincial past, for instance. Much of this reaction is more apparent than real. Just as the poet of *A rosa do povo* was rarely if ever a truly political animal, the 'older and wiser' man remains surprisingly subversive. His sonnets are not quite conventional in form, and his love poetry is about a doting 50-year-old poet who has fallen for a much younger woman: the facts of the case, which are plain enough in the poetry, became public after his death. These poems, some of them long (a page or two) and very ingenious in the formal sense, are among many readers' favourites: in them, the shapes and patterns we make of our lives seem to appear and disappear, in the poetry as in life.

His imaginary return to Itabira is not new in this poetry either. His identification with his home town, although it makes him one of the generation who lived in urban 'exile' from the countryside, defined by Roberto **Schwarz** as 'farmers of the air' (*fazendeiros do ar*), has a larger context, for Itabira has since the 1940s become the centre of a huge open-pit iron mine. From the 1942 'Viagem na família' (Travelling in the Family), he maintained a dialogue with his extended family, beginning with his father (who had died in 1931) but prolonged into a more distant past also. In every collection he returned to this theme, finally, in the 1968 *Boitempo* (Oxtime), dedicating a whole book to recalling life in Itabira early in the century.

Drummond's influence is hard to estimate, but it is huge. Along with Manuel **Bandeira**, he did more than anyone to bring erudite poetry close to everyday life and speech. He is very widely read, and posthumous collections, including some erotic verse, have sold very well. But he is difficult to imitate, because of his simplicity and technical skill. A civil servant for most of his life, he was also a prolific and popular journalist, mostly for the weekly columns known as ***crônicas*** published in the *Correio da Manhã* and the *Jornal do Brasil.*

Further reading

Andrade, C. Drummond de (1985) *Nova reunião*, Rio de Janeiro: Aguilar.

—— (1986) *Traveling in the Family: Selected Poems*, ed. T. Colchie and M. Strand, New York: Random House.

—— (1994) 'Song to the Man of the People Charlie Chaplin', trans. D. Treece, *Modern Poetry in Translation* 6: 43–9.

Gledson, J. (1981) *Poesia e poética de Carlos Drummond de Andrade*, São Paulo: Duas Cidades.
Gonzalez, M. and Treece, D. (1992) *The Gathering of Voices*, London: Verso.
Kinsella, J.M. (1997) 'Carlos Drummond de Andrade', in V. Smith (ed.), *Encyclopedia of Latin American Literature*, London: Fitzroy Dearborn, 38–41.
Lima, L.C. (1989) 'Carlos Drummond de Andrade', in C.A. Solé and M.I. Abreu (eds), *Latin American Writers*, New York: Scribners, 2: 957–74.
Sternberg, R. (1986) *The Unquiet Self: Self and Society in the Poetry of Carlos Drummond de Andrade*, Valencia: Albatros.

JOHN GLEDSON

Andrade, Mário Raúl de Moraes

b. 1893, São Paulo, Brazil; d. 1945, São Paulo

Critic, musicologist, ethnologist, writer and cultural administrator

One of Brazil's leading writers and **intellectuals**, best known for his rhapsodic novel ***Macunaíma*** (1928), at the age of 18 Mário de Andrade abandoned a course in commerce to study music and piano at the São Paulo Conservatory. By his mid-twenties he had already gained a reputation as a teacher and critic of art, music and poetry. A politely devastating critique of the literary establishment, 'Mestres do passado' (Past Masters), published in 1921 together with his first collection of poetry, *Há uma gota de sangue em cada poema* (There is a Drop of Blood in Every Poem), led fellow modernist Oswald de **Andrade** (no relation) to declare him 'my futurist poet'. Although he vigorously repudiated the title, he effectively confirmed his critical and artistic leadership of Brazil's modernist movement (see **Brazilian modernism**) with his next volume, *Paulicéia desvairada* (Hallucinated City), which appeared in the same year as São Paulo's momentous Modern Art Week (1922).

Andrade's theory of modernist poetics, expounded in the 'Extremely Interesting Preface' to *Paulicéia desvairada*, was set to work in wildly extended free verse compositions that assaulted the conservative complacency of Brazil's *belle époque* bourgeoisie in a defiantly surrealist and colloquial Portuguese, which evoked the painful yet tumultuous birth of a modern, European-style city in the tropics, a 'Gallicism bellowing in the deserts of America!'

This awareness of the contradiction at the heart of Brazilian modernity remained with Andrade, and by the mid-1920s, following the formal and linguistic iconoclasm of the Modern Art Week, he was leading the movement in its exploration of the wealth of rural and regional traditions which lay beyond the islands of urban development in the southeast. An extended journey through the country's north and northeast in 1927 produced the strongly folkloric poetry of *Clã do Jaboti* (Clan of the Tortoise), with its Utopian vision of an uncomplicated culture of 'indolence' and pure being among the rubber-tappers of the Amazon. The clash between that 'primitive' universe and the capitalist mentality of the city was played out in his most famous work, *Macunaíma*. This extraordinarily fertile period in Andrade's career, when his ethnomusicological researches also produced a pioneering *Ensaio sobre a música brasileira* (Essay on Brazilian Music) (1928) and *Compêndio da história da música* (Compendium of Music History) (1929), can best be seen as a multidisciplinary reflection on the dialectic between diversity and identity in Brazilian culture. When he wrote, in a poem of 1929, 'There are three hundred, three hundred and fifty of me/ But one day at last I will find myself', he was speaking as much of a national, as of a personal, dilemma.

The following year brought a political dimension to bear on this dilemma, as Getulio Vargas took power and the authoritarian, centralizing aspirations of the new regime clashed with São Paulo's determination to defend its regional autonomy. Despite an intellectual's scepticism about organized politics, the instinctive democrat Andrade felt a visceral identification with the socialist cause against the growth of the Far Right, something he expressed in the anguished, surreal language of the poem 'O carro da miséria' (The Wagon of Misery) in the mid-1930s.

Paradoxically, however, the emergence of a strongly centralized state seemed to offer Andrade the opportunity to turn his ideas for democratizing culture into reality in the public sphere. In 1935 he was appointed to São Paulo's Department of Culture where, as its director from 1937, he undertook the preliminary plans to establish a Department of National Historical and Artistic Heritage. The next two years saw a series of unprecedented initiatives in the cultural life of the city, all of them due to Andrade's vision and energy: a Society of Ethnology and Folklore; a Congress for the National Language in Song; the creation of children's parks with their own folk festivals; the first mobile library, music and record libraries; and the organization of free musical and dramatic performances at the Municipal Theatre, which opened its doors for the first time to working people.

However, in 1938, with the installation of a fully-fledged dictatorship in the shape of Vargas's Estado Novo and a drastic reform of the civil service, Andrade's cultural mission was cruelly cut short. Removed from his post as Municipal Director of Culture, he retreated into academic life in Rio de Janeiro and was eventually forced to cease his journalistic activities, spending the remaining years of his life hovering between illness and depression. One of his last, most outspoken public interventions, which angrily belies the general defeatism of this period, was a lecture published in 1942 under the title 'The Modernist Movement'. This was a severe critique of the avant-garde (see **avant-garde in Latin America**) generation which he had led in the 1920s, and of its failure to come down out of the ivory tower of experimentation and speculation into the real world and meet the challenge of social responsibility.

Yet Andrade's own career represented an incomparable example of the socially responsible artist/intellectual at work. It combined the painstaking dedication of the ethnographer dirtying his hands in the field, with the intellectual discipline of the library-bound researcher, the vision and initiative of the political activist with the poet's sensitivity to the language of individual experience. This grasp of the complex relationship between the particular and the general, between the detail and substance of cultural life and the larger picture, his intervention in such a range of disciplinary fields and his sober honesty in confronting the dilemmas of cultural change, make Mário de Andrade the single most enlightened commentator on his country's development, and one of the true pioneers of the art of cultural studies in Brazil.

Further reading

Andrade, M. de (1943) *Aspectos da literatura brasileira*, São Paulo: Martins.

—— (1965) *Aspectos da música brasileira*, São Paulo: Martins.

—— (1987) *Poesias completas*, São Paulo: Itatiaia.

—— (1988) *Macunaíma*, trans. R. Goodland, London: Carcanet.

Antelo, R. (1986) *Na ilha de marapatá: Mário de Andrade lê os hispano- americanos*, São Paulo: Ed. Hucitéc.

Duarte, P. (1971) *Mário de Andrade por ele mesmo*, São Paulo: Edart.

Lopez, T.P.A. (1972) *Mário de Andrade: Ramais e caminho*, São Paulo: Duas Cidades.

Moisés, M. (1989) 'Mário de Andrade', in C.A. Solé and M.I. Abreu (eds), *Latin American Writers*, New York: Scribners, 2: 771–80.

Schelling, V. (1997) 'Mário de Andrade', in V. Smith (ed.), *Encyclopedia of Latin American Literature*, London: Fitzroy Dearborn, 41–3.

DAVID TREECE

Andrade, Oswald de

b. 1890, São Paulo, Brazil; d. 1954, São Paulo

Writer and philosopher

Oswald de Andrade represents the Dionysian face of **Brazilian modernism**. His renovating impulse earned him his place as Brazil's most original avant-garde figure (see **avant-garde in Latin America**). And in evoking such a figure, the critic has no alternative but to use descriptions such as 'inventive', 'sarcastic', and 'irreverent genius of corrosive, libidinous and biting humour'.

Andrade was marked always by a creative will to transgress and oppose norms, be they literary, political or social. Few writers have maintained such a close connection between their life and their literary work. Fragments of his life were captured in characters such as João Miramar and Serafim (a name he liked to use himself), especially in *Un homem sem profissão – sob as ordens de mamãe* (A Man with No Profession – Under Mothers' Orders) (1954), written a few years before his death, in which he declared his passion and his insatiable curiosity for life and literature: 'I gather together everything, I add things up, I absorb'. His relationship with the world was, as he put it, anthropophagic; everything is devoured, to be later transformed into literary material.

Andrade's multiple personality makes him as different as it is possible to be from the salon literati. In the 1920s, he was a cosmopolitan intellectual (see **intellectuals**) responsible for the promotion of Brazilian modernism. It was he who discovered new young talents like Mário de **Andrade** (no relation), while his own work developed in a variety of genres; he was poet, novelist, playwright, essayist, writer of memoirs and a polemical journalist. His life and work were devoted to breaking literary and cultural traditions. Although he adopted infinitely varied genres and forms of expression, the nation (Brazil) is a constant in all the different manifestations of his art. Titles such as *Pau-Brasil* (Brazil Wood) (1925) or ***Antropofagia*** identify him immediately with Brazilian ideology. The national elements of his poetry and fiction, however, are opposed to a nineteenth-century rhetoric of nation-building tied to a Romantic exoticism of Brazilian landscape (as in José de Alencar), to the oppositional **civilization and barbarism** of Euclides da **Cunha** or to the representation of customs characteristic of realism and naturalism (as in Aluísio de **Azevedo**). Andrade's Brazilian adventure was based upon an avant-garde project with European, and particularly futuristic, roots. He looked towards both Brazil and Europe.

Andrade had to distance himself in order to understand his Brazil, to rediscover his roots and to propose a new poetic style; hence the journeys to Europe and the sojourns in Paris. Just as the anthropophagists devoured their enemies (not out of hunger, but out of a ritualistic desire to assimilate the best of the other), so Oswald proposed to 'devour' techniques of composition in order to produce something new.

During his first journey to Europe in 1912, Andrade made contact with the avant-garde, with the futurism of Marinetti, the cubism of Picasso and the poetic theories of Apollinaire. These theoretical principles, together with his own extraordinary intuition, produced the new poetry of *Pau-Brasil*. 'The forest is a school', he declared in his *Manifesto antropófago*, symbolically combining the autochthonous elements of the land with the knowledge he had gained in Europe.

These ideas were continued and developed in a far-reaching project whose theoretical foundations were laid in the *Manifesto antropófago*. The manifesto revealed how revolutionary his principles were, how directly connected with radical social transformation. The Utopian nation proposed by Andrade would be built on an alliance of natural man and twentieth-century technology. Liberated from the tyranny of labour, man would be free to return to the exercise of his natural idleness:

> In the supertechnological world to come, when the final barriers of Patriarchy have crumbled, man will be able to indulge his innate laziness, the mother of fantasy, invention and love. He will thus finally be restored, after his long period of negativity, to the synthesis of technical change which is civilization and natural life which is culture, to his ludic instincts ...

In this new society, the patriarchal, oppressive system that privileges the inherited rights of the patriarch's son would be abolished. In its place would arise the Matriarchy of Pindorama, which celebrates man's natural impulses in a classless society where all land is held in common. This was the anthropophagic culture, whose idealistic principles Andrade continued to explore and develop until the publication of *A crise da filosofia messiânica* (Crisis of Messianic Philosophy) in 1950.

Outstanding among Andrade's fiction is *Memórias sentimentais de João Miramar* (Sentimental Memoirs of João Miramar) (1924). His cinematographic prose captured the simultaneity of the real through montage and the superimposition of fragments. He emphasizes the dynamic, plastic elements of the scenes he narrates or describes. His roots in the avant-garde are evident in the interweaving of traditionally irreconcilable styles (prose, poetry, theatre, propaganda, and so on), the constant presence of humour and the satirical dimension that permeates the work, a violent critique of contemporary society. *Serafim Pont Grande*, although written in the 1920s, was not published until 1933; it represented the most radical extension of all his earlier propositions. It is a rebellious, transgressive text, realized through erotic humour and the exploration of the grotesque. The polemical character of these novels derives as much from their formal innovations as from their content. Both had to wait more than forty years for a second edition and for their recognition as major works. Together with Mário de Andrade's ***Macunaíma***, these books are the most important prose works of Brazilian modernism.

Andrade's avant-garde poetry and his innovative fiction are one of the most important and challenging legacies of contemporary Brazilian culture. His ideas continue to provoke reflection and admiration. The presentation in 1967 of his play *O rei da vela* (King of the Candle) produced its own revolution; the concrete poets (see **concrete poetry**) acknowledged him as one of their principal ancestors, while the 1960s *tropicalista* movement in music and cinema returned to anthropophagy and drew on its subversiveness and its corrosive and anarchic humour directed against bourgeois values.

Further reading

Andrade, O. de (1979) *Seraphim Grosse Pointe*, trans. K.D. Jackson and A. Bork, Austin, TX: New Latin Quarter Editions.

—— (1990–96) *Obras completas de Oswald de Andrade*, São Paulo: Globo, 23 vols.

Fonseca, M.A. (1990) *Oswald de Andrade: Biografia*, São Paulo: Art Editora/Secretaria do Estado da Cultura.

Jackson, K.D. (ed.) (1978) *A prosa vanguardista na literatura brasileira*, São Paulo: Ed. Perspectiva.

Nunes, B. (1979) *Oswald Canibal*, São Paulo: Perspectiva.

Schwartz, J. (ed.) (2000) *Oswald de Andrade: Obra incompleta*, Paris and São Paulo: Colección Archivos.

Silva, T.V.Z. da (1997) 'Oswald de Andrade', in V. Smith (ed.), *Encyclopedia of Latin American Literature*, London: Fitzroy Dearborn, 44–6.

Telles, G.M. (2002) 'Oswald de Andrade', in C. Solé and K. Müller-Bergh (eds), *Latin American Writers: Supplement I*, New York: Scribners. 31–54.

JORGE SCHWARTZ

Angel, Albalucía

b. 1939, Pereira, Colombia

Art critic, writer, journalist and singer

Angel's fiction is representative of the new narrative by women authors of the 1970s. Having moved to Paris in her early twenties, she published her first novel *Dos veces Alicia* (Alicia Twice Over) (1972) in Barcelona, Spain, where she met some of the writers of the **Boom**. Her second and best-known novel, *Estaba la pájara pinta sentada en el verde limón* (The Spotted Female Bird was Sitting on the Green Lemon Tree) (1982), titled after a children's rhyme, won an award in Colombia. Her third novel, *Misiá señora* (Madam Lady) (1983) is an ambitious and experimental work both in content and form.

Further reading

Angel, Albalucía (1983) *Estaba la pájara pinta sentada en el verde limón*, Barcelona: Argos Vergara.

García Pinto, M. (1988) 'Albalucía Angel', in *Women Writers of Latin America. Intimate Histories*, trans. Trudy Balch and M. García Pinto, Austin: University of Texas Press, 45–78.

MAGDALENA GARCÍA PINTO

Another Life

This autobiographical poem by Nobel Laureate Derek **Walcott** was written between 1965 and 1972 and published in 1973. The poem explores Walcott's childhood and early adulthood. Its focus, however, is not simply on describing his experiences with family, friends and acquaintances, but on exploring how those experiences engage questions of post-colonial Caribbean identity. Walcott vividly renders both the natural and human landscape of his boyhood Saint Lucia. Like much of his work, *Another Life* mixes meditations on the unique nature of Caribbean life with allusions to European texts. With the blossoming of Walcott's career and international acclaim in the 1980s and 1990s, *Another Life* has to some extent been overshadowed by his later works, particularly the epic poem ***Omeros*** (1990).

Further reading

Walcott, Derek (1982) *Another Life*, Washington, DC: Three Continents Press.

ROSANNE ADDERLEY

Antelo, Raúl

b. 1951, Buenos Aires, Argentina

Literary critic

An Argentine critic and essayist now living in Brazil, Antelo was educated in Buenos Aires before moving to São Paulo and later to Florianópolis. His marginal location on the academic map is also significant for his critical work. Thinking through the production of meaning, he reads literature and art as an allegory. Thus he does not limit himself to Brazilian or Latin American texts but thinks in terms of the networks and circuits through which discourses, figures and movements intercept and modify one another. Mário de **Andrade**, Le Corbusier and Oliverio **Girondo** have each given him an opportunity to develop one of the most original critical discourses of late twentieth-century Latin America.

Further reading

Garza, G. (1990) 'Identidade e a alteridade: Uma entrevista com Raul Antelo', *Dactylus* 10: 6–11.

Grandis, R. de (1995) 'La ficción crítica en los noventa: Nuevos textos, nuevas series: Posiciones y reacomodos (entrevista a Raul Antelo)', *Luso Brazilian Review* 32(1): 41–9.

GRACIELA MONTALDO

Anthony, Michael

b. 1932, Mayaro, Trinidad

Writer and historian

Considered one of Trinidad's foremost historians, Anthony travelled to England in 1955, where he worked in factories and as a telegraphist. His literary career began with contributions to the magazine *Bim*. His first novel, *The Games Were Coming*, was published in 1963; his most famous, *The Year in San Fernando*, in 1965. Other writings include short collections *Cricket in the Road* (1973), *Sandra Street and Other Stories* (1973) and *The Chieftain's Carnival and Other Stories* (1993), where each story is based on significant events in Trinidad's history. Much of his work after 1975 consists of historical research into his native island.

Further reading

Anthony, Michael (1992) *The Golden Quest: The Four Voyages of Christopher Columbus*, London: Macmillan Caribbean.

KEITH JARDIM

Antillano, Laura

b. 1950, Caracas, Venezuela

Writer

Antillano is a Venezuelan writer and educator whose work has been consistently focused on the concerns of women and children, within the specific historical and cultural frame of Venezuelan society. She is the daughter of a painter (mother) and a journalist, and her first collection of short stories *La bella época* (The Beautiful Age) (1969) was a mixture of memories with references to cinema, music, marketing, news, visual culture and performance. Further publications include *Un carro largo se llama tren* (A Very Long Car Is Called a Train) (1975),

Dime si dentro de ti no oyes tu corazón partir (Can You Hear Your Heart Leaving?) (1982) and *La luna no es de pan de horno* (The Moon Is Not Baked Bread) (1988).

VÍCTOR GALARRAGA OROPEZA

antipoetry

The term *antipoesía* or antipoetry belongs to the Chilean poet Nicanor **Parra**, although it had been used before by earlier poets, some belonging to the Latin American avant-garde movements (see **avant-garde in Latin America**). Parra's *antipoesía* was defined above all in his poetic practice; and though critics may continue to argue over its precise meaning, two elements seem clear. First, the poetic subject – the voice of the poetry – is antiheroic, insistent on the ordinariness of its experience ('Los vicios del mundo moderno' – The Vices of the Modern World, as one poem is entitled). Second, the language of the poetry eschews high rhetoric, elevated language and all elements of the sublime ('nosotros conversamos/ en el lenguaje de todos los días' – we speak in everyday language). Clearly iconoclastic, many have assumed that the implied opposite – the poetry to Parra's antipoetry – was that of Pablo **Neruda**. Others have seen it as a precursor to the *poesía conversacional* (conversational poetry) that dominated Latin American poetry of the 1960s and after.

Further reading

Grossman, Edith (1975) *The Antipoetry of Nicanor Parra*, New York: New York University Press.

MIKE GONZALEZ

Antología de la literatura fantástica

This polemical anthology was published in 1940 by Editorial Sudamericana. Edited by Jorge Luis **Borges**, Adolfo **Bioy Casares** and Silvina **Ocampo**, the anthology included an essay on the fantastic (see **fantastic literature**) by Bioy Casares that made clear that the editors were arguing for the genre, but also attacking the **socialist realism** and ***costumbrismo*** traditions in Spanish American literature. Most of the selections were short stories translated from English (and some from German); among the few Spanish American texts included in the first edition (others were stories by **Lugones** and Peyrou) was one of Borges's first major ***Ficciones***, the famous (and famously baffling) 'Tlön, Uqbar, Orbis Tertius', which appeared in the 1940 edition with a postscript dated 1947. The second edition of the anthology, published in 1965, included a significantly larger number of Spanish American texts, including **Bianco**'s great novella, *Sombras suele vestir* (Shadow Play) (1941), which had been written for the first edition but not finished in time for publication there, and stories by **Garro**, **Wilcock**, **Murena**, Ocampo and Bioy. The fact that there was much more to include was due to the influence of the anthology itself: **Cortázar**, in his essay on the fantastic, recognizes that it played a seminal role in the history of subsequent Spanish American fiction.

Further reading

Balderston, D. (2002) 'La *Antología de la literatura fantástica* y sus alrededores', *Casa de las Américas* 229: 104–10.

Borges, J.L., S. Ocampo and A. Biioy Casares (ed.) (1940) *Antología de la literatura fantástica*, Buenos Aires: Editorial Sudamericana.

—— (1988) *The Book of Fantasy*, intro. Ursula K. LeGuin. New York: Viking.

DANIEL BALDERSTON

Antoni, Robert

b. *c.*1955, Trinidad and Tobago

Writer

Antoni's successful first novel, *Divine Trace* (1991), won a Commonwealth Writers Prize for Best First Novel and is considered a landmark in Caribbean literature. *Blessed Is the Fruit*, his second novel, was published in 1997 to great acclaim. Senior editor of the literary journal *Conjunctions*, he is also associate director of the University of Miami's Caribbean Writers Summer Institute. He is currently a professor at the same university, where he teaches fiction writing and **magical realism**. Antoni has lived most of his life in the Bahamas.

Further reading

Antoni, Robert (1992) *Divina Trace*, Woodstock, NY: Overlook Press.

—— (2001) *My Grandmother's Erotic Folktales*, New York: Grove Press.

KEITH JARDIM

Antropofagia

A cultural theory and movement led by Brazilian Oswald de **Andrade** and dating from the publication of his *Manifesto antropófago* (Cannibalist Manifesto) in the movement's journal, ***Revista de Antropofagia***, in 1928. Four years previously, in his *Manifesto da Poesia Pau-Brasil* (Brazil Wood Poetry Manifesto), Andrade had proposed a flexible, dynamic model for Brazil's cultural development, illuminating the dialectic of forces – traditional and modern, indigenous and metropolitan – that had shaped the post-colonial condition. In part a response to the challenge of the crudely xenophobic nationalism of *verdeamarelo* (Greenyellowism) (see ***verdeamarelismo***) in the intervening years, Andrade now radicalized his earlier analysis by placing at its centre the very concept which had, in colonial discourse, most defined the Latin American 'Other' as primitive and barbaric – cannibalism.

Far from being the exclusive preserve of a peripheral, pre-modern culture, anthropophagy, argued Andrade, constituted 'The only law of the world. The masked expression of all individualisms, of all collectivisms. Of all religions. Of all peace treaties'. The Cannibalist impulse to absorb 'the sacred enemy ... to transform him into a totem' was thus reclaimed as a subversive, revolutionary force immanent, not only in Brazil's history of anti-colonial struggle, but also in the metropolitan world's desire to escape its own internal contradictions: 'But it wasn't crusaders that came. They were fugitives from a civilization that we are eating...' The re-appropriation and re-invention of Carnival and Christianity (in the form of Candomblé) by black Brazilians were manifestations of the anthropophagous instinct to invert the relationship between colonizer and colonized by 'digesting' imported values and re-synthesizing them in an autonomous form: 'We were never catechized ... We gave birth to Christ in Bahia'. They therefore prefigured not only a national, but a universal revolution, echoing the world-historic act of patricide depicted in Freud's *Totem and Taboo*. Ritualistically consuming the patriarchal body politic of Western civilization, its oppressive power would be neutralized and incorporated into the popular, indigenous and pre-industrial values of Andrade's matriarchal Utopia 'without complexes, without madness, without prostitutions and without penitentiaries'.

During the brief fourteen months of its existence, the Cannibalist movement, and especially its journal, *Revista de Antropofagia*, provided an important pole of attraction for some of the most radically experimental artists of the decade, including Tarsila do Amaral, Carlos Drummond de **Andrade** and Raul Bopp. ***Macunaíma***, the prose narrative of Mário de **Andrade**, was acclaimed the Cannibalist masterpiece and, although arguably more pessimistic in outlook, his work nevertheless shared a similar concern with the questions of acculturation, cultural hybridity and the subversive potential of so-called 'primitive' cultures. The potential repercussions of *Antropofagia* were cut short by the reaction against avant-garde experimentation from 1930 onwards. But Oswald de Andrade's ideas were 'rediscovered' in the mid-1960s by the Concretists and Tropicalists, who found their blend of nationalism and internationalism, their synthesis of the archaic and the modern, of 'high' and 'low' culture, a refreshing alternative to the mechanical populism and traditionalism that dominated contemporary cultural politics.

Further reading

Andrade, O. de (1991), *"Cannibalist Manifesto" by Oswald de Andrade'*, trans. L. Bary, *Latin American Literary Review* 19(31): 35–47.

Helena, L. (1983) *Uma literatura antropofágica*, Fortaleza: Universidade Federal do Ceará.

Johnson, J.R. (1987) 'Tupy or not Tupy: Cannibalism and Nationalism in Contemporary Brazilian Literature and Culture', in J. King (ed.), *Modern Latin American Fiction: A Survey*, London: Faber & Faber, 41–59.

DAVID TREECE

Arango, Gonzalo

b. 1931, Andes, Colombia; d. 1976, Tocancipá, Colombia

Poet

Arango was the founder of the Colombian poetic movement ***Nadaísmo***, whose anti-institutional aesthetics reflected existentialist (see **existentialism**) influences as well as Arango's personal crisis of religious belief. In 1958, he published his first *Manifiesto nadaísta* (Nadaísta Manifesto); followed by another in 1962. His first poems appeared in two anthologies in 1963: *13 poetas nadaístas* and *De la Nada al Nadaísmo* (From Nothingness to Nadaísmo). Three more collections followed, including *Providencia* (Providence) (1972) and *Fuego en el altar* (Fire on the Altar) (1974). In his later years he distanced himself from his *nadaísta* colleagues, accusing them of a desperate nihilism.

Further reading

Arango, Gonzalo (1963) *Sexo y saxofón; cuentos*, Bogotá: Ediciones Tercer Mundo.

—— (2001) *Teatro*, Bogotá: Intermedio.

MIGUEL A. CARDINALE

Arango, Luis Alfredo

b. 1935, Totonicapán, Guatemala

Writer

Poet, narrator, and founding member of *Nuevo Signo* (New Sign), Arango represented indigenous peoples realistically, and was one of the best writers of his generation (winning the **Asturias** literary prize in 1988). In Totonicapán, Arango was a rural school teacher who cultivated direct ties with oppressed Indian communities. He represented their experience and values in expressive poems and stories that exhibit a remarkable sense of humour and a balance between lyricism and epigrammatic wit. Among his books are *El amanecido: O cargando el arpa* (Up at Dawn: or The Harp Corner), *Archivador de pueblos* (The People's Archivist), *Lola dormida* (Lola Asleep), *Después del tango vienen los moros* (After the Tango, the Moors) and *El volador* (The Flyer).

Further reading

Arango, Luis Alfredo (1988) *Después del tango vienen los moros*, 1a ed. del X aniversario de RIN-78, Guatemala: Grupo Literario Editorial 'RIN-78'.

—— (1992) *El país de los pájaros*, Mexico: SEP.

MARC ZIMMERMAN

Aranha, Graça

b. 1868, São Luiz de Maranhão, Brazil; d. 1931, Rio de Janeiro, Brazil

Writer

Graça Aranha (born José Pereira da Graça Aranha) was already famous for his novel *Canaã* (Canaan) (1902) by the time of his participation in the famous Semana da Arte Moderna (Modern Art Week) in São Paulo in 1922, the founding moment of **Brazilian modernism**. A member of the Brazilian Academy of Letters since its founding in 1896, he broke with the institute in 1924 when he gave a speech 'O espírito moderno' (The Modern Spirit), which represented a break with the cultural institutions of the past.

Further reading

Aranha, G. (1969) *Obra completa*, ed. A. Coutinho, Rio de Janeiro: Instituto Nacional do Livro.

Aiex, A. (1975) 'Graça Aranha and Brazilian Modernism', in M.H. Forster (ed.), *Tradition and Renewal: Essays on Twentieth-century Latin American*

Literature and Culture, Urbana: University of Illinois Press.
Daniel, M.L. (1997) 'José Pereira da Graça Aranha', in V. Smith (ed.), *Encyclopedia of Latin American Literature*, London: Fitzroy Dearborn, 46–7.

DANIEL BALDERSTON

Araújo, Helena

b. 1934, Bogotá, Colombia

Writer

The daughter of a diplomat, Araújo spent her childhood and adolescence in Colombia and Brazil. During the late 1950s she established herself as a literary critic and journalist, contributing to the news weekly *Semana* (Week) and other publications. In 1971 she moved to Lausanne, Switzerland, to serve as an academic, centring her research on Latin American **women's writing**. Her work includes short stories, a novel, *Fiesta en Teusaquillo* (A Party in Teusaquillo) (1981), and two books on literary criticism: *Signos y mensajes* (Signs and Messages), published in 1976, and *La Scherezada criolla* (The Native Scherezade), published in 1989.

Further reading

Araújo, Helena (1970) *La 'M' de las moscas (relatos)*, Bogotá: Ediciones Tercer Mundo.
—— (1989) *La Scherezada criolla. Ensayos sobre escritura femenina latinoamericana*, Bogotá: Edición Universidad Nacional de Colombia.

HÉCTOR D. FERNÁNDEZ L'HOESTE

Arce de Vázquez, Margot

b. 1904, Caguas, Puerto Rico; d. 1990, Hato Rey, Puerto Rico

Critic

Margot Arce was instrumental in the creation and growth of modern literary criticism in Puerto Rico. She did a doctorate in Madrid, studying with Américo Castro and Tomás Navarro Tomás, and completing a dissertation on the Spanish Renaissance poet Garcilaso de la Vega, then returned to direct the department of Hispanic Studies at the University of Puerto Rico for many years. Her critical work on the poetry of her friend Gabriela **Mistral** (1958) helped establish Mistral's work as worthy of serious study. Much of her criticism is focused on modern Puerto Rican writing, including studies of Tomás Blanco, Luis **Lloréns Torres** and Luis **Palés Matos**.

Further reading

Arce de Vázquez, Margot (1964) *Gabriela Mistral, the Poet and her Work*, New York: University Press.
—— (1966) *Lecturas puertorriqueñas; prosa*, Sharon, CT: Troutman Press.

DANIEL BALDERSTON

Arce Leal, Manuel José

b. 1935, Guatemala City; d. 1985, Paris, France

Writer

One of the founders of the Moira poetry group and polemical journalist/poet, Arce wrote surrealist plays (see **surrealism**) attacking the consumerism of Guatemala's rising middle class and the 1960s extrajudicial executions. His urban, existentialist 'anti-poetry' revealed him to be a master of subjective lyricism. The Guatemalan crisis of his final years led to highly polemical poems such as *Guatemala* (1982), published in Paris, and to a body of journalistic essays collected in *Diario de un escribiente* (A Scribe's Diary) (1988). Exiled for his anti-military writings, yet dubbed the conscience of his country, Arce died of cancer in 1985.

Further reading

Arce Leal, Manuel José (1970) *Los episodios del vagón de carga (anti-pop-emas)*, Guatemala: Editorial Universitaria, Universidad de San Carlos de Guatemala.

MARC ZIMMERMAN

Archivos

The 'Archivos' collection is the product of a multilateral agreement between various academic organizations in Argentina, Brazil, Colombia, Spain, France, Italy, Mexico and Portugal. Directed by Amos Segala, Archivos began publishing its collection of the most representative literary works of Latin America and the Caribbean in 1984, brought together under the umbrella of UNESCO . It is a collection of critical, analytical editions, including the text with its variants, followed by studies of the context in which the text was produced, of the reception of the work, as well as supporting documents and interpretative writings. The object of the enterprise is to associate genetic criticism with the other current critical currents, thus providing exhaustive reference editions.

Further reading:

1899–1999: Vida, obra y herencia de Miguel Angel Asturias, catalogue with discussion of history of the collection, Paris: UNESCO.

JULIO PREMAT

Arciniegas, Germán

b. 1900, Bogotá, Colombia; d. 1999, Bogotá

Essayist and historian

For his conspicuous cultural contribution, Arciniegas has been called 'Universal Colombian'. In addition, in 1989, the Americas Society awarded him the title Man of the Americas. A member of Los Nuevos, a group of Colombian intellectuals who were born in the first decades of this century, he advocated the modernization and socio-political advancement of his country. Arciniegas earned a degree in Law, and while a university student, he founded the Federación de Estudiantes de Colombia (Colombian Students' Federation). As a student leader, he advocated academic freedom in the classroom and educational reform. When elected a representative in the Congress, he proposed a bill to reform the university system. In 1928, he was named director of the editorial section of the newspaper *El Tiempo*, for which he wrote a column for some seventy years (his newspaper articles are estimated to total some 15,000).

Arciniegas started his diplomatic career as vice consul in London in 1929. He was also Colombian ambassador to Italy, Israel, Venezuela and the Vatican City. Arciniegas was elected to the Congress several times, and was twice minister of education. He was a professor at Columbia and several US universities. At the Universidad de los Andes, in Bogotá, Arciniegas for several years directed the Cátedra de las Américas course on which he invited distinguished thinkers of the Americas and Europe to lecture. He was instrumental in the founding and leadership of the Latin American branch of the Congress for Cultural Freedom.

Arciniegas's thought is found in numerous articles and essays. He took a strong interest in studying the peoples and cultures of the Americas with an emphasis on the sociocultural interelationships among the American, the European and the African worlds. He viewed the New World in a dynamic and progressive way that he thought created favourable conditions for freedom and democracy. In contrast, the rise of dictatorships in Latin America has been one of his major concerns. *Entre la libertad y el miedo* (The State of Latin America) (1952) discusses the historic background that made possible the rise of dictators such as Perón and Odría. Other works include *El estudiante de la mesa redonda* (The Student of the Round Table) (1932), *América, tierra firme* (Latin America, Terra Firma) (1937), *Biografía del Caribe* (Biography of the Caribbean) (1945), *Colombia, itinerario de la Independencia* (Colombia, the Road to Independence) (1969), *América en Europa* (America in Europe) (1975) and *Bolívar y la Revolución* (Bolívar and the Revolution) (1984). His works for an English-speaking audience include an anthology of excerpts from Latin American classics, *The Green Continent* (1944); in the introduction to this text Arciniegas argued: 'It is not in the light of the present but of the future that the importance of the Latin-American nations must be evaluated'.

The obituary for Arciniegas in *El Tiempo* asks: 'What was Arciniegas: A politician? A diligent polemicist? A historian? A journalist? The discoverer of a literary continent?' It answered by saying that he was all of these and more.

Further reading

Arciniegas, G. (1990) *Tierra firme y otros ensayos*, Caracas: Biblioteca Ayacucho.

Cobo-Borda, J.G. (1990) *Germán Arciniegas: 90 años escribiendo: Un intento de bibliografía*, Bogotá: Universidad Central/Instituto Colombiano de Estudios Latinoamericanos y del Caribe.

—— (ed.) (1990) *Una visión de América: La obra de Germán Arciniegas*, Bogotá: Instituto Caro y Cuervo.

Suárez-Torres, J.D. (1989) 'Germán Arciniegas', in C.A. Solé and M.I. Abreu (eds), *Latin American Writers*, New York: Scribners, 2: 897–901.

MIGUEL A. CARDINALE

Arenas, Reinaldo

b. 1943, Holguín, Cuba; d. 1990, New York City, USA

Writer

The international success of Arenas's memoir *Antes que anochezca* (Before Night Falls) (1992) has renewed interest in the work of one of the most polemical Cubans of recent times. Until his death from AIDS, Arenas wrote novels, short stories, poems and essays. Among his narrative works, the best known are *Celestino antes del alba* (Singing from the Well) (1967), *El mundo alucinante. Una novela de aventuras* (The Ill-Fated Peregrinations of Fray Servando) (1969), *Otra vez el mar* (Farewell to the Sea) (1982), and the story collections *Con los ojos cerrados* (With Closed Eyes) (1972) and *Termina el desfile* (The Parade's Over) (1981). Most of his essays, and his long poem *El central* (The Sugar Mill) (1981), document the repressive conditions under which Arenas lived in Cuba. As part of the first post-revolutionary generation, Arenas was always a contentious political liability for the regime and was tireless and unyielding in his dissidence.

Born in the provinces to a poor family, Arenas joined the Rebel army in 1958. He lived in Havana from 1962, where he also dedicated himself to writing. He was a finalist in the Cirilo Villaverde prize for narrative in 1965, but began to have problems with the government in 1973, in part due to his homosexuality but mostly because Arenas responded to Cuban censorship by sending his manuscripts abroad for publication. He was imprisoned in El Morro for a time, and lived in a general state of poverty and disaffection until he left Cuba clandestinely through the Mariel boatlift in 1980. His major work completed in exile was the *Pentagonía* (1967–91), a sequence of five novels which give an account of the personal and political struggles of Cubans during the Republic and after the Revolution; the quintet comprises *Cantando en el pozo* (Singing from the Well) (1967), *El palacio de las blanquísimas mofetas* (The Palace of the White Skunks) (1980), *Otra vez el mar* (Farewell to the Sea) (1982), *El color del verano* (The Colour of the Summer) (1991) and *El asalto* (The Assault) (1991). Arenas was a tireless innovator, like many Latin American writers of the 1960s, but his sense of experimentation went beyond the much-touted **magical realism**. Like Virgilio **Piñera**, he created a sense of the absurd that does not conceal its roots in a certain kind of despair. It is for the particular tone of anger guided by furies that Arenas will be remembered, both in Cuba and abroad, as well as for his ability to represent a defiant subjectivity besieged by networks of power.

Further reading

Ette, O. (ed.) (1992) *La escritura de la memoria*, Frankfurt: Vervuert Verlag.

Hernández-Miyares, J. and P. Rozencvaig (eds) (1990) *Reinaldo Arenas: Alucinaciones, fantasías y realidad*, Glenview, IL: Scott Foresman Montesinos.

Lugo Nayario, F. (1995) *La alucinación y los recursos literarios en las novelas de Reinaldo Arenas*, Miami: Universal.

Negrín, M.L. and M. Soloterevsky (1997) 'Reinaldo Arenas', in V. Smith (ed.), *Encyclopedia of Latin American Literature*, London: Fitzroy Dearborn, 48–52.

Salgado, C.A. (2002) 'Reinaldo Arenas', in C. Solé

and K. Müller-Bergh (eds), *Latin American Writers: Supplement I*, New York: Scribners, 55–72.

Sánchez, R. (ed.) (1994) *Reinaldo Arenas: Recuerdo y presencia*, Miami: Universal.

Soto, F. (1990) *Conversación con Reinaldo Arenas*, Madrid: Betania.

—— (1994) *Reinaldo Arenas: The 'Pentagonía'*, Gainesville: University Presses of Florida.

Valero, R. (1991) *El desamparado humor de Reinaldo Arenas*, Miami: Iberian Studies Institute, University of Miami.

JOSÉ QUIROGA

Arévalo Martínez, Rafael

b. 1884, Guatemala City; d. 1975, Guatemala City

Writer

A major *modernista* (see **Spanish American modernism**) poet and fiction writer, Arévalo is best known for his psychological novels and 'psycho-zoological tales', which caricature national figures by mixing human and animal traits; the most famous is 'El hombre que parecía un caballo' (The Man Who Looked Like a Horse) about Arévalo's friendship with Porfirio **Barba-Jacob**. His two 1914 autobiographical novels, *Una vida* (A Life) and *Manuel Aldano*, highlighted the central themes of twentieth-century Guatemalan literature – the Indian and imperialism. Arévalo's later work explores the impact of national dictatorships – for example, his 1939 chronicle-biography of Estrada Cabrera, *¡Ecce Pericles!* (1945), and his novels *Hondura* (1947) and *Ubico* (published posthumously in 1984).

Further reading

Arévalo Martínez, Rafael (1959) *Obras escogidas: Prosa y poesía; 50 años de vida literaria*, Guatemala City: Editorial Universitaria.

—— (1997) *El hombre que parecía un caballo y otros cuentos*, ed. Dante Liano, Paris: Colección Archivos.

Martin, G. (1997) 'Rafael Arévalo Martínez', in V. Smith (ed.), *Encyclopedia of Latin American Literature*, London: Fitzroy Dearborn, 52–3.

MARC ZIMMERMAN

Argentina

Argentina at the beginning of the twentieth century was a country that had undergone major economic and demographic changes since 1860. Sponsored by the government, there had been large-scale immigration from the Middle East and Europe, with the majority arriving from Spain and Italy. In a few decades, the demographics of the country changed dramatically, particularly in the cities of Buenos Aires, Rosario and Cordoba and in the wet grasslands of the pampas where many of them settled.

Economically, Argentina became integrated into an expanding capitalist system as a provider of agricultural goods such as cereals and the products of cattle-raising, namely beef and leather. It embarked on a process of modernization with the construction of a vast railway network, a state education system that substantially reduced illiteracy levels, the creation of a telephone and telegraph system and an incipient industrialization based on agriculture. At the same Buenos Aires was transformed from a village into a major cosmopolitan city whose land-owning upper bourgeoisie did all it could to mimic the lifestyles of the European capitals, and particularly of Paris.

None of this occurred without profound social conflict, of course; the immigrants circulated socialist and anarchist ideas and the first trade unions were formed to defend workers' rights and interests. A middle class was also in formation, which had enjoyed an education and now demanded political representation and changes in what was seen as a corrupt, aristocratic regime.

Modernization also affected the cultural sphere. What Beatriz Sarlo, after Bourdieu, calls 'the autonomous field of literature' was beginning to take shape and the professional writer, as someone who made a living from their intellectual and cultural activity, was beginning to emerge to take the place of the 'amateur writer', who was often a politician or a diplomat devoting their leisure time to writing. The journal *Nosotros*, founded in 1907 by Alfredo Bianchi and Roberto Giusti, published much of the work of this new group.

At the same time the educated elite reacted against immigration and the new cosmopolitanism by devoting its efforts to the recovery of the threatened national tradition. It was this cultural nationalism that produced courses in the study of Argentine literature at the University of Buenos Aires in 1913, organized by Ricardo **Rojas**, who was also responsible for the first *Historia de la Literatura Argentina* (1917–22). His work placed gaucho literature at the centre of the canon of national literature, in particular José Hernández's *Martín Fierro*, which he saw as the literary reflection of the national spirit. Leopoldo **Lugones**, the emblematic figure of the time and an ultraconservative influence until his death in 1938, argued, in a series of lectures in 1913, that the poem represented the foundation on which to build a national literature.

By the 1920s however, gaucho writing had reached its limits or become embedded in popular cultural practices such as the circus, the serial novel and popular music; in literature modernism and social realism were becoming the dominant aesthetic modes. Manuel **Gálvez**, Hugo **Wast**, Ricardo Payró and Benito Lynch were the Argentine inheritors of Russian realism and French naturalism.

After 1920, and with the appearance of the literary avant-garde movements, Argentine literature evolved between two conflicting tendencies: a persistent realism that served the reformist or revolutionary purposes of the political vanguard, and those currents that proposed the formal renewal of literary language, with no pretension to reflect reality, and which were represented by the writers who gathered around the journal ***Martín Fierro***.

In 1921, Jorge Luis **Borges** returned from Europe, where he had been in contact with the emerging avant-garde, and introduced and disseminated the ideas of *ultraismo* in Argentina. The young writers whose concern was to explore and develop a 'new sensibility' grouped around him – Oliverio **Girondo** and Leopoldo **Marechal** were among the founder members of the Florida group (see **Boedo vs Florida**). It was Girondo who wrote the group's manifesto, published in the journal *Martin Fierro*; its design and format, using illustrations, reproductions and photographs, broke with the more austere style of *Nosotros*. Its tone was playful and satirical and openly hostile to the aesthetics of modernism, and it produced an authentic revolution both in writing and in its approach to art.

Yet the Argentina avant-garde stands out for what Sarlo calls its moral and political 'moderatism' as well as its re-elaboration of the national tradition, particularly in the work of Borges who, in the poetry he published during this period (*Fervor de Buenos Aires*, *Luna de enfrente*), attempts to link that tradition with an avant-garde sensibility. By contrast the Boedo group – Leónidas Barletta, Roberto **Mariani**, Elías Castelnuovo – continued to write in a realist mode, their political commitment expressed in works of denunciation and political education, which also extended to the publication of classic works at accessible prices and the creation of journals such as *Claridad* and *Los pensadores*.

At the same time there were important antecedents to future renewal in narrative. In 1926, Ricardo **Güiraldes** published *Don Segundo Sombra* and Roberto **Arlt** his *El juguete rabioso*; despite their very different themes and aesthetics, both novels were highly innovative. Guiraldes explores national themes, but in a language that clearly displays the influence of avant-garde experimentation, while Arlt, in an original urban picaresque work, goes beyond the limits of a national literary language by incorporating a curious heteroglossia that echoes the range of oral registers in the speech of Buenos Aires on the one hand, and the artificial style of translated literary classics, which the author had read, on the other.

In 1930, the radical president Hipólito Yrigoyen was overthrown and replaced in power by a group of ultra-conservative military officers; it was the beginning of what became known as the 'infamous decade' characterized by electoral fraud, economic corruption and the persecution of political opponents. In the same year Victoria **Ocampo** founded the journal ***Sur***, which would occupy a key place in

Argentine culture in the decades that followed. *Sur*, the first issue of which appeared in 1931, published the old Martinfierristas such as Borges and Girondo, but was also a platform for new writers like Eduardo **Mallea**, Silvina **Ocampo**, Adolfo **Bioy Casares** and Ezequiel **Martínez Estrada**. It was a cornerstone of modernization, disseminating new developments in European and North American literature in a cultural environment that felt increasingly oppressive as the government moved in an increasingly Catholic and conservative direction.

Against this background, and in the growing conviction that the efforts to build a liberal state had failed, there emerged an 'essay of national interpretation' through which intellectuals sought explanations for that failure. This body of writing includes Raúl **Scalabrini Ortiz** (*El hombre que está solo y espera)* (The Man Who Stands Alone and Waits) (1931), Martínez Estrada's *Radiografía de la pampa* (1933) and Mallea's *Historia de una pasión argentina* (History of an Argentine passion) (1937).

In this post-avant-garde period, two major new directions opened up in the area of fiction. The first was the explosion of the literature of fantasy, with works by Borges, Bioy Casares (*La invención de Morel,* (1940)) and Silvina Ocampo, joint editors of the celebrated ***Antología de la literatura fantástica*** (Anthology of Fantastic Literature) (1940). Beginning with *Bestiario* (1951), the stories of Julio **Cortázar** continued in the same current while embracing the heritage of **surrealism**.

The other new direction, which also embraced Borges and Bioy Casares, was the detective story, including those written jointly by them under the pseudonym Bustos Domecq. Indeed, in those years Borges was an emblematic figure who could not be ignored by anyone setting out as a writer. Themes such as national identity, the role of the writer, literary language, the issue of commitment, would all be addressed with reference to Borges, whether to follow him or to reject his ideas.

The period of the two successive Perón governments (1946–55) proved to be key to contemporary Argentine history. Perón's anti-intellectual populism drove most writers to turn against him: both the liberal group around *Sur* and those who belonged to the Left. The magazine ***Contorno*** (1953–59), while hostile to *Sur*, which was entering a period of decline, opened its pages to a range of intellectual currents – existentialism, psychoanalysis and the new readings of Marxism that reflected the modernizing impulse of the time. The magazine also offered new readings of Argentine literature, rejuvenating interest in writers such as Arlt and Marechal, the first marginalized because of his aesthetics, the second because of his political ideas.

The 1960s were marked above all by the Cuban Revolution, the suppression of Peronism and the Vietnam War; but it was also the period when new artistic avant-gardes emerged in the context of the modernization of culture. New debates arose around the responsibility of the writer in bourgeois society, realism and the experimental, the character of the traditional genres and the status of literature in a society in which it must necessarily confront its relations with other registers and practices, for example mass culture.

Three works in particular address and reflect these tensions – Julio Cortázar's ***Rayuela*** (Hopscotch) (1963), Rodolfo **Walsh**'s *Operación masacre* (1964) and Manuel **Puig**'s *La traición de Rita Hayworth* (Betrayed by Rita Hayworth) (1968).

The turbulent 1970s, which culminated in the bloody military dictatorship installed by military coup in 1976, produced a growing intellectual polarization. Many writers died or disappeared, others were forced into exile and those who remained were subject to rigid censorship. In 1982, the military government declared war on the United Kingdom over possession of the Malvinas; the Argentine defeat led to the fall of the dictatorship and the election of the Radical presidential candidate, Raúl Alfonsín.

Ricardo **Piglia**'s novel *Respiración artificial* (1980) not only testified to the survival of an intellectual tradition, but also suggested the possibility of articulating literary and critical traditions which had seemed antagonistic until then – Borges and Arlt, for example – while at the same time revising national history from its origins..

In the last twenty years of the century, the historical novel was a particularly rich field, offering new interpretations of the past which in their turn shed light on the present realities of Argentina. Martín Caparrós's *Ansay*, Tomás Eloy **Martínez**'s *La novela de Perón* (1985) and *Santa Evita* (1995), Fogwill's *Los pichiciegos* and Juan José **Saer**'s *El **Entenado*** (The Witness) (1983) figure among them.

Contemporary literary production is characterized by narrative experimentation and unconventional uses of the traditional genres (the urban novel, adventure stories and thrillers) or aesthetic schools (North American minimalism, socialist realism) in Aníbal Jarkowski's *Rojo amor* (Red Love) (1993), Martín Rejtman's *Privado rapado* (1992) and *Velcro y yo* (1996) and Miguel Vitagliano's *Posdata para las flores* (Postscript for the Flowers) (1991), *El niño perro* (The Dog Child) (1993) and *Los ojos así* (Eyes like This) (1996).

Further reading

Colas, Santiago (1994) *Postmodernity in Latin America: The Argentine Paradigm*, Durham, NC: Duke University Press.

Foster, D.W. (1982) *Argentine Literature: A Research Guide*, New York, Garland.

—— (1995) *Violence in Argentine Literature: Cultural Responses to Tyranny*, Columbia and London: University of Missouri Press.

—— (1998) *Buenos Aires: Perspectives on the City and Cultural Production*, Gainesville: University of Florida Press.

Jitrik, N. (ed.) (1999) *Historia critica de la literatura argentina*, Buenos Aires: Emecé, 3 vols published to date of a planned 11 vols.

King, John (1986) *Sur: A Study of the Argentine Literary Journal and Its Role in the Development of a Culture 1931–1970*, Cambridge: Cambridge University Press.

Masiello, Francine (2001) *The Art of Transition: Latin American Culture and Neoliberal Crisis*: Durham. NC and London: Duke University Press.

Montaldo, G. and G. Nouzeilles (2002) *The Argentina Reader*, Durham, NC: Duke University Press.

Sarlo, B. (1988) *Buenos Aires, una modernidad periférica*, Buenos Aires: Ed Nueva Visión.

Sarlo B. and C. Altamirano (1997) *Ensayos argentinos*, Barcelona: Ariel.

Zanetti, S. (ed.) (1980–86) *Historia de la literatura argentina*, Buenos Aires: Centro Editor de America Latina, 4 vols.

JOSÉ MARISTANY

Arguedas, Alcides

b. 1879, La Paz, Bolivia; d. 1946, La Paz

Historian, writer and sociologist

Almost all Arguedas's writings were marked by a determinist view that physical environment and race are the prevailing factors in society. Lacking faith in the people of Bolivia, he wrote from a profoundly pessimistic perspective, particularly in ***Pueblo enfermo*** (A Sick People) (1909) in which he berates Bolivia for its incapacity as a nation. He was acknowledged as an *indigenista* writer after the publication of his *Raza de bronce* (Bronze Race) (1916), although recent criticism has been less convinced of his *indigenista* credentials (see ***indigenismo***).

Further reading

Arguedas, A. (1920) *Historia de Bolivia: La fundación de la república*, Madrid: Editorial América.

—— (1959) *Obras completas*, Mexico: Aguilar.

—— (1988) *Raza de bronce; Wuata Wuara*, ed. Antonio Lorente Medina, Paris: Colección Archivos.

Aronna, M. (1999) *'Pueblos enfermos' : The Discourse of Illness in the Turn-of-the-century Spanish and Latin American Essay*, Chapel Hill: University of North Carolina.

Paz Soldán, E. (2002) 'The Indigenist Writer as a (Mis)translator of Cultures: The Case of Alcides Arguedas', in Daniel Balderston and Marcy E. Schwartz (eds), *Voice Overs: Latin American Literature and Translation*, Albany: SUNY Press, 170–81.

Prada-Oropeza, R. (1995) 'Presentación crítica de Alcides Arguedas', *Texto crítico* 1(1): 217–37.

Rodríguez Luis, J. (1980) *Hermenéutica y praxis del indigenismo: La novela indigenista de Clorinda Matto a José María Arguedas*, Mexico City: Fondo de Cultura Económica, 56–87.

MARÍA DORA VILLA GÓMEZ

Arguedas, José María

b. 1911, Andahuaylas, Peru; d. 1969, Lima, Peru

Novelist and ethnographer

Born in highland Peru, Arguedas spent his early childhood under the care of Quechua-speaking indigenous people. This formative encounter generated his lifelong dedication to communicating Peruvian indigenous experience and shaped his literary and ethnographic achievements, including folkloric studies and compilations, Spanish translations of Quechua poetry and his own poetry (written primarily in Quechua), and the short stories and five novels comprising his most widely read work. Arguedas's suicide in 1969 has been attributed partly to despair over the continued oppression of Peruvian Indians. In style and narrative perspective, however, his novelistic expression of these concerns constitutes a fundamental move away from traditional Spanish-American ***indigenismo***. While this artistic mode had often romanticized or stereotyped its subjects, Arguedas sought to represent indigenous worlds from within and to portray the shifting linguistic experience and complex, cross-cultural negotiations characterizing a multi-ethnic society. Arguedas's multifaceted work as a teacher, translator, ethnographer and literary creator constitutes a coherent and dynamic intellectual project.

Because his mother died before he was three and his father travelled the Andean *sierra* as an itinerant lawyer, Arguedas lived with Quechua servants. Joining his father as an adolescent, he witnessed the treatment of Indians under *latifundismo* and attended ethnically diverse schools. From 1931–37 he studied literature at Lima's Universidad de San Marcos, while working for the post office and, well into the 1940s, as a secondary school teacher. During the 1930s and 1940s, Arguedas published compilations and studies of Quechua literary, folkloric and musical materials, including the collections of indigenous music *Canto Kechwa* (1937) and the story and song anthology *Canciones y cuentos del pueblo quechua* (Song and Stories of the Quechua People) (1949). He published the story collection *Agua* (Water) in 1935 and the novel *Yawar Fiesta* in 1941. The latter presents a confrontation over bullfighting in a small Andean town and anticipates Arguedas's later narratives in its demonstration of cross-cultural interactions in the Andean world. These works also signal Arguedas's reluctant decision to write prose in Spanish and represent early efforts to render in Spanish the syntactical and lyrical qualities of Quechua. He would achieve this most effectively in ***Los ríos profundos*** (Deep Rivers) (1958).

Arguedas was most productive from the mid-1950s until his death in 1969. He earned a doctorate in ethnology in 1963 from San Marcos with a dissertation on *Las comunidades de España y del Perú* (The Communities of Spain and Peru) (1968). He was also a leader of national institutes and museums of culture, folklore and history; published extensively on Quechua ethnography, folklore and musicology; launched and collaborated in journals of Peruvian culture; and travelled to symposia to conduct research in Spanish America, Europe and the USA.

His critically acclaimed novel *Los ríos profundos* appeared in 1958. In this autobiographical novel of self-growth, an adolescent white Peruvian boy, raised among Quechua speakers, attends a provincial, religious boarding school populated by students of varied social and ethnic backgrounds. Shaped by the myths and lyrical worldviews recalled from childhood, the boy decodes the social hierarchies and injustices in the school and town, which together form a microcosm of Peru. Discerning cultural conflicts, he focuses particularly on the diverse conceptions of language held by various groups and identifies most strongly with rebellious *chola* (mestiza) women and Indian serfs.

Published in 1963, *El sexto* (The Sixth), like *Los ríos profundos*, presents a microcosmic view of Peruvian social problems, but in the more urban setting of an infamous Lima jail and through the eyes of a student political prisoner. By contrast, Arguedas's 1965 novel *Todas las sangres* (All the Bloods) creates a more panoramic narrative world that expands the struggle between two *sierra* brothers, an *hacendado* and a mine owner, to address class and ethnic conflicts between owners and workers, the Western and the indigenous, the *sierra* and the coast, and the ideologies of nationalism and capitalist modernity. Arguedas's unfinished final novel, *El zorro de arriba y el zorro de abajo* (The Fox From Above, The Fox From Below), explores the chaotic and developing coastal world of Chimbote, a town teeming with what he described as a 'human swarm' of multiple ethnic and social origins. In this most experimental of Arguedas's works, narrative portions juxtapose vanguardist images of a rapidly developing Chimbote with the non-Western, mythical worldview and expressive forms of the character who confronts it. Arguedas's personal diary entries interrupt these narrative portions to address the novel's composition and the author's suicidal thoughts.

While critics have focused on the novels, in his poetry of the 1960s (published posthumously as *Tembla-Katatay* (1972)), Arguedas realized a long-standing resolve to write in Quechua. His cultural project as a whole resists a critical privileging of the literary, as even the novels weave together narrative, poetic, ethnographic and musical motifs into a thick description of Andean experience. All of his work was shaped as well by the ardent commitment to demonstrate the creative richness of Andean verbal and musical art, and he fittingly dedicated his last novel to the poet Emilio Adolfo **Westphalen** and to his good friend, the Quechua-speaking musician and violinist Máximo Damián Huamani. Thus Arguedas's literary and ethnographic work constitutes a remarkable, lifelong search for effective communication and reconciliation among the contentious elements that marked his own life and that shape the modern Peruvian experience of rapid cultural change.

Further reading

Arguedas, J.M. (1990) *El zorro de arriba y el zorro de abajo*, ed. E. Fell, Paris: Archivos.

Cornejo Polar, A. (1973) *Los universos narrativos de José María Arguedas*, Buenos Aires: Losada.

Larco, J. (ed.) (1976) *Recopilación de textos sobre José María Arguedas*, Havana: Casa de las Américas.

Lienhard, M. (1981) *Cultura popular andina y forma novelesca: Zorros y danzantes en la última novela de Arguedas*, Lima: Latinoamericana.

Márquez, I.P. (1997) 'José María Arguedas', in V. Smith (ed.), *Encyclopedia of Latin American Literature*, London: Fitzroy Dearborn, 65–7.

Ortega, J. (1989) 'José María Arguedas', in C.A. Solé and M.I. Abreu (eds), *Latin American Writers*, New York: Scribners, 3: 1131–8.

Rodríguez Luis, J. (1980) *Hermenéutica y praxis del indigenismo: La novela indigenista de Clorinda Matto a José María Arguedas*, Mexico City: Fondo de Cultura Económica, 122–226.

Rowe, W. (1996) *Ensayos arguedianos*, Lima: Sur.

Vargas Llosa, M. (1996) *La utopía arcaica: José María Arguedas y las ficciones del indigenismo*, Mexico City: Fondo de Cultura Económica.

VICKY UNRUH

Argueta, Manlio

b. 1936, San Salvador, El Salvador

Writer

Manlio Argueta is one of the best-known and most widely read Central American writers. His novel *Un día en la vida* (1980), translated as *One Day of Life* (1983), is a chronology of one day in the life of a Salvadoran family involved in the bloody struggles of the 1970s and 1980s. This novel has the urgency of the ***testimonio***, and challenges both literary genres. Argueta has published six novels, three books of poetry and numerous articles. Due to his political activities he lived in Costa Rica for twenty-one years, but is currently living in El Salvador.

Further reading

Argueta, M. (1985) *One Day of Life*, trans. B. Brow, New York: Aventura.

—— (1987) *Cuzcatlán: Where the Southern Sea Beats*, trans. C. Hansen, New York: Random House.

—— (1998) *Little Red Riding Hood in the Red Light District: A Novel*, Willimantic, CT: Curbstone Press.

Boland, R.C. (1997) 'Manlio Argueta', in V. Smith

(ed.), *Encyclopedia of Latin American Literature*, London: Fitzroy Dearborn, 68–70.

NICASIO URBINA

Arias, Arturo

b. 1950, Guatemala City

Writer

A US-based Guatemalan novelist, critic and professor, Arias publishes literary, historical and theoretical studies on Central American and Guatemalan themes. In his 1979 novel, *Después de las bombas* (After the Bombs) (1990), he portrays the effect of the 1954 intervention on his generation. *Itzam Na* (1981) describes the turbulent life of teenagers educated in Guatemala City's 'best' high schools but caught up in political violence, while his epic novel *Jaguar en llamas* (Jaguar in Flames) (1989) takes four characters through the major events of Guatemalan history. These works show Arias's concern with Guatemalan history and novelistic form. He has recently edited an important collection of essays on the controversies surrounding Rigoberta Menchú's testimony.

Further reading

Arias, Arturo (2001) *The Rigoberta Menchú Controversy*, Minneapolis: University of Minnesota Press.

MARC ZIMMERMAN

Aridjis, Homero

b. 1940, Michoacán, Mexico

Writer and green activist

Aridjis is a poet and narrator who has long held an important place in Mexican letters. He studied journalism and was a member of the literary workshop of Juan José **Arreola**, winning the prestigious Xavier **Villaurrutia** prize in 1964. Collaborator and contributor to a compilation of contemporary Mexican poetry *Poesía en movimiento* (Poetry in Motion) (1966) along with Octavio **Paz**, Alí Chumacero and José Emilio **Pacheco**, Aridjis has served the Mexican government as a cultural attaché in Holland and as ambassador to Switzerland. A recurrent concern in his creative work is the destruction of the environment. He currently leads the Grupo de los Cien, a green activist group.

Further reading

Aridjis, Homero (2000) *La montaña de las mariposas*, Mexico City: Alfaguara.

EDUARDO SANTA CRUZ

Ariel and arielismo

Since the 1900 publication of José Enrique **Rodó**'s essay *Ariel*, this term has been identified with an aesthetic, and sometimes political, movement associated with Rodó's characterization of Latin American cultures. The essay, like works by Sarmiento and **Martí**, has been seen as an essential key in the Latin American search for identity. In *Ariel*, directed at the youth of Latin America, Rodó claims that Latin cultures are more spiritual and less materialistic or pragmatic than Anglo-Saxon cultures, as well as more appreciative of beauty. For him, the ethereal spirit of Ariel from Shakespeare's *The Tempest* represents the Latin or Mediterranean cultural heritage in contrast to the barbaric and materialist cultures represented by Caliban. Because its publication followed shortly on the 1898 defeat of Spain in the Spanish-American War, many also have interpreted *Ariel* as a reaction to the increasing hegemony of the US in Latin American affairs. Rodó also clearly reacts negatively to the pressures of positivistic thought, so influential in the region (especially in Mexico, Brazil, Argentina and Uruguay), and to the changing nature of society amidst growing urbanization and industrialization. Like Matthew Arnold, Rodó questions how high culture is to survive in a mass society. Rodó has often been criticized for not considering the indigenous past and contemporary indigenous cultures as part of the spiritual matrix of Latin American values.

While initially *arielismo* was associated with an aesthetic based on spiritualism and elitism (Rodó directed himself in a refined style to a male audience in the context of a teacher–student relationship), it was subsequently transformed into a broader-based intellectual movement which called for a greater sense of identity for Latin America and for greater acknowledgement of the humanities. Young intellectuals grouped together throughout the continent to react against positivist and materialist values. The important group Ateneo de la Juventud in Mexico included Alfonso **Reyes**, the brothers Caso, Diego Rivera as well as other important figures. Although the group dissolved shortly after the beginning of the Revolution, many of its principal figures later became the principal architects of the cultural programmes of the revolutionary governments which sought to vindicate Mexico's own cultural history, particularly its indigenous roots. *Arielismo* sometimes merged with other more political currents and was also influential in the university reform movements of the first decades of the century.

In addition to its Mexican adherents, other writers who have been associated with the tendency are Mariano **Picón Salas** and Pedro **Henríquez Ureña** who continued the essay form in seeking a definition of the qualities of Latin American culture. Others have reworked or questioned the terms of Rodó's propositions, such as his compatriot Alberto **Zum Felde**, José Carlos **Mariátegui**, Luis Alberto **Sánchez**, and, most famously, Roberto **Fernández Retamar**, whose *Calibán* (1971) reread *The Tempest* through another lens, identifying the people of Latin America with Caliban and their oppressors with Ariel and Prospero.

Further reading

Ardao, Arturo (1950) *Espiritualismo y positivismo en el Uruguay*, Mexico City: Fondo De Cultura Económica.

González Echevarría, R. (1985) 'The Case of the Speaking Statue: *Ariel* and the Magisterial Voice of the Latin American Essay', in *The Voice of the Masters: Writing and Authority in Modern Latin American Literature*, Austin: University of Texas Press, 8–32.

Rodó, José Enrique (1988) *Ariel*, Austin: University of Texas Press.

Rodríguez Monegal, Emir (1957) *Introducción; Obras completas de Rodó*, Madrid: Aguilar.

—— (1976) *Ariel/Motivos de Proteo*, ed. Carlos Real de Azúa, Caracas: Biblioteca Ayacucho.

DANIEL BALDERSTON AND GWEN KIRKPATRICK

Arlt, Roberto

b. 1900, Buenos Aires, Argentina; d.1942, Buenos Aires

Writer

One of Spanish America's first urban novelists, Arlt (born Roberto Godofredo Christophersen Arlt) is known for his gritty but somewhat surreal portrayals of Buenos Aires, best exemplified in his 1929 novel, *Los siete locos* (The Seven Madmen), and its 1931 sequel, *Los lanzallamas* (The Flamethrowers). The memorable characters of these novels propose to found an anarchist Utopia funded by an income from prostitution. Arlt worked as a journalist for the newspapers, *El Mundo* and *Crítica*; his journalistic columns were collected in several volumes of *Aguafuertes* (Watercolours), some first collected in 1933 but others still coming to light more than a half-century after the author's death. He also wrote for the theatre and worked as an amateur inventor. Associated with members of both the Boedo and Florida groups (see **Boedo vs Florida**), Arlt – a writer whose work is open to anarchism and proletarian writing as well as to the avant-garde movements (see **avant-garde in Latin America**) – has been championed in recent years by Ricardo **Piglia**, often celebrated as one of the essential protagonists of Argentina's modernity.

Further reading

Amícola, J. (1994). *Astrología y fascismo en Roberto Arlt*, Rosario: Beatriz Viterbo.

Arlt, R. (1981) *Obra completa*, Buenos Aires: C. Lohlé.

—— (1984) *The Seven Madmen*, trans. Naomi Lindstrom, Boston: Godine.

—— (2000) *Los siete locos; Los lanzallamas*, ed. Mario Goloboff, Paris: Colección Archivos.
González, H. (1996) *Arlt, política y locura*, Buenos Aires: Colihue.
Hayes, A.W. (1989) 'Roberto Arlt', in C.A. Solé and M.I. Abreu (eds), *Latin American Writers*, New York: Scribners, 2: 881–6.
Jordan, P. (1997) 'Roberto Arlt', in V. Smith (ed.), *Encyclopedia of Latin American Literature*, London: Fitzroy Dearborn, 70–3.
Martínez, V.J. (1991) *The Semiotics of a Bourgeois Society: An Analysis of the Aguafuertes porteñas by Roberto Arlt*, Potomac, MD: Scripta Humanistica.

DANIEL BALDERSTON

Armas Alfonzo, Alfredo

b. 1921, Clarines, Venezuela; d. 1990, Caracas, Venezuela

Writer and journalist

An impressive display of narrative mastery distinguishes Armas Alfonzo's crónicas (see **crónica**) and fiction. His book *El osario de Dios* (God's Ossuary) (1969) is regarded as one of the most solid works in Venezuela's short story tradition and laid the basis for subsequent narrative explorations of time and language in the mid-twentieth century. In 1970 he was awarded the National Prize for Literature. His works include *Los cielos de la muerte* (Death's Heavens) (1949), *Cada espina* (Each Thorn) (1989) and *Los desiertos del ángel* (The Deserts of the Angel) (1990). He also had a long career as a journalist.

Further reading

Alegre, Atanasio *et al.* (1987) *Una valoración de Alfredo Armas Alfonzo*, Cunamá, Sucre, Venezuela: Centro de Actividades Literarias José Antonio Sucre/Consejo Nacional de la Cultura.
Armas Alfonzo, A. (1976) *Cuentos*, Havana: Casa de las Américas.
Various authors (2002) *Alfredo Armas Alfonso ante la crítica*, Caracas: Monte Avila.

VÍCTOR GALARRAGA OROPEZA

Arraíz, Antonio

b. 1903, Barquisimeto, Venezuela; d. 1962, Westport, Connecticut, USA

Poet and journalist

In 1924 the critics discovered Arráiz's poetic work *Áspero* (Harsh), perhaps the first avant-garde piece in Venezuelan poetic tradition (see **avant-garde in Latin America**). By then, Arraíz had already developed an outstanding career as a poet and journalist, and would soon be imprisoned for seven years after taking part in a mobilization against Juan Vicente Gomez's dictatorship. Later on he represented Venezuela in the United Nations, edited the journal *Ahora y después* (Now and After) and with Miguel **Otero Silva** founded *El Nacional*, one of the most widely read newspapers in Venezuela. The pioneering character of his work is not defined by any radical formal change but by an urgency of innovation and a virile affirmation of spirituality that have profoundly impacted later generations. Works include *Historia de Venezuela* (Venezuelan History), *Geografía de Venezuela* (Venezuelan Geography), *Vida ejemplar del Gran Mariscal de Ayacucho* (Ayacuchos's Exemplary Life), *Puros Hombres* (Pure Men) and the famous duo *Tío Tigre y Tío Conejo* (Uncle Tiger and Uncle Rabbit).

Further reading

Araujo, O. and O. Sambrano Urdaneta (1975) *Antonio Arráiz*, Caracas: Universidad Central de Venezuela.
Contribución a la bibliografía de Antonio Arráiz, 1903–1963 (1969) Caracas: Gobernación del Distrito Federal.

VÍCTOR GALARRAGA OROPEZA

Arráiz Lucca, Rafael

b. 1959, Caracas, Venezuela

Poet, journalist and editor

Arráiz Lucca belongs to a new generation of writers in Venezuela. His works include the collections

Balizaje (1983), *Terrenos* (Terrains) (1985), *Litoral* (Coast) (1991), *Pesadumbre de Bridgetown* (Sorrow in Bridgetown) (1992), *Batallas* (Battles) (1995), *Poemas ingleses* (English Poems) (1997) and *Reverón, 25 poemas* (Reveron, 25 poems) (1997), as well as several volumes of essays, including *Venezuela en cuatro asaltos* (Venezuela in Four Rounds) (1993). Director of Monte Avila Editores, he has prepared both an extensive anthology of Venezuelan poetry (1997) and the collection *Veinte poetas venezolanos del Siglo XX* (Twenty Venezuelan Poets of the Twentieth Century) (1998), in which he suggests a lyrical and existential understanding of human history during a war-torn period.

Further reading

Arráiz Lucca, R. (1999) *Antología poética*, Caracas: Monte Avila.

Rojo, V. (1996) *El infierno soy yo: Conversaciones con Rafael Arráiz Lucca*, Caracas: Editorial Panapo.

VÍCTOR GALARRAGA OROPEZA

Arrate, Marina

b. 1957, Santiago, Chile

Writer

Drawing on her experience as a psychologist and a critic, Arrate's writing constitutes an exploration of female identity, possibly the darkest area of Latin American experience. Within women's poetry and the variety of national poetic conventions, her voice stands out as a liberating project, with her themes of love and eroticism. Her works include *Este lujo de ser* (This Luxury of Being) (1986), *Máscara negra* (Black Mask) (1990), *Tatuaje* (Tattoo) (1992) and in 1996 an *Antología* which also includes *El hombre de los lobos* (The Wolf Man).

Further reading

Contreras, Marta (1993) 'Tatuaje de Marina Arrate y algunas disquisiciones sobre la poesía', *Acta Literaria*, 18: 183–9.

ELIANA ORTEGA

Arreola, Juan José

b. 1918, Ciudad Guzmán, Jalisco, Mexico; d. 2001, Guadalajara

Writer

An outstanding writer of stories and other short fictions, Arreola is as famous for his writing as for his public appearances, particularly on television, as a witty commentator on contemporary manners. Wit and humour (often quite a savage humour) characterize his writings, published in *Confabulario* (Confabulary) (1952), *Bestiario* (Bestiary) (1958) and *Palindroma* (Palindrome) (1964). Arreola is fascinated by language – at times this produces an elegant and restrained style, at times witty word play, and at others excessive and pretentious expression. But the link between his literary work and his public performance is a preoccupation with the spoken word, its sounds and rhythms, and its curious contradictions. His epigrams and sayings have been collected in two volumes, *La palabra educación* (The Word Education) (1973) and *Inventario* (Inventory) (1976).

Further reading

Arreola, Juan José (1995) *Obras*, Mexico City: Fondo de Cultura Económica.

Biriotti, M. (1997) 'Juan José Arreola', in V. Smith (ed.), *Encyclopedia of Latin American Literature*, London: Fitzroy Dearborn, 72–4.

Castañón, A. (1999) *El reino y su sombra: En torno a Juan José Arreola*, Mexico City: Ediciones del Ermitaño.

Cluff, R.M. and L.H. Quackenbush (1989) 'Juan José Arreola', in C.A. Solé and M.I. Abreu (eds), *Latin American Writers*, New York: Scribners. 3: 1229–36.

Poot Herrera, S. (1992) *Un giro en espiral: El proyecto literario de Juan José Arreola*, Guadalajara: Editorial Universidad de Guadalajara.

MIKE GONZALEZ

Arrigucci Jr, Davi

b. 1943, São João da Boa Vista, São Paulo, Brazil

Critic

One of the most influential critics of his generation, Arrigucci was trained by Antonio **Candido**. His approach is, if anything, more 'aesthetic' than that of his Marxist friend Roberto **Schwarz**. He has written on Spanish American topics (a book on **Cortázar** and excellent essays on **Rulfo** and **Borges**), but also enjoys writing about 'minor' aspects of Brazilian literature, journalism, memoirs, short stories, etc. It is fitting that his *Humildade, paixão e morte* (Humility, Passion and Death) (1990) is a study of Manuel **Bandeira**, who defined himself as a 'minor' poet.

Further reading

Arrigucci Jr, Davi (1990) *Humildade, paixäa o e morte: A poesía de Manuel Bandeira*, São Paulo: Companhia das Letras.

—— (1999) *Outros achados e perdidos*, São Paulo: Companhia das Letras.

JOHN GLEDSON

Arrom, José Juan

b. 1910, Holguín, Cuba

Critic

An outstanding scholar of Latin American literature, Arrom lived in the USA from an early age, graduating from Yale University. His historical and critical essays on Cuba and Latin America include *Historia de la literatura dramática cubana* (History of Cuban Drama) (1944), *El teatro en Hispanoamérica en la época colonial* (Hispanic American Theatre in the Colonial Era) (1956), *Esquema generacional de las letras hispanoamericanas* (Generational Model of Latin American Literature) (1963) and *En el fiel de América* (America in the Balance) (1985).

Further reading

Arrom, J.J. (1991) *Imaginación del Nuevo Mundo: Diez estudios sobre los inicios de la narrativa*, Mexico City: Siglo XXI.

WILFREDO CANCIO ISLA

Arrufat, Antón

b. 1935, Santiago de Cuba

Writer and dramatist

Arrufat's first poems were published in the magazine *Ciclón*. In 1968 his play *Los siete contra Tebas* (Seven Against Thebes) was awarded the **UNEAC** theatre prize, a decision which unleashed an intense public debate; Arrufat was marginalized and the work banned for fifteen years. His drama is collected in *Teatro* (1963) and *La tierra permanente* (The Permanent Earth) (1987). He has published volumes of poetry, a novel and short stories including *Mi antagonista y otras observaciones* (My Antagonist and Other Observations) (1963), as well as a personal testimony *Virgilio Piñera; entre él y yo* (Between Piñera and Me) (1994).

Further reading

Arrufat, Antón (1994) *Poesía y crítica: Virgilio Piñera*, Mexico City: Consejo Nacional para la Cultura y las Artes.

—— (2000) *La noche del aguafiestas*, La Habana: Editorial Letras Cubanas.

—— (2001) *La huella en la arena: Poemas reunidos*, La Habana: Ediciones Unión.

Barquet, J.J. (2002) *Teatro y Revolución Cubana: Subversión y utopía en Los siete contra Tebas de Antón Arrufat*, Lewiston, NY: E. Mellen Press.

Espinosa Mendoza, N. (2001) 'Los idus de Arrufat', *Encuentro de la Cultura Cubana* 20: 21–3.

Smith, V.A. (1990) 'Memorias del país de los muertos: Una lectura *de La caja está cerrada*, de Anton Arrufat', *Revista iberoamericana* 56(152–3): 1091–1102.

WILFREDO CANCIO ISLA

Arturo, Aurelio

b. 1909, La Unión, Colombia; d. 1974, Bogotá, Colombia

Poet

A representative figure of twentieth-century Colombian poetry, Aurelio Arturo belonged to the literary group 'Piedra y Cielo'. He began his career as a lawyer, and as a poet wrote for Colombian newspapers such as as *El Tiempo* and *El Espectador*. He received the National Poetry Award in 1965. Arturo's poetry follows Aristotle's lyrical principles. In his words, spirituality touches the borders of transcendentalism under the axiom that humankind communicates with its soul in a mystical experience. To Arturo, all individuals and all things are, at once, microcosms and macrocosms. The unifying power in the universe is love, a force that is present in his stanzas. The poet also sings to the average, simple man who is anonymous and hopes for a better life.

Further reading

Arturo, Aurelio (1992) *Morada al sur*, Santafé de Bogotá: Grupo editorial Norma, colección Cara y Cruz.

Ospina, William (1990) *Aurelio Arturo*, Bogotá: Procultura.

ALVARO BERNAL

Arvelo Larriva, Enriqueta

b. 1886, Barinitas, Venezuela; d. 1962, Barinitas

Poet

Considered today to be one of the founders of women's poetry in Venezuela and one of the country's principal avant-garde (see **avant-garde in Latin America**) poets, Enriqueta Arvelo was largely overshadowed during her lifetime by her brother Alfredo, himself a poet. Her writing is austere, erotic and spare. She spent most of her life in her native town, and wrote about love, the landscape of the Venezuelan plains (the *llanos*) and her own inner life. In 1958 she was awarded the Municipal Poetry Prize for her volume *Mandato del canto* (The Instruction to Sing).

Further reading

Arvelo Larriva, Enriqueta (1957) *Mandato del canto; poemas, 1944–1946*, Caracas.

JORGE ROMERO LEÓN

Asir, Revista

Asir was a Uruguayan cultural journal (1948–59) founded by Washington Lockhart and linked to the Generation of 1945. From no. 14 onwards its contributors included Montevideo intellectuals such as Domingo Bordoli and Líber Falco who steered it in a sort of existentialist spiritualist direction. *Asir* privileged rural writers like J.J. Morosoli and Francisco **Espínola**, but also published Felisberto **Hernández** and Carlos **Denis Molina**, and in later issues introduced a new generation of young poets. Ediciones Asir, its co-operative publishing imprint, included Carlos **Real de Azúa** and Angel **Rama** and published, among other works, **Onetti**'s *El infierno tan temido* (A Hell So Feared) (1962) and Denis Molina's *Lloverá siempre* (It Will Always Rain) (1967).

NORAH GIRALDI DEI CAS

Asis, Jorge

b. 1946, Buenos Aires, Argentina

Writer, journalist and diplomat

The fiction of Jorge Asis belongs within a realist current, the major representative of which is Roberto **Arlt**. He has published several highly successful novels, including *La manifestación* (The Demonstration) (1971), *Don Abdel Salim* (1972), *Flores robadas en los jardines de Quilmes* (Flowers Stolen from the Garden of Quilmes) (1980), *Carne picada* (Minced Meat) (1981), *Sandra, la trapera* (Sandra the Seller of Used Clothes) (1996), several of which have been translated into a number of languages. He has been Argentine ambassador to UNESCO and was a member of its Executive Committee between 1989 and 1994, and has also served as Minister of Culture and Ambassador to Portugal.

Further reading

Asis, Jorge (2000) *Del flore a Montparnasse; el sentido de la vida en el socialismo*, Buenos Aires: Editorial Sudamericana.

—— (2001) *Excelencias de la nada*, Buenos Aires: Sudamericana.

Burgos, N. (2001) *Jorge Asís: Los límites del canon*, Buenos Aires: Catálogos.

Maristany, J. (1995) 'Contestations ostentatoires et adhesion: *Flores robadas en los jardines de Quilmes* de Jorge Asis', *Imprévue* 1: 51–68.

GRACIELA MUSACHI

Assis, Joaquim Maria Machado de

b. 1839, Rio de Janeiro, Brazil: d. 1908, Rio de Janeiro

Writer

Brazil's most important writer and the finest novelist in Latin America during the nineteenth century, Machado de Assis explored the theme of urban life with irony and technical sophistication. Influenced by the self-conscious fiction of Laurence Sterne, Machado (as he is usually called) constructs a fictional world in which the characters are centrally concerned with their image in society. His finest novel, *Dom Casmurro*, inagurates the twentieth-century tradition of narrative experimentation in the region.

Born in Rio de Janeiro, then the Brazilian capital, to a Portuguese washerwoman and a mulatto house painter, Machado was acquainted from childhood with popular urban life, but also had contact with life in the upper strata of society through his godparents. The theme of race appears in his writing in rather oblique ways, but critics have seen a subtle abolitionist current in his work, and his last novel *Memorial de aires* (1908) registers the abolition of slavery in 1888. Machado's intellectual prominence earned him a central place in the cultural world of the late Brazilian Empire and the early Republic. In 1896 he founded the Brazilian Academy of Letters and was its president for the rest of his life.

His early career as a literary critic, particularly as a theatre critic, informed his later work, which often turns on dramatic motifs (most notably the Othello theme in *Dom Casmurro*). His lucid early essays include 'Instinto de nacionalidade' (1873), which anticipates Borges's argument in the 1951 essay 'El escritor argentino y la tradición' on the creative potential of the Latin American's peripheral position *vis á vis* the Western tradition: Machado, like Borges seventy years later, argues that the freedom and irreverence that come from this marginal position need to be wellsprings of the new literature. He also wrote three books of poetry in the 1860s and 1870s.

His first phase as a novelist is marked by romanticism. Works from this period are *Resurreição* 872), *A mão e a luva* (1874), *Helena* (1876) and *Iaiá Garcia* (1878). *Helena* demonstrates Machado's growing interest in the realist novel. His short stories also show a growing interest in narrative complexity, with a layering of narrative levels.

Machado's reputation rests primarily on a series of extraordinary novels, most notably *Memórias póstumas de Brás Cubas* (1881), *Quincas Borba* (1891), *Dom Casmurro* (1899) and *Esaú e Jacó* (1904). These novels are characterized by what John Gledson has called a 'deceptive realism', as psychological uncertainty undermines the telling of the story. *Memórias póstumas* is narrated from the grave, *Quincas Borba* bears the name of both a philosopher and a dog and *Dom Casmurro* is told by a narrator who is convinced that his youthful perception of the world – and particularly of his wife and his best friend – was radically mistaken. Machado expresses in these works a dark view of human nature, a view in which vanity and the thirst for fame twist the human character in ways that make it impossible to believe what people say or even what they do.

The most modern of nineteenth-century Latin American writers, Machado has been justly celebrated in recent years by Susan Sontag and many others. Motifs from his work have been echoed in numerous works of Brazilian literature and culture, with frequent adaptations for stage and screen. The haunting complexity of *Dom Casmurro* is among the high points of psychological fiction in modern literature.

Further reading

Assis, J.M. Machado de (1953) *Dom Casmurro*, trans. H. Caldwell, Berkeley: University of California Press.

—— (1959) *Obras completas*, Rio de Janeiro: Aguilar, 3 vols.

Caldwell, H. (1970) *Machado de Assis: The Brazilian Master and his Novels*, Berkeley: University of California Press.

Gledson, J. (1984) *The Deceptive Realism of Machado de Assis: A Dissenting Interpretation of Dom Casmurro*, Liverpool: Francis Cairns.

—— (1986) *Machado de Assis: Ficção e história*, São Paulo: Paz e Terra.

Schwarz, R. (1977) *Ao vencedor as batatas*, São Paulo: Duas Cidades.

—— (1991) *Un mestre na periferia do capitalismo: Machado de Assis*, São Paulo: Duas Cidades.

DANIEL BALDERSTON

astillero, El

Written by the Uruguayan writer Juan Carlos **Onetti** and published in 1961, *El astillero* (The Shipyard) is part of a series of novels and stories set in an imaginary town, Santa María, in the River Plate region. The naively enthusiastic protagonist, Larsen, returns to work for Petrus, the shipyard owner. With two other employees, Galvéz and Kunz, he maintains the illusion of a functional shipyard by studying decaying plans and paying imaginary bills. The facade slowly becomes an integral part of the characters. Onetti creates a ghostly feeling of unreality while appropriating realist conventions and the interior monologues of frustrated characters.

Further reading

Millington, M. (1985) *Reading Onetti*, Liverpool: Francis Cairns.

Onetti, Juan Carlos (1992) *The Shipyard*, London: Serpent's Tail.

VICTORIA RUÉTALO

Asturias, Miguel Angel

b. 1899, Guatemala City; d. 1974, Madrid, Spain

Novelist

A member of the same crucial generation of writers as Jorge Luis **Borges**, Alejo **Carpentier** and Pablo **Neruda**, Asturias was the first Latin American novelist to be awarded the Nobel Prize for Literature, in 1967, and is without a doubt the dominant literary figure of Guatemala and the most influential novelist in the history of Central America to date. Nevertheless, the last twenty years have seen a decline in interest in his work even though, curiously, *Hombres de maíz* (Men of Maize) (1949), a novel previously neglected by critics, is now routinely granted mastepiece status.

More than that of any other Latin American country except perhaps Peru, the history of Guatemala has been structured and dominated by what used to be called the 'Indian problem'. It is not surprising, then, that Asturias's entire oeuvre is similarly conditioned. His first major work was *Leyendas de Guatemala* (Legends of Guatemala), published in Madrid in 1930, a collection of stories based on the heterogeneity of Guatemala's cultural identity. These stories retain the capacity to surprise and delight which inspired a famous prologue by Paul Valéry when the French translation appeared in 1932. Moreover, they reveal an incipient consciousness which historians would later call post-colonial.

Asturias was born in Guatemala City, the eldest son of a lawyer who found it difficult to practise effectively during the savage dictatorial regime of Manuel Estrada Cabrera (1898–1920). His middle-class mother was forced to open a shop to make ends meet, and this humiliation had a radicalizing effect upon her son. Asturias took full part in university politics between 1917 and 1923, including the overthrow of Estrada in 1920; and like all Guatemalans, he experienced the great earthquake of 1917 which, he said, transformed the capital city and Guatemalan society and became one of the great symbols of revolution in his subsequent work.

Although radicalized by student politics, Asturias was still no revolutionary by the time he graduated. Admittedly, he did write Guatemala's first university thesis on the 'social problem of the Indian' in 1923, but it owed more to nineteenth-century race-based positivist sociology than to the new revolutionary doctrines of the twentieth century. His consciousness developed with extraordinary speed however, after his arrival in Paris in 1924, at one of the great cultural moments of Western history. Within ten years he had written more than 400 newspaper articles, translated the best-known Maya text *Popol Vuh* (Book of the Council) into Spanish (from French!), published *Leyendas de Guatemala* and, above all, completed what would become his most famous work, a historical and stylistic point of reference for Latin American literature as a whole, *El Señor Presidente* (The President) (1946), about the Estrada Cabrera era. The novel shows clearly the influence of **surrealism** on Asturias's language and technique, but its perceptions are used functionally to convey humanistic disbelief at the horrors of oppression and injustice.

El Señor Presidente would have to wait thirteen years for publication, from 1933, when Asturias returned to Guatemala, until 1946, when the work appeared in Mexico. The reason, ironically but unsurprisingly, was the existence of another US-backed dictatorship, that of Jorge Ubico (1931–44). Asturias lay as low as possible and worked on his most important novel, *Hombres de maíz*, which was eventually published in Buenos Aires. A difficult, complex and controversial work, *Hombres de maiz* traces the long, painful and uncompleted interaction between the Indian cultures which occupied Central America at the time of the sixteenth-century conquest and the Europeans who invaded and subjugated them. The work's relevance is enhanced by Asturias's prescient analysis of how European imperialism seeks to dominate not only other human beings but everything else, including nature, culture and thought itself.

In the 1950s, the era of literary engagement, Asturias devoted himself to political concerns through his controversial *Trilogía bananera* (Banana Trilogy), an interesting but not entirely successful amalgam of **magical realism** and **socialist realism** which documents US imperialism in Guatemala and prophesies revolutionary victory for the Guatemalan people. He also published *Weekend en Guatemala* (1956), a collection of stories protesting against the 1954 US-backed invasion of his country which sent him into exile.

In the 1960s he returned to his early interest in Guatemalan cultural syncretism, first with *Mulata de tal* (Mulatta) (1963) and later with *Maladrón* (The Bad Thief) (1969). Although lacking the full continental resonance of his first three works, these were novels of a remarkable freshness for a writer in his sixties, and Asturias continued the trend with *Tres de cuatro soles* (Three of Four Suns), published after his death in 1974. By that time, despite the Nobel Prize, his star was in decline, but he is likely to be remembered nonetheless as one of the most original Latin American voices of the twentieth century.

Further reading

1899/1999: Vida, obra y herencia de Miguel Angel Asturias, Paris: UNESCO.

Asturias, M.A. (1963) *The President*, London: Gollancz.

Brotherston, G. (1978) *The Emergence of the Latin American Novel*, Cambridge: Cambridge University Press.

Callan, R. (1968) *Miguel Angel Asturias*, Boston: Twayne.

Franco, J. (1989) 'Miguel Angel Asturias', in C.A. Solé and M.I. Abreu (eds), *Latin American Writers*, New York: Scribners, 2: 865–73.

Keightley, R. (1997) 'Miguel Angel Asturias', in V. Smith (ed.), *Encyclopedia of Latin American Literature*, London: Fitzroy Dearborn, 76–9.

Martin, G. (1989) *Journeys through the Labyrinth: Latin American Fiction in the Twentieth Century*, London: Verso.

Prieto, R. (1993) *Miguel Angel Asturias's Archeology of Return*, Cambridge: Cambridge University Press.

GERALD MARTIN

autobiography

In her book *At Face Value* (1991), Sylvia **Molloy** has observed that: 'whereas there are and have been a good many autobiographies written in Spanish America, they have not always been read autobiographically: filtered through the dominant discourse of the day, they have been hailed either as history or as fiction, and rarely considered as occupying a space of their own'. She examines, among others, autobiographical works by Victoria **Ocampo**, Mariano **Picón Salas** and José **Vasconcelos**. In all of them she observes a certain uneasiness about speaking about the private or the intimate: these are very largely the public lives of famous people, recorded for their contemporaries and for posterity. When they seem to be most intimate, she observes, instead of narrating the self (the hallmark of autobiography since Rousseau), these writers take refuge in telling the stories of their families or their ancestors: thus autobiography shades into **biography**.

Neruda's *Confieso que he vivido: Memorias* (translated simply as *Memoirs*) (1974), a work not discussed by Molloy, is a useful case in point. Assembled by Neruda (or perhaps by his heirs, since it was published posthumously) from bits of his journalism, this work contains profiles of his friends (and enemies) and of his times – life as a consul in Asia, the Spanish Civil War, exile in Mexico, his return to Chile – but it is surprisingly lacking in self-disclosure: it is as if Neruda put on the costumes that decorate his houses in Santiago and Isla Negra and never took them off. The great set piece that is at the centre of the book, the telling of his decision to join the Chilean Communist Party in 1945, is oddly distanced: Neruda tells of being asked by miners in the desert of northern Chile to read his poetry, and reports that his poetry has earned him the laurel crown of a worker who salutes him as a brother. He then reports: 'I entered the Chilean Communist Party on 15 July 1945'. The event is presented in an oddly flat way, as if its significance were given to him by others, not by his own decision.

The autobiographical impulse is strongly present in fictional works, including those of Felisberto **Hernández**, Ricardo **Güiraldes**, Virgilio **Piñera**, Clarice **Lispector**, José **Lezama Lima**, Molloy herself and Ricardo **Piglia**, as well as (more fleetingly) in the works of **Borges**, **Rulfo**, **Cortázar** and **Onetti**. To some extent, elements of self-disclosure which seem relatively lacking in many of the autobiographies are more fully present in these fictions, perhaps precisely because of the ruse that this is not the whole nor nothing but the truth. Another genre that flirts with autobiography is ***testimonio***, although here the life that is told is not being written by the one who experienced it (Rigoberta Menchú, Domitila Chungara, Esteban Montejo, Jesusa Palancares) but is being told to an other who writes (Elizabeth Burges-Debray, Moemi Viezzer, Miguel **Barnet**, Elena **Poniatowska**). This is obviously rather distant from the writing of one's own life, which involves self-definition or self-construction, and the negotiation with a reader about what can be told, about what is fit to print.

Further reading

Costa, E. de (1997) 'Autobiography', in V. Smith (ed.), *Encyclopedia of Latin American Literature*, London: Fitzroy Dearborn, 81–3.

Ellis, R.R. (2002) *They Dream Not of Angels but of Men: Homoeroticism, Gender and Race in Latin American Autobiography*, Gainesville: University Press of Florida.

Feal, R.G. (1986) *Novel Lives: The Fictional Autobiographies of Guillermo Cabrera Infante and Mario Vargas Llosa*, Chapel Hill: University of North Carolina Press.

Iglesia, C. (1996) *Islas de la memoria*, Buenos Aires: Cuenca del Plata.

Molloy, S. (1991) *At Face Value: Autobiographical Writing in Spanish America*, Cambridge: Cambridge University Press.

Prieto, A. (1966) *La literatura autobiográfica argentina*, Buenos Aires: Jorge Alvarez.

Rosa, N. (1990) *El arte del olvido*, Buenos Aires: Puntosur.

DANIEL BALDERSTON

avant-garde in Latin America

Until the late 1950s, the Latin American avant-garde was perceived as derivative of the European avant-garde, without recognition of its originality of influence on subsequent literary and artistic movements. With the exception of a few major figures, such as Pablo **Neruda**, César **Vallejo**, Vicente **Huidobro** and Nicolás **Guillén**, little attention had been given to the period that Peter Bürger has called, in his *Theory of the Avant-Garde*, the 'historic avant-garde' (between the early 1910s and the 1940s). The emergence of the Latin American novel, the so-called '**Boom**', in the early 1950s and 1960s, inspired an examination of its antecedents, and with it, an interest in understanding the Latin American avant-garde as a significant cultural development that gave voice to a relatively unified and distinctly Latin American art, also part of a larger international movement.

The international character of the Latin American avant-garde is due principally to the unprecedented flow of political ideas and aesthetic styles between different urban and regional centres and across national borders. This aesthetic and ideological cross-fertilization was made possible by the free movement of artists throughout Europe and the Americas and a steady migration towards the national capitals. Capital cities in Latin America, including Buenos Aires, Mexico City, Lima, Havana and Santiago de Chile, joined New York City and established European capitals in an international network with Paris at its centre. In addition to the formative voyage that Latin American artists ritually undertook to Europe, many avant-garde artists spent long periods there. Notable among these were **Borges**, who lived in Switzerland and Spain, Cesár Vallejo, who spent most of his adult life in Paris, and Oliverio **Girondo**, who made annual trips to Europe. At the same time, many Europeans made their way to South America, searching for inspiration for their artistic experiments. André Breton spent time among the Tarahumaras in Mexico, Blaise Cendrars lived in Brazil, while Guillermo de Torre lived in Argentina. Finally, Latin America avant-garde artists explored their own continent and made contacts with avant-garde artists from other Latin American countries and regions. Pablo Neruda, Pablo de **Rokha**, Oliverio Girondo and Carlos **Pellicer** illustrate this deliberate and conscious effort to explore Latin America and write about the cultural and aesthetic issues they encountered in their travels.

Along with increased ease of transatlantic travel, breakthroughs in communications technology contributed to the internationalism of the avant-garde movement. The telegraph, radio, cinema and flourishing print industries were seen as icons of a new era and a new and radically different spirit. New art forms emerged that sought to describe and consciously shape a new international reality, as well as challenge the traditional relationship between society, art and artist. The artist was seen as being in a formative relationship with society. Thus, in the symbolic universe of the arts, the arrival of the avant-garde represented the dissolution of ideological, political and cultural centrality, and with it the erosion of European dominance, which allowed for a more inclusive and relativistic view of cultural and historical phenomena.

The Latin American avant-garde was, however, more than an expression of the larger international movement. Vicky Unruh has pointed out that Latin American vanguardism was also 'autochthonous in its orientation, as artists interacted with European avant-garde currents in keeping with their own cultural exigencies'. The Latin American avant-garde affirmed its own distinctive identity, whether national, regional or continental. Nelson **Osorio** has explained this independence by defining the avant-garde as a product of specific Latin American socio-economic conditions. He understands it as a response to the anti-oligarchic spirit of the era and an expression of hope for political and ideological change. This is seen in the increased demand for political power by the nascent middle class, the working class, farmers, students and ethnic groups as well as a response to socialism, communist parties, anarchism, fascism and union-based philosophies.

One of the main characteristics that defines the Latin American avant-garde is a desire to break with the past, both politically and aesthetically. The *modernista* aesthetic no longer adequately described the New World at the beginning of this century.

The avant-garde defined itself in terms of a 'modern' sensibility, coupled with a desire to belong to 'modernity' (often, in Latin America, this was expressed as a longing) and, at times, to an almost futuristic world. The avant-garde artist can be understood as a vagabond, a wandering camera, an eye registering and commenting on the modern city and its technologies. The poetry of Girondo, Luis **Cardoza y Aragón**, Borges, Jorge **Carrera Andrade**, Manuel **Maples Arce** and others describes this new and changing architectural landscape of major Latin American cities together with their European counterparts.

Another important characteristic of the Latin American avant-garde was political activism and a commitment to social and political change. This was expressed in the revolutionary content of art works and in formal experimentation, both of which sought to recreate the world anew. Ideologically, art was viewed not as a mere reflection of society but as an active participant in shaping that society. By changing perceptions of the world, art could also change the world itself. Whether expressed in Marxist terminology, anti-colonial ideology or populist union-based thinking, the avant-garde engaged in a fight against *modernismo* (see **Spanish American modernism**) as an aesthetic form that stood for the ideology of the oligarchic political structure in power throughout most of Latin America. The murals of Diego Rivera, José Clement Orozco and David Alfaro Siqueiros, members of the League of Revolutionary Writers and Artists in Mexico, evidence a search to find an art that was both national and popular. Their explicit goals were to create art for the masses and serve the ideology of revolution. Other examples of social and political commitment in the avant-garde can be found in the formal experimentation and political content of works by Neruda, Vallejo, Magda **Portal**, Arturo Peralta (Gamaliel **Churata**) and the Afro-Caribbean poetry of Nicolás Guillén and Luis **Palés Matos**.

A third characteristic of the Latin American avant-garde is a continuous experimentation with form and content in the search for an ever-changing newness that better expresses the condition of modernity. Examples of this experimentation include destruction of the concept of beauty; harmony and unity in art through dislocation, parody and irony; elimination of a single narrator or cohesive poetic voice; hybridization of genres; interest in and the assimilation of popular or mass art (the circus, cabaret, recitals, film) as well as primitive or anonymous art; dismemberment of traditional poetic form (use of free verse, poems without stanzas, rhyme, traditional syntax or metre); the innovative use of typographical spaces on the page; the use of different physical and representational materials in montage; and the use of calligramatic and concrete poetry. Together, this experimentation reflected a general desire to destroy the concept of art as a bourgeois institution and artistic objects as possessions to be owned by individuals.

The fourth characteristic of the Latin American avant-garde is that the world it created and expressed was no longer governed by logic and reason. Formal experimentation led to descriptions of a reality understood or experienced as fragmented and discontinuous, without obvious psychic unity, and often with irrational foundations. The speaking subject was no longer a stable psychic unity but a shifting voice or point of view. The basic feeling expressed through its dislocated language was that of alienation from the world. The reader was integrated into the avant-garde text. The reader became the speaker's ally as seen in the multitude of avant-garde **manifestos** in which the voice fights against a common enemy (the old system, past literary school or poetic forms). At times the reader became the enemy attached or disregarded through an aggressive or totally cryptic language that did not concern itself with 'communicating' with the reader.

Finally, it is important to examine the Latin American avant-garde as a national phenomenon that had unique expressions in different parts of Latin America. While there was avant-garde activity throughout most of Latin America, the major vanguard centres were Buenos Aires, Mexico City, Lima, Havana and São Paulo. An examination of avant-garde activities specific to national centres illustrates the crucial importance of vanguard group activities and the journals in which art and ideas were published. Studying avant-garde at the national level also facilitates a better understanding of the relationship between individual artists, their specific socio-political contexts, and the national or regional ideological traditions within which they worked. This relationship is well illustrated by the Brazilian avant-garde, for example, notable for both its national expression in the incorporation of a non-academic 'Brazilian' language and for its cosmopolitan tendencies. After the centennial independence celebration of the Modern Art Week in São Paulo in 1922, a number of distinct and diverse vanguard groups appeared, located in different urban centers such as São Paulo, Rio de Janeiro, and Belo Horizonte and Cataguases in Minas Gerais. The 'Dinamista' group was led by Graça Aranha, who had a special interest in futurist elements such as movement, velocity and material and technical progress; the 'Primitivista' group was led by Oswald de **Andrade**; the 'nacionalista' group was located in São Paulo and published the journals *Verdeamarelo* (1926), *Anta* (1927) and *Bandeira* (1936); the 'Espiritualista' group was located in Rio de Janeiro; and the 'Desvairista' group was centred around the magnetic personality of Mário de **Andrade**. Also of note was the participation of three Brazilian women: cubist painter Anita Malfatti, whose 1917 show in São Paulo was considered scandalous; the painter Tarsila do Amaral, who participated in the '**Antropofagia**' group and published, along with her husband Oswald de Andrade, in its important journal ***Revista de Antropofagia*** (São Paulo, 1928–9); and the poet Cecília **Meireles**, who was associated with the magazine *Festa*.

The Argentine avant-garde was polarized between two groups. The Boedo group was working class and socialist, and primarily wrote prose, while the Florida group (associated especially with the journal ***Martín Fierro*** (1924–7)) was cosmopolitan, upper class and wrote mostly poetry (see **Boedo vs Florida**). In Peru, most vanguard activity was centred on the exceptional journal ***Amauta*** (1926–30), edited by José Carlos **Mariátegui**; it often dealt with the issue of ***indigenismo***. There were important national avant-gardes in most capitals of the continent. Two additional avant-garde journals played a critical role in the development of both a national and continental Latin American avant-garde: the Cuban ***Revista de Avance*** (1927–30) and the Costa Rican ***Repertorio americano*** (1919–59).

The 'historical' Latin American avant-garde can be understood as playing an important formative role in the remarkable experimentation of contemporary Latin American literature and art. The Boom narrative of the 1960s is directly indebted to the experimentation of the historical avant-garde, even through writers – among them Gabriel **García Márquez**, Julio **Cortázar**, Carlos **Fuentes** and others – have not always acknowledged their debt to prose works by Borges, Vallejo, Huidobro and María Luisa **Bombal**. Poetical avant-garde experimentation also anticipated some of the works of the Brazilian poesia concreta movement (see **concrete poetry**) of the 1950s and 1960s (especially the **Noigandres group**, which included the poets Augusto de **Campos**, Décio **Pignatari** and Haroldo de **Campos**), the Poema/Proceso group from Rio de Janeiro led by Wlademir Dias Pino, the Poesía para y/o Realizar of Edgardo Antonio Vigo and the Poesía Inobjetal of the Uruguayan Clemente Padín. All of these follow in the footsteps of the historical avant-garde in their experimentation with the visual aspect of poetry and notions of poetry as art, action and engagement.

Further reading

Ades, D. (1989) *Art in Latin America: The Modern Era 1820–1980*, New Haven: Yale University Press.

Espinosa, C. (ed.) (1990) *Corrosive Signs: Essays on Experimental Poetry*, trans. H. Polkinhorn, Washington, DC: Maisonneuve Press.

Forster, M.H. and K. David Jackson (1990) *Vanguardism in Latin American Literature: An Annotated Bibliographical Guide*, Westport, CT: Greenwood Press.

García Pinto, M. (1997) 'Avant-Garde', in V. Smith (ed.), *Encyclopedia of Latin American Literature*, London: Fitzroy Dearborn, 83–4.

Grünfeld, M. (1995) *Antología de la poesía latinoamericana de vanguardia*, Madrid: Hiperión.
Osorio, N. (1988) *Manifiestos, proclamas y polémicas de las vanguardia literaria hispanoamericana*, Caracas: Ayacucho.
Schwartz, J. (1991) *Las vanguardias latinoamericanas: Textos á programáticos*, Madrid: Cátedra; 2nd edn, Mexico City: Fondo de Cultura Económica, 2002.
Unruh, V. (1994) *Latin American Vanguards: The Art of Contentious Encounters*, Berkeley: University of California Press.
Verani, H. (1986) *Las vanguardias literarias en Hispanoamérica (Manifiestos, proclamas y otros escritos)*, Mexico City: Fondo de Cultura Económica.
—— (1996) *Narrativa vanguardista hispanoamericana*, Mexico City: UNAM.
—— (1996) 'The *Vanguardia* and its Implications', in R. González Echevarría and E. Pupo-Walker (eds), *Cambridge History of Latin American Literature*, Cambridge: Cambridge University Press, 2, 114–37.
Videla, G. (1994) *Direcciones del vanguardismo hispanoamericano*, Pittsburgh: Instituto Internacional de Literatura Iberoamericana.

MIHAI GRÜNFELD

Azevedo, Aluísio

b. 1857, São Luís do Maranhão, Brazil; d. 1913, Buenos Aires, Argentina

Novelist

Brazil's most important naturalist writer, Azevedo applied the lessons of Zola's clinical view of society to the life of lower-class Rio de Janeiro. His best-known novel was *O cortiço* (A Brazilian Tenement) (1896), a vivid picture of a racially diverse city of immigrants and ex-slaves. His fiction includes some of the first representations of female sexuality, including lesbianism, in Brazilian literature. (About the same time Adolfo Caminha depicted male homosexuality in *Bom Crioulo*, 1895.) His novel *O Mulato* (Mulatto) (1881) is concerned with the repressive space of Azevedo's native city in northern Brazil. Besides his four naturalist novels Azevedo wrote a number of romantic melodramas. He gave up writing in 1895 and became a diplomat.

Further reading

Azevedo, A. (1926) *A Brazilian Tenement*, trans. H.W. Brown, New York: R.M. McBride.
—— (1937–44) *Obras completas*, ed. N. da Silva, Rio de Janeiro: Briguiet, 12 vols.
—— (1990) *Mulatto*, trans. M.G. MacNicoll, Rutherford, NJ: Fairleigh Dickinson Press.
Haberly, D.T. (1997) 'Aluísio Azevedo', in V. Smith (ed.), *Encyclopedia of Latin American Literature*, London: Fitzroy Dearborn, 87–9.
Loos, D.S. (1963) *The Naturalistic Novel of Brazil*, New York: Hispanic Institute.
Mérian, J.-Y. (1988) *Aluísio Azevedo, vida e obra*, Rio de Janeiro: Espaço e Tempo.

DANIEL BALDERSTON

Azuela, Mariano

b. 1873, Lagos de Moreno, Jalisco, Mexico; d. 1952, Mexico City

Writer

A major novelist of the Mexican Revolution (see **novel of the Mexican Revolution**), Azuela's most famous work, *Los de abajo* (The Underdogs) (1925), first appeared in 1915 in El Paso, Texas, in serial form. It represented the Revolution as an increasingly directionless process taken over by power seekers and opportunists, echoing the disillusionment Azuela expressed in several other novels. A doctor and supporter of Francisco Madero, he joined Pancho Villa before withdrawing from politics. He wrote prolifically, usually in the same episodic realist style as his early work, apart from three experimental novels written, he claimed, as a challenge to critical fashions.

Further reading

Azuela, Mariano (1960) *Los de abajo: Novela de la Revolución Mexicana*, Mexico City: Fondo de Cultura Económica.

—— (1992) *The Underdogs*, Pittsburgh: University of Pittsburgh Press.

Herbst, G.R. (1977) *Mexican Society as Seen by Mariano Azuela*, New York: Abra.

Leal, L. (1971) *Mariano Azuela*, Boston: Twayne.

—— (1989) 'Mariano Azuela', in C.A. Solé and M.I. Abreu (eds), *Latin American Writers*, New York: Scribners, 2: 457–64.

McMurray, G. (1997) 'Mariano Azuela', in V. Smith (ed.), *Encyclopedia of Latin American Literature*, London: Fitzroy Dearborn, 89–92.

MIKE GONZALEZ

B

Baccino Ponce de León, Napoleón

b. 1947, Montevideo, Uruguay

Writer

Maluco (1989), his first novel, gained Baccino international acclaim and various prizes. Defying established histories, *Maluco* is a postmodern parodic reconstruction of the Magellan voyage, related by a buffoon through an extensive letter to King Charles V of Spain. Baccino's later novels *Un amor en Bangkok* (Love in Bangkok) (1994) and *Arte de perder* (The Art of Losing) (1995) are written in the same witty style. He has also published articles on Uruguayan writer Horacio **Quiroga**, cultural criticism for various newspapers and journals, and more than seventy short stories.

Further reading

Baccino Ponce de León, Napoleón (1989) *Maluco: La novela de los descubridores*, Ciudad de la Habana, Cuba: Ediciones Casa de las Américas.

VICTORIA RUÉTALO

Ballagas, Emilio

b. 1908, Camagüey, Cuba; d. 1954, Havana, Cuba

Poet

Associated with Cuba's major avant-garde literary journal, *Avance* (1927–30), Ballagas's first poems balanced a *modernista* aesthetic with an avant-garde vocabulary (see **avant-garde in Latin America**; **Spanish American modernism**). He then moved to 'pure poetry' (removed from social concerns), as represented by his first collection *Júbilo y fuga* (Jubilation and Flight) (1931) and by the celebrated *Cuaderno de poesía negra* (Black Poetry Notebook) (1934), his contribution to Afro-Cuban poetry. Ballagas's most effective poems are the elegies of *Sabor eterno* (Eternal Taste) (1938), love poems which lament the failure of a homosexual relationship. Although married with one son, Ballagas was homosexual; he was 'outed' in a 1955 essay by Virgilio **Piñera**.

Further reading

Armas, E. de (1997) 'Emilio Ballagas', in V. Smith (ed.), *Encyclopedia of Latin American Literature*, London: Fitzroy Dearborn, 93–4.

Ballagas, E. (1946) *Mapa de la poesía negra Americana*, Buenos Aires: Editorial Pleamar.

—— (1955) *Obra poética*, ed. C. Vitier, Havana: Ucar García.

Piñera, V. (1994) 'Ballagas en persona', in A. Arrufat (ed.), *Poesía y crítica*, Mexico City: Consejo Nacional para la Cultura y las Artes, 192–209.

Rice, A.P. (1966) *Emilio Ballagas, poeta o poesía*, Mexico City: Ediciones de Andrea.

—— (1989) 'Emilio Ballagas', in C.A. Solé and M.I. Abreu (eds), *Latin American Writers*, New York: Scribners, 3: 1081–7.

BEN A. HELLER

Balza, José

b. 1939, San Rafael, Delta Amacuro, Venezuela

Writer

Author of fiction, essayist, teacher and scholar, Balza is one of Venezuela's foremost writers. His first works were published in the 1960s; their experimental and psychological concerns explain why they represented a profound revision of the Latin American and Venezuelan narrative traditions. He founded and contributed to a number of important journals in the 1960s and 1970s – *En haa, CAL, Cultura universitaria, El falso cuaderno*. His novel *Marzo anterior* (The Previous March) won the 1966 Municipal Fiction Prize, and in 1978 his novel *D* earned him CONAC's Literary Prize. In 1991 he was awarded the Venezuelan National Prize for Literature.

Further reading

Aponte de Zacklin, L. (1996?) 'Escritura, exactitud y fascinación en la narrativa de Jose Balza', *Inti: Revista de literatura hispánica* 37–8: 171–7.

Balza, José (1982) *Un rostro absolutamente: Ejercicios narrativos, 1970–1980*, Caracas, Venezuela: Monte Avila.

—— (2000) *Percusión*, Caracas, Venezuela: Fundación Biblioteca Ayacucho.

Belrose, M. (1999) *Claves para descifrar la novelística de José Balza*, Caracas: FUNDARTE/Alcaldía de Caracas.

Berrizbeitiz, J. (1994) 'Jose Balza, la escritura como medio de conocimiento', *Revista iberoamericana* 60(166–7): 307–19.

JORGE ROMERO LEÓN

Banana Bottom

Written by the Jamaican Claude **McKay** and published in 1933, the novel *Banana Bottom* is set in a village deep in the hill country of Jamaica, and tells the story of Bita Plant, an intelligent black girl adopted by the zealous English missionaries Malcolm and Priscilla Craig. When, age 13, she is 'seduced' by the simple village musician, Crazy Bow, the Craigs send her to be educated in England. On her return, she is destined to marry their protégé Herald Newton Day, a smug theological student, but he is disgraced when found fornicating with a sheep and Bita settles for a traditional life on a smallholding, marrying Jubban, a local carter. McKay does not disguise the cultural differences the couple will have to face, but indicates that mutual respect will make the marriage work. It was a wedding of education and folk culture that McKay himself saw as the future of Jamaica.

The novel's title refers not to a person but to a fictional place. The estate of Banana Bottom and its local village Jubilee were created in the 1930s by Adair, a Scots émigré who liberated the slaves and sold them the land in smallholdings, marrying the blackest of them. This multiracial beginning gave rise to a distinctively Jamaican popular culture maintaining the best of African and European traditions and evolving its own customs and rituals. Music is at the centre of village life. The Craigs teach Bita Western music, and on her return her first act is to play the piano for the black choristers in the chapel. But McKay also portrays the alternative tradition of the village 'tea-meetings', with their folk-based dance music, and an African-based possession ritual. Bita learns from Squire Gensir, a white folklorist closely modelled on Walter **Jekyll**, McKay's own mentor, that art transcends cultural boundaries.

Written towards the end of McKay's life of exile, lived mainly in the USA, *Banana Bottom* is a loving recreation of his childhood rural island community, and a statement of his hopes for an independent Jamaica. Both for its vivid portrayal of a black heroine and its detailed account of Jamaican village life in the late nineteenth century, the novel was ahead of its time, and can be claimed as the first major novel in the English-speaking Caribbean.

Further reading

Ramchand, K. (1970) 'Claude McKay and *Banana Bottom*', *Southern Review* 4(1): 53–66.

LOUIS JAMES

Bandeira, Manuel

b. 1886, Recife, Brazil; d. 1968, Rio de Janeiro, Brazil

Poet

A central figure in Brazilian literature (see **Brazil**), Bandeira marks the aesthetic transition from late nineteenth-century to modern Brazilian poetry. In 1913, he was sent to a sanatorium in Switzerland for his tuberculosis and there came into contact with French symbolism, whose influence is obvious in his early work.

His first volumes *A Cinza das Horas* (Ashes of Time) (1917) and *Carnaval* (1919) represent a new kind of Brazilian poetry – simple, almost colloquial in style, it began to break with the Parnassian symbolism which had prevailed until then. His famous 'Os sapos' (The Toads), a satire of Parnassian formalism, belongs to that period and earned him the title of the 'John the Baptist of Brazilian modernism' from the young organizers of the Modern Art Week of 1922, even though he had not participated directly in those events (see **Brazilian modernism**). In *Ritmo Dissoluto* (Dissolute Rhythm) (1924) he explores the possibilities of free verse and incorporates prosaic themes into the lyric, establishing a new diction in modernist poetry. *Libertinagem* (Libertinage) (1930) is a work of maturity, marked by great aesthetic freedom and a varied style. His intimate, sometimes melancholic lyrics reflect his nostalgia; they are markedly humorous, rebellious and ironic, employ colloquial forms, explore Brazilian themes and reveal a great technical skill in free verse and rhyme.

After *Libertinagem*, Bandeira continued to purify his expression and his style, exploring themes of childhood and folklore, as in *Estrela da manhã* (Morning Star) (1936), *Mafuá do Malungo* (1948) and *Opus 10* (1952). *Estrela da tarde* (Evening Star) (1958) confirmed his versatility as he ventured into the realm of **concrete poetry**. *Estrela da vida inteira* (Star of a Whole Life) (1966) gathered all his work into a single volume.

The musical quality of his work led composers such as Villa-Lobos to set his work to music; its simplicity guaranteed for him a special place in Brazil, influencing many other poets. It is still read and recited by every subsequent generation.

Further reading

Arriguci Jr, Davi (1990) *Humildade, paixäao e morte: a poesia de Manuel Bandeira*, São Paulo: Companhia das Letras.

Bandeira, M. (1966) *Estrela da Vida Inteira*, Rio de Janeiro: José Olympio.

—— (1989) *This Earth, That Sky: Poems by Manuel Bandeira*, trans. C. Slater, Berkeley: University of California Press.

Dinneen, M. (1997) 'Manuel Bandeira', in V. Smith (ed.), *Encyclopedia of Latin American Literature*, London: Fitzroy Dearborn, 94–6.

Teles, G.M. (1989) 'Manuel Bandeira', in C.A. Solé and M.I. Abreu (eds), *Latin American Writers*, New York: Scribners, 2, 629–41.

VIVALDO A. SANTOS

Baquero, Gastón

b. 1918, Banes, Cuba; d. 1997, Madrid, Spain

Writer and journalist

Baquero's was a unique poetic voice. Many of his key poems, such as 'Testamento del pez' (The Fish's Testament) and 'Palabras escritas en la arena por un inocente' (Words Written in the Sand by an Innocent) appeared in ***Orígenes***. His columns for the *Diario de la Marina* in the 1940s were influential. In 1959 he went into exile in Spain, where he published several volumes of poetry and the essay collection *Indios, blancos y negros en el caldero de América* (Indians, Whites and Blacks in the American Melting Pot) (1991), expressing his belief in the mestizo character of Latin America.

Further reading

Baquero, Gastón (1998) *Poesía completa*, Madrid: Editorial Verbum.

—— (2001) *La patria sonora de los frutos (antología*

poética), ed. Efraín Rodríguez Santana, Havana: Editorial Letras Cubanas.

Ruiz Barrionuevo, C. (1995) 'Proyección de un origenista: Las invenciones de Gastón Baquero', *Revista Unión* 18: 40–4.

Vitier, C. (1958) 'Lección XIV: La visión poética de Gastón', in *Lo cubano en la poesía*, Havana: Ediciones Universidad Central de Las Villas/Úcar, 410–22.

WILFREDO CANCIO ISLA

Barba-Jacob, Porfirio

b. 1883, Santa Rosa de Osos, Colombia; d. 1942, Mexico City

Poet

Miguel Ángel Osorio Benítez adopted the pseudonym Barba-Jacob and travelled widely through Mexico and Central America and in Guatemala. He is remembered in **Lezama Lima**'s novel ***Paradiso*** as an early 'propagandist' for homosexuality. His friend, the Guatemalan Rafael **Arévalo Martínez**, based his short story *El hombre que parecía un caballo* (The Man Who Resembled a Horse) (1914) on Barba-Jacob's personality. Among his collections of poems are: *Rosas negras* (Black Roses) (1932), *Canciones y elegías* (Songs and Elegies) (1933) and *La canción de la vida profunda* (Song of the Deep Life) (1937). His *Poemas intemporales* (Timeless Poems) (1944) were published posthumously.

Further reading

Barba-Jacob, Porfirio (1958) *Poesías completas*, Bogotá: Editora Latinoamericana.

—— (1985) *Poemas*, Bogotá: Procultura, Presidencia de la República.

MIGUEL A. CARDINALE

Barnet, Miguel

b. 1940, Havana, Cuba

Writer

Barnet is probably best known for *Biografía de un cimarrón* (Autobiography of a Runaway Slave) (1966), based on the life of Esteban Montejo. Barnet originally interviewed him for ethnographic purposes, but the resulting first person narrative proved an ideal medium for giving voice to and empowering those individuals from marginalized social groups who could not write their own stories. The success of the ***testimonio*** in Latin America has produced some debate over whether the editing of oral narrative may counter the authority of the informant. Barnet currently holds an extremely influential position as director of the Casa Fernando Ortiz.

Further reading

Barnet, Miguel (1993) *The Autobiography of a Runaway Slave*, London: Macmillan Caribbean.

—— (2001) *Afro-Cuban Religions*, Princeton, NJ: Markus Wiener Publishers and Kingston, Jamaica: Ian Randle Publishers.

García Chichester, A. (1997) 'Miguel Barnet', in V. Smith (ed.), *Encyclopedia of Latin American Literature*, London: Fitzroy Dearborn, 96–8.

González Echevarría, R. (1985) '*Biografía de un cimarrón* and the Novel of the Cuban Revolution', in *The Voice of the Masters: Writing and Authority in Modern Latin American Literature*, Austin: University of Texas Press, 110–23.

JAMES BUCKWALTER-ARIAS

Barrenechea, Ana María

b. 1913, Buenos Aires, Argentina

Literary critic

A disciple of Amado Alonso and Pedro **Henríquez Ureña**, Barrenechea has produced key texts in linguistics and literary criticism. *La expresión de la irrealidad en la obra de Jorge Luis Borges* (The Expression of Unreality in the Work of Borges) (1957) is one of the first systematic explorations of **Borges**'s work. She introduced structuralism into the University of Buenos Aires, which she left when Onganía took power. Director of the Instituto de Filología and a member of the Spanish Academy, no Argentine critic can fail to acknowledge a debt to her.

Further reading

Barrenechea, Ana María (1965) *Borges, the Labyrinth Maker*, New York: New York University Press.

—— (1985) *El espacio crítico en el Discurso literario*, Buenos Aires: Kapelusz.

—— (2000) *La expresión de la irrealidad en la obra de Jorge Luis Borges y otros ensayos*, Buenos Aires: Ediciones del Cifrado.

DANIEL LINK

Barreto, Afonso Henriques de Lima

b. 1881, Rio de Janeiro, Brazil; d. 1922, Rio de Janeiro

Novelist

The most important Brazilian novelist in the period following the death of Machado de **Assis**, Lima Barreto is best known for his satirical novel *Triste fim de Policarpo Quaresma* (The Patriot) (1915; first published in serial form, 1911). Set in the period after the end of the Brazilian monarchy in 1889, this novel tells of the struggles of a naïve patriot, Policarpo Quaresma, during a period of civil war. Barreto's other works are marked by irony, black humour and a bleak view of human failings. He also wrote short stories and journalism.

Further reading

Barbosa, F. de A. (1989) 'Afonso Henriques de Lima Barreto', in C.A. Solé and M.I. Abreu (eds), *Latin American Writers*, New York: Scribners, 2: 565–73.

Barreto, A.H. de (1959–61) *Obra completa*, ed. F. de Assis Barbosa, São Paulo: Brasiliense.

Kinnear, J.C. (1974) 'The "Sad End" of Lima Barreto's Policarpo Quaresma', *Bulletin of Hispanic Studies* 51.

Oakley, R.J. (1997) 'Afonso Henriques de Lima Barreto', in V. Smith (ed.), *Encyclopedia of Latin American Literature*, London: Fitzroy Dearborn, 98–9.

DANIEL BALDERSTON

BARRETO, JOÃO PAULO ALBERTO COELHO *see* Rio, João do

Barreto Burgos, Chiquita (Amelia)

b. 1947, Colonia Dr Cecilio Báez, Paraguay

Writer

Chiquita Barreto Burgos is a prolific short story writer whose publications include three collections: *Con pena y sin gloria* (With Sorrow and Without Glory) (1990), *Con el alma en la piel: 9 relatos eróticos* (With the Soul on the Skin: 9 Erotic Tales) (1994) and *Delirios y certezas* (Delusions and Certainties) (1995). She is also a professor at the Universidad del Norte and collaborates with the Unión de Mujeres para Ayuda Mutua or UMPAM (Union of Women for Mutual Help) in Coronel Oviedo.

Further information

http://cervantesvirtual.com

TERESA MÉNDEZ-FAITH

Barrett, Rafael

b. 1876, Torrelavenga, Santader, Spain; d. 1910, Arcachon, France

Journalist and essayist

Barrett, a Spanish anarchist who is remembered particularly for his eloquent essays on Paraguay, did not come to South America until 1903, when he arrived in Buenos Aires. In Spain he had frequented intellectual circles but had published close to nothing. It was in the last seven years of his life, five of which were spent in Paraguay, that he wrote the books for which he is famous: *Lo que son los yerbales* (What the Yerba Mate Plantations Are)

(1910) and *El dolor paraguayo* (The Pain of Paraguay) (1911). His eloquent defence of the peons on the yerba mate plantations inspired later writers including Horacio **Quiroga** and Augusto **Roa Bastos**. He also wrote against the Church, against nationalism and against other forms of exploitation (including the oppression of women, blacks and Indians).

Further reading

Barrett, R. (1978) *El dolor paraguayo*, ed. M.A. Fernández, with intro. by A. Roa Bastos, Caracas: Biblioteca Ayacucho.

—— (1988–90) *Obras completas*, ed. F. Corral and M.A. Fernández, Asunción: RP Ediciones, 4 vols.

Lewis, T.K. (1997) 'Rafael Barrett', in V. Smith (ed.), *Encyclopedia of Latin American Literature*, London: Fitzroy Dearborn, 100–2.

Roa Bastos, A. (1981) *Rafael Barrett y la realidad paraguaya a comienzos del siglo*, Stockholm: Instituto de Estudios Latinoamericanos.

Yunque, A. (1929) *Rafael Barrett, su vida y su obra*, Buenos Aires: Claridad.

DANIEL BALDERSTON

Barroeta, José

b. 1942, Trujillo, Venezuela

Writer and lawyer

A prolific poet who belonged to the controversial 1960s generation, his voice and verse are those of a changing country, and attempt to signify the convergence of avant-garde aesthetics and the dramatic ideological struggle that characterized many classrooms and streets in Venezuela at that time. His poems account the memory of a nation that sees its own space dramatically reshaped with the coming of urban modernity. His *Obra poética* (Poetic Works) (2001) collects the titles: *Todos han muerto* (They Are All Dead) (1971), *Cartas a la extraña* (Letters to the Strange Woman) (1972), *Arte de anochecer* (Art of the Nightfall) (1975), *Fuerza del día* (Day Strength) (1985) and *Culpas del juglar* (The Minstrel's Guilt) (1996). He teaches at the Universidad de los Andes.

Further reading

Barroeta, José (2001) *Obra poética 1971–1996*, Mérida, Venezuela: Eds El Otro, El Mismo.

VÍCTOR GALARRAGA OROPEZA

Barros, Pía

b. 1956, Santiago, Chile

Writer

Barros's prose is centrally concerned with feminine identity, eroticism, cultural policy and politics. She also played an important role facilitating others: the writers of the Generation of 1980 were formed in her writers' workshops, and her publishing house 'Ergo Sum' published literary texts and book-objects containing narratives and graphic work by her pupils. Her works include short stories – *Miedos transitorios* (Transitory Fears) (1986), *A horcajadas* (Astride) (1995) and *Signos bajo la piel* (Signs under the Skin) (1995) – and a novel *El tono menor del deseo* (Desire in a Minor Key) (1991).

Further reading

Barros, Pía (1990) *A horcajadas*, Santiago: Mosquito editores.

Niebylski, Diana C. (1999) 'Semiologias del deseo en *Signos bajo la piel*, de Pía Barros', *Revista chilena de literatura*, Nov., 55: 67–83.

Pelage, Catherine (2000) 'Pía Barros y Diamela Eltit: Transgresion y literatura femenina en Chile', *La palabra y el hombre*, April–June, 114: 59–77.

ELIANA ORTEGA

Bartolomé, Efraín

b. 1950, Ocosingo, Chiapas, Mexico

Poet

Bartolomé is one of the most important contemporary poets from the southern Mexican state of Chiapas. His first work, *Ojo de jaguar* (Eye of the Jaguar) (1982), addressed the destruction of the

Lacandón jungle in Chiapas and marked the appearance of a mature ecological literature in Mexico. Although his subsequent poetry turned increasingly towards urban experience, esoteric themes and eroticism, Bartolomé returned to writing about Chiapas in his extended prose poem, *Ocosingo, diaro de guerra* (Ocosingo, War Diary) (1994), which offers a first-hand account of fighting between the Mexican Army and the Zapatista National Liberation Army from early January 1994. Bartolomé currently lives in Mexico City where he works as a psychotherapist.

Further reading

Argüelles, Juan Domingo (1997) *Diálogo con la poesía de Efraín Bartolomé*, Toluca, Mexico: Cuadernos de Malinalco.

Avendaño Chen, Esther R. (1994) '*Ojo de jaguar*, o la poética etnográfica', *Confluencia* 10 (1): 26–32.

Bartolomé, Efraín (1994) *Agua Lustral, poesía (1982–1987)*, Mexico City: Consejo Nacional Para la Cultura y las Artes.

—— (1994) *Ocosingo, diario de guerra*, Mexico City: Joaquín Mortiz.

BRIAN GOLLNICK

Bascom, Harold

b. 1951, Vergnoegen, Guyana

Writer

Bascom's acerbic, early novel, *Apata* (1986), confronts the effects of social and racial discrimination, documenting the life and death of the young fugitive Michael Rayburn Apata in 1959, which coincided with the Queen's visit to Guyana. Focusing on popular cultural and national themes, his plays at the National Cultural Centre in Georgetown were widely praised and awarded. In the 1990s several were presented again to considerable public acclaim. Bascom has also researched local mythical figures, and his illustrations about Indian immigration appear in the 1972 children's textbook, *Bound for Guyana* (Ministry of Education).

JILL E. ALBADA-JELGERSMA

Baugh, Edward Alston

b. 1936, Port Antonio, Jamaica

Poet and critic

A leading critic of Caribbean literature, Baugh edited the seminal *Critics of Caribbean Literature* (1978); equally important was his insightful and pioneering study of Derek **Walcott**, *Derek Walcott: Memory as Vision* (1978). He is also a well-known poet whose volume of poetry, *A Tale from the Rainforest*, was published in 1988. His writing uses varieties of language to explore the consequences of a colonial history. He is Professor of English at the University of the West Indies Mona Campus in Jamaica.

Further reading

Baugh, Edward Alston (2000) *It Was the Singing (poems)*, Toronto and Kingston, Jamaica: Sandberry Press.

MIKE GONZALEZ

Bayley, Edgar

b. 1919, Buenos Aires, Argentina; d. 1990, Buenos Aires

Writer

A member of the so-called 'Generation of 1940' Bayley rejected the prevailing neo-romantic and testimonial modes of his time. His very personal style, akin to **concrete poetry**, accorded poetry autonomy relative to other discourses and material reality. More than a genre, poetry for him was a category of the real. He wrote for poetry journals, as well as translating and writing occasional narrative and drama. His writings have a pure and disenchanted air, simple yet also aggressive, even brutal. The author of over twelve volumes, Bayley died poor, his talents unrecognized.

Further reading

Arias, J. (1986) 'El poeta es un cazador solitario: El argentino Edgar Bayley y su "Obra poetica" ', *Foro literario: Revista de literatura y lenguaje*, Montevideo, 15–16: 32–6.

Bayley, Edgar (1976) *Obra poética*, Buenos Aires: Corregidor.

SERGIO CHEJFEC

Bayly, Jaime

b. 1965, Lima, Peru

Writer

Bayly's three published novels reflect contemporary Peruvian society. *No se lo digas a nadie* (Don't Tell Anybody) (1994) – transferred to the cinema by Francisco Lombardi in 1998 – and *Fue ayer y no me acuerdo* (It was Yesterday, and I Don't Remember) (1995) include several episodes of homosexual and bisexual love. *Los últimos días de La Prensa* (The Last Days of La Prensa) (1996) narrate the final days of the newspaper, *La Prensa*, in the aftermath of a socio-political crisis in the Peru of the 1980s. *Yo amo a mi mamá* (I Love My Mummy) (1999) returns to themes of sexual repression among the Peruvian bourgeoisie. His most recent book is *La mujer de mi hermano* (My Brother's Wife) (2002). Bayly lives in Miami where he currently fronts a TV talk show.

Further reading

Bayly, Jaime (2000) *Los amigos que perdí*, Lima: Alfaguara.

—— (2002) *La mujer de mi hermano*, Lima: Editorial Planeta.

Escoubet Fernández, G.D. (1998) *Lectura de una construcción identitaria en No se lo digas a nadie de J. Bayly*, Montreal: Université de Montréal.

Ruiz Bravo, P. (2001) *Sub-versiones masculinas: Imágenes de los varones en la narrativa joven*, Lima: Centro de la Mujer Peruana Flora Tristán.

MIGUEL A. CARDINALE

Bedregal, Yolanda

b.1916, La Paz, Bolivia

Writer

Intimate feelings and everyday experience dominate the poetry of this Bolivian writer. Bedregal writes about a familiar urban world, the poor districts that produced the 'unknown soldier' (who probably fought in the Chaco War) described in her first book, *Naufragio* (Shipwreck) (1936). Her poems for children, such as *El cántaro del angelito* (The Little Angel's Pitcher) (1979), express her sympathy for the 'disabled heroes', the street children. Her novel *Bajo el oscuro solo* (Alone in the Darkness) (1971) won first prize in a Los Amigos del Libro competition.

Further reading

Bredegal, Yolanda (1984) *Bajo el oscuro sol*, La Paz: Editorial Los Amigos del Libro.

J.M. DE LA VEGA RODRÍGUEZ

Belaval, Emilio S.

b. 1903, Fajardo, Puerto Rico; d. 1973, San Juan, Puerto Rico

Writer

A lawyer who became a Supreme Court judge, Belaval is best known as a writer of plays and essays, but is particularly known for his three collections of short stories – *Los cuentos de la universidad* (Stories of the University) (1935), *Los cuentos para fomentar el turismo* (Stories to Promote Tourism) (1946) and *Los cuentos de la Plaza Fuerte* (Stories of the Old Fort) (1967) – in which he uses popular culture and language to create a **neo-baroque** text that can be seen as the direct precedent of some more recent Puerto Rican fiction, especially the works of Ana Lydia **Vega** and Luis Rafael **Sánchez** (who wrote his doctoral dissertation on Belaval).

Further reading

Belaval, Emilio S. (1977) *Los problemas de la cultura puertorriqueña*, Río Piedras, PR: Editorial Cultural.

Sánchez, L.R. (1979) *Fabulación e ideología en la cuentística de Emilio S. Belaval*, San Juan: Instituto de Cultura Puertorriqueña.

EFRAÍN BARRADAS

Bellatín, Mario

b. Mexico City, 1960

Novelist

Bellatín, who has spent much of his life in Peru but now lives in Mexico City, has burst on the literary scene in the last few years with the publication in quick succession of eight brief and intense novels. The best known of these is *Salón de belleza* (Beauty Parlor) (1999), a first-person narrative of a transvestite beautician who turns his beauty shop into a hospice for his associates who are dying of an unnamed illness (the reader inevitably thinks of AIDS) at the same time as the fish tanks in the shop are left to go stagnant. The mysterious relations between the dying friends and the dead and dying fish are richly allusive, as are the narrator's thoughts on death and life.

Bellatin's other work include *Flores* (Flowers) (2000), a novel about the consequences of the drug thalidomide when taken by pregnant women (Bellatín himself is missing an arm because of this medical scandal); *Poeta ciego* (Blind Poet) (1998), about a blind poet who is a sort of sect leader whose cult is based on hermetic practices and bizarre sexuality; and *Shiki Nagaoka: una nariz de ficción* (Shiki Nagaoka: A Book-Length Nose) (2001), about a Japanese photographer with an absurdly large nose.

Bellatín is active in literary circles in Mexico City and is closely associated with Sergio **Pitol** and Margo **Glantz**.

DANIEL BALDERSTON

Bellessi, Diana

b. 1946, Zavalla, Santa Fe Province, Argentina

Poet, essayist and translator

Bellessi has been important in articulating a space for the emergence of the female poetic voice. Her explorations of eroticism and her intense lyricism (she is often grouped with the **neo-baroque** poets) have earned her a distinctive position. Her poetry includes *Destino y propagaciones* (Destiny and Propagations) (1970), *Crucero ecuatorial* (Cruiser on the Equator) (1981), *Tributo del mudo* (Tribute of the Speechless) (1982), *Danzante de doblemáscara* (Double-Masked Dancer) (1985), *Eroica* (1988), *El jardín* (The Garden) (1992), *Sur* (South) (1998), and with Ursula LeGuin a bilingual co-edition *The Twins, the Dream: Two Voices* (1996). She has also translated US female poets in *Contéstame, baila mi danza* (Answer and Dance My Dance) (1984). Her cultural criticism (editorial board of ***Feminaria***, ***Diario de Poesía***, *Ultimo Reino*) and feminist cultural activism have resulted in publications such as *Paloma de contrabando* (Smuggled Dove) (1988), produced by prison workshops.

Further reading

Bellessi, D. and U. Le Guin (1996) *The Twins, The Dream – Two Voices: Poems*, Houston: Arte Público Press.

Ortega, E. (1996) 'Travesías Bellessianas', in *Lo que se hereda no se hurta: Ensayos de crítica literaria feminista*, Santiago: Cuarto Propio, 195–207.

GWEN KIRKPATRICK

Belli, Carlos Germán

b. 1927, Lima, Peru

Poet

One of Peru's leading contemporary poets, Belli's voice is very distinct from that of his contemporaries Antonio **Cisneros** and Javier **Sologuren**. Speaking through a tormented persona with a distinct private mythology, Belli both fascinates and disconcerts his readers. An almost comic rage gives his verse a prophetic power, while his private characters (for example, the cybernetic muse Anfriso Fisco) inhabit a space that is impossible to fix. The poet's performances are memorable for all who have seen them.

Further reading

Belli, C.G. (1988) *Antología personal*, Lima: CONCYTEC.
—— (1992) *Los talleres del tiempo: Verso escogido*, ed. P.W. Borgeson, Madrid: Visor.
Borgeson, P.W. (1997) 'Carlos Germán Belli', in V. Smith (ed.), *Encyclopedia of Latin American Literature*, London: Fitzroy Dearborn, 105–8.
Cánepa, M.A. (1971) *Lenguaje en conflicto: La poesía de Carlos Germán Belli*, Madrid: Editorial Orígenes.
Higgins, J. (1982) 'Poetry of Alienation', in *The Poet in Peru (Alienation and the Quest for a Super-Reality)*, London: Francis Cairns, 46–64.
Hill, W. Nick (1985) *Tradición y modernidad en la poesía de Carlos Germán Belli*, Madrid: Editorial Pliegos.

DANIEL BALDERSTON

Belli, Gioconda

b. 1948, Managua, Nicaragua

Writer

Known both for her political commitment and her erotic poetry, Belli has supported both national liberation and the struggle for women's rights in Sandinista and post-Sandinista Nicaragua. Her first book of poetry *Sobre la grama* (On the Grass) (1974) won a literary prize. In exile in Costa Rica from 1975, she returned with the 1979 Revolution to work in the Press and Propaganda Section of the government. She headed Daniel Ortega's successful election campaign in 1984. Her poetry, collected in *El ojo de la mujer* (Woman's Eye) (1991) and three novels, all show her concern with women, the poor and the oppressed.

Further reading

Belli, Gioconda (2002) *The Country under My Skin: A Memoir of Love and War*, New York: Knopf.
Hood, E.W. (1997) 'Gioconda Belli', in V. Smith (ed.), *Encyclopedia of Latin American Literature*, London: Fitzroy Dearborn, 108–9.

DEREK PETREY AND ILEANA RODRÍGUEZ

Benedetti, Mario

b. 1920, Paso de los Toros, Uruguay

Writer, essayist and critic

Since his first attempts as a poet and short story writer during the late 1940s, Mario Benedetti has successfully cultivated a wide range of literary genres, a fact that has contributed to his status as one of the most versatile writers of contemporary Latin America. The author of more than seventy titles, he is also one of the most prolific writers of his generation.

With his early poems, short stories and novels – for example, *Poemas de la oficina* (Office Poems) (1956), *Montevideanos* (1959 and 1962), and *La tregua* (The Truce) (1960) – Benedetti became a national best-seller and gained a reputation as a great humorist and shrewd analyst of the Uruguayan lower middle-class, depicting the existential dilemmas and moral feebleness of the many civil servants in the bureaucracy of a stagnant and decaying welfare state.

Together with some of the most influential contributors to the weekly *Marcha*, Benedetti became progressively more radical through the 1960s. His greater political involvement, his anti-imperialist attitude and a broader continental preoccupation can also be detected in his literary work from this period, in particular in his poetry and in a curious novel in verse form, *El cumpleaños de Juan Angel* (Juan Angel's Birthday) (1971), a work that twenty years later inspired the 'subcomandante' of Chiapas to adopt the name Marcos, the enigmatic guerrilla leader of the novel.

From 1973 until the mid-1980s, Benedetti lived in exile in Argentina, Peru, Cuba and Spain, and became the literary spokesman for Latin-Americans who had suffered political ostracism during the harsh dictatorships in the Southern Cone. Being a 'communicative writer', he also collaborated closely with composers and performers such as Alberto Favero, Nacha Guevara and Joan Manuel Serrat, who made his songs and poems even more familiar to Latin audiences.

The Uruguayan's literary work of the last two decades emphasizes the problems of exile and return from exile (for which he coined the term '*desexilio*'). Although more reflective in tone, he is still capable of humorous invention and of denouncing social injustice and moral corruption. Some of his best books from this period – the novel *Primavera con una esquina rota* (Spring with a Broken Corner) (1982), and the collection of short stories *Geografías* (Geographies) (1984) – also show a writer dedicated to formal experimentation, unusual combinations of prose and poetry, defamiliarization and play on words. Hs most recent book is *Buzón de tiempo* (1999).

Further reading

Benedetti, M. (1997) *Blood Pact and Other Stories*, Willimantic, CT: Curbstone Press.

Fornet, A. (ed.) (1976) *Recopilación de textos sobre Mario Benedetti*, Havana: Casa de las Américas.

Olivera Williams, M.R. (1989) 'Mario Benedetti', in C.A. Solé and M.I. Abreu (eds), *Latin American Writers*, New York: Scribners, 3: 1255–63.

Paoletti, M. (1995) *El aguafiestas. Mario Benedetti, la biografía*, Buenos Aires: Seix Barral.

Ruffinelli, J. (1997) 'Mario Benedetti', in V. Smith (ed.), *Encyclopedia of Latin American Literature*, London: Fitzroy Dearborn, 112–14.

JON ASKELAND

Benítez, Fernando

b. 1912, Mexico City

Writer

Benítez's distinguished journalistic career began in 1934. In the 1950s and 1960s he spearheaded the creation of weekly cultural magazines such as *La cultura en México* (in *¡Siempre!*), *La Jornada Semanal*, characterized by a new journalistic style combining in-depth interviews with chronicles and incisive criticism. Benítez's work on colonial history includes *La ruta de Hernán Cortés* (In the Footsteps of Cortes) (1950). His five-volume series of chronicles on *Los indios de México* (1967–81) combines travel narrative with anthropological and journalistic observations on the Indian tribes in various regions of the country. He was also Mexican ambassador to the Dominican Republic.

Further reading

Benítez, Fernando (1998) *Un indio zapoteco llamado Benito Juárez*, Col. Del Valle, Mexico City: Taurus.

CYNTHIA STEELE

Benítez Rojo, Antonio

b. 1931, Havana, Cuba

Writer

Benítez Rojo's first impact on Cuban literary circles came with the publication of his volume of short stories *Tute de Reyes* (A Trick of Kings), which won the 1967 **Casa de las Américas** prize. His next collection, *El escudo de hojas secas* (The Shield of Dry Leaves) (1968) won an award in the **UNEAC** literary competition. He edited (with Mario **Benedetti**) the anthology *Quince relatos de América Latina* (Fifteen stories from Latin America) (1970) and the important essay ***La isla que se repite*** (The Island That Repeats Itself) (1989). He currently lives in the United States.

Further reading

Benítez Rojo, Antonio (1992) *The Repeating Island: The Caribbean and the Postmodern Perspective*, Durham, NC: Duke University Press.

Campa, R. de la (1995) 'Mimicry and the Uncanny in Caribbean Discourse', in *Latin Americanism*, Minneapolis: University of Minnesota Press, 85–120.

Stavans, I. (1996) 'Carnaval de ideas: Una conversación con Antonio Benitez Rojo', *Apuntes postmodernos* 6(2)–7(1).

Zielina, M.C. (1992) *La africanía en el cuento cubano y puertorriqueño: Gerardo del Valle, Lydia Cabrera, José Luis González, Antonio Benítez Rojo, Carmelo*

Rodríguez Torres, Ana Lydia Vega, Miami: Ediciones Universal.

WILFREDO CANCIO ISLA

Bennett, Louise

b. 1919, Kingston, Jamaica

Writer, performer and broadcaster

One of the most respected poets working in the Jamaican dialect, Bennett has lectured in Africa, Europe and North America. Her collections of poems include: *Jamaica Labrish* (1966) and *Selected Poems* (1982). Her work is also available on records and cassettes. She began writing as a teenager, and has performed her poetry since 1938. She wrote for the *Gleaner* in Jamaica, and collected folklore material throughout the island. In 1945, she won a scholarship to the Royal Academy of Dramatic Art in London. She later worked for the BBC. She is a recipient of an MBE and many other awards.

Further reading

Bennett, Louise (1983) *Selected Poems*, Kingston, Jamaica: Sangster's Book Stores.

KEITH JARDIM

Berenguer, Carmen

b. 1942, Santiago, Chile

Poet

Berenguer is an active cultural figure and a poet of **neo-baroque** complexity. Her poetry begins as an allegorical depiction of the suffering of political minorities, and then moves on to elaborate a stark landscape of life in Santiago under military rule in *Huellas de Siglo* (Century Traces) (1986). The stress on wordplay in her next book unleashes the struggle of the female subaltern's voice (see **subaltern studies**) toward cultural empowerment, and in *Sayal de pieles* (Skin Tunic) (1994) it highlights the excruciating pain which AIDS inflicts upon the human body.

Further reading

Berenguer, Carmen (1987) *A media asta*, Santiago, Chile: Editorial Cuarto Propio.
—— (1993) *Sayal de pieles*, Santiago, Chile: F. Zegers.
—— (1999) *Naciste pintada*, Santiago Chile: Editorial Cuarto Propio.

OSCAR D. SARMIENTO

Berman, Sabina

b. 1952, Mexico City

Playwright, novelist and poet

One of the Mexico's most prominent contemporary playwrights, Berman is the first to have won the Premio Nacional de Teatro four times. Her plays are complex and provocative, with subject matter ranging from the conundrum of Trotsky's assassination in Mexico in 1942 in *Rompecabezas* (Puzzle) (1981), to the conquest of Tenochtitlán in *Aguila o sol* (Heads or Tails) (1985), to politics and machismo in contemporary Mexico in *Entre Villa y la mujer desnuda* (Between Villa and the Naked Woman) (1993). All of Berman's plays are prismatically structured, producing a multifaceted view of a central subject. Plays such as *Yanqui* (Yankee) (1979), *Rompecabezas*, *Herejía* (Heresy) (1983) and *El suplicio del placer* (The Agony of Ecstasy) (1985) are open-ended. They provide for a variety of different intepretations. This, of course, is not new. Any play with lasting power eschews the dogmatic and draws in its audience. The difference here is that Berman locates this confluence of possible interpretations within the characterizations themselves. In a Berman play, character is never fixed, but always fluid. The final effect of a Berman play is to produce a new-found awareness of our own sense of identity. We are shown just how fragile that identity can be, how provisional the sense of self can become. In *Yanqui* the most prominent character is Bill, the US citizen who suddenly appears to offer his services as handyman to a young couple living on the outskirts of Puerta Vallarta. Obviously undergoing some ill-defined turmoil, Bill provides a series of explanations about himself and why he is in Mexico. Each successive scene cancels out the identity previously established until we are left with a man who has so many identities that he has no identity. The only constant is his desire to establish a sense of self, to quiet the confusion raging within him. *Herejía* continues this exploration of identity with its depiction of a family of *conversos* who secretly continue to practice Judaism. Journeying to New Spain they establish a new life in Mexico only to be denounced to the Holy Inquisition by the spurned suitor of one of the female members of the family. The play's focus is the interplay between the family's exterior mask of Christian respectability and its internal commitment to Judaism. Berman has also refused to confine her own identity to the theatre. She has written for television, adapted *Entre Villa y la mujer desnuda* for film (directed by Berman herself and Isabelle Tardán in 1995), and directed a Mayan village of 250 inhabitants in her play *Arux*, about the Mayan dwarf-god. Her play, *Krisis* (1996), is a blatant attack upon the political corruption and cronyism of the PRI, Mexico's ruling party from the Mexican Revolution until 2000.

Further reading

Burgess, R.D. (1991) *The New Dramatists of Mexico, 1967–1985*, Lexington: University of Kentucky Press.

Cypess, S.M. (1993) 'Ethnic Identity in the Plays of Sabina Berman', in R. DiAntonio and N. Glickman (eds), *Tradition and Innovation. Reflections on Latin American Jewish Writing*, New York: State University of New York Press.

Eyring Bixler, J. (1997) 'The Postmodernization of History in the Theatre of Sabina Berman', *Latin American Theatre Review*, Spring, 30(2).

ADAM VERSÉNYI

Berry, James

b. 1924, Jamaica

Writer

A writer of poetry, short stories and children's fiction, Berry has lived in England since 1948. His *A Thief in the Village and Other Stories* (1988) is a collection of stories about life in contemporary Jamaica. *Ajeemah and His Son* (1992) recounts the story of Ajeemah and his son Atu, who in 1807 are kidnapped by slave traders and transported to neighbouring plantations in Jamaica, never to see each other again. The poems of *Everywhere Faces Everywhere* (1997) explore themes of growing up, nature, change, the magic of myths and a society unwilling to embrace diversity. In 1990, Berry received the Order of the British Empire in recognition of his writing achievements.

Further reading

Berry, James (1994) *Celebration Song: A Poem*, New York: Simon & Schuster Books for Young Readers.

KEITH JARDIM

beso de la mujer araña, El

El beso de la mujer araña, (Kiss of the Spider Woman) (1976) is Manuel **Puig**'s fourth novel which was circulated secretly in Argentina until the return of democracy (in 1984). It was adapted for theatre as a musical as well as a play and filmed by Héctor Babenco with William Hurt's brilliant performance as Molina. This ensured Puig's international recognition and ended his realist period.

Imprisoned in the same cell, two men converse. One is a left-wing activist, the other a homosexual; or, in terms of the current language, one is a 'guerrillero' (a guerrilla) the other a 'loca' (a queen). Each expresses to the other his fascination with his own worlds, governed by quite opposite values. Molina narrates and interprets to Valentin a series of classic films. Presumably their incarceration in one cell was part of a strategy to undermine Valentin's will and lead him to inform on his comrades – the 'loca' is part of the machinery of torture. But Molina and Valentin possess a similar integrity, and in the end Molina protects his cellmate. Under threat, he dissembles before the prison authorities, but he cannot and will not betray him. At some point, the worlds of the two men touch; when their bodies encounter each other, it is an act that goes beyond copulation. Molina is freed, and Valentin presses him to take a message to his comrades. At the end of the novel, both are dead.

Puig works with powerfully drawn social types – but he cuts into the comfortable and fluid narrative with profuse footnotes which document current discourses on the relations between sexuality and politics. In some sense the novel functions like a kind of television 'docudrama', with fictional segments illustrating ideas presented elsewhere by various 'talking heads', or a fictional programme with expert commentary.

If, in the context of contemporary literature, the novel was read as a folkloric representation of two typically Latin American social types within Argentina, Puig's text was one of the first literary representations of the repression of the 1970s. It took to its limit the use of dialogue to present plot and reclaimed a narrative method first employed by Roberto **Arlt** in his *El juguete rabioso* (The Angry Toy).

The subject matter of the novel would seem to exclude humour, but Manuel Puig's view of his characters is heavily ironic – they rush to occupy stereotypical aesthetic compartments which Puig subjects to a constant critique in all his work.

Further reading

Amícola, J. (1992) *Manuel Puig y la tela que atrapa al lector: Estudio sobre El beso de la mujer araña en su relación con los procesos receptivos y con una continuidad literaria contestaria*, Buenos Aires: Grupo Editor Latinoamericano.

Bacarisse, P. (1988) *The Necessary Dream: A Study of the Novels of Manuel Puig*, Cardiff: University of Wales Press.

Dabove, J. (1994) *La forma del Destino: Sobre El beso de la mujer araña de Manuel Puig*, Rosario: Beatriz Viterbo Editora.

Kerr, L. (1987) *Suspended Fictions: Reading Novels by Manuel Puig*, Urbana: University of Illinois Press.

Muñoz, E.M. (1987) *El discurso utópico de la sexualidad en Manuel Puig*, Madrid: Editorial Pliegos.

Puig, M. (2002) *El beso de la mujer araña*, ed. J. Amícola, with essays by J. Romero, G. Goldchluk, D. Balderston and others, Paris: Colección Archivos.

DANIEL LINK

best-sellers

The phenomenon of 'best-sellers' in Latin America is strongly related to the **Boom** of the late 1960s. Before that, Latin American literature had a limited circulation, and books were not articles of mass consumption; the *folletínes* (serials) were an exception in the 1920s and 1930s, but they belonged strictly to popular culture. The book becomes a commodity for the first time with the 'Boom'; indeed, for some critics the Boom itself is essentially a market phenomenon, rather than a genuine literary-cultural advance.

The 1960s brought new types of magazine such as *Primera plana*, *La Opinión* and *Marcha*, among others. They were the Latin American versions of *Life* or *Le Monde*, and signalled a modernization of cultural representation and criticism; their progressive, centre-left vision of society and culture radically changed the relationship between literature and public, in part by redefining the position of the writer within society. Writers became objects of new marketing strategies imported from the cultural industries of the USA and Europe. Interviews, mass-media visibility and best-seller lists began to attend the act of writing; writers became the new superstars.

The first edition of ***Rayuela*** (Hopscotch), by Julio **Cortázar**, published in 1965, had a print run of 4,000 copies; the book was reprinted in 1968, and half-a-million copies had been sold by 1973. The case of Gabriel **García Márquez**'s ***Cien años de soledad*** (One Hundred Years of Solitude) is even more revealing: the first edition of 25,000 copies in 1967 was followed by editions of 100,000 copies in subsequent years, with several reprints during a single year. Moreover, the success of one book guaranteed a market for the author's other work. Mass-media coverage of a book guaranteed success, as with the sexual scandal provoked in Argentina by *La traición de Rita Hayworth* (Betrayed by Rita Hayworth) by Manuel **Puig** and *Nanina* by Germán García, in 1968, both first novels by young novelists.

The 'Boom' formula still remains a guarantee of best-seller status – thus García Márquez's '**magical realism**' has become the model for success, especially since it opened a new international market for Latin American writers and publishers;

'magical realism' became Latin America's principal cultural export. The best-sellers of the 1980s and 1990s, like Isabel **Allende** and Laura **Esquivel**, recycled the 'magical realism' formula and combined it with feminine issues to win an expanding international audience. In this new context, the relationship with cinema is decisive: the success of ***Como agua para chocolate*** (Like Water for Chocolate) by Laura Esquivel was due, at least in part, to the film adaptation. This new articulation of literature and cinema has created new audiences and new possibilities for literary success.

Further reading

Fernández Moreno, C. (1972) *América Latina en su literatura*, Mexico City: UNESCO and Siglo XXI.

Shaw, D. (1997) 'Best-sellers', in V. Smith (ed.), *Encyclopedia of Latin American Literature*, London: Fitzroy Dearborn, 115.

Viñas, D. *et al.* (1981) *Más allá del boom: Literatura y mercado*, Mexico City: Marcha.

GABRIEL GIORGI

Bianchi, Soledad

b. 1948, Antofagasta, Chile

Critic

An important literary critic whose studies reflect a concern with literary theory and the historical context of literature positioned as cultural memory. After receiving her doctorate at the University of Paris, Bianchi taught in Chile and France, returning to the Universidad de Chile after a period in exile following the 1973 military *coup*. Her most important works include *Poesía chilena (Miradas-Enfoques-Apuntes)* (Chilean Poetry (Glances, Perspectives, Notes)) (1990) and her volume of interviews with members of the literary groups of the 1960s, *La memoria: Modelo para armar* (Memory: An Assembly Kit) (1995).

Further reading

Bianchi, Soledad (1995) *La memoria: Modelo para armar*, Santiago: Dirección de Bibliotecas, Archivos y Museos.

ELIANA ORTEGA

Bianco, José

b. 1908, Buenos Aires, Argentina;
d. 1986, Buenos Aires

Writer

Editor of ***Sur*** from 1938 to 1961, author of two extraordinary novellas, a novel and an important body of essays, and a distinguished translator, Bianco was one of the foremost men of letters of Argentina. Though his output of narrative fiction is modest, the two novellas, *Sombras suele vestir* (Shadow Play) (1941) and *Las ratas* (The Rats) (1943) are important examples of the fantastic (see **fantastic literature**) and of **crime fiction**, respectively. *Sombras suele vestir* was written for the famous ***Antología de la literatura fantástica*** but was not finished in time for the 1940 edition; it was, however, incorporated in the second edition (1965). His later novel, *La pérdida del reino* (The Loss of the Kingdom) (1972), on which he worked intermittently for decades, is a fascinating portrait of postwar Paris and Buenos Aires, and something of a *roman à clef.* As an essayist, Bianco wrote delightful pieces on **Borges**, **Bombal**, Victoria **Ocampo**, **Piñera**, Sarmiento, Bierce, Camus, and above all on Proust. His work with *Sur* over a period of more than twenty years was vital in establishing that journal as the foremost organ of imaginative literature in Spanish; before Bianco began as editor, the journal was largely given over to serious (and sometimes rather solemn) essays, but during his period it came to welcome the extraordinary new work of Borges, of Jean Genet and countless others. When Bianco went to Cuba in 1961 at the invitation of **Casa de las Américas**, Victoria Ocampo published an angry note in the magazine saying that Bianco had gone on his own and not as a representative of *Sur*; when he returned to Buenos Aires, he resigned. He then worked for several years at **EUDEBA**, the press of the University of Buenos Aires, where he directed the *Genio y figura* series of biographies (see **biography**). An extraordinary translator, his versions of Henry James, Giraudoux, Sartre, Stoppard, James Kirkwood, Genet and others are justly celebrated. A phrase from *Las ratas* exemplifies his lifelong fascination with the ambiguities of human experience:

> Perhaps we never really lie. Perhaps the truth is so rich, so ambiguous, and presides from such a distance over our modest human endeavours, that all interpretations can be interchanged, and that the best we can do to honor truth is to desist from the innocuous goal of knowing it.

Further reading

Bianco, J. (1988) *Ficción y reflexión*, Mexico City: Fondo de Cultura Económica.

—— (1983) *Shadow Play and The Rats: Two Novellas*, trans D. Balderston, Pittsburgh: Latin American Literary Review Press.

DANIEL BALDERSTON

Biblioteca Ayacucho

The Biblioteca Ayacucho, publishing arm of the Ayacucho Foundation, was established in 1974 by Presidential decree, under the government of Carlos Andrés Pérez, to commemorate the Battle of Ayacucho. Its object was to launch a collection of 500 titles to represent the civilizing, cultural and literary traditions of Latin America from pre-Hispanic times to the present. The list was drawn up in the light of discussions at the Seminario de Cultura Latinoamericana in 1976 and publication began the following year.

The Biblioteca's volumes include a prologue by a specialist critic and a detailed biographical, historical and cultural chronology as well as a bibliography at the end. In addition to the original collection, published in both hardback and paper, the Biblioteca has also produced complementary collections in different formats, like 'La expresión americana' (Expression of America) and 'Claves de América' (Keys to America).

Biblioteca Ayacucho was created by a group of internationally recognized Venezuelan and Latin American intellectuals, among them the Uruguayan critic Angel **Rama**, and José Ramón Medina and Oscar **Sambrano Urdaneta**, both members of its governing council, together with Oswaldo **Trejo**, Ramón J. Velásquez and Pascual Venegas Filardo.

Further information

http://www.cervantesvirtual.com/portal/Venezuela/biblioteca_ayacucho.shtml

JORGE ROMERO LEÓN

Biografía de un cimarrón

Biografía de un cimarrón (Autobiography of a Runaway Slave) is a novel by the poet and ethnologist Miguel **Barnet**, first published in 1966. Described by its author as a 'testimonial novel' (see ***testimonio***), it combines valuable anthropological insights and literary qualities, and goes well beyond a simple documentary transposition of reality. Its protagonist, Esteban Montejo, is a slave who became a freedom fighter (*mambí*) in the wars against Spanish colonialism. Through his peculiar vision of the world, he tells his own life story and recreates the world of the time. Widely translated, parts of the book were recorded in France by Jean Villard; it also inspired German composer Hans Werner Henze's opera *Cimarrón*.

Further reading

Barnet, Miguel (1968) *The Autobiography of a Runaway Slave*, New York: Pantheon.

González Echevarría, R. (1985) '*Biografía de un cimarrón* and the Novel of the Cuban Revolution', in *The Voice of the Masters: Writing and Authority in Modern Latin American Literature*, Austin: University of Texas Press, 110–23.

WILFREDO CANCIO ISLA

biography

Borges, in his eccentric 1930 book on the Buenos Aires poet Evaristo Carriego, notes: 'For an individual to want to have another individual discover memories that belonged only to a third person is an evident paradox. To resolve that paradox smoothly is the innocent desire of every biography.' Although many of the works of Domingo Faustino Sarmiento in the nineteenth century could be called biographies, and Ezequiel **Martínez Estrada** devoted himself in large measure to biographies of Horacio **Quiroga**, W.H. Hudson and José **Martí**, the genre is not one that has been much cultivated until recently in Latin America. In contrast to the English-speaking world, where important canonical works from Boswell and Carlyle to Lytton Strachey are biographical, there are few similar monuments in the Spanish and Portuguese tradition. Instead of the secular tradition of biography, the closest available model for centuries in the Iberian and Ibero-American world was the saint's life, hardly a promising model for the modern biography (however productive it might be for imaginative literature). In recent years, though, the market for biographies of celebrities has expanded, perhaps piqued by the successes of the genre in the English-speaking world.

In the 1960s, after being removed by Victoria **Ocampo** as editor of ***Sur*** for having visited revolutionary Cuba, José **Bianco** was invited by Boris Spivakow to work at **EUDEBA**, the press of the University of Buenos Aires, where he set up the series *Genio y Figura* (Character and Figure), which began publication in 1964 with a book on Rubén Darío, the *modernista* (see **Spanish American modernism**) poet. These compact volumes, less than two hundred pages in length, included illustrations (photographs of the author, of first editions and manuscripts, and of places important in the work) and an anthology of works, as well as a chronology. The main part of the book consisted of a biographical essay. The series included early biographies of **Borges**, **Neruda**, Alfonsina **Storni** and many others. Interestingly, though, the works are not packaged as biographies *per se* (any more than Borges's book on Carriego was fully a biography): though material was drawn together about the featured writer, the purpose was not to write a life of that person, or as Borges had mischievously pointed out in 1930, to evoke memories that belong neither to the biographer nor to the reader.

In contrast, recent years have seen an explosion of biographies, with Editorial Sudamericana and others publishing a whole series of works of this kind. Volodia **Teitelboim**, former social realist novelist and political figure in Chile, has devoted much of the last twenty years to biographies of Neruda, Gabriela **Mistral**, **Huidobro** and Borges. Similarly, Jorge **Edwards** had great success with his biography of Neruda. There are biographies on the market of Glauber Rocha, **Onetti**, **García Márquez**, Alejandra **Pizarnik** and countless others (although many major figures still have not been the subject of a biography). There are whole biographical industries around certain iconic figures: biographies of Eva Perón, Che Guevara and Frida Kahlo, to mention the three most obvious figures, have proliferated.

At the same time, novels that are almost biographies, or biographies that are almost novels, have also come into fashion. One of the more curious examples is Félix Luna's 'autobiography' of President Julio Argentino Roca, the figure who dominated Argentine politics from 1880 to 1904: Luna insists that his *Soy Roca* (I am Roca) (1989) is not a novel, yet the narration in the first person singular is clearly a novelistic device. (Silviano **Santiago** explored a similar device in his first person continuation of Graciliano **Ramos**'s prison memoirs.) Tomás Eloy **Martínez** has written novels that come close to being biographies of Juan Domingo Perón and of his second wife Eva. Sergio **Ramírez**, in *Margarita, está linda la mar* (Margarita, The Sea is Beautiful) (1998), has written a novel that is at least in part a biography of Rubén **Darío**.

Also of interest is the literary memoir. Margo **Glantz**'s *Las genealogías* (The Family Tree) (1981) is largely a memoir of the author's father, Jacobo Glantz, a Mexican-Yiddish poet and president of the Mexican Jewish Committee. José **Donoso**'s *Conjeturas sobre la memoria de mi tribu* (Conjectures About the Memories of My Tribe) (1996) is a biographical study of generations of ancestors.

Finally, it should be noted that there are elements of biography in the genre of the ***crónica*** (see for instance Carlos **Monsiváis**'s profiles of famous Mexican icons), which by virtue of its relative brevity escapes the trap of having to tell the whole of a life (and to base that telling on the documentary evidence), and in that of the ***testimonio***, which is to a large extent a displacement of the biographical impulse from the telling of elite or famous lives to the telling of less known ones (though *testimonio* also plays with the conventions of **autobiography**): see for instance Miguel **Barnet**'s *Biografía de un cimarrón* (oddly translated as *Autobiography of a Runaway Slave*) (1966).

Further reading

Borges, J.L. (1955) *Evaristo Carriego*, Buenos Aires: Emecé.

Bromwich, D. (1984) 'The Uses of Biography', *Yale Review*, Winter, 161–76.

Cockshut, A.D.J. (1974) *Truth to Life: The Art of Biography in the Nineteenth Century*, New York: Harcourt Brace.

DANIEL BALDERSTON

Bioy Casares, Adolfo

b. 1914, Buenos Aires, Argentina; d. 1999, Buenos Aires

Writer

Bioy Casares is best known as the writer of carefully constructed fantastic narratives (see **fantastic literature**), particularly the novels *La invención de Morel* (The Invention of Morel) (1940) and *El sueño de los héroes* (The Dream of Heroes) (1954) and the short stories of *La trama celeste* (The Celestial Plot) (1948). His friend **Borges** called the plot of *La invención de Morel* 'perfect'; its **science fiction** quality and mathematical rigor owe a great deal to one of Bioy's favourite writers, H.G. Wells. Bioy was also the author of an extensive body of other work, including diaries, **crime fiction** and screenplays. Most critics find his writing of the 1940s and 1950s, when he was working most closely with Borges, to be his most interesting.

Born into a wealthy and conservative landowning family, Bioy began to publish very young: he published four works of fiction before *La invención de Morel*. His first collaboration with Borges was on an advertising campaign for the yoghurt produced by Bioy's mother's family's dairy; for this campaign they invented an imaginary, and exceedingly long-lived, family. They would later collaborate on numerous works of crime fiction, most notably *Seis problemas para don Isidro Parodi* (Six Problems for Don Isidro Parodi) (1942), featuring an imprisoned amateur detective who is visited in his prison cell by all sorts of outlandish Buenos Aires characters. (This collaboration, under the pseudonyms H. Bustos Domecq and B. Suárez Lynch, also resulted in later parodies of modernist and avant-garde pretension.) They also co-edited two anthologies of detective stories, a very successful series of detective novels for Emecé that ran to hundreds of titles, and an anthology of gauchesque poetry for the **Fondo de Cultura Económica**. With Bioy's wife, the extraordinary Silvina **Ocampo**, Borges and Bioy edited the famous ***Antología de la literatura fantástica*** (Anthology of Fantastic Literature) (1940) and the *Antología poética argentina* (Anthology of Argentine Poetry) (1941). Bioy and Ocampo also co-authored a detective novel, *Los que aman, odian* (Those Who Love, Hate) (1946). Late in his life Bioy published excerpts from his diaries and commonplace books.

Bioy had a lifelong interest in the cinema, and his legacy in that medium is influential: both Leopoldo Torre Nilsson and Hugo Santiago made films based on several of his works. In Eliseo Subiela's *Hombre mirando el sudeste* (Man Looking Southeast) (1986) the protagonist quotes from *La invención de Morel*, an acknowledgement that the film is an adaptation of Bioy's novel.

One of the interesting questions is what Bioy would have been as a writer had it not been for his long association with Borges. Perhaps he would have been a light, humorous writer whose theme was the complications of love and sex. Instead, he tried his hand at a great variety of forms and weighty themes, was rewarded with many prizes, including the top prize in the Spanish-speaking world, the Cervantes Prize (1990), and yet somehow, oddly, seemed always a shadow of Borges, and also of the Bioy he might have been.

Further reading

Bioy Casares, A. (1964) *The Invention of Morel, and Other Stories*, trans. R.L. Simms, Austin: University of Texas Press.

—— (1988) *La invención y la trampa: Una antología*, Mexico City: Fondo de Cultura Económica.
—— (1994) *Selected Stories*, trans. S.J. Levine, New York: New Directions.
Camurati, M. (1989) 'Adolfo Bioy Casares', in C.A. Solé and M.I. Abreu (eds), *Latin American Writers*, New York: Scribner's, 3, 1201–08.
—— (1990) *Bioy Casares y el alegre trabajo de la inteligencia*, Buenos Aires: Corregidor.
—— (1997) 'Adolfo Bioy Casares', in V. Smith (ed.), *Encyclopedia of Latin American Literature*, London: Fitzroy Dearborn, 121–24.

DANIEL BALDERSTON

Bissoondath, Neil

b. 1955, Arima, Trinidad

Writer

A well-established writer of refreshingly sober and elegant prose, Bissoondath left Trinidad when he was eighteen to study in Toronto and later became a teacher in Canada. His first novel, *A Casual Brutality* (1988), is a profoundly disturbing and prophetic portrait of Trinidad's corruption, racism and violence. The book of short stories *On the Eve of Uncertain Tomorrows* (1990) continues his examination of the consequences of the continuing flight of Trinidadians from social disintegration. He departed from fiction with *Selling Illusions: The Cult of Multiculturalism in Canada* (1993), a controversial and often courageous review of Canadian policies.

Further reading

Bissoondath, Neil (2002) *Doing the Heart Good*, New York: Scribners and London: Simon & Schuster.

KEITH JARDIM

Bizzio, Sergio

b. 1956, Villa Ramallo, Argentina

Writer

Bizzio has written for Argentine cinema and television, and has published four novels, including *El divino convertible* (The Convertible Divine) (1990) and three volumes of poetry, *Paraguay* outstanding among them. But he is best known to the general public for his theatrical pieces, written with Daniel **Guebel**, which are considered exemplary in the new Argentine theatre. *La china* (The Girl) is a mixture of Argentine gaucho traditions, the theatre of the absurd and the colloquial (and obscene) language of television.

Further reading

Bizzio, Sergio (2001) *En esa época*, Buenos Aires: Emecé.

DANIEL LINK

black writing

Writing by black slaves and their descendants has been important in Latin America and the Caribbean since the middle of the nineteenth century, with some notable early figures being the Cuban poet and autobiographer Juan Francisco Manzano (1797–1854) and the Brazilian poet João da Cruz e Sousa (1861–98). In the 1920s and 1930s, under the influence of surrealism and its fascination with 'the primitive', poets, such as Luis **Palés Matos** and Nicolás **Guillén** cultivated what was called ***negrismo***, which had less to do with the race of the poet (Palés Matos was white) than with the theme (and often the rhythms) of the poetry. Meanwhile, in the Francophone world poets such as Aimé **Césaire**, Léon Gontran **Damas** and Léopold Senghor created the writings of ***négride***. Other significant writings about the African experience in the Americas are the novels and short stories of Manuel **Zapata Olivella** (Colombia), Quince **Duncan** (Costa Rica), Adalberto **Ortiz** and Nelson **Estupiñán Bass** (Ecuador) and Mayra **Santos Febres** (Puerto Rico). Contemporary poets of note are Derek **Walcott** (St Lucia), Nancy **Morejón** (Cuba), Kamau **Brathwaite** (Barbados) and **Mutabaruka** (Jamaica).

The *Afro-Hispanic Review*, published at Howard University in Washington, is a significant source of critical bibliography in this area. Notable critics who have worked on black writing in the Americas include Marvin Lewis, Lawrence Prescott, Ian Smart, David Brookshaw, Lorna Williams, Richard L. Jackson and Yvonne Captain.

Further reading

Brookshaw, D. (1986) *Race and Color in Brazilian Literature*, Metuchen, NJ: Scarecrow Press.

—— (1997) 'African-Brazilian Literature', in V. Smith (ed.), *Encyclopedia of Latin American Literature*, London: Fitzroy Dearborn, 11–12.

Jackson, R.L. (1979) *Black Writers in Latin America*, Albuquerque: University of New Mexico Press.

Lewis, M.A. (1987) *Treading the Ebony Path: Ideology and Violence in Contemporary Afro-Colombian Prose Fiction*, Columbia: University of Missouri Press.

Morales, J.L. (ed.) (1981) *Poesía afroantillana y negrista: Puerto Rico, República Dominicana, Cuba*, Río Piedras, PR: Universidad de Puerto Rico.

Smart, I.I. (1984) *Central American Writers of West Indian Origin: A New Hispanic Literature*, Washington: Three Continents Press.

—— (1997) 'African-American Literature: Central and South America' and 'African-Caribbean Literature', in V. Smith (ed.), *Encyclopedia of Latin American Literature*, London: Fitzroy Dearborn, 9–10 and 12–14.

Williams, L.V. (1994) *The Representations of Slavery in Cuban Fiction*, Columbia: University of Missouri Press.

DANIEL BALDERSTON

Blanco, Andrés Eloy

b. 1897, Cumaná, Venezuela; d. 1955, Mexico City

Poet, journalist and politician

In 1905 Blanco's family was forced into exile on Margarita Island due to their opposition to Cipriano Castro's government, and this perhaps marked the beginning of one of the most active careers in Venezuela's political and literary history. His sensitivity to people's voices and his active militant engagement won him an incomparable reputation within literary circles and led to his appointment as a diplomat. Very few poets have enjoyed the popular reputation of Blanco. His book *Poda* (1934), a collection of his work, includes 'El alma inquieta' (The Restless Soul), 'El río de las siete estrellas' (The River of The Seven Stars) and 'El limonero del Señor' (The Lord's Lemon Tree). He has also authored two of the most recited poems in Venezuelan oral tradition: 'La loca Luz Caraballo' (The Madwoman Luz Caraballo) and 'Píntame angelitos negros' (Paint Me Little Black Angels).

Further reading

Otero Silva, M. (1974) *Andrés Eloy Blanco: Homenaje en el LXXVIII aniversario de su natalicio*, Caracas: Ediciones del Congreso de la República.

Rivas Dugarte, R.A. (1997) *Andrés Eloy Blanco: Cronología mayor y bibliografía*, Caracas: Ediciones de la Comisión Presidencial y la Comisión Estadal del Estado Sucre.

Rodríguez, M.A. (1980) *La voz perenne de Andrés Eloy Blanco*, Caracas: Ediciones Centauro.

Subero, E. (1997) *Andrés Eloy Blanco: Fuentes para el estudio de su vida y su obra*, Caracas: Ediciones del Congreso de la República.

VÍCTOR GALARRAGA OROPEZA

Blanco, José Joaquín

b. 1951, Mexico City

Writer

Known primarily as a journalist and essayist who comments broadly and incisively on the contemporary Mexican scene, particularly that of Mexico City, Blanco is a prolific writer whose articles have appeared regularly in some of Mexico's leading newspapers and journals, including *La jornada*, *El Nacional*, *Unomásuno*, *Nexos* and *Siempre*. His contemporary chronicles and commentaries on Mexican culture are similar to the work of Carlos **Monsiváis**. They have been collected in several volumes, including *Cuando todas las chamacas se pusieron medias nylon* (When All Girls Wore Nylons) (1987) and *Se visten novias* (Specialists in Bridal Wear) (1993). He includes the gay community in his writings, as in his essay 'Ojos que da pánico soñar'

(Eyes That Could Terrify Dreams) (1979), one of the earliest Mexican texts on homosexual identity, and *Las púberes canéforas* (The Pubescent Canephoros) (1983), one of five novels he has published to date. Blanco's writings also include poetry and several volumes of literary criticism on both Mexican and foreign writers. His highly acclaimed screenplay, *Frida, naturaleza viva* (Frida, Still Life), on Frida Kahlo, written in collaboration with Paul Leduc, was awarded an Ariel in 1985.

Further reading

Blanco, José Joaquín (2000) *Poemas y elegías*, Mexico City: Cal y Arena.

EDUARDO GUÍZAR-ALVAREZ

Blanco Fombona, Rufino

b. 1874, Caracas, Venezuela; d. 1944, Buenos Aires, Argentina

Novelist, short story writer, essayist and poet

One of Venezuela's most prolific writers, Blanco Fombona also occupied a number of diplomatic posts under various governments. His opposition to and criticism of the governments of Cipriano Castro and Juan Vicente Gómez earned him a prison sentence and a long exile until Gómez's death in 1935. Under the influence of modernism (see **Spanish American modernism**) at first, and later of Nietzsche and naturalism, his work constitutes a fierce critique of the society of Caracas during the period of modernization at the end of the last century and the beginning of the twentieth.

Further reading

Gil López, E.J. (1989) 'La máscara de Rufino Blanco Fombona: Una aportación a la novela de dictadura', *Actas del X Congreso de la Asociacion de Hispanistas*, ed. A. Vilanova, Barcelona: Promociones y Pubs. Universitarias.

Hirshbein, C.Z. (1997) *Rufino Blanco Fombona y su pensamiento americanista*, Caracas: Universidad Central de Venezuela.

Pérez, G.S. (1989) 'Rufino Blanco Fombona', in C.A. Solé and M.I. Abreu (eds), *Latin American Writers*, New York: Scribners, 2, 503–11.

Rivas Dugarte, R.A. (1979) *Fuentes para el estudio de Rufino Blanco Fombona, 1874–1944*, Caracas: Centro de Estudios Latinoamericanos Rómulo Gallegos.

JORGE ROMERO LEÓN

Blinder, Oda

b. 1918, Curaçao, Netherlands Antilles; d. 1969, Curaçao

Poet

Oda Blinder (real name, Yolanda Corsen) published only one small collection of poetry, *Brieven van een Curaçaose blinde en andere gedichten* (Letters from a Blind Curaçaoan and Other Poems) (1968), during her lifetime. She published her first work in the literary magazine ***De Stoep*** in 1944 and continued to contribute until its demise in 1951. Her writings, preoccupied with unrequited love and often of a strong erotic nature, were generally written in Dutch and published posthumously in the Netherlands under the title *Verzamelde stilte* (Collected Silence).

AART G. BROEK

Block de Behar, Lisa

b. 1937, Montevideo, Uruguay

Literary critic

Block de Behar is Professor of Semiotics and Interpretative Theory at the Universidad de la República and, since 1996, head of its School of Communication Sciences. Her *El lenguaje de la publicidad* (The Language of Advertising) (1973) and *Una retórica del silencio* (A Rhetoric of Silence) (1984) are key texts, while her work on poetics includes *Una palabra propiamente dicha* (A Word Properly Speaking) (1994), in which she proposes a poetics of translation from a comparative perspective and addresses aspects of film theory. Her *Al margen de Borges* (Borges at the Margins) (1987) attests to the

Argentine writer's key aesthetic and epistemological role in her work.

Further reading

Block de Behar, Lisa (1994) *Una palabra propiamente dicha*, Mexico City: Siglo XXI.

—— (1999) *Borges, la pasión de una cita sin fin*, Mexico City: Siglo XXI.

CELINA MANZONI

Boal, Augusto

b. 1931, São Paulo, Brazil

Drama theoretician and playwright

Boal's fundamental aim, shared by other contemporary Brazilian dramatists, is to develop a popular theatre to serve as a vehicle for radical social change, a commitment clearly demonstrated in the plays about political struggle which he wrote from 1960 onwards, such as *Revoluçâo na América do Sul* (Revolution in South America) (1960). Having studied drama in the USA, Boal returned to Brazil in 1956 and worked with the Arena Theatre Group in São Paulo, which he later directed.

His most important work, however, has taken place at the level of theory and method. With Arena, he experimented with new techniques that sought to break with the conventions of the bourgeois drama that he saw as sterile and reactionary, and created a theatre of popular participation. He continued this work in exile between 1971 and 1985, when radical drama became impossible during Brazil's military dictatorship. His highly influential *Teatro do oprimido* (Theatre of the Oppressed) (1974) summarizes those experiences and shows how spectators can be turned into actors. The techniques employed encourage participants to think critically about their society and prepare them to become active agents in its transformation. Drawing inspiration from the theories of educator Paulo Freire, the work explains methods for breaking down the barrier between actors and the passive audience, so that the spectators participate in the dramatic action, take control of it and change its course as they see fit. Each course of action can then be critically evaluated to assess its consequences, as in 'forum theatre', where group members are invited to act out a particular problem and attempt to resolve it by trying a series of different solutions, each of which is then analysed. The aim is to empower the marginalized and oppressed, giving them the means to find their own solutions to social and personal problems. Boal believes that a truly popular theatre can function as a rehearsal for social action which can lead to real political change.

Since returning to Brazil in 1985, Boal has developed these techniques further. He has also written essays and novels, and has entered into politics as a prominent member of the PT and as city councillor for Rio de Janeiro (1992–6). His international recognition, however, rests on the theories and techniques of the Theatre of the Oppressed, which have been controversial but have had considerable international impact.

Further reading

Boal, A. (1979) *Theatre of the Oppressed*, London: Pluto Press.

—— (1995) *The Rainbow of Desire: The Boal Method of Theatre and Therapy*, London: Routledge.

Dinneen, M. (1997) 'Augusto Boal', in V. Smith (ed.), *Encyclopedia of Latin American Literature*, London: Fitzroy Dearborn, 124–6.

Schutzman, M. and J. Cohen-Cruz (eds) (1994) *Playing Boal: Theatre, Therapy, Activism*, London: Routledge.

MARK DINNEEN

Bobadilla, José Antonio

b. 1955, Santo Domingo, Dominican Republic

Writer

Poet, novelist and short story writer, Bobadilla belongs to the Generation of the 1980s. In 1984, he won a prize at Casa de Teatro (House of Theatre) with his novel *Ay, Janet, así no se puede* (Ay, Janet, It Cannot Be This Way). He has published the novels *Abalorios* (Beads) (1982) and *El jardín de*

Onan: Navajas y coronas de una solitaria historia de amor (Onan's Garden: Blades and Crowns for a Lonely Love Story) (1988). In his books, Bobadilla recovers Alejo **Carpentier**'s **neo-baroque** style to elaborate erotic plots.

FERNANDO VALERIO-HOLGUÍN

Boedo vs Florida

A literary polemic which began in Buenos Aires in 1924 and lasted little more than a year, Boedo vs Florida came to public notice through its publication in the review ***Martín Fierro*** (1924–27). At that time Florida was the city's most elegant street where the offices of the magazine promoting the avant-garde were to be found; Boedo was in a lower middle-class and working-class immigrant area where the magazine *Claridad*, representing the cultural Left, had its offices. They became the social, cultural and ethnic symbol of two aesthetic positions (the avant-garde and the realist school), but also the emblem of the problems that divided the cultural life of Argentina during the 1920s (see **avant-garde in Latin America**).

Further reading

Barletta, Leónidas (1967) *Boedo y Florida; una versión distinta*, Buenos Aires: Ediciones Metrópolis.

GRACIELA MONTALDO

Bolaño, Roberto

b. 1953, Santiago, Chile; d. 2003, Barcelona, Spain

Writer

Emerging as one of Chile's most significant younger writers, Bolaño lived in exile, first in Mexico and later in Spain, since the 1973 *coup*. Many of his works are largely set in Spain, albeit often with Latin American exiles as their central characters. His best known works include *La literatura nazi en América* (Nazi Literature in the Americas) (1996), *Estrella distante* (Distant Star) (1996) and *Llamadas telefónicas* (Telephone Calls) (1997). He has also published several books of poetry, and contributed regularly to the Spanish and Chilean press. He was a recent winner of the Rómulo Gallegos Prize.

Further reading

Bolaño, Roberto (2000) *Nocturno de Chile*, Barcelona: Editorial Anagrama.

—— (2000) *Tres*, Barcelona: El Acantilado.

Gras Miravet, D. (2000) 'Entrevista con Roberto Bolaño', *Cuadernos hispanoamericanos* 604: 53–65.

Vila Matas, E. (1999) 'Bolaño en la distancia', *Letras libres* 1(4): 74–7.

DANIEL BALDERSTON

Bolivia

It is part of the common sense of Bolivian historiography that its land-locked isolation explains the relatively late development of its cultural life. A different way of addressing the same problem might be to note that the majority of Bolivia's population was, and remains, Aymara- and Quechua-speaking – and that the majority of cultural practices would thus correspond to that section of the population, and in many cases be conducted in those languages. It is to popular culture that we would need to look for examples. From the point of view of a formal literary tradition, however, the small Spanish-speaking elite produced little in the way of culture, There were writers of prose in the late nineteenth century, including Ricardo **Jaimes Freyre**, who is far better known, however, as a *modernista* poet. Alcides **Arguedas**'s *Raza de bronce* (Bronze Race) (1919) is sometimes regarded as an *indigenista* novel, but his earlier *Pueblo enfermo* (A Sick People) (1909) exposes the novel's deterministic and racist foundations which betray little sympathy for the living Indian, as opposed to the idealized indigenous men and women of the past. Franz **Tamayo**, the historian and poet, shared many of those views, although he at times adopted a more paternalistic view. Jesús **Lara**'s *Surumi* (1943) and *Yanakuna* (1952) are outstanding representatives of a very different *indigenista* writing, more determinedly realist, vindicating indigenous rights and exploring their culture from within.

The situation of Bolivia's indigenous people was a clear representation of the inequalities and historical injustices that marked the nation's history. Two other themes serve to focus that cultural-historical critique. The Chaco War (1932–35) with Paraguay produced only the most pyrrhic of victories. The terrible human costs of the war were narrated by Augusto **Roa Bastos** in his *Hijo de hombre* (Son of Man) (1960), shown from the Paraguayan perspective, Augusto **Céspedes**, in his *Sangre de mestizos* (Blood of Mestizos) (1936) and Oscar **Cerruto** in his *Aluvión de fuego* (Fireflood) (1935) among others. A second repeated motif in Bolivian literature was the situation of the mining communities. If silver was the origin of Bolivia's wealth in colonial times, it was tin that produced most of its export earnings in the first half of the twentieth century. In neither case, of course, did that wealth devolve upon those who had produced it. Céspedes's factually based novel *El metal del diablo* (The Devil's Metal) (1946) recounts the life of Simón Patiño, the richest of the tin barons, and sets it against the life experience of the miners. Others had written about these mining regions – Jaime Mendoza's *En las tierras de Potosí* (In the Lands of Potosí) (1911) was imbued with the same positivist ideology as Arguedas, while Roberto Leyton's *Los eternos vagabundos* (The Eternal Wanderers) (1939) and Ren Poppe's short stories in *El paraje del Tío* (The Whereabouts of El Tio) (1985) express an explicit sympathy with the workers.

It was the miners union who were the most significant force in the Bolivian Revolution of 1952. In literary terms, it is Carlos Medinaceli who most clearly articulates the radical nationalist ideas that informed that movement, although he died three years before it occurred. Their most famous post-revolutionary expression was probably Marcelo **Quiroga Santa Cruz**'s *Los deshabitados* (The Uninhabited) (1957). Santa Cruz was a leader of the revolutionary movement, yet his literary work opened new directions away from social realism and towards a more philosophical, existentialist writing. Jaime **Sáenz**'s dark satires on urban life follow in his footsteps. Renato **Prada Oropeza** took the life and death of Che Guevara in Bolivia as the theme of his *Los fundadores del alba* (The Founders of the Dawn) (1969) which won a Cuban **Casa de las Américas** prize in that year, as did Pedro **Shimose**'s *Quiero escribir pero me sale espuma* (I Try to Write but I Foam at the Mouth) (1972) three years later.

The testimonial literature (see ***testimonio***) that emerged throughout the region in the 1970s and after was exemplified in Domitila Barrios de Chungara's narrative of life in the mining communities *Si me permiten hablar* (If I Am Allowed To Speak) (1977) and the work of the Taller de Historia Andina, which collected the life stories of many of Bolivia's most excluded people through the 1980s.

Further reading

Echeverría, E. (1973) *La novela social de Bolivia*, La Paz: Ed. Difusión.

Poppe, René (1983) *Narrativa minera boliviana*, La Paz: Eds Populares Camarlinghi.

Sanjinés, Javier (ed.) (1985) *Tendencias actuales en la literatura boliviana*, Minneapolis and Valencia: Institute of Ideologies and Literature.

JOSEFA SALMÓN

Bombal, María Luisa

b. 1910, Viña del Mar, Chile; d. 1980, Santiago, Chile

Writer

Bombal's fiction addresses two areas: experimentation with time, language and point of view; and the extent to which women's experiences transgress the cultural codes assigned to the 'feminine'. Within an ambiguous reality where the borders between life and death, imagined experiences and tangible reality are obscured, Bombal denounces the imbalances created by patriarchy. Using poetic imagery, in her novels *La última niebla* (The Final Mist) (1935) and *La amortajada* (The Shrouded Woman) (1938), she presents female characters who search for their own identity through intense eroticism and sensual contact with nature.

Further reading

Agosín, M.S. (1983) *Las desterradas del paraíso:*

Protagonistas en María Luisa Bombal, New York: Senda Nueva de Ediciones.
Alegría, F. (1989) 'María Luisa Bombal', in C.A. Solé and M.I. Abreu (eds), *Latin American Writers*, New York: Scribners, 3, 1111–17.
Bombal, María Luisa (1992) *La ultima niebla; El arbol; Las islas nuevas; Lo secreto: Textos completos*, Santiago de Chile: Editorial Andres Bello.
Gligo, A. (1985) *María Luisa (sobre la vida de María Luisa Bombal)*, Santiago: Editorial Andrés Bello.
Guerra-Cunningham, L. (1980) *La narrativa de María Luisa Bombal: Una visión de la existencia femenina*, Madrid: Playor.
Kostopoulos-Cooperman, C. (1988) *The Lyrical Vision of María Luisa Bombal*, London: Tamesis Books.
Sibbald, K.M. (1997) 'María Luisa Bombal', in V. Smith (ed.), *Encyclopedia of Latin American Literature*, London: Fitzroy Dearborn, 130–2.

LUCÍA GUERRA

Boom

Although they are unavoidable, literary labels tend today to have a bad press. So-called literary 'movements' or 'styles', the best-known Latin American example being the concept of '**magical realism**', are especially deprecated. Close behind magical realism as a critical bugbear – and equally difficult to exorcize – is the 'Boom', the name neither of a movement nor a style but of a particular literary moment, the one that saw the astonishing rise of the Latin American novel to world attention in the 1960s. Many critics have argued that the use of an economic – indeed commercial – term (and in English at that) was demeaning and alienating; some added that in any case the term was also misleading, that the Latin American novel in the 1960s was not noticeably different from what it had been in the 1940s and 1950s, and that any change was more in the mode of perception, so to speak, than in the object of study. To put it more crudely, the Boom was as much a marketing and public relations exercise as a literary phenomenon.

But this, of course, was precisely the point. There was in fact an explosion of interest in the Latin American novel from the early 1960s, which did indeed lead to an increased demand for the product, a demand which in its turn led to an expanded supply and a further spiral of interest. Moreover, four product leaders emerged to dominate the new market: Carlos **Fuentes**, Julio **Cortázar**, Mario **Vargas Llosa** and Gabriel **García Márquez**. Cortázar died in 1984, but the others are all still alive and remain indisputably the three leading novelists – the most prestigious literary brand names – of the continent almost forty years after the birth of the Boom. All are well known beyond the frontiers of Latin America, and all are in a position to make a living from their writing. Not even Jorge Luis **Borges**, Alejo **Carpentier** or Miguel Angel **Asturias**, giants from an earlier generation, could have dreamed of such favourable terms of trade when they first came to prominence during the 1940s and 1950s.

Critics differ in their explanation of the phenomenon. Clearly, the development of Latin American societies in the 1950s, with the generalized economic policy of import substitution, had led to the formation of a new, broader, university-educated continental middle class which was simultaneously nationalist and cosmopolitan in its tastes and ready for home-grown equivalents of international artistic commodities. The Boom novels were tailor-made to meet this demand. Politically, in the Cold War context, a wave of populist (Perón, Vargas) and quasi-revolutionary (Guatemala, Bolivia) regimes had paved the way for the most radical upheaval of all, that caused by the Cuban Revolution of 1959. This event put Latin America at the centre of world attention for the first time and gave writers and artists a choice of commitments, whether to Cuban-style revolutionary Marxism, US-style freedom and progress, or other points in between. There is no doubt that this temporary openness of horizons – to be negated almost absolutely by the 1970s – created an aesthetic moment of extraordinary fertility. This openness, this choice between alternatives, is clearly visible in both the subject matter and the structures of the canonical texts of the era. All are about the historical formation of Latin America, the relation between that history and other mythical versions, and the contribution of both to contemporary Latin American identity: they are the grand themes or –

as later critics would say, with pejorative intent – 'master narratives' of the great mestizo continent.

The Mexican Carlos Fuentes probably deserves credit as the inaugurator of what would come to be called the Boom. His *La región más transparente* (Where the Air is Clear) (1958), modelled on Dos Passos, may fairly be considered the first great novel of the new era, followed perhaps by Cortázar's *Los premios* (The Prizes) (1960). In 1962, Fuentes followed up with possibly his most important novel, *La muerte de Artemio Cruz* (The Death of Artemio Cruz), an existentialist (see **existentialism**) interpretation of the entire history of Mexico against the critical background of the recent Cuban Revolution. A year later, Cortázar published ***Rayuela*** (Hopscotch) (1963) which was not, as some have argued, the novel that began the Boom but undoubtedly the novel that confirmed, crystallized and characterized it; or, to put it another way, the novel that showed that there was a phenomenon in need of a name.

The name duly arrived. Critics argue as to who coined it, but regardless of who did, there is no doubt that the Boom's great publicist and propagandist was the Uruguayan critic Emir **Rodríguez Monegal**, who is inseparable from its trajectory, whether in the literary press or the halls of academe. Rodríguez Monegal went on to found the literary/cultural journal ***Mundo nuevo*** (1966–71), based initially in Paris, which had an extraordinary influence on Latin American literature in general and the Boom in particular until it collapsed in controversy, due in part to accusations of CIA funding. Meanwhile in Cuba, *Mundo nuevo*'s intellectual antagonist, ***Casa de las Américas***, founded during the first year of the Revolution, began its less ambiguous revolutionary mission which continues, somewhat precariously, to the present time. *Casa* had its own scandal during the same period with the so-called '**Padilla** affair', and the two cases give a good insight into the pressures brought upon writers and, more specifically, the extent to which it was impossible to avoid making political choices – whether inside or outside fiction – in the tempestuous Latin American situation after about 1967. In due course the writers of the Boom who, as well as being colleagues, were close friends in the 1960s, found themselves drifting apart in the 1970s. A comparison with their contemporaries the Beatles – another four-man group – proves to be more illuminating than would seem likely at first sight.

The youngest of the Boom writers was Mario Vargas Llosa, whose *La* ***ciudad y los perros*** (The Time of the Hero) appeared in 1962 and won a key literary prize in Spain (the influence of Spanish – particularly Catalan – publishers on the course of the Boom is a fascinating chapter in itself). Vargas Llosa was then age 26. Under immense pressure to repeat his remarkable achievement, he wrote the even more extraordinary *La casa verde* (The Green House) in 1966, and the monumental *Conversación en la Catedral* (Conversation in the Cathedral) in 1969. The influence of William Faulkner on Vargas Llosa is unmistakable, but the Peruvian takes Faulkner's techniques to lengths that even Faulkner never envisaged, with an audacity and a lucidity that astonished Latin America's new readers.

The central period of the brief moment that was the Boom was the intense stretch of time from 1963, and the appearance of *Rayuela*, to 1967, and García Márquez's ***Cien años de soledad*** (One Hundred Years of Solitude) – the Boom novel *par excellence*. Everyone agreed that *Rayuela* was something like 'Latin America's *Ulysses*'; appropriately enough, given that the Boom is best understood as the crystallization and culmination of Latin America's modernist movement dating back to the 1920s. But *Cien años de soledad* changed the entire perspective, making it clear at once that something much more far-reaching had occurred for which a quite different time frame was required; as almost everyone again agreed, *Cien años de soledad* was 'Latin America's *Don Quixote*'. Clearly, a brief literary moment which somehow conjoins a *Ulysses* with a *Quixote* is more than just a historical flash in the pan.

Many other writers and other literary phenomena were also active at this time. The Cuban exile Guillermo **Cabrera Infante** wrote the scintillating *Tres tristes tigres* (Three Trapped Tigers) (1967), which somehow became a novel of the Boom even though its politically incorrect author did not become a writer of the Boom. Some critics argue that there was a fifth Boom writer, the Chilean José **Donoso**, whose *El* ***obsceno pájaro de la noche*** (The Obscene Bird of the Night) appeared in 1970, as the moment began to fade in the face of a changing aesthetic horizon beneath a darkening political sky. Curiously enough, a more convincing candidate as fifth Boom writer, although taxonomically more problematical, would be the Spaniard Juan Goytisolo, whose own radical departures in the late 1960s had much in common with his leading Latin American contemporaries. He remained Spain's most important novelist at home and abroad into the 1990s, thirty years after the Boom.

Most intriguing perhaps for the historian, and less often noticed, is the fact that although the unparalleled success of the Boom writers sparked an explosion of literary activity, it evinced few direct imitations. If the Boom was, as we are arguing, the high point of modernism, the so-called post-**Boom**, which began in the late 1960s, was clearly postmodernist (see **postmodernism**). The best-known example is the constellation of Mexican writers of the late 1960s (José **Agustín**, Gustavo **Sainz**, Parménides García Saldaña and others) known as La **Onda** or 'New Wave', inspired less by traditional questions of politics and national identity than by rock music, drugs and urban alienation. However, individual writers such as the Argentinian Manuel **Puig** were already opening new avenues in the late 1960s with works such as *La traición de Rita Hayworth* (Betrayed by Rita Hayworth) (1968), based on Puig's fascination with the movies and the mass media generally. In that sense the end of the Boom, which some would put as early as 1970, marked by Donoso's *El obsceno pájaro*, and others as late as 1975, signalled by Fuentes's mammoth *Terra nostra*, was also the end of a monolithic belief in the novel as high art.

Ironically enough, and this too is rarely understood, the Boom writers all had not one but two careers, since they all became **post-Boom** writers as well. Indeed, Fuentes's *Cambio de piel* (A Change of Skin) (1967) and Cortázar's *62: Modelo para armar* (62: A Model Kit) (1968), both obviously 'post-Boom' and postmodernist in style, were in fact published at the height of the Boom itself. Vargas Llosa's *Pantaleón y las visitadoras* (Sergeant Pantoja's Special Service) (1973) and García Márquez's *El otoño del patriarca* (Autumn of the Patriarch) (1975) followed shortly behind and equally clearly represented new points of departure for their respective authors. No one since has achieved anything like the same authority as this quartet; and although many critics assert that loss of 'authority' is precisely what the postmodern era is all about and this is the reason no other writer has approached their unique combination of critical and commercial success, there is something rather hollow about the argument. Interestingly enough, however, the only writers who have managed since the 1960s to write convincingly 'decentred' works – in contrast with the original four's famously 'finished' works – are women, writers such as the Brazilian Clarice **Lispector** (the greatest Latin American novelist of the 1960s outside the Boom's boys' club) or the Chilean Diamela **Eltit**. Another woman, Isabel **Allende**, is the only writer to have achieved best-seller (see **best-sellers**) status comparable with the famous four.

Was the phenomenon known as the Boom an optical illusion, or did it indeed exist? The answer seems clear. The Boom was a uniquely charged moment, at what seemed at the time to be the confirmation of Latin America's passage from clinging underdevelopment to beckoning modernity, a transition we now see differently, as the transition between modernity and postmodernity; with Latin America as 'hybrid' and 'heterogeneous' as ever, still unjust and uneven, still stranded between so-called development and so-called underdevelopment. When the historians look back in the twenty-first century, they may well conclude that the novelists of the Boom brought a more critical and productive gaze to bear upon this problematic area than their successors, despite their market success and the controversial label which was accordingly attached to them.

Further reading

Donoso, J. (1977) *The Boom in Spanish American Literature: A Personal Account*, New York: Columbia University Press.

Martin, G. (1989) *Journeys through the Labyrinth: Latin American Fiction in the Twentieth Century*, London: Verso.

Mudrovcic, M.E. (1997) *Mundo Nuevo: Cultura y Guerra Fría en la década del 60*, Rosario: Beatriz Viterbo.

Rama, A. (ed.) (1981) *Más allá del boom: Literatura y mercado*, Mexico City: Marcha.

Rodríguez Monegal, E. (1972) *El boom de la novela latinoamericana*, Caracas: Tiempo Nuevo.

GERALD MARTIN

Boquitas pintadas

Manuel **Puig**'s second novel *Boquitas pintadas*, published in 1969, was subtitled 'a serial'; in fact, Puig did consider publishing it in instalments in a magazine. He also wrote the screenplay for Leopoldo Torre Nilsson's 1973 film adaptation. The story, told through a series of letters, concerns the (amorous) life of Juan Carlos, a small town Don Juan, whose excesses end in a mountain sanatorium where he is sent after contracting tuberculosis. There were three women in his life: Nené, now living in Buenos Aires with her husband and two children, who begins to write letters when she hears of his death; Mabel, whose provincial *savoir-faire* is set against the chaste Nené; and Raba, the servant. In her letters, Nené seeks information about her 'eternal love' Juan Carlos, whose sexual excesses, we learn in the end, were practised with Mabel. Her letters to Juan Carlos' mother are full of complaints about her husband and her peculiarly dull family life. But it is Celina, the dead lover's sister, who replies to the letters; she blames Nené for her brother's death, and her revenge is to send Nené's letter to her husband, who does absolutely nothing when faced with proof of his wife's lack of love.

The story does not evolve so straightforwardly in the letters that compose the book, of course. Narrated entirely through the words of its characters, Puig's novel is faithful to the conventions of the serial novel, but it is also an adaptation of Thomas Mann's *Der Zauberberg*. The relationship between realism and illusion, barely hinted at in the first novel, here appears crudely exposed through the more or less perverted 'quotation' of one of the features of that relation. Puig's narrative moves resolutely towards experimental, non-representational models which he deploys with great skill. *Boquitas pintadas* was a best-seller, like some of Puig's subsequent work.

However, behind the apparently sentimental plot there is a whole theory of social relations cloaked behind relations of knowledge. Raba, the most oppressed and ignorant of the three, is the one who gains most (socially) by the novel's end. In the mysterious mix of knowledge and power proposed in *Boquitas pintadas* lie many of the keys to understanding Puig's work.

Further reading

Muñoz, E.M. (1988) *Boquitas pintadas: Una zona de resistencia en el discurso novelístico de Manuel Puig*, Sacramento: Department of Foreign Languages, California State University.

DANIEL LINK

Borges, Jorge Luis

b. 1899, Buenos Aires, Argentina;
d. 1986, Geneva, Switzerland

Writer

The most influential Latin American writer of the twentieth century, Borges revolutionized the practice of the essay and the short story. His family (his parents and sister, the painter Norah Borges) spent the years of the First World War in Geneva, where he mastered German, French and Latin; English was the first language of his father and paternal grandmother, and the language of his first readings. His early work, in the *ultraísta* avant-garde movement that began in Spain in the early 1920s, was an urban poetry much influenced by German expressionism that sought intense and bare feeling. By the time some of these poems were collected in his first book, *Fervor de Buenos Aires* (Fervor for Buenos Aires) (1923), Borges was distancing himself from the European avant-garde. His initial book of essays, *Inquisiciones* (Inquisitions) (1925), explored philosophical themes and metaphor; it was followed by two more books of essays, *El tamaño de mi esperanza* (The Extent of My Hope) (1926) and *El idioma de los argentinos* (The Argentine Language) (1928), which were largely concerned with ***criollismo*** and cultural nationalism. Two other books of poetry, *Luna de enfrente* (Moon Across the Way) (1926) and *Cuaderno San Martín* (San Martín Copybook) (1929), expressed Borges's search for a philosophical poetry, and one that included a reflection on Argentine national culture and the urban space. These concerns also animated his biography of the Buenos Aires poet Evaristo Carriego (1930).

Apart from a few minor experiments during the 1920s, Borges began exploring short narrative in an audacious cultural supplement he edited with Ulises Petit de Murat in 1933–34, the *Revista multicolor de los sábados*, for Natalio Botana's newspaper *Crítica*. These portraits of murderers, gangsters, impostors and pirates were collected in 1935 as *Historia universal de la infamia* (Universal History of Infamy), a book that also includes his first person narrative of a Buenos Aires thug, the famous 'Hombre de la esquina rosada' (Man on Pink Corner). In 1936 he published a review of an apocryphal detective novel (supposedly published in Bombay); this text, 'El acercamiento a Almotásim' (The Approach to Al-Mu'tasim) inaugurated his experiments with **crime fiction** and with a new hybrid genre, somewhere between the essay and the short story (the *ficción*). The latter exploration led to two stories that have fascinated readers since their first publication: 'Pierre Menard, autor del Quijote' (Pierre Menard, Author of Don Quixote) (1939) and 'Tlön, Uqbar, Orbis Tertius' (1940). Startling examples of a new way of reading and writing, these texts were eventually collected in ***Ficciones*** (Fictions) (1944), along with several famous detective stories. The following collection of stories, *El aleph* (The Aleph) (1949), continued Borges's exploration of imaginary worlds, labyrinths, time and the adventures of reading.

Besides his work in *Crítica*, Borges also published hundreds of reviews in the popular family magazine *El Hogar*, mostly between 1936 and 1939, and thousands of articles, book reviews and film reviews in magazines such as ***Sur*** and in newspapers like *La Nación* and *La Prensa*. Always concerned with popular culture and with political questions, he expressed himself on many aspects of Argentine and Latin American culture, as well as on a bewildering variety of literary and philosophical figures from around the world. The quintessential book of Borges's learned essays is *Otras inquisiciones* (Other Inquisitions) (1952): playful and paradoxical, these essays range widely in their references, culminating in epigrammatic, often ironic, finales. If the stories of *Ficciones* and *El aleph* explore erudite philosophical or literary problems, so the essays of *Otras inquisiciones* often have a narrative turn, telling fascinating and tantalizing stories.

Borges's work of the 1940s and 1950s was complemented by a number of important polemical anthologies. The ***Antología de la literatura fantástica*** (Anthology of Fantastic Literature) (1940), edited with Adolfo **Bioy Casares** and Silvina **Ocampo**, was an oblique attack on the social realist tradition in Latin American writing (see **socialist realism**), suggesting that the writer's first obligation was to tell interesting and challenging stories. The same three collaborators also produced an *Antología poética argentina* (Argentine Poetic Anthology) (1941), while Borges and Bioy edited several anthologies of **crime fiction** and gauchesque poetry, and directed a very successful series of detective novels (mostly translated from English) for the Buenos Aires publisher Emecé.

In 1955, about the time of the fall of Juan Domingo Perón, whose government Borges had vociferously opposed, Borges lost most of his eyesight and was no longer able to read; ironically, as he was to comment in his 'Poema de los dones' (Poem of the Gifts), it was at this moment that he was named director of the National Library, a post he held until 1969. The need to dictate produced a series of changes in Borges's writing: he returned to poetry, particularly to traditional forms like the sonnet and to traditional meters, as they were easier to remember and then to dictate. Similarly, the stories he was to write in the latter part of his career had a less dense and bookish character, often aspiring to the direct quality that he admired in Kipling's early *Plain Tales from the Hills*. The most significant books of his later career are *El hacedor* (The Maker) (short prose and poems, 1960), *Elogio de la sombra* (In Praise of Darkness) (short prose and poems, 1969), *El informe de Brodie* (Brodie's Report) (stories, 1970), and *El libro de arena* (The Book of Sand) (stories, 1975). His numerous later publications also include an unusual book of travel writing by a blind traveller, *Atlas* (1984).

Borges's impact on the world of letters has been significant, although often resisted (particularly by younger Latin American writers). The work of **Cortázar**, **Piglia**, **Saer** and numerous others is in constant dialogue with Borges, as has also been the case outside of Latin America in the writings of Robbe-Grillet (France), Pynchon (USA), Ben Jelloun (Morocco), Rushdie (India and the UK), Shammas (Israel) and many more. Borges has also been a favourite reading for literary theorists from Gérard Genette to John Frow, particularly for his ideas that undermine a romantic notion of authorship and originality. The critical bibliography on Borges is by far the most extensive that exists on any Latin American writer, and continues to grow in an almost alarming way. He has been translated into countless languages; for the centenary of his birth, new English translations of his stories, selected poems and selected non-fiction were published.

Further reading

Balderston, D. (1986) *The Literary Universe of Jorge Luis Borges*, Westport, CT: Greenwood Press.

—— (1993) *Out of Context: Historical Reference and the Representation of Reality in Borges*, Durham, NC: Duke University Press.

Borges, J.L. (1998) *Collected Fictions*, New York: Viking.

—— (1999) *Selected Non-Fictions*, New York: Viking.

—— (1999) *Selected Poems*, New York: Viking.

Dunham, L. and I. Ivask (eds) (1971) *The Cardinal Points of Borges*, Norman: University of Oklahoma Press.

Fishburn, E. (ed.) (1998) *Borges and Europe Revisited*, London: University of London/Institute of Latin American Studies.

Foster, D.W. (1984) *Jorge Luis Borges: An Annotated Primary and Secondary Bibliography*, New York: Garland.

Helft, N. (1997) *Jorge Luis Borges: Bibliografía completa*, Buenos Aires: Fondo de Cultura Económica.

Molloy, S. (1994) *Signs of Borges*, Durham, NC: Duke University Press.

Sarlo, B. (1993) *Jorge Luis Borges: A Writer on the Edge*, London: Verso.

DANIEL BALDERSTON

Bosch, Juan

b. 1909, La Vega, Dominican Republic

Writer and politician

An acknowledged master of the Latin American short story, Juan Bosch published his first collection, *Camino real* (Royal Highway), in 1933. The stories describe the life of the peasants of the Cibao region of the Dominican Republic, among whom he had spent his childhood. *Dos pesos de agua* (Two Pesos-worth of Water) (1941), by contrast, addressed other themes and introduced an element of fantasy, although the writer's social concerns were always present. *Ocho cuentos* (Eight Stories) (1947) includes 'Luis Pié', which tells the tragic story of a Haitian immigrant worker in a sugar mill in the Dominican Republic. His *Cuentos escritos en el exilio* (Stories Written in Exile) (1962) and *Más cuentos escritos en el exilio* (More Stories) (1964) included some hitherto unpublished writings as well as other stories rewritten in a standard Spanish accessible to readers not familiar with the accents of Cibao. There were also two novels, one published in 1936, *La mañosa* (The Trickster), the other in 1975, *El oro y la paz* (Gold and Peace).

In addition to his literary work, Juan Bosch published several volumes of essays on politics, history and sociology – they included *Composición social dominicana* (Social Structure of the Dominican Republic) (1974), *De Cristóbal Colón a Fidel Castro: El Caribe frontera imperial* (From Columbus to Castro: The Caribbean as the Frontier of Empire) (1970), *Judas Iscariote, el calumniado* (Judas Iscariot: A Man Much Maligned) (1955) and *Trujillo: Causas de una tiranía sin ejemplo* (Trujillo: Causes of an Unparalleled Tyranny) (1961).

While recognized as a fine writer, Juan Bosch also played an extraordinarily significant role in Dominican political life. Exiled in Cuba during the Trujillo dictatorship, Bosch was one of the founders of the Partido Revolucionario Dominicano (PRD – Dominican Revolutionary Party) in 1941. He helped to prepare the Luperón invasion to overthrow the dictatorship in 1949; returning to the country in 1962, he was elected president in the first free elections since 1930. Seven months later, overthrown in a military *coup*, he was driven into exile once again.

On 24 April 1965, a civil war broke out over the demand for a return to the constitution approved under the Bosch government; the result of the war was the second US invasion of the Dominican Republic this century. Bosch stood again as a presidential candidate in the elections that took place under the gaze of the US Marines in 1966, but failed to win a majority; since then he repeatedly presented his candidature again in a series of elections beset by fraud and won in each case by Dr Joaquín Balaguer. In 1973 he left the PRD and founded the Partido de la Liberación Dominicana (Dominican Liberation Party), which entered government (1996–2000) under the presidency of Dr Leonel Fernández.

Further reading

Fernández Olmos, M. (1992) *La cuentística de Juan Bosch*, Santo Domingo: Alfa y Omega.

Montero, J. (1986) *La cuentística dominicana*, Santo Domingo: Bibliotcca Nacional.

FERNANDO VALERIO-HOLGUÍN

Bosi, Alfredo

b. 1936, São Paulo, Brazil

Critic

Bosi is Professor of Brazilian Literature at the University of São Paulo, and is considered one of Brazil's major literary critics. His writings seek out the humanist sense of art and the connections between poetry and philosophy. His best-known work, the *História concisa da literatura brasileira* (Concise History of Brazilian Literature) (1970), traces the course of Brazilian writing from its origins to the 1990s. *Dialéctica da colonização* (Dialectics of Colonization) (1992) is an encyclopedic study of Brazilian culture and colonization.

Further reading

Bosi, Alfredo (1978) *História concisa da literatura brasileira*, São Paulo: Editor Cultrix.

—— (1992) *Dialética da colonização*, São Paulo: Companhia das Letras.

MILTON HATOUM

Boullosa, Carmen

b. 1954, Mexico City

Novelist, poet and playwright

One of the most well-known, versatile and prolific writers of her generation, Bollousa possesses an immeasurable capacity to experiment with language, style and form. Since her first publication in 1978, a collection of poetry entitled *El hilo olvida* (The Thread Forgets), she has demonstrated her formalistic flexibility and talent by publishing in different genres: novel, short story, poetry and theatre. Boullosa is particularly deft at situating front-centre the body as a site of sensorial explorations of history, identity and eroticism, the main themes that are tightly woven in her writing. Her second novel, *Antes* (Before), won the much-coveted Premio Xavier Villaurrutia in 1989. Much of her work has been translated into different languages.

Further reading

Boullosa, Carmen (1987) *Mejor desaparece*, Mexico City: Océano.

—— (1989) *Antes*, Mexico City: Vuelta.

—— (1989) *La salvaja*, Mexico City: Fondo de Cultura Económica.

—— (1991) *Son vacas, somos puercos*, Mexico City: Era; trans. Leland H. Chambers, *They're Cows, We're Pigs*, Berkeley, CA: Grove Press/Atlantic, 1997.

—— (1992) *El médico de los piratas*, Mexico City: Siruela.

—— (1999) *Treinta años*, Mexico City: Alfaguara; trans. Geoff Hargreaves, *Leaving Tabasco*, Berkeley, CA: Grove Press/Atlantic, 2001.

Forné, Anna (2001) *La piratería textual: Un estudio hipertextual de Son vacas, somos puercos and El médico de los piratas de Carmen Boullosa*, Lund, Sweden: Romanska Institutionen, Lunds Universitet

LAURA G. GUTIÉRREZ

Brand, Dionne

b. 1953, Guayaguayare, Trinidad

Poet

Brand was one of the Caribbean intellectuals and artists who went to Grenada to contribute their talents to the revolution led by Maurice Bishop's New Jewel Movement. As a poet, she is fascinated by history and its implications and often counters dominant male perspectives with feminist/black woman/neo-colonial perspectives. Her publications include *Chronicles of the Hostile Sun* (1984), *Winter Epigrams and Epigrams to Ernesto Cardenal in Defense of Claudia* (1983), *Primitive Offensive* (1982), *Earth Magic* (1980) and *'Fore Day Morning* (1978).

Further reading

Brand, Dione (2000) *At the Full and Change of the Moon*, New York: Grove Press.

FUNSO AIYEJINA

Brandão, Ignácio de Loyola

b. 1936, Araraquara, Brazil

Writer

As a journalist in the late 1950s, Brandão wrote on political movements and social issues in Brazil for newspapers and magazines. His first novel, *Bebel que a cidade comeu* (The Bebel the City Ate), appeared in 1968 at the height of the military dictatorship. *Zero*, an experimental novel denouncing military repression, appeared first in Italy; when published in Brazil in 1974, it was immediately banned by the military. Brandão's fiction portrays Brazil's social and political reality with slang and journalistic language, different narrative genres and the disruption of chronological time.

Further reading

Brandão, Ignácio de Loyola (1999) *O homem que odiava a segunda-feira: Las aventuras possíveis*, São Paulo: Global.

CRISTINA FERREIRA-PINTO

Brathwaite, Kamau

b. 1930, Bridgetown, Barbados

Writer

Born at the height of the British colonial period, (Edward) Kamau Brathwaite studied history at Cambridge, then worked in Ghana as an education officer. African diaspora culture strongly informs his three-volume poem cycle *The Arrivants* (1973), first published as *Rights of Passage* (1967), *Masks* (1968) and *Islands* (1969). After early poems and plays (*Odale's Choice* (1967)), his poetic voice was already evident in the brilliant *Rights of Passage.*

Brathwaite's second trilogy, *Mother Poem* (1977), *Sun Poem* (1982) and *X/Self* (1987), explored Barbados's significance as maternal and then as paternal source. In *X/Self,* an individual whose name registers the loss of his ancestral name is imaged as the complex confluence of West Indian history and culture. Brathwaite's historical and cultural writing and poetry speak closely to one another (*X/Self* has historical footnotes). With *The Folk Culture of Jamaican Slaves* (1969), *The Development of Creole Society in Jamaica* (1971), *Contradictory Omens* (1974) and *History of the Voice* (1984), Brathwaite has contributed immensely to Caribbean revisioning of history.

African-centred music, from ritual drum chants to the blues and jazz (*Black and Blues* (1995)), reggae, calypso and dub (see **dub poetry**) from the Americas, centrally informs Brathwaite's aesthetic which explores the relation of scribal and oral culture. His autobiographical *Barabajan Poems* (1994) uses 'video style', a computer-generated visual language. His reworking of Caliban and his mother Sycorax, from Shakespeare's *The Tempest,* offers the computer, icon of Western technology, as a trope of anti-colonial resistance and post-colonial creativity. Brathwaite's 'proems', most recently the major *Dreamstories* (1994), *Zea Mexican Diary* (1994) and *Trench Town Rock* (1994), combine the compression of the poem with the narrative of prose.

Brathwaite has published nineteen collections of poems, four major 'proems', two volumes of plays and eight volumes of cultural criticism, as well as academic books and many articles and essays. He won the Neustadt International Prize for Literature in 1994.

See also: nation language

Further reading

Brathwaite, D.M. (1986) *EKB: His Published Prose and Poetry 1948–1986*, Kingston: Savacou Cooperative.

Brown, S. (ed.) (1995) *The Art of Kamau Brathwaite*, Bridgend: Poetry Wales Press.

Rohlehr, G. (1981) *Pathfinder: Black Awakening in the Arrivants of Edward Kamau Brathwaite*, Tunapuna: Gordon Rohlehr.

World Literature Today (1994) 'Kamau Brathwaite 1994: Neustadt International Prize for Literature', special issue, 68(4).

ELAINE SAVORY

Brazil

Latin America's largest and most populous country, Brazil's population is ethnically extremely diverse. It embraces 260,000 or so indigenous peoples speaking some 170 languages, some three and a half million immigrants in the twentieth century alone and the millions of Brazilians descended from the African slave populations brought to the Brazilian colony to work the sugar plantations. Indeed, arguably the single most important formative influence on the country's cultural developments has been the painful experience of physical and social dislocation and the creative responses it has produced.

Many of those encounters and creative dislocations are reflected in the language of the country itself – Brazilian Portuguese – shaped by inflections of African speech and vocabulary and the realities of the rural interior. When this interior began to make its presence felt in the burgeoning cities of Rio de Janeiro and São Paulo, the early twentieth century avant-garde saw it as an opportunity to advocate an authentic 'national-popular' culture. **Brazilian modernism** reflects this search in complex ways, and particularly in the writings of key figures of the movement such as Mário de **Andrade**, Oswald de **Andrade** and the poet Manuel **Bandeira**. The Modern Art Week (Semana de Arte Moderna) which they and others organized in February 1922 in São Paulo reflected both the central role of the city in a growing economy, and the revolutionary thinking of this new generation of artists – not only writers but painters and musicians and architects too, whose collaboration was one of the most dramatic and creative features of the Week.

The Modern Art Week was certainly a point of departure for a new generation of daring and innovative artists. They found vehicles in journals such as *Klaxon* and the Rio de Janeiro based magazine *Festa*, which published the early writings of Cecília **Meireles** (although she disclaimed modernism) and the scandalous erotic poetry of Gilka Machado. The most important of the magazines was Oswald de Andrade's ***Revista de Antropofagia***. Its first series (1928–29) included his *Manifesto Antropófago*; in this, as in his earlier *Manifesto da poesia pau-brasil* (Brazil Wood Poetry Manifesto), Andrade argued for a creative absorption, a 'cannibalizing' of European influences, as a prior condition for the creation of an authentic Brazilian tradition. The journal published the early poetry of Manuel Bandeira and Carlos Drummond de **Andrade**. But it also exposed ideological faultlines among its members which would evolve into two bitterly hostile currents in the course of the journal's second series, with a confrontation between the revolutionaries in the movements and the Catholic revivalists of Plínio **Salgado**'s 'verdeamerelista' movement which rapidly progressed in a neofascist direction. These very distinct politico-cultural positions defined themselves and hardened in the context of Getulio Vargas's 'Estado Novo' (1937–45).

The richness of its folk and oral traditions, and the ambivalences at the heart of Brazilian Modernism found expression in Mario de Andrade's ***Macunaíma*** (1928) and later in the extraordinarily rich linguistic universe of João Guimarães **Rosa**, who drew extensively on the popular ***literatura de cordel*** storytelling tradition and the ballads of the north east. Monteiro **Lobato**, by contrast, while a cultural modernist, rejected this use of the language of popular speech.

In a very different register, the outstanding novelist of the turn of the century in Brazil, Machado de Assis, turned an ironic and sharply modern eye on an emerging urban society and its contradictions, especially its excessive nationalism. Lima **Barreto**'s *Triste fim do Policarpo Quaresma* (translated as The Patriot) (1911) is a worthy successor. Euclides da **Cunha**'s *Os **sertões*** (Rebellion in the Backlands) (1902) belongs within a nineteenth-century tradition in its scale and overarching philosophical framework, but its setting – the Brazilian north-east – would provide the location for a **regionalist** novel born of an ideological commitment to the poor and the oppressed. Emerging in the 1930s, it brought to public attention writers like Rachel de **Queiroz** and José Lins do Rego whose *Menino de engenho* (Plantation Boy) (1932) inaugurated a cycle of novels set in the sugar plantations of the region. Outstanding among this body of work were the novels of Graciliano **Ramos** – *São Bernardo* (1934) and *Vidas secas* (Barren Lives) (1938), with its terse cinematic style. Arrested by Vargas, Ramos produced in 1953 his *Memorias do carcere* (Prison Memoirs) (1953). Yet the most famous writer of this generation, nationally and internationally, is undoubtedly Jorge **Amado**, whose prolific contribution to the literature of social protest and later to the evolution of a Brazilian variant of **magical realism** began with *Cacau* (Cocoa) (1933) and *Suor* (Sweat) (1934). His best known works internationally – *Gabriela cravo e canela* (Gabriela Clove and Cinammon) (1959) and *Dona Flor e sus deus maridos* (Dona Flor and Her Two Husbands) (1966) – belong to the second phase of his work.

In poetry, it was Carlos Drummond de Andrade who came to occupy a central place with collections like *Sentimento do mundo* (The Feeling of the World) (1940) and *A rosa do povo* (The People's Rose) (1945). By the early 1950s, however, the **concrete poetry** movement, with its emphasis on poetry as form and design, became increasingly dominant; its principal exponent were the **Noigandres group**, gathered around the journal of the same name, which included Augusto de **Campos** and his brother Haroldo de **Campos** as well as Décio **Pignatari**.

It might be argued that the inheritors of the popular-democratic artists of the 1930s, like Amado and Ramos, were to be found particularly in theatre by the early sixties, gathered around Augusto **Boal** and the work of companies like Teatro Oficina and the educational projects of Paulo Freire, as well as in the Centres of Popular Culture and the emerging Cinema Novo movement. Although not explicitly political in the same way, the national-popular impulse in João Guimarães **Rosa**'s extraordinary ***Grande sertão: Veredas*** (The Devil to Pay in the Backlands) (1956) is embedded in its language. The world of Clarice **Lispector**, by contrast, is urban and largely occupied by women, as in her *Lacos da familia* (Family Ties) (1960). In the same period, there emerged a school of poets strongly embedded in Catholicism for whom social purposes were alien to poetry; it embraces Jorge de **Lima**, Murilo **Mendes** and Ferreira **Gullar** among others.

The imposition of military rule after 1964, and particularly after 1968, repressed any attempt at a critical and engaged writing, and there emerged a more allusive and oblique register to elude censorship in the fiction of Antonio **Callado**, the theatre of Oduvaldo **Vianna Filho**, or the poetic song lyrics of Chico **Buarque** or Caetano Veloso. The mimeograph poets, a group that included Ana Cristina **César**, distributed their work in the streets, while magical realism provided an elusive version of the surrounding reality in the writings of Rubem **Fonseca** and Sergio **Sant'Anna** as well as the ironic register of Dalton **Trevisan**.

The military regime very consciously promoted mass culture, through organizations like the media conglomerate O Globo, and the official samba schools, to counter the more subversive notions of popular culture. Trevisan and Caio Fernando **Abreu**'s pastiches constitute critiques and challenges to that notion of the popular which could once again be voiced with the end of the military regime in 1984. But it seemed that the newer writings would return to the harsh realism that could unmask the realities of late twentieth-century urban life, as in Patricia Melo, or return to the regional, Milton **Hatoum**'s depictions of Amazonia, or Silviano **Santiago**'s journeys across sexual frontiers. At the same time, black writers have found an increasingly renonant voice through the work of groups like Quilombhoje.

Further reading

Candido, Antonio (1995) *On Literature and Society*, Princeton, NJ: Princeton University Press.

DiAntonio, Roberto (1989) *Brazilian Fiction: Aspects*

and Evolution of the Contemporary Narrative, Fayetteville: University of Arkansas Press.
Gonzalez, Mike and David Treece (1992) *The Gathering of Voices*, London: Verso.
Nist, J. (1967) *The Modernist Movement in Brazil: A Literary Study*, Austin: University of Texas Press.
Rowe, W. and Vivian Schelling (1992) *Memory and Modernity: Popular Culture in Latin America*, London: Verso.
Santiago, Silvano (2002) *The Space In-between: Essays on Latin American Culture*, Durham, NC: Duke University Press.
Schwarz, Roberto (1992) *Misplaced Ideas: Essays on Brazilian Culture*, London: Verso.
Sevcenko, N. (1992) *Orfeu extático na metropole*, São Paulo: Companhia das Letras.

DAVID TREECE AND MIKE GONZALEZ

Brazilian modernism

Brazilian modernism (1922–45) represents a sharp awareness of the modern which, in a lesser sense, refers back to Machado de Assis. In fact, in Rio de Janeiro in the late nineteenth century there were already identifiable elements of modernization: authoritarian centralization imposed by the empire, the reconstruction of the federal capital in the style of Haussman, migration to the cities generating the first *favelas* (whose name derives from the huts the army found in the northeast in the course of repressing a movement of anti-republican religious fanaticism) and the internationalization of investments in a society devoted to leisure and consumption. But in São Paulo, to coincide with the Independence Centenary, a kind of Armory Show, the Semana de Arte Moderna (Modern Art Week), opened in February 1922 in the Municipal Theatre. It brought together artists from different fields around a project which Mário de **Andrade**, one of its initiators, was to describe as the stabilization of a creative national consciousness. That was the essential question for the movement; the universal tenaciously pursued by modern enlightenment thought in its democratizing urge now had to give way to the multiple, creating in this way a tension between the singular and the general. The singular arose from a heroic moment for the avant-garde of São Paulo: the division of a cultured bourgeois public which, faced with this radical proposal, vacillated between paranoia and mystification. At the same time, through the estrangement of representations, a new public was to be created, one capable of accepting the free lyricism of Manuel **Bandeira**, the rhapsodic constructions of Villa-Lobos (*Bachianas brasileiras*) and Mário de **Andrade** (***Macunaíma***) (1928) or the cubist syntheses of João Miramar and Serafim Ponte Grande, the infamous heroes of Oswald de **Andrade**.

The general aspect, on the other hand, points to the cynical, mercantile aspect of every avant-garde movement and brought institutionalization, that is, official capitalization of a radical historicist effort to produce a new version of the Brazilian past (for example, with the rescue of the baroque style of Minas Gerais) which led to a reappraisal of the cultural diversity of the country. This stimulated an alliance between modernism and regionalism (see ***regionalismo***), but levelled out disharmonies and cacophonies at the local level. Within this tendency are included the work of Portinari (oscillating between committed 'Muralism' and a flattering portraiture), di Cavalcanti's frescoes depicting typical scenes of Bahia life and the search for less strident tones by composers such as Camargo Guarnieri and Erico Veríssimo. From this effort at modernist institutionalization there emerged a number of official institutions linked to the State under Getulio Vargas (National Book Institute, National Historic and Artistic Heritage Service, Embrafilme; institutions which more or less disappeared with the end of national-populist hegemony and the globalization of the 1990s) and there developed in São Paulo a strong internationalist current whose outstanding manifestations were, from the 1930s onwards, the University of São Paulo, and from the 1950s on, the São Paulo Bienale.

Attracted in its singular phase by the promises of futurist simultaneism and efforts at expressionist action, but marked too by orphic practices and corroded by integralista vertigo, Brazilian modernism turned in its general phase to a benevolent and euphoric reconstruction of itself through memoirs, which ensured its decline. The debate about its exhaustion (beginning prematurely in the 1930s) produced two currents of response: the 'Baudelairean' culturalism, not modernist but modern, of Murilo Mendes and liberation theology, and the 'Mallarmé-an' constructivism of the Utopian and the post-Utopian recognizable in the work of the concrete poets (see **concrete poetry**) such as Haroldo and Augusto de **Campos** or the musical *tropicalismo* of Caetano Veloso. The discontinuous memoirs of Milton **Hatoum** or the self-consciously fake memoirs of Silviano **Santiago**, as well as the stories of Rubem **Fonseca**, simulating forgetfulness, indicated a line of escape from the movement, a current of pre-individual singularities and impersonal individualities.

Further reading

Avila, A. (1975). *O Modernismo*, São Paulo: Perspectiva.

Martins, W. (1967) *O Modernismo (1916–1945)*, São Paulo: Editora Cultrix.

Nist, J. (1967) *The Modernist Movement in Brazil: A Literary Study*, Austin: University of Texas Press.

Pontiero, G. (ed.) (1969) *An Anthology of Brazilian Modernist Poetry*, Oxford: Pergamon.

Santiago, S. (1996) *Uma literatura nos trópicos?*, Durham, NC: Duke University Press.

Sevcenko, N. (1992) *Orfeu extático na metrópole*, São Paulo: Companhia das Letras.

RAUL ANTELO

Brechtian theatre

Bertolt Brecht (1898–1956) is the contemporary dramatist whose influence has been most pervasive in Latin American theatrical circles during the second half of the twentieth century. His plays and theoretical writings offered an innovative model shaped by Marxism that allowed for the representation of socio-cultural situations. Attracted by its political implications, several generations of playwrights enthusiastically adopted his well-known doctrine of the *Verfremdungseffekt* (alienation effect). Nonetheless, the results of Brecht's influence are neither a slavish imitation nor an acritical appropriation of successful devices prevailing in foreign theatre. On the contrary, his techniques underwent significant transformations and adjustments to fit the cultural history of Latin America.

From the theoretical point of view, a prominent place belongs to the Brazilian director Augusto **Boal**, who authored the influential *Teatro do oprimido* (Theatre of the Oppressed) (1975) and other texts internationally recognized as models for revolutionary theatre. In the Spanish-speaking world, the Colombian Enrique **Buenaventura** occupies a similar place. Founder in 1955 of what later became the Teatro Experimental de Cali (TEC), he wrote several plays combining Brecht with popular culture: the many versions of *En la diestra de Dios Padre* (On the Right Hand of God the Father) (1960), *Los papeles del infierno* (Documents from Hell) (1968) and the more distinctively Brechtian *La denuncia* (The Accusation) (1973), dealing with the exploitation and massacre of workers in 1928 by the United Fruit Company and the local government.

In the 1950s, plays written under the aegis of Brecht's didactic dramatology could be found everywhere in Latin America. *El tren amarillo* (The Yellow Train) (1954) by Guatemalan Manuel **Galich**, *Ida y vuelta* (Round Trip) (1955) by Uruguayan Mario **Benedetti** and *Historias para ser contadas* (Stories to be Told) (1957) by Argentine Osvaldo **Dragún** are celebrated examples of the use of theatre to achieve a deeper understanding of social reality. From this point on, Brechtian techniques – including the use of narrators, plot fragmentation, experimentation with masks, music and other expressive resources, and acting styles designed to avoid empathy with the public – have become staples for all major playwrights. Among many examples are *La paz ficticia* (The Fictitious Peace) (1960) by Luisa Josefina **Hernández**; *Un pequeño día de ira* (A Short Day of Anger) (1962) and *Yo también hablo de la rosa* (I Also Speak of the Rose) (1966) by Emilio **Carballido**; *El atentado* (The Assault) by Jorge **Ibargüengoitia**; *Yo, Bertolt Brecht* (I, Bertolt Brecht) (1966) and *Pirámide 179* (1969) by Máximo Avilés Blonda; *La pasión según Antígona Pérez* (The Passion According to Antigone Perez) (1968) by Luis Rafael **Sánchez**; *Santa Juana de América* (Saint Joan of America) (1975) by Andrés Lizárraga; and *Mil años, un día* (A Thousand Years, A Single Day) (1993) by Ricardo **Halac**.

Further reading

De Toro, F. (1987) *Brecht en el teatro hispanoamericano contemporáneo*, Buenos Aires: Galerna.
Pellettieri, O. (ed.) (1994) *De Bertolt Brecht a Ricardo Monti. Teatro en lengua alemana y teatro argentino*, Buenos Aires: Galerna.
Taylor, D. (1991) *Theatre of Crisis: Drama and Politics in Latin America*, Lexington: University Press of Kentucky.

DANIEL ALTAMIRANDA

Breeze, Jean 'Binta'

b. 1956, Hanover, Jamaica

Poet and dub performer

A scribal poet and a formidable 'dub' (see **dub poetry**) performer in a field dominated by men, Jean 'Binta' Breeze was briefly associated with Rastafarianism until she became disillusioned with the movement's gender politics. She migrated to England, where she performed with Linton Kwesi Johnson on the BBC's 'Poetry in Dub and Otherwise', wrote stage and screen plays, appeared in a film about her life, produced records (including *Riddym Ravings*, *Tracks* and *Riding on De Riddym*) and three collections of poetry. She has toured widely. *On the Edge of an Island* (1997) interweaves poems and short stories.

Further reading

Breeze, Jean 'Binta' (2000) *The Arrival of Brighteye and Other Poems*, Newcastle-upon-Tyne: Bloodaxe Books.

PAT DUNN AND PAMELA MORDECAI

Briceño Guerrero, José Manuel

b. 1929, Valera, Venezuela

Writer and philosopher

Briceño Guerrero is best known for his deliberations on Latin American cultural identity, exemplified by *El laberinto de los tres minotauros* (The Labyrinth of Three Minotaurs) (1996), which brought together his three major studies on the subject. Philosophy and philology, which he studied as a student, have remained central concerns of his work. He has also written several novels under the pseudonym of Jonuel Brique, such as *Triandáfila* (1967) and *Holadios* (1984), characterized by a poetic narrative style, and has had a distinguished academic career. Original in his thinking and in his style of writing, Briceño Guerrero was awarded Venezuela's national prize for literature in 1996.

Further reading

Briceño Guerrero, José Manuel (1981) *Europa y América en el pensar mantuano*, Caracas: Monte Avila.

MARK DINNEEN

Brierre, Jean Fernand

b. 1909, Jeremie, Haiti; d. 1992, Port-au-Prince, Haiti

Poet and dramatist

Brierre played an active role in the nationalist backlash against the US Occupation, at which time he established a reputation as a gifted poet of Haitian ***indigènisme***. He later served as Haiti's ambassador to Argentina but spent twenty five years in exile in Dakar, Senegal, because of his opposition to the Duvaliers. He was noted for his dramatic verse celebrating the heroes of Haitian Independence, the black diaspora and later such African-American artists as Langston Hughes, Paul Robeson and Marian Anderson. He is frequently anthologized as the poet of Haitian ***négritude*** because of his works *Black Soul* (1947) and *La Source* (The Source) (1956).

Further reading

Brierre, Jean Fernand (1947) *Black Soul*, Havana: Lex.

J. MICHAEL DASH

Brito, María Eugenia

b. 1950, Santiago, Chile

Writer

The topics of Brito's poetry are language itself, the inner dimensions of subjectivity, and female desire that trangresses the limits of static gender identity. They are the themes of her books *Vía Pública* (Public Highway) (1984), *Filiaciones* (Affiliations) (1986) and *Emplazamientos* (Defiances) (1993). Like other contemporary Chilean women writers, artists and critics (Diamela **Eltit**, Nelly **Richard** and Raquel **Olea** among them), Brito treats questions and issues raised by contemporary feminist and post-structuralist theories, as well as by the Latin American condition of her own writing.

Further reading

Brito, María Eugenia (1998) *Dónde vas*, Providencia, Santiago: Editorial Cuarto Propio.

LUIS E. CÁRCAMO-HUECHANTE

Britto García, Luis

b. 1940, Caracas, Venezuela

Writer

One of the most acclaimed Venezuelan writers of his generation, Britto García is best known for his fiction. He published his first works in the 1960s, but rose to prominence in 1970 with *Rajatabla*, a collection of short stories, characterized by humour and irony, which refer to political repression and violence. The narratives show the inclination for linguistic experiment which is central to his writing. His major work of fiction to date is his 1980 novel, *Abrapalabra*, which explores the cultural and political development of Venezuela through the present century. In 2000 he published a historical novel, *Piratas* (Pirates). A man of wide-ranging interests, he has also written plays, film scripts and several notable works of political analysis.

Further reading

Britto García, Luis (1980) *Abrapalabra*, Havana: Casa de las Américas.

Caldera, R. (1994) 'Transgresión y violencia en los cuentos de *Rajatabla*', *Cifra nueva: Revista de cultura* 2: 101–10.

Lasarte, F.J. (1991) '*Abrapalabra*, del mundo como escritura', *Revista iberoamericana* 155–6: 665–71.

Tomassini, G. (2000) 'Hipertextualidad y etica en *Rajatabla* de Luis Britto Garcia', *Cuento en red: Estudios sobre la ficcion breve* 2: n.p.

MARK DINNEEN

Brodber, Erna

b. 1940, St Mary, Jamaica

Novelist and social scientist

A meticulous scholar, Brodber also writes prose that is often highly poetic, like Kamau **Brathwaite**. Her first two novels, *Jane and Louisa Will Soon Come Home* (1980) and *Myal* (1988), both set out young women's self-healing and maturation within the context of a Caribbean society wounded by colonialism. Her third novel, *Louisiana* (1984), is a Jamaican-American woman's cultural journey into the collective history of black women.

Further reading

Webb, Barbara (1996) 'Erna Brodber', in B. Lindfors and R. Sander (eds) *Twentieth Century Caribbean and African Writers*, third series, Detroit: Gale Research, 57, 17–36.

ELAINE SAVORY

Brouard, Carl

b. 1902, Port-au-Prince, Haiti; d. 1965, Port-au-Prince

Poet

Perhaps the most notoriously bohemian and mystical of the Haitian *indigènisme* poets, Brouard established his reputation with early verse published in *La revue indigène* and from the outset, in the French tradition of the *poète maudit*, was obsessed by life in the slums of Port-au-Prince and Vodun religion. His most productive period was the 1930s and 1940s, before he drifted off into early senility. He became known as an ardent apologist for Haitian ***noirisme*** and was director of *Les Griots*, the journal of the ethnological movement.

Further reading

Berrou, R. (1975) *Deux poètes indigènistes: Carl Brouard et Émile Roumer*, Port-au-Prince: Editions Caraïbes.

Gaillard, R. (1966) *La destinée de Carl Brouard; essai accompagné de documents photographiques*, Port-au-Prince: H. Deschamps.

Knight, V.W. (1975) 'Carl Brouard: A Haitian "poete maudit" ', *Black Images: A Critical Quarterly on Black Arts and Culture* 4(3–4): 20–9.

J. MICHAEL DASH

Brown, Wayne

b. 1944, Woodbrook, Trinidad

Writer

Brown is an exceptionally talented and controversial critic, journalist, short story writer and teacher. He worked for the *Trinidad Guardian* between 1964 and 1995, but now writes for *The Independent*, which was founded in 1996. Brown distinguished himself early as a poet, winning the poetry prize at the Jamaica Independence Festival (1968), and the Commonwealth Poetry Prize (1972) for the collection *On the Coast*. Other books are: *Edna Manley: The Private Years, 1900–38* (1976); *21 Years of 'Poetry and Audience'*, as co-editor (1976); *Voyages* (1989); and *The Child of the Sea* (1990). He has also edited a selection of Derek **Walcott**'s poetry.

Further reading

Brown, Wayne (1975) *Edna Manley: The Private Years, 1900–1938*, London: Deutsch.

KEITH JARDIM

Brull, Mariano

b. 1891, Camagüey, Cuba; d. 1956, Havana, Cuba

Poet

Brull was a prominent member of the Cuban avant-garde movements of the day (see **avant-garde in Latin America**). Posted as a diplomat to various European cities, he was in close contact with contemporary European poets and translated Paul Valéry among others. His most famous contributions to poetry were the evanescent 'jitanjáforas', experiments in onamatopoeia and nonsense words: 'Filiflama alabe cundre/ ala olalúnea alífera/ alveolea jitanjáfor a/ liris salumba salífera'. He also wrote poetry in French.

Further reading

Brull, M. (1999) 'Three Poems and One Essay by Mariano Brull', trans. K. Müller-Bergh, M. Anania and B. Bergan, *Caribe: Revista de cultura y literatura* 2(1): 107–16.

—— (2000) *Poesía reunida*, ed. K. Müller-Bergh, Madrid: Cátedra.

DANIEL BALDERSTON

Bruma, Eddy

b. 1925, Suriname

Politician, poet and playwright

Bruma studied law in the Netherlands, became a politician and was an outspoken defender of the 1980 *coup d'état* in Suriname. As a leading member of the cultural movement **Wie eegie sanie**, he was a fervent advocate of the use of the native creole

Sranan Tongo, in which he published some poetry. His play *De geboorte van Boni* (The Birth of Boni) (1952), a eulogy of Maroon life, contributed to Wie eegie sanie's goal of reassessing Surinamese history from a local point of view.

AART G. BROEK

Brunet, Marta

b. 1901, Chillán, Chile; d. 1967, Montevideo, Uruguay

Writer

Brunet introduced the feminine experience into ***criollismo***. *Montaña adentro* (In the Heart of the Mountain) and *Bestia dañina* (Harmful Beast), both published in 1929, and *Humo hacia el sur* (Smoke in the South) (1946), placed in the landscape the discontent and rebellion of women. In Brunet's narratives, women see their hopes and expectations disappear because of social restrictions. Her work also renewed a nationalistic discourse, and looked at the effects of modernization upon Chilean culture, particularly the rural areas.

Further reading

Balart Carmona, Carmen (1999) *Narrativa chilena femenina: Marta Brunet*, Santiago de Chile: Santillana.

SANDRA GARABANO

Bryce Echenique, Alfredo

b. 1939, Lima, Peru

Writer

A respected and well-known Peruvian narrator since the 1970s, Bryce Echenique's first published volume of short stories, *Huerto cerrado* (Closed Orchard), was finalist for the 1968 **Casa de las Américas** prize. However, his great transatlantic success was his 1970 novel *Un mundo para Julius* (A World for Julius). Later came other humorous novels about the adventures of Latin American intellectuals in European exile, such as *La vida exagerada de Martín Romaña* (The Exaggerated Life of Martin Romaña) (1981) and *No me esperen en abril* (Don't Expect Me in April) (1995). Bryce also writes journalism for the Madrid paper *El País* and elsewhere. In 1993 he published *Permiso para vivir (Antimemorias)* (Permission to Live: Anti-Memoirs).

Further reading

Bryce Echenique, Alfredo (2000) *La historia personal de mis libros*, Lima: Fondo Editorial del Congreso del Perú.

—— (2001) *Tarzan's tonsillitis*, New York: Pantheon.

Ferreira, C. (2002) 'Alfredo Bryce Echenique', in C. Solé and K. Müller-Bergh (eds), *Latin American Writers: Supplement I*, New York: Scribners, 89–102.

Ferreira, C. and I.P. Márquez (eds) (1994) *Los mundos de Alfredo Bryce Echenique: Textos críticos*, Lima: Pontificia Universidad Católica del Perú, Fondo Editorial.

Krakusin, M. (1999) 'El retorno del protagonista: Mito y estructura en la novelistica de Alfredo Bryce Echenique', *Hispanófila* 125: 75–85.

Ortega, J. (1994) *El hilo del habla: La narrativa de Alfredo Bryce Echenique*, Guadalajara: Universidad de Guadalajara.

Páramo, M.L. (1996) 'Alfredo Bryce Echenique: La persona literaria y sentimental', *Especulo: Revista de estudios literarios* 2.

Wood, D. (1997) 'Alfredo Bryce Echenique', in V. Smith (ed.), *Encyclopedia of Latin American Literature*, London: Fitzroy Dearborn, 148–51.

JOSÉ ANTONIO MAZZOTTI

Buarque, Chico

b. 1944, Rio de Janeiro, Brazil

Writer

Chico Buarque is most widely known, both inside and outside Brazil, as a musician. He was a founding member of the MPB (Música Popular Brasileira) movement of the late 1960s, whose songs were marked by a subtle and poetic language which often veiled sharp social criticism. Less generally known outside the country is his work in theatre and his fiction. He adapted and staged classic works such as João Cabral do **Melo Neto**'s ***Morte e vida severina*** in 1966, and his *Opera do Malandro* (Hustler's Opera) (1978) was hugely popular. His first novel, *Fazenda modelo: Novela pecuária* (Model Farm: A Bovine Novel), described as 'an Orwellian allegory', was published in 1974. Subsequent fiction was published in the 1990s, and like *Estorvo* (Disturbance) (1991) and *Benjamim* (1995), is more poetic in tone and surreal in form, moving through shifting layers of narrative in an urban setting.

MIKE GONZALEZ

Buarque de Holanda, Heloisa (Helena Oliveira)

b. 1939, Ribeirao Preto, Brazil

Cultural critic

The 'marginal' poets of *26 poetas hoje* (26 Poets Today) were the subject of Holanda's 1979 doctoral thesis *Impressões de viagem* (Impressions on a Journey), which analysed the relationship between poetic language and politics in the 1960s and 1970s. She continued to explore the relations between culture and politics in other texts, while developing her own interests in newspaper and radio journalism and film production. She has played a key role in disseminating the cultural production of Brazilian women, organizing volumes on women film directors and silent screen actresses as well as *Ensaístas brasileiras* (Brazilian Women Essayists) (1993), in which she links them to the French and Anglo-American feminist theory which she introduced to Brazil.

Further reading

Buarque de Holanda, Heloisa (1979) *Impressões de viagem*, São Paulo: Ed. Brasiliense, Editora Rocco, 1992.

—— (1992) *¿Y nosotras latino americanas? Estudos sobre raça e gênero?*, São Paulo: Fundação Memorial da América Latina.

—— (1993) *Ensaístas brasileira*, Rio de Janeiro: Editora Rocco.

ADRIANA AMANTE

Buarque de Holanda, Sérgio

b. 1902, São Paulo, Brazil; d. 1982, São Paulo

Historian and literary critic

A key figure in the dissemination of modernist ideas in Brazil, Buarque was regarded, despite his youth, as the most sophisticated thinker of those associated with **Brazilian modernism**. In 1921 he moved from São Paulo to study law in Rio de Janeiro, and there became involved in artistic circles. However, he retained links with his native city and returned to attend the seminal Modern Art Week of 1922. He contributed to the São Paulo modernist journal *Klaxon* and was founding editor of the journal *Estética*, published in Rio de Janeiro from 1924. In 1929 he went to Germany as a correspondent for a São Paulo magazine and there attended Meinecke's courses at the University of Berlin and studied the work of the German historical school, writing critical essays on Kantorowicz, Sombart and Weber.

Returning to Brazil he published, in 1936, his best-known work – *Raízes do Brasil* (Roots of Brazil), a critical study of the Iberian origins of the authoritarian traditions of the Brazilian elite, their adaptation to the colonial context and to the Republic, and their institutionalization in the state. In that same year he began to work with French historian Henri Hauser. A volume of essays, *Cobra de vidro* (Glass Cobra), appeared in 1944, and in 1945 his classic historical study *Monções* analysed the river-borne expeditions out of São Paulo in the colonial period which led to the incorporation of the *sertões* (plains) of the interior into Brazilian territory, as well as the discovery of rich deposits of gold and gemstones. His *Caminhos e fronteiras* (Roads and Frontiers) (1957) continued the same theme. In the same year he produced another definitive work, *Visões do paraíso* (Visions of Paradise), on the projection onto America of European myths of the Garden of Eden. Between 1960 and 1972 he directed the collection *História geral da civilização brasileira* (General History of Brazilian Civilization). In 1969 he resigned from the University of São Paulo, where he had worked since 1956, in protest against the military government's incursion into the university. An original member of the Socialist Party in 1946, he was also a co-founder, in 1980, of PT, the Workers Party. His erudition, fine writing and analytical insights make Sérgio Buarque de Holanda a key point of reference for all contemporary Brazilian historiography.

Further reading

Nogueira, Arlinda Rocha (1988) *Sérgio Buarque de Holanda: Vida e obra*, São Paulo: Secretaria de Estado da Cultura, Universidade de São Paulo.

NICOLAU SEVCENKO

Buarque de Holanda Ferreira, Aurélio

b. 1910, Passo de Camarajibe, Brazil; d. 1989, Passo de Camarajibe

Writer and lexicographer

Part of the group around Graciliano **Ramos**, Holanda's most important work was editing the *Novo Dicionário da língua portuguesa* (New Dictionary of the Portuguese Language) (1975, republished 1986), popularly known as the 'Aurélio', which includes not only literary language but also the language of the mass media and popular songs. He published a book of stories, *Dois mundos* (Two Worlds) (1942), edited (with Paulo Rónai) an anthology of international short stories, *Mar de histórias* (Sea of Stories) (1945–63), and (with Alvaro Lins) *Roteiro literário do Brasil e de Portugal* (Literary Guide to Brazil and Portugal) (1956).

Further information

http://www.uol.com.br/aurelio

ADRIANA AMANTE

Buenaventura, Enrique

b. 1925, Cali, Colombia

Playwright and theatre director

Buenventura is a true renaissance man in the midst of the tensions of the twentieth century: playwright, director, actor, poet, theoretician, professor, artist, revolutionary and maestro. He is one of the pivotal figures of the New Popular Theatre movement in Latin America. In the 1950s he participated in the Independent Theatre movement of the Southern Cone. Shortly after, in 1955, he returned to Colombia to teach in the newly formed Theatre School within the Escuela de Bellas Artes in Cali. They recruited students for the school by placing an advertisement in the local newspaper. An eclectic group of twenty responded, among them workers, peasants and an elderly lady who could neither read nor write.

This group would eventually become the Teatro Experimental de Cali (TEC) under Buenaventura's direction. This was during Rojas Pinilla's dictatorship, a time in which Buenaventura was blacklisted by the military, which meant that he could not officially direct the Theatre School, even though he was its *de facto* director. He built the school and the group by going deeply into popular theatre, and by researching local folklore, dances, storytellers, popular literature, songs and music.

One of the first productions of the group was a 'nationalized' popular Nativity play in which the Massacre of the Innocents was closely tied to La Violencia in Colombia, with Herod represented as a tropical dictator. This 'nationalization' and re-elaboration of folk tales, plays, novels and short stories into a TEC style and vision would become trademark characteristics of the group. Later, they adapted Tomás Carrasquilla's *En la diestra de Dios Padre* (On God's Right Hand) for the theatre in a version that was widely acclaimed and won many prizes at the 1958 Bogotá Second Theatre Festival. Another of Buenaventura's and TEC's characteristics is the performing of a multiplicity of versions of the same play, as the interaction with the audience changes it and as the group and the author untiringly search for a new language of popular theatre.

The second version of *En la diestra de Dios Padre* was marked by Buenaventura's discovery of Brecht. Buenaventura admits that Brecht's influence was one of the causes of the failure of this second version of the play. However, he realized that this happened because they were applying Brecht in a way that Brecht himself would have hated: as a recipe, a formula (see **Brechtian theatre**). Freed from those formulaic constraints they were able to incorporate Brecht in a much more dynamic, 'nationalized' manner. Together with maestros such as Atahualpa del Cioppo from El Galpón in Uruguay, Buenaventura became an authority on Brecht in Latin America. Brecht was more than a simple influence; in a profoundly confluent quest, Buenaventura reinvented Brecht as he created a fiercely unique Latin American theatrical expression. The '*método de creación colectiva*' devised with TEC is a testament to this 'going beyond' of Brecht's original principles. The third version of *En la diestra de Dios Padre* incorporated the Mojiganga of the Antioquia peasants, a carnivalesque revision with on-stage musicians, masks and an 'abanderado' – a version that took the play away from realism. By going away from Brecht Buenaventura had in fact come closer to Brecht's theories.

With the period of 'nationalization of the classics' well underway, TEC would become known for producing its own versions of *Oedipus Rex*, *La Celestina*, *Ubu Roi* and the work of Molière, Lope de Vega, etc. In 1960 they were invited to the Theatre of Nations in Paris where they presented the second version of *En la diestra de Dios Padre* and Osvaldo **Dragún**'s *Historias para ser contadas* (Stories for Telling). This was their first international success – a success that consolidated their position in Colombia. Buenaventura did not return to Colombia for a while after this, instead staying in Paris for two years where he wrote *El requiem* (1961) and *La tragedia del Rey Christophe* (1962). While there he married Jacqueline Vidal, his lifelong companion and collaborator. Upon his return to Colombia, he began to write *La trampa* (The Trap) (1964) with TEC. This was the beginning of his questioning of the role of the individual author writing in isolation. Ethical and consequential, he attempted to relinquish his individual role as a playwright to create a new collective methodology, an actor's dramaturgy: '*El método de creación colectiva del TEC*'. This method circulated throughout Latin America, creating a veritable explosion of groups inspired by its empowering principles.

Rather than the hierarchical structure of traditional theatre, TEC advocated equality and a participatory ethics whereby the group's voice and viewpoint was present in each play that was created together. Given their ongoing militant criticism of the government, TEC and Buenaventura were expelled from the school in 1969. They had finally become an independent, non-official theatre, the now renamed Teatro Experimental de Cali. This is when Buenaventura and they dived even further into the history of their country, in particular, and of Latin America, in general. This was a true expropriation of history from the '*historiotenientes*', as he called them, to rescue history for a people's perspective and to accompany that history in the making through theatre. Plays such as his *Los papeles del infierno* (Documents from Hell), five sketches that include *La orgía* (The Orgy), were continued contributions in that direction. Others followed: *Soldados* (Soldiers), *La denuncia* (Denunciation), *Opera bufa*, *El encierro* (Round-Up) and *La estación* (The Station), among so many others.

Ever present at festivals and meetings throughout Latin America and the world, Enrique Buenaventura and TEC are true incarnations of a people's theatre where what is depicted on stage is inseparable from the way of life of its members, with all of its successes, pains and contradictions. Among his theoretical works are *'El arte nuevo de hacer comedias' y el nuevo teatro latinoamericano* (The 'New Art of Making Plays' and New Latin American Theatre), *La dramaturgia del actor* (Dramaturgy and the Actor), *Metáfora y puesta en escena* (Metaphor and *Mise-en-scène*), *El enunciado verbal y la puesta en escena* (The Verbal Utterance and *Mise-en-scène*) and *Notas sobre dramaturgia: Tema, mitema y contexto* (Notes on Dramaturgy: Theme, Mytheme and Context).

In 1990 (the year that TEC was disbanded)

Buenaventura wrote *Proyecto piloto* (Pilot Project), a dark, heartfelt look at a world running amok in a process of '*ratificación*' (becoming rats), a true dystopian view that seems to painfully disarticulate his previous position of Utopian revolutionary attachment. Nevertheless, this did not last, and in spite of the difficult process that groups such as TEC have had to endure in these postmodern, post-corporate times, Buenaventura continues to write and direct in his unfailing, profoundly ethical love affair with history and theatre.

Further reading

Buenaventura, E. (1990) *Teatro*, Mexico City: Siglo XXI.

Watson, M. (1976). 'Enrique Buenaventura's Theory of Committed Theatre', *Latin American Theatre Review* 9(2): 43–8.

MARINA PIANCA

Buitrago, Fanny

b. 1943, Barranquilla, Colombia

Writer

Novelist and playwright Fanny Buitrago is best known for her novel *Señora de la miel* (Mrs Honeycomb) (1993), an ironic story of the liberation of feminine desire, often compared to Laura **Esquivel**'s ***Como agua para chocolate*** (Like Water for Chocolate) for its sensual portrayal of food. Buitrago published her first novel, *El hostigante verano de los dioses* (The Tormenting Summer of the Gods), in 1963 and in 1964 was awarded the National Theatre Prize for her play *El hombre de paja* (The Straw Man). Buitrago portrays characters situated in the socio-cultural environment of the Caribbean; some of her novels are set in Colombia during the period of La Violencia.

Further reading

Arrington, T.R. (1997) 'Fanny Buitrago', in V. Smith (ed.), *Encyclopedia of Latin American Literature*, London: Fitzroy Dearborn, 151–2.

Buitrago, F. (2002) *Bello animal*, Bogotá: Seix Barral.

MIGUEL A. CARDINALE

Bullrich, Silvina

b. 1915, Buenos Aires, Argentina; d. 1989, Punta del Este, Uruguay

Writer

Bullrich explored the 'small human comedy' by weaving the psychological with the social in her narratives. Few Latin American 1950s writers were able to achieve a similar degree of popularity and financial success. In 1971 she received second prize in the National Award for *Los pasajeros del jardín* (The Travellers of the Garden); she resented this secondary accolade and described it in 'The Woman Writer in Latin America' as representative of the injustices against which women writers struggle. In addition to her short stories, novels and articles she also wrote ***crónica***, a biography and a television programme.

Further reading

Bullrich, Silvina (1986) *La Argentina contradictoria*, Buenos Aires: Emecé Editores.

FERNANDA A. ZULLO

Burgos, Julia de

b. 1914, Carolina, Puerto Rico; d. 1953, New York, USA

Poet

Although she published only two volumes of verse during her lifetime, Julia de Burgos (full name, Julia Constanze Burgos García) is recognized as one of Puerto Rico's finest poets. Born in a small village, into a large, impoverished family, her poems 'Río Grande de Loíza' and 'A Julia de Burgos' express a profound appreciation for the Puerto Rican landscape and a sense of herself as a strong, passionate woman. Despite her nationalism, she lived in New York from 1942 until her death. Her bicultural life and the intensity of her verse have made her a cultural icon of Puerto Rican identity, and an inspiring figure for later women writers such as Rosario **Ferré**.

Further reading

Burgos, Julia de (1997) *Song of the Simple Truth: Obra Completa Poética = The Complete Poems*, Willimantic, CT: Curbstone Press.

BEN A. HELLER

C

Caballero, Antonio

b. 1945, Bogotá, Colombia

Writer and journalist

Caballero is one of the most important political journalists in Colombia. His style is controversial and confrontational and he has a weekly column in the magazine *Semana* (Week), in which he frequently criticizes the Colombian oligarchy, imperialism and globalization. He is perhaps better known for his left-wing political views than his literary work. Caballero is considered an icon within the radical political movement that emerged from the ashes of the New Left. As a novelist, he wrote an excellent urban novel about Bogotá in which he comments on political and social problems of the generation born in the seventies via his main character, Escobar.

Further reading

Caballero, A. (1984) *Sin remedio*, Bogotá: Editorial Oveja Negra.

Valencia-Solanilla, C. (2000) '*El resto es silencio* y *Sin remedio*: La crisis de la modernidad en la novela urbana', in M.M. Jaramillo, B. Osorio and A.I. Robledo (eds), *Literatura y cultura: Narrativa colombiana del siglo XX*, Bogotá, Colombia: Ministerio de Cultura, II, 273–300.

ALVARO BERNAL

Caballero Calderón, Eduardo

b. 1910, Bogotá, Colombia; d. 1990, Bogotá

Writer

Author of over ten novels and eleven volumes of essays, Caballero Calderón was a major Colombian writer. His essay on *Don Quijote* demonstrates his knowledge of the Hispanic literary heritage from the *Poema de mío Cid* through the twentieth century. His novels *El cristo de espaldas* (Christ on his Back) (1952), *Siervo sin tierra* (Landless Servant) (1953) and *Manuel Pacho* (1962) are related to the civil war identified as La Violencia and have received substantial critical attention. *El buen salvaje* (The Good Savage) (1965), which received Spain's Nadal Prize in 1965, is a self-conscious work about a struggling novelist in Paris.

Further reading

Caballero Calderón, Eduardo (1963) *Obras*, Medellín: Bedout.

RAYMOND L. WILLIAMS

Cabichu'í 2

Cabichu'í 2 is a literary journal co-founded by Moncho Azuaga, Emilio Lugo and Ricardo de la Vega in 1989. Published semi-annually, *Cabichu'í 2* began as the platform for the poets of the Taller de Poesía Manuel Ortiz Guerrero (Manuel Ortiz Guerrero Poetry Workshop), who became known in the last stages of the Stroessner dictatorship (1955–89). It continued the work begun by Editora Taller (Workshop Publishing), which published some ten titles by Paraguayan poets.

Further information

http://www.anselm.edu/homepage/tmfaith/dic-cioc.html

TERESA MÉNDEZ-FAITH

Cabral, Manuel del

b. 1907, Santiago de los Caballeros, Dominican Republic; d. 1999, Santo Domingo, Dominican Republic

Poet

One of the initiators of black poetry in the Caribbean, del Cabral lived in Argentina, where in the 1940s he published *Trópico negro* (Black Tropics) (1941), *Compadre Mon* (Godfather Mon) (1943) and *Chinchina busca el tiempo* (Chinchina's Search for Time) (1945). In *Doce poemas negros* (Twelve Black Poems) (1935) and *Trópico negro* he explored Afro-Caribbean culture and social problems. *Compadre Mon* is an extensive poem in which humanity sings to the earth in search of its origins. In *Chinchina busca el tiempo*, del Cabral expressed his metaphysical concerns.

Further reading

Bajarlía, J.J. (1974) 'La poesía metafísica de Cabral', *Hispamérica* 8: 92–6.

Cabral, Manuel del (1957) *Antología clave*, Buenos Aires: Editorial Losada.

Echeverría, E. (1972) 'Sobre Manuel del Cabral, *El escupido*', *Revista iberoamericana* 78: 159–60.

FERNANDO VALERIO-HOLGUÍN

Cabrera, Lydia

b. 1899, Havana, Cuba; d. 1991, Miami, Florida, USA

Writer and ethnologist

A central figure in Afro-Cuban studies, Cabrera's study of Cuban folklore began under Fernando Ortiz before her move to Paris, where she continued her studies of the religion, myths and customs of black Cubans. At the same time she studied painting and became absorbed by Eastern religion. In Spain, she formed a close relationship with García Lorca.

Her first book, *Cuentos negros de Cuba* (Black Stories from Cuba) (1936), published in Cuba in 1940, recreated in twenty-two poetic prose pieces the experiences of a marginal population that nevertheless played a central role in the formation of Cuba's national culture. Her writing went beyond the transient interest in Afro-Cuban culture to capture the deeper spirituality of black Cubans, locating Caribbean mythology in a category of universal values.

Returning to Paris from Spain in 1938, she resumed her explorations of the surviving traditions of a population whose origins were in Africa and developed a careful and detailed study of the linguistic and anthropological aspects of black Cuban culture. The result was her most important work, *El monte* (1954), a Bible of Cuba's black culture. Its subtitle, 'Notes on the religions, music, beliefs and folklore of Afro-Cubans and the people of Cuba', indicates how thoroughly documented it was, and explains why it has become the definitive work on Santería.

Other works in the same vein followed: *Anagó, vocabulario Lucumí* (Anagó, Lucumí Vocabulary) (1957) and *La sociedad secreta abakuá narrada por viejos adeptos* (The Abakua Secret Society Narrated by Aged Members) (1959).

Cabrera went into exile in 1960, but continued to work on the material collected in previous years, producing a number of works including *Cuentos para adultos niños y retrasados mentales* (Stories for Childish Adults and Mentally Handicapped People) (1983) and *La medicina popular en Cuba* (Popular Medicine in Cuba) (1984).

Further reading

Castellanos, I. and J. Inclán (1987) *En torno a Lydia Cabrera (Cincuentenario de 'Cuentos Negros de Cuba') 1936–86*, Miami: Universal.

Davies, C. (1997) 'Lydia Cabrera', in V. Smith (ed.), *Encyclopedia of Latin American Literature*, London: Fitzroy Dearborn, 153–5.

Hiriart, R. (1978) *Lydia Cabrera: Vida hecha arte*, New York: Eliseo Torres.

Montenegro, N. (2002) 'Lydia Cabrera', in C. Solé and K. Müller-Bergh (eds), *Latin American Writers: Supplement I*, New York: Scribners, 119–31.

Quiroga, J. (2000) 'Queer Desires in Lydia Cabrera', in *Tropics of Desire: Interventions from Queer Latino America*, New York: New York University Press, 76–100.

Sánchez, R. (ed.) (1977) *Homenaje a Lydia Cabrera*, Miami: Universal.

WILFREDO CANCIO ISLA

Cabrera Infante, Guillermo

b. 1929, Gibara, Cuba

Writer

One of the leading contemporary writers of Latin America, Cabrera Infante has lived in self-imposed exile in Britain since the mid-1960s and is a vocal critic of Fidel Castro. His career began as a journalist with the popular magazine *Bohemia*. In 1954, under the pseudonym G. Cain, he became film critic for the journal *Carteles* and continued until the magazine ceased publication. He founded the Cinemateca de Cuba and was its president from 1951 to 1956; he was also editor of the literary magazine ***Lunes de Revolución*** throughout its existence. His disenchantment with the Cuban Revolution began with the conflict over the film *PM* (1961), an experimental journey through Havana nightlife which was censored by the Castro government (and which recently featured in the closing credits of the film *Before Night Falls*). After three years as a cultural attaché in Belgium, Cabrera Infante resigned his diplomatic post in 1965 and left Cuba to become resident in Europe.

Although he had won the occasional literary prize, early recognition of his work came with his *Así en la paz como en la guerra* (Rites of Passage) (1960), a volume of short stories set in pre-revolutionary Cuba. It was his novel *Tres tristes tigres* (Three Trapped Tigers) (1967) that brought him international recognition. This fabulous recreation of Havana at night revolves around the obsessive themes of his writing – nostalgia for the city, music, the cinema and joyful games with language. It offers a broad fresco of Cuban life and manners during the 1950s, evoked with irreverence, satirical wit and a narrative certainty which gives his work its great power.

Critics agree that *Tres tristes tigres* (its title taken from a children's tongue twister) is a key work of the Latin American literary **Boom** and a landmark in Cuban literature. His subsequent work has embraced several genres. *Vista del amanecer en el trópico* (View of Dawn in the Tropics) (1974) narrates the history of Cuba from the Discovery to the present through a series of vignettes. *O* (1975) is a collection of essays and articles on contemporary issues; *Ejercicios de esti(l)o* (Style Trials) (1976) is a series of experimental writings while *La Habana para una infanta difunta* (Infante's Inferno) (1979) is a novel.

Mea Cuba (My Cuba), published in 1992, brings together his political and critical writings; *Delito por bailar el chachachá* (1995), a volume of stories, and *Ella cantaba boleros* (She Sang Boleros) (1996), a narrative based on his earlier novels, followed. His passion for film is reflected in critical essays collected in *Un oficio del siglo veinte* (A Twentieth-Century Job) (1963) and *Cine y sardina* (Film and Sardines) (1997). He has also explored the history of the Cuban cigar in *Holy Smoke*, published in English in 1985.

In 1997 he won the Cervantes Prize for Literature.

Further reading

Aching, G. (2002) 'Specularity and the Language of Corpulence: Estrella's Body in Cabrera Infante's *Tres tristes tigres*', in *Masking and Power: Carnival and Popular Culture in the Caribbean*, Minneapolis: University of Minnesota Press, 101–25.

Cabrera Infante, G. (1999) *Assays, essays and other arts*, New York: Twayne.

MacAdam, A. (2002) 'Guillermo Cabrera Infante', in C. Solé and K. Müller-Bergh (eds), *Latin*

American Writers: Supplement I, New York: Scribners, 133–48.

Machover, J. (1996) *El heraldo de las malas noticias: Guillermo Cabrera Infante: Ensayo a dos voces*, Miami, FL.: Ediciones Universal.

Pereda, Rosa M. (1979) *Guillermo Cabrera Infante*, Madrid: Edaf.

Souza, R.D. (1996) *Guillermo Cabrera Infante: Two islands, many worlds*, Austin: University of Texas Press.

Volek, E. (1997) 'Guillermo Cabrera Infante', in V. Smith (ed.), *Encyclopedia of Latin American Literature*, London: Fitzroy Dearborn, 155–7.

WILFREDO CANCIO ISLA

Cabrujas, José Ignacio

b. 1937, Caracas, Venezuela; d. 1995, Margarita, Venezuela

Playwright, actor, screenwriter and essayist

Together with Román Chalbaud and Isaac **Chocrón**, Cabrujas founded El Nuevo Grupo, one of the most important theatre companies of the 1960s. His dramatic works have been performed frequently and some adapted for the cinema. It was on television, however, where Cabrujas made his particular mark, introducing major innovations into the genre of the television soap opera (*culebrón/telenovela*). Among his best-known plays are *Acto cultural* (A Cultural Act) and *El día que me quieras* (The Day You Love Me). His *telenovelas La señora de Cárdenas* (Mrs Cardenas) (1977) and *La dueña* (The Landlady) (1985) are classics of the genre.

Further reading

Cabrujas, José Ignacio (1990) *El día que me quieras y acto cultural*, Caracas: Monte Avila.

—— (1996) *La viveza Criolla. Destreza, mínimo esfuerzo o sentido del humor*, Caracas: Cátedra Fundación Sivensa-Ateneo de caracas.

JORGE ROMERO LEÓN

Cadenas, Rafael

b. 1930, Barquisemeto, Venezuela

Poet

One of Venezuela's most representative and widely read poets, Cadenas was associated with the post-Pérez Jiménez intellectual movements. His lyrical testimony *Los cuadernos del destierro* (Notebooks from Exile) (1960) celebrates the world as seen by a patient and obsessive observer and offers an ironic self-representation through sensual and reflective imagery. Since then his poetry has become increasingly concentrated and aphoristic, as in *Memorial* (1977) or *Gestiones* (Operations) (1992), which won him the Pérez Bonalde Poetry Prize. Cadenas has also published works straddling the line between poetry and aphorism, as well as volumes of essays.

Further reading

Cadenas, R. (2000) *Obra entera: Poesía y prosa, 1958–1995*, Mexico City: Fondo de Cultura Económica.

Rama, A. (1990) 'La experiencia en abismo de Rafael Cadenas', in *Ensayos sobre literatura venezolana*, Caracas: Monte Avila. 221–5.

Sucre, G. (1974) 'La metáfora del silencio', *Revista nacional de cultura* 216: 47–57.

RAFAEL CASTILLO ZAPATA

Cahier d'un retour au pays natal

Aimé **Césaire** began work on his lengthy lyric poem *Cahier d'un retour au pays natal* (Notes on a Return to the Homeland), a politically engaged meditation on a return to his native island of Martinique and a founding text of ***négritude***, in 1936 while still a student in Paris. Published for the first time in the review *Volontés* in 1939, the poem underwent numerous revisions and publications, of which the 1956 **Présence Africaine** edition is considered definitive. Despite Césaire's surrealist techniques, the poem includes autobiographical detail and vehemently denounces the historical problems of colonialism, slavery and poverty in Africa and the Antilles.

Further reading

Cesaire, A. (2000) *Notebook of a Return to the Native Land*, Middletown, CT: Wesleyan University Press.

Condé, M. (1978) *Cahier d'un retour au pays natal: Césaire: Analyse critique*, Paris: Hatier.

SCOTT A. COOPER

Caicedo, Andrés

b. 1953, Cali, Colombia; d. 1977, Cali

Writer

Caicedo was a respected Colombian novelist whose suicide is legendary in Colombian literary circles. One of the first writers interested in the multicultural and diverse world of large Colombian cities, his novels take place in Cali, Colombia (Colombia's third largest city). His characters are beings who navigate through drugs, nightclubs, prostitution, underground music and the outskirts of the city. Caicedo's most successful novel, *Qué viva la música* (Long Live Music) (1977) tells the story of an innocent young girl who involves herself in the underworld of Cali. His narrative introduces the tragedy of urban youth surrounded by anarchy, violence and corruption, a topic that has been recently rediscovered by new Colombian narrators.

Further reading

Caicedo, Andrés (1977) *Qué viva la música*, Bogotá: Instituto Colombiano de cultura, Santafé de Bogotá.

Cobo Borda, Juan Gustavo (1977) 'Andrés Caicedo: Narrador y crítico', *Magazín Dominical – El Espectador*, Bogotá, 22 May: 10.

Williams, Raymond (1983) 'Andrés Caicedo's ¡Qué viva la música!: Interpretation and the Fictionalized Reader', *Revista de estudios hispánicos* 1: 43.

ALVARO BERNAL

Cairo, Edgar E.

b. 1948, Paramaribo, Suriname; d. 2000, Amsterdam, the Netherlands

Writer and playwright

Cairo grew up in Suriname. His first publication was in Sranan Tongo, a Surinamese creole, but he later turned to Dutch and the local Surinamese variant of Dutch. In the 1970s and 1980s he was a very prolific writer, with over twenty-five publications of prose, poetry and drama, including the lengthy novels *Dat vuur der grote drama's* (That Fire of Great Dramas) (1982) and *Jeje Disi: Karakter's krachten* (A Character's Powers) (1980). He also became known for his lively reading sessions. Resident in the Netherlands, he was forced to stop writing due to psychological problems.

AART G. BROEK

Calderón, Teresa

b. 1955, La Serena, Chile

Poet

In the constrained conditions of the Pinochet regime (1973–90), Calderón's work addresses women's day-to-day experience and their dealings with masculine culture. Her language is colloquial and direct and charged with irony. Her first book, *Causas perdidas* (Lost Causes) was published in 1983. *Género femenino* (Feminine Gender/Genre) (1989) highlights her sense of identity as a woman. In the post-1990 Chilean democracy, however, her generation saw its opportunities for promotion and recognition expand. She won the prestigious Pablo Neruda Prize for Poetry in 1992.

Further reading

Calderón, Teresa *et al.* (1996) *Veinticinco años de la poesía chilena (1970–1995)*, Mexico City: Fondo de Cultura Económica.

LUIS E. CÁRCAMO-HUECHANTE

Caliban

Caliban, a rebellious island native enslaved by a colonizing Milanese Duke named Prospero in William Shakespeare's *The Tempest*, became a favourite symbol of revolutionary, anti-imperialist culture for Caribbean writers in the 1960s and early 1970s. The character's name is an anagram of 'cannibal', a word introduced to English shortly after Christopher Columbus dubbed the natives of the West Indies *caníbales*, mishearing the name *Caribes*, and saddled them with a reputation for eating human flesh. In *The Tempest*, Caliban is similarly characterized as a half-human savage. When the protagonist of the play, Prospero, tries to remind Caliban of all the latter owes him, including the use of language, Caliban responds with his most famous lines: 'You taught me language, and my profit on't/ Is, I know how to curse. The red plague rid you/ For learning me your language!' (I.ii.362–4).

The Tempest and Caliban were the subject of commentary for centuries, with Prospero cast in the role of civilizing force and Caliban as the barbarous savage in need of cultivation. But it was not until the Martinican psychoanalyst Frantz Fanon, in the midst of post-Second World War decolonization, critically reversed the traditional associations and values assigned to Prospero and Caliban that the latter began his late career as a poster boy for anti-imperialist revolutionary culture in the Caribbean. After Fanon's ***Peau noire, masques blancs*** (Black Skin, White Masks) (1952), the Barbadian author George **Lamming** devoted two chapters of his *Pleasures of Exile* (1992) to the play. Lamming, although clearly sympathetic to the plight of the colonized Caliban, nevertheless was unable to transform the figure into a symbol of defiant cultural appropriation. However, by the late 1960s, with the Cuban Revolution in full swing and several West Indian island nations savouring newly won independence, Lamming's compatriot Edward Kamau **Brathwaite**, in his poetry volume *Islands*, and the Martinican playwright and poet Aimé **Césaire**, in his *A Tempest: Adaptation of Shakespeare's 'The Tempest' by a Negro Theater*, decisively identified Caribbean culture with Caliban and stamped it with a revolutionary and anti-imperialist character.

Just a few years later, the Cuban poet and scholar Roberto **Fernández Retamar** inflected the imagery of Caliban with a Latin American tone in his 1971 essay *Caliban*. Retamar argued that Caliban, and the ferocious island Caribs he represented, were the true ancestors and symbols for the long tradition, only then finally victorious, of Latin American revolutionary anti-imperialism. He also challenged the long-prevailing view of José Enrique **Rodó**, the Uruguayan writer who in his 1900 essay *Ariel*, in the wake of US intervention in the War for Cuban Independence, associated the United States with what he saw as a brutish Caliban and Latin America with Ariel, the fairy spirit of *The Tempest* (see ***Ariel* and *arielismo***). Against this view, Retamar pointed out that Ariel, like Caliban, is the slave of the imperialist Prospero, but that unlike Caliban, Ariel faithfully obeys the master. More particularly, Retamar polemicized against some of the famous novelists of the so-called **Boom** for hitching their political wagons to the horse of US-sponsored, anti-Cuban propaganda (see ***Mundo nuevo***). With this polemic, Retamar ushered in his ringing final call for the Ariels, or **intellectuals**, of Latin America to humbly seek 'from Caliban the honour of a place in his rebellious and glorious ranks'.

Further reading

Césaire, A. (1992) *A Tempest*, trans. R. Miller, New York: Ubu Repertory Theater Publications.

Fanon, F. (1968) *Black Skin, White Masks*, trans. C.L. Markmann, New York: Grove Publishing.

Fernández Retamar, R. (1989) *Caliban and Other Essays*, trans. E. Baker, Minneapolis: University of Minnesota Press.

Fishburn, E. (1997) 'Caliban: America as the Other', in V. Smith (ed.), *Encyclopedia of Latin American Literature*, London: Fitzroy Dearborn, 158–9.

Hulme, P. (1992) *Colonial Encounters: Europe and the Native Caribbean, 1492–1797*, New York: Routledge.

Lamming, G. (1992) *The Pleasures of Exile*, Ann Arbor: University of Michigan Press.

SANTIAGO COLÁS

Callado, Antônio

b. 1917, Niterói, Brazil; d. 1997, Rio de Janeiro, Brazil

Writer

A career journalist, Callado distinguished himself with nine novels, although he also published eight volumes of plays, several of journalistic essays and one of short stories. Callado always displayed a deep historical and social consciousness, and was concerned with understanding and defining Brazilian identity. His novels address the question, 'What does it mean to be Brazilian?', dealing with elements constitutive of Brazilian society such as religion, education, politics and ethnicity. After his novel *Quarup* (filmed by Ruy Guerra) (1967), the military dictatorship (1964–85) and subsequent political problems were central to Callado's fiction.

Further reading

Ferreira-Pinto, C. (1985) *A viagem do herói no romance de Antônio Callado*, Brasília: Thesaurus.

CRISTINA FERREIRA-PINTO

Calzadilla, Juan

b. 1931, Altagracia de Orituco, Venezuela

Poet, painter and art critic

Founder of two of the main literary groups in Venezuela – *Sardio* and *El techo de la ballena* (Sardio, and Roof of the Whale) – Calzadilla published his first poems in 1954 and soon became a standard-bearer of urban, socially committed poetry. His verses are enriched by narrative elements and a dramatic unfolding of the lyric self. His literary activity has produced witty essays and fine translations. He has been included in several major anthologies, and has also built a solid career as a painter and art critic. His books include: *La Torre de los pájaros* (Tower of Birds) (1955), *Dictado por la jauría* (Dictated by Hounds) (1962), *Manual de extraños* (Stranger's Manual) (1965), *Malos modales* (Bad Manners) (1968), *Ciudadano sin fin* (Endless Citizen) (1970), *Oh Smog* (1978), *Minimales* (Minimals) (1992) and *Antología* (Anthology) (1993).

Further reading:

Silva, L. (1988) *Juan Calzadilla/Elfredo Silva Estrada. Dos poetas contrapuestos de la generación del 58*, Maracay: Casa de la Cultura.

VÍCTOR GALARRAGA OROPEZA

Cameron, Norman Eustace

b. 1903, New Amsterdam, British Guiana; d. 1983

Writer and historian

Cameron's broad intellectual curiosity was stimulated by boyhood travels throughout Guyana accompanying his father, a sanitary inspector. Although he studied and later lectured in mathematics, Cameron's early interest in hybrid Guyanese cultural practices informs his mature work, especially his two-volume *The Evolution of the Negro*, written in 1929 and 1934, the poetry anthology *Guianese Poetry* (1931), *Thoughts on Life and Literature* (1950) and *150 years of Education in Guyana* (1968). His play *The Price of Victory* (1965), written one year before Guyanese independence from Britain, recognizes the function of Yoruba culture and mythology in Afro-Guyanese syncretism.

Further reading

Cameron, Norman Eustace (1959) *Thoughts on the Making of a New Nation*, East Demerara, British Guiana: Argosy Co.

JILL E. ALBADA-JELGERSMA

Campobello, Nellie

b. 1900, Villa Ocampo, Durango, Mexico; d. 1986, Progreso de Obregón, Hidalgo

Novelist

Nellie Campobello is the only woman whose works form part of the canonical **novel of the Mexican Revolution**. She is also the most aesthetically and historically significant writer of this movement. Born María Francisca Luna in the northern Mexican state of Durango, Nellie was the oldest child of Rafaela Luna. She took the surname Campobello from the father of her sister Gloria, an Englishman with the last name Campbell Morton. Campobello's non-literary works are a biographical narrative on Pancho Villa and a treatise on Mexican folk dance, co-authored with her sister. Her literary works include several collections of poetry and two novels, *Cartucho* (1931) and *My Mother's Hands* (1938). The novels treat Campobello's memories from the period of the Mexican Revolution, which she describes from the highly eccentric vantage point of a young girl. Both *Cartucho* and *My Mother's Hands* make innovative use of fragmentary narration. In *Cartucho*, the fragmentary narrative form can be related to Campobello's intense reflection on social violence, which the novel treats in a disturbingly direct manner, devoid of the moral judgements that characterize many narratives about rural insurgency in Latin America. Perhaps more importantly, Campobello also engages with popular cultural forms, such as the *corrido* and etchings in the style of José Guadalupe Posada, and offers the incisive social critique contained in the genre novel of the Mexican Revolution. While most such novels contain the dynamics of popular rebellion within a nationalistic framework, *Cartucho* allows its characters and its depiction of the Villista movement to inhabit a militantly regional framework that functions to question the nationalism of the post-revolutionary state. *My Mother's Hands* is also written in a series of brief sketches, but is more lyrical in tone and more centrally focused on a feminine narrative space defined by the powerful axis of the mother–daughter relationship. The exclusion of strong paternal figures, in part a reflection of Nellie's non-relationship with her birth father, also generates one of the ways in which her literary work challenges the cultural norms of her time.

For many decades, Campobello was far better known in Mexico as a dancer than as a writer, and her books were long out of print in Spanish. As she advanced in age, Campobello's life became increasingly controlled by feckless assistants who apparently kidnapped her from her own home in 1986. She died shortly afterwards. Her tragic marginalization can perhaps best be measured by the fact that the exact conditions of her death went uninvestigated and unreported for over a decade. In recent years, her life and work are finally receiving the extended study they deserve.

Further reading

Campobello, Nellie (1940) *Apuntes sobre la vida militar de Pancho Villa*, Mexico City: Iberoamericana Publications.

——(1960) *Mis libros*, Mexico City: Compañía General de Editores.

—— (1988) *Cartucho /My Mother's Hands*, trans. Doris Meyer and Irene Mathews, Austin: University of Texas Press.

Campobello, Gloria and Nellie Campobello (1940) *Ritmos indígenas de México*, Mexico City: NP.

Good, C. (1997) 'Nellie Campoebello', in V. Smith (ed.), *Encyclopedia of Latin American Literature*, London: Fitzroy Dearborn, 161–2.

Martínez, Reynosa and Emilia Elena (1965) *Nellie Campobello y su obra literaria*, Mexico City: UNAM.

Mathews, Irene (1997) *Nellie Campobello. La centaura del Norte*, Mexico City: Cal y Arena.

Rodríguez, Blanca (1998) *Nellie Campobello. Eros y violencia*, Mexico City: UNAM.

BRIAN GOLLNICK

Campos, Augusto de

b. 1931, São Paulo, Brazil

Poet, critic and translator

One of the original Noigandres poets of the 1950s

(see **Noigandres group**), this key figure has stayed closest to the minimalist aesthetics of **concrete poetry**. He is known for experimental varieties of poetry involving colour, visual images and electronic media, as in *Viva Vaia Poesia 1949–1979* and *Despoesia* (1993). His criticism and translations have focused on innovations in Western lyrics. In other writings he was the first to recognize the poetry of MPB (Música Popular Brasileira) songs. His suggestive poem 'pós-tudo' (post-everything) (1984) sparked a polemic with Roberto **Schwarz** about **postmodernism** in Brazil. In the 1990s, he also began performing poetry with musical and video accompaniment.

Further reading

Campos, Augusto de (1997) *Os sertões dos Campos: Duas vezes Euclides*, Rio de Janeiro: Sette Letras.

CHARLES A. PERRONE

Campos, Haroldo de

b. 1929, São Paulo, Brazil; d. 2003, São Paulo

Poet, critic and translator

One of the key figures of Brazilian poetry and literary criticism in the second half of the twentieth century, Campos first achieved distinction as co-founder and theorist of the *Noigandres* journal (see **Noigandres group**) and of **concrete poetry**. He has pursued inventive impulses in lyric and sought the expansion of borders between literary genres. In addition to exploring new writing directions, he developed a creative method of translation called 'transcreation' (renderings of ancient Chinese poetry, the Book of Genesis, Dante, Goethe, Mayakovsky, Pound and Joyce). He broadened the horizons of criticism and literary theory in Brazil through rethinkings of salient unconventional works of national or European literature. His visits to the USA and Europe helped to establish a new presence for Brazilian literature in international circles.

In early concrete poems, Campos integrated verbal and visual effects through such techniques as fragmentation and the employment of white type on black backgrounds. He was the principal theorist of the rational 'orthodox' phase of concrete poetry (cf. the provocation of neo-concretism), as well as of the nationalist character of concretist experiments when they were assailed as alienated and foreign. His work on the poetry of Oswald de **Andrade** in the 1960s was essential for the re-evaluation of **Brazilian modernism**, as was his doctoral thesis, which diversified discussions of ***Macunaíma***. With this and other studies, Campos helped advance aspects of literary structuralism in the 1970s. Perhaps his most significant later contribution was the essay 'The Rule of Anthropophagy: Europe under the Sign of Devoration', which affirms an uncompromising, self-assertive role for Brazilian letters. In the 1980s, Campos also completed *Galáxias*, a decade-long experimental prose-poetry project. His rethinking of lyric produced the notion of the 'post-Utopian poem', informed by the implications of historical transformations, and the classically tinged long poem *Finismundo*.

Further reading

Campos, H. de (1976) *Xadrez de estrelas*, São Paulo: Perspectiva.

—— (1985) *A educaçâo dos cinco sentido*, São Paulo: Brasiliense.

—— (1986) 'The Rule of Anthropophagy: Europe Under the Sign of Devoration', *Latin American Literary Review* 14(27): 42–60.

—— (1992) *Os melhores poemas de Haroldo de Campos*, São Paulo: Global.

—— (1992) *Metalinguagem e outras metas: Ensaios de teoria e crítica literária*, Sño Paulo: Editora Perspectiva, 4th edn.

Perrone, C. (1996) *Seven Faces: Brazilian Poetry since Modernism*, Durham, NC: Duke University Press.

CHARLES A. PERRONE

Campos Menéndez, Enrique

b. 1914, Punta Arenas, Chile

Writer and statesman

Campos Menéndez is a prolific writer of fiction, biographies and essays. Born into one of the most prominent families of southern Chile, he has taken an active role in the political affairs of Chile, favouring the idea of guidance by an enlightened minority or intellectual elite. Campos was an ardent critic of the government of Salvador Allende and held several positions within the regime of Augusto Pinochet. In 1986, while acting as Chile's Ambassador to Spain, he was awarded the National Prize for Literature. Notable among his publications are the story collection *Sólo el viento* (Only the Wind) (1974) and the biography *Vida fuera la vida* (Life from Life) (1996).

Further reading

Campos Menéndez, Enrique (11976) *A Generation of Destiny*, Tempe: Center for Latin American Studies, Arizona State University.

ROBERTO CARLOS ORTIZ

Cândido, Antônio

b. 1918, Rio de Janeiro, Brazil

Literary critic

The most distinguished critic of his generation in Brazil, Antonio Candido de Mello e Souza began his career as a sociologist, and his approach to literature has always balanced the social context and the formal characteristics of the text. He studied at the Universidade de São Paulo in the 1930s with famous teachers such as Claude Lévi-Strauss and Roger Bastide, and in 1941 founded the review *Clima*. A long-time member of the Brazilian Socialist Party, he was courageous in his opposition to the military regime during the 1960s and 1970s. He has had an enormous influence on successive generations of pupils: he is the mentor of such critics as Roberto **Schwarz**, Jorge **Schwartz** and Davi **Arrigucci**. These virtues are also apparent in his prose, which is always clear and easy to read. He has worked hard to maintain links between Brazil and Spanish America, notably through his friendship with the Uruguayan critic Angel **Rama**.

Candido began his career in the press, writing reviews, and the great majority of his criticism consists of essays, by no means limited to Brazilian literature. His only major long work, the two-volume *Formação da literatura brasileira* (Formation of Brazilian Literature) (1959), is an account of the development of Brazilian national consciousness through literature, in the eighteenth and nineteenth centuries. He is notably free of nationalist bias, and is willing to see how Brazil has been influenced by European literature.

His essays vary in nature from academic articles to memoirs of friends and ancestors, and surveys of general topics. There is an excellent essay on Carlos Drummond de **Andrade**, for example, a powerful synthesis of the development of culture in Brazil in the 1930s, and an essay on literature and underdevelopment which ranges with enviable ease throughout Latin America. Some, notably 'Dialéca da malandragem' (The Dialectics of Roguery), which traces the figure of the *malandro* in a mid-nineteenth-century novel and identifies a whole tradition of work-shy pranksters in Brazilian literature, have had a pervasive influence.

Further reading

Candido, A. (1995) *Ensayos y comentarios*, trans. R. Mata Sandoval and M. Celada, Mexico City: Fondo de Cultura Económica.

– (1995) *On Literature and Society*, trans. H. Becker, Princeton, NJ: Princeton University Press.

JOHN GLEDSON

Canese, Jorge

b. 1947, Asunción, Paraguay

Poet and narrator

A medical doctor and professor, Canese is part of the 'Generation of 1970'. Among his numerous published books of poetry, *Paloma blanca, paloma negra* (White Dove, Black Dove) was one of the few books censored during the Stroessner dictatorship. He is also the author of the novel *Stroessner roto* (Stroessner Broken), and two collections of short stories. In 1995 he published *Apología a una silla de ruedas* (Apology to a Wheelchair), four brief satirical essays about the nation's problems.

TERESA MÉNDEZ-FAITH

Canto general

Canto general is the title of a 1950 book of epic poetry by the Nobel Prize-winner Pablo **Neruda**, the core of which is the retelling of the history of Chile and the Americas. Throughout its 500 pages, 320 poems and over 20,000 verses, *Canto general* (General Song) demystifies the dominant clichés of continental historiography to explore pre-Columbian civilizations and the social struggles of oppressed groups during periods of conquest, colonization, independence and modernization. In this sense, this monumental work offers a historical, social and political account of a collective and continental fate. His poetic discourse oscillates between moments of intense lyrical vibrancy such as '**Alturas de Macchu Picchu**' (Heights of Macchu Picchu) and texts strongly marked by the narration of concrete events.

As critic René de Costa has affirmed, both Octavio **Paz**'s *El laberinto de la soledad* (Labyrinth of Solitude) (1950) and Neruda's *Canto general* reflect the quest for cultural identity in modern Latin America after the periods of independence and nation-state building. Thus, Neruda's collection embodies a poetics of political alignment and prophecy by constructing a new historical vision of the Americas, denouncing the agents of oppression and praising the collective struggles for freedom and justice, the symbols of the popular culture, the heroes of the past and the possibility of an Utopian future for the continent. The poet becomes the voice of those who have been subjugated, namely indigenous groups, the working class and Third World nations.

Neruda began to write *Canto general* in 1940 while he was in Mexico; he completed it on 5 February 1949 in Chile. At that time he had to leave Chile secretly, escaping from the anti-communist repression of Gabriel González Videla's government. For this reason, the publication of *Canto general* was prohibited in Chile and the work was published instead in Mexico. The first Mexican edition (1950) was limited, but its successful reception led to a second printing of 5,000 copies and many more editions since.

Further reading

Costa, R. (1979) *The Poetry of Pablo Neruda*, Cambridge, MA: Harvard University Press.

Neruda, P. (1991) *Canto general*, trans. J. Schmitt, Berkeley: University of California Press.

Santi, E. (1982) *Pablo Neruda: The Poetics of Prophecy*, Ithaca, NY: Cornell University Press.

LUIS E. CÁRCAMO-HUECHANTE

Capécia, Mayotte

b. *c.* 1916, Carbet, Martinique; d. 1955, Paris, France

Writer

Firmly located within the landscape, culture and the religion of the island, between Catholicism and Vodun, Capécia's novels are innovative representations of the linguistic features of Martinican speech. Probably born as Lucette Ceranus, Capécia's two novels – *Je suis martiniquaise* (I am a Martinican Woman) (1948) and *La Négresse blanche* (The White Negress) (1950) – are narrated by mulatto Martinican women, who seek social mobility through relationships with French or 'béké', French creole men, and mixed blood offspring who can pass for white. Ironically, they confront the new affirmation of blackness in the French Caribbean, which led Capécia to further isolation and eventually a move to Paris.

Further reading

Capécia, Mayotte (11997) *I am a Martinican woman;*

& The White Negress: Two Novelettes, Pueblo, Colo.: Passeggiata Press.

JILL E. ALBADA-JELGERSMA

Carballido, Emilio

b. 1925, Córdoba, Mexico

Playwright and novelist

The most prolific and effective of Mexico's living dramatists, Carballido debuted with *Rosalba y los llaveros* (Rosalba and the Keyrings) (1950), directed by Salvador **Novo** at the Theatre of Bellas Artes. His courses and workshops have produced a number of new writers for the Mexican stage, but he has also written opera and ballet librettos and film scripts. In 1970 he became director of the School of Theatre Arts at the Fine Arts Institute in Mexico, and assistant director of the University of Veracruz Theatre Department (1974–6). In 1975 he founded the theatre journal *Tramoya*, specializing in works by new authors. He has received innumerable prizes and awards, but perhaps the most important recognition is that his works continue to be presented by amateur and professional companies. In addition he has written short stories, essays and novels, including *El Norte* (The North) (1958), *Los zapatos de fierro* (The Iron Shoes) (1976) and *Querétaro imperial* (Imperial Queretaro) (1994). His many plays range from *La zona intermedia* (The Intermediate Zone) (1950), one of his earliest, to *Un pequeño día de ira* (One Small Day of Rage) (1960–1), *Yo también hablo de la rosa* (I Also Speak of Roses) (1966), *Acapulco los lunes* (Acapulco on Mondays) (1970), *Tiempo de ladrones* (Time of Thieves) (1984), *Los esclavos de Estambul* (Slaves of Istanbul) (1991) and *Escrito en el cuerpo de la noche* (Written on the Body of the Night) (1996).

Further reading

Bixler, J.E. (1989) 'Emilio Carballido', in C.A. Solé and M.I. Abreu (eds), *Latin American Writers*, New York: Scribners, 3, 1289–94.

—— (1997) *Convention and Transgression: The Theater of Emilio Carballido*, London: AUP.

Peden, M.S. (1980) *Emilio Carballido*, Boston: Twayne.

Vásquez Amaral, M. (1975) *El teatro de Emilio Carballido*, Mexico City: Costa-Amic Editor.

TITO VASCONCELOS

Cardenal, Ernesto

b. 1925, Granada, Nicaragua

Poet, political activist and priest

Cardenal's poetic work opened a new direction in Latin American poetry that he himself described as *exteriorismo*, a poetry rooted in the rhetoric of speech – renouncing metaphor in favour of rhythm and the 'things of the world'. The witty imitations of his early collection, *Epigramas* (1961), linked love and politics with his own marginal involvement in the plot to overthrow the dictator Somoza in the failed April conspiracy of 1954. His *Hora cero* (Zero Hour) (1960) is what Steven White calls 'the quintessential Latin American political poem' – a narrative of Nicaraguan history interwoven with a visionary hope. In the intervening years, Cardenal had spent a key period in his life at the community of Gethsemani in Kentucky under the tutelage of Thomas Merton, the outstanding poet whose death would later move Cardenal to produce some of his finest writing. Although writing on secular themes was forbidden in the religious community, the spiritual commentaries written there and published as *Vida en el amor* (A Life in Love) (1970) give an insight into Cardenal's understanding of the relationship between religion and social revolution, later expressed in the principles of liberation theology. *Hora cero* and Cardenal's subsequent writings seek out the foundations of this new community of loving equals in history in *Homenaje a los indios Americanos* (Homage to the Indians of the Americas) (1969), in the example of Cuba (*En Cuba* (In Cuba) (1972)) and in the apocalyptic religious visions of *Salmos* (Psalms) (1964).

But Cardenal set out to create this community in

practice, on the island of Solentiname on the Lake of Nicaragua. At the same time, he gave his support to the FSLN in its struggle against the Somoza dictatorship, although he remained uneasy about the use of armed violence. Nonetheless, he allowed Solentiname to be used for the preparation of a Sandinista assault on a barracks at San Carlos; the dictator's revenge, in 1977, was to destroy Solentiname from the air. Cardenal then moved to Costa Rica and became an active advocate of the Sandinista cause, returning to Nicaragua after the Sandinista Revolution of 1979 to become Minister of Culture. From his new post he continued the work of Solentiname, creating poetry and art workshops for ordinary Nicaraguans (see **workshop poetry**). Some felt that Cardenal's adherence to a 'primitive' style pre-empted a more authentic creativity, but the materials gathered in the volumes called *El evangelio en Solentiname* (1976–8) leave little doubt as to the quality of both words and paintings. Cardenal's own perceptions of the Solentiname experience are gathered in *Nostalgia del futuro* (Nostalgia for the Future) (1984). His major but flawed poetic work of this era was *Cántico cósmico* (Cosmic Canticle) (1990), a sprawling volume whose eclecticism and embrace of all forms of knowledge may have been intended as a kind of *summum* but fails to achieve coherence. Coinciding as it does with the Sandinista electoral defeat, it may more significantly indicate a momentary loss of direction in the pursuit of the liberated community. The first volume of his memoirs, *Vida perdida* (A Lost Life), appeared in 1998. By this time, Cardenal had publicly split with the leadership of the FSLN and joined a new social-democratic grouping around Sergio **Ramírez**.

Further reading

Borgeson, P.W. (1984) *Hacia el hombre nuevo: Poesía y pensamiento de Ernesto Cardenal*, London: Támesis.

González-Balado, J.L. (1978) *Ernesto Cardenal, poeta, revolucionario, monje*, Salamanca: Ediciones Síeme.

West-Durán, A. (2002) 'Ernesto Cardenal', in C. Solé and K. Müller-Bergh (eds), *Latin American Writers: Supplement I*, New York: Scribners. 149–66.

White, S.F. (1997) 'Ernesto Cardenal', in V. Smith (ed.), *Encyclopedia of Latin American Literature*, London: Fitzroy Dearborn, 164–6.

Zimmerman, M. (1985) *Ernesto Cardenal: Flights of Victory/Vuelos de Victoria*, Maryknoll, NY: Orbis Books.

MIKE GONZALEZ

Cárdenas, Eliécer

b. 1950, Cañar, Ecuador

Writer

Cárdenas has rapidly, and justifiably, become one of Ecuador's most highly regarded novelists. He has produced a number of works and maintained a consistent standard. His main concerns have been to recuperate popular culture and address issues of personal and collective identity and transculturation (see **cultural theory**). His clear command of narrative technique and lyrical expression are evident in *Juego de mártires* (Martyrs' Game) (1977), *Polvo y ceniza* (Dust and Ashes) (1979), *Háblanos, Bolívar* (Speak to Us, Bolívar) (1983), *Las humanas certezas* (Human Certainties) (1985), *Diario de un idólatra* (Diary of an Idolater) (1990) and *Que te perdone el viento* (May the Wind Forgive You) (1993).

Further reading

Robles, M. (1986) 'To the Rescue of a Concealed History: Eliécer Cardenas' *Polvo y ceniza*', in D. Balderston (ed.), *The Historical Novel in Latin America: A Symposium*, Gaithersburg: Ediciones Hispamérica, 151–7.

MERCEDES M. ROBLES

Cardoso, Lúcio

b. 1913, Curvelo, Minas Gerais, Brazil; d. 1968, Rio de Janeiro

Novelist, poet, playwright and journalist

Cardoso is known particularly for his 1959 novel *Crônica da casa assassinada* (Chronicle of the Murdered House), a novel of decadence, cross-dressing and sexual ambiguity. His literary career begins in

1934 with the publication of his first novel; this was followed by two books of poems, several novellas, some film scripts and an autobiographical novel. He was close to Clarice Lispector. *Crônica da casa assassinada* was published near the end of his literary career; in 1962 he suffered a stroke. In his last years he devoted himself to painting. He was also a gifted translator, with important versions of *Moll Flanders*, *Ana Karenina*, *Pride and Prejudice* and other works. Several critics have claimed *Crônica* as Brazil's most significant gay novel after Adolfo Caminha's early *Bom Crioulo* (1895); an excellent edition of the novel was prepared by Mario Carelli.

Further reading

Albuquerque, S. (2002) 'Fictions of the Impossible: Clarice Lispector, Lúcio Cardoso and "Impossibilidade" ', in S.C. Quinlan and F. Arenas (eds), *Lusosex*, Minneapolis: University of Minnesota Press, 84–103.

Cardoso, L. (1991) *Crônica da casa assassinada*, ed. M. Carelli, Paris: Archivos.

Carelli, M. (1988) *Corcel de fogo: Vida e obra de Lúcio Cardoso*, Rio de Janeiro: Editora Guanabara.

Lopes, F.C. (1994) 'Cardoso, Lúcio', in D.W. Foster (ed.), *Latin American Writers on Gay and Lesbian Themes: A Bio-Critical Sourcebook*, Westport, CT: Greenwood Press, 102–5.

DANIEL BALDERSTON

Cardoza y Aragón, Luis

b. 1904, Antigua, Guatemala; d. 1992, Mexico City

Writer and art critic

The great vanguard poet of the Generation of 1920 along with **Asturias**, Cardoza was a key figure during the October Revolution (1944–54), editing *Revista de Guatemala*. Mixing lyricism, colloquialism, erudite symbolism and prosaic discourse, Cardoza distanced himself from poetic norms, becoming increasingly concerned with national identity and ***indigenismo*** as sources of spiritual revitalization. Cardoza also wrote political articles, essay books and art criticism. His principal prose works are *Guatemala, las líneas de su mano* (Guatemala, The Lines of its Hands) (1955), an essay on Guatemalan culture and history, and his memoirs, *El río: Novelas de caballería* (The River: Chivalry Novels) (1986). Following the 1954 *coup*, Cardoza lived in Mexico, where he was renowned as an art critic and essayist.

Further reading

Albízurez Palma, F. (1973) 'Luis Cardoza y Aragón', in *Estudios sobre literatura guatemalteca*, Guatemala City: Piedra Santa.

Cardoza y Aragón, L. (1976) *Guatemala: Las líneas de su mano*, Mexico City: Fondo de Cultura Económica.

—— (1977). *Poesías completas y algunas prosas*, Mexico City: Fondo de Cultura Económica.

Monterroso, A. (1988) 'Luis Cardoza y Aragón', *USAC: Revista de la Universidad de San Carlos* 3: 114–16.

MARC ZIMMERMAN

Carew, Jan

b. 1925, Agricola, Guyana

Novelist and cultural historian

Carew's first novels, *Black Midas* (1958) and *The Wild Coast* (1958), dealt with the racial politics of Guyana and were heavily influenced by the Marxism of Frantz Fanon. Having travelled and lived in many parts of the world, Carew's work is not limited to Caribbean themes. Russia is the setting for two 1964 novels – *Green Winter*, about an African student who travels there, and *Moscow Is Not My Mecca* – while Harlem is the setting for *The Last Barbarian* (1960). He has published poems, plays and several children's stories, such as *The Third Gift* (1974). Much of his scholarly writing – such as *Fulcrums of Change: Origins of Racism in the Americas and Other Essays* (1988), *Rape of Paradise: Columbus and the Birth of Racism in the Americas* (1994) and *Ghosts in Our Blood: With Malcolm X in Africa, England, and the Caribbean* (1994) – deals with issues of race in post-colonial societies. He is Professor Emeritus of African American Studies at Northwestern University.

Further reading

Carew, Jan (1994) *Ghosts in Our Blood: With Malcolm X in Africa, England, and The Caribbean*, Chicago: Lawrence Hill Books, distributed by Independent Publishers Group.

CAROL J. WALLACE

Caribbean literature

For the purposes of convenience, the literature of a series of small island countries are often grouped as literatures of the Spanish, Francophone, Dutch and English Caribbean, while this last is often called in English simply 'Caribbean literature'. Confusion arises due to the fact that the linguistic situation is vastly more complicated than the reference to the old European empires suggests (some of the islands in the 'Dutch Caribbean' are not Dutch-speaking and there are many French creole speakers in formerly British islands) and by the fact that the contemporary political situations vary widely, with many independent countries, some federations, some overseas territories and some colonies. There are many cultural ties across linguistic boundaries, yet cultural exchange (between Martinique and Haiti, say) may often pass through the metropolis (Paris, in this case). The collective history of Caribbean literature (cast in terms of comparative literary studies) edited by James Arnold (with Michael Dash, Ineke Phaf and Julio Rodríguez-Luis as co-editors) is the most comprehensive examination to date, but even this is divided according to the official languages of the former European colonies. While there are many cultural commonalities, there are also significant differences, making it difficult to give an adequate account of the area.

In English

Tom **Redcam**'s *Becka's Buckra Baby* (1903) was the first volume of his All Jamaica Library, a first attempt to create a body of writing rooted in the material realities and historical experience of the British Caribbean colonies. H.G. de **Lisser**'s historical romances could be seen as an attempt to recover, or rewrite, an often slightly idealized past – though as editor of the Jamaica *Gleaner* for forty years, he was also embedded in the current reality of the island's political life.

The first sustained attempts to capture the authentic voice of the islands, however, came with the post-Depression resistance and burgeoning nationalism throughout the region (not just the Anglophone parts of it) in the early 1930s. In Trinidad, the work of the Beacon group echoed the discontents and the new aspirations of the time; examples include the work of Alfred **Mendes**; Ralph **de Boissiere**'s *Crown Jewel* (written around 1935 although not published until the early 1950s); and C.L.R. **James**'s *Minty Alley* (1936) as well as his short stories of the time. James was a prolific and outstanding essayist: travelling across Europe and the Americas through the decade gave him a multi-layered perspective on both the internal life of the colonies and the colonial system evidenced in works such as *The Black Jacobins* (1938), his extraordinary study of the resistance of the Caribbean slaves.

Claude **McKay**'s ***Banana Bottom*** (1933), a key work of the time, was a rich and moving depiction of plantation life in nineteenth-century Jamaica; the writing of Guyanese writer Edgar **Mittelholzer** was an ambitious mural of the history and complex development of his multi-ethnic community. A similar impulse to recovery of the past, and the creation of a literature rooted in historical and current realities, led E.L. Crozier to found the influential magazine *Bim* (1942–), edited by Frank **Collymore**, and A.J. **Seymour** to launch ***Kyk-Over-Al*** in British Guiana under Ian **McDonald**'s editorship three years later. These journals would offer a space for younger poets and writers such as Martin **Carter**, Derek **Walcott** and Wilson **Harris**. But it was the BBC's radio programme *Caribbean Voices*, initially produced by Jamaican poet Una Marson, that gave them a bigger platform from which to launch the dialect poetry (of Claude McKay, Michael McTurk and Edward Cordle among others) which would evolve into the **dub poetry** of later years.

The 1940s were less fertile in prose fiction, although V.S. **Reid**'s *New Day* (1949) pointed ahead to a literature rooted in oral tradition which would emerge strongly after the 1960s. Indeed, many of the writers of the post-war generation (Reid was an exception) emigrated to Britain, partly in search of education, partly to involve themselves in the richer and more diverse cultural life of the metropolis. Yet the conflicts and doubts generated by emigration itself, by racism, and by the distance from home, are often at the heart of the work of George **Lamming** (*The Emigrants* (1954)), Samuel **Selvon** (*The Lonely Londoners* (1956)), V.S. **Naipaul** (*The Middle Passage* (1961)) as well as Edgar Mittleholzer and Andrew **Salkey**. Other novels of the fifties looked towards Africa (O.R. **Dathorne**'s *The Scholar Man* (1964), for example) or began to explore folk tradition, like Selvon's *A Brighter Sun* (1952) or Roger **Mais**'s *Brother Man* (1954).

Lamming's most famous novel, ***In the Castle of My Skin*** (1953), written before his departure for Europe, in a sense anticipated the recuperation of black history, both on the islands and in the slave trade, which provided themes for Geoffrey **Drayton**, Michael **Anthony**, Austin **Clarke**, John **Hearne**, Namba Roy and Ian **McDonald**.

In both poetry and prose, the multiplication of voices and accents signalled the growing pressure for independence across the British colonies. It was not only a representation of a plural and multilayered Caribbean society; it was also a demand for legitimacy and autonomy, both political and cultural, from the colonial metropolis. Jean **Rhys**'s ***Wide Sargasso Sea*** (1966) and the new creole poetry of Louise **Bennett**, Mervyn **Morris**, Wayne **Brown** and Denis **Scott** represent this development. V.S. Naipaul's *The Mimic Men* (1967) and his earlier *A* ***House for Mr Biswas*** (1961) are far more sceptical visions of this process of independence and self-discovery. Wilson Harris's ***Palace of the Peacock*** (1960) narrates this polyphony in a form that in some ways echoes the **magical realism** of the Latin American novel.

Language is at the centre of the cultural struggles of the colonial and post-colonial periods. Kamau **Brathwaite** and others' concept of '**nation-language**' located identity in the spoken language, in the rhythms and forms of orality, whose diversity is captured in his three-volume *The Arrivants* (1973) and which also found expression in the work of performance poets – Jean 'Binta' **Breeze**, Linton Kwesi Johnston, **Mutabaruka**, Pamela **Mordecai**, Christine **Craig**, Lorna **Goodison**, Grace **Nichols**, Paul **Keens-Douglas** and Mikey **Smith**. Earl **Lovelace**'s *The Wine of Astonishment* (1982) continued the project into prose.

Derek Walcott's ***Omeros*** (1990) was the culmination of a body of poetry which would be rewarded two years later with a Nobel Literature Prize which was as much an acknowledgement of the richness and maturity of Caribbean poetry as it was a tribute to Walcott's extraordinary body of writing. He draws together the forms and achievements of metropolitan writing and the language and experience of the Caribbean. Many other writers have searched for a submerged identity in the problematic and tense realities of the long struggle for independence – Erna **Brodber**, Zee **Edgell** and Jamaica **Kincaid** among them. But there is also a body of writing which, while executed abroad, resonates with the Caribbean voice – in Britain, Caryl **Phillips**, John **Figueroa** and John **Agard**; in the United States, Louis **Simpson**; in Canada, David **Dabydeen** among others.

In French

The Francophone Caribbean really has two twentieth-century histories. The first is the story of an impoverished Haiti, once France's most prosperous sugar colony until the slave insurrections of the early nineteenth century tore it painfully away from the metropolitan connection. The other is the experience of Guadeloupe and Martinique, colonies *d'outre mer* whose curious current status as 'overseas colonies' effectively ties them to a Paris that is still the economic, political and cultural reference point – although the problematic of that relationship has provided the theme of much of the islands' cultural production.

Haiti declared its independence in 1804. The coffee trade enriched the small, mostly light-skinned (mulatto) elite who disputed power amongst themselves while the majority black population laboured the land to produce the wealth that sustained the minority. The turmoil of political life, and the extreme poverty in which most Haitians lived, left little space for cultural activities. The Génération de la Ronde, whose iconic figure was the novelist Fernand Hibbert, took inspiration from the French Realist tradition. Ironically, however, it was the American military occupation of the country between 1915 and 1934 (as part of a strategy of domination of the Caribbean region) that sparked the first indigenous expressions, born of a more general 'turn to Africa' throughout the region, in Jean **Price-Mars**'s *Ainsi parla l'oncle* (This Is How Uncle Spoke) (1928) and with the publication of the *Revue indigène*. Together, these two events marked the beginning of ***indigénisme***. Perhaps the best-known and most influential of these writings was Jacques **Roumain**'s ***Gouverneurs de la rosée*** (Masters of the Dew) (1944). The novel was at once a depiction of peasant life in Haiti, with its language, its voodoo beliefs and its myths, and a Utopian vision of a community built on communist principles (Roumain was a founder member of the Haitian Communist Party in 1934). In the 1940s, Roumain's lyrical evocations of Haitian culture, married with the influence of **surrealism**, produced a new group of Haitian writers attuned to the new **magical realism** then emerging from writers such as Alejo **Carpentier** in Cuba. Most prominent among them were René **Depestre** and Jacques Stephen **Alexis**, whose ***Compère Général Soleil*** (Comrade General Sun) (1955) was a representative work of a movement that Alexis himself defined in a famous essay published in the journal ***Présence Africaine*** a year later. In all of these writers it is Africa and black culture that is the source of Haitian identity.

In 1957 François Duvalier, known as Papa Doc, took power. His tyranny, and his systematic persecution and torture of critics and opponents, meant that for nearly three decades Haitian culture flowered in exile. Marie Chauvet, for example, was forced to leave after the publication of her *Amour, colère et folie* (Love, Rage and Madness) in 1968; Anthony Phelps, Gérard Etienne (whose *Dezafi* (Defiance) was the only novel written entirely in Haitian creole), Depestre and Pierre Clitandre wrote from the diaspora of Haitian intellectuals. Very few writers continued to write under the shadow of Papa Doc, though Franketienne's *Spiralisme* movement did produce works of a resolutely apolitical character within the island. Other Haitian writers, most notably Dany **Laferrière** and Edwige Danticat (writing in English) began to address issues of exile and marginalization rather than evoking the world of Haiti.

When Papa Doc died in 1971 he was immediately succeeded by his 19-year-old son Jean-Claude, known as Baby Doc; although as brutal and repressive as his father, Baby Doc was less effective a tyrant and fissures began to open in the state until his overthrow in 1986. Yet for many Haitian writers, the difficulties of reconnecting with an impoverished, culturally deprived island society proved as difficult as living outside it, a theme explored by a number of writers, including Depestre, Emile Ollivier, Lilas Desquiron and Nadine Magloire, and in the pages of journals such as *Chemins critiques*, launched in 1986.

In Martinique and Guadeloupe, unlike Haiti, French was the uncontested language of culture as the century began. It was the Martinican Aimé **Césaire** who, together with Léopold Senghor of Senegal and Léon Gontran **Damas** of French Guyana, launched the hugely influential ***négritude*** movement in the early 1920s to recuperate and re-establish Africa as a source of cultural identity. Its ramifications spread through the Spanish and English-speaking Caribbean and into the black cultural movements of the United States. The key text of the movement, deeply expressive of its rage and passionate Africanism, was Césaire's ***Cahier d'un retour au pays natal*** (Notes on a Return to the Homeland), published in 1939. Césaire's influence on a younger group of writers, including Vincent **Placoly** and Xavier Orville, is undeniable.

Yet Césaire's concepts were not universally accepted, despite his enormous cultural authority. Taking their lead from an equally powerful presence in the debate, Edouard **Glissant**, a new generation of writers contested the African focus of *négritude*. For Raphael **Confiant**, Patrick **Chamoiseau** and the Guadeloupean Jean Bernabé, it was the Caribbean reality that would produce a new alternative identity. The idea, expressed in Glissant's famous essay *Le discours antillais* (Caribbean Discourse) (1981), laid the foundation for the ***créolité*** movement launched in a short, jointly authored essay published in 1989. Simone **Schwartz-Bart** was also influenced by the earlier debate; her novels, written in a literary and lyrical French, nevertheless embrace Créole as orality. Maryse **Condé**, probably Guadeloupe's most prolific writer, spent much of her life in Africa; through her writing she has engaged critically with themes of exile, *négritude* and *Créolité*, while not subscribing exclusively to any single school. The youngest writers, like Gisèle Pineau, remain concerned with the survival and resilience of a creole culture always under threat from the continuing dominance of French.

In Dutch, Papiamentu, etc.

Besides the political, economic and demographic bonds with the Netherlands, the official language, Dutch, creates an artificial impression of unity. On the Windward Islands, English is the common language. While literary output in English is limited, there is a substantial literature in Papiamentu, the native language of 90 per cent of the population of the Leeward islands, including Aruba, Bonaire and Curaçao. Writers in this native creole include Willem Eligio **Kroon** and Manuel Antonio Fray, among the earliest Papiamentu writers. A key figure in the development of Papiamentu as a literary language was Frank E. **Martinus**, editor of the magazine *Ruku* and himself author of four long novels and poetry in the language. Elis **Juliana** and Pierre **Lauffer**, editor of the important anthology *Di Nos* (Our Heritage) (1971) and possibly the best known and most widely read of all, were contributors to the journal *Simadán* published in Curaçao (1950–1). Written entirely in Papiamentu, it represented a reaction against the more venerable but more literary journal *De* ***Stoep*** (1940–51) whose contributors wrote mostly in Dutch – they included Silvio (Tip) **Marugg** and Oda **Blinder**, whose considerable reputation rested on the one slim volume of poetry published during her lifetime.

Literary production in all three of the languages, but especially in Papiamentu, tends to highlight island-bound topics, which some authors, especially those writing in Dutch, creatively deploy to reach a wider audience. The authors who write in Dutch have generally not moved to the Netherlands – in contrast to those from Suriname – but they do find their audience primarily in that country. An exception is René de **Rooy** of Suriname who, having written in *De Stoep*, moved to Mexico after Suriname became independent in 1975 and from there wrote his *Verworpen Vaderland* (Scrap the Fatherland) (1979), an angry indictment of the corruption of his own country.

In Suriname, where seventeen main languages are spoken, the majority speak the creole Sranan Togo. The literary and cultural movement **Wie eegie sanie** (Our Own Things) promoted the written language through the work of writers such as Eddy **Bruma** and Edgar Caro (who later moved on to write largely in Dutch). Other significant writers include translator and performance poet Nydia **Ecury** and poet and novelist Cecil P. de Hareth.

In Spanish

Although the islands of the Hispanic Caribbean – Cuba, the Dominican Republic and Puerto Rico – have possessed three different political systems, three distinct forms of governance and three distinct literary and cultural traditions since at least the early nineteenth century, there are many links between the three countries that justify us examining their literary tradition as one. The work of late nineteenth-century writers and patriots such as Eugenio María de Hostos and José **Martí** was known throughout the circum-Caribbean area, and the constant migratory flows between one island and the other – as well as from each of the islands to the United States – also allows us to view them as belonging to a common tradition. During the twentieth century in particular, writers have kept abreast of developments between one island and the other. For example, during the 1920s Luis **Palés Matos**'s Afro-Caribbean poems were read in Cuba, and Nicolás **Guillén** and his *Motivos de Son* (1930) read in Puerto Rico. In the 1930s, writers from Puerto Rico collaborated with Cuban magazines such as ***Revista de Avance*** and since the 1930s, Cuba and Puerto Rico have welcomed exiles from the Trujillo dictatorship.

Although the Spanish-American-Cuban War of 1898 affected principally Cuba and Puerto Rico, one could use the conflict as a starting point for twentieth-century Hispanic Caribbean literature. From that point of departure, one could also divide the century into at least three major time periods: the first, from 1898 to 1933–4; the second from 1933 to 1959; the third from the beginning of the 1960s until the contemporary period. During the first period, which concludes more or less with the collapse of the Machado dictatorship in Cuba, Cuban and Puerto Rican literature dealt with the aftermath of the collapse of the Spanish Empire. This is particularly clear in texts such as the Puerto Rican Antonio **Pedreira**'s ***Insularismo*** (1934) as well as in the later work of Manuel Zeno Gandía (1855–1930). The Machado dictatorship in Cuba sent two of its most important narrators into exile in Europe: Lino **Novás Calvo** and Alejo **Carpentier**. Even as the sugar boom of the 1920s changed the fabric of Havana's cityscape and society, it also produced some of the first important manifestations of Cuban art by the writers, as well as Ramón Guerra's *Azúcar y población en las Antillas* (Sugar and Population in the Caribbean) (1927).

While Machado's dictatorship in Cuba collapsed, Trujillo's in Santo Domingo remained intact, from 1930 to 1961. The second period, from 1933 to 1959, was marked by the consolidation of the experience of the literary and aesthetic avant-gardes, as these were linked to national frameworks. This is clear in the work of the Cuban José **Lezama Lima** and the journal ***Orígenes*** (1944–56), as well as in the work of other writers such as Virgilio **Piñera**, while in Puerto Rico there was the theatre of René **Marqués** and the narrative of Enrique Laguerre (1906–). During the 1940s and 1950s, both Cuba and Puerto Rico received well-known exiles from the collapse of the Spanish Republic: María Zambrano was a frequent guest in Cuba, associating herself with the Orígenes group, while Pablo Casals started an important festival in Puerto Rico and Juan Ramon Jiménez established residence in San Juan. The Cuban literary magazine *Orígenes* circulated both in Cuba as well as in Puerto Rico, although at the same time Santo Domingo was somewhat isolated due to the political repression of Trujillo. In Cuba, essays such as Fernando Ortíz's *Contrapunteo cubano del tabaco y el azúcar* (Cuban Counterpoint of Sugar and Tobacco) (1940) are important in order to understand national culture and history, while in Puerto Rico, writers such as Enrique Laguerre mixed social commentary with realistic narrative and drama reflected the growing migration to the United States, particularly in René Marqués's classic *La carreta* (The Cart) (1951). Some further exploration of the migratory literature produced by Puerto Ricans in New York falls outside the scope of this essay, but it should be noted that in the 1960s an important group of Niuyorican writers appeared in the urban context of New York, and that since then there has been an important movement of Cuban artists establishing magazines, bookstores and publishing houses in Miami.

Arguably, 1959–61 is the central year in Caribbean history, the year when everything changed, given the success of the Cuban Revolution of 1959. During the 1960s, the effects of the Cuban Revolution were felt throughout all the art, literature and music of the Hispanic Caribbean area. In Cuba, major literary journals established after the Revolution included ***Casa de las Américas*** and *Unión*; in Puerto Rico journals from this period included *Asomante* and *Sin nombre* (edited by Nilita **Vientós Gastón**) and ***Zona de carga y descarga*** (edited by Rosario **Ferré**). It is impossible to underestimate the profound effects that the Cuban Revolution had in the Caribbean area. Certainly, the political processes and art that followed the collapse of the Trujillo dictatorship in Santo Domingo owed much to the cultural impetus provided by the Cuban Revolution, and the emphasis in graphic art was also accompanied by novel developments in literature and music, particularly in the period directly prior to the US invasion of Santo Domingo in 1967. Some of the more important novels and literary works of the period were published as the result of work that had already been done in the 1950s, and even in the 1960s, including José Lezama Lima's ***Paradiso*** (1967) and Pedro **Mir**'s *Donde amaban las tierras comuneras* (Where They Loved The Common Land) (1978). A novel such as Guillermo **Cabrera Infante**'s *Tres tristes tigres* (Three Trapped Tigers) (1967) is a paean to the nightlife lost with the triumph of the Cuban Revolution, and the work of Heberto **Padilla**'s book of poems *Fuera del juego* (Outside the Game) (1968) certainly marked the political problems of the day. In Puerto Rico, the crisis of the colonial relationship also produced a crisis in terms of the subject of the literature produced. The work of Rosario **Ferré** is important in this regard, as well as the work of an openly queer writer such as Manuel **Ramos Otero**. Puerto Rico's entry into the broader circuits of literary production, however, occurred with Luis

Rafael **Sánchez**'s ***La guaracha del Macho Camacho*** (Macho Camacho's Beat) (1976), which serves as a point of demarcation between one kind of Puerto Rican literature and another. At the same time, the work of women writers in Puerto Rico such as Ana Lydia **Vega** produced a particularly sharp reading of a society at a point of crisis. Comparable visions in Cuba would have to wait until the 1990s, when the collapse of the Soviet Union threatened the socialist structure of Cuban society, and a new group of narrators and poets came to the fore, including Zoe Valdés (1959–) – the clearest epigone to Guillermo Cabrera Infante – and Ena Lucía Portela, whose stories are partly autobiographical representations of a woman who explores herself in social, sexual and political terms. More recently, literature in Cuba has been marked by a new crop of 'dirty realist' tales, which have been enormously successful as a market phenomenon in Spain; examples include Pedro Juan **Gutiérrez**'s *Trilogía sucia de La Habana* (Dirty Havana Trilogy) (1998) and Leonardo **Padura Fuentes**'s *Máscaras* (Masks) (1997). In Puerto Rico, the work of Mayra **Santos Febres** stands out as one that follows the work of Ana Lydia Vega, while newer narrators such as Pedro Cabiya have produced noteworthy and important novels. In Santo Domingo, the diasporic context has seen the appearance of the book of essays by Silvio Torres Saillant, *El retorno de las yolas* (The Return of the Yolas: Democracy, Diaspora and Dominican identity) (1999), as well as newer novelistic accounts such as Rita Indiana Hernández's *La estrategia de Chochueca* (2000).

At this point, pending the denouement of the Cuban situation, the Hispanic Caribbean can be said to be at a point of transition, and no new political or literary trends can be foreseen in the near future.

Further reading

In English

Benson, E. and L.W. Conolly (1994) *Encyclopedia of Post-Colonial Literatures in English*, London: Routledge.

Brown, Stewart (ed.) (1986) *Caribbean Poetry Now*, London: Hodder & Stoughton.

Burnett, P. (1986) *Penguin Book of Caribbean Verse in English*, Harmondsworth: Penguin Books.

Davies, C.B. and E. Savory (1990) *Out of the Kumbla: Caribbean Women and Literatures*, Trenton, NJ: Africa World Press.

Figueroa, John (1973) *Caribbean Voices*, Washington: R.B. Luce.

McDonald, I. and S. Brown (1992) *The Heinemann Book of Caribbean Poetry*, London: Heinemann.

Markham, E.A. (1989) *Hinterland: Caribbean Poetry from the West Indies and Britain*, Tarset, Northumberland, England: Bloodaxe Books.

In French

Arnold, James A. (1994–2001) *A History of Literature in the Caribbean*, Amsterdam and Philadelphia: Benjamins, 3 vols.

Arthur, Charles and J. Michael Dash (eds) (1999) *Libeté: A Haiti Anthology*, London: Latin America Bureau.

Dash, J. Michael (1981) *Literature and Ideology in Haiti 1915–1961*, London: Macmillan.

Dash, J.M. (1998) *The Other America: Caribbean Literature in a New World Context*, Charlottesville: University Press of Virginia.

Glissant, E. (1989) *Caribbean Discourse*, trans. J.M. Dash, Charlottesville: University Press of Virginia.

Ormerod, Beverley (1985) *An Introduction to the French Caribbean Novel*, London: Heinemann.

Regis, Antoine (1992) *La littérature franco-antillais*, Paris: Karthala

In Dutch, Papiamentu etc.

Berrian, Brenda F. and Aart Broek (eds) (1989) *Bibliography of Women Writers from the Caribbean*, Boulder: Lynn Rienner.

Gundagin, R. (1986) *De surinaamse literatuur*, Bergen op Zoom: Heeffer.

Rutgers, Wim (1994) *Schrijven is zilver, spreken is goud*, Utrecht: n.p.

—— (1996) *Beneden en boven de wind: Literatuur van de Nederlandse Antillen en Aruba*, Amsterdam: De Bezige Bij.

Van Kempen, M. (1995) *Spiegel van de Surinaamse poezie*, Amsterdam: Meulenhoff.

Voorhoeve, J. and Ursy M. Lichtfeld (1975) *Creole*

Drum: An Anthology of Creole Literature in Surinam, New Haven and London: Yale University Press.

In Spanish

Alcántara Almánzar, J. (1990) *Los escritores dominicanos y la cultura*, Santo Domingo: Amigo del Hogar.
Behar, Ruth (1995) *Bridges to Cuba*, Michigan, University of Michigan Press.
Beverley, John (ed.) (2002) 'From Cuba', special edition of *boundary 2* (Durham, Duke University Press) 29(3).
Díaz Quiñones, A. (1982) *El almuerzo en la hierba (Llorens Torres, Palés Matos, René Marqués)*, Rio Piedras, PR: Ed. Huracán.
Gelpi, J. (1993) *Literatura y paternalismo en Puerto Rico*, San Juan: Universidad de Puerto Rico.
Menton, Seymour (1975) *Prose Fiction of the Cuban Revolution*, Austin: University of Texas Press.
Pérez, L.A. (1999) *On Becoming Cuban: Identity, Nationality and Culture*, Durham, NC: Duke University Press.

MIKE GONZALEZ (ENGLISH SECTION)
J. MICHAEL DASH AND
MIKE GONZALEZ (FRENCH SECTION)
AART G. BROEK (DUTCH, PAPIAMENTU SECTION)
JOSÉ QUIROGA (SPANISH SECTION)

Carmagnola, Gladys

b. 1939, Guarambaré, Paraguay

Writer

Carmagnola's early work is considered 'children's poetry', but her poetry for adults includes *Lazo esencial* (Essential Bond) (1982), *A la intemperie* (Outdoors) (1984), *Igual que en las capueras* (Same As in the Farms) (1989), *Depositaria infiel* (Unfaithful Trustee) (1992) and *Un sorbo de agua fresca* (A Sip of Fresh Water) (1995). She has published eight books of poetry and various commemorative poetry collections. In 1996, she and Jacobo A. **Rauskin** shared the Premio Municipal de Literatura (Municipal Prize in Literature), the highest literary award in Paraguay.

TERESA MÉNDEZ-FAITH

Carpentier, Alejo

b. 1904, Lausanne, Switzerland; d. 1980, Paris, France

Writer

A founding figure in the new novel movement in both Cuba and Latin America, Carpentier also wrote journalism and essays on a wide range of topics. The son of a French father and a Russian mother, there is some doubt as to whether he was born in Cuba or at Lausanne in Switzerland. As a young man his education was largely in the hands of his father, who encouraged him to read the great works of French literature. In 1921 he entered the school of architecture of Havana University, but was obliged to abandon his studies to maintain his mother after his father's departure from the family home.

He began as a columnist and reporter for the newspaper *La Discusión* in 1922. Through the 1920s, Carpentier was linked to the **Grupo Minorista** and several avant-garde groups (see **avant-garde in Latin America**); his writings appeared regularly in magazines such as *Social* and *Carteles* as well as the review he helped to found, the ***Revista de Avance***. He also published poetry and wrote ballets with Afro-Cuban themes.

In 1928 Carpentier left for Paris, where he lived for the next eleven years, writing regular *crónicas* (see **crónica**) which took journalism from reportage into new areas of creative expression. From 1933 he also worked for radio and was a director of the Foniric studios, which produced state-of-the-art recordings. Carpentier's time in Paris was central in defining his ideas about both art and society. He wrote prolifically about his contacts with **surrealism** and other European artistic currents, which allowed him to see the American experience in a more profound way. 'Suddenly, like an obsession, I became absorbed by the idea of America', he wrote, describing this period of his life. He travelled across Europe, participating in the Congress in Defence of Culture which took place in Madrid in 1937, during the Spanish Civil War.

On his return to Cuba in 1939, Carpentier continued his journalism and produced radio programmes, beginning too the research that would culminate in his study of *La música en Cuba* (Music in

Cuba) (1946). He moved to Venezuela in 1945 and remained there, working in advertising, until his return to Cuba in 1959 after the Cuban Revolution. It was during this period that his reputation as a writer began to grow and his work become known more widely.

Carpentier had published his first novel, *Ecue Yamba O*, in 1933; it owed much to the novel of rural manners and, as its author later acknowledged, represented a failed attempt to capture the syncretic world of black Cubans. It was his story 'Viaje a la semilla' (Journey to the Seed) (1944) that marked a definitive change in his narrative conceptions; its culmination was the novel *El reino de este mundo* (The Kingdom of this World) (1949) and the formulation of his theory of '*lo* ***real maravilloso***' (marvellous realism).

If his excursion into the magical world of Haitian Vodun in 1943 was a determining factor in this evolution, his travels around the remoter corners of the Venezuelan savannah and the Upper Orinoco through 1947 and 1948 would complete his American worldview; out of that experience was born *Los* ***pasos perdidos*** (The Lost Steps) (1953), which earned him a central place in Latin American literature. The cycle of novels of this period ends with *El acoso* (The Siege) (1956), a text structured like a sonata and set in the political context of Cuba in the 1930s, and the volume of stories called *Guerra del tiempo* (Time War) (1958) and the novel *El* ***siglo de las luces*** (Explosion in a Cathedral) (1962), the result of another series of journeys.

When he returned to Cuba, Carpentier immersed himself in the profound changes which the country was undergoing. He produced less in the 1960s, having assumed several public posts and taken a leading role in the cultural institutions created by the new revolutionary government. In 1961 he was elected vice-president of **UNEAC**, and a year later appointed director of the Editora Nacional (the national publishing house). He travelled widely on official delegations while continuing to write for newspapers in Cuba, among them *El Mundo*, until his appointment as Cuban ambassador to Paris, where he lived and worked during his final years.

His late writings reaffirm the permanence, through time and changing circumstances, of an essentially baroque spirit in Latin American art, ideas expressed in the essays of *Tientos y diferencias* (Essays and Differences) (1964), *Razón de ser* (Reason for Being) (1976) and the posthumously published *La novela latinoamericana en vísperas de un nuevo siglo y otros ensayos* (The Latin American Novel on the Eve of a New Century and Other Essays) (1981). He also published the novels *Concierto barroco* (Baroque Concert) and *El recurso del método* (For Reasons of State) (both 1974), the epic novel *La consagración de la primavera* (The Rite of Spring) (1978) and *El arpa y la sombra* (The Harp and the Shadow) (1979). In 1977 he was awarded the Cervantes Literature Prize.

Further reading

Carpentier, A. (1956) *The Lost Steps*, trans. H. de Onís, New York: Knopf.

—— (1957) *The Kingdom of This World*, trans. H. de Onís, New York: Knopf.

—— (1963) *Explosion in a Cathedral*, trans. J. Sturrock, London: Gollancz & and Boston: Little Brown.

—— (1983) *Obras completas*, Mexico City: Siglo XXI.

González Echevarría, R. (1990) *Alejo Carpentier: The Pilgrim at Home*, Austin: University of Texas Press.

Larsen, N. (2001) 'Alejo Carpentier: Modernism as Epic', in *Determinations*, London: Verso, 115–26.

López Lemus, V. (ed.) (1985) *Entrevistas*, Havana: Editorial Letras Cubanas.

Márquez Rodríguez, A. (1970) *La obra narrativa de Alejo Carpentier*, Caracas: Universidad Central de Venezuela.

—— (1983) *Lo barroco y lo real maravilloso en la obra de Alejo Carpentier*, Mexico City: Siglo XXI.

Mûller-Bergh, K. (1972) *Alejo Carpentier. Estudio biográfico-crítico*, New York: Las Americas.

Padura, L. (1994) *Un camino de medio siglo: Carpentier y la narrativa de lo real maravilloso*, Havana: Editorial Letras Cubanas.

WILFREDO CANCIO ISLA

Carranza, María Mercedes

b. 1945, Santafé de Bogotá, Colombia

Poet and journalist

Carranzas's first book of poetry, *Vainas y otros poemas* (Things and Other Poems) (1972), communicates her disappointment with traditional poetry, and proposes instead to speak about contemporary issues in an irreverent manner. Her collections of poems include *Tengo miedo* (I Am Afraid) (1983) and *Hola, Soledad* (Hello, Loneliness) (1987). Carranza's journalistic writing has been published in the newspaper *El Siglo* and the journal *Semana*.

Further reading

Carranza, M.M. (1994) *De amor y desamor y otros poemas*, Bogotá: Grupo Editorial Norma.

MIGUEL A. CARDINALE

Carrera, Arturo

b. 1948, Coronel Pringles, Argentina

Poet

Carrera has published more than fifteen volumes of poetry. *La partera canta* (The Midwife Sings) (1982) and *Mi padre* (My Father) (1985) are intensely baroque in style, reminiscent of Mallarmé. *Arturo y yo* (Arthur and I) (1984), an absolutely fundamental work in the poetic panorama of twentieth-century Argentina, marks a move towards a 'neo-simplicity' that is precise and anything but naive. *Children's Corner* (1989), *La banda oscura de Alejandro* (Alexander's Obscure Band) (1994) and *El vespertilio de las parcas* (1997) have confirmed his reputation as a major poet. The recurrent themes of his work are rural life, children, the passing of time, desire and modernity.

Further reading

Carrera, Arturo (1992) *Teoría del cielo*, Buenos Aires: Planeta.

—— (2001) *Tratado de las sensaciones*, Valencia: Pre-Textos.

DANIEL LINK

Carrera, Margarita

b. 1929, Guatemala City

Writer, critic and professor

Carrera is known for her broad philosophical and psychological interests and has written poetry, essays and literary criticism. In *Del noveno círculo* (Of the Ninth Circle), written after the 1976 earthquake, she created a powerful image of Guatemalan reality modelled on Dante's *Inferno*, in which the personal and the national meet, anticipating 1980s Guatemalan feminism. In *Signo XX* (1986), a volume written before the emergence of Vinicio Cerezo, her Freudian tendencies transform specific forms of Guatemalan class domination and military oppression into characteristics of a modern civilization governed by a 'mindless malignity'.

MARC ZIMMERMAN

Carrera Andrade, Jorge

b. 1903, Quito, Ecuador; d. 1978, Quito

Writer

Carrera began his poetic career during the transition between *modernismo* (see **Spanish American modernism**) and the avant-garde (see **avant-garde in Latin America**). An endless traveller, his poetry registered the world imagistically in 'micrograms', a poetic form reminiscent of the epigram and the haiku. His early delight in the metaphorical and sensual yielded to the pre-eminence of the 'secret country' of the soul of contemporary man: anguish, solitude, death. His principal books of poetry are *Boletínes de mar y tierra* (Bulletins from Land and Sea) (1930), *La hora de las ventanas iluminadas* (The Time of Lit Windows) (1937), *Lugar de origen* (Native Country) (1945) and *Hombre planetario* (Planetary Man) (1959).

Further reading

Carrera Andrade, J. (2000) *Obra poética*, ed. R. Pacheco and J. Vásconez, intro. A. Querejata, Quito: Ediciones Acuario.
—— (2001) *Antología poética*, Mexico City: Fondo de Cultura Económica.
Córdova, H. (1986) *Itinerario poético de Jorge Carrera Andrade*, Quito: Casa de la Cultura Ecuatoriana.
Ojeda, E. (1971). *Jorge Carrera Andrade: Introducción al estudio de su vida y su obra*, New York: Eliseo Torres.
—— (2002) 'Jorge Carrera Andrade', in C. Solé and K. Müller-Bergh (eds), *Latin American Writers: Supplement I*, New York: Scribners, 167–85.
Spindler, W. (1997) 'Jorge Carrera Andrade', in V. Smith (ed.), *Encyclopedia of Latin American Literature*, London: Fitzroy Dearborn, 175–8.

HUMBERTO E. ROBLES

Carrión, Benjamín

b. 1898, Loja, Ecuador; d. 1979, Quito, Ecuador

Critic and writer

Carrión's contributions to the sociology of culture and literary tastes of twentieth-century Ecuador are inestimable. Founder of the Casa de la Cultura Ecuatoriana (Ecuador's House of Culture) in 1944, he set out to make accessible the national experience, from history and literature to music and folklore, with a particular emphasis on indigenous contributions to the creation of a collective identity. Some of his essays are collected in *Obras* (Works) (1981), while his polemical commitment to social justice is expressed in his *García Moreno: El Santo del Patíbulo* (García Moreno: The Gallows' Saint) (1959).

Further reading

Carrión, B. (1981) *América dada al diablo*, Caracas: Monte Avila.
—— (2001) *La patria en tono menor: Ensayos escogidos*, ed. Gustavo Salazar, Mexico City: Fondo de Cultura Económica.
Handelsman, M. (1989) *En torno al verdadero Benjamín Crrrión*, Quito: El Conejo.
Salazar, G. (1998) *Benjamín Carrión: Un rastreo bibliográfico*, Quito: Eskeletra Editores.

HUMBERTO E. ROBLES

Carter, Martin (Wylde)

b. 1927, Georgetown, British Guiana; d. 1997, Georgetown, Guyana

Poet and historian

Carter is one of the Caribbean's most important poets. His collection *Poems of Resistance* (1954) is about his experience in the anti-colonial struggle in British Guiana. He was imprisoned by the British for some months in 1953 because of his involvement with the early nationalist movement. Eventually he became Minister of Culture in a post-independence government (1967–70). Later he was writer in residence at several universities. A regular contributor to the journal ***Kyk-Over-Al***, his work develops a distinctive voice of rebellion and resistance and a strong sense of landscape and geography, as in *Poems of Shape and Motion* (1955).

Further reading:

McWatt, M. (1985) 'The Challenge of Space: Being and Consciousness in the Poetry of Martin Carter', in J. Jackson and J.B. Ellis (ed.), *West Indian Poetry*, St Thomas: College of the Virgin Islands, 143–52.
Robinson, J. (1986) ' "The root and the stone": The rhetoric of Martin Carter's *Poems of Resistance*', *Journal of West Indian Literature* 1: 1–12.

KEITH JARDIM

Cartey, Wilfred

b. 1931, Laventille, Trinidad; d. 1992, New York, USA

Teacher, critic, editor, poet and novelist

Cartey's critical and creative visions are informed by a commitment to the dignity of the African spirit. He published five critical works including *Whisper from a Continent* (1969), twelve volumes of poetry including *The House of Blue Lightning* (1973), one novel (*Oakman* (1989)) and edited several journals. He attended the University of the West Indies, Jamaica, and was a Fulbright-Hays scholar at Columbia University, where he also taught (1957–77) before becoming the first Martin Luther King, Jr. Distinguished Professor at Brooklyn College, City University of New York, a post he held until his death in 1992.

Further reading

Cartey, Wilfred (1991) *Whispers from the Caribbean: I Going Away, I Going Home*, Los Angeles: Center for Afro-American Studies, University of California.

FUNSO AIYEJINA

Casa de las Américas

An independent cultural organization whose purpose is to develop socio-cultural contacts between Cuba, the rest of the Caribbean and Latin America, Casa de las Américas was created by decree of the Revolutionary Government of Cuba on 28 April, 1959. Subsidized through most of its existence by the Cuban state, it became self-financing in some areas during the 1990s.

The organization set out to spread the message of the Cuban Revolution and break the political, economic and cultural siege to which Cuba was subjected during the sixties, when most Latin American countries severed diplomatic relations with the government of Fidel Castro. Its first director, Haydée Santamaría, brought in outstanding artists and intellectuals, from Cuba and elsewhere, who raised the organization's international profile and won for it a significant reputation in the Latin American cultural arena.

Its functions included the promotion of the whole range of Latin American cultural expressions, publishing books and recordings, organizing theoretical debates and art exhibitions, and developing links with cultural institutions across the world. Each area of work had a specific department within the Casa, outstanding among them a library containing 140,000 volumes and 8,400 periodical titles. The visual arts department researches the field and organizes temporary exhibitions in its Latin American Gallery. The resources of the collection Arte de Nuestra América (Art of Our America) include 6,000 works of art donated by artists, collectors and cultural organizations; they form part of the Casa's permanent collection exhibited in its headquarters as well as in the Hadyée Santamaría gallery, specializing in graphics and photography, and the Mariano gallery devoted to popular arts. It also offers the Joven Estampa prize for graphic artists aged under 35, and the Ensayo Fotográfico (Photographic Essay) prize, offered for the best collection of photographs reflecting Latin American reality.

The music department organizes recitals and concerts, for example the Festival de la Canción Protesta (Festival of Protest Song) in 1967, and possesses an important collection of donated sheet music, discs and tapes. It has its own record label, 'Música de esta América', and from 1970 onwards has published a monthly bulletin. Under its auspices a biennial prize is offered in the field of Latin American and Caribbean musicology.

The theatre department promotes exchanges of directors, actors and playwrights as well as offering drama and directors workshops. It presents works by Caribbean authors, organizes the Gallo de la Habana prize and produces the quarterly drama journal, *Conjunto*.

Its editorial department co-ordinates and designs Casa's various collections, including the publication of the prizewinners of its annual literary contest, the Literatura Latinoamericana collection of classic works, 'La Honda' for short stories and young writers, Nuestra América for essays and Nuestros Países for monographs), Valoración Múltiple, collections of essays on specific authors, and Colibrí for children's writers.

The Literary Research Centre produces anthologies and essay collections on specific authors and movements, and organizes programmes of lectures and the Archivo de la Palabra, an archive of spoken recordings by outstanding literary, artistic and political personalities. It publishes records and cassettes and the journal *Criterios*, in collaboration with **UNEAC** (the Cuban Writers Organization), and organizes the international literary competition, which is Casa de las Americas' most important activity. The competition was originally organized in the categories of poetry, novel, short story and essay; testimonial writing, writing for children and young people, and special prizes for Caribbean Anglophone and Francophone writers have all been added since then. The participation of important Latin American writers in the judging panels was testimony to the significance of the prizes. The early competitions, held during the period of consolidation of the Cuban Revolution, brought to Havana the intellectual elite of Cuba and Latin America. Later, debates about the social responsibilities of writers and disagreements over increasing dogmatism and censorship in Cuban cultural life at the beginning of the seventies led to a drastic reduction in the number of artists and intellectuals travelling to Havana for the prize competitions.

Although relatively independent, Casa de las Américas was never able to stand apart from the centralization of social and political power in Cuba, and has always served to execute official cultural strategies towards Latin America.

The journal *Casa de las Américas* (1960–) has had an undeniable impact on Latin American literary life, publishing important cultural and philosophical texts. Its editor since 1965 has been Roberto **Fernández Retamar**, who also took over the Presidency of the Casa in 1986 from painter Mariano Rodríguez. In 1979, the Caribbean Studies Centre of the Casa was created to encourage an expansion of research in that area, and to organize the publication of the journal *Anales del caribe.*

Casa has also established a Women's Studies programme which organizes courses and conferences, publishes anthologies of women's writing and seeks to contribute to knowledge of women's cultural and historical production in the region. It has a bookshop and a screen printing workshop which reproduces work by the key artists of the region.

Further reading

25 aniversario de Casa de las Américas 1959–1984 (1984) Havana: Casa de las Américas.

Campuzano, Luisa (1996) 'La revista *Casa de las Américas* 1960–1995', *Unión* (Havana), 24: 25–34.

Escajadillo, Tomás (1989) 'Una sólida casa', *Quehacer* 58(2): 96–101.

Frenk, Susan F. (1984) 'Two Journals of the 1960s, *Casa de las Americas* and *Mundo Nuevo*', *Bulletin of Latin American Research* 3(3): 83–93.

Lie, Nadia (1991) 'Casa de las Américas y el discurso sobre el intelectual (1960–71)', *Cuadernos americanos*, 5(28): 287–9.

Pogolotti, Graziela (1969) 'Introducción', in *Indice de la revista casa de las Americas (1960–67)*, Havana: Biblioteca Nacional José Marti.

WILFREDO CANCIO ISLA

Casaccia, Gabriel

b. 1907, Asunción, Paraguay; d. 1980, Buenos Aires, Argentina

Writer

The founder of contemporary Paraguayan narrative, Casaccia lived most of his life in Argentina, where he also wrote and published almost all his seven novels and two short story collections – *El guajhú* (The Howl) (1938) and *El pozo* (The Well) (1967) – and one play. A few days before his death, he finished the manuscript for his last novel, *Los Huertas* (The Huertas), published posthumously in 1981. His most important works are three novels: *La babosa* (The Gossiping Woman) (1952), *La llaga* (The Wound) (1964) and *Los exiliados* (The Exiles) (1966).

Further reading

Casaccia, G. (1983) *La Babosa*, Asunción: El Lector.

—— (1984) *Cuentos completos*, ed. F.E. Feito. Asunción: El Lector.

Feito, F.E. (1977) *El Paraguay en la obra de Gabriel Casaccia*, Buenos Aires: García Cambeiro.

TERESA MÉNDEZ-FAITH

Casaravilla Lemos, Enrique

b. 1889, Montevideo, Uruguay; d. 1967, Las Piedras, Uruguay

Poet

A controversial and rather isolated figure within

Uruguayan literature, Casaravilla published very little. His first volume of poetry, *Celebración de la primavera* (Celebration of Spring) (1913), was followed in 1920 by *Las fuerzas eternas* (The Eternal Forces) and ten years later by *Las formas desnudas* (Naked Forms) (1930). His unpublished work was later anthologized by Esther de Cáceres as *Partituras secretas* (Secret Scores) (1967), which, she argued, expressed his 'formal rigour'. Not all critics agreed; some felt that his work lacked literary value, while others found a unity of expression circling the conflict between asceticism and sensuality.

Further reading

Apratto, R. (1992) 'Casaravilla: La práctica de los sentidos', *Revista iberoamericana* 160–1: 947–52.

Casaravilla Lemos, E. (1967) *Partituras secretas*, Montevideo: Ministerio de Instrución Pública y Previsión Social.

CELINA MANZONI

Casartelli, Mario

b. 1954, Asunción, Paraguay

Poet and musician

By the early 1990s Casartelli had published five books of poetry, among them *Contrapunto* (Counterpoint) (1988) and, under the pseudonym Braulio Gamarra, *Monodia del verano* (Summer Monody) (1993). A singer and composer, in 1985 he recorded *Según el color del cristal* (According to the Colour of the Glass). In 1992 he won second prize in the José Asunción Flores national composition competition with his song 'A un hermano del futuro' (To a Brother of the Future). He is also a cartoonist for the afternoon newspaper *Ultima Hora*.

Further reading

Casartelli, Mario (1997) *La urdimbre del laurel*, Asunción: Arandura.

TERESA MÉNDEZ-FAITH

Casartellí, Victor

b. 1943, Puerto Pinasco, Paraguay

Poet

Victor Casartellí is the author of three books of poetry: *Todos los cielos* (All the Heavens) (1987), his first book; *La transparencia de los días* (The Transparency of the Days) (1990), which was awarded the 1990 El Lector Prize; and *La vida que vivimos* (The Life We Live) (1992). He also has had poems published in national and foreign literary journals and anthologies. He is director of the municipal library and was President of the Society of Paraguayan Writers.

Further reading

Casartellí, Victor (2001) *La emoción que no cesa*, Asunción: Arandura.

TERESA MÉNDEZ-FAITH

Casey, Calvert

b. 1924, Baltimore, Maryland, USA; d. 1969, Rome, Italy

Writer and critic

A member of the group of writers around *Ciclón* and later a contributor to ***Lunes de Revolución***, Casey moved to Havana in the late 1950s. The central themes of his fiction were displacement, frustration and the anguished search for personal identity. In Cuba he published the volume of stories *El regreso* (The Return) (1962) and brief essays in *Memorias de una isla* (Memoirs of an Island) (1964). The only surviving chapter of his unpublished novel *Piazza Margana* is regarded as a key text of Cuban homoerotic literature. He committed suicide in 1969.

Further reading

Casey, Calvert (1998) *The Collected Stories*, trans. John Polt, Durham, NC: Duke University Press.

WILFREDO CANCIO ISLA

Castellanos, Rosario

b.1925, Mexico City; d. 1974, Tel Aviv, Israel

Writer and feminist thinker

In an untitled manuscript published twenty-three years after her untimely death in 1974, which the editor titled *Declaración de fé* (Declaration of Faith) (1997) after an early poem, Rosario Castellanos traces the representation of women throughout the trajectory of Mexican cultural history, from classical Aztec and Maya literature, to Sor Juana, to the heroines of the Wars of Independence, to the poets of her own generation. Her own rich body of literary work – novels, short stories, poetry, plays and essays – remains unparalleled in the history of Mexican letters, for its simultaneous interrogation of the roots of oppression in internal colonialism, underdevelopment and the Mexican variants of the patriarchal family.

Having grown up amid the Mayan–ladino (white) apartheid of Chiapas, in a dysfunctional colonial family, Castellanos was exposed to both the burden of privilege and the pain of marginalization. The turning point in her life was the death of her younger brother, the only male heir and her parents' favourite; with his death, her parents withdrew from her all the more. In *Declaración de fé* she describes the Mexican family constellation that appears obsessively in her fiction: the distant, disenfranchised and ultimately weak patriarchal father; and the masochistic mother who uses her suffering to manipulate her husband and chain her son to her for life, while teaching her daughter to drink from the fountain of obedience and self-contempt.

The author became conscious of the import of her early experiences while writing her first, autobiographical, novel, *Balún-Canán* (The Nine Guardians) (1957). Feeling an acute intellectual and moral responsibility to address the Indian problem, Castellanos worked for the next several years with the National Indian Institute, in both Chiapas and Mexico City, helping to found a bicultural, travelling puppet theatre and a bilingual literary magazine which would serve as important precursors to the Mayan literary movement of the 1980s and 1990s. At the same time she began writing an unparalleled cycle of novels, short stories and poetry about the poisoning effect of colonial relations on all sectors of society in Chiapas – after *Balún-Canán* came *Ciudad real* (City of Kings) (1960), *Oficio de tinieblas* (The Book of Lamentations) (1962); *Los convidados de agosto* (The August Guests) (1964); and *Lívida luz* (Livid Light) (1960).

After her return to Mexico City in 1957, Castellanos's writings turned away from Chiapas' ethnic conflicts to satire of gender roles among the urban middle classes and analyses of female creativity. She became a Professor of Comparative Literature at the National Autonomous University of Mexico (UNAM), as well as a visiting professor at several US universities. At the same time, her literary and political prominence grew. She won a series of important literary prizes for her Chiapas cycle: the Premio Chiapas in 1958, the Premio Sor Juana Inés de la Cruz in 1961 and the Premio Xavier Villaurrutia in 1962. When Castellanos died in 1974, allegedly by accidental electrocution, she was serving as Mexico's ambassador to Israel. At the age of 49, she became the first woman to be buried in the Rotunda of Illustrious Men in Mexico City.

During these final years Castellanos continued to have a troubled personal life, as is evident in her *Cartas a Ricardo* (Letters to Ricardo), published in 1994. She was prone to depression and low self-esteem, and her marriage to the philosopher Ricardo Guerra soon went sour. However, the birth of their only child, Gabriel, following two miscarriages, seems to have brought her some measure of happiness, as did her lifelong love affair with literature.

In 1997, three years after they finally authorized the publication of her letters, Castellanos's ex-husband and son allowed the publication of both *Declaración de fé* and a long-lost novel manuscript that she had chosen not to publish, entitled *Ritos de iniciación* (Rites of Passage) (1997). The appearance of three new books by this major author, two decades after her untimely death, provided a rare opportunity for reassessment of her oeuvre.

Castellanos's poetic vocabulary follows a trajectory from the highly rhetorical and tragic, to the conversational and mordant. Similarly, her fiction progresses from autobiographical, lyrical and fragmented prose, to historical fiction, to urban satire. The best of her plays is the posthumously published feminist farce *El eterno femenino* (The Eternal Feminine) (1975). Much of Castellanos's writing is marked by a confessional tone, which perhaps helps to explain the ambivalence that many male critics have expressed towards her work, and the enthusiasm it tends to elicit in women readers.

Further reading

Ahern, M. (1989) 'Rosario Castellanos', in C.A. Solé and M.I. Abreu (eds), *Latin American Writers*, New York: Scribners, 3, 1295–1302.

Alarcon, N. (1992) *Ninfomanía: El discurso feminista en la obra poética de Rosario Castellanos*, Madrid: Editorial Pliegos.

Castellanos, R. (1988) *A Rosario Castellanos Reader*, ed. and trans. M. Ahern, Austin: University of Texas Press.

—— (1989) *Obras. I: Narrativa*, Mexico City: Fondo de Cultura Económica.

—— (1997) *Declaracion de fé. Reflexiones sobre la situación de la mujer en México*, Mexico City: Alfaguara.

—— (1998) *The Book of Lamentations*, trans. E. Allen, New York: Penguin.

—— (1998) *Obras. II: Poesía, teatro y ensayo*, Mexico City: Fondo de Cultura Económica.

Castillo, D. (1992) *Talking Back: Toward a Latin American Feminist Literary Criticism*, Ithaca, NY: Cornell University Press.

Franco, J. (1989) *Plotting Women: Gender and Representation in Mexico*, New York: Columbia University Press.

Grant, C. (1997) 'Rosario Castellanos', in V. Smith (ed.), *Encyclopedia of Latin American Literature*, London: Fitzroy Dearborn, 181–3.

López González, A. (1991) *La espiral parece un círculo*, Mexico City: Universidad Autónoma Metropolitana, Unidad Ixtapalapa.

O'Connell, J. (1995) *Prospero's Daughter. The Prose of Rosario Castellanos*, Austin: University of Texas Press.

CYNTHIA STEELE

Castilla, Manuel J.

b. 1918, Salta, Argentina; d. 1980, Salta

Poet

One of the exceptional lyric poets of northern Argentina, Castilla's poetry examines the indigenous world from within. The people, culture and nature of Salta and Chaco Provinces and the Bolivian mining regions are the central themes of his poetry. Castilla, together with his predecessor Juan Carlos Dávalos, is one of the few voices of the interior to earn the admiration of Buenos Aires and to have received important regional awards. Two of his most memorable books of poems are *Copajira* (Corrosive Mining Water) (1964) and *Triste de la lluvia* (Sad of Rain) (1977).

Further reading

Bilbao Richter, B. (1987) *Sueños y memoria en la poesía de Manuel J. Castilla*, Buenos Aires: Centro de Estudios Latinoamericanos.

Castilla, Manuel J. (2000) *Obras completas*, Buenos Aires: Corregidor.

Vehils, J. (1981) *Manuel J. Castilla*, Buenos Aires: Ediciones Culturale Argentinas.

MAGDALENA GARCÍA PINTO

Castillo, Abelardo

b. 1935, San Pedro, Buenos Aires, Argentina

Writer

An important contemporary writer, Castillo's stories appear alongside **Borges**, **Quiroga** and **Cortázar** on standard secondary school book lists. He won the **Casa de las Américas** prize in 1961, and in 1965 a jury that included Ionesco rewarded his play *Israfel*. Founder and editor of the literary journal *El escarabajo de oro* (The Golden Scarab), he has written two novels, *El que tiene sed* (He Who is Thirsty) (1985) and *Crónica de un iniciado* (Chronicle of an Initiate) (1991). His essays are collected in *Las palabras y los días* (Words and Days) (1988).

Further reading

Castillo, Abelardo (1997) *Cuentos completos: Los mundos reales*, Buenos Aires: Alfaguara.

Morello Frosch, M. (1979) 'Las panteras y el templo de Abelardo Castillo', *Hispamérica* 22: 97–8.

ENRIQUE FOFFANI

Castillo, Otto René

b. 1937, Quetzaltenango, Guatemala; d. 1967, Zacapa, Guatemala

Writer

Founder and best-known poet of the group Generación Comprometida (the Committed Generation), Castillo belonged to the Guatemala Workers' Party (PGT) and was frequently exiled. In El Salvador, he collaborated with Roque **Dalton** and others in a new 1960s revolutionary poetry. When he returned to the armed struggle in Guatemala, he and his *compañera* Nora Paíz were killed by army operatives. Castillo's poems, simple and lyrical, are filled with an idealism in which romantic love and death are treated as a function of revolutionary hope and sacrifice. He became an icon of revolutionary poetry, influencing Dalton, Leonel Rugama and many others.

Further reading

Castillo, Otto René (1970) *Clamor de América*, Buenos Aires: Ediciones Convergencia, distributed by DER.

—— (1982) *Informe de una injusticia*, Mexico City: Taller de Gráfica Popular.

MARC ZIMMERMAN

Castor, Suzy

b. 1936, Port-au-Prince, Haiti

Historian and social researcher

An opponent of the Duvalier dictatorship, Castor lived in exile in Mexico until she returned to Haiti in 1986, where, together with her husband Gérard Pierre-Charles, she founded the non-governmental organization Centre de Recherche et de Formation Economique et Sociale pour le Développement (CRESFED – Centre for Research and Economic and Social Education for Development). A specialist in the development of Haiti's grassroots organizations, she has written numerous books and articles in French and Spanish, in particular concerning the US occupation of Haiti (1915–34), Haiti's relations with the Dominican Republic and the women's movement in Haiti.

Further reading

Castor, Suzy (1983) *Migraciones y relaciones internacionales (el caso haitiano – dominicano)*, Mexico City: Facultad de Ciencias Políticas y Sociales, UNAM.

CHARLES ARTHUR

Castro, Tomás

b. 1959, Santo Domingo, Dominican Republic

Poet

Like other members of the literary group Taller Literario César Vallejo, Castro started publishing his poetry in magazines and journals in the early 1980s. He has won the Samuel Santana National Prize for Poetry and the University Poetry Prize. His most acclaimed book *Amor a quemarropa* (Pointblank Love) (1985), reprinted four times, is concerned with everyday images about love and despair and is reminiscent of Pablo **Neruda**'s *Veinte poemas de amor* (1924).

Further reading

Castro, T. (2000) *Poemas posbíblicos*, Dominican Republic: Ediciones El Pez Rojo.

FERNANDO VALERIO-HOLGUÍN

Castro Caycedo, Germán

b. 1940, Zipaquirá, Colombia

Journalist and writer

A prolific journalist and a columnist for several newspapers, Castro Caycedo began writing for *El Tiempo* and *El País* of Madrid. He became popular after producing a television news magazine called *Enviado especial* (Special Correspondent) during the 1970s and 1980s. He has written around fourteen books, all of them classified by critics as testimonials (see ***testimonio***). His works have always been related to the conflictive history of Colombia as exemplified by its violence, drugs and major social problems. In one of his most interesting recent works, *Colombia X* (1999), the author introduces the underground lives of some young people aged between 18 and 25, living in Bogotá and immersed in a confusing world led and ruled by globalization.

Further reading

Castro Caycedo, Germán (1998) *Obra completa*, Santafé de Bogotá: Editorial Planeta.

—— (2001) *Candelaria*, Santafé de Bogotá: Editorial Planeta.

ALVARO BERNAL

Castro Saavedra, Carlos

b. 1924, Medellín, Colombia; d. 1989, Medellín

Poet

Profoundly influenced by the writings of Pablo **Neruda**, Castro Saavedra's verse represents an important moment in Colombian poetry. Homeland, nature, love, the passage of time and internal strife are recurrent themes in his work. His verses capture the power of language to communicate the daily drama of existence. Castro Saavedra belonged to a generation of poets who began consciously to discuss Colombia's social problems. Castro Saavedra understood the relationship between mankind and the reality of social and political life of his country, along with its the great mysteries. He was a prolific artist who published several books and wrote in various Colombian newspapers.

Further reading

Abad-Gomez,-Hector (1979) 'Poetas colombianos: Carlos Castro Saavedra', *Nivel*, Mexico City, 193: 9–11.

Castro Saavedra, Carlos (1989) *La voz del viento*, Medellín: Editorial Universidad de Antioquia.

ALVARO BERNAL

CELCIRP

CELCIRP (Centre for the Study of the Literatures and Civilizations of the River Plate region) is an international centre based in France, which draws together specialists in the study of the cultural production of the countries of the River Plate region – Argentina, Paraguay and Uruguay. Founded in 1982 by Paul Verdevoye, Claude Cymerman and Nilda Díaz, CELCIRP organizes various academic and cultural activities, and in particular a biennial Congress. Between 1985 and 1997, CELCIRP published eighteen issues of its journal *Rio de la Plata*.

JULIO PREMAT

Central America

The six republics of Central America (including Panama) established their final frontiers at different points through the nineteenth century – the last was Panama, which declared its independence from Gran Colombia in 1903. Entirely agricultural, the small land-owning elite monopolized political power in the shifting state formations and alliances that characterized their first century of existence.

Change came with the expansion of export

agriculture – principally in coffee and bananas – in the 1880s and 1890s, as the expanding population of urban workers in the USA acquired the tastes of modernity. The traditional agricultural communities were robbed of their lands – and their source of food – as they were absorbed into the export sector by quasi-legal means at times, at others by force. Their populations would become an occasional workforce on the new estates, although the pattern varied slightly from country to country. In Costa Rica, for example, small farmers dominated the coffee sector, while the patterns on the banana-growing Atlantic coast followed that of the rest of the isthmus.

At the turn of the nineteenth and twentieth century, ***costumbrismo*** was dominant in the narrative, offering descriptions and sketches of rural and provincial life in a language peppered with localisms. In Costa Rica, Manuel González Zeledón was its best-known exponent. In El Salvador, the school lasted well into the twentieth century, expressed in the work of writers such as Arturo Ambrogi and José María Peralta Lagos. It could be argued that the group of Guatemalan writers who wrote with a degree of identification and sympathy about the old land-owning order belonged to that literary current, rather than to a later form of realism – Flavio Herrera's *La tempestad* (The Storm) (1935), Carlos Wyld Ospina's *La gringa* (1935) and Carlos Samayoa Chinchilla's *Madre Milpa* (Mother Maizefield) (1934) belong to this group.

The 1890s also witnessed the emergence of the innovative school of *modernismo*; its leading figure was a Nicaraguan, Rubén **Darío**, whose *Prosas profanas* (Profane Prose) (1896) was a founding text of the movement. In marked contrast to the *costumbristas*, the *modernistas* were resolutely cosmopolitan, taking their aesthetic line from, among others, the symbolists of late nineteenth-century France. In his *Cantos de vida y esperanza* (Songs of Life and Hope) (1905), Darío turned his attention to Latin America, emphasizing the spiritual in contrast to the materialism of an encroaching USA which had declared its interest in the southern continent through the Monroe Doctrine.

In Guatemala, the prose of Enrique **Gómez Carrillo** and Rafael **Arévalo Martínez** (particularly his famous story 'El hombre que parecía un caballo' (The Man Who Looked Like A Horse) (1914)) signalled the maturity of *modernismo*. In El Salvador, Francisco Gavidia's rich and contradictory body of writing included a strong *modernista* element, although Carlos Bustamante is generally regarded as the country's prime exponent of the movement.

The banana companies who would play such a key role in shaping the destiny of the isthmus were established there by the early 1900s. As their operations expanded, and they seized control directly or indirectly of increasing stretches of land, a new generation of dictators emerged to defend their interests from the heart of the State. Estrada Cabrera and later Ubico governed Guatemala for over forty years with a ruthlessness commemorated above all in Miguel Angel **Asturias**'s novel *El Señor Presidente* (1946) and the later Banana Trilogy.

The best-known fictional representation of the exploitation of the banana workers and the ferocious behaviour of the banana companies is *Mamita Yunai* (1941) by Carlos Luis **Fallas**, himself a union organizer on the plantations. In Costa Rica it marked a decade-long dominance of a genre of documentary social realism also followed by Joaquín Gutiérrez and Carmen **Lyra**. The classic Honduran novel in this genre is *Prisión verde* (Green Prison) (1950) by Ramón Amaya Amador, also a union organizer on the banana plantations. In Panama, the writing of José María Sánchez and César Candanedo reflect the same reality.

Paradoxically, perhaps, Central America is also the home of many outstanding figures in the avant-garde movements of the 1920s and 1930s (see **avant-garde in Latin America**), just as it had been key in the development of *modernismo* a couple of decades earlier. In Panama Rogelio **Sinán** is an outstanding and influential figure, while Nicaragua – one of Latin America's poorest countries – has nevertheless produced an extraordinarily rich crop of poets. José **Coronel Urtecho** was and remained a leading figure and a significant influence on the Granada group that included Pablo Antonio **Cuadra**, Salomón de la **Selva** and the extraordinary anti-*modernista* poet Ernesto **Cardenal**, who would be a central figure in Nicaraguan cultural life for the rest of the century as a poet, a spiritual teacher and as Minister of Culture in the Sandinista government of 1979–90.

Asturias was Guatemala's and probably Central America's leading novelist, his prose influenced and shaped as much by surrealism and the avant-garde as by his social commitment and concerns – both characterize his important exploration of indigenous life in *Leyendas de Guatemala* (1930), *El Señor Presidente* and *Hombres de maíz* (Men of Maize) (1949). His contemporary, Luis **Cardoza y Aragón**, was equally resistant to categorization in any one school, but his influence extended through poetry and fiction into literary and art criticism. When Guatemalan politics took a new and modernizing direction between 1944–54 under Arévalo Martínez and later Arbenz, Cardoza partipated actively in what was in a sense a brief cultural revolution encapsulated in the group caled Saker'ti, Kak'chiaquel Maya for 'Dawn'. The poet Carlos **Illescas**, playwright Manuel **Galich** and writers such as Mario **Monteforte Toledo** and Otto Raúl **González** were among those whose involvement in this period of social progress would result in exile when the Arbenz government was overthrown by a US-inspired coup in 1954.

In El Salvador, the 1932 'Matanza' – the massacre of Indian communities – inaugurated a period of repression and poverty in the countryside represented in the short stories of **Salarrué**, *Cuentos de barro* (Clay Short Stories) (1933), and in a less direct way in the visionary writing of Hugo **Lindo** and in the lyrical poetry of Claudia Lars, who sustained a lyrical and intimate feminist voice without losing sight of the wider social reality. In some sense, Claribel **Alegría** continues in a similar trajectory; although much of her later work was written in Nicaragua, she remains a poet engaged with her early experience in El Salvador.

In Costa Rica, which had escaped dictatorship and entered a period of consensual politics, Yolanda **Oreamuno**, Eunice **Odio** and Ana Istaru make up a generation of outstanding women poets.

In the context of a Central America whose twentieth-century experience was so often one of repression and dictatorship, it is not surprising that much literary debate concerns the relationship between politics and creativity. The debate in El Salvador centred on the work of Raúl Contreras and his alter ego Lydia Nogales, whose intense lyrical work eschewed politics; on the other hand there was a tradition of political poetry which linked Pedro Geoffroy Rivas directly to the work of the country's best-known political poet, Roque **Dalton**; they shared not only a politics but also an ironic and prosaic poetic style that also found echo in the poetry of Ernesto Cardenal in Nicaragua.

In the aftermath of the Cuban Revolution of 1959, literature entered the political struggle directly in several countries. Otto René **Castillo** and Roberto **Obregón** figured among the most talented writers of their era in Guatemala – and both were killed as a result of their political activities. Roque Dalton died, albeit in different circumstances, in El Salvador in the 1970s. Dictatorship informed the later work of the Honduran poet Roberto **Sosa**. Leonel Rugama was one of a number of much younger poets who died during the resistance to the Somoza dictatorship, finally overthrown in 1979 by a movement led by the Sandinistas. The new Sandinista administration put the poet Ernesto Cardenal at the head of a Ministry of Culture which began to actively encourage poetry among ordinary people – the result was the extraordinary **workshop poetry** that emerged throughout the succeeding decade. Other poets became active and prolific in the same period too, Gioconda **Belli**, Vidaluz **Meneses**, Rosario **Murillo** and Daisy **Zamora** prominent among them. In Guatemala Manuel José Arce's Nuevo Signo group, founded in 1968, announced a new direction, as did the irreverent and iconocalastic work of writers such as Arturo **Arias** and Dante **Liano**, much influenced by the post-1968 Mexican movement known as La **Onda**. The group also included Luis de Lión, whose posthumous novel (he disappeared in 1984) *El mundo principia en Xibalbá* (The World Begins at Xibalba) (1985), as well as his poetry, pointed ahead to the emergence of other Mayan writers such as Enrique Sam Colop and Humberto **Ak'abal**.

Through the 1980s, Central America – and particularly El Salvador, Guatemala and Nicaragua – was witness to a decade of repression and resistance between popular movements and local repressive forces financed and sustained by the USA. Inescapably, that struggle was the material with which most writers and artists worked. Sergio **Ramírez**, possibly Nicaragua's best short story writer, was vice president of the Sandinista government; Claribel Alegría (a Salvadorean although by now living in Nicaragua) or her countryman Manlio **Argueta** explored in poetry and prose the experience of a society torn by conflict, as did the Guatemalan poet Alaíde **Foppa**, herself one of its victims, and the authors of two outstanding testimonials, Rigoberta **Menchú** and Mario **Payeras**.

In Panama, a different experience has produced a rather different literature; yet the poets of the 1960s and 1970s, among them Ramón Oviero and Bertalicia Peralta and younger writers such as Manuel Orestes Nieto, have focused on the impact of the almost ninety year-long US occupation of the Canal Zone.

Finally, mention should be made of the first generation of Belizean artists – two outstanding women writers Zee **Edgell** and Zoila **Ellis** who, together with Quince **Duncan**, have set out to find a voice for a multicultural ex-colony with just two decades of experience behind it.

Further reading

Acevedo, Ramón Luis (1982) *La novela centroamericana*, Rio Piedras, PR: Ed. Universitaria.

Beverley, John and Marc Zimmerman (1990) *Literature and Politics in the Central American Revolutions*, Austin: University of Texas Press.

Liano, Dante (1992) *Ensayos de literatura guatemalteca*, Rome: Bulzoni.

Paredes, R. and M. Salinas Paguada (eds) (1987) *Literatura hondureña*, Tegucigalpa: Editores Unidos.

Sandoval de Fonseca, V. (1978) *Resumen de literatura costarricense*, San Juan: Ed. Costa Rica.

Sosa, Roberto (ed.) (1993) *Diálogo de sombras*, Tegucigalpa: Ed. Guaymuras.

White, Steven F. (1986) *Culture and Politics in Nicaragua*, New York: Lumen Books.

—— (1982) *Poets of Nicaragua: A Bilingual Anthology 1918–79*, Greensboro, NC: Unicorn Press.

Zavala, M. and Seidy Araya (1995) *La historiografía literaria en América Central (1957–87)*, San José: Ed. Fundación.

Zimmerman, Marc (1995) *Literature and Resistance in Guatemala*, Athens: Ohio University Press, 2 vols.

MIKE GONZALEZ

Cerruto, Oscar

b. 1912, La Paz, Bolivia; d. 1981, La Paz

Writer

Cerruto was one of the most important figures in contemporary Bolivian literature. A poet, short story writer and novelist, he introduced many innovations that superseded traditional notions about literature. Part of the Chaco Generation, a term referring to an ideological current emerging after the Chaco War (1932–35) which focused on a nationalist vision, his novel *Aluvión de fuego* (Fireflood) (1935) is representative of the period. His poetry and short stories are also important. Cerruto was a career diplomat.

Further reading

Cerruto, Oscar (1985) *Poesía*, Madrid: Ediciones de Cultura Hispánica.

—— (2000) *Aluvión de fuego*, La Paz, Bolivia: Plural Editores.

Mitre, E. (1986) 'Oscar Cerruto: La soledad del poder', in *El árbol y la piedra: Poetas contemporáneos de Bolivia*, Caracas: Monte Avila, 34–43.

MARÍA DORA VILLA GÓMEZ.

Césaire, Aimé

b. 1913, Basse-Pointe, Martinique

Poet and playwright

One of the founders of the ***négritude*** movement in Francophone literature, Césaire was also an important politician in his native Martinique. His poetry stands out as a culminating example of French modernism, while also occupying a preeminent place among twentieth-century texts of the African diaspora.

Césaire was born in Basse-Pointe in the north of Martinique, then a French colony, to a family of moderate means which valued formal education and high French culture. He attended the prestigious Lycée Schoelcher in Martinique's capital, Fort-de-France, where he met Léon Gontran **Damas**, from the French colony of Guyane, whose later collection of poetry, *Pigments* (1937), occupied an important place in the *négritude* movement. In 1932, Césaire was awarded a scholarship to study in France, where he met Léopold Senghor, poet and future president of Senegal, with whom he formed a lasting friendship; these two were the main forces behind the *négritude* movement. Césaire entered the Ecole Normale Supérieure in Paris in 1935 and obtained his diploma in 1939, with a thesis on the theme of the South in African-American literature. That same year he published his first and most influential work, ***Cahier d'un retour au pays natal*** (Notebook of a Return to The Native Land), in a small Paris magazine.

Césaire's meeting with Senghor was a psychological seismic shock. In Senghor, he found a representative of an African culture untainted by the negative images propagated by the French colonial system. It made possible Césaire's discovery of his own African-ness. Paris in the 1930s was in intellectual ferment. In vogue at this time were African and African-American art forms ranging from African sculpture to US blues and jazz. The writers of the Harlem Renaissance, particularly Claude **McKay** and Langston Hughes, enjoyed great success; they, along with young Haitian poets such as Jacques **Roumain**, were the proximate models for these young black Francophone poets. (Césaire was relatively untouched by the Afro-Cuban movement until after the war.) Senghor and Césaire read widely on African culture, particularly the anthropological works of Frobenius; they were also steeped in the poetic tradition of late nineteenth-century France – Rimbaud, Verlaine, Mallarmé – and the burgeoning modernist movements that capitalized on these predecessors. Part of the attraction of French modernism – particularly of **surrealism** – was its revolutionary stance, its will to contest the values of Western civilization. This also brought Césaire to Marxism, which had the added attraction of addressing the colonial question and of associating capitalist society with imperialism.

These intellectual avenues converge in the *Cahier*, written between 1936 and 1939 and revised numerous times thereafter. A long, impassioned, semi-autobiographical poem, it tells of the narrator's return to the island of his birth. The poem is a journey at the end of which the narrator accepts his people's history of suffering, his island geography, his body, his blackness. Hence the term *négritude*, by which Césaire meant the recognition of being black, and the acceptance of black history and culture.

Shortly before the Second World War, Césaire returned to Martinique and a post at the Lycée Schoelcher, teaching such future writers as Frantz Fanon, Edouard **Glissant** and Joseph **Zobel**. He also published the literary journal *Tropiques* from 1941–45, a key surrealist magazine of the time.

The end of the war in 1945 marked Césaire's entrance into politics, representing Martinique to the Constituent Assembly as a member of the Communist Party. Shortly thereafter he successfully introduced to the French Parliament legislation to turn the colonies of Martinique, Guadeloupe, Guyane and Réunion into departments of France, with full rights of citizenship. This move, prompted by a general post-war optimism, had sparked criticism from those advocating Martinican independence. Césaire himself quickly grew disillusioned with departmental status, especially given the French Parliament's turn towards the Right during the Cold War. Césaire also later broke with the Communist Party and formed his own party, the Parti Progressiste Martiniquais, which continues to play an important role in Martinican politics.

Césaire's reputation as a major surrealist poet was confirmed by the publication in 1946 of *Les armes miraculeuses* (The Miraculous Weapons), and by the subsequent publication of *Soleil cou coupé* (Solar Throat Slashed) (1948) and *Corps perdu* (Lost Body) (1950), this last illustrated by Picasso. Césaire also published in 1950 his influential essay, *Discours sur le colonialisme* (Discourse on Colonialism), a ringing condemnation of European colonialism and racism from a rather orthodox Marxist position. *Ferrements* (Ferraments) (1960) initiated a mature poetic phase, more accessible and moving, especially in the elegiac pieces devoted to Louis Delgres, Paul Eluard and others; this tone is also present in the later volume, *moi, laminaire* (i, laminaria) (1982).

Césaire was also a distinguished playwright, an activity allowing him a more direct communication with his public. His *La tragédie du roi Christophe* (The Tragedy of King Christophe) (1961–63) treats a historical figure from post-independence Haiti, while his last play, *Une tempête* (A Tempest) (1969), is a reworking of Shakespeare's *The Tempest*, which has provided much material for Caribbean writers interested in colonialism.

See also: Caliban

Further reading

Arnold, A.J. (1981) *Modernism and Negritude: The Poetry and Poetics of Aimé Césaire*, Cambridge, MA: Harvard University Press.

Césaire, A. (1976) *Oeuvres complètes*, Fort-de-France: Désormeaux.

—— (1983) *The Collected Poetry*, trans. C. Eshleman and A. Smith, Berkeley: University of California Press.

Ganderton, D. (1997) 'Aimé Césaire', in V. Smith (ed.), *Encyclopedia of Latin American Literature*, London: Fitzroy Dearborn, 187–90.

Irele, A. (ed.) (1994) *Cahier d'un retour au pays natal*, Ibadan: New Horn.

Kubayanda, J. (1990) *The Poet's Africa: Africanness in the Poetry of Nicolás Guillén and Aimé Césaire*, New York: Greenwood Press.

Pallister, J.L. (1991) *Aimé Césaire*, New York: Twayne.

BEN A. HELLER

César, Ana Cristina

b. 1952, Rio de Janeiro, Brazil; d. 1983, Rio de Janeiro

Writer

In the early 1980s César published her most important works: *Literatura não é documentação* (Literature is not Documentation), on the political ramifications of documentary film; and two volumes of poetry that contained powerful, political metaphors for lesbian voices – *Luvas de pelica* (Kid Gloves) (1980), and *A teus pés* (At Your Feet) (1982). César was an integral part of the 'Mimeograph Generation' (see **marginal poets**). She committed suicide after returning to Rio de Janeiro from studying abroad.

Further reading

César, Ana Cristina (1999) *Inéditos e dispersos: poesia, prosa*, Sñao Paulo: Instituto Moreira Salles: Editora Ática.

SUSAN CANTY QUINLAN

Céspedes, Augusto

b. 1903, Cochabamba, Bolivia

Writer

One of Bolivia's best-known writers, Céspedes is identified with Bolivian populism and with the intellectual currents that led to the Bolivian Revolution of 1952. *Sangre de mestizos* (Blood of Mestizos) (1936) is a group of eight linked stories about the suffering of the common soldiers in the Chaco War between Bolivia and Paraguay (1932–35). *El metal del diablo* (The Devil's Metal) (1946) is a fictive biography of the Bolivian tin baron Simón I. Patiño, and is thought to have contributed to the nationalization of the tin mines in the Revolution of 1952. Céspedes served in the Bolivian Congress in 1938 and 1944, and also worked in the diplomatic service, most notably as Bolivian ambassador to UNESCO in 1978.

Further reading

Céspedes, Augusto (1983) *Sangre de mestizos: Relatos de la Guerra del Chaco*, La Paz, Bolivia: Libreria Editorial Juventud.

Montenegro, R. (1983) 'Del personaje en *Sangre de mestizos* de Augusto Céspedes', in L. García Pabón and Wilma Torrico (eds), *El paseo de los sentidos (estudios de literatura boliviana contemporánea)*, La Paz: Instituto Boliviano de Cultural, 155–63.

Prada Oropeza, R. (1983), in L. García Pabón and Wilma Torrico (eds), *El paseo de los sentidos (estudios de literatura boliviana contemporánea)*, La Paz: Instituto Boliviano de Cultural, 165–97.

DANIEL BALDERSTON

Céspedes, Diógenes

b. 1941, Santo Domingo, Dominican Republic

Critic

Professor Céspedes is one of the few Dominican critics with a solid academic foundation in literature. Céspedes studied with the famous semiotician A.J. Greimas and with Henri Meschonnic and obtained his PhD from the University of Paris VIII. Among his most important books are *Seis ensayos sobre poética latinoamericana* (Six Essays on Latin American Poetics) (1983), *Estudios sobre literatura, cultura e ideologías* (Studies on Literature, Culture, and Ideologies) (1983) and *Lenguaje y poesía en Santo Domingo en el siglo XX* (Language and Poetry in Santo Domingo during the Twentieth Century) (1985). Since 1982 he has been the director of the journal *Cuadernos de poética* (Poetry Notebooks).

FERNANDO VALERIO-HOLGUÍN

Chahín, Plinio

b. 1959, Santo Domingo, Dominican Republic

Poet

With José **Mármol**, Dionisio de **Jesús**, Tomás **Castro** and Adrián **Javier**, Chahín belongs to the generation of the 1980s which originated around the Taller Literario César Vallejo, sponsored by the Department of Culture of the Universidad Autónoma de Santo Domingo. Chahín's first two books are *Consumación de la carne* (Consummation of the Flesh) (1986) and *Solemnidades de la muerte* (Solemnities of Death) (1991). Informed by Octavio **Paz**'s aesthetics, his poetry explores the metaphysics of everyday life and the power of words.

Further reading

Chahín, P. (2002) *Salvo el insomnio: cuentos*, Santo Domingo: Ediciones La Trinitaria.

FERNANDO VALERIO-HOLGUíN

Chamoiseau, Patrick

b. 1953, Fort-de-France, Martinique

Dramatist and novelist

A prominent contemporary French-Caribbean novelist inspired by Edouard **Glissant**, Chamoiseau wrote the *créoliste* manifesto *Eloge de la créolité* (In Praise of Créolité) with Jean Bernabé and Raphael **Confiant** in 1989 (see ***créolité***). His novels reveal a preoccupation with Fort-de-France's sub-culture of hustlers or *djobeurs* and are written in an interlect combining French and creole. His first successful novel *Chronique des sept misères* (Chronicle of Seven Miseries) (1986) dealt with the decline of Fort-de-France's vegetable market. After *Solibo Magnifique* (Solibo the Magnificent) (1988), he won the Prix Goncourt in 1992 for the novel *Texaco.*

Further reading

Aching, G. (2002) 'Turning a Blind Eye in the Name of the Law: Cultural Alienation in Chamoiseau's *Solibo Magnifique*', in *Masking and Power: Carnival and Popular Culture in the Caribbean*, Minneapolis: University of Minnesota Press, 126–52.

Chamoiseau, P. (2002) *Biblique des derniers gestes: Roman*, Paris: Gallimard.

Chamoiseau, P. and R. Confiant (1991) *Lettres créoles: Tracées Antillaises et continentales de la littérature 1635–1975*, Paris: Hatier.

J. MICHAEL DASH

Charry Lara, Fernando

b. 1920, Bogotá, Colombia

Poet

Charry is best known as a member of the Cántico and *Mito* groups, which greatly influenced the Colombian cultural scene during the 1940s and the 1950s. His poetry, lyrical and erotic, includes the 1949 *Nocturnos y otros sueños* (Nocturnes and other Dreams) and *Pensamientos del amante* (A Lover's Thoughts) (1981). His prose centres on the work of poet José Asunción Silva. Charry studied law and political science at the Universidad Nacional in

Bogotá, where he later served as director of Cultural Affairs; he was also director of the Radiodifusora Nacional de Colombia, a member of the Academia Colombiana de la Lengua and an honorary member of the prestigious Instituto Caro y Cuervo.

Further reading

Charry Lara, Fernando (1997) *Antologia poetica*, Bogotá: Editorial IGITUR.

HÉCTOR D. FERNÁNDEZ L'HOESTE

Chasqui

Chasqui is a journal of Latin American literature published since 1972 at Brigham Young University. Its title is a Quechua word used to designate the messengers of the Inca empire, but the journal is not particularly focused on the Andes or on indigenous questions. Edited for many years by Ted Lyon, it is currently directed by David William Foster. It publishes creative writing as well as articles and book reviews.

DANIEL BALDERSTON

Chaves, Raquel

b. 1938, Asunción, Paraguay

Writer

The author of social poetry in *La tierra sin males* (The World Without Evil) and of a series of mini-poems with a mythical-philosophical content – true Paraguayan haikus – in *Espacio sagrado* (Sacred Space) (1988), Chaves has also published *Todo es del viento: Siete viajes* (Everything Belongs to the Wind: Seven Trips) (1984). He received the 1977 Segundo Premio Municipal (Second Municipal Prize) for 'Ciudadalma' (City-Soul), an ecological text co-authored with Nila López.

TERESA MÉNDEZ-FAITH

Chávez Alfaro, Lizandro

b. 1929, Bluefields, Nicaragua

Writer

An important Nicaraguan novelist, Chávez Alfaro was born on the Atlantic coast of the country. In his literary production he discusses the ambivalence between the Atlantic and Pacific regions by reference to *mestizaje* and ***creolité***. His most important work, *Trágame tierra* (Swallow Me Earth) (1969), is a profound reflection upon land divided across ethnic lines and cultural traditions. He lived in Mexico and Costa Rica during the Somoza era, and during the Sandinista administration he was the National Librarian and the Nicaraguan ambassador to Hungary. He currently works at Managua National University.

Further reading

Chávez Alfaro, Lizandro (1985) *Trágame tierra*, Managua, Nicaragua: Ministerio de Cultura.

Espinoza Mondragón, B. (1977) 'Dos maneras de vivir y morir en *Trágame tierra*', *Cuadernos universitarios* (León) 21: 105–27.

DEREK PETREY AND ILEANA RODRÍGUEZ

Chejfec, Sergio

b. 1956, Buenos Aires, Argentina

Novelist

While distanced from the explicitly experimental, the texture of Chejfec's fiction addresses the limits of language, the minimalist events of daily life and the personal and generational tales that weave together to form the underside of history. Chejfec is as much at ease in recovering his Jewish roots as in reconstructing disquietingly fragmentary urban routines. His writings include *Lenta biografía* (Slow Biography) (1990), *Moral* (1990), *El aire* (Air) (1992), *El llamado de la especie* (The Call of the Species) (1997) and *Cinco* (Five) (1996). Chejfec has lived in Caracas since 1990, where he is currently managing editor of the leading journal *Nueva sociedad*.

Further reading

Chejfec, Sergio (2000) *Boca de lobo*, Buenos Aires: Alfaguara.

SAÚL SOSNOWSKI

Chen, Willi

b. 1934, Coura, Trinidad

Artist and writer

A prolific and multifaceted artist, Chen began publishing his stories of Trinidad life in the 1980s in journals and newspapers. His only collection to date, *King of the Carnival and Other Stories*, was published in 1982. Traditional in his literary style, his central theme is the encounter between cultures in the often harsh context of his native island; strangely, the Chinese community, into which he was born, rarely appears in his work. A painter and sculptor, he designed the Christ the Lord Roman Catholic Church in Marabella, Trinidad. He was awarded the National Hummingbird Medal for Art and Culture in 1989.

Further reading

Chen, W. (1988) *King of the Carnival and Other Stories*, London: Hansib.

KEITH JARDIM

Chihuailaf, Elicura

b. 1952, Temuco, Chile

Writer

Chihuailaf is a poet and thinker of the Mapuche people, Chile's largest indigenous group, who live primarily in the south-central regions of the country. He has translated the poetry of Pablo **Neruda** into Mapudungún, the Mapuche language, and published a bilingual edition of Neruda's work. For Chihuailaf, the power and richness of language are the most valuable legacy of his Mapuche ancestors. Chihuailaf's recent collection of poetry, *Azul* (Blue) (1996), touches upon the contradictions and hypocrisy of modernity in Latin America, which has not overcome race and class discrimination. He organized the Workshop for South American Writers of Indigenous Languages, held in Temuco, Chile, in 1996.

See also: indigenous literature

Further reading

Chihuailaf, E. (2000) *De sueños azules y contrasueños*, Santiago de Chile: Editorial Universitaria; Editorial Cuarto Propio.

AMALIA PEREIRA

children's literature

Latin American writers who have written important works of children's literature include Horacio **Quiroga**, Silvina **Ocampo**, Rosario **Ferré** and Monteiro **Lobato**. The poet, singer and writer Maria Elena **Walsh** is perhaps most famous for her children's literature and music. (One of her songs is sung – hauntingly – by the little girl in Puenzo's film, *La historia oficial* (The Official Story) (1985).) Until recently, there was no children's publishing market *per se*, except perhaps for magazines such as *Billiken*, but that has changed with the huge expansion in the field worldwide. There are now nearly 400 publishers specializing in children's literature, including more than 100 in Brazil. In contemporary Chile, half of the books published are for the children and youth market (compared to 20 per cent in Brazil, 9 per cent in Venezuela and 5 per cent in Argentina). Two prominent authors who specialize in the field today are Ana Maria Machado of Brazil and Graciela Montes of Argentina.

Further reading

Bravo Villasante, C. (1966) *Historia y antología de la literatura infantil iberoamericana*, Madrid: Doncel, 2 vols.

Smith, V. (1997) 'Children's Literature', in V. Smith

(ed.), *Encyclopedia of Latin American Literature*, London: Fitzroy Dearborn, 193–5.

DANIEL BALDERSTON

Chile

Two themes have been dominant in the cultural history of Chile through the twentieth century. The first is its ties to a Europe remote in space but economically dominant, as Chile has depended for most of the century on the nitrates and later the copper that provided the bulk of its export earnings. The second element is geography – the extraordinary diversity of Chile's landscape and its distance not simply from the controlling metropolis but also from the rest of Latin America.

While Luis Orrego Luco represents the *modernista* current in the country (see **Spanish American modernism**), the turn of the century is dominated by Chile's version of ***regionalismo***, ***criollismo***. Its most important representative, Mariano Latorre, describes the Chilean landscape in great detail in his novels – but sees its diversity as an obstacle to change. Eduardo Barrios explores the urban/rural relationship in novels such as *El hermano asno* (Brother Ass) (1922). Augusto **D'Halmar** is a key figure of this literary generation, but is less easy to categorize. His *Juana Lucero* (1902) is a novel in the style of Zola. Two years after its publication he was involved in a failed attempt to set up a Tolstoyan rural colony. His subsequent short stories, and his *La lámpara en el molino* (The Light at the Mill) (1914), locate him within a *modernista* current, with an emphasis on the psychological. And in 1924 he published *La pasión y muerte del cura Deusto* (The Passion and Death of Father Deusto), a very popular novel exploring the tensions between religious belief and homosexual desire. Although very different in subject matter, Baldomero **Lillo**'s short stories about the harsh life of the mining communities were also influenced by the writing of Emile Zola.

In poetry, *modernismo*'s influence was giving way by 1920 to a different kind of writing, characteristically direct, intimate and lyrical in expression. Pedro Prado was an important representative of this school, but its most profound exponent was certainly Gabriela **Mistral**, whose *Desolación* (1922), *Ternura* (Tenderness) (1924) and, later, *Tala* (Tree Felling) (1938) earned her a major literary reputation and an eventual Nobel prize for Literature in 1945. Although her work has its origin in her own experience, it is far more than simple provincial poetry, despite the directness of its language. Mistral travelled widely as a diplomat and a cultural ambassador; the loneliness reflected in her poetry is more often that of women, both within Chile and outside it.

Her contemporary, Pablo **Neruda**, is undoubtedly the better known of the two, although they share the accolade of a Nobel prize (Neruda received his in 1972, a year before his death). Neruda's *Veinte poemas de amor y una canción desesperada* (Twenty Love Poems and a Desperate Song) (1924) remain hugely popular. The first two books of *Residencia en la tierra* (Residence on Earth) collected his work over ten years spent in diplomatic posts around the world, culminating in Spain; it was often introspective, avant-garde and deeply personal. Within Chile, it was Vicente **Huidobro** who dominated the field of avant-garde poetry; his ***Altazor*** (1931) is a tour de force, a radical and disturbing evocation of the disintegration of language.

Pablo de **Rokha**, a deeply ideological writer, spared no criticism of his peers and as a result ensured his lifelong isolation from the mainstream of Chilean letters.

Nicanor **Parra**, begetter of *antipoesía* (see **antipoetry**), published his first works at the end of the 1930s; deliberately prosaic, thematically everyday and emotionally flat, they provided an antidote to the high rhetoric of Neruda which reached its pinnacle with the great historical narrative of the ***Canto general*** (A General Song) (1950). Parra's *Poemas y antipoemas* was published in 1954, followed by *La cueca larga* (The Long Cueca) (1958) and *Versos de salón* (1962). Of the same generation as Parra, the poetry of Gonzalo **Rojas** is powerful, sensual and overshadowed by the powerful external forces that shape human lives.

Although the next group of poets to emerge in this poetry-rich cultural environment began to publish in the 1960s, much of the work of Enrique **Lihn**, Miguel Arteche and others was shaped by the profound political changes that affected Chile through the 1970s and 1980s.

The figure of Manuel **Rojas** stands out among the writers of prose from the 1930s onwards. His *Hijo de ladrón* (Born Guilty) (1951) is a fine novel, existentialist in its preoccupations and rooted among Chile's poor and marginal population. Juan Marín's novels, for example *Paralelo 53 Sur* (1936), were didactic novels directed against foreign interests, while the stories of Francisco **Coloane** depict the lives of fishing and sealing communities, particularly in the far south of the country, the region around Tierra del Fuego. Marta **Brunet** explored the experience of women in Chile as did her younger colleague María Luisa **Bombal**. Carlos Droguett's *Eloy* (1960) was one of a series of novels narrating Chile's fraught history. Outstanding among the writers of this generation was José **Donoso**, whose novels are witty, cruel and challenging in their exploration of the terrains of exile and desire, as in *El lugar sin límites* (Hell Has No Limits) (1966) and *El* ***obsceno pájaro de la noche*** (The Obscene Bird of the Night) (1970).

In November 1970, Salvador Allende was elected to Chile's presidency as the representative of the Popular Unity coalition. The repercussions of the election of a radical reforming government were felt within the country and internationally. The period that followed was conflictive and tense, but also rich in cultural and political experiment; there was the emergence of a new public theatre, for example, as well as intense debates about the role of culture and cultural production in the new society. Antonio **Skármeta** published two books of short stories during the Allende period, while his *Soñé que la nieve ardía* (I Dreamt the Snow Was Burning) (1975), set in the last days of the Allende government, was written from exile in Argentina. His *Ardiente paciencia* (Burning Patience) (1985), concerning a relationship between a village postman and an ailing Pablo Neruda, was filmed twice, the second time in Italian as *Il Postino*, a film which won international acclaim.

The Allende government was overthrown in a violent military coup led by Augusto Pinochet on 11 September 1973. There followed a fifteen-year military dictatorship, during which all expressions of resistance or criticism were systematically repressed. Many of those who had supported Allende were imprisoned, murdered or sent into exile. It could be argued, indeed, that there are two Chilean literatures during those years – one evolving in enforced exile, the other produced under conditions of extreme repression within the country itself, and therefore characteristically elliptical and allusive. Isabel **Allende**'s *La casa de los espíritus* (House of the Spirits) (1982) won considerable international success for its lightly disguised account of Chilean history from a female perspective. Patricio **Manns**, José Donoso, Skárta and many others continued to write from exile. Within Chile, Raúl **Zurita**'s daring, experimental and challenging poetry complemented his work as a performance artist. Equally demanding, ironic and subversive were the prose works of Diamela **Eltit**, including *Por la patria* (For the Fatherland) (1986) and *Lumpérica* (LumpenAmerica) (1983). Her feminism found an echo and continuity in the writing of Ana María **Del Río**, Marcela Serrano and Pía **Barros**.

The newest voices in Chilean writing include those writing in the hitherto unfamiliar language of Chile's indigenous people, the Mapuche; Elicura **Chihuailaf** is a prominent representative. From a different perspective, Patricio Manns, Lautaro Yankas and Luis Vulliamy have explored in prose the history and experience of the Mapuche and other indigenous peoples. In the same period (the 1990s) Luis **Sepúlveda** has found an international readership for his stories about ethnicity and the environment. Recent gay writing is represented by Juan Pablo **Sutherland** and Pedro **Lemebel**.

Chile also has a rich theatrical history which continued, through groups like ICTUS and the Teatro del Silencio, even after the coup of 1973. And in the field of criticism, a distinguished history of literary interpretation embraces critics as different as **Alone**, during the 1930s and 1940s, and Nelly **Richard**, editor of the ***Revista de crítica cultural***.

Further reading

Concha, Jaime (1973) *Poesía chilena*, Santiago: Ed. Quimantú.
Goic, Cedomil (1991) *La novela chilena: Los mitos degradados*, Santiago: Ed. Universitaria.
Promis Ojeda, J. (1993) *La novela chilena del último siglo*, Santiago: Ed. La Noria.
Richard, Nelly (1998) *Residuos y metáforas: Ensayos de crítica cultural sobre el Chile de la transición*, Santiago: Ed. Cuarto Propio.

MIKE GONZALEZ

Chiriboga, Luz Argentina

b. 1940, Esmeraldas, Ecuador

Poet, essayist and novelist

Chiriboga's work explores themes of identity, Afro-centrism, female subjectivity and desire. Her 1994 novel, *Jonatás y Manuela*, narrates the story of three generations of women and their struggles under slavery. The novel retells the history of the independence period from an Afro-centric and feminine point of view, as it traces the relationship between the slave Jonatás and Manuela Sáenz, companion of Simón Bolívar. The novel problematizes the allegedly mestizo and Sierran foundations of Ecuadorian national identity. Other works include the novel *Bajo la piel de los tambores* (Beneath the Drum Skin) (1991), *La contraportada del deseo* (The Other Face of Desire) (1992, poetry) and *Escritores esmeraldeños: Raíces, biografía, producción y crítica* (Writers of Esmeraldas: Roots, Biography, Production and Criticism) (1995, essay). Her work is included in *Antología de narradoras ecuatorianas* (Anthology of Ecuadorean Women Writers) (1997) and *Between the Silence of Voices: An Anthology of Contemporary Ecuadorean Women Poets* (1997).

Further reading

Handelsman, Michael (1999) *Lo afro y la plurinacionalidad: El caso ecuatoriano visto desde su literatura*, University MS: Romance Monographs.

EILEEN WILLINGHAM

Chocano, José Santos

b. 1875, Lima, Peru; d. 1934, Santiago, Chile

Poet

One of the most colourful figures of the time, Chocano's life was full of political intrigue, treasure hunting, duels and prison sentences. He travelled widely, spending prison time in Guatemala and in Lima, until finally he was killed on a tram in Santiago by his partner in a treasure-hunting venture. A Byronic figure, his poetry was bombastic, feverish and wild. Often anti-imperialist and nationalist, he also published poems on the discovery of the New World, on the geography of the Americas, on the jungle and the Pacific Ocean and on Latin American identities. **Borges**, in his brilliant 'El arte de injuriar' (The Art of Invective) (1933), recalls a diatribe against Chocano by **Vargas Vila**. His memory now resides more in the lore about his life than in his verse, even the once famous *Alma América* (Soul America) (1906).

Further reading

Chocano, J.S. (1954) *Obras completas*, ed. L.A. Sánchez, Mexico City: Aguilar, 4 vols.
Meza Fuentes, R. (1935) *La poesía de José Santos Chocano*, Santiago: Universidad de Chile.
Sánchez, L.A. (1960) *Aladino; o, Vida y obras de José Santos Chocano*, Mexico City: Libro Mex.
Tamayo y Vargas, A. (1989) 'José Santos Chocano', in C.A. Solé and M.I. Abreu (eds), *Latin American Writers*, New York: Scribners, 2, 543–49.

DANIEL BALDERSTON

Chocrón, Isaac

b. 1930, Maracay, Venezuela

Playwright, essayist and novelist

Although he studied economics and international relations in the USA, Chocrón's major contribution to the culture of his country has been in the theatre and in prose fiction. His theatre pieces transcend the simple references to the national reality to present conflicts and passions of universal significance. In the 1960s he co-founded, with José Ignacio **Cabrujas** and Román Chalbaud, the Nuevo Grupo theatre company, and at the end of the 1980s formed the Compañía Nacional de Teatro. In 1963 he was awarded the Ateneo de Caracas prize for his *Animales feroces* (Fierce Animals), and in 1979 won the National Theatre Prize.

Further reading

Chocrón, I. (1966) *El nuevo teatro venezolano*. Caracas: Oficina Central de Información.

—— (2000) *Tap dance y otras piezas*, Caracas, Venezuela: Monte Ávila Editores Latinoamericana.

—— (1968) *Teatro*. Caracas: Imprenta Universitaria.

Azparren, L. (1979)' 'Isaac Chocrón: En busca de las pistas perdidas.' *El teatro venezolano y otros teatros*. Caracas: Monte Avila, 107–28.

Klein, D.A. (1987) "The Theme of Alienation in the Theatre of Elisa Lerner and Isaac Chocron', *Folio* 17: 151–66.

Vestrini, M. (1980) *Isaac Chocrón frente al espejo*, Caracas: Ed. Ateneo de Caracas.

JORGE ROMERO LEÓN

Churata, Gamaliel (Arturo Peralta)

b. 1897, Puno, Peru; d. 1969, Lima, Peru

Writer

Churata was the leading figure of the avant-garde movement in Puno, the provincial centre of 1920s vanguard activity in Peru, and editor of its journal *Boletín Titikaka*. Central to his agenda was the reconciliation of the indigenous Andean cultural tradition with the liberating forces of modernity. That project underlies *El pez de oro* (The Golden Fish) (1957), a long, hermetic book that employs surrealist techniques (see **surrealism**), generic mixing and a hybrid language combining Spanish with Quechua and Aymara in an attempt to fuse conflicting traditions into a cohesive whole.

Further reading

Ayala, José Luis (2000) 'Gamaliel Churata en la perspectiva ultraórbica del siglo XX', *Revista peruana de literatura, palabra en libertad*, 4.

Churata, G. (1971) *Antología y valoración*, Lima: Edicioines Instituto Puneño de Cultura.

—— (1957) *El pez de oro (Retablos de Layhkakuy)*, La Paz: Ed. Canata.

JAMES HIGGINS

Cien años de soledad

Probably the most successful novel to come out of Latin America, Gabriel **García Márquez**'s *Cien años de soledad* (One Hundred Years of Solitude) was published in 1967. The novel is set, like most of his writing, in the fictional community of Macondo. Macondo has several narrative functions: it stands for Colombia's particular experience and for Latin America's colonial history. The town is isolated and enclosed, and yet is subject to forces and changes that lie beyond the imprisoning frontiers that shape and determine its destiny. In precisely that sense, Macondo echoes the experience of a colonized world imagined and structured by a distant and unreachable metropolis. The 'hundred years' of the title is not exact time, but a metaphorical 'century' that embraces all of the key experiences of the region from Conquest through the military authoritarianism of the post-independence republics to the neo-colonialism practised by US capital; it chronicles, too, the acts of resistance (strikes and rebellions), the natural and man-made catastrophes, and the ultimate abandonment by those very colonial powers, leaving a Latin America that will ultimately be consumed in a final cataclysm.

Yet it is also an immensely funny book, its humour sustained by the exaggerated mythical actions of some of its key characters, the distortions and disturbances of time, the mockery of life and death. It is as if there were twin narratives at work – the first historical and linear, the second rooted in myth and legend, a kind of popular alternative history in which the inescapable truths of one world were reversed in another. It is this conjunction of narrative modes, this mutual reflection of history upon myth and vice versa, that is encapsulated in

García Márquez's own description of his method of writing as '**magical realism**'.

The encounter of opposites continues in other ways too: José Arcadio Buendía, patriarch of the family/clan whose family history evolves through the novel, spends most of his life bent on a search for the philosopher's stone, the scientific solution to the transformation of lead into gold and thus of nature into culture. His lifelong companion, Ursula, is profoundly sceptical about the enterprise, trusting instead to a different but equally present knowledge – the collective understanding of folk wisdom and collective experience sometimes described as 'magic' or even 'superstition'. This gives her gifts of both prophecy and healing and the capacity to move effortlessly between the two. That conflictive relationship between nature and culture, popular wisdom and science, is replayed in one way or another with each generation of the Buendías. But the problem seems to be that the secrets of scientific knowledge are held elsewhere and introduced piecemeal into the community, often by the travelling gypsy Melquíades, who brings ice and false teeth to the village.

Yet at the same time another power seems to govern the lives of this community and its members, a destiny symbolized by the pig's tail that Ursula knows will one day appear on the body of a Buendía child and mark the fulfilment of a curse; a judgement on some original sin, a fall from Eden that preceded the creation of Macondo. This, of course, is another (religious) narrative – and a prediction fulfilled in the final moments of the novel when knowledge immediately precedes destruction, in an uncanny echo of some of the fictions of Jorge Luis **Borges**. Yet, in the end, the narrative – the tale told – does remain as evidence of a history already lived and of a history to come, which will add its own account to the sum of myth and history that is Latin America.

Further reading

Bell, M. (1993) *Gabriel García Márquez: Solitude and Solidarity*, London: Macmillan.

García Márquez, G. (1970) *One Hundred Years of Solitude*, trans. G. Rabassa, New York: Harper & Row.

Ludmer, J. (1975) *Cien años de soledad: Una interpretación*, Buenos Aires: Editorial Sudamericana.

Martin, G. (1987) 'On Magical and Social Realism in García Márquez', in B. McGuirk and R. Cardwell (eds), *Gabriel García Márquez: New Readings*, Cambridge: Cambridge University Press.

Murray, P. (1997) 'Cien años de soledad', in V. Smith (ed.), *Encyclopedia of Latin American Literature*, London: Fitzroy Dearborn, 351–3.

Wood, M. (1990) *García Márquez: One Hundred Years of Solitude*, Cambridge: Cambridge University Press.

MIKE GONZALEZ

cinema and literature

The relationship between literature and the cinema has always been a complex and difficult one. Yet it has also frequently been symbiotic. There is no doubt, for example, that the avant-garde of the early twentieth century was excited by the moving image as much for its expressive content as for its identification with modernity. The Futurists and others attempted to capture speed and transformation using the techniques unleashed by Cubism and the revolt against representation; in the US novel, the influence of filmic language was obvious in the work of writers such as Scott Fitzgerald and Dos Passos, so often structured as a sequence of images.

Beyond the formal, the cinema as a cultural institution, its production of a star system and its creation of a new language of popular myth, was itself the subject for writing. And in the contrary direction, cinema excavated literature for themes, ideas and narratives with which to structure a new and different visual history.

The earliest cinema found its themes in literature; Martin Luis **Guzmán**'s *El compadre Mendoza* (1933) and Rafael Muñoz's *Vámonos con Pancho Villa*, both directed by Fernando de Fuentes, were the subject of early Mexican sound films. The Mexican Revolution, of course, would continue to be the favoured topic of Mexican cinema through the next two decades – and their sources would often be the **novela de la revolución Mexicana**. In Argentina, by contrast, early sound film was dominated by tango and the tango melodrama, just as much as early sound cinema in Brazil focused on music and musical performance.

Mexican cinema in the golden age of early sound seemed to derive its inspiration largely from song and popular myth. Yet Fernando de Fuentes, one of Mexico's most prominent commercial directors, made his own version of Rómulo **Gallegos**'s ***Doña Bárbara*** (in 1943) and adapted Dostoyevsky's novel to a Mexican setting for his own *Crimen y castigo* (Crime and Punishment) (1950). The stories of **indigenista** writer Francisco Rojas González provided the material for the outstanding collaborative documentary *Raíces* (Roots), released in 1955. A number of literary originals were adapted for the cinema in the 1960s, as directorial individuality increasingly marked a new era in cinema. Roberto Gavaldón, Alberto Isaac, Arturo Ripstein and the great Brazilian director Ruy Guerra each brought short stories by **García Márquez** to the screen, while Carlos Velo adapted Juan **Rulfo**'s masterpiece *Pedro Páramo* for the screen in 1966. José **Donoso**'s novel of shifting identities, *El lugar sin límites* (Hell Has No Limits) (released as a film in 1978), seemed particularly appropriate to the enigmatic and symbolic style of Arturo Ripstein, since the novel itself employed a restless and changing narrative perspective.

The 1960s were a particularly rich and fertile period for cinema. In Cuba, a new revolutionary cinema was created after 1959. Though its dominant style was the raw documentary mode of Santiago Alvarez, Tomás Gutiérrez Alea brought Edmundo **Desnoes**'s ***Memorias del subdesarrollo*** (Memories of Underdevelopment) to the screen in 1968 and towards the end of his life adapted a story by Senel **Paz** for his highly significant film *Fresa y chocolate* (Strawberry and Chocolate) (1993).

Brazil's cinema novo may have originated in the dominant realism of the previous decade, but it added to that a powerful mythic element, seeking not only the material reality of the Brazilian interior (and particularly the north east) but also its collective consciousness. In 1964, the military coup moved the political debate into more allusive cultural arenas – but it did continue, at least until the imposition of direct censorship after 1968. The movement's most successful film, ***Macunaíma*** (1969), directed by Joaquim Pedro de Andrade, revisited Mario de **Andrade**'s 1928 allegorical narrative of a return to origins in a journey through Brazil. Leon Hirzsman's *São Bernardo* (1972) similarly returned to Machado de Assis's classic novel to address the complex historical and political conflicts still active behind the mask of censorship. Nelson Pereira dos Santos adapted Graciliano **Ramos**'s *Vidas secas* (1963); his version of Ramos's *Memorias do cárcere* (Prison Memoirs), released in 1984, was the last expression of an important school of filmmaking. Bruno Barreto's adaptation of Jorge **Amado**'s *Dona Flor e seus dois maridos* (Dona Flor and Her Two Husbands) (1976) and Suzana Amaral' s *A hora da estrela* (The Hour of the Star) (1985), after Clarice **Lispector**'s novella, began to win an international audience for Brazilian film.

Argentina between 1976 and 1983, and Chile from 1973 to 1989, were both living under conditions of military dictatorship and extreme censorship. Much of its best cinema was realized in exile during those years. Fernando Solanas, for example, made *Los hijos de Fierro* (Martin Fierro's Sons) in 1972, building on the enigmatic ending of the great nineteenth-century national epic poem ***Martín Fierro*** by José Hernández, itself already filmed by Torre Nilsson in 1968. Aida Bortnik, a famous Argentine screenwriter who adapted Mario **Benedetti**'s novel *La tregua* (The Truce) for the screen in 1974 and Carlos **Fuentes**'s *Gringo viejo* in 1990, wrote the screenplay for Luis Puenzo's *La versión oficial* (The Official Story) (1984), the first of a number of post-dictatorship films which began to examine and analyse the experience of exile and dictatorship. Hector Babenco's film of Manuel Puig's *Kiss of the Spiderwoman*, with its brilliant central performance by William Hurt, brought the issue to an international audience in the same year. Eliseo Subiela's *Hombre mirando al sureste* (Man Looking South East) (1986), explored the same issues, and includes references to Adolfo **Bioy Casares**'s *La invención de Morel* (The Invention of Morel) (1940).

The late eighties saw the progressive withdrawal of state subsidies for cinema under market pressures and a search increasingly for projects that could attract a range of external sponsorship. The result was a series of internationally successful Latin American films. An early example was the adaptation of Chilean novelist Antonio **Skármeta**'s poignant novel about the last days of Pablo **Neruda** and his relationship with a local postman; *Ardiente paciencia* (Burning Patience) was originally filmed in Cuba with a Chilean cast, but it was its remake *Il Postino*, relocated to Italy, which brought international success and, ironically, a widespread interest in Neruda's poetry. In 1991, Laura **Esquivel**'s ***Como agua para chocolate*** (Like Water for Chocolate), set in and around the Mexican Revolution, was a massive success for her and director Alfonso Arau.

García Márquez's *Crónica de una muerte anunciada* (Chronicle of a Death Foretold), a Franco-Italian production directed by Francesco Rosi, was released in 1987 while Julio **Cortázar**'s story 'Las babas del diablo' was adapted as *Blow Up*, an iconic film by Antonioni. Alex Cox's adaptation of Borges's story *La muerte y la brújula* (Death and the Compass) was less successful, but the film version of Ariel **Dorfman**'s *Death and the Maiden* did approach its runaway success as a stage play. Few Latin American films, however, could claim the degree of international acceptance achieved by Walter Salles's *Central do Brasil* (Central Station) (1999) or *Cidade de Deus* (City of God), the adaptation of Paulo **Lins**'s 1997 novel of the same name.

Further reading

Chanan, M. (ed.) (1976) *Chilean Cinema*, London: BFI.

—— (ed.) (1985) *The Cuban Image: Cinema and Cultural Politics in Cuba*, London: BFI.

Johnson, Randal and Robert Stam (1995) *Brazilian Cinema*, New York: Columbia University Press.

Myerson, M. (1973) *Memories of Underdevelopment: The Revolutionary Films of Cuba*, New York: Grossman Publishers.

Martins, Laura M. (2002) *En primer plano: Literatura y cine en Argentina 1955–1969*, New Orleans: University Press of the South.

Podalsky, Laura (ed.) (2002) *Cine y literatura*, special issue of *Revista iberoamericana*, LXVII/199, April–June.

MIKE GONZALEZ

Cisneros, Antonio

b. 1942, Lima, Peru

Poet

Cisneros is the leading representative of the 1960s generation which renovated poetry in Peru through the use of more open forms, intertextual dialogue and an irreverent conversational manner, for example in *Canto ceremonial contra un oso hormiguero* (Ceremonial Song against an Ant-eater) (1968). Reflecting the spirit of the 1960s, his work deploys a devastating irony to subvert the conservative ethos of Peru's middle classes. At the same time, he seeks to establish a modern Peruvian and Third World identity by rewriting national history and defining himself in relation to the forces that have shaped his country.

Further reading

Bueno, R. (1992) 'Antonio Cisneros entre las aguas del Pacífico Sur', *Revista de crítica literaria latinoamericana* 35: 71–80.

Cisneros, A. (1996) *Poesía reunida, 1961–1992*, Lima: Editora Perú.

—— (1999) *Postales de Lima, Postales para Lima*, Buenos Aires: Ediciones Colihue.

García Pinto, M. (1997) 'Antonio Cisneros', in *Encyclopedia of Latin American Literature*, ed. V. Smith, London: Fitzroy Dearborn, 202–3.

Higgins, J. (1982) *The Poet in Peru (Alienation and the Quest for a Super-Reality)*, Liverpool: Francis Cairns, 65–88.

JAMES HIGGINS

city and literature

Urbanization is not solely a contemporary phenomenon in Latin America; the Spanish colonial administration constructed fine city centres from which to conduct the business of domination. The centres of Mexico, Quito, Lima, Cartagena and Potosí stand testimony to that. For the cultural historian, however, the relationship between literature and the city becomes significant and problematic at certain key points in the expansion of those ancient cities, and the growth of others, in the framework of modernity.

At the very beginning of the century, writers such as the Mexican Federico Gamboa and the Argentine Julián Martel were taking the Paris of the French Naturalists, and of Zola in particular, and relocating it to the newly expanding cities set in the export economies like Mexico City or a Buenos Aires in full and rapid transformation. It could be argued that the first writers of Buenos Aires were the early lyricists of tango, together with the dramatist Florencio **Sánchez**. Jorge Luis **Borges**, by contrast, in his 1923 volume of poetry *Fervor de Buenos Aires* sought in that same city a tradition that was in a sense prior to and stronger than the modern. In any event, the two loose artistic groupings that named themselves after the urban thoroughfares of Boedo and Florida were claiming the city from very different positions (see **Boedo vs Florida**). The writers of Florida celebrated its modernity aesthetically, yet in many ways remained ideologically rooted in a nostalgia for a more conservative nation defined, albeit differently, by writers such as Leopoldo **Lugones** and Ricardo **Güiraldes**. The Boedo group, meanwhile, were seeking a literary language of realism that could respond to the experience of the immigrant and working-class communities who could make no claim on the remembered city but only define the burgeoning metropolis in which they lived and worked. The outstanding urban novelist of the period is Roberto **Arlt**.

Elsewhere in Latin America, the definitive subordination of the rural to the urban was a longer and later process. In Mexico, Ecuador, Colombia and Peru, among others, the struggle for modernity – and for modernization – was enacted on the land through the 1920s and 1930s. The search for a national literary expression, therefore, was articulated there through a literature of rural conflict – principally the schools of ***indigenista*** writing.

The emergence at the centre of literary expression of the experience of urban living occurred at different moments in different countries. The nature of modernity and the material transformations that would shift the dynamic centre of the economy towards exports and industrialization, with the consequent growth of the modern city, was clarified in varied and changing circumstances. In Argentina, the definitive shift came at the turn of the century, as Buenos Aires emerged clearly as the focus of growth and change. One effect of that change, of course, was the emergence of what Angel **Rama** called 'the lettered city' – a class of urban intellectuals charged with shaping and defining this experience of modernity in cultural and aesthetic terms. In Mexico, a similar process began to occur as the Mexican Revolution affirmed a definitive shift of power towards a new political class centralized in the capital city. While the struggles on and for the land continued until the late 1930s, the emerging avant-garde was resolutely urban. The Estridentistas (see **Estridentismo**), for example, took their lead from the Italian Futurists in their celebration of the dynamic pace, the clamour and the technology of city life.

In 1941, the US publishers Farrar Straus held a competition to identify the 'great Latin American novel'. While the winner was Ciro **Alegría**'s *indigenista* novel *El mundo es ancho y ajeno* (Broad and Alien is the World), second place went to Juan Carlos **Onetti**'s *Tierra de nadie* (No Man's Land), whose setting was an alienated city reminiscent of John Dos Passos's New York in *Manhattan Transfer* (1926). In a sense, Onetti's tense and neglected urban landscape was a metaphor for the failed promise of the 'lettered city', the cosmopolitan centre of culture that Buenos Aires, and to a lesser extent Montevideo, were intended to represent. Vicente **Huidobro**'s extraordinary poetic work ***Altazor*** (1919–31) could perhaps be seen as a record of a similar disillusionment.

In the 1940s and 1950s a new period of urban expansion coincided with an era of economic growth and modernization. In the aftermath of the Crash of 1929, new policies of state-led growth began to be articulated by nationalist politicians such as Getúlio Vargas in Brazil, Lázaro Cárdenas in Mexico and Marcos Pérez Jiménez in Venezuela. The creation of import-substitution industries on the one hand, and the attempt to exercise control over raw materials and commodities directed to the export market on the other, drew increasing numbers towards the larger cities of the region and their surrounding industrial areas. By the 1950s, the larger Latin American cities were mushrooming, and the peripheral poor suburbs growing as people left the countryside to seek work in the metropolis in growing numbers.

A new generation of writers responded to these changes; Carlos **Fuentes**'s *La región más transparente* (Where the Air is Clear) (1958) was set in a growing Mexico City, while Julio **Cortázar**'s ***Rayuela*** (1963) was located mostly in Buenos Aires. Mario **Vargas Llosa**'s *La* ***ciudad y los perros*** (The

Time of the Hero) (1962) explored the tensions within a military high school as a reflection of those that cut across the wider society of Lima. These novels all reflected the sense of anomie and atomization in the new cities that Carlos Drummond de **Andrade** had earlier explored in collections such as *A rosa do povo* (The People's Rose) in 1945. There was a clear echo of his work in the poetry of Antonio **Cisneros** in Peru and indeed in the **antipoesía** of Nicanor **Parra** in Chile. For all of them the city was a kind of exile, a place of loss but with no feeling for a past to sustain its wandering residents.

In this period of transition and change, however, it was still the case that writers retained a certain right to criticize and protest; they were still seen to have a degree of public responsibility. Thus, the Mexican events of 1968, which culminated in the Three Cultures Square massacre of October 2 in that year, spurred intellectuals such as Octavio **Paz**, Carlos Fuentes and others to use their positions to denounce this act of naked repression. To that extent, the lettered city was still alive.

Yet there were changes occurring in urban society which would call that authority into question. It had to do, in part, with a redefinition of culture and cultural production itself. By the 1980s, Latin American cities had expanded into megalopolises. São Paolo and Mexico City vied for the title of the world's largest city, although the real number of urban inhabitants was always an estimate rather than an exact figure. At the same time the slums and shantytowns were forests of television aerials, signalling an exponential growth in mass popular culture. Manuel **Puig**, the Argentine novelist, addressed the way in which popular culture shaped consciousness in a series of novels – tango lyrics in ***Boquitas pintadas*** (Heartbreak Tango) (1969) and cinema in *El beso de la mujer araña* (Kiss of the Spider Woman) (1976). In Mexico José **Agustín** and the writers of La **Onda** spoke through the language of a new, nihilistic youth culture often reflected in rock music.

Laura **Esquivel**'s ***Como agua para chocolate*** (Like Water for Chocolate) (1989) was an enormous commercial success. Although its setting was rural, its form imitated the serial novels now so familiar both in print and in radio and television soap operas. It marked, too, a major shift through the 1980s, as literature increasingly leaned towards a commercial market dominated more and more by mass culture products. This was the urban culture that had been defined in a path-breaking 1995 work by Néstor García Canclini as 'hybrid cultures' – a merging of mass culture and traditional practices, of mass media and literature. In this cultural space, the authority of intellectuals gave way to the instantaneous (and transient) authority of the visual image. It was reflected in a new idiom in urban writing, a growing body of work set in the amoral world of the urban slum. Examples include the work of Patricia Melo and Paulo **Lins** in Brazil and Fernando **Vallejo**'s *La virgen de los sicarios* (Our Lady of the Assassins) (1994); Ricardo **Piglia**'s *La ciudad ausente* (Absent City) (1992); and the very difficult writing of Néstor **Perlongher**, in a kind of full body immersion in the cacophony of urban noise.

This milieu produced what might be seen as the first literary product of the new mass metropolis – the ***crónica***, sometimes referred to as 'chronicles of popular culture' by its most influential practitioners, particularly Carlos **Monsiváis** of Mexico, the Chilean Pedro **Lemebel** and, at an earlier stage, Clarice **Lispector** in Brazil.

Further reading

Foster, D.W. (1998) *Buenos Aires: Perspectives on the City and Cultural Production*, Gainesville: University of Florida Press.

Franco, Jean (2002) *Decline and Fall of the Lettered City: Latin America and the Cold War (Convergences)*, Cambridge, MA and London: Yale University Press.

García Canclini, Nestor (1995) *Hybrid Cultures*, Minneapolis: University of Minnesota Press.

Podalsky, Laura (2003) *Specular City: The Transformation of Culture, Consumption and Space after Perón*, Philadelphia: Temple University Press.

Rama, Angel (1996) *The Lettered City*, Durham, NC: Duke University Press.

Sarlo, Beatriz (1999) *Una modernidad periférica: Buenos Aires 1920 y 1930*, Buenos Aires: Ed. Nueva Visión.

—— (2001) *Scenes from Postmodern Life*, Minneapolis: University of Minnesota Press.

MIKE GONZALEZ

ciudad y los perros, La

Mario **Vargas Llosa**'s first novel, *La ciudad y los perros* (The Time of the Hero) was published in 1962 and won a prize from Seix Barral. The novel paints a harsh picture of a military school in Lima, presented as a microcosm of the fractious society of Peru. The Leoncio Prado military school establishes military discipline, but that discipline is the source of tension, violations of the rules and all sorts of intrigue among the school's students and staff. The all-male world of the school is riven by sexual tension as well as by authoritarianism, which operates in terms of masters and slaves. The novel is a *Bildungsroman* or novel of education, with the shifting narrators and fragmented narration that Vargas Llosa would use (perhaps to better effect) in his subsequent novels. The novel was adapted for the screen by Francisco Lombardi in 1986.

Further reading

Standish, Peter (1982) *Vargas Llosa: La ciudad y los perros*, London: Grant & Cutler in association with Tamesis Books.

Vargas Llosa, Mario (1965) *La ciudad y los perros*, Barcelona: Editorial Seix Barral.

DANIEL BALDERSTON

civilization and barbarism

A key term in Latin American cultural theory, 'Civilización y barbarie' was the original title of Domingo Faustino Sarmiento's 1845 biography of Juan Facundo Quiroga, a strongman or *caudillo* from the Argentine interior who had been assassinated a few years earlier. Sarmiento retold the life of Facundo as a vehicle for giving his views on the maladies of nation formation and cultural identity that afflicted Argentina in his time, and which he associated with atavism, a lack of curiosity about the outside world, isolation of local communities, ignorance and cultural inferiority. The solutions he proposed were improved education, transportation, communications and immigration, to 'cure' the maladies of life on the Argentine pampas and elsewhere in the vast country. In his view Buenos Aires and the ports of the Paraná river needed to become conduits for contact with (and immigration from) Europe, and greater cultural sophistication would cure the 'barbarism' or 'savagery' that was the product of isolation and internal turmoil.

'Civilization and barbarism' proved a powerful way of thinking about key problems of Latin American life, although even when echoed by intellectuals who were sympathetic to Sarmiento's formulation – one thinks of Euclides da **Cunha** in *Os **sertões*** (Rebellion in the Backlands) (1905), Alcides **Arguedas** in *Pueblo enfermo* (A Sick People) (1909) or Rómulo **Gallegos** in ***Doña Bárbara*** (1929) – there was an obvious problem with the idea that 'culture' or civilization came from somewhere else (the capital city, the major port or, ultimately, from Europe). The crisis of the model is perhaps most acute in *Os sertões*, as da Cunha is attentive to the horror of the notion of 'civilization' imposed at bayonet point or by cannon shot. In his account of the military campaigns against the messianic settlement of Canudos in the Brazilian interior, it seems that the only way to 'civilize' the fanatics of Canudos is to kill them all, suggesting deep problems with the model of civilization that drove the ideologues of the new Brazilian liberal republic.

In the 1960s, critiques of Sarmiento centred on dependency theory, with its questioning of the notions of cultural superiority and inferiority in relations between metropoles and peripheries. To give one example among many, Noé Jitrik's work on Sarmiento and on what he termed 'bipolarities' in Argentine thought (civilization/barbarism, country/city, **Boedo vs Florida**, etc.) were vexed by an inevitable circularity of argument. Much subsequent work in cultural theory, such as that of Angel **Rama**, Antônio **Cândido**, Roberto **Fernández Retamar** and Antonio **Cornejo Polar**, was based implicitly on these critiques of static ideas of 'civilization' and 'barbarism'. Beatriz **Sarlo**, in her work on Buenos Aires as a space of 'peripheral modernity', can also be considered a belated response to Sarmiento.

While Sarmiento's thoughts on 'civilization and barbarism' (and his later reflections on race, particularly in his later positivist works) are easy to critique today, his portrait of the gaucho and of that archetypal gaucho *caudillo* Facundo Quiroga make for one of the most lasting works of Latin American literature. One of the stunning contradictions of *Facundo* is the Byronic or daemonic power of the protagonist, and the ways in which Sarmiento's language is particularly vivid at the moment he evokes what he claims to most despise. Borges's 1925 poem 'El general Quiroga va en coche a la muerte' (General Quiroga Rides to Death in a Carriage) is just one example of the spellbinding power of Sarmiento's monumental and ultimately tragic conception of his anti-hero.

Further reading

Fishburn, E. (1997) 'Civilisation and Barbarism', in V. Smith (ed.), *Encyclopedia of Latin American Literature*, London: Fitzroy Dearborn, 204–5.

Salomon, N. (1984) *Realidad, ideología y literatura en el Facundo de D. F. Sarmiento*, Amsterdam: Rodopi.

Sarmiento, D.F. (1868) *Life in the Argentine Republic in the Days of the Tyrants or Civilization and Barbarism*, trans. M.P. Mann, New York: Hurd & Houghton; subsequent facsimile eds.

——(1977) *Facundo; o civilización y barbarie*, ed. and intro. N. Jitrik, Caracas: Biblioteca Ayacucho.

Sorensen, D. (1996) *Facundo and the Construction of Argentine Culture*, Austin: University of Texas Press.

DANIEL BALDERSTON

Clarke, Austin M.

b. 1934, St Matthias, Barbados

Novelist

Clarke's work addresses the problem of being Caribbean in Canada. He studied economics at the University of Toronto and has taught at several universities in the USA. For a time he worked as a broadcaster. He has lived in Toronto since 1955. He is author of six novels: a trilogy beginning with *The Meeting Point* (1967); and the story collections *When He Was Free and Young and He Used to Wear Silks* (1971), about Anancy, the mythical Caribbean trickster, *When Women Rule* (1985), and *Nine Men Who Laughed* (1986). He has written an autobiography, *Growing Up Stupid Under the Union Jack* (1980), and his essay, 'Exile', appears in the anthology *Altogether Elsewhere* (1994), edited by Marc Robinson. His most recent novel, *The Polished Hoe* (2003), is the story of a black matriarch on the fictional island of Bimshire (closely based on Barbados) whose murder of a white overseer is the occasion for a confession that is also a history of the island.

Further reading

Algoo Baksh, S. (1994) *Austin C. Clarke: A Biography*, Toronto; Barbados: ECW and University of the West Indies Press.

Baugh, E. (1980) 'Friday in Crusoe's City: The Question of Language in Two West Indian Novels of Exile', *ACLALS-Bulletin* 5.3: 1–12.

Clarke, A.M. (1999) *Pigtails 'n' Breadfruit: The Rituals of Slave Food, A Barbadian Memoir*, Toronto: Random House Canada.

KEITH JARDIM

Cliff, Michelle

b. 1946, Kingston, Jamaica

Writer

Born in Jamaica, Cliff grew up in New York. The prose poem *Claiming an Identity They Taught Me to Despise* (1980) and the novels *Abeng* (1984) and *No Telephone to Heaven* (1987) establish Cliff's central autobiographical theme of a light-skinned Jamaican's desire to claim her African heritage. Her *Land of Look Behind* (1985), prose poetry, and the powerful short stories of *Bodies of Water* (1990) explore issues of migration and fractured identity. The novel *Free Enterprise* (1993) mixes historical and fictional characters and deals with slavery in the USA and its aftermath.

Further reading

Brice-Finch, J. (1996) 'Michelle Cliff', in B. Lindfors and R. Sander (eds) *Twentieth Century*

Caribbean and African Writers, Detroit: Gale Research, third series, 157, 49–58.
Cliff, M. (1998) *The Store of a Million Items: Stories*, Boston: Houghton, Mifflin.

ELAINE SAVORY

Cobo Borda, Juan Gustavo

b. 1948, Santafé de Bogotá, Colombia

Poet, essayist and literary critic

In *La tradición de la pobreza* (Tradition of Poverty) (1980), Cobo Borda affirms that in the history of Colombian literature there are very few who really deserve to be called poets. His own poetry is often hilarious or sarcastic, or celebrates popular culture. Among his collections of poems are: *Consejos para sobrevivir* (Advice on Survival) (1974), *Ofrenda en el altar del bolero* (Offering on the Altar of Bolero) (1981) and *Todos los poetas son santos e irán al cielo* (All Poets are Saints and Will Go to Heaven) (1983).

Further reading

Cobo Borda, Juan Gustavo (1995) *Historia portátil de la poesía colombiana, 1880–1995*, Bogotá: TM Editores.

MIGUEL A. CARDINALE

Coelho, Paulo

b. 1947, Rio de Janeiro, Brazil

Writer

Latin America's best-selling New Age author (see **best-sellers**), Coelho became known around the world for *O alquimista* (The Alchemist) (1988), which has been translated into numerous languages. In his youth, he was committed several times to mental hospitals and subjected to electroshock treatments; he has used this experience as a vehicle to talk about the need for human beings to look for their destiny within. His first career was as a writer of rock lyrics for artists such as Elis Regina and others; some of his songs were considered subversive and he was imprisoned and tortured by the Brazilian military regime in 1974. His first book *O peregrino* (The Pilgrimage) (1987) was an account of his experience walking to the great medieval pilgrimage church of Santiago de Compostela in Galicia, Spain. He has published seven more books since then, selling over 23 million copies to date. He was invited to speak at the World Economic Forum in 1998 and 1999, and spoke on the need to respect spirituality and culture. In an interview with the BBC hosted by Tim Sebastian, broadcast in early 2000, he stated that 'When you want something the whole world conspires to help you get it'; his optimistic message has obviously been well received by many readers, although his writing has yet to be taken seriously by literary critics.

Further reading

Coelho, P. (2001) *Histórias para pais, filhos e netos*, São Paulo: Globo.

DANIEL BALDERSTON

Collins, Merle

b. 1950, Aruba, Netherlands Antilles

Poet, novelist and scholar

Collins's work addresses the Caribbean populations' diasporic foundations and experiences, which are representatively embodied by her life and career in the Caribbean, USA and UK. She explores these themes in works such as her 1992 poetry collection, *Rotten Pomerack*, and the 1995 novel, *The Colour of Forgetting*. Collins weaves the stories or sings the emotion of personal memories, which are narrated against the grain of official history by voices ranging freely over and on the back of oral traditions, myth, education, family and nation.

Further reading

Collins, M. (1995) *The Colour of Forgetting*, London: Virago Press.

JOHN D. PERIVOLARIS

Collyer, Jaime

b. 1955, Santiago, Chile

Writer

Collyer has published novels and short stories, including the novels *Infiltrado* (The Infiltrator) (1989), *Cien pájaros volando* (100 Birds Flying) (1995) and the collection of short stories *Gente al acecho* (People on the Prowl) (1992). He lived in Madrid, Spain from 1981 to 1991, when he returned to Chile. Once in Chile he contributed to the post-dictatorship renewal of writing and publishing, working as an editor at the publishing company Planeta Chilena and as a regular contributor to the leftist magazine *Apsi* and the newspaper *La Epoca*. The ironic and humorous stories included in *Gente al acecho* have won literary prizes in Spain, Cuba and Chile.

Further reading

Collyer, Jaime (1998) *La bestia en casa*, Santiago de Chile: Alfaguara.

AMALIA PEREIRA

Collymore, Frank

b. 1893, Woodville, Barbados; d. 1980, Woodville

Writer

As editor of the magazine *Bim*, Collymore played a central role in the growth and development of Caribbean literature from the 1940s onwards, publishing the work of George **Lamming** and Austin **Clarke** among many others. His acknowledged importance in that role, however, has unfortunately led to a neglect of his own writing; his five volumes of poetry, gathered in the *Collected Poems* (1968), and his short stories which, while set in the Caribbean, address issues of wider resonance – madness (in 'Shadows') (1942), loneliness ('Rewards and Chrysanthemum') (1961) and the power of atavistic forces (in his poem 'Hymn to the Sea' (1959)) for example.

Further reading

Barrat, H. (1990) 'The Short Stories of Frank Collymore', *Bim* 73.

Baugh, E. (1973) 'Frank Collymore: A Biographical Portrait', *Savacou* 7–8: 139–48.

Brown, L. (1978) *West Indian Poetry*, Boston: Twayne.

Collymore, F. (1957) *Notes for a Glossary of Words and Phrases of Barbadian Dialect*, Bridgetown, Barbados: Advocate Co.

—— (1968) *Collected Poems*, Bridgetown: Advocate.

MIKE GONZALEZ

Coloane, Francisco

b. 1910, Chiloe, Chile

Writer

Coloane's writing returns to the traditional themes of the struggle between man and nature in the southernmost part of Chile, in Patagonia, the southern seas and Tierra del Fuego, where he grew up. Moving to Santiago, he worked as a journalist and published his collections of stories *El último grumete de La Baquedano* (La Baquedano's Last Cabin Boy) and *Cabo de Hornos* (Cape Horn) (both 1941). The novel *Los conquistadores de la Antártida* (Conquerors of the Antarctic) (1945) and the collection of short stories *Tierra del fuego* (1956), among others, followed. In 1964 he was awarded the National Literature Prize.

Further reading

Coloane, F. (1999) *Cuentos completos*, Madrid: Alfaguara.

Droguett, C. (1974) 'Francisco Coloane, o la séptima parte visible', *Mensaje* 235: 620–30.

Petreman, D. (1987) *La obra narrativa de Francisco Coloane*, Santiago: Editorial Universitaria.

CELINA MANZONI

Colombia

The poetry of the early twentieth century in Colombia certainly developed under the influence and inspiration of José Asunción Silva, although he died in 1896 at the age of 31. Perhaps as a result of the violence endemic to Colombia's post-independence history, and particularly the opening years of the twentieth century, there is a pervasive sense of isolation and withdrawal among Colombian poets. The avant-garde writers, though largely unrecognized, built on Silva's legacy of symbolism and linguistic experiment. León **de Greiff**, for example, explored a range of formal and linguistic innovations in his *Libro de signos* (Book of Signs) (1930); so too did the poets of the Piedra y Cielo group, particularly Arturo Camacho Ramírez. Other members of this important, but largely unrecognized, group included Luis Vidales, Jorge Zalamea, Fernando **Charry Lara** and Aurelio Arturo.

José Eustacio **Rivera**'s *La vorágine* (The Vortex) (1924) is universally acknowledged as the classic prose work of Colombian literature. It is a slightly curious fusion of two traditions. On the one hand, it belongs within a tradition of ***regionalismo*** that represents the struggle between the human and nature as a prelude to development; on the other it is a representation of a highly modernist inner struggle within its protagonist, Arturo Cova. His contemporary Tomás Carrasquilla, by contrast, writes within a *costumbrista* (see ***costumbrismo***) mould of provincial realism, but without Rivera's powerful sense of the dynamics of change.

The works of José María **Vargas Vila** offer a critical view of the traditional provincial world, while Eduardo **Zalamea Borda**'s *Cuatro años a bordo de mí mismo* (Four Years Aboard Myself) (1934) narrates the tensions between rural and urban worlds.

In 1948, the popular Liberal Presidential candidate Jorge Eliécer Gaitán was murdered in Bogotá. Three days of rioting followed which then ignited (or re-ignited) simmering social and regional conflicts in both provincial cities and the countryside. The result was a fourteen-year period of armed confrontation across the country which came to be known as La Violencia. It was a time when political life entered into the kind of suspended animation represented in Gabriel **García Márquez**'s *La mala hora* (In Evil Hour) (1962) where the only change was a kind of permanent decay.

García Márquez was a member of the **Grupo de Barranquilla** and associated with the journal *Mito*; their collective work was a critique of the conservatism of the Colombian literary establishment and its hostility to international literary developments. Thus García Márquez, like the other members of the group, was an enthusiastic reader of William Faulkner, Virginia Woolf and Franz Kafka, from whom he derived that fusion of the real and the imagined later defined as **magical realism**. Macondo, the town at the centre of his series of novels the high point of which was ***Cien años de soledad*** (One Hundred Years of Solitude) (1967), was a fictional place based on the real lowland town of Aracataca. For García Márquez, the eruption of the banana companies into northern Colombia (chronicled in his first novel *La hojarasca* (Leafstorm) (1955) as well as in Alvaro Cepeda Samudio's *La casa grande* (The Big House) (1962)) and La Violencia were the key moments of Colombian history. Indeed, it was a reference point for a whole generation of Colombian artists – the poets of **Nadaísmo**, for example, responded with a kind of literary anarchism. Other writers also focused on the decade and a half of violence. Gustavo **Alvarez Gardeazábal**'s ***Cónres no entierran todos los días*** (1972) addresses its impact in the Cauca Valley while Jorge Eliécer Pardo looks at its effects in the Tolima region in *El jardín de las Hartmann* (The Garden of the Hartmann Women) (1978).

Other writers of this generation, such as Manuel **Mejía Vallejo**, Héctor Rojas Herazo, Pedro **Gómez Valderrama** and Alvaro **Mutis**, have created a significant body of fiction, and Mutis is also one of Colombia's premier poets.

It can hardly be said that violence has ceased to be a feature of Colombian society since the end of La Violencia. On the other hand, the new generation of writers emerging since the early 1970s has addressed different issues. R.H. **Moreno-Durán** began by writing a very dense, almost postmodernist prose before moving towards historical chronicles in the 1980s, while the poetry of Darío **Jaramillo Agudelo** has moved from the ironic tones of his early work towards a more intimate tone in the 1990s. Albalucía **Angel**'s work has evolved from an early concern with La Violencia towards feminist themes. Fanny **Buitrago**, for her part, derives her material, linguistic and social, from the popular cultural practices of

Colombia's Caribbean coast. Recently, new women writers have appeared in the national cultural landscape with interesting and new literary proposals such as Laura Restrepo and Consuelo Triviño. In recent times, a body of testimonial literature has appeared, including the work of Germán **Castro Caycedo**. The rediscovery of the city as a multicultural space engaged narrators from different generations such as Andrés Caicedo, whose *Qué viva la música* (Long Live Music) (1977), his only novel, was set in Cali, and Fernando **Vallejo**, whose highly successful novel *La virgen de los sicarios* (Our Lady of the Assassins) (1998) was made into a successful film, as well as the writers Luis Fayad, and Santiago Gamboa.

The **essay** has been a historically vital genre in Colombia, and remains so today. Germán **Arciniegas** and Otto **Morales Benítez** have been among the most productive: written in the tradition of the 'man of letters' rather than the specialist, their essays cover a broad range of topics, from the cultural to the historical and political. Colombian poet and literary critic Juan Gustavo **Cobo Borda** is the most recent intellectual joining this venerable tradition, publishing several wide-ranging volumes of essays. Another respected essayist in Colombian literary circles is Rafael **Gutiérrez Girardot**, whose interdisciplinary academic training allows him to approach literature as an encoding of political, philosophical and social imperatives.

Further reading

Echeverría, Rogelio (1992) *Antologia de la poesía colombiana*, Bogotá: Editorial Carlos Valencia Editores.

Giraldo, Luz Mery (2000) *Ciudades escritas*, Bogotá: Edición Convenio Andrés Bello.

—— (2000) *Narrativa colombiana: Búsqueda de un nuevo canon, 1975–1995*, Santa Fé de Bogotá: Centro Editorial Javeriano, Pontificia Universidad Javeriana.

Jaramillo, M.M. *et al.* (2000) *Literatura y cultura colombiana: Narrativa colombiana del siglo XX*, Bogotá: Ministerio de Cultura.

Williams, R. (1991) *The Colombian Novel: 1844–1987*, Austin: University of Texas Press.

RAYMOND L. WILLIAMS AND ALVARO BERNAL

Como agua para chocolate

Laura **Esquivel**'s *Como agua para chocolate* (Like Water for Chocolate) (1989) was an international phenomenon as both novel and film, and forms part of a best-selling boom in Latin American **women's writing** (see **best-sellers**). This woman-centred narrative focuses on three generations of land-holding female members of the de la Garza family, who reside on the Mexican side of the USA–Mexico border. A core section of this historical melodrama, largely set between 1895 and 1934, focuses on the period of the 1910 Mexican Revolution, the event that marks Mexico's entry into modernity. Unlike the traditional **novel of the Mexican Revolution**, in *Como agua para chocolate* the Revolution is of secondary importance; the focus is on how Tita breaks from the family tradition that the youngest daughter is obligated to remain unwed in order to care for her mother during her old age. The privileged site for social change in this film is within the domestic sphere. Tita's role as caretaker and carrier of tradition proves to be a vantage point in her quest to wed Pedro who, given Tita's unavailability, marries her older sister to be near his loved one. With the kitchen as centre of Tita's universe, her culinary skills give her power over family members and friends. Through food Esquivel employs magical realist techniques (see **magical realism**) to underscore the ritual function of food as a spiritual code for communication. Mexico, in this narrative, is associated with exotic and sensual food, given the narrative's structural organization around the cookbook genre; each chapter is preceded by a recipe. National gastronomic delights stand in for eminently consumable and exportable images of Mexico. The spatial focus on the kitchen underscores the maternal-feminine space *par excellence.* The Revolution provides the moment for representing shifting gender power relations and generational tensions. As of 1992, Esquivel's novel had been translated into over twenty-four languages. Its US publisher, Doubleday, issued the novel in both Spanish and English editions, both of which sold phenomenally well. *Like Water for Chocolate* was in the top ten *New York Times* best-seller list for thirty-nine weeks, making it the only Latin American novel to have remained among the top ten best-sellers for such an uninterrupted period.

Director Alfonso Arau's 1991 film adaptation was one of the Mexican film industry's biggest international successes of the 1990s. The film broke international box-office records and became one of the highest earning foreign language films in the USA, having grossed, as of 1996, $22 million on its theatrical release.

Further reading

Noriega, C. and S. Ricci *The Mexican Cinema Project*, Los Angeles: UCLA Film and Television Archives.

Wu, H. (2000) 'Consuming Tacos and Enchiladas: Gender and nation in *Como agua para chocolate*', in C. Noriega (ed.), *Visible Nations*, Minneapolis: University of Minnesota Press, 174–92.

SERGIO DE LA MORA

Companhia das Letras

Companhia das Letras is an important São Paulo publishing house, founded by Luís Schwarz in the late 1980s, which has set new standards for books with a broad-based academic appeal and has continually expanded in the 1990s. Its success is largely due to an intelligent choice of best-selling and 'prestige' titles and (an innovation in this type of publishing) an efficient and reliable system of payment to authors. Companhia das Letras has also taken initiatives such as paying authors of possible best-sellers stipends while they write, and promoting Brazilian literature abroad.

See also: best-sellers

Further information

http://www.companhiadasletras.com.br

JOHN GLEDSON

Compère Général Soleil

Compère Général Soleil (Comrade General Sun) (1955) was Jacques Stephen **Alexis**'s first novel, dealing with a 1937 massacre of Haitian cane-cutters in the Dominican Republic. Alexis practises a form of social realism in the detailed depiction of the misery of the protagonist, Hilarius Hilarion, and in his biting satire of the Haitian elite. The novel's views of Haitian culture are not dissimilar from those found in Jacques **Roumain**'s ***Gouverneurs de la rosée*** (Masters of the Dew) (1944), but Alexis's work is marked by a dense, episodic style that draws on Alejo **Carpentier**'s theory of *lo* ***real maravilloso*** (marvellous realism). In the story, the epileptic hero, ostracized because of his illness, becomes politicized in prison but pays with his life for his involvement in the cane-cutters' strike.

Further reading

Alexis, J.S. (1999) *General Sun, My Brother*, Charlottesville: University Press of Virginia.

Nourrisier, F. (1955) 'Jacques Stéphen Alexis: *Compère Géneral Soleil*', *Nouvelle Revue Française* 34: 787–8.

J. MICHAEL DASH

concrete poetry

Concrete poetry was an organized international avant-garde (see **avant-garde in Latin America**) movement of the 1950s and 1960s. The prime exponents of these experiments in lyric and spatial minimalism were the co-founders, Swiss-Bolivian poet Eugen Gomringer (b. 1924) and the **Noigandres group** of Brazil. The cosmopolitan movement owes much to productions and conceptualizations in Brazil, where *poesia concreta* evolved in three phases. In its initial years (1952–6), prime procedures included desentimentalization and visual shaping, including colourizing. 'Classical' or 'orthodox' material emerged during a second period (1956–61) that involved ultra-rational principles of composition and extensive theorization, including the manifesto 'pilot plan for concrete poetry' (see **manifestos**). In a third stage, from 1962 onwards, open notions of 'invention' led to different practices, from semantic variations to word collages and abstract designs with lexical keys. Several splinter-groups appeared: *neo-concretismo* (1957), the politically charged *poesia praxis* (1962) and the graphically oriented *poema processo* (1967). Of the original Noigandres trio, the later work of Augusto de **Campos** is the most influenced by the movement itself, which was over by the early 1970s. Non-denominational mixtures of words and text in the 1970s and 1980s which show the influence of concrete poetry, whether by original concrete poets or the next generation, can be placed under the rubric of 'intersemiotic creation'.

Since the 1960s, the term 'concrete poetry' has been used to refer to various kinds of alphabetic, verbal and semi-verbal experiments on the printed page, many of which fall short of the profoundly poetic and conceptual 'high' concretism of Brazil, which tried to reconcile social realities, formal research and advances in communication media, incorporating and anticipating technological progress in poetry.

The contributions of Spanish America to concrete poetry were limited. Gomringer wrote a few texts in Spanish, and Solt includes one Mexican artist. As the essays in the volume edited by Espinoza show, later related production in the River Plate region (for example, Clemente Padín) tends more towards visual poetry and other modes of experimentation.

Further reading

Espinosa, C. (ed.) (1990) *Corrosive Signs: Essays on Experimental Poetry (Visual, Concrete, Alternative)*, Washington DC: Maisonneuve Press.

Perrone, C. (1996) *Seven Faces: Brazilian Poetry since Modernism*, Durham, NC: Duke University Press.

—— (1997) 'Concrete Poetry', in V. Smith (ed.), *Encyclopedia of Latin American Literature*, London: Fitzroy Dearborn, 219–20.

Poetics Today (1982) special issue, 3(3).

Solt, M. (ed.) (1970) *Concrete Poetry: A World View*, Bloomington: Indiana University Press.

Williams, E. (1967) *An Anthology of Concrete Poetry*, New York: Something Else Press.

CHARLES A. PERRONE

Condé, Maryse

b. 1934, Pointe-à-Pitre, Guadeloupe

Writer

A novelist whose writing career began in 1976 with the publication of *Heremakhonon*, Condé has become one of the pre-eminent writers of the French Caribbean. Her work spans the African diaspora from West Africa to the Caribbean to the North American continent. In 1959 she married Mamadou Condé, an actor from Africa, and moved to the Ivory Coast. Her second novel, *Une saison à Rihata* (A Season at Rihata) (1981), is the story of an unhappy marriage between Marie-Hélène, far from her native home in Guadeloupe, and her African husband, Zek.

Condé's reputation was established with the publication of *Ségou* in 1984, which narrates the history of Africa on the eve of the slave trade. Her next novel, *Moi, Tituba, sorcière noire de Salem* (I, Tituba, Black Witch of Salem) (1986), creates a fictional narrative of the slave from Barbados who became the only black victim of the Salem witch trials. *Traversée de la mangrove* (Crossing the Mangrove Swamp) (1989) is a story of the mystery surrounding the death of a young outsider found face down in the mud near a small village in Guadeloupe. Whether they loved him, hated him or feared him, every villager has an opinion, and each holds a piece of the puzzle of his death. *Les derniers rois mages* (The Last Magi) (1993) is a story of exile and lost origins which tells of an African king, Behanzin, exiled to Martinique for his opposition to French colonialism. As the novel follows the lives of his offspring in the Caribbean and the USA, it paints a picture of the diversity of the African diaspora. *La migration des coeurs* (The Migration of Hearts) (1995) retells the Emily Brontë novel *Wuthering Heights*, setting the tale of obsessive love in nineteenth-century Guadeloupe and Cuba.

Condé received her doctorate in Comparative

Literature at the Université de Paris in 1975, her research focusing on black stereotypes in Caribbean literature. She spent many years teaching French in Guinea, Ghana and Senegal. Since 1995, she has taught French Caribbean Literature at Columbia University and divides her time between New York City and Guadeloupe. Richard Philcox, her second husband (she remarried in 1982), is the English translator of the majority of her novels.

Further reading

Kadir, D. (ed.) (1993) 'Focus on Maryse Condé', special issue of *World Literature Today* 67(4).

Perret, D. and M.-D. Shelton, (eds) (1995) 'Maryse Condé', special issue of *Callaloo* 18(3): 535–711.

Soirieau, M.-A. (1997) 'Maryse Condé', in V. Smith (ed.), *Encyclopedia of Latin American Literature*, London: Fitzroy Dearborn, 220–2.

CAROL J. WALLACE

Cóndores no entierran todos los días

Cóndores no entierran todos los días (They Don't Bury Condors Every Day) (1972), a novel by the Colombian writer Gustavo **Alvarez Gardeazábal**, exemplifies the literature of La Violencia, the brutal period following the assassination of Liberal leader Jorge Eliecer Gaitán on 9 April 1948. Amidst a fast-paced recollection of events, it narrates the story of León María Lozano, the head of the death squads of the Conservative party in the author's home town, Tuluá, a city near Cali in western Colombia. The 1984 film version, directed by Francisco Norden and starring Frank Ramírez, represents the first major international success of Colombian cinema, receiving awards at the Chicago, Huelva, Havana and Biarritz film festivals.

Further reading

Williams, R.L. (ed.) (1977) *Aproximaciones a Gustavo Alvarez Gardeazábal*, Bogotá: Plaza y Janés.

HÉCTOR D. FERNÁNDEZ L'HOESTE

Confiant, Raphael

b. 1951, Fort-de-France, Martinique

Novelist and essayist

The most outspoken member of the ***créolité*** movement, to whose manifesto, *Éloge de la créolité* (In Praise of *Créolité*) he also contributed, Confiant wrote his first novels entirely in creole. International success came, however, with a stream of novels written in a creative combination of French and creole, of which the best known are *Le nègre et l'amiral* (The Black Guy and the Admiral) in 1988, *L'allée des soupirs* (The Walkway of Sighs) in 1994 and *La vierge du grand retour* (The Virgin's Great Comeback) in 1996. His novels are as outrageously ribald as his essays are provocative, the most important of the latter being his critique of **Césaire**, *Aimé Césaire, une traversée paradoxale du siècle* (Aimé Césaire, A Paradoxical Journey Across the Century), in 1993.

Further reading

Chamoiseau, P. and R. Confiant (1991) *Lettres créoles: Tracées Antillaises et continentales de la littérature 1635–1975*, Paris: Hatier.

Confiant, Raphael (2001) *Brin d'amour: Roman*, Paris: Mercure de France.

—— (2001) *Dictionnaire des néologismes creoles*, Petit-Bourg, Guadeloupe: Ibis rouge and Presses universitaires créoles/GEREC-F.

J. MICHAEL DASH

Contemporáneos

The Contemporáneos were a group of young writers who in the 1920s rallied round the literary journal *Contemporáneos*, published in Mexico City from 1928 to 1931. They played an important role in the intense discussions that followed the 1910 Revolution, arguing for a cosmopolitan Mexican literature aware of its own roots but in touch with innovative international developments. Jaime **Torres Bodet**, Bernardo Ortiz de Montellano, José **Gorostiza**, Carlos **Pellicer** and Enrique González Rojo were the nucleus of the group; later members included Salvador **Novo**, Xavier **Villaurrutia**, Jorge Cuesta and Gilberto **Owen**. The group is considered one of the most distinguished in twentieth-century Mexican letters.

Further reading

Forster, M. (1964) *Los Contemporáneos, 1928–1932, perfil de un experimento vanguardista mexicano*, Mexico City: Ediciones de Andrea.

Maristany, L. (1992) *Contemporáneos: Poesías*, Madrid: Anaya.

Olea Franco, R. and A. Stanton (eds) (1994) *Los Contemporáneos en el laberinto de la crítica*, Mexico City: El Colegio de México.

Sheridan, G. (1985) *Los Contemporáneos ayer*, Mexico City: Fondo de Cultura Económica.

MERLIN H. FORSTER

Conti, Haroldo

b. 1925, Chacabuco, Argentina; d. 1976, place unknown

Writer

Conti's early work was largely descriptive; journeys and wanderings set in motion long, melancholy meditations on reality in his novels *Sudeste* (Southeast) (1962) and *En vida* (In My Lifetime) (1971). His later work brought changes in literary style which corresponded to the writer's growing political involvement; they increasingly embraced the exhilaration and richness of **magical realism**, as in his 1975 novel *Mascaró, el cazador americano* (Mascaró the Latin American Hunter). One year after its publication, he joined the list of Argentine writers who 'disappeared' during the Videla dictatorship.

Further reading

Conti, H. (1998) *Sudeste; Ligados*, Paris: Colección Archivos.

Restivo, N. and C. Sánchez (1986) *Haroldo Conti, con vida*, Buenos Aires: Nueva Imagen.

Romano, E. (1986) *Haroldo Conti: Mascaró*, Buenos Aires: Hachette.

JULIO PREMAT

Contorno

A combative journal associated with a group of angry young men that Emir **Rodríguez Monegal** called the *generación de los parricidas* (the generation of parricides), who were drawn to the Sartrean idea of *littérature engagée*. The names associated with the journal were David **Viñas** and his brother Ismael, Tulio Halperin Donghi, Adolfo Prieto, Noé **Jitrik**, Ramón Alcalde, Leon Rozitchner, Rodolfo **Kusch** and Juan José Sebreli, although eventually the Viñas brothers were the most directly involved. At the time of the founding of the journal, the group felt alienated in a society dominated by Peronism, and after the fall of Perón in 1955, Halperin Donghi published an article in the journal that traced continuities from fascism to Peronism; later, several of those who had been associated with *Contorno*, particularly the Viñas brothers, were drawn into the Peronist Left. The ten issues of the journal (which have been studied in a useful book by William Katra, *Contorno: Literary Engagement in Post-Peronist Argentina* (1988)) appeared at irregular intervals; *Contorno* also published a few books and pamphlets. The idea of the responsibilities of the intellectual to society evolved over time from 'engaged' literary criticism to political analysis and theory, and then to political action. In the final issues, Rozitchner and Ismael Viñas called on the middle-class intellectual (see **intellectuals**) to take a vanguard position in the coming proletarian revolution.

Further reading

Croce, M. (1996) *Contorno: Izquierda y proyecto cultural*, Buenos Aires: Colihue.

Katra, W.H. (1988) *Contorno: Literary engagement in post-Peronist Argentina*, Rutherford, NJ: Fairleigh Dickinson University Press.

DANIEL BALDERSTON

Contreras, Gonzalo

b. 1958, Santiago, Chile

Writer

Contreras's first novel *La ciudad anterior* (The City Before) (1991) was one of the best-selling novels published in Chile after the country's return to democracy. The novel, about a small-time arms dealer who travels to a mysterious town in the northern desert, alludes to Chile's politically repressive and violent recent past. It won *El Mercurio*'s literary competition in 1991. His *El nadador* (The Swimmer) (1995) is set in Santiago and deals with the upheavals experienced by a family living in a rapidly changing and modernizing country. Contreras's third novel, *El gran mal* (The Great Evil), was published in 1998.

Further reading

Contreras, Gonzalo (1995) *El nadador*, Mexico City: Aguilar, Altea, Taurus, Alfaguara.

AMALIA PEREIRA

Cony, Carlos Heitor

b. 1926, Rio de Janeiro, Brazil

Writer

A leading figure of the left-wing opposition to military rule in Brazil, Cony distinguished himself as a prolific novelist and essayist. He has written several regular columns in major national newspapers, including *Correio da Manhã* and *Folha de São Paulo*. His most acclaimed novel, *Pessach: A travessia* (Passover: The Crossing), from 1967, narrates the story of a novelist who joins the urban guerrilla movement on his fortieth birthday, a radical life change which parallels the gradual acceptance of his Jewish heritage.

Further reading

Cony, Carlos Heitor (2001) *Pilatos: Romance*, São Paulo: Companhia das Letras.

CHRISTOPHER DUNN

Copi

b. 1937, Buenos Aires, Argentina; d. 1987, Paris, France

Writer and actor

Copi (Raúl Damonte) was a member of an important Uruguayan-Argentine family (his grandfather was Natalio Botana, founder of the journal *Crítica*). His father was a diplomat, whose itinerant lifestyle meant that Copi spent most of his childhood in Europe. When Copi was 22, his father sought political asylum in the Uruguayan embassy in Paris, and Copi himself remained in France as well. Most of his writing, including theatre, short stories and several comics, the best known of which is *La mujer sentada* (Seated Woman), is in French. Copi's work, which used stereotypes of Argentine and gay culture, initiated a kind of Argentine minimalism as well as a new form of non-representational realism.

Further reading

Aira, C. (1991) *Copi*, Rosario: Beatriz Viterbo.
Tcherkaski, J. (1998) *Habla Copi: Homosexualidad y creación*, Buenos Aires: Galerna.
—— (2000) *Eva Perón*, Buenos Aires: Adriana Hidalgo Editora.

GRACIELA MONTALDO

Cornejo Polar, Antonio

b. 1936, Lima, Peru; d. 1997, Lima

Literary critic

A dominant figure in Andean studies, professor and rector of the Universidad Mayor de San Marcos, founder (1975) and editor of ***Revista de crítica literaria latinoamericana***, Cornejo Polar also wrote one of the earliest (1973) and best studies of José María **Arguedas**. While his sustained emphasis was on Peruvian authors, notably on *indigenista* writers, through several collections of essays he also built a systematic cultural approach to literary studies by focusing on 'heterogeneity' as a defining term for Latin American literatures.

Literature as a social act, and literary systems as historical categories, link him to critics such as Angel **Rama**, Antonio **Candido** and Agustín Cueva. After leaving Peru, he taught at the University of Pittsburgh and at the University of California-Berkeley.

Further reading

Cornejo Polar, A. (1989) *La novela peruana*, Lima: Horizonte.

—— (1994) *Escribir en el aire, ensayo sobre la heterogeneidad sociocultural en las literaturas andinas*, Lima: Horizonte.

—— (1997) *Los universos narrativos de José María Arguedas*, Lima: Horizonte.

D'Allemand, P. (2001) 'Antonio Cornejo Polar: Sobre la heterogeneidad cultura y literaria en la América Latina', in *Hacia una crítica cultural latinoamericana*, Lima: Latinoamericana Editores, 127–56.

Grandis, R. de (2000) *Unforeseeable Americas: Questioning Cultural Hybridity in the Americas*, Amsterdam: Rodopi.

Moraña, M. (ed.) (1998) *Indigenismo hacia el fin del milenio: Homenaje a Antonio Cornejo Polar*, Pittsburgh: Instituto Internacional de Literatura Iberoamericana.

Schmidt, F. (ed.) (2000) *Antonio Cornejo Polar y los estudios latinoamericanos*, Pittsburgh: Instituto Internacional de Literatura Iberoamericana.

SAÚL SOSNOWSKI

Coronel Urtecho, José

b. 1906, Granada, Nicaragua; d. 1994, San Juan, Nicaragua

Writer

Known as the founding father of Nicaraguan poetry, in the early 1920s, together with Luis Alberto Cabrales, Coronel founded the Vanguardista movement which also included Pablo Antonio **Cuadra** and Joaquín **Pasos**. He had a profound influence on several generations of poets, from the first avant-garde (see **avant-garde in Latin America**) writers to Gioconda **Belli** and Daisy **Zamora**. His works include translations, poems and short stories that use avant-garde and surrealist (see **surrealism**) techniques to explore the effects of urban living, although he himself spent much of his life living in relative isolation near the Costa Rican border. His political positions, before and after 1979, were always ambiguous.

Further reading

Coronel Urtecho, J. (1985) *Prosa reunida*, Managua: Editorial Nueva Nicaragua.

Tirado, M. (1983) *Conversando con José Coronel Urtecho*, Managua: Editorial Nueva Nicaragua.

White, S. (1993) *Modern Nicaraguan Poetry: Dialogues with France and the United States*, London and Toronto: Associated University Press.

DEREK PETREY AND ILEANA RODRÍGUEZ

Corretjer, Juan Antonio

b. 1908, Ciales, Puerto Rico; d. 1985, San Juan, Puerto Rico

Writer

A member of the Nationalist Party and a friend of Pedro Albizu Campos, Corretjer was also imprisoned in the USA and accused of being involved in political violence in Puerto Rico. He founded the Socialist League to secure independence for Puerto Rico by any means. His poetry addresses Puerto Rico's Amerindian and African roots, the history of the peasants and workers, the struggle for independence, his love for his companion Consuelo Lee, his people and his nation. His poem 'Oubao Moin' was put to music and has become an unofficial national anthem.

Further reading

Corretjer, J.A. (1977) *Obras completas: Poesía*, intro.

J.L. Vega, San Juan: Instituto de Cultura Puertorriqueña.
Medina López, R.F. (1984) *Juan Antonio Corretjer, poeta nacional puertorriqueño*, San Juan: Instituto de Cultura Puertorriqueña.

MARÍA CRISTINA RODRÍGUEZ

Cortázar, Julio

b. 1914, Brussels, Belgium; d. 1984, Paris, France

Writer

Born in Brussels to Argentine parents, Cortázar was educated in Buenos Aires. His earliest works (essays, stories and two novels) were only published after his death. Cortázar's search for a distinctly personal voice and a world of his own was conducted in solitude, until he moved to France in 1951. His *Bestiario* (Bestiary) was published in that year, and was followed five years later by *Final del juego* (End of the Game). These two collections of stories contained many of his best-known pieces – such as 'La noche boca arriba' (The Night Upside Down), 'Axolotl' and 'La casa tomada' (The Occupied House) – and signalled an original form of fiction in which our perceptions of time, space and identity are systematically destabilized. His constant questioning of reality led to increasingly sharp and fantastic representations of the world, as in the perfect stories that comprise the 1966 volume, *Todos los fuegos el fuego* (Fire is Every Fire). With ***Rayuela*** (Hopscotch), in 1963, Cortázar embarked on a body of writing that exasperated all formal inquiry and moved instead into metafiction and the rituals of initiation. As with so many avant-gardists, Cortázar's aesthetic questioning led him towards the Left in politics. His involvement with the Cuban Revolution began in 1962; in the 1970s he was active in solidarity work with the Sandinista Revolution and with the victims of repression in the Southern Cone. In *El libro de Manuel* (Manuel's Book), published in 1973, his political commitment became explicit for the first time, albeit still in the context of the author's customary concerns, characters and situations. In the volumes of stories published between 1977 and 1983 – *Alguien que anda por ahí* (There's Someone Walking Around out There), *Queremos tanto a Glenda* (We Love Glenda So) and *Deshoras* (Out of Time) – Cortázar set aside some of his aesthetic concerns in order to place the representation of historical violence at the centre of his fiction. At the time of his death, in Paris in 1984, Cortázar was one of Latin America's most widely read writers.

Cortázar's work could be defined as an attempt to express duplicity – two versions of reality, two identities (formed of mirror images and arising from the discovery of an intimate Other), two sets of moral values and often two spatio-temporal systems (or two mutually contradictory diegeses that mysteriously combine). That duplicity is expressed in fantastic tales such as 'La noche boca arriba', where a traffic accident in a modern city coincides with an incident during a War of Flowers in pre-Columbian Mexico. This duplicity provokes an often quasi-mystical search for synthesis (as in his novels, *Los premios* (Prizes) (1960) and *62 modelo para armar* (62: A Model Kit) (1968)), which, as so often, induces his hero to magically slip from one space–time to another through the syntagmatic flow of language. As the familiar readings are transformed into a self-reflective discourse, it becomes clear that Cortázar yearns for a lost Eden (called 'the island at mid-day', 'the kibbutz of desire' or the 'artificial sky' in some texts), for values long since lost. This explains his interest in primitive societies, infantile perception, surrealism, Jungian archetypes, music (as the expression of a meaning both before and beyond meaning) and in a magical thought rooted in a pre- or a-logical terrain. This search for Utopia explains the writer's ideological evolution from the kibbutz of desire to a commitment to socialist ideals. At the same time, the dialectics of rebellion and legality, of desire and frustration, operate in all of Cortázar's work through humour and game-playing, particularly in the short texts collected in *Historias de cronopios y famas* (1962). Following on from the absurd humour of Macedonio **Fernández** and the speculations of Jorge Luis **Borges**, Cortázar's work gave new impetus to fantastic literature, multiplying the doubts, fables, invasions and the terrors that desire can evoke, yet sustaining throughout a stylistic and formal rigour.

In the 1960s Cortázar's work found a passionate readership among a younger generation of Latin Americans who identified with the irreverence, the valorization of the imaginary, the rebellion and the yearning for (social, sexual and discursive) liberation expressed in these texts. Of the writers of his generation only Gabriel **García Márquez** enjoyed a similar reputation in both Latin America and Europe. The wealth of translations, the success of Antonioni's film *Blow-Up*, based on a story from the 1959 volume *Las armas secretas* (The Secret Weapons), and the inclusion of his writings on countless student reading lists have contributed to the growing interest in his work. And yet Cortázar did not influence subsequent generations of writers, perhaps because his political development provoked public criticism of him by both the nationalist Left and the conservative Right. The recent publication of his complete works, however, including a number of unpublished texts, variations and drafts, have generated an affectionate complicity and a general agreement that, despite their occasional ideological naïvety, his texts are still extraordinary.

Further reading

Alazraki, J. (1994) *Hacia Cortázar: Aproximaciones a su obra*, Barcelona: Anthropos.

Alonso, C. (ed.) (1998) *Julio Cortázar; New Readings*, Cambridge: Cambridge University Press.

Cortázar, J. (1994) *Cuentos completos*, Madrid: Alfaguara, 2 vols.

—— (1994) *Obra crítica*, ed. S. Yurkievich, J. Alazraki and S. Sosnowski, Madrid: Alfaguara, 3 vols.

Ivask, I. and J. Alazraki (eds) (1978) *The Final Island: The Fiction of Cortázar*, Norman: University of Oklahoma Press.

Ortiz, Carmen (1994) *Julio Cortázar: Una estética de la búsqueda*, Buenos Aires: Almageste.

Picón Garfield, E. (1989) 'Julio Cortázar', in C.A. Solé and M.I. Abreu (eds), *Latin American Writers*, New York: Scribners, 3, 1177–93.

Yurkievich, S. (1994) *Julio Cortázar: Mundos y modos*, Madrid: Muchnik.

JULIO PREMAT

Cortés, Alfonso

b. 1893, León, Nicaragua; d. 1969, Managua, Nicaragua

Poet

One of Nicaragua's most important poets, Alfonso Cortés suffered from schizophrenic episodes and was committed to the Managua Asylum for the Insane where he spent over twenty-five years. He was discovered by José **Coronel Urtecho** and Ernesto **Cardenal**, who published one of his books. Works he wrote during and in-between his mental episodes are extremely varied in quality, ranging from works derivative of modernism and Parnassianism to bizarre, highly creative poems that incorporate philosophical and metaphysical inquiries into space, time and self-knowledge that question the principles of Catholic beliefs. His intellectual rebellion prefigures the attitudes of subsequent generations of vanguardist and revolutionary poets.

Further reading

Cortés, Alfonso (1968) *Treinta poemas*, Managua: Editorial Mundial.

—— (1981) *El tiempo es hambre y el espacio es frío*, Managua: Ed. Americanas.

Cortés Bendaña, M.L. (1975) *Alfonso Cortés, biografía*, León: Ed. Hospicio.

Varela-Ibarra, J. (1977) *La poesía de Alfonso Cortés*, León: Editorial Universitaria.

DEREK PETREY AND ILEANA RODRÍGUEZ

Cossa, Roberto

b. 1934, Buenos Aires, Argentina

Playwright

In the context of the 1976–83 military dictatorships in Argentina, Cossa's work took up the challenge of producing a critical theatre. In 1977, his *La nona* (Granny) opened, playing for two years. Its central figure, a senile Italian immigrant grandmother, is the grotesque embodiment of the promise to immigrants to 'make it in America'. Cossa participated in the Teatro Abierto 1981 movement, defying government repression of the arts, with a play about Italo-Argentine exiles in Italy, *Gris de ausencia* (The Greyness of Absence). Both plays depict the destruction of the family by a dictatorship that touted the family as a sacred national institution.

DAVID WILLIAM FOSTER

costumbrismo

The description of ordinary life in a particular milieu, especially of provincial, regional or rural life, *costumbrismo* was a favourite genre in nineteenth-century Spanish literature (with such authors as Larra, Mesonero Romanos, Pereda and Fernán Caballero), and spread early in Spanish America. The 'cuadro de costumbres' (sketch of manners and customs) influenced classic nineteenth-century works such as Esteban Echeverría's *El matadero* (The Slaughterhouse) (published posthumously in 1871), often claimed as the first Spanish American **short story**, Sarmiento's *Facundo* (translated as *Life in the Argentine Republic in the Days of the Tyrants*) (1845) with its descriptions of life on the *pampas*, and Jorge Isaacs's *María* (1867), with its descriptions of life on a Colombian plantation. The genre survived at least until the middle of the twentieth century in areas whose national culture depended to some extent on the idealization of a rural past, such as Uruguay (the 'nativist' tradition) and especially Costa Rica, where large anthologies of *costumbrista* writing have been compiled, and where the genre forms an important component of the literary canon.

Further reading

Bueno, S. (ed.) (1987) *Costumbristas cubanos del siglo XIX*, Caracas: Biblioteca Ayacucho.

Castro Rawson, M. (1966) *El costumbrismo en Costa Rica*, San José: Editorial Costa Rica.

Goic, C. (1991) 'Costumbres y experiencia', in *Historia y crítica de la literatura hispanoamericana*, Barcelona: Editorial Crítica, 2: 147–77.

Watson, M. (1979) *El cuadro de costumbres en el Perú decimonónico*, Lima: Pontificia Universidad Católica del Perú.

DANIEL BALDERSTON

Cote Lamus, Eduardo

b. 1928, Cúcuta, Colombia; d. 1964, Cúcuta

Poet

Although he attended law school in Bogotá, Cote Lamus later studied Spanish philology in Salamanca, thanks to a Spanish government scholarship. During his time in Spain, he established himself as poet and befriended many intellectuals, including writer Vicente Aleixandre. He then served in diplomatic positions in Glasgow and Frankfurt. In 1957 he returned to Colombia and pursued an expeditious political career, serving as secretary of education, congressman, senator and governor for his province. He was one of the founding members of the magazine *Mito* (Myth), marking an important moment in Colombia's cultural scene in the 1950s. His most mature work reflects the influence of T.S. Eliot.

Further reading

Cote Lamus, Fernando (1976) *Obra literaria*, Bogotá: Instituto Colombiano de Cultura.

HÉCTOR D. FERNÁNDEZ L'HOESTE

Coutinho, Afrânio

b. 1911, Salvador, Bahia, Brazil; d. Rio de Janeiro, Brazil

Critic

Afrânio Coutinho introduced literary historiography and aesthetic analyses to Brazilian audiences more familiar with impressionistic criticism. A staunch New Critic, Coutinho did much to anthologize and republish literature and literary criticism throughout Brazil. Many of his anthologies are used as textbooks, including the *Enciclopédia de literatura brasileira* (Encyclopedia of Brazilian literature) (1971). Coutinho offered his personal library to students and scholars via the Oficina Literária Afrânio Coutinho (OLAC) in Rio de Janeiro, a tradition continued by his daughter Graça Coutinho de Goes. Gregory Rabassa's 1969 translation of *Introdução à literatura brasileira* (An Introduction to Brazilian Literature) introduced Coutinho's work to English-speaking audiences.

Further reading

Coutinho, A. (1965) *Antologia brasileira de literatura*, Rio de Janeiro: Editôra Distribuidora de Livros Escolares.
—— (1990) *Crítica y poética*, São Paulo: Editora Civilizacao Brasileira.
—— (1992) *Conceitos da literatura brasilera*, São Paulo: Editora Ediouro.
Miscelânea de estudos literários: Homenagem a Afrânio Coutinho (1984) Rio de Janeiro: Pallas.

SUSAN CANTY QUINLAN

Cozarinsky, Edgardo

b. 1943, Buenos Aires, Argentina

Filmmaker and writer

Although Cozarinsky is largely known in Europe for his experimental films, he has also published numerous books of essays, often based on his contributions to periodicals such as *La nación, primera plana*, *Tiempo de cine* and *Panorama*, and books of short stories including *Vudú urbano* (Urban Voodoo) (1985) and *La novia de Odessa* (The Fiancée from Odessa) (2001). The title story of the latter collection is an outstanding text on Jewish immigration to Argentina. A recent collection of his *crónicas* (see **crónica**) is *El pase del testigo* (The Travels of the Witness) (2000). He has also written a book of criticism on Henry James and edited a well-known collection of the writings of **Borges** on cinema (1974, expanded edition 1978).

Further reading

Cozarinsky, E. (2001) *La novia de Odessa*, Buenos Aires: Sudamericana.
—— (2000) *El pase del testigo*, Buenos Aires: Sudamericana.

DANIEL BALDERSTON

Craig, Christine

b. 1943, Kingston, Jamaica

Writer

Craig is a poet, short story writer and writer of children's books as well as a working journalist. Her first volume of poems, *Quadrille for Tigers* (1984), was very strong, with very assured poems articulating social, political, racial and gender tensions in subtle and original ways, such as her well-known 'Crow Poem' and 'All Things Bright . . .'. She has said that her poetry is most realistic when it is most obscure; her gift is for unusual images of complex feeling. Her story collection *Mint Tea* (1993) is of uneven quality but contains some vivid portraits of Jamaican women.

Further reading

Craig, Christine (1993) *Mint Tea and Other Stories*, Oxford: Heinemann.

ELAINE SAVORY

créolité

A literary and cultural movement, *créolité* advocates the use of creole and is centred on the diverse, multi-ethnic identity of Martinique. Begun in Martinique in the 1900s, the movement was shaped by Edouard **Glissant**'s theories. It is as much a reaction against the Europeanization of France's overseas departments as a reaction against ***négritude***. Its ideas are expressed in the 1989 manifesto *Éloge de la créolité* (In Praise of Créolité) by Jean Bernabé, Patrick **Chamoiseau** and Raphael **Confiant**, the polemical articles in the weekly magazine *Antilla* and in the novels of Chamoiseau, Confiant and the Guadeloupeans Ernest Pepin and Gisele **Pineau**.

Further reading

Chamoiseau, P. and R. Confiant (1991) *Lettres créoles: Tracées Antillaises et continentales de la littérature 1635–1975*, Paris: Hatier.

J. MICHAEL DASH

Crespo, Luis Alberto

b. 1941, Carora, Venezuela

Poet

Crespo's first book, *Si el verano es dilatado* (If Summer is Late) (1968), revealed a very particular poetic voice full of the resonances of provincial speech and populated by images of the arid and luminous landscapes of his native region. His poetry has kept faith with that diction, at once archaic and despairing and employing a symbolic vocabulary determined by experiences of distance, solitude, desert and the emptiness of space. In 1991, he published his first anthology, *Como una orilla* (Like a Shore), and he has published tirelessly ever since: other works include *Duro* (Hard) (1995), *Más afuera* (Further Out) (1995) and *Solamente* (Only) (1996).

Further reading

Palacios, Antonia (1989) *Ficciones y aflicciones*, Caracas: Biblioteca Ayacucho.

RAFAEL CASTILLO ZAPATA

crime fiction

The dominant paradigms of the crime fiction genre are embedded in British and US literary history and bear the ideological imprint of their respective social contexts. The puzzle-solving British whodunit developed in the nineteenth century as a formula that displays aberrant criminal behaviour against the framework of a basically stable and secure society. The hard-boiled model which surfaced in the 1920s in the USA works, in contrast, to expose a violent and corrupt society in which crime is all-pervasive and institutions are distrusted. Works of both types were translated and widely distributed in Latin America, where writers also began to appropriate the genre as early as the late nineteenth century. The centres of crime fiction writing in Latin America are Argentina, Brazil, Cuba and Mexico, although important examples have been produced elsewhere including Colombia, Peru and Chile.

Latin American crime fiction writers often produce works that deliberately undermine the conventions of the genre in order to raise fundamental questions about truth, political order and economic justice. One of the best-known detective tales from Latin America, 'La muerte y la brújula' (Death and the Compass) (1942) by Argentine author Jorge Luis **Borges**, is a metaphysical reflection on time and space. The solution-oriented aim of the genre breaks down in this anti-detective story that locates the co-ordinates of the puzzle in a universe characterized by paradox and limitlessness. Another challenge to the ordering principle of conventional crime fiction was developed by Argentine authors of the 1970s such as Ricardo **Piglia**, who adopted the hard-boiled model to comment on institutionalized violence and injustice. A satirical mode is also common throughout Latin American crime fiction, where examples can be found even in the otherwise generally didactic works that have flourished in post-revolutionary Cuba.

The association of crime fiction with popular or 'low' culture is apparent in the ambivalence with which the Latin American literary elite has regarded the genre, especially the hard-boiled school of detective fiction. Crime fiction has consequently developed in some contexts, especially Argentina, as a site at which the territories of high and low culture, and the social identities attached to them, are explored and negotiated. Recent decades have seen a shift in the way that the genre marks boundaries between elite and popular culture, in part because of a developing market abroad for crime fiction by Latin American authors. Mexico's Paco Ignacio **Taibo II** and Brazil's Rubem **Fonseca** are two writers whose works have been translated and distributed abroad, thus reversing the pattern of a virtually exclusive importation of texts.

Further reading

Biron, R. (2000) *Murder and Masculinity: Violent Fictions of Twentieth-Century Latin America*, Nashville: Vanderbilt University Press.

Lafforgue, J. and J.B. Rivera (eds) (1977) *Asesinos de papel*, Buenos Aires: Calicanto.

Medeiros e Albuquerque, P. de (1979) *O mundo emocionante do romance policial*, Rio de Janeiro: Francisco Alves.

Nogueras, L. (1982) *Por la novela policial*, Havana: Ediciones Unión.

Simpson, A. (1990) *Detective Fiction from Latin America*, Rutherford, NJ: Fairleigh Dickinson University Press.

—— (1997) 'Detective Fiction', in V. Smith (ed.), *Encyclopedia of Latin American Literature*, London: Fitzroy Dearborn, 256–8.

AMELIA SIMPSON

criollismo

A term derived from *criollo*, *criollismo* is used to refer to a regionalist tendency in Spanish American writing in the first decades of the twentieth century (see ***regionalismo***), often associated with certain currents of *modernismo* (see **Spanish American modernism**) (although some claim that the gauchesque poem ***Martín Fierro*** of 1872–9 and the serial novels of Eduardo Gutiérrez as earlier examples of the tendency, because of their affirmation of local culture). Used in 1902 by Ernesto Quesada in the polemical essay *El criollismo en la literatura argentina* (*Criollismo* in Argentine Literature), the term was used in the following decades to designate literature that represented the local or national culture (as opposed to that of the immigrant masses); it is employed in that way by **Borges** in his essays of the 1920s, particularly in those of *El tamaño de mi esperanza* (The Shape of My Hope) (1926). In Uruguay and southern Brazil, the same tendency is often called *nativismo*. *Criollismo* was also a dominant tendency in Colombian and Venezuelan literature in the same period. The term is notable for its ambiguities, however, since it is often used interchangeably with *arielismo* (see ***Ariel* and *arielismo***) and ***mundonovismo***, and to designate the so-called novela de la tierra (see **novel**).

Further reading

Castillo, H. (1962) *El criollismo en la novelística chilena; huellas, modalidades y perfiles*, Mexico City, Ediciones de Andrea.

Hernández de Norman, I. (1977) *La novela criolla en las Antillas*, New York: Plus Ultra Edition.

Prieto, A. (1988) *El discurso criollista en la formación de la Argentina moderna*, Buenos Aires: Editorial Sudamericana.

Ras, N. (1999) *Criollismo y modernidad: Un análisis formal de la idiosincrasia criolla*, Buenos Aires: Academia Nacional de Ciencias.

Rubione, A.V.E. (1983) *En torno al criollismo: 'El criollismo en la literatura argentina y otros textos'*, Buenos Aires: Centro Editor de América Latina.

DANIEL BALDERSTON

crónica (genre)

This term *crónica* is used today to refer to a genre that emerged during the late 1960s throughout Latin America as an intermediate form between journalism and literature, and which explores the everyday life of the people, their culture and social conventions in the urban context. Its texts are characteristically short, designed to be published in newspapers and magazines, although they are later usually collected in book form. The term *crónica* also identifies a historiographic tradition that flourished in antiquity and the Middle Ages, in which historical events are narrated in chronological order. The historical element is still significant in the *crónica*, which not only registers the avatars of everyday life, but also manifests an explicit inclination to uncover the origins of the present and to rescue its forgotten memories. Today's *crónica* has its antecedents in the nineteenth-century *cuadro de costumbres* (see ***costumbrismo***), a vignette in which urban characters and the everyday life of the nation are represented in their typicality, and in the *crónica* *modernista* from the turn of the century, where the *cronistas* – often poets such as **Martí**, **Darío** and Gutiérrez Nájera – mapped with literary sophistication the landscapes of the city and guided their readers through the good manners and taste defined by foreign, modern standards. The *crónica* – influenced by the 'New Journalism' of the USA – can be characterized by the central position of its writer as the source who narrates the facts, often appearing as a character in the text as well; by the narrativization and fictionalization of the events it portrays, thus creating a certain ambiguity between reality and fiction; by its descriptive intention (it recreates the atmosphere in which particular events have taken place); and by the significant presence of orality, both in the writer's language, which is close to spoken language, and in the direct speech of its characters. It is moreover a stylized text through which the *cronistas* address their readers in an individual and recognizable voice. The *crónica* assumes its purpose to be to express the contemporary culture of the city in its manifold manifestations. It often draws its imagery from popular and mass culture, which it incorporates in its language and form, and from emerging social movements. This is why it can be considered, in its widest sense, a report from the unofficial culture, appropriating and revealing the energy and creativity of the social forces from below and deriding and exposing, at the same time, the hypocrisy of political life and the social conventions of the elite and the middle classes. The *crónica* has developed strongly in Mexico, thanks in part to the efforts of its most renowned *cronista*, Carlos **Monsiváis**, who as well as producing a contemporary history of Mexican life in his several volumes of *crónicas*, has critically analysed the genre and anthologized it. Other *cronistas* include Pedro **Lemebel** in Chile and Jorge Martillo Montserrate in Ecuador. There is a related journalistic genre in Brazil, the *crônica*; famous practitioners in recent decades include Carlos Drummond de **Andrade** and Clarice **Lispector**.

Further reading

Egan, L. (2001) *Carlos Monsiváis*, Albuquerque: University of New Mexico Press.

Martillo Monserrate, J. (1999) *La bohemia en Guayaquil y otras historias crónicas*, Guayaquil: Archivo Histórico del Guayas.

Monsiváis, C. (1977) *Amor perdido*, Mexico City: Era.

—— (1978) *A ustedes les consta. Antología de la crónica en México*, Mexico City: Era.

—— (1997) *Mexican Postcards*, ed. and trans. J. Kraniauskas, London: Verso.

Moser, G.M. (1971) ' "The crônica": A New Genre in Brazilian Literature', *Studies in Short Fiction* 8(1): 217–29.

Nogueira, Armando *et al.* (1980 and 1981) *O melhor da crônica brasileira*, Rio de Janeiro: José Olympio Editora, 2 vols.

ESPERANZA BIELSA

Cuadra, José de la

b. 1903, Guayaquil, Ecuador; d. 1941, Guayaquil

Writer

Cuadra was a distinguished writer of the **Guayaquil Group**. His 'montuvian novel' *Los Sangurimas* (The Sangurimas) (1934) is a ground-breaking work, an early example of **magical realism**. His early work focused on the loves, nostalgia and yearnings of the petit-bourgeoisie of his native city. Later his writings concentrated on the urban marginal, the Indians and, principally, the inhabitants of the coast, the *montuvios*, a mixed race group about whom he wrote in *El montuvio ecuatoriano* (1937). He also wrote literary and sociological essays and biography. His major works are *Los monos enloquecidos* (Wild Monkeys) (1931), *Repisas* (Drawers) (1931) and *Horno* (Kiln) (1932).

Further reading

Carrión de Fierro, F. (1993) *José de la Cuadra, precursor del realismo mágico*, Quito: Ediciones de la Pontificia Universidad Católica del Ecuador.

Cuadra, J. de la (1938) *Guásinton; relatos y crónicas*, Quito: Talleres Gráficos de Educación.

Martínez, P.A. (1997) 'José de la Cuadra', in V. Smith (ed.), *Encyclopedia of Latin American Literature*, London: Fitzroy Dearborn, 233–5.

Robles, H.E. (1976) *Testimonio y tendencia mítica en la*

obra de José de la Cuadra, Quito: Casa de la Cultura Ecuatoriana.

HUMBERTO E. ROBLES

Cuadra, Pablo Antonio

b. 1912, Managua, Nicaragua; d. 2002, Managua

Writer

Director of several literary magazines, Cuadra began the review *Vanguardia* in 1930 with fellow Nicaraguan poet Octavio Rocha. He also worked with José **Coronel Urtecho** on the post-Vanguardist review *La reacción*. Although internationally educated and strongly influenced by French literature, his poetry stimulated modern Nicaraguan poets to search for that which is native to their own country, in a complementary stance to Rubén **Darío**'s internationalism. Cuadra's Vanguardist poetry, especially that of *Poemas nicaragüenses* (Nicaraguan Poems) (1934), paints Nicaragua as a mythical birthplace of heroes (most notably the mariner Cifar) in danger of destruction due to outside invasion. The characterization of the pre-Columbian indigenous societies of his homeland as primitive, idyllic, pre-capitalist and pre-Fall paradises prefigured the imagery used by Ernesto **Cardenal** in his works at Solentiname. Aside from the obvious invasion of the Spanish conquerors, the occupation of the country by US Marines between 1926 and 1933 also figures prominently in Cuadra's early work. He spent much time in the Nicaraguan countryside, and his knowledge of it is well used in his rich portrayals of the paradisical landscape.

Cuadra became a respected and established member of the Nicaraguan literary elite, and his service as long-time director of *La Prensa Literaria*, a literary supplement to the newspaper *La Prensa*, enabled several new poets to be introduced to the Nicaraguan reading public. He is considered the major influence in modern Nicaraguan poetry before Ernesto Cardenal. During the Somoza regime he was the *de facto* Minister of Culture. His opposition to the Sandinistas distanced him from his friends, particularly from Cardenal and Coronel Urtecho. In the post-Sandinista era, he was asked to run as a presidential candidate for the 1996 election, but declined the offer.

Further reading

Balladares, J. (1986) *Pablo Antonio Cuadra: La palabra y el tiempo, secuencia y estructura en su creación poética*, San José: Editorial Libro Libre.

White, S. (1993) *Modern Nicaraguan Poetry: Dialogues with France and the United States*, London and Toronto: Associated University Press.

DEREK PETREY AND ILEANA RODRÍGUEZ

Cuarto Propio

Cuarto Propio Press was founded in 1984, during the Pinochet dictatorship in Chile, by women **intellectuals** opposed to the military government. Its name recalls Virginia Woolf's famous essay, 'A Room of One's Own'. Cuarto Propio created a channel for women from any social and economic class to write and publish, but it has also published a wide variety of poetry, fiction and criticism by male and female authors from Chile and other countries that questions dominant ideologies and discourses. Cuarto Propio's stated purpose is to broaden cultural horizons in Chile by maintaining a non-commercial focus and publishing a multitude of viewpoints.

Further reading

http://www.cuartopropio.cl

Ortega, Eliana (1996) *Lo que se hereda no se hurta: Ensayos de crítica literaria, feminista*, Santiago de Chile: Editorial Cuarto Propio.

AMALIA PEREIRA

Cuentos fríos

Cuentos fríos (Cold Tales) (1956) is Virgilio **Piñera**'s most important collection of short stories, but was reprinted only once in Cuba (in 1964), undoubtedly because of the marginalization suffered by Piñera after the Cuban Revolution. The stories are set in a no-man's land, an ill-disguised mirror of society with systems of regimentation and repression imposed by self and others. In Piñera's world there is no meat in the city, so its inhabitants cut fillets from their own flesh; a woman's wedding album becomes an event dislocating notions of time and space. In Piñera's universe, the absurd collides with absolute logic.

Further reading

Piñera, V. (1988) *Cold Tales*, trans. Mark Schafer, Boulder: Erídanos Library.

—— (1999) *Cuentos completos*, Madrid: Alfaguara.

Molinero, R. (ed.) (2002) *Virgilio Piñera: La memoria del cuerpo*, San Juan: Editorial Plaza Mayor.

JOSÉ QUIROGA

cultural theory

The analysis of Latin American culture in the twentieth century has unfolded in the context of broader theoretical approaches to society and economy. In each of them, however, the central issue has been the dynamics of the historic colonial relationship, its continuities and transformations, and the conflictive and contradictory relationship between local and regional cultural expressions and metropolitan – and later global – cultural forms. By the end of the twentieth century, that debate was transformed by a process of globalization which seemed to undermine the notion that the terrain of struggle was the encounter between peripheral nation and metropolitan power. For that relationship, in the view of Néstor García Canclini, Jesús Martín-Barbero, J.J. Brunner and Norbert Lechner, for example, was now transmuted into an *internal* contradiction expressed in hybrid cultures which were at once fields of conflict and forms of resolution.

But the significance of that concept only becomes clear by first reflecting back on the evolution through the century of the theory of culture. At the heart of the debate that runs from the mid-nineteenth century to the early twentieth is the formula '**civilization and barbarism**'. Derived from the Argentine writer and politician Sarmiento's *Facundo* (1846), it returns in the early part of the twentieth century in works such as Rómulo **Gallegos**'s ***Doña Bárbara***, where the question of cultural development is posed as a struggle between atavistic and instinctual forces on the one hand and the civilizational impulse enshrined in European culture in the other. What is absent here is any sense of the organic relationship between the two factors. But the conclusion drawn from this simplistic characterization was that Latin America should find its way into the circle of civilization (there was only one) and control the instinct to barbarism.

This represents, quite clearly, a cultural theory legitimating conquest and colonization, whether the Spanish or the European variant, as a 'civilizational project'. As the twentieth century dawned, and the US claimed hegemony in the region, the theory of 'manifest destiny' would come to occupy the same terrain. Resistance to the presence of the newest imperialism expressed itself in the struggle to create nation-states – the truncated project begun with independence a century earlier – which possessed the economic capacity to endure. In the process – and it is the Mexican Revolution that marks the watershed – a new theory of culture emerges that can provide the cohesion required by the nation-building project. Its distinctness – its specificity – is derived from the long-buried indigenous or subordinated cultures, from national traditions and popular expression, fused with the modernizing impulse. The result is a theory of *mestizaje*, in one of several variants. In Mexico it is articulated by José **Vasconcelos**'s notion of 'la raza cósmica'; in Cuba by the recuperation of black culture expressed in the pages of Havana's *Diario de la Marina* which are headed 'Ideales de una raza', where Nicolás **Guillén**, among others, published his first poetry of ***négritude***. This notion of *mestizaje* or syncretism became a matter for long theoretical argument in the writing of Edourd **Glissant** and Aimé **Césaire** in the Francophone Caribbean and in the discussion of Fernando **Ortiz**'s notion of 'transculturation' later developed by Angel **Rama**. In Brazil, the **Antropofagia** movement embraced every area of art and culture in reversing the order of civilization – exoticizing the Brazilian interior as in the work of Sérgio **Buarque de Holanda**. For the Andean countries, ***indigenismo*** fulfilled a similar function, although more radical in its identification with the oppressed and hitherto invisible Quechua-and Aymara-speaking communities of the *sierra*. How radical it was as a project was the issue of fierce polemic between José Carlos **Mariátegui**, for whom its implication was a form of socialist organization based on Inca collectivism, and Haya de la Torre, whose APRA organization claimed Indian heritage but represented a broader populism in its political strategies. In Argentina and the River Plate region, and to some extent in Chile, that emblematic role was filled by the disputed figure of the gaucho or the urban immigrant whose realities and desires were expressed in the tango. Yet by the 1930s, when Latin America was suffering the effects of the Depression, more radical identifications with the oppressed were current – and the identities of ethnicity or tradition were replaced by the experiences of class addressed in the social realism of Ecuador's **Guayaquil Group** and the work of the Mexican Muralists, and in particular of Diego Rivera.

In the late 1930s the culture of nationhood arose again in a project for State led development expressed by the Estado Novo in Brazil and the Cárdenas regime in Mexico. In both cases a resurgent national culture provided a symbolic language with which to legitimate the political project and represent it credibly to every section of society. The unity of nation was expressed in an imagery transmitted in music – the ranchera in Mexico, the officialized samba of Brazil, the trova of Cuba – through the newly popular radio networks, and in the filmic spectacles of national unity exemplified by the Golden Age of Mexican cinema and the musical extravaganzas of Carmen Miranda. It was the peculiar power of Evita Perón that she brought the spectacle to politics, and the *radionovela* to reality before the rapt gaze of a newly arrived and disorientated layer of migrant workers who would become, at least in rhetorical terms, the very heart of the national dream.

After the Second World War the unified nation aspired to economic and political independence – the economic surge occasioned by the war and its aftermath produced a new economic theory exemplified by SELA. Led and organized by the State, and in the context of a continental market, the new nation-states could reach modernity. The failure of the industrialization project was manifestly the result of the exercise of hegemonic economic and political power by the USA – particularly in the wake of the Cuban Revolution of 1959, which had announced its project for independence precisely in those terms. The US domination of the world market, of the key commodities and of patterns of consumption, was mirrored in the proliferation of its cultural instruments – the growth of the commercial music industry, the birth of a television system dominated completely by US capital and technology, a film industry whose Hollywood production values made it impossible for an impoverished regional film industry to compete. The continental penetration of Disney products, for example, ensured the dissemination both of a fundamental anti-communism on the one hand, and a model of growth and success based on the American way, on the other.

The reintegration of Latin America into the US ambit politically, economically and ideologically was addressed and theorized by a new layer of **intellectuals** for whom the problem was not 'underdevelopment' – a failure of states to develop – but an international system of inequality whose mechanisms maintained and deepened the imbalance. This dependency theory – in the writings of Gunder Frank, Furtado and Cardoso – acknowledged that culture and ideology were key modes of control and discipline. As Armand Mattelart, co-author with Ariel **Dorfman**, of the seminal study *Para leer al Pato Donald* (How to Read Donald Duck) (1971), revealed in his researches, 'culture is not a light industry'. Control of news, of the new mass culture of pop music, television and Hollywood cinema, and the ability to define the aspirations and values of a whole society were potent and key weapons of domination. The fruit of that insight was the theory of cultural imperialism.

In the early 1970s, the concept of cultural imperialism responded to what, descriptively, seemed an obvious truth – television was still dominated by US programmes, although Globo and Televisa were growing into the conglomerates they would become in the next decade. International news distribution was overwhelmingly controlled by United Press and Reuters; the cinemas, despite attempts to impose a quota of national films in Brazil, for example, were full of American products, particularly the progeny of the Disney stable. US capital remained powerful, although venture capital and private financial institutions seemed increasingly centralized – particularly in Mexico and Chile – a high profile reinforced by the overpowering architecture of foreign-owned banks in most of the region's major cities. Salsa, a US-generated dance rhythm, was sweeping the Latin American music market before it.

Underpinning the argument, however, was a late version of the dependency thesis. The aspiration to independent development of the 1960s had clearly failed, the construction of the national state had arrested or begun to assume the distorted forms of a military authoritarianism whose national projects involved new forms of combination with foreign investors. The explanation offered by the cultural imperialism thesis was that the US used its economic, political and ideological power to subvert national independence; the analyses of the Chilean coup of 1973, for example, insisted on US involvement and curiously underplayed the leading role played by the Chilean bourgeoisie itself. The call for a New International Information Order, first mooted in 1976, was one response to the theory – and the result was the McBride Commission, set up a year later. But it did permit the reinvention of nationalism, despite its many failures, and the assertion that the central cultural contradiction was on the border between nation and imperialism, and that these were the protagonists of the cultural struggle. Roberto **Schwarz**'s concept of 'misplaced ideas', first proposed in 1977, developed a more sophisticated conception of the same conflict. The rediscovery of tradition and the excavation of the past for the foundations of national culture followed, although this often developed in exile, where the national intellectuals found themselves more often than not as the new military regimes expelled its critics. The political consequence, however, was a series of national coalitions created in exile and emerging in the early to mid-eighties in Central America, Chile, Argentina and Uruguay.

At the same time, however, changes in both the external reality and the theoretical explanation of it were laying the foundations of a transformation as profound as any that century. A new *modernity*, officially designated **postmodernism**, signalled a new economic globalization and a cultural metamorphosis. As John Beverley affirms, the thesis of modernity reflects a crisis of the national project in the face of the global reorganization of capital. Neo-liberal economic strategies increasingly subordinate the national state to administrative functions as international agencies impose the priorities of the world market. Most loans and aid programmes to the countries of the region in the eighties carry conditions which directly involve cuts in public spending. The Caribbean Basin initiative promoted by President Ronald Reagan, for example, like most aid packages of the period, was a joint public–private initiative. In Mexico the government of Miguel de la Madrid (1982–8) embarked on a massive privatization of state enterprises as a precondition for the closer integration of the regional economy eventually consolidated through the NAFTA agreement. The cultural industry was no different in that respect from any other branch of the economy; but privatization/marketization implied the simultaneous undermining of state-subsidized broadcasting and its public service ethos and the massive growth of the Latin American conglomerates such as Globo, Televisa, Manchete and Venevisión.

As Renato **Ortiz** argues throughout his work, this is a function of economic and market integration and of a new phase of economic growth – but not now in the context of a protected national market, rather as part of an alliance of powerful economic actors in a global context. Thus Televisa moves into the US context, serving a growing Hispanic audience; Globo beams across Latin America but also into Europe; and Venezuela conquers a large part of the niche market in *telenovelas*. The simple confrontation of imperialism and nation is swept away and replaced by the notion of an interconnected and interdependent system dominated by global patterns of consumption and production (symbolized perhaps by Ford's 'world car' whose components were produced in a number of different countries and assembled in yet another, or the '*maquiladora*' phenomenon, in which regional assembly plants produce goods for often distant markets – the Japanese factories on the Mexican–US border are a key example). The fall of the Berlin Wall in 1989 simply serves to reinforce the sense of a single and universal environment.

The cultural effects are undoubtedly extraordinarily far-reaching. Postmodernism enunciates the eclecticism of the new cultures, which merge high and low, the canon and the consumer good; the city as the favoured locus of the new culture no longer has a rural past to yearn for as it did in the 1950s, since the countryside itself is now a place of production for the market – paradoxically signified in the growth of the cocaine trade, an international commodity *par excellence*! In the urban space tradition and modernity mingle in an undifferentiated way – indigenous market traders wear Discmen, television reaches into the furthest corners, as witness the forest of aerials over the region's shanty towns, the globalization and reselling of Latin American music. The mass media provide the model for the new culture. More significant still is the appropriation by the market of the very language of liberation – 'empowerment', for example, now refers not to the emancipatory strategies for social classes or groups but to subjectivities and the freedom of choice.

Jesús Martín Barbero and Néstor García Canclini theorize and interrogate this new reality from the perspective of Latin America – and it is significant that they do not share the cultural pessimism of some of their contemporaries in the old metropolitan centres. The postmodern space does not allow national redefinitions perhaps – the national territorial frontiers are now shifting spaces. The primary advocates of the nation-state, the bourgeois beneficiaries of the old populist projects, are now partners with multinational financial institutions. But the new 'hybrid cultures' of which Canclini speaks are not simply new products, but spaces of conflict and contestation. Popular culture is not simply overwhelmed and domesticated, it also resists, reshapes and remakes even the products of the global market. The new technology serves to create a vast industry in pirated music, new identities replace the nation – youth culture, for example, which according to Barbero crosses frontiers and links resistances in constant merging and remaking of music in rap and roots samba and reggae. Local community radio reconnects with oral cultures as the technology for transmission becomes more simply available. It is a phenomenon that Canclini desribes as 'decollection' – the reordering of cultural products. Video permits the reconstruction of film, the rapid remote control reconstructs the TV image, and the new age of internet music will presumably permit new mosaics.

The dilemma is that in the crisis of representation and of politics that has marked the end of the twentieth century such resistances are by their nature fragmentary, local, sometimes transient – the Zapatista rebellion in Mexico is emblematic. The liberation of the majority of the region's population from want and despair, however, remains an urgent and ever-present need. The rediscovery of the common experience and the joint action is still a precondition for that project – and the categories that underpin such a strategy remain to find a language of common experience.

Further reading

Franco, J. (1999) *Critical Passions*, ed. Kathleen Newman and Mary Louise Pratt, Durham, NC and London: Duke University Press.

García Canclini, N. (1989) *Culturas híbridas: Estrategias para entrar y salir de la modernidad*, Mexico: Era.

Gollnick, B. (2003) 'Approaches to Latin American Literature', in Phillip Swanson (ed.), *The Companion to Latin American Studies*, London: Arnold Publishing, 107–21.

Martín Barbero, J. (1987) *De los medios a las mediaciones*, Barcelona: Ed. Gili.

Rama, A. (1982) *Transculturación narrativa en América Latina*, Mexico City: Siglo XXI.

Rowe, W. and Vivian Schelling (1991) *Memory and Modernity in Latin America*, London: Verso.

Schwarz, R. (1992) *Misplaced Ideas: Essays on Brazilian culture*, trans. J. Gledson, London: Verso.

Yúdice, G. (2002) *El recurso de la cultura*, Barcelona: Gedisa.

MIKE GONZALEZ

Cumper, Patricia

b. 1954, Kingston, Jamaica

Writer

A novelist and short story writer, Cumper is best

known as a dramatist; she has written extensively for radio, stage and screen in the Caribbean and Britain. Author of three series and a children's play for Jamaican radio, her popular 1987 black comedy, *The Fallen Angel and the Devil Concubine* was followed by a play with Sistren Theatre based on a Claude **McKay** story exploring nineteenth-century class prejudice, as well as a UNICEF-commissioned piece on ghetto violence. Since her move to England in 1993, she has written for theatre, radio and television.

Further reading

Cumper, Patricia (1998) *One Bright Child*, London: BlackAmber Books.

SITA DICKSON LITTLEWOOD

Cunha, Euclides da

b. 1866, Cantagalo, Rio de Janeiro, Brazil; d. 1909, Rio de Janeiro

Writer, engineer and journalist

Da Cunha is the author of one of the most extraordinary works of Latin American literature, *Os* ***sertões*** (Rebellion in the Backlands) (1902). Trained as a military engineer, he joined the Brazilian army's third and final expedition against the religious sectarians in Canudos in the backlands of Bahia; his original dispatches from 1897 were gathered in book form in 1939. Apart from *Os sertões*, written while he was supervising the construction of a bridge, da Cunha also wrote several works on geography.

Further reading

Cunha, E. da (1966) *Obra completa*, Rio de Janeiro: Aguilar, 2 vols.

Freyre, G. (1944) *Perfil de Euclides da Cunha e outros perfis*, Rio de Janeiro: José Olympio, 21–63.

Rabello, S. (1947) *Euclides da Cunha*, Rio de Janeiro: Casa do Estudante do Brasil.

DANIEL BALDERSTON

Cuzzani, Agustín

b. 1924, Buenos Aires, Argentina; d. 1987, Buenos Aires

Playwright, novelist and lawyer

Agustín Cuzzani's long and distinguished career in the Argentine arts included work in film, television and adaptations of foreign plays such as *Hair* and *Marat/Sade*. He is best known for his 'farce-satires', *Una libra de carne* (A Pound of Flesh) (1954), *El centroforward murió al amanecer* (The Centerforward Died at Dawn) (1955), *Los indios estaban cabreros* (The Indians Were Angry) (1957) and *Sempronio* (1957). All four plays mix highly farcical elements with biting satire relating to humanity's condition.

ADAM VERSÉNYI

D

Dabydeen, David

b. 1955, Berbice, British Guiana

Writer

Obtaining his PhD in eighteenth-century literature and art, Dabydeen sees the tension between insider and outsider (immigrant) as an impetus to exciting creativity in language, as suggested in the critical notes to his 1984 book of poetry, *Slave Song*, and in the play between Standard English and creole in his 1991 novel, *The Intended*. Born of Indo-Guyanese parents, he moved to England in 1969 and, despite adolescent difficulties, excelled academically at Cambridge and London University. As editor of the *Handbook for Teaching Caribbean Literature* (1988) and of *Across the Dark Waters: Indian Identity in the Caribbean* (1996), Dabydeen has promoted an appreciation of Caribbean literature and culture.

Further reading

Dabydeen, David (1994) *Turner: New & Selected Poems*, London: Cape Poetry.

—— (1997) *A Reader's Guide to West Indian and Black British Literature*, London: Hansib.

—— (1999) *A Harlot's Progress*, London: Jonathan Cape.

JILL E. ALBADA-JELGERSMA

Dalton, Roque

b. 1935, San Salvador, El Salvador;
d. 1975, place unknown, El Salvador

Poet

Although he wrote historical and critical essays, and a famous biography of the old communist, *Miguel Mármol* (1981), Dalton's literary reputation rests on his poetry. It is a poetry defined by its wit and humour, on the one hand, and its absolute commitment to human freedom, on the other.

From an early age Dalton was a political activist – he described his early experience in a wonderfully self-deprecating little poem 'Buscándome líos' (Looking for Trouble) in which his over-earnest responses at his first political meeting are gently parodied by his comrades and then his mother rebukes him when he is late for tea. But these sardonic poems directed at himself are not mere iconoclasm – Dalton's poetry humanizes the revolutionary Left to which he belonged, exposing its pomposities and its sectarianism, and in a sense rescuing the project for human liberation that is at the heart of the revolutionary project.

In that sense, the poetry has a didactic purpose specific to time and place. 'La segura mano de Dios' (God's Sure Hand) is narrated by the assassin of ex-dictator Hernández Martínez of El Salvador. And his *Historias secretas de Pulgarcito* (Secret Lives of Tom Thumb) (1974) is a brilliant eclectic narrative of the history of his country.

The poet Dalton also lived the life of Dalton the militant; the years of organization and the prison terms, the torture, the death sentence from which he escaped when an earthquake broke open the walls of his cell, the subsequent exile in eastern Europe, was recalled frequently in his poetry with a mixture of sadness and nostalgia.

Dalton spent most of the late 1960s and early 1970s in Cuba, preparing a guerrilla force for El Salvador (the ERP – the People's Revolutionary Army). Yet an armed-resistance organization, the FPL (People's Liberation Front), already existed under the leadership of a legendary political figure, Salvador Cayetano Carpio. It had mass support, based on Carpio's long years in the trade union movement. The ERP, on the other hand, was a collection of radical Christians and Guevarists, with little in the way of a base, dedicated to building a guerrilla cell or *foco* – which Dalton himself had criticized (in 'Maneras de morir' (Ways of Dying), for example) for its elitism and its contempt for popular organization.

When he did return to El Salvador in 1973, Dalton was stopped from assuming the leadership and, in the ensuing internal battles, was killed by his own comrades in 1975. The *Poemas clandestinos* (Clandestine Poems) were written during this period (although not published until 1980), while Dalton was living and working with the guerrillas. Written in a variety of voices, and through several personae, Dalton explores the nature of commitment and idealism. Why these pseudonyms? It was an offence punishable by torture or even death to carry the poetry of Roque Dalton; he was after all a leader of the armed opposition. Multiplying his words through a group of students, Dalton's voice remains unmistakable. These are not alternative personalities; nor are they mere entertainments. As 'Vilma Flores' put it in 'Sobre nuestra moral poética' (On Our Poetic Morality), 'Let's be clear, we are poets writing from underground – we're not comfortably and safely anonymous, but face to face with the enemy, attacking the system from our poetry'. In some ways they are Dalton at his least ironic and subtle – yet placed back within the body of his work they are just one (or several) of the faces of a poet, revolutionary, historian, organizer and thinker; and of a key figure in enriching the general understanding of what is meant by a poetry of transformation.

Further reading

Beverley, J. and M. Zimmermann (1990) *Literature and Politics in the Central American Revolutions*, Austin: University of Texas Press.

Dalton, R. (1980) *Poemas clandestinos*, San José, Costa Rica: EDUCA.

—— (1994) *En la humedad del secreto: Antología poética*, ed. Rafael Lara Martínez, San Salvador: Concultura.

García Verzi, H. (1986) *Recopilación de textos sobre Roque Dalton*, Havana: Casa de las Américas.

Shurow, J. (1997) 'Roque Dalton', in V. Smith (ed.), *Encyclopedia of Latin American Literature*, London: Fitzroy Dearborn, 247–51.

MIKE GONZALEZ

Damas, Léon Gontran

b. 1912, Cayenne, French Guiana;
d. 1978, Washington, DC, USA

Poet and essayist

A contemporary of Aimé **Césaire** and Leopold Senghor, Léon Damas was one of the founders of the ***négritude*** movement. He was one of the rare writers from French Guiana to achieve international success, as his first book of poems, *Pigments* (1937), articulated the themes of cultural exile and racial dispossession that were characteristic of *négritude*. This reputation for political militancy was further enhanced with his sharp critique of French colonialism, *Retour de Guyane* (Return from Guyane), in 1938. His deep interest in oral culture and folk history, stimulated by the Harlem Renaissance, was later manifested in a volume of folk tales translated into French, *Veillées noires* (Black Wakes), in 1943. After spending two years as Deputy for the Department of French Guyane, he travelled widely and spent his last years at Howard University in the USA.

Further reading

Damas, León Gontran (1961) *African Songs of Love, War, Grief & Abuse*, Ibadan: Mbari Publication.

—— (1972) *Pigments. Névralgies*, Paris: Présence africaine.

Racine, D. (1979) *Léon Gontran Damas, 1912–1978, Founder of Negritude*, Washington: University Press of America.
—— (1983) *Léon Gontran Damas, l'homme, l'oeuvre*, Paris: Présence africaine.

J. MICHAEL DASH

Darío, Rubén

b. 1867, Metapa, Nicaragua; d. 1916, León, Nicaragua

Poet

Born Félix Rubén García Sarmiento, Darío renamed himself to evoke more exotic predecessors, one of the first of many transformations he would undergo during his lifetime. Undisputed leader of major changes in poetic language, Darío also is representative of the changing status of the writer in Spanish American societies caught in the throes of modernization. In large part he earned his living as a journalist, like many other writers of his generation, and he published engaging chronicles of his stays in many Latin American and European capitals, especially Buenos Aires, Madrid and Paris. Although he practised various genres – the short story and the journalistic chronicle – above all he is known as a poet.

An oft-repeated truism is that a good reader can tell the difference between a poem in Spanish written before and after Rubén Darío. What sort of writer could create such massive changes in poetry? An answer can be found in the voracious incorporative nature of his relationship with literature and art. Convinced of the spiritual importance of poetic language, he sought out the perfect harmonies of music and spirit. 'Just as each word has a soul, every verse has an ideal melody, in addition to a verbal harmony' (preface to *Prosas profanas* (Profane Prose), 1896). By that time Darío had become a lightning rod for both adulation and scorn because of his and his followers' breaks with tradition. Scolded by a Spanish critic for indulging in 'the modern', Darío adopted proudly the label '*modernista*'. And without a doubt, he did want to be in the mainstream of international currents. He spent a great deal of his adult life in tension between his modest background and his desire to transcend everyday reality. He referred to himself as an 'intellectual aristocrat', and in the same preface cited above, he alludes to his mestizo heritage: 'Is there in my blood a drop of African blood, or of Chorotegan or Nagrandano Indian' despite his 'hands of a Marquis'? Conscious of Latin American realities, nonetheless he longed to inhabit the sublime worlds of art. Many of the changes in his poetry respond to the oscillations between his vocation and his necessary response to external issues.

Even during his early years in his provincial village, Darío showed the prodigious talent that would lead him around the world. A series of local recognitions led him to continue his career in Chile, where he worked as a journalist and there published the landmark *Azul* (Blue) (1888), a collection of poems and short stories. There he read the works of the French symbolists and formed friendships with other bohemian writers. The subject matter of *Azul* often displays Darío's predilection for the exotic, and he sought in myth, legend and forgotten medieval works the elaborate images he worked so intricately. Like a fine jeweller as well as an artist, Darío was a master craftsman of metrical and rhyme forms, reviving archaic Spanish forms and transforming French meters to Spanish. A highly charged eroticism, rendered in images more explicit than in recent poetic tradition, earned his works an air of scandal as well as mystery.

In later works, especially *Cantos de vida y de esperanza* (Songs of Life and Hope) (1905), Darío weaves a personal and artistic testimony to counter in part the criticisms aimed at his 'escapist' tendencies or his preference for the ornate and exotic. Its first poem, 'Yo soy aquel' (I am the other), recounts his personal and artistic development and acknowledges his detractors, in this case particularly José Enrique **Rodó**, an admirer of Darío's talents who also questioned his insistence on excess. The same volume includes poems of a more explicit political nature, especially the famous 'A Roosevelt' which denounces US intervention in Latin America and continues Rodó's attacks on US culture as materialistic and violent. Although Darío idealized French culture, his attachment to Spain and to his own country heightened during his later years. His 'Epístola a la senora de Lugones' is explicit in its nostalgia for a lost tranquillity and security and its unease in the increasingly technological world he was required to inhabit.

So complete was Darío's dominance of the poetic scene that later generations of poets found it necessary to rebel against his authority. Immediately succeeding generations, such as the vanguardist poets, set about dismantling the elaborate constructions of rhyme, meter and extended imagery that Darío had celebrated. If Darío's poetry represented elegance and eloquence, then subsequent poets would go against the grain by dropping rhyme and meter and adopting free verse, as well as integrating colloquial speech and topics of modernization in their works. Yet Darío's poetry continues to be a classic of Spanish literature, and his works are perhaps the most recited in public readings. As Octavio **Paz** described him in his essay 'The Siren and the Seashell', Darío was the 'founder' of all that was to come.

See also: Spanish American modernism

Further reading

Anderson Imbert, Enrique (1967) *La originalidad de Rubén Darío*, Buenos Aires: Centro Editor de América Latina.

Barcia, Pedro Luis (ed.) (1968) *Escritos dispersos de Rubén Darío recogidos de periódicos de Buenos Aires*, La Plata: Universidad de La Plata.

Concha, Jaime (1975) *Rubén Darío*, Madrid: Ediciones Júcar.

Darío, Rubén (1950) *Cuentos completos*, ed. with notes by Ernesto Mejía Sánchez, intro. Raimundo Lida, Mexico City: Fondo de Cultura Económica.

—— (1950) *Obras completas*, Madrid: Afrodisio Aguado, 5 vols.

—— (1952) *Poesía. Libros poéticos completos y antología de la obra dispersa*, ed. Ernesto Mejía Sánchez, intro. Enrique Anderson Imbert, Mexico City: Fondo de Cultura Económica.

—— (1954) *Poesías completas*, ed. and intro with notes by Alfonso Méndez Plancarte, Madrid: Aguilar S.A. de Ediciones.

—— (1977) *Poesía*, ed. Ernesto Mejía Sánchez, Caracas: Biblioteca Ayacucho.

Ellis, Keith (1974) *Critical Approaches to Rubén Darío*, Toronto, Ont.: University of Toronto Press.

Jrade, Cathy Login (1983) *Rubén Darío and the Romantic Search for Unity: The Modernist Recourse to Esoteric Tradition*, Austin: University of Texas Press.

Paz, Octavio (1965) 'El caracol y la sirena', in *Cuadrivio: Darío, López Velarde, Pessoa, Cernuda*, Mexico City: Joaquín Mortiz, 9–65.

Rama, Angel (1970) *Rubén Darío y el modernismo (circunstancia socioeconómica de un arte americano)*, Caracas: Ediciones de la Biblioteca de la Universidad Central de Venezuela.

Rodó, José Enrique (1931) *Hombres de América (Montalvo, Bolívar, Rubén Darío)*, Barcelona: Cervantes.

Zavala, Iris M. (1989) *Rubén Darío bajo el signo del cisne*, Río Piedras, PR: Editorial de la Universidad de Puerto Rico.

GWEN KIRKPATRICK

Dathorne, Oscar Roland

b. 1934, Georgetown, British Guiana

Writer, scholar and critic

Dathorne is one of the most influential figures in the development of a Caribbean ethic and identity in the post-colonial literary world, explored through fiction, poetry and literary criticism. He received a prestigious scholarship to Guyana's Queen's College and studied there, hoping to become a teacher, but his life changed when his father lost his job and the family emigrated to England. This disruptive but fruitful transition is reinvented in his first novel, *Dumplings in the Soup* (1963), which details the lives of colonials trying to make it in the metropole.

Dathorne's subsequent life experiences continued to inform his creative and critical work. After earning a certificate of education from the University of London, Dathorne travelled to Nigeria to teach at Amadou Bello University, where he began the interrogation with his heritage that frames his entire corpus. His second novel, *The Scholar Man* (1964), is an early manifestation of the literary subgenre that explores the dilemmas of Afro-Caribbean writers who attempt to come to terms with their African heritage, For Dathorne, as for others of his generation, the fit is not comfortable. Neither European nor African, the

West Indian writer, according to Dathorne, must carve out a place for his/her Caribbean self.

Dathorne's inquiry into his African heritage has also led him to become one of the major critics of the Caribbean. With his edited collections of Caribbean and African literatures and his critical anthologies, Dathorne has helped develop the corpus of African and diaspora literature. His most significant critical work to date is *The Dark Ancestor: The Literature of the Black Man in the Caribbean* (1981), an exhaustive study of the growing body of work in that field.

Dathorne is a Professor of English at the University of Kentucky and still remains an active scholar and writer. He is editor of the *Journal of Caribbean Studies*, and, reflecting upon his experiences at an American university, he has published a critical anthology, *In Europe's Image: The Need for American Multiculturalism* (1994). Dathorne's most recent text is *Worlds Apart* (2001).

Further reading

Dathorne, O.R. (1969) *African Poetry for Schools and Colleges*, London: Macmillan.

—— (1994) *Imagining the World: Mythical Belief Versus Reality in Global Encounters*, Westport, CT: Bergin & Garvey.

—— (1996) *Asian Voyages: Two Thousand Years of Constructing the Other*, Westport, CT: Bergin & Garvey.

—— (2001) *Worlds Apart: Race in the Modern Period*, Westport, CT: Bergin & Garvey.

GAY WILENTZ

Dávila Andrade, César

b. 1918, Cuenca, Ecuador; d. 1967, Caracas, Venezuela

Writer

Dávila Andrade's works figure among the most important in the literature of Ecuador, particularly his *Boletín y elegía de las mitas* (Report and Elegy for the Mitas) (1967), with its adventurous use of language and its creation of new epic forms. His early poetic works include *Canción a Teresita* (A Song to Teresita) (1946). He went on to publish more poetry and three volumes of stories including *Abandonados en la tierra* (Abandoned on Earth) (1952) and *Cabeza de gallo* (Cock's Head) (1966). He taught university in Caracas, where he committed suicide in 1967.

Further reading

Crespo, M.R. (1980) *Tras las huellas de César Dávila Andrade*, Cuenca: Departamento de Difusión Cultural, Universidad de Cuenca.

Dávila Andrade, C. (1984) *Obras completas*, Cuenta: Pontificia Universidad Católica del Ecuador/ Banco Central.

—— (1993) *Poesía, narrativa, ensayo*, Caracas: Biblioteca Ayacucho.

Liscano, J. (1967) 'El solitario de la gran obra', *Zona franca* 45.

CELINA MANZONI

D'Costa, Jean

b. 1937, St Andrew, Jamaica

Writer

A linguistic scholar specializing in Caribbean language, literary critic and writer of fiction for young people, D'Costa is the author of the highly successful 1975 adventure story, *Escape to Last Man Peak*, which has gone through thirteen reprintings. Her novels and short stories for children draw on a highly skilled and sensitive use of Jamaican lore and language varieties, with imaginative plots set in closely observed, realistic settings. D'Costa has also published lucid essays on Roger **Mais** and Jean **Rhys**, some poems and made substantial contributions to the historical linguistics of Caribbean creole. She taught English language and literature at the University of the West Indies for fifteen years before moving to Hamilton College, New York.

Further reading

D'Costa, J. and B. Lalla (1989) *Voices in Exile*, Tuscaloosa and London. University of Alabama Press.

—— (1990) *Language in Exile: Three Hundred Years of Jamaican Creole*, Tuscaloosa: University of Alabama Press.

BRIDGET JONES

de Boissiere, Ralph A.C.

b. 1907, Trinidad

Novelist

Ralph de Boissiere's first novel, *Crown Jewel* (1952), is considered one of the most important novels of the Caribbean region. It tells the story of the Butler riots in the oilfields of southern Trinidad during the 1930s. Other novels include *Rum and Coca-Cola* (1956), about the US occupation of Trinidad during the Second World War, which de Boissiere has called 'the first real blow to British prestige'; and *No Saddles for Kangaroos* (1964), based on his experiences in Australia working for General Motors during a period of strong anti-communist sentiment. De Boissiere left Trinidad and Tobago in 1947 and has since lived in Melbourne, Australia. His novels have been translated into eight languages, including Chinese.

Further reading

Birbalsingh, F.M. (1970) 'The Novels of Ralph de Boissiere', *Journal of Commonwealth Literature* 9: 104–8.

de Boissiere, Ralph A.C. (1952) *Crown Jewel*, London: Allison & Busby.

—— (1956) *Rum and Coca Cola*, London: Allison & Busby.

KEITH JARDIM

De Greiff, León

b. 1895, Medellín, Colombia; d. 1976, Santafé de Bogotá, Colombia

Poet

As a poet De Greiff developed a very personal style without attaching himself to any particular literary tendency. His work concentrates on four major themes: nature, love, the mysteries of life (death, loneliness, madness), and poetry and art itself. His major work is collected in eight volumes, each one identified subsequently with a subtitle indicating the numerical order from *Tergiversaciones. Primer mamotreto* (Distortions: First Big Book) (1925) to *Nova et Vetera. Octavo Mamotreto* (Nova et Vetera: Eighth Big Book) (1973). De Greiff never became involved directly in politics, but he would identify himself as a left-wing liberal.

Further reading

Alape, A. (ed.) (1995) *Valoración múltiple sobre León de Greiff*, Bogotá: Ediciones Universidad Central and Havana: Casa de las Américas.

De Greiff, L. (1991) *Baladas y canciones*, Bogotá: El Ancora Editores.

—— (1993) *Obra poética*, Caracas: Biblioteca Ayacucho.

—— (1995) *Relatos*, Bogotá: El Ancora Editores.

MIGUEL A. CARDINALE

de la Parra, Teresa

b. 1889, Paris, France; d. 1936, Madrid, Spain

Writer and essayist

Teresa de la Parra's 1924 novel *Ifigenia*, like her letters and essays, are texts out of their time. Her story of 'a young lady who writes because she is bored' in the patriarchal Caracas of the late nineteenth century is as eccentric as her relationships (her impossible loves, her ambiguous friendships with women). She developed an autobiographical register as the key strategy for delineating the strong feminine voice that emerges in her second novel *Memorias de Mamá Blanca* (1929). Her intellectual activity was intense; she was involved in a number of political and cultural movements in her country. In the context of the aesthetic experiments of the avant-garde (see **avant-garde in Latin America**), de la Parra attempted a different kind of break with tradition – the creation of an anomalous voice. In the 1990s, feminist readings have taken her out of the context of ***costumbrismo*** in which she had always been read and explored her interrogation of gender. She died of tuberculosis in Spain.

Further reading

Bosch, V. (1983) *Lengua viva de Teresa de la Parra. Relectura de la obra de Teresa de la Parra*, Caracas: Editorial Pomaire.

de la Parra, T. (1992) *Obra escogida*, Caracas: Monte Avila.

—— (1993) *Mama Blanca's Souvenirs*, trans. H. de Onís and F. Fornoff, Pittsburgh: University of Pittsburgh Press.

—— (1996) *Las memorias de Mamá Blanca*, Paris: Colección Archivos.

García Chicester, A. (1997) 'Teresa de la Parra', in V. Smith (ed.), *Encyclopedia of Latin American Literature*, London: Fitzroy Dearborn, 630–2.

Garrels, E. (1987) *Las grietas de la ternura: Nueva lectura de Teresa de la Parra*, Caracas: Monte Avila.

Mata-Kolster, E. (1989) 'Ana Teresa de la Parra Sanojo', in *Latin American Writers*, ed. C.A. Solé and M.I. Abreu, New York: Scribners, 2, 717–20.

Molloy, S. (1995) 'Disappearing Acts: Reading Lesbian in Teresa de la Parra', *¿Entiendes? Queer Readings, Hispanic Writings*, Durham, NC: Duke University Press.

Rosa, R. and D. Sommer (1995) 'Teresa de la Parra: America's Womanly Soul', in *Reinterpreting the Spanish American Essay: Women Writers of the 19th and 20th Centuries*, ed. D. Meyer, Austin: University of Texas Press, 115–24.

GRACIELA MONTALDO

Debrot, Nicolaas

b. 1902, Bonaire, Netherlands Antilles; d. 1981, Laren, the Netherlands

Politician, writer and critic

Nicolaas (Cola) Debrot studied medicine and law before turning to politics in the 1950s. In the 1960s, he became the first Governor-General of the Netherlands Antilles to have an Antillean background. He was a poet, novelist, short story writer, literary critic and essayist, who generally wrote in Dutch. Hardly anyone leaves secondary school in the Netherlands Antilles without having read his short first novel *Mijn zuster de negerin* (My Sister the Negro) (1935), in which he focuses on inter-ethnic relations, a topic which remained a central preoccupation in his work.

AART G. BROEK

del Paso, Fernando

b. 1935, Mexico City

Novelist

Fernando del Paso is one of the leading Mexican novelists of the past thirty years. He is the author of three monumental, linguistically experimental novels exploring national history, including the railroad workers' movement of 1958–59, the 1968 student movement and the French occupation of Mexico by the Austrian Archduke Maximilian and the Empress Carlota. His first novel, *José Trigo* (1970), was followed by *Palinuro de México* (1977) and *Noticias del imperio* (News of the Empire) (1987). Most recently, del Paso has experimented with a modern detective novel, *Linda 67, Historia de un crimen* (Linda 67, Story of a Crime) (1995).

Further reading

Borsó, V. (2002) 'Fernando del Paso', in C. Solé and K. Müller-Bergh (eds), *Latin American Writers: Supplement I*, New York: Scribners, 187–99.

Del Paso, F. (1989) *Palinuro of Mexico*, trans. E. Plaister, London: Quartet.

Fiddian, R. (1981) '*Palinuro de México*: A World of Words', *Bulletin of Hispanic Studies* 58.

—— (2000) *The Novels of Fernando del Paso*, University Press of Florida.

Stavans, I. (1997) 'Fernando del Paso', in V. Smith (ed.), *Encyclopedia of Latin American Literature*, London: Fitzroy Dearborn, 635–6.

CYNTHIA STEELE

Del Río, Ana María

b. 1948, Santiago, Chile

Writer

Del Río has published two short story collections and four novels including *Oxido de Carmen* (Carmen's Oxide) (1986) and *Tango Abierto* (Open Tango) (1995). An admirer of Chilean writer José **Donoso**, she is interested in writing about 'what is unspoken' in the lives of Chilean women of all ages. She lived in the USA from 1987–91 and afterwards taught literature and writing in universities in the northern Chilean cities of Arica and Iquique.

Further reading

Del Río, A.M. (1996) *La esfera media del aire*, Santiago de Chile: Aguilar Chilena de Ediciones.

AMALIA PEREIRA

Delgado, Susy

b. 1949, San Lorenzo, Paraguay

Poet

An important bilingual poet, Susy Delgado has been published in Spanish – *Algún extraviado temblor* (Some Misplaced Tremor) (1986), *El patio de los duendes* (The Fairies' Patio) (1991) and *Sobre el beso del viento* (On the Kiss of the Wind) (1995) – and Guarani – *Tesarái mboyvé* (Spanish translation *Antes del olvido* (Before Oblivion)) (1987). With degrees in media and sociology, Delgado is also a journalist for the newspaper *La nación*. She has received a number of national and international literary prizes.

Further reading

Delgado, S. (1999) *Ayvu membyre = hijo de aquel verbo*, Asunción: Arandura Editorial: Ediciones Colihue Mimbipa.

TERESA MÉNDEZ-FAITH

Denis Molina, Carlos

b. 1918, San José, Uruguay; d. 1983, Montevideo, Uruguay

Writer

Poet and novelist best known for his work in theatre, Denis Molina was an actor in, and artistic director of, the Teatro Solís. *Orfeo* (Orpheus) (1949), with Margarita Xirgu in the leading role, brought him early success. His absurd and poetic vision was expressed in several plays, including *Soñar con Ceci trae cola* (Dreaming of Ceci has After-Effects) (1983); performed at the Comedia Nacional while he was gravely ill, this play satirized the situation under Uruguay's military dictatorship and imagined a different future. His magical realist novel, *Lloverá siempre* (It Will Always Rain) (1950), occupied a central place in Uruguayan fiction (see **magical realism**).

Further reading

Denis Molina, C. (1981) *Lloverá siempre*, Montevideo: Biblioteca.

NORAH GIRALDI DEI CAS

Depestre, René

b. 1926, Jacmel, Haiti

Writer

Like his contemporary Jacques Stephen **Alexis**, Depestre was born during the US occupation of Haiti and was influenced by the Marxism of Jacques **Roumain**. He was one of the student leaders of *La Ruche* who, inspired by the visit of Andre Bréton, helped to overthrow the government in 1946. While in Paris as a student in the 1950s, he was drawn to the ideas of the communist poet Louis Aragon. This meant the beginning of a nomadic life for Depestre, who eventually returned home in 1957 after spending three years in Latin America where he became close friends with writers such as Nicolás **Guillén**, Pablo **Neruda** and Jorge **Amado**. Threatened by Duvalier's regime, he left for Cuba just after Fidel Castro's takeover of the country and stayed for twenty years. Eventually, at odds with the Cuban government, he left in 1979 to work for UNESCO in Paris, and has lived in the south of France since his retirement in 1986.

Depestre's first collections of poems *Etincelles* (Sparks) (1945) and *Gerbe de Sang* (Spray of Blood) (1946) were exuberant celebrations of youthful revolt influenced by the lyricism of Paul Eluard. While most of his 1950s poems were little more than Marxist tracts, the later poems, especially *Mineral noir* (Black Ore) (1956) and *Journal d'un animal marin* (Diary of a Sea Creature) (1964), reveal a fuller range of themes, from lyrical love to wry evocations of exile. Anti-US politics become apparent in his Cuban writing with the publication of the dramatic poem *Un arc en ciel pour l'occident chretién* (A Rainbow for the Christian West) (1967) and *Poète à Cuba* (Poet in Cuba) (1976). These years also represent an explicit critique of Haitian ***noirisme*** and a shift in interest to fiction. The short stories in *Alleluia pour une femme jardin* (Hallelujah for a Garden Woman) in 1973 celebrate the theme of erotic adventure, not favourably viewed by Depestre's Cuban hosts. Similarly, the anti-Duvalierist *roman à clef Le mat de cocagne* (Festival of the Greasy Pole) (1979) associates political dictatorship with sexual repression and imagines Vodun as a salutary source of sexual and political liberation. Eroticism has become more pronounced in his fiction since his move to Paris. *Hadriana dans tous mes rêves* (Hadriana in My Every Dream) is written in the tradition of *lo* ***real maravilloso*** (marvellous realism) and was awarded the Prix Renaudot in 1988. It is the first of an erotic trilogy, the second of which is a collection of tales, *Eros dans un train chinois* (Eros on a Chinese Train) (1990).

Further reading

Couffon, C. (1986) *René Depestre*, Paris: Seghers.

Dayan, J. (1977) *A Rainbow for the Christian West*, Amherst, MA: University of Massachusetts Press.

Soirieau, M.-A. (1997) 'René Depestre', in V. Smith (ed.), *Encyclopedia of Latin American Literature*, London: Fitzroy Dearborn, 255–6.

J. MICHAEL DASH

Desnoes, Edmundo

b. 1930, Havana, Cuba

Writer

Desnoes is the author of novels including *No hay problema* (No Problem) (1961) and ***Memorias del subdesarrollo*** (Memories of Underdevelopment) (1965) as well as critical essays collected in *Lam: azul y negro* (Lam: Blue and Black) (1963) and *Punto de vista* (Point of View) (1967). He studied and worked in New York before returning to Cuba after the Cuban Revolution, where he contributed to the newspaper *Revolución* and its cultural supplement *Lunes de Revolución*. From 1965 to 1970 he was a member of the editorial board of the journal ***Casa de las Américas***. He currently lives in the USA.

Further reading

Desnoes, Edmundo (1990) *Memories of Underdevelopment*, New Brunswick: Rutgers University Press.

WILFREDO CANCIO ISLA

D'Halmar, Augusto

b. 1882, Santiago, Chile; d. 1950, Santiago

Writer

D'Halmar, the pseudonym of Augusto Thomson, was a Utopian writer who wrote of the yearning for a new social order. In 1904 he and other writers tried to form a 'Tolstoyan colony' in southern Chile, but the attempt failed and he returned to Santiago to form a similar group in San Bernardo. At the core of this project was a return to nature which reflected the naturalist aesthetics of D'Halmar and many of his Latin American contemporaries (such as José Eustacio **Rivera** or Ricardo **Güiraldes**). He was the first recipient of the National Prize of Literature for Chile, in 1942. His novel *La pasión y muerte del cura Deústo* (The Passion and Death of Father Deusto) (1924) is one of the first Latin American novels to deal with homosexual love.

Further reading

D'Halmar, A. (1934) *Capitanes sin barco; novelas*, Santiago de Chile: Ediciones Ercilla.

—— (1970) *Obras escogidas*, Santiago de Chile: Editorial Andrés Bello.

Lockhart, D.B. (1997) 'Augusto D'Halmar', in V. Smith (ed.), *Encyclopedia of Latin American Literature*, London: Fitzroy Dearborn, 258–60.

Molloy, S. (2000) 'Of Queens and Castanets: *Hispanidad*, Orientalism, and Sexual Difference', in C. Patton and B. Sánchez-Eppler (eds), *Queer Diasporas*, Durham, NC: Duke University Press, 105–17.

LUIS E. CÁRCAMO-HUECHANTE

Di Benedetto, Antonio

b. 1922, Mendoza, Argentina; d. 1986, Buenos Aires, Argentina

Writer

Di Benedetto stands at the opposite extreme from regionalist writing (see ***regionalismo***). His novels and short stories are characteristically anti-naturalist and laconic, speculating on questions of logic and identity within a framework of fantastic writing (see **fantastic literature**) influenced by **Borges**. His avant-garde concerns led him to techniques close to the French *nouveau roman*, as in the stories of *El juicio de Dios* (God's Judgment) (1975). His novel *El hacedor de silencio* (The Silence Maker) (1964) uses noise as the starting point for a metaphysical exploration, while a historical novel set in colonial Paraguay (*Zama* (1956)) employs distance in time as an opportunity to explore existential issues.

Further reading

Di Benedetto, A. (1999) *Cuentos claros*, Buenos Aires: Adriana Hidalgo Editora.

—— (2000) *Mundo anima; el cariño de los tontos*, Buenos Aires: Adriana Hidalgo Editora.

Ricci, G. (1978) 'Aproximacion a la obra de Antonio Di Benedetto', *Nueva Crítica* 1: 85–104.

JULIO PREMAT

Diario de Poesía

Diario de Poesía is a poetry journal in tabloid form appearing four times a year. Founded in 1986 and edited in Buenos Aires by poet Daniel Samoilovich, it is divided into 'Information', 'Creative Writing' and 'Essay' sections, all three embracing poetry written in languages other than Spanish. Its translations of poetry and critical essays comprise a major contribution. Its newspaper format suggests an effort to popularize poetry, underlining the fact that a poem can be a news event; it also dates, documents and preserves poetry in the collective memory. Issue 38, published in 1996, provides a full index of its first ten years.

Further reading

Samoilovich, D. (1991) *La Ansiedad Perfecta*, Buenos Aires: Ed. de la Flor.

—— (1997) *Superficies Iluminadas*, Madrid: Hiperión.

ENRIQUE FOFFANI

Diáspora(s)

A literary group and journal, the principal members of Diaspora are Rolando Sánchez Mejías, Carlos Alberto Aguilera, Ismael González Castañer, Rogelio Saunders, José Manuel Prieto, Ricardo Alberto Pérez, Pedro Márquez de Armas and Radamés Molina. Most of them are living now out of Cuba, in Europe and Mexico City, although they published their first works in Havana from the late eighties onwards.

Founded as a group in 1993, they define themselves as 'una avanzadilla (sin) táctica de guerra' (a little movement (without) tactics of war) (*Diáspora(s)* # 1, 1997). Among their goals are 'to write a short story as if it were one, a poem as if it were one, an essay as if it were one; a novel as if it were one, etc'. and to 'terrorize Cuban Literature through the Concept'. As part of the writing process, they do not avoid ideology and politics from a critical perspective, and this lack of reticence puts them in a difficult situation with respect to the official institutions of the Cuban cultural system. Diaspora(s) journal is published clandestinely in

Havana with the help of friends inside and outside of the country. On its pages appear works by Diáspora(s) members and by national and international authors whose ideas do not have much space in the official journals.

JESÚS JAMBRINA

Díaz, Jesús

b. 1941, Havana, Cuba; d. 2001, Madrid, Spain

Writer and filmmaker

Díaz is perhaps the most controversial Cuban writer moulded by the direct influence of the Cuban Revolution. His book *Los años duros* (The Hard Years) won the **Casa de las Américas** short story prize in 1966, helping to create what was then called 'La narrativa de la violencia' (the narrative of violence). This narrative tries to represent the revolutionary armed struggle from the viewpoint of the protagonists. Some of the writers who practised such tendencies were viewed with suspicion by the government during the first years of the Cuban Revolution, but by the 1980s their works had been accepted completely.

Díaz's novel *Las iniciales de la tierra* (The Initials of Earth) is widely considered his best work. Published in Havana in 1985, although written a decade earlier, it narrates the story of a candidate for membership in the Communist Party who has written his self-criticism in order to be able to join the organization. Due to the revolutionary orthodoxy of his fellows and his own hesitation in taking on the role of hero, neither he nor the readers are sure if he will be finally accepted as a new member. The public and the critics recognized the excellence of the novel and it is now widely read and taught. Another important novel is *Las palabras perdidas* (The Lost Words) (1992).

With his essay 'Los anillos de la Serpiente (The Serpent's Rings) (1992) Díaz, exiled in Europe in 1990, distanced himself from official ideology and began a process of self-criticism that led him to describe his own disappointment with the communist system. The latter is a theme especially visible in his last novels, which include *Dime algo sobre Cuba* (Tell Me Something About Cuba) (1998) and *Siberiada* (2000). *Las cuatro fugas de Manuel* (Manuel's Four Escapes) (2002), published posthumously, is an exploration of Díaz's dramatic transition from being a strong supporter of the Communist Party to his feelings of dislocation in exile.

Through the years, Díaz also founded important cultural journals including *Pensamiento crítico* (Critical Thought) (1967), *El caimán barbudo* (The Bearded Alligator) (1966) and *Encuentro de la cultura cubana* (Encounter with Cuban Culture) (1996), all of them important in Cuban literary and cultural history. As a filmmaker, he directed several documentaries and films among which *55 hermanos* (55 Brothers) (1978) and *Lejanía* (Distance) (1985) are particularly outstanding. Both of these films deal with the return of Cuban exiles to Cuba at a time when this was a taboo subject for many both inside and outside the country; in these films (made in Cuba), Díaz's treatment was in accord with the official view.

Further reading

Brotherton, J. (1995) 'Rewriting the Revolution: Jesus Díaz's *Las iniciales de la tierra*', *Journal of Iberian and Latin American Studies*, Dec., 1(1–2): 69–81.

Rodriguez Vivaldi, A.M. (2001) 'Jesus Díaz: El cine como texto y pretexto para la literatura', *Atenea* 21(1–2): 125–36

JESÚS JAMBRINA

Díaz, Jorge

b. 1930, Rosario, Argentina

Playwright

In 1959, Díaz began to work with ICTUS in Chile, the group that would stage many of his plays. With them, he would also work as an actor and stage designer. Originally located within the theatre of the absurd movement, his plays have branched in many directions He has written several children's plays and many scripts for radio and television. Twice winner of the coveted Tirso de Molina prize, his plays include *Introducción al elefante y otras zoologías* (Introduction to the Elephant and other Zoologies) (1968), *Mata a tu prójimo como a ti mismo* (Kill Thy

Neighbour as Thyself) (1977) and *Ayer sin ir más lejos* (Yesterday to Go No Further) (1986).

Further reading

Díaz, J. (1978) *Teatro*, Santiago: Nascimento.

Monleón, J. (ed.) (1967) *Jorge Díaz*, Madrid: Taurus.

Woodyard, G. (1976) 'Jorge Díaz and the Liturgy of Violence', in L.F. Lyday and G. Woodyard (eds), *Dramatists in Revolt: The New Latin American Theatre*, Austin: University of Texas Press, 59–76.

—— (1989) 'Jorge Díaz', in *Latin American Writers*, ed. C.A. Solé and M.I. Abreu, New York: Scribners, 3, 1393–7.

MARINA PIANCA

DÍAZ ARRIETA, HERNÁN *see* Alone

Díaz Quiñones, Arcadio

b. 1940, Mayagüez, Puerto Rico

Literary critic

Díaz Quiñones has devoted many articles to the writing of history and to the role of intellectuals in Hispanic-Caribbean society during the nineteenth and twentieth centuries. His publications include *Conversación con José Luis González* (A Conversation with José Luis **González**) (1976) and *La memoria rota: Ensayos de cultura y política* (Broken Memory: Essays on Culture and Politics) (1993). He directs the series 'La Nave y el Puerto' for Ediciones Huracán in San Juan, which has published work by Tomás Blanco, Cintio **Vitier** and Mario **Vargas Llosa** among others. He taught at the University of Puerto Rico before taking a position as Professor of Spanish at Princeton University in 1983.

JUAN CARLOS QUINTERO HERENCIA

Díaz Rodríguez, Manuel

b. 1871, Caracas, Venezuela; d. 1927, New York, USA

Writer, physician and politician

Díaz Rodríguez studied medicine, and in 1891 became a physician. However, it was not science that would make him famous. One of the most important fiction writers in **Spanish American modernism**, his writings include *Confidencias de Psíquis* (Psyche's Secrets) (1896), *Cuentos de color* (Colour Tales) (1899) and his most important novel *Idolos rotos* (Broken Idols) (1901), written when his father passed away and he had to take over the administration of the family farm. His work also comprises *Sangre patricia* (Noble Blood) (1902), the essay 'Camino de perfección' (Path to Perfection) (1910) and 'Sermones líricos' (Lyrical Sermons) (1918). During his lifetime he held positions as administrative director of Universidad Central de Venezuela, minister, senator, diplomat and governor.

Further reading

Castro, J.A. (1988) *Narrativa modernista y concepción del mundo*, Caracas: Comisión Presidencial para el Bicentenario del Natalicio del General Rafael Urdaneta.

Dunham, L. (1959) *Manuel Díaz Rodríguez, vida y obra*, Mexico City: Ediciones de Andrea.

VíCTOR GALARRAGA OROPEZA

Díaz Solís, Gustavo

b. 1920, Guiria, Sucre, Venezuela

Writer

Although he published little, Díaz Solís was undoubtedly a major influence on generations of short story writers. A lawyer and university professor, he occupied a number of important university posts. Having studied English and US literature in Washington and Chicago, he published his first writings in the journal *Contapunto* as well as *Elite*, ***Revista nacional de cultura***, *Fantoches* and others. His brief stories are built around strong and often subconscious emotions such as death, desire and conflict. He also has an important body of translations of Romantic and modern poetry from English. In 1996 he won the National Literature Prize.

Further reading

Araujo, O. (1988) 'La lección de Díaz Solís', in *Narrativa venezolana contemporánea*, Caracas: Monte Avila.

Díaz Solís, G. (2002) *Cuentos escogidos*, Caracas: Monte Avila.

Sambrano Urdaneta, O. (1963) 'Los cuentos de Gustavo Díaz Solís', *Revista nacional de cultura* 158–9: 39–58.

JORGE ROMERO LEÓN

Diego, Eliseo

b. 1920, Havana, Cuba; d. 1994, Mexico City

Writer

Originally a member of the **Orígenes** literary group, Diego was more influenced by his readings of the Spanish Golden Age lyric and English poetry and prose (especially the fantastic) than he was by his early association with Juan Ramón Jiménez or José **Lezama Lima**. His poetry and stories were always superbly crafted and luminously simple, combining affection for everyday things with a profound reverence for the (frustrated) promise of the Republican era of Cuban history. After the 1959 Revolution, Diego stayed in Cuba, working at the National Library, and later at the Union of Cuban Artists and Writers (**UNEAC**). He died in Mexico after receiving the Juan Rulfo Prize.

Further reading

Diego, E. (1999) *En otro reino frágil*, Havana: Ediciones UNIÓN.

—— (2002) *Obra poética*, Havana: Ediciones UNIÓN.

Febles, J. (1997) 'Eliseo Diego', in V. Smith (ed.), *Encyclopedia of Latin American Literature*, London: Fitzroy Dearborn, 260–2.

Sainz, E. (ed.) (1991) *Acerca de Eliseo Diego*, Havana: Ediciones Letras Cubanas.

BEN A. HELLER

DIEGO, ELISEO ALBERTO *see* Alberto, Eliseo

Diez de Medina, Fernando

b. 1908, La Paz, Bolivia; d. 1990, La Paz

Writer

One of the most prolific writers of twentieth-century Bolivian literature, Diez de Medina often used literature for political purposes. He wrote poetry, essays, drama, a novel, biographies and a history of Bolivian literature. Despite his vast output, current criticism does not consider him of theoretical significance as a philosopher or a sociologist. He was famous for his polemical newspaper articles and played a prominent role in politics, filling both government and diplomatic posts. He investigated and idealized the mythology of the Aymara.

Further reading

Díez de Medina, F. (1947) *Thunupa: Ensayos*, Buenos Aires: Imprenta López.

—— (1969) *Mateo Montemayor*, La Paz: Los Amigos del Libro.

Francovich, G. (1956) *El pensamiento boliviano en el siglo XX*, Mexico City: Fondo de Cultura Económica.

MARÍA DORA VILLA GÓMEZ

Discépolo, Armando

b. 1887, Buenos Aires, Argentina; d. 1971, Buenos Aires

Playwright

Discépolo is one of the founding figures of contemporary Argentine drama. The son of Italian immigrants, Discépolo devoted most of his works to the abyss between the promised prosperity of the New World and the reality of immigrant life. He developed a theatrical language called ***grotesco criollo*** in which details of plot, character and interpersonal relations are marked by profound contradictions and a strident despair, providing audiences with a sense of the monstrous underbelly of vaunted national prosperity.

Further reading

Discépolo, A. (1969) *Obras escogidas*, ed. D. Viñas, Buenos Aires: Jorge Alvarez, 3 vols.

—— (1987, 1990) *Obras escogidas*, ed. O. Pelletieri, Buenos Aires: Galerna, 2 vols.

Kaiser-Lenoir, C. (1977) *El grotesco criollo: Estilo teatral de una época*, Havana: Casa de las Américas.

Pelletieri, O. (1990) *Obra dramática de Armando Discépolo*, Buenos Aires: Galerna.

DAVID WILLIAM FOSTER

discours antillais, Le

Published in 1981, *Le discours antillais* (Caribbean Discourse) is a monumental essay collection which established Edouard **Glissant**'s reputation as the major Caribbean theorist of the post-war, post-***négritude*** period. As the title suggests, the book is both a discourse on the Caribbean and a study of Caribbean discursive practices. In dense and wide-ranging essays, Glissant addresses Caribbean history, cultural resistance, a poetics of landscape and his theory of *antillanité.* He theorizes that the Caribbean islands are typified by an irreducible creole diversity, threatened in Martinique because of departmentalization. The region, he argues, possesses an exemplary indeterminacy in a world increasingly dominated by cultural archipelagos.

Further reading

Britton, Celia (1999) *Edouard Glissant and Postcolonial Theory: Strategies of Language and Resistance*, Charlottesville: University of Virginia Press.

Campa, R. de la (1995) 'Mimicry and the Uncanny in Caribbean Discourse', in *Latin Americanism*, Minneapolis: University of Minnesota Press, 85–120.

Glissant, Edouard (1992) *Caribbean Discourse: Selected Essays*, Charlottesville: Caraf Books.

—— (1997) *Poetics of Relation*, Ann Arbor: University of Michigan Press.

J. MICHAEL DASH

Disla, Reynaldo

b. 1956, Cotuí, Dominican Republic

Playwright

Disla belongs to the generation of the 1980s. His 1985 play *Bolo Francisco* won the **Casa de las Américas** prize. He was also recognized at Casa de Teatro (House of Theatre) for his play *La muerte aplaudida* (The Applauded Death). He has acted in forty-two plays, pioneered puppet theatre for children and founded several theatre groups, such as Texpo and Los Teatreros. In his plays, Disla uses new experimental techniques to express social conflicts. Influenced by **Brechtian theatre**, Disla is always looking for interaction between audiences and actors.

Further reading

Disla, Reynaldo (1985) *Bolo Francisco*, Havana: Casa de las Américas.

FERNANDO VALERIO-HOLGUÍN

Dobru, R.

b. 1935, Suriname; d. 1983, Suriname

Writer and politician

Dobru (real name Robin Raveles) was a political activist, politician and literary author from the 1960s until his death. He is the author of one the best-known poems in Sranan Tongo, 'Wan bon' (One Tree), which appeared in his 1965 debut poetry collection *Matapi: Poewema.* His poetry and prose writing was greatly influenced by Cuban and Chinese communist ideology and his strong nationalist feelings. A selection of his poetry, *Boodschappen uit de zon* (Messages from under the

Sun) was published by a Dutch publishing house in 1982.

AART G. BROEK

Doña Bárbara

Doña Bárbara is Rómulo **Gallegos**'s best-known and most emblematic novel, published in Spain in 1929 for fear of government censorship, and for years regarded as a comprehensive image of a rural Venezuela facing modernization. The novel's principal figure was regarded by Venezuela's 'civilizers' as the fascinating and fearsome symbol of a savage and hostile region which rejected the benefits of progress – the dark interior clinging to its old barbaric habits. The book became, and remains, a canonical text. The film adaptation, directed by Mexican Fernando de Fuentes, with María Félix in the title role, added little to the novel but did project Félix into the limelight.

Further reading

Dunham, Lowell (1974) *Rómulo Gallegos: An Oklahoma Encounter and the Writing of the Last Novel*, Norman: University of Oklahoma Press.

Gallegos, Rómulo (1942) *Doña Bárbara*, New York: F.S. Crofts & Co.

—— (1948) *Doña Bárbara*, trans. R. Malloy, Magnolia, MA: Peter Smith.

González Echevarría, R. (1985) '*Doña Bárbara* Writes the Plain', in *The Voice of the Masters: Writing and Authority in Modern Latin American Literature*, Austin: University of Texas Press, 33–63.

VERONICA JAFFÉ

Donoso, José

b. 1924, Santiago, Chile; d. 1996, Santiago

Writer

Donoso is one of Latin America's most important novelists and a key figure in the emergence of a 'new' Latin American novel that moves beyond realism. Born into an upper-middle class family, Donoso from childhood rejected the rituals and aspirations of the Chilean bourgeoisie. In 1943 he dropped out of school, and two years later, unable to hold a job for more than a few months, he travelled to Magallanes, the southern tip of Chile, and then through Patagonia to Buenos Aires working as a shiphand and a dockhand. In 1947 he returned to Chile, finished high school and studied English at university. Two years later he received a scholarship to study at Princeton University under Allen Tate. This was when Donoso developed his fascination with the works of Henry James. His first short stories, 'The Poisoned Pastries' and 'The Blue Woman', were published in *MMS*, a Princeton literary review.

At first sight, *Coronación* (Coronation) (1956) offers a traditional realistic depiction of urban society and an existentialist hero in Andrés Abalos. Yet, the novel's final scene is the threshold of his future fiction. The grotesque figure of the old and feeble Elisa Abalos, dressed in rags as a queen by her old drunken maids, creates the atmosphere of a bizarre carnival which transgresses the realist mode.

In Donoso's subsequent novels, all centres of power enter into conflict and are displaced by the margins. Thus, in *El **lugar sin límites*** (Hell Has No Limits) (1966), the homosexual Manuela is the destabilizing axis, erasing the official borders delimiting the 'masculine' and the 'feminine'. Dressed as a woman, old Manuela's grotesque body sensually performs a Spanish dance and seduces his/her 'manly' audience in the whorehouse: a carnivalized version of the bourgeois family. Arturo Ripstein later brilliantly adapted it for the screen.

In his account of the Latin American **Boom**, Donoso describes how national regionalisms were left behind and became cosmopolitan under the influence of **Asturias**, **Bioy Casares**, **Borges** and particularly **Carpentier**, whose writings on the baroque suggested to him that the distorted and excessive considerably increased the possibilities of the novel.

In *El **obsceno pájaro de la noche*** (The Obscene Bird of the Night) (1970), he elaborates the baroque through the opposition of order and chaos, through a proliferation of masks, multiple identities and deforming mirror reflections and stories which annul the possibility of a centre or unity. Significantly, both houses in the work are unconventional spaces: the House of Spiritual Exercises is a maze of closed corridors and patios filled with the surplus possessions of wealthy families, not only objects but old women who were former servants; La Rinconada, on the other hand, has been converted into a monstrous asylum to protect and imprison Boy, a deformed child whose parents could also be any of the characters. Boy's body is described as chaos and disorder, as a different but worse form of death and, in his monstrosity, he is the other who threatens any power exerted upon society, artistic forms or language. Therefore he must be silenced and suppressed like the female characters who represent waste, witchcraft and the irrational. Symbolically, Humberto's writing, attempting an orderly biography of Jerónimo, becomes a chaotic polyphony of displaced voices; the narrator as centre of consciousness and unity is reduced to zero, to a confined body wrapped up in burlap and consumed by fire.

Games in Donoso's novels are always a source of transgression. In *Este domingo* (This Sunday) (1967), children's games momentarily subvert bourgeois prescriptions; in *Casa de campo* (A House in the Country) (1978), they lead to torture and evil, to the removal of all fences and invasion by the natives and the primitive forces of nature. To some extent an allegory of dictatorial power in Chile, the novel also ironically dismantles the rules of fiction. Between order and insurrection, the narrator playfully tears away the veils of orderly configurations to show their deceitful nature.

In 1981, after seventeen years of voluntary exile, Donoso returned to Chile. His experiences abroad constitute an underlying motif in *La misteriosa desaparición de la marquesita de Loria* (The Mysterious Disappearance of the Little Marquise of Loria) (1980) whose Nicaraguan protagonist is viewed by Spaniards as a primitive symbol of Latin America. The Marquise, like the mysterious dog, is the indomitable force that surpasses even the transgressive quality of the erotic and can only be re-encased in rumour and legend. Exile in *El jardín de al lado* (The Garden Next Door) (1981) represents identity as a split self, both in terms of a national territory and a mythical lost paradise. *La desesperanza* (Curfew) (1988) shows the return to one's own land, now under military dictatorship. Swaying between the present and the past, both the protagonist and Chile itself, in spite of the abuse of power, maintain a multiple reality submerged in dreams and magic within a landscape of natural wonders which remain impervious to the horrors of military rule.

Further reading

Adelstein, M. (1990) *Studies on the Works of José Donoso: An Anthology of Critical Essays*, Lewiston, NY: Edwin Mellen.

Cerda, C. (1988) *José Donoso: Originales y metáforas*, Santiago: Planeta.

Donoso, J. (1977) *Personal History of the Boom*, New York: Columbia University Press.

Goic, C. (2002) 'José Donoso', in *Latin American Writers: Supplement I*, ed. C. Solé and K. Müller-Bergh, New York: Scribners, 201–16.

Kerr, L. (1997) 'José Donoso', in V. Smith (ed.), *Encyclopedia of Latin American Literature*, London: Fitzroy Dearborn, 267–70.

McMurray, G. (1979) *José Donoso*, Boston: Twayne.

Mandri, F. (1995) *José Donoso's House of Fiction: A Dramatic Construction of Time and Place*, Detroit: Wayne State University Press.

Swanson, P. (1988) *José Donoso: The 'Boom' and Beyond*, Liverpool: Francis Cairns.

LUCÍA GUERRA

Donoso Pareja, Miguel

b. 1931, Guayaquil, Ecuador

Writer

A truly 'postmodern' writer who has broken new paths for Ecuadorean letters, Donoso Pareja's works masterfully address exile and the search for identity, the complexities of memory and forgetfulness, the essence of invention and the creative process, eroticism and the demystification of sexual norms. Donoso Pareja is also a cultural activist –

director of writers' workshops, editor of magazines and classics, journalist and literary critic. His principal works include *Nunca más el mar* (Never Again the Sea) (1981), *Todo lo que inventamos es cierto* (Everything We Invent is True) (1990), *Ultima canción del exiliado* (The Exile's Latest Song) (1994) and *Hoy empiezo a acordarme* (Today I Begin to Remember) (1995).

Further reading

Donoso Pareja, M. (1982) *Nunca más el mar*, Quito: Editorial El Conejo.

—— (2001) *La muerte de Tyrone Power en el Monumental del Barcelona*, Quito: Eskeletra Editorial.

HUMBERTO E. ROBLES

Dorfman, Ariel

b. 1942, Buenos Aires, Argentina

Writer and critic

Born in Buenos Aires and Chilean by choice, after the electoral triumph of Salvador Allende in 1970 Dorfman participated actively in the Popular Unity administration. The construction of a peaceful road to socialism in Chile marked his life in a definitive way. The *coup* by Augusto Pinochet forced him to leave the country and become an exile in France, Holland and eventually the USA where he works as a professor, literary critic and journalist.

Imaginación y violencia en América Latina (Imagination and Violence in Latin America) (1970), a volume of critical essays, was followed by the publication of *Para leer el Pato Donald* (How to Read Donald Duck: Imperialist Ideology in the Disney Comic) (1971), co-written with Armand Mattelart, which was an important contribution to the intellectual debate on the mass media. In the context of the 1970s, the book was a challenge for those critics who felt that the importance of critical work is directly proportional to its object. In that sense, the work dismantled not only the axioms of the Disney industry but certain presumptions about high culture, and presented a project for the creation of a new national and popular culture.

His first novel, *Moros en la costa* (Hard Rain) (1973), stands in the tradition of the search for the new initiated by the vanguard of the 1920s and followed by the **Boom** of the Latin American novel. It is an attempt to deepen the debates about the possibility of a revolutionary literature and in that sense is reminiscent of ***Rayuela*** by Julio **Cortázar**. If *Moros en la costa* is the novel about the revolutionary process, *Viudas* (Widows) (1981) narrates the experience of a military *coup* and of exile. A year later, Dorfman published his third novel, *La última canción de Manuel Sendero* (The Last Song of Manuel Sendero) (1982). Two voices resonate in the novel – that of Manuel Sendero and that of his grandfather – voices that interweave to the point of becoming one single voice. Grandson and grandfather refuse to be born, given the political circumstances that await them. This work presents a radical departure in the novelistic style of Dorfman, as it presents a new way of understanding political commitment, calling into question ideas of representation, partisan ethics and even the notion of exile and homeland.

Máscaras (Masks) (1988) explores the subject of State violence, continuing and further exploring the trend begun in *Manuel Sendero*, and with sly humour delivers a work open to diverse readings and interpretations. His play, *La muerte y la doncella* (Death and the Maiden), has been successful in several languages, and was made into a film in 1995 with Ben Kingsley and Sigourney Weaver, directed by Roman Polanski. Subsequent works include the novel, *Konfidenz* (1995), and an autobiography, *Looking South, Heading North* (1998).

Further reading

Claro-Mayo, J. (1981) 'Dorfman, cuentista comprometido', *Revista iberoamericana* 114–15: 339–45.

Dorfman, A. (1998) *Heading South, Looking North: A Bilingual Journey*, London: Hodder & Stoughton.

—— (1991) *Some Write to the Future: Essays on Contemporary Latin American Fiction*, trans. George Shivers with the author, Durham, NC and London: Duke University Press.

Oropesa, S. (1992) *La obra de Ariel Dorfman*, Madrid: Pliegos.

Walker, J. (1997) 'Ariel Dorfman', in V. Smith (ed.),

Encyclopedia of Latin American Literature, London: Fitzroy Dearborn, 270–2.

SANDRA GARABANO

Dragún, Osvaldo

b. 1929, Entre Ríos, Argentina

Playwright

Beginning with the Teatro Independiente, Dragún later co-founded the Teatro Abierto. In *La peste viene de Melos* (The Plague Comes from Melos) (1956), he sought the origins of a conflictive present in the past. The bulk of his work – ranging from *Historias para ser contadas* (Stories to be Read Aloud) (1956), to *¡Arriba corazón!* (Lift Up, My Heart) (1987) – explores individual alienation in everyday life. His theatre, realist in intent, employs a metaphorical discourse and a reflective estrangement.

Further reading

Schmidt, D. (1976) 'The Theater of Osvaldo Dragún', in L.F. Lyday and G. Woodyard (eds), *Dramatists in Revolt: The New Latin American Theater*, Austin: University of Texas Press, 37–58.

Woodyard, G. (1989) 'Osvaldo Dragún', in *Latin American Writers*, ed. C.A. Solé and M.I. Abreu, New York: Scribners, 3, 1377–82.

STELLA MARTINI

Drayton, Geoffrey

b. 1924, Christchurch, Barbados

Writer

Drayton is the author of two novels. *Christopher* (1959), grounded in his Caribbean childhood, is the story of an imaginative child, a white son of the planter class of Barbados, whose father resents his dependence on his wife's money. The male adult world of the father, along with the resentment he extends to his son, taints the joys of childhood, especially the relationship between Christopher and his black nanny, Gip. *Zohara* (1961) is the story of a Spanish village where superstition and fear lead to the murder of the 14-year-old protagonist. Drayton has also written poetry. He has a degree in economics from Cambridge University, England and lived for many years in England and Canada before retiring to live in Spain.

Further reading

Drayton, Geoffrey (1972) *Christopher*, London: Heinemann Educational.

CAROL J. WALLACE

dub poetry

Dub is a performance poetry, rhythmically aligned with reggae or ska bass beats. Its language is the language of the Jamaican street; its content the experience of the most oppressed members of that society – but it is also their cry of protest. In the Caribbean the dub poets are 'orators as well as poets' – like Louise **Bennett**, in an earlier generation, and later Jamaican poets such as **Mutabaruka** (recorded on *Any Which Way Freedom* (1989), for example), or Mikey **Smith**, who was murdered age 29 but who had already established a reputation with his album, *Mi Cyaan Believe it* (1982), or Grenada's Paul **Keens-Douglas**. Dub was brought to Britain and adapted to the Caribbean diaspora by poets such as Linton Kwesi Johnson, Benjamin Zephaniah and Pepsi Poet.

Further reading

Cooper, C. (1995) *Noises in the Blood: Orality, Gender and the 'Vulgar' Body of Jamaican Popular Culture*, Durham, NC: Duke University Press.

MIKE GONZALEZ

Duncan, Quince

b. 1940, Limón, Costa Rica

Writer

Duncan was born and raised in Limón, a province with a large Afro-Caribbean population. Deeply conscious of these African roots and of his own

Jamaican descent, in his short stories and anthologies Duncan explores the problems of black people both within the hostile Latin society of Costa Rica and throughout the whole of the African diaspora. In addition to his treatment of the racial and linguistic marginalization of Costa Rican blacks, Duncan's strong interest in the syncretism of West African and European Protestant religious traditions is of particular note.

Further reading

Duncan, Quince (1978) *La paz del pueblo*, San José: Editorial Costa Rica.

—— (1979) *Final de calle*, San José: Editorial Costa Rica.

SCOTT A. COOPER

E

Ecuador

Much of Ecuadoran literature reflects the economic and social realities of the multicultural nation. The **Guayaquil Group**, a writers' collective formed in the 1930s to narrate the plight of the coastal inhabitants, and the work of Jorge **Icaza**, author of the social realist indigenist novel *Huasipungo* (The Villagers) in 1934, continue to influence Ecuadorian writers. Nelson **Estupiñán Bass**'s *Cuando los guayacanes florecieron* (When the Guayacan Trees Bloomed) (1954) depicts the folkloric rhythms and lyrics of the Afro-Ecuadoran population on the coast, as does Antonio Preciado's poetry. Jorge Enrique **Adoum**'s narrative, poetry and essays explore the complex personal and international stature of an Ecuador which is no longer provincial and isolated. His innovative novel *Entre Marx y una mujer desnuda* (Between Marx and a Naked Woman) (1976) wrestles with problems of narrative form as well as depicting the drama of intellectual introspection. Eliécer **Cárdenas**'s *Polvo y ceniza* (Dust and Ashes) (1979) recounts the deeds of a bandit who battles the landowners in southern Ecuador, becoming a legendary figure. *La linares* (The Linares Woman) (1975), written by Iván **Egüez**, depicts the heady world of politics where a beautiful woman brings down a president.

Women writers also address the cultural constructs of nation; most notable is the literary group 'Mujeres del Atico' (Women of Atico), who maintain a literary salon and publish editorial pieces in the Guayaquil newspaper *El Telégrafo* (The Telegraph). Internationally recognized for her novels is Alicia **Yánez Cossío**, the author of *Bruno, Soroche y los tíos* (Bruno, Soroche and the Uncles) (1972) and *La cofradía del mullo del vestido de la virgen Pipona* (The Religious Brotherhood of the Shell Garment of the Virgin Pipona) (1985), novels which blend a controlled magic realism and Catholic lore with the sharp irony and wit reflective of the region. An interesting historical novel that looks at the struggle for independence from the viewpoint of an Afro-Ecuadoran woman is Luz Argentina **Chiriboga**'s *Jonatás y Manuela*. Certainly, one of the more notable innovations in the literary scene is the publication of two books of poetry in Quichua by the Otavalan Indian Ariruma Kowii, *Mutsuctsurini* (1988) and *Taisik* (1993).

Ecuadoran writers and artists receive support and exhibition space in the national and regional branches of the Casa de la Cultura Ecuatoriana (the Ecuadorian National Endowment for the Arts). A number of books emerged in the latter part of the 1990s which returned to the question of national identity. These included Jorge Enrique Adoum's *Ecuador: Señas particulares* (Ecuador, Identifying Features) (1997) and Miguel **Donoso Pareja**'s *Ecuador: Identidad o equizofrenia* (Ecuador, Identity and Schizophrenia) (1998).

Further reading

Ansaldo Briones, C. (ed.) (1993) *Antología del cuento ecuatoriano*, Guayaquil: Universidad Católica Santiago de Guayaquil/Universidad Andina Simón Bolívar.

Jaramillo, G. (1992) *Indice de la narrativa ecuatoriana*, Quito: Editora Nacional.

Polit Dueñas, G. (ed.) (2001) *Crítica literaria ecuatoriana: Antología*, Quito: FLACSO-Ecuador.
Robles, H. (1988) *La noción de vanguardia en el Ecuador. Recepción–trayectoria–documentos. 1918–1934*, Guayaquil: Casa de la Cultura Ecuatoriana.
Wishnia, K.J.A. (1999) *Twentieth-Century Ecuadorian Narrative: New Readings in the Context of the Americas*, Lewisburg, PA: Bucknell University Press.

REGINA HARRISON

Ecury, Nydia Maria Enrica

b. 1926, Aruba

Actor, director and poet

Ecury moved to Curaçao in the 1950s, where she translated plays by Paso, Williams, Genet and Shakespeare into the creole Papiamentu. She is an actress and director, as well as the author of various collections of poetry, including the 1984 bilingual edition of *Kantika pa Mama Tera/Songs for Mother Earth*. Ecury has been strongly opposed to the consolidation of female stereotypes and to the relegation of women to the periphery of public life. She has been a performing artist of Papiamentu poetry at numerous literary festivals both inside and outside the Caribbean.

AART G. BROEK

Edgell, Zee

b. 1940, Belize City

Novelist and activist

The foremost writer of Belize, Edgell's first novel *Beka Lamb* (1982) is autobiographical and relates the problems of a young creole girl maturing into adulthood to the growing pains of a country struggling for independence. After travelling widely abroad, Edgell was appointed director of the Women's Bureau in the new country of Belize (1981). Out of this experience came her second novel, *In Times like These* (1991). Currently a professor at Kent State University, Edgell's most recent novel, based on a historical incident, is *The Festival of San Joachim*, in which she examines domestic abuse and the mestizo community in Belize.

GAY WILENTZ

Edwards, Jorge

b. 1931, Santiago, Chile

Writer

Edwards started his writing career in 1952 with the publication of a collection of short stories entitled *El patio* (The Backyard). Against the background of the simple situations of everyday life, the child protagonists obliquely experience the authoritarian regime of the adults, their lack of communication and the ineffectiveness of the bourgeois system. Although *Gente de la ciudad* (City People) (1961) and *Las máscaras* (Masks) (1967) present bureaucrats and urban adults leading an empty and pedestrian life, the same tensions created by the social and economic regimes are present. Edwards has been defined as an author of few themes and multiple elaborations on the conflict between conventionalized roles and defeated masks.

After completing his law studies at the University of Chile and at Princeton, Edwards began a career in diplomacy. In 1970, Salvador Allende sent him to Cuba from where, after three months and for no explicit reason, he was expelled. This experience led him to write *Persona non grata* (1973), a testimonial account of the economic difficulties of the Cuban Revolution and the problems of a political power which represses independent artistic creation and jails writers such as Heberto **Padilla**.

Edwards's novels *Los convidados de piedra* (The Stone Visitors) (1978), *El museo de cera* (The Wax Museum) (1981) and *La mujer imaginaria* (The Imaginary Woman) (1985) are, in a sense, a chronicle of the decadence and re-articulation of oligarchic power in Chile. The narrator is a *voyeur* who, with distance and irony, envelops the characters' voices and perspectives. Within this frame, past and present merge in a temporal line where each period retroactively sheds light onto the present. Thus, in *Los convidados de piedra*, although the plot centres on the bourgeois ritual of a birthday celebration for an aristocrat, time extends back to 1890, the critical year preceding the Revolution of 1891, and the subsequent regeneration of the oligarchy. According to Edwards's ideology, Chilean history has been dominated by the anachronistic power of colonial aristocracy, a concept symbolized by the Marquis de Villa-Rica, who detained social change by sculpturing reality into wax.

In 1971, Edwards worked with Pablo **Neruda** as cultural attaché in Paris, and his memoirs of Neruda entitled *Adiós, Poeta* ... (Farewell, Poet ...) (1990) won the III Comillas Prize sponsored by Tusquets Editores. He was awarded the National Prize for Literature in Chile in 1995.

Further reading

Balboa Echeverría, M. (1989) 'Jorge Edwards', in C.A. Solé and M.I. Abreu (eds), *Latin American Writers*, New York: Scribners, 3, 1399–1403.

Costa, E. de (1997) 'Jorge Edwards', in V. Smith (ed.), *Encyclopedia of Latin American Literature*, London: Fitzroy Dearborn, 283–4.

Moody, M. (1985) 'Chile and *El museo de cera*', *Chasqui* 14(3): 37–42.

Otero, J. (1990) 'Subjetividad y mito como modos narrativos en *Persona non grata*', *Confluencia* 5(2): 47–53.

Rodríguez, M.A. (1988) '*La mujer imaginaria*: Una reflexión de Jorge Edwards sobre la historia chilena reciente', *Revista de filología* 4: 225–39.

Rojas Piña, B. (1992) '*El anfitrión* de Jorge Edwards: Reescritura de mitos en el contexto de la dictadura y el exilio chilenos', *Chasqui* 21(1): 77–91.

—— (1994) 'El narrador en *El museo de cera* de Jorge Edwards', *Acta literaria* 19: 69–85.

LUCÍA GUERRA

Edwards Bello, Joaquín

b. 1887, Valparaíso, Chile; d. 1968, Santiago, Chile

Writer and journalist

A keen observer of Latin American culture, Edwards's chronicles, travel diaries and memoirs offer valuable insights on all aspects of life, from politics to fashion. As an aristocrat who despised the values of his social class, he presents in his novels *El inútil* (The Loser) (1910) and *El roto* (The Down and Out) (1920), a morbid microcosm of poverty, denouncing the injustices of the Chilean rich in the 1920s. Esmeraldo, a main character in several of Edward's works, is a countertext of the *roto*, the national symbol which reconstructs men from the lower classes as brave, strong and adventurous. He represents the Chilean working classes.

Further reading

Calderon, A. (1968) 'Joaquín Edwards Bello: Ocho conversaciones', *Atenea* 45(166): 11–20.

—— (1981) 'El bisabuelo de piedra: Entrevista postuma a Joaquín Edwards Bello', *Atenea* 443–4: 261–7.

Silva Castro, R. (1968) 'Joaquín Edwards Bello y Daniel de la Vega, prosistas chilenos', *Revista hispanica moderna* 34: 791–8.

LUCÍA GUERRA

Egüez, Iván

b. 1944, Quito, Ecuador

Writer

Egüez was at the forefront of every aspect of the cultural scene in Ecuador, from the creation of avant-garde publications to the establishment of his own publishing house, Abrapalabra. In his own work, his command of technique, psychological insight, and unique use and manipulaton of language are outstanding, as well as his biting humour, experimentation and incursions into the world of the sensual. His major publications are *La Linares* (The Linares Woman) (1976), *El poder del gran señor* (The Grand Lord's Power) (1985) and *Historias leves* (Light Stories) (1994).

HUMBERTO E. ROBLES

Eguren, José María

b. 1874, Lima, Peru; d. 1942, Lima

Poet and plastic artist

Eguren lived a secluded life due to poor health, and his need to rest for long periods of time allowed him to become a voracious reader. His main influences were the English pre-Raphaelites and the French symbolists. His poetry, collected in *Poesías* (1929), relies on a symbolic system of suggestions, impressions and correspondences that link the perceptions of the real world to the imaginary. He evokes dreamlike, misty atmospheres through subdued and nuanced colours. He also wrote poetic prose and essays collected in 1959 under the title *Motivos estéticos* (Aesthetic Motifs).

Further reading

Eguren, J.M. (1974) *Obras completas*, ed. R. Silva Santisteban, Lima: Mosca Azul.

Elmore, P. (1989) 'José María Eguren', in C.A. Solé and M.I. Abreu (eds), *Latin American Writers*, New York: Scribners, 2, 513–18.

Rebaza-Soraluz, L. (1997) 'José María Eguren', in V. Smith (ed.), *Encyclopedia of Latin American Literature*, London: Fitzroy Dearborn, 285–6.

MAGDALENA GARCÍA PINTO

Eichelbaum, Samuel

b. 1894, Domínguez, Entre Ríos, Argentina; d. 1967, Buenos Aires, Argentina

Writer and dramatist

Eichelbaum's plays accurately reflect his self-portrait as 'a maniac of introspection'. He is best remembered for *Un guapo del 900* (A Turn-of-the-Century Tough Guy) (1940), a commercial success which also earned him Argentina's National and Municipal Prizes. *Un guapo del 900* profiles a figure who 'cultivates courage' and whose sense of honour and justice confronts established political and legal interests. In his over thirty plays, mostly centred on the middle classes, intellectual curiosity crafted his characters. The balance he struck between recognizable Argentine characters and individual idiosyncracies served to redirect his country's theatre away from strictly realistic scenarios.

Further reading

Cruz, J. (1962) *Samuel Eichelbaum*, Buenos Aires: Ediciones Culturales Argentinas.

Eichelbaum, S. (1959) *Las aguas del mundo*, Buenos Aires: Ediciones del Carro de Tespis.

—— (1967) *Un guapo del 900; las aguas del mundo*, Buenos Aires: Ediciones Culturales Argentinas.

—— (1969) *Un patricio del 80*, Buenos Aires: Talía.

Quackenbush, L.H. (1989) 'Samuel Eichelbaum', in C.A. Solé and M.I. Abreu (eds), *Latin American Writers*, New York: Scribners, 2, 797–801.

SAÚL SOSNOWSKI

Eielson, Jorge Eduardo

b. 1924, Lima, Peru

Writer and painter

Eielson has been active in a broad variety of genres (poetry, novels, theatre, happenings) and media (he is also a fine painter). His poetry has a spiritual bent, telling of what he has called 'esculturas subterráneas' (underground sculptures). One remarkable poem, 'Primera muerte de María' (Mary's First Death (1949), also the title of a 1988 novel by Eielson), is Joseph's account of the death of the Virgin Mary; other poems concern Don Quixote, figures from Greek mythology and the *Chanson de Roland*. His 1971 novel *El cuerpo de Giuliano* (Julian's Body) is an erotic exploration of sexual ambiguity. Since 1948 he has lived in Europe, largely in Rome.

Further reading

Chirinos, E. (1998) *La morada del silencio: Una reflexión sobre el silencio en la poesía a partir de las obras de Westphalen, Rojas, Orozco, Sologuren, Eielson y Pizarnik*, Lima: Fondo de Cultura Económica.

Eielson, J.E. (1989) *Poesía escrita*, Mexico City: Vuelta.

Silva Santisteban, R. (1989) 'Un tema recurrente

en la poesía de Eielson', in *Escrito en el agua*, Lima: Editorial Colmillo Blanco, 325–54.
Sologuren, J. (1988) 'La poesía viva y consumada de Jorge Eduardo Eielson', in *Gravitaciones y tangencias*, Lima: Editorial Colmillo Blanco, 277–80.

DANIEL BALDERSTON

Electra Garrigó

Electra Garrigó is a play written in 1941 by Virgilio **Piñera** and presented for the first time by the Prometeo group in 1948 under the direction of Francisco Morín. The play translates classical tragedy into a Cuban context, desanctifies mythological characters and develops a parody full of comic reference and verbal brilliance. Clytemnestra's death occurs when she eats a huge papaya, and the ancient chorus is replaced by a typical Guantanamera. This piece inaugurates modern theatre in Cuba and introduces a new way of conceiving scenic space. The work itself is a penetrating exploration of what elements comprise Cuban identity.

WILFREDO CANCIO ISLA

Elizondo, Salvador

b. 1932, Mexico City

Writer

Elizondo's highly reflective narrative texts, essays and contributions to literary, film and cultural journals and radio programmes mark him out as one of the leading authors of his generation. His first and most celebrated novel, *Farabeuf* (1965), has often been associated with the French *nouveau roman* and deals mainly with time, eroticism and the act of writing. His deep reflections on these subjects became a trademark. His texts are always constructed with utmost rigour and irony. He received the Xavier Villaurrutia Prize (1965) and the Mexican National Prize for Letters (1990).

Further reading

Bell, S.M. (1981) 'Literatura crítica y crítica de la literatura: Teoria y práctica en la obra de Salvador Elizondo', *Chasqui* 11(1): 41–52.
—— (1986) 'Postmodern Fiction in Spanish America: The Examples of Salvador Elizondo and Nestor Sánchez', *Arizona Quarterly* 42(1): 5–1.
Curley, D. (1997) 'Salvador Elizondo', in V. Smith (ed.), *Encyclopedia of Latin American Literature*, London: Fitzroy Dearborn, 291–2.
Elizondo, S. (1991) 'Teorias', *Vuelta* 15(177): 45–7.
—— (1992) *Farabeuf*, trans. from the Spanish by John Incledon, Garland Library of World Literature in Translation vol. 2, New York: Garland Publishing.
Malpartida, J. (1998) 'Salvador Elizondo, él escriba', *Insula* 618–19: 20–2.

JUAN PELLICER

Ellis, Zoila

b. 1957, Dangriga, Belize

Writer and environmental lawyer

One of an emerging literary community in Belize, whose foremost writer is also a woman (Zee **Edgell**), Ellis grew up in the Garifuna community, a group tied closely to its African roots. Her collection of short stories, *On Heroes, Lizards, and Passions* (1980), explores the lives of Belizeans, with their passions and inter-ethnic prejudices, both at home and in the USA. In addition to her short stories, Ellis has also published poetry in the CAFRA collection, *Creation Fire* (1990), edited by Ramabai **Espinet**. With degrees in law and development studies, Ellis works as a development consultant and environmental lawyer while continuing her writing.

GAY WILENTZ

Eltit, Diamela

b. 1949, Santiago, Chile

Writer and performance artist

One of Chile's most talented contemporary writers, Eltit, together with poet Raúl **Zurita** and the visual artist Lotty Rosenfeld, was a member of the performance art group CADA, which staged art events critical of political and social realities under the military regime of Augusto Pinochet. Eltit has published several novels, including *Lumpérica* (1983), *Por la patria* (For the Fatherland) (1986), *El cuarto mundo* (The Fourth World) (1988), *Vaca sagrada* (Sacred Cow) (1991) and *Los vigilantes* (The Vigilantes) (1995). She has also published a testimonial work, *El padre mío* (My Father) (1989), and collaborated with photographer Paz Errázuriz on the book *El infarto del alma* (The Soul's Heart Attack) (1994). Her work has been described as poetic and experimental in its approach to themes like women and the body, tyranny, violence, rebellion and writing. Her writings problematize the Spanish language and the Chilean dialect, and use them in inventive, non-representational and non-referential ways. Her novels combine genres such as poetry, drama and narrative, and incorporate practices from the literary vanguard, the **neo-baroque**, psychoanalysis and film. *Lumpérica* and *Por la patria* exploit multiple art forms (painting, video art, performance art) and literary forms (poem, narrative, dramatic text) and connect writing and visual expression.

El cuarto mundo and *Los vigilantes* challenge traditional concepts of the family and social institutions modelled on the patriarchal family. The fragmentation produced by the multiple narrative voices of her texts – both rational and coherent and irrational and unconscious – is one technique for subverting structures of domination and established order. Characters use multiple systems of expression, including conscious and unconscious voices, the language of the body, and writing. In *Los vigilantes* the creative process is the protagonist's only means of salvation from a repressive and violent world. Writing becomes the sole way she can order and give meaning to her existence. Through her style and subject matter, Eltit engages readers in a complex exploration of the violent struggle for representation on the social, sexual and cultural margins of Latin America.

Eltit won a Guggenheim fellowship in 1985. In 1992–93 she was cultural attaché at the Chilean embassy in Mexico. She often lectures at US universities.

Further reading

Brito, E. (1990) *Campos minados: Literatura post-golpe en Chile*, Santiago: Cuarto Propio.

Eltit, D. (1992) *On Literary Creation*, Niwot: University Press of Colorado.

Lértora, J.C. (ed.) (1993) *Una poética de literatura menor*, Santiago: Cuarto Propio.

Maíz-Peña, M. (1997) 'Diamela Eltit', in V. Smith (ed.), *Encyclopedia of Latin American Literature*, London: Fitzroy Dearborn, 293–4.

Uribe, O.T. (1995) 'Breves anotaciones sobre las estrategias narrativas en Lumpérica, Por la patria y El cuarto mundo de Diamela Eltit', *Hispanic Journal* 16(1): 21–37.

AMALIA PEREIRA

Emar, Juan

b. 1893, Santiago, Chile; d. 1964, Santiago

Writer

Juan Emar (Alvaro Yáñez Bianchi) was the intellectual power behind the Chilean avant-garde movements of the early 1920s. He is one of the innovative forces behind the new narrative, texts which interrogate language and expose its inadequacies in communicating a reality. His texts suggest but never explain, enunciating the impossibility of narration, de-realizing the nominal world, questioning reality and its logic. His works include *Ayer, Un año y Miltín* (Yesterday, One Year and Miltin) (1934–35), *Diez* (Ten) (1937) and *Umbral* (Threshold) (1977).

Further reading

Brodsky, P., P. Lizama and C. Pina (1990) 'Ausencia-presencia de Juan Emar', *Escritura* 15(29): 199–213.

Coddou, M. (1997) 'Bibliografía de Juan Emar', *Inti: Revista de literatura hispánica* 46–7: 309–16.

Espinoza Orellana, M. (1987) 'La obra de Juan Emar', *Literatura chilena: creación y crítica* 11(2(40)): 2–5.

ELIANA ORTEGA

Engels, Christiaan Joseph Hendrikus

b. 1907, Rotterdam, The Netherlands; d. 1980, Curaçao, Netherlands Antilles

Writer, painter and musician

Engels established his medical practice on Curaçao in 1937, and there began to write a poetry of free association, characterized by its idiosyncratic syntax and personalized imagery. He was publisher and editor of the literary magazine *De* ***Stoep***. His later prose and essays dealt with the pre-Columbian indigenous continental and island cultures. He also turned to painting and music. He was founder of the Curaçao Museum, a centre of artistic activities and exhibitions in the 1950s and 1960s. As a composer and pianist, he was a member of the Curaçao Philharmonic Orchestra.

AART G. BROEK

Enigma of Arrival, The

In *The Enigma of Arrival* (1987) V.S. **Naipaul** breaks new ground in his continuing exploration of the dilemmas of the post-colonial writer. Proustian and symbolic, the novel probes the meaning of time, decay and renewal through circular reflections in which Naipaul's own thinly fictionalized life is viewed by an alter ego or implicated in parallel biographies. Embodying Naipaul's own quest to understand his life through writing, the novel becomes a meditation on the nature of art itself.

Divided into two halves and five parts, the novel takes its title from a surrealist painting by de Chirico, named by Apollinaire, which reflects the mystery of stasis and movement. Returning to the wharf to rejoin his ship, the traveller finds 'There was no mast above the walls of the wharf. No ship. His journey – his life's journey – had been made'. The first section, 'Jack's Garden', is set in Wiltshire, Naipaul's home for much of his life in England. Here he becomes familiarized with the landscape and natives of this most English of landscapes. In 'Ivy', the focus moves from the life of the labourer (Jack) to the squirearchy. The owner of the manor refuses to have the ivy removed because he likes it, a motif of a refusal to change. Naipaul perceives that England's past culture relates to his own roots in rural India, where a feudal system also held within it the principle of decay. Yet his new awareness of history leads him forward from a vision of loss to one of recurring patterns within cultural change.

Opening the second half of the novel, 'The Journey' relates a dual passage, Naipaul's physical voyage to Europe, and the writings through which he had journeyed towards understanding the permanent realities beneath transience. In the penultimate chapter, 'Rooks', the author juxtaposes his own life in writing with the unfulfilled career and early death of Alan, an English alter ego. He finds he cannot make his own cultural connection between life and writing until he finally confronts his Indian roots in Trinidad. This is intimated in the epilogue, 'The Ceremony of Farewell', where the author returns to Trinidad for his sister's death and cremation, and the Hindu belief in reincarnation hints at Naipaul's final 'arrival' at his awareness of cultural continuity. As the book ends, he hurries away to begin writing it. A slow, poetic, suggestive work, the final meaning of the book eludes any synopsis and remains, as the title indicates, an 'enigma'.

Further reading

Jussawalla, F. (ed.) (1997) *Conversations with V.S. Naipaul*, Literary Conversations Series, Jackson: University Press of Mississippi.

Mustafa, F. (1995) *V.S. Naipaul*, Cambridge Studies in African and Caribbean Literature 4, Cambridge: Cambridge University Press.

Phillips, C. (ed.) (1999) *Extravagant Strangers: A Literature of Belonging*, New York: Vintage Books.

Theroux, P. (1998) *Sir Vidia's Shadow: A Friendship across Five Continents*, Boston: Houghton Mifflin Co.

LOUIS JAMES

entenado, El

El entenado (The Witness) (1983), by Juan José **Saer**, relates the story of the only survivor of the Solís expedition to the Río de la Plata (River Plate) and his capture by the Charrúa Indians. The experience of living with them for several years transforms the cabin boy and his attitudes. One of the novel's central passages is an anthropophagic banquet, which provides an opportunity for a discussion about otherness. *El entenado* gives access in its turn to Jean de Léry's *Journey to the Land of Brazil, Also Called America*, Montaigne's essay 'On Cannibals' and Oswald de **Andrade**'s *Manifesto antropófago*.

MARÍA JULIA DAROQUI

Escoffery, Gloria Blanche

b. 1923, Gayle, Jamaica

Painter and writer

Escoffery explains a fierce attachment to her birthplace as a result of 'the nationalist fervor emanating from the Manleys and affecting young people of my generation'. During the 1950s, she contributed poetry to the BBC's *Caribbean Voices* and was a critic for the programme. She was a regular contributor to *Bim* and other literary journals, and her poems appeared in several anthologies. In the 1980s she worked as a regular columnist for the *Daily Gleaner* and was art critic for the *Jamaica Journal*. The 1988 collection *Loggerhead* revived interest in her poetry.

SANDRA COURTMAN

Escudero, Gonzalo

b. 1903, Quito, Ecuador; d. 1971, Brussels, Belgium

Poet

Among the leaders of the avant-garde in Ecuador, Escudero's early *modernista* (see **Spanish American modernism**) poetry evolved in a metaphorical direction under the influence of futurism, cubism and **surrealism**. His later works turned towards **existentialism** and the Spanish classics in search of serenity and harmony. *Poesía* (Poetry) (1965) is a compendium of his poems. He also wrote one of the few examples of avant-garde drama in Ecuador, the surrealist-inspired *Paralelograma* (Parallelogram) (1936). His *Justicia para el Ecuador* (Justice for Ecuador) (1968) is a plea for an understanding of Ecuador's position on the border disputes with Peru.

Further reading

Alemán, H. (1953) 'Gonzalo Escudero', in *Presencia del pasado*, Quito: Editorial Casa de la Cultura.

Escudero, G. (1965) *Obras completas*, Quito: Casa de la Cultura Ecuatoriana.

Fernández, Maria del Carmen (1992) 'Gonzalo Escudero y la vanguardia ecuatoriana', in Juana Alcira Arancibia (ed.), *Literatura del mundo hispáco: VIII Simposio Internacional de Literatura, Quito: Universidad San Francisco de Quito, 30 July–3 Aug 1990*, Westminster, CA: Instituto Literario y Cultural Hispánico.

HUMBERTO E. ROBLES

Espinet, Ramabai

b. 1948, Princes Town, Trinidad and Tobago

Writer

An Indo-Trinidadian-Canadian poet, fiction writer, academic and activist in the women's movement, Espinet is best known for her anthology of poetry *Nuclear Seasons* (1991). Her writing addresses the specificities of Indo-Caribbean culture, indentureship and the experiences of women of the Indian diaspora. Her poetry and her collaborative experimental poetry/dance/performance piece 'Indian Robber Talk' synthesize elements of Indian, Indo-Caribbean and Afro-Caribbean folk traditions to develop a hybrid Caribbean feminist aesthetics sensitive to cultural diversity. With the support of the Caribbean Association for Feminist Research and Action, in 1990 Espinet edited *Creation Fire*, an anthology of poetry by 121 contemporary women from throughout the Caribbean. The anthology is significant for gathering the individual creative expressions of both well-known and unpublished women poets, creating a public archive and a collective context for the poetry.

Further reading

Espinet, R. (1989) 'The Invisible Woman in West Indian Fiction', *World Literature Written in English* 29(2): 116–26.

Mehta, B.J. (1999) 'Indo-Trinidadian Fiction: Female Identity and Creative Cooking', *Alif* 19: 151–84.

Puri, S. (1997) 'Race, Rape, and Representation: Indo-Caribbean Women and Cultural Nationalism', *Cultural Critique* 36: 119–63.

SHALINI PURI

Espínola, Francisco

b. 1901, San José, Uruguay; d. 1973, Montevideo, Uruguay

Writer

Espínola was a skilled **short story** writer. His inventive and witty stories of *Raza ciega* (Blind Race) (1926) and *El rapto y otros cuentos* (The Kidnapping and Other Stories) (1950) are rooted in the popular culture of the River Plate region. He wrote theatre criticism for several newspapers, and his own play *La fuga en el espejo* (Escape into the Mirror) was produced in 1937. His gifts as a storyteller brought him fame as a radio and television performer, and he received the National Literature Prize in 1961. His unpublished articles and stories were collected in several volumes published in 1984–5.

Further reading

Espínola, F. (1980) *Cuentos completos*, Montevideo: Arca.

Maggi, C. (1968) *Paco Espínola*, Montevideo: Centro Editor de América Latina.

Mántaras Loedel, G. (1986) *Francisco Espínola: Época, vida y obra*, Montevideo: La Casa del Estudiante.

CELINA MANZONI

Espínola, Lourdes

b. 1954, Asunción, Paraguay

Writer

Although a dentist by profession, Espínola has written poetry from an early age. She followed her first book *Visión del Arcángel en once puertas* (Vision of the Archangel in Eleven Doors) (1973) with others which have won two international literary prizes; works include *Almenas del silencio* (Parapets of Silence), *Ser mujer y otras desventuras* (Being a Woman and Other Misadventures), a bilingual English–Spanish edition, *Tímpano y silencio* (Harmonica and Silence) and *Partidas y regresos* (Departures and Returns), with a prologue by Augusto **Roa Bastos**. Her *La estrategia del caracol* (The Snail's Strategy) was adapted for cinema by Sergio Cabrera.

TERESA MÉNDEZ-FAITH

Espinosa, Norge

b. 1972, Santa Clara, Cuba

Poet and playwright

One of the most prominent of the young Cuban poets, Norge Espinosa was among the first to experiment with homosexual themes in the late 1980s, with his widely anthologized poem 'Vestido de Novia' (Dressed as a Bride), written when he was but a teenager. He has published *Las breves tribulaciones* (The Brief Tribulations) (1992), *Los pequeños prodigios* (The Little Prodigies; children's poetry) and *Estategias del páramo* (Bleak Plateau Strategies) (2000), and has written several plays, including *Romanza del lirio* (Romance of the Lily) and *Sarah's*. He has also developed cultural presentations and is a prolific lecturer, as well as book and theatre critic. He has worked closely with El Público, one of the most acclaimed theatre groups of the 1990s in Havana, and has organized events on gay and lesbian culture in Cuba.

Further reading

Espinosa. N. (2002) 'I, Charlotte, comme il faut',

trans. D. Balderston and C. Merrill, *Iowa Review* 32: 69–75.

CÉSAR PÉREZ

Esquivel, Laura

b. 1949, Mexico City

Novelist

Esquivel is best known as the author of ***Como agua para chocolate***: *Novela de mensuales con recetas* (Like Water for Chocolate: A Novel in Monthly Instalments) (1989), a best-selling novel which has sold over 300,000 copies in Spanish and more than a million in English, and was made into a hit movie of the same title directed by Alfonso Arau. Her second novel, *La ley del amor* (The Law of Love) (1996), is set in the Mexico City of 2200 and its protagonist is an astroanalyst whose patients' psychological problems are caused by acts they committed in previous lives. This New Age, multimedia novel is marketed with a CD including opera arias by Puccini, salsa music and comics.

Further reading

Esquivel, L. (1989) *Como agua para chocolate*, Mexico City: Planeta.

—— (1994) *Like Water for Chocolate*, trans. Carol Christensen and Thomas Christensen, Englewood Cliffs, NJ: Prentice Hall.

García-Serrano, M.V. (1995) 'Como agua para chocolate de Laura Esquivel: Apuntes para un debate', *Indiana Journal of Hispanic Literatures* 6–7: 185–205.

Saltz, J. (1995) 'Laura Esquivel's *Como agua para chocolate*: The Questioning of Literary and Social Limits', *Chasqui* 24(1): 30–7.

Shaw, D. (1997) 'Laura Esquivel', in V. Smith (ed.), *Encyclopedia of Latin American Literature*, London: Fitzroy Dearborn, 117–18.

Valdes, M.E. (1995) 'Verbal and Visual Representation of Women: Como agua para chocolate/ Like Water for Chocolate', *World Literature Today* 69(1): 78–82.

CYNTHIA STEELE

essay

Latin America has produced a rich body of creative and critical essays, particularly works that reinterpret social representations, symbols, metaphors and concepts and show the relationship between intellectuals and the social ethos. Some authors, such as **Arciniegas**, have taken its origin back to the very moment of the discovery and conquest of America; others, like Arturo Andrés Roig, have found the origins of the Latin American essay in Romanticism and journalistic practices linked to the circulation of new ideas in the eighteenth and nineteenth centuries. For writers such as José Guilherme **Merquior**, by contrast, it is *modernismo* (see **Spanish American modernism**) and the emergence of a layer of **intellectuals** that explain the essay's origin.

The essay, in its contemporary form, is clearly linked to the world of books, newspapers, intellectuals and to the maturing of the conditions for the emergence of a public that Eduardo Nicol described as 'la generalidad de los cultos' (cultured people in general). The century opened with the essays of José **Martí**, Rubén **Darío**, Manuel **González Prada** and José Enrique **Rodó**, and the Ateneo de la Juventud generation in Mexico. For these writers, positivist universalism had entered into a profound crisis, and they turned instead to an exploration of Iberoamerica's relations with the Latin and Anglo-Saxon worlds.

The theme of 'civilization versus barbarism' (see **civilization and barbarism**), first addressed in the nineteenth century by Sarmiento and in subsequent writings by Alcides **Arguedas** and Euclides da **Cunha** among others, which shared a negative vision of *mestizaje* and the rural world, were now overtaken by a new current of ideas. One group of writers developed the Shakespearean symbolism of **Caliban** and Ariel (see ***Ariel* and *arielismo***) first from a Latinist point of view (in Darío and Rodó) and later from a frankly anticolonialist perspective in the work of Roberto **Fernández Retamar** and Leopoldo Zea. Other writers sought out the specificity of Latin American experience, like **Lezama Lima** in *La **expresión americana*** (American Expression) and Alejo **Carpentier** with his idea of '*lo **real maravilloso***'.

In the 1940s, Latin Americanist thought that stressed a unity of origin and destiny re-emerged with Pedro **Henríquez Ureña**, Alfonso **Reyes** and Germán Arciniegas; it reopened questions about the relations between Latin America and Spain and between Latin America and the USA, and became increasingly concerned with the tension between the local and the universal (Jorge Cuesta, Jorge Luis **Borges**, Octavio **Paz** and Carlos **Fuentes** are examples). Essayists such as Ezequiel **Martínez Estrada**, José Carlos **Mariátegui**, Guillermo Francovich and the Octavio Paz of *El laberinto de la soledad* (The Labyrinth of Solitude) (1950) share a concern to explore national characteristics; others, like Arturo **Uslar Pietri**, Mariano **Picón Salas**, Luis Alberto **Sánchez** and Germán Arciniegas, continued to develop the Latin Americanist current set in train by the Mexican José **Vasconcelos** and reflected in journals like ***Repertorio americano*** and *Cuadernos americanos*.

Avant-garde aesthetic ideas opened new directions in the essay (see the work of César **Vallejo**, Luis **Cardoza y Aragón**, Aimé **Césaire**, Miguel Angel **Asturias** and Lezama Lima). Today, Latin American critical writing appears in synchrony with developments elsewhere in the world. It increasingly shares common frontiers with poetry and narrative (Cuesta, Borges, Ernesto **Sábato**, Paz, Fuentes); with philosophy (where the influence of José Ortega y Gasset and José Gaos on the relationship between ideas and circumstance particularly influenced Leopoldo Zea), or thinkers such as Francisco Romero, Adolfo Sánchez Vázquez, Eduardo Nicol and Luis Villoro); with the ***crónica*** (Elena **Poniatowska**, Carlos **Monsiváis**); with anthropology (Fernando Ortiz, Gilberto Freyre, Darcy Ribeiro); with the exploration of popular culture and the impact of mass media (Beatriz **Sarlo**, Néstor García Canclini); with social science, education and history (José Luis Romero, Gregorio Weinberg, Enrique Krauze and Roger Bartra); with economics (José Medina Echavarría, Daniel Cosío Villegas, Jesús Silva Herzog, Raúl Prebisch); and with literary criticism (Enrique **Anderson Imbert**, Angel **Rama**, Antonio **Cornejo Polar**, Antonio **Candido**, Julio **Ortega**, Juan José **Saer**, Roberto **Schwarz**). The works of Alfonso Reyes, Jorge Luis Borges, Julio **Cortázar**, Octavio Paz, Mario **Vargas Llosa** and Tomás Segovia will continue to represent the essay at the frontiers of its possibilities.

Further reading

Earle, P.G. (1997) 'The Essay', in V. Smith (ed.), *Encyclopedia of Latin American Literature*, London: Fitzroy Dearborn, 296–8.

Levy, K.L. and K. Ellis (1970) *El ensayo y la crítica literaria en Iberoamérica*, Toronto: University of Toronto/Instituto Internacional de Literatura Iberoamericana.

Meyer, D. (ed.) (1995) *Reinterpreting the Spanish American Essay: Women Writers of the 19th and 20th Centuries*, Austin: University of Texas Press.

—— (1995) *Rereading the Spanish American Essay: Translations of 19th and 20th Century Women's Essays*, Austin: University of Texas Press.

Oviedo, J.M. (1990) *Breve historia del ensayo hispano"americano*, Madrid: Alianza Editorial.

—— (1996) 'The Modern Essay in Spanish America', in R. González Echevarría and E. Pupo-Walker (eds), *Cambridge History of Latin American Literature*, Cambridge: Cambridge University Press, 2, 365–423.

Skidmore, T.F. (1996) 'The Essay: Architects of Brazilian National Identity', in R. González Echevarría and E. Pupo-Walker (eds), *Cambridge History of Latin American Literature*, Cambridge: Cambridge University Press, 3, 345–61.

Skirius, J. (1981) *El ensayo latinoamericano*, Mexico City: Fondo de Cultura Económica.

Stabb, M.S. (1967) *In Quest of Identity: Patterns in the Spanish American Essay of Ideas 1890–1960*, Chapel Hill: University of North Carolina Press.

—— (1994) *The Dissenting Voice: The New Essay of Spanish America, 1960–1985*, Austin: University of Texas Press.

LILIANA WEINBERG

Estévez, Abilio

b. 1954, Havana, Cuba

Writer

Estévez's play *La verdadera culpa de Juan Clemente Zenea* (Juan Clemente Zenea's Real Guilt) won the

UNEAC drama prize in 1984 and is considered one of the most important works of contemporary Cuban theatre. His other theatrical pieces include *Perla marina* (Deep-Sea Pearl) (1993), *Santa Cecilia* (1994) and *La noche* (The Night) (world premiere in 1996), which won the 1994 Tirso de Molina prize. He has written short stories, published in *Juego con Gloria* (A Game with Glory) (1987), a volume of poetry, *Manual de las tentaciones* (The Handbook of Temptations) (1989), and two successful novels, *Tuyo es el reino* (Thine is the Kingdom) (1997) and *Los palacios distantes* (2002).

Further reading

Estévez, A. (1999) *Thine is the Kingdom*, trans. D. Frye, New York: Arcade Publishing.

WILFREDO CANCIO ISLA

Estorino, Abelardo

b. 1925, Unión de Reyes, Cuba

Playwright and theatre director

A major figure in the new Cuban theatre movement of the 1960s, Estorino's *El robo del cochino* (The Stolen Pig) (1961) and *La casa vieja* (The Old House) (1964) offer vivid and critical insights into the reality of Cuban family life and social behaviour. Other works in the same vein include *Los mangos de Caín* (Cain's Mangos) (1964), *Ni un sí ni un no* (Neither Yes nor No) (1979), *Morir del evento* (To Die of the Event) (1983) and *Parece blanca* (She Looks White) (1994). As a director, he has worked primarily with Teatro Estudio.

Further reading

Estorino, A. (1975) 'El robo del cochino', in Carlos Solórzano (ed.), *El teatro hispanoamericano contemporáneo (tomo ii)*, Colección popular.61, Mexico City: Fondo de Cultura Económica.

—— (1997) *Vagos rumores y otras obras*, La Habana: Editorial Letras Cubanas.

Woodyard, G. (1983) 'Estorino's Theatre: Customs and Conscience in Cuba', *Latin American Literary Review* 11(22): 57–63.

WILFREDO CANCIO ISLA

Estridentismo

Estridentismo was the first clearly defined Mexican vanguardist group, whose suggestive designation and aggressive **manifestos** revealed an initial influence of European futurism and dadaism. Its central figure was Manuel **Maples Arce**, who wrote most of the early 1920s manifesto broadsides (for example, 'Actual No. 1', from 1921, and 'Manifesto No. 2', from 1923) and was the motivating force behind the combative literary journals *Irradiador* (1923) and *Horizonte* (1926–27), the principal group publications. Other group members were the poets Germán List Arzubide and Luis Quintanilla and prose writers Arqueles Vela, Xavier Icaza and Salvador Gallardo.

Further reading

List Arzubide, G. (1926) *El movimiento estridentista*, Xalapa: Ediciones de Horizonte.

Schneider, L.M. (1985) *El estridentismo: México, 1921–1927*, Mexico City: UNAM.

MERLIN H. FORSTER

Estupiñán Bass, Nelson

b. 1912, Súa, Esmeralda, Ecuador

Writer

A poet inspired by the Afro-Ecuadorean culture of his native province of Esmeraldas, Estupiñán Bass's early work in particular is framed by the philosophy of ***negrismo***, and characterized by its use of popular rhythms and forms. *Las tres carabelas* (Three Caravelles) (1973) gathers together his poetry, short stories and theatre.

The African community of Esmeraldas was ostensibly established when seventeen men and women from a wrecked Spanish ship escaped into the jungle in 1553 and created an 'Indo-African-Ecuadorean community'. The community grew with the addition of new members from the wreck of a slave ship in 1600 and escaped slaves from surrounding plantations. The population expanded again in the nineteenth century as a result of booms in rubber and gold. Yet two centuries earlier, Esmeraldas was already referred to as 'the black Republic'. The failure of a series of expeditions to dominate the area allowed the growth of interactions among whites, blacks and Indians reflected in poetry combining literary forms and rhythms derived from the Spanish tradition with African elements; the result is a dynamic and unique culture.

Estupiñán Bass also wrote novels set in this cultural space, the first of which was *Cuando los guayacanes florecían* (When the Guayacanes were in Bloom) (1954). Other novels, like *Senderos brillantes* (Bright Paths) (1974), belonged within the political novel tradition of the 1930s, although the writer introduced new narrative techniques. *Las puertas del verano* (Gates of Summer) (1978) and *Bajo el cielo nublado* (Under a Cloudy Sky) (1981) belong to the same genre, though some critics have located the latter within a magical realist tradition (see **magical realism**). *El crepúsculo* (Dusk) (1992) is a thriller.

In all his work, Estupiñán Bass brings to a long tradition of social protest writing the additional element of an attack on racism. The protagonist of *El último río* (The Last River) (1966), for example, adopts what Frantz Fanon called a 'white mask', rejecting his origins and denying his roots. His impotence and ultimate madness express the insoluble contradition between oppressor and oppressed, black and white incarnated in a single character. One critic has described the novel as 'the first black novel of Ecuador', superior even to Adalberto **Ortiz**'s *Juyungo* (1943).

Further reading

Richards, H.J. (1997) '*El crepúsculo* de Nelson Estupiñán Bass, crisol de técnicas narrativas', in *Cultura: Revista del Banco Central del Ecuador* 1, Quito.

CELINA MANZONI

EUDEBA

The University of Buenos Aires Publishing House (EUDEBA) was founded in 1958 as a mixed public–private enterprise. Under Boris Spivakow's direction it played a key role in disseminating a range of new works and ideas, translating hitherto unknown works into Spanish, publishing the work of local authors and contributing to the **Boom**. EUDEBA was taken over when the university was occupied by the military government in 1966, and Spivakow then formed the Centro Editor de América Latina (CEAL). With the return of democracy in 1973, EUDEBA briefly flowered under Arturo Jauretche until the State took control of it for the second time in 1975.

Further reading

www.eudeba.com.ar

Maunás, D. (1995) *Boris Spivakow: Memoria de un sueño argentino*, Buenos Aires: Colihue.

PABLO KREIMER

Eulálio, Alexandre

b. 1932, Rio de Janeiro, Brazil; d. 1988, São Paulo, Brazil

Literary critic

One of the most curious, encylopedic and sensitive minds of his generation, Eulálio only began university teaching in 1979. Before that he was a journalist, editor of the *Revista do livro*, and a diplomat in Venice. His work is enormously varied: it consists mostly of essays, many of which were published posthumously as *Livro involuntário* (Involuntary Book) (1993). He had a special interest in the city of Diamantina, Minas Gerais, where his family was from, and in the plastic arts. His only book was on the Swiss poet Blaise Cendrars' journey to Brazil in the 1920s.

JOHN GLEDSON

existentialism

French philosophical and literary movement that had great impact on Latin American writing during the 1950s and 1960s. After the split between its two principal figures, Jean Paul Sartre and Albert Camus, their Latin American followers also took separate paths for a time: Camus was one of Victoria **Ocampo**'s heroes and was featured in ***Sur***, while Sartre influenced León Rozitchner and others in the ***Contorno*** group, as well as the young **Vargas Llosa**. Other writers close to existentialism's central concerns – alienation, the search for meaning, the need for ethical and political engagement – included Juan Carlos **Onetti** and Virgilio **Piñera**, although this may be somewhat coincidental as they were interested in these issues before the works of Camus and Sartre were much known outside France. A figure who has adhered to the tenets of existentialism since his early days, and who now, at the beginning of the twenty-first century, perhaps deserves the title of the Last Existentialist, faithful to these ideas long after they passed out of fashion, is Ernesto **Sábato**.

Further reading

Adams, M.I. (1975) *Three Authors of Alienation: Bombal, Onetti, Carpentier*, Austin: University of Texas Press.

García Losada, M.I. (1999) *La filosofía existencial en la Argentina: Sus introductores*, Buenos Aires: Plus Ultra.

Fernandes, J. (1986) *O existencialismo na ficção brasileira*, Goiânia: Editora da Universidade Federal de Goiás.

DANIEL BALDERSTON

expresión americana, La

An essay collection published in 1957 by the Cuban writer José **Lezama Lima**, *La expresión americana* (American Expression) is a seminal contribution to the debate on Latin American identity, and a brief yet startlingly original cultural history of Latin America. Lezama proposes a theory of interpretation which allows for American culture to translate or transfigure inherited cultural elements, thus creating new forms in dialogue with a different, shaping landscape. The first and quintessential Latin American artistic movement, the American Baroque, is an expression of this landscape; it is also a hybrid cultural expression, product of a dialogue between African, indigenous New World and European cultures.

Further reading

Yurkievich, S. (1991) '*La expresión americana* o la fabulación autóctona', *Revista iberoamericana* 154: 43–50.

BEN A. HELLER

F

Fallas, Carlos Luis

b. 1909, Alajuela, Costa Rica; d. 1966, San José, Costa Rica

Writer

One of Latin America's most important social realist writers, Fallas's novel *Mamita Yunai* (1941) describes the life and conditions of workers on Costa Rica's banana plantations. As a young man he worked on the United Fruit Company's plantations on his country's Atlantic coast, became a union organizer and joined the Communist party. In 1934 he was among the leaders of a national banana workers' strike, an experience that provided the core material for his most famous novel. The novel was rejected by the judges of the 1941 Farrar Rinehart prize (eventually won by Ciro **Alegría**), presumably on the grounds that it was too explicitly propagandistic. Nonetheless, it was widely read and imitated by other 'proletarian writers' in subsequent years. Through the last twenty years of his life, Fallas was centrally involved in national politics and in a struggle with José Figueres for recognition of the Communist Party, of which he was a leading member. He continued to write, but without repeating the success of his first work.

Further reading

Aguilar, M. (1983) *Carlos Luis Fallas, su época y sus luchas*, San José, CR: Editorial Porvenir.

Arroyo, V.M. (1973) *Carlos Luis Fallas*, San José, CR: Ministerio de Cultura Juventud y Deportes.

Fallas, C.L. (1941) *Mamita Yunai*, San José, CR: Editorial Costa Rica.

Picado, M. (1987) 'Carlos Luis Fallas: Visión de conjunto', *Revista iberoamericana* 53(138–9): 219–31.

Solera, R. (1970) 'Carlos Luis Fallas: El novelista de su propia vida', *Hispania* 53: 403–10.

MIKE GONZALEZ

fantastic literature

Although most famously associated with **Borges**, **Bioy Casares** and **Cortázar**, fantastic literature has much earlier roots in Latin America. The Argentine writer and scientist Eduardo Ladislao Holmberg (1852–1937), influenced by E.T.A. Hoffmann, wrote Gothic stories that play on a tension between scientific and spiritual thinking. Leopoldo **Lugones**, in the stories of *Las fuerzas extrañas* (The Strange Forces) (1906), also reflects an interest in the occult; this collection includes the famous stories 'La lluvia de fuego' (The Rain of Fire), 'Yzur' and 'Los caballos de Abdera' (The Horses of Abdera). Alfonso **Reyes**, Horacio **Quiroga**, Manuel Peyrou and Santiago Dabove were other practitioners of the fantastic.

Without doubt, however, the modern tradition of the fantastic in Latin America begins in 1940 with the publication of the ***Antología de la literatura fantástica*** by Borges, Bioy Casares and Silvina **Ocampo**. In tandem with Bioy's novel *La invención de Morel* (Morel's Invention) (1940), which appeared with a preface by Borges, and the Borges stories that culminated in ***Ficciones*** (1944), the anthology set out to show Latin American writers, and the reading public, that a distinct literature distant from the dominant social realist tradition was possible. The Borges story 'Tlön, Uqbar, Orbis Tertius' was the boldest Latin American work included in the first edition of the anthology, and it was celebrated by Bioy in the preface as an example of a new literary genre. The second edition of the anthology, published in 1965, included works by Cortázar, **Murena**, **Wilcock**, **Garro** and **Bianco**.

Julio Cortázar was, after Borges, the most important Latin American practitioner and theorist of the fantastic. His 'Sentimiento de lo fantástico' (The Feeling of the Fantastic) in *La vuelta al día en ochenta mundos* (Around the Day in Eighty Worlds) (1967), and the comments on the fantastic in 'Del cuento breve y sus alrededores' (On the Short Story and Environs) in *Ultimo round* (Last Round) (1969), focused on the psychological effects of the fantastic (following Poe, whose work Cortázar had translated) instead of focusing on the formal structures that had interested Borges and Bioy Casares.

The tradition of the fantastic in Spanish America has been studied by Ana María **Barrenechea** and Oscar **Hahn**; the Brazilian tradition, particularly the work of Murilo **Rubião**, has been studied by Jorge **Schwartz**. The fantastic, particularly the form cultivated in Argentina, is sometimes confused with so-called **magical realism** (and with **Carpentier**'s '*lo* ***real maravilloso***'), but at least in general terms the Argentine version was more controlled and cerebral, while **García Márquez** and his successors preferred flashier effects.

Further reading

Balderston, D. (2002) 'La *Antología de la literatura fantástica* y sus alrededores', *Casa de las Américas* 229: 104–10.

Hahn, O. (1978) *El cuento fantástico hispanoamericano en el siglo XIX*, Mexico City: Premiá.

—— (1990) *El cuento fantástico hispanoamericano en el siglo XX*, Santiago: Editorial Universitaria.

König, I. (1984) *La formación de la narrativa fantástica hispanoamericana en la época moderna*, Frankfurt: Peter Lang.

Wheelock, C. (1980) 'Fantastic Symbolism in the Spanish American Short Story', *Hispanic Review* 48: 415–34.

DANIEL BALDERSTON

Fariña, Soledad

b. 1943, Antofagasta, Chile

Poet

Fariña's writing insistently explores a series of unanswerable questions: how to express a sexuality denied, how to recuperate a pre-Columbian culture long suppressed, and how to discover the Latin American dimension of language. She has published three volumes of poetry: *El primer libro* (The First Book) (1985), *Albricia* (Good News) (1988) and *En amarillo oscuro* (In Dark Yellow) (1994), which have been studied and translated. She graduated in political science from the University of Chile, and in philosophy and letters from the University of Stockholm.

Further reading

Ortega, E. (1996) 'Fénix-Camaquén: El *Amarillo Oscuro* de Soledad Fariña', in *Lo que se hereda no se hurta: Ensayos de crítica literaria feminista*, Santiago: Cuarto Propio, 209–16.

—— (1996) 'Viaje a la otra palabra: *Albricia* de Soledad Fariña', in *Lo que se hereda no se hurta: Ensayos de crítica literaria feminista*, Santiago: Cuarto Propio, 191–4.

ELIANA ORTEGA

Feijóo, Samuel

b. 1914, San Juan de los Yeras, Cuba; d. 1992, Santa Clara, Cuba

Writer, artist and ethnologist

Director of the Department of Folklore Studies at Cuba's Central University of Las Villas, Feijóo's research into the traditions and customs of rural Cuba was fundamental to the development of ideas in this field. His published work included *El girasol sediento* (The Thirsty Sunflower) (1963) and *Poeta en el paisaje* (Poet in the Landscape) (1966) and a popular novel *Juan Quinquin en Pueblo Mocho* (1964), later filmed by Julio García Espinosa. Self-taught, he contributed regularly to journals including *Carteles* and ***Orígenes***; in 1958 he became director of his university's publishing house and editor of its journal *Islas*.

Further reading

Feijóo, S. (1982, 1984) *Crítica lírica*, Havana: Editorial Letras Cubanas.

—— (1984) 'African Influence in Latin America: Oral and Written Literature', in Manuel Moreno-Fraginals (ed.) and Leonor Blum (trans.), *Africa in Latin America: Essays on History, Culture, and Socialization*, New York and Paris: Holmes & Meier; UNESCO.

—— (1984) *Poesía: Antología*, Havana: Editorial Letras Cubanas.

Kersten, Raquel (1984) 'Samuel Feijoo: Un poeta cubano', *Hispamérica: Revista de literatura*, April, 13(37): 87–94.

WILFREDO CANCIO ISLA

Feminaria

Feminaria, a semi-annual feminist journal of theory, criticism and literature, is a pioneer publication on women's issues. Founded in Buenos Aires in 1988, and directed by Lea Fletcher, its editorial board (Fletcher, Diana **Bellessi**, Alicia Genzano, Jutta Marx and Diana Maffía) receives contributions internationally, with translation directed by María Averbach and frequent cartoons by Diana Raznovich. Most issues include six sections: essays on social and cultural theory and criticism, annotated and/or specialized bibliography, art, humour, notes and interviews, and 'Feminaria literaria' which combines creative and critical works.

Further reading

feminaria@fibertel.com.ar

Fletcher, L. (1994) *Mujeres y cultura en la Argentina del siglo XIX*, comp, Buenos Aires: Feminaria Editora.

GWEN KIRKPATRICK

Feria, Lina de

b. 1945, Santiago de Cuba

Poet

One of the most representative figures of the Cuban poetry of the revolutionary period, Feria's poems emphasize individual experience over collective whilst maintaining a Utopian view of history. This characteristic has made her an important influence for the new generations of writers, particularly her first book *Casa que no existía* (The House That Did Not Exist) (1967). De Feria was one of the poets censored by the official cultural politics from the late sixties until the late eighties when her writing started to be published again. She has obtained the National Critics Award for *A mansalva de los años* (Safe from the Years) (1991), *El Ojo Milenario* (The Millenial Eye) (1996) and *Los rituals del inocente* (The Rituals of the Innocent) (1997). She has also published *Espiral en tierra* (Spiral on Earth) (1991), *A la llegada del delfín* (When the Dolphin Arrives) (1998), *El libro de los equívocos* (The Book of Misunderstandings) (2001) and *El rostro equidistante* (The Equidistant Face) (2001). She has been included in several anthologies both inside and outside Cuba.

Further reading

Alonso Estenoz, A. (1997) 'Casa que sí existía', *Casa de las Américas* 209.

Bejel, E. (2001) 'The Search for an Elided Voice', in *Gay Cuban Nation*, Chicago: University of Chicago Press, 181–8.

Feria, Lina de (1967) *Casa que no existía*, Havana: UNEAC, Premio David.

Fowler, V. (1997) 'La tarea del poeta y su lenguaje en la poesía cubana reciente', *Casa de las Américas* 215: 11–25.

Prats Sariol, J. (1990) 'Prólogo', in Lina de Feria

(ed.), *A mansalva de los años*, Havana: Ediciones Unión.

JESÚS JAMBRINA

Ferland, Barbara

b. 1919, Spanish Town, Jamaica

Poet and songwriter

A member of a circle of young writers and artists, including Derek **Walcott** and V.S. **Naipaul**, Ferland became a contributor to the BBC's *Caribbean Voices*. As a songwriter, she collaborated with Louise **Bennett** on a collection of Jamaican folk songs and wrote songs for the first all-Jamaican pantomime, *Busha Bluebeard* (1949). Ferland's song 'Evening-Time' is still used as Radio Jamaica's signature tune. Her poetry, sharpened to knife-point, was published in anthologies and in the journals *Bim* and *Focus*. She received the Sir Robert Barker Prize for Lyric Poetry (1952) and in 1994 published the collection *Without Shoes I Must Run*.

SANDRA COURTMAN

Fernández, Macedonio

b.1874, Buenos Aires, Argentina; d. 1952, Buenos Aires

Writer

One of Argentina's outstanding writers, Fernández's reputation is partly attributable to **Borges**, for whom he was simply an intellectual (see **intellectuals**), and partly due to Fernández's well-known distaste for publishing his own works (most of which were published posthumously by his son and others). Both are false. Borges's views are disproved by Fernández's rich body of work – stories, poems, novels, letters, essays which he called his 'papers' (*papeles*). His *Museo de la novela de la Eterna* (Museum of the Novel of the Eternal), posthumously published in 1967, is the expression of an avant-garde which does not distract itself with unrealizable Utopias but sees the novel itself as the distraction rendered Utopia. Fernández constructs all his work in opposition to the aesthetics of **Lugones**, which is why the *ultraísta* movement of the 1920s (see ***ultraismo***) adopted him as an emblematic progenitor. He was a fine poet and author of one of the most beautiful erotic poems in Spanish, 'Elena Bellamuerte', an extraordinary thinker hostile to all systems of thought, and a humorist of genius. He and his wife Elena de Obieta are evoked in Ricardo Piglia's novel *La ciudad ausente* (The Absent City) (1992).

Further reading

Borinsky, A. (1987) *Macedonio Fernández y la teoría crítica*, Buenos Aires: Corregidor.

Englebert, J.A. (1978) *Macedonio Fernández and the Spanish American New Novel*, New York: New York University Press.

Fernández, M. (1974–1989) *Obras completas*, Buenos Aires: Corregidor.

García, G.L. (1975) *Macedonio Fernández: La escritura en objeto*, Buenos Aires: Siglo XXI.

Lindstrom, N. (1989) 'Macedonio Fernández', in C.A. Solé and M.I. Abreu (eds), *Latin American Writers*, New York: Scribners, 2, 483–91.

Obieta, A. de (1999) *Macedonio: Memorias errantes*, Buenos Aires: Manuel Pamplín Editor.

Piglia, R. (ed.) (2000) *Diccionario de la novela de Macedonio Fernández*, Buenos Aires: Fondo de Cultura Económica.

Salvador, N. (1997) 'Macedonio Fernández', in V. Smith (ed.), *Encyclopedia of Latin American Literature*, London: Fitzroy Dearborn, 304–5.

ENRIQUE FOFFANI

Fernández, Pablo Armando

b. 1930, Central Delicias, Holguín, Cuba

Writer

An outstanding exponent of the Cuban school of 'conversational poetry', Fernández worked and lived in the USA until 1959, when he returned to Cuba. He was a leading figure in ***Lunes de Revolución*** and an editor of the journal ***Casa de las Américas***. He wrote several volumes of poetry, and his novel *Los niños se despiden* (The Children Say Farewell) won the 1968 Casa de las

Américas prize for fiction. He subsequently published two more novels and a volume of short stories, *El talismán y otras evocaciones* (The Talisman and Other Evocations) (1994).

Further reading

Benedetti, M. (1971) 'Pablo Armando o el desafío subjetivo', *Crítica cómplice*, Havana: Instituto Cubano del Libro, 94–104.

Fernández, P.A. (1984) *Campo de amor y de batalla*, Havana: Editorial Letras Cubana.

—— (1988) *El sueño, la razón*, Havana: UNEAC.

Lopez Lemus, V. (1988) 'Palabras a Pablo Armando', in *Palabras del trasfondo*, Havana: Editorial Letras Cubanas, 267–79.

WILFREDO CANCIO ISLA

Fernández Moreno, Baldomero

b. 1866, Buenos Aires, Argentina; d. 1950, Buenos Aires

Poet

One of the most beloved of Argentine poets, Fernández Moreno's work (characterized as *sencillismo*, an aesthetic of simplicity) is born of a critique of **Spanish American modernism**, although Fernández Moreno was a contemporary of the *modernistas* and his poetry is in dialogue with theirs. A poet of the city, his writings evoke a rapidly changing Buenos Aires, its objects, the life of its streets. In this respect he has affinities to Evaristo Carriego (1883–1912) and to Borges's poems on Buenos Aires in the 1920s. Borges in fact remarks on Fernández Moreno's ability to look at the city around him, although he himself rejected the creed of *sencillismo*. Fernández Moreno's son César was also a well-known poet.

Further reading

Carilla, E. (1973) *Genio y figura de Baldomero Fernández Moreno*, Buenos Aires: EUDEBA.

Fernández Moreno, B. (1969) *Obra poética (Antología)*, ed. and intro. by H.J. Becco and M.D. Iturralde, Buenos Aires: Huemul.

Fernández Moreno, C. and M. Fernández Moreno (1961) *Bibliografía de Fernández Moreno*, Buenos Aires: Instituto de Literatura Argentina, Universidad de Buenos Aires.

Monteleone, J. (1986) 'Baldomero Fernández Moreno; poeta caminante', *Cuadernos hispanoamericanos* 429: 79–96.

DANIEL BALDERSTON

Fernández Retamar, Roberto

b. 1930, Havana, Cuba

Writer

A poet, Fernández Retamar is regarded as one of the most important exponents of the school of 'conversational poetry' which included Fayad Jamis, Pablo Armando **Fernández** and Heberto **Padilla** among others. One of the younger poets associated with the **Orígenes** group, Retamar's first volume of poetry, *Elegía como un himno* (Elegy Like a Hymn), was published in 1950. In 1952 he won the National Poetry Prize with *Patrias* (Homelands). Having graduated from Havana University, he continued his studies at the Sorbonne and in London, before becoming cultural attaché at the Cuban embassy in Paris in 1960. He continued to publish works of poetry including *En su lugar poesía* (In its Place, Poetry) (1961), *Con las mismas manos* (With the Same Hands) (1962) and *Que veremos arder* (We'll Watch it Burn) (1970). His *Juana y otros poemas personales* (Juana and Other Personal Poems) (1980) won the Ruben Darío Latin American Poetry prize and *Aquí* (Here) (1994) was awarded the Pérez Bonalde Poetry Prize. Retamar has also produced several books of essays, among them *Calibán* (1971) and *Para una teoría de la literatura latinoamericana* (Towards a Theory of Latin American Literature) (1975). He is well known for his research on the work of the nineteenth-century poet and politician José **Martí**, developed through numerous talks, articles and anthologies as well as his own *Introducción a José Martí* (Introduction to José Martí) (1978).

Fernández Retamar has played an important role as editor of literary journals such as *Nueva revista cubana* and *Unión*, and particularly as editorial director of **Casa de las Américas**, a post he has held since 1965. Since 1986 he has been the president of the Casa.

Further reading

Arcos, J.L. (ed.) (2001) *Orbita de Roberto Fernández Retamar*, Havana: Ediciones UNION.

Benedetti, Mario (1971) 'Fernández Retamar; poesía desde el cráter', in *Crítica cómplice*, Havana: Instituto del Libro.

Fernández Retamar, R. (1962) *Con las mismas manos 1949–62*, Havana: Ediciones Unión.

Fornet, A. (ed.) (2001) *Acerca de Roberto Fernández Retamar*, Havana: Editorial Letras Cubanas.

Pogolotti, Graziela (1963) 'La poesía de Fernández Retamar', *Unión* 2(5/6): 111–17.

Vitier, Cintio (1952) 'Roberto Fernández Retamar', in *Cincuenta años de poesía cubana (1902–1952)*, Havana: Ministerio de Educación.

WILFREDO CANCIO ISLA

Fernández Spencer, Antonio

b. 1922, Santo Domingo, Dominican Republic; d. 1995, Santo Domingo

Poet

Poet, literary critic, professor and diplomat, Fernández Spencer first published his poems in ***Poesía sorprendida*** (Poetry Surprised) in 1944 and later founded the poetry journal *Entre las soledades* (Amid Loneliness). He studied in Spain, where he won prizes for *Bajo la luz del día* (In the Daylight) (1953) and *Diario del mundo* (World Diary) (1970). After returning to Santo Domingo, he founded the Colección Arquero (Archer Collection). His poetry is influenced by the mysticism of the Spanish poets such as Santa Teresa de Jesús and San Juan de la Cruz.

Further reading

Fernández Spencer, A. (1981) 'Lo más real de la realidad en la poesía de Manuel Joglar Cacho', *Nueva estafeta* 36: 68–71.

—— (1989) 'Ecuatorial: Obra maestra', *Cuadernos hispanoamericanos* 471: 59–71.

FERNANDO VALERIO-HOLGUÍN

Ferré, Rosario

b. 1938, Ponce, Puerto Rico

Writer

A controversial and prolific feminist writer, Ferré was born into a wealthy family and was educated mostly in the USA. She began her literary career in the late 1960s, when she founded an illustrated literary magazine, ***Zona de carga y descarga***, with other young writers such as Manuel **Ramos Otero**, as an outlet for their controversial stories. Her first book, *Papeles de Pandora* (Pandora's Papers) (1976), is a collection of experimental short stories incorporating elements from popular culture, and deliberately contrasting upper- and lower-class worlds. These stories revolve around women from different social stations who face love, marital bondage and sexuality. Among the most acclaimed pieces are 'Cuando las mujeres quieren a los hombres' (When Women Love Men), and 'La muñeca menor' (The Youngest Doll). Her second work, *Sitio a Eros* (Eros under Siege) (1980), is a collection of essays on distinguished women artists like Virginia Woolf, Jean **Rhys**, Sylvia Plath, Julia de **Burgos** and Tina Modotti. One essay addresses the importance of journal or diary writing for women.

Fábulas de la garza desangrada (Fables of the Bleeding Heron) (1982) is a book of long poems of remarkable figural beauty. Her main concern is the process of subverting the figuration of classical and contemporary feminine myths, including Julia de Burgos, the Puerto Rican poet much admired by Ferré, and many writers from this Caribbean island. Her other works include *Maldito amor* (Sweet Diamond Dust) (1986), a novel that reconstructs the wealthy life and the demise of the Puerto Rican land-owning class. It is the story of three generations marking three crucial periods in Puerto Rico's history: the arrival of US capital, the decline of traditional agriculture, and the development of a new industrial urban culture. The theme of the Latin American family and the problem of class is explored in most of Ferré's fiction to date.

In addition, she has written essays on Julio **Cortázar**, on Spanish classics including Sor Juana Inés de la Cruz, and on Felisberto **Hernández**. In the 1990s she published a short story entitled *Las dos Venecias* (The Two Venices) (1992) and *The House in the Lagoon* (1995) in English. As well as several volumes of children's books which draw on oriental fables, Germanic fairy tales and American Indian legends, she also helped her politician father, Luis Ferré, write his memoirs. She published another novel in 1999, *Eccentric Neighborhoods*.

Further reading

Fernández Olmos, M. (1987) 'Luis Rafael Sánchez and Rosario Ferré: Sexual Politics and Contemporary Puerto Rican Narrative', *Hispania* 70.

—— (1990) 'Rosario Ferré', in D. Marting (ed.) *Contemporary Women Authors of Latin America: A Bio-Bibliographical Source Book*, New York: Greenwood Press.

García Pinto, M. (1991) 'Interview with Rosario Ferré', in *Women Writers of Latin America. Intimate Histories*, trans. Trudy Balch and M. García Pinto, Austin: University of Texas Press, 81–103.

Gascón Vera, E. (1995) '*Sitio a Eros*: The Liberated Eros of Rosario Ferré', in Doris Meyer (ed.), *Reinterpreting the Spanish American Essay: Women Writers of the 19th and 20th Centuries*, Austin: University of Texas Press, 177–87.

López-Baralt, M. (2002) 'Rosario Ferré', in C. Solé and K. Müller-Bergh (eds), *Latin American Writers: Supplement I*, New York: Scribners, 217–31.

Murphy, M. (1997) 'Rosario Ferré', in V. Smith (ed.), *Encyclopedia of Latin American Literature*, London: Fitzroy Dearborn, 308–10.

Ortega, E. (1996) 'Escritura de mujer de letras: En torno al ensayo de Rosario Ferré', in *Lo que se hereda no se hurta: ensayos de crítica literaria feminista*, Santiago: Cuarto Propio, 167–79.

MAGDALENA GARCÍA PINTO

Ferrer, Renée

b. 1944, Asunción, Paraguay

Writer

Ferrer is one of the most prolific writers of her generation and has won various prestigious national and international prizes. *La voz que me fue dada (Poesía 1965–1995)* (The Voice That Was Given to Me (Poetry 1965–1995)) is a sort of personal poetic anthology. Her narrative works include *Los nudos del silencio* (The Knots of Silence) (1988), her first novel and *Desde el encendido corazón del monte* (From the Burning Heart of the Hill Country) (1994), a book of ecological tales which won the First Prize of UNESCO and the Fundación del Libro at the 1995 Feria del Libro (Book Fair) of Buenos Aires. She is also the author of several books of poems and stories for children.

TERESA MÉNDEZ-FAITH

Ficciones

A famous collection of short stories by Jorge Luis **Borges**, published in 1944. The first half of the book first appeared as *El jardín de senderos que se bifurcan* (The Garden of Forking Paths) (1941–42) and included the extraordinary and innovative stories 'Pierre Menard, autor del Quijote' (Pierre Menard, Author of Don Quixote) (1939) and 'Tlön, Uqbar, Orbis Tertius' (1940), both of which appeared first in the journal ***Sur***, as well as the innovative work of **crime fiction** that gave the volume its name. In 1944 a second half was added, entitled 'Artificios' (Artifices), which included the stories 'Funes el memorioso' (Funes the Memorious), 'La forma de la espada' (The Shape of the Sword), 'La muerte y la brújula' (Death and the Compass) and 'El milagro secreto' (The Secret

Miracle). (Additional stories were added to the second edition of *Ficciones* in 1956.)

Ficciones was a title that implied an aesthetic programme for Borges, including the elements of a highly self-conscious fiction (including a dizzying degree of fictions within fictions), a distancing from the social realist style that dominated the period, and the cultivation of seemingly minor genres such as crime fiction, **science fiction** and the fantastic (see **fantastic literature**). The programme was outlined by Adolfo **Bioy Casares** in his 1940 preface to the ***Antología de la literatura fantástica*** (Anthology of Fantastic Literature), in which Bioy notes that Borges has just created a new kind of fantastic literature in his story 'Tlön, Uqbar, Orbis Tertius', and in Borges's 1940 preface to Bioy's *La invención de Morel* (Morel's Invention), which expresses a preference for plot over character. In Borges's own case, this permitted a radically new kind of fiction, first realized fully in 'Pierre Menard', in which a French symbolist poet rewrites – word for word – certain passages of Cervantes's *Don Quixote*, an event whose full implications must be divined by the reader.

Borges's use of the term *ficciones* was probably derived from John Dewey's division (in his library classification system) of literature into fiction and non-fiction; the English substrate adheres to the word, which acquired the status of a neologism in Spanish, closely associated with Borges's practice. Ironically, however, the stories of *Ficciones* are profoundly involved with the 'non-fictional' realms of philosophy, history and politics. Borges's stories have dazzled readers for decades, have been the focus of a vast amount of critical work, and have revolutionized the practice of the short story.

Further reading

Balderston, D. (1993) *Out of Context: Historical Reference and the Representation of Reality in Borges*, Durham, NC: Duke University Press.

Shaw, D.L. (1990) 'Jorge Luis Borges: Ficciones', in Philip Swanson (ed.), *Landmarks in Modern Latin American Fiction*, London: Routledge.

DANIEL BALDERSTON

Fierro, Enrique

b. 1942, Montevideo, Uruguay

Writer

A prolific poet, Fierro has published twenty-five books of poems; *De la invención* (About Invention) (1964) was his first. His poetry, representative of the vitality of recent Uruguayan poetry, is constructed on a system of references that reveal his vast cultural and literary knowledge, marked by a skilful use of humour and irony. He has held the post of Director of the National Library of Montevideo, and since 1989 has taught at the University of Texas at Austin. He is married to the poet Ida **Vitale**.

Further reading

Carignano, D. and S. Yurkievich (1988) 'Detrás de toda fábula: Entrevista a Enrique Fierro', *Rio de la Plata/Culturas* 7: 63–72.

Fierro, Enrique (1968) *Los poetas del 45*, Montevideo and Buenos Aires: Centro Editor de América Latina.

Olivera Williams, M.R. (1988) 'Poesía del exilio', *Revista hispánica moderna* 41(2): 125–40.

Verani, H.J. (1983) 'El fragmento como texto: La poesía de Enrique Fierro', *Studi di letteratura ispano americana* 13–14: 131–40.

MAGDALENA GARCÍA PINTO

Figueroa, John J.M.

b. 1920, Kingston, Jamaica; d. 1998, London, England

Poet

James T. Livingston has called John Figueroa 'perhaps the most classical of West Indian poets'. Long a believer in an eclectic approach to art, Figueroa agreed with the Latin poet Terence that 'nothing human is alien to me'. His poetry collections are *Blue Mountain Peak* (1943), *Love Leaps Here* (1962) and *Ignoring Hurts* (1976). Figueroa taught at London University and was a professor of education at the University of the West Indies from

1957 to 1973. He also held academic posts in Nigeria and in various British institutions. He has published many essays on educational and literary topics, and edited the first substantial anthology of Caribbean poetry, *Caribbean Voices*.

Further reading

Figueroa, J.J.M. (1973) *Caribbean Voices*, Washington, DC: R.B. Luce.

—— (1974) 'Poetry and the Teaching of Poetry', in John H. Dorenkamp (ed.), *Literary Studies in Memory of Francis A. Drumm*, Worcester, MA: College of the Holy Cross and Wetteren, Belgium: Cultura Press, 207–27.

Figueroa, J.J.M. *et al.* (1979) *Caribbean Writers: A Bio-Bibliographical-Critical Encyclopedia*, Washington, DC: Three Continents.

KEITH JARDIM

Filho, Adonias

b. 1915, Itajuípe, Bahia; d. 1990, Ilhéus, Bahia

Writer

Adonias Aguiar Filho grew up in the *cacau* region in southern Bahia, where several of his narratives are set (for example, *Corpo vivo* (Living Body) (1962)). His fiction melds the social concerns of the regionalist novel (see ***regionalismo***) with psychological and existential introspection. Many of his characters are caught in a blind struggle against destiny in a nightmarish, seemingly godless world where they must rely only on their own instincts. Narratives such as *O forte* (The Fortress) (1965) and the short stories of *Léguas da promissão* (The Leagues of Promise) (1968) are written in a densely poetic, elliptical style that juxtaposes multiple levels of time and space.

Further reading

Castro, S. (1991) 'Literatura e Ideologia em Adonias Filho', *Rassegna Iberistica* 40: 15–32.

Filho, A. (1969) *Memories of Lazarus*, trans. F. Ellison, Austin: University of Texas Press.

—— (1973) 'O romance: Um testemunho', *Jornal de letras* 277(Cad. 2): 7.

Reis, R. (1997) 'Adonias Filho', in V. Smith (ed.), *Encyclopedia of Latin American Literature*, London: Fitzroy Dearborn, 311–12.

Simões, M. (1981) 'Introdução à Narrativa de Adonias Filho', *Studi di letteratura ispano americana* 11: 73–89.

RANDAL JOHNSON

Filloy, Juan

b. 1894, Córdoba, Argentina; d. 2000, Córdoba

Writer

Trained as a lawyer, Filloy privately published several works in the 1930s for a very limited public. When some of them were republished by Paidos in the 1990s, including *¡Estafen!* (Con Them) (1932) and *Op Oloop* (1934), Filloy became the great 'discovery' of the time, though **Cortázar** had already referred to him in ***Rayuela***. He is recognized as a great master of parody and illusive realism. The new interest in his work led other important works to be republished, among them *La Potra* (1973), *Vil-y-vil* (1975) and *La purga* (The Purge) (1992). Filloy is a particularly skilful coiner of palindromes, some of them in a satirical vein. His long silence as a writer is explained by the fact that he became a judge in 1968.

Further reading

Aguinis, M. (2000) 'Juan Filloy, 1894–2000: La libertad seductora', *La Nación, suplemento cultura* 23 July: 1–2.

Flores, F.G. (1994) 'Provinciano universal', *La Nación, suplemento cultura* 31 July: 1–2.

Gowland, M. (1994) 'Doctor en mundología', *La Nación, suplemento cultura* 7 Aug.: 4.

—— (1995) 'El hombre de los tres siglos: Entrevista con Juan Filloy', *La Nación, suplemento cultura* 3 Sept.: 3.

Renella, P. (2001) 'Juan Filloy: Contrastes y desmesuras alrededor de un mito', in Fernando O. Reati and Miriam Pino (eds), *De centros y periferias en la literatura de Córdoba*, Córdoba, Argentina: Rubén Libros.

ENRIQUE FOFFANI

Flores, Angel

b. 1900, Barceloneta, Puerto Rico; d. 1994, New York, USA

Critic

A prolific critic of Hispanic literature, Flores's career spans several decades and the breadth of his knowledge several centuries and two continents. Flores taught and wrote in several US institutions, including Rutgers University and Cornell. He published criticism on Spanish Golden Age literature, and edited numerous anthologies of Spanish and Latin American literature from the Middle Ages to Pablo **Neruda**. Flores also translated works of Hispanic literature, including Pablo Neruda's 1935 *Residencia en la tierra* (Residence on Earth) (1946) and Esteban Echeverría's 1871 *El matadero* (The Slaughter House) (1959).

Further reading

Flores, A. (1959) *Historia y antología del cuento y la novela en Hispanoamérica*, New York: Las Americas.

—— (1975) *Bibliografía de escritores hispanoamericanos, 1609–1974*, New York: Gordian Press.

—— (1984) *Expliquémonos a Borges como poeta*, Mexico City: Siglo XXI.

—— (1992) *Spanish American Authors: The Twentieth Century*, New York: Wilson.

CATHERINE DEN TANDT

Florit, Eugenio

b. 1903, Madrid, Spain; d. 1999, Miami, Florida, USA

Writer

An outstanding lyric poet of his generation, Florit lived in Cuba from the age of 14. A member of the **Revista de Avance** group, he moved to New York in 1940 but collaborated with the Cuban **Orígenes** group and wrote for its magazine. He also co-edited *Revista hispánica moderna* in New York with Federico de **Onís** and Angel del Río. His many works, from *Trópico* (1930) to *A pesar de todo* (Despite Everything) (1987), present a poetry of existential concerns, marked by a sense of man's essential solitude and characterized by serenity and rich language.

Further reading

Florit, E. (1991–2001) *Obras completas*, ed. Luis T. González del Valle and Roberto Esquenazi Mayo, Boulder: Society of Spanish and Spanish-American Studies, 6 vols.

Jiménez, J.O. (1979) 'Introducción a la poesía de Eugenio Florit', *Círculo* 8: 7–26.

Nuñes, A.R. (1991) 'Eugenio Florit: Retrato de un poeta', *Círculo* 20: 7–23.

Saa, O. (2000) 'Eugenio Florit: Poeta de la ecuanimidad', *Círculo* 29: 126–34.

WILFREDO CANCIO ISLA

Fondo de Cultura Económica

The Fondo de Cultura Económica (FCE) constituted the cornerstone of twentieth-century Mexican publishing. Founded in 1934 by Daniel Cosío Villegas and Eduardo Villaseñor with subsidies from government offices and private investments, the FCE has vigorously promoted Latin American culture. Through Spanish translations, the FCE made available important titles in history, anthropology and the social sciences. In the 1950s it became a major institution for Mexican literature and culture with two new collections: 'Letras Mexicanas' introduced new writers and 'Colección pular' promoted reading with inexpensive paperbacks. At the same time, FCE began publishing the complete works of canonical figures such as Alfonso **Reyes**.

Under Daniel Cosío Villegas's direction from 1934 to 1948, the FCE took advantage of the expertise of **intellectuals** exiled during and after the Spanish Civil War of 1936–39. Former FCE employees later founded other publishing houses. Joaquín Díez-Canedo left the FCE and founded

Joaquín Mortiz because he wanted to create a strictly literary publishing house, but Arnaldo Orfila Reynal's tenure marked an important and radical change at FCE. As director from 1948 to 1965, Orfila Reynal modernized the company's literary profile while the **Boom** in the Spanish American novel was emerging. In 1965, after publishing a Spanish translation of Oscar Lewis's *The Children of Sánchez*, he was dismissed from the FCE. He later went on to form Siglo XXI. State intervention in the FCE has created managerial tensions since then. The 1982 Mexican debt crisis profoundly affected the publishing industry, and further exacerbated financial constraints at the FCE. Although FCE has remained a key Mexican publisher in the 1980s and 1990s, institutional histories by Víctor Díaz Arciniega have underscored the difficult mission of a cultural firm that must respond to governmental guidelines, remain financially solvent, and also strive to maintain independent criteria for judging cultural values.

Further reading

http://www.fce.com.mx/

Díaz Arciniega, V. (1994) *Historia de la casa: Fondo de Cultura Económica (1934–1994)*, Mexico City: Fondo de Cultura Económica.

Zaid, G. (ed.) (1985) *Daniel Cosío Villegas: Imprenta y vida pública*, Mexico City: Fondo de Cultura Económica.

DANNY J. ANDERSON

Fonseca, Rubem

b. 1925, Juiz de Fora, Minas Gerais, Brazil

Writer

One of Brazil's most eminent living writers, and arguably one of the masters of the **short story** on the continent, Fonseca focuses on raw and often painful aspects of reality, though his writing sometimes has a playful and humorous quality even as it deals with very brutal and sordid events. A splendid example of this tendency is his story 'A matéria do sonho' (The Stuff of Dreams), in *Lúcia McCartney* (1969), narrated by a solitary young man whose fantasy life has been taken in hand by a social worker who has provided him with an inflatable sex doll; the humour in the story is provided by the lists of the narrator's readings, which range wildly through high and low culture, and by the contrast between his earnest efforts at self-improvement and the equally earnest, but somehow more misguided, efforts to 'solve' the alleged problem of his solitude. The stories included in *Feliz ano novo* (Happy New Year) (1975) and *O cobrador* (The Collector) (1979) consolidated Fonseca's reputation as one of Brazil's foremost writers, while taking an acid, violent look at the fractured worlds of the rich and the poor. Several of his subsequent books have been highly regarded novels. *A grande arte* (High Art) (1983) is an accomplished thriller, interspersed with instructions on the use of firearms. *Bufo & Spallanzani* (1985) is based on the life of an eighteenth-century Italian biologist, while *Vastas emoções e pensamentos imperfeitos* (Vast Emotions and Imperfect Thoughts) (1990) plays with the life story of the Russian writer, Isaac Babel (1894–1941). *Agosto* (August) (1990) is an eloquent examination of the moment in Brazilian history marked by the suicide of Getúlio Vargas. Some of Fonseca's work has been translated into Spanish and English, but his powerful writing is not yet as well known outside Brazil as it deserves to be.

Further reading

Ballantyne, Christopher J. (1986) 'The Rhetoric of Violence in Rubem Fonseca', *Luso-Brazilian Review* 23(2): 1–20.

Fonseca, R. (1987) *High Art*, trans. E. Watson, New York: Harper & Row.

—— (1990) *Buffo and Spallanzani*, trans. C.E. Landers, New York: Dutton.

Silva, Deonisio da (1996) *Rubem Fonseca: Proibido e consagrado*, Rio de Janeiro: Relume-Dumara.

Vieira, N.H. (1997) 'Rubem Fonseca', in V. Smith (ed.), *Encyclopedia of Latin American Literature*, London: Fitzroy Dearborn, 317–18.

Xavier, Elódia (1987) 'Rubem Fonseca: O conto depurado', in *O conto brasileiro e sua trajetória*, Rio de Janeiro: Padrão, 119–32.

DANIEL BALDERSTON

Foppa, Alaíde

b. 1914, Barcelona, Spain; d. 1980, Guatemala

Writer

Foppa grew up in Italy, married Guatemala politician Mario Solórzano and took Guatemalan citizenship. Exiled in Mexico after the 1954 coup, she developed a feminist radio programme in the late 1970s for UNAM which highlighted the oppression of Mayan women. Foppa published her first collection of feminist poems in Mexico in 1970, *Elogio de mi cuerpo* (Eulogy to My Body), and helped to edit the journal *Fem.* Her poetry is intensely lyrical, not always overtly political and not as strident as that of younger women poets. Kidnapped and presumably murdered upon her return to Guatemala in 1980, she is a symbol of women's participation in Guatemalan resistance.

Further reading

Foppa, A. (1968) 'Realidad e irrealidad en la obra de Miguel Angel Asturias', *Cuadernos americanos* 156: 53–69.

—— (1969) 'Maquialveo y el Príncipe', *Revista de la Universidad de México* 23(9): 25–9.

—— (1975) 'Matta: Lo visivo, lo crítico, lo visionario', *Revista de bellas artes* 20: 2–4.

MARC ZIMMERMAN

Forde, A.N.

b. 1923, Barbados

Writer

A multifaceted writer, Forde has published a one act play, *The Passing Cloud* (1966), a poetry collection, *Canes by the Roadside* (1951), and edited the anthology *Talk of the Tamarinds* (1971). He is well known as a teacher, and has had his work broadcast by the BBC. During the heyday of the Barbados literary magazine *Bim*, Forde was one of its editors, contributing stories, poems and essays to it and other journals. His riveting poetic short story, 'Sunday with a Difference', is included in the anthology *From the Green Antilles* (1966).

KEITH JARDIM

Fornet, Ambrosio

b. 1932, Bayamo, Oriente, Cuba

Writer

Narrator, essayist and editor, Fornet headed the Arte y Literatura publishing house, part of the Cuban National Publishers and later of the National Book Institute, between 1964 and 1971. Educated in the USA and Spain, he was the Cuban delegate to the International PEN Conference at Abidjan, Ivory Coast in 1967; the following year he was secretary of Commission III at the Havana Cultural Congress. His writings have appeared in *Carteles*, ***Lunes de Revolución***, ***Casa de las Américas***, *Unión* and *Revolución y cultura*, as well as in several anthologies and his own volumes of stories and essays.

Further reading

Fornet, A. (1967) *Antología del cuento cubano contemporáneo*, Mexico City: Era.

——(1987) *Alea, una retrospectiva crítica*, La Habana: Editorial Letras Cubanas.

—— (1993) 'Las máscaras del tiempo en la novela de la Revolución Cubana', *Casa de las Américas* 33(191): 12–24.

—— (1997) 'Briding Enigma: Cubans on Cuba', *South Atlantic Quarterly* 96(1).

JOSÉ ANTONIO EVORA

Franqui, Carlos

b. 1921, Cifuentes, Cuba

Writer and journalist

Of working-class origins, Franqui joined the struggle against the dictatorship of Fulgencio Batista at an early age, and suffered imprisonment and exile as a result. In 1955 he created *Revolución*, the underground journal of the 26th of July

Movement led by Fidel Castro. In 1958 he joined the armed struggle in the Sierra Maestra and became director of the rebel radio station, Radio Rebelde. In 1959, with the victory of the Cuban Revolution, he became editor of *Revolución* and was the inspiration behind its cultural supplement, ***Lunes de Revolución***, until 1963, when he was dismissed. In 1968 he assisted in the organization of the Cultural Congress in Havana, and shortly thereafter went into exile in Italy. In 1993 he moved to Puerto Rico. His publications include *El libro de los doce* (The Book of the Twelve) (1966), about the development of the guerrilla war in Cuba, *Retrato de familia con Fidel* (Family Portrait with Fidel) (1981) and *Vida, aventura y desastres de un hombre llamado Fidel* (The Life, Adventures and Disasters of a Man Called Fidel) (1988). He subsequently founded and edited *Carta de Cuba*, a bulletin publishing reports from independent Cuban journalists.

Further reading

Clark, S.J. (1999) 'Retrato de familia con Fidel: Las memorias de un revolucionário exiliado', *Caribe* 2(1): 44–58.

WILFREDO CANCIO ISLA

Fresán, Rodrigo

b. 1963, Buenos Aires, Argentina

Novelist

Fresán's first work of fiction, *Historia argentina* (Argentine History), a collection of fifteen short stories, was published in 1991 and stayed on the best-seller list for several months. His first novel, *Esperanto* (1995), has been praised by critics. His fiction production to date is rounded out by the short stories *Vida de santos* (Saints' Lives) (1993), some journalistic notes, *Trabajos manuales* (Manual Labour) (1994) and the novels *La velocidad de las cosas* (The Speed of Things) (1998) and *Mantra* (2001). In his works there is a sort of collage that creates a cosmopolitan imagination in which contemporary mass-culture mythologies co-exist with the literary traditions of the avant-garde (see **avant-garde in Latin America**).

Since 1984 Fresán has worked as a journalist. His articles appear frequently in the Argentine newspaper *Página 12* and in various Mexican and Spanish papers. He writes about food, music, books and film. At present he lives in Barcelona.

JOSÉ J. MARISTANY

Fuentes, Carlos

b. 1928, Panama City

Writer

Fuentes is one of the leading Hispanic-American literary figures of the twentieth century, associated with the so-called **Boom** of the 1960s. His numerous works include novels and short stories as well as plays and essays. Because of his eloquence and his deep understanding of the present and past reality of Latin America, he has come to be regarded, mainly in the USA, as a sort of spokesman for the subcontinent.

The son of a Mexican diplomat, Fuentes was born in Panama City and lived in Quito, Montevideo and Rio de Janeiro before attending primary school in Washington, DC. He attended secondary school in Santiago, Buenos Aires and Mexico City. He studied law at the Institut des Hautes Études Internationales in Geneva (1950) and at the National University of Mexico (UNAM) (1951). He was secretary to the Mexican delegation to the International Law Commission of the United Nations in Geneva (1951) and Director of Cultural Affairs at the Mexican Ministry of Foreign Affairs (1957). His literary awards have included the Xavier Villaurrutia Prize (1975), the Rómulo Gallegos Prize (1977), the Mexican National Prize for Letters (1984) and the Cervantes Prize (1987).

His main contribution to Hispanic-American literature may be found among his narrative texts as well as in his essays. Conscious of the traditions born out of his special background that includes the heritages of Hispanic, English and French cultures and literatures, his writings are rooted in Cervantes and Quevedo, in Shakespeare and Joyce, in Flaubert and Balzac, as well as in Dostoevsky and Thomas Mann.

Los días enmascarados (Masked Days), a collection

of six short stories, marked his literary debut in 1954. 'Chac Mool', the first story, is now regarded as a small masterpiece of the fantastic genre. His first novel, *La región más transparente* (Where the Air is Clear) (1958), is a portrait of Mexico during the 1950s, particularly of Mexico City and its multi-levelled middle class. Its experimental character with regard to language and new novelistic forms was acclaimed as the breakthrough of a most promising young narrative talent. But it was *La muerte de Artemio Cruz* (The Death of Artemio Cruz) (1962) that established its author as a first-class novelist. Many regard this novel as Fuentes's masterpiece. It is the story of the social and economic rise – and corruption – of a man who participated in the Mexican Revolution; it can be read as the history of the corruption of the Revolution. This novel's remarkably dynamic narrative includes, among other devices, interior monologues, juxtaposing of narrative points of view, masterful handling of time as well as first, second and third-person narration, all within the memory of the dying protagonist. All this is carried out using extremely realistic language. The novel projects ethical meaning through a most accomplished aesthetic virtuosity.

Aura (1962) and *Cumpleaños* (Birthday) (1970) are two short novels related by their intertextuality and by their common themes: identity and time. The story in the novel *Cambio de piel* (A Change of Skin) (1967) takes place in Cholula, a pre-Hispanic religious centre, during the 1960s. It has been suggested that the central role played by history in *Aura* and the tense co-existence of Cholula's past with the characters present in *Cambio de piel*, paved the way towards Fuentes' most ambitious project – the rewriting of Hispanic history in his monumental novel *Terra nostra* (1975).

The novel *Cristóbal nonato* (Christopher Unborn) (1987) represents a chaotic and apocalyptic portrait of Mexico at the end of the twentieth century. This text's most outstanding acomplishment might be the pyrotechnical nature of its language based on hallucinating plays of words sustained throughout the text by different means: witty puns, double meanings – above all related to sexual power – creative blendings of Spanish and English words producing new meanings, and so on.

As an essayist, Fuentes has also produced brilliant texts. Within the field of literary criticism, *La nueva novela hispanoamericana* (The New Hispanic American Novel) (1969), and *Valiente mundo nuevo* (Brave New World) (1990) study the historic context and significance of modern Hispanic-American novelists. *Myself with Others* (1981) is a collection of short essays that also includes autobiographical information. In order to mark the Columbian quincentenary of the European discovery of America, he published *El espejo enterrado* (The Buried Mirror) (1992). It is a didactic description, with eloquent commentary, of the development of Hispanic culture from the Middle Ages until today, both in the Iberian peninsula and in the Americas. He has also made a television series of the same title.

Fuentes's literary texts reveal the privileged point of view of a Mexican who grew up both in Mexico and abroad, a Mexican who can look at his own country from the vantage point of the USA and France – where he seems to feel at home – as well as from that of the more familiar Argentina and Chile. This heightened perspective is an asset as well as a handicap; at times Mexico is rendered picturesque and even touristy in his writings. However, Fuentes is consistently sympathetic to progressive causes in Latin America.

Further reading

Boldy, S. (1997) 'Carlos Fuentes', in V. Smith (ed.), *Encyclopedia of Latin American Literature*, London: Fitzroy Dearborn, 327–31.

Brody, R. and C. Rossman (eds) (1982) *Carlos Fuentes: A Critical View*, Austin: University of Texas Press.

Faris, W.B. (1983) *Carlos Fuentes*, New York: Ungar.

Fuentes, C. (1985–9) *Obras completas*, Mexico City: Aguilar.

—— (1988) *Myself and Others: Selected Essays*, New York: Farrar, Straus.

Gyurko, L.A. (2002) 'Carlos Fuentes', in C. Solé and K. Müller-Bergh (eds), *Latin American Writers: Supplement I*, New York: Scribners, 233–48.

Van Delden, M. (1998) *Carlos Fuentes, Mexico and Modernity*, Liverpool: Liverpool University Press.

JUAN PELLICER

Fuguet, Alberto

b. 1964, Santiago, Chile

Writer

Fuguet is the author of the short story collection *Sobredosis* (Overdose) (1990), and the novels *Mala Onda* (Bad Vibes) (1991), *Por Favor Rebobinar* (Please Rewind) (1994) and *Tinta Roja* (Red Ink) (1997). From 1993–95 he was literary editor of the youth supplement *Zona de Contacto*, published weekly by *El Mercurio*, Chile's largest newspaper. Narrating in a realistic style the decadent pastimes of upper-class urban teenagers, *Sobredosis* and *Mala Onda* were best-sellers and raised controversy in Chilean literary circles. In particular, *Mala Onda*, the great moral novel of the 1980s, repudiates Chile's social climate during the Pinochet dictatorship. In 1996 he co-edited the controversial short story anthology ***McOndo***, which celebrates the postmodern and 'Americanized' lifestyle of Latin American yuppies. He has been unstinting in his criticism of earlier Latin American novelists, particularly of their political and social commitments.

Further reading

Hargrave, K. and G. Smith-Seminet (1998) 'De Macondo a McOndo: Nuevas voces en la literatura latinoamericana', *Chasqui* 27(2): 14–26.

Lorenzi, A. (2001) 'In Search of Lost Time: Intellectuals, Media, and Narrative', in Edmundo Paz-Soldan, Debra A. Castillo and David William Foster (eds), *Latin American Literature and Mass Media*, New York: Garland Publishing.

O'Connell, P.L. (2001) 'Narrating History through Memory in Three Novels of Post-Pinochet Chile', *Hispania* 84(2): 181–92.

Palaversich, D. (2000) 'Rebeldes sin causa: Realismo mágico vs. realismo virtual', *Hispamérica* 29(86): 55–70.

AMALIA PEREIRA

Futoransky, Luisa

b. 1939, Buenos Aires, Argentina

Writer

The piercing, deconstructing humour of Futoransky's novels (for which she has been called a female Woody Allen) combines in her poetry with a lyrical but pitiless vision of loneliness in an alien world. A poet and a novelist, she lived in Japan and China before moving to Paris in 1981. She has published six volumes of poetry and the novels *Son cuentos chinos* (Those Are Chinese Tales) (1983), *De Pe a Pa (o de Pekín a París)* (From Peking to Paris) (1986) and *Urracas* (Magpies) (1992). She won the order of Chevalier des Arts et Lettres of France, and a Guggenheim Fellowship in 1991.

Further reading

Beard, L.J. (1997) 'A is for Alphabet, K is for Kabbalah: Luisa Futoransky's Babelic Metatext', *Intertexts* 1(1): 25–39.

—— (1998) 'La sujetividad femenina en la metaficción feminista latinoamericana', *Revista iberoamericana* 64(182–3): 299–311.

García-Pinto, M. (1999) 'Las movadas del exilio: La poesía de Luisa Futoransky', *Confluencia* 14(2): 3–11.

Schwartz, M.E. (1999) *Writing Paris: Urban Topographies of Desire in Contemporary Latin American Fiction*, Albany: State University of New York Press.

FLORINDA F. GOLDBERG

G

Gaitán Durán, Jorge

b. 1925, Pamplona, Colombia; d. 1962, Guadaloupe, French Antilles

Poet, essayist and literary critic

The son of a well-off family, in the 1950s Gaitán lived in Paris, where he studied cinematography. In 1955, he founded *Mito*, a magazine and intellectual movement which also included Eduardo **Cote Lamus**, Hernando Valencia Goelkel and Jorge Eliécer Ruiz. Gaitán's poetry has a predominantly tragic tone, with reflections on life, death and love. His collections of poems include *Insistencia en la tristeza* (Insistence on Sadness) (1946), *Asombro* (Amazement) (1951), *Amantes* (Lovers) (1954) and *Si mañana despierto* (If I Wake Up Tomorrow) (1961). A political activist, Gaitán fought against Rojas Pinilla's dictatorship.

Further reading

Gaitán Durán, J. (1960) *Sade. Textos escogidos y precedidos por un ensayo: El libertino y la revolución*, Bogotá: Ediciones Mito.

—— (1975) *Obra literaria de Jorge Gaitán Durán*, Bogotá: Colcultura.

Jursich Duran, M. and R.E. Serrano (1992) 'Trípco', *Boletín cultural y bibliográfico* 29(30): 33–55.

Restrepo Forero, G.A. (1991) 'Esta presencia ausencia', *La palabra y hombre* 77: 183–8.

Romero, A. (1984) 'Los poetas de Mito', *Revista iberoamericana* 50(128–9): 689–755.

MIGUEL A. CARDINALE

Galeano, Eduardo

b. 1940, Montevideo, Uruguay

Writer

To call Eduardo Galeano a 'writer' merely hints at his prodigious talents, for he practices his craft with remarkable versatility as an essayist, journalist, novelist, historian, and social and political commentator. He has even tried his hand at children's story-telling, publishing *La piedra arde* (The Hot Stone) in 1987. The blurb for *Guatemala: País ocupado* (Guatemala: Occupied Country) (1967) credits Galeano, before deciding to become a writer, with having earned his keep, among other activities, 'as a bill collector, commercial artist, caricaturist, stenographer, bank clerk and fashion page artist'. Periods working in Uruguay for the weeklies *El Sol* and *Marcha*, and the daily *La Época*, preceded his exile in 1973 to Argentina, where he founded and edited *Crisis*. After a second period of exile, this time in Spain (1977–85), Galeano returned to his native Montevideo.

His best-known works are *Las venas abiertas de América latina* (Open Veins of Latin America) (1971), and the trilogy ***Memoria del fuego*** (Memory of Fire) (1982 and 1985). The former is bold, assertive, sweeping in its scope, quick-paced and urgently written – the view of an agitated young man; the latter is nuanced, tender, contemplative in tone, slow-moving and meticulously wrought – the vision of a patient, mature mind. Both, however, are passionate and heartfelt, for Galeano wants nothing to do with the dry fabrications that purport to be objective and neutral about depicting a Latin

American reality which for him is as inspiring and dignified as it is demoralizing and tragic.

As a prose stylist, Galeano's mastery of the vignette is unparalleled in Latin American writing. He is economical with words, blessed with a keen ability to pare things down to the quick; the reader is left marvelling at how much can be said with so little text. Galeano's vignette style was well established by the time he published his second novel *Días y noches de amor y de guerra* (Days and Nights of Love and War) (1978), but it flourished and became his literary trademark with *Memoria del fuego*. Since then Galeano has authored three books in which the vignette is the preferred, characteristic mode: *El libro de los abrazos* (The Book of Embraces) (1989), *Las palabras andantes* (Walking Words) (1993) and *El fútbol: A sol y sombra* (Football: Light and Shade) (1995), which he also illustrated himself. Two anthologies, *Nosotros decimos no* (We Say No) (1989) and *Ser como ellos y otros artículos* (To Be Like Them and Other Articles) (1992) showcase his journalism.

Further reading

Galeano, E. (1973) *Open Veins of Latin America*, trans. Cedric Belfrage, New York: Monthly Review Press.

—— (1985–8) *Memory of Fire*, New York: Pantheon Books, 3 vols.

Palaversich, D. (1995) *Silencio, voz y escritura en Eduardo Galeano*, Frankfurt-am-Main: Bibliotheca Ibero-Americana.

Wood, D. (1997) 'Eduardo Galeano', in V. Smith (ed.), *Encyclopedia of Latin American Literature*, London: Fitzroy Dearborn, 335–7.

W. GEORGE LOVELL

Galich, Franz

b. 1951, Guatemala City

Writer

Primarily a short story writer, Galich lives in Nicaragua, where he also engages in committed editorial activity. His 1989 collection, *La princesa de ónix* (The Princess of Onyx), plays off references to modernist fantasy. Although referring to the conquest and to recent Guatemalan and Nicaraguan history, he breaks free of the influence of **Asturias** and **Cardoza y Aragón** and the themes of land and regionalism, instead being reminiscent of **Monterroso Bonilla**. Galich's tone is playful, critical and ironic, but the violence in his stories points to the violence of his country.

Further reading

Galich, F. (1979) *Ficcionario inédito*, Guatemala: Editorial Rin.

—— (1989) *La princesa de ónix y otros relatos*, Guatemala: Editoria Impacto.

—— (1995) *Huracán corazón del cielo*, Managua: Signo Editores.

—— (1995) '*Miguel Angel Asturias* casí novela de Luis Cardoza y Aragón: Estudio de una obra de Cardoza y Aragón sobre Asturias: La indigenidad de ambos', *Istmica* 2: 24–34.

MARC ZIMMERMAN

Galich, Manuel

b. 1913, Guatemala City; d. 1984, Havana, Cuba

Writer

The best-known playwright of Guatemala's Generation of 1930, a student leader in 1944 and a political force in the 1944–54 period, Galich eventually went to Cuba where he helped establish the testimonial genre (see ***testimonio***) and where he lived until his death in 1984. His most famous testimonial book is *Del pánico al ataque* (From Panic to Attack) (1949), about the student uprising against the Ubico regime. He also wrote *Por qué lucha Guatemala. Arévalo y Arbenz: Dos hombres contra un imperio* (Why Guatemala Struggles. Arévalo and Arbenz: Two Men Against an Empire) (1958), one of the best volumes about the revolutionary period.

Further reading

Galich, M. (1983) 'El pensamiento martiano en la

guerrilla guatemalteca', *Casa de las Américas* 23(138): 109–12.
—— (2001) *Del pánico al ataque*, Guatemala: Editorial Universitaria.
Marceles Daconte, E. (1984) 'Manuel Galich: La identidad del teatro latinamericano', *Latin American Theatre Review* 17(2): 55–63.

MARC ZIMMERMAN AND LINDA J. CRAFT

Gallegos, Rómulo

b. 1884, Caracas, Venezuela; d. 1969, Caracas

Writer and politician

The best-known and most widely read Venezuelan twentieth-century writer, Gallegos's ethical and political concerns centred on the need to transform the country and overcome its backwardness. From his journalistic articles to novels which became emblematic of the confrontation between **civilization and barbarism**, like ***Doña Bárbara*** (1929), which brought him international fame, *Cantaclaro* (1934) and *Canaima* (1935), Gallegos viewed writing as an instrument of social transformation. He made a logical move into politics, founding the Acción Democrática party in 1936, becoming a deputy and finally being appointed President of the Republic in 1948, although he was deposed in November of that year by a military junta.

Further reading

Díaz-Seijas, P. (1980) *Rómulo Gallegos ante la crítica*, Caracas: Monte Avila.
Gallegos, R. (1991) *Doña Bárbara*, Mexico City: Ed. Espasa-Calpe.
—— (1992) *Canaima (Colección Archivos, N. 20)*, ed. Charles Minguet, Pittsburgh: University of Pittsburgh Press.
—— (1998) *Doña Bárbara*, Denver: Continental Book Co.
Rodríguez Alcalá, H. (1979) *Nine Essays on Rómulo Gallegos*, Riverside: University of California Press.
Ruffinelli, J. (1989) 'Rómulo Gallegos', in C.A. Solé and M.I. Abreu (eds), *Latin American Writers*, New York: Scribners, 2, 603–10.
Shaw, D.L. (1997) 'Rómulo Gallegos', in V. Smith (ed.), *Encyclopedia of Latin American Literature*, London: Fitzroy Dearborn, 338–40.

RAFAEL CASTILLO ZAPATA

Gallegos Lara, Joaquín

b. 1911, Guayaquil, Ecuador; d. 1947, Guayaquil

Writer

Gallegos Lara was a member of the **Guayaquil Group** and co-author of ***Los que se van**, cuentos del cholo y del montuvio* (The Vanishing Ones: Stories about the Cholo and the Montuvio) (1930). An almost mythical figure, with severe physical disabilities, he was regarded as the ideologue and best critical mind of his generation. He advocated a literature in favour of the proletariat and downtrodden. His novel, *Las cruces sobre el agua* (Crosses on the Water) (1946), transcends his social realism and effectively depicts the city prior to and during the 1922 labour uprising in Guayaquil.

Further reading

Gallegos Lara, J. (1956) *Cuentos completos*, Guayaquil: Casa de la Cultura.
—— (1981) *Obras escogidas*, Quito: Casa de la Cultura Ecuatoriana.
Pérez, G.R. (1970) 'Tres narradores de la Costa del Ecuador', *Revista interamericana de bibliografía* 20: 169–90.

HUMBERTO E. ROBLES

Galvão, Patricia

b. 1910, Sao João da Boa Vista, Brazil; d. 1962, Santos, Brazil

Writer

Joining the movement led by Oswald de **Andrade** in 1929, Galvão became the muse of anthropophagy. In 1931 she joined the Communist Party, but due to political differences she used the pseudonym Mara Lobo when writing her first 'proletarian novel' *Parque Industrial* (Industrial Park) (1933). She was also Pagú, the mysterious poet Solange Sohl, and Ariel when writing social chronicles. In 1945 she co-founded the anti-Stalinist journal *Vanguarda socialista* (Socialist Vanguard). From 1952 she devoted herself to theatre. She was the first female political prisoner in Brazil . Hers were also the first translations into Portuguese of works by Ionesco and Beckett, poems by Valéry and Apollinaire, and of Joyce's *Ulysees*.

See also: Antropofagia

Further reading

Bloch, J.H. (1986) 'Patricia Galvão: The Struggle against Conformity', *Latin American Literary Review* 14(27): 188–201.

Galvão, P. (1993) *Industrial Park: A Proletarian Novel*, trans. Elizabeth Jackson and K. David Jackson. Lincoln: University of Nebraska Press.

Marshall, T. (1996) 'Marxist Feminism in Brazil', *Romance Notes* 36(3): 283–92.

ADRIANA AMANTE

Gálvez, Manuel

b. 1882, Paraná, Argentina; d. 1962, Buenos Aires, Argentina

Writer

Gálvez was a Catholic and nationalist writer who, despite his ideology, wrote some of the most ambiguous social novels of Argentina, even publishing one of them – *Nacha Regules* (1919) – in the socialist newspaper *La Vanguardia*. The intense ambiguity of his social novels has led critics to include him in the movement known as critical realism. Alongside Ricardo Olivera he founded the journal *Ideas*, which promoted the nationalist credo of the turn of the century. Many of his texts deal with the newly visible tango world. He fought with fervour for the institutional organization of **intellectuals**.

Further reading

Jiménez, L.A. (1990) *Literatura y sociedad en la narrativa de Manuel Gálvez*, Buenos Aires: Peña Lillo.

—— (1993) 'Bibliografía seleccionada y comentada sobre Manuel Gálvez (1882–1962)', *Revista interamericana de bibliografía* 43(4): 571–610.

Kisnerman, P. (1964) *Bibliografía de Manuel Gálvez*, Buenos Aires: Fondo Nacional de las Artes.

Lichtblau, M.I. (1989) 'Manuel Gálvez', in C.A. Solé and M.I. Abreu (eds), *Latin American Writers*, New York: Scribners, 2, 585–9.

Payá, C. and E. Cárdenas (1978) *El primer nacionalismo argentino: Manuel Gálvez y Ricardo Rojas*, Buenos Aires: Peña Lillo.

Walker, J. (1986) 'Manuel Gálvez y la soledad argentina', *Norte Sul* 9(22).

—— (1997) 'Manuel Gálvez', in V. Smith (ed.), *Encyclopedia of Latin American Literature*, London: Fitzroy Dearborn, 341–3.

FLORENCIA GARRAMUÑO

Gambaro, Griselda

b. 1928, Buenos Aires, Argentina

Playwright, novelist and short story writer

Perhaps the most important contemporary woman playwright in Latin America, Gambaro's plays are forceful investigations of the physical and psychological violence that have historically characterized Argentinian political and daily life. Her early plays such as *Los siameses* (Siamese Twins) (1967) and *El campo* (The Camp) (1968) have frequently been analysed in terms of Artaud's 'Theatre of Cruelty' or Martin Esslin's definition of the 'Theatre of the Absurd'. In its depiction of socially, psychologically and physically deformed characters, however, Gambaro's work is directly rooted in the Argentinian ***grotesco criollo*** pioneered by Armando **Discépolo** (1887–1971) and Defillipis Novoa (1889–1930). Intricately constructed, Gambaro's plays confront the myriad ways in which the forces of daily existence can serve to delimit and destroy our dreams and aspirations.

In 1977 during the 'Dirty War', Gambaro's novel *Ganarse la muerte* (To Win One's Death) was banned by then president Jorge Rafael Videla. Equivalent to a death threat, the extraordinary decree forced Gambaro to flee to Spain where she remained until 1980. Her plays from that period of exile, such as *Decir sí* (Say Yes), *La malasangre* (Bitter Blood) (1982) and *Antígona furiosa* (Furious Antigone) (1986), increasingly investigate the repercussions of complicity with repressive regimes and the terror they engender. The manner in which they do so is diverse. *La malasangre* draws upon the iconography of nineteenth-century dictator Juan Manuel de Rosas, and *Antígona furiosa* upon classical material to critique the military junta of the 1970s. Some of her plays, such as *Información para extranjeros* (Information for Foreigners) (1972), have yet to be performed in Argentina. Her plays of the 1990s, *Penas sin importancia* (Unimportant Sorrows) (1991), *Atando cabos* (Loose Ends) (1991), *La casa sin sosiego* (House without Calm) (1991) and *Es necesario entender un poco* (A Little Understanding is Crucial) (1994), take her work in new directions, reflecting the altered social and political context since the fall of the military junta.

Further reading

Boling, B. (1998) 'Reenacting Politics: The Theater of Griselda Gambaro', in Catherine Larson and Margarita Vargas (eds), *Latin American Women Dramatists: Theater, Texts, and Theories*, Bloomington: Indiana University Press.

Contreras, M. (1997) 'Diagnosis teatral: Una aproximación a la obra dramática de Griselda Gambaro', *Acta Literária* 22: 19–25.

Costa, E. de (1997) 'Griselda Gambaro', in V. Smith (ed.), *Encyclopedia of Latin American Literature*, London: Fitzroy Dearborn, 343–5.

Feitlowitz, M. (1990) 'Griselda Gambaro', *BOMB* 32: 53–6.

Gambaro, G. (1992) *Information for Foreigners: Three Plays by Griselda Gambaro*, trans. M. Feitlowitz, Evanston, IL: Northwestern University Press.

Jehenson, M.Y. (1999) 'Staging Cultural Violence: Griselda Gambaro and Argentina's "Dirty War"', *Mosaic* 32(1): 85–104.

Mazziotti, N. (ed.) (1989) *Poder, deseo y marginación: Aproximaciones a la obra de Griselda Gambaro*, Buenos Aires: Puntosur Editores.

Picon Garfield, E. (1989) 'Griselda Gambaro', in C.A. Solé and M.I. Abreu (eds), *Latin American Writers*, New York: Scribners, 3, 1323–8.

Taylor, D. (1991) *Theatre of Crisis: Drama and Politics in Latin America*, Lexington: University of Kentucky Press.

Trastoy, B. (2000) 'Madres, marginados y otras víctimas: El teatro de Griselda Gambaro en el ocaso del siglo', in Osvaldo Pellettieri (ed.), *Teatro argentino del 2000*, Buenos Aires: Galerna/Fundación Roberto Arlt.

ADAM VERSÉNYI

García Calderón, Ventura

b. 1887, Lima, Peru; d. 1959, Paris, France

Writer

Best known as a short story writer, García's first book of short stories, *Dolorosa y desnuda realidad* (Painful and Naked Reality) (1914), was shaped by *modernismo* (see **Spanish American modernism**). His greatest success was a short story collection of neo-realist inspiration, *La venganza del cóndor* (The Condor's Revenge) (1924), which directly addressed the status of Peruvian Indians during the Republican era. He wrote literary criticism and also published *Cuentos peruanos* (Peruvian Short Stories) (1952) and several volumes in French, including *Danger de mort* (Danger of Death) (1926) and *Couleur du sang* (Colour of Blood) (1931).

Further reading

Aviles Ramirez, E. (1974) 'Le souvenir de Ventura García Calderón', *Nouvelle revue des deux mondes* 122–6.

Delgado, L.H. (1947) *Ventura García Calderón*, Lima: Latino América Editores.

García Calderón, Ventura (1924) *La venganza del cóndor*, Madrid: Mundo latino.

—— (1938) *The White Llama*, London: The Golden Cockerel Press.

—— (1989) *Obra literaria selecta*, Caracas: Biblioteca Ayacucho.
March, K.N. (1997) 'Ventura García Calderón', in V. Smith (ed.), *Encyclopedia of Latin American Literature*, London: Fitzroy Dearborn, 346–7.

JOSÉ ANTONIO MAZZOTTI

García Márquez, Gabriel

b. 1927, Aracataca, Colombia

Novelist

Gabriel García Márquez was born in 1927 (not 1928, as is usually believed) in a small town in northern Colombia surrounded by US-owned banana plantations. From this humble and conflictive background he rose in due course to become the most admired and widely read novelist of Latin America, and perhaps the most universally celebrated literary figure from the Hispanic world since Cervantes.

Immediately after his birth, the young García Márquez was placed with his grandparents and brought up by them until the age of nine. He lived in a household full of women, with the exception of his grandfather, who had been a colonel in the army of the Liberal Party during Colombia's catastrophic War of the Thousand Days (1898–1901). This historical background, together with a notorious massacre of fruit company workers by the Colombian army near Aracataca in 1928, inspired much of what García Márquez would come to write in later decades; all of it framed by the experience of life in a household criss-crossed by the conflicting narratives of history, folklore and superstition.

After the death of his grandfather in 1937 ('nothing of importance ever happened to me after his death'), the young García Márquez was sent away to school in Barranquilla and then to Zipaquirá, near the capital Bogotá. Here he first became aware of the vast cultural difference between the tropical Caribbean coastlands where he was born and the stiff, chilly culture of the Andean regions from where the country was governed. By 1948 he was an unenthusiastic law student in Bogotá – one who had already published a couple of well-reviewed stories – when the 'Bogotazo' took place: Jorge Eliecer Gaitán was murdered and his enraged supporters set fire to the centre of the city, setting off La Violencia. García Márquez abandoned his studies, fled to Cartagena and became a journalist. By 1955 he had worked not only in Cartagena but also in Barranquilla – as a member of the so-called **Grupo de Barranquilla** of artists and intellectuals – and in Bogotá, had written literally hundreds of essays and articles, and had become one of his country's most admired newspapermen. He had also published his first novel, *La hojarasca* (Leafstorm) (1955), based on childhood memories of Aracataca filtered through the influence of William Faulkner. His home town had lost its name, however, and taken on a name that would resonate through world literature: Macondo.

García Márquez travelled to Europe in 1955 to study cinema – a lifelong obsession – in Italy and then moved to Paris, where he wrote one of the most perfect short novels by a Latin American, *El coronel no tiene quien le escriba* (No One Writes to the Colonel), not published until 1961. From Paris he moved to Venezuela in 1958, the year he married his childhood sweetheart, and from there to New York where he worked as a press officer for the new Cuban Revolution. In 1961 he took up residence in Mexico and worked in advertising and film, scripting, among others, *Tiempo de morir* (Time to Die) (1965) and Arturo Ripstein's *Opera prima*, and appearing in Alberto Isaac's *En este pueblo no hay ladrones* (In This Town There Are No Thieves) (1964). Finally, in 1965, he began work on the novel that would make him both famous and rich, ***Cien años de soledad*** (One Hundred Years of Solitude). When published in Buenos Aires in 1967, this unique novel caused a sensation which gave García Márquez the kind of fame and glamour only usually associated with matinee idols, sporting heroes or bullfighters. He became known by his nickname, Gabo, moved to Barcelona and settled down, despite the uproar, to write again. The result, in 1975, was *El otoño del patriarca* (The Autumn of the Patriarch), a quite different kind of novel but another startling success. It told the tale of the rise and fall of a brutal Caribbean dictator and staged two of the writer's fundamental obsessions: love and power. That same year he published his first book of collected stories, featuring particularly the ones from his best collection, *Funerales de la Mamá Grande* (Big Mother's Funeral), which had appeared without much fanfare in 1962.

In the later 1970s García Márquez took up residence in Mexico again, and devoted himself to political writing. By now he was the best-known Latin American celebrity supporting the Cuban Revolution, and he became a personal friend of Fidel Castro. In 1981 he eventually published another short novel, *Crónica de una muerte anunciada* (Chronicle of a Death Foretold), and in 1982 became one of the most popularly acclaimed winners of the Nobel Prize, thus emulating two of his most admired models, Faulkner and Hemingway.

Nothing, however, could dent García Márquez's extraordinary concentration: 1986 saw the appearance of *El amor en los tiempos del cólera* (Love in the Time of Cholera), one of the most popular of all his books, and in 1989 he published *El general en su laberinto* (The General in his Labyrinth), his astonishingly audacious interpretation of the last months in the life of the great Simón Bolívar. In recent years his creativity has been undimmed: *Del amor y otros demonios* (Of Love and Other Demons) appeared in 1994, the scintillating *Noticia de un secuestro* (Report of a Kidnapping) in 1996, a documentary narrative surveying Colombia's horrific contemporary situation. In 2002 he published *Vivir para contarla* (Living to Tell the Tale), the first volume of a planned three-volume autobiography.

No Latin American writer in the twentieth century has ever combined critical and popular success in the way that García Márquez has succeeded in doing. The unique status of *Cien años de soledad* has tended to associate him with the 'magical realist' label (see **magical realism**), but his work is in fact marked by an extraordinary commitment to the everyday lives and beliefs of quite ordinary Colombians. Similarly, those who expect that a writer who is a socialist will write tub-thumping novels are invariably surprised by these wise, humorous but somewhat pessimistic, albeit life-enhancing, narratives. The explanation lies partly in the history of Colombia, partly in his memories of his grandfather, and partly in a still-more ancient influence: that of Sophocles, who gives a hint perhaps that García Márquez, despite his celebrity status, was always searching for a more timeless, classical profile.

Further reading

Bell-Villada, G. (1990) *García Márquez: The Man and his Work*, Chapel Hill: University of North Carolina Press.

McGuirk, B. and R. Cardwell (1987) *Gabriel García Márquez: New Readings*, Cambridge: Cambridge University Press.

McMurray, G. (ed.) (1987) *Critical Essays on Gabriel García Márquez*, Boston: G.K. Hall.

—— (1989) 'Gabriel García Márquez', in C.A. Solé and M.I. Abreu (eds), *Latin American Writers*, New York: Scribners, 3, 1329–45.

McNerney, K. (1989) *Understanding Gabriel García Márquez*, Columbia: University of South Carolina Press.

Martínez, P.S. (ed.) (1969) *Recopilación de textos sobre García Márquez*, Havana: Casa de las Américas.

Minta, S. (1987) *García Márquez: Writer of Colombia*, New York: Harper & Row.

Palencia-Roth, M. (2002) 'Gabriel García Márquez', in C. Solé and K. Müller-Bergh (eds), *Latin American Writers: Supplement I*, New York: Scribners, 249–68.

Vargas Llosa, M. (1971) *Gabriel García Márquez: Historia de un deicidio*, Barcelona: Barral.

GERALD MARTIN

García Marruz, Fina

b. 1923, Havana, Cuba

Poet and literary critic

An early member of the literary group **Orígenes**, together with her husband, the poet and critic Cintio **Vitier**, García has not received much critical attention, due perhaps to her diffidence and the overshadowing presence of other Orígenes poets. Her poetry is nevertheless first-rate, combining attention to worldly detail with metaphysical (at times religious) investigation. After the Revolution, she combined Christian and socialist values in her poetry and solid and perceptive critical essays. She is especially noted for her research into the works of

José **Martí**, much of it undertaken in collaboration with Vitier.

Further reading

Arcos, J.L. (ed.) (1990) *En torno a la obra poética de Fina García Marruz*, Havana: UNEAC.

Davies, C. (1997) 'Fina García Marruz', in V. Smith (ed.), *Encyclopedia of Latin American Literature*, London: Fitzroy Dearborn, 355–7.

García Marruz, F. (1984) *Poesías escogidas*, ed. J. Yglesias, Havana: Editorial Letras Cubanas.

Hernández, W. (1997) 'Entre Orígenes y la revolución: Introducción a la poesía de Fina García Marruz', *Monographic Review* 13: 340–54.

Ramírez, A. (1992) 'Textualidades en la obra poética de Fina García Marruz', *Linguística y literatura* 13(21): 95–104.

BEN A. HELLER

García Monge, Joaquín

b. 1881, Desamparados, Costa Rica; d. 1958, San José, Costa Rica

Writer

García was editor throughout most of his life (1919–58) of the important cultural review ***Repertorio americano***. He published his first novel, *El moto*, in 1900; others followed in the 1910s and 1920s. Part of the anti-imperialist intelligentsia, in 1913 he founded a cultural centre with the *arielist* (see ***Ariel* and *arielismo***) idea of educating workers. After retiring from his post as director of the National Library in 1936 for political reasons, he devoted himself to his editing work.

Further reading

Bonilla, A. (1965) 'La obra literária y de acercamiento cultural de don Joaquín García Monge', *Revista interamericana de bibliografía* 15: 3–16.

García Monge, J. (1959) *Tres novelas: El moto*, San Salvador: Ministerio de Cultura, Departamento Editorial.

—— (1974) *Obras escogidas*, San José: EDUCA.

—— (1983) *Cartas selectas de Joaquín García Monge*, San José: Editorial Costa Rica.

Henkin, A.B. (1968) 'A Critical Study of the Life and Works of Joaquín García Monge', *Dissertation Abstracts* 29: 602A.

Mora Rodríguez, A. (1989) *El ideario de Joaquín García Monge*, San José: Editorial Costa Rica.

JUSSI PAKKASVIRTA

García Ponce, Juan

b. 1932, Mérida, Mexico

Writer

García Ponce's work incorporates various genres, including the novel, short story and theatre. He is also a prolific art and literary critic. He has made an enormous contribution to Mexican literary culture through his teaching in the Universidad Nacional Autónoma de México (UNAM) and his editorial involvement with numerous literary magazines, including ***Revista mexicana de literatura***. Ponce's fiction is primarily concerned with the evocation of the female, and his 1963 collection of short stories, *La noche* (Night), is a haunting exploration of the destructive nature of relationships. His work has received many prestigious prizes, including the Premio Nacional de Literatura in 1990.

Further reading

García Ponce, J. (1993) *La noche*, Mexico City: Ediciones Era.

—— (1994) *The House on the Beach*, trans. Margarita Vargas and Juan Bruce-Novoa, Austin: University of Texas Press.

—— (1997) *Cuentos completos*, Barcelona: Seix Barral.

Letona Ibarra, F. (2000) 'La concepción literária de Juan García Ponce', in Rosaura Hernández Monroy and Manuel F. Medina (eds), *Pensamiento y crítica: Los discursos de la cultura hoy*, East Lansing: Michigan State University, University of Louisville, Centro de Cultura Casa Lamm.

Martínez Morales, J.L. (ed.) (1998) *Juan García Ponce*

y la generación del medio siglo, Veracruz, Mexico: Universidad Veracruzana.
Peña, L.H. (1997) 'Juan García Ponce', in V. Smith (ed.), *Encyclopedia of Latin American Literature*, London: Fitzroy Dearborn, 357–8.

NUALA FINNEGAN

García Romero, Rafael

b. 1957, Santo Domingo, Dominican Republic

Writer

Like many others from the Generation of the 1980s, García Romero was a member of the César Vallejo Literary Workshop. He started publishing poetry in the Literary Section of the *La Noticia* newspaper. In 1991 he won Third Prize in the Casa de Teatro Literary Contest for the short story 'Y así llegaste tú, Aurora' (And You Arrived Like That, Aurora), written in collaboration with René Rodríguez Soriano and Ramón **Tejada Holguín**. Besides his 1983 volume of short stories *Fisión* (Fission), this prolific writer has published three other books.

Further reading

García Romero, R. (1983) *Fisión*, Santo Domingo: Impresos Urgentes.
—— (1986) *El agonista*, Santo Domingo: Ediciones de la Biblioteca Nacional.
—— (1995) *Historias de cada día*, Santo Domingo: Ediciones Cedibil.
—— (1999) *Obras narrativas juntas*, Santo Domingo: Consejo Presidencial de Cultura Colección Fin de Siglo.

FERNANDO VALERIO-HOLGUÍN

GARCÍA SARMIENTO, FÉLIX RUBÉN *see* Darío, Rubén

Gardea, Jesús

b. 1939, Ciudad Delicias, Mexico

Writer

A prolific novelist and short story writer, Gardea is self-taught and one of the very few Mexican writers whose literary world is outside the urban environment. He withdrew from his dentistry practice in 1983 in order to pursue his true vocation, having won the 1980 Xavier Villaurrutia Award for his short story collection *Septiembre y los otros días* (September and Other Days). Two recurrent themes in Gardea's prose are death and solitude, and they often occur in the imaginary and ironically named town of Placeres (Pleasures), where an atmosphere of **existentialism** prevails.

Further reading

García García, J.M. (1987) 'La geografía textual de "Placeres" ', *Plural* 17(1 (193)): 55–6.
Gardea, J. (1980) *Septiembre y los otros días*, Mexico City: Premio Villarrutia.
—— (1998) *Juegan los comensales*, Mexico City: Editorial Aldus.
—— (1998) *Stripping Away the Sorrows from This World*, trans. Mark Schafer, Mexico City: Editorial Aldus.
Valenzuela, J.P. (1990) 'La muerte y la soledad en los cuentos de Jesús Gardea', *Dissertation Abstracts International* 50(8): 2509A.

EDUARDO SANTA CRUZ

Garmendia, Julio

b. 1898, El Tocuyo, Venezuela; d. 1977, Caracas, Venezuela

Writer, journalist and diplomat

One of the most valued short story writers of Venezuelan literature, Garmendia is considered the first avant-garde creator of his generation. His entire body of work is brief and full of irony, a lucid attempt to release Venezuelan literature from the realism within which it had been trapped. Closely related to the so-called Generation of 1928, he served as a diplomat, assigned to the Venezuelan Embassy in Paris, and later to the Consulates in Genoa, Copenhagen and Norway. His famous story 'La tienda de muñecos' (The Puppet Shop) was published in 1923. He was awarded the Municipal Prize for Prose for his story 'La tuna de oro' (The Golden Tuna) in 1951, and in 1972 he was honoured with the National Prize for Literature. In 1979, posthumously, *La hoja que no había caído en su otoño* (The Leaf That Did Not Fall in Autumm) was published along with some other previously unpublished stories.

Further reading

Garmendia, J. *et al.* (1968) *Aquí Venezuela cuenta*, Montevideo: Arca.

Garmendia, Julia (1980) *Ante la crítica*, Caracas: Monte Avila.

Sambrano Urdaneta, O. (1999) *Del ser y del quehacer de Julio Garmendia*, Caracas: Monte Avila.

Tedesco, I. (1982) *Julio Garmendia y José Rafael Pocaterra: Dos modalidades del cuento en Venezuela*, Caracas: Academia Nacional de la Historia.

VÍCTOR GALARRAGA OROPEZA

Garmendia, Salvador

b. 1928, Barquisimeto, Venezuela; d. 2001, Caracas, Venezuela

Short story writer, novelist and scriptwriter

Co-founder in the 1950s of the literary group and journal *Sardío*, Garmendia then split from it to form, with others, the **Techo de la Ballena** group. He won the National Prize for Literature in 1973. From *Los pequeños seres* (Little People) (1959) onwards, Garmendia cast his sharp, existential and hyper-realist eye on the city of Caracas and its inhabitants. He was also the writer of one of Venezuela's best soap operas (*culebrón*), *La hija de Juana Crespo* (Juana Crespo's Daughter), as well as adaptating two novels by Rómulo **Gallegos**, ***Doña Bárbara*** and *Pobre negro* (Poor Black).

Further reading

Brushwood, J.S. (1977) 'Cinco novelas de Salvador Garmendia: El impacto sobre los hábitos perceptivos', *Hispania* 60: 884–9.

Garmendia, S. (1993) 'Por qué escribo', *Inti: Revista de literatura hispánica* 37–8: 263–72.

—— (1998) 'Arte y oficio de contar', *Encuentro Internacional Narradores de Esta América*, ed. Jorge Cornejo Polar, Lima: Universidad de Lima.

JORGE ROMERO LEÓN

Garro, Elena

b. 1920, Puebla, Mexico; d. 1998, Cuernavaca, Mexico

Writer

By the early 1960s, on the basis of two plays, a novel and a short story collection, Elena Garro had established herself as one of the leading Mexican women writers of the twentieth century. After studying humanities briefly at UNAM in 1936, Elena Garro studied dance and worked as an actress and choreographer at the Teatro de la Universidad, under the direction of Julio Bracho. In 1937 she married the poet Octavio **Paz** and together they worked with the International Brigades in the Spanish Civil War. Garro began writing journalism and theatre upon their return to Mexico in 1938 and during their sojourns in New York and Paris. She wrote her classic short story collection, *La semana de colores* (The Week in Colours) (1960), and her most famous novel, *Los recuerdos del porvenir* (Recollection of Things To Come) (1963), while she was hospitalized in a sanatorium in Berne, southern France. The novel went on to win the Xavier Villaurrutia Prize, and was adapted for the screen by Arturo Ripstein. A saga of the Cristero Wars told by an entire community, the novel's stories revolve around the loves of the Cristero generals and their mistresses. The novel has recently been the subject of criticism by Jean Franco and Debra Castillo.

La semana de colores was an equally original book of short stories, which included the masterpiece 'La culpa es de los tlaxcaltecas' (It's the Fault of the Tlaxcaltecas). Here Garro again explores female subjectivity, as a neglected bourgeois wife, *c.*1960, finds happiness by running off with an Aztec warrior, with the complicity of her maid. As this plot suggests, Garro was among the first Mexican authors to make extensive use of **magical realism**, through the fantasy life of imaginative little girls, alienated housewives and resourceful prostitutes and *campesinos* – all marginal characters.

During her years in Paris, Garro had a month-long affair with the Argentine writer Adolfo **Bioy Casares**, followed by an intimate correspondence that lasted two decades. Shortly after Paz and Garro returned to Mexico City in 1948, their daughter Helene was born; the two would be inseparable for five decades. Between 1951 and 1958 the family lived in Japan, and in New York from 1959 to 1963. Back in Mexico again, Garro wrote the play, *Felipe Angeles* (1979), on the life of the revolutionary general, as well as several film scripts and the trilogy, *Un hogar sólido* (A Solid Home) (1958). These works earned her a reputation as a major playwright, as well as a writer of fiction.

Ever the strong-willed individualist, Elena Garro made herself *persona non grata* in Mexican intellectual circles beginning in 1968, when she and her daughter Helene, taken to a student meeting by Carlos **Monsiváis**, publicly accused leaders of the movement of collusion with the government. Subsequently she was accused of naming names to government officials (a charge that she steadfastly denied). When they began receiving anonymous death threats, she and her daughter went into self-imposed exile, first in New York, then, from 1974 to 1984, in Madrid and Paris. During this period Garro published her memoirs of the Spanish Civil War, *Memorias de España*, and the novel, *Andamos huyendo Lola* (Let's Make a Run for It, Lola) (1980), revolving around the themes of persecution and the mother–daughter bond.

Garro finally returned to Mexico twenty years later, and in 1994 she settled, with her daughter and five cats, in a cramped apartment in Cuernavaca. She died of a heart attack, brought on by emphysema, four years later, in poverty and relative obscurity.

During the final years of her life Garro published a series of minor novels written during the 1960s: *Un corazon en un bote de basura* (A Heart in a Garbage Can) (1996), *Un traje rojo para un duelo* (A Red Dress for a Duel) (1996) and others. The year 1999 saw the appearance of the posthumous novel, *Mi hermanita Magdalena* (My Little Sister Magdalena) (1999); still other unpublished manuscripts may well follow.

Scandal has always trailed Garro, from her denunciation of the student leaders in 1968, to her daughter's current conflict with University of New Mexico professor Patricia Rosas over intellectual property rights to Garro's unpublished manuscripts and personal photograph collection. As Carlos Monsiváis wrote shortly after her death, Garro was controversial and contradictory – and a great writer.

Further reading

Balderston, D. (1989) 'The New Historical Novel: History and Fantasy in *Los recuerdos del porvenir*', *Bulletin of Hispanic Studies* 66(1): 41–6.

Bradu, F. (1987) *Señas particulares, escritora: Ensayos sobre escritoras Mexicanas del siglo XX*, Mexico City: Fondo de Cultura Economica.

Franco, J. (1989) *Plotting Women. Gender and Representation in Mexico*, New York: Columbia University Press.

Garro, E. (1979) *Recollections of Things to Come*, trans. Ruth L.C. Simms, Austin: University of Texas Press.

—— (1997) *First Love and Look for My Obituary: Two Novellas*, trans. David Unger, Willamantic, CT: Curbstone Press.

Méndez Rodenas, A. (2002) 'Elena Garro', in C. Solé and K. Müller-Bergh (eds), *Latin American Writers: Supplement I*, New York: Scribners, 269–88.

Rubio, P. (1997) 'Elena Garro', in V. Smith (ed.), *Encyclopedia of Latin American Literature*, London: Fitzroy Dearborn, 362–3.

Stoll, A.K. (ed.) (1990) *A Different Reality: Studies on the Work of Elena Garro*, Lewisburg, PA: Bucknell University Press.

Winkler, J. (2000) *Light into Shadow: Marginality and Alienation in the Work of Elena Garro*, New York: Peter Lang.

CYNTHIA STEELE

gay male literature

The 1990s witnessed a concerted effort, primarily by Euro-American scholars, to track a gay male literary heritage. The differences in sexual systems within and among Latin American countries make the application of Euro-American gay identity politics problematic and uneven because the social construction of male homosexuality in Latin America differs from its US and European counterparts. Few Latin American countries can claim a gay liberation movement like the US model. In Mexico, for example, men who exclusively play the role of penetrator with other men do not necessarily lose their heterosexual identity. Luis **Zapata**, Mexico's most prominent gay novelist, refuses the ghettoized classification of his novels as gay literature.

Despite these differences and tensions, the category of gay male literature in Latin America exists, on a minor scale, as a marketing category and as an object of inquuiry. The pioneer text addressing male homosexual practices is Adolfo Caminha's Brazilian naturalist novel *Bom-Crioulo* (Bom-Crioulo: The Black Man and the Cabin Boy) (1895), where male–male sexuality is racialized as a psycho-sexual aberration since the emancipated seaman slave is the tragic victim of his uncontrollable desires for the nubile blonde cabin boy. Other early texts belonging to the tragic homosexual genre include the Chilean Augusto **D'Halmar**'s *La pasión y muerte del cura Deusto* (The Passion and Death of Father Deusto) (1924) and Mexico's *El diario de José Toledo* (The Diary of José Toledo) (1964) by Manuel Barbachano Ponce. Both conclude with the lead character's suicide, the first due to the priest's unreconcilable and unarticulated erotic attachment to his younger protégé, while in the latter, unrequited love leads to the tragic denouement. In José **Donoso**'s ***El lugar sin límites*** (Hell Has No Limits) (1966), socio-economic power relations are played out through gender and sexual roles, where the transvestite brothel owner La Manuela and her sadistic, hyper-masculine suitor Pancho are in varying degrees both victims of compulsory heterosexuality. Authoritarian dictorships give rise to texts which link political repression to questions of sexual choice and liberation, as are the cases with Cuba's Senel **Paz**'s *El lobo, el bosque y el hombre nuevo* (The Wolf, the Forest, and the New Man) (1991), adapted for the screen as *Fresa y chocolate* (Strawberry and Chocolate) (1993), and Manuel **Puig**'s *El* ***beso de la mujer araña*** (Kiss of the Spider Woman) (1976). Politically less repressive than the aforementioned national contexts, Luis Zapata's *Las aventuras, desventuras y sueños de Adonis García, el vampiro de la colonia Roma* (The Adventures, Misadventures and Dreams of Adonis Garcia: Vampire of the Roma District) (1979) celebrates male homosexual urban subcultures through the figure of a Mexico City hustler.

Further reading

Balderston, D. (1999) *El deseo, enorme cicatriz luminosa*, Caracas: excultura.

Bergman, E. and P.J. Smith (eds) (1995) *¿Entiendes? Queer Readings, Hispanic Writings*, Durham, NC: Duke University Press.

Foster, D.W. (1991) *Gay and Lesbian Themes in Latin American Writing*, Austin: University of Texas Press.

—— (ed.) (1994) *Latin American Writers on Gay and Lesbian Themes: A Bio-Critical Sourcebook*, Westport, CT: Greenwood Press.

Molloy, S. and R.M. Irwin (1998) *Hispanisms and Homosexualities*, Durham, NC: Duke University Press.

SERGIO DE LA MORA

Gayoso, Milia

b. 1962, Villa Hayes, Paraguay

Writer

A regular contributor to newspapers such as *El Día*, Gayoso's first published journalism appeared in the university journal *Turú*. She has published four short story collections: *Ronda en las olas* (Serenade in the Waves) (1990), *Un sueño en la ventana* (A Dream in the Window) (1991), *El peldaño gris* (The Grey Stair) (1993) and *Cuentos para tres mariposas* (Stories for Three Butterflies) (1996).

TERESA MÉNDEZ-FAITH

Gelman, Juan

b. 1930, Buenos Aires, Argentina

Poet

Gelman's poetry has a quality of exalted speech, touching directly on events of this world, public and private, yet speaking of them with passion and (sometimes) rage. In eloquent poems such as 'Bellezas' (Beauties) and 'Arte poética' (The Art of Poetry) (1973), he attacks the static ideas of poetry that he associates with the work of Octavio **Paz**, José **Lezama Lima** and Alberto **Girri**. For Gelman, poetry is 'como un martillo la realidad/ bate/ las telitas del alma o corazon' (like a hammer reality/ beats/ on the tissues of the soul or the heart.) His work includes ardent poems on the Cuban Revolution, beautiful lyrics of love, translations from imaginary English and Japanese works, lyrics in Ladino (the language of Sephardic Jewry after the expulsion from Spain in 1492) and a moving letter to his late mother. A central figure in the Montoneros, Gelman was exiled to Italy and then to Mexico, where he still resides, after members of his family were killed by the military. In 1988, in a book-length series of interviews with Roberto Mero, he was frank in his self-critique and in a review of the errors of the Argentine Left of the 1970s. The Ladino poems of *Dibaxu* (Below) (1985) are very popular, and have been set to music. An extraordinary poet and a complex man, Gelman (who won the Juan Rulfo prize in 2000) is revered and widely read in a country where he has chosen not to live.

Further reading

Canaparo, C. (1997) 'Juan Gelman', in V. Smith (ed.), *Encyclopedia of Latin American Literature*, London: Fitzroy Dearborn, 363–6.

Dimo, E. (1993) 'Una voz nacida del silencio: Conversación con Juan Gelman', *Chasqui* 22(2): 109–13.

Gelman, J. (1994) *Dibaxu*, Barcelona: Editorial Seix Barral.

—— (1997) *Incompletamente*, Barcelona: Editorial Seix Barral.

—— (1997) *Unthinkable Tenderness: Selected Poems*, trans. Joan Lindgren, Berkeley: University of California Press.

Gomes, M. (1997) 'Juan Gelman en la historia de la poesía hispanoamericana reciente: Neorroamticismo y neoexpresionismo', *Revista iberoamericana* 63(181): 649–64.

DANIEL BALDERSTON

Gerbasi, Vicente

b. 1913, Canoabo, Venezuela; d. 1992, Caracas, Venezuela

Poet

In Gerbasi's exceptional poetry, the magnificent flora and fauna of his home region in northern Venezuela merge with the twilight world of the poetry of Novalis and others. His work is at once sensual and meditative, portraying through word and rhythm a real or imaginary landscape reconstructed from memory and dream. His 1945 volume *Mi padre el inmigrante* (My Father the Immigrant) was the first in a series of fine works, including *Los espacios cálidos* (Warm Spaces) (1952), *Edades perdidas* (Lost Ages) (1981) and *Iniciación en la intemperie* (Initiation in the Storm) (1990).

Further reading

Charry Lara, F. (1992) 'La poesía de Vicente Gerbasi', *Revista Casa Silva* 5: 63–70.

Gerbasi, V. (1970) *Antología poética*, Caracas: Monte Avila.

Gúzman, P. (1994) 'Vicente Gerbasi, moderno: Nuestro único padre es el morir', *Revista iberoamericana* 60(166–7): 47–59.

'Homenaje a Vicente Gerbasi' (1984) *Poesía*, special issue dedicated to Vicente Gerbasi, 11(3–4 (62–3)).

Iribarren Borges, I. (1972) *La poesía de Vicente Gerbasi*, Caracas: Tiempo Nuevo.

RAFAEL CASTILLO ZAPATA

Gerchunoff, Alberto

b. 1883, Proscuroff, Ukraine; d. 1949, Buenos Aires, Argentina

Fiction writer, essayist, poet and journalist

Born in a *shtetl* (small town with mainly Jewish population) in the Ukraine, Gerchunoff emigrated in 1890 with his family to Argentina, settling first in the Jewish colony of Moisés Ville, Santa Fe, and later in Rajil, Entre Ríos. The memory of his early rural experiences formed the basis of his most famous work, *Los gauchos judíos* (The Jewish Gauchos), published in 1910 in commemoration of the Centenary of Independence. This series of stories offers an elegiac vision of life on the *pampas*, showing immigrants and *criollos* in harmonious co-existence in spite of the occasional hint of under-lying prejudices. Gerchunoff's wide range of interests is reflected in his novels and approximately two thousand essays dealing with such topics as love, nationality, politics, literature and Judaism. His fictional writings include evocative studies of Heine and Spinoza. His admiration for Cervantes led to the publication of *Nuestro señor Don Quijote* (Our Lord Don Quixote) (1913), *La jofaina maravillosa* (The Enchanted Pitcher) (1922) and the posthumous *Retorno a Don Quijote* (Return to Don Quixote, prologue by **Borges**) (1951). There is also an autobiographical account in *Entre Ríos, mi país* (Entre Rios, My Country) (1950) and *El hombre importante* (The Important Man) (1934) offers a humorously critical portrayal of the nascent democratic politics of his day.

Gerchunoff became one of Argentina's leading cultural figures, making accessible through his essays and lectures some of Europe's most important writers as well as the poetry of **Darío** and other modernist (see **Spanish American modernism**) poets. He was remembered, by Borges among others, for his elegant turn of phrase both as conversationalist and as a prose writer. Gerchunoff combined his literary activities with being a prolific journalist: he wrote for a variety of newspapers but is identified mainly with *La Nación*, for which he was an easily recognizable leader writer, and where he wrote justly famous obituaries over a period of forty years. Gerchunoff exemplifies the immigrant who became totally assimilated into and accepted by his adoptive country while maintaining a faithful interest in his own cultural past.

See also: Jewish writing

Further reading

Aizenberg, E. (2002) *Books and Bombs in Buenos Aires: Borges, Gerchunoff and Argentine Jewish Writing*, Hanover: University Press of New England.

Gover de Nasatsky, M.E. (1976) *Bibliografía de Alberto Gerchunoff*, Buenos Aires: Fondo Nacional de las Artes.

Jaroslavsky de Lowy, S. (1957) *Alberto Gerchunoff: Vida y obra – Bibliografía – Antología*, New York: Hispanic Institute.

EVELYN FISHBURN

Gesta Bárbara

Gesta Bárbara was a journal which provided a platform for two generations of Bolivian writers. Founded in 1918, its first ten issues were published in Potosí. Twenty years later, in 1948, the second series began publication, although it only ran to four issues. Both series published poetry of group members as well as essays and articles by contemporary writers, among them Carlos Medinaceli, Gamaliel **Churata** and Armando Alba, who could be described as the founders of Bolivian literary criticism.

J.M. DE LA VEGA RODRÍGUEZ

Giardinelli, Mempo (Oscar)

b. 1947, Resistencia, Chaco, Argentina

Writer

A journalist and commentator, Giardinelli's first creative writings were poetry and short stories, but he is best known as a novelist. He was awarded the Rómulo Gallegos literary prize in 1993 for his novel *Santo oficio de la memoria* (The Holy Office of Memory), and the Mexican National Award in 1983 for *Luna caliente*, published in English as *Sultry Moon* (1998). He founded the short-story magazine,

Puro cuento, in 1986 and was its editor until it closed in 1992. In 1976, Giardinelli went into exile in Mexico after his novel, *Toño tuerto rey de ciegos* (One-Eyed Tony, King of the Blind), was pulped by the publishing house for political reasons. He returned in 1990 to live in his home town of Resistencia. He has published articles, essays and stories in newspapers and magazines throughout the world, and his works have been translated into a dozen languages.

Further reading

Giardinelli, M. (1983) *Luna caliente*, Buenos Aires: Prometeo Libros.
—— (1991) *Santo oficio de la memoria*, Calí, Colombia: Norma.
—— (2000) *The Tenth Circle*, trans. Andrea G. Labinger, Pittsburgh: Latin American Literary Review Press.
Marcos, J.M. (1983) 'La narrativa de Mempo Giardinelli', *Escritura* 8(16): 217–22.
Ruffinelli, J. (1997) 'Mempo Giardinelli', in V. Smith (ed.), *Encyclopedia of Latin American Literature*, London: Fitzroy Dearborn, 367–8.
Torres, V.F. (1987) 'El trabajo literário de Mempo Giardinelli', *La palabra y el hombre* 61: 89–94.

ANDREW GRAHAM-YOOLL

Gil Gilbert, Enrique

b. 1912, Guayaquil, Ecuador; d. 1973, Guayaquil

Writer

A member of the **Guayaquil Group** and co-author of ***Los que se van***, *cuentos del cholo y el montuvio* (The Vanishing Ones. Stories about the Cholo and the Montuvio) (1930), Gil Gilbert saw literature as a vehicle for social protest, but this does not detract from his considerable lyrical powers. *Nuestro pan* (Our Daily Bread) (1943), his most famous novel, was first runner up to the Farrar & Reinhart prize won in 1940 by Ciro **Alegría**'s *El mundo es ancho y ajeno* (Broad and Alien is the World). Other works include *Yunga* (Jungle) (1933) and *Relatos de Emmanuel* (Emmanuel's stories) (1939).

Further reading

Gil Gilbert, E. (1942) *Nuestro pan*, Guayaquil: Libería Vera.
—— (1943) *Our Daily Bread*, trans. Dudley Poore, New York: Farrar & Rinehart.
Pérez, G.R. (1970) 'Tres narradores de la Costa del Ecuador', *Revista interamericana de bibliografía* 20: 169–90.

HUMBERTO E. ROBLES

Gilkes, Michael

b. 1933, Georgetown, British Guiana

Playwright

Gilkes's plays typically combine realism and surrealism, dance and music, to explore the multiracial identity of the Guyanese peoples. *Couvade* is based on an Amerindian ritual associated with birth, and was chosen to represent Guyana at the first CARIFESTA of 1972. He is also an actor and producer. As an academic, Gilkes has lectured in Britain, the USA, Guyana and in Barbados, his adopted home. He is a leading interpreter of Guyanese writers Wilson **Harris** and Edgar **Mittelholzer**.

Further reading

Gilkes, M. (1974) *Couvade*, Trinidad and Jamaica: Longman Caribbean.
—— (1975) *Wilson Harris and the Caribbean Novel*, Trinidad and Jamaica: Longman Caribbean.
—— (1981) *The West Indian Novel*, Boston: Twayne.
—— (2002) *Jonestown: And Other Poems*, Leeds, UK: Peepal Tree Press.

LOUIS JAMES

Gilroy, Beryl

b. 1924, Berbice, British Guiana

Writer, educator and clinical psychologist

Gilroy went to England in 1951 and became the first black headmistress in her North London borough. Taking a PhD in psychology, she opened a private counselling clinic in London for black women. Her multifaceted experience underlies her writing, including the autobiographical *Black Teacher* (1976), poetry and short stories, and fiction, of which *Frangipani House* (1986) won a GLC prize for Black Literature. *Stedman and Joanna – A Love in Bondage* (1991) and *Inkle and Yarico* (1996) are historical fiction.

Further reading

Dance, D.C. (1998) 'Beryl Gilroy: A Bio-Literary Overview', *MaComere* 1: 1–3.

Gilroy, B. (1976) *Black Teacher*, New York: Cassell.

—— (1986) *Frangipani House*, Portsmouth, NH: Heinemann.

—— (2002) *The Green Grass Tango*, Leeds, UK: Peepal Tree Press.

Poynting, J. (1998) 'A Writer at the Height of Her Powers: Three Recent Novels by Beryl Gilroy', *MaComere* 1: 4–7.

LOUIS JAMES

Girondo, Oliverio

b. 1891, Buenos Aires, Argentina;
d. 1967, Buenos Aires

Poet

Girondo was the most daring and experimental poet of his generation. A typical 1920s cosmopolitan dandy, his commitment to the artistic avant-garde (see **avant-garde in Latin America**) was expressed through the journal ***Martín Fierro***, which he co-edited. In its fourth issue, his 'Martín Fierro Manifesto' (see **manifestos**) defined the contours of this most representative avant-garde journal, and Girondo himself became its central figure. His first two volumes, *Veinte poemas para ser leídos en el tranvía* (Twenty Poems to Read on the Tram) (1922) and *Calcomanías* (Transfers) (1925), reveal the cosmopolitan gaze of the poet moving through the shifting space and time of a traveller's guide. The first book moves between the cities of Europe and America; the second is devoted to Spain, but in both the poetry portrays an alienated, fragmented and grotesque society. Girondo's writings are marked by corrosive humour, reinforced by the accompanying coloured cartoons drawn by the author himself.

The 1930s mark the end of the aestheticizing experimentalism of a whole generation. *Espantapáros (al alcance de todos)* (Scarecrow Within Everybody's Reach) (1932) opens with a two-coloured calligram of the scarecrow of the title. The volume consists of twenty-four prose-poem vignettes, an inner exploration mixing elements of **surrealism** with expressionist despair. Girondo abandons the cubo-futurism of his early work and combines word games with a wild, highly sexual imagination. *Interlunio* (Interlune) (1937), dedicated to the writer who later became his wife, Norah **Lange**, is more sombre. The *feísmo* (ugliness) of his previous work is further accentuated here through the terrifying engravings of Lino Spilimbergo. Europe and urban culture are now called into question and rejected, to the detriment of both the *pampa* and the Argentine *arrabal*. The cow, now one of the totems of Girondo's poetry, appears here for the first time. The 'there' of Europe, now old and broken, yields to a 'here' that is Argentina, rural and infinite.

The last of Girondo's poetic revolutions began with *Persuasión de los días* (Persuasion of Days) (1942), and ran through to one of the finest works of poetry in Spanish, *En la masmédula* (Into the Moremarrow) (1954). The radicalism of this work located him within the tradition of Vicente **Huidobro**, César **Vallejo** and **concrete poetry**. The explosion and estrangement of the word, the immersion in the materiality of language, make this final work one of the key texts of Argentine poetry.

Further reading

Girondo, O. (1968) *Obras completas*, Buenos Aires: Losada.

—— (1999) *Obra completa*, Madrid: Archivos.

Nóbile, B. de (1972) *El acto experimental*, Buenos Aires: Losada.

Pellegrini, A. (1964) *Oliverio Girondo*, Buenos Aires: Eds Culturales Argentinas.

Pío del Corro, G. (1976) *Oliverio Girondo: Los límites del signo*, Buenos Aires: Fernando García Cambeiro.

Schwartz, J. (1993) *Vanguardia y cosmopolitismo en la década del veinte*, Rosario: Beatriz Viterbo.
Wilson, J. (1997) 'Oliverio Girondo', in V. Smith (ed.), *Encyclopedia of Latin American Literature*, London: Fitzroy Dearborn, 368–9.

JORGE SCHWARTZ

Girri, Alberto

b. 1919, Buenos Aires, Argentina; d. 1991, Buenos Aires

Poet

An outstanding poet and translator (of Wallace Stevens and John Donne, among others), Girri's considerable body of work begins with *Playa sola* (Lonely Beach) (1946). His poetry is a constant reflection upon the poetic act itself, a concern further explored in his critical essays (particularly in his important *Notas sobre la experiencia poética* (Notes on the Poetic Experience) (1983)) and his regular contributions to ***Sur***, *La Nación* and *Correo Literario*. His poetry explores the various dimensions of experience, artistic as well as everyday, with a sharp eye and a laconic tone.

Further reading

Girri, A. (1977–84) *Obra poética*, Buenos Aires: Corregidor, 4 vols.
—— (1983) *Notas sobre la experiencia poética*, Buenos Aires: Losada.
Running, T. (1990) 'Alberto Girri: Poesía sobre poesía', *Letras* 21–2: 53–63.
Vitale, I. (1975) 'Alberto Girri, poeta de lo real', *Sin nombre* 5(3): 65–9.
Wilson, J. (1997) 'Alberto Girri', in V. Smith (ed.), *Encyclopedia of Latin American Literature*, London: Fitzroy Dearborn, 370–1.
Yurkievich, S. (1981) 'Alberto Girri: Fases de su creciente', *Hispamérica* 10(29): 99–105.
—— (2002) 'Alberto Girri', in C. Solé and K. Müller-Bergh (eds), *Latin American Writers: Supplement I*, New York: Scribners, 289–302.

ENRIQUE FOFFANI

Gladwell, Joyce

b. 1939, St Catherine's, Jamaica

Writer

Gladwell's ground-breaking autobiography *Brown Face Big Master* (1969) exposes her struggle to maintain Christian faith within the stifling colonial atmosphere of a Jamaican boarding school and traces the psychological implications of moving from rural Jamaica to London University and her mixed marriage. Gladwell's second autobiography is unpublished. She currently works as a family therapist and freelance journalist in Canada.

Further reading

Courtman, S. (2001) 'Portrait of a West Indian Woman as a Young Writer in England', *Wasafiri* 33: 9–14.

SANDRA COURTMAN

Glantz, Margo

b. 1930, Mexico City

Critic and novelist

The most eminent literary critic of her generation and a highly original novelist, Glantz has also done public service at the National Institute of Fine Arts (INBA) (1983–86) and as cultural attaché to the Mexican Embassy in London (1986–88). In her autobiographical novel *Las genealogías* (The Geneologies) (1981), Glantz recounts her experiences growing up in an intellectual and artistic Jewish immigrant family in Mexico City during the 1940s. In *Síndrome de naufragios* (Shipwreck Syndrome) (1984), Glantz draws on her incisive readings of chronicles of the Conquest, and in *Apariciones* (Apparitions) (1996) she explores the mystical raptures of a colonial nun. Much of her early criticism of Mexican literature focused on nineteenth- and twentieth-century Mexican narrative, including La **Onda** (a term she invented), but in recent years she has published important collections of essays and editions on the Conquest, La Malinche and colonial nuns. Glantz was awarded the Magda Donato Prize in 1982 and the Xavier Villaurrutia Prize in 1984. She received her PhD in Literature from the Sorbonne in 1958, and from 1959 to 1995 she held a UNAM chair in Mexican Literature. Drawing on her remarkable erudition in Mexican and European cultural history, much of Glantz's criticism has been influenced by contemporary French philosophers, including Barthes, Bachelard and Bataille, in their reflections on eroticism, the body, gender and society.

Further reading

García Pinto, M. (1991) 'Margo Glantz', in *Women Writers of Latin America. Intimate Histories*, trans. Trudy Balch and García Pinto, Austin: University of Texas Press, 105–22.

Glantz, M. (1991) *The Family Tree*, trans. S. Bassnett, London: Serpent's Tail.

—— (1981) *Las genealogías*, Mexico City: Aguilar.

Jörgensen, Beth E. (1995) 'Margo Glantz, Tongue in Hand', in Doris Meyer (ed.), *Reinterpreting the Spanish American Essay: Women Writers of the 19th and 20th Centuries*, Austin: University of Texas Press, 188–96.

Maíz-Peña, M. (1997) 'Margo Glantz', in V. Smith (ed.), *Encyclopedia of Latin American Literature*, London: Fitzroy Dearborn, 371–3.

CYNTHIA STEELE

Glissant, Edouard

b. 1928, Sainte Marie, Martinique

Writer

It is because of the reputation of writers such as Edouard Glissant that Martinique is called the island of intellectuals. He and his contemporary Frantz Fanon are the best known of the generation that came after Aimé **Césaire**. Like Fanon, he was educated at the Lycée Schoelcher and later left for Paris after participating in Césaire's electoral campaign. His early poems were dense meditations on landscape that were remarkably different from work by his contemporaries. His first book of essays, *Soleil de la conscience* (Sun of Consciousness) (1956), set out his definition of the Caribbean as diverse and constantly changing, as opposed to the more ideologically static picture derived from ***négritude*** and Marxism. *La **lézarde*** (The Ripening), which won the Prix Renaudot in 1958, and *Le quatrième siècle* (The Fourth Century) (1965) brought him to prominence because of their original treatments of Martinican space and history and their refusal to be restrained by generic conventions.

After spending nineteen years in Paris, during which time he produced enthusiastic reviews of the work of writers as diverse as St John **Perse**, Victor Segalen, William Faulkner and Alejo **Carpentier**, and became involved in anti-colonial politics through the Front Antillo-Guyanais formed with Paul Niger, he returned to Martinique in 1965 and founded the Institut Martiniquais d'Etudes. By inviting artists such as Matta from Chile and Cárdenas from Cuba, and with the publication of the magazine *Acoma*, Glissant tried to counter the rapid Europeanization of Martinique, which had become a French département in 1946. His bleak view of Martinique's future as a département is recorded in the 1975 novel, significantly entitled *Malemort* (Undead). In 1980 he left Martinique to become the editor of the *UNESCO Courier* in Paris. In the following year he published his well-known and influential *Le **discours antillais*** (Caribbean Discourse) and the novel *La case du commandeur* (The Driver's Cabin). By this time, he had established himself as the major Caribbean theorist of the post-***négritude*** period. His most recent novels, with the untranslatable titles *Mahagony* (1987) and *Tout monde* (1993), continue to explore the themes and characters of his early fiction. Similarly, his theoretical work *Poétique de la Relation* (Poetics of Relating) in 1990 and *Faulkner, Mississippi* (1996) further develop his theories of a Caribbean and New World identity.

Further reading

Baudot, A. (1993) *Bibliographie annotée d'Edouard Glissant*, Toronto: Ed. du Gref.

Caistor, N. (1997) 'Edouard Glissant', in V. Smith (ed.), *Encyclopedia of Latin American Literature*, London: Fitzroy Dearborn, 373–4.

Case, F.I. (1973) 'The Novels of Edouard Glissant', *Black Images* 3–4: 3–13.

Campa, R. de la (1995) 'Mimicry and the Uncanny

in Caribbean Discourse', in *Latin Americanism*, Minneapolis: University of Minnesota Press, 85–120.
Dash, J.M. (1995) *Edouard Glissant*, Cambridge: Cambridge University Press.
Glissant, E. (1989) *Caribbean Discourse*, trans. J.M. Dash, Charlottesville: University Press of Virginia.
Radford, D. (1982) *Edouard Glissant*, Paris: Seghers.

J. MICHAEL DASH

GODOY ALCAYAGA, LUCILA *see* Mistral, Gabriela

Goldenberg, Jorge

b. 1941, Buenos Aires, Argentina

Playwright

Goldenberg's play *Relevo 1923* (Changing of the Guard, 1923) (1975), about a political assassination by a foreign anarchist during a period of strikes in Patagonia, raised a difficult topic during the military dictatorship. Goldenberg's theme responded to an official rhetoric which blamed 'foreign infiltrators' for alleged subversion. With the return to institutional democracy, Goldenberg wrote *Knepp* (1983), which addressed the issue of State terror and the disappearance of dissidents during the dictatorship. He has written extensively for film, including for María Luisa Bemberg's last film, *De eso no se habla* (We Don't Talk about Such Things) (1983) and Sergio Cabrera's *Ilona llega con la lluvia* (Ilona Comes with the Rain) (1996).

Further reading

Foster, D.W. (1991) '*Krinksy* de Jorge Goldenberg y la identidad étnica argentina', *Latin American Theatre Review* 24(2): 101–5.
—— (1993) '*Krinsky*: A Play of Argentine Ethnic Identity', *Yiddish* 9(MJS Annual. VIII/2): 19–23.
Glickman, N. and G. Waldman (eds) (1996) *Argentine Jewish Theatre: A Critical Anthology*, Lewisburg, PA: Bucknell University Press.
Goldenberg, Jorge (1975) *Relevo 1923*, La Habana: Casa de las Américas.
—— (2000) *Knepp; Sería más sencillo*, Buenos Aires: Teatro Vivo.
Ostergaard, A.G. (1975) '*Relevo 1923*: Discurso metateatral: Análisis de la enunciación', Caravelle: *Cahiers du monde hispanique et luso brésilien*, 41: 63–80.

DAVID WILLIAM FOSTER

Gomes, Alfredo Dias

b. 1922, Salvador, Bahia, Brazil; d. 1999, São Paulo, Brazil

Playwright

A key figure in modern Brazilian theatre, Gomes's work is inspired by conflicts between idyllic rural life and corrupt urban life. His most famous play, *O pagador de promessas* (Journey to Bahia) (1962), was adapted for the screen by Anselmo Duarte and won Brazil's first Golden Palm Award at the Cannes Film Festival. Much of his work of the 1960s and 1970s was satirical, inspired by the severe political repression during the military dictatorship. *O santo inquérito* (The Holy Inquisition) (1966) and *O bem-amado* (The Beloved) (1977) are most often viewed as contemporary allegorical and morality plays. Gomes has also written many important *telenovelas* for TV Globo, among them *Roque Santeiro* (1986).

Further reading

Bailey, D.S. (1972) '*Pagador de Promessas*: A Brazilian Morality Play', *Latin American Theatre Review* 6(1): 35–9.
Gomes, A.D. (1962) *O pagador de promessas*, Rio de Janeiro: Editora Ediouro-Tecnoprint.
—— (1977) *O bem-amado*, Rio de Janeiro: Editora Ediouro-Tecnoprint.
Lyday, L.F. (1976) 'The Theater of Alfredo Dias Gomes', in Leon F. Lyday and George W. Woodyard (eds), *Dramatists in Revolt: the New Latin American Theater*, Austin: University of Texas Press.
Mazzara, R.A. (1969) 'Alfredo Dias Gomes, Social Commentator and Artist', *Latin American Theatre Review*, 2(2): 41–59.

SUSAN CANTY QUINLAN

Gómez, Ana Ilce

b. 1945, Masaya, Nicaragua

Poet

Ana Ilce Gómez is one of the most refined and polished lyrical poetic voices of Nicaraguan poetry. Her perfection in form is praised highly by her peers. Because she is not a member of the ruling elite, Gómez is rarely included in public events. She studied journalism at the National Autonomous University of Managua (UNAM), and has worked for the National Bank for many years. She was active in the Sandinista Association of Cultural Workers (ASTC). Her work concentrates on the repressive effect that Catholicism, capitalism and patriarchy created in 1970s Nicaragua. She is a single mother and resides in her home town, commuting to work daily. Only two books of poems of hers have been published and she has literally burned her lesser works rather than see them in print.

SILVIA CHAVES AND ILEANA RODRÍGUEZ

Gómez Carrillo, Enrique

b. 1873, Guatemala City; d. 1927, Paris, France

Writer

Gómez Carrillo was famous for his voluminous **travel writing** and journalism, especially his impressions of Europe and the Orient. One of the significant prose writers of **Spanish American modernism**, his lush style evoked places far from his readership in Latin America, sometimes with a teasing sensuality, as in some of his crónicas (see **crónica**) from Japan (and many of those on Paris). Part French, he spent much of his life in France or at least in the orbit of French culture; his last published work was *La nueva literatura francesa* (New French Literature) (1927). He also wrote numerous chronicles about the battlefields of the First World War and a three-volume autobiography.

Further reading

Gómez Carrillo, E. (1919–23) *Obras completas*, Madrid: Editorial Mundo Latino, 27 vols.

Kronik, J. (1989) 'Enrique Gómez Carrillo', in C.A. Solé and M.I. Abreu (eds), *Latin American Writers*, New York: Scribners, 2, 465–9.

Mendoza, J.M. (1946) *Biografía de Enrique Gómez Carrillo*, Guatemala City: Tipografía Nacional, 2 vols.

DANIEL BALDERSTON

Gómez Valderrama, Pedro

b. 1923, Bucaramanaga, Colombia; d. 1995, Bogotá, Colombia

Writer and diplomat

A recognized writer whose prose is concerned mainly with historical facts such as the process of colonization of certain rural areas of Colombia. His novel *La otra raya del tigre* (The Tiger's Other Stripe) (1977) describes the adventures of a German settler who, looking for fortune, arrives in Colombia. Gómez Valderrama includes elements of **magical realism** in his narrations and establishes settings built through dualisms, for example ruralism and progress, barbarism and civilization. Some of his other works are *La nave de los locos y otros relatos* (The Ship of Fools and Other Stories) (1984) and his poetry text *Biografía de la campana* (Biography of the Bell) (1946).

Further reading

Gómez Valderrama, Pedro (1992) *La otra raya del tigre*, Bogotá: Alianza Editorial.

ALVARO BERNAL

Gonzalez, Anson

b. 1934, Mayo, Trinidad

Writer

Gonzalez was editor and publisher of *The New Voices*

(1973–93), a journal of creative writing and essays which he financed almost entirely himself. He anthologized poems and stories by other writers, inaugurated World Poetry Day in 1979 in the Caribbean, and taught at primary, secondary and university levels in Trinidad and the region. His publications include *Collected Poems 1964–1979* (1979), *Moksha: Poems of Light and Sound* (1988) and *Merry-Go-Round and Other Poems* (1992). In 1996, the University of Miami Caribbean Writers' Institute honoured him with a lifetime achievement award for contributions to Caribbean art and culture.

KEITH JARDIM

González, José Luis

b. 1926, Santo Domingo, Dominican Republic; d. 1996, Mexico City

Writer

González is an emblematic contemporary writer whose concern with exile reflects a common Caribbean experience. Born to a Puerto Rican father and a Dominican mother, he began his journey into exile when the family moved to Puerto Rico, fleeing from hurricane Zenón and the Trujillo dictatorship. He completed his university studies on the island, where he met the Dominican *émigré* Juan **Bosch** who encouraged him to write. By the time he moved on, in 1946, he had already published two volumes of short stories, *En la sombra* (In the Shadows) (1943) and *Cinco cuentos de sangre* (Five Stories of Blood) (1945). His writing was concise in style and tense in narrative; his rural themes and concern for the social suffering of the peasantry suggested a link with the work of Emilio S. **Belaval**.

González travelled widely in North America and Europe, pursued postgraduate studies in political science in New York, and lived in Prague. *El hombre de la calle* (Man in the Street) (1948) marked the first representation of urban conflicts in Puerto Rican literature. The brief story, 'La carta' (The Letter), for example, addresses the issue of Puerto Rican heteroglossia, exploring in its two paragraphs the class and cultural gulfs that divide this US colony. In 1954, while residing in Guanajuato, Mexico, he published *En este lado* (On this Side), a collection of stories including 'En el fondo del caño hay un negrito' (There's a Black Boy at the Bottom of the Pipe). The setting of his writing was now the marginal communities around the great cities of Latin America, and his theme the tragic consequences of the move from rural to urban worlds.

His open commitment to Marxism precipitated his decision to renounce US citizenship; in solidarity, Mexico made him a citizen of that country. The US government's refusal to allow him into Puerto Rico confirmed his exile status. He remained a participant, albeit at a distance, in the political life of the island. He continued to write stories, novels and essays, developing new themes and concerns: the peasant who becomes a marginal worker in *La galería* (The Gallery) (1972); the involvement of young men in the Korean and Vietnam Wars in *Mambrú se fue a la guerra* (Mambru has Gone to War) (1973); the changes in the nature of agricultural production on the coast and in the mountains in *La balada de otro tiempo* (Ballad of Another Time) (1978); the US occupation of Puerto Rico in 1898 in *La llegada* (The Arrival) (1978). The question of Puerto Rican cultural identity is explored in two volumes of essays, *El país de cuatro pisos* (The Four-Storey Country) (1980) and *Una visita al cuarto piso* (A Visit to the Fourth Floor) (1986). No bureaucratic obstacle could deny José Luis González his citizenship, for he has established his identity as a writer.

Further reading

Díaz Quiñones, A. (1977) *Conversación con José Luis González*, Río Piedras, PR: Ediciones Huracán.

González, J.L. (1980) *El país de cuartro pisos y otros ensayos*, Río Pedras, PR: Ediciones Huracán.

—— (1992) *Todos los cuentos*, Mexico City: UNAM.

—— (1993) *Puerto Rico: The Four-Storeyed Country and Other Essays*, Princeton, NJ: M. Wiener.

Ruscalleda Bercedóniz, I.M. (1979) *Textos de/sobre José Luis González*, Xalapa: Universidad Veracruzana.

MARÍA JULIA DAROQUI

González, Otto Raúl

b. 1921, Guatemala City

Writer

A founding member of Grupo Acento and director of its journal, González was a key literary voice in the 1944 Revolution and the years that followed. With the intervention of 1954, he fled to Mexico where he wrote political poetry with strong Nerudean inflections (see **Neruda, Pablo**), even as he turned toward erotic poetry, fiction and other forms. He won the Miguel Angel Asturias national prize for literature in 1990, and has been able to visit his native country in recent years. Among his many works are his 1943 landmark collection, *Voz y voto del geranio* (Voice and Vote of the Geranium), reprinted in his *Poesía fundamental* (Fundamental Poetry) (1967).

Further reading

González, O.R. (1943) *Voz y voto del geranio*, Guatemala: Ediciones Acento.

—— (1978) 'Poesía contemporánea de Guatemala, los poetas de "Nuevo signo"', *Cuadernos americanos* 221: 174–87.

—— (1986) 'Los talleres de poesía', *Plural* 15(8 (176)): 48.

—— (1995) *Poesía fundamental 1943–1967*, Guatemala: Universidad de San Carlos de Guatemala.

—— (2001) *Oír con los ojos*, Guatemala: Editorial Universitaria.

MARC ZIMMERMAN

González de Alba, Luis

b. 1944, Charcas, San Luis Potosí, Mexico

Writer and activist

While a student and professor of psychology at UNAM, González de Alba became a leader of the 1968 student movement; he was arrested after the massacre of students by the army at Tlatelolco Square in Mexico City on 2 October. After several months in Lecumberri Prison he was exiled to Chile, experiences he recounts in *Los días y los años* (The Days and the Years) (1971). Returning to Mexico, he published a weekly newspaper column on scientific and political issues in the newspaper *La Jornada* and became a leading advocate for gay rights. He has published short stories, fiction, essays, poetry and drama.

Further reading

González de Alba, L. (1971) *Los días y los años*, Mexico City: Era.

—— (2000) 'Historia de una derrota católica: Un viejo litigio', *Nexos* 23(266): 31–40, 42, 44–5.

CYNTHIA STEELE

González Delvalle, Alcibíades

b. 1936, Ñemby, Paraguay

Writer

A polemical writer and playwright, González Delvalle has explored elements of Guarani folklore and Paraguayan history in plays such as *El grito del luisón* (The Cry of the Werewolf) (1972) and *Perú Rimá* (1987). His *San Fernando*, based on the 1865–70 War of the Triple Alliance, was banned on the eve of its premiere in 1975 and again in 1989. He also wrote *Nuestros años grises* (Our Grey Years) (1985) and *Función Patronal* (Patron Saint Function) (1980), a *costumbrista* (see ***costumbrismo***) novel.

Further reading

González Delvalle, A. (1980) *Función patronal*, Paraguay: Ediciones NAPA.

TERESA MÉNDEZ-FAITH

González León, Adriano

b. 1931, Valera, Venezuela

Writer

González León wrote perhaps the most renowned Venezuelan novel of the last fifty years: *País portátil* (Portable Country) (1968). A piece of work showing a fervent artistic vocation and the need to elaborate an adhesion to the leftist trends of those years, the novel is a clever and honest testimony of urban guerrilla struggle. His earlier work included the short story collections *Las hogueras más altas* (The Highest Bonfires) (1957) and *Linaje de árboles* (Lineage of Trees), *Crónicas del rayo y de la lluvia* (On Lighting and Rain) (1998) and two collections of poems *Hueso de mis huesos* (Bones of My Bones) (1997) and *Damas* (Ladies) (1998).

He has taught at the Universidad Central de Venezuela and served as cultural attaché to the Venezuelan embassy in Spain. His most recent novel, the 'old man's novel' *Viejo*, was published in 1995.

Further reading

Lasarte, F. (1980) '*Las hogueras más altas* y el proceso de la narrativa renovadora', *Escritura* 5(9): 117–65.

López Alvarez, L. (1991) *Literatura e identidad en Venezuela*, Barcelona: PPU.

Vidal, A. (1968) 'González León, un escritor, una novela', *Marcha* 1407 (21 June): 29–30.

VÍCTOR GALARRAGA OROPEZA

González Prada, Manuel

b. 1844, Lima, Peru; d. 1918, Lima

Essayist

González Prada was Peru's most important *pensador* or social thinker of the late nineteenth and early twentieth centuries, a master of the genre of the **essay**. An important figure in the devastated Peru that followed the Chilean occupation during the War of the Pacific (1879–84), González Prada devoted himself to organizing a literary club and then a liberal political party, the National Union. While in Europe, from 1891 to 1898, he attended classes given by Ernest Renan and others and published his first important book, *Pájinas libres* (Free Pages) (1894), published in Paris using an emended orthography. After returning to Peru he involved himself once more with the National Union before breaking with it and announcing his conversion to anarchism. His attacks on clericalism, political corruption and scandals in government, and his fervent defence of manual workers and the Indians, culminated in his publication of *Horas de lucha* (Hours of Battle) (1908). From 1912 until his death (with one interruption due to a military *coup*), he served as director of the National Library in Lima.

González Prada's essays were vital to the analysis of social problems in Peru. He proposed a plan of social and moral reconstruction, short on details but inspirational for those that followed (including, most obviously, José Carlos **Mariátegui**). A poet as well as an essayist, he revitalized political discourse with the sharpness of his expression and the passion of his commitments. His most famous (albeit unfinished) essay, 'Nuestros indios' (Our Indians) (1904), added to a posthumous edition of *Horas de lucha* (in 1924), is eloquent in its defence of the Indians' right to conduct their own struggle.

González Prada's prose was an inspiration to the later writers of ***indigenismo*** and to socialist and anarcho-syndicalist thinkers. His early poems pre-date some of the innovations that were associated with **Spanish American modernism** in their search for perfect poetic form. His essays on spelling and language use were important for defenders of a Spanish-American linguistic norm that differed from the Spanish norm. Eclectic, passionate and energetic, Gonzá-z Prada's writing still has great force a century later.

Further reading

Blanco Fombona, R. (1966) *Crítica a la obra de González Prada*, with an essay by J.C. Mariátegui, Lima: Fondo de Cultura Popular.

Chang-Rodríguez, E. (1957) *La literatura política de González Prada, Mariátegui y Haya de la Torre*, Mexico City: Ediciones de Andrea.

—— (1989) 'Manuel González Prada', in C.A. Solé and M.I. Abreu (eds), *Latin American Writers*, New York: Scribners, 1, 263–88.

González Prada, M. (1976) *Pájinas libres y Horas de lucha*, Caracas: Biblioteca Ayacucho.

—— (1985–8) *Obras*, ed. and intro. L A. Sánchez, Lima: Petroperú, 5 vols.
Sánchez, L.A. (1976) *Mito y realidad en González Prada*, Lima: Villanueva.

DANIEL BALDERSTON

González Tuñón, Raúl

b. 1905, Buenos Aires, Argentina; d. 1974, Buenos Aires

Poet

Poet of the city of Buenos Aires, González Tuñón shared with Jorge Luis **Borges** a preoccupation with the literary representation of the suburbs. Although at first associated with the group Florida (see **Boedo vs Florida**), his political commitments distanced him from the group's purely aesthetic concerns and he became aligned with a more politicized international avant-garde. With their fractured and miscellaneous structure, his poems show an immigrant Buenos Aires in rapid transformation. They were rediscovered by the politicized poets of the 1970s (like Juan **Gelman**), were made into tangos (sung by the Cuarteto Cedrón) and were celebrated by Beatriz **Sarlo** in her book, *Una modernidad periférica: Buenos Aires 1920 y 1930* (1988).

Further reading

Barletta, L. (1974) 'Homenaje a Raúl González Tuñón', *Contempora* 1: 2–9.
González Tuñón, R. (1995) *La calle del agujero en la media-Todos bailan*, Buenos Aires: Planeta.
Mirkin, Z. (1991) *Raúl González Tuñón: Cronista, rebelde y mago*, Buenos Aires: Instituto Literário y Cultural Hispánico.
Salas, H. (1978) 'Raúl González Tuñón: "Un modo de tutear a Díos" ', *Cuadernos hispanoamericanos* 334: 89–102.
Sarabia, R. (1992) 'Raúl González Tuñón: Poesía ciudadana y tono conversacional', *Hispanic Journal* 13(2): 323–44.

FLORENCIA GARRAMUÑO

Goodison, Lorna

b. 1947, Kingston, Jamaica

Poet

The best-known woman poet of the Anglophone Caribbean, Goodison's poetry is concerned with personal space, freedom and spirituality as well as social justice. She has a remarkably fluid and sensuous poetic voice developed through *Tamarind Season* (1980), *I Am Becoming My Mother* (1986), *Heartease* (1988), *Selected Poems* (1992) and *To Us, All Flowers Are Roses* (1995). She writes in a range of registers from Jamaican creole to international English; her work, like that of Derek **Walcott**, is both Caribbean-centred and international. Her short stories *Baby Mother and the King of Swords* (1990) depict gender relations in Jamaican culture.

Further reading

Baugh, E. (1990) 'Lorna Goodison in the Context of Feminist Criticism', *Journal of West Indian Literature* 4(1): 1–13.
Goodison, L. (1993) *Selected Poems*, Ann Arbor: University of Michigan Press.
—— (1995) *To Us, All Flowers Are Roses*, Champaign-Urbana: University of Illinois Press.
—— (2001) *Travelling Mercies*, Toronto: McClelland & Stewart.
Narain, D.D. (1990) 'Interview with Lorna Goodison', *Wasafiri* 11: 20–4.

ELAINE SAVORY

Gorodischer, Angélica

b. 1928, Buenos Aires, Argentina

Writer

Something of a cult writer among **science fiction** enthusiasts, Gorodischer's novels have won prizes in Argentina and abroad. Her writing is characterized by its subtle play with gender, particularly as it is embedded in language, and by its concern with women's domestic worlds and their relationship to men. The stories of *Bajo las jubeas en flor* (Under the Flowering Jubea Trees) (1973) and novels such as

Trafalgar (1979), *Kalpa imperial* (1983) and *Prodigios* (Prodigies) (1994) combine humour with great narrative skill.

Further reading

Balboa Echeverría, M. and E. Gimbernat-González (1995) *Boca de dama: La narrativa de Angélica Gorodischer*, Buenos Aires: Feminaria.

Ferman, C. (1997) 'Mujeres, cuento fantástico y ciencia ficción: Los poblados márgenes de la literatura argentina: Una entrevista con Angélica Gorodischer', *Osamayor* 4(10): 45–54.

Gorodischer, A. (1983) *Kalpa imperial*, Barcelona: Alcor.

—— (ed.) (1994) *Mujeres de palabra*, San Juan, PR: Editorial de la Universidad de Puerto Rico.

Juzyn Amestoy, Olga (1998) 'La narrativa fantástica de Angélica Gorodischer: La mirada "femenina" y los límites del deseo', *Letras femeninas*: 87–96.

SANDRA GASPARINI

Gorostiza, Carlos

b. 1920, Buenos Aires, Argentina

Playwright and theatre director

Gorostiza began his career with Teatro Independiente, where his play *El puente* (The Bridge) (1949) renewed theatrical discourse, presenting class conflicts in a convincing colloquial language, and influenced the new realist playwrights of the 1960s. Later works exhibited a more mature realism, symbolic language and some elements of the grotesque. His plays *El pan de la locura* (Bread of Madness) (1958), *Los prójimos* (Fellow Men) (1966), *Los hermanos queridos* (Dear Brothers) (1978), *El acompañamiento* (The Accompaniment) (1981) and *Aeroplanos* (Aeroplanes) (1990) reflect on Argentine identity and the complexity of human relationships. He also participated in Teatro Abierto.

Further reading

Flawia de Fernández, N.M. and O.R. Steimberg de Kaplan (1986) 'Cuerpos presentes de Carlos Gorostiza: De los mitos a la identidad nacional', *Rio de la Plata: Culturas* 3: 113–20.

Gorostiza, C. (1969) *¿A qué jugamos?* Buenos Aires: Editorial Sudamericana.

—— (1984) *Páginas de Carlos Gorostiza*, Buenos Aires: Editorial Celtia.

—— (1990) 'Perspectivas: Cincuenta años de una relación con el Teatro Cervantes', *La Nación, suplemento literario* 4 March: 2.

—— (1993) *El pan de la locura*, Argentina: Colihue.

—— (1995) *El reloj de Baltasar; comedia en tres actos*, Buenos Aires: Losange.

Montes Huidobro, M. (1992) 'Poder o no poder: La argentinidad según Carlos Gorostiza', in Juana A. Arancibia and Zulema Mirkin (eds), *Teatro argentino durante El Proceso (1976–1983)*, Buenos Aires: Vinciguerra.

Szoka, E. (1993) 'Acá, Ionesco sería un autor costumbrista: Entrevista con Carlos Gorostiza', *Gestos* 8(15): 147–54.

STELLA MARTINI

Gorostiza, José

b. 1901, San Juan Bautista (now Villahermosa), Tabasco, Mexico; d. 1973, Mexico City

Poet

Gorostiza is the author of one of the classic works of Mexican poetry, *Muerte sin fin* (Endless Death) (1935). A member of the generation of **Contemporáneos**, his early poems were published in *Contemporáneos* and the *Revista de la Universidad Nacional*. He also wrote other remarkable poems, essays and 'synthetic dramas' such as *Ventana a la calle* (Window on the Street) (1924). During **Vasconcelos**'s tenure at the Education Ministry, Gorostiza edited the magazine *El Maestro* (The Teacher) and contributed to *Lecturas clásicas para niños* (Classic Readings for Children). A career diplomat from 1935 to 1965, he was awarded the National Literature Prize in 1968.

Further reading

Biriotti, M. (1997) 'José Gorostiza', in V. Smith

(ed.), *Encyclopedia of Latin American Literature*, London: Fitzroy Dearborn, 380–1.
Gelpí, J. (1984) *Enunciación y dependencia en José Gorostiza: Estudio de una máscara poética*, Mexico City: UNAM.
Gorostiza, J. (1988) *Poesía y poética*, Paris: Colección Archivos.
Marrero-Henríquez, J.M. (1990) 'La creación del poema en "Muerte sin fin" de José Gorostiza', *Syntaxis* 23–4: 121–8.
Morales, C.J. (1999) 'José Gorostiza y las vanguardias poéticas', *La palabra y el hombre* 109: 59–74.
Pacheco, J.E. (1989) 'José Gorostiza', in C.A. Solé and M.I. Abreu (eds), *Latin American Writers*, New York: Scribners, 2: 923–31.

LILIANA WEINBERG

Gouverneurs de la rosée

Published posthumously in 1944, *Gouverneurs de la rosée* (Masters of the Dew) the masterpiece of Haitian ***indigénisme***, has been translated into a dozen languages and filmed twice (once as *Cumbite* (1964) by Tomás Gutiérrez Alea). Written while Jacques **Roumain** was chargé d'affaires in Mexico, it is a political parable that tackles the hardships of rural Haiti and an anthropologically accurate picture of peasant culture. The novel offers a Utopian vision of peasant solidarity and a renewal of culture through collective labour which is preached by the protagonist Manuel who returns from cutting cane in Cuba to his drought-stricken village.

Further reading

Gaillard, R. (1966) *L'universe romanesque de Jacques Roumain*, Port-au-Prince: Henri Deschamps.
Prat, M. (1986) *Gouverneurs de la rosée, Jacques Roumain: Analyse critique*, Paris: Hatier.
Roumain, J. (1944) *Gouverneurs de la rosée*, Port-au-Prince: Imp. de l'Etat.
—— (1947) *Masters of the Dew*, New York: Reynal & Hitchcock.

J. MICHAEL DASH

Gramcko, Ida

b. 1924, Puerto Cabello, Venezuela;
d. 1994, Caracas, Venezuela

Poet, playwright, essayist and journalist

Together with Enriqueta **Arvelo Larriva** and Ana Enriqueta **Terán**, Gramcko may be considered a pioneer of modern women's poetry in Venezuela. Her considerable poetic and dramatic work embraces symbolic, psychological and even folkloric themes; in short, the whole range of archetypes of Venezuelan imaginary. A graduate of the Universidad Central of Venezuela, where she subsequently taught, Gramcko contributed to a number of important journals and newspapers including *El Nacional* (she was its first leader writer, from 1943–46), *El Universal*, ***Revista nacional de cultura***, *Cultura universitaria* and ***Repertorio americano*** (Costa Rica).

Further reading

Castillo, S. (1992) 'La revisión de un mito: *María Lionza* de Ida Gramcko', in Elizabeth Schön *et al.* (eds), *Las risas de nuestras medusas: Teatro venezolano escrito por mujeres*, Caracas: Fundarte, 13–17.
Gerbasi, V. (1942) 'Umbral', *Revista nacional de cultura* 33: 138–9.
Gramcko, I. (1948) *Umbral*, Mexico City: Orbe.
—— (1956) *María Lionza*, Barquisimeto: Nueva Segovia.

JORGE ROMERO LEÓN

Grande sertão: Veredas

Grande sertão: Veredas (The Devil to Pay in the Backlands) (1956), by João Guimarães **Rosa**, is recognized as one of the high points of contemporary Latin American fiction. It has been translated into several languages, but its verbal experimentation and wealth of neologisms have stimulated a number of new versions, most recently a new French translation.

The plot of the novel addresses struggles between *jagunços* (north-eastern bandits), vengeance and the love affair between Riobaldo and Diadorim. Riobaldo, the novel's narrator-protagonist, is a man who seeks in memory and reflection a way to deny the existence of the Devil, with whom he makes a pact when he is looking for ways of overcoming Hermógenes, 'lord of all cruelty'. The work is inspired by chivalric novels and feudal epics, in which the sacred and the profane, and good and evil, co-exist.

Underpinning the epic is the conflict between the Narrator-Hero and the *sertão* (north-eastern backlands), between the I and the World. For Guimarães Rosa's narrator, the *sertão* is a metaphor for the wider world with all its moral, religious and philosophical conflicts. 'The *sertão* is everywhere' or 'The *sertão* is the size of the world', the author says. This huge area, which embraces the interior of several Brazilian states, becomes in this novel the scenario of a complex literary construction whereby poetry and myth fuse to both veil and reveal a global vision of existence. The contradictions and contrasts between the primitive rustic world of the *sertão* and the urban-industrial world can be sensed in Riobaldo's references to the people who will hear his stories. According to Alfredo **Bosi**, the conflict between hero and world does not disappear in this novel; it is resolved by a pact between men and the origin of these tensions – the Other, the Reverse Side of the world. The dialectics of the plot are not processed through an analysis of psychic fractures nor through the mimesis of local groups and types, but rather through the assiduous interaction of the character with an omnipresent natural-cultural Whole – the *sertão*.

Further reading

Bosi, A. (1988) *Céu, inferno*, São Paulo: Ediciones Atica.

Campos, H. de (1967) *Metalinguagem de outras metas*, São Paulo: Ediciones Vozes.

Candido, A. (1964) *Tese e ántitese*, São Paulo: Cia Ed. Nacional.

Galvão, W. (1972) *As formas do falso*, São Paulo: Ediciones Perspectiva.

Reis, R. (1997) 'Grande sertão: Veredas', in V. Smith (ed.), *Encyclopedia of Latin American Literature*, London: Fitzroy Dearborn, 400–1.

Rosa, J. Guimarães (1958) *Grande sertão: Veredas*, Rio de Janeiro: José Olympio.

—— (1963) *The Devil to Pay in the Backlands*, trans. J.L. Taylor and H. de Onís, New York: Knopf.

Schwarz, R. (1981) *A seréia e a desconfiado*, Rio de Janeiro: Ediciones Paz e Terra.

MILTON HATOUM

Griffero, Ramón

b. 1955, Santiago, Chile

Playwright

Griffero founded the Teatro de Fin de Siglo in 1984 in an abandoned warehouse. In his plays performed in the late 1980s – *Historias de un galpón abandonado* (Stories of an Abandoned Warehouse), *Cinema Utoppia*, *99 La Morgue* – he responded creatively to the limitations of working as an artist within an oppressive military regime. To work around censorship, his plays de-emphasized the text and instead experimented with performance spaces, sets and presentation styles. His 1995 play *Río Abajo* (Downriver), with sets by Herbert Jonckers, gives an irreverent yet sensitive view of the world of Santiago's tenement dwellers.

Further reading

Bravo Elizondo, P. (1986) 'Ramón Griffero: Nuevos espacios, nuevo teatro', *Latin American Theatre Review* 20(1): 95–101.

AMALIA PEREIRA

grotesco criollo

A dramatic form derived from the *sainete* which had been typical of Argentine drama since the nineteenth century. Its tragic, despairing vision of the world is simultaneously expressed in dramatic and comic situations full of absurd characters and deep ironies. Metaphorically, it decries the few possibilities open to newly arrived immigrants. In 1923 Armando **Discépolo** described his own play *Mateo* as 'grotesque'. In the 1930s, 'the infamous decade', the grotesque permeates the lyrics of tangos, films and literature. In the 1970s it returns again, particularly in the work of Roberto **Cossa**, in acerbic descriptions of everyday life and its uncertainties, which in their turn produce immorality, despair and madness.

Further reading

Kaiser-Lenoir, C. (1977) *El grotesco criollo: Estilo teatral de una época*, Havana: Casa de las Américas.

Viñas, D. (1973) *Grotesco, inmigración y fracaso*, Buenos Aires: Corregidor.

NORA MAZZIOTTI

Grupo de Barranquilla

The Grupo de Barranquilla (Barranquilla Group) was a group of intellectuals – Álvaro Cepeda Samudio, Alfonso and José Félix Fuenmayor, Germán Vargas, Bernardo Restrepo Maya, Gabriel **García Márquez** and Alejandro Obregón – which emerged in 1940 with the arrival of Ramón Vinyes, an erudite Catalan, at the Colombian port of Barranquilla and lasted into the late 1950s. Their written production, issued in *Crónica* (Chronicle), the group's publication, and other media, is made up mostly of journalistic articles. In these, they harshly chastise the literary establishment of Bogotá, the Colombian capital, for its isolation, conventionalism and lack of acceptance of international literary influences. The group and its leader are gently caricatured in García Márquez's ***Cien años de soledad*** (One Hundred Years of Solitude) (1967).

Further reading

García Márquez, G. (2002) *Vivir para contarla*, New York: Knopf.

HÉCTOR D. FERNÁNDEZ L'HOESTE

Grupo Minorista

An intellectual movement emerging out of improvised gatherings in Havana during the early twenties, Grupo Minorista rapidly became the cultural and political epicentre of the epoch. Led by young left-wing intellectuals, its 1927 manifesto – the Declaración Minorista – expressed a spirit of rebellion against distortions of the Cuban cultural heritage and demanded changes in national political life. It had no organ of its own, but its members wrote regularly in journals such as *Social*, *Carteles* and the cultural supplement of the *Diario de la Marina*. Internal political and ideological tensions led to its collapse at the end of the decade.

WILFREDO CANCIO ISLA

guaracha del Macho Camacho, La

La guaracha del Macho Camacho (Macho Camacho's Beat) is a novel by the Puerto Rican Luis Rafael **Sánchez**, first published in Buenos Aires in 1976. Its title came from a popular song which is heard blasting out in the background throughout the novel. It was significant that this text should first have found acceptance outside its natural context, and equally significant that in the same year René **Marqués**, the most authoritative voice in Puerto Rican culture, published his novel *La mirada* (The Look) in Puerto Rico. Sánchez's novel had to wait for recognition until the early 1980s, when it coincided with the discursive break with the 'pessimist' canon.

In the novel, a prostitute, a corrupt politician, a retarded hydrocephalic child, a poor woman and a frusrated society lady meet for the purpose of creating the national saga of Puerto Rican *guachafita* (disorder). It is as if uninhibited sexuality, disorder and muddle are merely simulations whose purpose is to avoid confronting the existential problem; Sánchez's metafictional proposal seeks to find in humour and parody a secure refuge not only for these miserable beings, but also for the readers, who are as impotent and defenceless as the characters of the novel, and perhaps as the narrator himself, who invites his audience to join him in watching this grotesque tragicomedy.

Voices that intercept and quote one another, people in danger, popular culture, bourgeois clichés, intertextualities, slogans and warnings, all meet in the space of orality. For what finds expression in each chapter of *La guaracha* is the project of speaking in Puerto Rican, all of whose voices and accents find a place in its fictional heterogeneity. Sánchez constructs a metafictional cultural artefact, in which the co-existence of multiple languages permits him to develop a theory of Caribbean linguistic hybridism. Ana Lydia **Vega**, Juan Antonio Ramos and Edgardo **Rodríguez**, among others, have shared Sánchez's aesthetic project to set in train a new narrative.

These oppressed sectors who take the pages of the novel by storm are not the stereotypical figures of pre-industrial tradition, but serve to throw into relief the inequalities that have arisen within society itself. Faced with the impossibility of creating a new order, however, all that is left is laughter, carnival and the affirmation that 'life's great'.

Further reading

Barradas, E. (1981) *Para leer en puertorriqueño: Acercamiento a la obra de Luis Rafael Sánchez*, Rio Piedras, PR: Ed. Cultural.

Gelpi, J.G. (1993) *Literatura y paternalismo en Puerto Rico*, Rio Piedras, PR: Editorial de la Universidad de Puerto Rico.

Ramos, J. (1982) '*La guaracha del macho Camacho:* texto de cultura puertorriqueña', *Texto crítico* 8(24–5): 171–83.

MARÍA JULIA DAROQUI

Guardia, Gloria

b. 1940, Panama City

Writer

An important Panamanian writer, Guardia's *El último juego* (The Final Game) (1977) is a complicated experimental novel, critical of Panamanian dependency on the USA and political corruption. The plot deals with the terrorist kidnapping of a group of politicians by a guerrilla commando. Through several narrative voices, Guardia portrays the alienation and solitude of her characters in a world inundated by propaganda, consumerism and money. She has also published an important critical work on Pablo Antonio **Cuadra**, and numerous articles. She lives in Colombia.

Further reading

Camargo, A.M. (2001) 'El dilema humano frente al social, a través del tema del canal en *El último juego* de Gloria Guardia', *South Eastern Latin Americanist* 44(4): 51–61.

Guardia, G. (1977) *El último juego*, San José: Editorial Universitaria.

—— (1999) *Libertad de llamas*, Mexico City: Plaza y Janés.

NICASIO URBINA

Guarnieri, Gianfrancesco

b. 1934, Milan, Italy

Playwright and actor

One of Brazil's most important playwrights and an extraordinary actor, Guarnieri was born into a family of talented classical musicians who emigrated to Brazil in 1936. He began his professional career as an actor in São Paulo, at the newly founded Teatro de Arena (1953) in 1956. In 1958 he premiered his first play there, the realist political thriller *Eles não usam black tie* (They Don't Wear Black Tie). When Leon Hirszman adapted Guarnieri's play for the screen in 1981, Guarnieri co-wrote the script, updating the story to the politically turbulent 1970s. He also gave a fine performance as one of the protagonists, Otávio, a long-time leftist disturbed by the rising militancy of a new generation of activists including his own son. Guarnieri has continued writing for the stage and television, most recently (in 1999) starring in his own play, *Anjo na contramão* (Angel Going the Wrong Way) (co-written with his son, Cacau Guarnieri), in São Paulo.

Further reading

Guarnieri, G. (1966) *Eles não usam black-tie; peça em 3 atos e 6 quadros*, Sáo Paulo: Editora Brasiliense.

—— (1976) *Ponto de partida: Fábula em um ato*, São Paulo: Editora Brasiliense.
—— (2001) *O melhor teatro*, compiled by Décio de Almeida Prado, São Paulo: Global Editora.

ANA M. LÓPEZ

Guayaquil Group

A literary group consisting of Demetrio **Aguilera Malta**, José de la **Cuadra**, Joaquín **Gallegos Lara**, Enrique **Gil Gilbert** and Alfredo **Pareja Diezcanseco**. Its defining features were: a socialist-inspired exposé of socio-economic abuses; a literature rooted in popular culture; Freudianism; a grotesque vision of the world; and a concern with anthropology and indigenous culture. The Guayaquil Group is considered a forerunner of **magical realism**.

See also: Los que se van

Further reading

Adoum, J.E. (1984) *La gran literatura ecuatoriana del 30*, Quito: Editorial El Conejo.
Heise, K. (1975) *El Grupo de Guayaquil: Arte y técnica en sus novelas*, Madrid: Playor.

HUMBERTO E. ROBLES

Guebel, Daniel

b. 1956, Buenos Aires, Argentina

Writer

Guebel's first novel was *Arnulfo o los infortunios de un príncipe* (Arnulfo, the Misadventures of a Prince) (1987), but recognition as an accomplished and imaginative writer came with the Emecé Prize for *La perla del emperador* (The Emperor's Pearl) in 1990. Many have compared his work to that of César **Aira**. Guebel is also a journalist and a dramatist. His collaborations with Sergio Bizzio have been important and innovative contributions to Argentine theatre; they include *El amor* (Love), in which different love situations are resolved in sudden and dramatic scenes.

Further reading

Carricaburo, N. (1997) '*La perla del emperador* de Daniel Guebel y la teoría del Big Bang', *Letras* 35–6: 59–68.
Guebel, D. (1990) *La perla del emperador*, Buenos Aires: Emecé.
Zeiger, C. (2000) 'Guebel, o los infortunios de un escritor', *Radar libros* 30 April.

DANIEL LINK

Guedes, Lino

b. 1897, Campinas, São Paulo, Brazil; d. 1951, Campinas

Writer

Lino Guedes was a leading figure in black literary circles in Campinas and São Paulo during the 1920s and 1930s. He was editor-in-chief of the Afro-Brazilian newspaper in Campinas, *Getulino* (1923–24), and a frequent contributor to São Paulo's *Clarim d'Alvorada* (1924–35), which was an important vehicle for black social and political mobilization. He published eight volumes of poetry which dramatized the historical and contemporary tribulations of Afro-Brazilians. His poems about black communities of the *cortiços* (urban slums) in São Paulo register an early attempt to versify the colloquial speech of Afro-Brazilians.

Further reading

Malinoff, J. (1982) 'Poetry for the People: Lino Guedes and Black Folk Style in Early Twentieth-Century Afro-Brazilian Verse', *Research in African Literatures* 13(3): 366–82.

CHRISTOPHER DUNN

Guerra, Lucía

b. 1942, Santiago, Chile

Writer and critic

Guerra's work builds upon early Chilean feminist discourses. Her novel *Más allá de las máscaras* (Beyond the Masks) (1984) looks at women in history, and explores the hardships faced by women in a culture where even language is inherited from men. In her fiction and criticism, Guerra warns against feminist discourses centred on women's perspectives alone, particularly where, as in Latin America, men have also been subjected to colonization. Her *La mujer fragmentada: Historias de un signo* (The Fragmented Woman: Stories of a Sign) won the 1994 **Casa de las Américas** prize. Her critical work on María Luisa **Bombal** is of great importance.

Further reading

Guerra, L. (1986) *Más allá de las máscaras*, Pittsburgh: Latin American Literary Review Press.

Meuser, F. (1996) 'Lucía Guerra: Her Own Creative Voice', *Romance Languages Annual* 8: 573–5.

SANDRA GARABANO

guerrilla poetry

This is not an easy body of work to categorize, since its defining and unifying feature is neither aesthetic nor geographical, but political. Yet it is a recognizable group of writings, occurring simultaneously in time (largely in the 1960s) and disparately in space (from Central America to Peru). And it does present common characteristics, both in expression and register, and in the general circumstances of its conception and unfolding.

The Cuban Revolution of 1959 resonated throughout Latin America, and seemed to promise the possibility of confronting the economic and political power of the USA from a position of material weakness but moral strength. The success of Cuba's 26 July movement in bringing down the dictatorship of Fulgencio Batista, despite its limited numbers and primitive armament, validated the guerrilla method as a strategy for anti-imperialist struggle. Articulated by Ernesto Che Guevara in his manual *Guerrilla Warfare* (1963), it suggested that conviction, moral rectitude and the tactics of 'armed propaganda' could bring down even a militarily well-endowed and supported dictatorship.

For many young revolutionaries this provided the solution to their sense of isolation from the mass movement. Idealism and vision, the Cuban example suggested, could compensate for the lack of social forces at their disposal. And it is that idealism and vision which is expressed, and ideally so, in poetry. There is also a sense that this was a peculiarly male enterprise. There were, of course, women included among the guerrillas, but it was only in Central America in the struggles of the 1980s that females came to occupy key leadership roles in the armed struggle.

In Peru, the young poet Javier **Heraud** joined the ELN (National Liberation Army) in 1963. His economical, lyric poetry, written before his death in 1963, aged 21, expressed both his idealism and his belief in the redemptive power of words and armed struggle. Otto René **Castillo** was killed in Guatemala at the age of 31, in 1967, his legacy a collection of work including the iconic poem 'Vámonos patria a caminar' (Walk with Me My Country). In Nicaragua, the young students who joined the Sandinista Liberation Front to fight the dictatorship of Anastasio Somoza were imbued with the same self-belief. Many died in the struggles that culminated in Somoza's overthrow in 1979, among them Ricardo Morales, Leonel Rugama and Fernando Gordillo. Others, such as Gioconda **Belli**, lived to translate their convictions into support for a political project in power.

The poetry of Roque **Dalton**, a leader of the guerrilla movement in El Salvador, is more complex and varied than most of the guerrilla poets. Dalton came from a previous generation, and his poetry has a characteristically ironic and prosaic quality and an obviously satirical tone that suggests an idealism tempered by a richer and more uneven political experience. Dalton died in 1975 at the hands of dissident members of his own organization.

Idealism and a visionary quality were by no means limited to these young poets who died tragically young; nor were hope and conviction their monopoly. Indeed, poetry has often proved the most appropriate means for expressing Utopian hopes and humane aspirations. The guerrilla poets are one expression of those qualities.

Further reading

Benedetti, Mario (1980) *Poesía trunca*, Madrid: Visor.

Gonzalez, Mike and David Treece (1992) *A Gathering of Voices*, London: Verso.

Gott, Richard (1970) *Guerrilla Movements in Latin America*, London: Thomas Nelson.

Márquez, Robert (ed.) (1974) *Latin American Revolutionary Poetry*, New York: Monthly Review Press.

MIKE GONZALEZ

Guido, Beatriz

b. 1922, Rosario, Argentina; d. 1988, Madrid, Spain

Writer

Guido's fiction focuses obsessively on the decline of the Argentine upper classes and oligarchy. She summarized the relationship between history and fiction in her work with the formula 'to lie the truth'. Private, claustrophobic spaces such as home are her preferred locations, in which young people struggle through violent sexual rites of passage. Her husband, film-maker Leopoldo Torre Nilsson, adapted several of her works for the screen, for example *La casa del ángel* (The House of the Angel) (1957) and *La caída* (The Fall) (1959).

Further reading

Díaz, G.J. (1988) 'El nacionalismo argentino en la novelística de Beatriz Guido', *Alba de América* 10–11: 101–8.

Osorio, E. (1991) *Beatriz Guido*, Buenos Aires: Planeta.

SILVANA DASZUK

Guillén, Nicolás

b. 1902, Camagüey, Cuba; d. 1989, Havana, Cuba

Poet

Often considered the 'national poet' of Revolutionary Cuba, Guillén is one of the most important poets of the African diaspora and a central figure in the Latin American poetic canon. His poetry belongs to two traditions, ***negrismo*** or 'poesía negra', and social poetry, while also drawing on the rich tradition of Spanish verse.

Born in the year Cuba was officially declared independent, Guillén came from a relatively well-to-do family of Afro-Cuban ancestry, but his father, a high-ranking politician and newspaper editor, was assassinated in 1917 in a political reprisal, and Guillén was forced to take over financial responsibility for the family. His early poetry was primarily within the *modernista* vein. Later he was influenced by the avant-garde (see **avant-garde in Latin America**) aesthetics of poets such as Federico García Lorca and Langston Hughes, who explored popular traditions and colloquial diction. Guillén's first book of poems, *Motivos del son* (1930), represents Afro-Cuban speech while capturing the rhythmic form of the 'son', a popular music form combining African and Spanish elements. By his second collection, *Sóngoro cosongo* (1931), he called this 'mulatto poetry', emphasizing the transculturation (see **cultural theory**) central to the formation of a new Cuban culture. Guillén continued to write in this form throughout the 1930s and 1940s, giving voice to the under-represented and mounting an anti-imperialist critique in *West Indies, Ltd.* (1934), *Cantos para soldados y sones para turistas* (Songs for Soldiers and Sons for Tourists) (1937) and *El son entero: Summa poética, 1929–1946* (1947). He also embraced leftist politics, becoming a member of the Communist Party of Cuba, supporting the Republicans in the Spanish Civil War and attending the anti-fascist Second International Conference of Writers for the Defense of Culture in Madrid in 1937, with fellow Latin American poets César **Vallejo**, Pablo **Neruda**, Octavio **Paz** and others. Like Vallejo and Neruda, he published a collection of poems about the conflict, *Poema en cuatro angustias y una esperanza* (Poem in Four Anguishes and a

Hope) (1937). In the next two decades Guillén adopted an increasingly critical stance toward the Cuban government (dominated by the dictator Fulgencio Batista), which resulted in his exile in 1953. He returned in 1959, three weeks after the triumph of the Revolution.

Guillén played a leading role in the cultural politics of the Cuban Revolution as president of the newly formed Union of Writers and Artists of Cuba (**UNEAC**); his full endorsement of the Utopian urge of the Revolution is evident in his 1964 *Tengo* (I Have). Guillén's later work, especially *Diario que a diario* (Daily Diary) (1972), shows his always mordant sense of humour and ardent anti-imperialism, while also bringing poetry into critical contact with the discourse of history, through the integration of snippets of newspaper articles, advertisements and official documents.

Further reading

Ellis, K. (1983) *Cuba's Nicolás Guillén: Poetry and Ideology*, Toronto: University of Toronto Press.

Guillén, N. (1972) *Man-Making Words: Selected Poems*, trans. R. Márquez and D.A. McMurray, Amherst: University of Massachusetts Press.

Kubayanda, J. (1990) *The Poet's Africa: Africanness in the Poetry of Nicolás Guillén and Aimé Césaire*, New York: Greenwood Press.

Kutzinski, V.M. (1989) 'Nicolás Guillén', in C.A. Solé and M.I. Abreu (eds), *Latin American Writers*, New York: Scribners, 2, 947–55.

Smart, I. (1997) 'Nicolás Guillén', in V. Smith (ed.), *Encyclopedia of Latin American Literature*, London: Fitzroy Dearborn, 391–3.

Williams, L.V. (1982) *Self and Society in the Poetry of Nicolás Guillén*, Baltimore, MD: Johns Hopkins University Press.

BEN A. HELLER

Güiraldes, Ricardo

b. 1886, Buenos Aires, Argentina;
d. 1927, Paris, France

Writer

Güiraldes immortalized the gaucho legend in his 1926 novel *Don Segundo Sombra*, a classic of Argentine literature (adapted for the screen by Leonardo Favio). His tale of the rite of passage of the 14-year-old Fabio from *guacho* (orphan) to gaucho and then to landowner boss has been labelled a *bildungsroman*, a tale of apprenticeship and development under the tutelage of the seasoned gaucho Don Segundo. The novel evokes the disappearing rural world of the gauchos and is a remembrance of an idealized pastoral world in which individualism, patriarchy, freedom and nature are superior values. **Borges** has called the novel an elegy rather than an epic: '*DSS* seeks to compensate for that loss by recalling vigorous tales of old'. Güiraldes's novel is central to the debates within Latin American vanguardism concerning nativist writing and cosmopolitan influences, as well as the reformulation of national traditions throughout Latin America. Later critics (for example, J. **Ludmer**) have shown what is at stake in Güiraldes's depoliticizing of the guachesque tradition and the significance of Fabio's transformation from displaced orphan to aristocratic landowner. His nostalgic evocation of the disappearing life of the pampas became an Argentine national myth, particularly notable for its portrait of gaucho life and reproduction of vernacular speech. *DSS* is considered one of Latin America's most important regionalist novels of the early twentieth century, particularly notable for its experimental style.

Prior to the success of *Don Segundo Sombra*, Güiraldes published poetry (*El cencerro de cristal* (The Glass Bell)) (1915) and fiction (*Cuentos de muerte y de sangre* (Stories of Death and Blood), 1915; *Raucho*, 1917; *Xaimaca*, 1923) and was a senior member of the avant-garde groups associated with ***Proa*** and ***Martín Fierro***. Belonging to a wealthy Argentine family, Güiraldes was a cosmopolitan, travelling the world – Europe, Asia, Latin America and the Caribbean – with long residences in Paris.

Further reading

Alonso, C. (1990) 'Don Segundo Sombra', in *The Spanish American Regional Novel: Modernity and Autochthony*, Cambridge: Cambridge University Press, 79–108.

Battistessa, A.J. (1987) *Ricardo Güiraldes. En la huella spiritual y expresiva de un argentino (1886–1986)*, Buenos Aires: Corregidor.
Castagnino, R.H. (1989) 'Ricardo Güiraldes', in C.A. Solé and M.I. Abreu (eds), *Latin American Writers*, New York: Scribners, 2, 619–27.
Güiraldes, R. (1995) *Don Segundo Sombra*, critical edition in English with essays by Alberto Blasi, Noé Jitrik, Gwen Kirkpatrick, Francine Masiello, Ernesto Sábato, Beatriz Sarlo and P.O. Steiner, trans. Patricia Owen Steiner, ed. Gwen Kirkpatrick. Pittsburgh and London: University of Pittsburgh Press/UNESCO-Colección Archivos.
Jitrik, Noé (1968) 'Ricardo Güiraldes', in *Capítulo. La Historia de la literatura argentina*, Buenos Aires: CEAL, 265–88.
Leland, C.T. (1986) 'The Failure of Myth: Ricardo Gúiraldes and *Don Segundo Sombra*, in *The Last Happy Men: The Generation of 1922. Fiction, and the Argentine Reality*, Syracuse, NY: Syracuse University Press, 119–47.
Sarlo, B. (1988) *Una modernidad periférica. Buenos Aires 1920 y 1930*, Buenos Aires: Nueva Visión.

GWEN KIRKPATRICK

Gullar, (José Ribamar) Ferreira

b. 1930, Sao Luis do Maranhão, Brazil

Poet

A member of the Generation of 1945, Gullar published *A luta corporal* (The Corporal Struggle) in 1954. Two years later he participated in the first exposition of **concrete poetry** in São Paulo. However, the abstract notion of the visual soon gave way to the sensuality of the word, and Gullar went on to found the neo-concrete movement. Gullar's interest in popular culture and the social function of poetry was sparked in the 1960s when he directed the Fundação Cultural (Cultural Foundation). Always polemical, he has contributed to the social, political and historical reintegration of Brazilian culture as poet, playwright, art critic and president of FUNARTE during José Sarney's presidency.

Further reading

Gullar, (José Ribamar) Ferreira (1954) *A luta corporal*, Rio de Janeiro: Civilização Brasileira.
—— (1968) *Por você, por mim*, Rio de Janeiro: Sped.
—— (1987) *Toda poesía (1950–1987)*, Rio de Janeiro: José Olympio Editora.
—— (1989) *Poemas escolhidos*, Rio de Janeiro: Ediouro.
Guyer, L. (1987) 'An Interview with Ferreira Gullar', *Discurso Literário* 5(1): 27–41.
—— (1997) 'Ferreira Gullar', in V. Smith (ed.), *Encyclopedia of Latin American Literature*, London: Fitzroy Dearborn, 405–7.
Kovadloff, S. (1988) 'Ferreira Gullar: Poesía y persona', *Cuadernos hispanoamericanos* 461: 61–76.

PEGGY SHARPE

Gusman, Luis

b. 1944, Buenos Aires, Argentina

Writer

Gusman was a founding member of the artistic avant-garde of the 1970s, grouped around the journal *Literal*. In 1973 he published 'El frasquito' (The Little Bottle), a story rightly acclaimed for the power of its writing, and which many have associated with the work of Osvaldo **Lamborghini**. His ten published works include *En el corazón de junio* (In the Heart of June) (1983), his autobiography *La rueda de Virgilio* (Virgil's Wheel) (1988) and *La música de Frankie* (Frankie's Music) (1993).

Further reading

Balderston, D. (1988) 'Latent Meanings in Ricardo Piglia's *Respiración artificial* and Luis Gusman's *En el corazón de junio*', *Revista canadiense de estudios hispánicos* 12(2): 207–19.
Gusman, L. (1983) *En el corazón de junio*, Buenos Aires: Editorial Sudamericana.
Link, D. (1985) 'Sobre Gusman, la realidad y sus parientes', *Filología* 20(1): 197–212.

DANIEL LINK

Gutiérrez, Pedro Juan

b. 1950, Matanzas, Cuba

Writer

It was the *Trilogía sucia de La Habana* (Dirty Havana Trilogy) of 1998 that first brought Gutiérrez to public notice internationally. Although he has lived in Havana all his life, and published poetry there, the *Trilogía* was first published abroad. Its characteristic 'dirty realism' and explicit sexual language earned it a kind of cult status. Its picture of Havana in 1994, crumbling and apocalyptic, explains the disapproval of Cuban literary authorities. His second novel *El rey de la Habana* (The King of Havana) was published in 1999 and chronicles the short and tragic life of two young lovers in the same crumbling and corrupted city. His third, *Animal tropical* (Tropical Animal) (2000), translated into English in 2003, was published in Cuba in the same year. Its central character is once again Pedro Juan, a journalist whose life closely parallels that of its author.

Further reading

Clark, Stephen (2003) 'El rey de Centro Habana; conversación con Pedro Juan Gutiérrez', available at www.librusa.com/entrevista7.htm.

MIKE GONZALEZ

Gutiérrez Girardot, Rafael

b. 1928, Sogamoso, Colombia

Literary critic

The most prominent Colombian intellectual figure of his generation, Gutiérrez Girardot studied philosophy, literature and sociology in Spain and Germany. As a literature professor, he taught at the universities of Cologne, Munster, Bochum and Bonn in Germany. In 1970, he founded the Hispanic Studies department at the University of Bonn, where he is currently a professor. His deep and analytical capacity to approach texts allows him to establish different and interesting connections with brilliant assertiveness. In 2002, Gutiérrez Girardot received the Alfonso Reyes International Award for his outstanding academic career. He has written several works and essays on Alfonso **Reyes**, Hegel and dialectics, Heidegger, Kafka and **Borges**, and has translated Nietzsche, Hölderlin, Friedrich and Janoska-Bendl. One of his most polemical articles, 'América sin realismos mágicos' (America without Magical Realisms) (1989), questions the traditional and endemic **post-Boom** view of Latin American literature.

Further reading

Gutiérrez Girardot, Rafael (1989) *Hispanoamérica: Imágenes y perspectivas*, Bogotá: Temis.

—— (1990) *La formación del intelectual hispanoamericano en el siglo XIX*, series no. 3, University of Maryland at College Park: Latin American Studies Center.

—— (1992) *Provocaciones*, Bogotá: Fundación Editorial Investigar/Fundación Nuestra América Mestiza.

—— (1994) *Cuestiones*, Mexico City: Fondo de Cultura Económica.

—— (1996) 'Moriré callando', in *Tres poetisas judías: Gertrude Kolmar, Else Lasker-Schüler, Nelly Sachs*, Barcelona: Montesinos.

ALVARO BERNAL

Guy, Rosa

b. 1928, Diego Martin, Trinidad

Novelist

Taken as a child to Harlem in 1932, Rosa Guy (Rosa Cuthbert) grew up there and participated in the Harlem Renaissance. She writes primarily for children and young adults, and has published thirteen major works of fiction as well as a play, and edited a collection of writings by young African-Americans of the 1960s. In the 1940s she worked with the American Negro Theater and was influenced by the revolutionary politics of black *Garveyites*, Martin Luther King, Jr, and Malcolm X. In 1951 she became the founding president of the Harlem Writers' Guild and began writing seriously.

Her first novel, *Birds at My Window*, was published in 1966.

Further reading

Guy, R. (1990) 'The Human Spirit', in Selwyn R. Cudjoe (ed.), *Caribbean Women Writers: Essays from the First International Conference*, Wellesley: Calaloux, distributed by the University of Massachusetts Press.

—— (2001) *Birds at My Window*, Minneapolis: Coffee House Press.

FUNSO AIYEJINA

Guzmán, Augusto

b. 1903, Cochabamba, Bolivia; d. 1994, Cochabamba

Writer

Productive in almost every literary genre, Guzmán wrote novels, essays, criticism and biography. *La sima fecunda* (The Fruitful Abyss) (1933), a novel set in the valleys of Cochabamba, and *Prisionero de guerra* (Prisoner of War) (1937), which addresses the problems of prisoners during the Chaco War, are his best-known works. He is also the author of a number of critical approaches to Bolivian literature. His essays often address religious issues, a topic rarely discussed in Bolivia, as in his *El Cristo viviente* (The Living Christ) (1981).

Further reading

Echevarría, E. (1977) *La novela social en Bolivia*, La Paz: Difusión.

Francovich, G. (1956) *El pensamiento boliviano en el siglo XX*, Mexico City: Fondo de Cultura Económica.

Guzmán, A. (1973) *Panorama de la novela en Bolivia*, La Paz: Amigos del Libro.

—— (1982) *Biografías de la literatura boliviana*, Cochabama: Los Amigos del Libro.

—— (1983) *El ensayo en Bolivia*, Cochabama: Los Amigos del Libro.

MARÍA DORA VILLA GÓMEZ

Guzmán, Martín Luis

b. 1887, Chihuahua, Mexico; d. 1976, Mexico City

Writer

A participant in the Mexican Revolution (1910–17), Guzmán was also one of its principal chroniclers (see **novel of the Mexican Revolution**). He was associated with the intellectual movement known as the Ateneo de la Juventud and worked with the Madero government, resigning his post when it was overthrown by Victoriano Huerta in 1913. From his youth, Guzmán was an active political journalist, and was personally acquainted with most of the leading actors in the Revolution – including Venustiano Carranza (whom he criticized bitterly) and Pancho Villa – who appear in his novels. He spent several periods in political exile in the USA (1916–20) and Spain (1915–16, 1925–36), where he adopted Spanish citizenship to show solidarity with the Republican government. While in Spain he contributed to several Madrid newspapers and later joined the editorial board of *El Sol* and *La Voz*. On returning to Mexico he played an important role as the founder of a publishing house and as editor of the journals *Romance* and *Tiempo*. Having been a strong critic of the post-Revolutionary regime, Guzmán ended his life as a senator for the official party.

Guzmán's first book, published in 1915 in New York, was *La querella de México* (The Mexico Debate), a powerful reflection on the lack of direction in the Mexican Revolution after the fall of Díaz. His major novel, *La sombra del caudillo* (The Shadow of the Chief) (1929), was originally published in instalments in Mexican and foreign newspapers, as was his memoir of life during the Revolution, *El águila y la serpiente* (The Eagle and the Serpent) (1928), which gained him a wide audience. In the first novel, Guzmán chronicles the events of the period 1913–15, when various political factions were disputing the control of the nation. The second work exposed the bloody power struggle between the politicians who had inherited the revolutionary mantle but not its democratic and revolutionary ideals. It was Pancho Villa who fascinated Guzmán, and who provided the inspiration for his most ambitious work, *Memorias de Pancho*

Villa (Pancho Villa's Memoirs), written in the first-person from the perspective of Villa. This work was published in four volumes between 1936 and 1951. Despite his dedication, Guzmán never successfully found the form or the language that could express the particular characteristics of Villa's elusive figure. While revered as a writer of the Mexican Revolution, Guzmán is today under-appreciated as one of the most polished prose writers in Mexican literature and one of Latin America's early innovators in describing urban experience.

Further reading

Abreu Gómez, E. (1968) *Martín Luis Guzmán*, Mexico City: Empresas Editoriales.

Guzmán, M.L. (1965) *The Eagle and the Serpent*, trans. H. de Onís, New York: Dolphin Books.

—— (1965) *Memories of Pancho Villa*, Austin: University of Texas Press.

Gyurko, L.A. (1989) 'Martín Luis Guzmán', in C.A. Solé and M.I. Abreu (eds), *Latin American Writers*, New York: Scribners, 2, 655–62.

McMurray, G.R. (1997) 'Martín Luis Guzmán', in V. Smith (ed.), *Encyclopedia of Latin American Literature*, London: Fitzroy Dearborn, 410–11.

Rutherford, J. (1971) *Mexican Society during the Revolution: A Literary Approach*, Oxford: Clarendon Press.

RAFAEL OLEA FRANCO AND BRIAN GOLLNICK

H

Hahn, Oscar

b. 1938, Iquique, Chile

Poet

Hahn combines the literary language of the classic Spanish tradition with colloquial expressions and elements of contemporary lyric poetry in poetic and philosophical explorations of love and death. His works include *Mal de amor* (Love Breaks) (1981), *Imágenes nucleares* (Nuclear Images) (1983), *Estrellas fijas en un cielo blanco* (Fixed Stars in an Open Sky) (1989) and *Versos robados* (Stolen Verses) (1995). His work has been translated by James Hoggard as *The Art of Dying* (1987, *Love Breaks* (1991) and *Stolen Verses* (2001). He teaches at the University of Iowa.

Further reading

Hahn, 0. (2001) *Magias de la escritura*, Santiago, Chile: Editorial Andres Bello.

—— (2002) *Apariciones profanas*, Madrid: Hiperión.

Lastra, P. (2002) *El arte de Oscar Hahn*, Lima: Santo Oficio.

Nemes, G. (1977) 'Entrevista a Oscar Hahn', *Prismal/Cabral* 1: 47–51.

Rosado, G. (1987) 'La poesía de Oscar Hahn', *Atenea* 455: 149–57.

ELIANA ORTEGA

Halac, Ricardo

b. 1935, Buenos Aires, Argentina

Playwright

Halac's plays – *Soledad para cuatro* (Solitude for Four) (1961), *Estela de madrugada* (Dawn Trail) (1965) and *Fin de diciembre* (End of December) (1965) – are within the critical realist tradition, nourished by the discontent, solitude and frustration of the middle class. Later he adopted in his work a style akin to the ***grotesco criollo*** to explore the crisis of a couple (in *Segundo tiempo* (Second Half) (1976)) or of a family (*Un trabajo fabuloso* (A Great Job) (1980)) through parody and humour. He has also written scripts for television series such as *Compromiso* and the investigative programme *Yo fui testigo* (I Was a Witness).

Further reading

Glickman, N. (1990) 'Entrevista con Ricardo Halac', *Latin American Theatre Review* 23(2): 55–61.

Halac, Ricardo (1962) *Soledad para cuatro*, Buenos Aires: Talía.

—— (1991) *Teatro de Ricardo Halac, Tomo 1*, Buenos Aires: Ediciones Corregidor.

—— (2000) *Teatro*, Buenos Aires: Corregidor.

Woodyard, G. (1998) 'Making America or Making Revolution: The Theatre of Ricardo Halac in Argentina', in Richard Boon and Jane Plastow (eds), *Theatre Matters: Politics, Culture and Performance*, Cambridge: Cambridge University Press.

NORA MAZZIOTTI

Halley Mora, Mario

b. 1926, Coronel Oviedo, Paraguay

Writer

Author of more than fifteen published plays including the two volumes of *Teatro paraguayo* (Paraguayan Theatre), Halley is the most prolific Paraguayan playwright of the twentieth century. He was also chief editor of the newspaper *Patria* during the Stroessner regime, radio librettist during the 1950s, script writer (as Alex) of the first Paraguayan Guarani comic strips, and editor of the newspaper *La Unión* (1990s). Among his many novels, *Ocho mujeres y las demás* (Eight Women and the Rest) was hailed as the most widely read novel of 1994 in Paraguay.

Further reading

Halley Mora, M. (1990) *La quema de Judas*, Asunción: Editorial Comuneros.

—— (1994) *Ocho mujeres y los demás*, Asunción: Editorial El Lector.

—— (1996) *Amor de invierno*, Asunción: Editorial El Lector.

Vallejos, R. (1971) *La literatura paraguaya, como expresión de la realidad nacional*, Asunción, Editorial 'Don Bosco'.

TERESA MÉNDEZ-FAITH

Hamilton, Judith

b. 1952, Spanish Town, St Catherine, Jamaica

Poet

Belonging to the 'new' generation of Caribbean poets, Hamilton claims Mervyn **Morris** and the late poets Anthony **McNeill** and Dennis **Scott** as influences. Morris's legacy is economy and craft: Hamilton's poems are brief, recalling haiku. Scott's gift is careful lineation and the occasional surreal image, and McNeill's is whimsy, the spare power of images, Jamaica-talk as 'noise in the street'. Hamilton's work has appeared in anthologies such as *Focus 1983*, *From Our Yard* and *Caribbean New Voices I*. *Rain Carvers* (1992) was her first collection.

PAT DUNN AND PAMELA MORDECAI

Harris, Claire

b. 1937, Port-of-Spain, Trinidad

Poet

Claire Harris's major preoccupations in her generally experimental poetry include racism, minority rights and expatriation. Author of five collections of poetry; her *Fables from the Women's Quarters* (1984) won the Americas' regional award of the Commonwealth Poetry Prize (1985). Her writing has been influenced by a wide range of writers, especially European surrealists and prose poem writers. Harris studied at University College, Dublin, Ireland; the University of the West Indies, Jamaica; and the University of Nigeria, Nsukka. She emigrated to Calgary, Alberta, Canada in 1966 in order to teach. She has travelled extensively and participated in community literary activities in Canada.

Further reading

Harris, C. (1986) 'Poets in Limbo', *A Mazing Space: Writing Canadian Women Writing*, Edmonton: Longspoon.

Reid, M. (1984) 'Choosing Control: An Interview with Claire Harris', *Waves* 13(1): 37–41.

FUNSO AIYEJINA

Harris, Wilson

b. 1921, New Amsterdam, British Guiana

Writer

A visionary and original novelist, Harris left school at 17 to become a land surveyor and led a number of expeditions into the jungle of British Guiana between 1941 and 1953. These jungle expeditions were extremely important to Harris and his later work. So profound were his experiences that conventional forms of fiction proved inadequate to their expression; so too did poetry, which seemed too limited to render fully a fantastical Amerindian culture. He turned, therefore, to poetic prose to present the spirit of Amerindian mythology in conflict with the European conquerors.

Indeed, Harris seems to suggest that we cannot become truly civilized until we examine thoroughly, and with empathy, the nature of existence in the pre-Columbian world and the tragedies inflicted on its humanity and natural history. The result is a narrative that is sometimes difficult but at the same time a testimony to the possibility of a universal spiritual revival. His twenty novels include *Heartland* (1964), *Age of the Rainmakers* (1971), *Resurrection at Sorrow Hill* (1993) and *Jonestown* (1997).

Further reading

Drake, S.E. (1986) *Wilson Harris and the Modern Tradition: A New Architecture of the World*, New York: Greenwood Press.

Gilkes, M. (1975) *Wilson Harris and the Caribbean Novel*, London: Longman.

Harris, W. (1988) *The Palace of the Peacock*, London: Faber & Faber.

—— (1993) *Resurrection at Sorrow Hill*, London: Faber & Faber.

James, C.L.R. (1965) *Wilson Harris: A Philosophical Approach*, St Augustine, Trinidad: University of the West Indies.

Maes-Jelinek, H. (ed.) (1991) *Wilson Harris: The Uncompromising Imagination*, Sydney: Dangaroo Press.

KEITH JARDIM

Haseth, Carel P. de

b. 1950, Curaçao, Netherlands Antilles

Writer and politician

A chemist by profession, de Haseth has written both in Dutch and in Papiamentu. In his poetry collection in the native creole language, *Poesia venená* (Venomous Poetry) (1985), and a short novel, *Katibu di shon* (A Master's Slave) (1988), he depicted Curaçao society as ethnically mixed. This involved him in serious debates with those who tended to privilege Afro-Caribbean people and their socio-cultural aspects as more authentically Curaçaoan. Since 1994 he has been a full-time politician.

AART G. BROEK

Hasta no verte Jesús mío

Elena **Poniatowska**'s second book, *Hasta no verte Jesús mío* (Until I See You, My Lord) (1969), is a testimonial narrative (see ***testimonio***) tracing the long, hard life of Jesusa Palancares, a slightly fictionalized version of Josefina Bórquez, a feisty washer-woman and former *soldadera* living in a Mexico City shanty town during the 1960s. (For a photograph of Josefina Bórquez and the youthful Poniatowska in 1963, see Steele 1992.)

The contours of Jesusa's life mirror those of the modern Mexican peasantry and sub-proletariat, from the impoverished, violent patriarchal countryside of the Porfiriato, to the alienated individuals of the Mexican Revolution, and on to the ranks of survivors, mainly women and children, who flooded into Mexico City's slums after the Revolution. Jesusa's lingering sense of betrayal and disappointment, and her unsatisfying professional and family life, echo the failures of the Revolution to meet the needs of the country's impoverished masses.

This is the first of many texts in which Poniatowska fashions a unique narrative voice, combining the ideolects of a multitude of poor Mexicans she has known, from every region of the country. On the surface this use of popular dialect to address progressive socio-political themes, by a daughter of the European nobility, seems highly contradictory. In fact this contradiction constitutes the core of the hybrid originality of this text and of testimonial narrative in general. As she describes in an autobiographical essay originally published in ***Vuelta*** in 1978, 'And here's to you, Jesusa', Poniatowska has always managed to negotiate, if at some personal cost, between her mother's world and that of Jesusa Palancares; between a cocktail party at the French Embassy and a hovel in one of Mexico City's most wretched slums. Poniatowska again wrote eloquently about this poignant and difficult balancing act, that of the committed intellectual woman in a developing country, in an essay on the death of Jesusa Palancares that is included in her collection of essays on Mexican women, *Luz y luna, las lunitas* (Light and the Moon, Little Moons) (1994).

Further reading

Jorgensen, B. (1994) *The Writing of Elena Poniatowska*, Austin: University of Texas Press.

Kerr, L. (1992) 'Gestures of Authorship: Lying to Tell the Truth in Elena Poniatowska's *Hasta no verte Jesús mío*', in *Reclaiming the Author: Figures and Fictions from Spanish America*, Durham, NC: Duke University Press.

Poniatowska, E. (1969) *Hasta no verte Jesús mío*, Mexico City: Ediciones Era.

—— (1978) 'Hasta no verte Jesús mío: Jesusa Palancares', *Vuelta* 24: 7–9; English translation in Doris Meyer (ed.), *Lives on the Line*, Berkeley: University of California Press, 1988.

—— (1994) *Luz y luna, las lunitas*, Mexico City: Ediciones Era.

Risse, K. (1997) 'Following the Procession: Dialogue with the Significant Other in Elena Poniatowska's *Hasta no verte, Jesús mío*', *Romance Review*, Fall; 7: 45–52.

Sommer, D. (1999) *Proceed with Caution, When Engaged by Minority Writing in the Americas*, Cambridge, MA: Harvard University Press.

Steele, C. (1992) 'Gender, Genre and Authority', in *Politics, Gender, and the Mexican Novel, 1968–1988: Beyond the Pyramid*, Austin: University of Texas Press.

Villalobos, J.P. (1995) 'La problematización feminista en *Hasta no verte Jesus mío*', in M. Alegría de la Colina *et al.* (eds), *Nuevas ideas; viejas creencias: La cultura mexicana hacia el siglo XXI*, Azcapotzalco, Mexico: Universidad Autonoma Metropolitana, Azcapotzalco, 281–91.

CYNTHIA STEELE

Hatoum, Milton

b. 1952, Manaus, Brazil

Novelist

Few Brazilian writers have explored the intersections and disjunctions between the locally and ethnically specific and the national and global dimension as has Milton Hatoum in his two novels, *Relato de um Certo Oriente* (The Tree of the Seventh Heaven) (1989), which received the 1989 Jabuti Prize, and *Amazonas, palavras e imagens de um rio entre ruínas* (Amazonia, Words and Images of a River among Ruins) (1979). Without relying on facile notions of *mestizaje* or syncretism, Hatoum recreates his Arabic background in a dense and multi-layered chronicle of the 1920s Christian and Muslim Lebanese immigration to the Amazonian city of Manaus.

Further reading

Mata, R. (1996) 'El orient de una novela', *Remate de Males*, 16: 101–8.

CÉSAR BRAGA-PINTO

Hearne, John

b. 1926, Montreal, Canada; d. 1994, Kingston, Jamaica

Writer

Hearne is a significant, if atypical, figure in the post-war development of the West Indian novel. Living mainly in London and Paris, he published five novels of which *Voices Under the Window* (1954) and *Land of the Living* (1961) remain the finest. In these, Hearne explored the role of the middle-class liberal on the imaginary island of Cayuna, based on Jamaica. In 1962 he returned to Jamaica and became Head of the Creative Arts Centre at Mona. His fine last novel, *The Sure Salvation* (1981), set on a slave ship, explores the historical roots of conflict in the Caribbean.

Further reading

Binder, W. (1984) 'Subtleties of Enslavement: An Interview with the Jamaican Writer John Hearne', *Komparatistische Hefte* 9–10: 101–13.

Cartey, W. (1969) 'The Novels of John Hearne', *Journal of Commonwealth Literature* 7: 45–58.

Hearne, J. (1982) *The Sure Salvation*, New York: St Martin's Press.

—— (1985) *Voices Under the Window*, London: Faber & Faber.

LOUIS JAMES

Heath, Roy

b. 1926, Georgetown, British Guiana

Novelist

Roy Heath grew up in Georgetown, where all his novels are set, although in 1951 he settled in London. His first novel, *A Man Come Home* (1974), revealed a disturbing vision in which detailed realism thinly masks the tensions of a claustrophobic Guyanese society, which develops into violence in *The Murderer* (1978), a *Guardian* fiction prize-winner. *From the Heat of the Day* (1979) began a three-part saga of a Georgetown family. *Kwaku* (1982), a tragi-comedy with a trickster hero, reflects a Guyana in social disintegration. *Shadows Round the Moon* (1990) is his autobiography.

Further reading

Heath, R. (1980) *From the Heat of the Day*, New York: Schocken Books.

—— (1993) *The Murderer*, New York: Persea Books.

—— (1997) *Kwaku*, London: Marion Boyars.

McWatt, M. (1990) 'Wives and Other Victims in the Novels of Roy A.K. Heath', in *Out of the Kumbla: Caribbean Women and Literatures*, Trenton, NJ: Africa World Press.

LOUIS JAMES

Helman, Albert (Lou Lichtveld)

b. 1903, Paramaribo, Suriname; d. 1996, Hilversum, the Netherlands

Writer, historian and diplomat

The first and most prolific writer from Suriname to publish in Dutch, Helman went to the Netherlands in his teens, but later worked in Suriname. He represented the Netherlands at the United Nations in New York, travelled widely and spent his final years in the Netherlands. His writing reflects his wide travels, but he is best remembered for his novels and short stories from Suriname. He was awarded an honorary doctorate from the University of Amsterdam for his literary and scholarly achievements, among which his 1983 critical historiography of the Guyanas, *De foltering van Eldorado* (The Torturing of El Dorado), is outstanding.

Further reading

Rutgers, W. (1982) 'Caribbean Plantation Literature in Dutch', *Germanic Notes* 13(2): 19–22.

AART G. BROEK

Hendriks, Arthur Lemiére

b. 1922, Kingston, Jamaica

Poet and broadcaster

In 1950 Hendriks began a career developing broadcast services in the Caribbean. From 1961 he was General Manager of the Jamaican Broadcasting Corporation, and in the 1960s he was director of Thompson Television in Bermuda, before finally settling in England. A writer of both short stories and verse, he is best known for his volumes of poetry, *On this Mountain* (1965), *These Green Islands* (1971) and *Muet – Poems* (1972). Elegant, precise and objective, his work is marked by a simple clarity and reflects an inner peace uncharacteristic of most contemporary Jamaican verse.

LOUIS JAMES

Henriquez, May

b. 1915, Curaçao, Netherlands Antilles

Writer and sculptor

A poet and short story writer in Papiamentu as well as the author of two studies about the idiomatic contributions of the Sephardic Jews to Papiamentu, Henriquez (née Alvarez-Correa) has also translated works by Molière, Shakespeare, Shaw and Sartre into Papiamentu, thus contributing substantially to the development of the dramatic arts in Curaçao. After studying in Paris with Zadkine, she also distinguished herself as a sculptor. As a member of the Board of Supervisory Directors of the Maduro & Curiel's Bank, she was instrumental in the bank's extensive support for local arts.

AART G. BROEK

Henríquez Ureña, Camila

b. 1894, Santo Domingo, Dominican Republic; d. 1973, Santo Domingo

Writer

Like her brother Pedro **Henríquez Ureña**, Camila spent most of her life outside the Dominican Republic. She obtained her PhD in Cuba, where she founded the Lyceum and the Instituto Hispano-Cubano de Cultura. She taught literature in Cuba and in the USA. As a feminist, Camila participated actively in conferences and associations. Some of her works, such as *Feminismo y otros temas sobre las mujeres en la sociedad* (Feminism and Other Subjects on Women in Society), were published posthumously in the 1980s.

Further reading

Henríquez Ureña, Camila (1982) *Estudios y conferencias*, Ciudad de La Habana: Editorial Letras Cubanas.

FERNANDO VALERIO-HOLGUÍN

Henríquez Ureña, Max

b. 1885, Santo Domingo, Dominican Republic; d. 1968, Santo Domingo

Writer

Like his brother Pedro **Henríquez Ureña**, Max was a fiction writer, historian, literary critic and professor. Among his most important books are *Panorama histórico de la literatura dominicana* (Historical Overview of Dominican Literature) (1945) and his *Breve historia del modernismo* (Brief History of Modernismo) (1954). He lived in Cuba, Mexico and Puerto Rico for many years, was a minister and diplomat during Trujillo's dictatorship, and taught literature at the Universidad Autónoma de Santo Domingo and Universidad Nacional Pedro Henríquez Ureña.

Further reading

Henríquez Ureña, M. (1954) *Breve historia del modernismo*, Mexico City: Fondo de Cultura Económica.

—— (1960) *De Rimbaud a Pasternak y Quasimodo: Ensayos sobre literaturas contemporáneas*, Mexico City: Fondo de Cultura Económica.

FERNANDO VALERIO-HOLGUÍN

Henríquez Ureña, Pedro

b. 1884, Santo Domingo, Dominican Republic; d. 1946, Buenos Aires, Argentina

Writer

Poet, literary critic, linguist and professor, Henríquez Ureña came from an intellectual family: his maternal grandfather and his mother were both poets. His father, Francisco Henríquez y Carvajal, was an educator and President of the Dominican Republic. His brother Max **Henríquez Ureña** and his sister Camila **Henríquez Ureña** were also important writers.

From 1900 onwards, Pedro lived in the USA, Spain, Cuba, Mexico and Argentina. A friend of Alfonso **Reyes** and José **Vasconcelos**, he influenced an entire generation of young **intellectuals** and promoted the foundation of the Escuela de Altos Estudios at the Universidad de México. He founded the Centro de Estudios Históricos (Center for Historical Studies) with Ramón Menéndez Pidal in Spain. He taught at the Universidad de La Plata in Argentina, where he became friends with Jorge Luis **Borges** and Ernesto **Sábato**.

Henríquez Ureña started his career writing poetry, which he abandoned in order to focus on criticism. His early poems were collected in the 1946 book *Poesías juveniles* (Juvenile Poems). In the early twentieth century, he published *Ensayos críticos* (Critical Essays) (1905), *Horas de estudio* (Study Hours) (1910) and *La enseñanza de la literatura* (The Teaching of Literature) (1913). As an *americanista*, his most important books are *La utopía de América* (The Utopia of Hispanic America) (1925) and *Seis ensayos en busca de nuestra expresión* (Six Essays in Search of Our Expression) (1928). In these books, Henríquez Ureña assesses diverse aspects of Latin American cultural identity.

Henríquez Ureña also contributed to the study of Latin American Spanish with his book *El español en Santo Domingo* (Spanish Language of Hispanic America) (1940) and *Observaciones sobre el español de América* (Observations on Hispanic American Spanish) (1921). His book *Gramática castellana* (Castillian Grammar) (1938–39), published with Dámaso Alonso, was used in Latin American schools for many decades.

Further reading

Alvarez, S. (1981) *La magna patria de Pedro Henríquez Ureña. Una interpretación de su americanismo*, Santo Domingo: Editora Taller.

Anderson Imbert, E. (1989) 'Pedro Henríquez Ureña', in C.A. Solé and M.I. Abreu (eds), *Latin American Writers*, New York: Scribners, 2, 597–601.

Borges, J.L. (1960) 'Prologue', in P. Henríquez Ureña, *Obra crítica*, Mexico: Fondo de Cultura Económica.

Céspedes, D. (1983) 'Pedro Henríquez Ureña: Lingüística y poesía', in *Seis ensayos sobre poética latinoamericana*, Santo Domingo: Biblioteca Taller.

Henríquez Ureña, M. (1950) *Pedro Henríquez Ureña*, Ciudad Trujillo: Librería Dominicana.

Henríquez Ureña, P. (1960) *Obra crítica*, Mexico City: Fondo de Cultura Económica.

—— (1976–80) *Obras completas*, Santo Domingo: Universidad Nacional Pedro Henríquez Ureña, 9 vols.

—— (1998) *Ensayos*, Paris: Colección Archivos.

Sábato, E. (1979) 'Pedro Henríquez Ureña', in *Apologías y rechazos*, Barcelona: Editorial Seix y Barral.

FERNANDO VALERIO-HOLGUÍN

Heraud, Javier

b. 1942, Lima, Peru; d. 1963, Puerto Maldonado, Peru

Poet

Killed in a confrontation between a guerrilla group and the Peruvian army, Heraud left behind a small but very promising body of lyric poetry (published in Cuba in 1967 as *Poemas*); by his life and example he also shared in the mythology of the 'guerrilla poets' (see **guerrilla poetry**). Those who joined the guerrilla groupings in Latin America in the 1960s were almost all from educated, middle-class backgrounds; Heraud, with others of his generation such as the Guatemalan Otto René **Castillo**, wrote of their conviction and idealism. In Heraud's case, his poetry was set in emblematic landscapes, unsullied and open to transformation.

Further reading

Espejo, O. (1997) 'Contribución a la bibliografía de Javier Heraud', *Revista iberoamericana* 63(180): 509–23.

Goloboff, F.M. (1973) 'Javier Heraud: La palabra en su límite', *Hispamérica* 4–5: 41–7.

Heraud, J. (1973) *Poesías completas*, Lima: Campodónico Ediciones.

Toledo Sande, L. (1978) 'La voz interrumpida de Javier Heraud', *Casa de las Américas* 108: 11–20.

MIKE GONZALEZ

Herbert, Cecil

b. 1924, Belmont, Trinidad

Poet, teacher and land surveyor

Although he has published very little recently, in the past Herbert contributed many poems to major journals such as *Bim*, *Tamarack Review*, *Caribbean Quarterly*, and a number of anthologies. His output continues to stand up to rigorous critical scrutiny and has been collected as *The Poems of Cecil Herbert* (1981), edited by Danille Gianetti. Herbert's poetry is distinguished by a sensuous and celebratory approach to the landscape. He attended Queen's Royal College, Port-of-Spain, before training with the Royal Air Force in Moncton, Canada. After the war, he became a land surveyor, returning to Trinidad to practise.

FUNSO AIYEJINA

Hercules, Frank Elton Mervyn

b. 1917, San Fernando, Trinidad; d. 1996, Roosevelt Island, New York, USA

Novelist

Hercules has published three novels and one book of non-fiction, a study of racism in the USA – *American Society and Black Revolution* (1972). His works *Where the Humming Bird Flies* (1961) and *On Leaving Paradise* (1980) focus on colonialism and Caribbean reactions to it. As with his non-fiction, his third novel, *I Want a Black Doll* (1967), also examines racism in the USA. Educated in Trinidad and England where he read law at Middle Temple, London during the Second World War, he emigrated to the USA where he engaged in business, becoming a US citizen in 1959.

FUNSO AIYEJINA

Hernández, Felisberto

b. 1902, Montevideo, Uruguay; d. 1964, Montevideo

Writer

Hernández has a unique place in Latin American fiction and his work defies categorization. His first two books bore titles that made a point of their anonymity: *Fulano de tal* (So and So) (1925) and *Libro sin tapas* (Book Without Covers) (1928). Hernández always enjoyed the admiration of a small and select group, thus sometimes he saw himself as an impostor, while at other times he was bitterly ironic about the world's refusal to recognize him. This ambivalence was reflected in his themes. For many years, Hernández was read as the memorialist of a bucolic Montevideo, yet he was only really interested in memory as a mode of consciousness, alongside madness (a distracted consciousness) and identity (experiential consciousness). His style was distracted and concentrated and his syntax peculiar and idiosyncratic. A solitary pioneer, like the Argentine novelist with whom he is often compared, Roberto **Arlt**, recognition came only posthumously. Both writers exemplified the self-taught, struggling individual, incarnating the rising middle class, and shared an air of illusion and failure.

For more than a decade, Hernández was a concert pianist touring small rural towns, accompanying silent films and giving school recitals; sometimes he would follow the concert with talks on subjects such as: 'What artists do with feelings'. When he occasionally ran out of money on a tour he would sell the piano to get home. Hunger was an obsessive topic in his work; he wrote as if feeding on the past, with a hedonism that invades memory and evokes the past. There are echoes in his work of the ideas of Carlos Vaz Ferreira, a Socratic figure whose discussion circles Hernández attended. Jules **Supervielle** stimulated, advised and admired him, helping him to find his own register somewhere between the symbolic and the allegorical. Hernández often visited his friend Alfredo Cáceres at Montevideo's Pilardevó psychiatric hospital, where he observed with aesthetic interest various cases of madness, which enabled him to use his writing to explore deviant behaviour. In this respect, as in his view of hunger, poverty and marginality, Hernández was a kind of residual positivist, although he only addressed questions of individual identity.

In his fifties, Hernández became a devotee of Western films. He lived on a meagre municipal wage earned doing trivial tasks, perfected his own shorthand system and participated in a virulent anti-communist radio campaign.

See also: *Hortensias, Las*

Further reading

Echavarren, R. (1981) *El espacio de la verdad; Práctica del texto en Felisberto Hernández*, Buenos Aires: Editorial Sudamericana.

Giraldi Dei Cas, N. (1975) *Felisberto Hernández, del creador al hombre*, Montevideo: Ediciones Banda Oriental.

Hernández, F. (1967–74) *Obras completas*, Montevideo: Editorial Arca, 6 vols.

—— (1983) *Obras completas*, ed. M.L. Puga, Mexico City: Siglo XXI, 3 vols.

—— (1993) *Piano Stories*, trans. L. Harss, New York: Marsilio.

Panesi, J. (1993) *Felisberto Hernández*, Rosario: Beatriz Viterbo.

Rocca, P. (2002) 'Felisberto Hernández', in C. Solé and K. Müller-Bergh (eds), *Latin American Writers: Supplement I*, New York: Scribners, 303–16.

San Román, G. (1997) 'Felisberto Hernández', in V. Smith (ed.), *Encyclopedia of Latin American Literature*, London: Fitzroy Dearborn, 413–15.

Sicard, A. (ed.) (1977) *Felisberto Hernández ante la crítica actual*, Caracas: Monte Avila.

SERGIO CHEJFEC

Hernández, Juan José

b. 1932, Tucumán, Argentina

Writer

Hernández's writing includes poetry and prose, but his best work has been in the field of short stories: *El inocente* (The Innocent) (1965), *La favorita* (The Favoured Woman) (1977) and *La señorita Estrella y otros cuentos* (Miss Star and Other Stories) (1982). In 1971 he published his novel *La ciudad de los sueños* (The City of the Dreams). Unifying elements in his structurally complex fictions are provincial culture and the ambiguities of childhood. Hernández has won many prizes and has been recognized by the best writers of Latin America.

Further reading

Amar Sánchez, A.M. (1983) 'Juan Jose Hernandez: La constitucion de un nuevo referente', *Revista iberoamericana* Oct.–Dec., 49(125): 919–27.

Corvalán, O. (1974) 'Juan Jose Hernandez and His City of Dreams', *International Fiction Review* 1: 138–40.

Hernández, J.J. (1965) *El inocente*, Buenos Aires: Editorial Sudamericana.

—— (1977) *La favorita*, Caracas: Monte Avila.

—— (2001) *Desiderátum: Obra poética*, Buenos Aires: Adriana Hidalgo Editora.

CRISTINA GUZZO

Hernández, Luisa Josefina

b. 1928, Mexico City

Playwright and novelist

A teacher and translator as well as a writer, Hernández has taught at the Theatre School of the Mexican Institute of Fine Arts and the National University of Mexico. Her plays include *Aguardiente de caña* (Cane Liquor) (1951), *Los frutos caídos* (Fallen Fruit) (1955), *Los huéspedes reales* (The Royal Guests) (1958), *Los duendes* (The Spirits) (1963), *La paz ficticia* (The Fictional Peace) and *Apócrifa* (Apocrypha) (1980) as well as translations of Shakespeare, Christopher Fry, Dylan Thomas and Jerzy Kawalerowicz. She has also written novels, among them *La noche exquisita* (Exquisite Night) (1965) and *Nostalgia de Troya* (Nostalgia for Troy) (1970).

Further reading

Hernández, Luisa (1958) *Los huéspedes reales; obra en diez cuadros*, Xalapa: Universidad Veracruzana.

—— (1994) *En una noche como ésta*, Mexico City: Plaza y Valdés: Consejo Nacional para la Cultura y las Artes.

—— (2000) *El galán de ultramar; la amante; Fermento y sueño; y, Tres perros y un gato*, Xalapa: Universidad Veracruzana.

Rulfo, J. (1964) 'Los palacios desiertos', *Books Abroad* 38: 294.

TITO VASCONCELOS

Hernández Núñez, Angela

b. 1960, Jarabacoa, Dominican Republic

Writer

Hernández Núñez appeared on the Dominican cultural scene with her 1980 essay *Emergencia del silencio* (Emerging from the Silence), which revealed her sympathy with the Pluralismo group's call for a literature distanced from its social function. Her poetry in *Tizne y Cristal* (Soot and Glass) (1987) and *Arce espejada* (The Mirrored Maple) (1994) sustained that idea. *Masticar una rosa* (Chewing a Rose) (1993) completed her aesthetic project; this consists of brief stories paying homage to little people overwhelmed by the bustle of urban life and the hectic pace of modernization.

Further reading

González, C. (2000) 'An Interview with Angela Hernández Núñez', *Callaloo*, Summer, 23(3): 999–1010.

Paravisini Gebert, L. (2000) 'Allotropes: The Short Stories of Angela Hernández Núñez', *Callaloo*, Summer, 23(3): 983–6.

MARÍA JULIA DAROQUI

Herrera, Darío

b. 1870, Panama City; d. 1914, Valparaíso, Chile

Writer

Herrera travelled to Buenos Aires in 1898 to associate with the great modernist poet, Rubén **Darío**. He published work in *La Nación* and *El Mercurio de América*. Poet, storyteller, essayist, chronicler and literary critic, he is the best known modernist of Panama outside his native country, combining cosmopolitan flair with the modernist aesthetic. His work is known for its moderation, modesty and a melancholy that avoids the overly dark and desperate. His best short stories were collected in *Horas lejanas* (Distant Hours) (1903), but most of his work remains unpublished.

Further reading

Miró, R. (1947) 'Apuntes sobre Darío Herrera', *Teoría de la patria*, Buenos Aires: Amorrortu.

NORMAN S. HOLLAND

Herrera Luque, Francisco

b. 1927, Caracas, Venezuela; d. 1990, Caracas

Psychiatrist, novelist, historian and essayist

In the early 1960s the first of his controversial writings on the psychology of the Venezuelan – *Los viajeros de Indias* (The Travellers to the Indies) – appeared, and from then on his essays and historical novels have figured consistently among the best-selling works of national literature (see **best-sellers**). A graduate in medicine from the Central University of Venezuela in 1953, he went on to study neuropsychiatry in Madrid. He taught for many years at the Central University, where he set up the School of Psychiatry. Later he was Venezuelan ambassador to Mexico.

Further reading

Pineda, H. (1982) 'Francisco Herrera Luque: Siquiatra novelista', *Afro Hispanic Review* 1(3): 13–16.

JORGE ROMERO LEÓN

Herrera y Reissig, Julio

b. 1875 Montevideo, Uruguay; d. 1910 Montevideo

Poet

Herrera y Reissig was a striking poetic innovator. He parodically subverted *modernismo*'s excesses with his stylistic innovation, explicit and parodic eroticism and the startling nature of his metaphors. Noted for his brilliance and eccentricity, Herrera exaggerated and defied both poetic and social convention. His dislocations of an inherited poetic language through startling juxtapositions and neologisms inspired subsequent poets such as Ramón **López Velarde** and César **Vallejo**. His attention to the powerful visual nature of physical and erotic description shows his ties to his contemporaries' (especially naturalist writers) emphasis on the physical environment and the role of madness and sickness. Some of Herrera's preference for shock tactics of denunciation or exhibitionism reflected his aspirations to bohemianism or decadentism. Yet his preoccupation with his heart condition and his frustration in the face of a changing social structure also explain some of his extremes.

A member of the Uruguayan 'Generation of 1900', Herrera y Reissig was a contemporary of **Rodó**. Born into an aristocratic but not wealthy family, he spent part of his early life in rural settings, a topic which would reappear in some of his poetry. In contrast with Rodó's call for a cultivation of an interior spiritual world, Herrera flaunts the counter-stance, an assertion of physicality and excess, characteristics which mark his poetry and prose as well. Notions of delirium and automatic writing are associated with his writings; the disjointed voices, slippage between subject and object, dissolve the contours of an aestheticized, interior world. Inspired by **Lugones**'s *Los crepúsculos del jardín* (Twilight of the Parks), Herrera produced a book in a similar vein, *Los parques abandonados* (The Abandoned Parks) (1919). He carried the sensuality and ironies of Lugones's work to a different level, emphasizing the grotesque and sadomasochism. This hermetic and shocking vein would appear again in a later work, *La torre de las esfinges* (The Tower of the Sphinxes). Another volume, *Los éxtasis de la montaña* (The Ecstasies of the Mountain) (1910/1943), consisted of sonnets on a pastoral theme, generally more traditional but also with disturbing entrances of unfamiliar elements. He also published a number of essays, as well as the unpublished *Psicopatología de los uruguayos o los nuevos charrúas* (Psychopathology of the Uruguayans or, The New Charrúas), a work that mocks almost every aspect of Uruguayan life and national character (he called Montevideo 'Tontovideo').

Herrera y Reissig, along with his younger compatriot Delmira **Agustini**, clearly anticipates many of the changes in later poetry, particularly the appearance of the grotesque, physical explicitness and the almost frenzied exaggeration of poetic convention that announced its dissolution.

See also: Spanish American modernism

Further reading

Amestoy Leal, B. (1991) *Poética de lo imaginario: La mujer y su configuración imaginaria en la poesía de Julio Herrera y Reissig*, Montevideo: Trilce.

Herrera y Reissig, J. (1961) *Poesías completas y páginas en prosa*, ed. and intro. R. Bula Píriz, Madrid: Aguilar.

—— (1978) *Poesía completa y prosa selecta*, ed. A. Migdal, intro. I. Vilariño, Caracas: Biblioteca Ayacucho.

Kirkpatrick, G. (1989) *The Dissonant Legacy of Modernismo: Lugones, Herrera y Reissig and the Voices of Modern Spanish American Poetry*, Berkeley: University of California Press.

Vilariño, I. (1974) *Julio Herrera y Reissig*, Montevideo: Técnica.

GWEN KIRKPATRICK

Hibbert, Fernand

b. 1873, Miragoàne, Haiti; d. 1928, Port-au-Prince, Haiti

Novelist and playwright

Part of the *Génération de la Ronde* (comprising Frédéric Marcelin, Justin Lhérisson, Antoine Innocent and Hibbert) which preceded Haitian ***indigènisme***, Hibbert's fiction depicts Haitian life in the years leading up to the US occupation of 1915. Ironic and sceptical, he provides a sharp critique of the class divisions of Haitian life in such works as *Les Thazar* (The Thazars) (1907), in which the heroine prefers a German to a Haitian husband. He often turns his satirical wit to financial schemes and political chicanery.

Further reading

Chirol, M.M. (1997) 'Fernand Hibbert', in V. Smith (ed.), *Encyclopedia of Latin American Literature*, London: Fitzroy Dearborn, 420–2.

Gindine, Y. (1975) 'Satire and the Birth of Haitian Fiction (1901–1905)', *Caribbean Quarterly* 21(3).

Hibbert, F. (1988) *Esquisses d'hier, tableaux d'aujourd'hui*, Port-au-Prince: Deschamps, 7 vols.

DANIEL BALDERSTON

Hidalgo, Alberto

b. 1897, Arequipa, Peru; d. 1967, Buenos Aires, Argentina

Poet

Hidalgo was a pioneer of avant-garde poetry (see **avant-garde in Latin America**), first in his native Peru and then in Buenos Aires, where he settled in 1919. His artistic credo, defined as *simplismo* (simplism) and expounded in the 1925 book of the same name, involved the reduction of poetry to its essentials. He was particularly innovative in his experiments in typographical arrangement, notably in the 1928 collection *Descripción del cielo* (Description of Heaven).

Further reading

Hidalgo, A. (1967) *Antología personal*, Buenos Aires: Centro Editor de América Latina.

Núñez, E. (1968) 'Alberto Hidalgo o la inquietud literaria', *Letras* 80/1: 149–52.

O'Hara, E. (1987) 'Alberto Hidalgo, hijo del arrebato', *Revista de crítica literaria latinoamericana* 13(26): 97–113.

Reedy, D.R. (1987) 'Soi un bardo nuevo de concepto i de forma: La poesía futurista de Alberto Hidalgo', *Discurso literario* 4(2): 485–95.

JAMES HIGGINS

Hijo de hombre

Published in Buenos Aires in 1960 (rev. 1982), Augusto **Roa Bastos**'s first novel, *Hijo de hombre* (Son of Man), won the Losada novel prize for the previous year. It has since become a recognized classic of Latin American literature. As in subsequent novels, in *Hijo de hombre* Roa Bastos scrutinizes intellectual commitment (see **intellectuals**). The text of the novel is a found manuscript in which the military man Miguel Vera, its narrator and central character, tests himself as both storyteller and man of action; finding himself wanting in both respects he, apparently, commits suicide. The story he tells is thus one of betrayal. He fails as a narrator, for example, in comparison to Macario, the old Guarani-speaking peasant storyteller of his youthful days in the countryside. Having left the community for Asunción and become a man of the State, his representational skills betray him and his narrative becomes, he feels, inauthentic. Subsequently, as a committed man of action, he cannot betray the State and class he now serves. Instead, in a drunken moment, he betrays his peasant companions. Through Vera the novel thus stages the relation of misunderstanding and conflict between State institutions – such as the Church and the military – and the '*pueblo*'. Indeed, the heroic acts of the latter serve as a critical counterpoint to the former. In this way the novel becomes a dense network of stories representing the violent effects of capitalist modernization (Macario, for example, dies with the arrival of the railway) as well as of cultures of resistance. Culminating with the Chaco War – in which all participate, nearly all die and from which very few benefit – *Hijo de hombre* also addresses the contradictory logics of sacrifice.

Further reading

Foster, D.W. (1970) 'Nota sobre el punto de vista narrativo en *Hijo de hombre*', *Revista iberoamericana* 73: 643–50.

Montero, J. (1976) 'Realidad y ficción en *Hijo de hombre*', *Revista iberoamericana* 95: 267–74.

Roa Bastos, A. (1988) *Son of Man*, trans. R. Caffyn, New York: Monthly Review Press.

JOHN KRANIAUSKAS

hijo pródigo, El

El Hijo Pródigo appeared from 1943 to 1956. Its founding editor was Octavio Barreda, with Xavier **Villaurrutia** and Octavio **Paz** playing leading roles. A polemical publication in the tradition of ***Contemporáneos***, it sought to bring current international ideas on literature and the arts to Mexico. Those writing for *El Hijo Pródigo* often felt that Mexico had become too isolated culturally after the Revolution, and that its cultural development was thwarted by socialist realism and populism. (For instance, the art of Rufino Tamayo was defended in its pages against the charge that it was not as Mexican as the work of Rivera, Orozco and Siqueiros.) The magazine published translations of works by T.S. Eliot, Jean Giraudoux and many others, and works by Mexican writers including Rodolfo **Usigli**, Samuel Ramos, Ermilo Abreu Gómez, Antonio Castro Leal and Leopoldo Zea.

Further reading

El Hijo Pródigo (1983) Facsimile edition, Mexico City: Fondo de Cultura Económica, 7 vols.

Vento, Arnold C. (1978) *El hijo pródigo; A Critical Index of XX Century Mexican Thought*, Albuquerque, NM: Pajarito.

DANIEL BALDERSTON

Hill, Errol

b. 1922, Port-of-Spain, Trinidad

Dramatist

For Hill, theatre had a central role to play in the development of a national culture – and, in the case of Trinidad, that necessarily implied a marriage between theatre and carnival, the most important of indigenous performing arts. Hence his work with calypsonian Mighty Sparrow and choreographer Beryl McBurnie. His *Man Better Man* (1964) is built around the ritual of stick-fighting; its language, as in most of his plays, evokes the calypso form. His critical writings and essays express a lifelong dedication to the creation of a Caribbean theatrical tradition.

Further reading

Greer, P. (1973) *Why Pretend? A Conversation about the Performing Arts with Errol Hill*, San Francisco: Chandler & Sharp Publishers.

King, B. (1997) 'West Indian Performing Arts and the Rockefeller Foundation 1957–1963: The West Indian Arts Festival, The Little Carib, and Errol Hill', in M. Delrez *et al.* (eds), *The Contact and the Culmination*, Liège, Belgium: L3-Liège Language and Literature, 259–70.

Shafee, S.A. (1996) 'Song, Dance and Drum': Theatrics of African and Black Drama', *Indian Journal of American Studies*, Summer, 26(2): 36–44.

MIKE GONZALEZ

Hippolyte, Kendel

b. 1952, St Lucia

Writer and theatre director

Considered one of the outstanding popular Caribbean poets of his generation, Hippolyte's writings have appeared frequently in anthologies. Much of his early work employed the once-fashionable **nation language**. A graduate of the University of the West Indies, Hippolyte teaches literature and drama in Castries, St Lucia. He has edited *Confluence: Nine Saint Lucian Poets* (1988) and *So Much Poetry in We People* (1990), an anthology of performance poetry from the Eastern Caribbean. His own collections of poems include: *Island in the Sun – Side Two* (1980), *Bearings* (1986) and *The Labyrinth* (1993). In 1984 he co-founded The Lighthouse Theatre Company with his wife Jane **King**.

Further reading

Fido, E.S. (1987) 'Island & Overseas: Visions', *Journal of West Indian Literature* 1(2): 58–64.

Rohlehr, G. (1985) 'The Problem of the Problem of Form', *Caribbean Quarterly* 1.

KEITH JARDIM

Hispamérica: Revista de literatura

Hispamérica: Revista de literatura is an academic journal founded in 1972 by Saúl Sosnowski. It appears three times per year. *Hispamérica* took advantage of the enormous interest in Latin American literature in the 1960s and the early 1970s to establish a dialogue between North

American Latin Americanists and Latin American **intellectuals**. The journal focuses primarily upon twentieth-century literature, and each issue also contains poetry and fiction, occasional dramatic texts by well-known writers, interviews with important figures and reviews. Although the content is heavily Argentine/Uruguayan, the journal continues to be one of the best in the field of Latin American literary and cultural studies.

Further reading

Sosnowski, Saúl (1999) *La cultura de un siglo; América Latina en sus revistas*, Buenos Aires: Editorial RUBAISEN.

DAVID WILLIAM FOSTER

Hodge, Merle

b. 1944, Calcutta Settlement, Trinidad

Fiction writer and essayist

One of the Caribbean's best-known Anglophone women writers, her first novel *Crick, Crack Monkey* (1970), explores the clash of cultural values in the upbringing of a young girl in Trinidad; her second, *The Life of Laetitia* (1993), presents these conflicts through the eyes of Laetitia and her Indian friend Anjanee. Hodge is well known for her essays on the condition of the Caribbean, especially in relation to women's roles, and for her extensive writing on the importance of creole for the Caribbean person. Widely travelled, she always returns to Trinidad to write and teach.

Further reading

Balutansky, K.M. (1989) 'We Are All Activists: An Interview with Merle Hodge', *Callaloo* 12(4): 651–62.

Gikandi, S. (1990) 'Narration in the Post-Colonial Moment: Merle Hodge's *Crick Crack Monkey*', in I. Adam and H. Tiffin (eds), *Past the Last Post: Theorizing Post-Colonialism and Post-Modernism*, Calgary: University of Calgary Press.

Hodge, M. (1990) 'Challenges of the Struggle for Sovereignty: Changing the World versus Writing Stories', in S. Cudjoe (ed.), *Caribbean Women Writers: Essays from the First International Conference*, Wellesley: Calaloux.

GAY WILENTZ

Holst, Gilda

b. 1952, Guayaquil, Ecuador

Writer

Holst was one of an outstanding group of women writers appearing on Guayaquil's literary scene during the 1980s, many of them the product of the literary workshop directed by Miguel **Donoso Pareja**. Collectively, their work emphasized the conflicts between reality and desire, a sense of alienation and the plight of being female in a society intolerant of deviations from expected behavioural norms. Holst's stories are illustrative, exploring the question of literal and metaphorical power, authority and transgression, gender inequality and the lack of tenderness. Works she has published are *Más sin nombre que nunca* (More Nameless Than Ever) (1989) and *Turba de signos* (A Mass of Signs) (1995).

Further reading

Garcís Serrano, M.V. (1995) ' "Palabreo" de Gilda Holst o el nuevo "feminismo" latinoamericano', *Alba de América* 13(24–5): 343–54.

MERCEDES M. ROBLES

Hopkinson, Slade

b. 1934, New Amsterdam, British Guiana

Poet, playwright, actor and teacher

An actor of remarkable versatility, Hopkinson has worked with the leading playwrights of the region. He founded the Caribbean Theatre Guild Company in Trinidad in 1970. He embraced the Muslim faith and took the name Baakoo Abdul-Rahman. He has published both plays and collections of poetry, including *The Onliest Fisherman* (1957), *A Spawning of Eels* (premiered, 1968), and *The Friend* (1976). Educated in British Guiana,

Barbados and Jamaica, Hopkinson has lived and worked across the Caribbean region and now resides in Toronto, Canada.

FUNSO AIYEJINA

Hortensias, Las

Las Hortensias is a novella by the Uruguayan writer Felisberto **Hernández**, first published in 1949. Narrated in the third person (unusually for Hernández), it tells the story of Horacio, a married man who collects slightly larger than life-size rubber dolls. The dolls, displayed in glass cases or arranged in various scenarios, are initially integrated into the life of the couple. Horacio encourages the manufacturer to perfect one of these dolls – Hortensia, a replica of his wife – to the point where it reproduces human skin and body temperature. Unexpected passions are evoked by the dolls, which produce marital conflict and later lead Horacio into madness.

Further reading

Andreu, J.L. (1977) '*Las Hortensias*, o los equívocos de la ficción', in A. Sicard (ed.), *Felisberto Hernández ante la crítica*, Caracas: Monte Avila, 9–59.

Hernández, F. (1997) 'The Daisy Dolls', trans. L. Harss, *The Oxford Book of Latin American Short Stories*, ed. Roberto González Echevarría, Oxford University Press.

LILIANA ZUCCOTTI

Hosein, Clyde

b. 1940, Couva, Trinidad

Short story writer

Hosein's collection of stories *The Killing of Nelson John* (1980) offer a panorama of Caribbean life and characters which is at once socially conscious and deeply ironic. His short story 'Crow' is included in *The Penguin Book of Caribbean Short Stories* (1996). Having studied in London, Hosein worked for Radio Trinidad and the *Trinidad Guardian* before emigrating to Toronto, where he has remained to study film direction and to work with the Canadian Broadcasting Company.

KEITH JARDIM

House for Mr Biswas, A

An acclaimed novel by Trinidad-born V.S. **Naipaul** published in 1961. Mr Biswas, loosely based on the author's father, is a Trinidadian Indian, a descendant of indentured labourers who came from the sub-continent after the abolition of slavery. A man with aspirations to greater things, he is a failed writer who ends up devising lurid stories for a local tabloid before being put in charge of the paper's 'Deserving Destitutes' fund, which brings him into daily contact with the misery of the poor of colonial Trinidad. Mr Biswas's own poverty is a central concern of the novel, and he is frequently forced to rely on the largess of his wife's large and all-controlling family, the Tulsis. As part of this feuding and over-crowded household, Mr Biswas struggles to maintain his sense of manhood, waging his own small war against the Tulsis, winning small victories and suffering daily humiliations.

The first half of the novel is set in the sugar-cane fields of rural Trinidad, a luxuriant and unforgiving environment in which Mr Biswas's constant existential questioning leads to a mental breakdown. The question of individual and social identity on an island colonized first by the Spanish, then by the British, to which migrants came from Europe, Africa, India and China, is often articulated in racial terms in Naipaul's work. His colonial subjects experience profound feelings of rootlessness and find themselves at the mercy of arbitrary swings of history.

The second half takes place in the capital city to which Mr Biswas comes by accident. Port-of-Spain represents the hope of a more fluid society, in which Mr Biswas can get a day's work sign-painting at a newspaper's office and end up a journalist. However, fate repeatedly frustrates ambition and, by middle age, Mr Biswas transfers this ambition on to the education of his son. In fact, two of Mr Biswas's children manage to win scholarships to London, part of a new generation that will play a crucial part in the nation-building after independence. It is the success guaranteed by a metropolitan education that saves the family from penury and allows Mr Biswas to keep the ridiculously flawed house he has at last managed to buy and which represents his own solution to the issue of inheritance in a post-colonial society.

Further reading

Celestin, R. (1996) *From Cannibals to Radicals: Figures and Limits of Exoticism in V.S. Naipaul*, Minneapolis: University of Minnesota Press.

Levy, J. (1995) *V.S. Naipaul: Displacement and Autobiography*, New York and London: Garland.

Thieme, J. (1987) *The Web of Tradition: The Uses of Allusion in V.S. Naipaul's Fiction*, London: Hansib.

Weiss, Timothy (1992) *On the Margins: The Art of Exile in V.S. Naipaul*, Amherst: University of Massachusetts Press.

LORRAINE LEU

Huerta, Efraín

b. 1914, Guanajuato, Mexico; d. 1982, Mexico City

Poet

From his first volume of poetry, *Absoluto amor* (Absolute Love) (1935), Huerta focused on the many faces of love. Many of his poems were inspired by his passionate love–hate relationship with Mexico City. He translated into poetic language the sordid reality of everyday life and the anonymous voices of the city's streets. The 'poemínimos' or 'minimal poems' of his later years were full of wit and irony. In his poetry and his public activity, he expressed his solidarity with the oppressed and all those fighting for national liberation.

Further reading

Aguilar Melantzon, R. (1983) 'Efraín Huerta and the New School of Mexican Poets', *Latin American Literary Review* 11(22): 41–55.

—— (1990) 'Efraín Huerta en la poesía mexicana', *Revista iberoamericana* 56(151): 419–30.

González Pages, A. (1977) 'Efraín Huerta: Perfil del poeta vivo', *Plural* 67: 56–67.

EDITH NEGRÍN

Huidobro, Vicente

b. 1893, Santiago, Chile; d. 1948, Cartagena, Chile

Poet

The polemical Huidobro was Latin America's foremost poet of the avant-garde (see **avant-garde in Latin America**). He wrote both in Spanish and French, experimented in poetry, theatre and film, founded his own literary movement (creationism) and was not only Latin America's roving cultural ambassador to Paris but also perhaps its first performance artist. He apparently staged his own kidnapping in Paris at the hand of British imperialist agents. Even if Huidobro's life should not obscure the dazzling metaphors of his poetry, a cursory reading is in order here, for language as well as the staging of authenticity was one of Huidobro's most important themes.

Born to an aristocratic Chilean family, Vicente García Huidobro Fernández realized early on the importance of juicy polemics. One of his first books, *Pasando y pasando* (Going On and On) (1914) – confiscated by the authorities and burned by members of his family – opened with a much too premature autobiographical essay titled 'Yo', in which he proceeded to systematically debunk Jesuit schools, despotic priests, the Catholic Church, Spanish poetry and prominent critics. In Santiago, Huidobro was already making fun of futurism, writing calligrammatic poems and planting the seeds of future **manifestos**. In 1917 he took his young wife and children to Paris. He collaborated with the review *Nord–Sud* – the most important cubist journal – and wrote a number of his books in French: *Horizon Carré* (Squared Horizon) (1917), *Hallali* (1918), *Tour Eiffel* (1918) and *Saisons choisies* (Chosen Seasons) (1921). Juan Gris helped him with the language, Pablo Picasso drew his portrait and Tristan Tzara published his poetry. From Paris to Madrid, from Santiago to Zurich, Huidobro edited magazines, gave interviews and announced collaborations – which never materialized – with friends Stravinsky, Pound, Picasso, Tzara, Nijinsky and the Ballets Russes. The increasing power and prestige of his polemical darts – against André Breton and Pablo **Neruda**, among many others – prematurely took him out of the picture, and he returned to Chile, was a candidate for President on a reformist platform, lost the election, and finally settled into a kind of dejected discontent.

Through it all, he left what is perhaps one of the most baffling and interesting poems in the Spanish language: ***Altazor*** (1919–31), in which language is a transparent piece of clockwork allowing the reader to peer into its own mechanisms. It is a final epitaph for the heroic avant-garde.

Further reading

Camurati, M. (1980) *Poesía y poética de Vicente Huidobro*, Madrid: Cambeiro.

Concha, J. (1980) *Vicente Huidobro*, Madrid: Júcar.

De Costa, R. (1975) *Vicente Huidobro y el creacionismo*, Madrid: Taurus.

—— (1984) *Vicente Huidobro: The Careers of a Poet*, Oxford: Clarendon Press and New York: Oxford University Press.

Forster, M.H. (1989) 'Vicente Huidobro', in C.A. Solé and M.I. Abreu (eds), *Latin American Writers*, New York: Scribners, 2, 755–64.

Quiroga, J. (2002) 'Translating Vowels, or, The Defeat of Sounds', in D. Balderston and M. Schwartz (eds), *Voice Overs: Latin American Literature and Translation*, Albany: SUNY Press, 164–9.

Schwartz, J. (1978) 'Vicente Huidobro o la cosmópolis textualizada', *Eco* 202:1.

Yúdice, G. (1978) *Vicente Huidobro y la motivación del llenguaje*, Buenos Aires: Galerna.

JOSÉ QUIROGA

Hutchinson, Lionel

b. 1923, St Michael, Barbados

Writer

A novelist who spent much of his working life in government service, Hutchinson is known primarily for two novels. *Man from the People* (1969) is a bluntly comic portrayal of politics during the 1960s after the Barbados Labour Party of Grantley Adams was swept from office in favour of the Democratic Labour Party. *One Touch of Nature* (1971) is a commentary on race relations and on the people known in Barbados as 'Red Legs', descendants of the white slaves and indentured servants displaced by black slavery. Long considered failures and degenerates, they were not even offered the paternalistic sympathy sometimes offered to blacks. The novel's central character, Harriet Jivenot, believes that she is entitled to a better life and scorns East Indians, blacks and her own 'Red Legs' community.

Further reading

Salick, R. (1985) 'Lionel Hutchinson: Barbados' Forgotten Novelist', *Bim* 69.

CAROL J. WALLACE

Hyatt, Charles

b. 1931, Kingston, Jamaica

Writer

Hyatt's early career unfolded in theatre and, above all, in radio, where he worked with the BBC on the development of a vernacular theatre, based largely on the oral storytelling tradition in which Hyatt was a consummate performer, as in his portrayal of Pa Ben in Trevor **Rhone**'s play, *Old Story Time* (1981). His own stories and memories are collected in his volume of tales, *When Me Was a Boy* (1989).

MIKE GONZALEZ

I

Ibáñez, Roberto

b. 1907, Montevideo, Uruguay; d. 1978, Montevideo

Writer

An elegant and musical poet, Ibáñez's central concerns were the human tragedy, lost childhood, love and death and the solitude of the poet. He won the first **Casa de las Américas** Poetry Prize in 1961. Ibáñez was a scholar with a large unpublished bibliography and a controversial critic who famously engaged in public debate with Emir **Rodríguez Monegal**. He was responsible for many years for the literature programmes studied in his country's schools; he was also Uruguay's first Socialist deputy. One famous poem, 'Balada de tu nombre' (Ballad of Your Name), was written for his wife Sara de **Ibáñez**.

Further reading

Bordoli, D.L. (1958) 'La poesía de Roberto Ibáñez', *Asir* 38.

Supervielle, J. (1939) 'La poesía de Roberto Ibáñez', *France-Amérique Latine* 136.

NORAH GIRALDI DEI CAS

Ibáñez, Sara de

b. 1909, Chamberlain, Uruguay; d. 1971, Montevideo, Uruguay

Poet

Sara de Ibáñez combined national historical themes, often of an epic cast – 'Canto a Montevideo' (Hymn to Montevideo) (1941), 'Artigas' (1952) – with intensely lyrical poetry on topics of universal importance, such as war, the apocalypse, death, nature and love – 'Canto' (1940), 'Pastoral' (1948), 'Apocalípsis' (1970). She often used traditional verse forms, like the sonnet, as well as freer verse forms. Her *Poemas escogidos* (Selected Poems) (1974) contains selections from all her works. De Ibáñez is part of an outstanding generation of Uruguayan female poets including Juana de **Ibarbourou**, Dora Isella Russell, Esther de Cáceres, Selva Márquez, Clara Silva, Concepción Silva and Susana **Soca**.

Further reading

Ibáñez, R. (1973) *Anticipo, umbral y envío en Canto póstumo de Sara de Ibáñez*, Buenos Aires: Editorial Losada.

Ibáñez, S. de (1991) *Sara de Ibáñez: Antología crítica*,

ed. J. Arbeleche and G. Mántaras, Montevideo: Signos.

—— (1974) *Poemas escogidos*, Mexico City: Siglo XXI.

GWEN KIRKPATRICK

Ibarbourou, Juana de

b. 1892, Melo, Uruguay; d. 1979, Montevideo, Uruguay

Poet

Crowned in 1929 as 'Juana of America', this young poet began her work within the avant-garde (see **avant-garde in Latin America**). However, her voice is very distinct: seductive, spontaneous, fresh and modest. In a reaction to modernism, she glorifies everyday objects while giving them a marvellous and mysterious air. In her first book, *Las lenguas de diamante* (Diamond Tongues) (1919), she demonstrated this tendency to sentimental and innovative expression. However, by 1950, with the appearance of collections such as *Perdida* (Lost), she took on a more sombre and melancholic voice.

Further reading

Agostín, M. (1989) 'Juana de Ibarbourou', in C.A. Solé and M.I. Abreu (eds), *Latin American Writers*, New York: Scribners, 2: 803–7.

Brenes-García, A.M. (1997) 'Juana de Ibarbourou', in V. Smith (ed.), *Encyclopedia of Latin American Literature*, London: Fitzroy Dearborn, 431–2.

Ibarbourou, J. de (1960) *Obras completas*, ed. D. Isella Russell, Madrid: Aguilar.

Silva Silvera, A. (1980) 'Introducción a la poesía de Juana de Ibarbourou', *Cultura* 68–9: 192–203.

Videla de Rivero, G. (1995) 'Recordando a Juana de Ibarbourou', *Boletín de la Academia Argentia de Letras* 60(235–6): 113–33.

VICTORIA RUÉTALO

Ibargüengoitia, Jorge

b. 1928, Guanajuato, Mexico; d. 1983, Madrid, Spain

Writer

Ibargüengoitia is the most important satirical novelist of post-revolutionary Mexican literature. The author of numerous works of fiction, plays, essays and journalistic chronicles, Ibargüengoitia is most famous for his historical novels, which criticize dominant versions of Mexican history while avoiding hopelessness or cynicism. Although twice winner of the prestigious **Casa de las Américas** prize, Ibargüengoitia never achieved the international fame of authors such as Carlos **Fuentes** or Juan **Rulfo**. Nonetheless his work helped to maintain a long tradition of social satire in Mexican letters and he remains a beloved figure in his homeland. He died tragically in the same plane crash that took the lives of noted art critic and novelist Marta **Traba**, her husband Ángel **Rama** and the Peruvian poet and novelist Manuel **Scorza**.

Further reading

Campbell, F. (1989) 'Ibargüengoitia: La sátira histórico-política', *Revista iberoamericana* 148–9: 1047–59.

Canaparo, C. (1997) 'Jorge Ibargüengoitia', in V. Smith (ed.), *Encyclopedia of Latin American Literature*, London: Fitzroy Dearborn, 432–4.

Ibargüengoitia, J. (1983) *The Dead Girls*, trans. A. Zatz, New York: Avon.

—— (1984) *Two Crimes*, trans. A. Zatz, New York: Avon.

—— (1986) *The Lightning of August*, trans. I. del Corral, New York: Avon.

Leñero, V. (1989) *Los pasos de Jorge*, Mexico City: Joaquín Mortiz.

BRIAN GOLLNICK

Icaza, Jorge

b. 1906, Quito, Ecuador; d. 1978, Quito

Writer

Icaza's controversial *Huasipungo* (The Villagers) (1934), his first novel, exposed the terrible living conditions of Indians and the complicity of Church and Government. His characteristically shocking style used images of the grotesque, popular speech and a tone of protest. Icaza is usually located within the ***indigenista*** trend in Latin American literature, but he was more interested in the psychological and social complexes of the mestizo; his novel *El chulla Romero y Flores* (The Half-Breed Romero y Flores) (1958), for example, is a penetrating study of the concerns with race, appearance and culture that haunt the Ecuadorean experience.

Further reading

Corrales Pascual, M. (1989) 'Jorge Icaza', in C.A. Solé and M.I. Abreu (eds), *Latin American Writers*, New York: Scribners, 3: 1063–8.

—— (1988) *El Chulla Romero y Flores*, Paris: Colección Archivos.

Icaza, J. (1964) *The Villagers*, trans. P. Dulsey, Carbondale: Southern Illinois University Press.

March, K.N. (1997) 'Jorge Icaza', in V. Smith (ed.), *Encyclopedia of Latin American Literature*, London: Fitzroy Dearborn, 434–5.

Rodríguez Luis, J. (1980) *Hermenéutica y praxis del indigenismo: La novela indigenista de Clorinda Matto a José María Arguedas*, Mexico City: Fondo de Cultura Económica, 88–110.

HUMBERTO E. ROBLES

Illescas, Carlos

b. 1919, Guatemala City

Writer

One of the most talented poets of the Generation of 1940, Illescas joined the opposition against Ubico and participated in the 1944 uprising and the ten years of social agitation which followed, often working on an ad hoc basis with members of writer groups Acento and Saker-ti, without joining one group or the other. After the intervention of 1954, he lived in exile in Mexico, where he wrote several books and film scripts, working for various years at Universidad Nacional Autónoma de México and contributing to Mexico's intellectual life.

MARC ZIMMERMAN

In the Castle of My Skin

Published in 1953, *In the Castle of My Skin* established the reputation of its author George **Lamming**, and was a landmark text in the emergence of West Indian literature in the 1950s. The novel was based on Lamming's own experience of life in a Barbadian village between 1927 and 1950, when he emigrated to England. At the centre is the story of 'G', his early relationship with his mother, his schooling, his discussions with his friends, and his growing away from his roots as he enters secondary school. From early boyhood, G's sensitive and artistic individuality is in conflict with the intimacy of the village, and the story objectifies the tensions common to **intellectuals** in a colonized society who gain Western education at the cost of losing their communal roots. The novel ends with G leaving the island for further education abroad.

Yet the work is not a conventional autobiography. Lamming has written that it is not about an individual but a community, and this is mediated through a loose, open-ended narrative form that moves across a range of styles, from poetic prose to dramatic speech and reportage. Opening with G's seventh birthday, his experience merges with that of the village as a whole, which itself finds a voice in two elder figures, 'Ma' and 'Pa', whose long dialogues explore in poetic prose its history and concerns. The limestone island itself is vividly recreated with its landscape, weather, customs, food and speech. Because the novel takes place across the formative period when Barbados moved from traditional rural life to an individualistic materialism and towards political independence, G's coming of age coincides with similar changes on the island.

The novel begins with a scathing analysis of British colonialism as mediated through education, where the school children are regimented in squads and taught only English history, and the remains of the plantation society are embodied in the landowner Creighton in his house on the hill. The activities of Mr Slime, a schoolmaster dismissed for sexual misconduct, introduce the land sales which deprive the villagers of their traditional rights, and towards the end of the novel the political riots of the 1940s anticipate national independence.

The work was a revelation to contemporary West Indian writers. Edward Kamau **Brathwaite**, also from Barbados, was one whom it enabled to find his native idiom. Its penetrating critique of colonialism was recognized by the Kenyan author Ngügï wa Th'iongo, who called it 'one of the great political novels in modern "colonial" literature'. Jean-Paul Sartre republished it in his series *Les Temps Modernes*.

Further reading

Munro, I. (1971) 'The Theme of Exile in George Lamming's *In the Castle of My Skin*', *World Literature Written in English* 20: 51–60.

Nair, S. (1996) *Caliban's Curse. George Lamming and the Revisioning of History*, Ann Arbor: University of Michigan Press.

LOUIS JAMES

Indianismo

Indianismo is a representation produced by non-Indians in which the Indian appears as an exotic motif or as a source of nostalgia. When Christopher Columbus wrote his Diary (1492–93) he became the first Indianista by default. Believing that they had landed in India, Columbus and his crew gave the name 'Indians' to the human beings they saw and captured in the Caribbean. Indianista representations abounded during the colonial period; however, Indianismo refers specifically to texts written by non-Indian authors especially during the nineteenth century. This literature exploited Indian themes while ignoring the injustices suffered by the real Indian populations; indeed, its development is related to the reception of European Romanticism in Latin America represented by Chateaubriand's novel *Atala* (1801). Latin American Romantic novelists wrote interracial love stories in which Indians and their environments were represented exotically and located in a remote past. On the one hand, most Indian characters were depicted as savages who practised strange customs and rituals; on the other hand, a few isolated Indians were configured as 'noble savages' who lived in idyllic landscapes. Several of the *bons savages* at the end of the novels turned out to be mestizos or even white *criollos*, who only looked Indian because they had been raised by Indians.

It is not coincidental that Indianismo was most prevalent during the nineteenth century, when national states had just been established in Latin America. In the new national orders, the remaining Indian populations had two options: noble savages could be integrated into the new nation by becoming civilized, while the untameable savages would be eliminated. The canon of Indianista works includes *Cumandá* (1879) by the Ecuadorean Juan León Mera, *Enriquillo* (1882) by the Dominican Manuel de Jesús Galván and *Tabaré* (1888) by the Uruguayan Juan **Zorrilla de San Martín**. In the twentieth century there were still some residues of Indianista perspective, but it is almost impossible to find a significant Indianista text (see for example **Saer**'s ***El entenado***).

Indianismo is almost always confused with ***indigenismo***. The latter term derives from *indígena* (indigenous) and was coined in order to avoid the wrong use of the term Indian. Unlike Indianismo, the most important feature of *indigenismo* is its desire to offer political representation in favour of the contemporary indigenous population of the Americas.

Further reading

Brookshaw, D. (1997) 'Indianism: Brazil', in V. Smith (ed.), *Encyclopedia of Latin American Literature*, London: Fitzroy Dearborn, 437–9.

Harrison, R. (1997) 'Indianism: Spanish America', in V. Smith (ed.), *Encyclopedia of Latin American Literature*, London: Fitzroy Dearborn, 439–40.

Meléndez, C. (1934) *La novela indianista en Hispanoamérica*, Madrid: Hermando.

Sommer, D. (1991) *Foundational Fictions*, Berkeley: University of California Press.

JUAN ZEVALLOS AGUILAR

indigènisme

A radical literary movement of the 1920s, Haitian *indigènisme* was created as a response to the nationalist backlash against US occupation. Influenced by Charles Maurras and ethnologist Jean **Price-Mars**, the *indigènistes* criticized Haiti's Francophile elite and demanded that literature be grounded in an identifiably national reality. Their literary organ was the short-lived *La revue indigène* (1927–28), edited by Emile **Roumer** with the collaboration of poets Jacques **Roumain**, Carl **Brouard**, Philippe Thoby-Marcelin and Normil Sylvain. *Indigènisme* was similar to other movements in the Americas such as the Harlem Renaissance, Afro-Cuban writing and ***indigenismo***.

J. MICHAEL DASH

indigenismo

Indigenismo is an artistic movement that seeks to represent and emphasize the marginalized and exploited position of Indian peoples throughout Latin American history. The movement was most influential in the Andean region, Central America and in Mexico. Although the commitment of artists to Indian cultures extends beyond the flourishing of *indigenismo* proper, the label is more usually assigned to the wave of revolutionary and egalitarian ideologies during the first half of the twentieth century.

It was the Peruvian essayist José Carlos **Mariátegui** who in his ***Siete ensayos de interpretación de la realidad peruana*** (Seven Interpretive Essays on Peruvian Reality) (1928) established the scope of literary *indigenismo*. While so-called '**Indianismo**' is more related to an exotic, folkloric or sentimental depiction of the Indians, *indigenismo*, according to Mariátegui, is committed to the representation of the social and economic forces which intervene in their exploitation and subjection. An *indígena* literature, Mariátegui adds, one produced and consumed by the Indians themselves, has not yet been written. Mariátegui's classification reveals the paradoxes of *indigenismo*, since it constructs the split between the usually urban, educated and Spanish-speaking artists and the subjects they intend to represent. Most of this early *indigènista* literature is inscribed within Western narrative conventions, written in a non-Indian language and abounding with didactic passages and lexical explanations for the uninformed reader; this literature can be conceived of as alien to Indian cultures and as responding to the assimilative interests of the modern nation.

The precursor of the *indigènista* novel is *Aves sin nido* (Birds without a Nest) (1889) by Peruvian writer Clorinda Matto de Turner. *Raza de Bronce* (People of the Sun) (1916), by the Bolivian Alcides **Arguedas**, *Huasipungo* (The Villagers) (1934), by the Ecuadorian Jorge **Icaza**, and *El mundo es ancho y ajeno* (Broad and Alien is the World) (1941), by the Peruvian Ciro **Alegría**, are among the most important works of the movement. The novels combine the depiction of scenes and characters in the vein of ***costumbrismo*** with naturalist and realist narrative causality. The inclusion of novels influenced by European modernism within the scope of *indigenismo* has been a subject of disagreement. The novels of José María **Arguedas**, Rosario **Castellanos**, Miguel Angel **Asturias** and Manuel **Scorza** are good examples of this trend, which has been called *neo-indigenismo*. These novels abandon representational or mimetic paradigms and an emphasis on social inequality in favour of a more general inquuiry into Latin American identities through the filter of an Indian cosmovision.

A recent book by Vargas Llosa on José María Arguedas, *La utopía arcaica*, is a sign that *indigenismo* is still polemical. In addition, with the emergence of **indigenous literature** written by contemporary indigenous writers, Mariátegui's prediction that some *indigènista* writing would become dated is undoubtedly true.

Further reading

Favre, H. (1998) *El indigenismo*, Mexico: Fondo de Cultura Económica.

Kaliman, R.J. (1994) 'Unseen Systems: Avant-garde Indigenism in the Central Andes', in D. Jordan (ed.), *Regionalism Reconsidered: New Approaches to the Field*, New York: Garland, 159–83.

Kristal, E. (1987) *The Andes Viewed from the City: Literary and Political Discourse on the Indian in Peru, 1848–1930*, New York: Peter Lang.

Masferrer, K.E. (1981) *Indice general de Boletín ingenista y noticias indigènistas de America, 1940–1980*, Mexico: Instituto Indigènista Interamericano.

Moraña, M. (ed.) (1998) *Indigenismo hacia el fin del milenio: homenaje a Antonio Corejo Polar*, Pittsbugh, PA: Instituto Internacional de Literatura Iberoamerica.

Prieto, R. (1996) 'The Literature of Indigenismo', in R. Gonzalez Echevarria and E. Pupo-Walker (eds), *The Cambridge History of Latin American Literature*, Cambridge: Cambridge University Press, 2, 138–63.

Rodríguez Luis, J. (1980) *Hermenéutica y praxis del indigenismo: La novela indigènista de Clorinda Matto a José María Arguedas*, Mexico City: Fondo de Cultura Económica.

Vargas Llosa, M. (1996) *La utopía arcaica: José María Arguedas y las ficciones del indigenismo*, Mexico City: Fondo de Cultura Económica.

FERNANDO J. ROSENBERG

indigenous literature

The concept of indigenous literature was created by literary historians and historiographers in order to integrate Indian cultural production into both national and Latin American literatures. The most important collections of indigenous literature contain texts in languages of the most developed pre-Columbian civilizations and their successors. In other words, indigenous literatures are the collections of recorded compositions created by Aztecs, Incas and Mayans. The forms of recording include alphabetic writing, non-alphabetic writing and devices of human memory in Indian, European and a mixture of European and Indian languages. The studies of indigenous literatures acknowledge the following periods: pre-Columbian, colonial, republican and contemporary. The main sources of the pre-Columbian period are mesoamerican codices and inscriptions in Nahuatl and Mayan languages. The codices and the inscriptions include hieroglyphic and visual systems to register knowledge on paper and other materials. The reconstruction of the pre-Columbian period was also based on texts written during colonial times. The texts of the colonial and republican periods include documents written by Indians in Amerindian languages but using the Roman alphabet, for example that of Fernando Alvarez Tezozómoc who wrote his *Crónica Mexicayotl* (*c.*1609) in Nahuatl, or Guamán Poma de Ayala who wrote *Nueva corónica y buen gobierno* (1613) (translated as Letter to a King) in a mixture of Spanish and Quechua. There are texts written by mestizos such as Inca Garcilaso de la Vega who translated Quechua oral tradition into Spanish in his *Comentarios Reales* (Royal Commentaries) (1609), and Europeans such as Fray Fernandino de Sahagún who together with a group of Indian specialists wrote the earliest ethnography about Aztec culture in Nahuatl, Latin and Spanish from 1545 to 1580, or the Spanish priest Francisco de Avila who led an Indian group to compile Quechua oral tradition during the Catholic Campaign of *extirpación de idolatrías* (extirpation of idolatries) later collected in *Dioses y hombres de Huarochiri* (Gods and Men of Huarochiri) (*c.*1598).

In addition to collaborative/testimonial texts and transcriptions of oral tradition, both the republican and the contemporary period include textual production in Spanish and indigenous languages by indigenous authors. In the nineteenth century, production in indigenous languages included letters, proclamations and communiqués, but in the twentieth century, and especially during the last thirty years of it, the textual corpus by indigenous authors has grown to include genres more immediately recognizable as literary, including dramas, short stories, poetry and at least one novel (*El tiempo principia en Xibalbá* (Time Begins in Xibalbá) (1985), by the Guatemalan writer Luis de Lión). A significant amount of this literature has been produced in writing workshops with non-Indian writers as facilitators (see **workshop poetry**).

In addition to linguistic issues, these works raise significant questions of genre. The most important work produced by indigenous authors in indigenous languages has been in genres associated with oral tradition, especially drama and poetry. For example, the members of the Maya theatre company in

Chiapas, Mexico, **Sna Jtz'ibajom** (and its feminist offshoot, Fomma) work within a tradition established by Mexico's National Indigenous Institute, which in the 1950s promoted a Maya puppet troupe performing works written in collaboration with the well-known intellectual Rosario **Castellanos**. However, granted that poetry is the genre most closely aligned with oral tradition, it is not surprising that the most prominent Indian writers are poets, such as the renowned Quiché poet Humberto **Ak'abal** (Guatemala) and the Mapuche poet Elicura **Chihuailaf** (Chile). Works by Ak'abal and other Indian poets are often published in bilingual editions which are accessible to a wider reading public, and together with other trends, such as testimonial narratives and auto-ethnographic writings, these texts by indigenous authors are extending a counter-tradition of Indian writings which draws from the dominant, Hispanic literary history while profoundly questioning its ability to express national or cultural identity.

Further reading

Adorno, R. (1996) 'Cultures in Contact: Mesoamericana, the Andes, and the European written tradition', in R. Gonzalez Echevarría and E. Pupo-Walker (eds), *The Cambridge History of Latin American Literature*, Cambridge: Cambridge University Press, 1, 33–57.

Bareiro Saguier, R. (1980) *Literatura Guaraní del Paraguay*, Caracas: Editorial Ayacucho.

Bendezú, E. (1993) *Literatura Quechua*, Caracas: Biblioteca Ayacucho, 2nd edn.

Segala, A. (1990) *Literatura náhuatl. Fuentes, identidades, representaciones*, Mexico City: Grijalbo.

Sodi, D. (1990) *La literatura de los Mayas*, Mexico City: Joaquín Mortiz.

Vázquez, J.A. (1977) 'The Field of Latin American Indian Literatures', *Latin American Indian Literatures* 1: 1–33.

JUAN ZEVALLOS AGUILAR AND BRIAN GOLLNICK

indio ecuatoriano, El

Pío **Jaramillo Alvarado**'s fundamental and pioneering book *El indio ecuatoriano* (The Indian in Ecuador), on the indigenous question in Ecuador, was first published in 1922 and reprinted repeatedly thereafter. Although its author considered it a matter of absolute necessity that the Indian should be incorporated into white–mestizo culture, the work is a dramatic denunciation of the continuing practice of *concertaje*, or imprisonment for debt, and of the unequal distribution of land which disregarded the rights of indigenous communities.

Further reading

Carrión, B. (1977) 'Pío Jaramillo Alvarado', in *Plan del Ecuador*, Guayaquil: Casa de la Cultura Ecuatoriana, 103–40.

RAÚL VALLEJO

Ingram, Kenneth Everard Niven

b. 1921, St Ann, Jamaica

Bibliographer and poet

Alongside poets such as George Campbell, Una Marson and Vivian **Virtue**, Ingram helped to indigenize Jamaican poetry. He attended Jamaica College and the University of London. His poems and short stories of the 1940–44 period formed part of the creative nationalistic surge influenced by Edna Manley and the 'Drumblair' circle; he has a small (unpublished) body of poetry from the post-1944 years. A librarian with strong research interests, his output is mainly in bibliography. Although his work appears in anthologies and serials (*Focus*, *Public Opinion*, *Life and Letters*), no collection of his poetry or fiction exists.

PAT DUNN AND PAMELA MORDECAI

Instituto Caro y Cuervo

Founded in 1944 in Bogotá under the directorship of Father Félix Restrepo, the Instituto Caro y Cuervo's primary objectives were to prepare a scholarly Spanish-language dictionary and to collect the writings of the two nineteenth-century

Colombian scholars after whom it was named. The *Diccionario de construcción y régimen de la lengua castellana* was completed and published in eight volumes in 1994. The institute had already published a number of other dictionaries of Latin American Spanish, and its journal, *Thesaurus*, has provided a forum for scholarly debate on issues of linguistics and philology since its initial publication in 1947. The institute now contains departments of cultural history and literature, and the Andrés Bello Centre devoted to training Latin American philologists and lexicographers. In May 1998 an exhibition commemorating the institute's work was organized at the **Casa de las Américas** in Havana.

Further reading

http://www.caroycuervo.edu.co

Zéndegui, G. (n.d.) *Santuario de la lengua española: el Instituto Caro y Cuervo*, n.p.

MIKE GONZALEZ

Instituto Internacional de Literatura Iberoamericana

The Instituto Internacional de Literatura Iberoamericana was founded in 1938 in Mexico City by a group of professors of Latin American literature that included Arturo **Torres-Ríoseco**, Concha Meléndez, John Englekirk and Francisco Monterde (with the backing of Alfonso **Reyes** and Pedro **Henríquez Ureña**), and began to publish the *Revista iberoamericana* in the following year; the first issue opened with obituaries for Leopoldo **Lugones** and Alfonsina **Storni**. Since then, the Instituto has regularly held international conferences and has published the journal, volumes of conference proceedings and other books, including in recent years compilations in honour of Angel **Rama** and Antonio **Cornejo Polar**. From 1955 until his death in 1991, the *Revista iberoamericana* was edited by the Argentine poet and critic, Alfredo Roggiano, and for almost all of that time (and in the years since) the Instituto has been based at the University of Pittsburgh. The journal and publication series are currently directed by Mabel Moraña. The *Revista* has published special issues on **Borges**, José María **Arguedas**, **Vallejo**, **Huidobro** and other major figures, as well as on the literature of individual countries and topics of current interest (women's writing, colonial literature, *fin de siècle* literature and sexuality).

Further reading

www.pitt.edu/~iili/

Martin, G. (ed. and intro.) (2002) *Revista iberoamericana: Antología conmemorativa*, *Revista iberoamericana* 200.

DANIEL BALDERSTON

Insularismo

Puerto Rican essayist Antonio S. Pedreira's *Insularismo* (Insularity) (1934) was part of a series of extended essays that purported to diagnose a national pathology, a tradition that was related to so-called *arielismo* (see ***Ariel* and *arielismo***). A significant example from Spain was José Ortega y Gasset's *España invertebrada* (Invertebrate Spain) (1921); other examples include Alcides **Arguedas**'s *Pueblo enfermo* (Sick People) (1909) on Bolivia and Samuel Ramos's *El perfil del hombre y de la cultura en México* (Profile of Man and Culture in Mexico) (1934). Pedreira's essay, as its title implies, took its guiding metaphor from geography; Puerto Rico's geography, as well as its continued colonial status (four hundred years under Spanish rule, and then US occupation), made it isolated and docile. (The idea of Puerto Rican docility was taken up in a later essay by René Marqués, 'El puertorriqueño dócil' (The Docile Puerto Rican) (1962).) Pedreira was a defender of Puerto Rico's Hispanic identity, which sometimes coloured his observations on the presence of black culture on the island, and on its lost indigenous culture, with an unmistakable racism. He was also rather dismissive of the island's popular culture. His essay has been in print since its publication, with many editions by the Instituto de Cultura Puertorriqueña, and is considered one of the central texts of the Puerto Rican canon; at the same time, Pedreira's analysis and conclusions have been questioned (or perhaps demolished) by critics such as Juan Flores and Juan Gelpí.

Further reading

Flores, J. (1979) *Insularismo e ideología burguesa*, Río Piedras, PR: Ediciones Huracán.

Gelpí, J. (1993) *Literatura y paternalismo en Puerto Rico*, Río Piedras, PR: Universidad de Puerto Rico.

DANIEL BALDERSTON

intellectuals

The public intellectual has long played a prominent role in Latin American society. As analysed by the Uruguayan critic Angel **Rama** in *La ciudad letrada* (The Lettered City) (1984), the figure and role of the elite writer has been debated for a hundred years. The intense debates around issues of social justice of the last several decades have often been led by figures who are in opposition to governments and official cultural institutions. Green activism, gay and lesbian movements, indigenous rights movements, liberation theology and liberation philosophy as well as diverse women's movements have been organized by and centred around public intellectuals.

One example of a public intellectual is the Mexican writer and social commentator Carlos **Monsiváis**, who has made cameo appearances as himself in Mexican soap operas, has appeared in strip cartoons and was even called 'a frumpy Mexican Woody Allen' in the *New York Times* account of the funeral of Octavio **Paz**. Latin America has a long tradition of politicians who are intellectuals, often writers, including such eminent figures as Domingo Faustino Sarmiento, José **Martí**, Rómulo **Gallegos**, Juan **Bosch**, Ernesto **Cardenal**, Sergio **Ramírez**, Rosario **Castellanos**, Luis Alberto **Sánchez** and Elena **Poniatowska**. The experience of Cardenal, Ramírez and others in contemporary Nicaragua suggests, however, that in what Angel Rama called 'the city of letters' relations between the intellectual and the State are often uneasy and being renegotiated. (This process continues with such figures as Subcomandante Marcos in Chiapas, but also just as uneasily with intellectuals in positions of power recently such as Fernando Henrique Cardoso in Brazil and José Joaquín Brunner in Chile.)

The intellectual, considered as an identity category, was first used as a noun in late nineteenth-century France, and circulated almost immediately in Spanish and Portuguese. Writers of the *modernista* group in Spanish America (see **Spanish American modernism**) clearly considered themselves an elite class whose function was to articulate social issues and to design the future of society. This tendency is most famously associated with José Enrique **Rodó**'s essay *Ariel* (1900), which led to the tradition called *arielismo* (see ***Ariel* and *arielismo***). The professionalization of the writer in the first three decades of the twentieth century, and the writer's dissociation from the patronage system and movement into journalism and/or diplomacy (the Mexican writer Carlos **Fuentes** is a prominent case in point), created a new social space in which the writer as public intellectual mediated between the national bourgeoisie and the aspiring middle classes. Prefiguring the political movements of the 1960s and 1970s, writers often wrote on behalf of the dispossessed, for example in the *indigenista* novel and *negrista* poetry (see ***indigenismo***; ***negrismo***). Similarly, the painters of the Mexican Muralist and Andean *indigenista* groups cast themselves as spokespeople for the illiterate and undereducated masses, considered unable to speak for themselves. This notion appears forcefully in works such as José Carlos **Mariátegui**'s ***Siete ensayos*** (Seven Essays on Peruvian Reality) (1928) and Pablo **Neruda**'s '**Alturas de Macchu Picchu**' (Heights of Macchu Picchu) (published in *Canto General* (1950)).

After the Cuban Revolution artists and intellectuals, of whatever political stripe, were expected to take political positions of leadership on the social issues of the day. A famous example of this phenomenon was the **Casa de las Américas** debate including Mario **Benedetti**, Julio **Cortázar** and Mario **Vargas Llosa** on the role of the intellectual in the Revolution, out of which emerged a hard-line position from which Vargas Llosa and others quickly and loudly dissociated themselves, particularly after the **Padilla** case, arguing the necessity for the intellectual's independence from the State. By the time the Nicaraguan poet Ernesto Cardenal occupied the post of Minister of Culture in the Sandinista revolutionary government, the fractures in the traditional political movements had made clear that this established role was no longer sufficient. Emergent in the late 1970s, in a response both to authoritiarian leftist tendencies and the explicit repression of dictatorships, the new social movements of Latin America became the vital centre of political activity by the end of the next decade. New social movements (theorized by Ernesto Laclau) are distinguished from their predecessors not only by the content of their ideologies and worldviews, but also by the ways in which the ideas of the movements are materialized and disseminated – often sidelining the traditional intellectuals in favour of spokespersons whose qualifications included life experience and representativity.

Further reading

D'Allemand, P. (2001) *Hacia una crítica cultural latinoamericana*, Lima: Latinoamericana Editores.

González, C. (ed.) (1979) *Cultura y creación intelectual en América Latina*, Mexico City: Siglo XXI.

Laclau, E., and Mouffe, C. (1985) *Hegemony and Socialist Strategy*, London: Verso.

Lasarte, J.V. (ed.) (2001) *Territorios intelectuales: Pensamiento y cultura en América Latina*, Caracas: Fondo Editorial La Nave Va.

Marichal, J. (1978) *Cuatro fases de la historia intelectual latinoamericana (1810–1970)*, Madrid: Fundación Juan March/Cátedra.

Miller, N. (1999) *In the Shadow of the State. Intellectuals and the Quest for National Identity in 20th Century Spanish America*, London: Verso.

Rama, A. (1984) *La ciudad letrada*, Hanover, NH: Ediciones del Norte; English translation, John Charles Chasteen, *The Lettered City*, Durham, NC: Duke University Press. 1996.

Zea, L. (ed.) (1986) *América Latina en sus ideas*, Mexico City: Siglo XXI.

DANIEL BALDERSTON

invención de América, La

Edmundo O'Gorman's 1958 book *La invención de América* (The Invention of America) contributed to the debate about the impact of the Spanish arrival in America. Rejecting the idea of 'conquest', 'creation' or 'discovery', O'Gorman argued that from an ontological perspective America was an invention of the Western mind. The arrival in the new continent destabilized European perceptions of the world, requiring the modification of existing paradigms of understanding and explanation. Other Latin American writers adopted this approach; Carlos **Fuentes**'s *Terra Nostra* (1975) betrays O'Gorman's influence. Most Latin American **intellectuals** approached the 1992 Columbian quincentenary with a new formulation however: 'the encounter of two worlds'.

Further reading

Gonzalez, M. (1997) 'The Invention of America', in V. Smith (ed.), *Encyclopedia of Latin American Literature*, London: Fitzroy Dearborn, 33–5.

O'Gorman, E. (1961) *The Invention of America: An Inquiry into the Historical Nature of the New World and the Meaning of its History*, Bloomington: Indiana University Press.

ALEJANDRA LAERA

isla que se repite, La

La isla que se repite (The Repeating Island) is a key work of Latin American literary criticism by Antonio **Benítez Rojo**, published in the USA in 1989 and in a revised version in 1998 in Spain. From a postmodernist perspective (see **postmodernism**), the author proposes a new reading of the Caribbean world through its history, sociology, economics, anthropology and art. It is presented as a complex island bridge asymmetrically connecting South and North America and interwoven into the chronology of great moments in world history. Divided into three sections – Society, The Writer and The Book – the essay explores everything from the rich African religious and cultural traditions to the role of historical and literary figures.

Further reading

Benítez Rojo, Antonio (1992) *The Repeating Island: The Caribbean and the Postmodern Perspective*, Durham, NC: Duke University Press.

Bromberg, S.H. (1996) 'The New Story of the Caribbean: Quantum Mechanics and Postmodern Theory in Antonio Benitez Rojo's *La isla que se repite: El Caribe y la perspectiva posmoderna*', *Ometeca* 3–4: 142–53.

Campa, R. de la (1995) 'Mimicry and the Uncanny in Caribbean Discourse', *Latin Americanism*, Minneapolis: University of Minnesota Press, 85–120.

Spitta, S. (1997) 'Transculturation, the Caribbean, and the Cuban-American Imaginary', in F. Aparicio and S. Chávez-Silverman (eds), *Tropicalizations: Transcultural Representations of Latinidad*, Hanover: University Press of New England, 160–80.

WILFREDO CANCIO ISLA

Izaguirre, Boris

b. 1965, Caracas, Venzuela

Writer

Writer, chronicler and *enfant terrible* of the 1980s, Izaguirre began publishing a weekly column, 'Animal de frivolidad' (Frivolous Animal) in *El Nacional* in 1982 under the direction of Tomás Eloy **Martínez**. Throughout the 1980s he collaborated in José Ignacio **Cabrujas**'s *telenovelas*, *La dama de rosas* (Lady with the Rose) and *Señora*. Both productions were considered a turning point in the Venezuelan television industry. After his collaboration with Cabrujas, Izaguirre worked as a scriptwriter for co-productions in Argentina and Spain. His first novel, *El vuelo de los avestruces* (The Flight of the Ostriches) (1992), is a portrayal of the city's gay life, and was the second highest selling book of the year. As of the late 1990s Izaguirre is living in Spain and writing for TV and magazines.

JACINTO FOMBONA

J

Jackman, Oliver

b. 1929, Black Rock, St Michael, Barbados

Writer

A successful lawyer and newspaper columnist, Jackman's literary reputation is based on one short story, 'A Poet of the People' (1970) and one novel *Saw the House in Half* (1974), in addition to a series of poems published in the literary magazine *Bim*. The novel is concerned with themes of the West Indian in exile. The story is a more concise, and often considered superior, version of the novel. Jackman studied law at Sir Hugh Wooding Law School in Trinidad and was a member of the diplomatic corps in Washington DC from 1967 to 1984.

CAROL J. WALLACE

Jaffé, Verónica

b. 1957, Caracas, Venezuela

Writer and translator

Jaffé is one of the most renowned female writers dedicated to translating into Spanish the poetry of other women. She received her doctoral degree in linguistics and literature from the Ludwig-Maximilian-Universität in Munich and has written many articles on literary translation; she also teaches in Venezuela, Europe and the USA. She is the editor of the magazine *El libro actual* and director of Angria Editions, one of the new alternative poetry publishers in Venezuela. Author of three collections of poems, *El arte de la pérdida* (The Art of Loss) (1991), *El largo viaje a casa* (The Long Way Home) (1994) and *La versión de Ismena* (Ismena's Version) (2002), her prose works range from literary interpretation, theoretical reflections on language and culture, and Venezuelan literature and history.

VÍCTOR GALARRAGA OROPEZA

Jaimes Freyre, Ricardo

b. 1868, Tacna, Peru; d. 1933, Banfield, Argentina

Poet and historian

Jaimes Freyre, Bolivia's most important exponent of *modernismo* (see **Spanish American modernism**), was born in Peru, and served as ambassador in the USA, Chile and Brazil, before dying in Argentina; he also served as Bolivia's representative to the League of Nations. His most important book of poems, *Castalia bárbara* (Savage Castalia) (1899), appeared originally with an enthusiastic preface by Leopoldo **Lugones**. Similarly, **Borges** remarks in his lectures on poetry that one of the most striking poems in Spanish is the first poem in Jaimes Freyre's book, which begins: 'Peregrina paloma imaginaria/ Que enardeces los últimos amores;/ Alma de luz, de música y de flores,/ Peregrina paloma imaginaria' (Imaginary wandering dove/ that inflames the last loves;/ soul of light, of music and of flowers,/ imaginary wandering dove), a haunting stanza which has the lightness and the effervescent qualities of flight. Fascinated by Norse mythology, some of Jaimes Freyre's best poems refer to the violent and strange world of the Norse gods. He was also the author of a famous book on Spanish versification (1912), some short stories and several books of history, including a history of the Argentine city of Tucumán.

Further reading

Arrington, M.A. (1997) 'Ricardo Jaimes Freyre', in V. Smith (ed.), *Encyclopedia of Latin American Literature*, London: Fitzroy Dearborn, 444–6.

Carilla, E. (1967) *Ricardo Jaimes Freyre*, Buenos Aires: Ediciones Culturales Argentinas.

Cortés, D.A. (1989) 'Ricardo Jaimes Freyre', in *Latin American Writers*, ed. C.A. Solé and M.I. Abreu, New York: Scribners, 419–23.

Jaimes Freyre, R. (1957) *Poesías completas*, ed. F. Díez de Medina, La Paz: Ministerio de Educación y Bellas Artes.

—— (1969) *Modernismo y 98 a través de Ricardo Jaimes Freyre*, Madrid: Gredos.

DANIEL BALDERSTON

James, Cyril Lionel Robert

b. 1901, Tunapuna, Trinidad; d. 1989, Brixton, England

Writer

C.L.R. James was one of the Caribbean's most creative intellectual, artistic and political figures. A Marxist, he wrote fiction and drama, sports journalism, history, philosophy, literary and cultural criticism, and political pamphlets, and was a tireless supporter of revolutionary causes throughout the world. Born of well-educated, black, bourgeois parents in the then-English colony of Trinidad, James began his career as a fiction writer and a cricket reporter; the game remained a lifelong love and the basis around which he organized his autobiographical reflections on sport, colonial politics, art and society in *Beyond a Boundary* (1962). In often-neglected short stories such as 'La Divina Pastora' and 'Triumph' and in his novel *Minty Alley* (1936), James brought the techniques of modern European narrative to bear on the gritty reality of West Indian slums, focusing particularly on the problems and resources of women.

In 1932, James embarked upon a quarter-century odyssey through Britain and the USA, during which time he produced some of his most remarkable written work and established himself as one of the Marxist tradition's most original revolutionary thinkers. This period included *The Black Jacobins* (1938), a still classic study of the 1793 slave revolt in Saint Domingue which led to Haitian independence in 1804. Ten years later, James published *Notes on Dialectics*, a close, critical reading of Hegel grounded in, as James put it, a critical review of the 'labour movement from 1789', and focusing particularly on the theory and practice of Marx and Lenin. In 1950, James published *State Capitalism and World Revolution*. This work, critical of both Stalinism and the Trotskyist Fourth International, established James as a forceful and independent thinker in international Marxism. Yet James did not devote himself only to Marxist political theory and practice. While in jail on Ellis Island facing deportation hearings, he also wrote *Mariners, Renegades, and Castaways* (1953), a creative and succinct study of Herman Melville's *Moby Dick*, analysing the relations between the novel's narrator, the ship's captain and its expert 'Third World crew'. This work, in turn, grew out of notes and essays on American culture and politics that were only published, as *American Civilization*, five years after his death.

Mariners, with its focus on the Third World, also presaged James's active involvement in revolutionary decolonization in Africa, the Caribbean and Latin America, as well as among African-Americans in the USA. During the 1950s and 1960s, James visited many Africa nations (he wrote a full-length study of the revolution in Ghana) and Cuba, as well as major inner cities in the USA. He also returned to Trinidad for a brief period beginning in 1958, attempting to shape the future of the soon-to-be-independent nation. It was this work – political organization, lectures, pamphleteering on an international scale – which occupied James for most of the last quarter-century of his life.

Further reading

Buhle, P (ed.) (1986) *C.L.R. James: His Life and Work*, London and New York: Alison & Busby.

Farred, G. (ed.) (1996) *Rethinking C.L.R. James*, Oxford: Blackwell.

James, C.L.R. (1989) *The Black Jacobins: Toussaint L'Ouverture and the Santo Domingo Evolution*, New York: Vintage.

—— (1992) *The C.L.R. James Reader*, Oxford: Blackwell.

—— (1993) *Beyond a Boundary*, Durham, NC: Duke University Press.

—— (1993) *American Civilization*, Oxford: Blackwell.

SANTIAGO COLÁS

Jara, Cronwell

b. 1950, Piura, Peru

Writer

Jara exemplifies a new development in the Peru of the 1970s and 1980s: the emergence of writers from lower-class backgrounds whose work seeks to give their class a voice and a history. His 1989 novel *Patíbulo para un caballo* (Scaffold for a Horse), the story of a shanty town's fight against eviction, is a foundational myth of the marginalized masses' conquest of a space in national society.

Further reading

Jara C. (1998) 'Por qué escribo? Para qué escribo?', in J. Cornejo Polar (ed.), *Encuentro internacional narradores de esta América*, Lima: Universidad Católica de Lima.

JAMES HIGGINS

Jaramillo Agudelo, Darío

b. 1947, Santa Rosa de Osos, Colombia

Poet and novelist

A student of law and economics, Jaramillo began by writing intellectual and ironic poetry, but later switched to more intimate poems of love. Most of his poetry has been gathered in two volumes, both published in 1992: *Antología poética* (Poetic Anthology) and *Cuánto silencio debajo de esta luna* (So Much Silence under This Moon). He has also published a novel, *Cartas cruzadas*.

Further reading

Cobo Borda, J.G. (2000) 'Carta de Colombia: Mario Rivero, Darío Jaramillo y cuatro veces el futuro', *Cuadernos hispanoamericanos* 603: 123–6.

Shaw, D.L. (1988) 'Dario Jaramillo's *Cartas cruzadas* (1995) as a Post-boom Novel', *New Novel Review: Nueva Novela/Nouveau Roman Review*, Fall, 5(1): 19–35.

MIGUEL A. CARDINALE

Jaramillo Alvarado, Pío

b. 1884, Loja, Ecuador; d. 1968, Loja

Essayist, jurist, sociologist, journalist, educator and legislator

Jaramillo Alvarado's landmark 1922 essay, *El indio ecuatoriano*, reprinted numerous times, aimed to expose the miserable conditions endured by Ecuador's indigenous population, their bondage in a system of forced labour (*concertaje*) and their alienation from the rest of the nation. In this essay and in his historical works (notably, *La presidencia de Quito*) (1938), Jaramillo Alvarado traced the historical and juridical bases of Ecuador's national identity. His topics of investigation included land tenure and use, Ecuador's territorial sovereignty, legal history and ethnography. The founder of the Instituto Indigenista del Ecuador, he maintained links with *indigenistas* in other countries.

Further reading

Carrión, B. (1977) 'Pío Jaramillo Alvarado', in *Plan del Ecuador*, Guayaquil: Casa de la Cultura Ecuatoriana, 103–40.

EILEEN WILLINGHAM

Jaramillo Levi, Enrique

b. 1944, Colón, Panama

Writer

Although best known internationally for his short stories, including *Duplicaciones* (Duplications and Other Stories) (1973) and *The Shadow: Thirteen Stories in Opposition* (1996), Jaramillo is also a poet and essayist. He has also edited two anthologies, one in conjunction with Chambers entitled *Contemporary Short Stories from Central America* (1994) and the other being *When New Flowers Bloomed: Short Stories by Women Writers from Costa Rica and Panama* (1991). In addition, he founded and edited the influential Panamanian literary and cultural magazine *Maga*. He was educated at the local university, at the University of Iowa and at the Universidad Nacional Autónoma de México.

Further reading

Birmingham Pokorny, E.D. (ed.) (1993) 'Las realidades de Enrique Jaramillo Levi: Una entrevista', *Confluencia* 8–9(2–1): 185–98.

—— (1996) *Critical Perspectives in Enrique Jaramillo Levi's Work: A Collection of Critical Essays*, Miami: Universal.

Quiros Winemiller, B. (1990) 'Enrique Jaramillo Levi: Un autor que cuenta', *Chasqui* 19(2): 85–91.

NORMAN S. HOLLAND

Jauretche, Arturo

b. 1901, Lincoln, Buenos Aires Province, Argentina; d. 1974, Buenos Aires

Writer

In 1935, Jauretche founded FORJA (the Radical Orientation Force of Argentine Youth) with Raúl **Scalabrini Ortiz** and Luis Dellepiane, launching him on a career as a nationalist intellectual. FORJA was virulently anti-imperialist and strongly critiqued the liberal basis of Argentina's state and intellectual formation. After the rise of Perón (1943–45), Jauretche became a prominent Peronist intellectual, publishing such works as *Libros y alpargatas: Civilizados o bárbaros* (Books and Slippers: Civilized and Savages) (1983) and *El medio pelo en la sociedad argentina* (The Middle-Brow in Argentine society – or, as Nicolas Shumway has translated it, *Pretense and Social Climbing*) (1966) and the satirical *Manual de zonceras argentinas* (Guide to Argentine Follies) (1968).

DANIEL BALDERSTON

Javier, Adrián

b. 1967, Santo Domingo, Dominican Republic

Poet

One of the best poets from the younger generations in Santo Domingo, Javier is a former member of the Literary Circle Domingo Moreno Jimenes and the Franklin Mieses Burgos Poetry Workshop. He was only 21 years old when his book *El oscuro rito de la luz* (The Dark Rite of Light) (1989) won first prize in a contest. In *Bolero del esquizo* (The Bolero of the Schizoid) (1994), Javier returns to the simplicity of bolero lyrics to explore the split nature of **postmodernism**.

FERNANDO VALERIO-HOLGUÍN

Jekyll, Walter

b. 1849, Sussex, England; d. 1929, Jamaica

Folklorist and translator

Educated at Harrow and Cambridge, Walter Jekyll was in succession a priest and a music teacher, before in 1892 settling in the Blue Mountain region of Jamaica, partly for health reasons. His musical training and experience gained in travelling Europe and Scandinavia, fostered his interest in popular Jamaican music, dance and folklore, of which his collection *Jamaican Song and Story* (1907) is still a standard source. He was responsible for encouraging Claude **McKay** to write his groundbreaking verse in the Jamaican idiom, and appears, thinly disguised, in McKay's 1933 novel ***Banana Bottom***.

Further reading

Cobham, Rhonda (2000) 'Jekyll and Claude: The Erotics of Patronage in Claude McKay's *Banana Bottom*', in C. Patton and B. Sánchez-Eppler (ed.), *Queer Diasporas*, Durham, NC: Duke University Press, 122–53

LOUIS JAMES

Jesús, Dionisio de

b. 1959, Cevicos, Dominican Republic

Poet

Dionisio de Jesús studied philosophy and letters at the Universidad Autónoma de Santo Domingo, and his first poems appeared in magazines and anthologies in the early 1980s. Among other books, he has published *Axiología de las sombras* (Axiology of the Shadows) (1984) and *Oráculo del suicida* (Oracle of the Suicide) (1985). Although he works in marketing and advertising, he has continued writing and trying to integrate his professional experience into his poetry. His book *Homus Advertiser* (1996) points to the existential struggle of modern man.

FERNANDO VALERIO-HOLGUÍN

Jesús, Maria Carolina de

b. 1914, Sacramento, Minas Gerais, Brazil; d. 1977, São Paulo, Brazil

Writer

Granddaughter of slaves, illegitimate daughter who never knew her father, shanty dweller who made a precarious living gathering waste paper for sale, Maria Carolina de Jesús had a moment of great and unexpected fame when the journalist Aurélio Dantas edited the writings that she had put down in thirty-five notebooks and helped her publish *Quarto do despejo* (Trash Room, translated as *Child of the Dark*) (1960). The book went through numerous editions in Brazil and was translated into some thirty languages. She also published a novel, *Casa de alvenaria* (Brick House) (1961). A posthumous collection of her short stories, *Diário de Bitita* (Bitita's Diary) (1986), was based on interviews with French journalists. Her writing was celebrated for her simple allegories, parables in the manner of St Francis of Assisi, which told the truth about oppression, class and political struggle.

Further reading

Arrington, M.S., Jr (1993) 'From the Garbage Dump to the Brick House: The Diaries of Carolina Maria de Jesús', *South Eastern Latin Americanist* 36(4): 1–12.

Jesús, M.C. de (1960) *Quarto de despejo*, Rio de Janeiro: A Noite.

—— (1997) *I'm Going to Have a Little House: The Second Diary of Carolina Maria de Jesús*, trans. M.S. Arrington, Jr and R.M. Levin, Lincoln: University of Nebraska Press.

Vogt, C. (1983) 'Trabalho, pobreza e trabalho intelectual: Carolina Maria de Jesús', in Roberto Schwarz (ed.), *Os pobres na literatura brasileira*, São Paulo: Brasiliense, 204–13.

DANIEL BALDERSTON

JESÚS, PEDRO DE *see* López Acosta, Pedro de Jesás

Jewish writing

In the first half of the twentieth century, Jewish writing in Latin America – of which Alberto **Gerchunoff**'s *Los gauchos judíos* (The Jewish Gauchos of the *Pampas*) (1910) is the classic example – dealt mostly with the forging of a new identity combining Jewishness with various national identities. In recent decades, most Jewish writers have continued with the same basic subject, although the procedure has been reversed: starting from well-established national identities, they search for their Jewish roots and for the components shared by both. In some cases, this was a result of traumatic historical experiences such as dictatorship and repression in their native countries.

It is not sufficient to define Jewish writing by the explicit presence of Jewish themes, or by the writer's

Jewish self-identification or origin. It seems more accurate to look for its specificity in the focus on experiences shared by both Jews and Latin Americans – exile, survival in a hostile environment, multiple allegiances, marginality and a complex identity which should not be foregone in favour of cultural homogeneity: 'Jewish writers want to conjugate their own verb within the collective, polyphonic text of Latin American letters' (Senkman 1983). S. Sosnowski (1987b) defines it as a 'hyphenated' literature which 'must be read on two fronts at once'; this very fact 'negates the homogeneity of the continent' and therefore 'contributes to the central debates of Latin American literature'.

Increasing awareness of Jewish writing as a specific though integrated literary space within Latin American literature has produced many books and articles on the subject, and has led to the creation in 1985 of the International Association of Jewish Writers in Spanish and Portuguese, and its literary review *Noaj*. The Association is based in Jerusalem, with some 120 members living in the Americas, Europe and Israel. Several international conferences on Jewish writing in Latin America have taken place in various countries, and special sections have been devoted to it in conferences on general Latin American studies. Moacyr **Scliar** of Brazil, Margo **Glantz** of Mexico, Teresa **Porzencanski** of Uruguay, Luisa **Futoransky** and Sergio **Chejfec** of Argentina exemplify these trends.

Further reading

DiAntonio, R. and N. Glickman (eds) (1993) *Tradition and Innovation. Reflections on Latin American Jewish Writing*, Albany: SUNY Press.

Kalechofsky, R. (ed.) (1980) *Echad: An Anthology of Latin American Jewish Writings*, Marblehead, MA: Micah Publishing.

Landis, J.C. and N. Glickman (eds) (1992) *Argentine Jewish Literature – A Selection*, Flushing and New York: Queens College Press.

Lindstrom, N. (1989) *Jewish Issues in Argentine Literature*, Columbia: University of Missouri Press.

Lockhart, D.B. (ed.) (1996) *Latin American Jewish Writers: A Critical Dictionary*, New York: Garland.

Sadow, S.A. (ed.) (1999) *King David's Harp: Autobiographical Essays by Jewish Latin American Writers*, Albuquerque: University of New Mexico Press.

Senkman, L. (1983) *La identidad judía en la literatura argentina*, Buenos Aires: Pardés.

Senkman, L. and F.F. Goldberg (eds) (1987–) *Noaj – Literary Review*, Jerusalem: International Association of Jewish Writers in Spanish and Portuguese.

Sosnowski, S. (1987a) *La orilla inminente. Escritores judíos argentinos*, Buenos Aires: Legasa.

—— (1987b) 'Latin American Jewish Literature: On Ethnic and National Boundaries', *Folio* 17: 1–8.

FLORINDA F. GOLDBERG

Jitrik, Noé

b. 1928, Rivera, Province of Buenos Aires, Argentina

Critic and writer

Considered one of the most knowledgeable commentators on Latin American literature, Jitrik's critical writings are notable for their polemical quality, upholding the spirit of his early work in ***Contorno*** (although he later broke with co-editor David **Viñas**). His best-known essays include studies of Domingo Faustino Sarmiento, **Lugones**, **Güiraldes**, **Arlt**, **Borges**, **García Márquez**, **Vallejo**, **Carpentier** and numerous others. His writings on literary theory focus on practices of reading. He has also written poetry, short stories and novels, notably *Mares del sur* (Southern Seas) (1997). He has taught in Argentina, France, Mexico and the USA. Until recently he headed the Instituto de Literatura Hispanoamericana at the University of Buenos Aires, and is heading up a twelve-volume critical history of Argentine literature.

Further reading

Aguilar, G. and G. Lespada (1997) 'Prólogo', in N. Jitrik (ed.), *Suspender toda certeza: Antología*, Buenos Aires: Biblos, 9–16.

Brescia, P. (2002) 'De aflicciones, travesias y deseos: Conversación con Noé Jitrik', *Revista iberoamericana* 68(198): 187–93.

Jitrik, Noé (1970) *Ensayos y estudios de literatura argentina*, Buenos Aires: Editorial Galerna.
—— (1983) *Muerte y resurrección de Facundo*, Buenos Aires: Centro Editor de America Latina.
—— (1999) *Vertiginosas textualidades*, Mexico City: Coordinación de Difusión Cultural, Dirección de Literatura/UNAM.
—— (2000) *Los grados de la escritura*, Buenos Aires: Manantial.

DIEGO BENTIVEGNA

Joaquín Mortiz

Joaquín Mortiz is a Mexico City publishing house founded in 1962 by Spanish immigrant Joaquín Díez-Canedo. It specialized in works by Mexican authors (including Rosario **Castellanos**, Elena **Garro** and Carlos **Fuentes**), promoted cosmopolitan writings by authors associated with the ***Revista mexicana de literatura*** and introduced young Mexican writers associated with La **Onda**. In 1983 the company joined Planeta Chilena, a Spanish transnational publishing group, and in 1995 the founder's daughter, Aurora Díez-Canedo Flores, left the firm and ended the family's tradition as the arbiters of taste at Joaquín Mortiz.

DANNY J. ANDERSON

John, Errol

b. 1924, Port-of-Spain, Trinidad; d. 1988, London, England

Playwright and actor

John's lively, unflinching representations of the struggles of slum-dwellers are based on the city of his birth. A leading member of several amateur groups in the 1940s, his early, one-act plays, *How Then Tomorrow* (1947) and *The Tout* (1949), established his style as a playwright drawing on speech and song. Moving to London in 1951, disappointment with the minor roles offered to him as a black West Indian urged him to complete his major three-act work, *Moon on a Rainbow Shawl*, internationally recognized winner of the 1957 *Observer* playwriting award.

JILL E. ALBADA-JELGERSMA

Jones, Marion (Marion Glean O'Callaghan)

b. 1934, Woodbrook, Trinidad

Novelist

The author of *Pan Beat* (1973), a novel about steel band and the involvement of women in its development, and *J'Ouvert Morning* (1976), which examines middle-class predicaments in a society with a colonial heritage, Jones is preoccupied with issues of alienation and the claustrophobic ethos of island/colonial societies, race and poverty. She was educated in Trinidad (one of the first two women to be admitted to the Tropical School of Agriculture, St Augustine), the USA, and England, in library science and social anthropology.

Further reading

Maloy, F. (1978) ' "The Ellaville Special": Marion Jones and Her Fiddle', *Devil's Box* 12(4): 50–3.

FUNSO AIYEJINA

Jorge Alvarez, Editorial

One of Argentina's most important publishing houses between 1964 and 1972, when the country experienced a publishing boom led by the internal market, and the books of Argentine writers and the novelists of the **Boom** began to sell massively. Jorge Alvarez was one of the publishers who nourished this expanding market, producing, for example, the short stories of Rodolfo **Walsh**. The company also published a number of very successful thematic anthologies and the *crónicas* (Reports) on the bourgeoisie, on communication, on Latin America, on Cuba etc., as well as some lighter, more trivial topics, such as the Reports on Christmas. Alvarez later became a producer of rock concerts.

PABLO ALABARCES

Jorge Cardoso, Onelio

b. 1914, Calabazar de Sagua, Cuba;
d. 1992, Havana, Cuba

Writer

One of Cuba's most important short story writers, Jorge Cardoso worked for many years as a rural schoolteacher, journalist and scriptwriter for radio and television. Recognition came in 1945, when his story 'Los carboneros' (The Charcoal Burners) won the national literary prize. Later volumes – *El cuentero* (The Storyteller) (1958) and *El caballo de coral* (The Coral Horse) (1960) – confirmed his skilful use of popular language and culture, and the deep humanism characteristic of his work. He wrote a number of children's stories, and produced several more volumes of stories including *Caballito blanco* (Little White Horse) (1974).

Further reading

Bueno, S. (ed.) (1988) *Onelio Jorge Cardoso*, Havana: Casa de las Américas.

García Ronda, D. (1990) 'Onelio Jorge Cardoso: Cubania y universalidad', *Revista iberoamericana* 56(152–3): 993–9.

Hernández Azaret, J. (1982) *Algunos aspectos de la cuentística de Onelio Jorge Cardoso*, Santiago de Cuba: Ediciones Oriente.

Jorge Cardoso, O. (1981) *Cuentos completos*, Madrid: Ediciones de la Torre.

Prada Oropeza, R. (1988) *Poética y liberación en la narrativa de Onelio Jorge Cardoso*, Xalapa: Universidad Veracruzana.

Turton, P. (1979) 'Onelio Jorge Cardoso, Writer of the Cuban Revolution', in J. Griffiths and P. Griffiths (eds), *Cuba: The Second Decade*, London: Writers & Readers.

MARÍA IRENE FORNÉS

José Olympio

José Olympio is the name of the Rio de Janeiro publishing house founded in 1931. The publisher of many classics of Brazilian literature, including João Guimarães **Rosa**, Graciliano **Ramos**, Clarice **Lispector** and Carlos Drummond de **Andrade**, José Olympio is perhaps best known in Portugal and Brazil for its compact editions of the complete works of the Portuguese writers Eça de Queiroz and Fernando Pessoa and of numerous Brazilians including Joaquim Maria Machado de **Assis**, the great late nineteenth-century novelist, Carlos Drummond, Manuel **Bandeira**, Cecília **Meireles** and numerous others.

Further information

https://www.joseolympio.com.br/index2.html

DANIEL BALDERSTON

Journal of West Indian Literature

Twice-yearly publication of the Departments of English of the University of the West Indies, the journal started up in 1986. During the 1960s, members of the University's Faculty of Education and English Departments began to devise courses centred on West Indian literature and to press for the teaching of work by West Indian authors in regional schools, where previously their work had been subsumed into the study of 'Black' or 'Commonwealth' literature; the journal was representative of this move. Its emblem is Anancy, the folktale trickster, a character who epitomizes the ambivalences and ironies of West Indian identity.

Further information

http://humanities.uwichill.edu.bb/LLL/Lits/JournalsJWIL.htm

LORRAINE LEU

Juarroz, Roberto

b. 1925, Coronel Dorrego, Argentina;
d. 1995, Buenos Aires, Argentina

Poet

The originality of Juarroz's poetry is suggested by *poesía vertical* (vertical poetry), the constant title of all his collections from *Poesía vertical* (1958) to

Décimotercera poesía vertical (Thirteenth Book) (1993). All his writing is an intermittent journey in one direction, its language wholly consistent with this developing exploration. Juarroz graduated from the University of Buenos Aires, where he remained as lecturer and head of department. He was a fine translator and critic, and from 1958 to 1965 edited the journal *Poesía = poesía.*

Further reading

Bassetti, C. and K. Lohner (1986) 'Entrevista a Roberto Juarroz', *Letras* 15–16: 17–21.

Juarroz, R. (1991) *Poesía vertical*, Madrid: Visor.

Merwin, W.S. (1988) 'Roberto Juarroz: Fifteen Poems Translated and Introduced by W.S. Merwin', *The American Poetry Review* 17(1): 23–6.

ENRIQUE FOFFANI

Juliana, Elis

b. 1927, Curaçao, Netherlands Antilles

Poet, short story writer and artist

From the early 1950s onwards, Juliana has contributed extensively to Papiamentu literature, with over a dozen collections of poetry and short stories (some for children) to his name, including the four volume *Organisashon Planifikashon Independensia* (Organisation Planning Independence) (1979, 1981, 1983 and 1989). He cultivated as no other the intrinsic rhythmic and tonal aspects of the language, while also developing his interest in the Afro-Caribbean lifestyles of his people. In addition, Juliana distinguished himself in the visual arts, with various international exhibitions, and in ethnography, specializing in local folklore and the oral tradition.

AART G. BROEK

K

Kamenszain, Tamara

b. 1947, Buenos Aires, Argentina

Poet and essayist

Distinguished as a writer by her precision of poetic language and critical perception, Kamenszain explores memory, childhood, literature, Argentine life and Jewish tradition in spare and stylized patterns. Her texts are described by Sylvia **Molloy** as 'spectacles, as ceremonies, dazzling yet not indecipherable'. Kamenszain studied philosophy at the University of Buenos Aires. Resident in Mexico during Argentina's military dictatorship, she published there a major study on Latin American poetry, *El texto silencioso* (1983). Her books of poetry include *De este lado del Mediterráneo* (On This Side of the Mediterranean) (1973), *Los no* (The nos) (1977), *La casa grande* (The Big House) (1986), *Vida de living* (Sitting-room Life) (1991), *La edad de la poesía* (The Age of Poetry) (1996) and *Tango Bar* (1998).

Further reading

Lindstrom, N. (1996) 'Female Divinities and Story-Telling in the Work of Tamara Kamenszain', *Studies in Twentieth Century Literature* 20(1): 221–33.

Panesi, J. (1993) 'Banquetes en el living: Tamara Kamenszain', *Hispamérica* 22(64–5): 167–75.

GWEN KIRKPATRICK

Karlik, Sara

b. 1935, Asunción, Paraguay

Writer

A resident of Chile and prolific short story writer and novelist, Karlik has published five collections of short stories and three novels. In the short story genre her books include *Entre ánimas y sueños* (Between Spirits and Dreams) (1987), *Demasiada historia* (Too Much History) (1988) and *Efectos especiales* (Special Effects) (1989). Her novels include *Los fantasmas no son como antes* (Ghosts Are Not Like Before) (1989), *Juicio a la memoria* (Judgment to Memory) (1990) – which won the 1990 Premio Planeta (Planeta Prize) and the 1991 Premio Sésamo – and *Desde cierta distancia* (From a Certain Distance) (1991).

Further reading

Peiro Barco, J.B. (2001) 'El cuento femenino paraguayo después de Josefina Pla', *Cuento en Red: Estudios Sobre la Ficción Breve*, Fall, 4.

TERESA MÉNDEZ-FAITH

Kartún, Mauricio

b. 1946, Buenos Aires, Argentina

Playwright

In his plays *Chau Misterix* (1980), *La casita de los viejos* (The Old People's House) (1982), *Cumbia morena cumbia* (Cumbia, Brown Girl, Cumbia) (1983), the latter presented by Teatro Abierto, Kartún explored the construction of fantasies through the recreation of the world of children and their relations with adults. He rediscovered elements and characters from the *sainete* and other popular cultural practices (carnival, dances and touring '*criollo*' actors) in *El partener* (1988). He has won a number of prizes and is well known for his teaching of dramaturgy and script writing.

Further reading

Freire, S., R. Cossa and M. Kartún (1993) 'La dramaturgía: Un género en extinción?', *La Nación, suplemento literario*, Sept., 12: 6.

Kartún, M. (1993) 'Dramaturgía', *Revista del ateneo puertorriqueño* 3(8): 102–8.

—— (1999) *Teatro*, Buenos Aires: Corregidor.

NORA MAZZIOTTI

Keens-Douglas, Paul

b. 1942, Silver Mill, San Juan, Trinidad

Storyteller

Since 1974 in Trinidad, Keens-Douglas has concentrated on preserving, performing and developing Caribbean storytelling, poetry and oral traditions, with emphasis on Eastern Caribbean vernacular. He has created a host of memorable characters including Tanti Merle, Vibert, Slim, Sugar George and Dr Ah-Ah who populate his seven volumes of stories, twelve albums and videos. He is founder/producer of Trinidad's Tim Tam Storytelling Show and the annual Carnival Talk Tent which gives a variety of Caribbean performers, including younger folk artists, an opportunity to enact oral traditions.

Further information

Talk and More Talk (1999) Videorecording, Port-of-Spain, Trinidad and Tobago.

JOHN H. PATTON

Kellman, Anthony

b. 1958, Barbados

Writer and editor

Kellman is best known as a poet: his two collections *Watercourse* (1990) and *The Long Gap* (1996) were widely praised. His only novel, *The Coral Rooms* (1994), is a beautiful and disturbing examination of guilt, materialism and corruption on a post-colonial Caribbean island. As in his poems, his rendering of nature and landscape is profound. Editor of the first full-length US anthology of English-speaking Caribbean poetry, *Crossing Water* (1992), in 1997 he edited a Caribbean section of *Atlanta Review*. He is Professor of English and Creative Writing at Augusta State University in Georgia, USA.

Further reading

Kellman, A. (1993) 'The Revisionary Interior Image: A Caribbean Author Explores His Work', *Studies in the Literary Imagination* 26(2): 101–10.

KEITH JARDIM

Kempadoo, Peter (Lauchmonen)

b. 1926, Port Mourant, Guyana

Writer

Kempadoo's innovative narrative is framed by his experience of rural Indo-Guyanese society. Although he has worked in publishing, journalism, broadcasting and teaching, Kempadoo is widely recognized for two major novels, both published in London under his pseudonym Lauchmonen. In *Guiana Boy* (1960), the narrative voice of an Indo-Guyanese boy documents in simple detail the episodes of rural life which comprise his culture, engaging the reader by interweaving local and creole expressions. *Old Thom's Harvest* (1965) focuses on religious and ethnic practices in the life of a rural family.

JILL E. ALBADA-JELGERSMA

Khan, Ismith

b. 1925, Port-of-Spain, Trinidad

Writer

Like the character Jamini in his best-known novel *The Jumbie Bird* (1961), Khan was greatly influenced by his grandfather, a leader of the 1884 Hosay Rebellion, in which Muslims clashed with colonial authorities over the annual parade to commemorate early martyrs of Islam. The novel examines questions of identity and nation confronted by Trinidadian Indians ranging from former indentured labourers who dream of repatriation and rely on memory to deal with the experience of their dislocation, to first and second generations born on the island, whose culture becomes inevitably more hybrid. Other works include *The Obeah Man* (1964) and *The Crucifixion* (1987).

Further reading

Lacovia, R.M. (1972) 'Ismith Khan and the Theory of Rasa', *Black Images* 1(3–4): 23–7.

LORRAINE LEU

Kincaid, Jamaica

b. 1949, St John's, Antigua

Writer

Born Elaine Potter Richardson, to an Antiguan father and a mother of half-Carib descent who was from Dominica, Kincaid left Antigua in 1966 to become an au pair in New York. She made contact with a major writer from the *New Yorker* and, in 1973, adopted her writing name. By 1976 she was a staff writer for the magazine. Her stories *At the Bottom of the River* (1983) establish her very clear, highly professional literary style. She received acclaim for her work, including *Annie John* (1985), in which she captured a laconic, feisty, unselfconscious and highly perceptive young female voice which signified the struggle of Caribbean women to transcend colonization and its constructions of race, class and gender.

Her polemical essay on Antigua, *A Small Place* (1988), and her novels *Lucy* (1991) and *Autobiography of My Mother* (1996), while admired for their literary polish, have received mixed reviews and critical responses. Like Jean **Rhys**, Kincaid is a fine stylist and an emotionally and politically disturbing writer, not easily summed up in terms of political affiliations, but often co-opted by critics for their own political constructions. Like V.S. **Naipaul** and Rhys, she left the Caribbean at a young age and made her mark in prominent literary circles in the metropolis. Like Naipaul again, to whom she has been compared, Kincaid in *A Small Place* turns a savagely critical gaze on her birthplace, focusing on tourism and corruption, and has thus provoked some resistance. *Autobiography of My Mother* was the first Kincaid text to receive a largely negative reception. In this text, the characteristic terseness of the Kincaid protagonist – young and female – carries no self-questioning and seems to dull, in its relentless note of anger, the complexities of the other characters also.

Further reading

Andrade, Susan Z. (1996) 'Jamaica Kincaid', in B. Lindfors and R. Sander (eds), *Twentieth Century Caribbean and African Writers*, third series, Detroit: Gale Research, 157, 131–9.

Ferguson, M. (1994) *Jamaica Kincaid: Where the Land Meets the Body*, Charlottesville, VA: University Press of Virginia.

ELAINE SAVORY

King, Hugh B.N.

b. *c.*1953, Old Harbour, Jamaica

Playwright, producer, actor, director and screenwriter

King has produced his plays in North America and Europe, although their subject matter is firmly focused on the burning social issues in Jamaican life. His first play, *The Resurrection of Jonathan Digby*, first performed in Jamaica in 1977, examined the crisis of absentee fatherhood. Others, such as *Nightwork* (1978), deal with violent abuse and prostitution, topics often made palatable for the stage by comic situations and island humour emerging from the wit and cadences of Jamaican speech. King also manages his own production and graphics companies.

JILL E. ALBADA-JELGERSMA

King, Jane

b. 1952, Castries, St Lucia

Writer

Jane King's prize-winning poetry has been published in several regional and international anthologies, for example *Confluence: Nine Saint Lucian Poets* (1988). Her own collections include *Fellow Traveller* (1994), winner of the James Rodway Memorial Prize, and *In the Centre* (1993). She is also co-founder of The Lighthouse Theatre Company with her husband, Kendel **Hippolyte**. She is a lecturer in English at Sir Arthur Lewis Community College, Castries.

KEITH JARDIM

Koenders, Julius G.A.

b. 1886, Suriname; d. 1957, Suriname

Writer

An ardent defender of his native tongue Sranan Tongo and its cultural heritage, Koenders published the monthly *Foetoeboi* (Messengerboy) in Sranan Tongo and Dutch, which appeared for ten years between 1946 and 1956. He was virtually the sole contributor to the magazine, with numerous articles on education, Afro-Surinamese cultural heritage, politics and language. He was a primary school teacher in Suriname and, as he used to emphasize, the grandson of slaves.

AART G. BROEK

Kordon, Bernardo

b. 1915, Buenos Aires, Argentina

Writer

A social realist writer best known for his short stories on the plight of marginal individuals, Kordon's material is drawn from the urban underbelly, and like most social realists, he writes in a direct and forceful manner. His cinematographic style (many of his narratives have been turned into films) and use of colloquialisms make his texts highly readable, especially as they are totally free of the omniscient preachiness of other social realists. Kordon has also published five books on China and an anthology of Chinese writing.

Further reading

Rivera, J.B. (1983) 'Bernardo Kordon: Escorzo de un narrador argentino', *Cuadernos hispanoamericanos* 398: 372–85.

DAVID WILLIAM FOSTER

Kovadloff, Santiago

b. 1942, Buenos Aires, Argentina

Writer

Although known mainly as an essayist and cultural journalist, Kovadloff has also written poetry, children's stories and is a distinguished translator of poetry. *La nueva ignorancia* (New Ignorance) (1992), *El silencio Primordial* (Primordial Silence) (1993) and *Lo irremediable* (Irreparable, Irretrievable) (1996), his three most important collections of essays, deal with subjects ranging from the topical to the metaphysical and demonstrate an original and polemical mind.

Kovadloff is a regular contributor to the newspapers *La Nación* and *La Prensa* and appears regularly on television. In 1992 he received Argentina's highest literary prize, the Premio Nacional de Literatura Argentina.

Further reading

Altamiranda, D. (1998) 'Las armas y las letras: Respuesta de los intelectuales a la guerra sucia', *Chasqui: Revista de literatura latinoamericana*, May, 27(1): 23–32.

Darlin, S. (1973) 'Santiago Kovadloff habla de la "poesia contemporánea del Brasil" ', *Revista de cultura brasilena* 35 (Madrid): 85–96.

Kovadloff, S. (1982) 'Impopularidad de la poesía', *Quimera* 25: 59–61.

EVELYN FISHBURN

Kroon, Willem Eligio

b. 1886, Curaçao, Netherlands Antilles; d. 1949, Curaçao

Writer and activist

Working as an independent commercial artist, in the 1920s Kroon was also one of the first novelists writing in the native creole Papiamentu. He strongly defended Roman Catholicism in his novels, poetry and local journalism. In the 1930s, however, he clashed severely with the local Roman Catholic mission. Although he never left the Church, he stopped defending it in his writing. From the 1930s onwards he was also very active in the gradual rise of labour unions on the island.

AART G. BROEK

Kusch, Rodolfo

b. 1922, Buenos Aires, Argentina; d. 1979, Buenos Aires

Writer

Writing in several genres, Kusch focused on Argentine reality and the question of the 'essence' of America. Through marginal characters and settings and an appeal to popular ideas, he opposed liberal historiography with a celebration of 'barbarism'. Close to historical revisionism, in *La muerte del Chacho* (The Death of Chacho) (1960) he argued that 'civilization' was a false option. In *Credo rante*, a play first presented in 1958, and in *La leyenda de Juan Moreira* (The Legend of Juan Moreira) (1960), he mobilized elements of the popular imaginary.

Further reading

Fares, Gustavo (1992) 'La filosofía del mito: Rodolfo Kusch y Juan Rulfo', *Journal of Interdisciplinary Literary Studies* 3(2): 179–95.

SANDRA GASPARINI

Kyk-Over-Al

An annual literary magazine founded in 1945 in British Guiana by A.J. **Seymour**, the name *Kyk-Over-Al* refers to a still existing Dutch fort (*c.*1616) on the island of the same name. Under Ian **McDonald**'s directorship (1984–), the magazine became one of the most distinguished literary publications of the Caribbean region, publishing writers such as Derek **Walcott**, Martin **Carter** and Wilson **Harris**. According to Seymour, it was meant to build an awareness of the Guyanese people's 'intellectual and spiritual possibilities', which it has done by giving voice to resident West Indian and exiled writers. A special fiftieth anniversary edition was edited by Ian McDonald in 1995.

Further reading

Allsopp, R., I. McDonald and A.J. Seymour (1970) *The Literary Tradition in Guyana*, Georgetown: The National History and Arts Council of Guyana.

Brathwaite, E.K. (1966) '*Kyk-Over-Al* and the Radicals', *New World*, Guyana Independence Issue, 55–7.

Seymour, A.J. and I. McDonald (eds) (1986) 'Anthology of Selections from *Kyk-Over-Al* (1945–1961)', *Kyk-Over-Al*, 33–4.

KEITH JARDIM

L

Labrador Ruiz, Enrique

b. 1902, Sagua La Grande, Cuba;
d. 1991, Miami, Florida, USA

Writer

A poet, short story writer, essayist and novelist, Labrador Ruiz's '*gaseiforme*' (gasiform) fiction, as he called it, were fragmentary fictions whose innovative quality prefigures the **Boom** of the 1960s. A journalist and travelling salesman, his volumes of stories include *Trailer de sueños* (Dream Trailer) (1949) and *El gallo en el espejo* (The Rooster in the Mirror) (1953), considered by many as classics of the Cuban short story, and *Cuentos* (Stories) (1970). Among his novels are *El laberinto de sí mismo* (Labyrinth of Himself) (1933) and *La sangre hambrienta* (The Hungry Blood) (1950), which brought him the National Novel Prize. In 1976 he left Cuba for Miami and published his essays in *El pan de los muertos* (Bread of the Dead) (1988) and *Cartas a la carte* (Letters à la carte) (1990).

Further reading

Alba Buffill, E. (1993) 'Significación de Labrador Ruiz en las letras de Hispanoamérica', *Círculo* 22: 29–37.

Bueno, S. (1964) 'Trayectoria de Labrador Ruiz', in *Temas y personajes de la literatura cubana*, Havana: Ediciones Unión.

Labrador Ruiz, E. (1970) *Cuentos*, Havana: UNEAC.

—— (1983) *El laberinto de sí mismo*, New York: Senda Nueva de Ediciones.

Montero López, O. (1990) 'Entrando en el laberinto: Introducción a Enrique Labrador Ruiz y la novela de la dialéctica personal', *Lucero* 1: 69–76.

Piñera Llera, H. (1985) 'Enrique Labrador Ruiz: Patriarca de las letras cubanas', *Círculo* 14: 57–9.

WILFREDO CANCIO ISLA

Lacrosil, Michèle

b. 1915, Guadeloupe

Writer

Lacrosil's first two novels – *Sapotille et le serin d'argile* (Sapotille and the Clay Canary) (1960) and *Cajou* (1961) – are narrated by a female mulatto protagonist whose struggles in the face of persistent patriarchal discrimination recall the earlier work of Martinican Mayotte **Capécia**. Subjects of their discourse, but objects of men's violence, the protagonists seek flawed solutions in suicide and the predictable flight to Paris respectively. The multiple points of view of Lacrosil's third novel, *Demain Jab-Herma* (1967), offer a less bleak outcome of the racial and social tensions in Guadeloupe, as the title suggests: the black protagonist Jab-Herma will have his day.

Further reading

Ojo Ade, F. (1993) 'Color, Class and Gender in Michèle Lacrosil's Novels', *The Literary Griot* 5(2): 25–50.

Smith, R.P., Jr (1974) 'Michèle Lacrosil: Novelist with a Color Complex', *French Review* 47: 783–90.

JILL E. ALBADA-JELGERSMA

Ladoo, Harold

b. 1945, Couva, Trinidad; d. 1973, Trinidad

Writer

An extraordinary and tragic figure, Ladoo (known as 'Sonny') emigrated to Canada in 1968, studying by day and working at night to support his family. In 1972, his graduation year, he published the uncompromising *No Pain Like This Body*, a novel following the trials of a rice-growing family faced with a hostile Nature, alcoholism and extreme poverty. Their completely uncontrived, bare dialect reflects the limited possibilities of their lives. The novel is rarely studied – perhaps because it is genuinely distressing reading. Ladoo's own life was cut short during a research trip to Trinidad, where he was attacked and left for dead in a ditch. The novel *Yesterdays* (1974) was published posthumously.

Further reading

Early, L.R. (1976) 'The Two Novels of Harold Ladoo', *World Literature Written in English* 15: 174–84.
Ladoo, H. (1987) *No Pain Like This Body*, Portsmouth, NH: Heinemann.
Such, P. (1978) 'The Short Life and Sudden Death of Harold Ladoo', *Bim* 63: 205–13.
Wyke, C.H. (1982) 'Harold Ladoo's Alternate Worlds: Canada & Carib Island', *Canadian Literature* 95: 39–49.

LORRAINE LEU

Laferriere, Dany

b. 1953, Port-au-Prince, Haiti

Writer

A journalist under François Duvalier, Laferriere left for exile in Montreal in 1978 where he published his first bawdy, satirical novel *Comment faire l'amour avec un nègre sans se fatiguer* (How to Make Love to a Black Man without Getting Tired) (1985), a scandalous best-seller and major film. His next work, *Eroshima* (1987), was in the same vein. He later moved to Miami and published in 1991 a novel about growing up in Haiti, *L'odeur de café* (An Aroma of Coffee), followed by two more autobiographical novels. A recent novel again returns to Haiti, *Pays sans chapeau* (Land without a Hat) (1996).

Further reading

Coates, C.F. (ed.) (1999) 'Dany Laferriere: Fiction Writer: A Special Section', *Callaloo* 22(4): 901–49.
Delas, D. (2001) 'Dany Laferriere: Un ecrivain en liberte', *Notre librairie* 146: 88–90.

J. MICHAEL DASH

Lafourcade, Enrique

b. 1927, Santiago, Chile

Writer

Noted for his use of irony and black humour, Lafourcade wrote several novels, including *Frecuencia modulada* (Modulated Frequency) (1968) and *Palomita blanca* (Little White Dove) (1971), later filmed by Raúl Ruiz. He is a frequent author of the genre ***crónica*** in *El Mercurio*, one of which, *Salvador Allende* (1973), was published as a book. He went into exile for a time. His other work includes *La fiesta del rey Acab* (King Acab's Party) (1959), a satire on Dominican dictator Trujillo, *El gran taimado* (Great Cunning) (1984), indirectly about Pinochet, and *Hoy está solo mi corazón* (Today My Heart Is Lonely) (1990). He is also a fixture on Chilean television.

Further reading

Lichtblau, M. (1973) 'The Dictator Theme as Irony in Lafourcade's *La fiesta del Rey Acab*', *Latin American Literary Review* 2(3): 75–83.
Morello Frioli, C. (1982) 'Enrique Lafourcade, Premio de Literatura María Luisa Bombal', *Nueva revista del Pacífico* 22: 17–20.

CELINA MANZONI

Laleau, León

b. 1892, Port-au-Prince, Haiti; d. 1979, Petionville, Haiti

Writer

A writer and diplomat, Laleau was sympathetic to ***indigènisme*** even though he more conservatively clung to the techniques of French Parnassianism. His most prolific period was in the 1930s, when he published his best-known collection of poems *Musique nègre* (Black Music) (1931). He never belonged to any movement, but his reputation grew with the inclusion of some of his stylized evocations of national or racial themes in Leopold Senghor's 1948 anthology of black writing. He was also known in Haiti as a novelist for *Le Choc* (The Shock) (1932) which chronicled life during the Occupation.

J. MICHAEL DASH

Lamborghini, Osvaldo

b. 1940, Buenos Aires, Argentina; d. 1985, Barcelona, Spain

Writer

From his first text *El fiord* onwards, Lamborghini flew in the face of all the prevailing currents in an Argentine literature absorbed with the definition of identity. His writing is 'illegible' because of its obscenity, the violence of its scenes, its opposition to representation, and its foul language. It is illegible because of its destruction of the narrative and because its texts are a kind of collage of pieces of paper, scribblings and doodles. His poetics is one of the most original and innovative of the century; its lines of writing only began to be taken up at the end of the 1980s by writers like César **Aira** and Alan **Pauls**.

Further reading

Astutti, A. (2001) *Andares clancos: Fábulas del menor en Osvaldo Lamborghini, J. C. Onetti, Rubén Darío, J. L. Borges, Silvina Ocampo y Manuel Puig*, Rosario, Argentina: Beatriz Viterbo Editor.

Lamborghini, O. (1988) *Novelas y cuentos*, intro. C. Aira, Buenos Aires: Ediciones del Serbal.

GRACIELA MONTALDO

Lamming, George

b. 1927, Carrington, Barbados

Writer

George Eric Lamming was a prominent figure in the London West Indian literary movement during the 1950s. His first work, ***In the Castle of My Skin*** (1953), has attracted a wide readership, and the seven novels he has written to date along with such critical work as *The Pleasures of Exile* (1992) have assured his place in the Caribbean 'canon'. Lamming taught in Trinidad, and emigrated in 1950 to Britain. This experience sharpened his awareness of his colonial upbringing, which was explored, evocatively and critically, in *In the Castle of My Skin*. While *Castle* ended with 'G' leaving his home island, *The Emigrants* (1954) portrays West Indians from different areas voyaging to England on the ironically named 'Golden Image', for each is searching for the fulfilment denied him at home. They discover a new shared identity as 'West Indians', but in England they find only confusion and the novel, dominated by scenes of darkness, ends with a brawl in a club.

Set on the composite Caribbean island of San Cristobal immediately before independence, *Of Age and Innocence* (1958) is a political novel where 'age' is represented both by the reactionary forces surrounding the white chief of police and by Ma Shepherd, spokeswoman for the traditional black folk. The 'innocents' are boys, African, Indian and English, the multicultural society of the future. Between them stands Shephard, the popular leader who, although emotionally unstable, holds the key to the island's future. His mysterious murder leaves that future in the balance. *Season of Adventure* (1960) takes place immediately after independence, and concerns Fola, the coloured step-daughter of Piggott, the chief commissioner of police. Fola has a moment of vision in a Vodun ceremony which turns her away from her adoptive culture to search for her true father among common people of the Forest Reserve. Piggott's murder leads to their violent repression by the police, and the drums, the expression of their communal spirit, are smashed. This eventually provokes a rebellion, and the novel ends with qualified hope for the future.

Water with Berries (1971) returns to the immigrant scene some twenty years later. The title refers to Caliban's words in *The Tempest*, but the setting is Prospero's island, England, and the Calibans are three West Indian artists, working out their search for an independent identity amid increasing violencc. In *Natives of My Person* (1971), set in the sixteenth century, a slave ship retraces the Middle Passage without slaves, hoping to create an ideal society, but the expedition is doomed by the moral failure of the captain and the crew. The women of the expedition, sent on ahead, express a qualified hope for redemption. A complex, poetic work, drawing on historical sources but creating a timeless exploration of the colonial dilemma, it is arguably Lamming's finest work to date.

Further reading

Jonas, J. (1990) *Anancy in the Great House*, New York: Greenwood Press.

Nair, S. (1996) *Caliban's Curse: George Lamming and the Revisioning of History*, Ann Arbor: University of Michigan Press.

Pouchet Paquet, S. (1982) *The Novels of George Lamming*, London: Heinemann.

Thiong'o, N.W. (1973) 'George Lamming and the Colonial Situation', *Homecoming*, New York: Lawrence Hill, 127–44.

LOUIS JAMES

Lange, Norah Berta

b. 1906, Buenos Aires, Argentina;
d. 1972, Buenos Aires

Writer

An *ultraista* poet (see ***ultraismo***), Lange wrote for several Argentine avant-garde publications. Her first volume of poetry, *La calle de la tarde* (Afternoon Street) (1925), was recommended by her friend Jorge Luis **Borges**. Lange's novels – *Cuarenta y cinco días y treinta marineros* (Forty-five Days and Thirty Sailors), *Personas en la sala* (People in the Room) and *Los dos retratos* (Two Portraits) – are the work of a solid and individual writer. Together with Oliverio **Girondo**, her partner since 1930, she was the point of contact between artists and intellectuals from Argentina and abroad. *Cuadernos de infancia* (Childhood Notebooks) (1937), her autobiography, is her best-known work.

Further reading

Dominguez, N. (1996) 'Literary Constructions and Gender Performance in the Novels of Norah Lange', in A. Brooksbank Jones and C. Davies (eds), *Latin American Women's Writing: Feminist Readings in Theory and Crisis*, New York: Oxford University Press.

Miguel, M.E. de (1991) *Norah Lange*, Buenos Aires: Planeta.

Rosman Askot, A. (1997) 'La mise en scène de la escritura: La obra narrativa de Norah Lange', *Monographic Review/Revista monográfica* 13: 286–97.

Sibbald, K.M. (1997) 'Norah Lange', in V. Smith (ed.), *Encyclopedia of Latin American Literature*, London: Fitzroy Dearborn, 466–8.

ADRIANA AMANTE

Lara, Jesús

b. 1898, Muela, Cochabamba, Bolivia;
d. 1980, Cochabamba

Writer

A poet, novelist and essayist, Lara participated as a private soldier in the Chaco War (1932–33). His first language was Quechua, and he was a member of the Bolivian Communist Party – and its candidate for the vice presidency in 1956. An *indigenista* intellectual (see ***indigenismo***; **intellectuals**), he wrote prolifically from 1957 onwards, when his *Tragedia del fin de Atahuallpa* (The Tragedy of Atahualpa's Death) was published. His twenty or so published works include a

Diccionario Quechua (1978), writings on the Inca empire and Quechua literature, several novels set in the Cochabamba valley, the biography of the guerrillero Inti Peredo, who died beside Che Guevara in 1967, and *Repete* (1978) about the Indians in the Chaco War.

Further reading

Muñoz, W.O. (1986) 'La realidad boliviana en la narrativa de Jesús Lara', *Revista iberoamericana* 52(134): 225–41.

XIMENA MEDINACELI

Larreta, Antonio

b. 1922, Montevideo, Uruguay

Playwright and theatre director

Founder of the Teatro de la Ciudad de Montevideo (TCM) in 1960, which was at the centre of a brilliant period in theatre, Larreta was instrumental in bringing to Uruguay some of the best international plays, which he translated, adapted and directed.

His version of Lope de Vega's *Fuenteovejuna* was a particular milestone. In 1972 he won the coveted **Casa de las Américas** prize in theatre for his play, *Juan Palmieri*, but it was censored by the military dictatorship; however, it did première in Buenos Aires in 1973. Exiled in Spain, Larreta wrote a number of film and TV scripts, made a film, *Nunca estuve en Viena* (I was Never in Vienna) (1988) and published a novel, *Volavérunt* (1980), which won the Planeta prize in 1980. Currently he alternates his residence between Spain and Uruguay. In Montevideo he founded the Teatro del Sur where he has returned to directing and acting.

Further reading

Campanella, H. (1982) 'Antonio Larreta in Exile', *Index on Censorship* 11(1): 29–30.

MARINA PIANCA

Larreta, Enrique

b. 1873, Buenos Aires, Argentina; d. 1961, Buenos Aires

Writer

Larreta is known particularly for the historical novel *La gloria de don Ramiro* (The Glory of Don Ramiro) (1908), a recreation of the Spain of Philip II and one of the prose monuments of **Spanish American modernism**. Written in an archaic, ornate style, this novel was studied in depth by the Spanish philologist Amado Alonso in a 1942 book and mentioned by **Borges** in the important essay 'La postulación de la realidad' (The Postulation of Reality) (1930). Larreta's other works include a novel of gaucho life, *Zogoibi* (1926), historical studies, travel writings and a book of poems. The Argentine ambassador in France during the First World War, he was close to Maurice Barrès. His house and collections of Spanish art form the basis of a museum in Buenos Aires.

Further reading

Alonso, A. (1942) *Ensayo sobre la novela histórica: el modernismo en La gloria de don Ramiro*, Buenos Aires: Instituto de Filología.

Arrington, M.S. (1997) 'Enrique Larreta', in V. Smith (ed.), *Encyclopedia of Latin American Literature*, London: Fitzroy Dearborn, 468–70.

Ibieta, G. (1986) *Tradition and Renewal in La gloria de don Ramiro*, Potomac, MD: Scripta Humanistica.

Larreta, E. (1924) *The Glory of Don Ramiro*, trans. L.B. Walton, New York: Dutton.

Lupi, A. (1989) 'Enrique Larreta', in C.A. Solé and M.I. Abreu (eds), *Latin American Writers*, New York: Scribners, 2, 471–6.

DANIEL BALDERSTON

Laso, Margarita

b. 1963, Quito, Ecuador

Poet and singer

A talented popular singer with considerable interpretative skill, Laso is also gaining a reputation as a poet. Her works *Erosonera* (Erorhythms) (1991), *Queden en mi lengua mis deseos* (Let My Desires Remain on My Tongue) (1994) and *El trazo de las cobras* (The Cobras' Path) (1997) reveal rich erotic images and experimental rhythms. The exaltation of the body, nature and the recovery of the plenitude of fulfilled, unrestricted love underline the subversive and liberating force of the erotic in a repressive society. Her poetry combines the concrete and the cosmic, so that reality and desire can become one.

MERCEDES M. ROBLES

Lastra, Pedro

b. 1932, Quillota, Chile

Writer

Lastra is a university professor at State University of New York at Stony Brook (1972–95), literary scholar and poet. From 1966 to 1973 he directed the influential collection Letras de Américas (Letters of America) at Editorial Universitaria. He has studied rigorously the nineteenth-century Spanish American short story and the most distinguished Latin American contemporary narrators. In *Noticias del extranjero* (Travel Notes) (1996), Lastra deploys a concise and incisive language to reveal the ghost-like existence of the poet and his immediate surroundings.

Further reading

Lastra, Pedro (1982) *Noticias del extranjero*, Mexico City: Premiá Editora.

—— (1987) *Relecturas hispanoamericanas*, Santiago: Editorial Universitaria.

—— (1987) *Leído y anotado: Letras chilenas e hispanoamericanas imágenes encuentros*, Santiago: Editorial Universitaria.

OSCAR D. SARMIENTO

Lauer, Mirko

b. 1947, Zatec, Czech Republic

Writer

Living in Peru from his early years, Lauer became known as a poet with his first collection, *En los cínicos brazos* (In the Cynical Arms) (1966). Later came *Ciudad de Lima* (City of Lima) (1968), *Santa Rosita y el péndulo proliferante* (Little Saint Rose and the Proliferating Pendulum) (1972), *Bajo continuo* (Basso continuo) (1975) and others. He is also a noted researcher on popular visual arts and contemporary literature. His journalistic work appears in the editorial pages of the Lima social democratic newspaper *La República*.

Further reading

Ortega, J. (1982) 'Mirko Lauer', *Hispamérica* 11(32): 49–63.

JOSÉ ANTONIO MAZZOTTI

Lauffer, Pierre A.

b. 1920, Curaçao, Netherlands Antilles; d. 1981, Curaçao

Writer

The best-known author writing in Papiamentu, Lauffer has a dozen collections of poetry and short stories to his name. He edited the first anthology of Papiamentu literature, *Di Nos* (Our Literary Heritage) (1971), and wrote essays on the history of Papiamentu writing. He focused on traditional social and cultural patterns of Curaçao society, while criticizing the industrialization and Westernization of the island. He was a master at deploying the tonal and rhythmic patterns of Papiamentu and defended the use of archaic or little known words and phrases.

Further reading

Eustatia, M. (1986) *Catalogus van werken van Pierre*

Lauffer 1942–1986, Curaçao: Universiteit van de Nederlanse Antillen, Uitgave no. 30.
Lauffer, P.A. (1971) *Di nos, antologia di nos literatura*, Willemstad: Boekhandel Salas.
—— (1971–74) *Un selekshon di palabra i ekspreshon*, Curaçao: St Augustinus Boekhandel, 2 vols.

AART G. BROEK

Laurel

Laurel: Antología de la poesía moderna en lengua española is an ambitious and controversial anthology of Spanish and Spanish American poetry, prepared by the Mexican poets Xavier **Villaurrutia** and Octavio **Paz** and the Spanish poets Emilio Prados and Juan Gil Albert, and published in 1941 by Editorial Séneca in Mexico City. Thirty-seven poets are included, with a portrait sketch, brief bio-bibliographical information and some dozen texts for each figure. León Felipe and Pablo **Neruda** refused to have their works included, apparently because of animosity toward José Bergamín of Séneca or other organizers.

MERLIN H. FORSTER

Leal, Rine

b. 1930, Havana, Cuba; d. 1996, Caracas, Venezuela

Theatre critic

Leal's career as journalist and critic began in the Havana daily *Pueblo* and the magazines *Carteles* and *Bohemia* in 1954. In 1959 he became theatre critic for *Revolución* and was a founder of its supplement ***Lunes de Revolución***. His critical essays and historical research included *En primera persona* (First Person) (1967) and the most thorough history of Cuban theatre from its origins until 1902, published as the two-volume *La selva oscura* (The Dark Forest) (1975, 1982). In 1995 he edited *Cinco autores* (Five Authors), an anthology of Cuban exile drama.

Further reading

Leal, R. (1986) 'Problemas metodológicos de la investigación teatral (una aproximación)', *Universidad de La Habana* 227: 289–301.
—— (1993) 'Asumir la totalidad del teatro cubano', *OLLANTAY Theater Magazine* 1(2): 26–39.
Piñera, V. (1990) *Teatro inconcluso*, ed. R. Leal, Havana: Unión de Escritores y Artistas de Cuba.

WILFREDO CANCIO ISLA

Lee, Easton

b. 1931, Trelawny, Jamaica

Playwright and poet

Lee's early plays are based on improvisations from the period when, as drama officer, he worked with groups across Jamaica. He has worked in radio and television, producing (live) and directing his plays, *Paid in Full* (1965) and *Born for the Sea* (1962–65). In 1988 he received the Institute of Jamaica's Silver Musgrave Medal. Also an actor and poet, Lee was educated in Jamaica, thereafter studying theatre in the USA and communications in the UK. His first book of poetry, *From Behind the Counter: Poems from a Rural Jamaican Experience*, was published in 1998.

PAT DUNN AND PAMELA MORDECAI

Lee, John Robert

b. 1948, St Lucia

Poet and teacher

A graduate of the University of the West Indies, Jamaica, Lee worked for several years in theatre, radio and television. Since 1979 he has been active in the Christian Ministry, teaching, preaching and writing a weekly Christian column for the main local newspaper. His collections of poetry include: *Vocation* (1975), *Dread Season* (1978), *The Prodigal* (1983), *Possessions* (1984), *Saint Lucian* (1988) and *Clearing Ground* (1991). Lee is also a drama critic and librarian and he has compiled a bibliography of St Lucian literature.

Further reading

Gilkes, M. (1992) 'Confluences: Reconciling Life and Language – The Poetry of John Robert Lee', *Wasafiri* (July–August).

KEITH JARDIM

Leeuwen, Willem Christiaan Jacobus van

b. 1922, Curaçao, Netherlands Antilles

Writer

A practising lawyer in Venezuela and Curaçao, in 1947 van Leeuwen (nicknamed Boeli) made his literary debut as a poet, but soon turned to prose writing in Dutch. He is the author of five novels, which address the position of white creole elites and interracial relationships in Antillean society, such as in *De rots der struikeling* (The Rock of Offence) (1959), which is also available in Spanish as *La piedra de la tropieza* (1964). His later novels, including *Het teken van Jona* (The Sign of Jonah) (1988), show a preoccupation with social outcasts and their struggles to survive.

Further reading

Coemans-Eastatia, M.W.R. and H.E. Coomans (eds) (1991) *Drei Curaçaose Schrijvers in veelvoud: Boeli van Leeuwen, Tip Marugg, Frank Martinus Arion*, Zutphen: de Walburg Pers.

AART G. BROEK

Lemebel, Pedro

b. 1952, Santiago, Chile

Writer and performance artist

Lemebel set out to legitimize homosexuality in Chile through writing and public performances. In 1987 he and Francisco Casas formed Las Yeguas del Apocalipsis. His first book, *Incontables* (Tales Not to Be Told) (1986), presents writing as a transvestite act which displaces homosexual desire. In his urban *crónicas* (see **crónica**) *La esquina es mi corazón* (My Heart is the Street Corner) (1995), a postmodern *flâneur* walks the city, exposing the underlying poverty and social marginalization behind its neoliberal facade. Gay people from poor suburbs become tragic kitsch symbols of waste and injustice. *Loco afán* (Crazy Eagerness) (1996) depicts AIDS victims in Chile.

Further reading

Blanco, F. and J.G. Gelpi (1997) 'El desliz que desafia otros recorridos: Entrevista con Pedro Lemebel', *Nomada* 3: 93–8.

Del Pino, A.M. (1998) 'Chile: Una loca geografía o las crónicas de Pedro Lemebel', *Hispamérica* 27(80–1): 17–28.

Lemebel, Pedro (1997) *La esquina es mi corazón: crónica urbana*, Providencia, Santiago: Editorial Cuarto Propio.

—— (1997) *Loco afán: Crónicas de sidario*, Santiago: LOM Ediciones.

—— (1998) *De perlas y cicatrices: Crónicas radiales*, Santiago: LOM Ediciones.

—— (2001) *Tengo miedo torero*, Santiago: Editorial Planeta Chilena.

LUCÍA GUERRA

Leñero, Vicente

b. 1933, Guadalajara, Mexico

Writer

Although a novelist and non-fiction writer, Leñero is best known as a principal innovator in contemporary Mexican drama. He began a distinguished career as a writer in the late 1950s, and first won recognition in 1963 when Seix Barral Publishers (Barcelona) awarded the Biblioteca Breve Prize to his novel *Los albañiles* (The Construction Workers). The novel modified the conventions of detective fiction and portrayed class tensions among a group of construction workers, an architect and a police detective assigned to investigate the murder of a night watchman.

Although his other 1960s novels were characterized by highly self-referential narrative games, in the 1970s two other central concerns became explicit: religion and non-fiction writing. In *El evangelio de Lucas Gavilán* (The Gospel According to Luke Crow) (1979), Leñero created a Mexican version of the Gospel of Luke following the tenets of liberation theology. In *Los periodistas* (The Journalists) (1978) he recounted his experience during the government-orchestrated ousting of Julio Scherer García and other journalists from the daily *Excélsior* in 1976. He has published nine novels, both fiction and non-fiction.

Leñero is also the author of more than sixteen plays, often adapting his own novels. His documentary drama *El juicio* (The Trial) (1971) was based on court transcripts and represented the 1928 trial of two Catholics for the murder of President-elect Alvaro Obregón. A later play, *Martirio de Morelos* (Morelos's Martyrdom) (1981), explored historical interpretation through the biography of the nineteenth-century Independence War patriot. *Nadie sabe nada* (No One Knows Anything) (1988), subtitled a 'thriller', used simultaneous actions on a divided stage to address the problems of Mexican journalism and political corruption. Leñero's mastery of dialogue and dramatic structure also led to cinematic collaborations. He adapted a story by Guadalupe Loayza for Alejandro Pelayo's 1993 biographical film about actress Miroslava Stern, *Miroslava*, and he set a novel by Naguib Mahfouz in contemporary Mexico City for Jorge Fons's 1996 film *El callejón de los milagros* (The Alley of Miracles).

Also an active journalist, Leñero directed the women's magazine *Claudia* (1969–72), the weekly supplement of *Revista de revistas* for *Excélsior* (1972–76) and, with Julio Scherer García, founded the weekly magazine *Proceso*, for which he has served as associate director or vice-president since 1976.

Further reading

Anderson, D. (1989) *Vicente Leñero: The Novelist as Critic*, New York: Peter Lang.

Corona, I. (2000) 'Periodismo, sociedad civil y discurso contestatario en *Los periodistas* de Vicente Leñero', *Arizona Journal of Hispanic Cultural Studies* 4: 23–42.

Rodríguez Perez, A.M. (2000) '*El evangelio de Lucas Gavilán*: Vicente Leñero's Adaptation of the Gospel to Contemporary Mexico', *Italia francescana* 27(1–2): 73–83.

DANNY J. ANDERSON

Lerner, Elisa

b. 1932, Valencia, Venezuela

Writer

A member of the Sardio group, Lerner's prose is among the most elegant and caustic in contemporary Venezuelan literature. Writer of a number of successful plays, especially *Vida con mamá* (Life with Mother) (1975), she is the most cultured and merciless chronicler of post-Pérez Jiménez Venezuela. Her reviews and *crónicas* (see **crónica**) use apparently trivial events and issues to draw a critical map of contemporary reality. *Una sonrisa detrás de la metáfora* (The Smile behind the Metaphor) (1969), *Yo amo a Columbo* (I Love Columbo) (1983) and *Cronicas ginecológicas* (Gynaecological Chronicles) (1984) are samples of her way of seeing and describing Venezuela.

Further reading

Klein, D.A. (1987) 'The Theme of Alienation in the Theatre of Elisa Lerner and Isaac Chocron', *Folio* 17: 151–66.

RAFAEL CASTILLO ZAPATA

lesbian literature

Lesbian literature as a genre is a recent addition to literary studies, although its literary practice is not. Like most issues related to homosexuality, it had been forbidden or 'in the closet'; however, lesbian writing is coming out strongly through the publication of texts and the attention of contemporary readers and scholars. Partly as one of the many paradigmatic shifts spurred by feminist scholarship in the humanities, lesbian literature engages authors, readers, fictional characters and language itself in a discussion around homosexuality, whether the problematics are the inscription of ambiguity in suppressing sexual identity as dictated by cultural heterosexual norms, bringing out unexposed homosexual identities or confronting sexual identities in the interaction of private and public spheres.

Still at the early stages of its development as a genre, lesbian literature has gained recognition as an important expressive system, mainly by the quality of the fiction and poetry abundantly produced and published in recent years. Excellent representative works of lesbian literature are *En breve cárcel* (Certificate of Absence) (1981) by Argentine novelist and critic Sylvia **Molloy**; the fiction and poetry of Cristina **Peri Rossi**, from Uruguay; the work of Puerto Rican poet and literary critic Luz María **Umpierre**; the writings of Alejandra **Pizarnik**; *La rompiente* (The Breakwater) (1987) and *Monte de Venus* (Mount of Venus) by Reina Roffé; the poetry of Magaly Alabau, Ana Cristina **César** and Nancy Cárdenas; and the novels of Rosamaría Roffiel. In addition to studies of lesbian literature published in the last quarter of the twentieth century, a new and important development in this field of inquuiry is the rereading of canonical women of letters whose lesbianism was denied or never addressed. Two examples of the latter are recent critical writing on Gabriela **Mistral** and Teresa **de la Parra**.

Among the issues that are of concern to lesbian literature are the construction of the lesbian body, the erotic function of the female gaze, the fear of dismemberment, lesbianism and exile, homosexuality and Latin American identity, cross-dressing, lesbian subjectivity and self-figuration, and lesbian representation.

Further reading

Balderston, D. and D.J. Guy (ed.) (1997) *Sex and Sexuality in Latin America*, New York: New York University Press.

Bergmann, E.L. and P.J. Smith (eds) (1995) *¿Entiendes? Queer Readings, Hispanic Writings*, Durham, NC: Duke University Press.

Fiol-Matta, L. (2002) *Gabriela Mistral, Queer Mother for the Nation*, Minneapolis: University of Minnesota Press.

Foster, D.W. (1991) *Gay and Lesbian Themes in Latin American Writing*, Austin: University of Texas Press.

Martínez, E.M. (1996) *Lesbian Voices from Latin America*, New York: Garland.

Menéndez, N. (1997) '*Garzonas y feministas* in Cuban Women's Writing of the 1920s: *La vida manda* by Ofelia Rodríguez Acosta', in D. Balderston and D.J. Guy (eds), *Sex and Sexuality in Latin America*, New York: New York University Press, 174–89.

MAGDALENA GARCÍA PINTO

Letras libres

A direct heir of Octavio Paz's ***Vuelta*** and founded in 1999, *Letras libres* is a monthly literary and cultural magazine under the directorship of the historian, writer and cultural impresario Enrique Krauze. Intent on being recognized as an important cultural voice of the Spanish-speaking world, pages of the journal feature writers and intellectuals of national and international calibre. *Letras libres* aims to be a 'plural' venue of current thought and expression, as long as it is rigorous and high-quality work. In an attempt to extend its reach beyond the Mexican borders, it simultaneously launched a web version and, in 2001, became an international magazine, now concurrently published in Spain.

LAURA G. GUTIÉRREZ

Levrero, Mario (Jorge Varlotta)

b. 1940, Montevideo, Uruguay

Writer

A writer educated in the marginal genres – **science fiction**, **crime fiction**, serials – Levrero was influenced by Lewis Carroll, the surrealists and Felisberto **Hernández**. His fictions centre around the permanent transformations of space and objects (as in 'Capítulo XXX' (Chapter XXX), winner of the 1984 Más Allá Prize or 'La máquina de pensar de Gladys' (Gladys's Thinking Machine) (1970)), and on non-linear time, as in the stories of *Todo el tiempo* (All the Time) (1982). *Nick Carter* (1975), a novel published under his own name, parodies serials and detective novels.

Further reading

Capanna, P. (1997) 'Las fases de Levrero', *Inti: Revista de literatura hispánica* 45: 299–303.

Levrero, M. (1992) 'Entrevista imaginária con Mario Levrero', *Revista iberoamericana* 58(160–1): 1167–77.

SANDRA GASPARINI

Lezama Lima, José

b. 1910, Havana, Cuba; d. 1976, Havana

Poet, novelist and essayist

A major poet and one of the most original thinkers Latin America has produced, Lezama is best known for his **neo-baroque** novel ***Paradiso*** (1966). His work, known for its ludic sensuality and allusive density, was also a model of hermeticism, influencing many younger writers such as Severo **Sarduy**. His analyses of Latin American culture, in the essays of *La* ***expresión americana*** (American Expression) (1957), are a fundamental contribution to the debate on Latin American identity, while his ideas on aesthetics, which he termed a 'poetic system of the world', comprise a complex if fragmentary philosophy.

Lezama Lima led a life of apparent tranquillity and simplicity, never straying far from his native Havana. His family was middle class; his father was a military man who rose to the rank of colonel in the Cuban army before his untimely death aged 33. The young, asthmatic Lezama turned early to literature, and was a precocious reader. The loss of his father marked the young boy indelibly; much of his subsequent work, in particular *Paradiso*, can be seen as a creative response to the absence of the father. Lezama graduated with a law degree from the University of Havana and worked for some time at a Havana prison. After the Cuban Revolution he became vice president of **UNEAC**, the Cuban Union of Writers and Artists, and later worked in a library. He lived with his mother until her death in 1964, then married a close family friend who cared for him until his death in 1976. Lezama was widely known to be homosexual; sexuality in general is central to his work, and the issue of homosexuality is the subject of several important passages of both *Paradiso* and its continuation, *Oppiano Licario* (1977).

Belying its calm exterior, Lezama's life was one of great intellectual activity and creation. Beginning in the late 1930s and continuing over the next twenty years, he edited a series of literary magazines culminating in ***Orígenes*** (1944–56), one of the most important journals of its time in the Spanish-speaking world. It published original contributions from authors worldwide, and was also a cohesive forum for an extended group of Cuban writers, musicians and artists, most of whom shared a certain belief – albeit unorthodox in the case of Lezama – in Catholicism. Lezama himself first burst upon the Cuban literary scene with *Muerte de Narciso* (Death of Narcissus) (1937), a long poem which startled readers with its lush images and Gongorist syntax. He followed with *Enemigo rumor* (Enemy Rumour) (1941), *Aventuras sigilosas* (Discreet Adventures) (1945) and *La fijeza* (Fixity) (1949), this latter containing a series of important prose poems providing an early glimpse of the 'poetic system'. *Dador* (Giver) (1960) contains some of his most arcane and philosophical poems, influenced by his readings in world religion and mythology, while his posthumous *Fragmentos a su imán* (Fragments to His Magnet) (1977) includes his most direct and moving poetry. The publication of *Paradiso* – a semi-autobiographical *bildungsroman*, or novel of education – created a scandal in Cuba due to its baroque complexity and erotic passages, and earned Lezama a central place among the authors of the '**Boom**' in Latin American narrative. Lezama also published four books of essays, among them the important *La expresión americana*.

In the 1940s and 1950s, Lezama and the other writers and artists of *Orígenes* attempted to create an autonomous realm for art, seeing that cultural activity as a form of Utopian resistance to the dictatorial regime of Fulgencio Batista, under whom governmental corruption and political violence flourished. After the 1959 Revolution, however, many leftist critics accused the Orígistas of escapism. Lezama's own relationship with the Revolutionary government – problematic during the decade of the 1960s – took a turn for the worse after the **Padilla** Affair of 1971. Named for supposedly counter-revolutionary attitudes in Heberto Padilla's 'self-critique', Lezama was largely prohibited from publishing in the years leading to his death. He was only 'recuperated' officially by the Cuban government in the late 1980s and 1990s; one sign of this change in the official attitude is his treatment in the film *Fresa y chocolate* (Strawberry and Chocolate) (1993), where he figures as the gay protagonist's most important cultural hero.

Lezama Lima's 'poetic system', not a traditional philosophical system but a collection of ideas and quotations from diverse sources, views the world through the lens of aesthetics, privileging the irrational and the idea of a poetic causality. The most novel aspect of this system is Lezama's idea of the 'imaginary era', where he attempted to articulate a necessary relation between artistic creations and society, and to offer a new way of thinking about history. Lezama's poetic system is complemented by his reflection upon American cultural identity – what he called 'American expression' – centring on his notion of the American baroque as a hybrid product of a dialogue between European, African and New World cultures.

Further reading

Chiampi, I. (1989) 'José Lezama Lima', in C.A. Solé and M.I. Abreu (eds), *Latin American Writers*, New York: Scribners, 3: 1125–30.

Cruz-Malavé, A. (1994) *El primitivo implorante: El 'sistema poético del mundo' de José Lezama Lima*, Amsterdam: Rodopi.

Heller, B. (1997) *Assimilation/Generation/Resurrection: Contrapuntal Readings in the Poetry of José Lezama Lima*, Lewisburg, PA: Bucknell University Press.

Levinson, B. (1996) *Secondary Moderns: Mimesis, History, and Revolution in Lezama Lima's 'American Expression'*, Lewisburg, PA: Bucknell University Press.

Lezama Lima, J. (1974) *Paradiso*, trans. G. Rabassa, New York: Farrar, Straus & Giroux.

—— (1975–77) *Obras completas*, Mexico: Aguilar.

Pellón, G. (1989) *José Lezama Lima's Joyful Vision*, Austin: University of Texas Press.

BEN A. HELLER

lézarde, La

La lézarde (The Ripening) is the first novel by Edouard **Glissant**, previously known for his poetry, and winner of the Prix Renaudot in 1958. Written during the heyday of the *nouveau roman*, it is Glissant's most conventional novel and inaugurates a series of narratives with recurring characters and dealing with Martinican society, landscape and history. Based on Aimé **Césaire**'s 1945 election campaign, the plot centres on a group of political activists who hire a stranger to kill an assassin who threatens to upset their candidate's victory. Very much a poet's novel, it is less about politics than the group's self-discovery in a landscape dominated by the winding folds of the Lézarde river.

Further reading

Miller, E.S. (1978) 'The Identity of the Narrator in Edouard Glissant's *La Lézarde*', *South Atlantic Bulletin* 43(ii):17–26.

J. MICHAEL DASH

Liano, Dante

b. 1948, Chimaltenango, Guatemala

Writer and critic

A founding member of the writers' publishing group RIN-78, Liano has published an impressive collection of stories and two novels. The first, *El lugar de su quietud* (The Place of Quietness) (1989), is an experimental treatment of several events in Guatemalan history; the second, *L'uomo di Montserrat* (The Man from Monserrat) (1994), is the Italian version of Liano's only recently published Spanish-language novel dealing with military-guerrilla conflicts. Among his critical works, *La palabra y el sueño: Literatura y sociedad en Guatemala* (Word and Dream: Literature and Society in Guatemala) (1984) is a major study of national literature. He lives in Italy, where he teaches and edits the journal *Centroamericana*.

Further reading

Liano, D. (1984) *La palabra y el sueno: Literatura y sociedad en Guatemala*, Rome: Bulzoni.

MARC ZIMMERMAN

Lihn, Enrique

b. 1929, Santiago, Chile; d. 1988, Santiago

Writer

Known primarily as a poet, although he wrote narrative and drama as well, Lihn's work falls within a frame of '**antipoetry**', or at least what he himself called 'a poetry sceptical of itself'. His poem, 'Porque escribí' (Because I Wrote), from the collection *Poesía de paso* (Poetry in Passing) (1966), is a sort of anti-manifesto, a gentle self-parody of the poet as hero. The conversational language adds to the irony of his writing – for his protagonists are fragile, vulnerable beings. An experimental artist, Lihn was often involved in performance poetry and organized encounters between different sorts of text. Remaining in Chile after the 1973 *coup*, his satire became far darker in the context of repression, as in *El Paseo Ahumada* (Ahumada Avenue) (1983) and the texts gathered posthumously in *Diario de muerte* (Death Diary) (1989).

Further reading

Foxley, C. (1996) 'Poesía de Enrique Lihn en el contexto de la modernidad', *Inti: Revista de literatura hispánica* 43–4: 75–85.

Hill, W.N. (1990) 'Enrique Lihn critica la meta-poesía', *Alba de América* 6(14–15): 29–40.

Lastra, P. (1990) *Conversaciones con Enrique Lihn*, Santiago: Atelier.

Lihn, E. (1978) *The Dark Room and Other Poems*, trans. J. Cohen *et al.*, New York: New Directions.

Rebaza-Soraluz, L. (1997) 'Enrique Lihn', in V. Smith (ed.), *Encyclopedia of Latin American Literature*, London: Fitzroy Dearborn, 479–81.

Travis, C.M. (2002) 'Beyond the Vanguardia: The Dialectical Voice of Enrique Lihn', *Romance Quarterly* 49(1): 61–74.

MIKE GONZALEZ

Lillo, Baldomero

b. 1867, Lota, Chile; d. 1923, San Bernardo, Chile

Novelist and short story writer

Lillo was one of the most important Latin American followers of naturalism, the school of novelistic writing founded by Emile Zola in France and characterized by a clinical look at social problems. Lillo is best known for his stories of the hard lives of Chilean miners, *Sub terra* (1904). His subsequent collection, *Sub sole* (1907), is more varied in topic, including stories of miners, Indians, some humorous stories and some stories influenced by *modernismo* (see **Spanish American modernism**). The most widely anthologized of his stories is 'La compuerta número 12' (Hatch No. 12) from *Sub terra*, the tragic story of an 8-year-old miner.

Further reading

Brown, D. (1950) 'A Chilean *Germinal*: Zola and Baldomero Lillo', *Modern Language Notes* 65: 47–51.

Lillo, B. (1968) *Obras completas*, ed. R. Silva Castro, Santiago: Nascimento.

Walker, J. (1997) 'Baldomero Lillo', in V. Smith (ed.), *Encyclopedia of Latin American Literature*, London: Fitzroy Dearborn, 482–4.

DANIEL BALDERSTON

Lima, Jorge de

b. 1895, União, Alagoas, Brazil; d. 1953, Rio de Janeiro, Brazil

Writer

Although he also wrote novels, Lima is best known as a poet. His early verses were symbolist and Parnassian, but in the 1920s he assimilated the innovations of **Brazilian modernism**. His major preocupation was the search for spiritual values exemplified in his religious poetry, including *Tempo e eternidade* (Time and Eternity) (1935). His most popular work is the more accessible *negrista* poetry (see ***negrismo***) celebrating the vivacity of Afro-Brazilian culture such as *Poemas negros* (Black Poems) (1947).

Further reading

Dias, A. (1990) 'O Movimento Modernista e o Poeta Jorge de Lima no Nordeste Brasileiro', *Letras* 4(37): 15.

Lima, J. de (1958) *Obra completa*, Rio de Janeiro: Aguilar.

Nunes, C. (1989) 'Jorge de Lima', in C.A. Solé and M.I. Abreu (eds), *Latin American Writers*, New York: Scribners, 2, 765–70.

Stegagno Picchio, L. (1985) 'Jorge de Lima: Universal Poet', *Portuguese Studies* 1: 151–67.

MARK DINNEEN

Lindo, Hugo

b. 1917, La Unión, El Salvador; d. 1985, San Salvador, El Salvador

Writer

A superb example of the Latin American *pensador*, a blend of thinker, writer and statesman, Lindo contributed to the cultural and political life of El Salvador as poet, writer, critic, journalist, diplomat and lawyer. His famous short story collection, *Guaro y champaña* (Moonshine and Champagne) (1957), presents a complex world in which the fantastic and the psychological play prominent roles. His only novel, *El anzuelo de Dios* (God's Hook) (1963), reveals religious and metaphysical concerns as well as *costumbrista* (see ***costumbrismo***) tendencies. His poetry is refined, idealistic and intellectual, in contrast to the more political texts of his Salvadoran contemporaries.

Further reading

Miller, E.G. (1981) 'Retracing the Translation Process: Hugo Lindo's Only the Voice', *Translation Review* 7: 32–40.

LINDA J. CRAFT

Lins, Osman

b. 1924, Pernambuco, Brazil; d. 1978, São Paulo, Brazil

Writer

Lins's most innovative works, *Nove, Novena* (Nine, Novena) (1966) and *Avalovara* (1973), represent for the critic Antonio **Candido** key moments of modernity in contemporary Brazilian literature. His style fuses lyricism with rigour, or, as one character in his story 'Um ponto no Circulo' (A Point on the Circle) puts it, 'the balance between life and rigor, between disorder and geometry'. In São Paulo, he also taught literature and published journalistic chronicles. His first novel, *O visitante* (The Visitor) (1955), was followed by a volume of stories *Os gestos* (Gestures) (1957) and *O fiel e a pedra* (The Loyal Man and the Stone) (1961).

Further reading

Andrade, A.L. (1987) *Osman Lins: Crítica e criação*, São Paulo: Hucitec.

Frizzi, A. (ed.) (1995) 'Osman Lins', special edition devoted to the author, *The Review of Contemporary Fiction* 15(3): 155–222.

Nitrini, S. (1987) *Poéticas em confronto: Nove, novena e o novo romance*, São Paulo: Hucitec.

MILTON HATOUM

Lins, Paulo

b. 1958, Rio de Janeiro, Brazil

Novelist and poet

With the publication of his novel, *Cidade de Deus* (City of God) (1997), Paulo Lins was hailed as an important emerging voice in Brazilian literature. The novel is set in Cidade de Deus, a neighbourhood established on the urban periphery of Rio de Janeiro in the mid-1960s to house displaced communities after the demolition of several hillside shanty towns. It documents the sexual, racial, generational and cultural politics of this community in a context of abject cruelty and violence generated by the rise of drug trafficking during the 1970s, the emergence of heavily armed gangs vying for control of the trade and the actions of corrupt security forces motivated by vengeance and greed. Lins culled much of the material used in the novel when he worked as a research assistant for Alba Zaluar, an urban anthropologist who has worked extensively in the *favelas* of Rio de Janeiro.

CHRISTOPHER DUNN

Liscano, Juan

b. 1915, Caracas, Venezuela; d. 2001, Caracas

Writer and folklorist

A profoundly spiritual writer, Liscano's sometimes controversial critical and artistic practices have occupied a central place in Venezuela's literary life, particularly through his editorship of the influential journal ***Zona franca*** (1964–83) and his work with publisher **Monte Avila**. Early researches into the folk culture of the coastal regions of his country nourished a search for the pre-Hispanic sources of religious thought which is reflected in his early poetry. As director of the Servicio de Investigaciones Folclóricas, he was also closely identified with the nationalist ideas of Rómulo **Gallegos**, whose presidency ended in a military *coup* which led Liscano into exile for ten years. His work of that period, like the epic *Nuevo mundo Orinoco* (1959), returns to earlier cosmic themes but within a framework of existentialist concerns (see **existentialism**). Returning from exile in 1958 his poetry took a more lyrical and frequently erotic direction, while as a critic he became increasingly involved in both political and cultural debates with a new, more radical generation reflected, but only in a muted way, in *Zona franca*. By the late 1960s, in both his critical essays and his poetry, it becomes clear that Liscano's central preoccupation is the spiritual bankruptcy of contemporary society, in Venezuela and beyond.

Further reading

Cobo Borda, J.G. (2001) 'Juan Liscano (1915–2001)', *Alba de América* 20(37–8): 49–50.

Liscano, J. (1989) 'Sobre poeta y poesía', *Poesía* 13(3(74)): 1–6.

—— (1994) 'Vista de la poesía venezolana', in *La poesía nueva en el mundo hispánico: Los últimos años*, Madrid: Visor.

Machado, A. (1987) *El apocalipsis según Juan Liscano: Conversaciones*, Caracas: Publicaciones Seleven.

Rodríguez Ortiz, O. (ed.) (1990) *Juan Liscano ante la crítica*, Caracas: Monte Avila.

MIKE GONZALEZ

Lispector, Clarice

b. 1920, Tchetchelnik, Ukraine; d. 1977, Rio de Janeiro, Brazil

Writer

Lispector, who arrived in Brazil with her immigrant parents as an infant, often reflected on the consequences of having become a native speaker of Portuguese, rather than of another language more conducive to an international readership. Yet through other circumstances – the recent interest in **women's writing** and in the writing of the Jewish diaspora (see **Jewish writing**) – she became one of the better known and most translated Brazilian writers of the twentieth century.

After a difficult childhood, Lispector studied law and worked as a reporter for a Rio daily as one of the first women journalists in Brazil. In 1944 she published her first novel, *Perto do coração selvagem* (Near to the Wild Heart), which won a prize and attracted much critical attention. The title and epigraph are drawn from James Joyce, and the novel offers an introspective portrait of a headstrong and artistically inclined young woman. Soon after, Lispector, married by then to diplomat Maury Gurgel Valente, left Brazil to live abroad for most of the next fifteen years, mainly in Switzerland and the USA, with sojourns in Italy and England.

The two novels she published while living abroad, *O lustre* (The Lamp) (1949) and *A cidade sitiada* (The Besieged City) (1949), continue the introspective lyrical mode, where attention focuses on fluctuations of feeling and the course of perceptions rather than plot. While living in the United States (1952–59), Lispector published a collection of short stories (*Alguns contos*) (Some Stories) (1952), which includes some of her better known pieces (such as 'Love' and 'Family Ties') in the genre where she has written her most brilliant and influential work. In 1959 Lispector separated from her husband and returned to Rio de Janeiro with her two sons.

In the almost two decades until her death, Lispector became a well-known literary figure in Brazil, publishing five novels and five collections of short stories, although she did not lead a conventional literary life. Her fiction of the early 1960s, such as the short stories of *Laços de família* (Family Ties) (1960) and the novels *A maçã no escuro* (The Apple in the Dark) (1961) and *A paixão segundo G. H.* (The Passion According to G.H.) (1964), are among her most important works. They are written in an original, often strange language, dense with paradoxes, unusual phrases and abstract formulations that tease and elude the rational intelligence. The characters, mostly women, ponder metaphysical questions about their place in existence and in the universe as well as more immediate questions about their place in a constrictive social order.

During the 1960s and 1970s, Lispector also published four picture books for children and engaged in various journalistic activities: a newspaper column for women (published under a pseudonym), a series of interviews with writers and other **intellectuals** for a mass circulation weekly (later collected in *De corpo inteiro* (Full Length) (1975)), and, most significantly for her fiction, a weekly series of columns or *crónicas* (see **crónica**), this time in her own name, for an important Rio daily, the *Jornal do Brasil*, from 1967 to 1973. A selection of these *crónicas* was published posthumously as *A descoberta do mundo* (1984) (Discovering the World (1992)). It could be argued that these newspaper columns and her imaginative engagement with writing for a more diverse readership contributed to the radical changes in her writing during her last eight years. In the novels and short stories published in the 1970s, Lispector's characters are no longer mainly middle class; she experiments with self-referential narrators and with farcical plots and parodies of her earlier introspective and well-wrought fiction. *A hora da estrela* (1977) (The Hour of the Star) (1986), the short novel she published a month before her death, has as its protagonist an impoverished young woman from the north east trying to make her way as a typist in the urban jungle of Rio de Janeiro. This novel, with its failed Cinderella plot, farcical humour and touches of lyrical gentleness, was the basis for a successful film directed by Suzana Amaral in 1986.

Although Lispector was acclaimed early on as an extraordinary writer, it was only twenty years after the publication of her first novel that a book-length study of her work appeared in Brazil. Several early critics read Lispector in the context of **existentialism**, tracing affinities between the philosophical ideas in her fiction and those of Heidegger, Kierkegaard, Camus and Sartre. Other critics analysed aspects of her style: her use of the epiphany and of rhetorical devices such as internal monologue. More recently, questions of gender, poststructuralism and **postmodernism** have been brought to bear upon her text. Lispector was singled out as one of the two Brazilian writers (alongside Guimarães **Rosa**) belonging to the so-called **Boom** of Latin American fiction in the 1960s. In the 1970s, 1980s and 1990s, she emerged as an object of more extensive international attention in the wake of feminist criticism and of the French writer Hélène Cixous's celebration of her work as a model of *écriture feminine.*

The many autobiographical and semi-autobiographical self-figurations in Lispector's fiction and *crónicas* have given rise to a parallel critical interest in 'Lispector herself'. Praised by her contemporaries as a beautiful, strange and mysterious woman, she has become as compelling a figure as any of her fictional characters. Cixous, who did much to promote translations of her work in France, wrote critical texts haunted by an intense bond with Lispector. The first full-length biography of Lispector was published in Brazil in 1995, and in 1996 novelist Ana Miranda wrote a fictionalized biography in which fragments of her texts are made to appear as accounts of her life. Occupying a secure place among Lispector's gallery of characters that variously depict what it meant to be a woman, including a woman artist, in mid-twentieth-century Brazil – the constrictions one encountered, the vistas that could open up – 'Lispector herself' is perhaps Lispector's most fascinating creation.

Further reading

Cixous, H. (1990) *Reading with Clarice Lispector*, Minneapolis: University of Minnesota Press.
Fitz, E. (1985) *Clarice Lispector*, Boston: Twayne.
Nunes, B. (1989) *O drama da linguagem: Uma leitura de Clarice Lispector*, São Paulo: Ática.
Peixoto, M. (1994) *Passionate Fictions: Gender, Narrative and Violence in Clarice Lispector*, Minneapolis: University of Minnesota Press.
Pinto, C.F. (1990) *O Bildungsroman femenino: Quatro exemplos brasileiros*, São Paulo: Perspectiva, 77–108.
Severino, A. (1989) 'Clarice Lispector', in C.A. Solé and M.I. Abreu (eds), *Latin American Writers*, New York: Scribners, 3: 1303–9.
Yannuzzi, A. (1997) 'Clarice Lispector', in V. Smith (ed.), *Encyclopedia of Latin American Literature*, London: Fitzroy Dearborn, 484–5.

MARTA PEIXOTO

Lisser, H.G. de

b. 1878, Falmouth, Jamaica; d. 1944, Kingston, Jamaica

Novelist

De Lisser was particularly well known for his novels of Jamaican politics, as well as his knowledge of West Indian history and understanding of the Jamaican dialect. His ten books include *Jane's Career* (1914), *Susan Proudleigh* (1915), *The White Witch of Rose Hall* (1929), *The Arawak Girl* (1958), *The Cup and the Lip* (1956) and *Under the Sun* (1937). A journalist and a prominent figure in Jamaican society, he was editor of the Jamaica *Gleaner* for forty years, and also published a magazine called *Planter's Punch*.

Further reading

Morris, M. (1979) 'H.G. De Lisser: The First Competent Caribbean Novelist in English', *Carib* 1: 18–26.

KEITH JARDIM

List Arzubide, Germán

b. 1898, Puebla, Mexico; d. 1998, Mexico City

Writer

An important participant in Mexican **Estridentismo**, List Arzubide contributed along with Manuel **Maples Arce** to many of the **manifestos** published in the early 1920s, and was listed as editor of *Horizonte* (1926–27), one of the group's principal journals. His early volumes, *Esquina* (Corner) (1923) and *El viajero en el vértice* (The Apex Traveler) (1926), were substantial contributions to the Estridentista poetry style; *El movimiento estridentista* (The Estridentista Movement) (1926), a curious mix of prose and verse dedicated to Huitzilopoxtli, the Aztec god of war, proposed an idiosyncratic profile of the entire movement.

Further reading

Benedet, S.M. (1999) 'Modernidades estridentistas: El movimiento estridentista de Germán List Arzubide', *La palabra y el hombre* 112: 69–72.

MERLIN H. FORSTER

literary criticism

The practice of literary criticism in Latin America is linked to the construction of cultural paradigms or models. It became an independent activity at the beginning of the twentieth century, coinciding with the emergence of professional **intellectuals**. It was their task to write the first national histories of literature and to organize the literary corpus of each country or region as the nation-states of the region and their attendant nationalisms began to consolidate. Thus education could be reorganized around a canon of literary works – the national classics. At the same time a small but active market for Latin American writing began to emerge in the context of expanding cities with a vigorous intellectual life. New journals and publishing houses were established, and the press made it possible to keep up to date with innovations in Europe and North America.

Against this background, critical texts which took literary works as their immediate object, quickly generalized the discussion to embrace the questions of the national and regional 'identity' whose values and nature were 'represented' in fiction. This was the role played by literary critics like Pedro **Henríquez Ureña**, for example.

During the 1960s, literary criticism became significant once again. As the work of Jorge Luis **Borges** won an international reputation and the writing of Julio **Cortázar**, Mario **Vargas Llosa**, Carlos **Fuentes**, Gabriel **García Márquez** and José **Donoso** began to make its impact, the literature and art of Latin America began to attract considerable international attention.

The new political situation in Latin America created by the Cuban Revolution of 1959 and the left-wing liberation movements emerging in every country, made the region a focus for international expectations. In fact the politicized atmosphere of the 1960s throughout the Third World opened a space where, it was hoped, the questions that the traditional cultures (especially those which had engendered Nazism and Fascism) had proved incapable of articulating, still less of resolving, might finally be answered. The Latin American critics provided access to the new third world literature by offering creative critical writings which established the connection between the literary texts and the reality of their growing reading public.

Angel **Rama** stands out as a representative figure in this process. He began his career in the magazine *Marcha*, published in Montevideo, which played a key role in stimulating the intellectual ambience by publishing debates, new readings from the past, launching collections of books, educating the young and engaging in a constant dialogue with writers, artists, musicians and cultural leaders. Of his vast body of work, it is probably his volume *La ciudad letrada* (The Literate City) (1984), a work still unfinished when he died, and his writings on Spanish American modernism which are his most important legacy to subsequent generations.

Many of the major critics of the 1960s worked in similar ways, laying the basis for the critical and speculative writing of the generations that followed. Among them the work of David **Viñas** is fundamental, for he read culture through marginal texts, iconographies and documents and saw their connection to law and power. Antonio **Cornejo Polar** and Antonio **Candido** played equally important roles in politicizing and revising Latin American culture from a critical point of view, opening new areas of visibility. Their texts mark the culmination of one model of the literary critic, erudite and capable of producing a global vision of the continent. Later generations have chosen to work on specificities, on fragments of the cultural complex; many have abandoned militant activity in favour of another kind of political intervention – the deconstruction of cultural hegemonies.

See also: postmodernism

Further reading

Gollnick, B. (2003) 'Approaches to Latin American Literature, in Phillip Swanson (ed.), *The Companion to Latin American Studies*, London: Arnold, 107–21.

González, A. (1996) 'Literary Criticism in Spanish America', in R. González Echevarría and E. Pupo-Walker (eds), *Cambridge History of Latin American Literature*, Cambridge: Cambridge University Press, 2, 425–57.

Jackson, K.D. (1996) 'Literary Criticism in Brazil', in R. González Echevarría and E. Pupo-Walker (eds), *Cambridge History of Latin American Literature*, Cambridge: Cambridge University Press, 3, 329–43.

Klahn, N. and W.H. Corral (eds) (1991) *Los novelistas como críticos*, Mexico City: Fondo de Cultura Económica, 2 vols.

Lasarte, J.V. (ed.) (2001) *Territorios intelectuales: Pensamiento y cultura en América Latina*, Caracas: Fondo Editorial La Nave Va.

Nuevo texto crítico (1994) Special issue on literary criticism in Latin America, issue 14–15.

Pagano, A.S. (1997) 'Literary criticism', in V. Smith (ed.), *Encyclopedia of Latin American Literature*, London: Fitzroy Dearborn, 490–2.

Rama, A. (1984) *Las máscaras democráticas del Modernismo*, Montevideo: Fundación Internacional Angel Rama.

Revista de crítica literaria latinoamericana (1990) Special issue on literary criticism in Latin America, issue 32–3.

Sosnowski, S. (ed.) (1997) *Lectura crítica de la literatura americana*, Caracas: Biblioteca Ayacucho, 4 vols.

GRACIELA MONTALDO

literary histories

The beginning of the contemporary epoch coincides with a crisis that called into question the great totalizing literary histories of the nineteenth century. It is no coincidence that the most important surveys of national literature (such as Sílvio **Romero**'s *Historia de la literatura brasileira*) belong to the nineteenth century, or that the last of them (like Ricardo Rojas's *Historia de la literatura Argentina*) appeared early in the twentieth. The crisis was engendered by the rejection by the avant-garde (see **avant-garde in Latin America**) of the totalizing, causal, nationalist and organic models by which a nation's greatness was reflected in its literature. The new approaches set out to go beyond the nationalistic and scientific schema of nineteenth-century literary histories. Pedro **Henríquez Ureña**'s *Seis ensayos en busca de nuestra expresión* (Six Essays in Search of Our Expression) (1928) and *Las corrientes literarias en la América Hispánica* (Literary Currents in Spanish America) (1945) were founding texts of this new criticism. In Brazil, Antonio **Candido**'s influential *A formação da literatura brasileira* (Formation of Brazilian Literature) (1959) presented a sociological vision of two periods in Brazilian letters: the Enlightenment and romanticism. A 1983 conference in Campinas, Brazil, addressed the redefinition of the genre according to the formulations suggested by Henríquez Ureña, Angel **Rama** and Antonio Cándido (the papers were published under the title, *La literatura latinoamericana como proceso* – Latin American Literature as Process). The co-ordinator of these discussions, Ana **Pizarro**, compiled *Palavra, literatura e culture* (Word, Literature and Culture), a three-volume history of literature that fell short of its declared purposes, as the editor herself recognized. Nonetheless, the project was significant for its inclusion of Brazil and of minor literatures. The Chilean critic Cedomil Goic also proposed a renewal of the genre with his *Historia y crítica de la literatura hispanoamericana* (History and Criticism of Hispanic American Literature) (1988), applying the ideas of Henríquez Ureña and the model developed by Francisco Rico in his history of Spanish literature. These works identified critical problems central in 1980s debates: the construction of traditions, the relationship between dominant and subaltern systems and the periodization criteria appropriate for the literature of Latin America and the Caribbean.

Further reading

Cándido, Antonio (1988) *O método crítico de Silvio Romero*, São Paulo: Ed. USP.

Franco, J. (1969) *An Introduction to Spanish-American Literature*, Cambridge: Cambridge University Press.

González Echevarría, R. (1996) 'A Brief History of the History of Spanish American Literature', in R. González Echevarría and E. Pupo-Walker (eds), *Cambridge History of Latin American Literature*, Cambridge: Cambridge University Press, 1, 7–31.

Nunes, B. (1996) 'The Literary Historiography of Brazil', in R. González Echevarría and E. Pupo-Walker (eds), *Cambridge History of Latin American Literature*, eds. Cambridge: Cambridge University Press, 3, 11–46.

Oviedo, J.M. (1995–2002) *Historia de la literatura hispanoamericana*, Madrid, Alianza, 4 vols.

Pizarro, Ana (ed.) (1985) *La literatura latinoamericana como proceso*, Buenos Aires: CEAL.

GONZALO AGUILAR

literatura de cordel

Like other Latin American countries, Brazil has a strong tradition of popular narrative poetry used by the rural and urban poor to communicate their vision of the world. For many centuries, this verse existed only in oral form, but in the late nineteenth century some popular poets in Brazil started to produce small chapbooks or *folhetos* of their poems on simple hand presses (similar in format to earlier European pamphlet poetry) which they sold in the streets and markets. The poet would often display his *folhetos* on a length of string between two posts, and the poetry thus became known as *literatura de cordel*, 'literature on a string'.

The origins of Brazilian popular poetry can be traced back to the ballad or *romancero* tradition in the Iberian Peninsula. In the Brazilian north east – where socio-economic structures and many aspects of traditional rural life associated with them were relatively slow to change – popular poetry proved to be most vigorous and enduring. Later, migrants from the Northeast disseminated the poetic tradition throughout the country, and the *folheto* began a new phase of production and diffusion.

Cordel literature was at its most dynamic during the 1950s when it was created, produced and distributed by the rural and urban poor. Before the spread of radio and television, the *folheto* functioned as a type of popular journalism, reinterpreting regional, national and even international events according to the worldview of those disadvantaged sectors. To the traditional themes inherited from the Iberian *romancero* tradition, such as the power of religious faith and the adventures of popular chivalric heroes, were added new topics of concern to the poet and his/her community, for example land struggles, government corruption, inflation and pollution. It is this capacity of *cordel* literature to respond to the problems affecting the poet's community that largely explains why it remained such a dynamic form of popular expression for so many decades.

The process of *folheto* production has declined since the 1960s, largely as a result of the gradual erosion of traditional patterns of life in the north east. The *literatura de cordel* printed today reveals significant changes both in content and format, but it continues to provide inspiration for many Brazilian writers, among them Jorge **Amado** and Ariano **Suassuna**, who perceive it as the embodiment of the experience and worldview of the population of the north east. The covers of *folhetos* have traditionally been illustrated with woodcuts by graphic artists such as José Borges.

Further reading

Antologia da literatura de cordel (1978) Fortaleza: Secretaria Cultura, 2 vols.

Arantes, A. (1982) *O trabalho e a fala*, São Paulo: Kairós.

Dinneen, M. (1996) *Listening to the People's Voice*, London: Kegan Paul International.

Slater, C. (1982) *Stories on a String*, Berkeley CA: University of California Press.

—— (1996) 'Brazilian Popular Literature (the *literatura de cordel*)', in R. González Echevarría and E. Pupo-Walker (eds), *Cambridge History of Latin American Literature*, Cambridge: Cambridge University Press, 3: 315–27.

MARK DINNEEN

literature

In Latin America, literature had a key role to play in the process/project of emancipation, revolution and resistance both to imperialism and to capitalism in general. Angel **Rama** and Antonio **Candido**, for example, saw literature as a liberating project; in the 1960s, the discussions that took place concerning the responsibility of the writer, committed writing and the relationship between literature and revolution took as their starting point a common anti-capitalist ethos already identified in earlier writers as different among themselves as Juan **Rulfo**, Graciliano **Ramos** and Miguel Angel **Asturias**. These different projects sometimes sought their legitimacy in *el pueblo*, the people, and sometimes in the 'nature' of Latin America. But whatever their point of view, all of these different narratives legitimized literature as an emancipatory practice.

One of the least studied factors contributing to the loss of legitimacy of this emancipatory narrative was the Cold War, and its surreptitious translation by both sides into the field of culture. On the one hand the promotion of 'cultural freedom' and the autonomy of art, on the other 'reality' and 'commitment', became the opposing banners under which the antagonists fought. East and West appropriated cultural values in the service of their cause – indeed both had successfully done so at an earlier stage. During the 1930s, the 'proletarian moment' in both North and South America, and Russian cultural criteria ('**socialist realism**', for example) prevailed. After the Second World War, the USA launched a powerful campaign to disseminate 'Western' values across the world.

One of its instruments, the Congress for Cultural Freedom, constantly referred to the value of 'universality'; this tended to exclude any literature or art that was excessively local or regional, although in some cases, notably William Faulkner, João Guimarães **Rosa** and Gabriel **García Márquez**, this regionalism could be and was presented as a variant of universal themes already prefigured in classical mythology. The biographical, referential and contextual elements were simply disregarded. One critic, for example, argued that you could appreciate Jorge Luis **Borges** without knowing anything about Argentina. Beatriz **Sarlo** responded by noting that while Borges could be read as a universal writer from an aesthetic point of view, with the positive implication that it was a right of all Latin American artists to work within any and every tradition, what was lost was the connection to specifically Argentine traditions that Borges himself considered so important. The same argument was conducted in the visual arts, praising those Latin American artists who had adopted the 'international style'.

What is important here is not a conspiracy theory, but that Latin America was drawn into someone else's battles. While one side proposed an apolitical avant-garde, the other argued for an ill-defined realism and later, after the Cuban Revolution, for a vanguard whose logic led to guerrilla warfare. From the 'Western' point of view, abstractionism quickly merged into a transnational marketplace; on the other side, and despite the attempts by both Cuba and Nicaragua to democratize culture, neither country succeeded in its aesthetic project.

The shadow conflict was played out in the pages of ***Mundo nuevo*** on the one hand and ***Casa de las Américas*** on the other – and it allowed no middle ground. And yet the writing of the 1960s reveals an astonishing quantity and variety that escapes the parameters of the debate. Writers and artists were critics, teachers and creators, and they developed new theories that went beyond the East–West dichotomies in their defence of literature and literary values. With hindsight, the limitations of their proposals are obvious – the analogy between artistic freedom and national emancipation, a subject almost always constituted as masculine. Yet it was poets and novelists who offered the most interesting theoretical perspectives of the time, and who went furthest to overcome the manichaean character of politics. In *El arco y la lira* (The Bow and the Lyre) (1957), for example, Octavio **Paz** elaborated a theory of poetry and a critique of the avant-garde. The first exhaustive study of García Márquez was by Mario **Vargas Llosa**, and it is the Mexican novelist, Carlos **Fuentes**, who wrote the first book on the new novel, *La nueva novela hispanoamericana* (The New Spanish American Novel) (1969). Julio **Cortázar** wrote important essays on the short story, painting, politics and writing, and a defence of **surrealism**. Fuentes and Vargas Llosa also wrote about Cervantes and Flaubert, respectively, exercising their right to intervene in discussions within the cultural metropolis. It was Paz who introduced the ideas of Lévi-Strauss and Oriental literature to Latin America, Augusto **Roa Bastos** and José María **Arguedas** who recuperated oral cultures, David **Viñas** who offered fundamental documentary research into the frontier wars and Severo **Sarduy** and José **Lezama Lima** who explained and defended the **neobaroque**. There is no parallel anywhere else in the world for this new critical writing that broke free of the straitjacket of the Cold War to offer a range of ideas of literary value, from Lezama Lima's exaltation of poetry to Cortázar's Utopian project. What everyone agreed on was the value of literature: it is fire (Vargas Llosa), passion (Clarice **Lispector**), an alternative to the official language (Fuentes), revolutionary (Cortázar). What they all share, too, is their representation of Spanish America and Brazil in the global culture.

It is not my intention to idealize the **Boom** (with its alarming suggestion of marketing and sales), but rather to underline the fact that at least in the early 1960s a critical theory was to be found in literary texts and essays in literary criticism rather than in the academy. The situation changed in the 1970s, for several reasons. First, the national question that structured many of the novels of the Boom became compromised in many cases by military governments that imposed censorship and repression, and marginalized whole sectors of the population.

Second, Cuba no longer represented Utopia, and instead of developing a new aesthetics, it increasingly narrowed the limits of what was permissible within the Revolution. Third, the development of the mass media meant that the printed word was no longer seen as the only means of gaining access to modernity (see **cultural theory**).

The Cold War in Latin America was not only conducted against communism, but also against any and every effort, however misguided, to seek regional solutions that might have compromised the process of globalization. Among the failures were numbered the many projects for the democratization of culture, from the writing workshops (see **workshop poetry**) to bilingualism, from local theatre groups to national cinema. Yet, whatever the outcome, the 1960s saw a number of windows open, while the two decades that followed witnessed the triumph of military regimes in the Southern Cone, civil war in Central America and the advent of neo-liberalism. In this period literature ceased to be 'relevant', and when the question of the value of literature is again addressed it is under more difficult and embattled conditions than during the 1960s. For while the Cold War destroyed and de-legitimized certain positions of opposition, neo-liberalism has shown itself capable of an absorption so complete that it can destroy all opposition by embracing it.

The seduction of the market is nothing new; it was already an issue in nineteenth-century Europe. In 1958, Jorge **Amado**'s *Gabriela cravo e canela* (Gabriela Clove and Cinammon) was an instant best-seller. In 1966 Carlos Fuentes announced in an interview in *Mundo nuevo* that he had broken with the Cuban Revolution, and that 'we are now up to our necks in the rat race, as subject as any gringo or Frenchman to the world of competition and status symbols, of neon and Sears-Roebuck, washing machines, James Bond movies or tins of Campbell's Soup. The Graceful Epiphany of Art is dead'. This was an era that began with Fuentes's *Cambio de piel* (A Change of Skin) (1967), Vargas Llosa's *Pantaleón y las visitadoras* (Sergeant Pantoja's Special Service) (1973) and García Márquez's *telenovela* scripts. In Latin America, as elsewhere, cultural studies arose as the walls of the literary city collapsed. It had always had a strong interdisciplinary tradition: witness the links between literature and anthropology in the work of Asturias and Arguedas for example; the theorization of mass culture starting from sociology, anthropology and communications but going far beyond the schema of cultural imperialism in important research projects by Néstor García Canclini in Mexico and Jesús Martin Barbero in Colombia. At the same time, literature was beginning to embrace mass culture as an essential component of the modern experience, as novels such as José Emilio **Pacheco**'s *Las batallas en el desierto* (Battles in the Desert) (1981), the writings of La **Onda** in Mexico and the work of Manuel **Puig** were to demonstrate, our memories, our individual histories, our common points of reference are formed by comics, television programmes and popular music.

Mass culture is the culture of the majority; rap has brought poetry to millions and discussions about what goes on in soap operas are part of daily culture for millions, be they academics or workers. The impulse of European cultural studies to see mass culture and daily life as practices that were not wholly susceptible to control and manipulation, and could therefore become sites of resistance, yielded in the USA to their appropriation by academic institutions seeking novelty and publishing opportunities. The result was that the reasonable assertion that culture was not about literature alone led to a proliferation of studies and anthologies that discredited the original notion. A possible response came from a group of academics, many of them Latin American specialists, who have opposed the elitism of the institutions of literature by seeking the value of texts in the ethics of a responsibility towards the subjugated classes. Thus John Beverley, in his *Against Literature* (1993), has suggested that it is not a question of destroying literature but of broadening its base so that it is more open to solidarity and love. In contrast to the novel of the Boom, the ***testimonio*** is a 'democratic and egalitarian narrative', although the genre provides an insufficient body of work to provide a paradigm. *Me llamo Rigoberta Menchú* (I, Rigoberta Menchú) (1984) is the work most often cited, and for Beverley it represents the possibility of a new relationship, of complicity and identification with popular causes, between reader and narrator. It calls into question the role of the writer and the function of literature itself, Beverley argues, and represents the beginning of a post-fictional literature that reflects an emerging popular-democratic culture. Others have argued that Rigoberta is the agent rather than the representative of the collective, and that *testimonio* is a practice rather than a representation. Whatever the conclusion, it is clear that literature's loss of legitimacy has provoked a search for new criteria outside the literary metropolis.

Some critics have called into question this approach to narrative. Beatriz Sarlo, for example, writing from Argentina, expresses the problem thus:

> Modernity combined the pedagogical ideal with a display of symbolic goods in the market that would have been unimaginable previously. One unexpected result was that the market and the cultural industry subverted the basis of authority on which it would have been possible to conceive an educative paradigm in the realm of aesthetics. The contradiction was rapidly identified by those who saw that 'industrialized art' spelled death for the refined values of the cultural elites. The market, inevitably, introduced quantitative criteria that often contradicted the aesthetic judgments of artists and critics, and suggested that the establishment of qualitative values was not the task of the market. Thus art loses its sanctified status as a perfectly logical result of modernization.

Sarlo herself maintains a nostalgia for the historical avant-garde and sees the present as evidence of decline. But I see the problem rather as a different crisis, which bears names such as 'the collapse of paradigms', '**postmodernism**', etc.

In Latin America the reaction to this pragmatism has generated among certain writers and artists a new concept of the aesthetic linked to marginality and exclusion. The new aesthetics shares the aversion to totalizing theories, plays with fragmentation and sometimes employs non-canonical forms like the ***crónica***. In the recent *crónicas* of Carlos **Monsiváis** in Mexico and Pedro **Lemebel** in Chile, both very different from each other, there is an attempt to capture the multiple fleeting rituals through which people attempt to impose order on chaos (Monsiváis) or the archaeological traces of a recent past (Lemebel). What they represent is an aestheticizing of mass culture. Perhaps the strongest arguments in favour of a 'refractory' aesthetics are to be found in the Chilean journal, ***Revista de crítica cultural***, edited by Nelly **Richard**. The journal is unique in its insistence that art and literature transgress not simply by an inversion of terms, but through quotation, parody and exchange of categories and discourses. It is not a question of 'saving literature', but rather of valorizing documents, behaviours, art, texts, anything that calls into question from the periphery the narratives which continue to legitimate the centre.

Further reading

Franco, J. (1969) *An Introduction to Spanish American Literature*, Cambridge: Cambridge University Press.

Gonzalez, M. and D. Treece (1992) *A Gathering of Voices: The Poetry of Contemporary Latin America*, London: Verso.

Martin, G. (1990) *Journeys through the Labyrinth*, London: Verso.

Pupo-Walker, E. and Gonzalez Echeverría, R. (1996) *The Cambridge History of Latin American Literature*, Cambridge: Cambridge University Press.

JEAN FRANCO

llano en llamas, El

El llano en llamas (The Burning Plain) (1953) by Mexican writer Juan **Rulfo** is a collection of stories written in a laconic, austere language inspired by the speech of Jalisco peasants but re-elaborated to both reveal and transcend its origins in a perfect balance of poetry and realism. The characters are overwhelmed by a religion shot through with fatalism and resignation, because, as Carlos **Monsiváis** explains, 'secular experience creates a collective capable only of seeing heaven and earth within the confines of their daily life – no longer the "beyond" but rather the "forever present" '. In the story 'Luvina', Rulfo presents a devastated village inhabited by women in mourning, an early version of the Comala of his novel ***Pedro Páramo***. The radical ambiguity of Rulfo's texts, full of silences and allusions, express the hermetic nature of these people and landscape, left barren by nature and history until it is no more 'than a lightning flash, a duststorm of the dead'.

Further reading

Kooreman, T.E. (1972) 'Estructura y realidad en *El llano en llamas*', *Revista iberoamericana* 79: 301–6.

Rulfo, J. (1971) *The Burning Plain*, trans. G. Schade, Austin: University of Texas Press.

Sommers, J. (ed.) (1974) *La narrativa de Juan Rulfo: Interpretaciones críticas*, Mexico City: SEP/Setentas.

MARGO GLANTZ

Lloréns Torres, Luis

b. 1878, Collores, Puerto Rico; d. 1944, Puerto Rico

Poet

Champion of pan-Latin Americanism against burgeoning North American imperialism, Lloréns Torres was a leading poet of Puerto Rican *modernismo* (see **Spanish American modernism**), and founder (1913) of an important Caribbean outlet for *modernista* writing, the *Revista de las Antillas* (Review of the Antilles). His poems, such as 'Canción de las Antillas' (Song of the Antilles) (1913) and 'Velas épicas' (Epic Sails) (1913), are imbued with a sensuous appreciation of the colours, smells and vernacular rhythms of the Caribbean he paradoxically claims both as an exotic outpost of Hispanic culture and as an independent homeland.

Further reading

Caraballo Vida de Abreu, D. (1971) 'La prosa de Luis Lloréns Torres', *Revista de estudios hispánicos* 1(3–4): 81–91.

Luna, N. (1999) 'Paisaje, cuerpo e historia: Luis Lloréns Torres', *Torre* 4(11): 53–78.

Marrero, C. (1974) 'América en la poesía de Lloréns Torres', *Revista/Review Interamericana* 4: 308–21.

JOHN D. PERIVOLARIS

Lobato, Monteiro

b. 1882, Tabauté, São Paulo State, Brazil; d. 1948, São Paulo

Writer

A major modernizing force in Brazilian literature, Lobato (born José Bento Monteiro Lobato) was tireless in founding presses and magazines, promoting regional and **children's literature**, writing cultural journalism and bridging the gaps between Brazil and Spanish America. Best known for his regionalist (see ***regionalismo***) stories about the coffee-producing area of São Paulo State, Lobato created a peasant character, Jeca Tatú, who has become one of the familiar archetypes in Brazilian popular culture. A founder and editor of the *Revista do Brasil* (1916–25), Lobato was later associated with the newspaper *O estado de São Paulo*. His children's literature is set on a coffee plantation, the 'Sítio do picapau amarelo' (Yellow Woodpecker Farm), which is inhabited by a series of memorable characters. Lobato was an enthusiastic supporter of Juan Domingo Perón and resided in Buenos Aires for part of his last years. His complete works were published in thirteen volumes in 1946–47.

Further reading

Dezotti, M. and L. Silva (1999) 'Fábulas de Lobato: A teoria e a prática de um gênero', *Estudos lingüísticos* 28: 455–9.

Landers, V.B. (1983) 'Monteiro Lobato e o Modernismo', *Dissertation Abstracts International* 43(11): 3611A.

Penteado, J. and R. Whitaker (2000) 'The Children of Lobato: The Imaginary World in Adult Ideology', *Bookbird* 38(2): 18–22.

DANIEL BALDERSTON

López, Luis Carlos

b. 1879, Cartagena, Colombia; d. 1950, Cartagena

Poet

López seldom left Cartagena, where he is considered a local treasure; he visited Bogotá once and served twice as consul, in Munich in 1928 and Baltimore in 1937. His work bears his pictorial bent; his poems are finely crafted vignettes, portraits of life in Cartagena spiced with sarcasm and ironic humour. Although López exercised free verse, thematically, he is considered beyond the influence of **Spanish American modernism**. Nicknamed *El Tuerto* (One-Eyed) and the oldest of eleven brothers, his days at medical school were interrupted by civil war, and he soon turned to managing the family business.

Further reading

Bazik, M.S. (1977) *The Life and Works of Luis Carlos López*, Chapel Hill: University of North Carolina Press.

Garavito, F. (1981) 'Luis Carlos López', *Boletín cultural y bibliográfico* 18(2): 87–97.

Zubiria, R. (1988) 'Luis Carlos López: "Un primer clásico de nuestra literatura" ', *Noticias culturales* 37: 1–6.

HÉCTOR D. FERNÁNDEZ L'HOESTE

López Acosta, Pedro de Jesús

b. 1970, Fomento, Cuba

Writer and critic

De Jesús is one of the most innovative authors of his generation. Publications include *Sibilas en Mercaderes* (Sibyls on Mercaderes Street) (1999) and *Cuentos frígidos* (Frigid Tales) (2002). Thematically, his works explore the representation of the post-revolutionary subject, especially through issues considered taboo by the official cultural politics until recent years, for example, sexuality, in all its different variants (hetero, gay, lesbian and bisexual). He also focuses on formal topics such as intertextuality and writing itself, bringing together the national and international literary traditions, from Virginia Woolf to Virgilio **Piñera**, from Ronald Barthes to Reinaldo **Arenas**. He has published several essays on Severo **Sarduy**.

Further reading

Jesús, P. de (1999) *Sibilas en Mercaderes*, Havana: Editorial Letras Cubanas.

—— (2002) *Frigid Tales*, San Francisco: City Lights Books.

JESÚS JAMBRINA

López Albújar, Enrique

b. 1872, Chiclayo, Peru; d. 1966, Lima, Peru

Writer

López Albújar made a significant contribution to the development of Peruvian narrative with two works produced during the 1920s. *Cuentos andinos* (Andean Tales) (1920), although limited by Western preconceptions, prepared the way for later *indigenista* (see ***indigenismo***) fiction by its realistic portrayal of the Indian peasantry. *Matalaché* (1928), a historical novel depicting slave-owning society on the eve of independence, is consciously traditional in manner and form but echoes **Mariátegui** by using history to question the foundations on which modern Peru is built.

Further reading

Castro Urioste, J. (1998) 'Ambigüedades, mestizaje y tensiones irresueltas en la narrativa indigenista de Enrique López Albújar', in M. Moraña (ed.), *Indigenismo hacia el fin del milenio: Homenaje a Antonio Conejo-Polar*, Pittsburgh, PA: Instituto Internacional de Literatura Iberoamericana.

Cornejo, R.E. (1961) *López Albújar, narrador de América*, Madrid: Anaya.

Gayol Mecias, M. (1979) '*Matalaché*: Dos temas y tres personajes', *Casa de las Américas* 114: 141–6.

March, K.N. (1997) 'Enrique López Albújar', in

V. Smith (ed.), *Encyclopedia of Latin American Literature*, London: Fitzroy Dearborn, 493–4.

JAMES HIGGINS

López-Colomé, Pura

b. 1952, Mexico City

Poet

With her first collection of poetry, *El sueño del cazador* (1985), López-Colomé began to carve a space as one of the prominent voices of her generation. Since then, with poetry that evokes images of rhythmic stillness, she has inserted herself into a poetic tradition where the ubiquitous poetic meditations on memory and faith – in her sparse language – are rendered unique. López-Colomé is also a distinguished translator. She has translated into Spanish, among others: Samuel Beckett, H.D., Gertrude Stein and Virginia Woolf. Her literary criticism has been published in national and international literary magazines and cultural supplements, including a regular column for the newspaper *Unomásuno.*

Further reading

López-Colomé, Pura (1985) *El sueño del cazador*, Mexico City: Cuarto Menguante Editores.

—— (1989) *Un cristal en otro*, Mexico City: Ediciones Toled.

—— (1994) *Aurora*, Mexico City: Ediciones del Equilibrista.

—— (1997) *Intemperie*, Mexico City: Ediciones Sin nombre.

—— (1999) *Eter es*, Mexico City: CONACULTA, Col. Práctica Mortal.

—— (2002) *No Shelter: The Selected Poems of Pura López-Colomé*, trans. Forrest Gander, St Paul, MN: Graywolf Press.

LAURA G. GUTIÉRREZ

López Ortega, Antonio

b. 1957, Punta Cardón, Venezuela

Writer and cultural promoter

López Ortega is an intellectual dedicated to promoting Venezuelan culture and traditions throughout the country and abroad. His first novel *Ajena* (2001), which he started writing while studying Latin American literature in Paris in 1983, has recently been published and has encountered favourable comments. It depicts a girl from Caracas who constructs her very intimate reality through an epistolary relationship in which the reader becomes an intruder and accomplice at the same time. He has also published several short story collections: *Cartas de relación* (Letters of Relation) (1982), *Calendario* (Calendar) (1985), *Naturalezas menores* (Minor Natures) (1991) and *Lunar* (Lunar) (1999). Currently he is director of an important cultural foundation and his writing often appears in major Venezuelan newspapers.

Further reading

López Ortega, A. (1998) *Moonlit: Stories*, trans. Nathan Budoff, Cambridge: Lumen Editions.

VÍCTOR GALARRAGA OROPEZA

López Velarde, Ramón

b. 1888, Jerez, Zacatecas, Mexico; d. 1921, Zacatecas

Poet

The finest poet of rural and small-town Mexico, López Velarde's unique voice – tender, seemingly simple, vulnerable – is one of the most important in Spanish American poetry in the period following *modernismo* (see **Spanish American modernism**). One of his poems, 'Suave patria' (Sweet Country), has been set to music and its name has even been bestowed on a tequila. His impressionistic poems of the impact of the Mexican Revolution on his region are striking: understated, they nonetheless register the ways in which the Revolution changed the poet's world. Many of his later poems concern an impossible love with a muse whom he calls Fuensanta.

Further reading

López Velarde, R. (1990) *Obras*, ed. J.L. Martínez, Mexico City: Fondo de Cultura Económica.
Pastén, J.A. (1997) 'Ramón López Velarde', in V. Smith (ed.), *Encyclopedia of Latin American Literature*, London: Fitzroy Dearborn, 494–6.
Paz, O. (1965) 'El camino de la pasión', in *Cuadrivio. Darío. López Velarde. Pessoa. Cernuda*, Mexico City: Joaquín Mortiz, 67–130.
Phillips, A.W. (1962) *Ramón López Velarde, el poeta y el prosista*, Mexico City: INBA.
—— (1989) 'Ramón López Velarde', in C.A. Solé and M.I. Abreu (eds), *Latin American Writers*, ed. New York: Scribners, 2, 663–70.

DANIEL BALDERSTON

Los que se van

Los que se van, cuentos del cholo y del montuvio (The Vanishing Ones. Stories about the Cholo and the Montuvio) was the full title of a collection of short stories published in 1930 by Demetrio **Aguilera Malta**, Joaquín **Gallegos Lara** and Enrique **Gil Gilbert**. It is agreed by critics that the volume marked the emergence of a new style in Ecuadorean literature, a movement that came to be called the **Guayaquil Group** and included José de la **Cuadra** and Alfredo **Pareja Diezcanseco**.

Further reading

Adoum, J.E. (1984) *La gran literatura ecuatoriana del 30*, Quito: Editorial El Conejo.
Heise, K. (1975) *El Grupo de Guayaquil: Arte y técnica en sus novelas*, Madrid: Playor.

HUMBERTO E. ROBLES

Losada, Alejandro

b. 1936, Buenos Aires, Argentina;
d. 1985, Havana, Cuba

Critic

Losada's intense and fertile research into Latin American culture was cut short by his death in an aeroplane accident while flying from Havana to Managua; he was then directing a social history of Latin American literature. Until his death he was Director of Latin American Institute of the Free University of Berlin, where he was Professor of Languages and Literature and leader of a research team. His many publications include *La literatura en la sociedad de América Latina I: Los modos de producción entre 1750–1980* (Literature in Latin American Society: Modes of Production between 1750 and 1980) (1980).

Further reading

D'Allemand, P. (2001) 'Alejandro Losada: Hacia una historia social de las literaturas latinoamericanas', in *Hacia una crítica cultural latinoamericana*, Lima: Latinoamericana Editores, 85–126.
Losada, A. (1985) ' "Nueva novela" y procesos sociales en América Latina', *Texto crítico* 10(31–2): 246–70.
Morales Saravia, J. (ed.) (1986) *La literatura en la sociedad de América latina*, Lima: Latinoamericana.
Ventura, R. (1987) 'Alejandro Losada: Literatura e Sociedade na América Latina', *Revista de crítica literaria latinoamericana* 13(26): 7–23.

CELINA MANZONI

Losada, Editorial

Editorial Losada is the publishing house founded in Buenos Aires by a Spanish exile, Gonzalo Losada, in 1940. It soon established itself as the prime publishing house for writers associated at once with regionalist concerns (see ***regionalismo***) and with international solidarity. Its list included the emerging work of Miguel Angel **Asturias**, José María **Arguedas**, Ciro **Alegría** and others associated with ***indigenismo***. It was also the publisher for decades of the works of Pablo **Neruda** and of the great Spanish poet (exiled for many years in Buenos Aires) Rafael Alberti. Among others, it published Estela Canto, Olga **Orozco**, Silvina **Ocampo** and Virgilio **Piñera**. Still going today, years after the death of its founder, Losada is still a significant publisher (with a beautiful bookstore in Buenos Aires), though largely due to the prestige of its older list.

Further information

http://www.editoriallosada.com/

DANIEL BALDERSTON

Lovelace, Earl

b. 1935, Toco, Trinidad and Tobago

Writer

One of the Anglophone Caribbean's foremost writers, Lovelace belongs to the generation that came of age with Trinidadian independence in 1962. The lyrical realism of his novels, short stories and plays portrays the cultural forms and the struggles for personhood of Trinidad's folk as they negotiate the pressures of colonial education, the law, political opportunism, poverty and modernization. His 1979 novel *The Dragon Can't Dance* is a Caribbean classic. A critical tribute to Trinidad's lumpen proletariat, it uses carnival as a motif for exploring conflicting processes of self-creation, cultural co-optation and Utopian resistance to capitalist values of ownership. In 1997 Lovelace received the Commonwealth Writers Prize for his novel *Salt*, a multi-generational novel which continues his poignant and sometimes gently humorous explorations of the Trinidadian people's struggles for a freedom that remains elusive.

Further reading

Aching, G. (2002) 'Dispossession, Nonpossession and Self-Possession: Postindependence Masking in Lovelace's *The Dragon Can't Dance*', in *Masking and Power: Carnival and Popular Culture in the Caribbean*, Minneapolis: University of Minnesota Press, 51–72.

Sankar, C. (1998) 'Earl Lovelace: Unsettled Accounts', *Américas* 50(1): 38–43.

Sunitha, K.T. (1992) 'The Discovery of Selfhood in Earl Lovelace's Fiction', *Commonwealth Novel in English* 5(1): 27–37.

Thomas, H.N. (1991) 'From 'Freedom' to 'Liberation': An Interview with Earl Lovelace', *World Literature Written in English* 31(1): 8–20.

SHALINI PURI

Loynaz, Dulce María

b. 1903, Havana, Cuba; d. 1997, Havana

Poet

A prolific writer, Loynaz published over eight volumes of poetry, a novel, *Jardín* (Garden) (1951), and a collection of travel pieces, *Viaje a Tenerife* (A Trip to Tenerife) (1958). Daughter of a general in the Cuban Liberating Army against the Spanish and sister of the poet Enrique Loynaz Muñoz, her poems were first published in the Cuban newspaper *La Nación* in 1920, and later in journals as diverse as *Social*, *Grafos*, *Revista bimestre cubana* and ***Orígenes***. She was president of the Academia Cubana de la Lengua (Cuban Academy of Language) and won Cuba's National Literary Award in 1987 and the 1992 Premio Miguel de Cervantes in Spain.

Further reading

Behar, R. (1997) 'Dulce María Loynaz: A Woman Who No Longer Exists', *Michigan Quarterly Review* 36(4): 529–37.

López Cruz, H. (1999) 'Bibliografía fundamental de y sobre Dulce María Loynaz', *Boletín del instituto de investigaciones bibliográficas* 4(1–2): 249–72.

O'Connor, J. (2002) 'Absolute Solitude: The Prose Poetry of Dulce María Loynaz', *PN Review* 28(3): 29–31.

Smith, V. (1997) 'Dulce María Loynaz', in V. Smith

(ed.), *Encyclopedia of Latin American Literature*, London: Fitzroy Dearborn, 497–9.

LÁZARO LIMA

Ludmer, Josefina

b. 1939, San Francisco, Córdoba Province, Argentina

Literary critic

A university professor at Yale University, Ludmer's writings are indispensable for any student of Latin American literature – *Cien años de soledad: Una interpretación* (One Hundred Years of Solitude: An Interpretation) (1972); *Onetti: Los procesos de construcción del relato* (Processes of Construction of the Short Story) (1977). Her most important work, *El género gauchesco. Un tratado sobre la patria* (The Gaucho Genre. A Treatise on the Motherland) (1988), draws on literary criticism, anthropology, history and psychoanalysis to analyse the constitution of a canon of Argentine literature that stretches from Hidalgo to **Lamborghini**. This work is a key innovative text in Argentine cultural criticism.

Further reading

Ludmer, Josefina (1972) *Cien años de soledad: Una interpretación*, Buenos Aires: Editorial Tiempo Contemporáneo.

—— (1977) *Onetti: Los procesos de construcción del relato*, Buenos Aires: Editorial Sudamericana.

—— (2002) *The Gaucho Genre: A Treatise on the Motherland*, Durham, NC: Duke University Press.

DIEGO BENTIVEGNA

lugar sin límites, El

José **Donoso**'s novel *El lugar sin límites* (Hell Has No Limits), published in 1966, introduces into Latin American literature a ground-breaking narrative about how male homosociality, (homo)sexuality, homophobia and misogyny function in relation to complex traditional patriarchal structures. Set in a forgotten rural town in Chile, the novel focuses on the erotically shared power relations between the male transvestite brothel owner La Manuela, the prostitute La Japonesa, their daughter, La Japonesita, Pancho, a hypervirile worker who desires both father and daughter, and don Alejo, the local large-scale landholder.

The brothel and the transvestite's body are the privileged spaces for examining social and political structures as well as the limits of gender and sexual categories. *El lugar sin límites* was adapted for the screen in 1977 by Mexican director Arturo Ripstein with a screenplay co-written by Manuel **Puig** (not credited). A critical and commercial success, Ripstein's representation of the dilemmas of homoerotic desire is a cult classic, especially for the sympathetic portrayal of La Manuela, played by Roberto Cobo, who made his film debut in Luis Buñuel's *Los olvidados* (1950) as the adolescent delinquent el Jaibo. The deadly kiss between La Manuela, dressed in a red with white polka dot flamenco dress, and Pancho, stands as an ironic landmark in relation to the spectacle of Mexico's virile heterosexual national image.

Further reading

Cerda, C. (1997) *Donoso sin límites*, Santiago: LOM Ediciones.

Donoso, J. (1999) *El lugar sin límites*, Madrid: Cátedra, Letras Hispánicas.

Sifuentes Jáuregui, B. (1997) 'Gender without Limits: Transvestism and Subjectivity in *El lugar sin límites*', in D. Balderston and D.J. Guy (eds), *Sex and Sexuality in Latin America*, New York: New York University Press, 44–61.

SERGIO DE LA MORA

Lugo Filippi, Carmen

b. 1940, Ponce, Puerto Rico

Writer

Part of a group of **intellectuals** who in 1970 discarded the 'literary pessimism' and 'linguistic Hispanism' characteristic of Puerto Rican nationalist rhetoric, Lugo Filippi's writing displays humour and sharp wit, a distancing parody and a clear acknowledgement of the island's heteroglossic reality. Written with Ana Lydia **Vega**, *Vírgenes y mártires* (Virgins and Martyrs) (1981) is her most important collection of short stories.

Further reading

Méndez, J.L. (1983) 'Sobre *Virgenes y mártires*', *Sin nombre* 14(1): 61–7.

MARÍA JULIA DAROQUI

Lugones, Leopoldo

b. 1874, Villa de Santa María del Río Seco, Argentina; d. 1938, El Tigre, Argentina

Writer

A good friend of Rubén **Darío**, Lugones was to be Argentina's most important *modernista* poet. In his *magnum opus*, *Lunario sentimental* (Sentimental Calendar) (1909), however, he would transgress many assumptions and principles of Spanish American *modernismo* (see **Spanish American modernism**) and write in an experimental vein that anticipated the work of the avant-garde writers of ***Martín Fierro*** and ***Proa***, who admired his handling of metaphor but repudiated his pronounced deference to rhyme. During the following decades, Lugones's poetry evolved towards more traditional forms and themes, an evolution running parallel with the development of his ideological position: sympathizing with anarchism and socialism in his younger days, he was to end up an ultra-conservative if not fascistic nationalist, who did not hesitate to participate in the conspiracy that led to the military *putsch* of 1930. Alienated and isolated, he committed suicide in a secluded hotel in the delta of El Tigre (near Buenos Aires).

Lugones was an extremely prolific and versatile writer. Besides poetry he wrote various volumes of short stories (mostly in the fantastical mode) and countless articles, essays and studies on a great variety of political, historical, biographical, educational, religious, literary and cultural subjects. His universal knowledge, his conversion to tradition and his independent nature are only a few of many links with **Borges**, the co-author with Bettina Edelberg of *Leopoldo Lugones* (1955). And yet, Lugones's work lacks the sophisticated irony and the subdued melancholy of Borges's and is, in the end, more virtuosity than penetrating.

Further reading

Forster, M.H. (1989) 'Leopoldo Lugones', in C.A. Solé and M.I. Abreu (eds), *Latin American Writers*, New York: Scribners, 2, 493–502.

Jitrik, N. (1960) *Leopoldo Lugones: Mito nacional*, Buenos Aires: Ediciones Palestra.

Kirkpatrick, G. (1989) *The Dissonant Legacy of Modernism: Lugones, Herrera y Reissig, and the Voices of Modern Spanish American Poetry*, Berkeley: University of California Press.

Lockhart, D.B. (1997) 'Leopoldo Lugones', in V. Smith (ed.), *Encyclopedia of Latin American Literature*, London: Fitzroy Dearborn, 499–501.

Lugones, L. (1952) *Obras poéticas completas*, Madrid: Aguilar.

—— (1979) *El payador y antología de poesía y prosa*, ed. G. Ara, Caracas: Biblioteca Ayacucho.

Martinez Estrada, E. (1968) *Leopoldo Lugones: Retrato sin tocar*, Buenos Aires: Emecé.

MAARTEN STEENMEIJER

Lunes de Revolución

Lunes de Revolución was a weekly cultural supplement of the newspaper *Revolución*, published in tabloid form between March 1959 and November 1961. Its 129 issues covered every area of cultural, artistic and political life in Cuba and internationally. Its impact on national life was demonstrated by its circulation of over 500,000 per issue, a success unequalled before or since in the Cuban media.

The magazine was as innovative and polemical as the period in which it was produced, providing a space where free discussion on cultural identity could be conducted, a process marked by contingency and a constant struggle between different tendencies and currents of ideas. From issue 23 it was edited by Guillermo **Cabrera Infante**, assisted by Pablo Armando **Fernández**. Raúl Martínez was responsible for its design from the outset, becoming art editor from issue 74. Contributors included Virgilio **Piñera**, Antón **Arrufat**, Rine **Leal**, Calvert **Casey**, José A. Baragaño and Heberto **Padilla**.

The wide range of positions and opinions held by both its editorial team and its team of contributors symbolized the network of ideological and generational contradictions which co-existed during the first three years of the Castro regime. Its first editorial defined the eclectic and contestatory spirit in which the project was conceived: 'We are not a literary group; we are just friends of a similar age. We have no political ideology in common, though we do not reject some ways of interpreting reality – we are referring, for example, to dialectical materialism, psychoanalysis or **existentialism**.'

The work of *Lunes* embraced a terrain much wider than journalism, becoming the focus of other confrontations in Cuban cultural life. It promoted a number of important projects, like the Ediciones R publishing house, the 'Lunes en TV' programme and visits to Cuba by many international figures. However, Fidel Castro's 1961 speech 'Palabras a los intelectuales' (Words to the Intellectuals) pointed to the publication's imminent closure.

The topics most frequently addressed were literature and politics; in total 543 people wrote for *Lunes*, of whom more than thirty were Cuban. It published poems, stories and extracts from novels and essays, as well as devoting a large amount of space to Cuban theatre, reproducing one-act plays and fragments of other works. It also produced several monographs on Third World countries, events in history and prominent artists and writers. Its final issue (in November 1961) was a special number devoted to Pablo Picasso.

Further reading

Cabrera Infante, G. (*c.* 1999) *Assays, Essays and Other Arts*, New York: Twayne.

WILFREDO CANCIO ISLA

Lynch, Marta

b. 1925, Buenos Aires, Argentina;
d. 1985, Buenos Aires

Writer

Marta Lynch wrote seven novels and nine collections of short prose before her suicide. *La alfombra roja* (The Red Rug) (1962) is a jaundiced view of a presidential campaign, which drew on her experience with Argentine president Arturo Frondizi. *Al vencedor* (To the Victor) (1965) is a bleak look at the lives of two young men returning from military service. *La señora Ordóñez* (Mrs Ordonez) (1967) chronicles the empty life of a working-class girl who marries into the bourgeoisie. *El cruce del río* (River Crossing) (1972) tells the story of a *guerrillero* and his politically active mother. *Un árbol lleno de manzanas* (A Tree Filled with Apples) (1974) is a love story about politics, or vice versa. *La penúltima versión de la Colorado Villanueva* (The Penultimate Version of Red Villanueva) (1978) is another chronicle of middle-class family life and its disintegration during times of political crisis. *Informe bajo llave* (Report under Lock and Key) (1983) tells of a woman's sexual obsession. Lynch's short stories, like her novels, are stylistically sophisticated variations on the themes of loneliness, sex and politics.

Further reading

Esquível, M. (1988) 'Marta Lynch: Novelista por naturaleza', *Tragaluz* 2(13): 17–19.
Moya Raggio, E. (1988) 'Conversación con Marta Lynch', *Letras femeninas* 14(1–2): 104–11.
Paley de Francescato, M. (1975) 'Marta Lynch', *Hispamérica* 10: 33–44.

AMY KAMINSKY

Lyra, Carmen

b. 1888, San José, Costa Rica; d. 1949, Mexico City

Writer

The first major Costa Rican female writer, Lyra lost

her position as a school teacher when her writing turned from sentimental *modernismo* to political denunciation. In 1930 she joined the Communist Party. Lyra came to view literature as an instrument of social protest and revolution, and was one of the earliest writers to criticize the fruit companies in her *Bananos y hombres* (Banana Trees and Men) (1931). Costa Ricans best remember her for her children's narratives, *Los cuentos de mi Tía Panchita* (Stories from Aunt Panchita) (1920), which blended popular stories with 'universal' folktales.

Further reading

Horan, E.R. (2000) *The Subversive Voice of Carmen Lyra: Selected Works*, Gainesville: University Press of Florida.

LINDA J. CRAFT

M

Macunaíma

Mário de **Andrade**'s prose 'rhapsody' *Macunaíma* (1928) was published amid a critical debate within the modernist movement (see **Brazilian modernism**) regarding the country's cultural identity and development. Andrade's fantastical narrative, recounting the 'primitive' anti-hero's odyssey from the Amazon to São Paulo and back, is testimony to Brazil's wealth of popular and regional cultures, as well as a complex and sober commentary on the dilemmas of modernity and development and the prospects for survival of traditional identities and ways of life.

Andrade drew on many sources, but owed much to German traveller Theodor Koch-Grünberg's *Myths and Legends of the Taulipange and Arekúna Indians* (1916). Koch-Grünberg's Makunaima ('the great wicked one') supplied Andrade with the crucial paradox of the book's subtitle, 'the hero without any character'. While debates raged about 'national character', often using the language of scientific racism, Andrade celebrated the exploits of an ethnic chameleon, black, indigenous, blonde and blue-eyed, whose moral, psychological and even linguistic inconsistency mocked Brazil's official Order and Progress ideology. An enemy of Order, like his real-life urban counterpart, the Brazilian 'hustler' or *malandro,* Macunaíma is infuriatingly irresponsible, yet irresistibly subversive.

Andrade saw identity not as a stable category but as an open-ended process of becoming, hybrid and transcultural. He appeared to share this dialectical perspective with Oswald de **Andrade**, who seized on the book as the masterpiece of his cannibalist movement, **Antropofagia**; the subsequent rift between the two, however, suggested profound differences in their prognosis for Brazil's cultural development. The overwhelming defeatism with which *Macunaíma* concludes suggests, not the revolutionary cannibalist synthesis envisaged by Oswald, but a more pessimistic scenario in which the Brazilian capacity for adaptation also renders him vulnerable to marginalization and acculturation, and to being devoured by the world around him.

This was the perspective of Joaquim Pedro de Andrade's 1969 film adaptation which, in updating the setting to reflect the atmosphere of the economic miracle, foregrounded the theme of consumer capitalism. A product of the Tropicália movement and of the third phase of Cinema Novo, Andrade's film captured this carnivalesque atmosphere using the resources of the commercial cinema – colour, elaborate sets and a large cast – together with elements of Brazil's genre of musical comedy, the *chanchada.* In a further adaptation in 1978, this time for the stage, experimental dramatist Antunes Filho made ingenious use of actors and stage choreography to convey the narrative's rhapsodic flux. Its success on repeated international tours over the following decade suggests that Andrade's text and its popular trickster hero will remain a crucial and enduring source of reflection on Brazil's cultural development.

Further reading

Andrade, M. de (1988) *Macunaíma: O herói sem sem*

nenhum caráter, Ed. Telê Porto Ancona Lopez and Paris: Colección Archivos.
—— (1988) *Macunaíma*, trans. R. Goodland, London: Carcanet.
Johnson, R. (1978) 'Macunaíma as Brazilian Hero', *Latin American Literary Review* 38–44.
Proença, M.C. (1969) *Roteiro de Macunaíma*, Rio de Janeiro: Civilização Brasileira.

DAVID TREECE

Madariaga, Francisco

b. 1927, Buenos Aires, Argentina

Poet

Madariaga might well be considered one of the most important poets of the late twentieth century, were his work more widely known. In 1987, the Fondo de Cultura Económica published his complete works under the suggestive title *El tren casi fluvial* (The Almost Riverborne Train); it included ten volumes, from *El pequeño patíbulo* (The Little Scaffold) of 1954 to *Resplandor de mis bárbaras* (Light of My Barbarians) of 1985. The setting of his work is the province of Corrientes, its central theme the tension between urban and rural, expressed through bilingualism. Guarani scans its rhythms and its worldview, producing a strange everyday experience.

Further reading

Cobo Borda, J.G. (1985) 'Francisco Madariaga', *Poesía* 11(5 (64)): 37–40.
Madariaga, F. (1987) *El tren casi fluvial: Obra reunida*, Mexico City: Fondo de Cultura Económica.

ENRIQUE FOFFANI

Magaña, Sergio

b. 1924, Tepalcatepec, Mexico; d. 1990, Mexico City

Playwright

A major figure in twentieth-century Mexican theatre, Magaña wrote a small number of carefully crafted and profound plays exploring the themes of liberty, power and despair in the modern world.

Magaña learned his dramatic skills from Salvador **Novo**, Fernando Wagner, Seki Sano and Rodolfo **Usigli** (although he later distanced himself from Usigli) and worked with outstanding dramatists such as Luisa Josefina **Hernández** and Emilio **Carballido**, who was also a member of the Filosofía y Letras Theatre Group at UNAM which first performed Magaña's *La noche transfigurada* (The Transfigured Night) in 1947. Recognition came in 1951 with the premiere of *Los signos del Zodíaco* (The Signs of the Zodiac), directed by Salvador **Novo**.

The central theme of Magaña's work is liberty. His protagonists face dilemmas in their struggle to overcome fear and repression, sometimes succeeding and sometimes failing. He examines the power relations between individuals in a microcosm representative of more complex social and historical realities.

Schooled in the realist mould, only half his work is written in that way. He also wrote pieces involving many individuals in a kind of mural, as well as intense and concentrated monologues, such as *El reloj y la cuna* (The Clock and the Cradle) (1952). He worked in all dramatic forms, from tragedy to political commentary, and pioneered musical theatre in Mexico – in the US style – with *Rentas congeladas* (Frozen Rents) (1960), *El mundo que tú heredas* (The World You Inherit) (1970) and *Santísima* (1980). He composed the music for all these works, as well as a number of songs.

Magaña's work can be grouped in several cycles: his urban cycle embraces *Los signos de Zodíaco* (The Signs of the Zodiac) (1951), *El pequeño caso de Jorge Lívido* (The Little Case of Jorge Lívido) (1958) and *Los motivos del lobo* (Motives of the Wolf) (1965); another cycle is set in pre-Columbian and Conquest times – *Moctezuma II* (1953), *Cortés y la Malinche* (better known as *Los argonautas* (The Argonauts)) (1967) and *Los enemigos* (The Enemies) (1984). Magaña also wrote theatre for children, including *El viaje de Nocresida* (Nocresida's Travels) (1952), written with Carballido, and *El anillo de oro* (The Golden Ring) (1960). Other important works include *Ensayando a Molière* (Rehearsing Molière) (1966), *El que vino a hacer la guerra* (The Man who Came to Make War) (1972) and *La última diana* (The Last Reveille) (1984).

Magaña combined writing with theatre criticism and classes at the Theatre School of Mexico's National Institute of Fine Arts. He also wrote film scripts, a book of stories *El ángel roto* (Broken Angel) (1946) and a novel, *El molino del aire* (The Windmill) (1953). In later years he began to create an archive of his own work at the Rodolfo Usigli Centre for Theatre Research and Documentation. His work has yet to be collected in a complete works; most of it remains dispersed in journals.

Further reading

Magaña, S. (1985) *Moctezuma II, Cortés y la Malinche*, Mexico: Mexicanos Unidos.

—— (1990) *Los enemigos*, Mexico: Mexicanos Unidos.

EDUARDO CONTRERAS SOTO

Magdaleno, Mauricio

b. 1906, Zacatecas, Mexico; d. 1986, Mexico City

Writer

Several years spent living in one of Mexico's poorest regions provided rich material for Magdaleno's novels, notably *El resplandor* (Sunburst) (1937). He organized the avant-garde group Teatro Ahora with Bustillo Oro and became an exceptional screenwriter, working closely with the director Emilio 'El Indio' Fernández, cinematographer Gabriel Figueroa and stars such as Dolores Del Rio, María Félix and Pedro Armendáriz. Magdaleno wrote numerous novels, short story collections, biographies and essays. During the administration of Adolfo López Mateos, he played a prominent role as senator and Under-secretary for Cultural Affairs.

Further reading

Campos, J. (1966) 'Del corrido al cuento: Mauricio Magdaleno', *Insula* 21(230): 11.

Magdaleno, Mauricio. (1937) *El resplandor*, Mexico City: Ediciones Botas.

—— (1944) *Sunburst*, NY: Viking Press.

CYNTHIA STEELE

Maggi, Carlos

b. 1922, Montevideo, Uruguay

Writer

Considered the most important playwright of the 'Generation of '45', Maggi is also a respected essayist and fiction writer. His major plays include *La trastienda* (The Back Store) (1958), *La noche de los ángeles inciertos* (The Night of the Uncertain Angels) (1960), *La gran viuda* (The Great Widow) (1961), *El baile del cangrejo* (The Crab's Dance) (1971), *Frutos* (Fruit) (1985) and *Un cuervo en la madrugada* (A Blackbird at Dawn) (1989). He has also ventured into film and television, and won, in 1962, the Brussels Film Festival grand prize for his film *La raya amarilla* (The Yellow Line) (1962). His essays include *Gardel, Onetti y algo más* (Gardel, Onetti, and More) (1964) and *Los militares, la televisión y otras razones de uso interno* (The Military, Television and Other Matters for Internal Use) (1986).

Further reading

Benedetti, M. (1988) 'Carlos Maggi y su meridiano de vida', in *Literatura uruguaya del siglo XX*, Montevideo: Arca.

Quackenbush, L.H. (1975) 'Theatre of the Absurd, Reality, and Carlos Maggi', *Journal of Spanish Studies* 3: 61–72.

Szoka, E. (1989) 'Carlos Maggi: Sobre su teatro', *Dactylus* 9: 11–14.

MARINA PIANCA

magical realism

Coined by art critic Franz Roh in 1925 to describe German post-expressionist painting, this term was adopted and popularized by Latin American fiction writers and critics after it declined in Europe. Its literary meaning has changed radically and is still debated. Since the mid-1970s, it has been widely associated with the style or narrative mode of novels such as Alejo **Carpentier**'s 1949 *El **reino de este mundo*** (The Kingdom of This World), Miguel Angel **Asturias**'s 1949 *Hombres de maíz* (Men of Maize), Juan **Rulfo**'s 1955 ***Pedro Páramo*** and Gabriel **García Márquez**'s 1967 ***Cien años de soledad*** (One Hundred Years of Solitude). Similar authors of this period include the Ecuadorian Demetrio **Aguilera Malta** and Brazilian João Guimarães **Rosa**. The style is characterized by storytelling from a primitivist viewpoint that challenges modern Western norms. The authors draw from the worldview of tribal societies of Indian, African or archaic Christian origin, as well as their fusion known as syncretism. Myth, magic and superstition are presented as normal everyday realities in Latin America, while common aspects of technology, modernity and Western rationality are naively regarded with suspicion and disbelief. Due in part to the recent international influence of Latin American fiction, magical realism is now considered a worldwide phenomenon.

Its meaning within Latin American criticism has undergone three major stages. It was first adopted by dramatist Rodolfo **Usigli** (1940) and critics Alvaro Lins (1944) and José Antonio **Portuondo** (1952) to signify the opening of traditional realism to new poetic, psychological and existential tendencies then in vogue – particularly among writers of the Southern Cone (Argentina, Uruguay and Chile). A second stage began with Angel **Flores**'s influential article of 1955 which defined the term as a 'mixture of reality and fantasy', citing Kafka as precursor and **Borges** as initiator. This broad definition, including any deviation from traditional realism, gave rise to a debate never fully resolved. Yet in the 1970s, French criticism distinguished 'the fantastic' as a genre (see **fantastic literature**), indirectly narrowing the scope for magical realism. No longer confused with the fantastic, and with psycho-existentialist literature out of vogue, magical realism came to be regarded as modernist anthropological fiction sympathetically portraying the surviving magical worldview of 'primitive' folk – particularly in the Caribbean and the larger 'Afro-Indian zone'. The enormous success of *Cien años de soledad* reinforced that conception, as this novel became a sort of model and trademark for magical realism internationally.

The primitivist conception of magical realism originates, however, with Italian writer Massimo Bontempelli, who proposed since 1926 a 'realistic precision and magical atmosphere', claiming the dawn of a new era in which modern artists must be 'primitives with a past' and discover the surreal in reality itself. His friend, Venezuelan writer and diplomat Arturo **Uslar Pietri**, defined magical realism in Venezuelan fiction as a 'realism of primitives' (1948). Uslar, who befriended Asturias and Carpentier in 1920s Paris, must have been the link whereby the concept passed to Latin America. The three participated in surrealism's cult of primitive art. After returning home, Asturias, inspired by Mayan myths of his native Guatemala, would refer to his own work as magical realism. In turn, Carpentier would coin his own related term: *lo real maravilloso americano* (the marvellous American real) (see ***real maravilloso, lo***). Carpentier criticized French **surrealism** for invoking the marvellous in disbelief by means of artificial recipes such as the 'chance encounter' of objects never to be found together in reality. He considered European primitivism false in comparison to the primitive realities of Latin America, where the marvellous was found daily and throughout history in a natural 'authentic' state, by virtue of the chance encounter of disparate cultures and the syncretism of Indian, African and Christian beliefs. He concluded that 'the sensation of marvellous presupposes a faith'. Carpentier's 'marvellous real' has been immensely influential, not just as a literary concept, but as a matter of Latin American identity and expression.

The marvellous real, however, is not quite synonymous with magical realism, nor with the concoction 'marvellous realism' proposed by some. Carpentier could not admit an '-ism' at all, because he claimed the marvellous was in Latin American reality itself, not in the technique of storytelling. Yet, his concept served to justify magical realism as a form of expression rooted in regional identity; therefore claiming to be 'authentically' Latin American, not another imitation of Western (or Northern) models. Carpentier and Asturias have been criticized for claiming a mystical connection with the primitive essence of Latin American reality. As faith in their foundational literary myth eroded, authors such as Rulfo and García Márquez engaged magical realism frankly as an artful distortion of reality, bordering on parody and caricature. There is no pretence that the supernatural events in their novels should be taken at face value; rather, they suggest an allegorical interpretation of Latin American history and culture. This movement toward greater artificiality underscores more recent novels like Isabel **Allende**'s 1982 *La casa de los espíritus* (The House of the Spirits), Mario **Vargas Llosa**'s 1987 *El hablador* (The Storyteller) and Laura Esquivel's 1989 ***Como agua para chocolate*** (Like Water for Chocolate). Film versions of Allende's and Esquivel's novels have further popularized the style.

Further reading

Angulo, M.-E. (1995) *Magic Realism: Social Context and Discourse*, New York and London: Garland.

Chiampi, I. (1980) *O realismo maravilhoso: Forma e ideologia no romance hispano-americano*, São Paulo: Editora Perspectiva.

Menton, S. (1998) *Historia verdadera del realismo mágico*, Mexico City: Fondo de Cultura Económica.

Parkinson Zamora, L. and W. Faris (eds) (1995) *Magical Realism: Theory, History, Community*, Durham, NC and London: Duke University Press.

Rowe, W. (1997) 'Magical Realism', in V. Smith (ed.), *Encyclopedia of Latin American Literature*, London: Fitzroy Dearborn, 506–7.

ERIK CAMAYD-FREIXAS

Mais, Roger

b. 1905, Kingston, Jamaica; d. 1955, Kingston

Writer

Called 'the spokesman of emergent Jamaica' by Jean **D'Costa** in a critical essay of 1978, Mais was arrested and imprisoned for six months in 1947 for an essay titled 'Now We Know', an attack on British colonialism. He started writing his first novel in prison; it was published nine years later. His subsequent writings included *And Most of All Man* (short stories and verse, 1939), *Face and Other Stories* (short stories and verse, 1942), *The Hills Were Joyful Together* (novel, 1953), *Brother Man* (novel, 1954) and *Black Lightning* (novel, 1955). He died of cancer in Jamaica after travelling for three years in Europe. He left a fourth, unfinished novel.

Further reading

Davies, B. (1974) 'The Novels of Roger Mais', *International Fiction Review* 1: 140–3.

Hawthorne, E.J. (1989) *The Writer in Transition: Roger Mais and the Decolonization of Caribbean Culture*, New York: Peter Lang.

Mais, R. (1966) *The Three Novels of Roger Mais*, intro. Norman Manley, London: Jonathan Cape.

Williamson, K. (1967) 'Roger Mais: West Indian Novelist', *Journal of Commonwealth Literature* 2: 138–47.

KEITH JARDIM

Mallea, Eduardo

b. 1904, Bahía Blanca, Argentina; d. 1982, Buenos Aires, Argentina

Writer

Mallea's works exude a chauvinistic nationalism and a fervent search for the Hispanic roots of Argentine society. He devoted many of his writings – *La bahía del silencio* (The Bay of Silence) (1940), *Historia de una pasión argentina* (History of an Argentine Passion) (1937) and *La ciudad junto al río inmóvil* (The City by the Unmoving River) (1936) – to analysing the 'essence' of Argentine nationality. He was on the editorial board of the influential journal ***Sur*** and director of the literary supplement of the conservative newspaper *La Nación*.

Further reading

Lewald, H.E. (1977) *Eduardo Mallea*, Boston: Twayne.

Lichtblau, M.I. (ed.) (1985) *Eduardo Mallea ante la crítica*, Miami: Universal.

—— (1967) *El arte estilístico de Eduardo Mallea*, Buenos Aires: Goyanarte Editor.

—— (1989) 'Eduardo Mallea', in C.A. Solé and

M.I. Abreu (eds), *Latin American Writers*, New York: Scribners, 3: 981–90.
Mallea, E. (1961) *Obras completas*, Buenos Aires, Emecé, 2 vols.
—— (1967) *All Green Shall Perish*, London: Calder & Boyars.
Polt, J.H.R. (1959) *The Writings of Eduardo Mallea*, Berkeley: University of California Press.
Sierra, E. (1989) 'Notas para una relectura de Eduardo Mallea', *Inter-American Review of Bibliography* 39(3): 301–10.
Walker, J. (1997) 'Eduardo Mallea', in V. Smith (ed.), *Encyclopedia of Latin American Literature*, London: Fitzroy Dearborn, 507–9.

FLORENCIA GARRAMUÑO

Mañach, Jorge

b. 1898, Sagua la Grande, Cuba; d. 1961, San Juan, Puerto Rico

Writer

A leading member of Cuba's **Grupo Minorista** and founder of the ***Revista de Avance***, Mañach was a central figure in Cuba's cultural life through the 1930s. He was a journalist and editor of *Acción* (1934–35). In 1940 he returned to Cuba after five years exile in the USA and was elected to the Constituent Assembly. He taught at Havana University and presented the influential television programme *Ante la prensa* (Meet the Press). His many writings include the highly-praised biography *Martí el apóstol* (Martí the Apostle) and *Teoría de la frontera* (Theory of the Frontier) (1970), a posthumous collection of his lectures. A famous essay of his, *Indagación del choteo*, (1928), analyses a kind of Cuban humour.

Further reading

Alvarez, N.E. (1979) *La obra literaria de Jorge Mañach*, Madrid: Porrua.
—— (1989) 'Jorge Mañach Robato', in C.A. Solé and M.I. Abreu (eds), *Latin American Writers*, New York: Scribners, 2: 831–6.
Pérez Firmat, G. (1998) 'Jorge Mañach: Elements of Cuban Style', *Caribe* 1(1): 10–25.

WILFREDO CANCIO ISLA

manifestos

Taken most broadly, a manifesto is a public declaration of principles or beliefs, and its often aggressive presentation can bear on politics, religion, philosophy or the arts. Most commonly associated with literary schools or periods, literary manifestos abounded in the twentieth century, perhaps because of the political and cultural turbulence surrounding the First World War. Rubén **Darío**'s well-turned introduction to his seminal *Prosas profanas* (Profane Songs) (1896), representative of the refined language and ivory tower escapism typical of turn-of-the-century **Spanish American modernism**, was a predecessor.

A glance at the compilations of texts by Hugo Verani (1986), Nelson **Osorio** (1988) and Jorge **Schwartz** (1991) reveals that some forty literary manifestos or manifesto-like pronouncements appeared during the 1920s. **Avant-garde** figures and groups were in evidence in almost all nations, but the most significant manifestos were produced in the larger cultural centres. For example, the Chilean Vicente **Huidobro** and his *creacionismo* provided the earliest Latin American examples of avant-garde position-taking; his verse manifesto 'Arte poética' (Ars Poetica) (1916) and the multiple texts included in *Manifestes* (1925) are important representations of Huidobro's ideas. In Argentina, the most significant examples are the *Prisma* mural broadsides, written in 1921 and 1922 by Jorge Luis **Borges** and others, and the declamatory ***Martín Fierro*** manifesto, written by Oliverio **Girondo** and published in 1924. In Brazil, the argumentative tone was even more marked. Mário de **Andrade**'s 'Prefácio Interesantíssimo' (Most Interesting Preface) (1922) was a manifesto-like introduction to a long experimental poem; Oswald de **Andrade**'s 'Manifesto Pau-Brasil' (Brazilwood Manifesto) (1924) made a noisy case for new poetry in local terms. The most unusual such pronouncement in Brazil, and perhaps in all of Latin America, was Oswald de Andrade's 'Manifesto Antropófago' (Cannibalist Manifesto) (1928) (see ***Antropofogia***). Organized in fifty numbered segments and dated the '374th Year of the Swallowing of Bishop Sardinha', Andrade poked fun at antiquated European traditions (for example, the third section reads 'Tupi or not tupi, that is the question', a clever parody of Hamlet's words), which needed to be devoured and used as an energy source for new creations. Finally, Mexican **Estridentismo** produced several aggressive manifesto texts during the 1920s. The first – 'Actual, Núm. 1' (Current, No. 1, 1921), written by Manuel **Maples Arce** and pasted on downtown walls in the city of Puebla – recommended drastic action: 'Chopin to the electric chair!' A second proclamation by Maples Arce and others was entitled 'Manifiesto estridentista núm. 2' (Second Stridentist Manifesto) (1923) and equated the movement with manhood and strength: 'To be a stridentist is to be a man. Only the eunuchs are not with us. We'll put out the sun with a single sweep of our hats!'

Manifestos of the visual arts are included in an appendix to Dawn Ades's *Art of Latin America* (1989), the most famous being Siqueiros's manifesto of the Mexican Muralist movement. Of note in the 1960s and 1970s were the film manifestos associated with the New Latin American Cinema, especially those by Grupo Cine Liberación, Julio García Espinosa and Jorge Sanjinés.

Further reading

Osorio, N. (1988) *Manifiestos, proclamas y polémicas de la vanguardia literaria hispanoamericana*, Caracas: Biblioteca Ayacucho.

Schwartz, J. (1991) *Las vanguardias latinoamericanas*, Madrid: Cátedra; 2nd edn, Mexico City: Fondo de Cultura Económica, 2002.

Unruh, V. (1994) *Latin American Vanguards: The Art of Contentious Encounters*, Berkeley: University of California Press.

MERLIN H. FORSTER

Manns, Patricio

b. 1937, Bío Bío province, Chile

Writer and musician

Best known as a composer and singer, Manns's songs reflect his own lifelong political commitment; but they are far from 'pamphlet songs' – their lyrics are poetic and dense. Some, notably 'Cuando me acuerdo de mi país' (When I Remember my Country), have become unofficial anthems of the dispersed Chilean exile community. He is also a poet, novelist, essayist, writer of plays and for the screen, and the biographer of the musical mentor of his generation (*Violeta Parra* (1986)). His book of poems *Memorias de Bonampak* (Memories of Bonampak) (1995) is a neo-*indigenista* work that seeks to speak for the oppressed Maya people (see ***indigenismo***). His novel, *El corazón a contraluz* (The Heart in Silhouette) (1996), is about a historical figure, Julio Popper, a Jewish adventurer in southern Chile who links up with an Ona Indian girl in Tierra del Fuego. Manns has lived in France since 1973.

Further reading

Manns, Patricio (1967) *De noche sobre el rastro*, Santiago: Editorial Universitaria, Sociedad de Escritores de Chile.

—— (1999) *El desorden en un cuerno de niebla*, Buenos Aires: Emecé Editores.

DANIEL BALDERSTON

Maples Arce, Manuel

b. 1900, Papantla, Veracruz, Mexico; d. 1981, Mexico City

Poet and diplomat

The central figure in Mexican **Estridentismo**, Maples Arce wrote most of the group's manifestos and was the moving force behind its principal journals, *Irradiador* (1923) and *Horizonte* (1926–27). His own Estridentista poetry collections, *Andamios interiores* (Interior Scaffolding) (1922), *Urbe* (Metropolis) (1924) and *Poemas interdictos* (Prohibited Poems) (1927), reveal strong ties to the futurist and cubist avant-garde (see **avant-garde in Latin America**). *Memorial de la sangre* (Blood Memorial) (1947) gathers his more mature poetry. Maples Arce entered Mexico's foreign service in 1935, and held consular and ambassadorial posts in Europe, Latin America and elsewhere.

Further reading

Escalante, E. (2000) 'Modernidad y resistencia a la

modernidad en los poemas de Manuel Maples Arce', in J. Duran, R. Hernández Monroy and M.F. Medina (eds), *Los discursos de la cultura hoy*, East Lansing: Michigan State University; University of Louisville; Centro de Cultura Casa Lamm.

Maples Arce, M. (1981) *Las semillas del tiempo: Obra poética 1919–1980*, ed. and intro. R. Bonifaz Nuño, Mexico City: Fondo de Cultura Económica.

Sinán, R. (1959) *Los valores humanos en la lírica de Maples Arce*, Mexico City: Conferencia.

MERLIN H. FORSTER

Maran, René

b. 1887, Fort-de-France, Martinique; d. 1960, Paris, France

Novelist

Born of French-Guyanese parents in Martinique, René Maran is considered an important precursor to ***négritude*** and the first major writer from French Guiana. He spent little time in his homeland, however, and was educated in Bordeaux, France. He later spent thirteen years as a colonial administrator in Bangui in Central Africa, where he wrote his most famous novel *Batouala*, which won the Prix Goncourt in 1921. It was a vigorous critique of French colonialism in Africa, and eventually hostile reaction to the novel caused Maran to leave the French colonial service. He was celebrated as the father of *négritude*, but was also criticized as a deeply ambivalent *assimilée* by Frantz Fanon for a later novel, *Un homme pareil aux autres* (A Man like Any Other) (1947).

Further reading

Hausser, Michel (1975) *Les deux Batouala de René Maran*, Bordeaux: SOBODI.

Hommage à René Maran (1965) Paris: Présence Africaine.

Maran, R. (1958) *Poèmes (1909–1957)*, Paris: Présence Africaine.

Nwezeh, E.C. (1978) 'René Maran: Myth and Reality', *Odu* 18: 91–105.

J. MICHAEL DASH

Marechal, Leopoldo

b. 1900, Buenos Aires, Argentina; d. 1970, Buenos Aires

Writer

Marechal's most important novel, *Adán Buenosayres* (1948), anticipated many of the formal innovations introduced years later. *Megafón o la guerra* (Megaphone or War) (1970) and *El banquete de Severo Arcángel* (1965) completed the trilogy. Marechal was also a poet, essayist and playwright. The extraordinary coherence of his work is not solely due to a poetics which turns to symbolism and to a myth in which man is seen as transcendence and religion as restitution; he also deploys generic significations: theatricality in the novel, the epic in poetry, the intrinsic correspondence between fiction and essay, the nationalization of epic figures such as 'Adam' Buenosayres and 'Antígone' Vélez. In the 1940s and 1950s, Marechal was a prominent Peronist intellectual.

Further reading

Cheadle, N. (2000) *The Ironic Apocalypse in the Novels of Leopoldo Marechal*, London: Támesis.

Jozef, B. (1997) 'Leopoldo Marechal', in V. Smith (ed.), *Encyclopedia of Latin American Literature*, London: Fitzroy Dearborn, 510–11.

Marechal, L. (1997) *Adán Buenosayres*, ed. J. Lafforgue and F. Colla. Paris: Colección Archivos.

Maturo, G. (1989) 'Leopoldo Marechal', in C.A. Solé and M.I. Abreu (eds), *Latin American Writers*, New York: Scribners, 2, 887–96.

Navascués, J. de (1992) *Adán Buenosayres: una novela total (Estudio narratológico)*, Pamplona: Editorial Universitaria de Navarra.

Salas, H. (2000) 'Carta de Argentina: Memoria de Leopoldo Marechal', *Cuadernos hispanoamericanos* 601–2: 229–35.

ENRIQUE FOFFANI

marginal poets

The marginal poets were a group of young underground Brazilian poets of the mid-1970s. Their colloquial informality and epigrammatic representation of a fragmented, subjectivized world is reminiscent of the 1920s modernists (see **Brazilian modernism**). However, the marginals' grimly ironic tone spoke of a different social atmosphere: they wrote of the violence, alienation and anonymity of the darkest years of military rule following the collapse of the economic miracle. Struggling to operate outside the constraints of commercial publishing and state censorship, the 'mimeograph' poets, as they were also known, sought out their readers directly, distributing their work in cinema queues, bars and bookshops. While much of the generation's output was ephemeral, it did produce some of the most distinctive and original voices of the 1970s and 1980s, such as Francisco Alvim, Cacaso, Chacal and Ana Cristina **César**.

Further reading

Simon, I.M. and V. Dantas (1992) 'Bad Poetry, Worse Society', in G. Yúdice, J. Flores and J. Franco (eds), *On Edge: The Crisis of Contemporary Latin American Culture*, Minneapolis: University of Minnesota Press,141–59.

DAVID TREECE

Mariani, Roberto

b. 1892, Buenos Aires, Argentina; d. 1946, Buenos Aires

Writer

Mariani's *Cuentos de la oficina* (Stories from the Office) (1925) achieved a literary balance between a purist position and the idea of social responsibility which separated the Boedo and Florida literary groups in Argentina (see **Boedo vs Florida**). His posthumously published novel *La cruz nuestra de cada día* (The Cross We Bear Every Day) (1955) revealed narrative qualities and formal concerns which set him apart from other writers of the Boedo school. In July 1924, in an open letter to the magazine ***Martín Fierro*** called 'Martín Fierro y yo', he criticized those poets who failed to honour the name in the journal's title.

Further reading

Leland, C.T. (1987) *The Last Happy Men: The Generation of 1922, Fiction and the Argentine Reality*, Syracuse: Syracuse University Press.

CELINA MANZONI

Mariátegui, José Carlos

b. 1894, Moquegua, Peru; d. 1930, Lima, Peru

Writer and journalist

One of the most original and creative Marxists of Latin America, Mariátegui's writings cover a vast array of topics from world politics and sociology to surrealism and literary criticism. His book ***Siete ensayos de interpretación de la realidad peruana*** (Seven Interpretative Essays on Peruvian Reality) (1928) is one of the most widely read and translated works of Latin American sociology.

Born in southern Peru, he spent his childhood in Lima and Huacho. A bone disease kept him home from school, but he educated himself. Because of his family's deteriorating economic situation, he started working in a Lima printing house at the age of 14. He worked as linotypist for the newspaper *La Prensa*, and between 1912 and 1914 wrote articles as 'Juan Croniqueur'. He moved in Peruvian intellectual circles, and in 1916 began to write about poetry, literature, theatre and general cultural issues for other newspapers.

In 1919 Mariátegui founded the newspaper *La Razón* with César Falcón, and also the short-lived weekly *Nuestra Epoca*. After the Russian Revolution of 1917 he took a growing interest in socialist ideas, and these new publications showed him moving more clearly towards Marxism. During the social agitation of 1918–19 in Peru he, like Víctor Raúl Haya de la Torre, called for ideological co-operation among intellectuals, workers and students.

La Razón and its editors fiercely attacked Augusto B. Leguía's government, and in late 1919 Mariátegui was forced to accept Leguía's travel grant for Europe. He worked in Italy as a journalist, where he also had the status of cultural attaché. In Europe he became a convinced Marxist, and started to develop his own socialist interpretations for Peru and Latin America. Among those who influenced him were Italian Marxists and leftist intellectuals such as Labriola and the syndicalist ideas of Georges Sorel. Some even claim that Mariátegui represents a 'Nietzschean Marxism', because of his unorthodox southern European socialist contacts. His three years in Europe also affected Mariátegui in a different sense, as his medical condition improved in the southern Italian climate.

Returning to Peru in early 1923, Mariátegui devoted himself to journalism and also, increasingly, to political activity. He lectured in the Popular Universities and became the leading young intellectual of Lima's Marxist circles. In 1924 his illness worsened and his left leg was amputated. This did not, however, prevent his search for new kinds of solutions to the social and economic problems of Latin America. On the contrary, it seemed that after the amputation, Mariátegui became even more determined to develop his ideas for a socialist Peru. Mariátegui founded with his brother a new printing house, Minerva, while he simultaneously prepared the publication of a new monthly magazine, ***Amauta***.

The years 1926 to 1930 were very productive for Mariátegui, who was editing *Amauta* and contributing to many Peruvian and Latin American magazines and journals. In 1928 he completed his famous *Siete ensayos*, which presented Mariátegui's original Marxist interpretations of a range of issues, most famously the Indian problem and land reform. Mariátegui's political involvement began in the labour movement. When Haya de la Torre founded APRA in Mexico in 1924, Mariátegui sympathized with the idea of a continental anti-imperialist movement, but from 1927 onwards, the two young political leaders chose different ideological paths. Haya's united front theory was problematic for Mariátegui; he sought a more class-based political movement. In 1928 they disagreed openly: Haya accused Mariátegui of 'European thinking' (Marxism) unsuitable for Latin America, while Mariátegui began to organize a class-conscious socialist party. In many respects, the ideological dispute between Haya and Mariátegui symbolizes the divisions within the Latin American Left at the end of the 1920s.

In 1928, Mariátegui founded the Confederación General de Trabajadores del Perú (General Confederation of Peruvian Workers), which later became the most important centralizing force in the Peruvian labour movement. That same year Mariátegui began to publish a bimonthly newspaper *Labor* which, unlike *Amauta*, was directed at Peruvian workers.

In 1930, the shadow of Mariátegui's life, the malignant tumour in his left thigh, took its toll. He died on 16 April. Although his life was short, Mariátegui's legacy was considerable. His Marxism was always free of one-dimensional extremisms and dogmatism. He studied pre-Columbian cultures seriously and developed with Luis Valcárcel, for the first time in Peru, what might be called a 'non-paternalistic ***indigenismo***'. Indeed, Mariátegui was one of the first Latin American intellectuals to criticize the elitist Eurocentrism of Latin American thinking, challenging **Arielist** idealism in his famous essay '¿Existe un pensamiento latinoamericano?' (Is There a Latin American Thought?).

Mariátegui's revolutionary thinking has subsequently been used for many political purposes. The modern Peruvian guerrilla movement Sendero Luminoso (Shining Path) took its name from Mariátegui's sentence 'Marxism–Leninism will open the shining path for the future', although Mariátegui would hardly have supported its ideology or violent actions.

Further reading

Chang Rodríguez, E. (1983) *Poética e ideología en José Carlos Mariátegui*, Madrid: José Porrúa Turanzas.

—— (1989) 'José Carlos Mariátegui', in C.A. Solé and M.I. Abreu (eds), *Latin American Writers*, New York: Scribners, 2, 791–96.

Chavarría, J. (1979) *José Carlos Mariátegui and the Rise of Modern Peru: 1890–1930*, Albuquerque: University of New Mexico Press.

D'Allemand, P. (2001) 'José Carlos Mariátegui: Más allá de "El proceso de la literatura" ', in *Hacia*

una crítica cultural latinoamericana, Lima: Latinoamericana Editores, 25–58.
Flores Galindo, A. (1989) *La agonía de Mariátegui*, Lima: Instituo de Apoyo Agrario.
Gonzalez, M. (1997) 'José Carlos Mariátegui', in V. Smith (ed.), *Encyclopedia of Latin American Literature*, London: Fitzroy Dearborn, 513–14.
Mariátegui, J.C. (1989) *Seven Interpretative Essays on Peruvian Reality*, Austin: University of Texas Press.
—— (1981) *Obras completas*, Lima: Editorial Minerva.
Meseguer Illán, D. (1974) *José Carlos Mariátegui y su pensamiento revolucionario*, Lima: Instituto de Estudios Peruanos.
Quijano, A. (1991) *José Carlos Mariátegui: Textos básicos*, Lima: Fondo de Cultura Económica.
Vanden, H. (1986) *National Marxism in Latin America: José Carlos Mariátegui's Thought and Politics*, Boulder, CO: Lynne Rienner Publications.
Wiesse, M. (1959) *José Carlos Mariátegui: Etapas de su vida*, Lima: Empresa Editora Amauta.

JUSSI PAKKASVIRTA

Marinello, Juan

b. 1898, Jicotea, Las Villas, Cuba; d. 1977, Havana, Cuba

Writer

As a leading critic in the 1920s, and a member of the **Grupo Minorista** and founder of the ***Revista de Avance***, Marinello belonged to both the political and the artistic vanguard. In 1934 he edited *Masas*, organ of the Cuban Anti-Imperialist League, and the Communist journals *La Palabra* and *Mediodía*. Jailed for political reasons in the 1930s, he went into exile in Mexico. In 1948 he was presidential candidate for the PSP (Communist Party), becoming Rector of Havana University in 1962. His writings include several studies on José **Martí**, product of a lifetime of research.

Further reading

Antuña, M.L. and J. García-Carranza (1975) *Bibliografía de Juan Marinello*, Havana: Editorial Orbe.
Castellanos, O. (1983) 'Entrevista con Juan Marinello', *Casa de las Américas* 23(137): 122–9.
James, A. (1988) 'Juan Marinello: Escritor americano', *Santiago* 69: 69–83.
Marinello, J. (1977) *Ensayos*, Havana: Editorial Arte y Literatura.
—— (1977) *Poesías*, Havana: Editorial Arte y Literatura.
Recopilación de textos sobre Juan Marinello (1979) Havana: Casa de las Américas.

WILFREDO CANCIO ISLA

Mármol, José

b. 1960, Santo Domingo, Dominican Republic

Poet

A celebrated young poet, Mármol was the centripetal force for the 1980s postmodern generation, which opposed the aesthetics and the political programme of the Generation of 1965. Mármol has won the following prizes: the National Prize of Poetry for *La invención del día* (The Invention of the Day) (1989), the Pedro Henríquez Ureña Prize for *Lengua del paraíso* (Language of Paradise) (1992) and the Casa de Teatro Prize for *Deus ex machina* (1994). Informed by the philosophy of Nietzsche and the poetry of Octavio **Paz**, Mármol's work points to a conceptual reflection on mankind.

Further reading

Mármol, José (1988) 'Meditaciones en torno a la poesía dominicana de los años ochenta o la apertura del poetizar como pensar', *Cuadernos de poética*, Santo Domingo, Jan.–April;, 5(14): 5–25.

FERNANDO VALERIO-HOLGUÍN

Marqués, René

b. 1919, Arecibo, Puerto Rico; d. 1979, San Juan, Puerto Rico

Writer and playwright

A prolific writer, Marqués's literary work is

dominated by moralizing allegories which tend to separate the logic of social processes and the subjectivities he represents. A sometimes strident *telurismo* (integrated vision of man and nature) dominates his literary discourse, through which Marqués often expressed his clear anti-imperialism.

Marqués graduated from the Agricultural College at Mayagüez in 1942, and worked for two years in Puerto Rico's Department of Agriculture. In 1946 he studied literature at the Universidad Central de Madrid, and sent a series of articles called 'Chronicles of Spain' to the newspaper *El Mundo*. Returning to Puerto Rico in 1947, he continued to write newspaper articles and won a Journalism Prize awarded by the Instituto de Cultura Puertorriqueña (Institute of Puerto Rican Culture). In 1948 he became editor and leader writer of the *Diario de Puerto Rico* and published his play *El hombre y sus sueños* (Man and His Dreams) in the journal *Asomante*. A Rockefeller Foundation Fellowship allowed him to go to New York to study theatre at Columbia University and Piscator's Dramatic Workshop.

Returning to Puerto Rico in 1950, he began work in the Education Ministry and directed its publishing operations. In 1951, with the encouragement of Nilita **Vientós Gastón**, he founded the Teatro Experimental del Ateneo Puertorriqueño. A Guggenheim grant enabled him to write his first novel. His reputation was established with his plays *La carreta* (The Cart) (1951) and *Los soles truncos* (Cut-Down Suns) (1958), a volume of short stories, *En una ciudad llamada San Juan* (In a City Called San Juan) (1960) and his novel *La víspera del hombre* (The Eve of Man) (1958), which won the Ateneo Puertorriqueño Prize for 1958 and the William Faulkner Foundation prize in 1962. His essays were collected in *El puertorriqueño dócil* (The Docile Puerto Rican) in 1962 and *Ensayos 1955–1966* (Essays) in 1966. His last novel, *La mirada* (The Look) (1976), was not as well received by critics as his earlier work, but is of interest for its exploration of homoeroticism.

Further reading

Barradas, E. (1977) 'El machismo existencial de René Marqués', *Sin nombre* 8(3): 69–81.

Colecchia, F. (1997) 'René Marqués', in V. Smith (ed.), *Encyclopedia of Latin American Literature*, London: Fitzroy Dearborn, 517–18.

Díaz Quiñones, A. (1982) *El almuerzo en la hierba*, Río Piedras, PR: Ed. Huracán.

Gelpí, J. (1993) *Literatura y paternalismo en Puerto Rico*, Río Piedras, PR: Universidad de Puerto Rico.

Marqués, R. (1969) *The Oxcart*, trans. C. Pilditch, New York: Scribners.

Pilditch, C.R. (1977) *René Marqués: A Study of His Fiction*, New York: Plus Ultra.

Reynolds, B.H. (1989) 'René Marqués', in C.A. Solé and M.I. Abreu (eds), *Latin American Writers*, New York: Scribners, 3, 1237–46.

Rodríguez Ramos, E. (1979) 'Aproximación a una bibliografía: René Marqués', *Sin nombre* 10(3): 121–48.

JUAN CARLOS QUINTERO HERENCIA

Márquez Rodríguez, Alexis

b. 1931, Barinas, Venezuela

Literary critic

Márquez Rodríguez has devoted his life to critical writing on Venezuelan and Latin American writers such as Alberto Arvelo Torrealba, Rómulo **Gallegos**, Miguel **Otero Silva** and, above all, Alejo **Carpentier**. He wrote for many years in *El Nacional* and was director of **Monte Avila** publishing house during the 1990s. In 1966 he won the Caracas Municipal Prose Prize for his *Aquellos mundos tersos* (Those Terse Worlds).

Further reading

Márquez Rodríguez, A. (1991) 'Raíces de la novela histórica', *Cuadernos americanos* 28: 32–49.

Romero, A., A. Márquez Rodríguez, and A. López Ortega (eds) (1994) 'La literatura venezolana', *Revista iberoamericana* 60(166–7).

JORGE ROMERO LEÓN

Marshall, Paule

b. 1929, New York, USA

Writer

Marshall's finely crafted stories are important contributions to the collective narrative of pan-African peoples, and especially women, in their post-colonial journey towards repairing the damage wrought by colonialism, racism, sexism and class divisions. Her first novel, *Browngirl, Brownstones*, (1959) is a young Barbadian-American girl's journey to self-discovery. *Soul Clap Hands and Sing* (1961) contains four pieces of short fiction – 'Barbados', 'Brazil', 'Brooklyn' and 'British Guiana' – connected by their sensitive portraits of ageing men as well as by the alliterative titles of the stories and their pan-African milieu. *Reena and Other Stories* (1983, 1985) includes Marshall's very important essay 'From the Poets in the Kitchen', about the inheritance of verbal skills from her mother's circle. In the novels *The Chosen Place, The Timeless People* (1969) and *Praisesong for the Widow* (1983) she develops a major theme in her work: the spiritual survival of African peoples in the Americas through their rituals, especially dance.

Further reading

Boyce Davies, C. (1996) 'Paule Marshall', in B. Lindfors and R. Sander (eds), *Twentieth Century Caribbean and Black African Writers*, third series, Detroit: Gale Research, 192–202.

Callaloo (1983) Special issue on Paule Marshall.

ELAINE SAVORY

Martí, José

b. 1853, Havana, Cuba; d. 1895, Dos Ríos, Cuba

Poet, novelist and essayist

Writer, revolutionary leader and symbol of Cuba's struggle for independence, José Martí continues to be an important influence in Latin American thought and literature. His 1891 essay 'Nuestra América' (Our America) outlines in a series of vivid metaphors many of the dilemmas of Latin America's mixed cultural heritage. This essay, which forecast some of José Enrique's **Rodó**'s characterizations of Latin American culture, is an impassioned call to fellow Latin Americans to re-evaluate their notions of '**civilization and barbarism**' and to correct the injustices against African Americans and indigenous peoples. Calling for a return to 'our Greece and our Rome', the pre-Colombian cultures existing in America previous to the conquest, he asks Latin Americans to leave their slavish dedication to all things European and to acknowledge their multiple identities. Metaphors of nature, so prominent in Martí's work, here shape the many elements of the essay, as does the notion of the family as a metaphor of community. 'Nuestra América' has been reclaimed at different moments of Latin American history and continues to be one of Martí's best-known works.

Imprisoned and then exiled to Spain (1871–74), at age 17, by Cuba's colonial authorities, early on Martí was forced to adopt exile from Cuba for political reasons. After studying in Spain, Martí lived in Mexico, Guatemala and Venezuela, with brief returns to Cuba. After 1881 he was based in New York until he died in Cuba whilst on a military expedition against Spanish forces. Author of a vast number of publications, as a writer he is revered particularly as a poet and **cronista**, although he also cultivated the **novel**, **children's literature**, and the more extensive **essay**. Like many writers of his generation Martí depended on his journalistic work for financial support, but in his case journalistic writing also served as a platform for the campaign for Cuban independence and a redefinition of Latin America.

Martí is one of the most influential and innovative poets of Latin America. In his lifetime he published two books of poetry, *Ismaelillo* (1882) and *Versos sencillos* (Simple verses) (1891); posthumous collections include *Versos libres* (Free Verse) and *Flores del destierro* (Flowers of Exile) (1933). *Ismaelillo*, dedicated to his infant son, introduces a lighter and more playful tone to the poetry of the moment. *Versos sencillos* has had even greater resonance because of its incorporation of popular verse forms – the octosyllable of oral tradition and the redondilla form – as well as its initial poem, the straightforward confessional tone of which has entered the popular realm through musicalizations ('Guantanamera') and recitations. The vivid imagery of the collection, the directness of tone and the abbreviated process of image-making (sometimes cinematographic in its rapidity) represented a new start for Latin American poetry. Sometimes associated with **Spanish American modernism**, Martí's range is actually more expansive and is difficult to limit to any single aesthetic tendency. His later work, particularly *Versos libres*, experimental in their abandonment of rhyme, sometimes hermetic, reflect another side of his poetic persona and technique.

In prose Martí was a master of the *crónica*, a genre that flourished with the expansion of the periodical. The majority of these *crónicas* were published or dispatched from New York, and his observations on North American culture, from Coney Island to Buffalo Bill and Walt Whitman, are fascinating insights into his thoughts as well as into relations between the US and Latin America. A harsh critic of the USA and its race towards modernization, at the same time Martí was able to appreciate some of its positive aspects and local traditions.

Martí published under the pseudonym Adelaida Ral the novel *Amistad funesta* (A Deadly Friendship) (1885), also known as *Lucía Jerez*, which reflects the literary mannerisms of its day, a style less accessible to the modern reader than his rapid and lively chronicles. He also founded a children's magazine, *La edad de oro* (The Golden Age) (1889), which included translations as well as original pieces.

Martí as writer is inseparable from his passionate struggle for Cuban political independence and a renewal of Latin American culture. Tireless organizer and speaker, he travelled widely, especially to Florida and the Caribbean, organizing support for the Revolution. Unfortunately he did not live to see his Cuba free itself from Spanish colonialism. He died in 1895, whilst taking part in a military expedition against Spanish forces. For his patriotic passion, his untiring mission to free his homeland and his verbal art, Martí is often called 'The Apostle', revered both inside and outside Cuba.

Further reading

Kirkpatrick, Gwen (1989) *The Dissonant Legacy of Modernismo*, Berkeley: University of California Press.

Martí, José (1963–6) *Obras completas*, Havana: Editora Nacional de Cuba, 27 vols.

Ramos, Julio (2000) *Divergent modernities*, Durham, NC: Duke University Press.

Rotker, Susana (2000) *The American Chronicles of José Martí*, Hanover, NH: University Press of New England.

Schulman, Ivan (1969) *Martí, Darío y el modernismo*, Madrid: Ed. Gredos.

Vitier, Cintio (ed.) (1978) *José Martí: Obra literaria*, Caracas: Biblioteca Ayacucho.

GWEN KIRKPATRICK

Martín Fierro

Martín Fierro was a cultural and literary magazine published between 1923 and 1927 dedicated to promoting European **avant-garde** ideas, in an effort to regenerate and modernize Argentina's cultural and social life. The magazine took its name from José Hernández's poem *Martín Fierro* (1872, 1879). It included essays on the plastic arts, architecture, and literary movements and debates about the future of Argentine civilization. The eclectic Florida group of intellectuals were its principal contributors (see **Boedo vs Florida**). The magazine never resolved the inherent contradiction between promoting a national cultural movement and dedication to a 'universalized' art.

Further reading

Barletta, L. (1967) *Boedo y Florida; una versión distinta*, Buenos Aires: Ediciones Metrópolis.

González Lanuza, E. (1961) *Los Martinfierristas*, Buenos Aires: Ediciones Culturales Argentinas.

Revista Martín Fierro (1995) Facsimile edition, ed. H. Salas, Buenos Aires: Fondo Nacional de las Artes.

THOMAS EDSALL

Martínez, Tomás Eloy

b. 1934, Tucumán, Argentina

Writer and critic

Martínez won international recognition with the publication in 1996 of the English translation of his novel *Santa Evita* (1995), which coincided with the controversies surrounding the production and release of the film *Evita* (1996), Alan Parker's adaptation of the musical written by Andrew Lloyd Webber and Tim Rice and starring international superstar Madonna in the title role. The novel was important in momentarily internationalizing the political and sexual fascination for Eva Perón that until the mid-1990s had been an Argentine cultural phenomenon. Indeed, *Santa Evita* is in many ways a compilation of the many myths that have fed and reproduced that national obsession.

Santa Evita may be best read as a companion piece to Martínez's earlier and better work, *La novela de Perón* (The Peron Novel), published in 1985. Both novels combine aspects of meta-historical fiction (as practised, for example, by his one-time screenplay writer colleague, Augusto **Roa Bastos**) and the journalistic narration of real political events (as exemplified, in Argentina, by Rodolfo **Walsh**). This compositional combination is then inflected thematically in the texts in the form of an exploration of the processes whereby figures of political authority become the organizing principles of private fantasy. This is what the author means when he says that he writes 'intimate history'.

Martínez has also written *La pasión según Trelew* (The Trelew Passion) (1973) and *La mano del amo* (The Master's Hand) (1991). In 1974, after a bomb explosion in the offices of the newspaper *La Opinión*, where he worked, Martínez left Argentina for exile in Venezuela. Since the mid-1980s he has worked as a university professor in the USA.

Further reading

Fares, G. (1999) 'Historia y literatura en Argentina: *Santa Evita* de Tomás Eloy Martínez', in J. Cruz Mendizabal and J. Fernández Jiménez (eds), *Visión de la narrativa hispánica: Ensayos*, Indiana: Indiana University of Pennsylvania.

Salem, D. (1999) 'Historia, memoria y testimonio: Reflexiones sobre la obra de Tomás Eloy Martínez', *Alba de América* 17(32): 345–52.

Shumway, N. (2002) 'Tomás Eloy Martínez', in *Latin American Writers: Supplement I*, ed. C. Solé and K. Müller-Bergh, New York: Scribners, 333–44.

Steimberg de Kaplan, O. (1999) 'El problema de la verdad en la nueva novela histórica: La obra de Tomás Eloy Martínez', *Alba de América* 17(32): 187–95.

JOHN KRANIAUSKAS

Martínez Estrada, Ezequiel

b. 1895, Santa Fe, Argentina; d. 1964, Bahia Blanca, Argentina

Writer

A completely original figure in Argentine culture, Martínez Estrada developed a manner of writing interpellated by its context but resistant to all the clichés of his time. His two major books of essays ***Radiografía de la pampa*** (X-ray of the *Pampa*) (1933) and *Muerte y transfiguración de Martín Fierro* (Death and Transformation of Martin Fierro) (1948) explore the question of national identity conceived as displacement and failure to adapt; for him it is the external view – W.H. Hudson, gaucho literature and the writings of English travellers – that constructs Argentine literature, yet the reality is quite different. At a time when the crisis of political institutions of the 1930s and the irruption of Peronism in the 1940s required a positive national response, Martínez Estrada approached politics as a way of thinking culture, combining it with arguments from social psychology to form a highly polemical discourse.

Further reading

Burgos, N. (1995) 'Martínez Estrada inédito: Entre lo confesional y lo doliente: Cartas personales a su esposa', *Alba de América* 13(24–25): 129–48.

Earle, P.G. (1971) *Prophet in the Wilderness: The Works of Ezequiel Martínez Estrada*, Austin: University of Texas Press.

Garasa, D.L. (1989) 'Ezequiel Martínez Estrada', in

C.A. Solé and M.I. Abreu (eds), *Latin American Writers*, New York: Scribners, 2, 809–13.

Maharg, J. (1977) *A Call to Authenticity: The Essays of Ezequiel Martínez Estrada*, Oxford: University of Mississippi, Romance Monographs.

Martínez Estrada, E. (1951) *El mundo maravilloso de Guillermo Enrique Hudson*, Mexico City: Fondo de Cultura Económica.

—— (1981) *Radiografía de la pampa*, ed. L. Pollman, Paris: Colección Archivos.

—— (2001) *Sarmiento; meditaciones sarmientinas; los invariantes históricos en el Facundo*, Rosario, Argentina: Beatriz Viterbo Editora.

GRACIELA MONTALDO

Martínez Moreno, Carlos

b. 1917, Colonia del Sacramento, Uruguay; d. 1986, Mexico City

Writer

A contemporary of Juan Carlos **Onetti** and Mario **Benedetti**, Martínez Moreno's thematic range was marked by a pessimistic outlook on the failure of human relationships and of social progress. Often satirical in his approach to other artists and writers, the intertextual references in his writings are complex. He also wrote literary essays on Montevideo, the Uruguayan Generation of 1900, Latin American **avant-garde** movements and theatre criticism.

Further reading

Odber, P. (1997) 'Carlos Martínez Moreno', in V. Smith (ed.), *Encyclopedia of Latin American Literature*, London: Fitzroy Dearborn, 528–9.

Ruffinelli, J. (1985) 'Carlos Martínez Moreno, la energía que no cesa', in *Palabras en orden*, Xalapa: Universidad Veracruzana.

Stone, K.V. (1994) *Utopia Undone: The Fall of Uruguay in the Novels of Carlos Martínez Moreno*, Lewisburg, PA: Bucknell University Press.

DANIEL BALDERSTON

Martins, Wilson

b. 1921, São Paulo, Brazil

Literary critic

While Martins admits that socio-historical background may play a role in literature, he does not believe that this information has any place in the evaluation of a specific work. He insists on judging a work of literature solely and exclusively by its paramount literary merit, its aesthetic quality. Martins lived for over twenty-five years outside Brazil until he retired from his professorship at New York University and returned to Curitiba, Paraná. Best known for his work on **Brazilian modernism** and his extensive history of the Brazilian intellectual class, he is parodied in Silviano **Santiago**'s novel *Stella Manhattan*.

Further reading

Fody, M., II (1980) 'Wilson Martin's History of the Brazilian Mind', *World Literature of Today* 54: 243–5.

Martins, Wilson (1966) *Teatro brasileiro contemporáneo*, New York: Appleton-Century-Crofts.

—— (1971) *The Modernist Idea; A Critical Survey of Brazilian Writing in the Twentieth Century*, New York: New York University Press.

—— (1983) *A crítica literária no Brasil*, Rio de Janeiro: F. Alves.

—— (1996) 'Brazilian Literature in the Nineties', *Review* 53: 5–7.

Pestana, A. (1991) 'O último dos críticos, Wilson Martins: "A critica de jornal acabou por causa do Afranio Coutinho" ', *Minas Gerais, suplemento literario* 24(1161): 8–10.

SUSAN CANTY QUINLAN

Martinus (Arion), Frank E.

b. 1936, Curaçao, Netherlands Antilles

Writer

Martinus founded and edited the socio-literary magazine *Ruku* (1969–71) and has written poetry in Dutch and Papiamentu as well as four lengthy novels in Dutch, including *Dubbelspel* (Double Play) (1973) and *De laatste vrijheid* (The Final Freedom) (1995). A linguist, he specialized in creole languages and became a fervent defender of Papiamentu. In his literary work and essays, he has been critical of the continuing political, economic and cultural dependence of the Dutch Antilles on the Netherlands.

Further reading

Coemans-Eastatia, M.W.R. and H.E. Coomans (eds) (1991) *Drei Curaçaose Schrijvers in veelvoud: Boeli van Leeuwen, Tip Marugg, Frank Martinus Arion*, Zutphen: de Walburg Pers.

Rowell, C.H. (1998) 'An Interview with Frank Martinus Arion', *Callaloo* 21(3): 538–41.

Yoder, H. (1982) 'Righting Wrongs with Words: The Caribbean Dilemma of Frank Martinus Arion', *International Fiction Review* 9(1): 22–6.

AART G. BROEK

Marugg, Silvio Alberto

b. 1923, Curaçao, Netherlands Antilles

Writer

'Tip' Marugg is the author of three novels in Dutch, including *De morgen loeit weer aan* (Again the Roar of Dawn) (1988), in which solitude, death, alcohol and sexuality are given pivotal roles. He published his first poetry in the literary magazine *De* **Stoep**, and later, the collection *Afschuw van Licht* (Abhorrence of Light) (1976). Marugg is also the author of a dictionary of erotic words and phrases in Papiamentu. He worked in public relations at a large refinery on the island, from which he retired at an early age.

Further reading

Broek, A.G. (1990) 'Tip Marugg tussen het Nederlands en het Papiamentu', *Preludium* 6(4): 3–21.

Coemans-Eastatia, M.W.R. and H.E. Coomans (eds) (1991) *Drei Curaçaose Schrijvers in veelvoud: Boeli van Leeuwen, Tip Marugg, Frank Martinus Arion*, Zutphen: de Walburg Pers.

AART G. BROEK

Mastretta, Angeles

b. 1949, Puebla, Mexico

Novelist

Mastretta has created a publishing sensation with her novels and short stories about the loves of aristocratic provincial women in the early twentieth century. Her first novel, *Arráncame la vida* (Tear Out of My Life) (1985) (translated as *Mexican Bolero*), broke social taboo by telling the story of a revolutionary general's feisty wife and her extramarital affair. It was followed by the short story collection *Mujeres de ojos grandes* (Big-Eyed Women) (1990), loosely based on the stories of Mastretta's great aunts; the essay collection *Puerto libre* (Free Port) (1993), in which Mastretta discusses her ambivalent relationship to feminism; and the well-received novel *Mal de amores* (Love Sickness) (1996).

Further reading

Malloy, C. (1997) 'La escritura de Angeles Mastretta: Memorias a la deriva', in S.E. Vejar (ed.), *La otredad: Los discursos de la cultura hoy*, Mexico City: Universidad Autonoma Metropolitana-A.

Roffe, R. (1999) 'Entrevista con Angeles Mastretta', *Cuadernos hispanoamericanos* 593: 77–90.

CYNTHIA STEELE

Mata Gil, Milagros

b. 1951, Caracas, Venezuela

Writer

One of the most successful of Venezuela's women writers, both in terms of sales and critical recognition, Mata Gil is also among the most frequent winners of literary prizes. She, together with Ana Teresa **Torres** and Laura **Antillano**, represents an important current of renewal in contemporary Venezuelan writing. She is a journalist and professor and has filled an important cultural role, particularly in the south of the country.

Further reading

Barreto, Juan (1997) 'Disolverse y enmascararse: La poética en *Mata el caracol* de Milagros Mata', *Cifra-Nueva*, Nov., 5–6: 193–201.

Mata Gil, M. (1993) 'El espacio de la nostalgia en la escritura venezolana', *Inti: Revista de literatura hispánica* 37–8: 23–8.

Torres, A.T. (1997) 'Para leer a Milagros Mata Gil', *Cifra nueva* 5–6: 139–55.

ALICIA RÍOS

Mateo, Andrés L.

b. 1946, Santo Domingo, Dominican Republic

Writer

Like many **intellectuals** of his generation, Mateo was profoundly affected by the US invasion of the Dominican Republic in 1965 and its social and cultural repercussions. One result was the creation of a series of literary and intellectual groupings, including La Isla (The Island), founded by Mateo among others. Its ideas informed Mateo's first novel *Pisar los dedos de Dios* (Stepping on God's Fingers) (1979), where he represents two kinds of existence, one indifferent to the creation of a dictatorship, the other besieged by violence. He has also published *Mito y cultura en la Era de Trujillo* (Myth and Culture during Trujillo's Era) (1993), a cultural studies analysis of intellectuals during Trujillo's dictatorship.

FERNANDO VALERIO-HOLGUÍN

Mattos, Tomás de

b. 1947, Montevideo, Uruguay

Writer

Although trained as a lawyer and born in Montevideo, Mattos lives in northern Uruguay, which also provides the setting for his fiction. His many short stories have appeared in three collections, and his first novel *Bernabé, Bernabé* (1988) was a best-seller. Combining epistolary and manuscript forms, it describes the foundation of Tacuarembó by Colonel Don Bernabé Rivera and the subsequent massacre of the Charrúa Indians. The central character, a nineteenth-century female historian, gives voice to another silenced sector, women in science. The problems of national identity, aristocratic Uruguayan society and the civilization–barbarism dichotomy (see **civilization and barbarism**) are all addressed in this historical tale.

Further reading

Lanes, R. (1996) 'El (re)descubrimiento encanto de la fábula patria: *Bernabé, Bernabé* de Tomas de Mattos', *Romance Languages Annual* 8: 515–20.

Mattos, T. de (1998) 'Testimonio', in *Encuentro internacional narradores de esta América*, Lima: Universidad de Lima: Fondo de Cultura Económica.

Stewart, L. (2000) 'Forgetting Amnesia: Tomás de Mattos's *Bernabé, Bernabé* and Uruguayan Identity', *Revista canadiense de estudios hispánicos*, Winter, 24(2): 383–96.

VICTORIA RUÉTALO

Maya, Rafael

b. 1897, Popayán, Colombia; d. 1980, Bogotá, Colombia

Poet

Raised in western Colombia, Maya attended law school in Bogotá and frequented the capital's intellectual circles (see **intellectuals**). In the early 1920s he worked for the magazine *Cromos* (Prints), and in 1925 formed part of Los Nuevos (The New Ones), a group opposing the cultural predominance of the previous literary generation. He held various public offices, including the position of house representative for the Conservative Party, president of the Universidad Pedagógica, and in 1956, UNESCO representative in Paris. His poetry is best described as neo-classical, proudly evincing its affinity to Virgil.

Further reading

Boletín cultural y bibliográfico (1982) Special edition devoted to Rafael Maya, 19(1): 5–40.

Mejía Velilla, D. (1997) 'Recordando la poesía de Rafael Maya', *Boletín de la Academia Colombiana* 47(195): 29–32.

HÉCTOR D. FERNÁNDEZ L'HOESTE

Mayo, Hugo

b. 1898, Manta, Ecuador; d. 1988, Guayaquil, Ecuador

Poet

Hugo Mayo (Miguel Augusto Egas) was a leading poet of the avant-garde (see **avant-garde in Latin America**) who digested and promoted all the '-isms', from dadaism and *creacionismo* to *ultraísmo* and **Estridentismo**. He edited several important avant-garde magazines, including *Síngulus* (1921), *Proteo* (1922) and *Motocicleta* (1924). His poetry has still to be collected; it is scattered in local newspapers and prestigious international journals such as *Ultra* and ***Amauta***. *El zaguán de aluminio* (The Aluminum Threshold) (1981), an incomplete and imprecise collection of some of his avant-garde poems, is the only text that he allowed to be published. In the late 1920s Mayo was drawn towards ***indigenismo***, but his later work became increasingly personal.

Further reading

Mayo, H. (1979) *Poemas*, ed. and intro. R. Pesántez Rodas, Guayaquil: Casa de la Cultura.

—— (1982) *El zaguán de aluminio*, ed. J. Velasco Mackenzie and D. Osorno, Guayaquil: Casa de la Cultura.

MERCEDES M. ROBLES

McAndrew, Wordsworth

b. 1936, Georgetown, British Guiana

Poet

Beginning as a radio announcer, broadcaster and producer, McAndrew interwove elements of both Afro-Guyanese and Indo-Guyanese folklore, myth and the creole language in his broadcasts, which he later assembled in the 1979 folklore manual *OOIY.* While acclaimed poems such as 'Ole Higue' (Old Hag, a skinless vampire) are steeped in superstition and written for performance, McAndrew's poetry also makes an easy shift to standard English and traditional lyrical forms. His poems have appeared in several anthologies; his major collections are *Blue Gaulding* (1958), *Selected Poems* (1968) and *More Poems* (1970).

JILL E. ALBADA-JELGERSMA

McDonald, Ian

b. 1933, St Augustine, Trinidad

Writer

His only novel, *The Hummingbird Tree* (1969), won the Royal Society of Literature Prize for best regional novel and was adapted for television by the BBC in 1992. The novel explores friendship, youth, class and race in colonial Trinidad and evidences the poet he later became: his love of landscape and mood, his interest in history and the lives of people who live close to the land.

Mercy Ward (1988), his first collection of poems, is humane yet disturbing in its examination of death. The terminally ill patients are like landscapes we all hope to avoid. But we rejoice in the events of their lives: loves, friendships, accomplishments, hopes and desires. His second collection of poems, *Essequibo*, was published in 1992 and won the Guyana Prize for Poetry that year. Most of the poems deal with some aspect of the natural history of Guyana. It is obvious McDonald knows and loves the flora, fauna and people of these forests and riverscapes. He is always gentle and deeply respectful, seeing beauty in a grain of river sand and the gleam of a toucan's eye. He is the humble priest without religion, who understands how and why, in a place where creation lets its imagination flourish unhindered, even death can be beautiful.

In 1984 McDonald was instrumental in

reviving ***Kyk-Over-Al***, the Guyanese literary journal. *Jaffo the Calypsonian*, his third collection of poems, appeared in 1994. McDonald has co-edited anthologies of poetry, is a columnist with *Stabroek News* and was regional chairman (Canada and the Caribbean) on the panel of judges for the 1991 Commonwealth Writers' Prize. In 1986 he received Guyana's National Honour, the Golden Arrow of Achievement. In 1997, for his contribution to Caribbean literature, the University of the West Indies awarded him an honorary doctorate.

One of the Caribbean's most accomplished poets and citizens, McDonald was educated at Queen's Royal College in Port-of-Spain, Trinidad, and at Cambridge University, England, but has lived and worked in Guyana since 1955. He holds directorships in several companies, and is administrative director of the Guyana Sugar Corporation.

Further reading

Rohlehr, G. (1974) 'Introduction', in I. McDonald, *The Hummingbird Tree*, London: Heinemann.

Singh, Vishnudat (1989) 'The Indian in the Trinidadian Novel', in F. Birbalsingh (ed.), *Indenture & Exile: The Indo-Caribbean Experience*, Toronto: TSAR, 148–58.

KEITH JARDIM

McFarlane, Basil

b. 1922, St Andrew Parish, Jamaica

Poet and critic

Son of J.E. Clare **McFarlane** and brother of R.L.C. **McFarlane**, Basil McFarlane spent his life in Jamaica except for two years in the Royal Air Force (1944–46). After returning to Jamaica he joined the civil service. He was a sub-editor at *The Daily Gleaner* in 1955, and worked as a journalist with Radio Jamaica during the early 1960s. He has written art and film criticism. *Jacob and the Angel and Other Poems* appeared in the Miniature Poets Series (Georgetown, British Guiana) in 1952.

PAT DUNN AND PAMELA MORDECAI

McFarlane, John Ebenezer Clare

b. 1894, Spanish Town, Jamaica; d. 1962, Kingston, Jamaica

Poet and politician

Founder of the Poetry League of Jamaica in 1923, McFarlane compiled anthologies such as *Voices from Summerland* (1929) and *A Treasury of Jamaican Poetry* (1950), published five collections between 1918 and 1957, and became Jamaica's Poet Laureate in 1952. McFarlane's poetry is not particularly noteworthy except perhaps for 'The Black Peril', a 1920s poem defending Ethiopians and blacks from a British journalist's racist vituperation. A distinguished civil servant, McFarlane was the first Jamaican financial secretary. His sons, Basil and R.L.C. **McFarlane**, are also poets.

PAT DUNN AND PAMELA MORDECAI

McFarlane, R.L. Clare

b. 1925, Kingston, Jamaica

Poet

McFarlane was a member of a generation of poets, including Basil **McFarlane**, George Campbell, Una Marson, Ken **Ingram** and Vivian **Virtue**, which helped to indigenize Jamaican poetry. Brother of Basil and son of J.E. Clare **McFarlane**, he was educated in Jamaica, going abroad to study at the University of London and Howard University. Returning to Jamaica, he joined the civil service, later turning to teaching. He has published several collections of poetry, the earliest being *Selected Poems 1943–1952* (1953), and the most recent, *A Gift of Black Mangoes (Poems 1989–95)* (1995).

PAT DUNN AND PAMELA MORDECAI

McKay, Claude

b. 1890, Clarendon Parish, Jamaica; d. 1948, Chicago, Illinois, USA

Writer

A Jamaican writer closely associated with the Harlem Renaissance, McKay had already published his poetry, especially two volumes of 'dialect' verse, before leaving for the US in 1912. Always hard-up, he travelled widely, using his experiences to portray black and cosmopolitan low-life with zest and sympathetic intelligence in novels such as *Home to Harlem* (1928) and in short stories. He wrote for the radical press in the USA and in London, and was fêted when he visited the Soviet Union in 1922–23, but always retained an independent stance towards racial and political dogmatism. A poignant nostalgia for rural Jamaica emerges in his 1933 novel ***Banana Bottom***, but his militant poetry and celebration of black working-class values have had the widest impact, notably on the ***négritude*** movements.

Further reading

Gayle, A. (1972) *Claude McKay: The Black Poet at War*, Detroit: Broadside Press.

Giles, J. (1976) *Claude McKay*, Boston: Twayne.

Griffin, B. (2002) 'Claude McKay (1890–1948)', in E. Nelson (ed.), *African American Autobiographers: A Sourcebook*, Westport, CT: Greenwood Press.

McKay, C. (1963) *Selected Poems of Claude McKay*, New York: Harcourt Brace.

Ojo Ade, F. (1996) 'Claude McKay: The Tragic Solitude of an Exiled Son of Africa', in *Of Dreams Deferred, Dead or Alive: African Perspectives on African-American Writers*, Westport, CT: Greenwood Press.

BRIDGET JONES

McNeill, Anthony

b. 1941, Kingston, Jamaica; d. 1995, Jamaica

Poet

One of the finest and most original poets of his generation, McNeill's early collections *Hello Ungod* (1971), *Reel from 'The Life Movie'* (1975) and *Credences at the Altar of Cloud* (1979) explored existential (see **existentialism**) and religious questions. Born into a family of Jamaican politicians, McNeill's work addressed a variety of other subjects, from the Rasta cult to the writing of poetry itself, as his thematically arranged volume *Reel from 'The Life Movie'* (1975) makes clear. He was joint editor, with Neville Dawes, of the anthology *The Caribbean Poem* (1976).

Further reading

Mordecai, M. (1970) 'Interview by Martin Mordecai with Anthony McNeill', *Jamaica Journal* 4.

KEITH JARDIM

McOndo

This anthology of short stories expresses the disapproving view of a group of young Latin American writers who were born during the 1960s and who have taken issue with the stereotype of exotic and magical Latin America represented in some way by Gabriel **García Márquez**'s Macondo. This McOndo has to do more with contemporary technology, superhighways, Mac computers and globalization – in other words, the *sui generis* cohabitation between premodernity and modernity in Latin American life. Edited by the controversial writer and journalist Alberto **Fuguet** and his colleague Sergio Gómez, this collection of short stories by eighteen tyro writers was launched, ironically, at a branch of McDonald's in Santiago in 1996.

Further reading

Fuguet, A. and S. Gómez (1996) *McOndo*, Barcelona: Grijalbo Mondadori.

ALVARO BERNAL

McWatt, Mark

b. 1947, Georgetown, British Guiana

Poet and critic

A poet whose work has been published in various journals and anthologies, as well as in *Interiors* (1988), much of McWatt's poetry describes the people and places of the Guyanese interior where he grew up. He received his doctorate from Leeds University in England and is senior lecturer in literature at the Barbados campus of the University of the West Indies, where he teaches and researches West Indian literature and post-colonial literature in English. In addition to contributing critical articles to journals such as the *Journal of West Indian Literature*, he has edited a critical volume, *West Indian Literature and Its Social Context* (1985).

CAROL J. WALLACE

Medina, Enrique

b. 1937, Buenos Aires, Argentina

Writer

With almost two dozen books to his credit, including novels, chronicles, short stories and a play, Medina is Argentina's leading proponent of dirty realism. His first work, *Las tumbas* (The Tombs) (1973), remains his most famous; it has been widely translated and was adapted for the screen by Javier Torre, Leopoldo Torre Nilsson's son, in 1991. *Las tumbas* uses the setting of a boy's reformatory to explore the construction of violent social subjects in the context of Argentine society. Medina was heavily censored by the dictatorships between 1976 and 1983. More recently, he is best known for his columns in the daily *Página 12* and his *El escritor, el amor y la muerte* (1998) (The Writer, Love and Death).

Further reading

Foster, D.W. (1997) 'The Dirty Realism of Enrique Medina', *Arizona Journal of Hispanic Cultural Studies* 1: 77–96.

Lorente Murphy, S. (1996) 'El discurso de la dictadura y la narrativa de Enrique Medina: Oposición o copia?', *Alba de América* 14(26–27): 173–80.

DAVID WILLIAM FOSTER

Meireles, Cecília

b. 1901, Rio de Janeiro, Brazil; d. 1964, Rio de Janeiro

Poet

Considered the most important woman poet in Brazil, Meireles was greatly influenced by the symbolist poet Cruz e Sousa and created a uniquely personal and spiritual adaptation of symbolism's techniques, themes and forms. Meireles considered her work to be free of modernist (see **Brazilian modernism**) or nationalistic influences, yet she absorbed much from her contacts with the Catholic poets of the review *Festa* and with Indian and oriental spiritualism. Seldom recognized is the fact that she was one of the pioneers of Brazilian folklore studies and produced gifted ethnographic drawings.

Further reading

Igel, R. (1989) 'Cecília Meireles', in C.A. Solé and M.I. Abreu (eds), *Latin American Writers*, New York: Scribners, 2, 915–22.

Laurito, I.B. (1984) 'Cecília Meireles: No 20 Aniversário da Morte', *Colóquio/Letras* 79: 65–6.

Lockhart, M.A. (1997) 'Cecília Meireles', in V. Smith (ed.), *Encyclopedia of Latin American Literature*, London: Fitzroy Dearborn, 536–7.

Meireles, C. (1972) *Obra poética*, Rio de Janeiro: Aguilar.

SUSAN CANTY QUINLAN

Mejía Vallejo, Manuel

b. 1923, Jericó, Antioquia, Colombia, d. 1998, El Retiro, Antioquia

Writer

Mejía Vallejo is best known for his fiction dealing with the 1950s La Violencia, for example the stories of *Tiempo de sequía* (Drought Time) (1957) and his most recognized novel, *El día señalado* (The Appointed Day) (1964). The rural area of Antioquia is the setting for many of his novels. He has published twenty books of fiction as well as essays, and was awarded the Rómulo **Gallegos** Prize in 1989. His later novels include *Aire de tango* (Tango Tune) (1973), a work structured around tangos (see **tango**), as popular in Medellín as in Buenos Aires, and *La casa de las dos palmas* (The House with Two Palm Trees) (1989).

Further reading

Corbatta, J. (2000) 'Recordando a Manuel Mejía Vallejo: El hombre y su obra', in M.M. Jaramillo, B. Osorio, and A.I. Robledo (eds), *Literatura y cultura: Narrativa colombiana del siglo XX*, Bogotá, Colombia: Ministerio de Cultura.

Florez Ruíz, L.C. (1998) 'Recuerdos de Manuel Mejía Vallejo', *Revista Universidad de Antioquía* 253 (supplement): 39–41.

Hernández, C. (2000) 'Manuel Mejía Vallejo', *Casa Grande*: 48–54.

RAYMOND L. WILLIAMS

Melo Neto, João Cabral de

b. 1920, Recife, Brazil; d. 1999, Rio de Janeiro, Brazil

Poet

João Cabral was brought up on sugar plantations in the Brazilian north east, and often took the landscape and society of the area as the subject of his poetry. He moved to Rio de Janeiro in 1942, and in 1947 began a diplomatic career which took him to many parts of the world, notably Spain in the 1950s. In the landscapes of Andalusia and Castile he found an analogue for the hard, rocky terrain of his native Brazilian interior, and in the work of medieval and modern poets, the kind of concreteness and solid realism he admires. He stands out from the generally mediocre formalism of the so-called Generation of 1945 and has been lionized by the concretists (see **concrete poetry**), although his poetic project has very little to do with theirs. After retirement he lived in Rio de Janeiro.

His poetry began with a problematic exploration of his subconscious, in which images float in a vacuum, out of interpretive reach. However, from the mid-1940s onwards he turned to a rigorously objective style, in long poems centring on the river Capibaribe, which reaches the sea at Recife. The culmination of this series was the verse play ***Morte e vida severina*** (The Death and Life of a Severino) (1955), subtitled *Auto de natal* (A Pernambucan Christmas play). His most popular work, it became a resounding success in the 1960s when it was set to music by Chico **Buarque**, and made into a film. Its central character is a *retirante* (refugee), in flight from drought in the interior, who follows the river to its mouth in search of a decent life, only to encounter various types of death in the areas – the *sertão*, the sugar plantations and the city – he passes through. It is a sharp denunciation of repressive social conditions, although it does end with a kind of celebration of new birth in the riverside slums. Cabral was always discreetly left-wing in his politics.

His objectivism continued in the 1960s, enclosed now in tight, short lyrics in *Educação pela pedra* (Education by Stone) (1966). More recently, he wrote a play about the early nineteenth-century rebel, Frei Caneca.

Further reading

Melo Neto, J.C. de (1975) *Poesias completas*, Rio de Janeiro: José Olympio.

—— (1980) *A Knife All Blade or Usefulness of Fixed Ideas*, trans. K.S. Keys, Camp Hill, PA: Pine Press.

—— (1994) *Selected Poetry 1937–1990*, ed. D. Kadir, trans. E. Bishop, Hanover, NH: University Press of New England.

Peixoto, M. (1983) *Poesia com coisas*, São Paulo: Perspectiva.

Reckert, S. (1986) 'João Cabral: From *Pedra* to *Pedra*', *Portuguese Studies* 2: 166–84.
Reis, R. (1997) 'João Cabral de Melo Neto', in V. Smith (ed.), *Encyclopedia of Latin American Literature*, London: Fitzroy Dearborn, 537–8.
Zenith, R. (2002) 'João Cabral de Melo Neto', in C. Solé and K. Müller-Bergh (eds), *Latin American Writers: Supplement I*, New York: Scribners, 103–18.

JOHN GLEDSON

Melville, Pauline

b. 1948, Guyana

Writer

Melville grew up in England, and worked as an actress while writing her accomplished prize-winning first collection of short stories, *Shape Shifter* (1990). She has a keen ear for accent and nuance of voice in characters from Britain and the Caribbean. She utilizes the supernatural in clever, contemporary ways which draw on Caribbean traditions, and has a sure comic touch. Her second novel, *The Ventriloquist's Tale* (1998), deals with Amerindian culture in Guyana.

Further reading

Morris, M. (1993) 'Cross-Cultural Impersonations: Pauline Melville's *Shape-Shifter*', *ARIEL* 24(1): 79–89.

ELAINE SAVORY

Memoria del fuego

Memoria del fuego is the title of a trilogy by the Uruguayan writer Eduardo **Galeano** comprising *Los nacimientos* (Genesis), *Las caras y las máscaras* (Faces and Masks) and *El siglo del viento* (Century of Wind), written during his exile in Spain (1977–85). It renders the history of the Americas from the pre-Columbian beginnings until 1984, in classic Galeano vignettes that collapse myriad events and circumstances into skilfully crafted evocations of time and place. The author's poetic eye catches larger cultural meanings by paying careful attention to detail. The narrative effect of Galeano's 1,164 vignettes is cumulative and sustained, offering a rich appreciation of the diverse land and life of the Americas past and present. The English-language version of the trilogy, superbly translated by Cedric Belfrage, won Galeano the American Book Award in 1989.

W. GEORGE LOVELL

Memorias del subdesarrollo

Tomás Gutiérrez Alea's film *Memorias del subdesarrollo* (Memories of Underdevelopment) (1968) is based on a short novel of the same name by Edmundo Desnoes, published in 1965. Set in Havana, its protagonist is Sergio, a young man from a wealthy Havana family, the rest of whose members chose exile in Miami after the Cuban Revolution of 1959. Sergio's monologue in the novel and in the film examines the effects of the Revolution – the collapse of traditional institutions, the enshrining of a new way of thinking which judges everything that 'the rich' produce as pernicious, even if it is simply common sense, and as correct everything that comes from 'the poor', even if it is an attitude of scorn and insolence.

Further reading

Desnoes, Edmundo (1990) *Memories of Underdevelopment*, New Brunswick: Rutgers University Press.

JOSÉ ANTONIO EVORA

Mendes, Alfred Hubert

b. 1897, Port-of-Spain, Trinidad; d. 1981, Bridgetown, Barbados

Writer

Born of middle-class Portuguese parents and educated in England, Mendes fought in Flanders during the First World War and returned to Trinidad in 1920, inspired with socialist ideals by the Russian Revolution. In the 1930s he became a prominent member of the group associated with *The Beacon* (1931–35), a radical journal advocating

Trinidad's cultural independence. He wrote some fifty short stories as well as two novels, *Pitch Lake* (1934), concerning the rise and fall of an ambitious young Portuguese man in Trinidad society, and *Black Fauns* (1935), an account of life among the island's yard folk.

Further reading

Levy, M. (ed.) (2000) 'With Alfred H. Mendes in New York, 1936', in F. Asals and P. Tiessen (eds), *A Darkness That Murmured: Essays on Malcolm Lowry and the Twentieth Century*, Toronto: University of Toronto Press.

LOUIS JAMES

Mendes, Murilo

b. 1901, Juiz de Fora, Brazil, d. 1975, Lisbon, Portugal

Poet

One of Brazil's leading poets, although not associated with the groups that constituted **Brazilian modernism**, Mendes wrote of spiritual anguish, of war and of the great baroque city of Ouro Preto. Manuel **Bandeira** wrote a poem that defined Mendes as someone who reconciles opposites and Raúl **Antelo** has written of his peculiar mysticism that focuses on the figure of Christ as dandy. Mendes ran away from school in Rio in 1917 to see a performance by Nijinsky, which he credited with awakening in him his artistic vocation. A close friend of the modernist painter Ismael Nery, the latter's death in 1934 precipitated a spiritual crisis. Late in his life he wrote the *Murilogramas*, his attempts at **concrete poetry**.

Further reading

Araújo, I.C. do (1972) *Murilo Mendes*, Petrópolis: Vozes.

Guimarães, J.C. (1986) *Murilo Mendes*, Rio de Janeiro: Nova Fronteira.

Mendes, M. (1994) *Poesía completa e prosa*, Rio de Janeiro: José Olympio.

White, S.F. (1997) 'Murilo Mendes', in V. Smith (ed.), *Encyclopedia of Latin American Literature*, London: Fitzroy Dearborn, 538–40.

DANIEL BALDERSTON

Méndez Ballester, Manuel

b. 1909, Aguadilla, Puerto Rico

Writer

Méndez's first published work was the historical novel *Isla cerrera* (Closed Island) (1937), but he is best known as a playwright who has played a major role in shaping twentieth-century Puerto Rican drama. His initial plays, *El clamor de los surcos* (The Noise from the Ditches) (1940) and *Tiempo muerto* (Dead Time) (1940), exemplify the social realism of the 1930s. After experimenting formally and thematically in subsequent plays, he returned to Puerto Rican themes with *Encrucijada* (Crossroads) (1958). In later plays – *Bienvenido, Don Goyito* (Welcome, Don Goyito) (1966), *Los cocorocos* (1977) – and in his regular columns in the island's press, he satirizes contemporary Puerto Rican society.

Further reading

Quiles Ferrer, E. (1985) 'Don Manuel Méndez Ballester', *Intermédio de Puerto Rico* 1(1 (3–4)): 54–60.

VÍCTOR F. TORRES

Meneses, Guillermo

b. 1911, Caracas, Venezuela; d. 1978, Margarita, Venezuela

Writer

Chronicler of the city of Caracas, Meneses was a contributor to the journal *Elite*, the *Papel Literario* (Literary Supplement) of *El Nacional* and the ***Revista nacional de cultura***, and in the 1960s he was a founder of the journal *CAL*. His work is marked by **existentialism**, introspection and the exploration of memory. Several of his works have been adapted for cinema, including *La balandra Isabel*, *La mano junto al muro* (The Hand by the Wall) and *El mestizo José Vargas*. He also occupied a number of important civic and diplomatic posts.

Further reading

Corbalán, L. (1982) 'Guillermo Meneses: Lo otro como doble', *Hispamérica* 11(31): 79–84.
Lasarte Valcarcel, J. (1994) 'Nacionalismo populista y desencanto: Poéticas de modernidad en la narrativa de Guillermo Meneses', *Revista iberoamericana* 60(166–7): 77–96.
Zacklin, L. (1985) *La narrativa de Guillermo Meneses*, Caracas: Dirección de Cultura.

JORGE ROMERO LEÓN

Meneses, Vidaluz

b. 1944, Matagalpa, Nicaragua

Writer

A major poet whose work often deals with the simple realities of everyday living, Meneses maintained her revolutionary commitment to the FSLN without losing her Christian faith. Before the Sandinista Revolution of 1979, she was secretly involved with the Sandinistas when her father, a general in Somoza's National Guard and Nicaraguan ambassador to Guatemala, was executed by the Sandinistas. She responded by reaffirming her staunch solidarity with the poor while refusing to renounce her father. After 1979, she became National Librarian and Vice Minister of Culture, working closely with Ernesto **Cardenal**. She is currently Dean of Humanities at the Central American University (UCA).

SILVIA CHAVES AND ILEANA RODRÍGUEZ

Merquior, José Guilherme

b. 1941, Rio de Janeiro, Brazil; d. 1991, Boston, Massachusetts, USA

Literary critic

A prolific critic, Merquior spent much of his career as a diplomat, in Europe and Spanish America. As well as producing a useful short history of Brazilian literature to the end of the nineteenth century, and a book on Carlos Drummond de **Andrade**, he published numerous collections of essays. His position (set out most completely in a book on Rousseau and Weber) was determinedly liberal, and he often became involved in polemics with those to the Left of him. He was a determined opponent of many modern theorists, including Western Marxists, Foucault and Lacan.

Further reading

Coelho, J.F. (1994) 'Merquior Versificador', *Colóquio/Letras* 131: 201–2.
Lafer, C. (1994) 'Evocando José Guilherme Merquior', *Colóquio/Letras* 131: 199–200.

JOHN GLEDSON

Mexico

Modern Mexico begins with a revolution officially declared on 20 November 1910. In fact, it was not a single process but the coming together of several conflicts and social discontents. Francisco Madero, who launched the original manifesto, wanted the removal of the Porfirio Díaz dictatorship and the establishment of a functioning liberal democracy. But he did not address the deeper structural causes of inequality and corruption. In February 1911, the rural insurrection set in motion in Morelos by Emiliano Zapata addressed the land question directly, and raised a banner of agrarian reform in an agricultural economy increasingly dominated by major foreign and domestic interests who controlled crops such as sugar. The domination of Mexico by Europe and, increasingly, the USA was cultural and intellectual as well as economic, and the nationalism that underlay the Mexican Revolution would shape the thinking of a post-revolutionary culture.

There were straws in the wind even before 1910. The intellectuals of the Ateneo de la Juventud, which included artists, writers, critics and philosophers, were united in their opposition to the 'scientific' positivist doctrines adopted by the Porfiriato. But many writers of their own generation, particularly poets of the *modernista* school, had already emphasized intuition, sensuality and the aesthetic as the core of their poetic code. The *Revista azul* was the first of two key *modernista* journals published in Mexico; it was edited by Amado **Nervo** and Manuel Gutiérrez Nájera, themselves outstanding figures in the movement . The *Revista moderna*, for its part, spanned a development from aestheticism to a greater emphasis on psychological issues, an increasing experimentalism and a great social awareness among some of the poets summed up in Enrique González Martínez's poem beginning with the famous line 'Tuércele el cuello al cisne' (Strangle the Swan), written in 1911. The other outstanding poet of the group around the journal was Ramón **López Velarde**, whose short life and small amount of published work (only *La sangre devota* (Pious Blood) (1916) and the daring and innovative *Zozobra* (Anguish) (1919) were published in his lifetime) belie his key role as a bridge between the *modernistas* and the avant-garde writers of the 1920s, among them José Juan **Tablada**, Carlos **Pellicer**, José **Gorostiza**, Xavier **Villaurrutia** and the **Contemporáneos**. López Velarde's influence, his use of everyday language, his melancholy, echo through later poets too, such as Efraín **Huerta** and Jaime **Sabines**. Not all the avant-garde poets responded in the same way to modernity: the Estridentista group (see **Estridentismo**), for example, owed much to Italian futurism and its celebration of the modern city.

The novelists of the late nineteenth century were, in their majority, concerned with provincial life and a 'realism' that was concerned to represent an unchanging reality. Federico Gamboa, on the other hand, while often presented as a disciple of Zola, used naturalism as a more forceful critical instrument in his *Santa* (1903), a representation of a corrupt and decadent Mexico City under the Porfiriato.

The Mexican Revolution was as sharp a dividing line in cultural life as it was a signal for the end of the Porfiriato and the emergence of a new state. Curiously the period of social conflict itself (1910–17) produced only one major work reflecting on the process, Mariano **Azuela**'s *Los de abajo* (The Underdogs) (1915), first published in instalments, represented the Revolution as a cyclical process in which violence overwhelmed its initial noble purposes. That reflected Azuela's own experience as an early supporter of Madero, and his subsequent disillusionment. The structure and narrative method of Azuela's novel – its episodic structure and urgent, economic style – came to characterize a body of writing about the Revolution known collectively as the *novela de la Revolución Mexicana* (see **novel of the Mexican Revolution**). These works included Martín Luis **Guzmán**'s *El águila y la serpiente* (The Eagle and the Serpent) (1928), whose central figure was Pancho Villa, Nellie **Campobello**'s *Cartucho* (Bullet) (1931) and work by Rafael F. Muñoz and José Mancisidor among others.

In a sense the novel of the Mexican Revolution formed part of a foundational writing, an epic of the new state which emerged in Mexico after 1917, the primitive violence from which order emerged. It was, after all, contemporaneous with José **Vasconcelos**'s *Ulises criollo* (A Mexican Ulysses) (1935) – in a sense an autobiographical illustration of the qualities and characteristics of *La raza cósmica* (The Cosmic Race) about which he had written in a 1928 volume. These writings are contributions to a wider debate about Mexican-ness to which the essays of Alfonso **Reyes** were also a contribution. The Cristero wars, the background to Graham Greene's *The Power and the Glory*, were also the theme of several novels, representing the ideological struggles that were the birth pangs of the new state. It was a subject Elena **Garro** would return to later in her magical realist novel *Los recuerdos del porvenir* (Recollection of Things To Come) (1963). The presidency of Lázaro Cárdenas (1934–40) represents a high point of nationalist fervour and radicalism, as well as the moment of consolidation of the new state. The Mexican Revolution itself again became a theme of writings of the time, as in Gregorio López y Fuentes's *Tierra* (Land) (1931), while Mauricio **Magdaleno**'s *El Resplandor* (Sunburst) (1937) was one of a number of novels and short stories in the *indigenista* (see ***indigenismo***) mould which depicted the life of oppressed indigenous communities just as Cárdenas was embarking on a significant programme of land redistribution.

The end of Cárdenas's presidency marked a new phase in Mexico's process of modernization. Although radically nationalist in rhetoric, the succession of six-year presidencies after 1940 embarked on industrialization under the control of a Revolutionary Institutional Party (PRI) with a virtual monopoly of power. Agustín **Yáñez**'s *Al filo del agua* (On the Edge of the Storm) (1947) described an immediately pre-revolutionary, provincial Mexico that was dark and repressed; the arrival of Halley's Comet in 1910, which ends the book, clearly presages a brighter future. Juan **Rulfo**'s masterpiece, ***Pedro Páramo*** (1955), like the earlier stories of *El **llano en llamas*** (The Burning Plain) (1953), are in many ways a bitter epitaph to a disappointed hope of revolution in the countryside. This deeply critical reflection on the Revolution would find further expression in Carlos **Fuentes**'s *La muerte de Artemio Cruz* (The Death of Artemio Cruz) (1962). The title of his earlier novel, *La región más transparente* (Where the Air is Clear) (1958), is an ironic commentary on the sprawling growth of Mexico City – one effect of the new economic direction Mexico was taking.

In poetry, the avant-garde evolved towards more self-consciously national concerns in magazines such as ***Taller***, which are perhaps now remembered principally for publishing the early work of Octavio **Paz**, poet, critic and essayist and undoubtedly one of the central figures in Mexican literature. *Libertad bajo palabra* (Freedom on Parole) (1949) assembles his work from the 1930s, embracing the period of his participation in the Spanish Civil War (1936–39) and the time when the influence of **surrealism** was most apparent in his concept of poetry as an 'invention of Language'. More influential, perhaps, was his meditation on Mexican language and culture in *El laberinto de la soledad* (The Labyrinth of Solitude) (1950). He returned to the themes of that essay nineteen years later, with a postscript, *Posdata* (1970), a reflection on cyclical violence written in the aftermath of the massacre of protesting students at Tlatelolco, Three Cultures Square, in Mexico City on 2 October 1968.

The trauma of that event, which violently terminated the protest movement of that year on the eve of the Mexico City Olympics, and of the repression that followed, resonated through the literature of Mexico for several years thereafter. José **Revueltas**, writer of fiction and a lifelong political activist, was a relentless critic of the Mexican regime. He was imprisoned in the 1940s, an experience that informed his *El luto humano* (Human Grief) (1943); he returned to the theme in the post-Tlatelolco atmosphere with *El apando* (Solitary) (1969), a brutal account of dehumanization, and an allegory for the state of Mexico at the time.

A public figure and commentator, Carlos Fuentes's rich and multi-layered prose explored the Mexican reality also, from *Cambio de piel* (A Change of Skin) to the sprawling *Cristóbal Nonato* (Christopher Unborn) (1987). His *Los ojos de Laura Díaz* (The Eyes of Laura Diaz) (2000) revisited the Mexican century, and perhaps his own Artemio Cruz, in an ambitious historical sweep. Although Fuentes was perhaps Mexico's most acknowledged novelist, nationally and internationally, the work of Juan José **Arreola**, Rulfo and of Elena **Poniatowska** also stands out, although Poniatowska's best-known works hover between biography, investigative journalism and fiction, particularly her highly successful *Hasta no verte Jesús mío* (Until I See You My Lord) (1969), *La noche de Tlatelolco* (Massacre in Mexico) (1971) and *Tinísima* (1992), her biography of photographer Tina Modotti.

Although she died in 1974 in a freak accident, the stature of Rosario **Castellanos** has grown since her death, as a feminist, an unsentimental narrator of the realities of indigenous life in Chiapas and as a poet of intimate pain. In more recent times, a number of outstanding women novelists have followed her – Angeles **Mastretta**, Margo **Glantz**, Sabina **Berman**, María Luisa **Puga** and, the most commercially successful of all, Laura **Esquivel**, whose ***Como agua para chocolate*** (Like Water for Chocolate) (1989) sold over 300,000 copies in Spanish alone and was transferred with great acclaim to the screen.

The 1970s produced a very different reaction to the tragic events of the 1960s. La **Onda** was a movement of young writers based largely in Mexico City; they invented a street language born of rock and roll and an increasingly alienated youth culture. Although its main representatives, José **Agustín** and Gustavo **Sainz** had very uneven literary careers after the 1970s, La Onda did widen and diversify the language of literature and blur the divisions between elite and popular culture. That was also the project implicit in the urban *crónicas* (see ***crónica***), sometimes described as 'dispatches from the underground', of which Carlos **Monsiváis** is the outstanding exponent. It is a difficult genre to define – but that is perhaps its definition. Monsiváis moves with very little apparent effort in and out of popular and mass culture, finding there the forces that shape and reflect a dominant ideology but also provide a locus of resistance to it. While the form is not peculiar to Mexico, it is most penetrating and diverse there. Cristina **Pacheco** has chronicled in writing as well as in the mass media, the lives of ordinary people in the city, Guadalupe Loaeza trains her eye on the middle classes, while Juan Villoro narrates the everyday. Whilst very distant from the *modernista crónicas* or the explorations of the life of the elite in Salvador **Novo**'s *crónicas* of the thirties, forties and fifties, together they provide a sort of unofficial history of Mexican society as seen from below.

Among the poets of the latter part of the twentieth century, José Emilio **Pacheco** stands out, with his delicate ironies and sense of a corrosive time, as in his *No me preguntes cómo pasa el tiempo* (Don't Ask Me How the Time Goes By) (1969); he was also the author of a highly praised novella, *Las batallas en el desierto* (Battles in the Desert) (1981), which sees a rapidly changing Mexico City as symbolic of the swiftly moving stream of history. Homero **Aridjis**'s more apocalyptic vision moved him increasingly in the direction of ecological activism. Both were among the collaborative authors of a key anthology, *Poesía en movimiento* (Poetry in Movement) (1966), in which Octavio Paz, in a foreword, defined Mexican poetry by its very changing dynamic.

The last decade of the twentieth century was a time of deepening economic and political crisis. In 1994 the Zapatista rising in Chiapas returned the question of land and indigenous rights to the centre of political life. It produced a rich analytical literature, as well as new literary expressions, for example the work of Jesús **Morales Benítez** and Efraín **Bartolomé** as well as the fables written by Subcomandante Marcos himself. Corruption, growing violence and resistance to the power monopoly of the PRI produced deep social tensions as the century ended, which the election of the first non-PRI President, Vicente Fox, in 2000, did little to alleviate.

Further reading

Brushwood, J. (1989) *Narrative Innovation and Political Change in Mexico*, New York: Peter Lang.

Castillo, Debra A. (1998) *Easy Women: Sex and Gender in Modern Mexican Fiction*, Minneapolis and London: University of Minnesota Press.

Duncan, J. Ann (1986) *Voices, Visions and a New Reality: Mexican Fiction Since 1970*, Pittsburgh: University of Pittsburgh Press.

Fernandez, J. and Norma Klahn (eds) (1987) *Lugar de encuentro: Ensayos críticos sobre poesía mexicana actual*, Mexico City: Katún.

Foster, Merlin and Julio Ortega (eds) (1986) *De la crónica a la nueva narrativa: coloquio sobre Literatura mexicana*, Mexico City: Oasis.

Irwin, R.I. (2003) *Mexican Masculinities*, Minneapolis, University of Minnesota Press.

Joseph, G.M. (2003) *The Mexico Reader: History, Culture, Politics*, Durham, NC: Duke University Press.

Monsiváis, Carlos (1997) *Mexican Postcards*, London: Verso.

Sommers, Joseph (1968) *After the Storm: Landmarks of the Modern Mexican Novel*, Albuquerque: University of New Mexico Press.

Steele, Cynthia (1992) *Politics, Gender and the Mexican Novel 1968–1988: Beyond the Pyramid*, Austin: University of Texas Press.

MIKE GONZALEZ

Mir, Pedro

b. 1913, San Pedro de Macorís, Dominican Republic; d. 2000, Santo Domingo, Dominican Republic

Writer

While exiled in Cuba during Trujillo's dictatorship, Mir published his 1949 poem 'Hay un país en el mundo' (There is a Country in the World) which delineates the history of the Dominican Republic. In the early 1950s, Mir published another extensive poem 'Contracanto a Walt Whitman' (Countersong to Walt Whitman), in which he tries to respond to Whitman with the collective 'we' of exploited workers. Also important is his 1978 novel *Cuando amaban las tierras comuneras* (When Communal Lands were Loved), depicting the period between the two US invasions of the Dominican Republic (1916 and 1965).

Further reading

di Pietro, G. (1994) 'Pedro Mir, poeta comprometido', *Cuadernos de poética* 8(24): 33–49.

Ortega, J. (1991) 'Pedro Mir, poeta dominicano', *La palabra y el hombre* 77: 269–77.

FERNANDO VALERIO-HOLGUÍN

Miró, Ricardo

b. 1883, Panama City; d. 1940, Panama City

Poet

Born while Panama was still part of Colombia, Miró studied painting in Bogotá, Colombia before political events there forced him to interrupt his studies and return to his homeland. With the creation of the republic, a new literary era began to which he contributed actively. His poems served to unify national feelings; in 'Patria' (Homeland) he speaks in a late romantic voice of his country and its scenery. He became the national poet, and the annual Panamanian literary prize bears his name. On his centenary (1983), the National Institute of Culture published his complete works in two volumes: *Poesía* (Poetry) and *Novela y cuento* (Novels and Stories).

Further reading

Alvarado de Ricord, E. (1973) *Aproximación a la poesía de Ricardo Miró*, Panama City: Editora de la Nación.

Miró, R. (1984) *Obra literaria*, Panama City: Ed. Mariano Arosemena, 2 vols.

Rodríguez, M.A. (1956) *Estudio y presentación de los cuentos de Ricardo Miró*, Panama City: Editora Panamá-América.

NORMAN S. HOLLAND

Mistral, Gabriela

b. 1889, Vicuña, Chile; d. 1957, Hempstead, New York, USA

Poet

The first Latin American Nobel Prize winner for Literature (1945), Mistral's great contribution to poetry derives from her care and skill with the word. She signed her early work with her own name (her real name was Lucila Godoy Alcayaga), until she won the highest award at the Juegos Florales (Floral Games) in Santiago with her 'Sonetos a la muerte' (Sonnets to Death) (1914), and began to use the pseudonym Gabriela Mistral. In 1920 she began a career in education which took her around Chile and all of the Americas. In 1922 she was invited by the then Education Secretary José **Vasconcelos** to participate in Mexico's educational reform. Her *Lecturas de mujeres* (Readings for Women), published in Mexico in 1923, was a key text for the artistic, social and spiritual education of young Latin American women, whom she saw as her 'spiritual family'. The publication of *Desolación* (Desolation) (1922) in New York brought her international recognition. Travelling to Europe for the first time in 1924, she published in Madrid a small volume of poems, *Ternura* (Tenderness), which included her cradle songs, folkloric poems, games and riddles.

Returning to Chile in 1925, she was named secretary of one of the League of Nations' American sections the following year, beginning a diplomatic career that culminated in 1935 when she was named consul for life. Her travels were interrupted briefly in 1938 when she returned to Chile, and her volume *Tala* was published in Buenos Aires. This was Mistral's own favourite, because it contained 'the root of her Indoamericanism'. One poem in the volume, 'La flor del aire' (Flower of the Air), she described as a manifesto of her key concerns: the link between creation and passion, nature and mother earth, the centrality of the feminine; deep religiosity and a devotion to all living beings; the tensions in creativity; and the nature of poetry itself.

The Nobel Prize was followed by others in recognition of her humanitarian and literary activities. *Lagar*, published in Santiago in 1954, further developed her constant concerns; the search for a poetic language adequate to a complex Latin American identity expressed through the body and sensibility of a woman. Her language is rooted in the classics, in Spanish and Latin American baroque and in the writing of Martí – as she put it, 'old language, new ideas'. She tested each of the experimental schools and moved on, but her preoccupation with the language of her country and of her childhood was constant. When she died after a long illness, she named the companion of her later life, Doris Dana, as her executor and donated all her royalties to the children of Monte Grande, the village where she grew up.

Further reading

Arrigoitia, L. de (1989) *Pensamiento y forma en la prosa de Gabriela Mistral*, San Juan: Ed. de la Universidad de Puerto Rico.

Fariña, S. and R. Olea (eds) (1990) *Una palabra cómplice: Encuentro con Gabriela Mistral*, Santiago, Chile: Isis Internacional/Casa de la Mujer La Morada.

Fiol-Matta, L. (2002) *Gabriela Mistral, Queer Mother for the Nation*, Minneapolis: University of Minnesota Press.

Goic, C. (1989) 'Gabriela Mistral', in C.A. Solé and M.I. Abreu (eds), *Latin American Writers*, New York: Scribners, 2, 677–91.

Horan, E. (1994) *Gabriela Mistral: An Artist and Her People*, Washington: Organization of American States.

Mistral, G. (1961) *Selected Poems of Gabriela Mistral*, ed. and trans. D. Dana, Baltimore: Johns Hopkins University Press.

—— (2003) *Selected Poems of Gabriela Mistral*, trans. Ursula K. LeGuin, Albuquerque: University of New Mexico Press.

—— (2003) *Selected Prose and Prose Poems*, ed. and trans. S. Tapscott, Austin: University of Texas Press.

Rubio, P. (1995) *Gabriela Mistral ante la crítica; bibliografía anotada*, Santiago, Chile: Dirección de Archivos y Museos.

ELIANA ORTEGA

Mittelholzer, Edgar Austin

b. 1909, New Amsterdam, British Guiana; d. 1965, London, England

Writer

Of his twenty-three novels and two non-fiction books, the novels *A Morning at the Office* (1950), which looks carefully at five hours of race and class in Trinidad; *My Bones and My Flute* (1955), probably one of the best ghost stories ever written; and *The Life and Death of Sylvia* or *Sylvia* (1953), show Mittelholzer's descriptive powers at their best. He had an obsessive interest in Oriental occultism and psychical research. His mental deterioration became obvious in later novels like *The Wounded and the Worried* (1962) and *The Harrowing of Hubertus* (1954). He eventually committed suicide by setting himself on fire.

Further reading

Gilkes, M. (1979) 'Edgar Mittelholzer', in B. King (ed.), *West Indian Literature*, London: Macmillan.

Seymour, A.J. (1968) *Edgar Mittelholzer: The Man and His Work*, Georgetown, Guyana: National History & Arts Council.

KEITH JARDIM

***MODERNISMO* BRASILEIRO** *see* Brazilian modernism

***MODERNISMO*, SPANISH AMERICAN** *see* Spanish American modernism

Molina, Enrique

b. 1910, Buenos Aires, Argentina; d. 1997, Buenos Aires

Writer

An older member of the 1940 generation influenced by **surrealism**, Molina's poetry evoked the world of childhood and daily life, respecting the capacity of simple domestic objects to preserve traces of human history. In the 1950s he edited *A partir de 0. Revista de poesía y antipoesía* (Starting from Zero: Review of Poetry and Antipoetry), reviving the surrealist strand earlier espoused by Aldo **Pellegrini**. His novel *Una sombra donde sueña Camila O'Gorman* (A Shadow Where Camila O'Gorman Dreams) (1984) narrates the tragic love story of Camila and the priest Ladislao Gutiérrez.

Further reading

Espejo, E. (ed.) (1991) *Enrique Molina: Antología poética*, Madrid: Visor Libros.

Molina, E. (1979) *Obra poética*, Caracas: Monte Avila.

—— (1983) *Páginas de Enrique Molina (seleccionadas por el autor)*, intro. D.L. Garasa, Buenos Aires: Celtia.

Sefami, J. (1994) 'Itinerário de memorias: Entrevista con Enrique Molina', *Chasqui* 23(2): 143–9.

Zonana, V.G. (1994) 'La elegía funeral en los poetas del 40: Enrique Molina', *Revista de literaturas modernas* 27: 239–57.

MAGDALENA GARCÍA PINTO

Molinari, Ricardo E.

b. 1898, Buenos Aires, Argentina; d. 1996, Buenos Aires

Poet

Molinari belonged to the Argentine avant-garde (see **avant-garde in Latin America**) group represented by the magazine ***Martín Fierro***. His writings are informed not only by ***ultraísmo*** and **surrealism** but also by the classical Hispanic tradition. His poetry frequently combines metaphysical concerns with an interrogation of the American condition. The landscape of the *pampas* is presented in some of his poems as a lyrical space. He was awarded, among other distinctions, the Premio Nacional de Literatura in 1958. The collection of poems, *Las sombras del pájaro tostado* (The Shadows of the Brown Bird) (1974), encompasses his numerous books.

Further reading

Herrera, R.H. (1995) 'La muerte en la llanura: La poesía de Ricardo E. Molinari', *La Nación, suplemento literario*, 12 March: 8.

Molinari, R. (1983) *Páginas de Ricardo E. Molinari seleccionadas por el autor*, Buenos Aires: Celtia.

Pousa, N. (1961) *Ricardo E. Molinari*, Buenos Aires: Ediciones Culturales Argentinas.

Roggiano, A.A. (1988) 'Ricardo E. Molinari y la vanguardia poética argentina', *Mundi* 2(4): 3–13.

—— (1989) 'Ricardo E. Molinari', in C.A. Solé and M.I. Abreu (eds), *Latin American Writers*, New York: Scribners, 2: 837–44.

FERNANDO J. ROSENBERG

Molloy, Sylvia

b. 1938, Buenos Aires, Argentina

Writer

Molloy is one of the most insightful contemporary Latin American literary critics, and a creative writer of remarkable originality. Educated in Buenos Aires and at the Sorbonne in Paris, she later emigrated to the USA where she has taught at Princeton, Yale and is currently the Albert Schweitzer Professor of the Humanities at New York University.

Her critical career began with *La Diffusion de la littérature hispanoaméricaine en France* (The Dissemination of Spanish American Literature in France) (1972), written for her doctoral degree. A great admirer of Jorge Luis **Borges**, her *Las letras de Borges* (Signs of Borges) (1979) deals with the uncanny in Borges, exploring the fragile nuances and fragmentations in Borges's speaking subject. Her study *At Face Value: Autobiographical Writing in Spanish America* (1991) looks at the paradoxical nature of narratives that attempt the impossible task of telling their own story and has had considerable impact on how **autobiography** is understood in contemporary culture. She co-edited a valuable anthology, *Women's Writing in Latin America* (1991) with Sara Castro-Klarén and Beatriz **Sarlo**, including, among others, authors such as Gabriela **Mistral**, Raquel de **Queiroz**, Norah **Lange**, Blanca **Varela**, Nancy **Morejón**, Hebe de Bonafini and Lourdes Arizpe.

As a writer of fiction, she first experimented with short stories published in the literary journals of Buenos Aires. While writing her study on Borges, she also began *En breve cárcel* (Certificate of Absence) (1981), a third-person novel exploring the narrator's confinement in the prison house of love and language. Its protagonist and narrator unveils a love triangle among three women that brings to the protagonist despair and a deep sense of emptiness. It is a narrative search for self and the recovered memories of childhood that haunt the character in her most vulnerable moments of uncertainty. The craft of the novel and the thematics of lesbian love have elicited a long list of critical studies that have hailed it as 'the most notable lesbian novel to date in Latin American literature'.

In 2002 she published to great acclaim a second novel, *El común olvido*. The gay male narrator of this novel returns to Buenos Aires from New York City after his parents' death. A stunning recreation of a lost Buenos Aires, this novel delves into the uncertainties of social memory.

Further reading

García Pinto, M. (1991) 'Sylvia Molloy', in *Latin American Women Writers: Intimate Histories*, Austin: University of Texas Press, 105–43.

Kaminsky, A. (1993) 'Sylvia Molloy's Lesbian Cartographies: Body, Text and Geography', in *Reading the Body Politic: Feminist Criticism and Latin American Women Writers*, Minneapolis: University of Minnesota Press, 96–114.

Martínez, E. (1996) 'Lesbian Eroticism and the Act of Writing: Sylvia Molloy's *Certificate of Absence*', in *Lesbian Voices from Latin America*, New York: Garland, 143–66.

Molloy, S. (1989) *Certificate of Absence*, trans. D. Balderston and S. Molloy, Austin: University of Texas Press.

—— (1991) *At Face Value: Autobiographical Writing in Spanish America*, Cambridge: Cambridge University Press.

—— (1994) *Signs of Borges*, trans. O. Montero, Durham, NC: Duke University Press.

MAGDALENA GARCÍA PINTO

Monar, Rooplall

b. 1945, Lusignan Estate, East Coast Demerara, British Guiana

Writer

One of the few Guyanese writers permanently resident there, his novel, *Janjhat* (Peepal Tree) (1989), and three collections of short stories, *Backdam People* (1985), *Estate People* (1994) and *High House and Radio* (1992), are considered to be some of the best stories on Guyanese Indian life. His collection of poems, *Koker*, was published in 1987 and won the Guyana Prize for poetry that year, one of several prizes he has won. Monar has been a teacher, an estate bookkeeper, a journalist and a healer.

KEITH JARDIM

Monsiváis, Carlos

b. 1938, Mexico City

Writer

One of the foremost authorities on Mexican literature and popular culture in the last third of the twentieth century, Carlos Monsiváis is the most important cultural critic and humorist in a generation of Mexican **intellectuals** which includes José Emilio **Pacheco**, Sergio **Pitol**, and Elena **Poniatowska**. Monsiváis rose to prominence through cultural journalism, editing the Mexico City weekly *La cultura en México* (the supplement to *Siempre*) from 1972 to 1987. A truly public figure, he publishes essays in all of Mexico City's major newspapers and magazines, including the column 'A mi madre, bohemios' (To my Mother, Bohemians) in the newspaper *La Jornada*. He is also a regular television commentator.

Monsiváis's writings encompass the entire range of Mexican art and culture, and include major contributions on literary history, popular culture, the politics of nationalism, film, sexuality, and the visual and plastic arts. Within this broad field of study, he is perhaps best known as the premier chronicler of daily life in Mexico City. As early as 1966, Emanuel Carballo noted that Monsiváis was destined to inherit this role from Salvador **Novo**. However, where Novo chronicled the rise of Mexico City to become the centre of a major industrial economy, Monsiváis has chronicled the capital's struggles through a long series of political, economic, and ecological crises. Beginning with the student movement in 1968, Monsiváis has written on diverse social phenomena, including the 1985 earthquake which devastated Mexico City, the celebrations of Mexican football/soccer fans, the struggles for indigenous self-determination in Juchitán, Oaxaca and efforts to reform Mexico's labour movement.

Despite the difficult history Monsiváis has chronicled, his work is far from pessimistic. A highly synthetic thinker, Monsiváis's writings are always in touch with the latest trends in cultural theory but simultaneously engaged with the quotidian experience of popular culture. He never loses sight of the larger structures of power which overdetermine many aspects of commercial culture, but Monsiváis developed as an intellectual in the 1970s, when the leftist intelligentsia of Latin America began to absorb the writings of Antonio Gramsci. In keeping with a generally Gramscian approach to cultural history, Monsiváis has always defended popular culture as a powerful reservoir for alternative nationalist sentiments corrosive to the chauvinistic or authoritarian forms of nationalism promoted by Mexico's single-party state. A central feature of Monsiváis's engagement with popular culture on this level is his own acerbic sense of humour, which celebrates the liberating elements of kitsch while maintaining an ironic distance from the rapid-fire world of fashion, consumption and changing style. His broad-ranging analyses have included foundational essays on personalities across the spectrum of Mexican culture, ranging from politics (Fidel Velásquez), humour (Cantinflas, Jis y Trino), literature (Salvador Novo, Juan **Rulfo**, José **Revueltas**), music (Agustín Lara, José Alfredo Jiménez, Luis Miguel, Gloria Trevi), art (David Alfaro Siqueiros, Jesús Helguera), film (Irma Serrano, María Félix, Dolores Del Rio) and boxing (Julio César Chávez).

Unlike many other prominent intellectuals of his generation, Monsiváis has maintained an independent position as a professional writer and has never worked in any state-run institution.

Further reading

Egan, L. (2001) *Carlos Monsiváis*, Albuquerque: University of New Mexico Press.

Monsiváis, C. (1966) *Carlos Monsiváis*, intro. E. Carballo, Mexico City: Empresas Editoriales.

—— (1997) *Mexican Postcards* trans. and intro. J. Kraniauskas, London: Verso.

Mudrovcic, M.E. (1998) 'Cultura nacionalista v cultura nacional: Carlos Monsiváis ante la sociedad de masas', *Hispamérica* 79: 29–39.

BRIAN GOLLNICK

Monte Avila

A state-owned company founded in 1968, Monte Avila is Venezuela's largest publisher, and one of the biggest in Latin America. It is run without a profit-making objective, and the prices of its publications have always been kept low in order to make them as accessible as possible. That policy, and the quality of its publications, account for its good reputation throughout Latin America. It has played a valuable role in the mass production of educational texts for all levels, but its vast output covers a wide range of disciplines, including literature and the arts, philosophy, history and the social sciences. Its director until recently was Alexis **Márquez Rodríguez**.

Further information

http://www.analitica.com/biblioteca/monte_avila/default.asp

MARK DINNEEN

Montealegre, Jorge

b. 1954, Santiago, Chile

Poet

Montealegre's poetic itinerary starts with the paradoxical circumstances of Chilean exile life during the 1970s in Europe in *Exilios* (Exiles) (1983), continues with the excruciating life conditions of Santiago shanty-town dwellers after Pinochet's 1973 *coup d'état* in *Título de Dominio* (Certificate of Entitlement) (1980), and becomes a sharp critical view of the social and ideological transformations produced by the return to democracy in *Bien común* (Common Share) (1995). His keen eye for cultural contradictions reveals itself constantly as punning and wordplay.

OSCAR D. SARMIENTO

Montecino, Sonia

b. 1954, Santiago, Chile

Writer and anthropologist

Montecino's work is focused on issues of Chilean feminine identity, ranging from the essays *Mujeres de la tierra* (Women of the Earth) (1984) and *Madres y huachos: Alegorías del mestizaje chileno* (Mothers and Chileans: Allegories of Chilean Mestizaje) (1991), to the novel *La revuelta* (The Revolt) (1988), which focuses on the conflictive situation of women and their responses to dictatorial political oppression. She directs the Women's Studies Programme at the University of Chile.

Further reading

Montecino, S. (1992) 'El mundo indígena en la Chile de hoy: Temor y tension de una presencia', *Hispamérica* 21(61): 87–93.

ELIANA ORTEGA

Monteforte Toledo, Mario

b. 1911, Guatemala City

Writer, politician and sociologist

Monteforte made a significant contribution to Guatemalan fiction by representing indigenous and *ladino* perspectives. Expelled from the University of San Carlos for his opposition to Ubico, he studied in Paris in the 1930s and then returned to live in the countryside to experience Indian culture. His psychological, populist and social realist narratives avoid the romanticizing and posturing of picturesque ***indigenismo***. His two 1948 novels, *Anaite* and *Entre la piedra y la cruz* (Between the Rock and the Cross), are among his best written and richest. Monteforte was Vice President under Arévalo in the 1940s, but resigned, anticipating future dissent within the Left.

Further reading

Arias, A. (1970) *Ideología, literatura y sociedad durante la revolución guatemalteca 1944–1954*, Havana: Casa de las Américas.

Menton, S. (1960) 'Mario Monteforte Toledo y el arte de novelar', in *Historia crítica de la novela guatemalteca*, Guatemala: Editorial Universitaria, 244–76.

Rokas, N.W. (1986) 'Bibliografía crítica selecta de Mario Monteforte Toledo', *Inter-American Review of Bibliography* 36: 29–38.

MARC ZIMMERMAN AND LINDA J. CRAFT

Montejo, Eugenio

b. 1938, Caracas, Venezuela

Poet

Montejo's first volume, *Elegos* (1967), won him an immediate reputation as a poet of landscape and of experience. His most emblematic book, *Terredad* (1978), brilliantly reflects his capacity to embrace the world through the simplest of language and the most serene of images. Montejo resists any temptation to exuberance and offers images of rural and urban landscapes whose constitutive essence reveal themselves to the poet's penetrating glance. The core of his poetry, therefore, is temperate, colloquial, almost philosophical, as is obvious in other works such as *Trópico absoluto* (Absolute Tropics) (1982), *Alfabeto del mundo* (Alphabet of the World) (1986) and *Adiós al siglo XX* (Farewell to the 20th Century) (1992), now collected in a single *Antología* (1996). Montejo also wrote under a number of heteronyms a range of other volumes including *La guitarra del horizonte* (The Guitar of the Horizon) (1991) and *El hacha de seda* (The Silk Axe) (1995). *La ventana oblicua* (The Oblique Window) (1974) and *El taller blanco* (The White Workshop) (1996) include the bulk of his essays.

Further reading

Eyzaguirre, L. (1993) 'Eugenio Montejo: Poeta de fin de siglo', *Inti: Revista de literatura hispánica* 37–8: 123–32.

Lastra, P. (1984) 'El pan y las palabras: Poesía de Eugenio Montejo', *Inti: Revista de literatura hispánica* 18–19: 211–28.

Montejo, E. (1988) *Alfabeto del mundo*, Mexico City: Fondo de Cultura Económica.

—— (1998) 'Poesía venezolana: Valija de fin de siglo', *Inti: Revista de literatura hispánica* 48: 53–64.

RAFAEL CASTILLO ZAPATA

Montenegro, Carlos

b. 1900, Puebla del Caraminal, Spain; d. 1981, Miami, Florida, USA

Writer

Montenegro was a merchant seaman and itinerant worker throughout Central America and the USA before spending twelve years in jail (1919–31) in Havana. There he began to write and became a communist. Throughout the 1930s he edited several socialist newspapers, including *La Palabra* and *Hoy*. He went into exile in 1959. He wrote short stories, but his finest literary achievement is *Hombres sin mujer* (Men without Women) (1938), a brutal novel about Cuban prison life and an early approach to the theme of homosexuality. The novel was only republished in Cuba in 1995.

Further reading

Pujals, E.J. (1980) *La obra narrativa de Carlos Montenegro*, Miami: Universal.

WILFREDO CANCIO ISLA

Montero, Mayra

b. 1952, Havana, Cuba

Writer

Born in Cuba but living in Puerto Rico since childhood, Montero's fiction is sustained by the Afro-Caribbean world. The suffocating magical world of Vodun is the setting for her first collection of stories, *Veintitrés y una tortuga* (Twenty-Three and a Turtle) (1981). Her first novel, *La trenza de la hermosa luna* (The Plait of the Beautiful Moon) (1987), retains the Haitian setting and follows the crisis of an individual returning to his land and beliefs. In *Tú, la oscuridad* (You, Darkness) (1995), the work of a herpes specialist in Haiti is interrupted by the shadow of death and violence. *Como un mensajero tuyo* (The Messager) (1998) takes place during Enrico Caruso's visit to Havana in 1920 and set against a background of Santería rites.

Further reading

Prieto, J.M. (2000) 'Mayra Montero', trans. M. Harss, *BOMB* 70: 86–90.

Toral Aleman, B. (2001) 'Reescribiendo el Caribe: Entrevista a Mayra Montero', *Caribe* 4(1): 58–66.

MARÍA JULIA DAROQUI

Monterroso Bonilla, Augusto

b. 1921, Guatemala City, d. 2003, Mexico City

Writer

Guatemala's most famous author after Asturias, and one of the many writers exiled after the fall of the Arbenz government in 1954, Augusto 'Tito' Monterroso spent his mature life in Mexico. He wrote several collections of fables which broke with the realistic dimensions of the Guatemalan prose tradition and won him an international reputation. One famous story consists of a single sentence: 'When he woke up the dinosaur was still there.' Monterroso's stories are characterized by whimsy, irony, allegory and intellectual probing with little overt social content, although there are some obvious and famous exceptions: for example, in his story of multinational, imperialist and CIA intervention in Latin America, 'Mister Taylor'.

Further reading

Campos, M.A. (ed.) (1988) *La literatura de Augusto Monterroso*, Mexico City: UNAM.

Masoliver, J.A. (1997) 'Augusto Monterroso', in V. Smith (ed.), *Encyclopedia of Latin American Literature*, London: Fitzroy Dearborn, 562–3.

Monterroso, A. (1971) *The Black Sheep and Other Fables*, trans. W. Bradbury, New York: Doubleday.

—— (1995) *Complete Works and Other Stories*, trans. E. Grossman, Austin: University of Texas Press.

Ruffinelli, J. (ed.) (1976) *Monterroso*, Xalapa: Universidad Veracruzana.

—— (2002) 'Augusto Monterroso', in C. Solé and K. Müller-Bergh (eds), *Latin American Writers: Supplement I*, New York: Scribners, 345–61.

MARC ZIMMERMAN AND LINDA J. CRAFT

Monti, Ricardo

b. 1944, Buenos Aires, Argentina

Playwright

Monti's productions in the 1970s were expressly political and synonymous with rupture and the search for a new theatrical language. *Una noche con el Sr. Magnus e Hijos* (One Night with Mr Magnus and Sons) (1970) and *Historia tendenciosa de la clase media argentina* (Tendentious History of the Argentine Middle Class) (1971) set out to unmask social hypocrisies. From *Visita* (Visit) (1977) to *Una pasión sudamericana* (A South American Passion) (1989), he continued to comment upon society, although less vehemently. Re-elaborating ***grotesco criollo*** and the theatre of the absurd, his poetic plays were staged on sinister sets, often employing masks and found objects.

Further reading

Arlt, M. (2000) 'Ricardo Monti: Hacía un teatro epifánico', in O. Pellettieri (ed.), *Teatro argentino del 2000*, Buenos Aires: Galerna, Fundación Roberto Arlt.

Driskell, C.B. (1979) 'Conversación con Ricardo Monti', *Latin American Theatre Review* 12(2): 43–53.

Monti, Ricardo. (1971) *Una noche con el Sr. Magnus & hijos*, Buenos Aires: Talía.

—— (1972) *Historia tendenciosa de la clase media argentina, de los extraños sucesos en que se vieron envuelto*, Buenos Aires: Talía.

—— (1993) *Una pasión sudamericana; Una historia tendenciosa*, Ottawa: Girol Books.

STELLA MARTINI

montuvio ecuatoriano, El

An essay by José de la **Cuadra**, *El montuvio ecuatoriano* (The Montuvio of Ecuador) (1937) is a study of the *montuvio*, the archetypical inhabitant of the coastal area of Ecuador, and the inspiration for much of the literature produced by the members of the **Guayaquil Group**, particularly de la Cuadra himself. The book presents geographical, sociological, anthropological and ethnic information about the *montuvio*, the product of a mixture of three races: 60 per cent Indian, 30 per cent black and 10 per cent white. The essay interprets the *montuvio*'s literary history, as well as his criminal, political and mythical tendencies.

Further reading

Cuadra, J. de la (1996) *El montuvio ecuatoriano*, Quito: Universidad Andina Simón Bolívar.

HUMBERTO E. ROBLES

Moraes, Vinícius de

b. 1913, Rio de Janeiro, Brazil; d. 1980, Rio de Janeiro

Playwright, poet, song lyricist and critic

One of Brazil's best-loved public figures, Vinícius de Moraes famously combined the careers of diplomat, poet, songwriter, lover of women and professional drinker, with a bohemian *joie de vivre* whose popular instincts made of him a distinctive voice of democratic opposition to the post-1964 military regime. His early poetry, influenced by the neo-Catholicism of the 1930s modernists (see **Brazilian modernism**), shared Manuel **Bandeira**'s preoccupation with the tensions between the worldly and the divine, the erotic and the spiritual. But with his 1943 volume, *Elegias*, that balance had shifted definitively towards the blend of sensuality and simple colloquialism for which Moraes is known today.

By the 1940s he had also begun a successful career as a film critic, writing over a hundred reviews and columns for Rio de Janeiro newspapers between 1941 and 1952, and unleashing a public debate about the industry on the occasion of Orson Welles's visit to Brazil in 1942. A period of residence as vice-consul in Los Angeles between 1946 and 1950 enriched his contact with the worlds of cinema and popular music, particularly jazz, and following his return to Brazil these experiences took him along a new creative path.

In 1956 he met the young composer Tom Jobim and collaborated with him on the musical score for the stage play *Orfeu da Conceição*, the story of which he had already sold to the French film producer Sacha Gordine. Following the success of the play, in 1957 Gordine and director Marcel Camus finally went ahead with the film version, *Black Orpheus*, for which Moraes and Jobim added new songs, such as 'A Felicidade' (Happiness). With the release of a further Jobim–Moraes collaboration, 'Chega de saudade' (No More Longing) by singer-guitarist João Gilberto in 1958, the arrival of the new wave in Brazilian popular music, bossa nova, was assured, along with Moraes's role as its leading lyricist.

While Moraes's partnership with Jobim produced many of the classic gems of the movement, such as 'Insensatez' (Foolishness), 'O Grande Amor' (The Great Love) and 'Garota de Ipanema' (The Girl from Ipanema), many of his two hundred or more compositions were the fruit of other collaborations, with Carlos Lyra, Edu Lobo, Toquinho and Baden Powell, for instance. The partnership with Baden Powell marked Moraes's commitment to the politicized protest song movement of the early 1960s, before the military *coup*, and to its counterpart in the field of poetry, *Violão de Rua* (Street Guitar). More perhaps than any other artist of the period, it was Moraes who exemplified how the composer's art could shape the literary language of the lyric tradition to the rhythms of popular speech and music whilst avoiding either crude condescension or doctrinaire artificiality. In that sense, he set a demandingly high standard for the subsequent MPB (Música Popular Brasileira) generation of popular songwriters, having guaranteed them an unprecedented level of respect and prestige as artists as well as entertainers.

Further reading

Alonso, D. and A. Crespo (1964) 'Poemas de Vinicius de Moraes', *Revista de cultura brasileña* 3: 225–40.

Brandellero, S. (1997) 'Vinícius de Moraes', in V. Smith (ed.), *Encyclopedia of Latin American Literature*, London: Fitzroy Dearborn, 564–5.

Moraes, V. de (1976) *Obra poética y prosa*, ed. A. Coutinho, Rio de Janeiro: José Aguilar.

—— (1991) *Livro de letras*, São Paulo: Companhia das Letras.

Silva, D.F. de (1959) 'A temática da poesia de Vinícius de Morais', *Diálogo* 11: 15–26.

DAVID TREECE

Morales Benítez, Otto

b. 1920, Riosucio, Colombia

Essayist

One of Colombia's foremost essayists, Morales Benítez has published over thirty books. He appeared on the cultural scene in 1940s Medellín as director of the cultural magazine *Generación*, one of the earliest to promote modern international authors. His essays since the 1950s address *mestizaje* as the essence of Latin American identity, participatory democracy as the solution for Colombian political crises, and the importance of political, labour and agricultural reform. He has been one of the most vigorous and effective voices for liberal humanism in Colombia.

Further reading

Escobar Mesa, A. (1999) 'Otto Morales Benítez, poeta de la autenticidad mestiza', *Boletín de la Academia Colombiana* 50(203–4): 65–73.

Landinez Castro, V. (ed.) (1998) *Obras de Otto Morales Benítez, I: Caminos del hombre en la literatura*, Madrid: Instituto Caro y Cuervo.

Morales Benítez, Otto (1988) *Propuestas para examinar la historia con criterios Indoamericanos*, Bogotá: Tercer Mundo Editores.

—— (1998) *Obras*, Bogotá: Instituto Caro y Cuervo.

RAYMOND L. WILLIAMS

Morales Bermúdez, Jesús

b. 1947, San Cristóbal de Las Casas, Chiapas, Mexico

Novelist

Morales Bermúdez is the most important contemporary novelist from the southern Mexican state of Chiapas. His writings mark a dramatic new engagement with indigenous orality. His first novel, *Memorial del tiempo, o vía de las conversaciones* (Memorial of Time, or the Road of Conversations) (1987), is written in *castilla*, the dialect of Spanish spoken in Chiapas by native speakers of indigenous languages. *Ceremonial* (1992) develops this idiosyncratic dialect towards a more standard Spanish to narrate the experience of Maya peasants who moved to the jungles of Chiapas in the 1960s. As such, it documents an important antecedent to the Zapatista National Liberation Army. Recently Morales Bermúdez has written a history of literature in Chiapas and essays related to his experiences as a social organizer during the 1970s.

Further reading

Gollnick, Brian (1999) 'El Ciclón de Chiapas: El desarrollo reciente del indigenismo chiapaneco', *Revista de crítica literaria latinoamericana* 49: 199–216.

Medina, Rubén (1997) 'Hacia la liquidación del indigenismo en México: Una hipótesis en torno a Chiapas y *Memorial del tiempo*', *Siglo XX/20th Century* 109–29.

Morales Bermúdez, Jesús (1984) *On o'tian, antigua palabra ch'ol*, Mexico City: Universidad Autónoma Metropolitana, Unidad Azcapotzalco.

—— (1987) *Memorial del tiempo, o vía de las conversaciones*, Mexico City: Insituto Nacional de Bellas Artes.

—— (1992) *Ceremonial*, Mexico City: Consejo Nacional Para la Cultura y Las Artes/Gobierno del Estado de Chiapas.

—— (1994) *Por los senderos de lo incierto: Antología personal*, Tuxtla Gutiérrez, Chiapas: Universidad de Ciencias y Artes del Estado de Chiapas.

—— (1997) *Aproximaciones a la poesía y la narrativa de Chiapas*, Tuxtla Gutiérrez, Chiapas: Universidad de Ciencias y Artes del Estado de Chiapas.

Steele, Cynthia (1993) 'Indigenismo y posmodernidad: Narrativa indigenista, testimonio, teatro campesino y video en el Chiapas secular', *Revista de crítica literaria latinoamericana* 38: 249–60.

BRIAN GOLLNICK

Morales Santos, Francisco

b. 1940, Ciudad Vieja, Sacatepéquez, Guatemala

Poet

Founding member of the group Nuevo Signo (New Sign), Morales has also been the group's organizer, promoter and meta-commentarist. Also a founding member and first president of the Comunidad de Escritores Guatemaltecos (Community of Guatemalan Writers), he has anthologized national poetry and published several of his own books of poetry. Throughout his work, Morales has sought forms with a specifically Guatemalan flavour, has concentrated on social as well as erotic and sentimental themes, and always alludes to Guatemala's multiple problems and identities.

Further reading

Morales Santos, F. (1983) *Los nombres que nos nombran: Panorama de la literatura guatemalteca de 1782 a 1982*, Guatemala City: Tip. Nacional

—— (1990) 'Signos de identidad de la poesía guatemalteca', *Hispamérica*, April, 19(55): 73–91.

MARC ZIMMERMAN AND LINDA J. CRAFT

Mordecai, Pamela Claire

b. 1942, Kingston, Jamaica

Writer

Mordecai is a poet (producing both adult and prize-winning children's poetry), editor, publisher and academic. *Journey Poem* (1989) demonstrated a strong poetic voice, sensuous, accomplished in form, written largely in Jamaican-accented English. *de Man* (1995) portrays in Jamaican creole the witnessing of the Crucifixion by two Jamaicans, one a middle-aged maid in the service of Pontius Pilate's wife and one an old carpenter, taught by Joseph. Mordecai's academic work and publishing have contributed greatly to the development of Caribbean women's writing (see **Caribbean literature**).

Further reading

Savory, E. (1996) 'En/gendering Spaces: The Poetry of Marlene Nourbese Philip and Pamela Mordecai', in Georgina M. Colville (ed.), *Contemporary Women Writing in the Other Americas*, vol. 2, Lampeter: Edwin Mellen.

ELAINE SAVORY

Morejón, Nancy

b. 1944, Havana, Cuba

Poet

One of the most important poets of post-revolutionary Cuba, Morejón was born in Los Sitios, a poor neighbourhood of Havana. Her poetry deals with issues of race and gender, as well as evoking the scenery, rhythms and people of her island. Her first volume of poetry, *Mutismos* (Silences), was published in 1962 and she has published more than a dozen collections of poems since, as well as volumes of essays and criticism. Morejón is also a scholar of Francophone and English-speaking Caribbean literature and directs the Centro de Estudios del Caribe at **Casa de las Américas** in Havana.

Further reading

Behar, R. and L. Suárez (1995) 'Two Conversations with Nancy Morejón', trans. D. Frye, in R. Behar (ed.), *Bridges to Cuba/Puentes a Cuba*, Ann Arbor: University of Michigan Press.

Davies, C. (1997) 'Nancy Morejón', in V. Smith (ed.), *Encyclopedia of Latin American Literature*, London: Fitzroy Dearborn, 565–7.

Morejón, N. (2003) *Looking Within: Selected Poems 1956–2000*, ed. J.M. Cordones-Coda, Detroit: Wayne State University Press.

West, A. (1996) 'The Stone and Its Images: The Poetry of Nancy Morejón', *Studies in Twentieth Century Literature* 20(1): 193–219.

CAROL J. WALLACE

Moreno-Durán, R.H.

b. 1946, Tunja, Colombia

Writer

One of the most talented Colombian writers of the 1970s, Moreno-Durán is an urban and urbane novelist. After the hermetic modernist trilogy *Femina Suite – Juego de damas* (Checkers) (1977), *El toque de Diana* (Reveille) (1981) and *Finale capriccioso con Madonna* (Finale capriccioso with Madonna)

(1983) – he published *Los felinos del Canciller* (The Chancellor's Cats) (1985), an accessible chronicle of an aristocratic Colombian family. He is also the author of essays on Latin American literature, *De la barbarie a la imaginación* (From Barbarism to Imagination) (1976), and memoirs of Latin American writers, *Como el halcón peregrino* (Like the Peregrine Falcon) (1995).

Further reading

Bermúdez, M.T. (2000) 'Entrevista a R.H. Moreno Durán', *Enfocarte* 1(5).

Utley, G.J. (2000) 'R.H. Moreno-Durán y la narrativa colombiana actual', in M.M. Jaramillo, B. Osorio and A.I. Robledo (eds), *Literatura y cultura: Narrativa colombiana del siglo XX*, Bogotá: Ministerio de Cultura.

RAYMOND L. WILLIAMS

Morisseau-Leroy, Félix

b. 1912, Grand-Gosier, Haiti

Poet, playwright and novelist

Morisseau-Leroy was a major creator and advocate of the literature in Haitian creole (*kreyòl*), with such works as *Antigone en créole* (1953) and *Roua Kréon* (1978), both adaptations of the Greek stories to modern Haiti. The latter work was an attack on the regimes of Papa Doc Duvalier and his son. His most important poetry collection is *Diacoute* (Satchel) (1953); besides his writings in Haitian creole he also published several collections of poetry in French. His poems are critical of exoticizing views of Haiti and include celebrations of political figures such as Nkrumah and Salvador Allende.

Further reading

Hoffman, L.-F. (1997) 'Félix Morisseau-Leroy', in V. Smith (ed.), *Encyclopedia of Latin American Literature*, London: Fitzroy Dearborn, 567–9.

Morisseau-Leroy, F. (1983) *Dyakout 1, 2, 3, ak twa lòt poèm*, Miami: Jaden Kreyòl.

DANIEL BALDERSTON

Moro, César

b. 1903, Lima, Peru; d. 1956, Lima

Writer

As a surrealist poet and painter, Moro (born Alfredo Quíspez Asín) found his native Lima hostile to his aspirations as a gay artist; it was he who first described the city as 'Lima, the horrible'. In Paris in 1925 he joined the surrealists and published his first poems. Returning to Lima in 1934, he provoked new hostilities by espousing a **surrealism** that advocated total freedom of body and soul. In 1938 he left for Mexico City, where he met Xavier **Villaurrutia** and Agustín Lazo and co-organized the First Exhibition of Surrealist Art in Mexico City (1940). His writing, mostly in French, has recently been rediscovered by students of gay literature.

Further reading

Altuna, E. (1994) 'César Moro: Escritura y exilio', *Revista de crítica literaria latinoamericana* 20(39): 109–25.

García Pinto, M. (1997) 'César Moro', in V. Smith (ed.), *Encyclopedia of Latin American Literature*, London: Fitzroy Dearborn, 569–70.

—— (2000) 'La vida escandalosa de César Moro: Autorrepresentación, exilio y homosexualidad', in D. Balderston (ed.), *Sexualidad y nación*, Pittsburgh: Instituto Internacional de Literatura Iberoamericana, 271–82.

Martos, M. (1998) 'La poesía de César Moro', in *Encuentro Internacional de Peruanistas: Estado de los estudios historico-sociales sobre el Peru a fines del siglo XX, I-II*, UNESCO, Lima: Universidad de Lima.

Moro, C. (1976) *The Scandalous Life of César Moro*, ed. and trans. P. Ward, New York: Oleander Press.

Oviedo, J.M. (1977) 'Sobre la poesía de César Moro', *Lexis* 1: 101–5.

MAGDALENA GARCÍA PINTO

Morris, Mervyn

b. 1937, Kingston, Jamaica

Poet

The poems of Morris's first volume of poetry, *The Pond* (1973), range in subject from love and family to race politics and the colonial past. Awarded the 1976 Silver Musgrave Medal for poetry from the Institute of Jamaica, his subsequent volumes of poetry include *On Holy Week* (1976), *Shadowboxing* (1979) and *Examination Centre* (1992). Morris's critical writings include the essays published as *Is English We Speaking and Other Essays* (1999). He currently teaches English at the Mona, Jamaica campus of the University of the West Indies and has edited several collections, including *Voiceprint: An Anthology of Oral and Related Poetry from the Caribbean* (1989) and *The Faber Book of Contemporary Caribbean Short Stories* (1990).

Further reading

Morris, M. (1992) 'Behind the Poems', *Journal of West Indian Literature* 5(1–2): 65–74.

Mordecai, P. (1994) ' "The Labels Pin Them down": An Interview with Mervyn Morris', *Matatu* 12: 63–76.

CAROL J. WALLACE

Morte e vida severina

Written by the Brazilian poet João Cabral de **Melo Neto** and published in 1956, *Morte e vida severina* (Death and Life of a Severino) is subtitled *Auto de natal* (A Pernambucan Christmas play), recalling the popular, originally medieval Iberian tradition of one-act nativity plays in verse. However, Melo Neto critically reworked this dramatic structure in order to reflect on the oppressed condition of a north-eastern peasantry marginalized by Brazil's post-war drive for industrialization, something anticipated in the title's inversion of the customary sequence of life and death (is death to precede, or prevail over, the hope of a better life?).

The everyman Severino's cultural and linguistic universe combines the elemental figures of the hostile landscape of the semi-feudal rural interior (stone, drought, violence and death) with the stoic religiosity of a popular Catholicism rooted in the promise of salvation beyond the grave. Contrary to the didactic, propagandistic approach of much of the protest art from the 1960s which it pre-dates, Melo Neto instead submits the language of this universe to a dialectical process of interrogation, uncovering successive layers of meaning to arrive at an enriched and transformed consciousness of both word and world. By fusing in a single dramatic structure the biblical pilgrimage towards the miracle of Jesus's birth with the migrant's grim journey towards the coast in search of water, work and redemption, Melo Neto is able to expose in parodic form how the illusory faith in divine salvation is mirrored by the false secular promises of economic development.

Thus the 'rosary' of Severino's journey, the fragile thread of a dried-up riverbed punctuated by a succession of lifeless towns and villages, leads unremittingly through a litany of deaths (the arbitrary murders of peasants at the hands of greedy land barons, the slow grind of exploitation which swallows the plantation worker into the soil denied to him in life) that convince Severino that his pilgrimage to the city is nothing less than the road to his own funeral. Yet as he despairingly contemplates his suicide, the 'miraculous' birth of a sickly child in a riverside slum confronts him with the spectacle of man's stubborn resistance, the creative possibilities born out of his continual struggle to wrest life from seemingly exhausted material conditions.

Given this grimly materialist approach to the human struggle for survival and its deconstruction of the language of false promise employed by state and religion, it is not hard to understand the success of *Morte e vida severina* in the stage version performed across Brazil in the early years of the military dictatorship, with the musical settings composed by songwriter Chico **Buarque**. Walter Avancini's powerful 1980s screen adaptation for TV Globo, filmed on location in the states of Bahia and Pernambuco, further exploited the text's contemporary resonances by combining a professional cast with actors drawn from the local communities, and intercutting scenes from the drama with documentary footage of rural and urban poverty.

Further reading

Gonzalez, M. and D. Treece (1992) *The Gathering of Voices: The Twentieth-Century Poetry of Latin America*, London: Verso, 253–8.

Kadir, D. (1994) *João Cabral de Melo Neto, Selected Poetry 1937–1990*, Middletown, CN: Wesleyan University Press, 84–97.

Melo Neto, J.C. de (1980) *Morte e vida severina e outros poemas em voz alta*, Rio de Janeiro: José Olympio.

DAVID TREECE

Moura, Clovis Steiger de Assis

b. 1925, Almarante, Piaui, Brazil

Poet, historian and sociologist

Moura pioneered the application of Marxism to the study of Brazilian slave rebellions, denounced racism in *Brasil: Raízes do protesto negro* (Brazil: Roots of the Black Protest) (1983) and defended a militant sociology that links scientific practice with social change in *Sociologia do negro brasileiro* (Sociology of the Afro-Brazilian) (1988). He also examined the presence of racial prejudice in popular literature, founded the literary magazine *Jacuba* in Juazeiro, Bahia, edited the newspaper *O Momento* in Salvador, wrote for São Paulo newspapers and contributed in 1954 to the literary magazine *Fundamentos*, founded by writer and publisher Monteiro **Lobato**.

PEGGY SHARPE

Movimento Armorial

The aim of the Movimento Armorial, founded by Ariano **Suassuna** in Recife in 1970, was to create erudite art forms inspired by the traditions of popular music, songs, poetry and engravings of the rural north east of Brazil. Suassuna chose the word 'Armorial', referring to the book used to record the coat of arms of aristocratic families, to symbolize an ideal traditional and unified *sertão* culture. By evoking the wide range of heraldry, insignia and emblems created by popular artists, it linked the aristocratic with the popular, and the past with the present.

At its height in the mid-1970s, the movement included some eighty artists practising literature, music and graphic art. All those involved shared an interest in the popular culture of the backlands (or *sertão*), and the belief that, through the assimilation of its cultural forms, a truly national high art could be produced which would represent a Brazilian worldview and would be resistant to the degrading and standardizing effect of mass culture. The differences between Armorial art and the popular art upon which it was based are immediately evident. More refined and polished, the work of the Armorial artists did not aim to reproduce popular art forms, but to recreate them for a different public. The centrepiece of the movement was the Armorial orchestra, which remodelled traditional rhythms of the *sertão* into more sophisticated melodies, while writers such as Maximiano Campos, Janice Japiassu and Suassuna himself used the themes, characters, tone and imagery characteristic of ***literatura de cordel*** as the essential ingredients of their work.

The participants in the movement avoided any political implications and emphasized instead the fantastic and mystical qualities of regional popular expressions. A conservative approach to popular culture lay at the heart of Armorial art. Much of it was characterized by Arcadianism, exalting the simplicity of traditional rural life. The artists were selective in choosing their examples of popular culture, generally favouring more archaic forms and traditional themes such as messianism, banditry and folkloric legends, whilst ignoring contemporary urban popular culture.

The use which Armorial artists made of rich, popular material gave their work originality and vibrancy, but also produced contradictions. Despite their assertion that they were working with cultural values and expressions still existing in north-eastern Brazil, the nature of their work made it difficult to avoid a tendency towards the picturesque, and a strong air of nostalgia for a way of life felt to be under threat of extinction. The popular material presented in Armorial art often appears as folklore linked to a past age rather than as a living, dynamic force.

Further reading

Dinneen, M. (1996) *Listening to the People's Voice*, London: Kegan Paul International.

Slater, C. (1976) 'Folklore and the Modern Artist: The North East Brazilian Movimento Armorial', *Luso-Brazilian Review* 16 (2).

MARK DINNEEN

Mujica Láinez, Manuel

b. 1910, Buenos Aires, Argentina; d. 1984, Cruz Chica, Córdoba, Argentina

Writer

An Argentine novelist and journalist, some of Mujica Láinez's literary production explores European themes, as in *Bomarzo* (1962), a novel that served as text for the homonymous opera with music by Ginastera which received the Kennedy Prize in 1964. He also wrote about Buenos Aires, mostly in historical novels. *Misteriosa Buenos Aires* (Mysterious Buenos Aires) (1971), a collection of short stories, is his most celebrated work about the city.

Further reading

Carsuzán, M.E. (1962) *Manuel Mujica Láinez*, Buenos Aires: Ediciones Culturales Argentinas.

Cruz, J. (1978) *Genio y figura de Manuel Mujica Láinez*, Buenos Aires: EUDEBA.

Roffé, R. (2001) 'Entrevista a Manuel Mujica Láinez', *Cuadernos hispanoamericanos* 612: 107–16.

ALVARO FERNÁNDEZ-BRAVO

Mundo nuevo

Mundo nuevo was a cultural journal, first edited by Emir **Rodríguez Monegal** and published in Paris (1966–68), and later by Horacio Daniel Rodríguez in Buenos Aires (1968–71). Considered the official journal of the **Boom**, *Mundo nuevo* created a space which overcame the marginality and isolation of previous Latin American generations by inserting Latin American culture into an international context and de-emphasizing national boundaries. The journal set out to affirm the creative freedom of each writer while highlighting the continent's unity.

Political controversy arose in 1967 when the *New York Times* exposed a link between the 'Congress for Cultural Freedom' and the CIA. *Mundo* was financed by the Ford Foundation through an organization called ILARI (Instituto Latinoamericano de Relaciones Internacionales), associated with the anti-Communist Congress. This link suggested that any organization receiving funding from the Congress was in fact receiving funding from the CIA and was consequently a puppet of its cultural imperialism.

Rodríguez Monegal, the overseeing and omnipotent editor, responded with a denunciation of the CIA and defended the independence of the journal, claiming that culture must be free of politics. In his defence, he asked that if such ideological boundaries were enforced, why was the magazine banned in such politically different environments as Brazil, Argentina, Spain and Cuba? However, the political debate was not that simple. For example, an article criticizing Cuba's politics was published in the first issue while another favouring Cuba was rejected. This event sparked controversy and created enemies, especially in Cuba's **Casa de las Américas**. Nevertheless, this did not keep *Mundo* from publishing the work of political artists such as Pablo **Neruda**, Nicanor **Parra**, Carlos **Fuentes** and Gabriel **García Márquez**.

According to Rodríguez Monegal, *Mundo* was based in Paris because it was a cultural capital of Latin America, with many Latin American writers, and because it suited *Mundo*'s project of demarginalization. When the journal moved to Buenos Aires in 1968, Rodríguez Monegal resigned. Under the editorship of Horacio Daniel Rodríguez, the journal took a definite anti-communist stance. The quality and quantity of the writing deteriorated until its loss of funding and closure in 1971.

Further reading

Mudrovcic, M.E. (1997) *Mundo nuevo: Cultura y guerra fría*, Rosario, Argentina: Beatriz Viterbo.

VICTORIA RUÉTALO

mundonovismo

A literary term coined by the Chilean critic Francisco Contreras in 1917 to express his opposition to **Spanish American modernism** and his preference for an emphasis on the daily life of people in the New World. It has been used most frequently with regard to such works as José Eustacio **Rivera**'s *La* ***vorágine*** (The Vortex) (1924), Ricardo **Güiraldes**'s *Don Segundo Sombra* (1926) and Rómulo **Gallegos**'s ***Doña Bárbara*** (1929). These works have been designated *novelas de la tierra* (novels of the earth) by Arturo **Torres-Ríoseco**, and the latter term is favoured by critics such as Jean Franco and Carlos Alonso. Cedomil Goic, however, prefers the term *mundonovismo*, because he uses it to categorize not only novels of rural life such as those mentioned above but also urban novels that emphasis local roots or ***regionalismo***.

Further reading:

Contreras, F. (1919) 'El mundonovismo', in *La varilla de virtud*, Santiago: Casa Editorial Minerva, 101–15.
Marinello, J. (1959) *Sobre el modernismo: Polémica y definición*, Mexico City: UNAM.

DANIEL BALDERSTON

Murena, Héctor A.

b. 1923, Buenos Aires, Argentina; d. 1975, Buenos Aires

Writer

It was through his essays that Murena's ideological propositions became well known; a disciple of Ezequiel **Martínez Estrada**, he wrote within the interpretative current concerned to define 'the national'. Polemical texts such as *El pecado original de América* (America's Original Sin) (1954) presented his liberal cosmopolitanism and revealed his links to the journal ***Sur***, for which he wrote. Set in a liberal humanist framework, his arguments were aimed at those **intellectuals** who radicalized their positions during the first Peronist governments.

Further reading

Cristófalo, A. (1999) 'Murena, un crítico en soledad', in S. Cella (ed.), *La irrupción de la crítica*, 1. 10, *Historia crítica de la literature argentina*, Buenos Aires, Emecé, 105–23.
Frugoni de Fritzsche, T. (1985) *Murena: Un escritor argentino ante los problemas del país y de su literatura*, Buenos Aires: Taladriz.
Jiménez, J.O. (1976) 'Héctor A. Murena (1923–1975)', *Revista iberoamericana* 95: 275–84.
Lagos, M.I. (1989) *H.A. Murena en sus ensayos y narraciones: De lider revisionista a marginado*, New York: Maitén.
Martínez Palacio, J. (1968) 'La obra del argentino H.A. Murena', *Insula* 23: 1, 10; 4, 10.
Murena, Héctor A. (1954) *El pecado original de América*, Buenos Aires: Sur.
—— (1959) *El escándalo y el fuego*, Buenos Aires: Editorial Sudamericana.

SANDRA GASPARINI

Murillo, Rosario

b. 1951, Managua, Nicaragua

Poet

In her youth, Murillo was a leading member of the Grada group, which brought together avant-garde painters, poets and musicians. In the 1960s, she joined the Grupo Ventana founded by Sergio **Ramírez** and Fernando Gordillo. After the 1979 Sandinista Revolution she headed the Sandinista Association of Cultural Workers (ASTC) and edited *Ventana*, the cultural section of *Barricada*, from where she criticized the popular poetry workshops (see **workshop poetry**) led by Minister of Culture

Ernesto **Cardenal**. A controversial presence in Nicaraguan politics, Rosario Murillo was married to Sandinista president Daniel Ortega.

Further reading

Laurilla, M. (1988) 'Entrevista con Rosario Murillo', *Discurso literario* 6(1): 83–95.

White, S. (1986) 'An Interview with Nicaragua's First Lady: Rosario Murillo', *Third Rail* 7: 72–5.

SILVIA CHAVES AND ILEANA RODRÍGUEZ

music and literature

At first sight it might seem that music and literature are the most separate of the arts. While writing in whatever genre reworks the language of social communication common to those who read and those who do not, the musical code appears to be esoteric and inaccessible to a simple act of translation in the way that even some visual art still lends itself to interpretation through language. And yet music – I do not refer here to song, of course – does evoke emotional responses and buried memories in ways that have often defied theory. This capacity to awaken collective cultural reactions is as true of 'art music' as it is of popular forms; as true of instrumental music as it is of song, whose lyrics may often articulate, or attempt to articulate, the content of a shared consciousness.

Writers often deploy those references and mobilize those responses, sometimes for example by using evocative song titles or lyrics precisely for their capacity to situate experience in time and place and social class. And it is equally true that certain kinds of popular music are equally self-conscious in their deployment of literary language and reference. The great tango lyricists, for example, such as Enrique Santos Discépolo, Alfredo Le Pera and Homero Manzi deserve a place among Latin America's lyric poets. Their language owes much to the kind of *fin-de-siècle* melancholy echoed in the early work of Rubén **Darío** and other *modernistas*. And their sense of urban alienation is not so distant from the life of Buenos Aires as depicted in the writing of urban novelists such as Roberto **Arlt**. Agustín Lara, the undisputed monarch of the bolero, evokes an equally nostalgic world of love and disappointment in many of his enormously popular ballads. And the Mexican collective imaginary was very largely shaped in the 1930s and 1940s by a vision of rural Mexico and the Revolution crafted by the cinema of the so-called Mexican Golden Age and the songs that accompanied this, sung by legends of the era such as Pedro Infante, Jorge Negrete and María Félix.

Indeed, many writers have explored the way in which the imagery of song lyrics has served to shape consciousness and ways of seeing the world. Manuel **Puig**, for example, explored the issue in several of his novels, most notably *Boquitas pintadas* (Heartbreak Tango) (1969). In a different genre, the urban *crónicas* (see ***crónica***) of Mexican writer and cultural commentator Carlos **Monsiváis** frequently find points of reference and sources of meaning in popular culture in the lyrics of popular songs and their performers.

Popular music was a key source for Nicolás **Guillén**, whose poetry took its form, rhythm and language from Cuban popular song, as acknowledged in his early collection *Motivos de son* (Themes from the *Son*) (1930) and in much of his later work. Other writers of the ***negrismo*** movement, including Puerto Rican poet Luis **Palés Matos** and the Uruguayan writer and scholar Ildefonso **Pereda Valdés**, also found inspiration in the musical traditions of the black populations of the region.

Indigenismo, the intellectual movement which defended the rights of indigenous communities and celebrated their hitherto unacknowledged cultural traditions, extended beyond the written word. It was equally devoted to the recuperation of indigenous musical traditions and its instruments and songs. Outstanding in this respect among writers was the work of José María **Arguedas**, whose ethnographic activities included the recovery of Andean folklore and music. He returns time and again in his creative writing to the centrality of music as an expression of the historical culture of the *sierra*, particularly in a key chapter of his most important novel *Los* ***ríos profundos*** (Deep Rivers) (1958). Many other novelists and poets have also acknowledged this relationship.

Music would play a central part in the popular theatre movements of the 1930s and later of the 1960s and 1970s across Latin America – Peru's

Cuatro Tablas theatre group and Colombia's La Candelaria may serve as examples of a characteristic register of popular theatre, with their consistent and imaginative use of music and dance. And in the early years of the military dictatorship in Brazil, the portrayal of elemental forces at work in the north east in João Cabral do **Melo Neto**'s ***Morte e vida severina*** (Death and Life of a Severino) (1956) was brought to the stage with musical settings by Chico **Buarque**, to enormous success.

The relationship between literature and popular song is often more direct and explicit. Songs have provided titles for a number of works of literature: Angeles **Mastretta**'s *Arráncame la vida* (Tear Out My Life, translated as Mexican Bolero) (1985), Carlos **Monsiváis**'s *Amor perdido* (Lost Love) (1977) and Severo **Sarduy**'s *De dónde son los cantantes* (Where Do Singers Come From) (1967) are examples. The world of music and musicians has provided both theme and setting for a number of writers. Luis Rafael **Sánchez**, in *La* ***guaracha del Macho Camacho*** (Macho Camacho's Beat) (1976) and *La importancia de llamarse Daniel Santos* (The Importance of Being Called Daniel Santos) (1988), sees the popular culture of his native Puerto Rico as sites of resistance, with language and music as its instruments and expression; he has also written widely on music. Mayra **Santos Febres**'s *Sirena Silena* (2000) tells the tale of a transvestite chanteuse. Guillermo **Cabrera Infante**'s *Tres tristes tigres* (translated as Three Trapped Tigers) (1967) is set in the twilight world of pre-revolutionary Havana shaped by music, cinema and popular culture; his continuing interest in the popular music of Cuba is evidenced by the titles of later volumes of his stories, for example *Delito por bailar el chachachá* (It's a Crime to Dance the Chachacha) (1995) and *Ella cantaba boleros* (She Sang Boleros) (1996). Julio **Cortázar** used music in his writings in a number of ways; in some of his short stories ('Clone', for example) the structure is derived from musical forms. His story 'El perseguidor' (The Persecutor) (from the 1967 collection of the same title) was inspired by the life of jazz musician Charlie Parker; indeed jazz figures frequently in his work as a kind of metaphor for a free and spontaneous existence.

The Cuban novelist Alejo **Carpentier** was the author of a definitive work on Cuban music, *La música en Cuba* (Music in Cuba) (1946), reflecting his lifelong interest in music and dance on which he wrote widely. Several of his novels and books of stories do in fact take their titles from musical works: *El acoso* (The Siege) (1956) which is set during a concert, *Concierto barroco* (Baroque Concert) (1974) and *La consagración de la primavera* (The Rite of Spring) (1978) are examples. The Brazilian *modernistas* also worked across genres, actively encouraging the collaboration of writers, musicians and artists. Mário de **Andrade**, one of its leading lights, was briefly a Professor of Music and Aesthetics at the São Paulo Conservatory and worked with the Ministry of Culture in the early 1930s on the reform of music education. He published a *Pequena história da música* (Short History of Music) in 1942, but a promised larger opus on Brazilian music was never completed. Tropicalia in 1960s and 1970s, while primarily a popular music movement, produced in the work of Chico Buarque and Caetano Veloso among others a new poetic voice in its song lyrics.

The new song movements of the 1960s and after produced a body of song lyrics that were themselves poetic; thus the characteristically metaphorical and allusive songs of Cuban Silvio Rodríguez or the novelist and poet Patricio **Manns** in Chile. The work of many poets was memorably set to music in this period, including poems by Alfonsina **Storni**, Mario **Benedetti**, Pablo **Neruda**, César **Vallejo** and the Nicaraguan Gioconda **Belli**. The poetry of Silvina **Ocampo** was given musical settings by Alberto Ginasterra while in another genre, his opera *Bomarzo* was based on a 1962 novel by Manuel **Mujica Laínez**, who also wrote the libretto. Ricardo **Piglia**'s 1992 novel *La ciudad ausente* (The Absent City) was also adapted for the operatic stage by Gerardo Gandini. The outstanding musician Astor Piazzola collaborated with Jorge Luis **Borges** on a number of recordings of the latter's work. In the Anglophone Caribbean, poetry merged with music and performance to create the **dub poetry** of Louise **Bennett**, Mikey **Smith**, Linton Kwesi Johnson and others.

Further reading

Aparicio, Frances (2002) *Musical Migrations: Transnationalism and Cultural Hybridity in Latin/o America*, New York: Palgrave Macmillan.

Benítez Rojo, A. (1997) 'Significación del ritmo en la estética caribeña', in J. Becerra and L. Fiet. (eds), *Caribe 2000: Definiciones, identidades y culturas regionales y/o nacionales*, Río Piedras, PR: Facultad de Humanidades, Universidad de Puerto Rico, 9–23.
Carpentier, Alejo (2002) *Music in Cuba*, Minneapolis: University of Minnesota Press.
Castro, Donald A. (1991) *Argentine Tango as Social History*, Ceredigion: Edwin Mellen Press.
Collier, S. (1993) *Tango: The Dance, the Song, the Story*, London: Thames & Hudson.
Castillo Zapata, R. (1990) *Fenomenología del bolero*, Caracas: Monte Avila.
Dunn, Christopher (2001) *Brutality Garden: Tropicalia and the Emergence of a Brazilian Counterculture*, Chapel Hill: University of North Carolina Press.
Jackson, Irene (1985) *More Than Drumming: Essays on African and Afro-Latin Music and Musicians*, Westport, CT: Greenwood Press.
Manuel, Peter (1995) *Caribbean Currents: Caribbean Music from Rumba to Reggae*, Philadelphia: Temple University Press.
Mateo, M. (1982) *Del bardo que te canta*, Havana: Editorial Letras Cubanas.
Olsen, Dale A. and Daniel E. Sheehy (2000) *Garland Book of Latin American Music*, New York and London: Garland.
Otero Garabís, J. (2000) *Nacion y ritmo: 'Descargas' desde el Caribe*, Río Piedras, PR: Ediciones Callejón.
Quintero Herencia, A.G. (1998) *Salsa, sabor y control: Sociología de la música tropical*, Mexico City: Siglo XXI.
Steward, Sue (1999) *Música: The Rhythm of Latin America*, London: Thames & Hudson.
Zavala, I.M. (1991) *El bolero: Historia de un amor*, Madrid: Alianza.

MIKE GONZALEZ

Mutabaruka

b. 1952, Kingston, Jamaica

Poet and dub performer

Born Allan Hope, Mutabaruka was raised a Catholic but became a Rastafarian in his teens. By the 1970s he was writing and performing, long before being associated with Mikey **Smith** and Oku Onoura. A *tour de force* on stage, Mutabaruka feeds off audience response, entertaining by his irreverent commentaries, as well as by his poetry. Early works include *Outcry* (1973), *Sun and Moon* (with Faybiene) (1976) and *Mutabaruka: The First Poems (1970–79)* (1980); his later work is mostly recordings, many of which include poetic texts. As with other dub poets (see **dub poetry**), his is a poetry of protest; but it is also introspective, romantic and exhortatory.

Further reading

Morris, M. (1996) 'Mutabaruka', *Critical Quarterly* 38(4): 39–49.

PAT DUNN AND PAMELA MORDECAI

Mutis, Alvaro

b. 1923, Santafé de Bogotá, Colombia

Poet and novelist

As a child, Mutis lived in Belgium but returned frequently to his parents' *hacienda* in Colombia; as a young man he became a lasting friend of Gabriel **García Márquez**. His childhood experiences are reflected extensively in his work. Mutis's fictional characters, especially those of European descent, suffer regular identity crises and have a desperate view of the world in which they live. Among the most representative of his works are his poem *Un bel morir* (A Beautiful Death) (1989) and his novel *Maqroll el gaviero* (Maqroll the Lookout). In 1997 Mutis was awarded the Premio de Príncipe de Asturias literary prize. Since 1956, he has lived in Mexico.

Further reading

Caistor, N. (1997) 'Alvaro Mutis', in V. Smith (ed.), *Encyclopedia of Latin American Literature*, London: Fitzroy Dearborn, 571–2.
Canfield, M.L. (2002) 'La poética de Alvaro Mutis', *Cuadernos hispanoamericanos* 619: 35–42.

Mutis, A. (1985) *Obra literaria: Poesía (1947–1985)*, Bogotá: Procultura.

—— (1985) *Obra literaria: Prosas*, Bogotá: Procultura.

Mutis, S. (ed.) (2000) *Alvaro Mutis: De lecturas y algo del mundo (1943–1997)*, Barcelona: Seix Barral.

Palencia-Roth, M. (2002) 'Alvaro Mutis', in C. Solé and K. Müller-Bergh (eds), *Latin American Writers: Supplement I*, New York: Scribners, 363–80.

MIGUEL A. CARDINALE

N

Nadaísmo

More than a literary movement, Nadaísmo began as an irreverent gesture directed against Colombia's most traditional institutions – Catholicism and grammar. Its members came from the middle and lower-middle classes; they were young and shared literary and artistic concerns. The group gathered in Medellín around Gonzalo Arango, signatory of the first *Manifiesto Nadaísta* in 1958, the inspiration for which undoubtedly was the avant-garde iconoclasts of the early part of the century – although in Colombia they had been notable by their absence. Poets formed the core of the group (Arango himself, Jaime Jaramillo Escobar, Eduardo Escobar, Jotamario Arbeláez, Elmo Valencia, Darío Lemos, Amílcar Osorio), although some of them also wrote short stories and novels; the group also embraced the visual arts (Pedro Alcántara) and film (Diego León Giraldo). But all of them shared a prosaic intention, colloquial speech and humour. In the mid-sixties Arango withdrew from the group to concentrate on political activity; other Nadaísta survivors continue to write and work in the same way.

Futher reading

Galeano, Juan Carlos (1993) 'El Nadaísmo y "La Violencia" en Colombia', *Revista iberoamericana*, July–Dec., LIX(164–5): 645–58.

Jaramillo Agudelo, Dario (1984) 'La poesía nadaísta', *Revista iberoamericana*, July–Dec., L(128–9): 757–98.

O'Hara, Edgar (1993) 'Nadaísmo, bibliografia reciente', *Boletín cultural y bibliografico*, XXX(33): 3–42.

Romero, Armando (1988) *El Nadaìsmo o la búsqueda de una vanguardia perdita*, Bogotá: Tercer Mundo.

Valencia Goelkel, Hernando (1965) 'El triunfo del Nadaísmo', *Eco* XI, 3, 63 (July): 292–305.

OSCAR ALBERTO TORRES DUQUE

Naipaul, Seepersad

b. 1906, Longdenville, Caroni, Trinidad; d. 1953, Port-of-Spain, Trinidad

Journalist and novelist

Seepersad Naipaul is best known as the father of V.S. **Naipaul** and the fictional model for the eponymous hero of latter's ***A House for Mr Biswas*** (1961). Although of the pundit caste, he began life as a sign-painter. In 1929 he became a reporter on the *Trinidad Guardian*. In 1943 he published locally *The Adventures of Gurudeva*, short stories which, as V.S. Naipaul noted, provide 'a unique record of the Indian or Hindu community in Trinidad in the first half of the twentieth century', pioneering creative writing in the area.

Further reading

Firth, K. (1989) 'Seepersad Naipaul's Short Fiction: The Reductive World of Trinidad's First Generation East Indians', in J. Bardolph (ed.), *Short*

Fiction in the New Literatures in English, Nice: Fac. des Lettres & Sciences Humaines.

LOUIS JAMES

Naipaul, Shiva

b. 1945, Port-of-Spain, Trinidad; d. 1985, London, England

Writer

While still in his twenties, Naipaul won several literary prizes for *Fireflies* (1971), his first novel. In some of the most beautiful writing of his generation, Naipaul exposed the dishonesty and corruption he saw in political and religious leaders in works such as *Black and White* (1980), which analyses the mass suicide of the Jim Jones community in Guyana. *Fireflies* and the later novel *A Hot Country* (1983) address themes of exile and alienation. An outstanding short story writer, as the collection *Beyond the Dragon's Mouth* (1984) clearly shows, he suffered in part from unfair comparisons with his brother V.S. **Naipaul**.

Further reading

Maja Pearce, A. (1985) 'The Naipauls on Africa: An African View', *Journal of Commonwealth Literature* 20(1): 111–17.

Racker, D. (1995) 'Shiva Naipaul: Fragmented Traces as Material for Fictive Stereotypes', *West Virginia University Philological Papers* 40: 50–5.

KEITH JARDIM

Naipaul, V.S. (Vidiadhar Surajprasad)

b. 1932, Chaguanas, Trinidad

Writer

Although Naipaul's first novels were criticized as imitative of English literary models, they were innovative works initiating a highly individual strand of West Indian writing. The grandson of a Brahmin immigrant from the Punjab, and son of Seepersad **Naipaul**, a journalist and writer, Vidia found the intellectual world of Trinidad stifling. He won a scholarship to read English Literature at Oxford and vowed not to return to Trinidad. Subsequently, freelancing for the BBC, recollections of his Trinidad childhood prompted the short stories collected in his first work (although it was his third work to be published), *Miguel Street* (1959), portraying a gallery of idiosyncratic characters in a poor area of Port-of-Spain through the affectionate humour of a growing boy.

The Mystic Masseur (1957) and *The Suffrage of Elvira* (1959) turned a satirical eye on his home island as it emerged into independence. The first work charts the rise of Ganesh Ramsumair from a village masseur with assumed magical power to 'G. Ramsay Muir', eminent politician, by playing on popular superstition. The second is a hilarious account of a village election manipulated by bribes, colour prejudice and rural gullibility. These and *The Middle Passage* (1961), a mordant account of a Caribbean tour, aroused hostile reactions in the West Indies. In the same year, however, he published *A* ***House for Mr Biswas*** (1961). Drawing on a thinly fictionalized account of his father's life, and charting two generations of an East Indian family, Naipaul created a tragicomic saga in which the eponymous hero surmounts poverty, exploitation and ill luck to achieve a precarious independence and self-respect. It remains his most sympathetic novel.

This work was followed by *Mr Stone and the Knight's Companion* (1963), the short stories of *A Flag on the Island* (1967) and his major novel, *The Mimic Men* (1967). Moving between England and an imaginary Caribbean island called Isabella, Ralph Kripalsingh rises from island real estate to political power in the newly democratic island state. Within its interwoven stories and themes, Naipaul portrays the 'mimic' futility of West Indian society.

With the three novellas of *In a Free State* (1971), Naipaul looked outwards to Africa, the USA and Latin America. He also increasingly explored the interface between journalism and fiction. *Guerillas* (1979) was based on an actual rape and murder by revolutionaries that he had reported in an article. *A Bend in the River* (1979) paralleled *A Congo Diary* (1980), telling of an East Indian shopkeeper attempting to survive in a thinly disguised Zaire. Published seven years later, *The* ***Enigma of***

Arrival (1987) appeared to signal a retreat from narrative fiction. *A Way in the World* (1994) interwove Columbus's historical voyage to the Caribbean, revolutionary movements in Cuba and East Africa and personal memories to further explore the interrelationship of factual and imaginative truth.

Naipaul's many honours include the Trinity Cross from Trinidad (1989) and an English knighthood (1990). In 2001 he won the Nobel Prize for Literature.

Further reading

Hamner, R.D. (1973) *V. S. Naipaul*, Boston: Twayne.

—— (ed.) (1977) *Critical Perspectives on V. S. Naipaul*, Washington: Three Continents Press.

Mustafa, F. (1995) *V.S. Naipaul*, Cambridge: Cambridge University Press.

Theroux, P. (1972) *V. S. Naipaul: An Introduction to his Work*, London: Heinemann.

White, L. (1975) *V. S. Naipaul: A Critical Introduction*, London: Macmillan.

LOUIS JAMES

Najlis, Michele

b. 1946, Granada, Nicaragua

Poet

A Sandinista militant during the Somoza regime, Najlis published her first book of political poetry, *El viento armado* (The Armed Wind), in 1969. It was followed by the poetry and fiction of *Augurios* (1980), the satirical, feminist short prose of *Ars combinatoria* (1989), and the collected journalism chronicling the Sandinista years of *Caminos de la estrella polar* (Roads to the Pole Star) (1990). Najlis's later poetry is a spiritual exploration of an individual deeply marked by the secular world, a Jewish poet who works in a profoundly Christian environment.

Further reading

Cohen, H. (1993) 'Juego, luego existo: Najlis' ars combinatoria,' *Hispanic Journal*, Fall, 14(2): 69–81.

Kaminsky, A. (1995) 'The Poet after the Revolution: Intertextuality and Defiance in Michele Najlis's *Cantos de Ifigenia*', *Latin American Literary Review*, July–Dec., 23(46): 48–65.

AMY KAMINSKY

Nalé Roxlo, Conrado

b. 1898, Buenos Aires, Argentina; d. 1971, Buenos Aires

Writer

Nalé Roxlo's eclectic writings are a unique fusion of poetry and humour. He was first recognized in 1923 for his poem *El grillo* (The Cricket); later for his contributions to the satirical literary magazine ***Martín Fierro*** and humorous sketches and articles signed 'Chamico' and 'Alguien' (Someone). Nalé Roxlo also contributed to the activities of the Teatro Independiente in Buenos Aires with such plays as the much-praised 1941 *La cola de la sirena* (The Mermaid's Tail).

Further reading

Calvetti, J. (1998) 'Conrado Nalé Roxlo', *Boletín de la Academia Argetina de Letras* 63(249–50): 345–55.

Nalé Roxlo, C. (1970) *Antología apócrifa*, ed. and intro. M.L. Lacau, Buenos Aires: Kapelusz.

Ruíz Díaz, A. (1981) 'Como recuerdo a Nalé Roxlo', *Boletín de la Academia Argentina de Letras* 46(179–82): 153–63.

Tull, J.F., Jr (1967) 'El teatro breve de Nalé Roxlo', *Duquesne Hispanic Review* 6(1): 37–40.

FERNANDA A. ZULLO

Narain, Harry

b. 1950, Essequibo, British Guiana

Writer

Narain's reputation as a writer of short stories is based on a single volume of stories, *Grass-Root People*, published in 1981 by the Cuban **Casa de las Américas** publishing house. Its thirteen stories portray the harsh everyday life of rural Guyana, capturing the creole dialect. Raised on a rice farm, Narain became a school teacher but returned to the farm in 1978. The first story of the collection is in the form of a letter to the 'Comrade Prime Minister' from 'Rice Farmer', describing the powerlessness of the small Indo-Guyanese farmer caught between senseless government policies and the wealthy landowners, and is a barely veiled criticism of the autocratic government of Forbes Burnham. The ironic title of the volume suggests that the socialist propaganda of the Marxist government is at odds with its treatment of the 'grass-root people'.

CAROL J. WALLACE

Naranjo, Carmen

b. 1930, Cartago, Costa Rica

Writer

Costa Rica's most important contemporary novelist, Naranjo is also recognized for her poetry and essays. Her first book was *Canción de la ternura* (Song of Tenderness) (1964). *Diario de una multitud* (Diary of a Crowd) (1974) brought her international fame. Other important titles are: *Los perros no ladraron* (The Dogs Didn't Bark) (1966) and *Ondina* (1983), a collection of short stories dealing with gender representation, homosexual and heterosexual love, and power. She has been Costa Rican ambassador to Israel and director of EDUCA.

Further reading

Helmuth, C. (1996) 'Carmen Naranjo', *Hispamérica* 25(74): 47–56.

Martínez, L.I. (1987) *Carmen Naranjo y la narrativa femenina en Costa Rica*, San José: EDUCA.

Vallejos Ramírez, M.A. (1994) 'Un día en la vida de Carmen Naranjo', *Tropos* 20: 71–7.

NICASIO URBINA

Nassar, Raduan

b. 1935, Pindorama, São Paulo, Brazil

Writer

Nassar is regarded as one of Brazil's most important contemporary writers, despite having published only three short volumes: *Lavoura arcaica* (Archaic Ploughing) (1975), *Um copo de cólera* (A Glass of Rage) (1978) and his story *Menina a caminho* (A Girl on the Road), published privately in 1994. The brief but intense novel *Um copo de cólera* narrates the breakdown and reconciliation of a married couple; the title refers to the enraged conversations of the protagonists. It offers a microcosm of the rural society of the interior of São Paulo province.

Further reading

Pellegrini, T. (1997) 'Raduan Nassar: Masculino e Feminino, Contemporâneo', *Brasil/Brazil* 17: 9–26.

MILTON HATOUM

nation language

Nation language is an emergent Caribbean creole blending European, African and other languages, developed after European conquest and the destruction of Amerindian cultures and languages. According to Edward Kamau **Brathwaite**, who coined the term, nation language derives from the submerged language used by slaves to inform the English imposed upon the Caribbean psyche. Its lexicon may be based in English, but its contours, rhythms and timbres are closely related to the African aspects of the Caribbean experience. Brathwaite comments that it is 'inconceivable' for any Caribbean author writing in English today to not be influenced by this 'submerged/emergent' linguistic structure.

Further reading

Foster, C.Y.W. (1999) 'Motives to Speak Jamaican Patwah: A Rhetorical Analysis of National Identity through the Use of Nation Language', *Dissertation-Abstracts-International,-Section-A:-The-Humanities-and-Social-Sciences*, May; 60(11): 3844 DAI No.: DA9951144, Degree Granting Institution: University of Miami.

GAY WILENTZ

Nazoa, Aquiles

b. 1920, Caracas, Venezuela; d. 1976, Caracas

Writer and journalist

Born to a very poor family, at age 12 Nazoa began working to help support his family. He worked at many different occupations: carpenter, phone operator and clerk. As a packer for the newspaper *El Universal* he learned typography and proof-reading. In 1945 his book *El transeúnte sonreído* (The Smiling Passerby) inaugurated his literary talent. He frequently collaborated in journals such as *Élite*, *Fantoche* and *El Morrocoy Azul*. In 1948 he was awarded the National Prize for Journalism and two years later his book *Marcos Manure* was made into a feature film. Most of his work was collected in *Humor y amor* (Humor and Love) (1970). In 1967 he was awarded the Municipal Prize for Literature. His prose reflects the values and beliefs of the lower popular classes. He died in a car accident.

Further reading

Blanco Sánchez, B. (1989) *Visión parcial de Aquiles Nazoa*, Caracas: Imprenta Nacional.

Nazoa, A. (1978) *Obras completas*, Caracas: Universidad Central de Venezuela.

Subero, E. (1962) *La obra poética de Nazoa*, Caracas: Tipografía Vargas.

VÍCTOR GALARRAGA OROPEZA

negrismo

Negrismo is a Latin American movement that developed, mainly in poetry, between 1926 and 1940. Its purpose, in parallel to ***indigenismo***, was to recuperate the roots and traditions of countries with a large black population in order to redefine their national identity. Europe at the time was calling into question the hierarchical vision of a rational Western 'civilization' and a more intuitive and sensual 'primitive world'. In the arts, this questioning was reflected in avant-garde (see **avant-garde in Latin America**) movements and in a renewed search for identity.

Negrismo was not only racial; its concerns were also social, which is why it included white, mulatto and mestizo as well as black poets. In this sense it was quite different from its equivalents in the USA and West Indies (the Harlem Renaissance for example) or the French West Indies and some parts of Africa, which produced ***négritude***. The starting point for the movement were the early works of Nicolás **Guillén**, *Motivos de son* (Son Motifs) (1930) and *Sóngoro cosongo* (1931).

The main features of the poetry of *negrismo* were, at the thematic level, the re-evaluation of black (North and South) American customs and traditions, describing their rhythmic dances and their sensuality, the effect of music and drumming in producing religious ecstasy, and their integration into a tropical landscape not unlike that of Africa. But it was also concerned with protesting the exploitation and oppression to which peoples were subject, which they did by describing the daily life of the poorest sections of society.

These historical and socio-political issues were expressed through images that were highly original in their sensuality and synaesthesia, like the fusion of fruits, colours, textures, tastes, scents, climate, vegetation, the parts of the human body and the forms and sounds of musical instruments, all of them specific to Latin America. The rhythms, although they were basically the traditional metres of Spanish poetry, integrated the percussive elements of Afro-American music. The accents of traditional Castilian verse were modified to recreate the mulatto forms of popular music – son, rumba, guaguancó and others. Repetitition – of words, sounds, lines, accents – was a common device, as was the use of words of African origin and of nonsense words or *jitanjáforas* which onomatopetically reproduced the sounds of musical instruments while also alluding to religious rituals.

The protest extended from local issues to embrace the exploited throughout the world, and the opposition black/white was transformed into a unity of black and white. Many *negrista* poems have become part of the body of popular song, losing their author together with the solemnity which often accompanies poetry. Its chief exponents include Guillén, Emilio Ballagas, Luis **Palés Matos**, Ildefonso **Pereda Valdés** and Nicomedes Santa Cruz.

Further reading

González, J.L. and M. Mansóur (1976) *Poesía negra de América (antología general)*, Mexico City: Era.
Mansóur, M. (1973) *La poesía negrista*, Mexico: Era.

MONICA MANSÓUR

négritude

An international cultural and intellectual movement begun in Paris in the 1930s by scholars from French-speaking Africa and the Caribbean, in broadest terms, the idea of *négritude* rested on the notion that people of African descent, in Africa and throughout the world, possessed a shared cultural heritage. The movement acknowledged and criticized the fact that people of European descent either ignored, misunderstood or denigrated that unique heritage. The movement's founders argued that blacks themselves should embrace, promote and disseminate their culture. These leaders also linked the embrace of their African heritage with political and economic goals such as ending colonialism and racial discrimination, and securing opportunities for success and prosperity for black populations, especially in Africa and the Caribbean. The movement also criticized mulattoes (and blacks) of the middle and upper classes who rejected their common heritage with the black masses and embraced only European or Western culture.

However, as an artistic and social movement *négritude* by no means rejected all things European. On the contrary, the founders were significantly influenced by European thinkers and European ideas, most notably surrealism and communism. The three main founders were Aimé **Césaire** of Martinique, Léon **Damas** of French Guiana (Guyane) and Leopold Senghor of Senegal. Most scholars cite the beginning of the movement as the publication of *Légitime défense* by a group of students from Martinique, in Paris in 1932. This polemical essay criticized the Western capitalist world and the inferior place which that world assigned to non-white cultures. The founders of *négritude* took direct inspiration from this text. Other important publications included the *négritude* journal *L'etudiant noir* (The Black Scholar), published in Paris, and the magazine *Tropiques*, published by Césaire in Martinique. Of all the voluminous literary works associated with the *négritude* movement, Césaire's epic poem, ***Cahier d'un retour au pays natal*** (Notes on a Return to the Homeland), published in 1939, is probably the most famous. It was in this poem that the term '*négritude*' first appeared in print.

Although the height of the movement arguably occurred around the mid-twentieth century, its ideas continued to influence scholars and artists many decades later. Indeed, Lilyan Kesteloot, one of the foremost historians of the movement, even refers to different 'generations' of *négritude* writers. It is also important to note that some of the ideas expressed by *négritude* had appeared in the work of some black Francophone writers even before the 1930s. This is particularly true in the case of Haiti, with publications such as the *Revue indigene* and the work of scholar Jean **Price-Mars**. *Négritude* also shared common theories with the US Harlem Renaissance. In fact, some *négritude* scholars and artists communicated with writers of that North American movement.

Further reading

Jones, E. (1971) *Voices of Negritude: The Expression of Black Experience in the Poetry of Senghor, Césaire and Damas*, Valley Forge: Hudson.
Kesteloot, Lilyan (1991) *Black Writers in French: A Literary History of Negritude*, trans. Ellen Conroy Kennedy, Cambridge: Harvard University Press; first edition, 1968.
Ménil, R. (1981) *Tracées: Identité, négritude, esthétique aux Antilles*, Paris: Robert Laffont.

ROSANNE ADDERLEY

neo-baroque

Neo-baroque (*neobarroco*) is a term used particularly with regard to the Cuban writers José **Lezama Lima** and Severo **Sarduy**, both of whom were fascinated by the baroque of the Spanish Golden Age and of colonial Spanish America. Beginning with his long poem 'Muerte de Narciso' (Death of Narcissus) (1937), Lezama sought to outdo the difficult seventeenth-century poet Luis de Góngora in density of allusion, tormented syntax and verbal obscurity. Sarduy, in his essay 'Barroco' (Baroque) (1974), studied the connections between the scientific revolution and the baroque. Another Cuban writer who showed an interest in the baroque was Alejo **Carpentier**, particularly in *Concierto barroco* (Baroque concerto) (1974). Néstor **Perlongher**, the Argentine poet, proposed to import the Caribbean neo-baroque to the River Plate region, and in honour of the muddy colour of that river-estuary proclaimed his adherence to the 'neobarroso' (neo-muddy). An anthology of neo-baroque poetry, featuring both the *neobarroco* and the *neobarroso*, is *Medusario* (Medusaur) (1996), edited by Roberto Echavarren, José Kozer and Jacobo Sefamí.

Further reading

Echavarren, Roberto, José Kozer and Jacobo Sefamí (eds) (1996) *Medusario: Muestra de poesiá latinoamericana*, Mexico City: Fondo de Cultura Económica.

DANIEL BALDERSTON

Neruda, Pablo

b. 1904, Temuco, Chile; d. 1973, Isla Negra, Chile

Poet

The embodiment of the poet as a public figure, Neruda (born Neftalí Reyes) is probably Latin America's best-known and most widely read poet – and one who has repeatedly found new audiences, the last a posthumous one rediscovering his writing through the international success of the film, *Il postino*, based on Antonio **Skármeta**'s novel, *Ardiente paciencia* (Burning Patience) (1985).

Enormously prolific, Neruda's poetry embraces the most public forms and the most intimate of lyrics. His earliest work, however, was still deeply concerned with landscape – most famously in the *Veinte poemas de amor y una canción desesperada* (Twenty Love Poems and a Desperate Song) (1924) where the sexual encounter is also a journey into a landscape. Born the son of a railway worker, Neruda entered Chile's diplomatic service and in 1925 was sent to the Far East. His work over the next ten years was collected in the first two (of three) volumes of *Residencia en la tierra* (Residence on Earth). These poems are in stark contrast to his later work – private, intense and above all absorbed with the solitude of the poet in a world constantly on the verge of destruction. The poem, 'Walking Around', is testimony to this crisis. A transfer to Barcelona in 1933 and, particularly, to Madrid in 1935 brought Neruda to a crossroads – aesthetic as well as political. It was impossible in the conflictive atmosphere of the Spanish Republic on the edge of Civil War to deny politics – Neruda, after all, was a regular companion of García Lorca, Rafael Alberti, Luis Buñuel and others at this time – or the public responsibility of artists. The outbreak of the Civil War on 18 July 1936 produced an artistic decision that marked the rest of Neruda's life – the determination to assume the responsibilities of a public poet, to set experience and emotion in the context of history. 'Explico algunas cosas' (I Explain a Few Things) is almost a personal manifesto in these terms – 'You will ask/ what happened to the lilies . . . . Come and see the blood in the streets'. The years that followed were a period of intense political activity that largely shaped his poetry of the time, like *España en el corazón* (Spain in My Heart) (1937) and the writings gathered in *Tercera residencia* (1947). Contingent, sometimes pamphleteering writings, they are products of the moment and rarely survive it; after all, these were moments of vigorous campaigning for the Chilean Popular Front (1938) and a time as consul in Mexico, one of whose more inglorious moments was Neruda's provision of diplomatic papers for the Muralist Siqueiros after the latter's attempt on the life of Leon Trotsky.

Neruda joined the Communist Party officially in 1945, although he had for some years functioned as a close fellow traveller; elected a senator in the same year, the 1947 *ley maldita* (evil law) banning the Party forced him (like many others) into hiding. It was during that period (1947–49) that Neruda wrote his great ***Canto general*** (General Song) (1950), a sweeping panorama of Latin America's history, geography and contemporary reality whose direction is set out in the first five cantos of the first section. Here Neruda embarks upon a 'rediscovery' of the continent, a renaming of its many parts and a rewriting of Latin America's history from the perspective of the nameless 'Juans' (John Stonecutter, John Railsplitter) whose labour forged both Indian and Spanish America. In that sense the 'song' of the title is an epic, a foundational narrative for a post-colonial Latin America.

From the sometimes rhetorical flavour and linguistic richness of the *Canto general* Neruda moved to a very different tone and language: the *Odas elementales* (Elementary Odes), published in three volumes from 1951 to 1957, addressed the simpler aspects of the daily life of ordinary people – 'Old socks', 'Tomato', 'Onions' – in which beauty and poetic power were also to be found. These were hugely popular in the public readings that Neruda offered in factories and stadia around Chile. But these were also the years of the tender love poetry of *Los versos del capitán* (The Captain's Verses), privately published in 1952.

Neruda continued to write prolifically and in a range of moods – as his confidently titled 1962 volume, *Plenos poderes* (Fully Empowered), suggested. By now he was a prominent political figure as well as a major poet. In the run up to the 1970 elections he was nominated as the Communist Party's presidential candidate, although he withdrew when his party joined the Unidad Popular coalition that supported the successful candidacy of Salvador Allende. Briefly Chilean ambassador to France, Neruda spent the last years of his life at Isla Negra, his home on the Pacific coast southwest of Santiago. The award of the Nobel Prize in 1971 produced a famous acceptance speech and the phrase that would haunt his final hours – 'we must wait with a burning patience'. He died a few weeks after the military *coup* that overthrew the Popular Unity government. Fearful that his funeral would provide an opportunity for protest demonstrations the government of Pinochet attempted to prevent his burial in Santiago. But they failed in the attempt, and it seemed fitting that the only public demonstration permitted by the military for many years should have been the funeral of this poet who had always tried to speak with the voice of the people.

Further reading

de Costa, R. (1979) *The Poetry of Pablo Neruda*, Cambridge, MA: Harvard University Press.

Duran, M. and M. Safir (1981) *Earth Tones: The Poetry of Pablo Neruda*, Bloomington: Indiana University Press.

Felstiner, J. (1980) *Translating Neruda: The Way to Macchu Picchu*, Stanford, CA: Stanford University Press.

Rodríguez Monegal, E. (1966) *El viajero inmóvil*, Buenos Aires: Losada.

Neruda, P. (1974) *Five Decades: Poems*, trans. Ben Bellitt and Alastair Reid, New York: Grove Press.

—— (1977) *Memoirs*, trans. H. St. Martin, New York: Farrar, Straus.

—— (1999–2002) *Obras completas*, ed. H. Loyola, Barcelona: Círculo de Lectores, 5 vols.

Santí, E.M. (1982) *Pablo Neruda: The Poetics of Prophecy*, Ithaca: Cornell University Press.

Teitelboim, V. (1991) *Neruda: An Intimate Biography*, trans. Beverley J. deLong-Tonelli, Austin: University of Texas Press.

MIKE GONZALEZ

Nervo, Amado

b. 1870, Tepic, Nayarit, Mexico; d. 1919, Montevideo, Uruguay

Poet and novelist

Nervo was a literary celebrity of his time, editor of the *Revista moderna*, one of the most important journals of **Spanish American modernism**. Upon his unexpected death in Montevideo, his body was accompanied back to Mexico by ships from Argentina, Uruguay, Cuba and the USA, and his funeral in Mexico City was an occasion for mass mourning. Nervo's poems expressed his spiritual quests and the conflict between religious and carnal concerns; some of his later poems reveal his fascination with Eastern religions. He also published several novels, one of which, *Juana de Asbaje* (1910), concerned the life of the famous

Mexican poet and nun Sor Juana Inés de la Cruz (1651–95).

Further reading

Dauster, F. (1989) 'Amado Nervo', in C.A. Solé and M.I. Abreu (eds), *Latin American Writers*, New York: Scribners, 1, 425–9.

Durán, M. (1968) *Genio y figura de Amado Nervo*, Buenos Aires: EUDEBA.

Molloy, S. (2003) 'Sentimental Excess and Gender Disruption: The Case of Amado Nervo', in R.K. Irwin, E.J. McCaughan and M. Rocío Nasser (eds), *The Famous 41: Sexuality and Social Control in Mexico, 1901*, New York: Palgrave Macmillan, 291–306.

Nervo, A. (1962) *Obras completas*, ed. F. González Guerrero and A. Méndez Plancarte, Madrid: Aguilar.

Reyes, A. (1937) *Tránsito de Amado Nervo*, Santiago: Ercilla.

DANIEL BALDERSTON

Neto, Torquato

b. 1944, Teresina, Piauí, Brazil; d. 1972, São Paulo, Brazil

Poet and lyricist

Anguished poet of the Brazilian counterculture, Torquato Neto (full name Torquato Pereira de Araújo Neto) became a cult figure following his suicide at a young age. After coming to Salvador in the early 1960s, he became acquainted with Caetano Veloso and Gilberto Gil, whom he later joined in São Paulo. He wrote the lyrics to several Tropicalista songs including 'Geléia Geral' (General Jelly), 'Marginália II' and 'Domingou' (Sunday). Shortly before his death he played the vampire in Ivan Cardoso's underground film '*Nosferatu no Brasil*'. An excellent collection of his work is *Os últimos dias de Paupéria* (The Last Days of Poverty) (1973).

Further reading

Branco, J. (1975) 'Torquato: O Afinador dos Tristes', *Minas Gerais, suplemento literario* 14 June: 3.

CHRISTOPHER DUNN

Nichols, Grace

b. 1950, Georgetown, British Guiana

Teacher, journalist, novelist and poet

In both her poetry and fiction, Nichols focuses on women characters in an attempt to acknowledge the contribution of women, especially Caribbean women, to human civilization and the struggle for survival. Her long poem *I is a long memoried woman* (1983) won the Commonwealth Poetry Prize, has been adapted for film, and inspired a full-length radio drama on BBC. She has also published a semi-autobiographical novel, *Whole of a Morning Sky* (1986). A primary school teacher and journalist, she travelled extensively in the hinterland of Guyana before emigrating to England in 1977.

Further reading

Nichols, G. (1990) 'The Battle with Language', in S.R. Cudjoe (ed.), *Caribbean Women Writers: Essays from the First International Conference*, Wellesley: Calaloux, distributed by the University of Massachusetts Press.

FUNSO AIYEJINA

noche de los asesinos, La

La noche de los asesinos (The Criminals) is a two-act play written in 1964 by José **Triana** and awarded the 1965 **Casa de las Américas** prize. The play presents three characters who exchange roles and attitudes while acting out an imaginary ritual of parricide. The single set is transformed into various locations, metaphors for the many contradictions within each individual. The piece enacts the tragedy of a purification through death that is also a liberating exorcism. The characters relive their family conflicts and rebel against their tyrannical parents. This complex and profound cry for freedom has found an echo across the world, having been staged in more than thirty countries.

Further reading

Campa, R.V. de la (1979) *José Triana: Ritualización de la sociedad cubana*, Minneapolis: Institute for the Study of Ideologies and Literature.

Neglia, E.G. (1980) 'El asedio a la casa: Un estudio del decorado en *La noche de los asesinos*', *Revista iberoamericana* 110–11: 139–52.

Triana, J. (1971) 'The Criminals', in G. Woodyard (ed.), *The Modern Stages in Latin America: Six Plays*, New York: Dutton.

WILFREDO CANCIO ISLA

noche de Tlatelolco, La

Elena **Poniatowska**'s third book, a classic of Latin American testimonial literature (see ***testimonio***), was published in Spanish in 1971, and Helen R. Lane's English translation appeared in 1975 and was reprinted in 1992. It is the definitive literary treatment of the Mexican student movement of 1968 and its brutal repression by the Mexican government in the Plaza of Three Cultures, or Tlatelolco, in Mexico City. On 2 October 1968, the Mexican army surrounded a peaceful meeting with tanks, ambushing the unarmed participants, killing some 300 and wounding countless others. Subsequently they attempted to cover up their actions, burning bodies and accusing the students of having instigated the assault. This all occurred immediately before the Olympic Games were scheduled to open in the Mexican capital; the presence of international reporters helped to disseminate news of the massacre. Nevertheless, Secretary of State Luis Echeverría, who gave the order to open fire, became Mexico's next president.

At the time Poniatowska was a journalist and housewife with progressive sympathies but no history of political activism. After survivors of Tlatelolco came to her with their stories, Poniatowska's literary and political trajectory changed dramatically. Since then, she has adopted a passionately committed stance and addressed controversial issues in her work, including urban guerrillas, disappeared political prisoners, indigenous and feminist activists, victims of substandard housing and government corruption in the 1985 earthquake, the international brigades in the Spanish Civil War, etc.

Massacre in Mexico consists of a chorus of voices, ranging from students to soldiers to nurses, to the students' families, conveying the euphoria, anti-authoritarianism and democratic impetus of the mass mobilizations, as well as the bitter sense of betrayal and disillusionment following 2 October. Of particular poignancy are the testimonies of anguished mothers searching in vain for their children's bodies and finding, in their place, piles of bloody shoes. These descriptions anticipate the oral histories of the Madres de Plaza de Mayo in Argentina, and mothers of disappeared political prisoners in Chile and Central America during the 1970s and 1980s.

After Tlatelolco, leaders of the student movement were imprisoned, then exiled from Mexico. In recent years, as the tenth, twentieth and thirtieth anniversaries of the movement have approached, a number of important literary works and political analyses have appeared, as well as Jorge Fons's film. *Rojo amanecer* (Red Dawn) (1989), which draws heavily on dialogue from *Massacre in Mexico*, In 1998, in the midst of another, more prolonged student strike, the journalist and former student leader Luis **González de Alba**, author of the testimonial novel *Los días y los años* (The Days and the Years) (1971) and one of Poniatowska's key informants for her own book, publicly accused Poniatowska of plagiarism. This ignited a debate about the responsibilities of the testimonial writer, one that could not have occurred three decades earlier, when the genre was in its infancy.

Further reading

Campos, M.A. and A. Toledo (ed.) (1996) *Poemas y narraciones sobre el movimiento estudiantil de 1968*, Mexico City: Universidad Nacional Autónoma de Mexico.

Jorgensen, B. (1994) *The Writing of Elena Poniatowska*, Austin: University of Texas Press.

Poniatowska, E. (1975) *Massacre in Mexico*, trans. H. Lane. New York: Viking Press.
Schaefer, C. (1992) *Textured Lives: Women, Art, and Representation in Mexico*, Tucson: University of Arizona Press.

CYNTHIA STEELE

Nogueras, Luis Rogelio

b. 1945, Havana, Cuba; d. 1986, Havana

Poet and novelist

One of a group of young writers linked to the journal, *El caimán barbudo*, Nogueras's first volume of poetry, *Cabeza de zanahoria* (Carrot Head) (1967), announced an original and innovative poetic voice whose characteristic was a colloquial language unlike the previous generation of poets of the 1950s and the early years of the Cuban Revolution His subsequent works, including *Imitación de la vida* (Imitation of Life), which won the 1981 **Casa de las Américas** prize, and *Las palabras vuelven* (Words Return) (1994), confirmed his skill and wit, and his often disconcerting poetic allusions. He was a pioneer of **crime fiction** in Cuba: his titles include *Y si muero mañana* (And if I Die Tomorrow) (1977) and *Nosotros los sobrevivientes* (We Survivors) (1983).

Further reading

Padrón Nodarse, F. (1986) 'Un silencio que alguien oyo . . .: Sobre la poesía de Luis Rogelio Nogueras', *Universidad de La Habana* 228: 253–69.
Prada Oropeza, Renato (1987) 'Estructura y significación en *Y si muero mañana*', *Texto crítico* 13(36–7): 68–78.

WILFREDO CANCIO ISLA

Noigandres group

A group of poets based in São Paulo during the 1950s, the Noigandres group included Augusto de **Campos**, Haroldo de **Campos**, Décio **Pignatari** and others. Noigandres is a Provençal word whose meaning had baffled Romance philologists who studied the troubadors. It appears in *The Cantos of Ezra Pound*, where the Brazilian poets (working on a translation of Pound) discovered it. Noting both the scholarly mystery surrounding the word and the prestige of the US poet, they adopted 'noigandres' as an emblem of artistic adventure and made it the title of their own journal of experimental lyric and **concrete poetry** (published 1952–62).

Further reading

Campos, A. de, H. de Campos and D. Pignatari (1975) *Teoria da poesia concreta*, São Paulo: Livraria Duas Cidades.
Campos, H. de (1977) *Ruptura dos gêneros na literatura latinoamericana*, São Paulo: Perspectiva.

CHARLES A. PERRONE

noirisme

Generally seen as a Haitian form of ***négritude***, this late 1930s movement proposed a racialist view of culture and politics. It was provoked by the racial resentment created during the American occupation, and initially inspired by the views on cultural authenticity propounded by Jean **Price-Mars** in his 1928 work *Ainsi parla l'oncle* (So Spoke the Uncle). Its views were promoted in the journal *Les Griots* (1938–40), started by Louis Diaquoi, Lorimer Denis and François Duvalier, and to which the writers Carl **Brouard** and Magloire St Aude were frequent contributors. *Noirisme* was criticized by both Marxists and conservatives, but became the State ideology in 1957 when François Duvalier became president.

J. MICHAEL DASH

Nosotros

Published in Buenos Aires from 1907 to 1943, *Nosotros* was edited by Alfredo Bianchi and Roberto Giusti. It was the most canonical of the influential literary and cultural reviews of the period. Its lasting influence was due in part to the presence of a new reading public concomitant with the rise of the middle classes. It brought together a group of mostly social realist writers and intellectuals associated with the Boedo literary group (see **Boedo vs Florida**). The influence of *Nosotros* was so great that it gave its name to a generation of writers – also called the 'Generación del Centenario' – that grouped together some of the most important writers of the period, such as Manuel **Gálvez**, Evaristo Carriego and Alfonsina **Storni**.

Further reading

Ardissone, E. and N. Salvador (1971) *Bibliografía de la revista Nosotros (1907–1943)*, Buenos Aires: Fondo Nacional de las Artes.

Ulla, N. (ed.) (1969) *La revista Nosotros*, Buenos Aires: Galerna.

FLORENCIA GARRAMUÑO

Novás Calvo, Lino

b. 1905, La Coruña, Spain; d. 1983, Miami, Florida, USA

Writer

Novás Calvo's novel *Pedro Blanco, el negrero* (Peter White, the Slaver) (1933) is an acknowledged precursor of **magical realism**. His two volumes of stories, *La luna nona* (Grandma Moon) (1942) and *Cayo Canas* (1946), include some of the first **crime fiction** written in Cuba. His characters and plots are characteristically violent. Novás Calvo's family emigrated to Cuba when he was seven; as a young writer he joined the **Grupo Minorista**. He was a correspondent in Spain during the Spanish Civil War and editor of the magazine *Bohemia* until he left Cuba in 1960.

Further reading

Gutiérrez de la Solana, A. (1984) 'In memoriam de Lino Novás Calvo', *Círculo* 13: 7–10.

Roses, L.E. (1986) *Voices of the Storyteller: Cuba's Lino Novás Calvo*, New York: Greenwood Press.

Souza, R.D. (1981) *Lino Novás Calvo*, Boston: Twayne.

WILFREDO CANCIO ISLA

novel

The Latin American novel gets a relatively late start in the early nineteenth century, with important romantic works including Jorge Isaacs's *María* (1867) and José Alencar's *Iracema* (1865); Doris Sommer has argued that the novel of this period is centrally concerned with nation formation, though that is sometimes concealed as romance. The finest nineteenth-century novelist was Brazil's Joaquim Maria Machado de Assis (1839–1908), known for such psychological masterpieces as *Dom Casmurro* (1899). An important tradition in the novel from Clorinda Matto de Turner's *Aves sin nido* (Birds without a Nest) (1889) through the works of Alcides **Arguedas**, Jorge **Icaza**, Ciro **Alegría**, Miguel Angel **Asturias**, José María **Arguedas** and Rosario **Castellanos**, was ***indigenismo***, concerned with the representation of the oppressed indigenous population, particularly in the Andes and in Mexico and Guatemala. Another cycle of works was concerned with rural life: Ricardo Güiraldes's *Don Segundo Sombra* (1926) on the life of the gaucho, José Eustacio **Rivera**'s ***La vorágine*** (The Vortex) (1924) and numerous other works, sometimes called the *novela de la tierra* (novel of the earth). Brilliant Brazilian examples of this regionalist (see ***regionalismo***) tendency are Graciliano **Ramos**'s *São Bernardo* (1934) and *Vidas secas* (Barren Lives) (1938), and João Guimarães **Rosa**'s monumental ***Grande sertão: Veredas*** (The Devil to Pay in the Backlands) (1956). The novel of modern urban life begins with Oswald de **Andrade**, Roberto **Arlt** and Juan Carlos **Onetti**. A special case, intensely experimental, oneiric and, at the same time, rooted in the particularities of place, is Juan **Rulfo**'s great novel ***Pedro Páramo*** (1955).

The Latin American novel in the 1960s came into vogue thanks largely to the international success of Julio **Cortázar**'s ***Rayuela*** (Hopscotch) (1963) and, on a much greater scale, Gabriel **García Márquez**'s ***Cien años de soledad*** (One Hundred Years of Solitude) (1967). With José **Donoso**, Carlos **Fuentes** and Mario **Vargas Llosa**, these writers were considered to be part of an international **Boom** in Latin American writing; what they had in common was a taste for (sometimes rather pedestrian) experimentation in fiction. This Boom is generally not considered to include writing in Portuguese and the various languages of the Caribbean, but this period witnessed the emergence of Antonio **Callado**, V.S. **Naipaul**, Edouard **Glissant** and others. The experimental tradition reached its highest point with Augusto **Roa Bastos**'s ***Yo el supremo*** (I the Supreme) (1974), a spectacular monologue (mostly) by José Gaspar Rodríguez de Francia, the dictator who ruled Paraguay from 1814 to 1840.

Subsequent developments have included the novels of Manuel **Puig**, who played brilliantly with the conventions of the serial novel and the romantic film, Juan José **Saer**, known for his intense, knotty constructions, reminiscent of Onetti in their sustained concern with a group of characters and a particular place on the Paraná river, and Clarice **Lispector**, a famous novelist of introspection. Other notable novelists of recent years include Ricardo **Piglia**, Rubem **Fonseca**, Sergio **Pitol**, Roberto **Bolaño**, Cristina **Peri Rossi** and Patrick **Chamoiseau**

Further reading

Alonso, C. (1990) *The Spanish American Regional Novel: Modernity and Autochthony*, Cambridge: Cambridge University Press.

—— (1996) 'The *criollista* novel', in R. Gonzalez Echevarría and E. Pupo-Walker (eds), *The Cambridge History of Latin American Literature*, Cambridge: Cambridge University Press, 2, 195–211.

Fuentes, Carlos (1969) *La nueva novela hispanoamericana*, Mexico City: Joaquín Mortiz.

Lafforgue, Jorge (ed.) (1972, 1974) *Nueva novela latinoamericana*, Buenos Aires: Editorial Paidós, 2 vols.

Martin, Gerald (1989) *Journeys through the Labyrinth: Latin American Fiction in the Twentieth Century*, London: Verso.

Pellón, G. (1996) 'The Spanish American Novel: Recent Developments, 1975 to 1990', in R. Gonzalez Echevarría and E. Pupo-Walker (eds), *The Cambridge History of Latin American Literature*, Cambridge: Cambridge University Press, 2, 279–301.

Pope, R. (1996) 'The Spanish American Novel from 1950 to 1975', in R. Gonzalez Echevarría and E. Pupo-Walker (eds), *The Cambridge History of Latin American Literature* , Cambridge: Cambridge University Press, 2, 226–77.

Sommer, Doris (1991) *Foundational Fictions: The National Romances of Latin America*, Berkeley: University of California Press.

DANIEL BALDERSTON

novel of the Mexican Revolution

It is generally accepted that the Mariano **Azuela** novel *Los de abajo* (The Underdogs), published in 1916 (although first appearing in serial form in 1915), was the first novel of the Mexican Revolution. It was written while the military and political conflicts that followed the overthrow of the dictatorship of Porfirio Díaz in February 1911 were still being fought out. The official end of that process occurred a year after the publication of Azuela's novel, in 1917, with the passage of a new Constitution for Mexico. A new state now existed, replacing the *Porfiriato* and resting on basic principles of national sovereignty and political democracy.

Los de abajo, however, is a novel of deep disillusionment. Azuela had been a follower of Francisco Madero, whose 1910 pamphlet on the presidential succession argued for free elections, universal suffrage and the non-re-election of the Head of State. But while Madero and his followers had aspired to political reform, the fall of Porfirio had unlocked a series of class and regional conflicts which could no longer be repressed: the movement led by Emiliano Zapata represented the demand for land by the peasants and the indigenous communities, for example. The period 1911–17 also witnessed a series of power struggles among political and military leaders. For Azuela, this represented the disintegration of the Revolution into violence and destruction – a process which the novel depicts.

The bulk of novels of the Mexican Revolution, however, were written after the events they narrate. Indeed, collectively they represent the creation of a sort of literature of foundation, an epic account of the struggles that gave birth to the new Mexican state. What Martín Luis **Guzmán**'s *El águila y la serpiente* (The Eagle and the Serpent) (1928), Nellie **Campobello**'s *Cartucho* (1931), Rafael F. Muñoz's *Vámonos con Pancho Villa* (Let's Go With Pancho Villa) and Gregorio López y Fuentes's *Tierra* (Land) (1931) and *Mi General* (The General) (1934) have in common is both their subject matter and their style.

Each of the novels of the Mexican Revolution narrate events and episodes of the military struggle: Muñoz and Guzmán write from the perspective of the armies of Pancho Villa; López y Fuentes about the Zapatista movement. But all share an episodic structure, a terse style which is economic in description and propelled by action, and an objective and amoral narrative standpoint. They function as a series of tableaux in a process whose outcomes and purposes are of less interest than its restless rhythm of change. As literature turned in the late 1930s in Mexico towards an increasingly critical examination of the society brought into being by that Revolution, the moral neutrality of the novel of the Mexican Revolution ceased to be appropriate.

In 1962, in *La muerte de Artemio Cruz* (The Death of Artemio Cruz), Carlos **Fuentes** returned to the founding epic of the Revolution from the perspective of a corrupted revolutionary ideal. It could stand as an epilogue to the *novela de la revolución mexicana*.

Further reading

Castro Leal, A. (1971) *La novela de la revolución Mexicana*, Mexico: Aguilar.

Dessau, Adalbert (1986) *La novela de la revolución mexicana*, Mexico City: Fondo de Cultura Económica.

Rutherford, John (1996) 'The novel of the Mexican Revolution', in R. Gonzalez Echevarria and E. Pupo-Walker (eds), *Cambridge History of Latin American Literature*, Cambridge: Cambridge University Press, 2, 213–25.

Sommers, Joseph (1968) *After the Storm: Landmarks of the Modern Mexican Novel*, Albuquerque: University of New Mexico Press.

MIKE GONZALEZ

Novo, Salvador

b. 1904, Mexico City; d. 1974, Mexico City

Writer

Known for a small body of brilliant poetry and a vast corpus of *crónicas* (see ***crónica***), Novo was one of Mexico's most prominent **intellectuals** of the post-revolutionary period. With Xavier **Villaurrutia**, known from secondary school but who remained a close friend to the end of Villaurrutia's life, and a circle of other friends (Carlos **Pellicer**, Jaime **Torres Bodet**, Jorge Cuesta, Gilberto **Owen** and Bernardo Ortiz de Montellano), Novo published several magazines, including ***Contemporáneos***, which gave the group its name. In association with Villaurrutia, Cuesta, Celestino Gorostiza and Antonieta Rivas Mercado, Novo founded the Teatro Ulises, the beginnings of modern theatre in Mexico City. After a tempestuous period in the civil service, during which time he was persecuted by members of the Estridentista group (see **Estridentismo**) for his fairly public homosexuality, Novo became the unofficial *cronista* (chronicler) of Mexico for several decades, eventually being named official *cronista* of Mexico City.

Novo's poetry explores the themes of love and solitude, expressing homoerotic love without quite declaring it as such. (A collection of sonnets published almost secretly, however, celebrates adventures with policemen, taxi drivers and others.) The most memorable of his slim output of poems are the free-verse poems of *Nuevo amor* (New Love) (1933), of which one of the best known is 'Junto a tu cuerpo totalmente entregado al mío' (Next to Your Body Totally Surrendered to Mine). Novo was also the author of ferocious satirical poetry, most notably 'La Diegada', in which he calls Diego Rivera a 'Búfalo Vil' (Vile Buffalo, pronounced Buffalo Bill).

Novo's prose writings include **travel writing**, essays on literature, photography, boxing, Mexico City, politics and countless other topics, and a scandalous autobiography. *Return Ticket* (1928) is the record of travels in western Mexico (and a reflection on tourism), while *Continente vacío* (Empty Continent) (1935) tells of a trip to South America, which includes an important encounter with

Federico García Lorca in Buenos Aires. *Nueva grandeza mexicana* (New Grandeur of Mexico) (1951) is presented as a gloss on a famous poem about Mexico City by Bernardo de Balbuena (written in 1599). *Las aves en la poesía castellana* (Birds in Spanish Poetry) (1952), written when he was invited to join the Mexican Academy of Letters, is a learned treatise from the time when Novo was fired from the government service. His posthumous autobiography, *La estatua de sal* (The Statue of Salt) (1998), is a memoir of his and Villaurrutia's scandalous youth, with hilarious incidents involving Pedro **Henríquez Ureña** and many others; it could not be published until all of those mentioned were dead, finally appearing with a brilliant preface by Carlos **Monsiváis**, which reflects on the importance of homosexuality for Novo's work.

Novo's *crónicas* have been collected by José Emilio **Pacheco** in three huge volumes, *La vida en México en el período presidencial de Lázaro Cardenas* (Life in Mexico during the Presidential Term of Lázaro Cárdenas) (1964) and similar titles for the terms of Manuel Avila Camacho and Miguel Alemán (1965 and 1967). Another work of interest is *Las locas, el sexo, los burdeles* (Queens, Sex, Brothels) (1972), which begins with the defiant sentence: 'Hubo siempre locas en México' (There were always queens in Mexico).

At the end of his life, Novo was a celebrity who played the role of the dandy to the hilt, and who expressed strong disapproval of the student movement that culminated in the massacre at Tlatelolco in October 1968. In the decades after his death, his importance as a writer has been recognized, and his works have been carefully collected and republished, although his output was so vast that some portions have yet to be brought together. A building he owned in Coyoacán is now the Teatro el Hábito, the premier venue for political theatre in Mexico City, run by Jesusa Rodríguez and Liliana Felipe; as he looks down from a portrait, one imagines his delight that the traditions of political satire and of audacious modern theatre are alive and well.

Further reading

Monsiváis, C. (1977) 'Salvador Novo: Los que tenemos unas manos que no nos pertenecen', in *Amor perdido*, Mexico City: Era. 265–96.

—— (2000) *Salvador Novo: Lo marginal en el centro*, Mexico City: Era.

Novo, S. (1991) *Antología personal: Poesía, 1915–1974*, Mexico City: Consejo Nacional para la Cultura y las Artes.

—— (1996) *Viajes y ensayos*, Mexico City: Fondo de Cultura Económica.

—— (1998) *La estatua de sal*, intro. Carlos Monsiváis, Mexico City: Consejo Nacional para la Cultura y las Artes.

DANIEL BALDERSTON

Nueva revista de filología hispánica

Journal founded in 1947 at the Colegio de México, with the support of Alfonso **Reyes** and Daniel Cosío Villegas. It continued the fruitful work of the original *Revista de filología hispánica*, edited at the Buenos Aires Instituto de Filología by Américo Castro and Amado Alonso, which had made an important contribution to the study of Hispanic languages and literature. Currently edited by Antonio Alatorre, *Nueva revista* maintains its original philological perspective, enriched now by contributions on literary theory and the study of indigenous languages.

Further information

http://www.univ-tlse2.fr/amlat/Sommaires/filologia/nue.htm

RAFAEL OLEA FRANCO

Nuevo texto crítico

Building on the excellent record of *Texto crítico*, Jorge **Ruffinelli**'s move from the Universidad Veracruzana to Stanford University prompted the launch of *Nuevo texto crítico* in 1988. This twice-yearly publication includes an editorial board that grew over the years from a few Stanford colleagues to an international list of notable critics. *Nuevo texto crítico* maintains the initial drive of *Texto* *crítico*; it has incorporated critical discourses and foci of the American academy and interest in feminism, music, film, and Puerto Rican and Chicano literatures. Monograph issues (for example, on Rigoberta Menchú and Rodolfo **Walsh**) and the publication of major symposia frequently replace general issues.

SAÚL SOSNOWSKI

Número

A Uruguayan journal published in two series – 1949–55 and 1963–64 – and acknowledged for its interest in contemporary art and ideas, its cosmopolitanism and its intellectual rigour. The founding group of Emir **Rodríguez Monegal**, Idea **Vilariño** and Manuel Claps was later joined by Mario **Benedetti**. The review published translations of Eliot, Pinter and Queneau among others, as well as unpublished writings by **Borges**, Manuel **Rojas**, **Sábato**, Alfonso **Reyes** and **Bioy Casares**. But it was only the second series that emphasized Latin America, after Carlos **Martínez Moreno** joined the editorial board. Vilariño, meanwhile, resigned over the journal's apolitical stance. There were severe disagreements over Rodríguez Monegal's opposition to the Cuban Revolution; many board members resigned, refusing the takeover offer from the Congress for Cultural Freedom.

NORAH GIRALDI DEI CAS

Núñez, Enrique Bernardo

b. 1895, Valencia, Venezuela; d. 1964, Caracas, Venezuela

Writer

Novelist, journalist and chronicler of Caracas, Núñez is today considered one of the key figures in modern Venezuelan literature and one of the most important innovators in the genre the Venezuelan novel, particularly for his novel *Cubagua* (1931). A graduate in medicine and law from the Universidad Central de Venezuela, he was also a journalist, contributing to *El Nuevo Diario*, *La Esfera*, *El Universal* and *El Nacional* as well as the important avant-garde (see **avant-garde in Latin America**) journals *Billiken*, *Actualidad* and *Elite*. His two novels, *Cubagua* and *Galera de Tiberio* (Tiberius's Galley), address the theme which obsesses him – the mythic and historic roots of memory and time.

Further reading

Araujo, O. (1980) *La obra literaria de Enrique Bernardo Núñez*, Caracas: Monte Avila.

Barradas de Tovar, A. (1976) 'Notas sobre Enrique Bernardo Núñez: Teórico y renovador de la novelística venezolana', *Letras* 32–3: 13–26.

Britto García, L. (1999) 'Enrique Bernardo Núñez: Novelista, filósofo de la historia, utopista', in S.M. Steckbauer (ed.), *La novela latinoamericana entre historia y utopia*, Eichstätt, Germany: Katholische Universitat Eichstätt.

Subero, E. (ed.) (1970) *Contribución a la bibliografía de Enrique Bernardo Núñez*, Caracas: Gobernación del Distrito Federal.

JORGE ROMERO LEÓN

O

Obregón Morales, Roberto

b. 1940, San Antonio Suchitepéquez, Mazatenango, Guatemala; d. 1970, Guatemala, place unknown

Writer

A member of the Generación Comprometida (Committed Generation) and then Nuevo Signo (New Sign), Obregón began writing under the sway of the PGT (Guatemalan Workers' Party) and studied in the Soviet Union. Returning to Guatemala, he wrote poetry which explored his interest in the relations between Guatemalan indigenous traditions and revolutionary ideology. After joining the radical group MR-13 de Noviembre, Obregón was 'disappeared' by Salvadoran soldiers in the Guatemalan–Salvadoran border area on 6 July 1970. Obregón translated his politics into a culturally rich poetic opus, marked, especially in its final stages, by a sense of his imminent death.

Further reading

Morales Santos, F. (1983) *Los nombres que nos nombran: Panorama de la literatura guatemalteca de 1782 a 1982*, Guatemala: Tip. Nacional.

Obregón Morales, R. (1999) *El adiós y el retorno*, Guatemala: Editorial Oscar de León Palacios.

MARC ZIMMERMAN AND LINDA J. CRAFT

obsceno pájaro de la noche, El

One of the key works of the **Boom**, José **Donoso**'s great novel, *El obsceno pájaro de la noche* (Obscene Bird of Night), published in 1970, takes its title from a strange letter from Henry James Sr to his sons, William (the philosopher) and Henry (the novelist), which proclaims that 'life is no farce' and that the 'natural inheritance of everyone who is capable of spiritual life is an unsubdued forest where the wolf howls and the obscene bird of night chatters'. The sprawling novel is primarily set in a decaying old mansion in central Santiago, Chile, now inhabited by strange nuns and the hidden progeny of patrician families. An aesthetic of deformation takes the monstrous as its norm, an operation completed by the novel's shifting narrators, who speak from the perspective of the monstrous, the androgynous and the eccentric.

Further reading

Magnarelli, S. (1977) '*El obsceno pájaro de la noche*: Fiction: Monsters and Packages', *Hispanic Review* 45: 413–19.

Martínez, N. (1980) '*El obsceno pájaro de la noche*: La productividad del texto', *Revista iberoamericana* 110–11: 51–65.

Pujals, J.A. (1981) *El bosque indomado donde chilla el obsceno pájaro de la noche: Un estudio sobre la novela de José Donoso*, Miami: Universal.

Swanson, P. (1990) 'José Donoso: *El obsceno pájaro de*

la noche', in *Landmarks in Modern Latin American Fiction*, London: Routledge.

DANIEL BALDERSTON

Ocampo, Silvina

b. 1903, Buenos Aires, Argentina;
d. 1993, Buenos Aires

Writer

One of Argentina's most exciting and disturbing writers, Ocampo has been overshadowed by her more famous sister, Victoria **Ocampo**, and her husband, Adolfo **Bioy Casares**. Thus her work has not received the exposure and critical acclaim that it deserves.

The youngest of six daughters, she was originally a painter, influenced by de Chirico who was her teacher in Paris. Together with Bioy Casares and **Borges**, Ocampo edited an anthology of fantastic literature (***Antología de la literatura fantástica***) (1940), which played a determining role in the subsequent direction of Argentine literature. Ocampo's work consists mainly of poetry and short stories. Unlike the more abstract intellectual fictions of Borges and Bioy, Ocampo's stories focus on the everyday reality of middle-class life, although disconcertingly without the reassurance of a predictable moral or causal framework. The hallmark of her narrative is its acceptance of the bizarre and the inexplicable as constitutive elements of a reality in which love and revenge, evil and innocence, coexist naturally. Many of her stories provocatively blur accepted categories, overturning the hierarchies of power. With a hint of sadism, servants, seamstresses and the elderly relish revenge, as in 'Las esclavas de las criadas' (The Slaves of the Maids) (1959), though their motivation is often love for someone they feel has been wronged. Her 'cruel stories' do not represent children as innocent but rather as the naïve yet unconcerned, unreflecting agents of malevolence and spite. In stories such as 'La boda' (The Wedding), 'Las fotografías' (The Photographs) and 'La casa de los relojes' (The Clock House), the innocent language and unencumbered naïvety of the child narrator contrast starkly with the horrendous events that are being told. Her stories illustrate the tensions between the complex amoral reality of childhood and its mythification in a moral discourse.

Ocampo's humour ranged from gentle to the most extreme black humour. She was a pioneer who broke the traditional moulds of writing about everyday reality.

Further reading

Balderston, D. (1997) 'Silvina Ocampo', in V. Smith (ed.), *Encyclopedia of Latin American Literature*, London: Fitzroy Dearborn, 593–4.

Klingenberg, P. (1999) *Fantasies of the Feminine: The Short Stories of Silvina Ocampo*, Lewisburg, PA: Bucknell University Press.

Mangin, A. (1996) *Temps et écriture dans l'oeuvre narrative de Silvina Ocampo*, Toulouse: Presses Universitaires du Mirail.

Ocampo, S. (1982) *La furia y otros cuentos*, Madrid: Alianza.

—— (1988) *Leopoldina's Dream*, trans. D. Balderston, Toronto: Penguin Books.

—— (1991) *Las reglas del secreto*, ed. M. Sánchez, Buenos Aires: Fondo de Cultura Económica.

Tomassini, G. (1995) *El espejo de Cornelia: La obra cuentística de Silvina Ocampo*, Buenos Aires: Editorial Plus Ultra.

Ulla, N. (1982) *Encuentros con Silvina Ocampo*, Buenos Aires: Editorial de Belgrano.

EVELYN FISHBURN

Ocampo, Victoria

b. 1890, Buenos Aires, Argentina;
d. 1979, Buenos Aires

Writer and essayist

Ocampo was famous as a woman intellectual, as a patron of arts and culture, and as founder of the magazine ***Sur***. Born into an influential elite family, she was educated informally but rigorously by a series of French and English governesses. Her first language was French, and she often translated her own writing into Spanish. Her marriage in 1912 to Luis B. Estrada was a disaster; her lasting and intense relationship with Julián Martínez, however, remained secret, a sign of her continuing respect for social and family conventions. In 1930, she founded, edited and financed the journal *Sur*, which she envisaged as an intellectual bridge between two worlds that she identified with equally: Europe and Latin America. The journal continued for forty years and played a crucial role, particularly in its early years, in Latin American intellectual circles. Its contributors included **Borges**, **Bioy Casares**, Silvina **Ocampo**, Eduardo **Mallea**, Hector A. **Murena**, Ernesto **Sábato** and other Argentine intellectuals, collectively known as the *Sur* Group.

Active as a translator, Ocampo maintained friendships with musicians, philosophers and writers in Europe and North America whom she included in her cultural project, publishing their works under the *Sur* imprint which she founded in 1933. Between 1935 and 1951 she published four volumes of her *Testimonios*, which included autobiographical notes, travel diaries etc., and *El viajero y una de sus sombras* (The Traveller and One of His Shadows) (1951) and *Lawrence de Arabia y otros ensayos* (Lawrence of Arabia and Other Essays) (1951).

In the early 1950s she was awarded the Medal of Honour of the Argentine Society of Writers in recognition of her defence of traditional liberal values like freedom of thought. She was briefly imprisoned as a result of her opposition to Perón's government. These events confirmed Ocampo's and her group's place as the 'moral alternative' to the successive Peronist governments. She completed her *Autobiografía* in 1953, but it remained unpublished until her death; it was later published between 1979 and 1984 in six volumes and reprinted several times, providing access to the most interesting part of her career as a writer. Six more volumes of her *Testimonios* appeared between 1954 and 1977 as well as *Virgina Woolf en su diario* (Virginia Woolf in Her Diaries) (1954), *Juan Sebastian Bach el hombre* (Bach the Man) (1964), *La bella y sus enamorados* (Beauty and her Lovers) (1964) and *Diálogos* (1969) with Borges and Mallea. In 1977, two years before her death, she was inducted into the Argentine Academy of Letters.

Further reading

Arambel Guiñazu, M.C. (1995) ' "Babel" and *De Francesca a Beatrice*: Two Founding Essays by Victoria Ocampo', in D. Meyer (ed.), *Reinterpreting the Spanish American Essay: Women Writers of the 19th and 20th Centuries*, Austin: University of Texas Press, 125–34.

Bastos, M.L. (1989) 'Victoria Ocampo', in C.A. Solé and M.I. Abreu (eds), *Latin American Writers*, New York: Scribners, 2, 705–10.

Iglesia, C. (1996) *Islas de la memoria (sobre la Autobiografía de Victoria Ocampo)*, Buenos Aires: Cuenca del Plata.

King, J. (1997) 'Victoria Ocampo', in V. Smith (ed.), *Encyclopedia of Latin American Literature*, London: Fitzroy Dearborn, 595–6.

Ocampo, V. (1979) *Against Wind and Tide*, ed. and trans. with intro. D. Meyer, New York: G. Braziller.

Steiner, P.O. (1999) *Victoria Ocampo: Writer, Feminist, Woman of the World*, Albuquerque: University of New Mexico Press.

Vázquez, M.E. (1991) *Victoria Ocampo*, Buenos Aires: Planeta.

CRISTINA IGLESIA

Odio, Eunice

b. 1922, San José, Costa Rica; d. 1974, Mexico City

Poet

Odio's independent personality, talent and beauty made life in San José very difficult. After her first publications in Costa Rica, she moved north to Nicaragua and Guatemala, finally establishing herself in Mexico City, where she published most of her works and became friends with Yolanda **Oreamuno**. Her poems are difficult and hermetic, full of passion and beauty. She published six books of poetry, among them *Los elementos terrestres* (Terrestrial Elements) (1948), *Zona en territorio del alba* (Zone in the Dawn Territory) (1953) and *Tránsito de fuego* (Passage of Fire) (1957).

Further reading

Naranjo, C. *et al.* (1978) *Five Women Writers of Costa*

Rica: Short Stories, Beaumont: Asociación de Literatura Femenina Hispánica.
Odio, E. (1996) *Obras Completas*, San José: Editorial de la Universidad de Costa Rica.
Vallbona, R. (ed.) (2001) *La palabra inumerable: Eunice odio ante la crítica*, San José: Universidad de Costa Rica – Instituto Literario y Cultural Hispánico.

NICASIO URBINA

O'Donnell, Mario 'Pacho'

b. 1941, Buenos Aires, Argentina

Writer

A Lacanian psychoanalyst, O'Donnell produced several novels (including *Copsi* (1973)), volumes of short stories (*La seducción de la hija del portero* (The Seduction of the Doorman's Daughter) (1975)) and historical essays. His play *Lobo ... estás?* (Wolf ... Are You Ready?) (1982) was performed at the Teatro Abierto. In 1983 O'Donnell was Secretary of Culture of Buenos Aires, under the Unión Cívica Radical government. Under Menem's Peronist government he was a cultural attaché in Spain, and ambassador to Panama and Bolivia, and for a time National Minister of Culture.

Further reading

Magnarelli, S. (1986) 'Art and Audience in Pacho O'Donnell's *Vincent y los cuervos*', *Latin American Theatre Review* 19(2): 45–55.

FERNANDO RABOSSI

Olea, Raquel

b. 1944, Santiago, Chile

Critic

Olea was President of the Corporación para el Desarrollo de la Mujer (Women's Development Corporation) at La **Morada** and an important critic and literary theorist specializing in women's writing. She writes for the journals *El Canelo* and the ***Revista de crítica cultural*** as well as the newspaper *La Epoca*. Co-editor of *La palabra cómplice: Encuentro con Gabriela Mistral* (The Word as Accomplice: Encounters with Gabriela Mistral) (1990), she has also published a theoretical work on 1980s Chilean women writers entitled *Lengua de víbora* (Viper's Tongue).

Further reading

Olea, Raquel (1997) *Una palabra cómplice: Encuentro con Gabriela Mistral*, Santiago: Corporación de Desarrollo de la Mujer La Morada, Editorial Cuarto Propio.
—— (1998) *Lengua víbora: Producciones de lo femenino en la escritura de mujeres chilenas*, Santiago: Corporación de Desarrollo de la Mujer La Morada, Editorial Cuarto Propio.
—— (2000) *Escrituras de la diferencia sexual*, Santiago: LOM Ediciones/La Morada.

ELIANA ORTEGA

Oliver, María Rosa

b. 1900, Buenos Aires, Argentina; d. 1977, Buenos Aires

Writer

Oliver's memoirs are her most significant work. They include *Mundo, mi casa* (World, My House) (1965), *La vida cotidiana* (Everyday Life) (1969) and *Mi fe es el hombre* (My Faith is Man) (1981, posthumous). This trilogy portrays Argentina's cultural evolution throughout the century. Born into a traditional elite family, her public life was devoted to writing and social activism, despite being handicapped due to polio. Her political activities were focused on the women's movement and antifascist activism. She served as cultural adviser to the Roosevelt administration in the USA from 1942–44. She contributed frequently to the literary journal ***Sur***.

Further reading

Oliver, M. (1939) *Geografía argentina*, Buenos Aires: Editorial Sudamericana.
—— (1969) *La vida cotidiana*, Buenos Aires: Editorial Sudamericana.

—— (1965) *Mundo, mi casa; recuerdos de infancia*, Buenos Aires: Falbo Librero Editor.
González, E. (1997) ' "La tertulia de los viernes": Dos miradas, un espacio (Maria Rosa Oliver y Fernández Moreno)', *Segundas Jornadas Internacionales de Literatura Argentina*, Buenos Aires: Universidad de Buenos Aires.

ALVARO FERNÁNDEZ-BRAVO

Oliver Labra, Carilda

b. 1922, Matanzas, Cuba

Poet

Since her first book, *Preludio lírico* (Lyric Prelude) (1943), Oliver Labra has been a well-known poet in Cuba. *Al sur de mi garganta* (At the South of My Throat) (1950) won the National Poetry Prize, and explored the topics for which her poetry would become renowned – love and eroticism. Other themes appeared later, including patriotism, exemplified by 'Canto a la Bandera' (Song to the Flag) (1950) and *Canto a Martí* (Song to **Marti**) (1953); family (divided because of exile); and aspects of daily life in her home town, where she has always lived and hosted literary gatherings for decades. Her work was highly praised by Nobel Prize winners Gabriela **Mistral** and Pablo **Neruda**. Oliver Labra's other works include *Memoria de la fiebre* (Feverish Memory) (1958), *Desaparece el polvo* (Dust Disappears) (1984) (also available in English translation) and *Se me ha perdido un hombre* (I Have Lost a Man) (1992).

Further reading

Fernández Olmos, M. (1995–96) 'El erotismo revolucionario de las poetas cubanas', *Explicación de textos literarios* 24(1–2).
González Castro, V. (1997) *Cinco noches con Carilda*, Havana: Editorial Letras Cubanas.

ALFREDO ALONSO ESTENOZ

Olmos, Carlos

b. 1947, Chiapas, Mexico

Playwright

Olmos was the first Mexican dramatist to make gay themes a central part of his works (see **gay male literature** and **lesbian literature**). His enormously successful *El eclipse* (The Eclipse) (1990) used the apocalyptic overtones of beliefs about the eclipse to confront bourgeois morality regarding (homo)sexuality. *El dandy del hotel Savoy* (1989) has Oscar Wilde as its central figure. In these, and the earlier *El presente perfecto* (Present Perfect) (1982), Olmos exemplifies a growing postmodern identity politics in Mexico regarding same-sex desire and its challenge to the monolithic social and moral values that the culture of the Mexican Revolution, with its authoritarian *machismo* and idealized masculinism, sought to enforce.

Further reading

Olmos, C. (1983) *Teatro*, Xalapa: Universidad Veracruzana.
—— (1994) *Final de viernes: Teatro*, Tuxtla Gutiérrez: Universidad Autónoma de Chiapas.
Rosas Lopategui, P. (1994) 'La exploración onírica en Lenguas muertas de Carlos Olmos', *Latin American Theatre Review* 27(2): 85–101.

DAVID WILLIAM FOSTER

Olympio, José

b. 1902, Batatais, Brazil; d. 1990, Rio de Janeiro, Brazil

Publisher

One of Brazil's most influential and important publishers, Olympio 'discovered' many of Brazil's best-known writers. Age 15 he was employed by Casa Garraux, a book importing company in São Paulo. In the late 1920s he moved to Rio where, in 1930, he bought the 10,000-volume library of the deceased academic Alfredo Pujol. This became the stock of the José Olympio Bookshop, founded the following year. He began to publish writers such as José Lins do **Rego**, Guimarães **Rosa**, Graciliano **Ramos** and Jorge **Amado**. In all, he launched 608 Brazilian writers and published 25 million volumes.

Further information

www.joseolympio.com.br/

ANTONIO CARLOS VAZ

Omeros

Derek **Walcott**'s justifiably celebrated epic poem *Omeros* is titled by the Greek name for Homer. Walcott denies imitating the *Iliad* or the *Odyssey*. *Omeros* is his attempt to hear the names of people in their own context. Nevertheless, he uses names adapted from Greek myth for three major characters, Achille (Achilles), Hector and Helen, as well as including more minor Greek references. Walcott's graceful denial seems itself something of poetic licence, since he admits that the poem is written in a roughly hexametrical line with a terza rima form, borrowing from both Homer and Dante. But he clearly does not want critics to spend inordinate amounts of time trying to discover links with Homer when the intention of the poem is to depict St Lucia (the 'Helen' of the Caribbean).

Omeros is the blind, aged poet-seer who tells the tale; Achille is a fisherman, Hector a taxi driver and Helen a gorgeously attractive and entirely self-absorbed siren and feisty waitress. There are two ex-colonial British characters, the retired Major Plunkett and his wife Maud. In hurricane season, when he cannot often fish, Achille's friend Philoctete finds him 'landwork' on Plunkett's pig farm. The poem is divided into chapters, like a verse novel, and like a novel or a Homeric epic, works as much through character and story as through metaphor, line and rhythm. As a cultural symbol, *Omeros* establishes, just as Walcott's early plays did, that poor people in the Caribbean lead lives which can be considered heroic. Some of the poem is written in dialogue, like Walcott's early plays; it connects directly with the oral tradition in both English and French creole. In the Caribbean the poem, especially as musical performance, is much more popular than the novel. Walcott's epic is in fact a marvellous conversation between Caribbean ancestries which provokes a deeper understanding of the region's creative refiguring of Europe, Africa, Amerindian and other ethnic traditions.

Further reading

Bear, W. (ed.) (1996) *Conversations with Derek Walcott*, Jackson, MI: University Press of Mississippi.

Figueroa, J. (1995) '*Omeros*', in S. Brown (ed.), *The Art of Derek Walcott*, Bridgend: Seren Books.

Zoppi, I. (1999) 'Omeros, Derek Walcott and the Contemporary Epic Poem', *Callaloo* 22(2): 509–28.

ELAINE SAVORY

Onda, La

La Onda was a trend in Mexican narrative during the 1960s and 1970s initiated by José **Agustín** and Gustavo **Sainz**. In 1971, Mexican critic Margo **Glantz** associated this trend with the slang term *onda*, roughly translated as 'on the same wavelength' or 'in the groove'. Written by the generation that suffered the tragic Tlatelolco massacre of 1968, these works recounted the coming of age of middle-class male adolescents in Mexico City while rock-and-roll, recreational drugs and the sexual revolution were changing social mores. A self-conscious narrative style, it relied upon contemporary slang and debunked the solemn tone often associated with literary writing.

Further reading

Bruce Novoa, J. (1986) 'La Onda as Parody and Satire', in June C.D. Carter and Donald L. Schmid (eds), *José Agustín: Onda and Beyond*, Columbia: University of Missouri Press.

Carter, J.C.D. and D.L. Schmidt (eds) (1986) *José Agustín Onda and Beyond*, Columbia: University of Missouri Press.

Glantz, M. (1971) *Onda y escritura en México: Jóvenes de 20 a 33*, Mexico City: UNAM.

Gunia, I. (1994) '*¿Cuál es la onda?*': *La literatura de la* *contracultura juvenil en el México de los años sesenta y setenta*, Madrid: Iberoamericana.

Sánchez, A. (2001) 'Deserted Cities: Pop and Disenchantment in Turn-of-the-Century Latin American Narrative', in Edmundo Páz-Soldan and Debra Castillo (eds), *Latin American Literature and Mass Media*, New York: Garland.

DANNY J. ANDERSON

Onetti, Juan Carlos

b. 1908, Montevideo, Uruguay; d. 1994, Madrid, Spain

Writer

Uruguay's most important novelist, Onetti is known as the creator of an imaginary town, Santa María, and of the characters who inhabited it, in a series of novels and short stories published from 1950 to 1993. The first Uruguayan novelist to explore urban spaces, from his earliest works he broke with the rural or nativist tradition that dominated the literary scene. A master of the short story, he also wrote countless literary essays under a variety of pseudonyms. His work has had a strong impact throughout Spanish America and in Spain, where he lived for most of the last two decades of his life.

Onetti's first novella, *El pozo* (The Well) (1939), explored the anguish and alienation that would later be associated with **existentialism**. His highly experimental novel, *Tierra de nadie* (No Man's Land) (1941), relied on an unusual technique that he would develop more fully later, one of referring to characters obliquely by their physical characteristics and clothing, which makes the reader work hard to figure out who is who, but gives an odd satisfaction when one figures out how to recognize them. Other major works of the first period of Onetti's writing are the beautiful and tantalizing short story, 'Un sueño realizado' (A Dream Come True) (1941), the haunting 'Esbjerg, en la costa' (Esbjerg on the Sea) (1946) and 'La casa en la arena' (The House in the Sand) (1949).

The decisive moment in Onetti's writing comes in 1950 with the publication of *La **vida breve*** (A Brief Life). A frustrated writer, Brausen, invents a town, and later visits it; the characters who inhabit it include Larsen, among whose business ventures are Santa María's first brothel, and a not very successful doctor, Díaz Grey. In later works, Brausen becomes a shadow, invoked in formulas that in the world outside the text usually have to do with God, and a bronze statue of him with the inscription 'Brausen – Founder' graces the town square. Díaz Grey and Larsen return in a whole series of other novels of which the most famous are *El **astillero*** (The Shipyard) (1961) and *Juntacadáveres* (Corpse-Gatherer) (1964). Onetti makes a series of attempts to put an end to the saga of Santa María, most notably in *Dejemos hablar al viento* (Let the Wind Speak) (1979), but his characters continued to inhabit him to the end. His widow, Dorothea Muhr, relates that near the end he told her he could feel the characters circling the bed, in a sort of vigil; among his papers is a brief note from Larsen with affectionate greetings.

Onetti's innovations in the field of the short story and the novella were significant. In 'El infierno tan temido' (Hell Most Feared) (1957) he constructs a terrible story of failed love and revenge around a series of pornographic photographs that a reporter's estranged wife poses in and sends him, finally driving him to suicide. *Los adioses* (Goodbyes) (1954) is carefully constructed around the concealed identity of several of its central characters (the narrator not the least among them); in a response to one of his critics, Onetti invokes Henry James's *The Turn of the Screw*, and indeed the reader may experience a similar feeling of bafflement as the novella comes to an end. *Para una tumba sin nombre* (Toward a Nameless Grave) (1959) tells the strange story of two young men from Santa María who encounter a woman they know, now a beggar, who uses an old goat as a prop outside a Buenos Aires railroad. 'La cara de la desgracia' (The Face of Misfortune) (1960) is another masterpiece, the story of a self-absorbed man who encounters a young girl on a bicycle and confesses his troubles to her in a long speech that perhaps she never hears; the story ends with her battered body, and with the narrator suspected of her murder, although the reader cannot know anything for certain.

Onetti's literary hero, to whom he dedicated several essays, was William Faulkner, whose imaginary county in Mississippi has a great deal to do with the imaginary town on the River Plate. Other favourite writers included Louis Ferdinand Céline and Knut Hamsun. Somewhat aloof from such contemporaries as Felisberto **Hernández** (to whom he devoted an essay in which he called him a naïve writer) and **Borges** (even though Onetti's full name was Juan Carlos Onetti Borges), Onetti felt a greater kinship with Roberto **Arlt**.

Onetti lived for many years in Buenos Aires, where he worked in advertising (as he recalls in *La vida breve*, in which he appears briefly as a character). He returned to Uruguay in the 1960s, and there lived through the most tragic moment of his life in 1974. A member of a committee (others included Jorge Ruffinelli and Mercedes **Rein**) that awarded the journal *Marcha*'s literary prize to a story that the military government considered subversive, Onetti was imprisoned; when his health broke, he was confined to a mental hospital. Upon his release months later, his fourth wife Dolly took him to Spain, where he spent the rest of his life in bed (he was already given to reading, writing and living in bed in prior years, as in the filmed interview from 1973 made by Julio Jaimes and Jorge Ruffinelli). In 1978, he was awarded Spain's top literary prize, the Cervantes Prize; at that time, he chose to become a Spanish citizen.

Onetti's great importance as a novelist was widely recognized by the writers of the **Boom**, although he was older than they and suspicious of their fondness for publicity. The two great Uruguayan critics Emir **Rodríguez Monegal** and Angel **Rama** both tried to claim Onetti as their own; some years later it is clear that he was his own man. A powerful influence on numerous writers, his voice is sometimes mimicked by Ricardo **Piglia**, while Juan José **Saer**'s project of recreating the Zona of Santa Fe, Argentina, is an homage to the master.

Onetti's world is inhabited by failed, embittered men who live for their dreams and fantasies, many of which revolve around young, rather androgynous girls (as in the case of 'La cara de la desgracia'). *Los adioses* consists entirely of the interwoven fantasies of several of the characters, fantasies that focus on the former basketball player and his young daughter – or lover – or both. Even his last novel, *Cuando ya no importe* (When it Doesn't Matter Anymore) (1993), is focused on loss and fantasy. Onetti is one of Latin America's foremost writers, a bracing, often disturbing, always powerful voice.

Further reading

Ludmer, J. (1977) *Onetti: Los procesos de construcción del relato*, Buenos Aires: Sudamericana.

Millington, M. (1985) *Reading Onetti*, Liverpool: Francis Cairns.

Onetti, J.C. (1970) *Obras completas*, Madrid: Aguilar.

—— (1990) *Goodbyes and Stories*, trans. D. Balderston. Austin: University of Texas Press.

—— (1994) *Cuentos completos*, Madrid: Alfaguara.

Ruffinelli, J. (1997) 'Juan Carlos Onetti', in V. Smith (ed.), *Encyclopedia of Latin American Literature*, London: Fitzroy Dearborn, 596–8.

San Román, G. (ed.) (1999) *Onetti and Others*, Albany: State University of New York Press.

Verani, H.J. (1989) 'Juan Carlos Onetti', in C.A. Solé and M.I. Abreu (eds), *Latin American Writers*, New York: Scribners, 3, 1089–97.

DANIEL BALDERSTON

Onís, Federico De

b. 1885, Salamanca, Spain; d. 1966, Hato Rey, Puerto Rico

Critic

A noted literary critic and professor, Onís founded the Department of Hispanic Studies of the University of Puerto Rico, as well as the *Revista de estudios hispánicos* (1928). His teaching had a considerable influence on a generation of intellectuals, and he gained popular acclaim through a series of television lectures broadcast by WIPR-TV. Influenced in his early studies by Spain's 'Generation of '98', much of his critical work dealt with the work of noted Spanish writers such as Unamuno and Benavente. Onís joined the Spanish Department of Columbia University in 1916, remaining until 1954. In 1920, he founded the Hispanic Institute of the United States and became a leading force in introducing Hispanic literatures to US academia. After the fall of the Spanish Republic in 1939, Onís provided refuge for Spanish exiles and refused to return to Spain, although he travelled widely throughout the Hispanic world. His publications include *España en América* (Spain in America) (1955), and *Antología de la poesía española e hispanoamericana, 1882–1932* (Anthology of Spanish and Spanish American poetry) (1961).

Further reading

Alonso, A. (ed.) (1936) *Antología de ensayos españoles; notes and vocabulary by Antonio Alonso ... with a critical introduction by Federico de Onís*, Boston: DC Heath & Co.

Garcia Morales, A. (1998) 'Federico de Onís y el concepto de modernismo: Una revisión', *Revista iberoamericana* 64(184–5): 485–506.

Onís, F. (1961) *Antología de la poesía española e hispanoamericana, 1882–1932*, New York: Las Americas Pub. Co.

CAROL J. WALLACE

Oreamuno, Yolanda

b. 1916, San José, Costa Rica; d. 1956, Mexico City

Writer

An important feminist novelist, her novel *La ruta de su evasión* (The Route of Her Evasion) (1948) depicts the life of a woman subjected to domestic violence and patriarchal society. It preceded the feminist revolution, yet presented a clear vision of the social inequalities of women's life. Difficulties living in Costa Rica led her to emigrate to Guatemala and later to Mexico City, where her friendship with Eunice **Odio** began. Her first novel, *Por tierra firme* (On Solid Ground) (1940), won the 1940 Farrar and Reinhart award.

Further reading

Gold, J. (1990) 'Feminine Space and the Discourse of Silence', in Noël Valis and Carol Maier (ed.), *In the Feminine Mode: Essays on Hispanic Women Writers*, Lewisburg, PA: Bucknell University Press.

—— (1995) 'Yolanda Oreamuno: The Art of Passionate Engagement', in D. Meyer (ed.), *Reinterpreting the Spanish American Essay: Women Writers of the 19th and 20th Centuries*, Austin: University of Texas Press, 157–66.

Naranjo, C. *et al.* (1978) *Five Women Writers of Costa Rica: Short Stories*, Beaumont: Asociación de Literatura Femenina Hispánica.

Urbano, V. *et al.* (1978) 'Word Magic of the Costa Rican Writer, Yolanda Oreamuno', *Folio: Papers on Foreign Languages and Literature* 11: 149–58.

NICASIO URBINA

Oribe, Emilio

b. 1893, Melo, Uruguay; d. 1975, Montevideo, Uruguay

Writer

A poet at first, Oribe's *Poética y plástica* (Poetry and the Plastic Arts) (1930) explored the relationship between philosophy and poetry. In his subsequent work – *Teoría del Nous* (Theory of Nous) (1934), *El mito y el logos* (Myth and Logos) (1945) and *La dinámica del verbo* (Dynamics of the Word) (1953) – he developed a method in which philosophy was subordinate to lyrical expression. In other essays he approached the cultural problems of Uruguay and Latin America from a spiritualist perspective, which brought him close, in some senses, to the ideas of José Enrique **Rodó** and Carlos Vaz Ferreira.

Further reading

Albistur, J. (1992) 'Emilio Oribe, o la hoguera hecha estatua', *Revista iberoamericana* 58(160–1): 1001–13.

Crispo Acosta, O. (1963) 'Sobre la última manera del estilo de Emilio Oribe', *Revista nacional* 8: 103–5.

Oribe, E. (1953) *La contemplación de lo eterno; poemas*, Montevideo: Cuadernos nous.

—— (1944) *El pensamiento vivo de Rodó*, Buenos Aires: Editorial Losada.

CELINA MANZONI

Orígenes

The Cuban journal *Orígenes* was published by José Rodríguez Feo from 1944 to 1954 and edited by José **Lezama Lima**, the most important Cuban writer of the twentieth century. Because of the cultural and historical presence of the journal, its name distinguishes a group of Cuban writers known as the Orígenistas, including Cintio **Vitier**, Eliseo **Diego**, Fina **García Marruz** and others. *Orígenes* attempted, in the words of Cintio Vitier, to explore the particularities of '*lo cubano*' by making no concessions to 1940s debates on nationalism or cosmopolitanism, politics or aesthetics. *Orígenes* was deeply conservative but profoundly contemporary and open to all artistic currents. Rodríguez Feo's subsequent journal *Ciclón* was very critical of *Orígenes*.

Further reading

Cabanillas, J. (1995) 'La revista *Orígenes*: Cuba y el tema de la insularidad', in Carmen de Mora (ed.), *Diversidad sociocultural en la literatura hispanoamericana*, Sevilla: Universidad de Sevilla.

García Vega, L. (1987) *Los años de Orígenes*, Caracas: Monte Avila.

Ponte, A.J. (2002) *El libro perdido de los Origenistas*, Mexico City: Editorial Aldus.

Riccio, A. (1983) 'La revista *Orígenes* y otras revistas lezamianas', *Annali Istituto Universitario Orientale* 25(1): 343–90.

JOSÉ QUIROGA

Orozco, Olga

b. 1920, Toay, La Pampa, Argentina;
d. 1999, Buenos Aires, Argentina

Writer

Orozco shares the surrealist vision of the poets of the Generation of 1940, but unlike them her poetry deals with elements and themes drawn from religion, astrology, magic, alchemy and the Tarot. Among her important books are *Las muertes* (The Deaths) (1951), *Museo salvaje* (Wild Museum) (1974), *La noche a la deriva* (Drifting Night) (1984), *En el revés del cielo* (The Other Side of Heaven) (1987) and one collection of stories, *La oscuridad es otro sol* (Darkness is Another Sun) (1967). Her work speaks of death, ageing, anguish and memory; its political resonances have been of great interest to critics and readers.

Further reading

Colombo, S.M. (1983) *Metáfora y cosmovisión en la poesía de Olga Orozco*, Rosario, Argentina: Cuadernos Aletheia.

Grant, C. (1997) 'Olga Orozco', in V. Smith (ed.), *Encyclopedia of Latin American Literature*, London: Fitzroy Dearborn, 602–3.

Lojo, M.R. (1988) *Olga Orozco: La poesía como viaje heroico*, Buenos Aires: América Latina.

Nicholson, M. (2002) 'Olga Orozco', in C. Solé and K. Müller-Bergh (eds), *Latin American Writers: Supplement I*, New York: Scribners, 381–93.

Orozco, O. (1984) *Páginas de Olga Orozco seleccionadas por la autora*, ed. C. Piña, Buenos Aires: Celtia.

Torres de Peralta, E. (1987) *La poética de Olga Orozco: Desdoblamiento de Dios en máscara de todos*, Madrid: Playor.

MAGDALENA GARCÍA PINTO

Orozco Rosales, Efrén

b. 1905, Tulancingo, Hidalgo, Mexico

Playwright, director

Orozco Rosales's main contribution to Mexican performing arts was the 1927 *teatro de masas*, a series of large-scale spectacles that staged epic renderings of turning points in Mexico's history. He wrote around twenty plays for this format, including *Tierra y libertad* (Land and Freedom) and *Estampas de la revolución* (Images of the Revolution). With some 1,000 artists and technicians, he staged *El quinto sol* (The Fifth Sun) and *El sacrificio gladiatorio* (The Gladiatorial Sacrifice) for the inauguration of the UNAM's soccer stadium in the mid-1950s.

Further reading

Orozco, R.E. (1941) *La comisión organizadora del segundo Congreso inter-americano de turismo presenta: El mensajero del sol del prof. Efrén Orozco R., en el estadio nacional el 21 de septiembre de 1941 a las 11.30 hs. En honor a los asistentes a este congreso y al Cuarto panamericano de carreteras*, Mexico City: Talleres gráficos de la nación.

ANTONIO PRIETO-STAMBAUGH

Orphée, Elvira

b. 1924, Tucumán, Argentina

Writer

A prolific writer, Orphée is the author of several novels and collections of short stories. She moved to Buenos Aires when she was a young woman and studied literature at the University of Buenos Aires, and later in Paris. Childhood, a critical view of provincial social mores, rebelliousness and dissatisfaction are some of the recurrent features of Orpheé's fiction. Her 1966 novel *El aire tan suave* (Air So Sweet) has been hailed as a remarkable work. In her 1990 novel *La muerte y los desencuentros* (Death and Conflicts), Orphée revisits the themes explored in her other works, such as death and the impossibility of love.

Further reading

García Pinto, M. (1991) 'Elvira Orphée', in *Women Writers of Latin America. Intimate Histories*, trans. Trudy Balch and M. García Pinto, Austin: University of Texas Press, 145–61.

Garfield, E. (1985) *Women's Voices from Latin America: Interviews with Six Contemporary Authors*, Detroit: Wayne State University Press.

Orphée, E. (1984) *La última conquista de El Angel*, Buenos Aires: J. Vergara.

Slaughter, J. (1996) 'Torture and Commemoration: Narrating Solidarity in Elvira's Orphée's "Las viejas fantasiosas" ', *Tulsa Studies in Women's Literature* 15(2): 241–52.

MAGDALENA GARCÍA PINTO

Ortega, Julio

b. 1942, Chimbote, Peru

Writer and critic

First known as a poet, Ortega published *De este reino* (Of this Kingdom) (1964), *Tiempo de dos* (Time for Two) (1966), *Las viñas del moro* (The Vineyards of the Moor) (1968) and *Rituales* (Rituals) (1976) among others. It was his essays on Latin American literature that won him international recognition however, among them *La contemplación y la fiesta* (Contemplation and Feast) (1968), *Figuración de la persona* (The Person's Figuration) (1971) and *Crítica de la identidad* (Criticism of Identity) (1988). His narrative includes *Mediodía* (Noon) (1970), among others. He currently teaches at Brown University in the USA.

Further reading

Ortega, Julio (1984) *Acto subversivo*, Mexico City: Premiá.

—— (1994) *Ayacucho, Goodbye; Moscow's Gold*, Pittsburgh, PA: Latin American Literary Review Press.

—— (1999) *El combate de los ángeles: Literatura, género, diferencia*, Lima: Pontificia Universidad Católica del Perú.

—— (2000) *Caja de herramientas: Practicas culturales para el nuevo siglo chileno*, Santiago, Chile: LOM Ediciones.

JOSÉ ANTONIO MAZZOTTI

Ortiz, Adalberto

b. 1914, Esmeraldas, Ecuador

Writer and painter

The foremost Afro-Ecuadorian poet, Ortiz's work centres on the world of the black and mulatto in his native Esmeraldas, in north-western Ecuador. His novel *Juyungo* (1943) juxtaposes that historical referent with the lyrical and the magical. *Tierra, son y tambor* (Land, Song and Drums) (1945) collects poems inspired by the music and rhythms of his birthplace. In *El animal herido* (The Wounded

Animal) (1961), his poetry takes an antipoetic turn (see **antipoetry**). His novel *El espejo y la ventana* (The Mirror and the Window) (1967) concerns the existential predicaments of a black man. In Ortiz's paintings, the exuberant nature of his native province translates into brilliant colours, rendered with a 'naïf' technique reminiscent of the Haitian 'primitive painters'.

Further reading

Ortiz, A. (1959) *El animal herido: Antología poética*, Quito: Casa de la Cultura.

Planells, A. (1985) 'Adalberto Ortiz: El hombre y la creación literaria', *Afro-Hispanic Review* 4(2–3): 29–33.

HUMBERTO E. ROBLES

Ortiz, Juan L.

b. 1896, Gualeguay, Entre Ríos, Argentina; d. 1978, Paraná, Entre Ríos

Poet

Spending his life in the provincial solitude of Entre Ríos, far from official centres and institutions, Ortiz's huge body of work remains largely unknown, if not ignored, by high culture. *En el aura del sauce* (In the Willow's Shade) (1971) brings together almost all of his thirteen volumes of poetry, including his first collection, *El agua y la noche* (Water and Night), dated 1933 but written in 1924. His complete works, *Obra completa* (1996), include unpublished poetry and prose writings. His poetry is simple and hermetic, at once a celebration and an elegy; in it, nature becomes a landscape and a sign of his province, yet the page itself becomes a landscape too, an inescapable sign of modernity.

Further reading

Alonso, R. (1978) 'Juan L. Ortiz está vivo', *Texto crítico* 11: 194–7.

Canaparo, C. (1997) 'Juan L. Ortiz', in V. Smith (ed.), *Encyclopedia of Latin American Literature*, London: Fitzroy Dearborn, 605–7.

Ortiz, J. (1996) *Obra completa*, ed. S. Delgado, Santa Fe: Centro de Publicaciones, Universidad Nacional del Litoral.

Rowe, W. (2000) *Poets of Contemporary Latin America: History and the Inner Life*, Oxford: Oxford University Press.

Serra, E. (1976) *El cosmos de la palabra: Mensaje poético y estilo de Juan L. Ortiz*, Rosario, Argentina: Ediciones Noé.

Veiravé, A. (1984) *Juan L. Ortiz: La experiencia poética*, Buenos Aires: Carlos Lohlé.

—— (1974) 'La obra total de Juan L. Ortiz', *Hispanamérica* 3(8): 23–43.

ENRIQUE FOFFANI

Ortiz, Renato

b. 1947, Ribeirão Preto, Brazil

Cultural critic

A professor of sociology at the Federal University of Campinas, Ortiz's publications from the 1980s constitute an important critical reappraisal of the tradition of thinking on national identity in Brazil, in the light of the country's industrialization and internationalization. The new reality of a fully modern capitalist Brazil means, Ortiz argues, that what was previously thought of as a 'misplaced idea' (in the words of Roberto **Schwarz**), an unrealized project of modernity (see **cultural theory**), has now become the ideology of the established order, 'what we are', replacing the concept of Brazilian cultural identity as a complex of underdevelopment and inauthenticity. To be equal to its task, therefore, the new criticism, as Ortiz's more recent work demonstrates, must cease to view Brazilian culture as 'unique' and peripheral, approaching it instead from the perspective of the international culture industry as a whole, as one manifestation amongst many of a globalized system.

Further reading

Ortiz, Renato (1986) *Cultura brasileira e identidade nacional*, São Paulo: Brasiliense.

—— (1991) *A morte branca do feiticeiro negro: Umbanda e sociedade brasileira*, São Paulo: Editora Brasiliense.

—— (1996) *Mundialização e cultura*, São Paulo: Editora Brasiliense.
—— (2000) 'Diversidad cultural y cosmopolitismo', *Revista de Occidente*, Nov., 234: 7–28.

DAVID TREECE

Osorio, Nelson

b. 1938, Valdivia, Chile

Literary critic

A prolific and important Chilean critic, Osorio has published more than half a dozen books of criticism, among them *Manifiestos, proclamas y polémicas de la vanguardia literaria hispanoamericana* (Manifestos, Proclamations and Polemics of the Hispanoamerican Literary Avant Garde) (1988) and *Al margen de las letras* (On the Margin of Letters) (1994), and co-ordinated the three-volume *Diccionario enciclopédico de las letras de América Latina* (Encyclopedic Dictionary of Latin American Letters) (1995–98). In Chile he directed the series Ediciones Universitarias de Valparaíso (1971–73) and published his translations of critical works by Mukarovsky, Jakobson and others.

Further reading

Osorio, N. (1985) 'Rama y el estudio comprensivo de la literatura latinoamericana', *Texto crítico*, Jan.–Aug., 10(31–2): 24–32.
—— (ed.) (1995) *Diccionario enciclopédico de las letras de América Latina*, Caracas: Monte Avila/Biblioteca Ayacucho, 3 vols.
—— (1998) *Manifestos, proclamas y polémicas de la vanguardia literaria hispanoamericana*, Caracas: Biblioteca Ayacucho.

JUAN ARMANDO EPPLE

Ospina, William

b. 1954, Padua, Tolima, Colombia

Poet, literary critic and journalist

A great essayist and a major literary figure of contemporary Colombian intellectual life, Ospina has achieved renown for his outstanding poetry; he is also a respected translator and lecturer. Ospina lived in Europe between 1979 and 1981. In 1982, he received the National Poetry Award from the Instituto Colombiano de Cultura. Recently, he has focused his articles and essays on reflections about the future of Latin America, the armed conflict affecting his nation and the ambiguous and contradictory features of Colombian society. He has a weekly column in the magazine *Cromos* in which he discusses politics, literature and cultural issues.

Further reading

Barreras del Rio, C. (1996) 'William Ospina o el placer de la lectura', *Revista del atenéo puertorriqueño* 6(16–18): 296–313.
Ospina, W. (1995) *Too Late for Man: Essays*, Cambridge: Brookline Books.
—— (1999) *Las auroras de sangre: Juan de Castellanos y el descubrimiento poético de América*, Santa Fe de Bogotá: Ministerio de Cultura, Grupo Editorial Norma.
—— (2001) *La decadencia de los dragones*, Bogotá: Editorial Alfaguara.

ALVARO BERNAL

Ossott, Hanni

b. 1946, Caracas, Venezuela; d. 2002, Caracas

Writer and translator

One of the most lucid and important female voices in Venezuela, Ossott's writing keeps in close contact with the mysteries of existence and wanders along what Georges Bataille called 'the experience of limits'. In 1982 she published *Espacios de ausencia y de auz* (Spaces of Light and Absence) and in 1986 *El reino donde la noche se abre* (The Realm Where Night Opens Up). Her translations of D.H. Lawrence and Rainer María Rilke were widely admired. She taught at the Universidad Central de Venezuela. Her books include *Cielo, tu arco grande* (Sky, Your Great Arc) (1989), *Casa de agua y de sombras* (House of Water and Shadows) (1992) and *El circo roto* (The Torn Circus) (1996). In 1988 she was awarded the National Prize for Poetry. Her work displays a constant self-questioning and prompts many unanswered questions, creating a reflexive and desperate atmosphere.

VÍCTOR GALARRAGA OROPEZA

Otero Silva, Miguel

b. 1908, Barcelona, Anzoátegui State, Venezuela; d. 1980, Caracas, Venezuela

Writer

Otero Silva's adventurous life, full of incident due to his political involvements, became material for his fiction. Involved in an armed assault in Curaçao and an unsuccessful invasion of Venezuela in 1929 – experiences recounted in his novel, *Fiebre* (Fever) (1939) – and repeatedly exiled during the dictatorships of Gómez and Pérez Jiménez, he was elected senator in 1958, a period in which he was involved in the founding of CONAC. As a journalist, he published in *Elite* and other magazines, and was the principal founder of the newspaper, *El Nacional*, in 1943. His best-known novels are *Casas muertas* (Dead Houses) (1955) and *Oficina no. 1* (Office No. 1) (1961), on the decline of the Venezuelan rural economy and the beginnings of the oil boom; *Cuando quiero llorar no lloro* (When I Want to Cry I Can't) (1970), on the alienation of Venezuelan youth in the 1960s; and the historical novel, *Lope de Aguirre, príncipe de la libertad* (Lope de Aguirre, Prince of Freedom) (1979), about the early colonial adventurer. He also wrote poetry and theatrical works. He donated the money from one of his many prizes, the Lenin Peace Prize of 1980, to the building of a monument to Augusto César Sandino.

Further reading

Alvarez, J.B. (1997) 'Miguel Otero Silva', in V. Smith (ed.), *Encyclopedia of Latin American Literature*, London: Fitzroy Dearborn, 608–9.

Cano, J. (1969) 'Poesia de Miguel Otero Silva', *Insula: Revista bibliográfica de ciencias y letras* 24: 3.

Osorio, N. (1993) 'La historia y las clases en la narrativa de Miguel Otero Silva', *Casa de las Américas* 33(190): 34–41.

Otero Silva, M. (1977) *Prosa completa: Opiniones sobre arte y política*, Barcelona: Seix Barral.

Pacheco, C. (1994) 'Retrospectiva crítica de Miguel Otero Silva', *Revista iberoamericana* 60(166–7): 185–97.

DANIEL BALDERSTON

Oviedo, José Miguel

b. 1934, Lima, Peru

Writer and literary critic

Oviedo studied literature at Peru's Catholic University before becoming a professor in 1958. He was a literary critic for *El comercio* (1960–73) and Director of the Casa de la Cultura del Perú from 1970 to 1973. He has lived and worked in the USA since 1975. Although he has published several works of fiction, he is best known for his critical work, particularly on Peruvian writers such as Ricardo **Palma** and Mario **Vargas Llosa**. His writings include several anthologies of poetry and the short story as well as his *Historia de la literatura hispanoamericana* (History of Hispanic-American Literature) (1995).

Further reading

Oviedo, José Miguel (1991) *Breve historia del ensayo hispanoamericano*, Madrid: Alianza

—— (1992) *Antología crítica del cuento hispanoamericano del siglo XX*, Madrid: Alianza Editorial.

—— (1995) *Historia de la literatura hispanoamericana*, Madrid: Alianza Editorial.

CÉSAR SALAS

Owen, Gilberto

b. 1905, El Rosario, Sinaloa, Mexico; d. 1952, Philadelphia, Pennsylvania, USA

Writer and diplomat

One of the younger members of the **Contempor-**

áneos group, Owen moved to Mexico City in the early 1920s. He participated in several Contemporáneos group projects and published two experimental novels in 1925 and 1928. Owen left Mexico in 1928 to enter the Mexican foreign service, and had isolating periods of residence in the USA and South America. His two poetry collections appeared outside Mexico, the first in Buenos Aires and the second, his masterwork *Perseo vencido* (Perseus Defeated) (1948), in Lima.

Further reading

Boldridge, E. (1973) 'The Poetic Process in Gilberto Owen', *Romance Notes* 14: 476–83.

—— (1995) 'The Refabrication of Literary Personae in the Poetry of Gilberto Owen', *Revista de estudios hispánicos* 22: 109–19.

Moretta, E. (1985) *Gilberto Owen en la poesía mexicana: Dos ensayos*, Mexico City: Fondo de Cultura Económica.

Owen, G. (1953) *Poesía y prosa*, Mexico City: Impr. Universitaria.

Palacios, A. (1998) 'Gilberto Owen: Poeta de la quintaesencia', *Texto crítico* 4(6): 115–26.

MERLIN H. FORSTER

P

Pacheco, Cristina

b. 1941, Guanajuato, Mexico

Writer

Pacheco began as a newspaper journalist in 1960, and since the 1970s she has been widely recognized for her interviews with Mexicans from every walk of life and for her chronicles (see ***crónica***) and short stories. Since 1980 she has directed the television programme *Aquí nos tocó vivir* (It Was Our Lot to Live Here), a popular radio programme focusing on urban social problems, and written a weekly column for the leading newspaper *La Jornada*, called 'Mar de historias' (Sea of Stories). Pacheco has received the National Journalism Prize (1975, 1985), the Buendía Prize and the Prize of the Federation of Latin American Journalists. Her work has been collected in ten books, including *La rueda de la fortuna* (The Ferris Wheel) (1993).

Further reading

O'Connell, P. (2000) 'A Question of Genre: Discourse and Social Criticism in Cristina Pacheco's *Sopita de fideo* and *La rueda de la fortuna*', *Taller de letras* 28: 41–53.

Pacheco, C. *et al.* (1997) *A Necklace of Words: Stories by Mexican Women*, Fredonia: White Pine Press.

—— (2002) *Limpios de todo amor*, Mexico City: Océano.

Schaefer-Rodriguez, C. (1991) 'Embedded Agendas: The Literary Journalism of Cristina Pacheco and Guadalupe Lopaza', *Latin American Literary Review* 19(38): 62–76.

Valdes, M. (1991) 'La obra de Cristina Pacheco: Ficción testimonial de la mujer mexicana', *Escritura: Revista de teoría y crítica literarias* 16(31–2): 271–9.

CYNTHIA STEELE

Pacheco, José Emilio

b. 1939, Mexico City

Poet, fiction writer and literary essayist

Mexico's greatest living poet and its most erudite living intellectual, Pacheco is an unusually versatile and prolific writer who works alternately in the areas of poetry, the novel, the short story, translation and literary journalism. His first book of short fiction, *La sangre de Medusa* (Medusa's Blood) (1958), was highly rhetorical in style and, as the author acknowledges, strongly influenced by **Borges**, even as his early poetry was influenced by Octavio **Paz**. Subsequently Pacheco's prose style has increasingly approximated that of his conversational poetry, embracing verbal economy, understatement and irony.

While he belongs to the generation of Latin American writers that was profoundly affected by the anti-imperialism of the Cuban Revolution and the resistance to the war in Vietnam, Pacheco has always rejected the false patriotism and demagoguery of the so-called Institutionalized Mexican Revolution. Among his most famous poems is 'Alta traición' (High Treason), proclaiming loyalty to family, friends and place over the divisive abstractions of nationalism and ideology. From the beginning of his precocious career, Pacheco has read widely and voraciously in the Mexican literary and historical tradition, as well as that of of Spain, Latin America, France, England, the USA and the Classical world.

Pacheco's own literary works are pessimistic in tone but idealistic in outlook, exemplifying the humanism, universality and generosity that he finds absent in the world. His literary personae are typically sensitive souls reeling before accumulated evidence of universal egotism and cruelty, and of divine indifference to the suffering of humankind and nature.

Through his own family history, Pacheco was sensitized to both the tragedy and hypocrisy of modern Mexican history, and the continuing possibilities for ethical behaviour. During the battles of the generals following the armed phase of the Mexican Revolution, the writer's father, José María Pacheco, a federal attorney, was forced into retirement in 1927, when he refused to become an accomplice to the murder of the Presidential candidate Francisco R. Serrano. At the beginning of the century, Pacheco's paternal grandfather, a Cuban music teacher, had been exiled to Mexico by US imperialism at the end of the Ten Year War. José Emilio spent his childhood summers with his grandparents in Veracruz, where he also learned of the wounds to national pride left by the US Marines invasion of 1914. Back in Mexico City, he witnessed the chaotic mushrooming of the world's largest megalopolis and the deterioration of its elegant neighbourhoods, including his own Colonia Roma.

Veracruz and the Colonia Roma form the backdrop for much of Pacheco's fiction. His first novel, *Morirás lejos* (You Will Die Far From Here) (1967), is an experimental or new novel addressing the persecution of the Jewish people throughout world history. His second novel is *Las batallas en el desierto* (Battles in the Desert) (1981), about official corruption and globalization during the 1940s. Pacheco's short story collections, after *La sangre de Medusa* (Medusa's Blood) (1958), include *El viento distante y otros relatos* (The Distant Wind and Other Stories) (1963) and *El principio del placer* (The Beginning of Pleasure/The Pleasure Principle) (1972).

Since his first six books of poetry were collected in *Tarde o temprano* (Sooner or Later) (1980), Pacheco has published six more, including *Ciudad de la memoria* (City of Memory) (1989), *Miro la tierra* (I Watch the Earth) (1986) and *El silencio de la luna* (The Silence of the Moon) (1995). Also, he has collaborated on books with three leading Mexican visual artists: Francisco Toledo on *Un arco para el próximo milenio* (An Ark for the Next Millennium) (1993), with Vicente Rojo in *Escenarios* (Stage Settings) (1996) and Pablo Ortiz Monasterio in *La última ciudad* (The Final City) (1996).

Pacheco is famous for his anachronistic loyalty to the printed word, as well as for his perfectionism; he is constantly revising and bringing out new editions of his works. After dropping out of law school at the Universidad Nacional Autónoma de México (UNAM), Pacheco studied with the playwright Luisa Josefina **Hernández**, and then began making his living through literary journalism. Together with Carlos **Monsiváis**, he directed the literary supplement to the journal *Estaciones*. Subsequently he directed the office of Cultural Outreach at the UNAM, collaborated on *México en la cultura* (the cultural supplement to *Novedades*) and was chief editor of the *Revista de la Universidad de México* and *La cultura en México* (the supplement to *Siempre*).

Throughout the past two decades, Pacheco has written an acclaimed weekly column of book reviews and cultural history, *Inventario*, in the news magazine *Proceso*. He has worked as a researcher for the Seminar on the History of National Culture, at the National Institute of History and Anthropology (INAH), and teaches one semester a year at the University of Maryland. Since 1986, he has been a member of the Colegio Nacional (Mexico's version of the Academy of Arts and Sciences), for which he currently serves as president. Pacheco's numerous literary awards include the National Poetry Prize for *No me preguntes cómo pasa el tiempo* (Don't Ask Me How The Time Goes By) (1969); the Premio José Asunción Silva (for the best book of poetry published in Spanish between 1990 and 1995, *El silencio de la luna*); the Premio Xavier Villaurrutia; and the Premio Mazatlán.

Further reading

Dorra, R. (1986) *La literatura puesta en juego*, Mexico City: UNAM.

Jiménez de Baez, Y.D. and E.N. Moran (1979) *Ficción e historia. La narrativa de José Emilio Pacheco*, Mexico City: El Colegio de Mexico.

Pacheco, J.E. (1987) *Battles in the Desert and Other Stories*, trans. K. Silver, New York: New Directions.

—— (1987) *Selected Poems*, trans. T. Hoeksema, G. McWhirter and A. Reid, New York: New Directions.

—— (1997) *City of Memory and Other Poems*, trans. C. Steele and D. Lauer, San Francisco: City Lights.

Rebaza-Soraluz, L. (1997) 'José Emilio Pacheco', in V. Smith (ed.), *Encyclopedia of Latin American Literature*, London: Fitzroy Dearborn, 611–13.

Verani, H. (ed.) (1993) *La hoguera y el viento. José Emilio Pacheco ante la crítica*, Mexico City: Ediciones Era, 2nd edn.

CYNTHIA STEELE

Padilla, Heberto

b. 1932, Puerta de Golpe, Pinar del Río, Cuba; d. 2000, Montgomery, Alabama, USA

Poet

A major figure within the current of 'conversational' poetry in Cuba, Padilla's name is associated with the fate of his volume of poems *Fuera del juego* (Out of the Game) (1968), which won the UNEAC literary prize but was published with a foreword from its director denouncing the poems as counterrevolutionary. He was later imprisoned and socially marginalized. Once at liberty, Padilla left for the USA where for many years he edited the *Linden Lane Magazine*, devoted to Latin American culture in the USA. In the 1980s he published a novel, a memoir and a new book of poetry.

Further reading

Coleman, J. (2001) 'Padilla without Tears', *Review: Latin American Literature and Arts* 63: 8–9.

Gregory, S. (1990) 'Literature and Revolution in Cuba: The Padilla Affair', in Roy Boland and Alun Kenwood (eds), *War and Revolution in Hispanic Literature*, Melbourne: Voz Hispánica.

Kapcia, A. (1983) 'Culture and Ideology in Post-Revolutionary Cuba', *Red Letters: A Journal of Cultural Politics* 15: 11–23.

Padilla, H. (1990) *Self-Portrait of the Other*, New York: Farrar, Straus & Giroux.

—— (1991) *A Fountain, a House of Stone: Poems*, New York: Farrar, Straus & Giroux.

WILFREDO CANCIO ISLA

Padura Fuentes, Leonardo

b. 1955, Havana, Cuba

Novelist and essayist

Leonardo Padura Fuentes is perhaps the most popular living Cuban writer, thanks in great part to his series The Four Seasons: *Pasado Perfecto* (Past Perfect) (1991), *Vientos de Cuaresma* (Winds of Lent) (1994), *Máscaras* (Masks) (1997) and *Paisaje de Otoño* (Autumn Landscape) (1998), **crime fiction** in which the plot is a means to analyse the contradictions of contemporary Cuban society. He is a former investigative journalist and critic who at the inception of his career wrote several essays on Cuban and Latin American literature, especially on the works on Alejo **Carpentier**. One of his most recent works, *La novela de mi vida* (The Novel of My Life), is a historical novel based on episodes from the life of José María Heredia, Cuba's first major romantic poet (1803–39). Padura Fuentes has been awarded the Café Gijon Prize (in 1995) and the Hammett Prize (twice) for the best crime novels written in Spanish. Some of his works have been translated into French, English, Portuguese and Polish.

Further reading

Castells, R. (1998) 'La novela policíaca en la Cuba del período especial: *Pasado perfecto* de Leonardo Padura Fuentes', *South Eastern Latin Americanist*, Winter–Spring, 41(3–4): 21–35.

Pérez, J. (2002) 'Intertextuality, Homosexuality, Marginality and Circularity as Subversion in Novel Permutations of the Detective Genre', *Hispanófila*, May, 135: 73–88.

Rosell, S. (2000) 'La (re)formulación del policial cubano: La tetralogía de Leonardo Padura Fuentes', *Hispanic Journal*, Fall, 21(2): 447–58.
Smith, V. (1998) 'Leonardo Padura habla de sus libros', *Torre de papel*, Spring, 8(1): 105–17.

CÉSAR PÉREZ

Palace of the Peacock, The

The first novel by the Guyanese writer Wilson **Harris**, *The Palace of the Peacock* (1960) is a poetic, multi-layered work, bringing together Harris's wide and sometimes esoteric readings with his personal experience as a government surveyor of Guyana's jungle interior. It tells of a journey upriver to an immense waterfall in the South American heartland. But the expedition is a ghostly one, for the crew are retracing a previous journey in which all had died. At the centre of the novel they pass through a terrifying rapid, which merges with the persona of the Arawak woman they have taken as a guide, and the novel ends with the survivors climbing the living rock of the falls in which landscape has become transformed into a vision of harmony, 'the palace of the peacock'.

The story works on several levels. It is a vivid evocation of the presence of jungle and river, and the altered psychic state it creates in those who travel it, reflecting Harris's own experiences as a forest surveyor. Inseparable from the story is the narrative technique, as the highly individual prose style shifts from staccato narrative to poetic vision. The novel is also an account of the Guyanese peoples, for the crew contains representatives of all the main racial groups, Indian, African and various European nationalities. Each brings a particular gift to the expedition: the Indian has vigilance and spiritual insight; the African, Carol, has music. As the expedition moves up river they interact, undergo conflict, die and finally re-emerge in a spiritual unity.

The novel also explores the Guyanese past and future. At the beginning of the novel, Donne is shot by Mariella, the peasant girl he has exploited and beaten, reflecting the violence of the colonial encounter. As the journey progresses, Donne's character changes until he is able to see Mariella first as a 'mission station', a place of settlement, and finally as the visionary Madonna, the incarnation of divine love. Donne's name refers us to John Donne, the seventeenth-century writer and author of profane amorous verse, sermons and the Holy Sonnets. Harris's Donne also has two personae: the harsh administrator and expedition leader, and the spiritual alter ego who becomes his visionary 'eye' and the narrator of the story. The integration of the self, with its Jungian dimension, co-exists with an acceptance of 'the true substance of life', uniting the different races of Guyana with the aboriginal 'folk', in the spirit of the landscape.

Harris's work has interesting affinities with ***Los pasos perdidos*** (The Lost Steps) (1953) by the Cuban writer Alejo **Carpentier**, which also uses a journey into the South American interior as a quest for a psychic wholeness, but the two works are very different in style and form. *The Palace of the Peacock* established Harris as the most innovative of Anglophone West Indian writers.

Further reading

Dieke, I. (1999) 'Anagogic Symbolism in Wilson Harris's *Palace of the Peacock*', *CLA Journal* 42(3): 290–308.
Harris, W. (1960) *Palace of the Peacock*, London: Faber & Faber.
McDowell, J. (1991) 'The Duality of Language in *Palace of the Peacock*', *Commonwealth Novel in English* 4(1): 62–8.
Maes-Jelinek, H. (1976) *The Naked Design: A Reading of Palace of the Peacock*, Aarhus: Dangeroo Press.
Steele, F. (1997) 'Breaking Down Barriers as Genesis of a New Beginning in Wilson Harris's *Palace of the Peacock*', *Review of Contemporary Fiction* 17(2): 63–6.

LOUIS JAMES

Palacio, Pablo

b. 1906, Loja, Ecuador; d. 1947, Guayaquil, Ecuador

Writer

An outstanding representative of the narrative

avant-garde in Ecuador and Latin America (see **avant-garde in Latin America**), the dominance of a social protest literature in Palacio's native country prevented his works from being recognized until the late 1970s. His collection of short stories, *Un hombre muerto a puntapiés* (A Man Kicked to Death) (1927), and the novellas *Débora* (Deborah) (1927) and *Vida del ahorcado: Novela subjetiva* (The Hanged Man's Life: A Subjective Novel) (1932), contain ground-breaking features: open-ended structures, meta-literary practices, the disintegration of forms and corresponding decentring of traditions. Palacio, a socialist, also wrote several philosophical essays and a handful of poems.

Further reading

Donoso Pareja, M. (ed.) (1987) *Pablo Palacio: Valoración múltiple*, Havana: Centro de Investigaciones Literarias, Casa de las Américas.

Manzoni, C. (1994) *El mordisco imaginario: Crítica de la crítica en Pablo Palacio*, Buenos Aires: Editorial Biblos.

Martinez, E. (2001) *Before the Boom: Latin American Revolutionary Novels of the 1920s*, Lanham, MD: University Press of America.

Palacio, P. (1998) *Obras completas*, ed. W.H. Corral, Paris: Colección Archivos.

Pareja Diezcanseco, A. (1981) 'El reino de la libertad en Pablo Palacio', *Casa de las Américas* 22(127): 3–20.

Ruffinelli, J. (1979) 'Pablo Palacio: Literatura, locura y sociedad', *Revista de crítica literaria latinoamericana* 5(10): 47–60.

HUMBERTO E. ROBLES

Palacios, Antonia

b. 1904, Caracas, Venezuela; d. 2001, Caracas

Writer

Palacios's charming and poetic novel *Ana Isabel, una niña decente* (Ana Isabel, a Decent Girl) (1949) is obligatory reading for those wanting to understand the subtle changes that took place during the 1940s in Venezuela, narrated through the eyes of a girl who masters mysterious and lyrical elements. Her work reflects a vague melancholy inherited from Juan Vicente Gómez's dictatorship. The first woman to be awarded the National Prize for Literature, her short and dramatic stories and vivid poems feature an oppressive desolate atmosphere in which the lyric voice manages to move constantly between presence and memory. Her work includes *Crónicas de las horas* (Chronicles of the Hours) (1954), *Los insulares* (The Islanders) (1972), *París y tres recuerdos* (Paris and Three Memories) (1944) and *El largo día ya seguro* (The Long Safe Day) (1975).

Further reading

Latcham, R. (1962) 'La obra de Antonia Palacios', in *Carnet crítico: Ensayos*, Montevideo: Alfa, 66–71.

Liscano, J. (1973) 'Antonia Palacios', in *Panorama de la literatura venezolana actual*, Caracas: Publicaciones Españolas.

Rivera, F. (1976) 'De lo personal a lo mítico', *Revista nacional de cultura* 225: 13–20.

VÍCTOR GALARRAGA OROPEZA

Palacios, María Fernanda

b. 1945, Caracas, Venezuela

Poet and essayist

In the 1970s Palacios edited, together with José **Balza**, the journal *El falso cuaderno*. Her essays on Proust, Kafka, Thomas Mann, Teresa **de la Parra** and Tarkovsky constitute a serious and profound exploration of the relationship between the artist and the work. She edited the *Obras completas* (Complete Works) of Teresa de la Parra for the **Fondo de Cultura Económica** in Mexico. A graduate of the Universidad Central of Venezuela, where she later taught, she contributed to *El Papel Literario* (Literary Supplement) of *El Nacional*, and the journals ***Zona franca***, *Imagen* and ***Vuelta*** (Mexico).

Further reading

Palacios, M. (1984) 'La mujer y la casa', *Revista nacional de cultura* 4(255): 83–92.

JORGE ROMERO LEÓN

Palés Matos, Luis

b. 1898, Guayama, Puerto Rico; d. 1959, Santurce, Puerto Rico

Poet

The most enduringly popular of all Puerto Rican poets, Palés Matos was one of the first Latin American poets to explore in depth the African presence in Latin American culture. He is among the original creators of ***negrismo***, or *poesía negra*, practised later by poets such as Nicolás **Guillén**, Emilio **Ballagas** and Manuel del **Cabral**. Palés Matos's Afro-Antillean poetry was controversial from early on. In the 1930s many critics (even among those who praised him) accused him of overemphasizing African contributions to Puerto Rican culture. In later years others would accuse him of racism and exoticism, viewing with high suspicion a white middle-class poet's re-creation of Afro-Antillean experience. Nevertheless, some have seen him as an ironic mirror of a culture characterized by *mestizaje* and transculturation, and as a strong voice of anti-colonialism in an era of US domination of Puerto Rico.

Palés Matos moved to San Juan in 1921, where he supported himself through journalism and a number of bureaucratic positions, and finally as 'poet in residence' at the University of Puerto Rico. His *poesía negra* was extremely popular even before he published it in book form, a testament to its strong oral underpinning and to the oral nature of many **intellectual** fora (*tertulias* or salons, recitals, and so on) in the Puerto Rico of the early twentieth century. Yet not all of his poetry is of this genre. His first book, *Azaleas* (1915), reveals his early apprenticeship to the *modernista* (see **Spanish American modernism**) poetry of Rubén **Darío**, and Julio **Herrera y Reissig**. A voracious reader with an intense interest in the poetic revolutions taking Europe and the Americas by storm, he moved on to avant-garde experiments with onomatopoeia and neologisms, which later formed the basis for his *poesía negra*. While his *Tuntún de pasa y grifería* (1937/1950) is firmly within the vein of *poesía negra*, with its extreme rhythmicity, onomatopoeias and Afro-Antillean lexicon, his later poetry, partially collected in his *Poesía 1915–1956* (1957), surprises with its intimate, lyrical simplicity.

Further reading

Albada Jelgersma, J. (1997) 'La función del deseo por la mujer afroantillana en cuatro poemas de Luis Palés Matos', *Hispanic Journal* 18(2): 357–72.

Díaz Quiñones, A. (1982) *El almuerzo en la hierba*, Río Piedras, PR: Ediciones Huracán.

González-Pérez, A. (1987) 'Ballad of Two Poets: Nicolás Guillén and Luis Palés Matos', *Callaloo: A Journal of African American and African Arts and Letters* 10(2): 285–301.

—— (1989) 'Luis Palés Matos', in C.A. Solé and M.I. Abreu (eds), *Latin American Writers*, New York: Scribners, 2, 821–30.

Marzán, J. (1995) *The Numinous Site: The Poetry of Luis Palés Matos*, Madison, WI: Farleigh Dickinson University Press.

—— (1995) 'The Poetry and Antipoetry of Luis Palés Matos: From Canciones to Tuntunes', *Callaloo: A Journal of African American and African Arts and Letters* 18(2): 506–23.

Onís, F. de (1959) *Luis Palés Matos; vida y obra, bibliografía, antología*, Santa Clara, Cuba: Instituto de Estudios Hispánicos, Universidad Central de las Villas.

Palés Matos, L. (1995) *La poesía de Luis Palés Matos: Edición crítica*, ed. M. López-Baralt, Río Piedras, PR: Editorial de la Universidad de Puerto Rico.

BEN A. HELLER

Palm, Jules Ph. de

b. 1922, Curaçao, Netherlands Antilles

Writer and scholar

The translator of Shakespeare's *Midsummer Night's Dream* into Papiamentu, de Palm is also the author of a collection of short stories and two autobiographical novels, *Kinderen van de Fraters* (Children of the Brethren) (1986) and *Lekker warm, lekker bruin* (Nicely Warm, Nicely Coloured) (1990), which deal with how Afro-Antillean youngsters adapt to the exigencies of Dutch cultural patterns. He is also the editor of the standard encyclopedia of the Netherlands Antilles.

Further reading

Broek, A. (1983) 'Een studie, een roman en verhalen', *De Gids* 146(4): 307–11.

Versteeg, T. (1970) 'J. Ph. de Palm, Het Nederlands op de Curacaose school', *De Nieuwe Taalgids: Tijdschrift voor Neerlandici* 63: 74–7.

AART G. BROEK

Palma, Ricardo

b. 1833, Lima, Peru; d. 1919, Lima

Prose writer

Palma is known for the ten volumes of his *Tradiciones peruanas* (Peruvian Traditions), published in book form between 1872 and 1910 (although some had appeared in periodicals as early as 1851). The *tradiciones* are concerned especially with Lima in colonial times: with the intrigues among the principal families, the scandalous behaviour of the servants of the Church and the Crown, acts of generosity, betrayals and petty jealousies. His portrait of colonial Lima (especially during the eighteenth century) is evocative, his language familiar, his plots well-wrought. Not a professional historian but a teller of tall tales, Palma's work nevertheless is an eloquent recreation of the past. His son Clemente Palma was also a writer, although the son preferred fantastic tales. Both father and son worked out of the tradition of ***costumbrismo***, but had distinctive voices.

Further reading

Kneightley, R. (1997) 'Ricardo Palma', in V. Smith (ed.), *Encyclopedia of Latin American Literature*, London: Fitzroy Dearborn, 613–15.

Oviedo, J.M. (1965) *Genio y figura de Ricardo Palma*, Buenos Aires: EUDEBA.

—— (1989) 'Ricardo Palma', in C.A. Solé and M.I. Abreu (eds), *Latin American Writers*, New York: Scribners, 1, 221–8.

Palma, R. (1945) *The Knights of the Cape, and Thirty-seven Other Selections from the Tradiciones peruanas*, ed. and trans. H. de Onís, New York: Knopf.

—— (1977) *Cien tradiciones peruanas*, ed. J.M. Oviedo, Caracas: Biblioteca Ayacucho.

DANIEL BALDERSTON

Palmer, C. Everard

b. 1930, Kendal, Jamaica

Writer

One of the earliest and certainly the most prolific children's writer from the Anglophone Caribbean, Palmer was awarded the Institute of Jamaica's Silver Musgrave Medal in 1971. Educated in Jamaica and in Canada, whither he emigrated, Palmer has published over a dozen stories for children, most of them set in Jamaica. *A Dog Called Houdini* and *Houdini, Come Home* are set in Canada. His simple, exuberant stories, flavoured with humour and suspense, portray youngsters grappling with the exigencies of life. *My Father Sun-Sun Johnson*, published in 1974, was made into a film.

Further reading

Palmer, C.E. (1968) *Big Doc Bitteroot*, Indianapolis: Bobbs-Merrill.

—— (1970) *The Sun Salutes You*, Indianapolis: Bobbs-Merrill.

—— (1972) *A Cow Called Boy*, Indianapolis: Bobbs-Merrill.

PAT DUNN AND PAMELA MORDECAI

Palomares, Ramón

b. 1935, Boconó, Venezuela

Poet

A member of the Sardio group, Palomares is a key figure in contemporary Venezuelan poetry. His unique poetic voice reconstructs rural experience through language and memory; the archaic speech of the Venezuelan Andes region is the medium for the recuperation of myths and ancestral legends. His poetry is full of unexpected forms of speech, conversational rhythms and marvellous images. From *El reino* (The Kingdom) (1958), the book that brought his name to public notice, through *Paisano* (Countryman) (1964) and *Alegres provincias* (Cheerful Provinces) (1988), Palomares has remained a poet concerned with man in nature.

Further reading

Alfonzo, R. (1997) 'Ramón Palomares: Nueva visión de lo telúrico', *Cifra nueva: Revista de cultura* 5–6: 9–18.

Arellano, A. (1994) 'Oralidad y transculturación en la poesía de Ramón Palomares', *Revista iberoamericana* 60(166–7): 233–48.

Borgeson, P. (1990) 'Lo andino y lo universal en la poesía de Ramón Palomares', *Romance Languages Annual* 2: 349–57.

Palomares, R. (1958) *El reino. Poesía*, Caracas: Sardio.

RAFAEL CASTILLO ZAPATA

Pantin, Yolanda

b. 1955, Caracas, Venezuela

Poet

A member of the **Tráfico** group, Pantin's first volume *Casa o lobo* (House or Wolf) (1981) revealed the influence of **Gerbasi**, **Palomares** and **Crespo** in a dense language populated with complex autobiographical images. Her later work evolved in new directions, opening up to colloquial language and urban visions, and becoming more reflective, refined and ironic. As in *La canción fría* (The Cold Song) (1989), *El cielo de París* (The Sky of Paris) (1989) and *Los bajos sentimientos* (Low Feelings) (1993), *Correo del corazón* (Mail from the Heart) (1985) opened a new stage, focusing on every aspect of a woman's experience (mother, intellectual, Latin American) at century's end.

Further reading

Castillo-Zapata, Rafael (1993) 'Palabras recuperadas, la poesía venezolana de los ochenta: Rescate y transformación de las palabras de la tribu. El caso "Trafico" ', *Inti: Revista de literatura hispánica* 37–8: 197–205.

Pantin, Y. (1989) *El cielo de París*, Caracas: Pequeña Venecia.

—— (1989) *La canción fría*, Caracas: Editorial Angria.

—— (1993) 'De casa o lobo al cielo de Paris: El futuro imposible', *Inti: Revista de literatura hispánica* 37–8: 47–55.

—— (1998) *Enemiga mía: Selección poética (1981–1997)*, Madrid: Iberoamericana.

—— (1999) 'El poema que vendra', *Caribe* 2(2): 76–82.

RAFAEL CASTILLO ZAPATA

Paradiso

Published in 1966, *Paradiso* was the Cuban writer José **Lezama Lima**'s first novel. Its complexity and verbal daring have earned him frequent comparisons to Joyce and Proust. The semi-autobiographical *bildungsroman*, or novel of education, traces the family history and youth of José Cemí, a sensitive young man from Havana. The early chapters focus on the refined domestic life of this very creole family during the early years of the twentieth century, and particularly on Cemí's father, a military man who dies young in the presence of the enigmatic Oppiano Licario, who will later act as Cemí's spiritual guide. The father's death has a defining influence on the entire family; it means a downturn in the economic fortunes, as well as a ceaseless spiritual search to make his absence productive. The central chapters detail Cemí's university days and his friendship with a charismatic young student, Fronesis, and the high-strung Foción, a homosexual in love with Fronesis. These chapters at times approach the style of a Platonic dialogue between the three friends, while offering brilliant erotic scenes. After Fronesis leaves for Paris and Foción goes mad, Cemí discovers that

Oppiano Licario has died. He attends the wake and comes to understand his destiny as a writer.

Paradiso achieved notoriety for its **neo-baroque** style, its difficulty – which many viewed as out of step with the anti-elitist art promoted by the Cuban Revolution – and for its erotic scenes, both heterosexual and homosexual. Indeed, it was briefly censored by the Cuban government and was only restored to bookstores after Fidel Castro gave his personal permission. *Paradiso* is one of the most challenging novels of the '**Boom**' in Latin American narrative, and it is by far the best introduction to Lezama's aesthetics. It also provides a good summation of his thinking on Latin American cultural identity also set out in *La* ***expresión americana***. Finally, it is one of the few Latin American texts with a well-drawn homosexual character and a serious philosophical discussion of homosexuality. Lezama Lima was working on the continuation of *Paradiso* when he died in 1976; the unfinished sequel, *Oppiano Licario*, was published the following year.

Further reading

Bravo, V. (1992) *El secreto en geranio convertido: Una lectura de Paradiso*, Caracas: Monte Avila.

Lezama Lima, J. (1974) *Paradiso*, trans. G. Rabassa, New York: Farrar, Straus & Giroux.

—— (1988) *Paradiso*, ed. C. Vitier, Paris: Colección Archivos.

Pellón, G. (1989) *José Lezama Lima's Joyful Vision*, Austin: University of Texas Press.

Souza, R. (1983) *The Poetic Fiction of José Lezama Lima*, Columbia: University of Missouri Press.

BEN A. HELLER

Paraguay

The post-colonial history of Paraguay has been replete with political crises whose consequences have been both enduring and disastrous. In a country the bulk of whose nineteenth-century population were indigenous Guaraní speakers living in rural areas, the lack of a literature in Spanish is hardly to be wondered at. A sequence of dictatorships marked the nation's nineteenth century, culminating in the catastrophic War of the Triple Alliance of 1864–70. Unsurprisingly, the dominant writing of the latter years of the nineteenth century was concerned with history and the search for the fragments of a national identity. Writing about history, therefore, seems to have been the dominant mode at that time, albeit often in the framework of Romanticism. The twentieth century was equally attended by tragedy for Paraguay. The first writer of importance was the Spanish anarchist Rafael **Barrett**, who wrote searing accounts of the exploitation of workers in the yerba mate plantations. The Chaco War with Bolivia (1932–35) brought home the national reality with particular brutality; paradoxically it also produced the first realist narratives, prime among them Gabriel **Casaccia**'s *El guajhú* (The Howl) (1938), as well as Arnaldo Valdovinos's *Cruces de quebracho* (Wooden Crosses) (1934). The realist tradition continued with Casaccia's *La babosa* (The Gossiping Woman) (1952) and *El trueno entre las hojas* (Thunder in the Leaves) (1953), the first book of prose writings by Paraguay's outstanding writer Augusto **Roa Bastos**.

The post-Chaco War era also produced a generation of poets devoted to both personal exploration and literary modernization, the bulk of it in Spanish. The group of poets included Roa Bastos and Josefina **Plá**. Others of the same generation wrote in Guaraní, including Carlos Abente and Rosicrán (Narciso R. Colmán). The interregnum, however, was not to last, and with the Revolution of 1947 and the subsequent accession to power of Alfredo Stroessner, whose repressive and brutal dictatorship was to last from 1954 to 1989, Paraguayan literature became very largely a literature written in and often about exile. Casaccia's *Los exiliados* (The Exiles) (1966) focuses directly on that experience, while Roa Bastos's magnificent ***Hijo de hombre*** (Son of Man) (1960) explored the history of his country as pain and resurrection. He continues that project in the extraordinary ***Yo el Supremo*** (I the Supreme) (1974), which reconstructs a narrative of dictatorship as history and dream.

The realities of Stroessner's Paraguay are addressed by a number of exiled writers – Rubén Bareiro Saguier, Carlos Garcete and Juan Manuel Marcos among them – as well as Paraguay's outstanding poets Elvio **Romero** and Hérib

Campos Cervera. Many of them were contributors to a key literary journal published in the USA (and later in Paraguay), ***Discurso literario***.

Since it is these writers who have become more widely known, the overwhelming impression is that Paraguay virtually ceased to produce an internal literature. And it is certainly true that Stroessner exercised a ferocious direct censorship throughout his dictatorship, creating an atmosphere in which writers also censored themselves in anticipation of repression. Yet the remarkable thing is how much was written and published internally, albeit often in very limited editions. Josefina Plá and Francisco **Pérez-Maricevich**, and those gathered around the magazine *Criterio*, were among them. At the same time, writing in Guaraní (principally poetry) also continued; the poet Susy **Delgado** is a key figure in this movement. It is worth underlining the fact that Guaraní is not a minority language in Paraguay, unlike Quechua or Aymara in Peru or Bolivia. It is spoken by some two-thirds of the population, including those whose antecedents are not among the first nations. This explains the vitality of Guaraní writing, and the continuing significance of the Guaraní dramatist Julio Correa.

The end of the Stroessner dictatorship introduced an uneasy period of transition towards electoral democracy, but it also removed the suffocating censorship and allowed the exiles to return and their work to be made available, finally, to a younger generation that could now read the forbidden texts written within the country throughout that period. The result is a burgeoning new literature, often concerned with revisiting and exorcising those terrible years; works include Moncho Azuega's *Celda 12* (Cell No. 12) (1991) and Renée **Ferrer**'s *Desde el encendido corazón del monte* (From the Burning Heart of the Hill Country) (1994).

Further reading

Cardozo, Efraím (1987) *Apuntes de historia cultural de Paraguay*, Asunción: Universidad Católica.

Foster, D.W. (1978) *Augusto Roa Bastos*, Boston: Twayne.

Gausch, Fr. Antonio (1983) *El idioma guaraní: Gramática y antología de prosa y verso*, Asunción: Editiones Loyola.

Marcos, J.M. (1983) *Roa Bastos: Precursor del post-Boom*, Mexico City: Editiones Katún.

Méndez-Faith, Teresa (1985) *Paraguay: Novela y exilio*, Somerville, NJ: SLUSA.

—— (1994) *Breve diccionario de la literatura paraguaya*, Asunción: El Lector.

Rodríguez-Alcalá, Hugo (1970) *Historia de la literatura paraguaya*, Mexico City: Editiones de Andrea.

TERESA MÉNDEZ-FAITH AND MIKE GONZALEZ

Pardo Carugati, Dirma

b. 1934, Buenos Aires, Argentina

Writer and journalist

A teacher in secondary schools and universities in Asunción for three decades and a journalist with *La Tribuna* (1956–76), Pardo Carugati has also written two books of stories – *La víspera y el día* (The Eve and the Day) (1992) and *Cuentos de tierra caliente* (Stories from a Hot Land) (1999). One of her stories ('Baldosas negras y blancas' (Black and White Tiles)) was adapted for cinema and served as the script for the first Paraguayan film, *El secreto de la señora* (The Lady's Secret) (1989), honoured in international festivals in Havana in 1989 and Buenos Aires in 1993.

Further reading

Pardo Carugati, D. (1995) *La víspera y el día*, Edición digital de Mª Dolores Alcantud basada en la edición de Asunción, Paraguay: Editorial Don Bosco.

—— (1999) *Cuentos de tierra caliente*, Edición digital basada en la edición de Asunción, Paraguay: Intercontinental.

TERESA MÉNDEZ-FAITH

Pardo García, Germán

b. 1902, Choachí, Colombia; d. 1991, Mexico City

Poet

In his early years as a writer, Pardo was a member

of Los Nuevos and was influenced by *modernismo* (see **Spanish American modernism**). Born in Colombia. he lived in Mexico from 1932 onwards. While Pardo wanted to believe optimistically in the future of humanity, he was usually concerned with death and alienation in the present. He is the author of more than forty books of poetry. *U.Z. llama al espacio* (U.Z. Calls to Outer Space) (1954), one of his most representative works, is a desperate message about the lack of hope for humanity in the future.

Further reading

Irizarry, E. (1974) 'El poeta German Pardo García: Clásico, cósmico y americano', *Cuadernos americanos* 192: 243–9.

Pardo García, G. (1957) *Hay piedras como lágrimas*, Mexico City: Editorial Cultura.

—— (1961) *Treinta años de labor del poeta colombiano Germán Pardo García, 1930 a 1960*, Mexico City: Editorial Cultura.

—— (1979) 'Un auténtico binomio de grandes poetistas mexicanas', *Nivel* 204: 6–11.

MIGUEL A. CARDINALE

Pareja Diezcanseco, Alfredo

b. 1908, Guayaquil, Ecuador; d. 1993, Quito, Ecuador

Writer

One of the most productive members of the **Guayaquil Group**, Pareja's narrative constantly evolved; the sense of history, however, was always central. *El muelle* (The Dock) (1933), widely believed to be his best work, focuses on the economic crisis of 1929 in New York and Guayaquil. His other novels include *Baldomera* (1938) and *Las pequeñas estaturas* (Small Statures) (1970). His literary output increasingly has emphasized the psychological and existential. His historical writings include *La hoguera bárbara* (The Barbarous Bonfire) (1944) and *Historia del Ecuador* (History of Ecuador) (1956).

Further reading

Heise, K. (1973) *La evolución novelística de Alfredo Pareja Diezcanseco*, Buenos Aires and New York: Ed. La Libreria.

Pareja Diezcanseco, A. (1935) *La Beldaca, novela del trópico*, Santiago de Chile: Ediciones Ercilla.

—— (1945) *El muelle*, Mexico City: Edición Tezontle.

Ribadeneira, E. (1988) 'La obra narrativa de Alfredo Pareja Diezcanseco', *Revista iberoamericana* 54(144–5): 763–9.

HUMBERTO E. ROBLES

Parra, Esdras

b. 1937, Santa Cruz de Mora, Venezuela

Writer

Este suelo secreto: Poemas 1992–1993 is Esdras Parra's extraordinary reflection on her sex change, a stunning and often anguished series of poems on disquieting feelings of unease in a body, of pain and scars and the harrowing affirmation of selfhood. Parra, who began her career as a male short story writer with several collections including *Juego limpio* (Clean Game) (1968), which includes interesting stories about sexual ambiguity, was long-time editor of the Venezuelan magazine *Imagen* and a frequent contributor to the important Caracas daily *El Nacional.* After undergoing a sex change in London, Parra switched not just gender but genre, moving from the short story to poetry, not only in *Este suelo secreto* but also in *Antigüedad del frío* (The Antiquity of Cold) (2000).

Further reading

Bravo, V. (2000) 'Esdras Parra: El cuerpo, la memoria, la escritura', *El Nacional* online, Verbigracia 136.

Parra, E. (1995) *Este suelo secreto: Poemas 1992–1993*, Caracas: Monte Avila.

DANIEL BALDERSTON

Parra, Nicanor

b. 1914, San Fabian, Chile

Poet

The creator of *antipoesía* (see **antipoetry**), Parra has provoked a continuing debate as to what his poetry is *against*. In one sense, it is iconoclastic and frequently parodies recognized canonical literary forms. Yet this was equally true of other earlier poets such as **Huidobro**.

It has been suggested that the implicit 'enemy' is the rhetorical and flamboyant **Neruda** of, say, the ***Canto general*** (1950). And it is true that, from *Poemas y antipoemas* (1954) onwards, Parra's writing is a non-lyrical, prosaic – one might almost say anti-heroic – writing. It *registers* the world – catalogues it almost – as in 'Noticiario 1930' (News Bulletin 1930), but it neither celebrates nor condemns it. At the heart of Parra's work is a poetic persona – sometimes an *energúmeno*, a kind of Rumpelstiltskin figure who is cruel and bawdy and vulgar – and sometimes a kind of 'ordinary man in the street' – an *homme bourgeois moyen* who has no control over the world. This figure is exemplified in the long poem, *Soliloquio del individuo* (Soliloquy of the Individual). And sometimes he adopts the character of a kind of travelling ascetic, the Christ of Elqui, whose disquisitions are preserved in *Sermones y prédicas del Cristo de Elqui* (Sermons and Preachings of the Christ of Elqui) (1977).

None of these masks or doubles, of course, correspond to the brother of the great singer and folklorist Violeta Parra, or to the graduate in mathematics who was professor of theoretical physics at the University of Santiago for nearly forty years.

Parra's irreverence and black humour are directed against everyone; neither Left nor Right were spared the effect of his satirical scattergun. His *Artefactos* (1972) were sceptical (at best) of the government of Popular Unity in Chile (1970–73) and he appeared to take some perverse pleasure in the brutal *coup* that overthew Allende. His earlier visit to Richard Nixon's White House had in any event not endeared him to the Left. Yet his 1984 *Chistes Parra desorientar a la policía* (Parra's Jokes to Mislead Policemen) is clearly aimed at the Pinochet regime. And at times his work can also be poignant and lyrical, as in *Versos de salón* (1962).

An outstanding poet, an iconoclast and a radical individualist, his sceptical and aesthetically radical work has directly or indirectly influenced other poets, particularly those who sought an idiom for *poesía conversacional* during the 1960s.

Further reading

Grossman, E. (1975) *The Antipoetry of Nicanor Parra*, New York: New York University Press.

Montes, H. and M. Rodríguez (1970) *Nicanor Parra y la poesía de lo cotidiano*, Santiago, Chile: Pacífico.

Morales, L. (1990) *Conversaciones con Nicanor Parra*, Santiago, Chile: Editorial Universitaria.

Parra, N. (1969) *Obra gruesa*, Santiago, Chile: Editorial Universitaria.

—— (1985) *Hojas de parra*, ed. D. Turkeltaub, Santiago, Chile: Ganymedes.

—— (1985) *Antipoems: New and Selected*, ed. David Unger, trans. L. Ferlinghetti *et al.*, New York: New Directions.

Skármeta, A. (1989) 'Nicanor Parra', in C.A. Solé and M.I. Abreu (eds), *Latin American Writers*, New York: Scribners, 3: 1195–1200.

White, S.F. (1997) 'Nicanor Parra', in V. Smith (ed.), *Encyclopedia of Latin American Literature*, London: Fitzroy Dearborn, 628–9.

MIKE GONZALEZ

PARRA SANOJO, ANA TERESA *see* de la Parra, Teresa

PASO, FERNANDO DEL *see* del Paso, Fernando

Pasos, Joaquín

b. 1914, Granada, Nicaragua; d. 1947, Granada

Poet

Although he died without ever having left his native country, Joaquín Pasos was famous for his travel poetry. A part of the Vanguardia group, he spawned a genre of humorous rustic poetry called *poesía chinfónica*. His other works reflect the scatological influences of the First and Second World

War, and deal with journeys ending in the destruction of the human consciousness and life in general. His poem 'Canto de guerra de las cosas' (Song of the War of the Things) has been compared to Eliot's *The Waste Land.* His work remained unpublished until after his death.

Further reading

Bellini, G. (1993) 'Joaquín Pasos o el dolor de vivir', *Rassegna iberística* 46: 5–16.

Pasos, J. (1983) *Poemas de un joven*, Managua: Editorial Nueva Nicaragua.

Unruh, V. (1987) 'The Chinfonía burguesa: A Linguistic Manifesto of Nicaragua's Avant-Garde', *Latin American Theatre Review* 20(2): 37–48.

White, S. (ed.) (1982) *Poets of Nicaragua, a Bilingual Anthology, 1918–1979*, Greensboro: Unicorn Press.

—— (1985) 'Breve retrato de Joaquín Pasos', *Inti: Revista de literatura hispánica* 21: 67–73.

DEREK PETREY AND ILEANA RODRÍGUEZ

pasos perdidos, Los

Los pasos perdidos (The Lost Steps) (1953) is a key work of Latin American literature. The novel, by Alejo **Carpentier**, was inspired by the author's previous journeys into the Upper Orinoco region of Venezuela. The protagonist is a musician weary of modern society who travels into the jungle in search of his roots. His river journey, which takes him through different stages of civilization, becomes a philosophical exploration of time and history. The hero's search ends in failure; his journey back in time is an illusion. The author achieves the complete integration of character, milieu and action through a baroque language born of the need to express the Latin American reality.

Further reading

Carpentier, A. (1967) *Los pasos perdidos*, Madrid: Cátedra.

—— (1967) *The Lost Steps*, trans. Harriet de Onís, New York: Knopf.

Castells, R. (1994) 'The Hidden Intertext in Alejo Carpentier's *Los pasos perdidos*', *Confluencia: Revista hispánica de cultura y literatura* 10(1): 81–8.

Lynd, J. (1997) 'The Problem of Representing the Latin American Other: Alejo Carpentier's *El reino de este mundo* and *Los pasos perdidos*', *Romance Languages Annual* 9: 593–9.

WILFREDO CANCIO ISLA

Patterson, H. Orlando

b. 1940, Westmoreland, Jamaica

Writer and scholar

A leading authority on slavery, Patterson's *The Sociology of Slavery* (1967) was based on his doctoral research at London School of Economics. *The Children of Sisyphus* (1964), a novel examining modern life in Kingston's 'dungle', won first prize for fiction at the Dakar Festival of Negro Arts in 1966. *An Absence of Ruins* (1967) is also pessimistic, but *Die the Long Day* (1972), a historical novel celebrating the struggles of a woman slave, presents a brighter vision. Patterson taught briefly (1967–70) at his alma mater, the University of the West Indies, before leaving for Harvard. His output since then has been mainly academic.

Further reading

Jones, B. (1975) 'Some French Influences in the Fiction of Orlando Patterson', *Savacou: A Journal of the Caribbean Artists Movement* 11–12: 27–38.

Patterson, O. (1964) *The Children of Sisyphus*, London: New Authors Limited.

—— (1967) *An Absence of Ruins*, London: Hutchinson.

PAT DUNN AND PAMELA MORDECAI

Paula

Isabel **Allende**'s *Paula* (1995) is a deeply personal memoir of her daughter Paula, who died of porphyria while Allende kept vigil by her bedside. At one level it is autobiographical, in a similar way to many of Allende's other writings; at another it is an exploration of the relationship between mothers and daughters in history and in myth. Understandably enough, the style of the work tends towards the overwrought – as with the magical realist propensities of her earlier work (see **magical realism**). But the other presence in the book, Paula herself – who prior to her coma and death had embarked on a purifying spiritual journey of her own – insists upon simplicity and a kind of divestment of worldly clutter that acts as a counter to the narrator's rhetoric.

Further reading

Allende, I. (1995) *Paula*, trans. Margaret Sayers Peden, New York: Harper Collins Publishers.

Ewalt, M. (1999) 'Isabel Allende's Paula: The Writing Process and Self Discovery', *Torre de papel* 9(3): 26–38.

Perricone, C. (1998) 'Genre and Metarealism in Allende's Paula', *Hispania: A Journal Devoted to the Teaching of Spanish and Portuguese* 81(1): 42–9.

MIKE GONZALEZ

Pauls, Alan

b. 1959, Buenos Aires, Argentina

Writer

Paul's novels – *El pudor del pornógrafo* (The Shyness of the Pornographer) (1984), *El coloquio* (The Dialogue) (1990) and *Wasabi* (1994) – show a preoccupation with the specificity of writing in given political and aesthetic contexts. As a critic, his starting point is French literary theory; he has explored the issue of literary language, specifically the tension with 'orality', in the Argentine literary tradition and especially in non-canonical marginal literary traditions (such as the texts of Osvaldo **Lamborghini**, Manuel **Puig**, Pierre Klossowski, and the detective story). His study *Manuel Puig: La traición de Rita Hayworth* (1986) was an important reassessment of Puig's work.

Further reading

Pauls, A. (1984) *El pudor del pornógrafo*, Buenos Aires: Editorial Sudamericana.

—— (1986) *Manuel Puig: La traición de Rita Hayworth*, Buenos Aires: Librería Hachette.

—— (1990) *El coloquio*, Buenos Aires: Emecé Editores.

GABRIEL GIORGI

Pavlovsky, Eduardo

b. 1933, Buenos Aires, Argentina

Playwright

One of the most important Argentine playwrights, Pavlovsky has also acted in plays and films (such as Fernando Salamas's *La Nube* (Clouds) (1997)) and is a well-known psychoanalyst. His early works, like *Somos* (We Are) (1961) and *La espera trágica* (The Tragic Wait) (1964), were influenced by psychodrama and the theatre of the absurd. From *La mueca* (The Grimace) (1971) and *El señor Galíndez* (1973) onwards, he began to explore the connections between everyday life and feelings, between family and political violence. Banned and persecuted throughout the Process of National Reorganization, his plays *Pablo* (1985), *Potestad* (Father) (1987) and *Paso de dos* (Pas de Deux) (1990) explore the complex relationships between kidnappers and hostages. His work is notable for its constant experimentation and for its analytical and interpretative power.

Further reading

Dubatti, J. (2001) 'Eduardo Pavlovsky: El teatro del balbuceo', *Conjunto* 120: 62–9.

Lusnich, A.L. (2000) 'La dramaturgia de Eduardo Pavlovsky (1900–2000)', in O. Pellettieri (ed.), *Nuevas busquedas a fin de siglo*, Buenos Aires: Galerna; Fundacion Roberto Arlt, 55–65.

Pavlovsky, Eduardo (1997) *Teatro completo*, Buenos Aires: Atuel.

—— (1999) *Textos balbuceantes*, Buenos Aires: Ediciones Teatro Vivo.

—— (2001) *La ética del cuerpo: Nuevas conversaciones con Jorge Dubatti*, Buenos Aires: Atuel.

NORA MAZZIOTTI

Payeras, Mario

b. 1937, Chimaltenango, Guatemala; d. 1994, Mexico City

Writer

Payeras spent several years in the Guatemalan highlands as a guerrilla fighter, an experience he described in *Los días de la selva (1972–1976)* (Days of the Jungle: The Testimony of a Guatemalan Guerrillero) (1983), which won the **Casa de las Américas** prize for ***testimonio***. Later he wrote of his urban guerrilla experience. Living in exile in Mexico City, he also produced books on ecology and revolution and a poetry collection, *Poemas de la Zona Reina* (Poems of the Queen Zone) (1989), which reveals an imagistic style that projects his dialectical view of society.

Further reading

Duchesne, J. (1986) 'Las narraciones guerrilleras: Configuración de un sujeto épico de nuevo tipo', *Testimonio y literatura*, Minneapolis: Institute for Study of Ideologies and Literature.

Payeras, M. (1983) *Days of the Jungle: The Testimony of a Guatemalan Guerrillero, 1972–1976*, New York: Monthly Review Press.

—— (1996) *Asedio a la utopia: Ensayos políticos, 1989–1994*, Guatemala City: Magna Terra.

—— (1997) *Poemas de la Zona Reina, 1972–1974*, Guatemala City: Editorial Artemis Edinter.

MARC ZIMMERMAN

Paz, Octavio

b. 1914, Tlalpan, Mexico; d. 1998, Mexico City

Poet and critic

One of the most important writers of twentieth-century Latin American literature, the Mexican poet and essayist Octavio Paz (winner of the Nobel Prize in 1991) produced a body of work that is astounding for its sheer multiplicity. His poetry follows in the tradition of European modernism; his essays take into account both the cosmopolitan frenzy with which modernists rescued, devoured and created a world culture from the most disparate elements, as well as Mexico's own particular culture. Paz's allegiance was to the modern tradition and to the practice and theory of poetry, as seen in his most important essay, *Los signos en rotación* (Signs in Rotation) (1965). If, as a poet, Paz was more entrenched in the double vision of **surrealism**, as a poetry theorist he paid attention to phenomenology and delivered a trenchant critique of Lévi-Strauss's structuralism. It often seems as if no topic was ever far from Paz's mind. A roving ambassador of culture, he partook of Mexican history and aesthetics, Hindu and Buddhist religions, and Latin American art and politics.

Paz always argued that readers must take into account an explicit or implicit dialectics: the singular poet is always referenced by the community, the poetic text relates to political arguments surrounding it. Paz's own life became an allegorical figure of modernity: from his beginnings in Mexico as a solitary poet negotiating the distance between what he called a 'poetry of solitude' and a 'poetry of community', to his sudden political awakening while visiting Spain during the Spanish Civil War, and his condemnation of the Soviet system in Paris when news of Stalin's concentration camps filtered through to the West. In his most important collection of poetry, *Libertad bajo palabra* (Freedom on Parole) (1949), Paz chronicled (and, at times, substantially altered) the first stage of his poetic career. Conceived in the post-war period, this book grew like a tree through subsequent editions, climaxing with ***Piedra de sol*** (Sun Stone) (1957), perhaps Paz's most important and stunning poem.

Although *Libertad bajo palabra* is not necessarily chronological, critics agree that a different period of Paz's life began during the 1960s, when he worked for the Mexican state in the Far East and wrote *Ladera este* (East Slope) (1962–68), *Blanco* (White) (1967) and the prose poem *El mono gramático* (The Monkey Grammarian) (1974). Given the contentiousness of the 1960s in Latin America, it was to be expected that Paz, like many of his contemporaries, would comment on political issues. His political influence reached its climax when he resigned as Mexican Ambassador to India following the 1968 student massacre at Tlatelolco, and then wrote the essays collected in *El ogro filantrópico: Historia y política 1971–1978* (The Philanthropic Ogre: History and Politics 1971–1978) (1979), a detailed critique of the Mexican bureaucratic state. From the 1970s onwards his work was based on the magazine ***Vuelta***, itself perhaps one of the most influential contemporary Latin American literary journals.

Politically, Paz was a contentious figure. He openly condemned the Cuban Revolution for its excesses, rejecting the nuanced accommodations of his contemporaries. By the same token, he steered a clear political line in his critique of the Sandinista Revolution in Nicaragua, condemning the Sandinistas while at the same time decrying US policy in the region.

Paz's political opinions were not always well received or, according to Paz, well understood. His political conservatism was, on the surface, hard to reconcile with his experimental aesthetics. From the 1980s, Paz became not merely a Mexican poet and *homme de lettres* (in the Franco-Latin American tradition) but actually an institution and figurehead. Outside of Mexico his work is read as an explanation of Mexico to the West, while in Mexico proper he is seen as a public figure closely allied to the ruling power elite, a vision that culminated in the very public celebrations of his eightieth birthday that seemed to recall the pomp, splendour and literary brilliance of a long lost time. Later, Paz wrote a series of short memoirs and political tracts concerning important periods of his life: his visit to Spain during the Civil War, his sojourn in India for example. The public life of the intellectual was Paz's last focus, to the extent that it is virtually impossible to read him as a poet without taking into account the conflictive responses that his public figure has produced in Mexico: there are those who accuse Paz of singlehandedly monopolizing the Mexican literary scene, and those who see in him the most important Mexican writer of all time.

As befits a figure of his importance, the debate around Paz and his legacy is part and parcel of a work that has continually rewritten itself and assumed open multiplicity as its mode. Paz's poetry was grounded on the tensions between the individual and society, between the public and the private. Paz's vision speaks of a time when poetry was above all a space of knowledge and when poets were, in Shelley's sense, the 'unwritten legislators of the world'. More recent critics may take issue with Paz's notion of culture as translation, or with the idea of poetry as a fundamentally solitary activity. His major work on Mexico, *El laberinto de la soledad* (The Labyrinth of Solitude) (1950), has withstood countless revisions, not only by Paz himself but by others. Ultimately, the work itself will survive precisely to the extent that it is able to provoke and tease out conflictive interpretations and new avenues of critique. In spite of its apparently unruffled surface, Paz's poetry contains enough tension to withstand the test of time.

Further reading

Fein, J.M. (1986) *Octavio Paz; A Reading of His Major Poems, 1957–1976*, Lexington: University Press of Kentucky.

Gimferrer, P. (1980) *Lecturas de Octavio Paz*, Barcelona: Anagrama.

Phillips, I. (1972) *The Poetic Modes of Octavio Paz*, London: Oxford University Press.

Quiroga, J. (1999) *Understanding Octavio Paz*, Columbia: University of South Carolina Press.

Ruy Sánchez, A. (1989) 'Octavio Paz', in C.A. Solé and M.I. Abreu (eds), *Latin American Writers*, New York: Scribners, 3, 1163–76.

—— (1990) *Una introducción a Octavio Paz*, Mexico City: Joaquín Mortiz.

Santí, E.M. (1988) Prologue to *Libertad bajo palabra 1935–1957*, ed. E.M. Santí, Madrid: Cátedra.

—— (2002) 'Octavio Paz', in C. Solé and K. Müller-Bergh (eds), *Latin American Writers: Supplement I*, New York: Scribners, 395–401.

Sefamí, J., M. van Deelden and E. Volek (1997) 'Octavio Paz', in V. Smith (ed.), *Encyclopedia of Latin American Literature*, London: Fitzroy Dearborn, 637–43.

Sucre, G. (1975) 'Paz: La vivacidad, la transparencia', in *La máscara, la transparencia*, Caracas: Monte Avila.

Wilson, J. (1986) *Octavio Paz*, Boston: Twayne.

JOSÉ QUIROGA

Paz, Senel

b. 1950, Fomento, Cuba

Writer

Senel Paz established a reputation as a fiction writer with his short story collection *El niño aquel* (That Child), which won the 1979 Premio David from **UNEAC** (National Union of Cuban Writers and Artists). His screenplay for Tomás Gutiérrez Alea's 1993 film *Fresa y chocolate* (Strawberry and Chocolate), based on his own 1990 story 'El lobo, el bosque y el hombre nuevo' (The Wolf, the Forest and the New Man), garnered him an international reputation. Although Paz is a self-proclaimed beneficiary of the Cuban Revolution, the film generated interest in part because of the perception that it questioned official Party practices, especially its oppressive treatment of homosexuals.

Further reading

Barquet, J. (1995) 'Paz, Gutiérrez Alea y Tabio: Felices discrepancias entre un cuento, un guión y un film: *Fresa y chocolate*', *Fe de Erratas* 10: 83–6.

Bejel, E. (1989) 'Senel Paz', *Hispamérica: Revista de literatura* 18(52): 49–62.

Cruz-Malave, A. (1998) 'Lecciones de cubania: Identidad nacional y errancia sexual en Senel Paz, Martí y Lezama', *Revista de crítica cultural* 17: 58–67.

Paz, S. (1995) *Fresa y chocolate*, Navarra: Tzalaparta.

—— (1995) *Strawbery and chocolate*, trans. Peter Bush, London: Bloomsbury.

Resik, M. (1997) 'Writing is a Sort of Shipwreck: An Interview with Senel Paz', *South Atlantic Quarterly* 96(1): 83–93.

JAMES BUCKWALTER-ARIAS

Peau noire, masques blancs

Published in 1952 as *Peau noire, masques blancs* by Martinican psychiatrist, writer and revolutionary Frantz Fanon, the book was later translated as *Black Skin, White Masks*. It provided a searing analysis of black alienation in the aftermath of colonialism. A foundational text of colonial and post-colonial thinking, *Black Skin, White Masks* argued, in an evocative blend of social science and poetry, that the black man had internalized or 'epidermalized' white versions of black inferiority: 'For the black man there is only one destiny. And it is white'. Although he would radically alter this view in his 1961 *Les Damnés de la terre* (The Wretched of the Earth), *Black Skin, White Masks* advocated a reconciliation of the races through mutual understanding and self-recognition.

Further reading

Bergner, G. (1995) 'Who is that Masked Woman? Or, the Role of Gender in Fanon's Black Skin', *PMLA: Publications of the Modern Language Association of America* 110(1): 75–88.

Fanon, F. (1967) *Black Skin, White Masks*, trans. Charles Lam Markmann, New York: Grove Press.

Gibson, N. (1999) 'Thoughts about Doing Fanonism in the 1990s', *College Literature* 26(2): 96–117.

Otalvaro Hormillosa, S. (2001) 'Racial and Erotic Anxieties: Ambivalent Fetishization, from Fanon to Mercer', in John C. Hawley (ed.), *Postcolonial and Queer Theories: Intersections and Essays*, Westport, CT: Greenwood Press.

Verges, F. (1997) 'Creole Skin, Black Mask: Fanon and Disavowal', *Critical Inquiry* 23(3): 578–95.

CATHERINE DEN TANDT

Pedreira, Antonio S.

b. 1899, San Juan, Puerto Rico; d. 1939, San Juan

Essayist

Qualifying as a teacher in 1920, Pedreira graduated from the University of Puerto Rico in 1925 and then studied at Columbia University in New York. He then returned to the recently created Hispanic Studies Department at the University of Puerto Rico, eventually becoming its director. In

1929 he founded the journal *Indice*, a crucial discursive space for the Generation of 1930. In 1931 he began studies for a doctorate at the Universidad Central in Madrid. His long essay ***Insularismo*** (1934) is a pivotal reflective work in Puerto Rican intellectual life, one of the series of 'national pathologies' like Alcides **Arguedas**'s ***Pueblo enfermo*** in Bolivia; Juan Gelpí has studied its central place in what he calls the 'paternalist' canon of Puerto Rican literature. Pedreira's *Obras completas* (Complete Works) were published in 1970.

Further reading

Beauchamp, J. (1995) 'Los aterrizajes de Antonio S. Pedreira: El pretexto de *Insularismo*', *Revista de estudios hispánicos* 22: 253–67.

Díaz, L. (1992) 'La metáfora y la metonimia en el discurso y la ideología de Insularismo de Antonio S. Pedreira', *Revista del ateneo puertorriqueño* 2(4): 75–100.

Gelpí, J. (1993) *Literatura y paternalismo en Puerto Rico*, San Juan: Editorial de la Universidad de Puerto Rico.

Labrador Rodríguez, S. (1999) 'Mulatos entre blancos: Jose Celso Barbosa y Antonio S. Pedreira: Lo fronterizo en Puerto Rico al cambio de siglo (1896–1937)', *Revista iberoamericana* 65(188–9): 713–31.

Maldonado de Ortiz, C. (1974) *Antonio S. Pedreira: Vida y obra*, Río Piedras, PR: Editorial Universitaria, Universidad de Puerto Rico.

Pedreira, A. (1970) *Obras de Antonio S. Pedreira*, San Juan, PR: Instituto de Cultura Puertorriqueña.

JUAN CARLOS QUINTERO HERENCIA

Pedro Páramo

Pedro Páramo (1955), a novel by Mexican writer Juan **Rulfo**, was first published in fragments in various journals; the second extract appeared in the *Revista de la Universidad de México* as 'Los murmullos' (The Murmurs), the title Rulfo had originally chosen. The drafts published in the posthumous volume *Cuadernos* (Notebooks) (1994) show writing as carefully worked as the poetry of the great Peruvian César **Vallejo**: both stripped their language of any explanation or redundancy. The narrative and chronological discontinuity of the novel provides the necessary counterpoint for words and silences and creates a limitless space where, according to Rulfo, 'the dead have neither time nor space, they simply fade away'. Some early critics read the novel against the background of a now dead debate – regionalism (see ***regionalismo***) versus cosmopolitanism – although the argument persists when the novel is described as a precursor of **magical realism** or as an *indigenista* (see ***indigenismo***) work. Although influenced by the novelists of the Mexican Revolution (Mariano **Azuela**, Martín Luis **Guzmán** and others) (see **novel of the Mexican Revolution**), Rulfo broke with that tradition, creating a new form, language and a unique novelistic space, Comala, a region devastated by violence and inhabited only by souls in torment.

Further reading

Cohn, D. (1998) 'Paradise Lost and Regained: The Old Order and Memory in Katherine Anne Porter's Miranda Stories and Juan Rulfo's *Pedro Páramo*', *Hispanofila* 124: 65–86.

Espinosa Jácome, J. (1996) *La focalización inconsciente en Pedro Páramo*, Madrid: Pliegos.

Hernández de López, A. (1999) 'Pedro Páramo y Artemio Cruz: Dos personajes de la Revolución Mexicana', *Cuadernos americanos* 13(5(77)): 222–31.

Lespada, G. (1996) '*Pedro Páramo* o el poder de la escritura (Anfibología e incongruencia en la novela de Juan Rulfo)', *Literatura mexicana* 7(1): 61–78.

Rulfo, J. (1994) *Pedro Páramo*, trans. Margaret Sayers Peden, New York: Grove Press.

Sommers, J. (ed.) (1974) *La narrativa de Juan Rulfo: Interpretaciones críticas*, Mexico City: SEP/Setentas.

MARGO GLANTZ

Peix, Pedro

b. 1952, Santo Domingo, Dominican Republic

Writer

A prolific short story writer and novelist, Peix's

most celebrated work is *Las locas de la Plaza de los almendros* (The Mad Women from the Almond Tree Park), which won the 1977 National Prize. Together with Andrés L. **Mateo** and Tony **Raful**, he has broadcast the television programme *Peña de Tres* (Circle of Three) for many years. Unlike other writers from the 'Generación de Posguerra' (Postwar Generation), Peix has been more concerned with myth and fantasy than nationalism and social conflicts in his short stories. His writing shows the strong influence of Juan **Rulfo**.

Further reading

Peix, P. (1981) *El brigadier, o, La fábula del lobo y el sargento*, Santo Domingo: Alfa y Omega.

—— (1981) *La narrativa yugulada*, Santo Domingo: Alfa y Omega.

FERNANDO VALERIO-HOLGUÍN

Pellegrini, Aldo

b. 1903, Rosario de Santa Fe, Argentina; d. 1973, Buenos Aires, Argentina

Writer

In 1926 Pellegrini founded the first surrealist movement in Argentina (see **surrealism**) and published *Qué*, a short-lived journal. He also co-edited other magazines – *Ciclo*, *Letra y línea*, and *A partir de cero* – with Emilio A. **Westphalen** and César **Moro**. He wrote poetry and drama, the former published in *El muro secreto* (The Secret Wall) (1949) and *La valija de fuego* (The Suitcase of Fire) (1952). His anthology, *Antología de la poesía surrealista* (Anthology of Surrealist Poetry) (1961), contributed significantly to the dissemination of Latin American avant-garde poetry (see **avant-garde in Latin America**).

Further reading

Pellegrini, A. (1964) *Teatro de la inestable realidad*, Buenos Aires: Ediciones del Carro de Tespis.

—— (1965) *Para contribuir a la confusión general: Una visión del arte, la poesía y el mundo contemporáneo*, Buenos Aires: Ediciones Nueva Visión.

—— (1966) *New Tendencies in Art*, trans. Robin Carson, New York: Crown Publishers.

—— (1967) *Panorama de la pintura argentina contemporánea*, Buenos Aires: Paidós.

MAGDALENA GARCÍA PINTO

Pellicer, Carlos

b. 1899, Villahermosa, Tabasco, Mexico; d. 1977, Mexico City

Poet

The oldest of the Mexico City **Contemporáneos** group, Pellicer was also the most exuberant and colourful poet. In his early poetry volumes from the 1920s, such as *Hora y 20* (An Hour and 20) (1927), he developed a luxuriant tropical imagery. In somewhat later works, such as *Hora de junio* (June Hours) (1937) and *Práctica de vuelo* (Practice Flight) (1956), he turned to the more transcendental themes of death and religious faith. His last collections concentrated on Mexico's pre-Columbian history; Pellicer was instrumental in saving Tabasco's Olmec antiquities, and the museum of archaeology in Villahermosa bears his name.

Further reading

Melnykovich, G. (1979) *Reality and Expression in the Poetry of Carlos Pellicer*, Chapel Hill: Dept of Romance Languages, University of North Carolina.

Mullen, E. (1977) *Carlos Pellicer*, Boston: Twayne.

—— (1979) 'The Early Poetry of Carlos Pellicer', *Revista de estudios hispánicos* 13: 29–44.

Rivera Rodas, O. (1989) 'Metapoética vanguardista en Pellicer', *Texto crítico* 15(40–1): 53–67.

Zaid, G. (1989) 'Siete poemas de Carlos Pellicer', *Revista iberoamericana* 55(148–9): 1099–118.

—— (2001) 'Los años de aprendizaje de Carlos Pellicer', *Letras libres* 3(31): 18–20.

MERLIN H. FORSTER

Penteado, Darcy

b. 1926, São Roque, São Paulo State, Brazil; d. 1987, São Paulo

Writer and painter

One of Brazil's most prominent gay activists and writers, Penteado began his artistic career as a book illustrator and stage and costume designer. Included in Winston Leyland's anthologies of gay Latin American writing in 1979 and 1983, he formed part of the editorial collective of the Brazilian gay liberation magazine *Lampião*. His books of stories include *A Meta* (The Goal) (1976), *Crescilda e os Espartanos* (Crescilda and the Spartans) (1977) and *Teoremambo* (Theoremambo) (1979), with camp illustrations by the author. He also published a novel, *Nivaldo e Jerônimo* (Nivaldo and Jeronimo) (1981), on the theme of homosexuality and revolution. His career as a painter included participation in the Bienale de São Paulo and in collective shows at MASP, as well as exhibits in Europe and the USA. He died of AIDS in 1987.

Further reading

Foster, D.W. (1991) 'Duas modalidades de escrita sobre a homossexualidade na ficção brasileira contemporánea', in R. Reis (ed.), *Toward Socio-Criticism: Selected Proceedings of the Conference Luso-Brazilian Literatures, a Socio-Critical Approach*, Tempe: Center for Latin American Studies; Arizona State University, 55–65.

Penteado, Darcy (1991) *Nivaldo e Jerônimo*, Rio de Janeiro: Codecri.

DANIEL BALDERSTON

Pereda Valdés, Ildefonso

b. 1899, Tacurembó, Uruguay; d. 1996, Montevideo, Uruguay

Writer

Pereda Valdés published four books of avant-garde (see **avant-garde in Latin America**) poems between 1920 and 1929 depicting the life of black people in the River Plate region: *La casa iluminada* (The Illuminated House) (1920), *El libro de la colegiala* (The Schoolgirl's Book) (1922), *La guitarra de los negros* (The Guitar of Black People) (1926) and *Raza negra* (Black Race) (1929). He later wrote essays on the same topic, collected in *El negro rioplatense* (Black Population of the River Plate) (1937) and *El negro en Uruguay* (Black People in Uruguay) (1965). He remained intensely involved with avant-garde publications and was awarded the National Literature Prize in 1985.

Further reading

Neto, P. de C. (1955) *La obra afro-uruguaya de Ildefonso Pereda Valdés*, Montevideo: CEFU.

Pereda Valdés, I. (ed.) (1927) *Antologia de la moderna poesía uruguaya*, Buenos Aires: El Ateneo.

—— (1937) *El negro rioplatense, y otros ensayos*, Montevideo: C. García & Cía.

—— (1968) *Magos y curanderos: Medicina popular y folklore mágico*, Montevideo: Arca.

—— (1970) *Lo negro y lo mulato en la poesía cubana*, Montevideo: Ediciones Ciudadela.

Rodriguez Monegal, E. (1982) 'El olvidado ultraísmo uruguayo', *Revista iberoamericana* 48(118–19): 257–74.

CELINA MANZONI

Pereira, Lúcia Miguel

b. 1903, Barbacena, Brazil; d. 1959, Rio de Janeiro, Brazil

Writer

Although best known as a literary critic and essayist, having published two important books on Brazilian fiction – *Machado de Assis* (1936) and *História da literatura brasileira – prosa de ficção (de 1870 a 1920)* (1950) – Pereira is also the author of four novels with female protagonists, who are often torn between social traditions and new models of female behaviour. She also regularly published literary reviews and articles in newspapers such as *Correio da Manhã* and *Estado de São Paulo.*

Further reading

Marchant, E. (1991) ' "Lucia Miguel Pereira's Critical Discourse", IV Seminario Nacional Mulher e Literatura-Anais, Niteroi, Rio de Janeiro, 26 a 28 de agosto 1991', *Mulher e Literatura*, Niteroi, Brazil: Abralic.

—— (1999) *Critical Acts: Latin American Women and Cultural Criticism*, Gainesville: University Press of Florida.

Pereira, L. (1981) 'Retrato do Espirito', *Minas Gerais, suplemento literario* 14(783): 11.

—— (1988) *História da literatura brasileira: Prosa de ficção, de 1870 a 1920*, Belo Horizonte: Editora Itatiaia.

—— (1994) *Escritos da maturidade: Seleta de textos publicados em periódicos, 1944–1959*, Rio de Janeiro: Graphia.

Pinto, C.F. (1990) *O Bildungsroman femenino: Quatro exemplos brasileiros*, São Paulo: Perspectiva, 45–60.

CRISTINA FERREIRA-PINTO

Perera, Víctor

b. 1934, Guatemala City

Writer

Born of Sephardic Jewish parents from Jerusalem, Perera immigrated to the USA in 1946. A frequent contributor to journals including *The New Yorker*, *Harper's*, *New York Review of Books*, *Paris Review*, *The Nation* and *Partisan Review*, he has published a number of books. His works include *Rites: A Guatemalan Boyhood* (1986), *Unfinished Conquest: The Guatemalan Tragedy* (1993) and *The Cross and the Pear Tree: A Sephardic Journey* (1995). He has also translated and edited Víctor Montejo's *Testimony: The Death of a Guatemalan Village* (1987). He has taught writing and journalism at various US universities and colleges.

Further reading

Hunsaker, S. (1997) 'Nation, Family, and Language in Víctor Perera's *Rites* and Maxine Hong Kingston's *The Woman Warrior*', *Biography: An Interdisciplinary Quarterly* 20(4): 437–61.

Perera, V. (1973) *The Loch Ness Monster Watchers: An Essay*, Santa Barbara, CA: Capra Press.

—— (1986) *Rites: A Guatemalan Boyhood*, San Diego: Harcourt Brace Jovanovich.

—— (1993) *Unfinished Conquest: The Guatemalan Tragedy*, Berkeley: University of California Press.

Savin, A. (1998) 'The Burden and the Treasure: Víctor Perera's Sephardic Family Chronicle', *Prooftexts: A Journal of Jewish Literary History* 18(3): 225–37.

JUDITH MAXWELL

Pérez-Maricevich, Francisco

b. 1937, Asunción, Paraguay

Writer and critic

An important advocate of bilingualism (Spanish/Guarani) in Paraguay, Pérez-Maricevich is also a prolific creative writer. His published poetry includes *Paso de hombre* (Man's Steps) (1963), *Coplas* (Verses) (1970) and *Los muros fugitivos* (The Fugitive Walls) (1983); his short story 'El Coronel mientras agonizo' (The Colonel While I Die) (1963) has been frequently anthologized. His important writings on Paraguayan literature include *La poesía y la narrativa en el Paraguay* (Poetry and Narrative in Paraguay) (1969), *Pequeño diccionario de literatura paraguaya* (Short Dictionary of Paraguayan Literature) (1964–69, 1980) and *Los fuegos de la noche* (The Fires of the Night) (1985), a collection of Tupí-Guarani and Nivaclés myths.

Further reading

Pérez-Maricevich, Francisco (1969) *Breve antologia del cuento paraguayo*, Asunción: Ediciones Comuneros.

—— (1969) *La poesía y la narrativa en el Paraguay*, Asunción, Paraguay: Editorial del Centenario.

—— (1984) *Diccionario de la literatura paraguaya*, Asunción: Instituto Colorado de Cultura, distributed by F. Cooper.

—— (1988) *Panorama del cuento paraguayo*, Asunción, Paraguay: Tiempo Editora.

Pla, J. (1968) 'Narrativa paraguaya (Recuento de

una problemática)', *Cuadernos americanos* 159: 181–96.

TERESA MÉNDEZ-FAITH

Pérez Torres, Raúl

b. 1941, Quito, Ecuador

Writer

A committed writer who walks the line between dream and reality, Pérez Torres has edited several influential magazines, including *La Bufanda del Sol*, *Débora* and *Letras del Ecuador*, and is currently Director of the Nueva Editorial Casa de la Cultura Ecuatoriana. He has published some twelve books, among which the most accomplished are *Micaela y otros cuentos* (Micaela and Other Stories) (1974), *Musiquero joven, musiquero viejo* (Young Musician, Old Musician) (1978), *Teoría del desencanto* (Disenchantment's Theory) (1985) and *Sólo cenizas hallarás* (Only Ashes You Will Find) (1996). Most recently, Pérez Torres received the Juan Rulfo Prize (1994) and the Julio Cortázar Prize (1995).

Further reading

Pérez Torres, R. (1980) *En la noche y en la niebla*, Havana: Casa de las Américas.

—— (1981) 'El cuento ecuatoriano contemporáneo', *Casa de las Américas* 22(127): 167–70.

—— (1988) 'El oficio de escribir', *Revista iberoamericana* 54(144–5): 969–75.

—— (1996) *Sólo cenizas hallarás*, Quito: Casa de la Cultura Ecuatoriana 'Benjamin Carrion'.

Rodríguez, J. (1977) 'Raul Pérez Torres o el absurdo agónico', *Situación del relato ecuatoriano. Tomo I: Cincuenta opiniones y una discusion; Tomo II: Nueve estudios*, Quito: Eds de la Univ. Católica.

HUMBERTO E. ROBLES

Peri Rossi, Cristina

b. 1941, Montevideo, Uruguay

Writer

Peri Rossi is a prolific writer who has published several books of poems, collections of short stories and novels. Her central preoccupations are children, erotic love and the recurrent metaphor of a wreck, reflecting the political disintegration of Uruguay during the 1970s. From a working-class background, Peri Rossi was a teacher and journalist when she began to write poetry and short stories. During the repressive years of military rule in Uruguay, she joined a coalition of political parties of the Left, and was persecuted and exiled as a result. In 1972 she settled in Barcelona, Spain, where she now resides. Before leaving Uruguay she published several books of short texts: *Viviendo* (Living) (1963), *Los museos abandonados* (Abandoned Museums) (1968), *El libro de mis primos* (My Cousins' Book) (1969), *Indicios pánicos* (Panic) (1970) and *Evohé* (translated into English as *Evohe: Erotic Poems*) (1974), which caused a great scandal because of its erotic and lesbian themes.

Her imaginative range embraces both an essential solitude and human love, and in *Solitario de amor* (Solitary of Love) (1988) she explores the uterus as the source of that love: she believes that it is perhaps in this unique umbilical relation of naturally dependent bodies that Paradise Lost may be regained. Among her most admirable works are the short stories *El museo de los esfuerzos inútiles* (The Museum of Idle Efforts) (1983) and the novel *La nave de los locos* (The Ship of Fools) (1984).

Unlike many contemporary lesbian writers, she denies the existence of **lesbian literature**. However, in her most recent books, homosexuality is addressed openly. She also writes **fantastic literature**, a well-developed genre in the River Plate region. She has important connections with the narrative of Felisberto **Hernández** and Julio **Cortázar**, with whom she maintained a close friendship.

Further reading

Feal, R.G. (1995) 'Cristina Peri Rossi and the Erotic Imagination', in Doris Meyer (ed.), *Reinterpreting the Spanish American Essay: Women Writers of the Nineteenth and Twentieth Centuries*, Austin: University of Texas Press, 215–26.

Hughes, P. (1997) 'Cristina Peri Rossi', in V. Smith (ed.), *Encyclopedia of Latin American Literature*, London: Fitzroy Dearborn, 644–5.

Kaminsky, A. (1993) 'Cristina Peri Rossi and the Question of Lesbian Presence', in *Reading the Body Politic: Feminist Criticism and Latin American Women Writers*, Minneapolis: University of Minnesota Press, 115–33.

Peri Rossi, C. (1989) *The Ship of Fools*, trans. P. Hughes, London: Allison & Busby.

—— (1993) *A Forbidden Passion*, trans. M.J. Treacy, Pittsburgh: Cleis Press.

MAGDALENA GARCÍA PINTO

Perlongher, Néstor

b. 1949, Buenos Aires, Argentina;
d. 1992, São Paulo, Brazil

Writer

The **neo-baroque** signs interwoven in the poetry of Perlongher's six published volumes – *Austria-Hungría* (1980), *Alambres* (Wires) (winner of the Boris Vian prize in 1987), *Hule* (Rubber) (1989), *Parque Lezama* (Lezama Park) (1990), *Aguas Aéreas* (Waters in the Wind) (1992) and *El chorreo de las iluminaciones* (The Stream of Lights) (1992) – reveal one of the most original voices in contemporary Spanish American poetry. The eroticism of signs reverberates through the sexualized material in a poetics redolent of the works of **Lezama Lima** or Severo **Sarduy**. The aesthetics of perversion (Sade, Bataille) has its roots in an Argentine history transfigured through Perlongher's voice; examples include the story 'Evita vive' (Evita Lives) and the poem 'Cadáveres' (Corpses). Aligned to a neo-baroque aesthetic, Perlongher described his own work as *neobarroso*, 'the golden bubbles of Cuban baroque splashing their way into the estuary' (the River Plate), which he developed in an erudite introduction to his anthology *Caribe Transplatino* (a collection of the writings of Lezama Lima, Sarduy, José Kozer, Osvaldo **Lamborghini**, Arturo **Carrera**, Tamara **Kamenszain**, Perlongher himself, and others).

Perlongher's poetry explores an aesthetics of excess. His poetry overflows, lascivious and helicoidal, deliberately exposing erotic artificiality and the spiralling flow of images, leading in the last phase of his poetry to a search for mystical ecstasy ('Alabanza y exaltación del Padre Mario') (Praise and Exaltation of Father Mario). He spent the last ten years of his life in São Paulo teaching anthropology, working particularly in the area of sexuality. He published *O negócio do miché. Prostitução viril em São Paulo* (Male Prostitution in São Paulo) (1987) and *O que é Aids* (What is AIDS) (1987), as well as essays and interviews. In 1992, he won a Guggenheim award with a project for an 'auto sacramental' (a kind of miracle play), which remained incomplete.

Further reading

Perlongher, N. (1997) *Poemas completos: 1980–1992*, ed. R. Echavarren, Buenos Aires: Seix Barral.

—— (1997) *Prosa plebeya: Ensayos, 1980–1992*, Buenos Aires: Colihue.

Rosa, N. (1997) *Tratados sobre Néstor Perlongher*, Buenos Aires: Editorial Ars.

Siganevich P. and A. Cangi (1996) *Lúmpenes peregrinaciones: Ensayos sobre Néstor Perlongher*, Rosario, Argentina: Beatriz Viterbo.

Zapata, M. (1987) 'Néstor Perlongher: La parodia diluyente', *Inti: Revista de literatura hispánica* 26–7: 285–97.

JORGE SCHWARTZ

Perse, Saint-John

b. 1887, Pointe-à-Pitre, Guadeloupe;
d. 1975, Giens Peninsula, France

Poet

Born Alexis Saint-Leger Leger, Perse's sometimes obscure poetry expresses his nostalgia for Guadeloupe at the end of the plantation era. He published his first poems *Eloges* (Eloges and Other Poems) in 1911, followed by *Anabase* (Anabasis) in 1924 while a diplomat. After twenty years of silence and in exile from France during the Vichy government, he published *Exil* (Exile) in 1942, followed later by *Oiseaux* (Birds) (1963) and *Chant pour un Equinoxe* (Song for an Equinox) (1975). He received the Nobel Prize in 1960.

Further reading

Giménez, R. (1993) 'Two Epical Excursions: "Anabasis" and "Winds" by Saint-John Perse', *Panjab – University Research Bulletin (Arts)* 24(1): 133–42.

Little, R. (1993) 'Ponge's Hatred of Saint-John Perse: Further Evidence', *French Studies Bulletin: A Quarterly Supplement* 47: 14–17.

Rigolot, C. (2001) *Forged Genealogies: Saint-John Perse's Conversations with Culture*, Chapel Hill: University of North Carolina.

Sterling, R. (1994) *The Prose Works of Saint-John Perse: Towards an Understanding of His Poetry*, New York: Peter Lang.

Winspur, S. (1988) *Saint-John Perse and the Imaginary Reader*, Geneva: Droz.

York, R. (1996) 'Saint-John Perse, the Diplomat', *Claudel Studies* 23(1): 19–29.

ANNE MALENA

Perspectiva

A Brazilian publishing house founded in São Paulo in 1965 which has been directed for many years by Jaco Guinsburg., Perspectiva was known for many years as the prime publisher of works of literary theory in Portuguese, including translations of works by Umberto Eco, Roland Barthes, Tzvetan Todorov, and many others, as well as of the concrete poets (see **concrete poetry**). In fact, the design of the volumes' covers respected the font and layout that marks the poetry of the **Noigandres group**, especially that of Augusto de **Campos**. Guinsburg has also published important works of literary criticism, ranging from Davi **Arrigucci**'s study of **Cortázar** to Marta Peixoto's study of João Cabral de **Melo Neto** and the essays of Silviano **Santiago**. The company has also published works on art and architecture (including translations of Le Corbusier and studies of Brasília), numerous works on theatre and cinema, writings on Brazil by Blaise Cendrars and others, translations of thinkers from Hannah Arendt and Martin Buber to Erving Goffman and Thomas Kuhn, and works on development economics. Perspectiva has been important in bringing the work of Spanish American critics (Emir **Rodríguez Monegal**, Severo **Sarduy**, Ramón Xirau and others) to a Brazilian audience.

DANIEL BALDERSTON

Peru

In common with much of Latin America, the advent of *modernismo* (see **Spanish American modernism**) marked a new stage in Peruvian literature. In prose, Clemente Palma (the son of Peru's major nineteenth-century literary figure Ricardo **Palma**) wrote short stories imbued with a *fin de siècle* feeling, ironic, dark and often bizarre. His *Cuentos malévolos* (Malevolent Stories) were published in 1904. *Modernista* poetry had its precursor in Manuel **González Prada** whose influence was felt in so many ways by this first twentieth-century generation. Jose María **Eguren**, probably Peru's most important poet of the period, did not share González Prada's social concerns however; his work was closest to symbolism and its preoccupations were fundamentally aesthetic. Abraham **Valdelomar** moved away from the cosmopolitanism of his contemporaries to evoke a simple provincial life in his short stories.

If the Indian entered nineteenth-century Peruvian literature as a romanticized background figure in Clorinda Matto de Turner's *Aves sin nido* (Birds without a Nest) (1889), González Prada's virulent denunciations of colonialism opened the way towards a more socially aware writing. While the *Cuentos andinos* (Andean Stories) (1920) of Enrique **López Albújar** remain within a descriptive, *costumbrista* (see ***costumbrismo***) mould, the decade that followed produced a new writing about the Indian marked by solidarity and denunciation. The writings of José Carlos **Mariátegui** were both a reflection and a key influence on this new generation of *indigenistas*. His ***Siete ensayos de interpretación de la realidad peruana*** (Seven Interpretative Essays on Peruvian Reality) (1928) is a key text for understanding a generation schooled in the University Reform movement of 1919, hardened by the struggle against the dictatorship of Leguía, and informed by ***Amauta***, Mariátegui's journal which began publication in 1926. The journal published the work of César Falcón, Luis E.

Valcárcel and Gamaliel **Churata** among others, in militant defence of the Indian cause.

The 1920s also witnessed the emergence of a diverse and adventurous avant-garde movement whose echoes resonate through the rest of the century. César **Vallejo**'s two early collections, *Los heraldos negros* (The Black Heralds) (1918) and *Trilce* (1922), are emblematic works in their sense of a bewildered humanity facing the crisis of the old epistemology, the disintegration of language and the loss of all certainties. This response to modernity is not general, however; poets such as Alberto **Hidalgo** and Carlos Oquendo de Amat celebrate the advent of the modern. That festive element is largely absent from those avant-garde poets writing during the thirties. The characteristic note of Emilio Adolfo **Westphalen**'s poetry, for example, is melancholy and his work is intensely private; and César **Moro**'s voluntary exile in France, and his decision to write largely in French, may be seen as a repudiation of the Peruvian reality also. The repressive conditions of life through the forties produced two quite different responses among poets. One group sought a 'pure poetry' which was often highly innovative in form, perhaps as a withdrawal from reality as it was then; this group included Martín **Adán**, Javier **Sologuren** and Jorge Eduardo **Eielson**, as well as Blanca **Varela**. Another group, including Alejandro Romualdo and Juan Gonzalo Rose as well as, somewhat later, Washington Delgado, turned towards a more explicitly political poetry, or at least one which set personal experience within a social context.

In fiction, the legacy of the *indigenistas* of the 1920s found continuity in the social realism of prose writers such as Ciro **Alegría**. His early work described the life and conditions of the peasant communities, but his best-known work is the iconic *El mundo es ancho y ajeno* (Broad and Alien is the World) (1941), which describes a threatened Indian community that was in some senses analagous with Peru itself, as that country was described in the ideology of the Aprista party of which Alegría was a member. In some senses, both Alegría and José María **Arguedas** derived their vision from Mariátegui's conception of a national tradition rooted in a communitarian pre-Columbian world. Considered Peru's greatest novelist, Arguedas mounted a sustained critique of an ***indigenismo*** which, in his view, described an Indian spiritually incapacitated by colonialism and barely capable of feeling or reason. Arguedas's own work, as writer and ethnographer, captured the richness and sophistication of the Indian world, particularly in what is widely acknowledged as his masterpiece, *Los **ríos profundos*** (Deep Rivers) (1958). He was absorbed, however, by the problem of reconciling two worlds whose culture and language set them apart from each other; the despair he felt at the failure of his project to effect such an understanding, expressed in last book *El zorro de arriba y el zorro de abajo* (The Fox From Above, The Fox From Below) (1969) may well have contributed to his suicide in that year. Other writers did continue and develop the theme however, particularly Manuel **Scorza**, whose five-novel series *La guerra silenciosa* (The Silent War) (1970–79) explored the history of Indian struggle through the prism of **magical realism**.

A new generation of writers in the 1950s turned their attention increasingly to urban settings, and in particular to an expanding Lima; Enrique Congrains, Julio Ramón **Ribeyro** and Oswaldo Reynoso narrated the world that Sebastian Salazar Bondy would later describe as *Lima la horrible* (1964).

It was the city that provided the setting for the early novels of Peru's most internationally successful novelist, Mario **Vargas Llosa**, a success that began with his tale of a group of cadets at a Lima military school *La **ciudad y los perros*** (The Time of the Hero) (1962) and continued with *Conversación en la Catedral* (Conversation in the Cathedral) (1969). Alfredo **Bryce Echenique** also explored the urban middle-class universe in works beginning with *Un mundo para Julius* (A World for Julius) (1970). In subsequent years, Vargas Llosa's reputation grew as the novelists of the Latin American **Boom** were increasingly acknowledged on the international scene. His *La guerra del fin del mundo* (War of the End of the World) (1981) rehearses his central concerns about the circularity of history in the context of a nineteenth-millenarian rebellion in Brazil. That recuperation of a forgotten history, this time of the poorest sections of Peruvian society, was the theme also of works by Cronwell **Jara**, Gregorio Martínez and Miguel Gutiérrez.

A new generation in the 1960s confirmed the strength and diversity of poetry in Peru. The young guerrilla poet Javier **Heraud** was killed at an early age, but left a small and moving body of lyric poetry. Antonio **Cisneros** established his ironic, almost Whitmanesque register with his *Canto ceremonial contra un oso hormiguero* (Ceremonial Song against an Anteater) (1968), winner of the **Casa de las Américas** poetry prize that year and a ferocious attack on Peruvian bourgeois values. The same range of responses to an often alienated, and later, under Fujimori, a deeply repressive reality characterized the younger poets, including Carmen Ollé, José Watanabe, Marcela Dreyfus and Enrique Verástegui. Jaime **Bayly**, a television personality as well as a writer, is known for his novelistic explorations of youth culture, including drugs, homosexuality and bisexuality, and conflicts with the parent generation. In the field of theatre, the Cuatro Tablas group won a deserved reputation both nationally and internationally for its experimental techniques and its fusion of dance, music and performance art.

Further reading

Cornejo Polar, A. (ed.) (1981–82) *Literatura y sociedad en el Perúmero.*

Cornejo Polar, J. (1993) *Intelectuales, artistas y Estado en el Perú del siglo XX*, Lima: Universidad de Lima.

Elmore, Peter (1993) *Los muros invisibles: Lima y la modernidad en la novela del siglo XX*, Lima: Mosca Azul.

Foster, D.W. (1981) *Peruvian Literature: A Bibliography of Secondary Sources*, Westport, CT: Greenwood Press.

Higgins, James (1982) *The Poet in Peru*, Liverpool: Francis Cairns.

—— (1993) *Hitos de la poesía peruana siglo XX*, Lima: Milla Bartres.

Lauer, Mirko (1989) *El sitio de la literatura: Escritores y política en el Perú del siglo XX*, Lima: Mosca Azul.

Ortega, Julio (1988) *Crisis de la identidad: La pregunta por el Perú en su literatura*, Mexico City: Fondo de Cultura Económica.

Rodrígues Luis, (1980) Julio *Heremeneútica y praxis del indigenismo: La novela indigenista de Clordina Matto de Turner a José María Arguedas*, Mexico City: Fondo de Cultura Económica.

SARA CASTRO-KLAREN AND MIKE GONZALEZ

Peyrou, Manuel

b. 1902, Buenos Aires Province, Argentina; d. 1974, Buenos Aires, Argentina

Writer

Theatre and film critic for the newspaper *Crítica* and the literary supplement of ***La Prensa***, which he edited in the 1970s, Peyrou also wrote fantastic tales (see **fantastic literature**) and crime stories (see **crime fiction**) in the classic English mould. The title story of his prize-winning volume *La espada dormida* (The Sleeping Sword) (1945) was selected by **Borges** and **Bioy Casares** for their anthology *Los mejores cuentos policiales* (Best Crime Stories) (1943), which included only three Argentine writers. Peyrou's many volumes of writing included two novels, *La noche repetida* (The Repeated Night) (1953) and *Las leyes del juego* (Rules of the Game) (1959).

Further reading

Castagnino, R. (1983) 'Manuel Peyrou: El testimonio novelesco de una época argentina', *Revista de la Biblioteca Nacional* 2(3): 21–34.

Peyrou, M. (1967) *Marea de fervor*, Buenos Aires: Emecé Editores.

—— (1969) *El hijo rechazado*, Buenos Aires: Emecé Editores.

—— (1972) *Thunder of the Roses; A Detective Novel*, trans. Donald Yates, New York: Herder & Herder.

Peyrou, O. (1997) 'Manuel Peyrou, el hermano secreto de Borges', *Cuadernos hispanoamericanos* 562: 81–6.

ALEJANDRA LAERA

Pezzoni, Enrique

b. 1926, Buenos Aires, Argentina;
d. 1989, Buenos Aires

Literary critic

An innovative critic and teacher, Pezzoni was editor of the magazine ***Sur*** in the 1960s after **Bianco** was fired for visiting Cuba. Pezzoni introduced the ideas of Barthes, Kristeva and Lotman into an Argentine critical world dominated by philology and stylistics. A fine translator (of *Moby Dick*, *Lolita*, *Theorem*) and theorist of translation, he was also a pioneering teacher and exponent of literary theory in Argentina. His classes on Rubén **Darío**, **Borges** and **Vallejo** were examples of a rigour and elegance rarely seen in Argentine criticism. His writings have been gathered in the volume *El texto y sus voces* (The Text and Its Voices) (1986).

Further reading

Pezzoni, Enrique (1998) *El texto y sus voces*, Buenos Aires: Editorial Sudamericana.
—— (1999) *Enrique Pezzoni, lector de Borges: Lecciones de literatura 1984–1988*, Buenos Aires: Sudamericana.

DIEGO BENTIVEGNA

Philip, Marlene Nourbese

b. 1947, Tobago

Writer

Philip gave up her full-time law practice to write. In *Thorns* (1980), *Salmon Courage* (1983) and the prize-winning *She Tries Her Tongue, Her Silence Softly Breaks* (1988), she charts a poetic journey to find a demotic mother-tongue, rather than a dominating colonial father-tongue, increasingly experimenting with repetition, poetic lines and spatial arrangement. Her innovative prose poems such as *Looking for Livingstone* (1991), her novel for young people *Harriet's Daughter* (1988) and two volumes of cultural and political essays, *Frontiers* and *Showing Grit: Showboating North of the 44th Parallel*, raise crucial race and gender issues.

Further reading

Savory, E. (1996) 'Marlene Nourbese Philip', in B. Lindfors and R. Sander (eds), *Twentieth Century Caribbean and Black African Writers*, Detroit: Gale Research, 296–306, 3rd edn.

ELAINE SAVORY

Phillips, Caryl

b. 1958, Basseterre, St Kitts

Writer

Caryl Phillips was brought by his parents to England in the year of his birth, and he grew up in Leeds and studied at the University of Oxford. He has written scripts for film, plays, radio and television, among them the movie *Playing Away*, about a West Indian cricket team encountering the colonial behaviour of England. His novel *The Final Passage* (1985) won the Malcolm X Prize. Later novels include *Cambridge* (1992), *Crossing the River* (1994), *The Nature of Blood* (1997), *Higher Ground* (1989) and *A State of Independence* (1986). His collection of essays *The European Tribe* won the 1987 Martin Luther King Memorial Prize.

Further reading

De La Concha, A. (2000) 'The End of History. Or Is It? Circularity versus Progress in Caryl Phillips' *The Nature of Blood*', *Miscelanea: A Journal of English and American Studies* 22: 1–19.
Julien, C. (1997) 'The Diaspora and the Loss of Self in Caryl Phillip's Fiction: Signposts on the Page', *PALARA: Publication of the Afro Latin/American Research Association* 1: 98–105.
—— (1999) 'Surviving through a Pattern of Timeless Moments: A Reading of Caryl Phillips's *Crossing the River*', in Maria Diedrich, Henry Louis Gates, Jr and Carl Pedersen (eds), *Black Imagination and the Middle Passage*, New York: Oxford University Press.
Korkka, J. (1999) 'Language and Identity in Caryl Phillips's Fiction', in *Approaches to Narrative Fiction*, Turku, Finland: University of Turku.
Phillips, C. (1994) *Crossing the River*, New York: Knopf.

—— (2002) *A New World Order: Essays*, New York: Vintage Books.

KEITH JARDIM

Picón Salas, Mariano

b. 1901, Mérida, Venezuela; d. 1965, Caracas, Venezuela

Writer

An outstanding humanist scholar, historian and founder of the Faculty of Philosophy and Letters at the Universidad Central of Venezuela in 1946, Picón Salas was one of the group of **intellectuals** who shaped modern Venezuelan society after the death of dictator Juan Vicente Gómez in 1935. With a clear commitment to the recuperation of the traditional values of Venezuelan national culture, his autobiographical writings (see **autobiography**), histories – *Comprensión de Venezuela* (Understanding Venezuela) (1949) – and **literary criticism** – *Formación y proceso de la literatura venezolana* (Formation and Process of Venezuelan Literature) (1940) – are testimony to his reforming spirit.

Further reading

Fernández Romero, R. (2000) '*Viaje al amanecer* (1943), de Mariano Picón Salas: Infancia y utopia política', *Taller de letras* 28: 107–17.

Jaimes, H. (1998) 'Mariano Picón Salas y el discurso de la historia', *Revista hispánica moderna* 51(2): 327–40.

—— (1999) 'La historia y la autobiografía en los ensayos de Mariano Picón Salas', *Hispanófila* 125: 23–36.

Márquez Rodríguez, A. (1994) 'Mariano Picón Salas: El arte y la costumbre de pensar', *Revista iberoamericana* 60 (166–7): 31–45.

Morin, T. (1979) *Mariano Picón Salas*, Boston: Twayne.

Picón Salas, M. (1962) *A Cultural History of Spanish America. From Conquest to Independence*, Berkeley: University of California Press.

—— (1983) *Viejos y nuevos mundos*, Caracas: Biblioteca Ayacucho.

Sucre, G. (1989) 'Mariano Picón Salas', in C.A. Solé and M.I. Abreu (eds), *Latin American Writers*, New York: Scribners, 2, 903–8.

RAFAEL CASTILLO ZAPATA

Piedra de sol

Piedra de sol (Sun Stone) (1957), a poem of 584 free verse hendecasyllabic lines, is Octavio **Paz**'s most stunning poetic achievement. It joins the solitude of the individual poet to the ruined landscape of postwar Europe, fusing poetics and politics, eros and remembrance. It begins and ends in an unreal landscape of mirrored reflections, and the melancholic poetic voice produced by this exquisite form achieves a timelessness grounded in history: a linear poem that goes back over itself, a mandala of the universe, a notion also important for Paz's later *Blanco* (White) (1967). Because it paradoxically fashions its modernity in formal language (perfect hendecasyllables, for example), *Piedra de sol* is a thoroughly modern poem: a kind of historical and ahistorical machine that also comments on structure and text.

Further reading

Nelken, Z.E. 'Los avatares del tiempo en *Piedra de sol* de Octavio Paz', *Hispania* 51: 92–4.

Nugent, R. (1966) 'Structure and Meaning in Octavio Paz's *Piedra de sol*', *Kentucky Foreign Language Quarterly* 13(3): 138–46.

Pacheco, J.E. (1971) 'Descripción de *Piedra de sol*', *Revista iberoamericana* 74: 135–46.

Paz, O. (1962) *Sun Stone. Piedra de sol*, trans. M. Rukeyser, New York: New Directions.

JOSÉ QUIROGA

Piglia, Ricardo

b. 1940, Adrogué, Province of Buenos Aires, Argentina

Writer

One of Argentina's most eminent living writers, Piglia has argued that Argentinian literature is torn between the legacy of **Borges** and of **Arlt**; indeed, his own fiction owes a great deal to this tension. His extraordinary 1975 novella 'Homenaje a Roberto Arlt' (Homage to Roberto Arlt) is at once a complex work of criticism, an intense evocation of a lost world and a fascinating literary hoax. The novel ***Respiración artificial*** (Artificial Respiration) (1980) is the most important work to be published within Argentina during the terrible period of the Proceso. His work *La ciudad ausente* (The Absent City) (1992) is a fascinating tribute to Joyce and to Macedonio **Fernández**, and has been made into an important opera by Gerardo Gandini. Another novel, *Plata quemada* (Burnt Money) (1997), the controversial winner of the Planeta prize, recreates a famous bank robbery of 1965.

Piglia was active in the 1960s in *Los libros*, a leftist cultural journal, and he travelled to China in 1969. His first book of stories, called *La invasión* (The Invasion) (1967) in its Argentine edition and *Jaulario* (Cages) (1967) in its Cuban edition, won the coveted **Casa de las Américas** prize. The volume in which 'Homenaje a Roberto Arlt' appeared, *Nombre falso* (Assumed Name) (1975), was unfortunate in the timing of its publication (as Piglia remembers in a sad jest at the beginning of *Respiración artificial*) in the very violent and chaotic period of the end of Isabel Perón's presidency, in the months preceding the military coup of March 1976. Nevertheless, this volume, and particularly 'Homenaje', established Piglia as the foremost of the younger writers in the country.

Respiración artificial appeared near the end of the military period, and is a searing look at that worst of times. The first half of the novel consists in part of an epistolary exchange between Marcelo Maggi, a dissident historian, and his nephew Emilio Renzi, an aspiring novelist (and Piglia's alter ego: his full name is Ricardo Emilio Piglia Renzi). Much of that exchange centres on an invented political figure and writer in mid-nineteenth-century Argentina, Enrique Ossorio, one of whose projects is a futuristic novel entitled (ominously) *1979*; the 'letters from the future' transcribed in the novel are nightmarish accounts of the Buenos Aires in which the novel was written. The second half of the novel, after the nephew goes to the provincial city of Concordia in search of his uncle, consists mostly of a fascinating all-night conversation in a bar with the uncle's friends; as the night wears on, it becomes obvious (but is never stated directly) that the uncle has not made it to the meeting because he has been kidnapped and 'disappeared'. *Respiración artificial* won the Boris Vian Prize in 1981 and became something of a best-seller despite its tremendous complexity.

The recent *Plata quemada* is a very different kind of work. The bank robbery, and the subsequent flight of the group of robbers from Buenos Aires to Montevideo, where they are besieged by the police in a bloody shoot-out, is told in a direct way, albeit with subtle shifts in the narration. The novel won the Planeta prize but was immediately the subject of a controversy about whether it had been properly submitted to the jury; nevertheless, the fuss contributed greatly to its success.

Piglia has edited series of **crime fiction** for several publishing houses, and is the foremost champion of the 'hard-boiled' tradition in Argentina. His *La Argentina en pedazos* (Argentine in Bits) (1993) is a comic book version of Argentine classics (including works by Armando **Discépolo**, **Cortázar**, **Lugones**, **Borges**, **Puig** and **Arlt**), with illustrations by artists who work in comics. He has written the libretto for the Gandini opera *La ciudad ausente*, as well as film scripts for works by Babenco, Bemberg and others. There also exist several collections of his interviews. Sardonic, insightful, brilliant, Piglia is one of the central figures in intellectual debates in today's Argentina.

Further reading

Balderston, D. (2002) 'Ricardo Piglia', in C. Solé and K. Müller-Bergh (eds), *Latin American Writers: Supplement I*, New York: Scribners, 403–13.

Bratosevich, N. *et al.* (1997) *Ricardo Piglia y la cultura de la contravención*, Buenos Aires: Ediciones Atuel.

Díaz Quiñones, A. *et al.* (1998) *Ricardo Piglia:*

Conversación en Princeton, Princeton: Program in Latin American Studies.
Piglia, R. (1986) *Crítica y ficción*, Santa Fe: Universidad Nacional del Litoral; 2nd edn, 1990.
—— (1994) *Artificial Respiration*, trans. D. Balderston, Durham, NC: Duke University Press.
—— (1995) *Assumed Name*, trans. S. Waisman, Pittsburgh: Latin American Literary Review Press.

DANIEL BALDERSTON

Pignatari, Décio

b. 1927, São Paulo, Brazil

Writer

A dynamic figure in Brazilian arts and intellectual life since the 1950s, Pignatari co-founded the **Noigandres group** and helped conceptualize **concrete poetry**. The collected concrete and visual poems of *Poesia pois é poesia* (Poetry is After All Poetry) (1975), some informed by advertising, are among the best known internationally; examples include 'LIFE' and 'beba coca cola', a caustic satire of a universally known product. As a university professor in the architecture faculty of the University of São Paulo, Pignatari helped disseminate semiotics and contemporary theories during the 1970s and 1980s (discussed in *Contracomunicação* (Counter-Communication) (1971)). He has also produced very provocative experimental prose fiction.

Further reading

Medina, Cremilda (1984) 'Décio Pignatari, ao Ritmo da Taquigrafia do Romance', *Minas Gerais, suplemento literario*, 29 Sept., 19(939): 9.
Pignatari, D. (1974) *Semiótica e literatura*, São Paulo: Perspectiva.
—— (1977) *Poesia pois é poesia*, São Paulo: Editora Cultrix.
—— (1986) *O rosto da memória*, São Paulo: Brasiliense.
—— (1992) *Panteros*, Rio de Janeiro: Editora 34.
——(1998) *Cultura pó's nacionalista*, Rio de Janeiro: Imago.

CHARLES A. PERRONE

Pilgrim, Frank

b. 1926, Georgetown, British Guiana; d. 1989, Georgetown

Playwright

Pilgrim's literary career followed an unusually conservative path, as cultural representative of British Guiana in the CARICOM Secretariat and editor and drama critic for the *Guyana Chronicle*, a newspaper denounced as an instrument of governmental 'paramountcy'. Pilgrim's reputation as a playwright hinges on his major play *Miriamy*, first performed in 1962, which debunks bourgeois values, partly through the use of language, particularly regional accents, as markers of social standing and pretension. His radio plays, also satirical, include the series, 'The Jessamies', broadcast in the 1950s, the 1973 'Rain Stop Play' and the revue 'The Brink', staged in 1981.

Further reading

Pilgrim, F. (1963) *Miriamy: A West Indian Play in Three Acts*, Demerar, British Guiana: B.G. Lithographic.

JILL E. ALBADA-JELGERSMA

Pineau, Gisèle

b. 1956, Paris, France

Novelist

The most recent in a line of Guadeloupean female novelists, Pineau is unique in the predominantly male and Martinican ***créolité*** movement. She was not raised in the Caribbean as were **Confiant** and **Chamoiseau**, but in Paris. Instead of the university background of her male counterparts, she trained as a psychiatric nurse and has been practising in Guadeloupe since 1980. Less politically militant than her contemporaries, she first came to prominence with her prize-winning second novel *La grande dérive des esprits* (The Great Drifting of Spirits) in 1994 which evoked a magical world steeped in the beliefs of an oral creole culture. Her 1995 novel *L'espérance macadam* (The Macadam of Hope), centred on the lives of women, achieved great critical success.

Further reading

Licops, Dominique (1999) 'Origi/Nation and Narration: Identity as Epanouissement in Gisèle Pineau's *Exil selon Julia MaComere*', *Journal of the Association of Caribbean Women Writers and Scholars* (MaComere) 2: 80–95.

Pineau, G. (1997) *Guadeloupe découverte*, Fort-de-France: Fabre Domergue.

—— (1999) *La grande drive des esprits: Roman*, Paris: Serpent à plumes.

—— (2000) *Caraibes sur Seine*, Paris: Editions Dapper.

Suarez, Lucia M. (2001) 'Gisèle Pineau: Writing the Dimensions of Migration', *World Literature Today* 75(3–4): 9–2.

J. MICHAEL DASH

Piñera, Virgilio

b. 1912, Cárdenas, Cuba; d. 1979, Havana

Writer

Alongside José **Lezama Lima** and Alejo **Carpentier**, Virgilio Piñera is one of the most important Cuban writers of the twentieth century. His short stories, plays, longer narratives and poems present a universe where reality is seen through the prisms of the absurd and boundless despair. Piñera's deeply irreverent humour and his sense of the macabre comment upon what is termed the 'human condition' except that Piñera would have debunked this term as a cliché. Piñera was raised in a working-class family and never escaped a sense of financial strain. After a dispute with José Lezama Lima, he went to Argentina, where he met **Borges** and his circle, published in *Anales de Buenos Aires*, and befriended the Polish expatriate writer Witold Gombrowicz, who exerted an important influence on his work. One of the many anecdotes in Piñera's remarkable biography is that he, among others, translated Gombrowicz's *Ferdydurke* into Spanish without knowing a word of Polish. Piñera's novel, *La carne de René* (René's Flesh) (1952), owes much to Gombrowicz's sense of the absurd. Before the Cuban Revolution of 1959, Piñera had already produced a considerable body of work: aside from the aforementioned novel, he began his literary career as a poet, and his long poem, *La isla en peso* (1943), examines the crisis of Cuban culture in the early twentieth century. He also published a collection of stories, *Cuentos fríos* (Cold Tales) (1956) and plays such as *Electra Garrigó*, *Jesús* and *Aire frío* (Cold Air) (1959).

Piñera was also one of the guiding spirits of José Rodríguez Feo's journal *Ciclón*, published after the dispute that closed the venerable journal ***Orígenes***. In *Ciclón*, Piñera was able to polemicize freely. He published texts by Gide, Freud and de Sade, and brought homosexuality in literature out into the open. After 1959, Piñera wrote for the literary supplement ***Lunes de Revolución***. According to many sources, he was arrested on 11 October 1961 and spent a brief period in jail, due to revolutionary moralizing campaigns against homosexuals. From the late sixties until his death, Piñera was ostracized in his homeland; although seldom published, he continued writing clandestinely and reading for friends. Recently he has been 'rehabilitated', and his novel *La carne de René* published in Cuba for the first time. Piñera's sardonic humour and his irreverence have found favour in the work of a new generation that refuses to fall into the moralizing traps of the past.

Further reading

Aguilú de Murphy, Kaguel (1989) *Los textos dramáticos de Virgilio Piñera y el teatro del absurdo*, Madrid: Pliegos.

García Chicester, Ana (1992) 'Superando el caos: Estado actual de la crítica sobre la narrativa de Virgilio Piñera', *Revista interamericana de bibliografía* 43(1).

—— (1994) 'Virgilio Piñera', in David W. Foster (ed.), *Latin American Gay Literature: A Biographical and Critical Sourcebook*, Westport, CT: Greenwood Press.

González-Cruz, Luis F. (1990) 'Virgilio Piñera', in Julio A. Martínez (ed.), *Dictionary of Twentieth-Century Cuban Literature*, Westport, CT: Greenwood Press.

McQuade, Frank (1993) 'Making Sense out of Non-Sense: Virgilio Piñera and the Short Story of the Absurd', in John Macklin (ed.), *After Cervantes*, Leeds: Iberian Papers.

—— (1997) 'Virgilio Piñera', in V. Smith (ed.), *Encyclopedia of Latin American Literature*, London: Fitzroy Dearborn, 653–4.

Molincro, R. (ed.) (2002) *Virgilio Piñera: La memoria del cuerpo*, San Juan: Editorial Plaza Mayor.

Quiroga, José (1995) 'Fleshing out Virgilio Piñera from the Cuban Closet', in Emilie Bergmann and Paul Julian Smith (eds), *¿Entiendes? Queer Readings, Hispanic Writings*, Durham, NC: Duke University Press.

—— (2000) 'Outing Silence as Code: Virgilio Piñera', in *Tropics of Desire: Interventions from Queer Latino America*, New York: New York University Press, 101–23.

Torres, Carmen L. (1989) *La cuentística de Virgilio Piñera: Estrategias humorísticas*, Madrid: Pliegos.

JOSE QIUROGA

Piñon, Nélida Cuiñas

b. 1936, Rio de Janeiro, Brazil

Writer

In 1990 Piñon was elected as only the third ever women member of the Academia de Letras Brasileiras. In 1996 she was voted its first woman president and was awarded Mexico's prestigious Juan **Rulfo** Prize. She is the author of fourteen works of fiction and several books of essays.

Born of Portuguese, Spanish and Galician parentage, Piñon's writing draws heavily on this cultural heritage to create a fictional world that mirrors not only her own experiences, but those of other emigrant populations. Piñon recasts historical narrative so that the telling of tales reveals the experiences of marginalized persons and speaks to a broader audience.

Her writing indicates that one possibility for self-knowledge comes only after giving full voice to many different discourses. There are few other women writers in Brazil who have as deliberately and successfully incorporated open (historical) space into the framework of the novel. Her use of space almost always avoids closure and, thus, incorporates much more than a notion of the intimate; historical space is closely interwoven with narrative space and fact blended with a fantasized past in order to explain the present.

Piñon is uncomfortable with the label feminist writer, but it is from a profound self-knowledge that she is able to transmit the experience of alterity. She epitomizes the Brazilian woman's concern with the reconstruction of meaningful language in order to express what it means to be a woman and to give words, shape and form to her own reality.

Piñon is linked closely to such contemporary Spanish American writers as Gabriel **García Márquez**, Mario **Vargas Llosa**, Isabel **Allende** and Elena **Garro**; what differentiates her from them is this intentional manipulation of space to give specificity to a re-definition of that which is alien and female. In other words, Nélida Piñon attempts to rewrite both real and imagined Brazilian history in order to invent human intrigue. Space functions as a major protagonist, and it is through interaction with space that other characters achieve their own sense of identity and place.

Piñon's work is often a subversive reaction to oppressive Brazilian military governments; she does not address the actual problems encountered by the writer, such as censorship, exile or torture, but instead breaks with tradition in order to recapture communal space.

Further reading

García Pinto, M. (1997) 'Nélida Piñon', in V. Smith (ed.), *Encyclopedia of Latin American Literature*, London: Fitzroy Dearborn, 654–5.

Jozef, B. (1980). 'Nélida Piñon, a força da linguagem', in *O jogo mágico*, Rio de Janeiro: Editora José Olympio, 70–2.

Piñon, N. (1992) *Caetana's Sweet Song*, trans. H. Lane, New York: Knopf.

—— (1994) *The Republic of Dreams*, trans. H. Lane, London: Picador.

Teixeira, V.R. (2002) 'Nélida Piñón', in C. Solé and K. Müller-Bergh (eds), *Latin American Writers: Supplement I*, New York: Scribners, 415–31.

SUSAN CANTY QUINLAN

Pitol, Sergio

b. 1933, Puebla, Mexico

Writer

One of the most erudite and prominent narrators of his generation, Pitol's vocation for travelling and his cultural diplomatic assignments have familiarized him with remote cultures and literatures. His texts are mainly novels and short stories but also include literary criticism and translations from Polish, Russian, English and Italian, among others (see **translation in Latin America**). From his first novel, *El tañido de una flauta* (A Flute's Sound) (1972), through to his most mature work – *El desfile del amor* (Love's Parade) (1984), *Domar a la divina garza* (To Tame the Divine Heron) (1988) and *La vida conyugal* (Married Life) (1991) – Pitol exhibits humour, irony and a superb style. He has been awarded the Xavier **Villaurrutia** Prize (1981), the Mexican National Prize for Letters (1993) and the Juan Rulfo Prize (1999).

Further reading

Balza, J. *et al.* (2000) *Sergio Pitol: Los territorios del viajero*, Mexico City: Ediciones Era.

Costa, O. (1983) *Sergio Pitol*, Guanajuato: Gobierno del Estado de Guanajuato.

Edkins, A. (1997) 'Sergio Pitol', in V. Smith (ed.), *Encyclopedia of Latin American Literature*, London: Fitzroy Dearborn, 656–7.

Monsiváis, C. (2000) 'Sergio Pitol: El autor y su biógrafo improbable', *Letras libres* 2(14): 36–7.

Montelongo, A. (1998) *Vientres troqueles: La narrativa de Sergio Pitol*, Xalapa, Veracruz, Mexico: Universidad Veracruzana, Biblioteca.

JUAN PELLICER

Pizarnik, Alejandra

b. 1936, Avellaneda, Argentina; d. 1972, Buenos Aires, Argentina

Poet

The daughter of Russian Jewish immigrants, Pizarnik published her first book of poetry in 1955, and by her fourth volume, *Arbol de Diana* (Diana's Tree) (1962), was already considered among the outstanding Argentinian and Latin American poets. *Arbol de Diana* and *Los trabajos y las noches* (Works and Nights) (1965) represent the best of her distinctive style: short poems of compressed and intense expression, in which the empty page around the text is a signifier of the void in which the poetic voice struggles to find a sense to existence.

Pizarnik's imagery results from a surrealist (see **surrealism**) combinatory freedom and her control of composition and language: 'my desire [is] to make poems that are terribly exact despite my innate surrealism and to work with elements of interior shadows'. Some of her central symbols are the garden, the forest, childhood as paradise lost, the body, the house, the desert, thirst, shores, falling, and the colours blue, lilac, white and red. Distance is a capital motif, as her writing expresses the despairing separation from all good and an overwhelming longing for material and spiritual union with people and things.

The same search for sense through writing led to a different textual organization in *Extracción de la piedra de locura* (Extraction of the Stone of Folly) (1968) and the long prose poems of *El infierno musical* (Musical Hell) (1971). Her themes, however, are the same: loneliness, existential anguish, strangeness and alienation from her social environment, love (mostly as hope and loss), the precariousness of self, the seduction and dangers of silence, and above all, poetry as a longed for means of self-salvation. Though poetic beauty is conceived as the ultimate haven, her writing expresses the certainty of defeat and an unbearable despair, which very likely were among the reasons behind her mental instability and suicide in 1972.

Pizarnik was a gifted translator of French poetry,

and a subtle reader who wrote insightful articles on poetry and fiction. One of her critical essays became a book on its own right; in *La condesa sangrienta* (The Bloody Countess) (1971), on V. Penrose's *Erzébeth Bathory, La comtesse sanglante,* Pizarnik confronts the concurrence of evil and beauty which was also the keystone of one of her favorite authors, Lautréamont.

One of several anthologies of her works, *Textos de sombra y últimos poemas* (Texts of Shadow and Last Poems) (1985), is a compilation of late and unpublished texts, among them a series of prose texts in which intertextuality, play with words and obscenity combine in a mixture of violence and desperate humour which escapes any generic definition. Pizarnik's influence and importance in Latin American letters have been growing constantly.

Further reading

Goldberg, F.G. (1994) *Alejandra Pizarnik: 'Este espacio que somos'*, Gaithersburg: Hispamérica.

Graziano, F. (ed.) (1987) *Alejandra Pizarnik, A Profile,* trans. M.R. Fort, F. Graziano and S.J. Levine, Durango: Logbridge-Rhodes.

Lockhart, M.A. (1997) 'Alejandra Pizarnik', in V. Smith (ed.), *Encyclopedia of Latin American Literature,* London: Fitzroy Dearborn, 657–9.

Molloy, S. (1997) 'From Sappho to Baffo: Diverting the Sexual in Alejandra Pizarnik', in D. Balderston and D.J. Guy (eds), *Sex and Sexuality in Latin America,* New York: New York University Press, 250–8.

Piña, C. (1991) *Alejandra Pizarnik,* Buenos Aires: Planeta.

FLORINDA F. GOLDBERG

Pizarro, Ana

b. 1951, Santiago, Chile

Writer and critic

Pizarro was co-ordinator of a UNESCO project on the history of Latin American literature, which included *Hacia una historia de la literatura hispanoamericana* (Toward a History of Latin American Literature) (1987) and *La literatura latinoamericana como proceso* (Latin American Literature as a Process) (1985). These texts reflect on the complexity and cultural diversity of Latin America and challenge traditional historiography. Her first novel, *La luna, el vientre, el año, el día* (The Moon, the Womb, the Year and the Day) (1994), added her voice to the discourse on the Chilean diaspora that followed the *coup* of 1973.

Further reading

Pizarro, Ana (1994) *De ostras y caníbales: Reflexiones sobre la cultura latinoamericana,* Chile: Editorial Universidad de Santiago.

—— (1994) *La luna, el vientre, el año, el día,* Mexico City: Fondo de Cultura Económica.

—— (1994) *Sobre Huidobro y las vanguardias,* Santiago: Editorial Universidad de Santiago, Instituto de Estudios Avanzados.

SANDRA GARABANO

Plá, Josefina

b. 1909, Canary Islands, Spain; d. 1999, Asunción, Paraguay

Writer and art critic

Residing in Asunción since 1927, Plá dedicated her entire life to the artistic work of Paraguay and contributed enormously to its cultural development. More than sixty years of intense and constant writing have produced over fifty volumes, including poetry, from *El precio de los sueños* (The Price of Dreams) to *La llama y la arena* (The Flame and the Sand), and short story collections, among them *La muralla robada* (The Stolen Wall). In theatre, her work includes *Fiesta en el río* (Party in the River) and several pieces co-written with Roque Centurión Miranda. In addition, she has to her name several volumes of critical essays on Paraguayan culture.

Further reading

Plá, J. (1968) *El polvo enamorado,* Asunción: Ediciones Diálogo.

—— (1984) *Cambiar sueños por sombras*, Paraguay: Alcándara.
—— (1984) *Los británicos en el Paraguay, 1850–1870*, Asunción: Arte Nuevo Editores.
—— (1984) *Teatro paraguayo inédito*, Asunción: Mediterráneo.
—— (2002) *Los animales blancos y otros cuentos*, Santiago: LOM Ediciones.
Rodríguez Alcalá, H. (1968) 'Josefina Plá, española de América y de la poesía', *Cuadernos americanos* 4: 73–101.

TERESA MÉNDEZ-FAITH

Placoly, Vincent

b. 1946, Le Marin, Martinique; d. 1992, Fort-de-France, Martinique

Writer and activist

Placoly was a highly original thinker and writer of an intensely wrought prose. His output of essays, cultural journalism and fiction began with *La vie et la mort de Marcel Gonstran* (Life and Death of Marcel Gonstran) (1971), a study in alienation. Several of his plays recreate key episodes and figures in Caribbean history – Dessalines, Empress Joséphine, the French Revolution – or re-frame world dramas – like his créole *Don Juan* (1984). Placoly studied in Paris, taking an active part in left-wing student politics, before returning to Martinique to teach French language and literature. He was a member of the Groupe Révolution Socialiste on the Trotskyist left of the independentist parties.

Further reading

Kavaliunas, J. (1995) 'A la recherche de l'immortalité: Le paradoxe de la parole ecrite dans l'oeuvre de Vincent Placoly', *Francographies: Bulletin de la Société des Professeurs Français et Francophones d'Amérique* 2: 163–77.
Placoly, V. (1983) *Dessalines, ou, La passion de l'indépendance: Théâtre*, Havana: Casa de las Américas.
—— (1985) 'La Maison dans laquelle nous avons choisi de vivre', *La Quinzaine littéraire* 16–31; 436: 32–3.
Seguin-Cadiche, D. (2001) *Vincent Placoly: Une explosion dans la cathédrale*, Paris: L'Harmattan.

BRIDGET JONES

Pocaterra, José Rafael

b. 1890, Valencia, Venezuela; d. 1955, Montreal, Canada

Writer and diplomat

Jailed by the Gómez dictatorship in 1919, first in La Rotunda prison and later in the castle of Puerto Cabello, Pocaterra's prison experiences inspired one of the great pieces of testimonial writing (see ***testimonio***) in Venezuelan literature – *Memorias de un venezolano en la decadencia* (Memoirs of a Venezuelan in a Time of Decadence) (1936). All his work is characterized by a form of critical realism, as in *Cuentos grotescos* (Grotesque Tales) (1922) and *Panchito Mandefuá*. He lived in exile between 1922 and 1939, then returned to his country where he exercised important political and diplomatic functions for successive governments until his death in Canada.

Further reading

Herrera Guada, X. (1963) *José Rafael Pocaterra, vida y obra*, Valencia: Editorial París en América.
Pocaterra, J. (1956) *Obras selectas*, intro. M. Otero Silva, Madrid and Caracas: Ediciones Edime.
—— (1978) *Cuentos grotescos*, Caracas: Monte Avila.
Subero, E. (ed.) (1970) *Contribución a la bibliografía de José Rafael Pocaterra*, Caracas: Ediciones de la Gobernación del Distrito Federal.
Tejera, M. (1976) *José Rafael Pocaterra, ficción y denuncia*, Caracas: Monte Avila.

JORGE ROMERO LEÓN

Poesía sorprendida

Poesía sorprendida (Surprised Poetry) was a 1940s Dominican literary movement. It was influenced by international trends, especially late **surrealism**. The *poesía sorprendida* poets encoded their poetry to escape censorship during Trujillo's dictatorship.

The movement was especially significant for Dominican literature because it opened new modes of expression for subsequent generations. Among its best-known poets were Franklin Mieses Burgos, Freddy Gatón Arce, Antonio **Fernández Spencer**, Manuel **Rueda**, Aída Cartagena Portalatín and Rafael Amêrico Henríquez.

Further reading

Baeza Flores, A. (1977) *La poesía dominicana en el siglo XX: Historia crítica, estudio comparativo y estilístico: Generaciones y tendencias, poetas independientes, La poesía sorprendida, suprarrealismo, dominicanidad y universalidad, 1943–1947*, Santiago, República Dominicana: Universalidad Católica Madre y Maestra.

Olivera, O. (1988) 'Del ideal estético a la alusión patriótica en *La poesía sorprendida*', *Revista iberoamericana* 142: 213–27.

FERNANDO VALERIO-HOLGUÍN

poetry

Modernismo in Spanish America (see **Spanish American modernism**) marked the birth of a new poetic practice that drew on both formal and thematic innovations in France to generate renewal in Spanish-language poetry. Slightly later, in the early 1920s, **Brazilian modernism** produced its own radical vision of a peripheral modernity that encouraged the creative cannibalism of ***Antropofagia***. The extraordinarily innovative writing of Mário de **Andrade** and Oswald de **Andrade** perhaps found their equivalents in the avant-garde (see **avant-garde in Latin America**) currents that were emerging in Spanish America under a range of sobriquets – **Borges** representing Spanish ***ultraísmo*** in its Latin American variant; **Girondo** and Norah **Lange** among others producing innovative developments after **surrealism** in Argentina; **Huidobro** publishing one of the great poems of the moment – ***Altazor*** – in Chile; the **Contemporáneos** in Mexico exploring the autonomy of poetic language. A quite different direction was emerging in the poetry of the region at the same time – a poetry of social concerns and realist impulse, beginning perhaps with the poetry of ***négritude***) throughout the Caribbean, represented among others by Nicolás **Guillén**, Luis **Palés Matos**, Aimé **Césaire** and Nelson **Estupiñán Bass**, and evolving into a poetry of broader social concern and political protest whose products, by and large, did not enjoy a level of aesthetic achievement commensurate with their ideological passion.

The struggle between the uncertainty of the modern and the loss of the preserving myths of the past – family, tradition, community – is nowhere more powerfully or poignantly addressed than in the work of Peruvian poet, César **Vallejo**, from the crumbling language of *Trilce* (1923) to the ambiguous hopes of the posthumous *Poemas humanos* (Human Poems) of 1938. Like Vallejo, other Latin American poets had also seen the Spanish Civil War as a watershed – Guillén, Pablo **Neruda** and Octavio **Paz**, the outstanding Mexican poet who was also perhaps the region's most significant critic of poetry, among them. Paz was clearly left unconvinced by the promise of the Spanish Republic, and increasingly his own considerable poetic output reflected the division he articulated in a key essay between '*poesía de soledad*' and '*poesía de comunión*'; a poetry of solitude in the world as opposed to a poetry of communion in an imaginative poetic universe where opposites might be reconciled after a kind of sensual, aesthetic congress – it was what he later called, in his study of Claude Lévi-Strauss, the realm of culture.

After the political hopes of the 1930s came a period of reflection, in the intellectual explorations of the Mexican **Taller** group, for example, or the literary debates in ***Sur***. But the major poetic event of the 1940s was undoubtedly Pablo Neruda's great epic, ***Canto general*** (1950), written while Neruda was evading arrest after the banning of the Communist Party. Neruda's experiences in Spain proved to be a watershed, as his 1936 poem 'Explico algunas cosas' (I Explain a Few Things) testified. His earlier work was preoccupied with the survival of the self in an unstable world; after Spain, although he continued, as he did throughout his life, to write lyric love poetry, Neruda became a public poet addressing political and historical issues. *Canto general* represents a repossession of Latin American history; a journey of rediscovery. If

Canto general stands in a grand rhetorical tradition, Neruda's *Odas elementales* (1953) represented a new direction: a modest poetry, in form and language, whose subject matter was largely the smallest and simplest of everyday experiences – eating a salad, wearing warm socks, peeling an onion. Yet they were hugely popular among the large audiences Neruda attracted to his public readings.

Chile also produced a quite contrary poetic practice. The *antipoesía* (see **antipoetry**) of Nicanor **Parra** and others was prosaic in its thematic content and its language, and unheroic in its poetic voice – João Cabral de **Melo Neto**'s ***Morte e vida severina*** is an example of a similar impulse in Brazilian poetry. Some suggested that the poetry it opposed was the rhetorical excess of Neruda. In any event there was a clear connection between the work of Parra and the current of 'conversational poetry' (a term first used by Cuban poet **Fernández Retamar**) which linked the work of writers as different as Brazil's Carlos Drummond de **Andrade**, Nicaragua's Ernesto **Cardenal**, El Salvador's Roque **Dalton**, Argentina's Juan **Gelman** and the group of performance poets emerging in the English-speaking Caribbean through the 1950s and 1960s. But many of them were linked by their content as well as their language, and a conception of poetry as testimony that joined Dalton, Gelman, Francisco **Urondo**, Cardenal and others. In some cases such a concern with reality led directly to a political militancy that defined a group of writers of the 1960s known as the guerrilla poets (see **guerrilla poetry**) – **Heraud**, **Castillo** and Fernando Gordillo of Nicaragua among them.

There is a sense in which the history of Latin American poetry contains also an unheard voice – the voice of women. Cecília **Meireles** and Alfonsina **Storni**'s poetry was alive with a powerful and unfulfilled passion; so too in a different tone was the writing of 1945 Nobel Prize winner Gabriela **Mistral**, whose 'La maestra rural' (The Rural Schoolmistress) was described for so long as a work of provincial nostalgia rather than the moving and tragic expression it really is. The underestimated poetry of Rosario **Castellanos** (whose prose work is more widely known and acknowledged) joins the work of Luisa **Futoransky**, Ana Cristina **César** and the disturbing, sometimes wordless, writing of Alejandra **Pizarnik** in addressing the issue of power in language in the spaces that often fill the page.

New voices have been heard in the 1990s – voices of other silenced minorities, such as the Mapuches with whose voice Elicura **Chihuailaf** speaks in Chile; or other indigenous voices who speak in Guarani, Quechua or the Mayan of Guatemalan indigenous poet Humberto **Ak'abal**. And some of the profound pain of the loss of memory in the periods of dictatorship, of the uncertainty of a future dominated by a global imagery that threatens to fill the time we might otherwise have for reflection, has been explored in the work of the Chilean poets of recent years such as Raúl **Zurita**, Néstor **Perlongher** of Argentina or, in Mexico, José Emilio **Pacheco**, whose absorption with the transience of things and the permanence of the imaginative act seem particularly immediate in the context of a Mexico City now the largest and most contaminated urban environment in the world.

The poetry of the future is as open and uncertain as the future itself; but its poets may recall Luis **Cardoza y Aragón**'s reassurance: 'La poesía no envejece/ ... Siempre su realidad es profecía/ cada vez más próxima a su cumplimiento./ La poesía es la única prueba/ concreta de la existencia del hombre' (Poetry does not age/ ... its persistence is a prophecy/ closer to fulfilment as each day passes./ Poetry is the only concrete proof/ of man's existence).

Further reading

Gonzalez, M. and D. Treece (1992) *The Gathering of Voices*, London: Verso.

Kirkpatrick, G. (1989) *The Dissonant Legacy of Modernismo*, Berkeley: University of California Press.

Peixoto, M. (1996) 'Brazilian Poetry from 1900 to 1922', in R. Gonzalez Echevarría and E. Pupo-Walker (eds), *The Cambridge History of Latin American Literature*, Cambridge: Cambridge University Press, 3, 233–45.

Pontiero, G. (1996) 'Brazilian Poetry from Modernism to the 1990s', in R. Gonzalez Echevarría and E. Pupo-Walker (eds), *The Cambridge History of Latin American Literature*, Cambridge: Cambridge University Press, 3, 247–67.

Quiroga, J. (2996) 'Spanish American Poetry from

1922 to 1975', in R. Gonzalez Echevarría and E. Pupo-Walker (eds), *The Cambridge History of Latin American Literature*, Cambridge: Cambridge University Press, 2, 303–61.

Sucre, G. (1975) *La máscara, la transparencia*, Caracas: Monte Avila.

Yurkievich, S. (1971) *Fundadores de la nueva poesía latinoamericana*, Barcelona: Barral.

MIKE GONZALEZ

politics and literature

In some respects it is hard to imagine any Latin American literature that does not engage with the political reality of the region. Although many writers elect to turn their gaze away from the struggles for power or control that shape and define the daily reality of Latin America, their effects are hard to escape. Similarly, the deep divisions and inequalities that characterize society in every part of the continent are inescapable, even for those writers for whom they are not matters of artistic concern.

Nonetheless, there is an identifiable body of writing about politics on the one hand, and on the other literature informed by political beliefs and ideology. Although genre or school divisions are probably specious, it may be worth the attempt to separate the terms of that engagement in various ways.

The literature of political advocacy may embrace all those varieties of literary expression which employ aesthetic means to encourage attitudes to political events or social structures. A literature of nationalism, for example, may belong in this category, where it represents the struggle for nationhood as a literary motif. José **Martí** in Cuba might be an example. Elsewhere literature as an instrument of social agitation wears its colours more clearly on its sleeve. ***Indigenismo***, although it embraces a range of forms and emphases, promotes the cause of Latin America's first nations in the context of an exposure of their lack of representation, the social oppression to which they have been subjected, and the denial of their cultural traditions and expression. The Peruvian essayist José Carlos **Mariátegui** addressed all these issues in his influential ***Siete ensayos de interpretación de la realidad peruana*** (Seven Interpretative Essays on Peruvian Reality) (1928). The **Guayaquil Group** of Ecuador, to take but one example, illustrated that oppression with brutal realism in works such as Jorge **Icaza**'s *Huasipungo* (The Villagers) (1934) or the collectively authored ***Los que se van*** (The Vanishing Ones) (1930). This is not to say, of course, that these and other *indigenista* writers did not also explore other dimensions of indigenous experience – through myth, folklore, magic and so on – but that a defence of their cause and a vision of a different world were central to their representation. Ciro **Alegría**'s *El mundo es ancho y ajeno* (Broad and Alien is the World) (1941) may stand astride the genres, exploring the culture of the first nations of Peru while also addressing, in the latter half of the novel, the issue of organization and resistance as a dramatic impulse. There is a similar tension in the work of José María **Arguedas**, although a work such as *Todas las sangres* (All the Bloods) (1965) is manifestly a work of advocacy in its representation of the rising and struggles of indigenous peoples.

In the late 1920s, the cultural debates in the Soviet Union culminated in a definition of **socialist realism** which urged upon writers an obligation to speak for the oppressed and against the existing order. This, it was argued, was a creative as well as a political imperative – or rather, the division itself was an invention of bourgeois ideologies of art. Many were drawn to that rallying call, from the novelists of working-class life such as the Boedo group (see **Boedo vs Florida**) in Argentina to the **Estridentismo** movement in Mexico, which was influenced equally by the technological Utopianism of the Italian Futurists. Other poets of the avant-garde were impelled by the idea of the artist's social obligation; Rubén Martínez Villena of Cuba virtually abandoned his literary career for politics. Peruvian poet César **Vallejo** wrote a novel, *Tungsteno* (1931), in a social realist idiom yet expressed in much of his poetry a less trenchant and certain vision of the world. Jorge **Amado** also held to the practice of literature as exposure and denunciation – as in *Cacau* (1933) – although his work was rooted too in the black culture of Brazil which gave it a greater complexity in its realism. In the same way, Cuba's leading poet

Nicolás **Guillén**'s early work flowed from the popular culture of black Cuba, and reproduced its rhythms and (with varying success) its language. Yet it is with *West Indies, Ltd.* (1934) that Guillén assumed the responsibilities of the explicitly political poet. Two years later, face to face with the Spanish Civil War, Pablo **Neruda** acknowledged the public responsibility of the poet and of poetry. 'Why no more lilies' he asks (in the poem 'Explico algunas cosas' (I Explain a Few Things)); 'come and see the blood in the streets' is his answer. It would not be an exaggeration to say that, thereafter, Neruda becomes the archetypal political poet – not only because of the directly political content of much of his writing, but also in relation to the notion of the poet as a public performer. That public voice is then heard in a series of outstanding civic voices – Ernesto **Cardenal** in Nicaragua, Juan **Gelman** and Francisco **Urondo** in Argentina, Claribel **Alegría** and Roque **Dalton** in El Salvador among others.

Specific events and moments in twentieth-century Latin American history have posed the question of the relationship between politics and literature in quite stark and practical ways. The revolutions in Mexico (1910–17), Cuba (1959) and Nicaragua (1979), for example, challenged intellectuals and writers to place their skills and persuasive abilities at the service of a social project. Some found their place in the cultural revolutions – in Cuba, Guillén, **Fernández Retamar**, Cintio **Vitier** and the novelist and critic Alejo **Carpentier** addressed political issues to a greater or lesser degree in their work. The Cuban journal ***Casa de las Américas*** was an important vehicle for discussion about the relations between intellectuals, artists and the State. That discussion was reflected in two small but influential volumes – *El intelectual y la sociedad* (The Intellectual and Society) (1969) and the debate between Vargas Llosa, Julio **Cortázar** and Oscar Collazos in *Literatura en la revolución y revolución en la literatura* (Literature in the Revolution and the Revolution in Literature) (1971). The conservative journal ***Mundo nuevo***, published in Paris and almost certainly indirectly sponsored by the US government, was established in order to contest the journal's influence and the pro-Cuban positions it advocated. Not all Cuban writers were happy with the constraints that this implied; most notoriously, Heberto **Padilla** found the pressures of engagement to be inimical to artistic value and others, such as Reinaldo **Arenas**, were bitterly critical of the 'official' view of the role of intellectuals. In Nicaragua, a group of women including Gioconda **Belli** and Vidaluz **Meneses** spoke to a growing and enthusiastic audience for poetry mobilized by Ernesto Cardenal's Sandinista Culture Ministry. In the case of Mexico, it was visual artists rather than writers who made the principal contribution to the redefinition of public language. With the exception of Mariano **Azuela**, whose *Los de abajo* (The Underdogs) (1915) was in many ways a bitter critique of politics, most writers chose to record rather than engage directly with the events of the revolutionary period. It was not until the 1930s that the Mexican novel began to produce partisan responses to public events, in writers such as Gregorio López y Fuentes and Mauricio **Magdaleno**. Much later, in 1962, Carlos **Fuentes**'s novel *La muerte de Artemio Cruz* (The Death of Artemio Cruz) looked back at forty-five years of post-revolutionary Mexico with a critical eye – and in some ways revisited the themes of corruption that had informed a much earlier sceptical view of the Revolution and its aftermath, that of Martín Luis **Guzmán**'s *La sombra del caudillo* (The Shadow of the Chief) (1929).

There is an equally broad range of writing which casts a cynical eye on politics and politicians, as well as a literature informed by a more deeply conservative vision of political change. Plínio **Salgado** drew extreme right-wing conclusions from **Brazilian modernism** and went on to found Brazil's fascist Integralismo movement, and the Argentine poet Leopoldo **Lugones** moved towards increasingly ultra-nationalist positions in his later life. Two of the most prominent figures of the post-sixties literary world adopted active conservative positions. Octavio **Paz**, a Republican sympathizer during the Spanish Civil War, became a vocal critic of the Left and founded a journal, ***Vuelta***, which provided an important platform for right-wing thinkers. Mario **Vargas Llosa**, who had not previously participated in political life directly, although he was a prominent conservative spokesperson and journalist, stood as a presidential candidate in the Peruvian elections of 1990 on a neo-liberal platform, losing to Alberto Fujimori.

The election (1971) and subsequent violent overthrow (in 1973) of the Popular Unity government in Chile generated a broad cultural movement, particularly in music and theatre. But after 1973 political representation was largely restricted to the literature of exile, while the internal exploration of life in a repressive society was often conducted in extremely elliptical or symbolic ways – as in the writings of Diamela **Eltit**.

If certain key writers became involved at different stages in the political life of their country – Rómulo **Gallegos** in Venezuela, Aimé **Césaire** in Martinique, for example, – this was not by and large reflected directly in their literary production, which remained at the level of imaginative universes and symbolic explorations. Others – Urondo, Dalton, Alaída **Foppa** of Guatemala, and Javier **Heraud** of Peru, for example – were engaged directly in struggles against dictatorship which cost them their lives.

It remains a matter of intense and sustained debate whether the dynamics of public life can be attuned to the rhythms of the imagination. Some have argued that they are incompatible – that the demands of politics require a sharp definition of issues that literature might seek to explore in their complexity and contradiction. For others, it is precisely literature's role to illuminate public debate, especially at the point at which civic issues shape individual lives. It could be argued, for instance, that much of the body of writing subsumed under the heading of *literatura de* ***testimonio*** is an exploration of precisely that encounter. In the end, perhaps political writing is at its best when imaginative language is employed directly in the public arena in the advocacy of political causes, as in the work of writers such as Eduardo **Galeano** (Uruguay), Carlos **Monsiváis** and Elena **Poniatowska** in Mexico, or the political journalism of Gabriel **García Márquez**.

Further reading

Franco, Jean (2002) *Decline and Fall of the Lettered City*, Cambridge, MA and London: Harvard University Press.

Gonzalez, Mike and David Treece (1992) *The Gathering of Voices*, London: Verso.

Lie, N. (1991) *La revista cubana Casa de las Américas (1960–76)*, Leuven: Leuven University Press.

Mander, John (1969) *The Unrevolutionary Society: The Power of Latin American Conservatism in a Changing World*, New York: Knopf.

Miller, Nicola (1999) *In the Shadow of the State: Intellectuals and the Quest for National Identity in Twentieth Century Spanish America*, London: Verso.

Stoner Saunders, F. (2000) *The Cultural Cold War: The CIA and the World of Arts and Letters*, New York: New Press.

Vargas Llosa, Mario (1996) *Making Waves*, New York: Farrar, Strauss.

MIKE GONZALEZ

Poniatowska, Elena

b. 1932, Paris, France

Writer

Elena Poniatowska is arguably the most important woman writer in modern Mexico, if not in Latin America. A direct descendant of the Polish and Mexican aristocracies, she moved from Paris to Mexico City in 1942, and became a Mexican citizen in 1968, when her activism potentially placed her immigration status in question. She began her journalistic career by conducting daily newspaper interviews with intellectuals and celebrities. A selection of her hundreds of remarkable interviews is being published under the title, *Todo Mexico* (All of Mexico); so far five volumes have appeared.

Poniatowska quickly became known for her charming but naughty interviewing style, in which an appearance of ingenuity masks a pointed and often irreverent line of questioning. For instance, aboard the presidential airplane with Miguel de la Madrid in *Domingo Siete* (Sunday the 7th) she begins by fretting over a run in her nylons and technical problems with her tape recorder, eliciting a paternal response from the solicitous President; whereupon Poniatowska follows up with a hard-hitting question about the federal government's responsibility for Mexico's appalling levels of poverty and social inequality.

During the 1960s Poniatowska was the only

female member of a literary circle that included Fernando **Benítez**, José Emilio **Pacheco**, Carlos **Monsiváis**, Sergio **Pitol** and Juan José **Arreola**. Although her first, autobiographical novel, *Lilus Kikus*, was published in 1954, she was made famous by two books of testimonial literature (see ***testimonio***): *Hasta no verte Jesús mío* (Until I See You My Lord) (1969) and *La noche de Tlatelolco* (Massacre in Mexico) (1971). *Hasta no verte Jesús mío* follows closely the oral history of an embittered but feisty washerwoman, whose life reflects the contours of modern Mexican history, from the impoverished countryside of the Porfiriato to the ranks of the Mexican Revolution, and the subsequent massive immigration of unskilled workers, especially women, to Mexico City's slums and shanty towns. This is the first of many texts in which Poniatowska fashions a unique narrative voice, combining the ideolects of a multitude of popular Mexican characters she has known, from every region of the country. On the surface this powerful use of popular Mexican dialect, to treat controversial social and political themes, by a daughter of the European nobility, seems highly contradictory. In fact this contradiction constitutes the core of Poniatowska's hybrid originality. She has always managed to negotiate gracefully (if at some personal cost) between her mother's world and that of Jesusa Palancares or her own maid, to move from a cocktail party at the French Embassy to a hovel in one of Mexico City's most wretched shanty towns. Poniatowska has returned time and again to these divided class loyalties that mark her work and personality, most extensively and eloquently in her autobiographical novel, *La Flor de Lis* (1988).

La noche de Tlatelolco, the definitive literary treatment of the Mexican Student Movement of 1968, is a collage of voices describing the energy and enthusiasm of the movement's mass mobilizations, and the bitter disillusionment following the 2 October massacre at Tlatelolco, where some 300 civilians were killed. In 1998, as the thirtieth anniversary of the Student Movement approached, the journalist Luis **González de Alba**, a former student leader and one of Poniatowska's key informants, accused her of plagiarism, igniting a public debate about the responsibilities of the testimonial writer.

Affectionately referred to as the princess of the Mexican literary Left, for the past three decades Poniatowska has tirelessly championed progressive and subaltern political and social struggles, acting as Mexico's most public intellectual and producing a dizzying succession of essays, articles and books, many of them straddling the boundaries between biography, autobiography, fiction and oral history. Above all she has been drawn to the stories of creative and rebellious women of all social classes, from the painters Frida Kahlo and Angelina Beloff (*Querido Diego, te abraza Quiela* (Dear Diego) (1978)); to the photographer and communist militant Tina Modotti (*Tinísima* (1992)); to the socially and sexually assertive Zapotec women of Juchitan, Oaxaca (*Luz y luna las lunitas* (Light and the Moon, Little Moons) (1994)); to the female soldiers and camp followers of the Mexican Revolution (*Las soldaderas* (1999)). Poniatowska also wrote the definitive account of the massive earthquake of 1985, *Nada, nadie* (Nothing, Nobody) (1988). She has contributed prologues to dozens of books by women writers and artists, and has written the text for numerous books of photography, including several important ones by Mariana Yampolsky.

Winner of innumerable prizes, Poniatowska became a member of the National Association of Creative Artists in 1994, receiving a lifetime stipend from the federal government. With the possible exception of Carlos **Monsiváis**, no Mexican writer has had such a powerful impact on public attitudes toward the rights of women, the indigenous, the handicapped, political dissidents and the poor.

Further reading

García Pinto, M. (1991) 'Rosario Ferré', in *Women Writers of Latin America. Intimate Histories*, trans. Trudy Balch and M. García Pinto, Austin: University of Texas Press, 163–81.

Jorgensen, B. (1994) *The Writing of Elena Poniatowska*, Austin: University of Texas Press.

Poniatowska, E. (1975) *Massacre in Mexico*, trans. Helen R. Lane, New York: Viking Press.

—— (1987) *Dear Diego*, trans. Katherine Silver, New York: Pantheon.

—— (1988) 'And Here's to You, Jesusa', in Doris Meyer (ed.), *Lives on the Line: The Testimony of*

Contemporary Latin American Authors, Berkeley: University of California Press, 137–55.
—— (1995) *Nothing, Nobody: The Voices of the Mexico City Earthquake*, Philadelphia: Temple University Press.
—— (1996) *Tinísima*, trans. Katherine Silver, New York: Pantheon.
Poot Herrera, S. (2002) 'Elena Poniatowska', in C. Solé and K. Müller-Bergh (eds), *Latin American Writers: Supplement I*, New York: Scribners, 433–62.
Schaefer, C. (1992) *Textured Lives: Women, Art, and Representation in Mexico*, Tucson: The University of Arizona Press.
Sternberg, J. (ed.) (1991) *The Writer on Her Work, Vol. II: New Essays in New Territory*, New York: W.W. Norton & Co.
Volek, E. (1997) 'Elena Poniatowska', in V. Smith (ed.), *Encyclopedia of Latin American Literature*, London: Fitzroy Dearborn, 660–2.
Yampolsky, M. (1998) *The Edge of Time: Photographs of Mexico by Mariana Yampolsky*, prologue E. Poniatowska, Austin: University of Texas Press.

CYNTHIA STEELE

Ponte, Antonio José

b. 1964, Matanzas, Cuba

Writer

Antonio José Ponte is the most accomplished writer of the generation born in Cuba after the 1959 revolution. Trained as an engineer at the University of Havana (after being thrown out of the Faculty of Arts and Letters), he wrote mostly poetry in the 1980s, collected in 1997 as *Asiento en las ruinas*. He also published a number of essays, largely with the small semi-independent press Ediciones Vigía in Matanzas, notably *La lengua de Virgilio* (1985), which focuses on the figure of Virgilio **Piñera**, who had died in Havana in 1979 after a decade of being publicly silenced. Ponte's first book published outside of Cuba (and still unpublished in that country) was *Las comidas profundas* (1997), a meditation on the literary and cultural memory of food, which had become scarce in the 'Special Period in a Time of Peace' that followed the collapse of the socialist bloc in 1989. His essays, which have become steadily bolder in dealing with themes of political repression and its cultural consequences, are largely collected in *El libro perdido de los Origenistas* (2002), which includes important essays on Lorenzo García Vega, Piñera, José **Lezama Lima** and José **Martí** and others.

In the 1990s Ponte began publishing fiction; first the novella *Corazón de Skitalietz* (first published in French translation, 1997; Spanish original, 1998), the first and last of his narrative works to appear in Cuba, then a series of stories that have been collected in English (with *Skitalietz*) as *In the Cold of the Malecón* (2000) but have never been issued in book form in Spanish, then the somewhat lighter stories of *Cuentos de todas partes del Imperio* (2000), published in English as *Tales from the Cuban Empire* (2002). *Skitalietz* and the other stories in *In the Cold of the Malecón* deal with marginalized people living in the ruins of Havana. Ignoring altogether the heroic narratives of the Revolution, Ponte instead gives us the lives of people who live dazed in the aftermath of a disaster that they do not understand.

This intense focus on lives in ruins is developed further in Ponte's first novel to date, *Contrabando de sombras* (2002). Set largely in the Colón Cemetery of Havana, this is a story of gay outlaws and misfits that is traced over other underground lives in other historical periods. A powerful lyrical novel, *Contrabando de sombras* maps the subterranean life of a people finding – as in the title of Ponte's collection of poems – their place in the ruins.

Ponte's place in the literature of the Cuban Revolution is controversial. He is plain-spoken about his opposition to the cultural projects of the Cuban state and about the need for greater freedoms, and has been involved in various polemics with the Minister of Culture, the novelist Abel Prieto and with other cultural commissars. His most forceful critiques to date were published during the November 2002 Guadalajara Book Fair, which Ponte attended as an individual, unconnected to the large official Cuban delegation. In addition, his literature is marked by a corrosive irony and a deep scepticism about official cultural projects. In the introduction to his recent collection of essays, *El libro perdido de los Origenistas*, he writes: 'This could be considered a political book. A chronological ordering of the pieces in it would show how its author shook off little by little the fear of writing certain things, lost his caution and apprehension, became freer. Because it's worthwhile for someone who pays attention to historical censorship to heed self-censorship also, the hypochondriac version of censorship itself.'

Further reading

Ponte, Antonio José (2000) *In the Cold of the Malécon*, San Francisco: City Lights.

—— (2002) *Tales of the Cuban Empire*, San Francisco: City Lights.

Rodríguez, Néstor (2002) 'Un arte de hacer ruinas: Entrevista con el escritor cubano Antonio José Ponte', *Revista iberoamericana* 68(198): 179–86.

DANIEL BALDERSTON

popular culture and literature

As modernization progressed through Latin America's twentieth century, rural communities were swept away and urban centres swelled with the migrant populations expelled from the land. Not all went to the cities, of course; some became wage labour in the growing export agriculture sector, harvesting bananas or coffee or sugar. The resonances of that process were registered in a collective imagination that preserved a cultural memory as well as networks of traditions and practices that, while often suppressed, survived in indigenous languages, religious and cultural practices, music and folklore.

The echoes of that process of disruption and loss, and the resistance to it, constituted the point of contact between the printed word – literature – and a largely oral folk culture. In some cases, this was a conservative reaction, an idealization of a traditional order in the face of capitalist modernization; Ricardo **Güiraldes**'s famous Argentine novel *Don Segundo Sombra* (1926) or his contemporary Leopoldo **Lugones**'s fascination with the rural folk-singer, the *payador*, might serve as examples. Ironically, both were leading figures in the literary avant-garde. In Brazil, the *modernista* movement (see **Brazilian modernism**) captured the indigenous and colonial cultures of the past in a conflictive relationship with the dynamics of modernity. The unresolved contradictions found expression in Mário de **Andrade**'s ***Macunaíma*** (1928) and in Oswald de **Andrade**'s **Antropofagia** movement. Elsewhere in Latin America, the recuperation of orality and popular culture were often part of the construction of a national imaginary coincident with the building of new independent nation-states. The Afro-Cuban poetry of Nicolás **Guillén**, for example, or of Luis **Palés Matos** in Puerto Rico, were part of that process. Alejo **Carpentier** exploited much of that recovered memory in his 1943 novel *El reino de este mundo* (The Kingdom of this World). In the French-speaking Caribbean, this moment produced the writers of ***négritude*** such as Jacques **Roumain**, Jean **Price-Mars** in Haiti and outstanding works like Aimé **Césaire**'s ***Cahier d'un retour au pays natal*** (Notes on a Return to the Homeland) (1939). In Mexico, Ecuador and Peru, it was the rediscovery of an indigenous culture that provided the vocabulary of a new nationalism. José Carlos **Mariátegui** was its outstanding theorist, while Luis Valcárcel, Ciro **Alegría** and José María **Arguedas** were among its best-known literary voices. Miguel Angel **Asturias**'s *Leyendas de Guatemala* (Legends of Guatemala) (1930) and his subsequent translation of the Maya holy book, the *Popol Vuh*, established a central motif in his work. In Chile the poet and Nobel prize winner Gabriela **Mistral** was a devoted advocate for Latin America's first nations, her mantle taken up much later by the poet and composer Violeta Parra. In Mexico that recognition occurs over a historical period from the work of Mauricio **Magdaleno** in the 1920s and 1930s to the writings of Rosario **Castellanos**, like her *Balún-Canán* (The Nine Guardians) (1957), which were rooted in her home state of Chiapas in southern Mexico. The recovery of the hidden cultures of resistance extended to all those populations – indigenous, black, rural – whose collective memory had hitherto been inaccessible to a fundamentally urban and exclusively Spanish-speaking intelligentsia. In some ways the logic of that search led to ethnography on the one hand, and on the other the study of indigenous languages, for example in the work of Ricardo Pozas in Mexico, Jaime Dávalos in Bolivia and Gilberto Freyre in Brazil.

In a sense, the culmination of that process of rediscovering the popular imaginary was **magical realism**, and in particular, of course, the novels and stories of Gabriel **García Márquez**. His masterpiece, ***Cien años de soledad*** (One Hundred Years of Solitude) (1967), can be read as a dialogue between alternate histories and times, between the mythic time of popular memory and the chronology of narrative and history. The tensions between the two may illustrate a deeper and more enduring problem in the relationship of 'high' and 'low' cultures, literature and orality, individual and collective expression. In any event it is a problematic relationship; and the more so when both terms of the debate are subject to constant and profound transformations in the context of *mass* culture. For that is the terrain in which a created culture of consumption for the masses both contains and can ultimately undermine long-standing traditions of cultural resistance – and on the way, force a redefinition of popular culture. The difficulties of that process, and the problematic role of the intellectual within it, are well illustrated in the work and career of Brazilian author and playwright Ariano **Suassuna**. In a different sense, and although principally a movement in music, Tropicália in Brazil represented a complex and ironic response to mass culture, particularly in the song writing and poetry of Chico **Buarque** and Caetano Veloso.

Urban popular culture, the world of newspapers, radio, television, cinema and popular music, interpenetrated literature in the latter half of the century, although there was also a more elitist reaction against what were seen as the dilutions and reductions that popular culture implied. That is certainly the suggestion underpinning Mario **Vargas Llosa**'s very popular novel about a writer of radio soap operas, *La tía Julia y el escribidor* (Aunt Julia and the Scriptwriter) (1977). Manuel **Puig**, the Argentine novelist, has left a body of work whose protagonists explore their own reality *through* an imaginary world constructed by tango and radio soaps – the best known and most successful was *El* ***beso de la mujer araña*** (Kiss of the Spider Woman) (1976). And Puerto Rican writer Luis Rafael **Sánchez** produced two novels which took their theme from popular music – *La* ***guaracha del Macho Camacho*** (Macho Camacho's Beat) (1976) and *La importacia de llamarse Daniel Santos* (The Importance of Being Called Daniel Santos) (1988).

With Puig, literature crosses and re-crosses the boundaries between literature and mass culture. The issue of whether this is a journey into an area of *resistance*, in the same sense that an earlier generation had seen popular culture as a place of contestation, is a more vexing question. In one sense, the culture industry, explored critically by cultural analysts such as Armand Mattelart and Jesús Martin-Barbero, is a function of an urban society in which consumption creates false communities and illusory freedoms reinforced in many ways by cultural practices. Yet the relationship is often more complex and more contradictory, as the debate around hybridity and the work of Néstor García Canclini has revealed. For popular culture may also be a place of encounters and recreation, where new forms of cultural expression emerge born of the clash in urban space between practices. Thus literature may be drawn into the culture industry through, for example, the operation of literary prizes or a phenomenon of mass publishing; its structures may well reflect the habits of consumption in the mass market, as for example Laura **Esquivel**'s hugely successful ***Como agua para chocolate*** (Like Water for Chocolate) (1989). Yet it may also may be a site for pastiche or parody, in the work of performance artists such as Diamela **Eltit** in Chile or Jesusa Rodríguez in Mexico whose work constantly critiques and challenges the stereotypes and forms of conduct – for example, sexuality – that the mass market recommends.

There are many possible responses to a literature challenged by a mass market. One is to reaffirm the aesthetic over the popular, or the complexity and difficulty of the literary – Néstor **Perlongher** represents just such a challenge. Another is to develop a form of critical expression within the popular culture itself. The ***crónica*** as developed by Carlos **Monsiváis** in Mexico or Pedro **Lemebel** in Chile, for example, stands in a long tradition of critical expressions of resistance, escaping the labelling and consumerizing of literature by its brevity, its agility in moving between forms and genres, and its constant responsiveness to an immediate and shifting popular culture.

Further reading

Dunn, Christopher (2001) *Brutality Garden: Tropicalia and the Emergence of a Brazilian Counterculture*, Chapel Hill: University of North Carolina Press.

Franco, Jean (1999) *Critical Passions: Collected Essays*, ed. Mary Louise Pratt and Kathleen Newman, Durham, NC: Duke University Press.

—— (2002) *Decline and Fall of the Lettered City*, Cambridge and London: Harvard University Press.

García Canclini, Néstor (1995) *Hybrid Cultures: Strategies for Entering and Leaving Modernity*, Minneapolis: University of Minnesota Press.

Rowe, W. and Vivian Schelling (1991) *Memory and Modernity in Latin America*, London: Verso.

Sarlo, Beatriz (2001) *Scenes from Postmodern Life*, Minneapolis: University of Minnesota Press.

Schwartz, R. (1992) *Misplaced Ideas: Essays on Brazilian Culture*, London: Verso.

MIKE GONZALEZ

Porchia, Antonio

b. 1886, Coflenti, Calabria, Italy; d. 1968, Buenos Aires, Argentina

Writer

Porchia wrote and rewrote one book throughout his life, *Voces* (Voices), a book of aphorisms. In fact his 'voices' are fragments existing at the tenuous frontier between poetry and prose, enshrining a vision that illuminates the world. First published in 1943, his book became a best-seller. Porchia arrived in Argentina from Italy in 1902 and remained a humble immigrant all his life, working at the docks, weaving baskets and making prints. He was active in the Argentine trade union organization FORA, and was friends with several painters, including Quinquela Martín, and poets such as **Juarroz**, **Pizarnik**, **Girondo** and Aldo **Pellegrini**.

Further reading

Juarroz, R. (1975) 'Antonio Porchia o la profundidad recuperada', *Plural: Crítica, arte, literatura* 47: 32–6.

Porchia, A. (1969) *Voices*, trans. W.S. Merwin, Chicago: Big Table Pub. Co.

—— (1999) *Voces reunidas*, Mexico City: Universidad Nacional Autónoma de Mexico City: Coordinación de Humanidades.

ENRIQUE FOFFANI

Portal, Magda

b. 1901, Lima, Peru; d. 1992, Lima

Poet

Influenced by late nineteenth-century styles, Portal published *Ánima absorta* (Soul Absorbed in Thought) in 1924. Later came *Una esperanza y el mar* (One Hope and the Sea) (1928), for which she was recognized by José Carlos **Mariátegui** as one of the most outstanding Peruvian female poets of the moment, *Constancia del ser* (Constance of the Being) (1965), and other texts. She also wrote narrative prose: *La trampa* (The Trap) (1954), early essays in favour of a Peruvian feminism, *Hacia la mujer nueva* (Toward the New Woman) (1933) and political essays such as *Defensa de la revolución mexicana* (In Defence of the Mexican Revolution) (1931).

Further reading

Arrington, M. (1995) 'Magda Portal: Vanguard Critic', in *Reinterpreting the Spanish American Essay: Women Writers of the 19th and 20th Centuries*, Austin: University of Texas Press.

Grunfeld, M. (2000) 'Voces femeninas de la vanguardia: El compromiso de Magda Portal', *Revista de crítica literaria latinoamericana* 26(51): 67–82.

Portal, M. (1982) *La trampa*, Lima: Editorial Poma.

Reedy, D. (2000) *Magda Portal, la pasionaria peruana: Biografía intelectual*, Lima: Ediciones Flora Tristán.

Weaver, K. (1990) 'Magda Portal: Translation in Progress', *Translation Review* 32–3: 41–3.

JOSÉ ANTONIO MAZZOTTI

Portela, Ena Lucía

b. 1972, Havana, Cuba

Novelist and short-story writer

At the age of 25, Portela won the National Novel Prize, awarded by the Cuban Union of Writers and Artists (**UNEAC**), for her *El pájaro: Pincel y tinta china* (The Bird: Paintbrush and Chinese Ink) (1999). Her work deals with topics such as writing, sexuality and the life of the younger generation of intellectuals in Cuba. In the context of literature that openly reflects the social and political life of contemporary Cuba, Portela has distanced herself from testimonial (see ***testimonio***) writing and created a less immediate work. Her other books include the collection of short stories *Una extraña entre las piedras* (A Stranger among the Stones) (1999) and the novel *La sombra del caminante* (The Walker's Shadow) (2001).

Further reading

Bejel, E. (2001) *Gay Cuban Nation*, Chicago: University of Chicago Press, 188–95.

Cámara, Madeline (1997) 'Antropofagia de los sexos como "metáfora de incorporación" en "La urna y el nombre (cuento jovial)" de Ena Lucía Portela', *Torre de papel*, Fall, 7(3).

ALFREDO ALONSO ESTENOZ

Portuondo, José Antonio

b. 1911, Santiago de Cuba; d. 1996, Havana, Cuba

Critic

A theorist of Marxist aesthetics, Portuondo was editor of several journals including *La Gaceta del Caribe* (1944) and the weekly *Baraguá* (1938). He researched literary theory under Alfonso **Reyes** at the Colegio de México (1944–46). He was later Cuba's ambassador to Mexico (1960) and to the Holy See (1975), vice-president of the Cuban writers' union (**UNEAC**) and Director of the Institute of Literature and Linguistics of Cuba's Academy of Sciences. His extensive writings include *Estética y revolución* (Aesthetics and Revolution) (1963) and *La emancipación literaria de Hispanoamérica* (Latin America's Literary Emancipation) (1975).

Further reading

Portuondo, José Antonio (1944) *El contenido social de la literatura cubana*, Mexico City: El Colegio de México, Centro de Estudios Sociales.

—— (1975) *La emancipación literaria de Hispanoamérica*, Havana: Casa de las Américas.

—— (1979) *Itinerario estético de la Revolución cubana*, Ciudad de Havana and New York: Editorial Letras Cubanas.

—— (1980) *Martí, escritor revolucionario*, Havana: Editora Política.

—— (1984) *Teoría y crítica de la literatura*, Mexico City: CEESTEM: Editorial Nueva Imagen.

WILFREDO CANCIO ISLA

Porzencanski, Teresa

b. 1945, Montevideo, Uruguay

Writer and anthropologist

A central motif of Porzencanski's four published novels – *Invención de los soles* (The Invention of Suns) (1982), *Una novela erótica* (An Erotic Novel) (1986), *Mesías en Montevideo* (Messiah in Montevideo) (1989) and *Perfumes de Cartago* (Perfumes from Cartago) (1994) – is the encounter between different cultures in the Uruguayan urban context and the forging of new identities out of varied historical and mythical backgrounds. She also published a book of poetry (in 1967) and six volumes of short stories. A lecturer and researcher in anthropology and social work, Porzecanski has published eight books in these fields.

FLORINDA F. GOLDBERG

Pos, Hugo

b. 1913, Suriname; d. 2000, the Netherlands

Writer

Pos was a judge in Suriname and in the Netherlands and, although a poet and playwright throughout his working life, established his literary name only after his retirement in the mid-1980s. In his collections of short stories, mildly ironic and meticulous in style, Pos often fictionalizes accidental and everyday events of his youth in Suriname, and his experiences as a judge and traveller. In his 1995 autobiography *In triplo* (Tripartite), Pos grapples with the three major pillars of his identity: Suriname, the Netherlands and his Jewish background.

Further reading

Pos, H. (1981) 'Herinneringen', *Maatstaf* 29(6): 59–68.

AART G. BROEK

Posse, Abel

b. 1934, Córdoba, Argentina

Writer

Although outside the genre of the new Latin American novel, Posse's work shares the same fascination with historical and fantastic narratives. He has published a number of works, including *Daimon* (1981), *La reina del plata* (Queen of the River Plate) (1988), a complex reworking of the myths that surround the city of Buenos Aires, and *Los perros del paraíso* (The Dogs of Paradise) (1987), which won the Rómulo **Gallegos** prize. He has been much criticized for serving as a diplomat during the Argentine dictatorship (1976–83) and for his neo-Nazi ideas.

Further reading

Balderston, D. (1993) 'Abel Posse y *Los demonios ocultos*: ¿Otra vez el nazismo?', *Nuevo texto crítico* 6.11: 254–8.

Bowsher, K. (2002) 'Shipwrecks of Modernity: Abel Posse's "El largo atardecer del caminante" ', *Forum for Modern Language Studies* 38(1): 88–98.

Colomina Garrigos, L. (2001) 'La reescritura de la Historia y el peso de la conciencia historica en "El largo atardecer del caminante" de Abel Posse', *Tropos* 27: 7–20.

Posse, A. (1989) *The Dogs of Paradise*, trans. Margaret Sayers Peden, New York: Atheneum.

—— (2000) 'Un océano incesante', *La Nación, suplemento cultura* 16: 1–2.

—— (2001) *El inquietante día de la vida*, Buenos Aires: Emecé Editores.

Sims, R.L. (1997) 'Abel Posse', in V. Smith (ed.), *Encyclopedia of Latin American Literature*, London: Fitzroy Dearborn, 669–71.

SANDRA GARABANO

post-Boom

Post-Boom is a term coined by Emir **Rodríguez Monegal** to designate a group of writers representing a radicalization of the projects of the **Boom** of the 1960s. The group includes Severo **Sarduy**, Néstor Sánchez, Manuel **Puig** and Salvador **Elizondo**. Its main features are self-referential forms and experimentation with 'languages' and 'codes'. The 'post-Boom' novel therefore assimilates to writing new techniques and aesthetics/cultural codes from cinema, popular song, literary theory, popular literary genres and so on. The notion of post-Boom faded together with the Boom from which it originated, to be replaced by discussions about **postmodernism** in Latin American culture.

Further reading

Giardinelli, M. (1996) 'Reflections on Latin American Narrative of the Post-Boom', trans. A. MacAdam, *Review: Latin American Literature and the Arts* 52: 83–7.

Marcos, J.M. (1983) *Roa Bastos, precursor del post-Boom*, Mexico City: Katún.

Shaw, D. (1996) 'Three Post-Boom Writers and the Boom', *Latin American Literary Review* 24(47): 5–22.

—— (1998) *Reflections on Latin American Narrative of the Post-Boom*, Albany: State University of New York Press.

GABRIEL GIORGI

postmodernism

Postmodernism is a critical term with a maddening array of meanings. From its modest beginnings in the relatively narrow domain of post-war academic debates concerning literature in the USA to its widespread international currency today, the term has acquired layers of inflections and locally specific meanings that make any singular definition impossible. In relation to Latin America and the Caribbean also, postmodernism has been deployed in a variety of contexts and for very different purposes. Generally speaking, it refers to artistic, critical and theoretical works that address changes in the presuppositions, values or aims of modernization, modernity or modernism.

The term only gained widespread currency in the 1980s. In 1979, the French philosopher Jean-François Lyotard published *The Postmodern Condition: A Report on Knowledge*, in which he advanced the thesis that the 'postmodern condition' refers to humankind's contemporary 'incredulity toward meta-narratives'. Lyotard sought to capture the decreasing credibility of such Enlightenment ideals and institutions as reason, freedom, equality, democracy and communism. Then, in 'Modernity – An Incomplete Project', Jürgen Habermas, the German philosopher, attacked this view. Habermas countered Lyotard's view by arguing that the apparent incredulity toward modernity's metanarratives in fact derived not from modernity's excesses (for example, a mania for rationality expressed in a dehumanizing technological society), but rather from the one-sided development of modernity's initially twofold character. Western societies, Habermas argued, had only developed the impulse toward the acquisition of specialized knowledge about the world, forgetting about the Enlightenment's other imperative: to disseminate that knowledge. Given this, talk of postmodernity, of the end of rationality, seemed to Habermas misguided symptomatic reactions to the incomplete character of the project of modernity.

This philosophical debate may have established the broad currency of the term. But postmodernism already had a history when Lyotard and Habermas joined the debate. This history, densest in architectural circles and among literary critics, intersected with the terms of this philosophical exchange. In both architecture and literature, the term referred to democratizing stylistic shifts. In narrative, for example, critics observed a shift from the opaque, inward-looking and fragmented monuments of modernist fiction in the first part of the twentieth century to more conventional, and more playfully self-conscious, novels of the post-war era. Thematically, too, the individual psyche represented by modernists such as Virginia Woolf, William Faulkner or James Joyce gave way to the broad historical themes of novelists like Norman Mailer or John Dos Passos. In these debates, Latin American writers of the '**Boom**', like Gabriel **García Márquez** and Julio **Cortázar**, were assimilated into the category of postmodernism. Latin American specialists objecting to such categorizations frequently took one of two tacks. Some refused the category of the postmodern entirely, characterizing it as a foreign and therefore irrelevant category for understanding Latin American fiction. Others, such as Roberto González Echevarría, simply adopted the criteria defining the category but refined its application to Latin American fiction, especially that of the **post-Boom**.

Meanwhile, in the mid-1980s the US Marxist critic Fredric Jameson was gathering together the philosophical and artistic uses of the term 'postmodernism' and relating them all to social and economic developments since the end of the Second World War. In *Postmodernism, or The Cultural Logic of Late Capitalism*, Jameson argued, following the Belgian economist Ernest Mandel, that capitalism had entered a new phase after 1945, called 'late capitalism', characterized by its final penetration of both the Third World and the individual unconscious. For Jameson, postmodernism could be understood neither as a stylistic choice, which could then be subject to critical or moral approval or censure, nor as a simple artistic movement or period. Instead, Jameson described postmodernism, and the critical and theoretical commentary defining the term, as a symptom generated by the novel experiences produced by and within the latest phase of capitalist production.

Jameson had little to say about Latin America directly, but Latin Americanists such as George Yúdice, Neil Larsen and John Beverley, for whom the interdisciplinary and socially oriented criticism of Jameson came quite naturally, used Jameson's account as a point of departure for re-evaluating the use of the term postmodernism in the field of Latin American studies. Like Jameson, these critics sought to expand the term's relevance beyond period and style. However, by virtue of the specificity of their object of study – Latin American societies and cultures – they were forced to modify Jameson's conception of the postmodern. Specifically, Latin Americanists were forced to contend with the dramatically more uneven presence of those hallmarks of late capitalism and postmodernity that Jameson saw pervading Europe and the USA. Indeed, Latin Americanists made a significant contribution to the theory of postmodernity by insisting that the generalization of capitalism does not imply the homogenization of social and cultural experience, but in fact may imply rather the diversification of such experiences. Within the analyses of these critics, Latin American fiction, **poetry**, cinema and art, the region's political organizations, new social movements and economic activities all came to be scrutinized in relation to the general challenge posed by the assumptions of modernization, modernity and modernism by European and North American theorists.

More recently, Latin American intellectuals such as Norbert Lechner have taken the opportunity provided by the 'postmodernism debate', as it has come to be called, to reassess the character of modernity in Latin America. They ask: does progress, and its economic corollary, development, really represent the interests of the majority of Latin Americans? How well does representative democracy actually accommodate the multiple and often antagonistic political will of different groups in the region? And, more generally, what kind of purchase can European periodizing notions really gain on a terrain so deeply marked by the conflicts between Europeans and indigenous peoples?

Further reading

Beverley, J, J. Oviedo and M. Aronna (1995) *The Postmodern Debate in Latin America*, Durham, NC: Duke University Press.

Colás, S. (1994) *Postmodernity in Latin America: The Argentine Paradigm*, Durham, NC: Duke University Press.

Williams, R.L. (1995) *The Postmodern Novel in Latin America: Politics, Culture, and the Crisis of Truth*, New York: St Martin's Press.

Young, R.A. (ed.) (1997) *Latin American Postmodernisms*, Amsterdam: Rodopi.

SANTIAGO COLÁS

Prada Oropeza, Renato

b. 1937, Potosí, Bolivia

Writer and literary critic

Prada's first novel, *Los fundadores del alba* (The Founders of the Dawn), is a fictional account of the late 1960s guerrilla movement in Bolivia and was awarded, in 1969, both the Erich Guttentag Prize for the best novel and the international **Casa de las Américas** prize. As a literary critic, Prada has published books on discourse analysis, semiotics and narrative. He is a professor and researcher at the Universidad Veracruzana in Mexico, where he founded and directed the journal *Semiosis*.

Further reading

Blossman, M. (1995) 'El plurilinguismo de Renato Prada Oropeza en *Mientras cae la noche*', *Texto crítico* 1(1): 169–89.

Ferrufino, E. (1996) 'Renato Prada Oropeza: *Los fundadores del alba* y el conflicto social', *Bolivian Studies* 6(1): 144–53.

Ortega, J. (1973) *Letras bolivianas de hoy: Renato Prada y Pedro Shimose*, Buenos Aires: Fernando García Cambeiro.

Prada, A. (1995) 'Sobre *Mientras cae la noche* de Renato Prada Oropeza', *Texto crítico* 1(1): 191–205.

Prada Oropeza, R. (1971) *The Breach*, trans. Walter Redmond, Garden City, NY: Doubleday.

—— (2001) *El discurso – testimonio y otros ensayos*, Mexico City: Universidad Nacional Autónoma de México.

ISABEL BASTOS

Prado, Paulo da Silva

b. 1869, São Paulo, Brazil; d. 1943, Rio de Janeiro, Brazil

Writer and historian

One of the most important analysts of Brazilian social life between 1900 and 1920, Prado represented the state of São Paulo to European bankers from 1913–30 and presided over the Conselho Nacional do Café (National Council of Coffee) from 1931–32. Founder of the *Revista do Brasil*, the mouthpiece of nationalistic ideas, Prado was also director of the journal *Revista nova* with Mário de **Andrade** and Antônio de Alcântara Machado, was an active participant in the Modern Art Week in São Paulo (1922) and wrote the preface to Oswald de **Andrade**'s famous modernist manifesto (see **manifestos**).

Further reading

Prado, E. (1961) *A ilusão Americana*, São Paulo: Editôra Brasiliense.

PEGGY SHARPE

Présence Africaine

Founded in Paris in 1947 by Alioune Diop as a monthly journal of modern African letters, *Présence Africaine* has evolved into a quarterly journal and publishing house specializing in black African and Caribbean literatures in French. One of the foremost voices of the ***négritude*** movement, the journal has a dual focus on research on African culture and civilization and creative writings by Africans. In keeping with its anti-racist, anti-colonialist political orientation, *Présence Africaine* has been open from its inception to contributors of all races, a position reflected by its Committee of Patrons, which has included notable writers such as Camus, **Césaire**, Gide, Sartre and Senghor.

Further reading

Hill-Lubin, M. (1992) 'Présence Africaine: A Voice in the Wilderness, a Record of Black Kinship', in V.Y. Mudimbe (ed.), *The Surreptitious Speech: Présence Africaine and the Politics of Otherness*, Chicago: University of Chicago Press.

Howlett, J. (1977) *Index alphabétique des auteurs et des matières de la revue Présence Africaine*, Paris: Présence Africaine.

SCOTT A. COOPER

Price-Mars, Jean

b. 1876, Grande Rivière du Nord, Haiti; d. 1969, Petionville, Haiti

Ethnologist and essayist

One of Haiti's foremost intellectuals, Price-Mars, a physician, influenced Haiti's literary renaissance after the American occupation and the ***négritude*** movement in Paris. His early work was concerned with educational reform, but he became known for his criticism of the Haitian elite in his 1919 book *La vocation de l'élite* (The Elite's Vocation). His ethnological study *Ainsi parla l'oncle* (So Spoke the Uncle) (1928), a defence and illustration of Haiti's peasant culture, inspired various literary and cultural movements including ***indigenisme***, ***noirisme*** and *négritude*. In the backlash against the excesses of Duvalierism, Price-Mars was criticized for contributing to racial mystification.

Further reading

Antoine, J. (1981) *Jean Price-Mars and Haiti*, Washington, DC: Three Continents Press.

Depestre, R. (1968) 'Jean Price-Mars et le mythe de la négritude', *L'Homme et le societé* 7: 171–81.

Dorsinville, M. (1969) 'Jean Price-Mars', *L'Afrique littéraire* 4: 58–61.

Knight, V. (1975) 'Jean Price-Mars', *Black Images: A Critical Quarterly in Black Arts and Culture* 4(3–4): 4–19.

Price-Mars, J. (1983) *So Spoke the Uncle*, trans. M.W. Shannon, Washington, DC: Three Continents Press.

Robinson, C.A.F. (1997) 'Jean Price-Mars', in V. Smith (ed.), *Encyclopedia of Latin American Literature*, London: Fitzroy Dearborn, 675–6.

Shannon, M. (1996) *Jean Price-Mars, the Haitian Elite*

and the American Occupation, 1915–1935, Houndsmill: Macmillan Press.

J. MICHAEL DASH

Prince, Ralph

b. *c.*1938, Antigua

Short story writer and journalist

Prince's short stories have appeared in *Bim* and *Savacou*, including 'Ol Higue', a story dedicated to Frank **Collymore**. His short stories are scattered in newspapers throughout the Caribbean and have been broadcast on the BBC's 'Caribbean Voices' and published in various anthologies. His collection of stories called *Jewels of the Sun* (1979) celebrates nature with an unusual sense of romance.

KEITH JARDIM

prison writing

Prison is a place that many Latin American governments have used to contain and punish political dissidents; as such, it has also been a site for oppositional political challenges and resistance to authoritarian regimes of whatever ideological stance. There is no one kind of writing from behind prison walls: some works, such as Fidel Castro's famous 'History will absolve me', are speeches; others are memoirs that can be considered *testimonios* (see ***testimonio***); still others are fictionalized accounts, poetry and even song, like Víctor Jara's lyrics of hope while he was awaiting death in the National Stadium in Santiago, Chile. There is no single audience for prison writing either. Some works are directed at members of the writer's political organization to exhort followers to action or, like Ana Guadalupe Martínez's *Las cáncels clandestinas en el Salvador* (Clandestine Jails in El Salvador) (1978), to instruct them on how to survive prison life. Others call out to a national or even international readership, documenting abuses against human rights and proving the illegitimacy of the government that commits them.

Yet almost all of this writing, no matter how much its author disclaims literary intention or merit, reaches out beyond the specific case to capture profound human interactions and deep emotion. Newspaper editor Jacobo Timerman does this through words alone when he describes communication with another eye through the peepholes in the cell doors (*Prisoner without a Name, Cell without a Number* (1981)). On the other hand, guerrilla leader, Nidia Díaz, reports her political struggles in jail, but adds her drawings to her memoir, the images evoking the feelings that she has suppressed in the writing (*Nunca estuve sola* (I was Never Alone) (1988)).

In spite of the great variety in which former prisoners express their experiences – and there is even more than this if fiction about prison life were considered – prison writing is best characterized by its deeply political nature. The prisoner does not see her/himself only as an individual or the detention as a uniquely personal experience. To the contrary, even those writers who do not emphasize militancy in a party – Alicia Partnoy in her *The Little School* (1986), for instance – view their imprisonment as part of a repression that has attacked an entire generation or country. This creates solidarity with others in and outside of jail: to survive and to resist the social order that detains, tortures and kills its citizens. The writers' words are arms to expose injustices that are usually kept hidden and bring down the goverments that are based on them.

Further reading

Cayetano Carpio, S. (1979) *Secuestro y capucha en un pais del 'mundo libre'*, Costa Rica: Editorial Universitaria Centroamericana, Ciudad Universitaria Rodrigo Facio.

Costa, E. de (1997) 'Prison Writing', in V. Smith (ed.), *Encyclopedia of Latin American Literature*, London: Fitzroy Dearborn, 677–78.

Partnoy, A. (1988) *The Little School: Tales of Disappearance and Survival in Argentina*, London: Virago.

Timerman, J. (1981) *Prisoner without a Name, Cell without a Number*, New York: Knopf.

MARY JANE TREACY

Proa

One of the most important magazines of the **avant-garde in Latin America**, *Proa* was published in Buenos Aires by **Borges** and others. Its first incarnation, lasting only three issues, lasted from mid-1922 to mid-1923; during this period the editors were Borges and Eduardo González Lanuza, who used it to promote the avant-garde movement, ***ultraísmo***. The second incarnation, which is much better known and has been reproduced in part in facsimile editions, lasted from 1923 to 1926 and included fifteen issues, as well as some book publications. *Proa*'s editors during this second period were Borges, Brandán Caraffa, Ricardo **Güiraldes** and Pablo Rojas Paz, although Borges left the editorial group shortly before the demise of the journal. During this period *Proa* published such writers as Macedonio **Fernández**, Raúl **González Tuñón** and his brother Enrique, Roberto **Arlt**, Leopoldo **Marechal**, Roberto **Mariani** and numerous others, including members of what were later termed both the Florida and Boedo groups (see **Boedo vs Florida**); the painter Pedro Figari also participated, and Norah Borges provided many of the illustrations. Güiraldes funded the magazine while the younger poets set the tone. The publishing house, Editorial Proa, published Güiraldes's *Don Segundo Sombra* (1926), Borges's first books of essays and Macedonio Fernández's *Papeles del recienvenido* (Papers of the Newcomer) (1929). Roberto Alifano and others currently publish a journal of the same name in Buenos Aires, although its relation to the magazine of some seventy-five years earlier is tenuous at best.

Further reading

Giordano, C. (1987) 'La vanguardia en Argentina: Las revistas *Proa*, de Buenos Aires', *Rio de la Plata: Culturas* 4–6: 37–46.

Oberstar, D.L. (1980) 'Avant-garde Elements in the Prose Fiction of *Proa*', *Symposium* 34(2): 168–77.

DANIEL BALDERSTON

publishing

Through the *modernista* period at the beginning of the century, Latin American books were largely printed in Europe by presses such as Garnier et Frères in Paris, which was responsible for many of the publications of Rubén **Darío** and his contemporaries. With the rise of mass newspapers and magazines, publishers such as Anaconda and Claridad in Argentina, and Ariel in Brazil, began publishing for the local market. Particularly important in the rise of Latin American publishing were presses that published cheap, large editions, such as those that brought out the books of Horacio **Quiroga**, Roberto **Arlt** and the Brazilian north-eastern writers, like Jorge **Amado** and Graciliano **Ramos**. In post-revolutionary Mexico, the new government launched a whole range of new school textbooks and cheap popular editions of classics, and of contemporary works like those of Gabriela **Mistral**. Anarchist and socialist groups were also interested in producing cheap popular editions of classics and contemporary works. ***Sur*** founded a publishing house that mostly published writers who were associated with the magazine, or works in translation where the translator was such an associate. A phenomenon that occurred simultaneously was that of small avant-garde magazines such as ***Proa*** in Argentina and ***Contemporáneos*** in Mexico, which launched small presses that published their authors. (Early works by **Borges**, **Girondo** and many other avant-garde writers appeared in these series.)

The move toward the professionalization of publishing in the continent occurred largely with the displacement of Spanish exiles who founded publishing houses such as **Losada** and **Sudamericana** in Argentina and Porrúa in Mexico. Interestingly, the Spanish owner of Losada fostered the *mundonovista* (see ***mundovismo***) tendencies in the Spanish-American literature of the time, publishing authors like **Asturias**, **Icaza**, Ciro **Alegría** and others.

An important innovation during the 1940s was the founding of the **Fondo de Cultura Económica** in Mexico, with leadership by Pedro **Henríez Ureña** (in the Letras Americanas series), Alfonso **Reyes** and Daniel Cosío Villegas. With government support, the Fondo published Latin American classics such as the *Popol Vuh* and other indigenous works from early in the colonial period, an anthology of gauchesque poetry edited by Borges and **Bioy Casares**, new editions of **novels of the Mexican Revolution** (**Azuela**'s *Los de abajo* (The Underdogs), originally published in 1915) and contemporary works like **Paz**'s *Libertad bajo palabra* (Freedom on Parole) (1949) and **Rulfo**'s ***Pedro Páramo*** (1955). Other important presses include **Monte Avila** and **Biblioteca Ayacucho** in Venezuela, **Zig Zag**, **Quimantú** and, more recently, **Cuarto Propio** and Lom in Chile, **Perspectiva** and **Companhia das Letras** in Brazil, Siglo XXI, Era and **Joaquín Mortiz** in Mexico, **Jorge Alvarez** and Corregidor in Argentina, Arca in Uruguay and Amigos del Libro in Bolivia. The Centro Editor de América Latina, founded by Boris Spivakow, and Siglo XXI in Mexico, founded by Arnaldo Orfila Reynal, are important for bringing together notable groups of **intellectuals**. Heinemann is a leading publisher of Caribbean literature in English. Major university presses include those of the UNAM in Mexico, EDUCA in Central America and **EUDEBA** in Buenos Aires. An international scholarly publishing venture is Colección **Archivos**, sponsored by UNESCO and numerous cultural institutions in Iberia, Latin America and the Caribbean. The state-controlled Cuban publishing industry was focused for a brief period of effervescence after the Revolution around Ediciones R (associated with ***Lunes de Revolución***), but is now mostly dominated by Letras Cubanas and **Casa de las Américas**; a similar venture was Editorial Nueva Nicaragua in Sandinista Nicaragua.

Recent years have witnessed, in Latin America and the Caribbean as elsewhere, the growth of giant publishing empires. Seix Barral, Alfaguara and Planeta are Spanish publishing houses (all important for their Latin American publications) now belonging to the German publishing giant, Bertelsmann. In Brazil, local media empires that are now expanding to the surrounding companies include Globo and Abril. At the same time, there are small publishing houses related to new social movements such as feminism (Cuarto Propio, Feminaria).

Further reading

Simões, Célia Maria Braid Ribeiro and Maria Celeste Ferreira Cordeiro (1978) *Editoras Brasileiras e estrangeiras*, São Luís: Universidade Federal do Maranhão.

DANIEL BALDERSTON

Pucuna

An important magazine published irregularly in Quito during the 1960s, *Pucuna* (Blowgun) was the organ of a group of writers called 'Tzantzicos' (Head Shrinkers), who first appeared on the literary scene under the collective name of 'Umbral' (Threshold). Originally, the group consisted of Ulises Estrella, Fernando Tinajero, Marco Muñoz, Raúl Velasco and Bolívar Echeverría. Its basic form of expression was the **manifesto**, addressing issues such as the national cultural scene, the function of the artist in the creation and transformation of culture, the role of the collective in that transformation, and the radical break with tradition.

HUMBERTO E. ROBLES

Pueblo enfermo

Pueblo enfermo (A Sick People), published in 1909 by the writer-historian, Alcides **Arguedas**, is one of his most controversial essays because of its negative appraisal, according to some of his critics, of Bolivian society and politics. The author explains the political and social instability and the underdevelopment of the country through two factors. The first is the country's geography: the Andes mountains and Eastern jungles made it difficult to build roads and set up the railroad system needed for economic development in the early twentieth century when the country was dependent on tin exports. The second factor, according to Arguedas, was race. Following French thinker Gustave LeBon, he argued that the mixture of Indian and European races led to political and social instability and prevented the development of a homogeneous social body characteristic of more developed European nations. Arguedas's conception of Bolivian society is racially constructed; that is, the social psychology of the nation is formed by the Indian, mestizo and European. As summarized in the title of one of his chapters – 'Historical and Racial Corruption in Politics' – Arguedas's vision of Bolivian history was also based on race.

Informed by the positivist tendencies of nineteenth-century thinkers such as Sarmiento but relevant to the historical and social context of Bolivia, *Pueblo enfermo* established Arguedas as an interpreter of Bolivian society, albeit on the basis of an anti-nationalistic, pessimistic and racist commentary on Indian ethnicity and culture. Many Bolivian intellectuals such as Franz Tamayo and Tristan Marof, outraged by *Pueblo enfermo*'s interpretation of the Indian, wrote positive evaluations of the Indian in their respective works, *Creación de una pedagogía nacional* (The Creation of a National Pedagogy) (1910) and *La justicia del Inca* (Justice of the Inca) (1933).

Although condemned by critics as racist, *Pueblo enfermo* remains an important work which deals with the conceptions of race, society and nation, not only pertaining to a particular historical, political and social period, but also very much relevant to Bolivian society today.

Further reading

Arguedas, A. (1979) *Pueblo enfermo*, La Paz: Ediciones Isla.

Paz-Soldán, E. (2003) *Alcides Arguedas y la narrativa de la nación enferma*, La Paz: Plural.

Rivera-Rodas, O. (1993) '*Pueblo enfermo*: Los fracasos de la utopía y la historia', *Signos* 39–40 (May–Dec.): 41–67.

JOSEFA SALMÓN

Puga, María Luisa

b. Mexico City, 1944

Writer

Puga is a journalist and narrator whose works helped define a new period in Mexican literature. As a reporter, she has travelled and lived extensively outside of Mexico and her fiction often explores the experiences of women in unusual contexts. Her first novel, *Las posibilidades del odio* (The Possibilities of Hatred) (1978), is set in Kenya, and along with this thematic challenge to national literature, Puga's introspective prose brought new psychological depth to Mexican fiction. Her 1983 novel, *Pánico o peligro* (Fight or Flight) won the Xavier Villaurrutia prize in Mexico and uses interior monologue to combine the 1968 massacre of student protestors with the coming-of-age story of a working-class woman.

Further reading

De Beer, Gabriella (1996) 'María Luisa Puga', in *Contemporary Mexican Women Writers*, Austin: University of Texas Press, 11–57.

López, I.M. (1996) *Historia, escritura e identidad: La novelística de María Luisa Puga*, New York: Peter Lang.

Puga, María Luisa (1978) *Las posibilidades del odio*, Mexico City: Siglo XXI.

—— (1983) *Pánico o peligro*, Mexico City: Siglo XXI.

—— (1987) *Intentos*, Mexico City: Grijalbo.

Unruh, V. (2002) 'Puga's Fictions of Equivalence: The Tasks of the Novelist as Translator', in D. Balderston and M. Schwartz (eds), *Voice Overs: Latin American Literature and Translation*, Albany: SUNY Press, 194–203.

BRIAN GOLLNICK

Puig, Manuel

b. 1932, General Villegas, Province of Buenos Aires, Argentina; d. 1990, Cuernavaca, Mexico

Writer

Manuel Puig grew up in the small *pampa* town of

General Villegas, where the Hollywood movies in the local cinema were about the only way of escaping the utterly dull and oppressive way of life. Puig's enormous passion for the movies moved him to start a professional career in the film industry. In the 1950s he studied at the Centro Sperimentale di Cinematografia in Rome, became an assistant director and began to write film scripts. Realizing that none of these activities gave him the satisfaction and results he had expected, he gave up and tried his luck in literature. 'The stories I wanted to tell', Puig would recall, 'required the analytical possibilities of literature, not the synthetic ones of the cinema'.

Given this background, it was inevitable that cinema would play a crucial role in Puig's fiction. Emotionally disturbed by their repressive environment and detached from reality, some of Puig's most important characters find fulfilment in the dream world of the movies. The best-known is of course Molina, the protagonist of *El* ***beso de la mujer araña*** (Kiss of the Spider Woman) (1976), who projects his desires and doubts onto the film plots he tells his cellmate with great skill and fullness of detail. But the first such character is Toto Casals, the protagonist of Puig's first novel *La traición de Rita Hayworth* (Betrayed by Rita Hayworth) (1968). Experiencing the film world as reality and displaying a latent homosexuality, Toto is an admittedly autobiographical character. Just as he would do in his second novel, ***Boquitas pintadas*** (Heartbreak Tango) (1969), Puig fictionalized his youth experiences, reshaping General Villegas as Coronel Vallejos, a small, geographically and culturally isolated town with a rigid social and gender stratification and a suffocating, narrow-minded mentality. True emotions are repressed and, consequently, perverted by fantasies and illusions provoked and nurtured by the romantic and kitsch stereotypes represented in Hollywood movies, tangos, boleros, *radionovelas*, women's magazines and the like. Although Puig does not hesitate to reveal the pernicious effects of these cultural products, he is too much a devotee to condemn them. 'The escapist fantasies', Puig stated, explaining his ambiguous position, 'were the accomplices in the system, but also the oxygen of that community'.

Boquitas pintadas (adapted by the author for Leopoldo Torre Nilsson's movie) has the structure of a serial. Nevertheless, as in all Puig's novels, what is lacking is the presence of a narrator who might transmit the story and connect the various episodes with his unifying voice. Instead, the novel is constructed on the basis of the unmediated transmission of dialogues, interior monologues, dehumanized descriptions and a great variety of 'documents' (letters, case files, clippings, agendas, medical and police reports, tango and bolero lyrics, fragments of *radionovelas*). Appealing to what **Cortázar** has labelled the reader-accomplice, *Boquitas pintadas* creates the illusion of an objective point of view and deconstructs in an implicit, sophisticated way the discourses of certain forms of popular life and culture in Argentina during the 1930s and 1940s.

Following the path of real life (in 1946 he moved to Buenos Aires to attend high school and university), Puig changed the scenery in his third novel, *The Buenos Aires Affair* (1973, original title in English) – a 'detective novel', as the subtitle would have it – exchanging the *pampa* town of Coronel Vallejos for the metropolis. Another important new element is the psychoanalytical treatment of the two protagonists, Leo and Gladys. When they meet, both are marked by frustrated, lonely, distorted and perverted sexual experiences, reported in detail in the novel. Fearing and desiring violence, Gladys represents the passive, masochistic female, while Leo – full of violent memories and fantasies – is the dominant, sadistic male. Yet the references to the cinema, the collage structure and the absence of a commenting narrator links *The Buenos Aires Affair* with Puig's two preceding novels.

In *El beso de la mujer araña*, two men – the homosexual Molina and the revolutionary Valentín – share a prison cell. Molina represents female self-sacrifice, Valentín *machismo*. Confronted with each other, these two very different identities cross the bridge that separates them by understanding, accepting and even satisfying the needs and desires of the other. That is as far as they can get: in the end, each of them remains a prisoner of his role.

The bare set-up of *El beso de la mujer araña* made it very suitable for the theatre. Puig himself wrote an adaptation, deleting *force majeure* the numerous notes about homosexuality included in the novel which reveal the horrifying misunderstandings of homosexuality in academic circles. The play was successfully performed in many countries. Subsequently, a musical was made. But it was above all Héctor Babenco's film version – starring Hollywood stars William Hurt and Raúl Juliá – that turned *El beso de la mujer araña* into Puig's best-known work.

The two novels published after the psychoanalytically tinged *Pubis angelical* (Angelic Pubis) (1979) provoked a divergence of opinions. Some critics considered *Maldición eterna a quien lea estas páginas* (Eternal Curse on the Reader of These Pages) (1980) and *Sangre de amor correspondido* (Blood of Requited Love) (1982) to be among Puig's best works, while others were disappointed and reproached Puig with not writing fiction any more but merely transcribing real-life speech. It is true that both novels are based on conversations with real people Puig had in his places of residence at that time (New York and Rio de Janeiro, respectively). But these conversations were, of course, only used as raw material. And though the set-ups had become more sober, the theme remained the same: man as a captive of (self-)repressing roles and stereotypes which prevent him from being truly human and free.

In what was to be his last novel, *Cae la noche tropical* (Tropical Night Falling) (1988), Puig broke new ground, choosing two aged women as his main characters. Despite all the disillusions they have experienced and witnessed, they share a preoccupation with male affections with their adolescent and adult matches in Puig's preceding novels. *Cae la noche tropical* was published two years before the untimely death of this writer of a solid, fascinating oeuvre in which repressive patriarchal discourses and practices are laid bare in a way that is as original as it is penetrating.

Further reading

Amícola, J. (ed.) (1996) *Manuel Puig: Materiales iniciales para La traición de Rita Hayworth*, La Plata: Orbis Tertius/Centro de Estudios de Teoría y Crítica Literaria, Universidad Nacional de La Plata.

Bacarisse, P. (1988) *The Necessary Dream: A Study of the Novels of Manuel Puig*, Cardiff: University of Wales Press.

—— (1993) *Impossible Choices: The Implications of the Cultural References in the Novels of Manuel Puig*, Calgary/Wales: The University of Calgary and Wales Press.

Kerr, L. (1987) *Suspended Fictions. Reading Novels by Manuel Puig*, Urbana and Chicago: University of Illinois Press.

Levine, S.J. (2000) *Manuel Puig and the Spider Woman: His Life and Fictions*, New York: Farrar, Straus & Giroux.

Puig, M. (2002) *El beso de la mujer araña*, ed. J. Amícola, Paris, Colección Archivos.

MAARTEN STEENMEIJER

Punto de vista

Punto de vista is an Argentine literary journal founded by Beatriz **Sarlo** in March 1978 and one of the few outspoken voices during the Proceso, the 1976–83 dictatorship. Many of its initial contributors, such as Ricardo **Piglia** and Nicolás **Rosa**, had collaborated previously in *Los libros*, its immediate antecedent. Strongly permeated by political concerns, the end of dictatorship deprived the magazine of a common enemy, subsequently cracking the editorial coalition and redefining its policies. *Punto de vista* deals with broad cultural and social issues.

Further reading

(1978–) *Punto de vista*, Buenos Aires: Litodar.

ALVARO FERNÁNDEZ-BRAVO

Q

Queiroz, Rachel de

b. 1910, Fortaleza, Ceará, Brazil

Writer

Queiroz made her name as a writer aged just 20, with the publication in 1930 of *O Quinze* (The Year 1915). This work, protesting against the deprivation and injustices suffered by the poor of her native north-east Brazil, established her as one of the country's major social realist novelists (see **social realism**). Later works, such as *As Três Marias* (The Three Marias) (1963), shifted the emphasis away from the social towards the psychological. In a writing career lasting well over sixty years, Queiroz has written plays and *crônicas* (see **crónica**), produced many translations and is well known for her popular newspaper columns.

Further reading

Bruno, H. (1977) *Rachel de Queiroz: Crítica, biografia, bibliografia, depoimento, seleção de textos, iconografia*, Rio de Janeiro: Cátedra and Brasília: Instituto Nacional do Livro.

Ellison, F. (1989) 'Rachel de Queiroz', in C.A. Solé and M.I. Abreu (eds), *Latin American Writers*, New York: Scribners, 3, 1119–24.

Jozef, B. (1997) 'Rachel de Queiroz', in V. Smith (ed.), *Encyclopedia of Latin American Literature*, London: Fitzroy Dearborn, 695–6.

Pinto, C.F. (1990) *O Bildungsroman femenino: Quatro exemplos brasileiros*, São Paulo: Perspectiva, 60–76.

Queiroz, R. de (1963) *The Three Marias*, Austin: University of Texas Press.

—— (1984) *Dora, Doralina*, trans. D.S. Loos, New York: Avon.

MARK DINNEEN

Quilombhoje/Cadernos negros

In 1978 a group of Afro-Brazilian authors founded an annual journal, *Cadernos negros* (Black Notebooks) in São Paulo to publish their poetry and short stories. In 1980 they organized a cultural/literary group, Quilombhoje (from Quilombo, a settlement of runaway slaves, and *hoje*, today). Some of the founding members of the group, like Eduardo de Oliveira and Oswaldo de Camargo, dissociated themselves from *Cadernos negros* because of disagreements regarding the criteria used to select texts for publication. Quilombhoje hosts many literary and cultural activities which promote awareness of, and pride in, the Afro-Brazilian heritage.

Further reading

(1978–) *Cadernos negros*, São Paulo.

MARIA JOSÉ SOMERLATE BARBOSA

Quimantú, Editorial

Editorial Quimantú was a Chilean state publishing house established during the Presidency of Salvador Allende (1971–3) after the purchase of **Zig Zag**, the country's largest publisher. *Quimantú*, a Mapuche term meaning 'knowing (*kim*) the sun (*antu*)', signalled a state committed to protecting the national cultural heritage and making it available to the majority of the population. Quimantú began its publishing activities in 1972 with a programme of cheap and accessible books which were printed in large runs in the supportive context of the Popular Unity government. The result was an unprecedented commercial success, aided by low prices and high levels of employment; proof positive of what can be done in a society committed to overcoming social disparities in knowledge and culture.

The *Quimantú para todos* collection, for example, produced fifty-four volumes of world and Chilean literature in a single year. Three other collections also began publication in the same year: *Nosotros los chilenos* (We Chileans) set out to incorporate hitherto unacknowledged indigenous peoples and popular cultures; *Camino abierto* (Open Road) was devoted to analytical writings by the two largest Popular Unity parties, the Socialists and the Communists; and *Cuadernos de educación popular* (Popular Education Notebooks), directed by Marta Haernecker, set out arguments in support of Allende's proposals for social change.

At the end of 1972 new series were added, namely *Minilibros*, *Cordillera*, *Cuncunai* and *Documentos especiales*. *Minilibros* began by producing four outstanding pieces of world literature each month. In one year fifty-two works of fiction and two volumes of poetry were published, including Bécquer's *Poemas* and Antonio Machado's *Caminante no hay camino* (Traveller, There is no Road to Follow). The majority of Quimantú's publications were literary works or educational volumes; it never reached the point where it could begin to produce new work or promote a national literature.

Quimantú essentially catered to the internal market; it set up a highly successful sales network through newspaper kiosks on the one hand and trade unions and universities on the other. Sales people travelled the country and travelling exhibitions stimulated sales and interest in the poorer districts. Within a few months Quimantú achieved sales figures which would previously have taken years to reach. In the first five months of 1972, for example, it sold five million copies of its sixty-two titles, including the *Documentos especiales* and the *Cartillas de educación popular* (Popular Education Workbooks), many of which were distributed free.

Quimantú was immediately closed down by the new military government after September 1973. It reappeared under the title Editora Nacional Gabriela Mistral. Much of its stock was destroyed by the military government, and the rest was sold off as waste paper. In 1982, the Editora Gabriela Mistral passed into private hands.

EUGENIA NEVES

Quintero, Ednodio

b. 1947, Mérida, Venezuela

Writer

A forestry engineer and university professor who has always lived in his native Mérida, Quintero has written several fine stories, including 'Volveré con mis perros' (I'll Be Back with My Dogs) (1975) and 'La bailarina de Kachgar' (The Kachgar Dancer) (1991), and two novels, *La danza del jaguar* (Dance of the Jaguar) (1991) and *El rey de las ratas* (King of the Rats) (1994). His work was slow to find an audience, but when it did it was very successful. His prose, at times incisive and at times colloquial and simple, and his painful disturbing images, contribute to his reputation as one of Venezuela's oustanding contemporary writers. Quintero is co-organizer of the prestigious Mariano Picón Salas Literary Biennial.

Further reading

Puente Baldoceda, B. (1994) 'Itinerario de una poética narrativa en las obras de Ednodio Quintero', *Revista iberoamericana* 60(166–7): 337–50.

Quintero, E. (1994) 'La narrativa venezolana: Una isla flotante?', *Revista iberoamericana* 60(166–7): 141–53.

—— (2000) *El corazón ajeno*, Caracas: Grijalbo.

VERONICA JAFFÉ

Quintero, Héctor

b. 1942, Havana, Cuba

Playwright

A grasp of black humour and melodrama and skill in capturing popular types mark Quintero's work as both writer and director. His career began in radio and television before he moved into theatre, eventually becoming director of Havana's Teatro Musical. Early works such as *Contigo pan y cebolla* (With You, Bread and Onion) (1962) and *El premio flaco* (The Thin Prize) (1964) satirized Cuban family life in the 1950s. His later works, from *Mambrú se fue a la guerra* (Mambru's Gone to War) (1970) to *El lugar ideal* (The Ideal Place) (1997), provide a rich picture of daily life in Cuba.

Further reading

Quintero, H. (1980) *Teatro y revolución*, Havana: Editorial Letras Cubanas.

—— (1983) *Teatro*, Havana: Editorial Letras Cubanas.

—— (1990) *Antología de teatro cubano*, Havana: Editorial Pueblo y Educación.

WILFREDO CANCIO ISLA

Quiroga, Horacio

b. 1878, Salto, Uruguay; d. 1937, Buenos Aires, Argentina

Writer

Horacio Quiroga is the creator of the specific genre of the **short story** in Latin America – while his early stories betray the influence of Poe, he develops a structure and a thematic range that is entirely original. Yet there is a common thread from Poe to the Quiroga of his most famous stories, set in Misiones on the edge of the jungle. Both are fascinated by human beings living at the extremes – whether exploring the darker regions of the landscape of the mind or exposing the instincts and errors of human beings in the most extreme of circumstances. Thus, in the brief but powerful 'A la deriva', a man dying of a snake-bite lives out an illusion of survival, although the surroundings – the gorge through which the river flows, the birds flying over him – leave no doubt as to the inevitability of his fate; so it is with Mr Jones, the settler, in 'La insolación', where it is his own stubbornness that ensures sunstroke and a death that all his animals sense and anticipate. Only he seems oblivious.

On this frontier, man and animals co-exist in a single space – a space not yet defined as human or, any longer, as wild nature. It is the struggle between them for survival that is recounted in 'Anaconda', where man and snake are bitter enemies contesting a shrinking no man's land. But within the constraints of the place and time, there is room for decision and for error; sometimes it is human vanity or blindness that produces heroism – like the 'Pescador de vigas' who accepts a challenge to swim a fast, log-filled river in exchange for a wind-up gramophone.

The setting for these stories is the Misiones region, an area Quiroga himself knew well. Having visited Paris during his early twenties, Quiroga turned back to his own region when he joined an expedition to the Chaco area in 1903 as a photographer. He returned again the following year, this time as part of a project to colonize unoccupied lands. The project failed but he returned ten years later with his wife and children – this time to the town of San Ignacio in Misiones. He was in a sense a frontiersman, pushing back the limits of the social world and observing human beings *in extremis*. For Quiroga the short story corresponded to a world in which all experience was fragmentary and without a broader meaning. It was a world where tragedy occurred without drama; Quiroga's own life was full of personal tragedy, including his own suicide and those of several family members. Perhaps he saw this tragedy reflected in the unequal struggle between man and nature.

Quiroga's most important stories are to be found in *Cuentos de amor, de locura y de muerte* (Stories of Love, Madness and Death) (1917) and *Anaconda* (1921).

Further reading

Avaro, N. (2002) 'El relato de la "vida intensa" en los "cuentos de monte" ', in M.T. Gramuglio (ed.), *El imperio realista*, vol. 6 of *Historia crítica de la literatura argentina*, Buenos Aires: Emecé, 179–99.

Borgeson, P.W. (1997) 'Horacio Quiroga', in V. Smith (ed.), *Encyclopedia of Latin American Literature*, London: Fitzroy Dearborn, 697–9.

Flores, A. (ed.) (1976) *Aproximaciones a Horacio Quiroga*, Caracas: Monte Avila.

Quiroga, H. (1976) *The Decapitated Chicken and Other Stories*, trans. M.S. Peden, Austin: University of Texas Press.

—— (1993) *Todos los cuentos*, Madrid: Colección Archivos.

Rodríguez Monegal, E. (1968) *El desterrado: Vida y obra de Horacio Quiroga*, Buenos Aires: Losada.

Schade, G.D. (1989) 'Horacio Quiroga', in C.A. Solé and M.I. Abreu (eds), *Latin American Writers*, New York: Scribners, 2, 551–8.

MIKE GONZALEZ

Quiroga Santa Cruz, Marcelo

b. 1931, Cochabamba, Bolivia; d. 1980, Bolivia, place unknown

Writer and politician

As minister of mines, Quiroga nationalized the US Gulf Oil Company in 1969. Congressman and founder of the Socialist Party (PS-1) in 1971, he was its presidential candidate and instituted legal proceedings against ex-dictator Hugo Banzer for human rights abuses and corruption. Exiled in Chile and Mexico, he returned secretly to Bolivia in 1977. Murdered by paramilitary groups attacking the Bolivian Trade Union Federation (COB) in July 1980, his remains were never found, although the family received a box which was said to contain his ashes. His novel, *Los deshabitados* (The Uninhabited) (1957), marked a shift in Bolivian narrative from **social realism** to **existentialism**.

Further reading

Prada Oropeza, R. (1986) 'Los deshabitados: El círculo de la desolación', *Revista iberoamericana* 52(134): 127–38.

Quiroga Santa Cruz, M. (1980) *Los deshabitados*, La Paz: Los Amigos del Libro.

—— (1982) *Oleocracía o patria*, Mexico City: Siglo XXI.

WINSTON MOORE

R

Radiografía de la pampa

Radiografía de la pampa (X-Ray of the Pampa) is an interpretive essay on Argentine nationality by Ezequiel **Martínez Estrada** published in 1933. Texts of a similar kind appeared in Argentina throughout the 1930s. Martínez Estrada's analysis is completely negative; its central hypothesis concerns the 'false foundation' of the country, established on the basis of the rape of Indian women and the murder of their men. It is a rewriting of the thesis that Latin America was born out of an original violence which in Argentina took the form of the struggle between '**civilization and barbarism**' formulated by Sarmiento. The repressed violence re-emerges, making it impossible to construct a nation with an identity; thus it returns to the imitation of Europe. His ahistorical critique and powerful arguments find their political expression in his *Muerte y transfiguración de Martín Fierro* (Death and Transformation of Martin Fierro), published in 1948.

Further reading

Martínez Estrada, E. (1993) *Radiografía de la pampa*, ed. L. Pollman, Paris: Archivos.

Sarlo, B. (1984) 'El ensayo como forma del problema argentino: Una aproximación a "Radiografía de la pampa"', *Dispositio* 9(24–6): 149–59.

—— (1971) *X Ray of the Pampa*, Austin: U of Texas Press.

GRACIELA MONTALDO

Radrigán, Juan

b. 1937, Santiago, Chile

Playwright

Radrigán has written many plays focused on Chile's urban and rural poor. Since 1980 he has staged works both in theatres and community centres in shanty towns, trade unions and schools. In his plays the homeless, the alcoholics, the prostitutes, the elderly and the abandoned are witnesses of marginality and represent human survival in desperate conditions. In 1996 he presented the modern opera *El Encuentramiento*, about the encounter between the Spanish conquistadors and the native Chilean Mapuche people. Other well-known works include *Las brutas* (The Foolish Women) (1980) and *Hechos consumados* (Proven Facts) (1982).

Further reading

Boyle, C. (2001) 'Text, Time, Process and History in Contemporary Chilean Theatre', *Theatre Research International*, July, 26(2): 181–9.

Radrigán, Juan (1968) *El vino de la cobardía*, Santiago, Chile: Impresores Guerrero y Recabarren.

—— (1984) *Teatro de Juan Radrigán*, ed. M.L. Hurtado, J.A. Pina and H. Vidal, Minneapolis: CENECA, University of Minnesota.

Rojo, G. and S. Rojo (1989) 'Teatro chileno: 1983–1987: Observaciones preliminares', *Alba de América: Revista literaria*, July, 7(12–13): 159–86.

CAROLA OYARZÚN

Raful, Tony

b. 1951, Santo Domingo, Dominican Republic

Writer

Tony Raful (Antonio Raful Tejada) belongs to the Generación del 65 (Generation of 1965). With Andrés L. **Mateo** and Pedro **Peix**, he hosted the television programme *Peña de Tres* (Circle of Three). He has been a professor at the Universidad Autónoma de Santo Domingo and director of the National Library, and is deeply involved in politics. His most recent book of poetry is *Las bodas de Rosaura con la primavera* (Rosaura's Wedding with the Springtime) (1991). Most of his poetry evokes the 1965 war and other social conflicts, and is considered *panfletaria* or propagandistic.

FERNANDO VALERIO-HOLGUÍN

Rama, Angel

b. 1926, Montevideo, Uruguay; d. 1983, Madrid, Spain

Writer

Rama was one of the most vital contemporary cultural thinkers, whose untimely death in a plane crash (along with his wife Marta **Traba** and the writers Jorge **Ibargüengoitia** and Manuel **Scorza**) left a vacuum in Latin American thought. Rama first wrote poems, plays and novels. Later, he focused on reclaiming and evaluating Latin America's cultural past to explain its achievements and failures. As part of this task, he expended considerable effort on the dissemination of the literary production of writers less known or forgotten by canonical historiography. He played an active role in the influential cultural and political magazine *Marcha*, and in the publishing house Arca, both located in Montevideo, Uruguay. In 1970 he went into exile in Venezuela, where he founded and became general editor of the prestigious Venezuelan series **Biblioteca Ayacucho** and also edited the literary journal *Escritura*. Later he lived in Puerto Rico, the USA and finally in Europe until his death. His departure from the USA was forced by the State Department's denial of residence for his alleged communist ties.

Rama understood the task of the intellectual (see **intellectuals**) as a continuous process. He envisioned an America always alive, in a constant process of forging its cultural identity within an ideological, cultural and social grid of conflicting forces. Thus, the role of 'magister' of Latin American youth was central to his task. One of Rama's most stimulating ideas, inspired by José **Martí**'s Americanist spirit, was to think of Latin America as different cultural areas, forming a unified whole, yet preserving regional distinctiveness. Rama focused first on nineteenth-century cultural formation and development, focusing in particular on Martí, Rubén **Darío** and the forgers of Spanish American *modernismo* (see **Spanish American modernism**); in the last years of his life, he wrote on the newest narrative trends. He viewed Latin American narrative as a movement with multiple orientations, which originated in the 1920s against the regionalist novel of the first decades of the 1900s. In his *Rubén Darío y el Modernismo: Circunstancia socioeconómica de un arte americano* (Rubén Darío and Modernism: The Socioeconomic Circumstance of an American Art Form) (1970), Rama proposed a new reading of this artistic and literary movement, by examining the question of professionalization of the artist exemplified in Darío, thus establishing a new literary tradition that functioned as a coherent system of expression. His 1982 *Transculturación narrativa en América Latina* (Narrative Transculturation in Latin America) (1982) (Rama takes the term from Fernando Ortiz) explores the concept of cultural heterogeneity as a possible response and artistic solution to the difficulties arising from this heterogeneity, and the place of literature in cultural history. His *Literatura y clase social* (Literature and Social Class) (1983) was published posthumously, as was *La ciudad letrada* (The Lettered City) (1984), a watershed essay that analyses the function of cultural systems in Latin America.

Further reading:

Blixen, C. (1986) *Cronología y bibliografía de Angel Rama*, Montevideo: Fundación Angel Rama.

Casa de las Américas (1993) Special issue, July–Sept., 34(192).

Corona, I. (2001) 'Contesting the Lettered City: Cultural Mediation and Communicative Strategies in the Contemporary Chronicle in Mexico', in E. Paz Soldan and D.A. Castillo (eds), *Latin American Literature and Mass Media*, New York: Garland.

Campa, R. de la (1999) '*The Lettered City*, Power and Writing in Latin America', in *Latin Americanism*, Minneapolis: University of Minnesota Press, 121–48.

D'Allemand, P. (2001) 'Angel Rama: Literatura, modernización y resistencia', in *Hacia una crítica cultural latinoamericana*, Lima: Latinoamericana Editores, 59–84.

Díaz Caballero, J. (1991) *Angel Rama, o, La crítica de la transculturación*, Lima: Lluvia Editores.

Moraña, M. (ed.) (1997) *Angel Rama y los estudios latinoamericanos*, Pittsburgh, PA: Instituto Internacional de Literatura Iberoamericana.

Texto crítico (1985) Special issue, Jan.–Aug., 10(31–2): 24–32.

Zanetti, S. (1992) 'Angel Rama y la construcción de una literatura latinoamericana', *Revista iberoamericana* 58 (160–1): 919–32.

MAGDALENA GARCÍA PINTO

Ramchand, Kenneth

b. 1939, Cedros, Trinidad

Writer and critic

Ramchand's ground-breaking *The West Indian Novel and Its Background* (1970) contains outstanding interpretations of major West Indian writers such as Earl **Lovelace** and Wilson **Harris**. It was followed in 1976 by *An Introduction to the Study of West Indian Literature.* A visiting scholar in a number of universities in Britain and the USA, he became the first Professor of West Indian literature in 1984 at the University of the West Indies. His frequently controversial 'Matters Arising' column in *Trinidad Guardian* discusses political, economic and literary matters in the local dialect. A short-story writer in his own right, Ramchand's contribution to education and culture – as an academic, a creative artist and an independent senator – remains largely unrecognized in his own country.

Further reading

Ramchand, K. (1997) 'The West Indian Short Story', *Journal of Caribbean Literature*, Spring, 1(1): 21–33.

—— (2000) '"The West Indian Novel and Its Background" Thirty Years Later', *ARIEL: A Review of International English Literature*, Jan.–April, 31(1–2): 351–73.

KEITH JARDIM

RAMÍREZ GÓMEZ, JOSÉ AGUSTÍN *see* Agustín, José

Ramírez Mercado, Sergio

b. 1942, Masatepe, Nicaragua

Writer and statesman

A well-known prose writer and vice-president of the Sandinista government (1979–90), Ramírez continues to play an important cultural and political role in Nicaragua. His novel *Margarita, está linda la mar* (Margarita, the Sea is Beautiful), a novel about the life of Rubén **Darío**, intercut with the story of the assassination of Anastasio Somoza, won the 1998 Premio Alfaguara.

In 1960, while a law student at the University of León, he and Fernando Gordillo co-founded *Ventana* (Window), a group committed to both politics and literature which had a considerable influence on Nicaraguan cultural life. Ramírez became Director of the Consejo Superior Universitario Centroamericano (Superior Central America University Council (CSUCA)) and of the Editorial Universitaria Centro Americana (Central America University Publishing Company (EDUCA)). He later joined the *Grupo de los Doce*, a group of twelve prominent Nicaraguans publicly opposed to the Somoza dictatorship which later formed a transitional government between *Somocismo* and the Sandinista government of 1979 which he later joined. After the defeat of the Sandinistas and the election of Violeta Chamorro, Ramírez became head of the Sandinista Group in the National Assembly until he split from the group and formed a new alternative organization, the Movimiento Renovador Sandinista (Sandinista Renovation Movement), standing as its presidential candidate in the elections of 1996.

In his work, he uses irony to ridicule aspects of the colonial mentality, ***costumbrismo*** and gender roles, and to portray the politically corrupt practices of the Somoza dictatorship. He uses cinematic techniques to express the simultaneous realities of a polarized society; Flaubert's lessons on literary atmosphere inform his critical recreation of the petty and provincial way of life of small towns; his careful and delicate portrayal of popular characters attest to his political commitment; and his recurrent metaphor of light, a barely discernible dawn behind closed doors, connotes his hopes for a luminous future.

In *Castigo divino* (Divine Punishment) (1988), his masterpiece, he recreates the stifling atmosphere of the old colonial city of León. Erotic passion and criminal intrigues revise the universe of legality through the relationships between men and women and between the intimate and the social. By exacerbating the private, passion becomes public discussion. Ramírez's works have been reprinted in Nicaragua and have been translated into several languages. *De tropeles y tropelías*, a fable about Somoza's dictatorship, won the Venezuelan journal *Imagen*'s Latin American literary prize for short stories in 1971, and *Castigo divino*, the detective novelist writers' prize.

A student of the life and thought of Augusto C. Sandino, Ramírez collected and introduced Sandino's anti-imperialist and popular ideas in *El pensamiento vivo de Sandino* (1975).

Further reading

Beverley, J. and M. Zimmerman (1990) *Literature and Politics in the Central American Revolutions*, Austin: University of Texas Press.

Ramírez, S. (1994) *Cambios estéticos y nuevos proyectos culturales en Centroamerica: Testimonios, entrevistas y ensayos*, Washington: Literal Books.

Ruffinelli, J. and W. Corral (1991) 'Un diálogo con Sergio Ramírez Mercado: Política y literatura en una época de cambios', *Nuevo texto crítico* 4(8): 4–13.

Schaefer, C. (1987) 'La recuperación del realismo: *¿Te dio miedo la sangre?* de Sergio Ramírez', *Texto crítico* 36–7: 146–52.

DEREK PETREY AND ILEANA RODRÍGUEZ

Ramos, Graciliano

b. 1892, Quebrângulo, Alagoas, Brazil; d. 1953, Rio de Janeiro, Brazil

Writer

One of Brazil's most important writers of the twentieth century, Ramos is known for his eloquent novels of the interior of the Brazilian north east – *Vidas secas* (Barren Lives) (1938), about a family fleeing drought in the *sertão*, and *São Bernardo* (1934), a masterpiece about a ranch hand who fights his way up to become owner of the farm where he had worked. A journalist, director of the state printing office, then director of public instruction for the state of Alagoas, Ramos was jailed for a year during the Estado Novo, then released without ever having been charged. This experience resulted in his posthumous work, *Memórias do cárcere* (Prison Memoirs) (1953), which was later made into a film by Nelson Pereira dos Santos (who also made a film of *Vidas secas*, one of the classics of Brazilian Cinema Novo). Ramos joined the Communist Party of Brazil late in his life, and fell ill after a trip to the Soviet bloc.

Ramos's prose is spare, a literary recreation of common speech. *Vidas secas* is composed of a series of linked stories told from the points of view of the father, the mother, the children and the family dog. *São Bernardo* consists of the interior monologue of an insanely jealous husband; as in Machado de **Assis**'s *Dom Casmurro* years before, the jealousy is out of proportion to the scant motives the husband has. *São Bernardo* is also a fascinating work of metafiction, since its relatively unlettered narrator tries to learn the art of writing from his friends and associates, members of the local intelligentsia, whose prose is ridiculously ornate; his final product, the novel we are reading, is powerful for its blunt and plain-spoken quality.

Ramos is not as celebrated outside of Brazil as he deserves to be. His stylized rural speech, the human depth of the situation he describes and his passionate evocation of a region of the Brazilian interior are reminiscent of Juan **Rulfo**'s treatment of Jalisco. His writing is powerful in its representation of social problems, lyrical in its simplicity, intense in its emotional force.

Further reading

Abreu, M.I. (1989) 'Graciliano Ramos', in C.A. Solé and M.I. Abreu (eds), *Latin American Writers*, New York: Scribners, 2, 745–54.

Brayner, S. (1977) *Graciliano Ramos*, Rio de Janeiro: Civilizacao Brasileira/MEC.

Carvalho, C.D. (1978) *Ensaios Gracilianos*, Rio de Janeiro: Rio.

Mazzara, R.A. (1974) *Graciliano Ramos*, New York: Twayne.

Oliveira, C.L de. (1988) *Understanding Graciliano Ramos*, Columbia: University of South Carolina Press.

Ramos, G. (1961) *Obras completas*, São Paulo: Martins, 10 vols.

—— (1975) *São Bernardo*, trans. R. Scott-Buccleuch, London: Peter Owen.

—— (1961) *Barren Lives*, trans. R.E. Dimmick, Austin: University of Texas Press.

Silva, T.V.Z. da (1997) 'Graciliano Ramos', in V. Smith (ed.), *Encyclopedia of Latin American Literature*, London: Fitzroy Dearborn, 701–2.

Vincent, J.S. (1976) 'Graciliano Ramos: The Dialectics of Defeat', in H. Martins (ed.), *The Brazilian Novel*, Bloomington: Indiana University Press.

DANIEL BALDERSTON

Ramos Otero, Manuel

b. 1948, Manatí, Puerto Rico; d. 1990, Río Piedras, Puerto Rico

Writer

A short story writer and poet, Ramos Otero is considered an important member of Puerto Rico's 'Generation of the 70s', a group of younger writers, many of whom collaborated on the literary magazine ***Zona de carga y descarga*** (1972–75). His stories are like spiderwebs, with narratives that follow unexpected and diverging paths and tales that appear as elaborate traps. In *El cuento de la mujer del mar* (Story of the Woman from the Sea) (1979), arguably one of his best works, the narrative points to alternate realities where geography and time collapse. The stories are set in Puerto Rico as well as in New York, where Ramos Otero lived for many years.

Ramos Otero's choice of themes was always surprising and irreverent – ranging from prostitutes to society ladies, from illusions of love to sado-masochistic sex among men – and his style was one of narrative risk, with expressive tools that become weapons. In his ironic and lyrical world, disenchantment offers its own consolation. His writing, especially his poetry, validates the fluid and transitory over the static and unchanging. Ramos Otero helped to open up Puerto Rican discourse to the voices of the marginalized and selectively demolish the house of patriarchal culture in works such as *El libro de la muerte* (The Book of Death) (1985), where he pays homage to gay male culture. His last work, *Invitación al polvo* (Invitation to the Dust) (1991), published after his death from AIDS-related complications, offers readers the legacy of a poet ravaged by disease. Other works include *Concierto de metal para un recuerdo y otras orgías de soledad* (Brass Concert for a Memory and Other Orgies of Solitude) (1971) and *Página en blanco y staccato* (Empty Page and Staccato) (1987).

Further reading

Barradas, E. (1993) ' "Epitafios": El canon y la canonización de Manuel Ramos Otero', *La Torre: Revista de la Universidad de Puerto Rico* 7(27–8): 319–38.

Costa, M. (1991) 'Entrevista: Manuel Ramos Otero', *Hispamérica: Revista de literatura* 20(59): 59–67.

Cruz Malavé, A. (1993) 'Para virar al macho: La autobiografía como subversión en la cuentística de Manuel Ramos Otero', *Revista iberoamericana*, Jan.–June, 59(162–3): 239–63.

Rios Avila, R. (1998) 'Caribbean Dislocations: Arenas and Ramos Otero in New York', in S. Molloy and R. McKee Irwin (eds), *Hispanisms and Homosexualities*, Durham, NC: Duke University Press.

JOSÉ QUIROGA

Ramos Perea, Roberto

b. 1959, Mayagüez, Puerto Rico

Playwright

Ramos Perea is a prolific writer who has authored more than twenty plays in addition to his work in the theatre as actor, director and drama critic. He has played an outspoken role promoting the new generation of Puerto Rican dramatists. He has received playwriting awards from the Ateneo Puertorriqueño for *Módulo 104* (1983) and *Cueva de ladrones* (Den of Thieves) (1984). Another play, *Miénteme más* (Lie More to Me), was awarded the Tirso de Molina award in Spain (1992). He is also a journalist and has served as executive director of the Ateneo Puertorriqueño since 1986.

Further reading

Monge Rafuls, P. (1995) 'Entrevista al dramaturgo Roberto Ramos Perea sobre la actualidad del teatro puertorriqueño', *Revista del ateneo puertorriqueño*, Jan.–Dec., 5(13–15): 233–44.

Montañez, C.L. (1996) 'Los personajes femeninos en el teatro de Roberto Ramos Peres', *Revista del ateneo puertorriqueño*, Jan.–Dec., 6(16–18): 141–8.

Reynolds, B.H. (1987) 'Puertorriqueñidad: The Force Behind the Development of a Puerto Rican Theater', in A. Rodríguez de Laguna (ed.), *Images and Identities: The Puerto Rican in Two World Contexts*, New Brunswick: Transaction.

Romero, R.J. (1996) 'The Moon and the Gutter: Border, Women and Migration', *Discourse*, 1995 Fall–1996 Winter, 18(1–2): 84–106.

VÍCTOR F. TORRES

Ramos Sucre, José Antonio

b. 1890, Cumaná, Venezuela; d. 1930, Geneva, Switzerland

Poet

When originally published, Ramos Sucre's poetry – *La torre de Timón* (Timon's Tower) (1925), *Las formas del fuego* (The Forms of Fire) (1929) and *El cielo de esmalte* (The Enamel Sky) (1929) – was little read and barely understood. Rediscovered by the Sardio group in the 1950s, he began to be recognized for his modernist aesthetic and range of symbolic languages. The thematic universe of his poetry builds on evocation and quotations from literary and painted landscapes, and skilfully employs the drama and monologue form within the prose poem. His work has become paradigmatic of Venezuelan literary modernity.

Further reading

Castañón, A. (1998) 'José Antonio Ramos Sucre: Historia verdadera de dos ciudades', *Vuelta* 21(255): 52–6.

Ramos Sucre, J.A. (2001) *Obra poética*, ed. A.R. Hernández Bossio, Paris: Colección Archivos.

Rodríguez Silva, A. (1998) 'Hermeneútica y conocimiento en la poesía de Ramos Sucre', *Cifra nueva: Revista de cultura* 7: 105–12.

Tenreiro, S. (1994) 'Ramos Sucre y la crítica', *Revista iberoamericana* 60(166–7): 417–25.

RAFAEL CASTILLO ZAPATA

Raschella, Roberto

b. 1930, Buenos Aires, Argentina

Writer

Possibly the last and most sophisticated of Argentina's eccentric writers, Raschella belongs to a peculiar immigrant lineage. He places questions of language and ideology within the subjective universe of his characters. Working with fragmentary histories, their totality glimpsed in reiterated brief and imprecise dramatic motifs, Raschella's literary language embraces elements of Italian peasant language defiantly set within an admirable lyrical rhetoric, as in the novel *Diálogos en los patios rojos* (Dialogues on Red Patios) (1994). A schoolteacher for three decades, Raschella wrote criticism and a film script. After 1963 he turned to poetry, translation and fiction.

Further reading

Sarlo, B. (1998) 'Lugar de origen', *Punto de Vista: Revista de cultura*, Dec., 21(62): 33–6.

SERGIO CHEJFEC

Rascón Banda, Víctor Hugo

b. 1948, Uruáchic, Chihuahua, Mexico

Playwright

One of Mexico's foremost contemporary playwrights, Rascón Banda belongs to the *Nueva Dramaturgia* (New Drama) generation. His plays deal with a wide variety of issues: migration to the USA, in his 1979 *Los ilegales* (The Illegals); mine workers, in the poetic *Voces en el umbral* (Voices at the Threshold); wrestling, in *Máscara vs. Cabellera* (Mask versus Hair); and women's oppression, in *La fiera del Ajusco* (The Ajusco Beast). For the mid-1990s series 'Teatro clandestino' (Clandestine Theatre), seeking to reflect Mexico's immediate socio-political problems, he wrote *Los ejecutivos* (The Bank) and *Guerrero Negro*. Rascón Banda also writes theatre criticism for the weekly news magazine *Proceso*.

Further reading

Gann, M.S. (1991) 'El teatro de Víctor Hugo Rascón Banda: Hiperrealismo y destino', *Latin American Theatre Review*, Fall, 25(1): 77–88.

Rascón Banda, Víctor Hugo (1980) *Los ilegales: Nueva dramaturgia mexicana*, Mexico City: Dirección de Difusión Cultural, Departamento Editorial.

—— (1983) *Voces en el umbral: Nueva dramaturgia mexicana*, Mexico City: Dirección de Difusión Cultural, Departamento Editorial.

—— (1985) *Teatro del delito*, Mexico City: Editores Mexicanos Unidos.

—— (2000) *La mujer que cayó del cielo*, Mexico City: Escenología, A.C.

Sotelo, C.A. (1996) 'La preponderancia del espectáculo en el teatro méxicano: Las armas blancas de Víctor Hugo Rascón Banda', *Revista de literatura mexicana contemporánea*, Jan.–April, 1(2): 102–5.

ANTONIO PRIETO-STAMBAUGH

Rauskin, Jacobo A.

b. 1941, Villarrica, Paraguay

Poet

Author of several poetry books, Rauskin has also published some poems in both local and foreign magazines and literary anthologies. His poetic production includes, among others, the following titles: *Oda* (Ode) (1964), *Casa perdida* (Lost House) (1971), *Naufragios* (Shipwrecks) (1984), *La canción andariega* (The Wandering Song) (1991), *Alegría de un hombre que vuelve* (Happiness of a Man who Returns) (1992) and *La calle del violín allá lejos* (The Street of the Violin off in the Distance), his most recent book, published in 1996. Also in 1996, he and Gladys **Carmagnola** shared the Premio Municipal de Literatura (Municipal Prize in Literature), the highest literary award in Paraguay.

TERESA MÉNDEZ-FAITH

Rawet, Samuel

b. 1929, Klimontow, Poland; d. 1984, Brasília, Brazil

Writer

One of the few Brazilian writers to address the theme of immigration and uprootedness, Rawet is reminiscent of Jorge Luis **Borges** and Hermann Hesse. He intellectualizes the plight of the wandering Jew within the confines of Brazilian social reality, but his narrative voice makes him inaccessible to all but the most sophisticated reader. Since the 1990s, Rawet has increasingly become the subject of scholarly studies, especially works by Nelson Vieira. He also wrote several philosophical studies on the themes of homosexuality, alienation, anguish and conscience.

Further reading:

Secco, C.L.T. (1979) 'A metáfora do jogo em Samuel Rawet: Uma leitura do conto "O Jogo de Damas" ', *Minas Gerais, suplemento literario*, 31 March: 7.

Silverman, M. (1977) 'O motivo da viagem nas histórias dc Samucl Rawct', *Tempo brasileiro: Revista de cultura* 48: 72–7.

SUSAN CANTY QUINLAN

Rayuela

A novel by the Argentine writer Julio **Cortázar**, published in 1963, *Rayuela* became a major best-seller (see **best-sellers**), reprinted and translated innumerable times since then. One of the most representative works of the '**Boom**' of the 1960s, *Rayuela* has provoked passionate readings, yet it is revealing of the concerns of the time that the novel's reputation arises above all from its formal experimentation. The 'tablero de direcciones' (sign-board) with which it opens suggests two possible readings (the one linear and incomplete, the other following the chapters in a particular order foreseen by the author), while suggesting the possibility of multiple alternative readings as well. Through its three parts ('The other side', 'This side', 'On other sides') the novel follows a journey of initiation by an Argentine called Oliveira between two cities (Paris and Buenos Aires) and two women (la Maga and Talita), while at the same time presenting a personal view of the Bohemian lifestyle of a group of Latin Americans living in Paris.

The novel's title, *Rayuela* (Hopscotch), defines the writer's concerns and the creative direction in which he intends to move. The game of hopscotch suggests both a rite of passage (from earth into heaven) and a game which has transcendental dimensions; but it also alludes to a type of reading which 'jumps' chapters in order to find in another narrative order a truth that is impossible to communicate without these distortions and diversions. The novel attests to a constant estrangement, or critical distance, from the conventional relationships between language and reality. Cortázar assumes that the disruption of traditional forms of expression will allow a passage to other realities, for his 'reader-accomplice' is assumed to be familiar with the ideas of the text and the open work which were in circulation at the time (although in his work the metafiction is more the reflection of existential disorientation and the vital search than it is cultural speculation). To a fairly tenuous fictional line is added a challenge to traditional literature crystallized in the reflections of a character-reader called Morelli and in a series of quotations from different texts. All this defines *Rayuela* as a 'total' work, whose propositions look ahead to the ruptures of the late 1960s, and at the same time as a worldview and an unstable and paradoxical conception of literature itself. But the novel does not limit itself to calling reality and literature into question; some justly celebrated passages, like Berthe Trepat's concert, the death of baby Rocamadour and the scene in which Oliveira and Traveller put a board across the empty space between their apartments and have Talita go across it to get some nails for no obvious practical purpose, possess great evocative power and an undeniable lyricism. At another level, Cortázar continues and brings to a climax an Argentine tradition of looking at Paris, writing memorable descriptions of it and transforming its streets into a mythical terrain for Argentines in search of themselves.

Further reading

Barrenechea, A.M. and J. Cortázar (1983) *Cuadernos de bitácora de Rayuela*, Buenos Aires: Sudamericana.

Brody, R. (1976) *Rayuela*, *Critical Guides to Spanish Texts*, London: Grant & Cutler.

Cortázar, J. (1966) *Hopscotch*, trans. G. Rabassa, New York: Pantheon Books.

—— (1991) *Rayuela*, Madrid: Archivos.

Larsen, N. (1998) 'Cortázar and Postmodernity: New Interpretive Liabilities', in C.J. Alonso (ed.), *Julio Cortázar: New Readings*, Cambridge: Cambridge University Press.

JULIO PREMAT

Real de Azúa, Carlos

b. 1916, Montevideo, Uruguay; d. 1977, Montevideo

Historian and critic

In the course of his life, Real de Azúa embraced literary criticism and Uruguayan and Latin American history, as well as writing on sociology and political science. His political ideas evolved and changed substantially through time. In the 1930s he supported the Falange in Spain; in the 1950s he supported both traditional Uruguayan parties and in 1959 welcomed the Cuban Revolution; through the 1960s and 1970s his allegiances were with the Left.

He was a contributor to the magazine *Marcha* throughout its history (1948–74), professor of Latin American literature at the Artigas Teachers' Training Institute in Montevideo (1954–76), professor of political science at the Institute's Faculty of Economics and Management (1967) and visiting professor at Columbia (1973) and Yale (1975), among many other posts.

A specialist on the Uruguayan writer, José Enrique **Rodó**, he wrote the prologue for various editions of Rodó's *Ariel* and *Motivos de Proteo*. In 1964 he edited the *Antología del ensayo uruguayo contemporáneo* and the collection, *Capítulo oriental: La historia de la literatura uruguaya* (From the Eastern Bank: A History of Uruguayan Literature) in forty-four volumes, together with Carlos **Maggi** and Carlos Martínez Moreno.

His own writings include *Elites y desarrollo en América Latina* (Elites and Development in Latin America) (1969) and *Política, poder y partidos en el Uruguay de hoy* (Politics, Power and Parties in Contemporary Uruguay) (1971).

Further reading

Cotelo, R. (1987) *Carlos Real de Azúa de cerca y de lejos*, Montevideo: Ed. Nuevo Mundo.

Halperin Donghi, T. (1992) 'Carlos Real de Azúa: La ávida curiosidad por el mundo', *Revista iberoamericana* 58(160–1): 893–902.

Real de Azúa, Carlos (1965) *El mirador de Próspero*, Montevideo: Ministerio de Instrucción Pública y Previsión Social.

—— (1968) *La patria vieja: Selección*, Montevideo: Centro Editor de América Latina.

MARCO MAGGI

real maravilloso, lo

After Alejo **Carpentier** coined the term in the prologue to his 1949 novel ***El reino de este mundo*** (The Kingdom of this World), *lo real maravilloso* (marvellous realism) came to designate a specifically Latin American literary style characterized by bizarre images and events. Carpentier's original usage, however, did not define a literary category – such as **magical realism** – but a marvellous Latin American reality, which he believed literature could record. He contrasts this reality with a dull European experience that has exhausted its own mythologies, yet Carpentier's marvellous realism owes much to European movements, especially **surrealism**. Recently, critics have noted the imprecision of the term and questioned its usefulness.

Further reading

Chiampi, I. (1980) *O realismo maravilhoso*, São Paulo: Perspectiva.

Laguardia, G. (1986) 'Marvelous Realism/-Marvelous Criticism', in B.G. Chevigny and G. Laguardia (eds), *Reinventing the Americas: Comparative Studies of Literature of the United States and Spanish America*, New York: Cambridge University Press.

Llarena, A. (1997) *Realismo mágico y lo real maravilloso: Una cuestión de verosimilitud*, Gaithersburg, MD: Hispamérica.

Sánchez Molina, A.C. (1994) 'Lo real maravilloso americano y la estética de la recepción', *Revista de*

filología y lingüística de la Universidad de Costa Rica, July–Dec., 20(2): 59–72.
Vargas Llosa, M. (2000) 'Lo real maravilloso o artimañas literarias?' *Letras libres*, Jan., 2(13): 32–6.

JAMES BUCKWALTER-ARIAS

Reckord, Barrington (Barry)

b. 1926, Kingston, Jamaica

Playwright, essayist and director

A playwright and director, Reckord's works explore man–woman relationships in contexts where power dictates ugly socio-political dynamics. Born into a creative family (his brother Lloyd is a producer-director-actor, and his nephew Michael and niece Margaret are writers), Reckord read English on a scholarship at Cambridge. Returning to Jamaica in 1956, he taught there, in England and then at the University of Alberta. Some twelve Reckord plays have been produced, but only one has been published because he revises continually. He has published non-fiction – *Does Fidel Eat More Than Your Father: Conversations in Cuba* (1972) – and received a Guggenheim Fellowship.

PAT DUNN AND PAMELA MORDECAI

Reckord, Michael

b. 1943, Four Paths, Clarendon, Jamaica

Writer

Better known as a journalist and critic, Reckord is also a playwright, poet and short story writer with numerous stage plays, radio and television pieces, short stories and poems to his credit. Since 1964 his work has won many awards in Jamaica; he also won first prize for 'Dog Food' in a 1984 BBC short story competition and a Special Mention for poetry in 1986, also from the BBC. His poetry and story writing reflect his concern with current social issues and his interest in human relationships, while his radio, television and stage scripts, which include a pantomime, are often comic.

SITA DICKSON LITTLEWOOD

Redcam, Tom

b. 1870, Clarendon, Jamaica; d. 1933, London, England

Writer

Posthumously proclaimed the first Poet Laureate of Jamaica as editor of the *Jamaica Times*, Redcam (real name Thomas H. McDermott) took a leading role in Jamaican cultural circles, encouraging local writers including Claude **McKay** and initiating the cheap All Jamaica Library (1904–9) to popularize Jamaican fiction, to which he contributed *Becka's Buckra Baby* (1904) and *One Brown Girl and* – (1909). His poems were collected in *Orange Valley and Other Poems* (1951). While remaining largely Victorian in his style, he did much to pioneer a distinct tradition of Anglophone writing in Jamaica.

LOUIS JAMES

regionalismo

The term *regionalismo* (regionalism) refers to an artistic and cultural current emerging in the late nineteenth century in almost every country of Latin America. Literary regionalism has a strong political tone, setting out to draw marginal sectors of the population into the framework of the national State. It does so through the description of non-urban territories and customs, and by using local forms of speech, legitimizing (through the practice of writing) and incorporating into literate culture the practices of those within the national territory who are considered 'other'. Significantly, literary regionalism 'neutralized' practices other than those envisaged in the laws of the State by 'translating' them into the codes of the hegemonic culture.

It fell to the **intellectuals** to define a national identity by creating powerful shared symbols.

Costumbrista (see ***costumbrismo***) literature (which describes local customs) and regionalist writing have a decisive place in this process. In 'showing' difference, making it visible to the citizens of the national State, the novel in particular was able to suggest a territory unified despite its internal differences. The description of territories still outside the national consciousness (those numerous spaces yet to be absorbed by the State power as the twentieth century began) allowed a symbolic incorporation crucial in the process of national integration.

'Novels of the land', fictionalizing conflicts generally arising from questions of power, authority and alliances, usually set in the interior of the country, generally constitute the canon of Latin American national classics: Jorge Isaacs's *María* (1867), Alberto Blest Gana's *Martín Rivas* (1862), Clorinda Matto de Turner's *Aves sin nido* (Birds without a Nest) (1889), Mariano **Azuela**'s *Los de abajo* (The Underdogs) (1916), José Eustacio **Rivera**'s ***La vorágine*** (The Vortex) (1924), Ricardo Güiraldes's *Don Segundo Sombra* (1926) and Rómulo **Gallegos**'s ***Doña Bárbara*** (1929).

These novels postulate an identity and a regionalist perspective that coincides with the nation-building project; hence their fundamental role in the symbolic integration of Latin American nationalities. Two traditions meet in them; on the one hand, the political essays written by the *criollos* (Latin Americans of Spanish extraction) during the period of independence and the subsequent civil wars, and the writings of European travellers in Latin America; on the other, the constitution of the different Latin American cultural nationalisms towards the end of the nineteenth century.

These tendencies are first expressed in *Silvas americanas* (American Verses) (1823), in which the young Andrés Bello, exiled in London during the independence period, calls on 'Poetry' to abandon 'learned Europe' and move to America to sing of the natural beauties of the continent. The idea of *criollo* cultural identity that follows is rooted in Latin American nature and a programme for agricultural development, and is critical of the inequality and dehumanization of modern urban life. In 1845, in *Facundo*, Sarmiento argues that the relationship with the land (depopulated and inaccessible plains and forests) produces 'barbarous' people (nomadic, resistant to civilization, instinctive and violent). Only an enlightened liberal political programme would 'civilize' people. Within the recently independent republics the struggle developed in the polarization of country and city, expressed as the battle between **civilization and barbarism**.

These two seminal texts provided the framework within which Latin American culture evolved an interpretation of its political reality. Through romanticism and later through *costumbrismo*, Latin American literature fictionalized spaces and customs that were symptomatic of the radical differences in attitude of the independent republics towards Europe; but the polarization also represented the oppositions within them and especially the conflict between the city and the interior.

The *criollo* intellectuals, formed in a European mould, tried to find points of continuity and rupture with the Western tradition to which they felt they belonged. Literature (and art in general) played a key role in the process of constituting national traditions.

In a political sense, regionalism responded to the internal reorganization of the territorial frontiers of each newly independent nation; it responded too to the traditions of nomadic peoples, those without citizenship, who recognized only local laws and authorities. With the creation of the national State, the regions, with all their specificities, had to submit to the laws of the State, although the process was often accompanied by political violence.

Further reading

Alonso, C. (1990) *The Spanish American Regional Novel: Modernity and Autochthony*, Cambridge: Cambridge University Press.

Fuentes, C. (1969) *La nueva novela latinoamericana*, Mexico: FCE.

Leite, L.C.M. (1979) *Regionalismo e modernismo*, São Paulo: Atica.

Levy, K.L. (1995) 'En torno al regionalismo en su sentido más amplio', in D.V. Galvan, A.K Stoll and P. Brown Yin (eds), *Studies in Honor of Donal W. Bleznick*, Newark, DE: Juan de la Cuesta.

Reis, R. and M.A. Arrington (1997) 'Regionalism',

in V. Smith (ed.), *Encyclopedia of Latin American Literature*, London: Fitzroy Dearborn, 703–5.

GRACIELA MONTALDO

Rego, José Lins do

b. 1901, Pilar, Paraíba, Brazil; d. 1957, Rio de Janeiro, Brazil

Novelist

Most of Lins do Rego's writing records the life and associated culture of rural north east Brazil, especially that of the sugar zone. His nostalgia for much cherished traditions perceived to be disappearing under the impact of capitalist modernization shows the strong influence of the regionalist (see ***regionalismo***) thought of Gilberto Freyre. His most celebrated works are the five sugar cane-cycle novels of the 1930s and *Fogo morto* (1943), which are strongly autobiographical, and which, deeply marked by fatalism, trace the decline of the traditional sugar plantation. *Menino de engenho* (Plantation Boy) (1932) is a novel of early childhood which is particularly interesting in its portrayal of race and gender relations. Although they now seem somewhat antiquated, these works have made an important contribution to north-eastern regionalism.

Further reading

Chamberlain, B.J. (1989) 'José Lins do Rego', in C.A. Solé and M.I. Abreu (eds), *Latin American Writers*, New York: Scribners, 2, 909–13.

Coutinho, E. (1971) *José Lins do Rego: Antologia e critica*, Brasilia: Coordenada.

Coutinho, E.F. and A.B. de Castro, (eds), (1990) *José Lins do Rego*, Rio de Janeiro: Civilização Brasileira.

Daniel, M.L. (1997) 'José Lins do Rego', in V. Smith (ed.), *Encyclopedia of Latin American Literature*, London: Fitzroy Dearborn, 705–7.

Jordan, D.M. (1993) 'Regionalism, Nationalism, and Modernism: José Lins do Rego's *Fogo Morto*', in H. Ryan Ransom (ed.), *Imagination, Emblems and Expressions: Essays on Latin American, Caribbean, and Continental Culture and Identity*, Bowling Green, OH: Popular.

Kelly, J.R. (1972) 'An Annotated Bibliography of the Early Writings of José Lins do Rego', *Luso Brazilian Review* 9(1): 72–85.

—— (1979) 'José Lins do Rego and the Ideological Origins of Brazilian Northeastern Realism (1922–1932)', *Revista de estudios hispánicos* 13: 201–7.

Rego, J.L. do (1947) *Obras*, Rio de Janeiro: José Olympio, 11 vols.

—— (1966) *Plantation Boy*, trans. E. Baum, New York: Knopf.

MARK DINNEEN

Reid, Victor Stafford

b. 1913, Kingston, Jamaica; d. 1987, Kingston

Novelist

V.S. Reid worked as a farm overseer before turning to journalism. He travelled abroad but remained rooted in Jamaica, where he edited the radical journal *Public Opinion*. His novel *New Day* (1949) celebrated the first stage of Jamaican independence by recounting its history from the Morant Bay Rebellion to the present, in modified island speech and as seen by the island people. In *The Leopard* (1987), he attacked the British involvement in the Kenya Mau Mau emergency. He also wrote novels for children, inculcating pride in Jamaican history.

Further reading

Baugh, E. (ed.) (1987) 'Tribute to Vic Reid', *Journal of West Indian Literature* 2(1).

Reid, V.S. (1987) 'The Writer and His Work', *Journal of West Indian Literature* 2(1): 4–10.

LOUIS JAMES

Rein, Mercedes

b. 1931, Montevideo, Uruguay

Writer

A major figure in Uruguayan theatre, Rein was known for her own plays, including the important *El herrero y la muerte* (Death and the Blacksmith) (1982), written with Jorge Curi, and her translations of major European playwrights. A short story writer and novelist, she collaborated closely with Angel **Rama** and was jailed for her involvement with the journal *Marcha*. Her writing, and particularly her trilogy of novels culminating in *Marea negra* (Black Tide) (1996), metaphorically address the decline of Uruguayan society since the 1960s through technically complex and poetic expressionist texts. She is also an outstanding literary critic.

Further reading

Flori, M. (2001) 'Ficción uruguaya de posdictadura: Una conversación con Mercedes Rein', *Alba de América: Revista literaria*, July, 20(37–8): 687–92.

NORAH GIRALDI DEI CAS

reino de este mundo, El

The Cuban writer Alejo **Carpentier**'s *El reino de este mundo* (The Kingdom of this World) (1949) fictionalizes the history of Haiti between 1750 and 1820. The novel has no individual hero, and the plot develops in stages linked by minor characters such as the slaves Ti Noel and Solimán, and historical characters such as Pauline Bonaparte and Henri Cristophe. Carpentier stated that even minor details and characters in the novel are strictly historical, and several episodes and descriptions are based on research for his 1946 essay *La música en Cuba* (Music in Cuba). The main thrust of the story is to show a pattern of repetition involving power, submission and rebellion as part of humankind's endless struggle for happiness and fulfilment 'in the kingdom of this world'. Thus the history of Haiti in all its particularity symbolizes a universal human plight, marked by the intertextual relations of the novel's events and characters with Biblical episodes. The pattern of repetition also shapes the novel's structure, as many narrative components and motifs recur in the apparently independent episodes and produce significant reflections.

The novel's second characteristic is the blending of European and non-European cultures in Latin America, resulting in a new syncretic culture which, for Carpentier, constitutes the most peculiar result of the continent's conquest and colonization. Therefore, the story represents Latin American experience as a whole. In his foreword, which has become even more famous than the novel itself, Carpentier develops his thesis of Latin America as the realm of '*lo* ***real maravilloso***' (the marvellous real), a phenomenon foreign to the orderly and rational European vision of the world. This introduction is regarded as the basic statement of the **magical realism** which characterized and informed Latin American fiction in the 1960s and 1970s, and the novel itself is considered among the first works of this genre.

Further reading

Angulo, M.E. (1995) *Magic Realism. Social Context and Discourse*, New York: Garland.

Carpentier, A. (1970) *The Kingdom of this World*, trans. H. de Onis, New York: Collier Books.

—— (1975) *El reino de este mundo*, Buenos Aires: Librería del Colegio.

González Echevarría, R. (1977) *Alejo Carpentier: The Pilgrim at Home*, Ithaca, NY: Cornell University Press.

Speratti-Piñero, E. (1981) *Pasos hallados en El reino de este mundo*, Mexico City: Colegio de México.

Young, R.A. (1983) *Carpentier: El reino de este mundo, Critical Guides to Spanish Texts*, London: Grant & Cutler.

Zamora, L.P. and W.B. Faris (eds) (1995) *Magical Realism: Theory, History, Community*, Durham, NC: Duke University Press.

FLORINDA F. GOLDBERG

religion and literature

The Catholic Church figures large in the cultural history of Latin America. Until the nineteenth century its role as a pillar of the colonial order ensured that it would be represented as essentially oppressive and conservative. In many of the social realist writings of the 1920s and 1930s, for example, the Church appeared as part of an alliance of forces inhibiting and opposing progress. Thus in Jorge **Icaza**'s *Huasipungo* (1934), as one example among many, the priest is presented as an ally of the political establishment and the land-owning class. The Mexican Revolution (1910–17) directly challenged that nexus, and in the education programmes set in motion by José **Vasconcelos** during the period of construction of the new state, anti-clericalism was a core motif. The Cristero Wars in Mexico (1926–29) in many ways represented a Catholic counter-revolution, and produced their own literature; its most famous expression was Graham Greene's *The Power and the Glory*, but Jesús Goytortúa Santo's *Pensativa* (1928) was probably the best known of the local fictions set against the background of that conflict between Church and State.

In the transition to modernity, the Catholic Church clearly suffered a loss of its institutional power; but its influence and authority continues to pervade the ideological spaces in which Latin Americans live. Thus the power of the image of the Virgin and the spiritual centrality of the Church in a period of chaotic and uncertain transition offer symbolic anchors during times of change.

In that sense, the modernist writing of Latin America has often wrestled with the vacuum that the loss of that spiritual centre might imply – in the Mexican José **Gorostiza**'s seminal poem *Muerte sin fin* (Endless Death) (1935), for example, or in the anguished poems of César **Vallejo**'s *Trilce* (1922) in which God appears as an old man playing dice and as subject to the vagaries of fortune as the rest of humanity. It could be argued that the intense scepticism of Jorge Luis **Borges**'s ***Ficciones*** (Fictions) (1944) are in themselves responses to the absence of a divine project, which is supplemented by the human construction of illusory orders (as in 'The Circular Ruins'); perhaps the shipyard of Juan Carlos **Onetti**'s ***El astillero*** (1961) symbolizes the vacuum left by an absent God. The Cuban José **Lezama Lima**, by contrast, together with others of his generation, remained a philosophical Catholic, albeit deeply troubled by the sexual repression fostered by the Church, while Alfonsina **Storni**'s intense and often erotic poetry confronted repression and denial in bolder and more open ways.

The loss of moral direction and the absence of spiritual guidance is expressed in the stagnant water in the baptismal font at the beginning of Gabriel **García Márquez**'s novel *La mala hora* (The Evil Hour) (1961). For his native Colombia had experienced directly the corruption of an established Church increasingly identified with the ruthless administration of State power. But Colombia was also the point of origin for a new theology, embodied in the guerrilla priest Camilo Torres. This theology of liberation gave rise to a new rhetoric that fused the Utopian imaginary with a concept of critical solidarity, a public role for a religion that had chosen 'the option of the poor'. Ernesto **Cardenal**, the Nicaraguan poet, expressed both in his *Salmos* (Psalms) (1964), as did Cintio **Vitier**, the Cuban Catholic poet who found in the figure of Che Guevara an embodiment of a kind of revolutionary martyrdom. Cardenal's messianic vision found echoes among a generation of new writers and artists for whom religion now informed a revolutionary project; many of the young guerrilla poets (see **guerrilla poetry**) of the 1960s were influenced by these ideas.

But it was true also that that millenarian vision led many writers to return to other kinds of religious experience. Santería in Cuba and Candomblé and Umbanda in Brazil represented a popular and alternative religious community. Nicolás **Guillén** made frequent reference to it in his early poetry, as did Emilio **Ballagas** and Luis **Palés Matos** of Puerto Rico. In the move away from proletarian realism other writers found an alternative imaginary in black religion – René Zavaleta in *El Gran Burundú Burundá ha muerto* (The Great Burundú Burundá is Dead), for example, Alejo **Carpentier** in his novel ***El reino de este mundo*** (The Kingdom of this World) *(1943)* or Jorge **Amado** in *A tenda dos milagres* (The Tent of Miracles) (1969).

Popular religion has many other expressions, as the personal narratives of Rigoberta Menchú in Guatemala and Domitila **Barrios** in Bolivia reveal. By contrast, Elena **Poniatowska**'s account of a charismatic healer in a poor district of Mexico City, *Hasta no verte Jesús mío* (Until I See You My Lord) (1969), gives an insight into the symbolic universe of the growing numbers of Latin Americans involved with forms of charismatic or evangelical Protestantism. And the growing popularity of writers such as Paulo **Coelho** is testimony to the proliferation of New Age religions throughout the continent, but particularly in Brazil. But there are also critical visions of the phenomenon; one of the most amusing is Mario **Vargas Llosa**'s *Pantaleón y las Visitadoras* (Captain Pantoja and the Special Service) (1973). In 1981, the same author reworked Euclides da **Cunha**'s original account of the Canudos community (in *Os* ***sertões***) in his novel *La guerra del fin del mundo* (The War of the End of the World).

Margo **Glantz** has explored the experience of Jewishness, as have Moacyr **Scliar**, Luisa **Futoransky** and Sergio **Chejfec** among others. Milton **Hatoum** has set his writings among the Christian and Islamic communities of the Amazon region.

Liberation theology has also had a significant influence on theatre, particularly on those theatre movements of the 1960s and 1970s most influenced by Freire's ideas on the development of collective consciousness as a prelude to liberation.

Further reading

Calabrese, Elisa (ed.) (1975) *Ernesto Cardenal: Poeta de la liberación latinoamericana*, Buenos Aires: Fernando García Cambeiro.

Cardenal, Ernesto (1993) *Cosmic Canticle*, Willimantic, CT: Curbstone Press.

DiAntonio, R. and N. Glickmann (1993) *Tradition and Innovation: Reflections on Latin American Jewish Writing*, Albany: SUNY Press.

Rowland, C. (1999) *The Cambridge Companion to Liberation Theology*, Cambridge and New York: Cambridge University Press.

Versényi, Adam (1993) *Theatre in Latin America: Religion, Politics and Culture from Cortés to the 1980s*, Cambridge: Cambridge University Press.

MIKE GONZALEZ

repentistas

Repentistas are popular singers or poets of Brazil, especially in the north east, who improvise verses on a given subject to the accompaniment of a twelve-string guitar called a *viola*. Traditionally they perform publicly in pairs, each inventing a verse in turn, in poetic duels decided when one is unable to continue. They normally collect contributions from onlookers in a bowl placed in front of them. It remains a very dynamic form of popular expression and oral literature, and in recent decades *repentistas* have found new audiences in Brazil through television and radio performances.

Further reading

Arantes, A. (1982) *O trabalho e a fala*, São Paulo: Kairós.

Dinneen, M. (1996) *Listening to the People's Voice*, London: Kegan Paul International.

MARK DINNEEN

Repertorio americano

A continentally oriented Costa Rican bi-monthly cultural magazine (1919–59) edited in San José by Joaquín **García Monge**, *Repertorio americano* is considered one of the most representative magazines of Latin American culture, philosophy and literature. It included long essays, poems, literary criticism and translated articles. During the 1920s it also played an active anti-imperialist role, without excluding ideological disagreements: well-known Latin American and European **intellectuals** with various ideological and political positions debated on its pages. Due to the complete dedication of its editor and because the magazine never had censorship problems, it avoided the discontinuity common to similar magazines throughout Latin America.

Further reading

Henkin, A.B. (1971) 'Joaquin García Monge and His *Repertorio americano*, a Legacy of Andrés Bello', *Hispania* 54: 345–8.

Ortiz, M.S. (1990) 'Octavio Jiménez en el *Repertorio americano*: Una concepción de cultura', *Revista de filología y lingüística de la Universidad de Costa Rica* 16(1): 39–44.

JUSSI PAKKASVIRTA

Requena, María Asunción

b. 1915, Punta Arenas, Chile; d. 1986, Lille, France

Playwright

Requena's work gave theatrical expression to the extreme south of Chile, its legends and traditions, and its men and women. She found the 'intra-history' of this world in stories and chronicles and in the private epics of marginal people, like the first Chilean woman doctor Ernestina Pérez, protagonist of *El camino más largo* (The Longest Road), first presented by the University of Chile's Teatro Experimental in 1954. *Ayayema* (1964), premiered at the University of Concepción, showed people fighting for their land and for their indigenous comrades exploited by white man's greed.

Further reading

Echeverría, M.B. (1993) 'Memoria histórica y deseo: Espacio virtual del teatro de Asunción Requena e isidoro Aguirre', *Revista de estudios hispánicos* 20: 323–6.

Neghme Echeverría, L. (1994) 'Chiloé, cielos cubiertos (1972) y lagunas técnicas del teatro popular', *Revista chilena de literatura*, April, 46: 91–6.

Villegas, J. (1995) 'María Asunción Requena: Exito e historia del teatro', *Latin American Theatre Review*, Spring, 28(2): 19–37.

ELIANA ORTEGA

Respiración artificial

A 1980 novel by Ricardo **Piglia**, *Respiración artificial* (Artificial Respiration) was immediately recognized as an important reflection on Argentine history and culture. Published in Argentina, despite the censorship imposed by the Proceso de Reorganización Nacional, Piglia's novel was a complex response to the times. Piglia dedicates the novel to two of the disappeared, and one of the main characters is presumably kidnapped halfway through the book; its latter half is an all-night conversation during which the other characters try to hold on to his memory and his example. Piglia writes that it is important to write the history of defeats; it is clear that the brutal defeat of the Argentine Left in the 'dirty war' of the 1970s was on his mind. In a fascinating narrative ploy, most of the novel is cast as 'letters from the future' written in 1850; this is used to sustain a critical examination of key moments in the history of the Argentine nation and of the monstrous future (that is, the present of the novel's writing). The novel won the Boris Vian Prize and was a bestseller (see **best-sellers**) despite the density and elliptical nature of the writing.

Further reading

Balderston, D. (1988) 'Latent Meanings in Ricardo Piglia's *Respiración artificial* and Luis Gusman's *En el corazón de junio*', *Revista canadiense de estudios hispánicos* 12(2): 207–19.

Colas, S. (1994) *Postmodernity in Latin America: The Argentine Paradigm*, Durham, NC: Duke University Press.

Levinson, B. (1997) 'Trans(re)latinos: Dictatorship, Disaster and the "Literary Politics" of Piglia's *Respiration artificial*', *Latin American Literary Review* 25(49): 91–120.

Morello Frosch, M. (1985) 'Significación e historia en *Respiración artificial* de Ricardo Piglia', in H. Vidal (ed.), *Fascismo y experiencia literaria: Refleciones para una recanonización*, Minneapolis: Institute for the Study of Ideologies and Literature.

Newman, K. (1986) 'Historical Knowledge in the Post-Boom Novel', in D. Balderston (ed.), *The Historical Novel in Latin America*, Gaithersburg, MD: Hispamérica.

Piglia, R. (1994) *Artificial Respiration*, trans. D. Balderston, Durham, NC: Duke University Press.

DANIEL BALDERSTON

Revista chilena de literatura

Founded in 1970 by the Spanish Department of the Universidad de Chile in Santiago, with Cedomil Goic as its first editor, the *Revista chilena de literatura* survived the military dictatorship of the 1970s and 1980s, when many cultural institutions, especially those of the Universidad de Chile, were damaged or destroyed. It remains today one of the few Latin American journals devoted to world literature. Each of the twice-yearly issues contains critical articles, bibliographies, documentary material and book reviews. In general, its topics are weighted toward Chilean and Latin American literature. It is currently edited by Hugo Montes.

Further reading

http://www.uchile.cl/facultades/filosofia/revista_literaria/

Rosenfeld, K.C. (1991) 'La revista chilena de literatura: 1970–1985', *Revista chilena de literatura*, Nov., 38: 127–38.

DAVID WILLIAM FOSTER

Revista de Antropofagia

A cultural magazine appearing between May 1928 and August 1929, ostensibly as a vehicle for Oswald de **Andrade**'s ideas of cultural 'cannibalism', ***Antropofagia***. Publication was divided into two quite distinct series, called *dentições* ('milk teeth' and 'second set of teeth') in the humorous jargon of the movement.

The first *dentição* ran until February 1929 – edited by Antônio de Alcântara Machado and managed by Raul Bopp – in the form of ten monthly issues of an eight-sided tabloid. The first opened with the Andrade's Cannibalist *Manifesto* containing, at its centre, Tarsila do Amaral's primitivist painting *Aba-poru* (The Cannibal), which became the movement's central motif. In this phase, the magazine's 'Cannibalist' content was tokenistic, embracing poetry, fiction and essays on indigenist, nationalist and broadly modernist topics by authors who did not share Andrade's theoretical perspective, such as Manuel **Bandeira**. Alcântara Machado defended the eclecticism of this phase as a banquet of hostile allies, each cordially sinking his fork into his neighbour. In reality, these first issues of the magazine were a showcase for the latest modernist works, including Carlos Drummond de **Andrade**'s 'No meio do caminho', the opening chapter of Mário de **Andrade**'s ***Macunaíma*** and Bandeira's 'Noturno da Rua da Lapa'.

In the second *dentição*, directed alternately by Raul Bopp and Jaime Adour da Câmara, and edited by its 'butcher' Geraldo Ferraz, the magazine adopted a more polemical and propagandistic role. It now occupied a single, usually weekly, page in the then liberal broadsheet, *Estado de São Paulo*, until growing complaints forced the arrangement to be terminated. Space was given for Andrade and Oswaldo Costa to re-elaborate the *Manifesto*'s central themes, to define more clearly the ideological battle-lines and to celebrate the movement's success abroad. Growing internal dissent in the first *dentição* materialized into open attacks on the two currents most hostile to the revolutionary optimism of the *antropófagos* – the proto-fascist tendency, ***verdeamarelismo***, and the Catholic revivalists. Other contributions explored the political ramifications of Cannibalist theory, arguing for a totemic, tribal organization of society, defending the right of landless peasants to seize the property of absentee landlords and calling for new forms of anthropophagous government.

A promised third *dentição*, Cannibalist congress and banquet, research projects and a library, came to nothing; the movement did not long survive the magazine's closure. The modernist movement was now split along the ideological fault lines exposed within the *Revista de Antropofagia*. In the shadow of the economic and political crises which brought Getúlio Vargas to power, some contributors disappeared; others such as **Salgado**, became active on the far right, while Oswald de Andrade joined the Communist Party.

Further reading

Bopp, R. (1977) *Vida e morte da Antropofagia*, Rio de Janeiro: Civilização Brasileira.

Jackson, K.D. (1979) 'A View on Brazilian Literature: Eating the *Revista de Antropofagia*', *Latin American Literary Review* 7(13): 1–9.

Revista de Antropofagia (1976) facsimile edition, São Paulo: Metal Leve.

DAVID TREECE

Revista de Avance

Revista de Avance was an avant-garde journal published in Cuba from 1927 to 1930. Early editors included Juan **Marinello**, Alejo **Carpentier** and Jorge **Mañach**. The journal published poems, stories, essays and articles by Cuban and foreign writers. It also sponsored concerts of the music of hitherto unknown figures such as Alejandro García Caturla and Amadeo Roldán, and organized the historic 1927 Exposición de Arte Nuevo (New Art Exhibition), the first manifestation of modern Cuban painting. It devoted special issues to Lorca, Waldo Frank and **Mariátegui**. The journal also functioned as a publisher before ceasing to appear in the repressive climate created by the government of Gerardo Machado.

Further reading

Lesmes Albis, M. (1996) *Revista de Avance, o el delirio de originalidad americano*, Havana: Abril.

Manzoni, C. (1993) 'Vanguardia y nacionalismo: Itinerario de la *Revista de Avance*', *Iberoamericana: Lateinamerika, Spanien, Portugal* 17(1 (49)): 16–32.

Masiello, F. (1993) 'Rethinking Neocolonial Esthetics: Literature, Politics, and Intellectual Community in Cuba's *Revista de Avance*', *Latin American Research Review* 28(2): 3–31.

Ripoll, C. (1964) 'La *Revista de Avance* (1927–1930): Vocero de vanguardismo y portico de revolución', *Revista iberoamericana* 30: 261–82.

WILFREDO CANCIO ISLA

Revista de crítica cultural

Founded in Santiago in 1990 and edited by Nelly **Richard**, the *Revista de crítica cultura* played a major role in theorizing post-dictatorship cultures, particularly in Chile and the Southern Cone. A forum for transgressive and 'refractory' writing, the *Revista* opened its pages to contemporary debates on art, the university, feminism, **postmodernism**, democratization, gender and mass culture. Its contributors included writers, artists, philosophers and social scientists from Europe, the USA and Latin America, whose writing challenged disciplinary specialization. Defying the pragmatism which guides present-day neo-liberal societies, *Revista* has given space to those artists whose work complicates and transgresses generic boundaries.

Further reading

http://www.revista-de-critica-cultural.cl/

Vidal, H. (1993) 'Postmodernism, Postleftism, Neo-Avant-Gardism: The Case of Chile's *Revista de crítica cultural*', *Boundary 2: An International Journal of Literature and Culture*, Fall, 20(3): 203–27.

JEAN FRANCO

Revista de crítica literaria latinoamericana

Revista de crítica literaria latinoamericana is an academic journal founded by Antonio **Cornejo Polar** in 1975. The inaugural articles by Roberto **Fernández Retamar** and Alejandro **Losada**, as well as a distinguished international board, set a sustained progressive tone in its reading of Latin America's literary production. Published twice a year, it has maintained a Lima base; subsequently, addresses at Pittsburgh and UC-Berkeley were added to correspond to Cornejo Polar's academic appointments and institutional support. A mandatory reference journal, it has published as monographic sections or entire issues the results of major conferences and symposia that reflect on trends in Latin American theoretical and critical approaches with particular emphasis on cultural/historical venues. After Cornejo Polar's death, the journal moved to Dartmouth College under the editorship of Raúl Bueno. Cornejo Polar's widow, Cristina Soto, has continued to publish books in the associated publishing house, Latinoamericana Editores.

Further information

http://www.dartmouth.edu/~rcll/

SAÚL SOSNOWSKI

Revista mexicana de literatura

Revista mexicana de literatura was founded in 1955 under the editorship of Carlos **Fuentes** and Emmanuel Carballo. Later editors included Antonio Alatorre and, from 1960 onwards, Juan **García Ponce** and Tomás Segovia. In its first period it adopted a format similar to the *Nouvelle Revue Française* and a rigorous criterion of literary selection. It was responsible for disseminating US, French and English poetry as well as publishing work by Argentine and Mexican poets. Its contributors included Emilio **Carballido**, Jaime García Terrés, Ernesto Mejía Sánchez and Ramón Xirau, among others.

Further reading

Muñoz, M. (2000) 'La generación de la *Revista mexicana de literatura*, Esbozo mínimo de una aproximación', *La palabra y el hombre: Revista de la Universidad Veracruzana*, Jan.–March, 113: 83–9.

Novoa, B. (1988) 'Writing and the Visual Arts in Mexico: The Generation of Juan García Ponce', trans. A.J. MacAdam, *Review: Latin American Literature and Arts*, Jan.–June, 39: 5–13.

CELINA MANZONI

Revista nacional de cultura

The *Revista nacional de cultura* is a Venezuelan literary and cultural journal founded in 1938 by Mariano **Picón Salas**, and published regularly from that year until the present. Currently it is published by CONAC, the Venezuelan cultural funding agency, and headed by Oscar **Sambrano Urdaneta**. It publishes articles on literature, philosophy, the visual arts, music and related fields, and creative writing, particularly poetry. The *Revista nacional de cultura* has published work by Venezuelan writers such as Arturo **Uslar Pietri**, Vicente **Gerbasi**, Rómulo **Gallegos** and José **Balza**, as well as by writers from elsewhere in the region, including Leopoldo Zea, Octavio **Paz**, Benjamín **Carrión**, Alfonso **Reyes**, Julio **Ortega** and numerous others.

Further information:

http://www.celarg.org.ve/rumbo.htm

DANIEL BALDERSTON

Revolución, Ediciones

Ediciones Revolución (Ediciones R) was a publishing house founded in Cuba under the auspices of the newspaper *Revolución* (1959–65) and its editor Carlos **Franqui** to promote the work of new Cuban writers. The publishing house was decisively influenced by the group around the journal ***Lunes de revolución***, who helped to select works for publication and published some of their own under its imprint.

During its five years of existence, Ediciones Revolución published over 100 volumes in every genre. Although most of its authors were Cuban, some foreign writers were included in the list, among them Nathanael West, Juan Goytisolo, Claude Couffon and René **Depestre**. It also established the Ediciones R Prize for younger Cuban writers. Its catalogue includes many works of major significance, including Alejo **Carpentier**'s *El* ***siglo de las luces*** (Explosion in a Cathedral), Virgilio **Piñera**'s *Pequeñas maniobras* (Little Manoeuvres), Guillermo **Cabrera Infante**'s *Así en la paz como en la guerra* (In Peace as in War), Edmundo **Desnoes** *No hay problema* (No Problem), Onelio Jorge Cardoso's *Cuentos completos* (Complete Stories), Calvert **Casey**'s *El regreso* (The Return) and Pablo Armando **Fernández**'s *Toda la poesía* (Complete Poetry).

Ediciones R books were characterized by creative design and illustrations and daring typography and use of colour. The designers Raúl Martínez, Tony Evora and Santiago Armada (Chago) gave the collection a particular publishing style that influenced Cuban books in general. In the year that Ediciones R was closed down, Fidel

Castro set up Edición Revolucionaria in response to the urgent need for higher education textbooks, as the number of university students began to rise. Since many foreign writers and publishers refused to allow their books to be reprinted in Cuba, Castro declared education and knowledge to be a universal right and ordered textbooks to be printed for free distribution. This led Cuba to suspend the payment of royalties to both Cuban and foreign writers; payment was not resumed until 1977.

WILFREDO CANCIO ISLA

Revueltas, José

b. 1914, Durango, Mexico; d. 1976, Mexico City

Writer and politician

A prolific writer of novels, short stories and essays, as well as drama and film scripts, Revueltas was also an influential journalist and a left-wing activist; indeed he was one of Mexico's most important left-wing **intellectuals**. He was born into a large family; his father was a travelling salesman and his mother, the daughter of a miner, encouraged her children to follow artistic pursuits. His sister Rosaura became a well-known actress, and among his brothers, Fermín was an important painter and Silvestre an outstanding composer.

For economic reasons, Revueltas left school at an early age and educated himself in the libraries of Mexico City. At the same time he began work in a steel factory, where his contact with the workers fired his political concerns, leading him to join the political opposition. In 1929 he was arrested at a political meeting and spent six months in a reformatory; he then joined the Communist Party, banned between 1929 and 1934 during the presidency of Calles. Revueltas was active in revolutionary Marxist-Leninist organizations until his death. His commitment to the working-class cause brought sustained repression from the State, while his independence of thought and his critical attitude to Stalinism often brought him into conflict with others within the organizations to which he belonged. Expelled in 1943 from the Communist Party, in which he had been active for thirteen years, including two periods in prison on the Islas Marías (1932 and 1934), he joined Vicente Lombardo Toledano's Partido Popular in 1948, remaining there until 1955 when, after a fierce self-criticism, he was readmitted into the Communist Party. He was again ejected as a dissident in 1960. In that year he formed the Leninist *Liga Espartaco* (Spartacus League), from which he was expelled in turn in 1963. He participated in the 1968 movement as an independent intellectual, and was jailed after it was brutally crushed. He was released in 1971, and acknowledged by Mexican youth as the paradigm of the revolutionary intellectual.

Revueltas's fiction, probably his best work, comprises seven novels and three volumes of short stories. His writing is informed throughout by a socialist humanism permeated by Christian and existentialist concerns. His first novel, *Los muros de agua* (Walls of Water) (1941), recounts his prison experiences on the Islas Marías. *El luto humano* (Human Grief) (1943) is a synthesis of the history of twentieth-century Mexico. Its characters are peasants who represent all the oppressed and exploited of the nation. It is a highly symbolic work, imbued with the philosophy of 'lo mexicano' which some writers have associated with **existentialism**. The novel returns to some of the themes of the **novel of the Mexican Revolution**, but breaks with its traditional structure, introducing formal innovations derived from the modern European and North American novel. In these two novels, the Communists are positive characters, but in the next, *Los días terrenales* (Days on Earth) (1949), the author introduced characters deformed by Stalinism, echoing the internal conflicts within the Mexican Communist Party. The novel was bitterly criticized by his comrades.

Two minor novels followed, in which he tried to find a means of reconciliation with the Communist Party; then, in 1964, *Los errores* (The Errors) repeated his critique of dogmatism and deformation within both the Mexican and the Soviet parties. His last novel, *El apando* (Solitary) (1969), took a group of jailed common criminals as the symbol of a humanity locked in an existential prison. Revueltas's short stories address the same humanistic concerns, but are far less explicitly political. His most important essay, *Ensayo sobre un proletariado sin cabeza* (Essay on a

Headless Proletariat) (1962), set in train the analysis of political ideology in Mexico.

Between 1944 and 1975 Revueltas wrote twenty-six film scripts, including the screenplay for *El apando*, based on his own novel. The tensions and contradictions within Mexican communism in the twentieth century resonate throughout his work.

Further reading

Blanco, J.J. (1985) *José Revueltas*, Mexico City: Terra Nova CREA.

Murad, T. (1977–8) 'Before the Storm: José Revueltas and the Beginnings of the New Narrative in Mexico', *Modern Language Studies* 8: 57–64.

Revueltas, J. (1947) *El luto humano*, trans. H.R. Hays, *The Stone Knife*, New York: Reynal & Hitchcock.

—— (1981–7) *Obras completas*, Mexico City: Era, 26 vols.

—— (1987) *Obra literaria*, with epilogue by J. Agustín, Mexico City: Empresas Editoriales, 2 vols.

—— (1990) *Human Mourning*, Minneapolis: University of Minnesota Press.

—— (1991) *Los días terrenales*, ed. E. Escalante, Paris: Colección Archivos.

Ruffinelli, J. (1977) *José Revueltas: Ficción, política y verdad*, Xalapa: Universidad Veracruzana.

—— (2002) 'José Revueltas', in C. Solé and K. Müller-Bergh (eds), *Latin American Writers: Supplement I*, New York: Scribners, 463–77.

Slick, S. (1993) *José Revueltas*, Boston: Twayne.

EDITH NEGRÍN

Reyes, Alfonso

b. 1889, Monterrey, Mexico; d. 1959, Mexico City

Writer

Alfonso Reyes was a scholar of great erudition, poet and essayist. 'He was a man of letters ... I am not saying he was the first essayist, the first novelist, the first poet, but the first man of letters, at once reader and writer. A friend of Montaigne, Goethe, Stevenson and Homer, his spirit was gently open to all.' Thus wrote Jorge Luis **Borges** of Reyes, a Mexican writer with a Latin American vision and a universal vocation. His first poems were published in a newspaper in his home town of Monterrey. His real literary education, however, began when he became a member of the Ateneo de la Juventud, in Mexico City, and wrote for the *Revista moderna* and *Savia moderna*, both published in the Mexican capital. He was involved in the transformation of Mexico's Escuela Nacional Preparatoria, in the organization of talks and lectures, in the opening of the Escuela de Altos Estudios (School of Higher Studies) in 1910 and the founding of the Universidad Popular in 1912.

Although principally a poet, his first book *Cuestiones estéticas* (Aesthetic Questions) was a collection of essays published in Paris in 1911. It included his thoughts on the three Electras in Greek theatre, writings on aspects of medieval and Spanish Golden Age literature (his study of Góngora predates the rediscovery of the great Spanish poet by the peninsular Generation of 1927), and his perceptive critique of Mallarmé. His 'Paisaje en la poesía mexicana del siglo XIX' (Landscape in 19th Century Mexican Poetry) points ahead to his *Visión de Anáhuac* (1917), a series of tableaux which offer a fresco of Aztec Mexico on the eve of Conquest. This is the key work of his Madrid period (1914–24), when he became a scholar under Ramón Menéndez Pidal at the Centro de Estudios Históricos (Centre for Historical Studies). In the same period he published *El plano oblicuo* (The Oblique Plane) (1920), a collection of stories, and *Huellas* (Footprints) (1922), his first published collection of poetry. *Ifigenia cruel* (1924) marks the end of this period; it is a key book, for its references, symbols and masks relate to Greek tragedy at one level, but at another veil the poet's personal dramas.

Between 1913 and 1939 Reyes worked in the diplomatic service in Europe and Latin America. Returning to Mexico, he began to publish the works which would bring him his lasting reputation: *La crítica de la edad ateniense* (Criticism in the Athenian Age) (1941), *La antigua retórica* (Ancient Rhetoric) (1942), *La experiencia literaria* (The Experience of Literature) (1942) and *El deslinde; prolegómenos a la teoría literaria* (The Dividing Line, Prologomena to Literary Theory) (1944). In the latter years of his life he translated and recreated the verses of the *Iliad*. His abundant writings have been collected in a twenty-six-volume *Obras* (Works) and his personal collection is conserved as a comprehensive library.

Further reading

Conn, R.T. (2002) *The Politics of Philology: Alfonso Reyes and the Invention of the Latin American Literary Tradition*, Lewisburg, PA: Bucknell University Press.

Mejía Sánchez, E. (1966) *La vida en la obra de Alfonso Reyes*, Mexico City: Secretaría de Educación Pública.

Reyes, A. (1950) *The Position of America and Other Essays*, trans. H. de Onís, New York: Knopf.

—— (1955–92) *Obras*, Mexico City: Fondo de Cultura Económica, 26 vols.

—— (1964) *Mexico in a Nutshell and Other Essays*, trans. C. Ramsdell, Berkeley: University of California Press.

Robb, J.W. (ed.) (1981) *Por los caminos de Alfonso Reyes*, Mexico City: INBA.

—— (1989) 'Alfonso Reyes', in C.A. Solé and M.I. Abreu (eds), *Latin American Writers*, New York: Scribners, 2, 693–703.

RAFAEL OLEA FRANCO

Rhone, Trevor

b. 1940, Kingston, Jamaica

Playwright

Jamaica's most successful playwright, Rhone's numerous awards include the Institute of Jamaica's Gold Musgrave Medal. Painstakingly researched and rooted in Jamaican (sur)reality, his plays use humour and satire to explore oppression, cultural dispossession, black self-hate and survival. After training at Rose Bruford College, Sidcup, Kent, UK, he founded Theatre '77 (with Yvonne Clarke Brewster), mounting shows at the tiny Barn Theatre in Kingston. His published plays include *Smile Orange* (1981), *School's Out* (1980), *Old Story Time* (1981) and *Two Can Play* (1994). He has had major productions on three continents, and his screenplays have earned international plaudits, including *The Harder They Come* (1972) (with Perry Henzel).

Further reading

Frickey, P.M. (1992) 'Jamaica and Trinidad', in B. King (ed.), *Post-Colonial English Drama: Commonwealth Drama since 1960*, New York: St Martin's and Macmillan.

Gilbert, H. (1998) 'Responses to the Sex Trade in Post-Colonial Theatre', in L. Dale and S. Ryan (eds), *The Body in the Library*, Amsterdam: Rodopi.

Okagbue, O. (1990) 'Identity, Exile and Migration: The Dialectis of Content and Form in West Indian Theatre', *New Literature Review*, Summer, 19: 14–23.

Savory, E. (1995) 'Strategies for Survival: Anti-Imperialist Theatrical Forms in the Anglophone Caribbean', in J.E. Gainor (ed.), *Imperialism and Theatre: Essays on World Theatre, Drama and Performance*, London: Routledge.

PAT DUNN AND PAMELA MORDECAI

Rhys, Jean

b. 1890, Roseau, Dominica; d. 1979, Exeter, UK

Writer

Born Gwendoline Ella Williams, Rhys adopted her pseudonym for the publication of her first story 'Vienne' in Ford Madox Ford's *Translatlantic Review* in 1924. She left Dominica in 1907 to study theatre in London and in the mid-1920s became a professional writer, first in Paris and then in London. Her novels *Quartet* (1929), *After Leaving Mr McKenzie* (1931), *Voyage in the Dark* (1934) and *Good Morning Midnight* (1939) were well reviewed, but in the 1940s and 1950s Rhys's work was hardly read and she was even thought to be dead. ***Wide Sargasso Sea*** (1966) is her most evidently Caribbean novel, and it also made her very well known. For some time, however, she was seen simply as a British writer. Subsequently, she has been claimed by three groups of critics – modernists, feminists and Caribbeanists – although the best criticism combines all three.

Rhys is a superb stylist; her strength lies in her ability to delineate the inner world of her major characters, who are mostly but not always female, through highly effective dialogues and poetic techniques like compression, ellipsis and imagery. Her colonial white origins in conjunction with her experience as a working-class chorus girl and then professional writer make her fascinatingly contradictory in her constructions of race, gender, class and nationality, although she is always on the side of the marginalized. Posthumous publications include an autobiography, *Smile Please* (1979) and *Selected Letters* (1984).

Further reading

Angier, C. (1990) *Jean Rhys*, Boston: Little Brown.
Castro, J. (2000) 'Jean Rhys', *Review of Contemporary Fiction*, Summer, 20(2): 8–45.
Maurel, S. (1998) *Jean Rhys*, New York: St Martin's Press.
Rhys, J. (1984) *The Letters of Jean Rhys*, selected and edited by F. Wyndham and D. Melly, New York: Viking.
Savory, E. (1998) *Jean Rhys*, Cambridge: Cambridge University Press.

ELAINE SAVORY

Rial, José Antonio

b. 1911, San Fernando, Cádiz, Spain

Writer and dramatist

Imprisoned between 1939 and 1943 for his anti-Franco militancy, Rial emigrated to Venezuela in 1950 and eventually took Venezuelan citizenship. His writing covers a range of genres. He worked as a journalist for many years, has published essays on Latin American culture and has written several novels, the best known being *Venezuela imán* (Venezuela the Magnet) (1955), about European migration to Venezuela. He has been most successful as a dramatist, however, with plays such as *La muerte de García Lorca* (The Death of García Lorca) (1969) and *Bolívar* (1982). His plays are characterized by sharp social criticism and the psychological study of the characters.

Further reading

Cacheiro, M. (1991) 'La visión de Latinoamérica de José Antonio Rial', *Cuadernos americanos*, Nov.–Dec., 30: 225–8.
Nigro, K. (1990) 'History Grand and History Small in Recent Venezuelan Theatre: Rial's *Bolívar* and Cabrujas' *Acto cultural*', *Theatre Annual: A Journal of Performance Studies* 44: 37–46.

MARK DINNEEN

Ribeiro, Darcy

b. 1922, Montes Claros, Brazil; d. 1997, Brasília, Brazil

Anthropologist, educator, novelist and politician

One of the most productive and outspoken figures of Brazil's intellectual and public life, Ribeiro began his career as an ethnographer who soon became committed to the cause of Brazil's surviving indigenous communities. During the 1950s he worked within the state-run Indian Protection Service (FUNAI), under the inspiration of its legendary founder, the humanist Marshall Cândido Rondon. Besides creating the Museum of the Indian, Ribeiro's dedicated fieldwork amongst isolated tribal communites such as the Kadiuéu, Urubu and Kaapor led to his first publications, whose focus was the role of mythology in maintaining the communities' internal cohesion in the face of the shattering effects of inter-ethnic contact, not least with non-Indians.

The latter was the subject of a study commissioned by UNESCO in 1970 and originally intended to celebrate the successful assimilation of the indigenous population into Brazilian society. In fact, *Os Índios e a civilização* (The Indians and Civilization), published at the height of the military dictatorship, presented instead a devastating indictment of the failure of the state's integrationist policy, and a history of social and cultural disintegration and outright extermination. In 1979 Ribeiro combined his intimate knowledge of indigenous mythology and cultural practices with this critical vision of the Indians' current plight in a masterfully conceived novel, *Maíra*, which is constructed around the true story of a young Indian educated by missionaries in Europe, who tragically fails to rediscover his identity and role within the tribe of his birth. In the 1982 novel *Utopia selvagem* (Savage Utopia), Ribeiro revisited the entire tradition of literary reflections on Brazil's indigenous heritage, with an aggressively irreverent irony that is reminiscent of Mário de **Andrade**'s ***Macunaíma***.

Parallel to these literary activities, Ribeiro pursued an increasingly prominent public career in education, as founder and rector of the University of Brasília, and adviser to three reformist Latin American presidents: Salvador Allende, Velasco Alvarado and Brazil's João Goulart, serving as Minister of Education during the latter's 1961–64 administration. After a period in exile following the 1964 military *coup*, he became a leading member of Leonel Brizola's Democratic Labour Party (PDT), the political heir to the Vargas tradition of populist state intervention. Under Brizola's administration of the city of Rio de Janeiro during the mid-1980s, Ribeiro launched a daring project of purpose-built community schools, the CIECs, whose aim was to foster a concept of full-time integrated education extending beyond the classroom. One of his last political acts, in 1996, was to finalize an educational reform bill in Senate, prioritizing the role of the State as provider of free compulsory education, democratizing access at all levels and promoting extra-curricular support for school pupils. In 1995, already diagnosed with cancer, Ribeiro discharged himself from hospital in order to complete *O povo brasileiro* (The Brazilian People), his last, characteristically impassioned and grandiose reflection on his country's ethnic and social evolution.

Further reading

Columbus, C.K. (1989) 'Mother Earth in Amazonia and in the Andes: Darcy Ribeiro and José María Arguedas', in D. Philip and W. Aycock (eds), *Literature and Anthropology*, Lubbock: Texas Tech University Press.

DiAntonio, R.E. (1985) 'Darcy Ribeiro's *Maíra*: Fictional Transfiguration and the Failure of Cultural Pluralism', *Chasqui* 15(1): 11–18.

Lucas, F. (1993) 'Memoirs Told to the Mirror: Autran Dourado and Darcy Ribeiro', in Randal Johnson (ed.), *Tropical Paths: Essays on Modern Brazilian Literature*, New York: Garland.

Ribeiro, D. (1970) *Os Índios e a civilização: A integração das populações indígenas no Brasil moderno*, Rio de Janeiro: Civilização Brasileira.

—— (1985) *Maíra*, trans. E.H. Goodland and T. Colchie, London: Pan.

—— (1996) *O povo brasileiro: A formação e o sentido do Brasil*, São Paulo: Companhia das Letras.

DAVID TREECE

Ribeiro, João Ubaldo

b. 1941, Itaparica Island, Bahia, Brazil

Writer

One of Brazil's major contemporary writers, Ribeiro's work grows out of his regional background and island origin, but connects local events with the national and the global. His best-known novel, *Viva o povo brasileiro* (Long Live the Brazilian People) (1984), recreates three centuries of Brazilian history, weaving together episodes in Itaparica and Salvador with others that are set in Rio de Janeiro, São Paulo and Lisbon. Its hundreds of characters provide a vivid view of slavery and its legacies, of Candomblé and other popular religions, of the independence wars and the War of the Triple Alliance against Paraguay (1864–70), of the rise and fall of the plantation aristocracy, and of the rise of urban capitalism, all with a view to showing the constant oppression of the Brazilian people. Ribeiro's other works include: *Setembro não tem sentido* (September Makes No Sense) (1968); the raging narrative of a hired gun, *Sargento Getúlio* (Sergeant Getulio) (1971); *Ventecavalo e o outro povo* (Ventecavalo and the Other People) (1974), a collection of short stories; *Crónicas livro de histórias* (Book of Stories) (1984) and *O sorriso do lagarto* (The Lizard's Smile) (1989). Ribeiro is of interest for his reinvention of the political and historical **novel** and for his fresh take on the Brazilian regionalist tradition (see ***regionalismo***), which he parodies but to which he owes a great deal. Filmmaker Glauber Rocha wrote the preface to *Setembro não tem sentido* and Ribeiro dedicated *Viva o povo brasileiro* to his memory; they share an interest in experimental narrative, popular history and political liberation.

Further reading

DiAntonio, R. (1986) 'Chthonian Visions and Mythic Redemption in João Ubaldo Ribeiro's *Sergeant Getúlio*', *Modern Fiction Studies* 32–3.

Josef, B. (1997) 'João Ubaldo Ribeiro', in V. Smith (ed.), *Encyclopedia of Latin American Literature*, London: Fitzroy Dearborn, 712–14.

Ribeiro, J.U. (1989) *An Invincible Memory*, trans. by the author from *Viva o povo brasileiro*, New York: Harper & Row.

—— (1994) *The Lizard's Smile*, trans. C. Landers, New York: Atheneum.

Valente, L.F. (1993) 'Fiction as History: the Case of João Ubaldo Ribeiro', *Latin American Research Review* 28(1).

DANIEL BALDERSTON

Ribeyro, Julio Ramón

b. 1929, Lima, Peru; d. 1994, Lima

Writer

The author of three novels and over eighty short stories, Ribeyro was the major representative of the 1950s generation which modernized Peruvian fiction and prepared the ground for the new narrative of the 1960s. The best of his novels is the regionalist *Crónica de San Gabriel* (Chronicle of San Gabriel) (1960), which explores the decline of the land-owning class, but his forte was the **short story** and he has increasingly come to be recognized as one of Spanish America's foremost exponents of the genre. His simple, economical style exploits symbolism and figurative narrative patterns to enrich the basic realism of his texts, whose distinctive tone is a combination of humour and pathos.

Many of Ribeyro's stories explore the transformation of Peru occasioned by the modernization of the 1940s and 1950s, focusing particularly on identity crises suffered by sectors of the middle classes who find themselves unable to compete in the new society. At the same time Ribeyro has an eye for constants in national life and other stories highlight the perpetuation of deep-rooted divisions, attitudes and modes of behaviour, so that the overall image conveyed by his work is that of a country which remains fundamentally unaltered beneath a superficial veneer of change.

However, as is indicated by the fact that from 1954 onwards he established himself in Europe, Ribeyro was concerned to be more than a local writer and his work conveys a wryly pessimistic view of the human condition. Again and again his stories (some of which have been translated into English) portray characters who find their ambitions thwarted by an unpredictable world or see their illusions negated by an implacable reality. Others move away from specifically Peruvian settings to enter the terrain of the metaphysical in a manner reminiscent of **Borges**, posing inexplicable enigmas symbolic of the inscrutability of the world.

An all-round man of letters, Ribeyro also ventured into the essay and made a substantial contribution to the development of Peruvian theatre by authoring eight plays. Of these, the most important is *Vida y pasión de Santiago el pajarero* (Life and Passion of Santiago the Birdman) (1958, first staged 1960), which adapts the story of an eighteenth-century visionary who believed that he had discovered the secret of flight as an allegory of the situation of the artist in the backward cultural environment of the underdeveloped Third World.

Further reading

Higgins, J. (1991) *Cambio social y constantes humanos: La narrativa corta de Ribeyro*, Lima: Pontificia Universidad Católica del Peru.

Luchting, W. (1971) *Julio Ramón Ribeyro y sus dobles*, Lima: Instituto Nacional de Cultura.

—— (1988) *Estudiando a Julio Ramón Ribeyro*, Frankfurt: Vervuert.

Marquez, I. and C. Ferreira (eds) (1996) *Asedios a Julio Ramón Ribeyro*, Lima: Pontificia Universidad Católica del Perú, Fondo Editorial.

Zorrilla, Z. (1998) *Un miraflorino en París: Ribeyro, la tortuosa búsqueda del craft*, Lima: Lluvia Editores.

JAMES HIGGINS

Ricardo, Cassiano

b. 1895, São José dos Campos, São Paulo, Brazil; d. 1974, São Paulo

Poet and cultural activist

A late adherent to the modernist movement (see **Brazilian modernism**), the former symbolist poet Ricardo co-founded the mystical nationalist review *Novíssima*. The following year he launched the ***verdeamarelismo*** movement. The transfigured Amazonian landscape of his 1926 *Borrões de verde e amarelo* (Green and Yellow Impressions) embodies the nation's cosmic struggle to realize its destiny. Although anti-liberal and anti-capitalist like **Salgado**, Ricardo did not join the latter's fascist movement, Integralismo, but set up his own movement, Bandeira, whose theory he expounded in his *Marcha para Oeste* (March to the West) (1942). Ricardo continued to publish through the 1960s.

Further reading

Correa, N. (1970) *Cassiano Ricardo: O prosador e o poeta*, São Paulo: Conselho Estadual de Cultura.

Kovadloff, S. (1988) 'Cassiano Ricardo o el pesismismo combativo', *Cuadernos hispanoamericanos*, Sept., 459: 39–50.

Moreira, L.F. (1997) ' "All Silent ... Only One Signing": Contradictions in the Brazil of Cassiano Ricardo's *Martim Cererê*', *Cultural Critique*, Winter, 38: 107–35.

DAVID TREECE

Richard, Nelly

b. 1948, Caen, France

Critic

Chilean critic, founder and editor of the ***Revista de crítica cultural***, Richard became known internationally through her theoretical contribution to the postmodernist debate in Latin America, particularly her essays on art which were first published by Francisco Zegers, Santiago, as *Margins and Institutions* (1986) in a co-edition in English and Spanish. In *Masculino/Femenino: Prácticas de la diferencia y cultura democrática* (Masculine/Feminine: Practices of Difference and Democratic Culture) (1989) she situated feminist debates within a Chilean context; while arguing against 'women's writing' she took 'masculine' and 'feminine' to be binary terms in the struggle over signification and identified the feminine (and not woman) as the place of dislocation and possible transgression. *La insubordinación de los signos (cambio político, transformaciones culturales y poéticas de la crisis)* (The Insubordination of Signs (Political Change, Cultural and Poetic Transformations of the Crisis)) (1994) is both a review of aesthetic practices during and after the Pinochet regime and an exposition of those practices that challenges new and old totalizations.

Further reading

Huechante, L.E.C. (2001) 'MEDIAted Memory: Writing, Photography, and Performativity in the Age of the Image', in Edmundo Paz Soldán and Debra A. Castillo (eds), *Latin American Literature and Mass Media*, New York: Garland.

Richard, N. (1995) 'Cultural Peripheries: Latin America and Postmodernist De-Centering', in Michael Aronna, John Beverley and José Olviedo (eds), *The Postmodernism Debate in Latin America*, Durham, NC: Duke University Press.

—— (1996) 'Feminismo, experiencia y representación', *Revista iberoamericana*, July–Dec., 62(176–7): 733–44.

—— (1997) 'Intersectando Latinoamérica con el latinoamericanismo: Discurso académico y crítica cultural', *Revista iberoamericana*, July–Sept., 63(180): 345–61.

—— (1999) 'La cita de la violencia: Convulsiones del sentido y rutinas oficiales', *Punto de vista: Revista de cultura*, April, 22(63): 26–33.

JEAN FRANCO

Richmond, Angus

b. 1926, Georgetown, British Guiana

Writer

Having graduated from the University of London

in 1946, Richmond returned to London from British Guiana five years later and joined the immigrant West Indian literary community in London. His first novel, *A Kind of Living* (1978), traced inequalities between Guyanese urban social classes; its Spanish version earned Richmond the **Casa de las Américas** Award for Fiction. His 1988 short story 'Shame' tackled similar tensions within an Indo-Guyanese rural setting. His critical writing includes the prize-winning 1983 essay, 'The Sociology of the West Indian Novel in English'.

Further reading

Richmond, A. (1986) 'The Caribbean Writer and the Dynamics of Ideology', *Journal of Caribbean Studies*, Fall, 5(3): 233–47.

JILL E. ALBADA-JELGERSMA

Rights of Passage

Kamau **Brathwaite**'s first poetry collection *Rights of Passage* (1967) is an outstandingly original and poetically mature portrayal of the history and culture of African peoples in the New World. Brathwaite draws on considerable research in West Indian and African-American cultural and political history to construct a series of archetypal poetic personae. The form of each poem is thoughtfully related to its subject: 'Prelude' carries the origins of the long journey in Africa, 'Tom', 'All God's Chillun' and 'Didn't he ramble' revisions the notorious Uncle Tom figure, linking Africa with Europe's 'discovery' and claim of the Americas. Tom's agony is to have to compromise to survive, and to lose his children's respect in the process. Tom's descendants, scattered across the world, must find themselves by confronting history.

This volume, and the other two of the trilogy titled *The Arrivants* (*Masks* (1968) and *Islands* (1969)), gave voice to an immense collective experience, beginning in Africa and continuing through slavery, racism and colonialism, which is signified by music (Brathwaite theorized the importance of jazz in the West Indian novel in an essay contemporary with *Rights of Passage*). In this collection, he laid an important foundation for future work fusing African-derived musical forms and poetry.

ELAINE SAVORY

Riley, Joan

b. 1958, St Mary, Jamaica

Writer

Riley writes within the black/Caribbean tradition. She is distinguished by her harsh subjects: numbing accounts of the oppression of black women at home and abroad. Riley has never compromised rigorous honesty for critical approval. After an early education in Jamaica, in 1976 she read international relations at the University of Sussex, England. Of her four novels (*The Unbelonging* (1985), *Waiting in the Twilight* (1987), *Romance* (1988) and *A Kindness to the Children* (1992)), the last is controversial. Presenting religion and sex as exploitative forces, it considers incest in a small Jamaican rural community.

Further reading

Anievas-Gamallo, I.C. (1999) 'Race and Displacement in Joan Riley's *The Unbelonging: On Writing (and) Race in Contemporary Britain*', ed. and intro. F. Galvan and M. Bengoechea, Alcalá de Henares: Universidad de Alcala, 181–7.

Neumeier, B. (2001) *Crossing Boundaries: Joan Riley's No/Mad Women, Engendering Realism and Postmodernism*, ed. B. Neumeir, Amsterdam, Netherlands: Rodopi, 303–16.

PAT DUNN AND PAMELA MORDECAI

Rincón, Carlos

b. 1940, Bogotá, Colombia

Literary critic

Rincón's essays on literary criticism have been published in different periodicals in Colombia, for example *Mito*, *Tierra firme* and *Eco*, and in the newspaper *Junio*. A disciple of Werner Krauss in

Berlin, he became a professor at Centro de Estudios Latinoamericanos Rómulo Gallegos in Caracas, and more recently has taught in Berlin. *El cambio actual de la noción de literatura* (The Change in the Concept of Literature) (1978) was his first work published in Spanish.

Further reading

Rincón, Carlos (1978) *El cambio actual de la noción de literatura y otros estudios de teoría y crítica latinoamericana*, Bogotá: Instituto Colombiano de Cultura, Subdirección de Comunicaciones Culturales.

—— (1995) 'Posmodernismo, poscolonialismo y los nexos cartográficos del realismo mágico', *Neue Romania* 16: 193–210.

—— (1997) 'Streams out of Control: The Latin American Plot', in H.U. Gumbrecht (ed.), *Streams of Cultural Capital: Transnational Cultural Studies*, Stanford: Stanford University Press.

—— (1999) *García Márquez, Hawthorne, Shakespeare. De La Vega and Co. Unltd*, Bogotá: Instituto Caro y Cuervo.

MIGUEL A. CARDINALE

Rio, João do

b. 1881, Rio de Janeiro, Brazil; d. 1921, Rio de Janeiro

Writer and journalist

João do Rio, the pseudonym of João Paulo Alberto Coelho Barreto, was an important writer of *crônicas* (see ***crónica***) in *belle-époque* Rio de Janeiro. A dandy with a sharp eye for street scenes in the rapidly changing metropolis of his day, he was especially attentive to life on the margins. His work has been studied as an early example of gay writing in Brazil: full of intrigue, ironic, even somewhat camp. Raúl **Antelo** is one of several critics attentive to the remarkable qualities of Rio's urban chronicles.

Further reading

Antelo, R. (1989) *João do Rio: O dândi e a especulação*, Rio de Janeiro: Taurus-Timbre.

Magalhães Júnior, R. (1978) *A vida vertiginosa de João do Rio*, Rio de Janeiro: Civilização Brasileira.

Rio, J. do (1990) *Os melhores contos*, São Paulo: Global.

Rodrigues, J.C. (1994) 'Rio, João do', in D.W. Foster (ed.), *Latin American Writers on Gay and Lesbian Themes: A Bio-Critical Sourcebook*, Westport, CT: Greenwood Press, 359–61.

DANIEL BALDERSTON

ríos profundos, Los

José María **Arguedas**'s famous novel *Los ríos profundos* (Deep Rivers), first published by **Losada** in 1958, presents a boarding school in Abancay as a microcosm of the conflicts – ethnic, linguistic, class, cultural – with which Peruvian society is riven. Cast as a classical *Bildungsroman*, or novel of education, *Los ríos profundos* tells the story of Ernesto, the son of an itinerant lawyer who has been raised in a Quechua-speaking indigenous community, who is left by his father in the school, and there embarks on the difficult task of finding himself. His classmates include a panorama of the Andean elite, including some pupils who are strongly Indian in race but not in identification, children of the mestizo or misti and white elites, and Indians and others (like Ernesto) who strongly identify with the native culture. The novel contains famously lyrical descriptions of the river canyons of the Andes, as well as interesting ethnographic excurses (Arguedas was an anthropologist by training) on Quechua words and their significance for Andean culture, on the Quechua substrate of Andean Spanish, and on the cosmology of the Andean world. The novel was Arguedas's attempt to answer the questions he had posed in his earlier novel *Yawar Fiesta* (1941) and in the essay 'La novela y el problema de expresión en el Perú' (The Novel and the Problem of Expression in Peru) (1950) about how to express the fraught linguistic situation in the Andes. His solution in this novel was to break with the glosses and glossaries in the earlier *indigenista* novels (see ***indigenismo***) that had translated indigenous concepts into Spanish, instead altering his Spanish to help it evoke to some extent the structures and ways of thinking of

Quechua-speaking bilinguals and monolinguals. The novel includes a fascinating portrait of a small-scale revolt by the popular classes of Abancay, led by the *chicheras* (sellers of *chicha*, a fermented corn drink), against the land-owners, who sought to monopolize the trade in salt. It is also famous for its lyrical description of Andean music, particularly the power of the Andean harp. Partway through the novel, Ernesto evokes the sounds and sights around him, and comments: 'El hombre contempla indeciso el mundo así disputado' (Man contemplates such a disputed world uncertainly); his uncertainty, his search for his own (and his country's) identity, animate the novel.

Further reading

Arguedas, J.M. (1978) *Deep Rivers*, trans. F.H. Barraclough, Austin: University of Texas Press.

Cornejo Polar, A. (1973) *Los universos narrativos de José María Arguedas*, Buenos Aires: Losada.

Marín, G. (1973) *La experiencia americana de José María Arguedas*, Buenos Aires: García Cambeiro.

Rowe, W. (1971) *Mito e ideología en la obra de Arguedas*, Lima: Instituto Nacional de Cultura.

DANIEL BALDERSTON

Risco Bermúdez, René del

b. 1937, San Pedro de Macorís, Dominican Republic; d. 1972, Santo Domingo, Dominican Republic

Writer

During Trujillo's dictatorship, del Risco joined the clandestine political June 14th movement, and was subsequently persecuted and incarcerated. He founded the cultural group El Puño (The Fist) and won several awards from the literary contest La Máscara (The Mask). Although not a huge oeuvre – two poetry books and one collection of short stories – his work, especially *En el barrio no hay banderas* (In the Barrio There Are No Flags) (1974), has been very influential. Del Risco introduced to Dominican literature the Latin American **Boom**'s narrative techniques, especially **Cortázar**'s experiments.

Further reading

Sommer, D. (1980) 'Good-Bye to Revolution and the Rest: Aspects of Dominican Narrative since 1965', *Latin American Literary Review*, Spring–Summer, 8(16): 223–8.

FERNANDO VALERIO-HOLGUÍN

Risério, Antonio

b. 1953, Salvador, Brazil

Writer

Risério is an independent scholar and public intellectual who actively participated in the Brazilian counter-cultural movement of the 1970s. During this time he edited and contributed to several experimental poetry reviews, and wrote critical essays about popular music and literature. He has collaborated extensively with several famous MPB (Música Popular Brasileira) stars, notably Gilberto Gil, with whom he wrote and edited two books. In the 1980s he emerged as a prescient literary and cultural critic with books on the Afro-Bahian carnival, Dorival Caymmi, contemporary Brazilian poetry and the Bahian avant-garde of the 1950s.

CHRISTOPHER DUNN

Rivera, Andrés

b. 1928, Buenos Aires, Argentina

Writer

Rivera's militant working-class background (he was a textile worker) and political practice inform his literary production, particularly his earlier works. The decade-long silence he maintained during a period of military repression marked a significant shift in his work. Markers of Jewish-Argentine identity and the hidden aspects of Argentina's official history constitute defining components of his texts. His *La revolución es un sueño eterno* (The Revolution is an Eternal Dream) (1992) won the National Literature Prize. A furiously driven historical unveiling is more prevalent in his later writings – his *El farmer* (1996) has the nineteenth-century political leader Rosas as its central character. As others of his and the next generation have done, the gaze fixed on the formative years of the Republic has served to poignantly interpret the violence of their own days.

Further reading

García-Simón, D. (1999) 'Andrés Rivera o la excusa de la novela histórica', *Revista interamericana de bibliografía/Inter. American Review of Bibliography* 49(1–2): 187–93.

Luzzani, T. (1991) 'Una estética del desamparo: Ficción e historia durante la dictadura militar', *Río de la Plata* 11–12: 341–50.

SAÚL SOSNOWSKI

Rivera, Jorge B.

b. 1935, Buenos Aires, Argentina

Writer

Jorge Rivera's work embraces his writings on popular culture, teaching social science at the University of Buenos Aires and regular contributions to the media within and outside Argentina. His publications include: *La primitiva literatura gauchesca* (The First Gaucho Literature) (1968), *El escritor y la industria cultural* (The Writer and the Culture Industry) (1985), *La investigación en la comunicación social en Argentina* (Research in Social Communication in Argentina) (1986) and *Asesinos de papel. Ensayos sobre narrativa policial* (Paper Killers. Essays on Crime Fiction) (1996) with Jorge Lafforgue.

Further reading

Rivera, J.B. (ed.) (1977) *Poesía gauchesca*, Caracas: Biblioteca Ayacucho.

—— (1993) 'Periodismo y transición: De la recuperación pluralista al shopping comunicacional', *Cuadernos hispanoamericanos*, July–Sept., 517–19: 337–51.

CLAUDIA TORRE

Rivera, José Eustasio

b. 1888, Rivera, Colombia; d. 1928, New York, USA

Novelist and poet

Influenced by *modernismo* (see **Spanish American modernism**) and romanticism, Rivera's work portrays a powerful nature and its tragic impact on human lives. *Tierra de promisión* (Land of Promise) (1921), a collection of fifty-five sonnets, describes the Colombian landscape in the Amazon and the Llanos regions. In *La* ***vorágine*** (The Vortex) (1924), his most famous novel, the epic struggle of Arturo Cova is Rivera's pretext to describe the wild nature that absorbs and makes men as violent as itself, as well as to expose the exploitation suffered by the workers who extract latex from the rubber trees in the jungle.

Further reading

Arrington, M.A. (1997) 'José Eustasio Rivera', in V. Smith (ed.), *Encyclopedia of Latin American Literature*, London: Fitzroy Dearborn, 714–15.

Ordóñez, M. (1987) *La vorágine: Textos críticos*, Bogotá: Alianza Editorial.

Peña Gutiérrez, I. (1988) *Breve historia de José Eustasio Rivera*, Bogotá: Ed. Magisterio.

Rivera, J.A. (1935) *The Vortex*, trans. E.K. James, New York: Putnam.

Suárez-Torres, J.D. (1989) 'José Eustasio Rivera', in C.A. Solé and M.I. Abreu (eds), *Latin American Writers*, New York: Scribners, 2, 671–5.

MIGUEL A. CARDINALE

Roa Bastos, Augusto

b. 1917, Asunción, Paraguay

Writer

Paraguay's leading writer for the last four decades, Roa Bastos is the author of two of Latin America's most important novels, ***Hijo de hombre*** (Son of Man) (1960) and ***Yo el supremo*** (I the Supreme) (1974). He is also the author of poetry in Spanish and Guarani, the editor of an important collection of writings on the indigenous cultures of Paraguay, the author of some of the most haunting short stories (see **short story**) in the Spanish language and a public intellectual (see **intellectuals**) of great renown who has engaged major issues in his journalistic writings including the Columbian quincentenary, the failures of the truth commissions and the continuing need for social justice, the importance of indigenous and oral culture, and the dislocation produced by exile.

As an adolescent, Roa Bastos ran away from home and school to fight in the Chaco War, and later served as a war correspondent in London and Paris. Exiled from Paraguay in 1947 after a civil war in which Alfredo Stroessner emerged victorious (to rule for almost forty years), his career as a budding playwright was interrupted (although decades later he would adapt *Yo el supremo* for the stage). Instead, in exile in Buenos Aires in the late 1940s he wrote the intense bilingual poetry that was collected in 1983 as *El naranjal ardiente* (The Burning Orange Grove), which includes the section 'N'ane ne'eme' (In Our Tongue), a reflection on the complex relations in Paraguay between Spanish and Guarani, and between written and oral culture.

His first works of prose fiction were the short stories of *El trueno entre las hojas* (Thunder in the Leaves) (1953), which was followed by five more collections of short stories, the most notable of which is *Moriencia* (a neologism, perhaps The Experience of Dying) (1971), haunting stories told obliquely. In the first of these books, he provides a moving account of a hundred years of Paraguayan history from the end of the reign of the dictator Dr José Gaspar Rodríguez de Francia, who ruled the country from 1814 to 1840, through the War of the Triple Alliance, when Paraguay was defeated by a coalition composed of Argentina, Uruguay and Brazil (1865–70), through the Chaco War against Bolivia (1929–35), as well as a variety of civil wars.

Unfortunately Roa has never achieved such a high standard again. After some years of journalism, during which he produced little fiction, he has published a number of terrible novels in recent years, including *Vigilia del almirante* (The Admiral's Vigil) (1992) about Christopher Columbus, *El fiscal* (The Prosecuting Attorney) (1993), *Contravida* (Counterlife) (1994) and *Madama Sui* (1995), about a Japanese woman, an admirer of Evita Perón, who becomes the favourite of a Paraguayan dictator modelled on Stroessner. An odd example of the decline of Roa's powers is the inclusion in *El fiscal* of a short story that he had earlier published separately about the Argentine painter Cándido López, known for his paintings of the War of the Triple Alliance; a masterpiece when it was published as a separate story, it is strangely limp when included in the novel.

Roa Bastos will surely be remembered for *Hijo de hombre*, *Yo el supremo* and a few of the short stories. He has made an important contribution to the understanding of Paraguay in these books and in the collection *Las culturas condenadas* (Condemned Cultures) (1978), which brings together essays on the indigenous cultures of Paraguay by León Cadogan, Bartolomeu Meliá and others. (It also includes an anthology of songs and folk tales of the indigenous peoples.)

Roa Bastos left Argentina at the time of the Proceso, settling in France where he taught for many years at the University of Toulouse. He was awarded the Cervantes Prize by the Spanish government, and took Spanish citizenship when Stroessner revoked his Paraguayan citizenship. After the transition to democracy, he was able to return to Paraguay, first sporadically for the staging of the theatrical version of *Yo el supremo* and other projects, and then later to live. He currently resides in Asunción.

Further reading

Foster, D.W. (1978) *Augusto Roa Bastos*, New York: Twayne.

Marcos, J.M. (1989) 'Augusto Roa Bastos', in C.A. Solé and M.I. Abreu (eds), *Latin American Writers*, New York: Scribners, 3, 1209–13.

Roa Bastos, A. (1960) *Hijo de hombre*, Buenos Aires: Losada.

—— (1965) *Son of Man*, trans. R. Caffyn, London: Victor Gollancz, 1965.

—— (1974) *Yo el supremo*, Buenos Aires: Siglo XXI; critical edition by Milagros Esquerro, Madrid: Cátedra, 1983.

—— (ed.) (1978) *Las culturas condenadas*, Mexico City: Siglo XXI.

—— (1986) *I the Supreme*, trans. H. Lane, New York: Knopf.

Sosnowski, S. (ed.) (1986) *Augusto Roa Bastos y la producción cultural americana*, Buenos Aires: Ediciones de la Flor.
Vila Barnos, G. (1984) *Significado y coherencia del universo narrativo de Augusto Roa Bastos*, Madrid: Editorial Orígenes.
Weldt-Basson, H. (1993) *Augusto Roa Bastos's I the Supreme: A Dialogic Perspective*, Columbia: University of Missouri Press.

DANIEL BALDERSTON

Roach, Eric

b. 1915, Mount Pleasant, Tobago; d. 1974, Port-of-Spain, Trinidad

Writer

Although never collected during his lifetime, Roach's poetry was well known and widely read in Trinidad and Tobago through its publication in magazines and anthologies, and his regular contributions to the seminal journal, *Bim*. An activist with Eric Williams's People's National Movement, Roach withdrew in 1962 – the year of independence – and devoted himself entirely to journalism, returning to creative writing only in 1970, four years before his suicide. Roach's poetry celebrates the African roots of Caribbean culture, as well as the physical beauty of the Caribbean; it was edited by Kenneth **Ramchand** in 1991 as *The Flowering Rock: Collected Poems 1938–74*.

Further reading

Breiner, L.A. (1988) 'History, nature and people in the poetry of Eric Roach', *Journal of Commonwealth Literature* 1.

MIKE GONZALEZ

Roca, Juan Manuel

b. 1946, Medellín, Colombia

Writer

Belonging to the post-Nadaísta (see **Nadaismo**) generation of poets born in the 1940s, Roca began to publish in the 1970s. He is prolific, having published more than ten volumes of poetry and one of prose to date. His poetry combines a frank condemnation of the violence of Colombian society with moving and visual explorations of the themes of time and death. He has frequently collaborated with artists in the production of volumes combining poems and works of art, and has edited several anthologies containing thematic selections of poetry (for example, love poems and works by poets who have committed suicide).

Further reading

Melo, L.A. and G. Bernal Arroyabe (1989) 'Juan Manuel Roca: La poesía es una vocación de imposibles', *Casa de las Américas*, July–Aug., 30(175): 8–17.

BEN A. HELLER

Rodas, Ana María

b. 1937, Guatemala City

Writer

The third president of the Comunidad de Escritores (Writers Community), Rodas is a journalist and a daring feminist poet. In her 1974 *Poemas de la izquierda erótica* (Poems of the Erotic Left), she attacks *machismo* in its most sacred precinct, the militant and ever-so-virtuous Left, asserting herself as a Che Guevara of eros. In her 1993 poems, *La insurrección de Mariana* (The Insurrection of Mariana), about the CRN-URNG (Commission of National Reconciliation-Guatemalan National Revolutionary Union) peace dialogues, she addresses the relations between political and sexual marginalization, abuse and violence.

Further reading

Bollentini, Chiara (1998) 'La poesía de Ana María Rodas: La revolución socio-sexual en la Guatemala del patriarcado', *Confluencia*, Spring, 13(2): 156–68.
San Pedro,T. (1997) 'La palabra directa de Ana María Rodas o la negación de la estética poética

tradicional', *Istmica: Revista de la Facultad de Filosofía y Letras* 3–4: 196–20.

MARC ZIMMERMAN AND LINDA J. CRAFT

Rodó, José Enrique

b. 1871, Montevideo, Uruguay; d. 1917, Palermo, Italy

Writer

A major literary influence throughout the first half of the twentieth century, Rodó is best known for his landmark essay *Ariel* (1900), the widely read book which promoted a new vision of Latin American culture and its relation with the US (see ***Ariel* and *arielismo***). Framed as an address by a teacher to his students, the essay calls for a reflection on the spiritual qualities of 'Latinity' in opposition to 'Nordomania', the attraction to the technological progress and growing wealth of the USA. The intellectual movement of *arielismo* throughout Latin America called for more attention to spiritual, not material, matters and promoted idealism combined with an aristocratic concept of democracy. An elegant stylist, Rodó was also a major literary critic of his time, most famously for his perceptive critique of the poetry of Rubén **Darío**, who responded to Rodó's criticisms in the opening poem of *Cantos de vida y esperanza* (1905). A solitary and bookish man, Rodó lived outside the social mainstream of his native Uruguay, although through his political work and writings he was very much a force in his society.

Rodó's writing career began with his co-founding of a literary journal in 1895, and he subsequently added politics to his activities, as member of the Chamber of Deputies (1902–5 and 1908–14). His *Motivos de Proteo* (Motives of Proteus) (1909) continued his emphasis on classical themes and explored, through a series of parables, the development of ethical character and personality. Rodó's approach to the topic of personhood did not include the methodology of the newly emerged social sciences nor of fledgling psychoanalysis. Highly admired in its time, its elegant, highly wrought style, and its wealth of classical and Biblical references have made it less accessible to more contemporary readers. Its atemporal arguments do not continue the political and cultural arguments of *Ariel*.

Like most of his generation Rodó yearned to travel to Europe, especially Paris, as part of a cultural and spiritual pilgrimage. He travelled in 1916 as a correspondent for the magazine *Caras y caretas*, but died in Italy before reaching his goal.

Recent critics have turned their attention to Rodó's almost complete erasure of the body and eroticism in his writings on the self. This criticism reframes the nature of his cultural and aesthetic theories, and those of his *modernista* contemporaries, through the lens of misogyny and homoeroticism.

Further reading

Benedetti, M. (1966) *Genio y figura de José Enrique Rodó*, Buenos Aires: EUDEBA.

Montero, O. (1997) '*Modernismo* and Homophobia: Darío and Rodó', in D. Balderston and D.J. Guy (eds), *Sex and Sexuality in Latin America*, New York: New York University Press, 101–17.

Rodó, J.E. (1954) *Obras completas*, ed. E. Rodríguez Monegal, Madrid: Aguilar.

—— (1988) *Ariel*, trans. M.S. Peden, Austin: University of Texas Press.

San Román, G. (1997) 'José Enrique Rodó', in V. Smith (ed.), *Encyclopedia of Latin American Literature*, London: Fitzroy Dearborn, 720–2.

GWEN KIRKPATRICK

Rodrigues, Nelson

b. 1912, Rio de Janeiro, Brazil; d. 1980, Rio de Janeiro

Writer and playwright

Nelson Rodrigues lived most of his life in Rio de Janeiro, where he produced a voluminous body of writing that embraced theatre, novels, short stories, football reports, crime stories and memoirs; though the artist was visible in all of them. While his provocative and irreverent material attracted criticism and provoked debate, it was the writer who became known for his texts, for the words he coined that became part of Brazil's everyday speech, for his theatre and its adaptations for television and cinema. They were often the product of collaboration; he worked with Arnaldo Jabor to produce the film *Toda nudez será castigada* (All Nakedness Shall Be Punished) (1972), and with Antunes Filho, who directed many of his pieces for the theatre.

Universally acknowledged as a playwright, it was not in the theatre but in the press that Nelson Rodrigues lived out the most public part of a multifaceted life. His long journalistic career began age 13 when he began to write for the newspaper *A Manhã*, owned by his father. From then on, his complex life, full of tragic and unpredictable incidents, far surpassed any of his stories.

Since the innovative impact of the Semana de Arte Moderna (Modern Art Week) did not reach the theatre, it was only in 1940 when the theatre group Os Comediantes was formed under the Polish director Ziembinski, who was primarily responsible for developing an aesthetics of theatre in Brazil, that drama fell into line with the other arts there. A chance encounter between Rodrigues and the Polish director led to the presentation of the play *Vestido de Noiva* (Bridal Gown) in 1943, the moment that marks the beginning of modern Brazilian theatre.

Writing throughout the 1950s in *A vida como ela'é...* (Life as it is...), a daily section of the newspaper, Rodrigues began to develop another manner of writing. With a cast of young unemployed, street sellers and low-level clerks, and a Rio setting, these chronicles, like everything he wrote, described passions, crimes, funerals, incest and adultery. The public was fascinated and newspaper sales rose dramatically. His romantic novels, usually written under the pseudonym of Suzana Flag, were directed at an audience of women who enjoyed the complicated melodramatic plots and their interwoven gossip and tempestuous crimes of passion.

A controversial personality, considered a genius by some and a fool by others, evil and crazy by some and a moralist by others, Rodrigues left a series of unanswered questions about himself. Who was this theatrical revolutionary and political reactionary who turned all his sarcasm against the Brazilian Left and defended the military *coup* of 1964? Who was this writer who saw the bandit as a hero, little boys as low life, girls as whores, despair as a virtue and virtue as a punishment?

Further reading

Andrade, A.L. (1993) 'In the Inter(t)sex(t) of Clarice Lispector and Nelson Rodrigues: From Drama to Language', in R. Johnson (ed.), *Tropical Paths: Essays on Modern Brazilian Literature*, New York: Garland.

Castro, R. (1992) *O Anjo Pornográfico*, São Paulo: Companhia das Letras

Clark, F.M. (1991) *Impermanent Structures: Semiotic Readings of Nelson Rodriques' Vestido de Noiva, Album de Familia, and Anjo Negro*, Chapel Hill: Department of Romance Languages, University of North Carolina at Chapel Hill.

George, D.S. (2002) 'Nelson Rodrigues', in C. Solé and K. Müller-Bergh (eds), *Latin American Writers: Supplement I*, New York: Scribners, 479–91.

Lockhart, M.A. (1994) 'Beijo no Asfalto and Compulsory Heterosexuality', *Gestos: Teoría y Práctica del Teatro Hispánico*, April, 9(17): 147–58.

Magaldi, S. (1994) *Nelson Rodrigues/Teatro Completo*, Rio de Janeiro: Aguilar.

BERTA WALDMAN

Rodríguez, Reina María

b. 1952, Havana, Cuba

Poet

Since her first book, *La gente de mi barrio* (People from My Neighborhood) (1976), Rodríguez has enjoyed critical success both in Cuba and abroad. She is the only poet that has won the prestigious **Casa de las Américas** literary prize on two occasions: in 1984 with *Para un cordero blanco* (For a White Sheep), and in 1998 with *La foto del invernadero* (The Picture of the Greenhouse). Her poetry has evolved from an enthusiastic view of the Cuban revolutionary political process to a more sceptical reflection on it, and from a direct conversational language to a more metaphorical one. She is also well known for hosting a literary gathering, *La azotea* (The Terrace Roof), in her house through the 1990s. In addition she has founded a literary magazine *Azoteas.*

Further reading

Alonso Estenoz, A. (1998) 'El mundo como foto (en sepia)', *Casa de las Américas* 215.

Sánchez, O. (1990) 'Herencia, miseria y profecía de la más joven poesía cubana', *Revista iberoamericana* 56 (152–3).

ALFREDO ALONSO ESTENOZ

Rodríguez Alcalá, Guido

b. 1946, Asunción, Paraguay

Writer and critic

A lawyer by profession and a regular newspaper columnist, Guido Rodríguez Alcalá has published work in almost all genres. His books of poetry include *Apacible fuego* (Placid Fire) (1966), *Labor cotidiana* (Everyday Labour) (1979) and *Leviatán et cétera* (1981); he is the author of the novels *Caballero rey* (Caballero King) (1988) and *El rector* (The Principal) (1991) among others, and of three collections of short stories. His book-length essays include *Literatura del Paraguay* (Literature of Paraguay) (1980) and *Borges y otros ensayos* (**Borges** and Other Essays) (1995).

Further reading

Rodríguez Alcalá, Guido (1988) *Caballero Trey*, Asunción, Paraguay: RP Ediciones.

—— (1987) *Cuentos decentes*, Asunción, Paraguay: Criterio-Ediciones.

TERESA MÉNDEZ-FAITH

Rodríguez-Alcalá, Hugo

b. 1917, Asunción, Paraguay

Writer and critic

Hugo Rodríguez-Alcalá has published some fifty books. His critical writings include *El arte de Juan Rulfo* (The Art of Juan **Rulfo**) (1965) and *La incógnita del Paraguay y otros ensayos* (The Unknown Paraguay and Other Essays) (1987). He is the author of several volumes of short stories, including *La doma del jaguar* (The Taming of the Jaguar) (1995) and of poetry, including *La dicha apenas dicha* (The Joy Barely Expressed) (1967). Founder and first chair of the Department of Hispanic Studies at the University of California at Riverside, where he was active in running writing workshops, he taught in the USA for four decades before returning to Paraguay in 1982, where he has run writing workshops since 1983.

Further reading

Rodríguez-Alcalá, H. (1970) *Historia de la literatura paraguaya*, Mexico City: Ediciones de Andrea.

—— (1988) *Poetas y prosistas paraguayos y otros breves ensayos*, Asunción: Intercontinental Editores.

TERESA MÉNDEZ-FAITH

Rodríguez Juliá, Edgardo

b. 1946, Rio Piedras, Puerto Rico

Writer and essayist

Rodríguez Juliá mounts a permanent challenge to the text through the combination of different genres and modes of representation. His narratives fluctuate between the runaway baroque of his first novel *La renuncia del héroe Baltasar* (Resignation of the Hero Balthasar) (1974); the mortuary tales of *Las tribulaciones de Jonás* (Jonah's Tribulations) (1981) and *El entierro de Cortijo* (Cortijo's Funeral) (1983); his photographic record of the island's cultural memory in *Puertorriqueños: Álbum de la sagrada familia puertorriqueña* (Puerto Ricans: Album of the Puerto Rican Holy Family) (1990); his erotico-pornographic visual essay *Cámara secreta* (Secret Camera) (1994); and his detective novel *Sol de medianoche* (Midnight Sun) (1995).

Further reading

Franco, J. (1997) 'The Nation as Imagined Community', in A. McClintock, A. Mufti and E. Shohat (ed.), *Dangerous Liaisons: Gender, Nation, and Postcolonial Perspectives*, Minneapolis: University of Minnesota Press.

Perivolaris, J.D. (1999) 'Heroes, Survivors, and

History: Edgardo Rodríguez Juliá and Puerto Rico's 1898', *Modern Language Review*, July, 94(3): 691–9.

Ruiz Cumba, I. (1999) 'Edgardo Rodríquez Juliá y las paradojas de la (autor)idad narrative', *La Torre: Revista de la Universidad de Puerto Rico*, April–June, 4(12): 449–68.

Soto Crespo, R.E. (2002) ' "The Pains of Memory": Mourning the Nation in Puerto Rican Art and Literature', *MLN*, March, 117(2): 449–80.

MARÍA JULIA DAROQUI

Rodríguez Monegal, Emir

b. 1921, Melo, Uruguay; d. 1985, New Haven, Connecticut, USA

Literary critic

Emir Rodríguez Monegal was a prodigious literary critic, author or editor of forty books and countless articles. His controversial career lasted four decades. As an active writer, he participated in and edited a variety of literary journals: *Marcha* (1943–60), ***Mundo nuevo*** (1966–68), ***Número*** (1949–55, 1962–63). *Mundo nuevo*, although the most short-lived, caused the greatest controversy due to its alleged CIA links. Regardless of its politics, the journal was instrumental in promoting the 1960s literary **Boom** and has even been credited with its invention. The journal proposed to unite and demarginalize Latin American culture by including the work of such writers as Carlos **Fuentes**, Gabriel **García Márquez**, Clarice **Lispector**, Manuel **Puig**, Pablo **Neruda**, Julio **Cortázar** and José **Donoso**. In *El Boom de la novela latinoamericana* (The Boom of the Latin American Novel) (1972), Rodríguez Monegal suggests that the movement was more of a publicity venture than a literary event. The literary component of the movement had concrete roots in the 1940s novel. In *El juicio de los parricidas: La nueva generación argentina y sus maestros* (The Judgement of the Parricides: The New Argentine Generation and its Masters) (1956), he demonstrated Jorge Luis **Borges**'s importance and identified themes that would dominate literary debates in Latin America. His other books include works on Pablo Neruda, Eduardo Acevedo Díaz, Andrés Bello, José Enrique **Rodó** and Horacio **Quiroga**.

In 1968, after resigning from his position as editor of *Mundo nuevo*, Rodríguez Monegal entered the world of US academia, accepting a teaching position at Yale University. In an attempt to change the focus from the Peninsular emphasis that most Spanish departments had, he brought with him his vast knowledge of Latin American literature and of up-and-coming authors. His involvement and the continuity of his lifetime project to demarginalize Latin American literature led him to contribute to various US literary journals. Rodríguez Monegal's hard work in the Centre for Inter-American Relations (now the Americas Society), where he was the first editor of *Review*, a periodical dedicated to introducing Latin American writers to an English-speaking audience, is proof of his commitment. His fierce critic and enemy, Angel **Rama**, another Uruguayan, criticized him for ignoring the political realities of Latin America. Nonetheless, Rodríguez Monegal's contribution continues to influence contemporary literary studies.

Further reading

González Echevarría, R. (1986) 'Emir and the Canon: An Obituary Note', *Latin American Literary Review*, July–Dec., 14(28): 7–10.

Homenaje a Emir Rodríguez Monegal (1987) Montevideo: Ministerio de Educacion y Cultura.

Levine, S.J. (1990) 'Borges and Emir: The Writer and His Reader', in E. Aizenberg (ed.), *Borges and His Successors: The Borgesian Impact on Literature and the Arts*, Columbia: University of Missouri Press.

Rodríguez Monegal, E. (1987) *Borges: Una biografía literaria*, trans. A.T. Homero, Mexico City: Fondo de Cultura Económica.

Rodríguez Monegal, E. and E. Mario Santi (1980) *Pablo Neruda*, Madrid: Taurus.

Roggiano, A.A. (1986) 'Emir Rodríguez Monegal o

el crítico necesario', *Revista iberoamericana*, April–Sept., 52(135–6): 623–30.

VICTORIA RUÉTALO

Roemer, Astrid H.

b. 1947, Paramaribo, Suriname

Writer

A prolific poet, novelist, playwright and essayist in Dutch, Roemer's lengthy novels *Over de gekte van een vrouw* (About the Madness of a Woman) (1982) and *Levenslang gedicht* (Lifelong Poem) (1987) have been acclaimed for their stylistic experimentation and treatment of inter-racial relationships, female sexuality and the tense bonds between Suriname and the Netherlands. After the 1980 *coup d'état* in Suriname, she was very critical of the military regime. She has resided in the Netherlands since 1966.

Further reading

Rowell, C.H. (1998) 'An Interview with Astrid H. Roemer', *Callaloo: A Journal of African American and African Arts and Letters*, Summer, 21(3): 508–10.

AART G. BROEK

Rojas, Angel Felicísimo

b. 1909, Loja, Ecuador

Writer and critic

A member of the literary generation of 1930, his narratives are mainly set in the southern part of Ecuador. They express a sense of landscape, a penetrating social analysis and a humorous perspective tinged by a mild sense of melancholy. His major novels include *Banca* (Bench) (1938) and *El éxodo de Yangana* (Yangana's Exodus) (1949). He was also a critic, and his *La novela ecuatoriana* (The Ecuadorean Novel) (1949) is an indispensable critical tool.

Further reading

Calderón Chico, C. (1991) 'Angel F. Rojas', in *Tres maestros: Angel F. Rojas, Adalberto Ortiz y Leopoldo Benites Vinueza se cuentan a sí mismos*, Guayaquil: Casa de la Cultura, 5–100.

Jijón, C. (1983) 'Angel Felicísimo Rojas, un clérigo suelto del socialismo', *Vistazo* (Guayaquil) 377: 46–8.

Rojas, A.F. (1948) *La nueva novela ecuatoriana*, Mexico City: Fondo de Cultura Económica.

HUMBERTO E. ROBLES

Rojas, Gonzalo

b. 1917, Lebu, Chile

Poet

Gonzalo Rojas is a poet whose work is known for its dynamism, lyric power and eroticism. A miner's son, Rojas studied at Universidad de Concepción and the Universidad de Chile, where he formed ties with the group La Mandrágora. He received his first literary prize in 1946 for his first book *La miseria del hombre* (Man's Misery) (1948), and later the National Prize for Literature (Chile 1992), Premio Octavio Paz (1998) and Argentina's Premio José Hernández (1998) for his poetry, including *Contra la muerte* (Against Death) (1964), *Del relámpago* (On Lightning) (1981), *Antología del aire* (Anthology of the Air) (1991) and *Obra selecta* (Selected Works) (1997). Professor of the Universidad de Concepción, he also served under Salvador Allende as cultural attaché in China and Cuba. Expelled from Chile after the 1973 *coup*, he lived and taught in East Germany, Venezuela and the USA before returning to Chile.

Further reading

Coddou, M. (1984) *Poética de la poesía activa*, Madrid/Concepción: Lar.

—— (1986) *Nuevos estudios sobre la poesía de Gonzalo Rojas*, Santiago: Sinfronteras.

Earle, P.G. (1997) 'Gonzalo Rojas', in V. Smith (ed.), *Encyclopedia of Latin American Literature*, London: Fitzroy Dearborn, 722–4.

Giordano, E. (ed.) (1987) *Poesía y poética de Gonzalo Rojas*, Santiago: Ediciones del Maitén.
Rojas, G. (1988) *Antología personal*, Mexico City: UNAM.
—— (1988) *Schizotext and other poems. Esquizotexto y otos poemas*, trans. R.M. Cluff and L.H. Quackenbush, New York: Peter Lang.
Rojas, N. (1984) *Estudios sobre la poesía de Gonzalo Rojas*, Madrid: Playor.
Sefamí, J. (2002) 'Gonzalo Rojas', in C. Solé and K. Müller-Bergh (eds), *Latin American Writers: Supplement I*, New York: Scribners, 493–507.

GWEN KIRKPATRICK

Rojas, Manuel

b. 1896, Buenos Aires, Argentina; d. 1973, Santiago, Chile

Writer

Rojas published his first book of short stories in 1926 under the title *El hombre de ojos azules* (The Blue-Eyed Man). In 1951 he published his outstanding novel *Hijo de ladrón* (Born Guilty), a work characterized by a strong existentialist (see **existentialism**) and autobiographical tone. He directed the Chilean Writers' Association (1936–37) and lived several years in the USA, returning to Chile in 1964. His figure and his work are often identified with the generation of Latin American narrators of the 1920s whose works incorporated forms of **surrealism**.

Further reading

Concha, J. (1997) 'Manuel Rojas', in V. Smith (ed.), *Encyclopedia of Latin American Literature*, London: Fitzroy Dearborn, 724–5.
Cortés, D. (1986) *La narrativa anarquista de Manuel Rojas*, Madrid: Pliegos.
Goic, C. (1989) 'Manuel Rojas', in C.A. Solé and M.I. Abreu (eds), *Latin American Writers*, New York: Scribners, 2: 815–20.
Rodríguez Reeves, R. (1976) 'Bibliografía de y sobre Manuel Rojas', *Revista iberoamericana* 95: 285–313.
Rojas, M. (1955) *Born Guilty*, trans. F. Gaynor, New York: Library Publishers.
—— (1973) *Obras*, Madrid: Aguilar.
Román-Lagunas, J. (1986) 'Bibliografía de y sobre Manuel Rojas', *Revista chilena de literatura* 27–8: 143–72.

LUIS E. CÁRCAMO-HUECHANTE

Rojas, Ricardo

b. 1882, Tucumán, Argentina; d. 1957, Buenos Aires, Argentina

Writer and teacher

A prolific writer of poetry, essays and theatre, Rojas was also a journalist, critic and folklorist. His most famous works are *El santo de la espada* (The Saint with the Sword) (1933), filmed by Torre Nilsson in 1969, and *El profeta de la pampa* (The Prophet of the *Pampas*) (1945), but his most important work is *Historia de la literatura argentina* (History of Argentine Literature) (1917–21), then the first and most globalizing systematic critical study of the national literature. He created the Chair and the Institute of Argentine Literature at the University of Buenos Aires. In *Eurindia* (1924) he proposed the Indianism–exoticism dichotomy as a way of going beyond the opposition of **civilization and barbarism** formulated by Sarmiento.

Further reading

Becco, H.R. (1958) 'Bibliografía de Ricardo Rojas', *Revista iberoamericana* 23: 335–50.
Pagés Larraya, A. (1989) 'Ricardo Rojas', in C.A. Solé and M.I. Abreu (eds), *Latin American Writers*, New York: Scribners, 2, 591–5.
Payá, C. and E. Cárdenas (1978) *El primer nacionalismo argentino: Manuel Gálvez y Ricardo Rojas*, Buenos Aires: Peña Lillo.
Rojas, R. (1917) *La literatura argentina: Ensayo filosófico sobre la cultura en el Plata*, Buenos Aires: La Facultad.
—— (1945) *San Martín, Knight of the Andes*, trans. H. Brickell and C. Videla, Garden City, NY: Doubleday, Doran & Company, Inc.

ADRIANA AMANTE

Rojas Guardia, Armando

b. 1949, Caracas, Venezuela

Poet

Co-founder of the **Tráfico** group, Rojas Guardia's first volume of work, *Del mismo amor ardiendo* (With the Same Love Burning) (1979), brought immediate recognition for a poetry inspired by religion and his open homosexuality. These two aspects of his experience combined to produce a magnificent book – *El dios de la intemperie* (The God of Storms) (1985) – which sits on the frontier between diary, **autobiography** and philosophical essay. His poetry, charged with mysticism and eroticism, is built on an imaginary of everyday urban and domestic experiences on the one hand and an ornamental, sensual and reflective language on the other. In 1993 he produced his first *Antología poética*. He has also published essays and confessional pieces in *El caleidoscopio de Hermes* (Hermes' Kaleidoscope) (1989) and *El principio de la incertidumbre* (The Principle of Uncertainty) (1996).

Further reading

Ramírez Quintero, G. (1993) 'La poesía venezolana actual: Tres ejemplos', *Inti: Revista de literatura hispánica*, Spring-Fall, 37–8: 187–95.

Santaella, J.C. (1980) 'La poesía de Armando Rojas Guardia', *Zona franca: Revista de literatura*, May–Aug., 3(18): 21.

RAFAEL CASTILLO ZAPATA

Rokha, Pablo de (Carlos Díaz Loyola)

b. 1894, Licantén, Chile; d. 1968, Santiago, Chile

Poet

Usually associated with **surrealism**, Rokha's long poetic career outlived the avant-garde movements (see **avant-garde in Latin America**). His relationship with cultural institutions was always problematic, and he published his own work – some forty-two volumes of poetry and aesthetic criticism, of which *Los gemidos* (Sighs) (1922), a long and fragmentary prose song, marked a break in his poetic production. Although in general his work, including *Satanás* (Satan) (1924), *Ecuación* (Equation) (1929) and *Moisés* (Moses) (1937), was received with hostility or indifference, in 1965 he was awarded the National Literature Prize.

Further reading

Arenas, D. (1978) *Pablo de Rokha contra Neruda*, Buenos Aires: Galerna.

Ferrero, M. (1967) *Pablo de Rokha, guerrillero de la poesía*, Santiago: Editorial Univesitaria.

Lamberg, F. (1965) *Vida y obra de Pablo de Rokha*, Santiago: Zig Zag.

Nómez, N. (1988) *Pablo de Rokha: Historia, una escritura en movimiento*, Santiago: Ediciones Documentos

Rokha, P. de (1969) *Mis grandes poemas*, Santiago: Editorial Nascimento.

—— (1987) *Nueva antología*, ed. N. Nómez, Santiago: Sinfronteras.

—— (1990) *El amigo Piedra: Autobiografía*, Santiago: Pehuén Editores.

ALEJANDRA LAERA

Romeo-Mark, Althea

b. 1948, English Harbour, Antigua

Writer

A poet and short story writer, Romeo-Mark's work strives to capture the sounds and rhythms of Caribbean English. Raised in St Thomas, Virgin Islands, she says she was inspired to write by the storytelling of her father, Gilbert Romeo. She has published four collections of poems: *Beyond Dream: The Ritual Dancer* (1989), *Two Faces, Two Phases* (1984), *Palaver: West Indian Poems* (1978) and *The Silent Dancing Spirit* (1974). She has received awards for her poetry from the Virgin Islands Council on the Arts and from the Cuyahoga Writers Workshop. In 1995 she won second place in the Stauffacher's English Short Story Contest in Switzerland, where she currently resides and teaches.

CAROL J. WALLACE

Romero, Denzil

b. 1939, Barcelona, Venezuela

Writer and lawyer

Professor of the philosophy of education at the Instituto Pedagógico of Caracas, Romero is considered the leading writer of historical fiction in Venezuela, together with Francisco **Herrera Luque**. Translated into several languages, his novels, with their baroque descriptive style, have been **best-sellers** in his own country. His works include *La esposa del Dr Thorne* (Dr Thorne's Wife; novel) (1988) and *El invencionero* (The Book of Inventions; short stories) (1982). In 1983 he won the **Casa de las Américas** prize for *La tragedia del generalísimo* (The Tragedy of the Generalissimo) (1984).

Further reading

Rodríguez Ortiz, O. (1979) '*Infundios*, Denzil Romero', *Zona franca* 11: 59–60.

Santaella, J.C. (1988) 'Denzil Romero "soy un narrador que está dentro de la historia" ', *Imagen* 100: 3–5.

JORGE ROMERO LEÓN

Romero, Elvio

b. 1926, Yegros, Paraguay

Writer

A prolific versifier of the feelings of his people and one of the most prolific representatives of the avant-garde (see **avant-garde in Latin America**), Romero is Paraguay's best-known contemporary poet. A political exile in Buenos Aires since 1947, he has published most of his poetry there. Notable among his numerous books of poetry is *El poeta y sus encrucijadas* (The Poet and his Dilemmas) (1991), which earned him Paraguay's first Premio Nacional de Literatura (National Prize in Literature) in 1991. Romero's more than a dozen books of poetry have been translated in to more than ten languages; his writings have been widely praised, by Gabriela **Mistral** and Miguel Angel **Asturias**, among others.

Further reading

Rodríguez-Alcalá, H. (1988) 'En los sesenta años de Elvio Romero', in *Poetas y prosistas paraguayos y otros ensayos*, Asunción: Intercontinental Editores.

Romero, E. (1990) *Poesías completas*, Asunción: Ediciones Alcándara, 2 vols.

TERESA MÉNDEZ-FAITH

Romero, Sílvio

b. 1851, Lagarto, Sergipe, Brazil; d. 1914, Rio de Janeiro, Brazil

Literary critic

Romero was an intellectual pioneer in Brazil who strove to develop scientific methods of literary analysis. The best known of his numerous publications, *História da literatura brasileira* (History of Brazilian Literature) (1888), is Brazil's first work of modern literary history. Influenced by positivist, evolutionist and determinist theories, he sought to identify the characteristics of a distinctly national culture. He valued folk songs and stories, and the collections he published provided the foundation for the later work of, among others, Luis Câmara Cascudo.

Further reading

Cândido, A. (1963) *O método crítico de Sílvio Romero*, São Paulo: Universidade de São Paulo.

Guimarães, A. (1955) *Presença de Sílvio Romero*, Rio de Janeiro: Simões.

Haberly, D.T. (1997) 'Sílvio Romero', in V. Smith (ed.), *Encyclopedia of Latin American Literature*, London: Fitzroy Dearborn, 728–9.

Romero, S. (1945) *História da literatura brasileira*, Rio de Janeiro: José Olympio, 5 vols.

—— (1978) *Teoria, crítica e história literária*, ed. Antônio Cândido, São Paulo: Edusp.

—— (1982) *Ensayos literarios*, Caracas: Biblioteca Ayacucho.

MARK DINNEEN

Roopnaraine, Rupert

b. 1943, Kitty Village, Guyana

Poet, filmmaker, critic and politician

As co-leader of the Working People's Alliance, Roopnaraine (also Roopnarine) strives for national unity in the face of economic and environmental threats to Guyana, and racial divisions. In his 1988 book of criticism, *Web of October: Rereading Martin Carter*, Roopnaraine identifies, in his dual role as poet and activist, with Martin **Carter**, the revolutionary poet who called for Guyanese sovereignty in the face of British invasion. A similar approach, linking political statement and art, informs Roopnaraine's documentary film, *Land, Sea, Sea Wall* (1991), featuring actor Marc Matthews. Roopnaraine studied and obtained a doctorate in English at Cornell University.

JILL E. ALBADA-JELGERSMA

Rooy, René de

b. 1917, Suriname; d. 1974, Mexico

Poet

De Rooy published his first poetry in the literary magazine *De* ***Stoep***, which appeared in Curaçao. After mastering the local Dutch Antillean creole Papiamentu, he wrote a play and some poetry and was instrumental in promoting that language as a literary medium. He returned to Suriname in the late 1950s but left again in 1973, a deeply disillusioned man. He settled in Mexico and wrote *Verworpen vaderland* (Scrap My Homeland) (1979), a slightly fictionalized indictment of Suriname for its alleged moral decay.

AART G. BROEK

Rosa, João Guimarães

b. 1908, Minas Gerais, Brazil; d. 1967, Rio de Janeiro, Brazil

Writer

Born in the Brazilian interior, Guimarães Rosa graduated from Belo Horizonte as a doctor in 1930 and later worked as a medical officer in the provincial police. As a young man he showed a powerful aptitude for languages, and taught himself German and Russian. In his travels in the *sertão* (the backlands of the north east), Rosa heard and recorded the popular wisdom of the local cowboys, peasants, travelling salesmen, countrymen and women. His familiarity with the landscape and the way of life of the Brazilian north east provided the background and the material for his stories and novels. In 1934 he entered the Foreign Ministry and served as a diplomat in various European and Latin American countries. During the Second World War he was Brazil's Consul General in Hamburg. In 1942, when Brazil severed diplomatic relations with Nazi Germany, Guimarães Rosa was arrested and later freed in exchange for German diplomats detained in Brazil. He was elected to the Brazilian Academy of Letters in 1963, but only took up his seat in 1967, just three days before his death.

His first writings, the poetry collection *Magma* (1936), won a prize from the Brazilian Academy but was never published. In 1946 the rich language and dense symbolism of his collection of stories, *Sagarana*, marked an important step forward from the ***regionalismo*** that had dominated Brazilian writing during the 1930s and 1940s. Ten years later another story collection, *Corpo de baile* (Corps de Ballet), was followed by the novel, ***Grande sertão: Veredas*** (The Devil to Pay in the Backlands) (1956), which earned him recognition as one of Latin America's most important writers – critics compared him to **Borges**, Joyce, Carlo Emilio Gadda and William Faulkner among others. His writings, often narrated by the *capiaus*, or rural storytellers of the north east, pose metaphysical and existential questions, for his *sertão* is a place of travel that becomes the world; unlimited, embracing all other spaces, the near and the far, what the eye can see or what only the imagination could construct. The stories of *Corpo de baile* and *Sagarana* are linked to the idea of a wandering destiny. In one of his most famous stories, 'A terceira margem do rio' (The Third Bank of the River), a man leaves his family, floats off in a canoe and spends the rest of his life adrift on a journey that is a metaphor for alienation, an endless search and madness. The purpose of the journey sometimes coincides with the search for a solution to a moral or spiritual conflict, as in the story, 'A hora e a vez de Augusto Matraga' (Augusto Matraga's Time and Turn).

In Guimarães Rosa's *sertão*-world, poetry and myth fuse to create histories filled with magic and play; the ineffable and the ecstatic, the world of the unconscious and the pre-logical, reflections on time and destiny, the metamorphosis of men into animals, the pact or the stand-off between a man and the devil (as in his masterpiece, *Grande sertão: Veredas*) are all present.

The invention of this *sertão*-world, with its extraordinary range of linguistic and poetic resources – alliterations, ellipses, dislocations of syntax and a curious, archaic vocabulary – is Rosa's major triumph. The musicality of phrases, or often of individual words, the interaction of popular and erudite culture, the abolition of the frontier between prose and poetry and the numerous neologisms that he invents make Rosa's creative language one of the most extraordinary artistic creations of twentieth-century Latin American literature.

Further reading

Bolle, W. (1973) *Fórmula e fábula*, São Paulo: Ed. Perspectiva.

Bosi, A. (1988) *Céu, inferno*, São Paulo: Ed. Atica.

Campos, H. de (1967) *Metalinguagem*, Ed. Vozes.

Coutinho, E.F. (1989) 'João Guimarães Rosa, in C.A. Solé and M.I. Abreu (eds), *Latin American Writers*, New York: Scribners, 3: 1069–80.

Daniel, M.L. (1968) *João Guimarães Rosa: Travessia literária*, Rio de Janeiro: José Olympio.

—— (1997) 'João Guimarães Rosa', in V. Smith (ed.), *Encyclopedia of Latin American Literature*, London: Fitzroy Dearborn, 398–400.

Galvão, W. (1978) *Mitologia Rosiana*, São Paulo: Ed. Atica.

Nunes, B. (1969) *O dorso do tigre*, São Paulo: Ed. Perspectiva.

Rosa, J.G. (1963) *The Devil to Pay in the Backlands*, trans. J.L. Taylor and H. de Onís, New York: Knopf.

—— (1966) *Sagarana: A Cycle of Stories*, trans. H. de Onís, New York: Knopf.

—— (1968) *The Third Bank of the River and Other Stories*, trans. B. Shelby, New York: Knopf.

Schwarz, R. (1981) *A sereia e o desconfiado: Ensaios críticos*, Rio de Janeiro: Paz e Terra.

Vincent, J.S. (1978) *João Guimarães Rosa*, Boston: Twayne.

MILTON HATOUM

Rosa, Nicolás

b. 1939, Rosario, Argentina

Literary critic

Author of some of the basic texts of Argentine literary criticism, like his study of Sarmiento, *El arte del olvido* (The Art of Forgetting) (1990), Rosa is also largely responsible for introducing the ideas of Jacques Lacan into Argentine theoretical debates. He has also made significant contributions in the field of semiotics. Professor of Literary Theory at the University of Buenos Aires, a recent work is a volume of essays on the work of Néstor **Perlongher**, *Tratados sobre Néstor Perlongher* (1997).

Further reading

Rosa, N. (1992) 'Texto palimpsesto: Memoria y olvido textual', in K.A. Bluher and A. de Toro (eds), *Jorge Luis Borges: Variaciones interpretativas sobre sus procedimientos literarios y bases epistemológicas*, Frankfurt: Vervuert.

—— (1993) 'Veinte años después o la "novela familiar" de la crítica literaria', *Cuadernos hispanoamericanos*, July–Sept., 517–19.

DIEGO BENTIVEGNA

Rosenblat, Angel

b. 1902, Wengrow, Poland; d. 1984, Caracas, Venezuela

Literary scholar

In 1947 Rosenblat adopted Venezuela as his homeland after spending part of his youth in Argentina, Berlin, Paris and Madrid. A philologist, he dedicated his entire life to studying the complexities of Latin American Spanish. Few scholars have understood the Venezuelan people through their language as deeply as did Rosenblat in *Buenas y malas palabras* (Good and Bad Words) (1956). He initiated modern philological studies in Venezuela and also founded the Instituto de Filología Andrés Bello. Some of his works include *El castellano en España y el castellano en América* (Castillian in Spain and America) (1962) and *Lengua literaria y lengua popular en América* (Popular and Literary Language in America) (1969).

Further reading

Estudios filológicos y lingüísticos: Homenaje a Angel Rosenblat en sus 70 años (1974) Caracas: Instituto Pedagógico de Caracas.

Tejera, M.T. (1967) *Angel Rosenblat*, Caracas: Ediciones de la Facultad de Humanidades y Educación, Universidad Central de Venezuela.

VÍCTOR GALARRAGA OROPEZA

Rosencof, Mauricio

b. 1933, Florida, Uruguay

Playwright and writer

Rosencof was associated with the development of independent theatre groups such as El Galpón and Teatro del Pueblo in Montevideo who premiered his plays, including *Las ranas* (The Frogs) (1961) and *La valija* (The Suitcase) (1964). Other texts include a children's novel, *Vincha brava* (1993), and *Memorias del calabozo* (Memoirs from a Cell) (1987) with E. Fernández Huidobro. A leading member of the Tupamaros, Rosencof was imprisoned from 1972 to 1985. After his release he returned to the stage with works like *El combate del establo* (The Battle in the Stable) (1985), first presented in Stockholm and later in theatres around the world.

Further reading

Monleon, A. (1994) 'Mauricio Rosencof o el iluminador de sombras', *Primer acto*, Sept.–Oct., 255: 63–9.

Rosencof, M. (1992) 'Battle in the Barn', trans. L.B. Popkin, *The Kenyon Review*, Summer, 14(3): 129–45.

CELINA MANZONI

Roumain, Jacques

b. 1907, Port-au-Prince, Haiti; d. 1944, Mexico City

Writer

Haiti's best-known Marxist intellectual, Roumain dominates twentieth-century Haitian literature and ideas. Born into the Haitian elite, educated in Europe and fluent in several languages, Roumain rose to prominence as an activist in opposition to the American Occupation and as one of the founders of ***indigènisme***. He was both a nationalist determined to celebrate Haiti's folk culture, and cosmopolitan enough to want Haiti exposed to similar movements among Latin American and African-American writers. After forming the Haitian Communist Party in 1934 he was sent into exile in France, where he studied anthropology and travelled widely in leftist circles, establishing close contact with Langston Hughes, Pablo **Neruda** and Nicolás **Guillén**. He returned to Haiti in 1941, established the Institute of Ethnology and publicly criticized the Catholic Church's campaign against Vodun. He was made chargé d'affaires in Mexico in 1943, where he died one year later.

Roumain was the first of his generation to transcend *indigènisme*, using Marxism both to analyse Haitian culture and society and to counter *noiriste* racial essentialism (see ***noirisme***). His application of Marxist thought produced major essays on Haitian society, *L'analyse schématique* (Schematic Analysis) (1934); on the plantation South, *Les griefs de l'homme noir* (The Black Man's Grievances) (1939); and on Vodun, *Autour de la campagne anti-superstitieuse* (Concerning the Anti-Superstitious Campaign) (1943).

Despite his militancy during the Occupation, his early verse consists of stylized mood poems. His first prose works, *Les fantoches* (The Puppets) (1930) and *La proie et l'ombre* (The Victim and the Shadow) (1931), are bleak satires of the Haitian elite. His first treatment of the theme of peasant culture is the tragic novella *La montagne ensorcelée* (The Enchanted Mountain) (1931). Roumain's later works are epic evocations of proletarian revolt. The poems of *Bois d'Ebène* (Ebony Wood), written in the 1930s but published posthumously, are thundering appeals for working-class solidarity. The novel ***Gouverneurs de la rosée*** (Masters of the Dew), also published posthumously, is as much a poetic evocation of rural Haiti as a Utopian vision of rural solidarity.

Further reading

Cobb, M. (1979) *Harlem, Haiti and Havana: A Comparative Critical Study of Langston Hughes, Jacques Roumain, Nicolás Guillén*, Washington: Three Continents Press.

Dash, J.M. (1981) 'The Marxist Counterpoint', in *Literature and Ideology in Haiti 1915–1961*, London: Macmillan.

Dorsinville, R. (1981) *Jacques Roumain*, Paris: Présence Africaine.

Gaillard, R. (1966) *L'Universe romanesque de Jacques Roumain*, Port-au-Prince: Henri Deschamps.

Fowler, C. (1980) *A Knot in the Thread; The Life and Work of Jacques Roumain*, Washington, DC: Howard University Press.

Roumain, J. (1947) *Masters of the Dew*, trans. L. Hughes and M. Cook, New York: Reynal & Hitchcock.

—— (1972) *Ebony Wood*, trans. S. Shapiro, New York: Interworld Press.

—— (1995) *When the Tom-Tom Beats: Selected Prose and Poems*, trans. J. Fungaroli and R. Sauer, Washington, DC: Azul.

Sourieau, M.-A. (1997) 'Jacques Roumain', in V. Smith (ed.), *Encyclopedia of Latin American Literature*, London: Fitzroy Dearborn, 730–1.

J. MICHAEL DASH

Roumer, Emile

b. 1903, Jeremie, Haiti; d. 1988, Frankfurt, Germany

Poet

The first identifiably *indigèniste* work, Roumer's *Poèmes d'Haiti et de France* (Poems of Haiti and France) appeared in 1925. In fact, he was a founding member of ***indigènisme*** and edited its journal, *La revue indigène.* He played no part in subsequent literary movements, but continued to write technically accomplished but conservative poems in the *indigèniste* mode, later collected in a special issue of *Haiti Journal* (1947). The satirical poems of *Le caiman étoilé* (The Star-Spangled Alligator) (1963) are strongly anti-American. He became in his last years an ardent defender of Haitian creole, in which he wrote a number of sonnets.

Further reading

Berrou, R. (1975) *Deux poètes indigénistes: Carl Brouard et Émile Roumer*, Port-au-Prince: Editions Caraïbes.

J. MICHAEL DASH

Rubião, Murilo

b.1916, Carmo, Minas Gerais, Brazil; d. 1991, Belo Horizonte, Brazil

Writer

Rubião was a pioneer in the Brazilian short-story fantasy genre since the 1930s. In his work the fantastic, rather than breaking with reality, peacefully co-exists with realist narrative elements. Rubião produced only a small number of stories; obsessive and perfectionist, he rewrote more than he wrote. For more than thirty years he was almost unknown, until the re-publication of his short story 'O pirotécnico Zacarias' (Zacharias, the Firework Maker) in 1974 (first published in 1943) turned him into an almost overnight best seller. Today his work is distributed worldwide and widely translated.

Further reading

Arrigucci Jr., D. (1987) 'Minas, assombros e anedotas (os contos fantásticos de Murilo Rubião)', in *Enigma e comentário*, São Paulo: Companhia das Letras, 141–65.

Schwartz, J. (1981) *Murilo Rubião: A poética do uroboro*, São Paulo: Atica.

Zagury, E. (1971) 'Murilo Rubião, o contista do absurdo', in *A palavra e os ecos*, Rio de Janeiro: Vozes.

JORGE SCHWARTZ

rue cases-nègres, La

Published in 1950, the autobiographical novel *La rue cases-nègres* (Black Shack Alley) by Martinican author Joseph **Zobel** inspired a very successful film, *Sugar Cane Alley* (1983), by another Martinican, Euzhan Palcy. The novel recounts a childhood spent on a sugar cane plantation in the 1930s, where the only means of escape was to seek distinction in the colonial education system. Thus the protagonist José Hassam, first with the help of his grandmother M'man Tine in his native village and then with the help of his mother in Fort-de-France, masters French and the curriculum, obtaining the secondary diploma or baccalaureate. This apparent success story is tempered by the fact that, in order to avoid the drudgery of the cane field, José has to set himself apart from the world of his childhood, turn his back on his culture and his people, and consider exile in France. Having discovered the power of literature, and in particular of black writers such as Claude **McKay** and René **Maran**, José vows to keep telling the story of the black Caribbean people whose oral culture, industriousness and power of resistance Zobel celebrates throughout the novel.

The movie follows the novel closely but the cinematography, the filmic presence of other actors and a few narrative differences displace José's subjective point of view and contribute to a more ambiguous portrayal of José's educational journey and life in Martinique. For example, José becomes an orphan raised by his grandmother, who thus becomes a heroic figure. Although José's mother was not central in the novel, her struggle to help José through school suggested the possibility of collective sustained resistance. This narrative shift also means that, until he proves himself a brilliant student and is awarded a full fellowship, José is dependent on his grandmother and his world is restricted to the domestic environment she creates for both of them. In the novel he discovered Fort-de-France on his own, marvelling in its beauty and the poetic force of its shipyard workers, domestics and chauffeurs, whereas in the film, urban scenes are limited to their meagre lodging, the school and a few nearly deserted streets. The film was awarded the César Award for Best First Film at the Venice Film Festival and Darling Légitimus received the award for Best Actress for her portrayal of M'man Tine.

Further reading

Zobel, J. (1974) *La rue cases-nègres*, Paris: Présence Africaine; trans. K.Q. Warner, *Black Shack Alley*, London: Heinemann, 1980.

ANNE MALENA

Rueda, Manuel

b. 1921, Monte Cristi, Dominican Republic; d. 1999, Santo Domingo, Dominican Republic

Writer and musician

Poet, playwright, and short story writer, essayist and piano player, Rueda is one of the most versatile Dominican intellectuals. After studying music in Santiago, Chile and performing piano recitals, he joined the **Poesía sorprendida** (Surprised Poetry) group (the Dominican Republic's home-grown variety of **surrealism**) in 1951. He, with others, founded the poetry collection *La isla necesaria* (The Necessary Island). Among his many awards is the prestigious 1996 Tirso de Molina Prize for the play *Juana La Loca* (Queen Juana, The Mad Woman). In 1974, Rueda created the avant-garde movement 'El pluralismo' (Pluralism) (see **avant-garde in Latin America**). His most important poetry book is the spatially playful *Con el tambor de las islas. Pluralemas* (With the Drum of the Islands. Pluralemas) (1975).

FERNANDO VALERIO-HOLGUÍN

Ruiz Nestosa, Jesús

b. 1941, Asunción, Paraguay

Writer and photographer

Although Ruiz Nestosa has worked as a journalist for many years and has published short stories and novels since the 1970s, photography is his true love. He has had many shows, including a 1992 retrospective at the Museo Paraguayo de Arte Contemporáneo. His first novel, *Las musarañas* (The Shrews) (1973), was published in Buenos Aires. His other published works include *El contador de cuentos* (The Storyteller) (1980), a collection of five stories; *Los ensayos* (The Essays) (1982); and *Diálogos prohibidos y circulares* (Prohibited and Circular Dialogues) (1995). He has also written texts for musical compositions and photo exhibits by Luis Szarán.

Further reading

Marcos, J.M. (1987) 'Rodrigo Díaz-Pérez, Jesús Ruíz Nestosa y Helio Vera: Narrativa contracultural de los ochenta en el Paraguay', *Confluencia* Spring, 2(2): 53–61.

TERESA MÉNDEZ-FAITH

Rulfo, Juan

b. 1918, Apulco, Jalisco, Mexico; d. 1986, Mexico City

Writer

Rulfo's considerable reputation is based on few writings; one book of stories, *El* ***llano en llamas*** (The Burning Plain) (1953), a novel, ***Pedro Páramo*** (1955), and a film script which is really a novel, *El gallo de oro* (The Golden Cock), published in 1980 together with another script, *La fórmula secreta* (The Secret Formula), filmed in 1965 by Rubén Gámez. There are also fragments, like 'Un pedazo de noche' (A Piece of Night), written in 1940 as part of a novel, *Los hijos del desaliento* (Children of Despair), but later discarded, and 'La vida no es muy seria en sus cosas' (Life's Not Such a Serious Business), first published in 1945. Excerpts from *Pedro Páramo* appeared in various journals, including one entitled 'Los murmullos' (The Murmurs), Rulfo's original title for the novel. After his death, his notes were published as *Cuadernos* (Notebooks) (1994), essential materials for understanding this classic universal narrator and outstanding photographer.

Rulfo's father died in 1924, and his mother in 1930; he was left in the care of his grandmother, who sent him to an orphanage in Guadalajara, Jalisco, one of the centres of the Cristero Wars which were the final chapter of the Mexican Revolution. This conflict between religious groups and the government had a major influence on Rulfo's life and work. In 1934 he moved to Mexico City and in 1938 he began to write, although he published only fragments and the short stories later collected in *El llano en llamas*. In 1946 he found employment as a travelling salesman and began his important career as a photographer. In 1947 he married Clara Aparicio; they had four children. *Pedro Páramo*, two chapters of which were published first in journals. appeared in 1955. It was immediately translated into German by writer Mariana Frenk (1958) and later into several other languages. His stories have been filmed a number of times, including 'Talpa' in 1955 by Alfredo B. Crevenna and Gastón Melo, 'El despojo' (Pillage) in 1960, by Antonio Reynoso with a script by Rulfo himself, and 'Paloma herida' (Wounded Dove), directed by Emilio Fernández and co-written by Rulfo and the director. Roberto Gavaldón's *El gallo de oro* (The Golden Cock) (1964) was scripted by Carlos **Fuentes** and Gabriel **García Márquez**; it was later filmed again by Arturo Ripstein (1986). *Pedro Páramo* itself was directed in 1966 by Carlos Velo with script by Carlos Fuentes and Manuel Barbachano Ponce, and again in 1976 (under the title *El hombre de la media luna* (Half Moon Man)) with script by Rulfo and director José Luis Bolaños. Versions of other stories were directed by François Reichenbach and José Luis Serrato.

As his work became known, Rulfo began to speak and lecture in his own country and abroad;

for many years he worked for the Instituto Nacional Indigenista (National Indigenous Institute). In 1970 he received Mexico's National Literature Prize and in 1983 Spain's Príncipe de Asturias Prize. In 1980 he entered the Mexican Academy and in 1985 received an honorary doctorate from Mexico's National University (UNAM). His photographs are collected in the volume *Inframundo* (1980) with texts by José Emilio **Pacheco**.

Further reading

Esquerro, M. (1986) *Juan Rulfo*, Paris: L'Harmattan.

Estrada, J. (1990) *El sonido en Rulfo*, Mexico City: UNAM.

Larsen, N. (1990) 'Juan Rulfo: Modernism as Cultural Agency', in *Modernism and Hegemony: A Materialist Critique of Aesthetic Agencies*, Minneapolis: University of Minnesota Press, 49–71.

—— (2001) 'Rulfo and the Transcultural: A Revised View', *Determinations*, London: Verso, 137–42.

Leal, L. (1983) *Juan Rulfo*, Boston: Twayne.

—— (1989) 'Juan Rulfo, in C.A. Solé and M.I. Abreu (eds), *Latin American Writers*, New York: Scribners, 3, 1215–27.

Rulfo, J. (1967) *The Burning Plain and Other Stories*, trans. G. Schade, Austin: University of Texas Press.

—— (1983) *Inframundo* Hanover: Ediciones del Norte.

—— (1985) *Juan Rulfo*, special issue, vols 421/3, Madrid.

—— (1987) *Obras*, Mexico City: Fondo de Cultura Económica.

—— (1991) *Toda la obra*, ed. C. Fell, Paris: Colección Archivos.

—— (1994) *Pedro Páramo*, trans. M.S. Peden, New York: Grove Press.

—— (1994) *Cuadernos hispanoamericanos*.

Sommers, J. (ed.) (1974) *La narrativa de Juan Rulfo: Interpretaciones críticas*, Mexico City: SEP/Setentas.

MARGO GLANTZ

rural literature

The face of Latin American rural life was in process of profound transformation as the twentieth century began. The hacienda (or estancia or fazenda) and the plantation supplied the export products cultivated under oppressive conditions by a largely tied working population. These still existed in many places at the turn of the century. Sugar was still the main product of Cuba, Brazil and central Mexico; the Southern Cone supplied meat for a European market; Central America was supplying bananas and coffee. Bolivia by contrast was producing tin and Chile the nitrates used for fertilizer and explosives. All of these products were supplying a growing market in North America, and occupying increasing expanses of land to meet demand. The encroachment of the large landholders on communal lands produced deep conflict and resistance. In Mexico, Zapata's demand for 'land and liberty' was a core slogan of the Mexican Revolution; in Central America whole communities were progressively expelled from ancestral lands to become landless labourers on the growing estates. In the Andean region the search for mineworkers brought the labour contractors into the more remote villages, just as the largely foreign-owned mining companies increasingly took control of land as well as the sub-soil. All of these processes of change found their echo in literature.

The ***costumbrismo*** of the latter part of the nineteenth century chronicled an unchanging rural way of life. This did not usually embrace the indigenous communities however, who tended to live beyond the frontiers of the organized agricultural areas – although they often laboured under harsh conditions on the estates and farms. Many of the early twentieth-century writers about the countryside, however, were urbanized **intellectuals** reacting to the beginnings of change in the rural milieu by idealizing that community of the past. Thus, Chilean writers such as Mariano Latorre, Augusto **D'Halmar**, Mexican novelist José López Portillo y Rojas or the Argentina Alberto **Gerchunoff**, sought enduring values in rural life, as increasingly did Leopoldo **Lugones**. The dramatist Florencio **Sánchez**, by contrast, represented the conflicts between tradition and modernity that were erupting in the rural world at the turn of the century.

Thus writing about the land, often defined under the single rubric of ***regionalismo***, while rediscovering the enduring values which were to lay the foundation for ideas of national tradition, was often driven by contradictory impulses. Ricardo **Güiraldes**, for example, in his 1926 novel *Don Segundo Sombra*, discovered those values in the Argentine countryside. For Gabriela **Mistral**, too, the rural world was a source of certainties, although there are many moments in her writing when the isolation that is its condition of existence is a painful sacrifice, particularly for rural women. The land in José Eustacio **Rivera**'s famous novel *La **vorágine*** (The Vortex) (1924), by contrast, is a brutal and untamed nature inhibiting modernity, in the same way that Rómulo **Gallegos**'s eponymous heroine in ***Doña Bárbara*** (1929) symbolizes barbarous forces resisting change. In the stories of Horacio **Quiroga**, too, nature is an enemy, mutely resisting human encroachment at the frontiers of the social and the natural world. There is a sense, however, in Quiroga's work, in which that clash of forces is represented as a dialectic of change, just as it was in the work of Brazil's ***Antropofagia*** movement, inaugurated by Oswald de **Andrade** in 1928. Brazilian *regionalismo* belonged to the same decade of change, the 1920s; through the work of Rachel de **Queiroz**, Jorge **Amado**, José Lins do **Rego** and Graciliano **Ramos**, the Brazilian north east emerged as the scenario for a deeply humane but also angry literature. Lins do Rego's sugar cane cycle of novels, for example, describe a land where life is harsh and brutal and social relations reflect that relentless struggle for survival in corresponding ways.

While the setting for the writings of the *indigenista* (see ***indigenismo***) school is invariably rural, there is implicit in much of that writing – particularly for example in the work of Ciro **Alegría**, José María **Arguedas**, Manuel **Scorza**, Miguel Angel **Asturias** and Rosario **Castellanos** – a sense of a struggle over the meaning and value of the land. For the exploited indigenous people, land is part of the traditional continuum; for the landowners it is a commodity, as indeed is Indian labour, whose value is wholly economic.

The struggle for land remains at the core of the Latin American experience throughout the twentieth century; in its closing years, after all, the rising of the Zapatistas in Mexico was specifically linked to the question of land. In Central America, for example, history was made and unmade in rural settings. But beyond Amazonia there was little left to discover – and Eden had no place there. Rural life was often hard and poor, as the stories of writers as far apart as **Salarrué** in El Salvador and Francisco **Coloane** in Chile described. Yet from the 1940s onwards, as issues of national survival and development increasingly became questions of industrialization and technical change, the defining core of the nation-state became the burgeoning cities of the region. The countryside more and more became Macondo, an imaginary or imagined place, a shared past or an unfulfilled dream. At times, too, it became again a place of exile or a rediscovered wilderness beyond what was, increasingly, an urban hinterland.

Further reading

Alonso, C. (1990) *The Spanish American Regional Novel: Modernity and Autochthony*, Cambridge: Cambridge University Press.

Favre, H. (1998) *El indigenismo*, Mexico: Fondo de Cultura Económica.

Helena, L. (1983) *Uma literatura antropofágica*, Fortaleza: Universidade Federal do Ceará.

Martin, Gerald (1989) *Journeys through the Labyrinth*, London: Verso.

Morana, M. (ed.) (1998) *Indigenismo hacia el fin del milenio: Homenaje a Antonio Cornejo Polar*, Pittsburgh: Instituto Internacional de Literatura Iberoamericana.

Schwartz, Jorge (2000) *Oswald de Andrade: Obra incompleta*, Paris: Col. Archivos.

Schwartz, Roberto (1992) *Misplaced Ideas: Essays on Brazilian Culture*, London: Verso.

MIKE GONZALEZ

Russotto, Márgara

b. 1946, Sicily

Poet and translator

Devoted to research and literature on Latin American women's writing, Russotto earned a doctorate in comparative literature at the University of São Paulo (Brazil) and then became a professor at the Universidad Central de Venezuela, where she has taught Brazilian literature and gender studies since 1976. Awarded several literary and research prizes including a Fulbright scholarship in 1998, her books include *Restos del viaje* (Remains of a Journey) (1979), *Brasa* (Coal) (1979), *Viola d'amore* (1986) and *Épica mínima* (Minimal Epic) (1996), for which she won the Ramos Sucre International Poetry Prize. Other books include *Música de pobres y otros estudios de literatura brasileña* (Music for the Poor and Other Studies on Brazilian Literature) (1989), *Tópicos de retórica femenina* (Topics in Feminine Rhetoric) (1994) and *Bárbaras e ilustradas* (Barbarians and Educated Women) (1997).

VÍCTOR GALARRAGA OROPEZA

S

Sábato, Ernesto

b. 1911, Rojas, Province of Buenos Aires, Argentina

Writer

A writer whose life has informed much of his work as novelist and critic, Sábato was a pupil of Pedro **Henríquez Ureña**, a key figure in his life and in Argentine culture in general. He received his doctorate in Physics at the University of La Plata and then moved to Paris to work at the Curie Laboratories. The autobiographical elements that recur throughout his work suggest that the usual relationship between 'life and work' might be better expressed in his case as 'work and life', not just corroborating that biographical aspects appear in his writing, but also reading that biography in a more productive way than mere factual corroboration. Perhaps the key to his life is his crisis of confidence in both Marxism and science, both of which he abandoned in Paris in order to devote himself to literature. His writing, therefore, may then be seen as the problematic site of his crisis rather than of its resolution; in his work there is change, the transformation of the ideals he had abandoned in life. If his disillusionment originates in the empirical and is then transferred to the work, in the work it is still possible to find the positive and Utopian face of a still uncompromised ideal.

Sábato wrote three novels: *El túnel* (The Tunnel), published in 1948 (although an earlier text had appeared in the magazine ***Sur***), *Sobre héroes y tumbas* (On Heroes and Tombs) (1961) and *Abaddón el exterminador* (Abaddon the Exterminator) (1974), which won the prize for the best novel published in France two years later. Certain elements common to them all – itinerant characters, the centrality of existentialist angst (see **existentialism**), the presence of an enigmatic, sinister universe – might suggest they should be read as a trilogy. Thus in his novels communism becomes a search for hope, albeit presented as a 'metaphysical absurdity' in his second novel, while scientific rigour is transformed into the consistent lucidity of his characters such as Castel, Alejandra or even the character called Sábato in his last novel.

There is a close relationship between Sábato's novels and his essays. Just as a particular philosophy of existence emerges from the novels, traces of autobiography can be found in his essays, where he explores his own subjectivity, from *Uno y el universo* (One and the Universe) (1945) through his later collections *Heterodoxia* (1953), *Hombres y engranajes* (Men and Mechanisms) (1951) and *El escritor y sus fantasmas* (The Writer and his Phantoms) (1963). In all these writings he returns again and again to his faith in humanity, redemption through art and literature as a means of knowledge.

In 1984 Sábato responded, with other leading cultural figures, to the request of the then Argentine President Raúl Alfonsín to join CONADEP (the National Commission on the Disappeared). He now devotes himself to painting, and has presented several exhibitions.

Further reading

Cohen, H.R. (1989) 'Ernesto Sábato', in C.A. Solé

and M.I. Abreu (eds), *Latin American Writers*, New York: Scribners, 3, 1139–43.
Correa, M.A. (1971) *Genio y figura de Ernesto Sábato*, Buenos Aires: EUDEBA.
Giacoman, H.F. (1973) *Homenaje a Ernesto Sábato*, Boston: Twayne.
Keightley, R. (1997) 'Ernesto Sábato', in V. Smith (ed.), *Encyclopedia of Latin American Literature*, London: Fitzroy Dearborn, 737–42.
Oberhelman, H.D. (1970) *Ernesto Sábato*, Boston: Twayne.
Sábato, E. (1982) *On Heroes and Tombs*, trans. H. Lane, Boston: Godine.
—— (1988) *The Tunnel*, trans. M.S. Peden, New York: Ballantine.
Urbina, N. (1992) *La significación del género. Estudio semiótico de las novelas y ensayos de Ernesto Sábato*, Miami: Universal.

ENRIQUE FOFFANI

Sabines, Jaime

b. 1926, Tuxtla Gutiérrez, Chiapas, Mexico; d. 1999, Mexico City

Poet

One of the most widely read poets in Mexico, Jaime Sabines describes scenes of everyday life – an accident, a mugging, a love affair. His poetry belongs to no particular literary school but does anticipate the later themes of Beat poetry. His first book of poems, *Horal* (1950), immediately captured the notice of critics, who praised his work as instilling new power into Mexican poetry. *Recuento de Poemas* (Collected Poems) (1961), his first collected volume, presents four earlier books together with some new work. Other important works include *La señal* (The Signal) (1951), *Adán y Eva* (Adam and Eve) (1952), *Tarumba* (1956), *Diario Semanario y Poemas en Prosa* (Weekly Diary and Poems in Prose) (1961) and *Otro Recuento de Poemas 1950–95* (More Collected Poems) (1995).

Further reading

Campos, M.A. (2002) 'Jaime Sabines', in C. Solé and K. Müller-Bergh (eds), *Latin American Writers: Supplement I*, New York: Scribners, 509–16.
López, C. (1965) 'El mundo poético de Jaime Sabines', *Casa de las Américas* 30: 88–9.
Mansóur, M. (ed.) (1988) *Uno es el poeta: Jaime Sabines y sus críticos*, Mexico City: Secretaría de Educación Pública/CONAFE.
Sabines, J. (1979) *Tarumba: The Selected Poems of Jaime Sabines*, trans. P. Levine and E. Trejo, San Francisco: Twin Peaks Press.
—— (1995) *Places of Shadow*, trans. W.S. Merwin, Mexico City: Ediciones Papeles Privados.

EDUARDO GUÍZAR-ALVAREZ

Sáenz, Jaime

b. 1921, La Paz, Bolivia; d. 1986, La Paz

Writer

Surrealism dominates the work of Sáenz, even his late volumes *Recorrer esta distancia* (Travelling this Distance) (1973) and *Bruckner: Las tinieblas* (Mists) (1978). He never allowed his writing to be wholly automatic, however, and his work is always controlled. The free play of the psyche produces pure metaphors which sometimes defy the reader, for each is born in an involuntary 'act of genius'. His other works include the novel *Felipe Delgado* (1979) and the play *La noche del viernes* (Friday Night).

Further reading

Rivera Rodas, O. (1983–84) 'La poesía de Jaime Sáenz', *Inti.* 18–19: 59–82.
Sáenz, J. (1975) *Obra poética*, La Paz: Biblioteca del Sesquicentenario.
Taller Hipótesis (1985) 'Escribir antes y después de la muerte (sobre la obra poética de Jaime Sáenz)', *Revista iberoamericana* 134: 285–9.

J.M. DE LA VEGA RODRÍGUEZ

Saer, Juan José

b. 1937, Serondino, Argentina

Writer

The work of Saer consists of ten or more novels, various collections of essays, four books of short stories and one volume of poetry. It is a remarkably cohesive body of work, linked by a common spatial (and often temporal) framework, the so-called *Zona*, whose characters reappear from fiction to fiction and where events often continue from one text to another. The *Zona* corresponds to the area in and around the Argentine city of Santa Fé (although that is never acknowledged, thus preserving the specificity of the literary space) where Saer lived and worked for many years before moving to France in 1968 (where he still lives).

Saer's starting point was a critical reading of **Borges**, of the fictional possibilities of a narrative referring only to its own world, and a detailed knowledge of contemporary currents in literary theory, philosophy and psychoanalysis, allied to an assiduously poetic writing. Out of these components Saer has created a body of work that is emblematic of the potentialities, tensions and concerns of an Argentine writer at the end of the twentieth century. His first important work, the novel *Cicatrices* (Scars), appeared in 1969; its four independent stories, tangentially linked by a crime, exhausts the question of the representation of events, as well as exploring the implications of a 'writing of perception' which signals Saer's familiarity with the French *nouveau roman*. From these beginnings, Saer went on to novels which dramatized the 'impossibility of writing' – *El limonero real* (The Royal Lemon Tree) in 1974 and *Nadie nunca nada* (Nobody, Nothing, Never) in 1980, a rewriting of the story of the Spanish explorations of the Americas in the philosophical novel *El* ***entenado*** (The Witness) (1983) and a recreation of the historical *pampa* – *La ocasión* (The Opportunity) in 1987 – and on to a transgressive (both morally and in terms of genre) recreation of the crime novel in *La pesquisa* (The Event) in 1994.

In the work of Saer, intertextual references, the specificity of literary discourse and the obsessive questioning of representation set in motion an imaginary, fantastical process that renews the act of reading and creates what the writer calls 'unexpected mirages' (*espejismos inéditos*), while at the same time producing indirect and original fictional representations of the dramas of recent Argentine history (in the 1986 novel *Glosa* for example). The tension, the existential charge and the affective impact of his work is both evident and paradoxical; for in calling into question both literary discourse and the novel as a category, Saer has contributed to an unexpected regeneration of the genre.

Further reading

Balderston, D. (1997) 'Juan José Saer', in V. Smith (ed.), *Encyclopedia of Latin American Literature*, London: Fitzroy Dearborn, 742–3.

Canaparo, C. (1995) 'Interview with Juan José Saer', *Journal of Latin American Cultural Studies* 4(1).

Premat, J. (2002) *La dicha de Saturno: Escritura y melancolía en la obra de Juan José Saer*, Rosario, Argentina: Beatriz Viterbo Editora.

Romano, J. (2002) 'Juan José Saer', in C. Solé and K. Müller-Bergh (eds), *Latin American Writers: Supplement I*, New York: Scribners, 517–28.

Saer, J.J. (1986) *Juan José Saer por Juan José Saer*, Buenos Aires: Celtia.

—— (1990) *The Witness*, trans. M.J. Costa, London: Serpent's Tail.

—— (1993) *Nobody, Nothing, Never*, trans. H. Lane, London: Serpent's Tail.

—— (1995) *The Event*, trans. H. Lane, London: Serpent's Tail.

Stern, M. (1984) 'Juan José Saer: Construcción y teoría de la ficción narrativa', *Hispamérica* 13(37).

JULIO PREMAT

sainete

A significant genre in the theatre of the River Plate region between the late nineteenth century and the late 1930s, *sainete* was one of the first cultural expressions of the middle classes of Buenos Aires, Montevideo, Rosario and La Plata. It generated an entire cultural industry, supporting writers, companies of actors, new theatres and the establishment of new publishing houses. The most popular form was the '*género chico*' (the small genre), and within it the so-called *sainete criollo* which derived its main features from Spain, although it was progressively modified and adapted to the sociocultural reality of the River Plate. Like the zarzuela, the revue and other short pieces, it was presented in a multi-sketch form.

The development of the *sainete* was closely linked to urbanization and modernization, and above all to the arrival of important groups of immigrants from Europe and the Middle East. The immigrants, the majority of them Italian, Spanish and Polish, were forced into crowded urban slums called *conventillos*. The action of many *sainetes* takes place in the yard of a conventillo where the Italians (Genoese, Neopolitans, Calabrians) meet the Spaniards (Catalans, Basques, Andalusians) and other immigrants (Turks, Syrians, Russians, Jews). The works are short – a single act divided into three sketches – and often accompanied by tango dancing. Although centred around a melodramatic conflict of honour they often also had comic moments emerging from the immigrants' physical gestures and speech: actors spoke in *cocoliche*, a theatrical language parodying the immigrants' accents, or in *lunfardo*, the street language of pimps and petty criminals.

The *sainete* had many sub-genres, among them a more reflective variant closer to a theatre of identity – such as the plays of Carlos Mauricio Pacheco – which later led to what is called '*el* ***grotesco criollo***'. Another variant was more festive and overtly theatrical, as in the work of Alberto **Vacarezza**.

Although the *sainete* declined in the 1940s, many of its features persist in contemporary theatrical revue and on television, in the methods of comic acting and the structure of the sketch.

Further reading

Marco, S. *et al.* (1974) *Teoría del género chico criollo*, Buenos Aires: EUDEBA.

Pellarolo, S. (1997) *Sainete criollo/democracia/representación: El caso de Nemesio Trejo*, Buenos Aires: Corregidor.

Pellettieri, O. (1993) 'Actualidad del sainete en el teatro argentino', *Cuadernos hispanoamericanos*, July–Sept., 517–19: 421–36.

Rodríguez, M. (2000) 'Revista y modernidad (1890–1930)', in O. Pellettieri (ed.), *Indagaciones sobre el fin de siglo (teatro iberoamericano y argentino)*, Buenos Aires: Galerna, Fundación Roberto Arlt.

NORA MAZZIOTTI

St John, Bruce

b. 1923, St Michael, Barbados; d. 1995, Barbados

Poet

After a career as a teacher, St John began to develop oral poems in Barbadian creole, 'Bajan speech', from about the age of 50. *Bruce St. John at Kairi House* (1974), *Joyce and Eros and Varia* (1976) and *Bumbatak I* (1982) demonstrate his poetic skill. The records 'The Foetus-Pains' and 'The Foetus-Pleasures' (both 1973) present his accurate, creative interpretations of the tonality of the Bajan speech spoken during his childhood and on which his poetic form was founded. His poems express his opposition to colonial repression of Barbadian folk culture.

ELAINE SAVORY

St Omer, Garth

b. 1931, St Lucia

Writer

Long considered one of the Caribbean's best writers, St Omer's writing is cool and spare. It deals memorably with some of the more disturbing experiences in the colonial world, such as passivity, confusion and despair. His novels include *The Lights on the Hill* (1968), *Nor Any Country* (1969) and *J-, Black Bam and the Masqueraders* (1972). His short story, 'The Departure', appears in *The Penguin Book of Caribbean Short Stories* (1996). Educated in France and at the University of the West Indies, Jamaica, he taught in Ghana before going to the USA in the early 1970s, where he is now a university professor.

Further reading

Campbell, E. (1989) 'The Transmutation of Tragedy in the Fiction of Garth St. Omer', in A.L. McLeod (ed.), *Subjects Worthy of Fame: Essays on Commonwealth Literature in Honour of H. H. Anniah Gowda*, New Delhi: Sterling, 1–9.

Cousins, J. (1989) 'Symbol and Metaphor in the Early Fiction of Garth St. Omer', *Journal of West Indian Literature*, Sept., 3(2): 20–37.

KEITH JARDIM

Sainz, Gustavo

b. 1940, Mexico City

Writer

One of the young writers who, along with José **Agustín** and Parménides García Saldaña, were collectively referred to in the 1960s as La **Onda**, a term first coined by Margo **Glantz**, Sainz was the Xavier Villaurrutia Prize winner for his novel *La princesa del palacio de hierro* (The Princess of the Iron Palace) (1974). The discourse of La Onda was key in expressing the crisis of urban Mexican society, which culminated in the 1968 Tlatelolco massacre – an experience revisited in *Muchacho en llamas* (Boy in Flames) (1988). With *Gazapo* (1965) and *Obsesivos días circulares* (Obsessive Circular Days) (1969) Sainz proved that the 1960s narrative could, if only momentarily, express a new vision of the Mexican reality. He teaches at Indiana University in Bloomington, Indiana.

Further reading

Fernández, S.C. (1997) 'Gustavo Sainz', in V. Smith (ed.), *Encyclopedia of Latin American Literature*, London: Fitzroy Dearborn, 744–5.

Sainz, G. (1968) *Gazapo*, trans. H. St. Martin, New York: Farrar, Straus.

—— (1987) *The Princess of the Iron Palace*, trans. A. Hurley, New York: Grove Press.

EDUARDO SANTA CRUZ

Salarrué

b. 1899, Sonsonate, El Salvador; d. 1975, San Salvador, El Salvador

Short story writer

Born Salvador Salazar Arrué, Salarrué is considered to be the best Central American exponent of ***costumbrismo*** and ***indigenismo***. Although he published sixteen books, Salarrué is best known for *Cuentos de barro* (1933) (Clay Short Stories), a collection of simple narratives about the Izalco Indians in Sonsonate province. Love, death, injustice and destiny are his favourite motifs. He used colloquial language and regionalisms for characters who speak candidly, creating an atmosphere at once magical and cruel. He is also known for his *Cuentos de cipotes* (Children's Short Stories) (1945), in which he recreates scenes from Salvadoran life and its rich oral tradition.

Further reading

Acevedo, R.L. (1982) 'Salarrué, novelista o la esencial paradoja de la existencia', *La novela centroamericana*, Río Piedras, PR: Editorial Universitaria.

—— (1989) 'Salvador (Salarrué) Salazar Arrué', in C.A. Solé and M.I. Abreu (eds), *Latin American Writers*, New York: Scribners, 2, 875–9.

Gold, J.N. (1997) 'Salarrué', in V. Smith (ed.), *Encyclopedia of Latin American Literature*, London: Fitzroy Dearborn, 746–7.

Salarrué (1969–70) *Obras escogidas*, ed. and intro. H. Lindo, San Salvador: Editorial Universitaria de El Salvador.

—— (1977) *El ángel del espejo y otros relatos*, ed. and intro. S. Ramírez, Caracas: Biblioteca Ayacucho.

NICASIO URBINA

Salgado, Plínio

b. 1895, São Paulo, Brazil; d. 1975, São Paulo

Cultural activist, writer and political leader

Founder and leader of the Far Right wing of

Brazilian modernism ***verdeamarelismo***, and of Brazil's fascist party Integralismo, Salgado was the self-taught son of nationalistic farmers from the interior of São Paulo. He led the conservative wing of the São Paulo Republican Party following a split in 1924, and began to develop his ideas of national integration rooted in a mystical Indianismo. His theoretical and political writings are collected in *Literatura e política* (Literature and Politics) and *Despertemos a nação!* (Let Us Awaken the Nation!) (1935). His two messianic novels, *O Esperado* (The Awaited One) (1931) and *A Voz do Oeste* (The Voice from the West) (1934), rest on similar notions. He is better remembered as the ideologue of Brazil's most eccentric brand of reactionary politics, which he continued to advocate publicly in Congress into the 1970s.

Further reading

Dorea, A.G. (1980) *O romance modernista de Plinio Salgado.*, São Paulo: IBRAS/INL.

Prado, A.A. (1982) 'Literatura e integralismo: Um percurso ideólogico', *Minas Gerais: suplemento literario*, 22 May, 15(816): 8–9.

DAVID TREECE

Salkey, Andrew

b. 1928, Colón, Panama; d. 1995, Amherst, Massachusetts, USA

Writer

Salkey's collection of children's stories, *Anancy's Score* (1973) (based on the mythical Caribbean trickster Anancy), together with *Hurricane* (1964) and several other works for children, represent a major contribution to Caribbean children's literature. As a broadcast journalist for the BBC, Salkey did much to bring West Indian folk tales, myths and legends to an international audience. His many awards for writing include the 1955 Thomas Helmore poetry prize for the long poem *Jamaica Symphony*, a Guggenheim Fellowship (1960) for the novel *A Quality of Violence*, and the 1979 **Casa de las Américas** Poetry Prize for *In the Hills Where Her Dreams Live: Poems for Chile, 1973–1978.*

Further reading

Carr, B. (1968) 'A Complex Fate: The Novels of Andrew Salkey', in L. James (ed.), *The Islands in Between*, Oxford: Oxford University Press, 100–8.

Morris, M. (1986) 'Anansi and Andrew Salkey', *Jamaica Journal* 19.

Nazareth, P. (1986) 'The Fiction of Andrew Salkey', *Jamaica Journal* 19.

—— (1988) 'Sexual Fantasies and Neo-Colonial Repression in Andrew Salkey's *The Adventures of Catullus Kelly*', *World Literature Written in English* 28.

KEITH JARDIM

Salomão, Waly

b. 1944, Jequié, Bahia, Brazil

Poet

A key figure of the Brazilian counterculture, Waly Salomão has written several volumes of poetry, manifestos, essays and lyrics to songs recorded by Gal Costa, Gilberto Gil, Adriana Calcanhoto and other MPB (Música Popular Brasileira) performers. His 1972 collection of experimental poetry, *Me segura qu'eu vou dar um troço* (Hold Me 'Cause I'm Gonna Have a Fit), was a primary reference for *poesia marginal* (see **marginal poets**) and disaffected youth living through the most repressive phase of military rule who identified with the 'tune in, drop out' ethic of the so-called *desbunde.* In the early 1980s, he founded with Luciano Figueiredo the Projeto HO dedicated to the preservation and dissemination of Hélio Oiticica's work.

CHRISTOPHER DUNN

Sambrano Urdaneta, Oscar

b. 1929, Boconó, Venezuela

Literary critic and cultural administrator

Sambrano Urdaneta has dedicated much of his life to the study and teaching of Venezuelan literature and literary history. Since the 1950s he has published numerous studies and textbooks on the subject, being best known for his work on

Venezuelan poetry, and for forty years he taught literature in such institutions as the Pedagogical Institute and the Central University of Venezuela, both in Caracas. He has also worked for some of Venezuela's most important cultural organizations, serving as director of the Fundación la Casa de Bello and the Biblioteca Ayacucho, before being appointed President of CONAC (National Council for Culture) in 1995.

Further reading

Olivares Figueroa, F. (1961) '*Apreciación literaria* de Oscar Sambrano Urdaneta', *Revista nacional de cultura* 145–6: 253–5.

Paz Castillo, F. (1991) 'Oscar Sambrano Urdaneta', *Letras* (Caracas) 48: 25–8.

Rivas, R.A. (1991) 'Bibliografía y cronología de Oscar Sambrano Urdaneta', *Letras* (Caracas) 48: 29–57.

MARK DINNEEN

Sánchez, Florencio

b. 1875, Montevideo, Uruguay; d. 1910, Milan, Italy

Playwright

Born in Montevideo into a conservative and affluent family, Sánchez is attributed with having founded modern Uruguayan theatre. Along with José Enrique **Rodó**, Horacio **Quiroga**, Julio **Herrera y Reissig** and Delmira **Agustini**, Sánchez was a distinguished member of the 'Generación uruguaya del 1900'. This group of liberal, self-taught, non-conformist writers and intellectuals were concerned with all aspects of Uruguay as a nation and the different paths that the country could take. In the early twentieth century, in the capital, Montevideo, cultural activities, particularly theatre, were very much present and important aspects of social life. These activities grew in parallel with the urbanization, modernization projects, and the demographic shifts taking place. The intensity of theatrical activity is made evident not only because of the high presence of international (i.e., European) theatre companies, but also due to the high percentage of theatre consumers. As in other parts of Latin America, theatrical activity during this period was mostly reduced to 'foreign' or 'popular' performances. This coincided with Sánchez's entry into the theatrical world; his early incursion into theatre, both as an actor and then later as a playwright, explored the national character, in different settings (urban and rural) and among different social classes (lower classes and bourgeoisie). Among his most well-known plays, the following stand out: *Canillita*, *M'hijo el Dotor* – a piece from 1903 that introduces him as an important playwright – *La gringa*, *Barranca abajo*, *En familia*, *Los muertos*, *El conventillo*, *Los derechos de la salud* and *El cacique Pichuleo*. Important to note, however, is that since Sánchez's theatrical activities took him to different parts of Latin America, particularly Argentina where he lived in self-exile for a number of years, his place in theatre studies is better understood if he is also contextualized within *Ríoplatense* Theatre.

Sánchez is still considered one of the most important playwrights of Uruguay and his plays are still staged in theatres across that country, though not as often as in previous decades. His ambivalent position within the history of Uruguayan theatre or, better said, in the national consciousness, may explain why his plays are more often than not relegated to the stages of schools or amateur groups. However, there is no denying his 'official' position as there are numerous streets, theatres and prizes that honour him by carrying his name. In an attempt to extend his theatre beyond the Southern Cone region, Sánchez visited Italy in 1910, where he died of tuberculosis

Further reading

Castro, Griselda (1988) *Sainete: Análisis de la obra de Florencio Sánchez y Armando Discépolo*, Montevideo: Técnica.

Cruz, J. (1966) *Genio y figura de Florencio Sánchez*, Buenos Aires: EUDEBA.

Lafforgue, J. (1967) *Florencio Sánchez*, Buenos Aires: Centro Editor de América Latina.

Rela, W. (1973) *Repertorio bibliográfico sobre Florencio Sánchez*, Buenos Aires: Instituto de Literatura Argentina, Universidad de Buenos Aires.

Richardson, R. (1933) *Florencio Sánchez and the*

Argentine Theatre, New York: Instituto de las Españas en los Estados Unidos.
Sánchez, F. (1968–69) *Obras completas*, ed. and intro. J. Lafforgue, Buenos Aires: Schapire, 2 vols.

LAURA G. GUTIÉRREZ

Sánchez, Luis Alberto

b. 1900, Lima, Peru; d. 1994, Lima

Literary critic and politician

Sánchez was one of the most important figures of Peruvian intellectual (see **intellectuals**) and political life of the twentieth century. His first book, *Los poetas de la colonia* (The Poets of the Colony) (1921), revealed a precocious erudition as far as Peruvian literature was concerned. He joined the APRA (American Popular Revolutionary Alliance) party in 1930, and was exiled for his opposition to Sánchez Cerro's dictatorship in 1932 and again in 1934. During his years of exile in Chile, he wrote extensively in newspapers and began a series of literary biographies, the first being a biography of Manuel González Prada (1937). Later came *El Inca Garcilaso de la Vega, primer criollo* (Inca Garcilaso de la Vega, First Creole) (1939), *Una mujer sola contra el mundo* (A Woman Alone Against the World) (1942), *Aladino o vida y obra de José Santos Chocano* (Aladino, or Life and Works of José Santos Chocano) (1960), *El doctor océano* (Doctor Ocean) (1967), *Valdelomar, o la belle epoque* (Valdelomar, or the Belle Epoque) (1969) and others. His essays on cultural history located him in the mid-century debates about Latin American identity: *Balance y liquidación del 1900* (Final Account of the 1900 Generation) (1941) and *El Perú: Retrato de un país adolescente* (Peru: Portrait of an Adolescent Country) (1958) among others. However, his major contribution is *La literatura peruana: Derrotero para una historia cultural del Perú* (Peruvian Literature: Route for a Cultural History of Peru, in 5 volumes) (1950–65), in which he traces the origins of Peruvian literature from pre-Hispanic times and tries to define its national character within its social context. His assessments are often anecdotal and impressionistic. His memoirs, *Testimonio personal: Memorias de un peruano del siglo XX* (Personal Testimony: Memoirs of a Twentieth Century Peruvian, in 4 volumes) were published between 1969 and 1976.

Elected a member of the Chamber of Deputies in 1931 and in 1945–48, he was exiled again in 1948, returning to become Senator for Lima, 1963–68. During Alan García's administration (1985–90), he was First Vice-President of Peru.

Further reading

Chang-Rodriguez, E. (1983) *Homenaje a Luis Alberto Sánchez*, Madrid: Insula.
Galindo Vera, V. (1962) *Contribución a la bibliografía de Luis Alberto Sánchez*, Lima: Separata from *Boletín bibliográfico* 35(3–4).
Martínez, J.L. (1967) 'La obra de Luis Alberto Sánchez', *Libro de homenaje a Luis Alberto Sánchez en los 40 años de su docencia universitaria*, Lima: Universidad Mayor Nacional de San Marcos.
Sánchez, L.A. (1988) *La vida del siglo*, Caracas: Biblioteca Ayacucho.

JOSÉ ANTONIO MAZZOTTI

Sánchez, Luis Rafael

b. 1936, Humacao, Puerto Rico

Writer

Sánchez began his career as a playwright, and in 1968 achieved his first major success with *La pasión según Antígona Pérez* (The Passion According to Antígona Pérez), a retelling of the Antigone myth in an unidentified Latin American country. Two opposite currents characterize Sánchez's theatre: an existentialist (see **existentialism**) presentation of human anguish, as in *La espera* (The Wait) (1959), and a comic interest in life as a play with language, originally represented in *Farsa del amor compradito* (Farce of the True Love's Bargain) but best exemplified in *Quíntuples* (Quintuplets) (1985). This second characteristic also marks his fiction. In 1966 he published a collection of short stories, *En cuerpo de camisa* (Short Sleeves Unbuttoned) (1966), which marked a **neo-baroque** direction in his work, linking him with other important Spanish Caribbean writers proposing a similar aesthetics: Luis

Palés Matos, Emilio S. **Belaval**, Alejo **Carpentier** and Severo **Sarduy**, among others.

La ***guaracha del Macho Camacho*** (Macho Camacho's Beat) (1976), his first novel, was a major success and identified Sánchez as a '**post-Boom**' writer. Using different registers of oral Puerto Rican Spanish, he created a personal baroque speech full of puns and wordplays critiquing social conditions in his country. This project was continued in *La importancia de llamarse Daniel Santos* (The Importance of Being Called Daniel Santos) (1988), a text combining narrative and essayistic literary strategies. He called this work a *fabulación*, or hybrid text. In it, Sánchez presented a sampler of Spanish American languages and cultures in which Daniel Santos (1916–92), a popular singer from Puerto Rico known throughout Spanish America, serves as the unifying voice. In 1994 he published *La guagua áerea* (The Air Bus), a collection of essays and articles on Puerto Rican and Latin American social, political and literary issues. In his most important texts, Sánchez works with a neo-baroque camp aesthetics, which he has called *poética de lo soez* (the poetics of the sordid) to recover popular Latin American culture and to create works in which high and low culture, popular and standard languages are combined with humour to produce pleasurable texts that also function as tools for social criticism.

Further reading

Barradas, E. (1981) *Para leer en puertorriqueño: Acercamiento a la obra de Luis Rafael Sánchez*, San Juan: Editorial Cultural.

Fernández Olmos, M. (1987) 'Luis Rafael Sánchez and Rosario Ferré: Sexual Politics and Contemporary Puerto Rican Narrative', *Hispania* 70.

Hernández Vargas, N. and D. Caraballo Abreu (eds) (1985) *Luis Rafael Sánchez: Crítica y bibliografía*, Río Piedras, PR: Universidad de Puerto Rico.

Perivolaris, J. (1997) 'Luis Rafael Sánchez', in V. Smith (ed.), *Encyclopedia of Latin American Literature*, London: Fitzroy Dearborn, 749–53.

Sánchez, L.R. (1980) *Macho Camacho's Beat*, trans. G. Rabassa, New York: Pantheon.

Vázquez Arce, C. (1994) *Por la vereda tropical. Notas sobre la cuentística de Luis Rafael Sánchez*, Buenos Aires: Ediciones de la Flor.

Vélez, D.L. (1984) 'Class, Language and Literature: The Shift in Luis Rafael Sánchez's Narrative Style', *Bilingual Review* 11.

Zamora, L.P. (1983) 'Clichés and Defamiliarization in the Fiction of Manuel Puig and Luis Rafael Sánchez', *Journal of Aesthetics and Art Criticism* 41.

EFRAÍN BARRADAS

Sánchez Juliao, David

b. 1945, Lorica, Colombia

Writer

The short stories of Sánchez Juliao trivialize episodes of daily life, which he usually treats humorously. Some of his short stories, such as 'El Pachanga' (The Pachanga Man) and '¿Por qué me llevas al hospital en canoa, papá?' (Why Are You Taking Me to Hospital in a Canoe, Daddy?), were audiotaped, which made them accessible to a larger audience. He also wrote the novel *Pero sigo siendo el rey* (But I Am Still the King) (1983), based on the lyrics of popular Mexican songs, and which was itself the basis for a soap opera.

Further reading

Noriega, T.A. (1989) ' "Pero sigo siendo el rey': Musicalidad e intertextualidad del relato', *Revista letras* 38: 114–23.

MIGUEL A. CARDINALE

Sánchez Peláez, Juan

b. 1922, Altagracia de Orituco, Venezuela

Poet

Sánchez Peláez's work is one of the outstanding manifestations of **surrealism** in Latin America. His first book, *Elena y los elementos* (Elena and the Elements) (1952), began a poetic adventure marked by a fascination with women, eroticism and the flow of dreams, and a transparent language addressing sacred and mystical themes without becoming hermetic. The adventure continued through his subsequent books: *Rasgos comunes* (Common Features) (1975), *Por cual causa o nostalgia*

(For What Reason or Nostalgia) (1981) and *Aire sobre el aire* (Air on Air) (1989). *Poesía* (Poetry) (1993) gathered all his work together.

Further reading

Cuartin, P. (1994) 'Por los caminos de Animal de costumbre', *Cifra nueva: Revista de cultura,* May, 2: 9–20.

Leonardo, P. (1986) 'Juan Sánchez Peláez: Una poética bajo el látigo del oro', *Escritura: Revista de teoría y crítica literarias,* Jan.–June, 11(21): 101–44.

Marquez, A. (1994) 'Juan Sánchez Peláez: Otra lectura', *Revista iberoamericana,* Jan.–June, 60(166–7): 489–93.

Sánchez Peláez, J. (1985) *Poesía,* Caracas: Monte Avila.

RAFAEL CASTILLO ZAPATA

Sanín Cano, Baldomero

b. 1861, Rionegro, Antioquia, Colombia; d. 1957, Bogotá, Columbia

Literary critic

Publishing book reviews and literary essays for decades in the Colombian newspaper *El Tiempo* and in other periodicals, Sanín Cano was known for his acid wit, his firm commitment to humanist and liberal principles, and his wide-ranging literary and philosophical interests. His best-known work today is *Letras colombianas* (Colombian Literature) (1942), a survey of Colombian literature. Comparable to **Alone** (Hernán Díaz Arrieta) in Chile, he was famous in his day, but so much of his work is topical or occasional that it is no longer widely read.

Further reading

'Homenaje a Baldomero Sanín Cano' (1948) *Revista iberoamericana* 26.

Romera, A.B. (1958) 'Baldomero Sanín Cano', *Atenea* 130(379): 72–88.

Sanín Cano, B. (1980) *El oficio del lector,* ed. and intro. J.G. Cobo Borda, Caracas: Biblioteca Ayacucho.

DANIEL BALDERSTON

Santana, Rodolfo

b. 1944, Caracas, Venezuela

Dramatist and writer

Santana is one of Venezuela's most acclaimed twentieth-century playwrights. He rose to prominence in 1968, when his play *La muerte de Alfredo Gris* (The Death of Alfredo Gris) won him the first of numerous drama prizes. An interest in the metaphysical and in **science fiction** oriented his first plays, but from the 1970s onwards he developed a theatre of clear political commitment. His extraordinary productivity and continual experimenting made him one of the best-known figures in the Venezuelan theatre during its boom years of the 1970s and 1980s. The author of over seventy plays, Santana has also written a number of highly successful film scripts.

Further reading

Santana, R. (1986) *Teatro,* Caracas: Fundarte.

—— (1993) 'Obra para dormir', *Revista del ateneo puertorriqueña,* May–Aug., 3(8): 94–101.

MARK DINNEEN

Sant'anna, Affonso Romano de

b. 1937, Belo Horizonte, Minas Gerais, Brazil

Writer and critic

An acclaimed poet and critic, Affonso Romano de Sant'anna participated in the literary collective *Tendência,* which sustained a productive dialogue with the **concrete poetry** movement of São Paulo during the 1960s. In contrast to the formalist and experimental orientation of the concrete poets, Sant'anna remained committed to verse poetry dedicated to social and historical themes. His best-known poem, 'Que país é este?' (What Kind of Nation is This?) (1980), critiqued official repression and censorship under military rule, and raised questions about national identity as Brazil initiated a return to civilian rule. Sant'anna has also published numerous volumes of literary and cultural criticism, including his influential study, *Música popular e moderna poesia brasileira* (Popular Music and Modern Brazilian Poetry) (1978), which argues for understanding the tradition of Brazilian song within the canon of national poetry.

Further reading

Golin, C. (1991) 'Affonso Romano de Sant'anna: criação poética x teoria', *Brasil/Brazil: Revista de literatura brasileira/A Journal of Brazilian Literature* 6(4): 77–86.

CHRISTOPHER DUNN

Sant'Anna, Sérgio

b. 1941, Rio de Janeiro, Brazil

Writer and playwright

One of Brazil's most important contemporary writers and one of the least discussed outside the country, Sant'Anna is a master story teller influenced by the 1950s Beat Generation and the 1960s and 1970s counterculture. He attended the Iowa International Writing Program with José Emilio **Pacheco**, and there are striking similarities between the works of Mexico's La **Onda** and Sant'Anna's creation of new realities from Brazilian history. No subject is sacrosanct, and few escape Sant'Anna's sardonic wit.

Further reading

Dunn, C. (1998) 'Contrapontos fragmentários: Meta-ficção e produção simbólica em "O conceito de Joao Gilberto no Rio de Janerio" de Sérgio Sant'Anna', *Chasqui: Revista de literatura latinoamericana*, Nov., 27(2): 3–13.

Vieira, N.H. (1992) 'Sergio Sant'Anna: O espectaculo não pode parar', *Brasil/Brazil: Revista de literatura brasileira/A Journal of Brazilian Literature* 5(8): 81–92.

SUSAN CANTY QUINLAN

Santiago, Silviano

b. 1936, Formiga, Brazil

Writer

Santiago's 1981 text *Em liberdade* (At Liberty) – supposedly the diary of Graciliano **Ramos**, author of *Memórias da cárcere* (Prison Memoirs) written after his liberation – combines all of Santiago's activities as critic, essayist, literature professor and writer of fiction. He believes that literary criticism must have a provocative function and has found a way of decolonizing Latin American literature within its dislocated space. In *Stella Manhattan* (1985), about a group of Brazilians in New York during the military dictatorship, he explores that discontinuity, doubling the narrative voice and using the duality of grammatical gender to construct his protagonist Stella-Eduardo. Santiago is also known for his insightful essays on literature and culture, which have been collected in several volumes.

Further reading

Avelar, I. (1999) *The Untimely Present: Postdictatorial Latin American Fiction and the Task of Mourning*, Durham, NC: Duke University Press.

Jackson, K.D. (1993) 'The Prison-House of Memoirs: Silviano Santiago's *Em Liberdade*', in R. Johnson (ed.), *Tropical Paths: Essays on Modern Brazilian Literature*, New York: Garland.

Miranda, W.M. (1992) *Corpos escritos: Graciliano Ramos e Silviano Santiago*, São Paulo: Universidade de São Paulo; UFMG.

Quinlan, S.C. (2002) 'Cross-Dressing: Silviano Santiago's Fictional Performances', in F. Arenas and S.C. Quinlan (ed.), *Lusosex*, Minneapolis: University of Minnesota Press, 208–32.

ADRIANA AMANTE

Santos Febres, Mayra

b. 1966, Carolina, Puerto Rico

Writer

Short story writer and poet, Santos Febres continues into the 1990s the opening for women's literature created in previous decades by Rosario **Ferré**, Ana Lydia **Vega** and Mayra **Montero**. Using the method of the family photograph album, where a private iconography allows new significations of memory, the ten stories of *Pez de vidrio* (Glass Fish) (1991) fuse feminine social constructs and woman's imaginary identities. Her work has been published regularly in magazines since 1984; her two poetry collections, *Anamú y manigua* and *El orden escapado* (Order Escaped), both published in 1991, are reflections on the process of writing. Recent publications include *Urban Oracles: Stories* (1997) and her first novel, *Sirena Selena vestida de pena* (2000), a novel about a gay teenager who cross-dresses as a female singer.

Further reading

Birmingham Pokorny, E.D. (2000) 'Postcolonial Discourse and the Re-thinking of Gender, Identity, and Culture in Mayra Santos Febres's "Broken Strand" ', *Diaspora: Journal of the Annual Afro-Hispanic Literature and Culture Conference*, Spring, 10: 29–37.

Santos Febres, M. (1997) 'Salsa as Translocation', in Celeste Fraser Delgado and José Esteban Muñoz (eds), *Everynight Life: Culture and Dance in Latin/o America*, Durham, NC: Duke University Press.

MARÍA JULIA DAROQUI

Sarduy, Severo

b. 1937, Camagüey, Cuba; d. 1993, Paris, France

Writer

One of the most enigmatic authors of the '**Boom**' in Latin American narrative, Sarduy followed the **neo-baroque** tradition of the Cubans Alejo **Carpentier** and José **Lezama Lima**, matching them in verbal density and literary allusions and sharing their concern with Cuban (and Latin American) identity. He diverges from these masters in his iconoclastic attitude toward sexual identity and issues of representation (transvestism, simulacra, tattooing and so on).

Sarduy was born in a provincial city with a rich literary history. He moved to Havana in the 1950s to study medicine, but his studies were interrupted by the political disturbances of the Batista era. Sarduy was one of the few writers to take a firm stand in the movement against Batista, and he played an important role in the flurry of literary activity following the triumph of the Revolution. He received a fellowship from the new government to study art in Paris in 1959; after the fellowship expired, he stayed, preferring self-exile to the repression he would have experienced in Cuba as a homosexual and a writer.

The next two decades saw Sarduy involved in two of the most influential literary movements of the twentieth century: the Boom in Latin American narrative (in which he took part as novelist and as editor of the Latin American series of Éditions du Seuil), and the structuralist movement centred around the journal *Tel Quel*. Sarduy's first novel *Gestos* (Gestures) (1963), traditional in style and structure, did little to prepare his readers for the experimental nature of his second, now classic, novel *De donde son los cantantes* (From Cuba with a Song) (1967). The issue of Cuban identity is the central theme here; its division into three sections reflects the three ethnic components of the nation (and of Sarduy himself): Spanish, African and Chinese. His third novel, *Cobra* (1972), also explores issues of identity, but more in relation to sexuality.

Sarduy published four other novels, *Maitreya* (1978), *Colibrí* (Hummingbird) (1984), *Cocuyo* (1990) and the posthumous *Pájaros de la playa* (Beach Birds) (1993), as well as the autobiographical essays of *El Cristo de la rue Jacob* (1987). As a poet, Sarduy was a craftsman in the Baroque vein; among his best poems are profound meditations on death and homoerotic sensuality. Sarduy published four books of essays, including the important collection *Ensayos generales sobre el barroco* (General Essays on the Baroque) (1987), showcase of his complex theory of the Baroque, which integrated his interests in cosmology, Lacanian psychoanalysis and linguistics. He died of AIDS in 1993, never having returned to Cuba.

Further reading

Gil, L. (1997) 'Severo Sarduy', in V. Smith (ed.),

Encyclopedia of Latin American Literature, London: Fitzroy Dearborn, 753–4.
González Echevarría, R. (1987) *La ruta de Severo Sarduy*, Hanover, NH: Ediciones del Norte.
—— (1989) 'Severo Sarduy', in C.A. Solé and M.I. Abreu (eds), *Latin American Writers*, New York: Scribners, 3: 1437–44.
Montero, O. (1978) *The Name Game: Writing/Fading Writer in De donde son los cantantes*, Chapel Hill: University of North Carolina Press.
Ríos, J. (ed.) (1976) *Severo Sarduy*, Madrid: Fundamentos.
Rivero Potter, A. (ed.) (1998) *Between the Self and the Void: Essays in Honor of Severo Sarduy*, Boulder, CO: Society of Spanish and Spanish-American Studies.
Sarduy, S. (1975) *Cobra*, trans. S.J. Levine, New York: Dutton.
—— (1986) *Maitreya*, trans. S.J. Levine, Hanover, NH: Ediciones del Norte.
—— (1995) *Christ on the Rue Jacob*, trans. S.J. Levine and C. Maier, San Francisco: Mercury House.
—— (1999) *Obra completa*, ed. G. Guerrero and F. Wahl, Paris: Colección Archivos, 2 vols.

BEN A. HELLER

Sarlo, Beatriz

b. 1942, Buenos Aires, Argentina

Critic

Sarlo has written widely on all areas of literature, including popular romantic literature, the history of journalism and the mass media in Argentina, and cinema and mass culture in relation to artistic production and the role of intellectuals. Since 1978 she has edited the journal ***Punto de vista***. Her major works include *Una modernidad periférica: Buenos Aires 1920 y 1930* (Modernism on the Periphery) (1988) and the best-selling 1990s essay *Escenas de la vida posmoderna* (Scenes of Postmodern Life) (1994). She is also a screenwriter.

Further reading

D'Allemand, P. (2001) 'Beatriz Sarlo: Por una lectura de la pluralidad', in *Hacia una crítica cultural latinoamericana*, Lima: Latinoamericana Editores, 157–68.
Sarlo, B. (2001) *La batalla de las ideas (1943–1973)*, Buenos Aires: Ariel.
—— (2001) *Scenes from Postmodern Life*, Minneapolis and London: University of Minnesota Press.
—— (2001) *Tiempo presente: Notas sobre el cambio de una cultura*, Buenos Aires: Siglo veintiuno editores Argentina.

DANIEL LINK

Sarlos, Eduardo

b. 1937, Budapest, Hungary; d. 1998, Montevideo, Uruguay

Playwright and visual artist

Sarlos moved permanently to Montevideo in 1948. He qualified as an architect in 1971 and began his artistic work in 1979. His career as a playwright began in 1983 with *La pecera* (The Fish-Tank); his *Sarita y Michel* had its premiere in 1993. In the intervening years he wrote ten plays and won ten Uruguayan prizes. In 1994 he participated in the Biennale in Cuenca, Ecuador.

Further reading

Pignataro Calero, J. (1998) 'El dramaturgo Eduardo Sarlos', *Latin American Theatre Review*, Fall, 32(1): 177–82.

MARCO MAGGI

Savia

Savia (Energy) was a cultural and literary magazine published in Guayaquil during the late 1920s, an Ecuadorean *Vanity Fair*. The section entitled 'Periscopio literario' (Literary Periscope) provides a sense of how well informed the literati of Ecuador were about the cultural and intellectual activity of the Hispanic world and beyond. Many of the young Ecuadorean writers of the time published in *Savia*. Discussions about the nature and concept of the avant-garde were aired in its pages, as was the relationship between literature and society and the direction that Ecuadorean literature should follow.

HUMBERTO E. ROBLES

Scalabrini Ortiz, Raúl

b. 1898, Corrientes, Argentina; d. 1959, Buenos Aires, Argentina

Writer

Scalabrini Ortiz became famous in 1931 for his critique of Argentine liberalism, *El hombre que está solo y espera* (The Man Who is Alone and Waits), which critiqued liberal ideas for being out of touch with the 'spirit of the land', and said that the Argentine state built by the nineteenth-century liberals contradicted that spirit. He went on to found FORJA (Radical Orientation Force of Argentine Youth) in 1935 with Arturo **Jauretche** and Luis Dellepiane, and was considered one of the foremost intellectuals of Peronism. He supported Argentine neutrality in the Second World War, and was accused of harbouring pro-Nazi sentiments. His book of poetry *Tierra sin nada, tierra de profetas* (Land of Nothing, Land of Prophets) (1946) expressed his sympathy for Peronism. He also wrote extensively on the Argentine railway system, British penetration in the Argentine economy, foreign lending and national reconstruction. During the Malvinas War a major street in Buenos Aires, formerly called Canning after the British foreign minister, was renamed Scalabrini Ortiz.

Further reading

Shumway, N. (1994) 'Domingo Faustino Sarmiento: The Unnamed Presence in *El hombre que está solo y espera*', in Tulio Halperin Donghi *et al.* (eds), *Sarmiento: Author of a Nation*, Berkeley: University of California Press.

—— (1996) 'The Tribal Imagination: Raul Scalabrini Ortiz's Reconstruction of the Argentine Tribe That Never Was', *Annals of Scholarship: An International Quarterly in the Humanities and Social Sciences* 11(1–2): 83–101.

DANIEL BALDERSTON

Schwartz, Jorge

b. 1944, Posadas, Argentina

Critic and essayist

Though born in Argentina, Schwartz has lived in São Paulo since adolescence. He has played an outstanding role in the field of Latin American writing, emphasizing the right of Brazilian literature and culture to be included in the continental panorama. In this he continued the work of critics of an earlier generation, particularly Antonio **Candido**, Emir **Rodríguez Monegal** and Angel **Rama**. Having published a pioneering work on the fantasy narratives of Murilo **Rubião**, Schwartz turned his attention to the European and Latin American avant-garde of the 1920s and 1930s (see **avant-garde in Latin America**). His writings have become key reference works in the field.

Further reading

Schwartz, Jorge (1983) *Vanguarda e cosmopolitismo na década de 20: Oliverio Girondo e Oswald de Andrade*, São Paulo: Editora Perspectiva.

—— (2001) *Las vanguardias latinoamericanas: Textos programáticos y críticos*, Mexico City: Fondo de Cultura Económica.

BERTA WALDMAN

Schwarz, Roberto

b. 1938, Vienna, Austria

Literary critic and theorist

Schwarz is probably the most influential Brazilian literary critic of his generation. His parents fled from Europe when he was small, and he has lived in Brazil for most of his life. He is inspired by his mentor Antonio **Candido**'s sociological approach to literature and by European Marxist thought.

Schwarz's most influential idea, set out in his book on the nineteenth-century novelist Machado de Assis, *Ao vencedor as batatas* (The Winner gets the Potatoes) (1977), is that of 'idéias fora de lugar', or misplaced ideas. He argues that colonial and ex-colonial countries have often imported ideas along with other more tangible necessities, and that these ideas do not correspond necessarily to local realities. His main example is the liberal ideology of freedom, including the free labour market, imported into a Brazil still run on slave labour. This sets up a curious ideological comedy, for although the ideas are out of place, they are still influential and have a kind of life of their own. This is evident in the treatment of the intermediary class of dependents (*agregados/as*), who were theoretically free (not enslaved), but who in fact had very little practical room for manoeuvre. Their 'betters' had two available ideological systems to deal with them: they could blame them for their own misfortune, since they were 'free', or they could subject them via a more traditional paternalism, or 'favour' (a crucial word in Schwarz's vocabulary).

In his critical essays on nineteenth- and twentieth-century literature and film, Schwarz is very open to such ideological incongruities, in contexts such as the theatre and popular music of the 1960s, which often engaged in a kind of gesturing in place of the effective political action it was barred from, or the poetry of Oswald de **Andrade**, which is revealed as quite socially perceptive. He has also engaged in effective polemic with the concretists (see **concrete poetry**), whom he regards as proponents of a falsely optimistic internationalism. Although the notion of 'misplaced ideas' is easy to oversimplify, it has brought a new realism to the study of national identity throughout Latin America, a field in which Schwarz's ideas have also been influential.

Further reading

Arantes, P.E. (1992) *Sentimento da dialética na experiência intelectual brasileira: Dialética e dualidade segundo Antonio Candido e Roberto Schwarz*, São Paulo: Paz e Terra.

Larsen, N. (2001) 'Roberto Schwarz: A Quiet (Brazilian) Revolution in Critical Theory', in *Determinations*, London: Verso, 75–82.

Schwarz, R. (1977) *Ao vencedor as batatas*, São Paulo: Duas Cidades.

—— (1990) *Um mestre na periferia do capitalismo: Machado de Assis*, São Paulo: Duas Cidades.

—— (1992) *Misplaced Ideas: Essays on Brazilian culture*, trans. J. Gledson, London: Verso.

—— (1999) *Sequências brasileiras: Ensaios*, São Paulo: Companhia das Letras.

—— (2001) *A Master on the Periphery of Capitalism: Machado de Assis*, Durham, NC: Duke University Press.

JOHN GLEDSON

Schwarz-Bart, Simone

b. 1938, Charente-Maritime, France

Writer

Schwarz-Bart's novel *Pluie et vent sur Télumée Miracle* (The Bridge of Beyond) (1972) established her as one of the strongest feminist voices of the Francophone Caribbean. Growing up in Guadeloupe from the age of 3, her language was enriched by creole metaphors. Her works deal with Caribbean resistance to slavery, family breakdowns and economic stagnation. Concerned with genealogy and oral history, Schwarz-Bart's second novel *Ti-Jean L'horizon* (Between Two Worlds) (1979) and her play *Ton beau capitaine* (Your Handsome Captain) (1987), express the social and political malaise experienced by the people of Guadeloupe and the Caribbean.

Further reading

Busia, A.B.A. (1990) 'This Gift of Metaphor: Symbolic Strategies and the Triumph of Survival in Simone Schwartz-Bart's *The Bridge of Beyond*,' in C.B. Davies and E. Savory (eds), *Out of the Kumbla: Caribbean Women and Literature*, Trenton, NJ: Africa World Press, 289–301.

Sourieau, M.-A. (1997) 'Simone Schwarz-Bart', in V. Smith (ed.), *Encyclopedia of Latin American Literature*, London: Fitzroy Dearborn, 756–8.

Schwartz-Bart, S. (1981) *Between Two Worlds*, New York: Harper & Row.

—— (1982) *The Bridge of Beyond*, New York: Atheneum.

Wilson, E. (1992) 'History and Memory in *Un plat de porc aux bananes verts* and *Pluie et vent sur Telumée Miracle*', *Callaloo* 15(1): 179–89.

ANNE MALENA

science fiction

Science fiction writing in Latin America is closely related to the tradition of the fantastic and is often marked by **Borges**'s comment on the improper translation into Spanish of the term as '*Ciencia ficción*', with its Brazilian counterpart as '*Ficcão científica*' or '*Ficcão do tempo*'. Science fiction works in Latin America are often short stories or poetry, and tend to be less constricted by the pressures of mass marketing or pulp publishing than their counterparts in the English-speaking world. Historically, science fiction writing has had a strong tradition in the Río de la Plata region, and to a lesser extent in Mexico, Brazil and Castro's Cuba, with the occasional writer and fan clubs in other countries. In all, science fiction in Latin America can be mapped out through a corpus of texts that present a keen awareness of US and European canonical works of the genre, but very consciously strive to explore different issues related to the role of the region as a consumer, and not a producer, of technology. Latin American writers are often social scientists or humanists and seldom have a background in the so-called hard sciences.

Latin American proto-science fiction might be traced back to texts like *El viaje maravilloso del señor Nic Nac* (The Marvellous Journey of Mr Nic Nac) (1875) or 'Horacio Kalibán o los autómatas' (Horacio Kaliban and the Automatons) by Eduardo L. Holmberg (1852–1937) and to the work of Leopoldo **Lugones**, Horacio **Quiroga** and Macedonio **Fernández** in the Rio de la Plata. Some stories by Amado **Nervo** and the novel, *Mi tío Juan* (My Uncle Juan) (1920), by Francisco Urquizo (1891–1969) mark the beginnings of the genre in Mexico; while in Brazil texts such as *A liga dos planetas* (The League of Planets) (1923) by Albino Coutinho (1860–1940), *Amazonia misteriosa* (Mysterious Amazon) (1925) by Gastão Cruls (1888–1959) and *A filha do Inca* (The Inca's Daughter) (1930) by Menotti del Picchia (1892–1948) precede the popularizing work of Jerónimo Monteiro (1908–70) and that of the publicists Gumersindo Rocha Dorea, founder of GRD.

A number of Latin American science fiction works appeared in short-lived magazines like *Más allá* (1953–57) and *Revista de ciencia ficción y fantasía* (1977) in Argentina or *Magazine de ficção científica* (1970–71) in Brazil. The internet has allowed for a number of discussion groups among science fiction fans in Latin America, and the zine *Axxon* has appeared regularly. There are also a number of prizes, conventions and associations throughout the region, among which the Premio Puebla in Mexico has fostered a strong rebirth of the genre.

Further reading

Acosta, O. *et al.* (1970) *Primera antología de la ciencia ficción latinoamericana*, Buenos Aires: Rodolfo Alonso.

Goordon, B. and A.E. Van Vogt (eds) (1988) *Lo mejor de la ciencia ficción latinoamericana*, Buenos Aires: Hispamérica.

Hurtado, O. (ed.) (1968) *Cuentos cubanos de lo fantástico y lo extraordinario*, Havana: UNEAC.

Molinas Gavilán, Y. (1997) 'Science Fiction', in V. Smith (ed.), *Encyclopedia of Latin American Literature*, London: Fitzroy Dearborn, 760–1.

Souto, M. (ed.) (1985) *Ciencia ficción en la Argentina*, Buenos Aires: EUDEBA.

JACINTO FOMBONA

Scliar, Moacyr

b. 1937, Porto Alegre, Brazil

Writer

The grandson of Russian-born Jewish immigrants, Scliar turned to music, literature and the visual arts as an escape from the anti-Semitism prevalent during his childhood in Porto Alegre. A public health physician and a writer who still grapples with questions of national and cultural identity through short stories, novels and chronicles, Scliar combines the wit of his Jewish ancestry with a Kafkaesque imagination to produce award-winning collections, many of which have been translated into English by Eloah F. Giacomelli, among them *The Ballad of the False Messiah* (1985), *The Carnival of the Animals* (1985), *The Centaur in the Garden* (1984) and *The Volunteers* (1988). He has also written a literary history of medicine.

See also: Jewish writing

Further reading

Barr, L.B. (1996) 'The Jonah Experience: The Jews of Brazil According to Scliar', in Lois Baer Barr and David Sheinein (eds), *The Jewish Diaspora in Latin America: New Studies on History and Literature*, New York: Garland.

Igel, R. (1987) 'Jewish Component in Brazilian Literature: Moacyr Scliar', *Folio: Essays on Foreign Languages and Literatures* 17: 111–18.

Pirott Quintero, L.E. (2000) 'A Centaur in the Text: Negotiating Cultural Multiplicity in Moacyr Scliar's Novel', *Hispania*, Dec., 83(4): 768–78.

Sadow, S.A. (ed.) (1999) *King David's Harp: Autobiographical Essays by Jewish Latin American Writers*, Albuquerque: University of New Mexico Press.

PEGGY SHARPE

Scorza, Manuel

b. 1928, Lima, Peru; d. 1983, Madrid, Spain

Writer

Scorza's important series of five novels fictionalizing the dogged resistance of the peasants of Peru's Cerro del Pasco were collectively titled *La guerra silenciosa* (The Silent War) (1970–9) and were based on his own experience as general secretary of the peasant Movimento Comunal. Originally a poet, his first volume *Acta de remota lejanía* (Proceedings from a Remote Distance) was banned by the Odría dictatorship, as Scorza had been active in the opposition. *Las imprecaciones* (The Curses) was published in 1955 in Mexico, where Scorza was spending the first of several exiles. He was killed in the plane crash that also killed Angel **Rama**, Marta **Traba** and Jorge **Ibargüengoitia**.

Further reading

Aldaz, A.M. (1990) *The Past of the Future: The Novelistic Cycle of Manuel Scorza*, New York: Peter Lang.

Gonzalez Soto, J. (1998) 'Manuel Scorza: Apuntes para una biografía', *Revista de crítica literaria latinoamericana* 24(47): 259–79.

March, K.N. (1997) 'Manuel Scorza', in V. Smith (ed.), *Encyclopedia of Latin American Literature*, London: Fitzroy Dearborn, 761–3.

Scorza, M. (1977) *Drums for Rancas*, trans. E. Grossman, New York: Harper.

—— (1994) *Garabombo the Invisible*, trans. A.M. Aldaz, New York: Peter Lang.

MAGDALENA GARCÍA PINTO

Scott, Dennis

b. 1939, Kingston, Jamaica; d. 1991, New Haven, Connecticut, USA

Poet and dramatist

As a teacher of drama, a performer and a writer, Scott was profoundly influenced by **Brechtian theatre**, which offered a model for a committed and socially conscious theatre, such as that Scott himself produced. His poetry by contrast rests on a tension between an elegant, intellectual deployment of metaphor and verbal wit, on the one hand, and the language of Jamaican speech, on the other. The context of his writing, however, is always a deep social concern and a tone of protest – as in *Uncle Time* (1973) and *Dreadwalk: Poems 1970–78* (1982). His last work, *Strategies* (1989), seems preoccupied with death.

Further reading

Smith, I. (1979) 'Language and Symbol in the Poetry of Dennis Scott', *Carib.* 1: 27–38.

MIKE GONZALEZ

Scott, Lawrence

b. 1943, Trinidad and Tobago

Writer

One of the Caribbean's most talented short story writers, Scott originally went to England to become a Benedictine monk, but later left to do a degree in English. He has taught in London and Trinidad, and worked in the theatre in Trinidad. His novel *Witchbroom* (1993) met with considerable critical acclaim on both sides of the Atlantic and his poetry has been anthologized in *Caribbean New Voices 1*, edited by Stewart Brown. He won the Tom Gallon Award for his short story, 'The House of Funerals', which is included in his collection *Ballad for the New World and Other Stories* (1994). He currently lives in London.

Further reading

Dubois, D. (1999) 'In Search of a New Beginning for the New World in *Witchbroom* by Lawrence Scott', *Commonwealth Essays and Studies*, Autumn, 22(1): 81–8.

—— (2000) 'Guilt, Penance and Reconciliation in Lawrence Scott's *Witchbroom*', *Commonwealth Essays and Studies*, Autumn, 23(1): 43–50.

KEITH JARDIM

Sekou, Lasana M. (Harold H. Lake)

b. 1959, Aruba, Netherlands Antilles

Writer

Sekou is an essayist, dramatist and a prolific poet and short story writer whose English-language publications include *For the Mighty Gods* (1982), *Nativity* (1988) and *Mothernation* (1991). He moved to St Maarten at an early age, studied in the USA and established and manages the House of Nehesi Publishers in St Maarten. Well-versed in Afro-Caribbean poetics, he has been particularly concerned with the detrimental effects of colonialism and the present-day economic, political and cultural dominance of the USA in the Caribbean.

AART G. BROEK

Selva, Salomón de la

b. 1893, León, Nicaragua; d. 1969, Paris, France

Writer

In his youth, Salomón de la Selva moved to the USA and was adopted by a millionaire. He studied at Williams College and wrote his first book in English there, where he worked with poets, Stephen Vincent Bénet and Edna St Vincent Millay. Having served in the British Army during the First World War, he returned to the USA to work with union activist, Samuel Gompers. He moved back to Nicaragua and directed a campaign in the defence of Sandino in 1930. He spent the latter part of his life in Mexico. Eventually he decided to support the Somoza regime and worked in France as a diplomat until his death. His poems invoke a neo-classical mood, and his most famous works are odes to major figures in of the Americas such as Alexander Hamilton and Rubén **Darío**.

DEREK PETREY AND ILEANA RODRÍGUEZ

Selvon, Samuel

b.1923, San Fernando, Trinidad

Writer

Selvon's first novel, *A Brighter Sun* (1952), portrays aspects of colonial Trinidad during the Second World War, a distant event in the everyday life of the obscure village in the sugar cane belt where the protagonist Tiger is born and grows up. The locus of the novel shifts when, equipped with a small hut, two hundred dollars and a milking cow, Tiger begins his adult life with a child bride in a village near Port-of-Spain whose changing circumstances reflect encroaching modernizing projects, new racial configurations and the impact on social and economic life of the presence of American soldiers in Trinidad.

Tiger's hunger for education and self-improvement is in continuous conflict with his fight for survival. It is also the central concern of Moses, the main character of Selvon's seminal novel of West Indian immigration, *The Lonely Londoners* (1956), published six years after Selvon moved to England. The vagaries of immigrant life are captured brilliantly in the hopes and disappointments, struggles and celebrations of the novel's tragi-comic heroes. Facing racism, enduring hunger and bitter cold, most of the characters manage to scam their way from one meal and one dingy room to the next, living in picaresque fashion either off the goodwill of the West Indian immigrant community or by working the system as best they can.

The collection of stories *Ways of Sunlight* (1957) brings together the two main sources of Selvon's writing, with Part One set in Trinidad and Part Two set in London. The stories of the first half comment on and explain the immigration phenomenon. Life on the island is hard, although the islanders attempt to ease these hardships through humour, a characteristic indispensable for life in London. The London stories are less bleak than in Selvon's previous work; life is still a hustle, but song and dance, sport and male–female relationships provide increased interaction between West Indians and whites. There are moments of triumph and tenderness, which suggest hope in the ability of the indomitable West Indian spirit to adapt and survive without losing key aspects of identity.

Further reading

Nasta, S. (1988) *Critical Perspectives on Sam Selvon*, Washington, DC: Three Continents Press.

Wyke, C. (1991) *Sam Selvon's Dialectal Style and Fictional Strategy*, Vancouver: University of British Columbia Press.

LORRAINE LEU

Senior, Olive

b. 1941, Trelawny, Jamaica

Writer

Her first volume of poetry, *Talking of Trees* (1985), has strong correlations with her second, *Gardening in the Tropics* (1994); through powerful and unusual imagery, both explore the relation of nature to the human. Senior's stories, the prize-winning *Summer Lightning and Other Stories* (1987), *Arrival of the Snake Woman and Other Stories* (1989) and *Discerner of Hearts and Other Stories* (1995), are written often with a sharp wit, always with empathy for the complex realities of life for Jamaicans, and using Jamaican creole (see **nation language**) and Jamaican-accented international English.

Further reading

Flockemann, M. (1988) 'Asian Diasporas, Contending Identities and New Configurations: Stories by Agnes Sam and Olive Senior', *English in Africa*, May, 25(1): 71–86.

Pollard, V. (1988) 'An Introduction to the Poetry and Fiction of Olive Senior', *Callaloo* 3.

Rodriguez, L. (2000) 'Langue, parole, traduction: Balisage geolinguistique de "Summer Lightning" et "Country of the One Eye God" d'Olive Senior', *Palimpsestes* 12: 91–7.

ELAINE SAVORY

Señor Presidente, El

Miguel Angel **Asturias**'s famous novel was published in 1946 but written, according to its author, between 1922 and 1932. The paradigmatic example of the *novela de dictador* (dictatorship novel), it gives a demonic, almost oneiric view of a reign of terror. Based loosely on the dictatorship of Manuel Estrada Cabrera, who ruled Guatemala from 1898 to 1920, Asturias writes in poetic, incantatory prose of memorable characters known by nicknames such as Cara de Angel (angel face), Pelele (rag doll) and Terciopelo (velvet). Translated into many languages, *El Señor Presidente* established Asturias as one of Latin America's major writers, and anticipated later works by **Carpentier**, **García Márez**, **Roa Bastos** and others on the theme of dictatorship.

Further reading

Asturias, M.A. (1963) *The Presidente*, trans. F. Partridge, London: Victor Gollancz.

—— (2000) *El Señor Presidente*, ed. G. Martin, Paris: Colección Archivos.

Davies, L.H. (1997) 'El Señor Presidente', in V. Smith (ed.), *Encyclopedia of Latin American Literature*, London: Fitzroy Dearborn, 79–81.

Himelblau, J. (1973) '*El Señor Presidente*: Antecedents, Sources and Reality', *Hispanic Review* 41: 43–78.

Martin, G. (1970) '*El Señor Presidente* and How to Read It', *Bulletin of Hispanic Studies* 47: 223–43.

DANIEL BALDERSTON

Sepúlveda, Luis

b. 1949, Ovalle, Chile

Writer

Bodyguard to Salvador Allende, Sepúlveda was arrested and tortured after the military *coup* of September 1973 and imprisoned for two and a half years. Released into exile, he travelled throughout Latin America and was in Nicaragua during and after the Sandinista Revolution of 1979. In 1982 he moved to Germany where he still lives. His writings include *Un viejo que leía novelas de amor* (An Old Man Who Read Love Stories) (1992), *Patagonia Express* (1995), *Historia de un killer profesional* (1998) and *La última película de El Gordo y El Flaco* (Laurel and Hardy's Last Film) (1999).

Further reading

Cid Hidalgo, J.D. (1998) 'El acto de "leer" en *Un viejo que leía novelas de amor*: Aproximación a Luis Sepúlveda', *Atenea*, Jan.–June, 477: 241–7.

Lewis, B.L. (1999) 'Paths of Discovery: Escape and Return in Manuel Puig's *Los ojos de Greta Garbo* and Luis Sepúlveda's *Un viejo que leía novelas de amor*', *Publications of the Arkansas Philological Association*, Fall, 25(2): 23–31.

EUGENIA NEVES

sertões, Os

One of the most powerful works of Brazilian literature, Euclides da **Cunha**'s classic work of 1902 *Os sertões* (Rebellion in the Backlands) is an account of the Brazilian republican army's expeditions against a ragtag group of religious sectarians in the town of Canudos, Bahia, who were grouped around a prophet known to them as Antonio Conselheiro. Da Cunha, a military engineer by training and a positivist by belief, wrote his original dispatches from the battlefield in 1897; over the next five years he wrote and rewrote them feverishly. The final work was long, dense and searing; although it maintains the structure of a positivist discourse (discussion of the natural environment, human society, followed by an account of the individual case of Antonio Conselheiro and his followers in Canudos), it actually narrates a crisis of faith in positivism and in the liberal project of the new Brazilian republic. Few works of world literature tell more powerfully of a campaign of genocide; da Cunha's account, which initially springs from a paradigm not unlike Sarmiento's **civilization and barbarism**, ends up calling that ideology radically into question. There is a brilliant English translation of the novel by Samuel Putnam, while Mario **Vargas Llosa** retells the story of Canudos in his novel *La guerra del fin del mundo* (War of the End of the World) (1981); it has also been the subject of several films and other adaptations.

Further reading

Cunha, E. da (1985) *Os sertões*, ed. W.N. Galvão, São Paulo: Edusp.

—— (1985) *Rebellion in the Backlands*, trans. S. Putnam, New York: Viking.

Oliveira, F. de (1983) *Euclydes: A espada e a letra*, Rio de Janeiro: Paz e Terra.

DANIEL BALDERSTON

Seymour, Arthur James

b. 1914, Georgetown, British Guiana; d. *c.*1980s, Georgetown

Writer

One of the founders of West Indian literature, Seymour started the literary journal ***Kyk-Over-Al***, in British Guiana (now Guyana) in 1945, and edited it until 1961. He later revived it, with Ian **McDonald**, in the 1980s. Seymour recognized early the importance of language and the traditions of folk culture in building a national literature. In 1970 his key role in that process was acknowledged with the award of Guyana's Golden Arrow of Achievement. His own collections of poetry include *Sun's in My Blood* (1945), *Poetry in these Sunny Lands* (1945), *The Guiana Book* (1948) and *Images of Majority* (1978).

Further reading;

Christiani, J. (ed.) (1974) *A. J. Seymour: A Bibliography*, Georgetown, Guyana: National Library.

McLeod, A L. (1982) 'Tradition and Transition: A. J. Seymour and the Poetry of Guyana', *ACLALS Bulletin*, Ridge Singapore, Nov., 6(1): 42–54.

Seymour, A.J. (1980) *The Making of Guyanese Literature*, Georgetown: Guyana National Lithographic Co.

KEITH JARDIM

Shimose, Pedro

b. 1940, Riberalta, Bolivia

Poet

Arriving in La Paz in the 1960s with aspirations to become a journalist, Shimose, of Japanese descent, made his mark as the voice of the new poetry, first of all in popular songs. *Triludio en el exilio* (Trilude in Exile) (1961) opened new avenues of formal innovation, while *Poemas para un pueblo* (Poems for a People) (1968) explored new Bolivian and universal human dimensions. In 1972 he was awarded the **Casa de las Américas** poetry prize for *Quiero escribir pero me sale espuma* (I Try to Write But I Foam at the Mouth). Exiled in Spain since the 1970s, he has published *Reflexiones maquiavélicas* (Machiavellian Reflections) (1980) and *Bolero de Caballería* (Cavalry Bolero) (1985). He is also an art, cinema and theatre critic and a journalist.

Further reading

Chávez Taborga, C. (1974) *Shimose, poeta en cuatro estaciones*, Mérida, Venezuela: Universidad de loa Andes.

Hurtado Suárez, O.G. (1976) *Pedro Shimose y su obra*, Trinidad: Universidad Boliviana José Ballivián.

Ortega, J. (1973) *Letras bolivianas de hoy: Renato Prada y Pedro Shimose*, Buenos Aires: Fernando García Cambeiro.

Shimose, P. (1988) *Poemas*, Madrid: Playor.

J.M. DE LA VEGA RODRÍGUEZ

Shinebourne, Janice

b. 1947, Rosehall, British Guiana

Writer

Of East Indian and Chinese descent, Shinebourne grew up in rural surroundings before moving to Georgetown and then to London, where she now lives. Her two novels, *Timepiece* (1986) and *The Last English Plantation* (1989), explore the experiences of young women in Guyana. Both are contextualized by important periods in modern Guyanese history, the former set during troubled times of racial conflict in 1965, the latter during another politically turbulent time in the 1950s, when British troops arrived in the then British colony. Her stories have appeared in West Indian short story collections.

Further reading

Poynting, J. (1990) 'You Want to Be a Coolie Woman?': Gender and Ethnic Identity in Indo-Caribbean Women's Writing', in S.R. Cudjoe (ed.), *Caribbean Women Writers: Essays from the First International Conference*, Wellesley: Calaloux, 98–105.

Pyne Timothy, H. (1998) 'Language as Subversion in Postcolonial Literature: The Case of Two

Caribbean Women Writers', *MaComere: Journal of the Association of Caribbean Women Writers and Scholars* 1: 101–14

ELAINE SAVORY

short story

Horacio **Quiroga**, in his 'Decálogo del perfecto cuentista' (Ten Commandments for the Writer of Short Stories) (1927), recommends concision, intensity and narrow focus. These recommendations, learned from a reading of those whom Quiroga calls 'the masters' – Poe, Maupassant, Kipling and Chekhov – show that Quiroga had a conscious idea of the short story genre as something with its own laws and traditions, distinct from other kinds of narrative. Critics who have argued that the Latin American short story starts much earlier – Esteban Echeverría's 'El matadero' (The Slaughterhouse) (written around 1838, published posthumously in 1871) is often suggested as a starting point, or even earlier short narratives in the chronicles of the Conquest – have not convincingly shown that these earlier writers were as conscious of a short story genre. Quiroga experimented with point of view – he told the same plot in 'El hombre muerto' (The Dead Man) (1920) and 'Las moscas' (The Flies) (1923), once from the point of view of the dying man, then from that of the flies buzzing around his corpse. He was able to incorporate into the same story a narration of what happens and of what the characters think is happening and hope will happen, and still leave room for the reader to come to a conclusion or make a judgement on the events – and all of this in a very few pages. 'El hijo' (The Son) (1928) is one of Quiroga's most controlled experiments, and a masterpiece: the story tells of the son's setting out on a hunt full of hopes and of the father's imagining, waiting and final madness, and yet the reader is required to complete the tale.

If Quiroga was the inventor of the modern short story in Spanish America (Machado de Assis is the parallel figure in Brazil, somewhat earlier), then **Borges** was its most influential practitioner in the middle decades of the twentieth century. Like Quiroga, he was intensely conscious of the rules of the game: in his essay 'Los laberintos policiales y Chesterton' (Detective Mazes and Chesterton) (1936), he lays out six rules for the detective story, and his essay on Nathaniel Hawthorne makes clear the distinctions he sees between the short story and the novel. Yet he is also intensely involved in experimenting within the rigorous limits of the short story genre; his detective stories play with the rules he offers in the essay on Chesterton, without breaking them, while many other stories are written as if they were book reviews or some other genre, thus making the reader work out the generic conventions that apply. Borges was responsible in large measure for the popularity of the fantastic short story (see **fantastic literature**) and of **science fiction**, as well as of **crime fiction**.

Other notable practitioners of the short story genre are Mário de **Andrade**, Graciliano **Ramos**, João Guimarães **Rosa**, Clarice **Lispector** and Rubem **Fonseca** in Brazil; Julio **Cortázar**, Silvina **Ocampo**, Adolfo **Bioy Casares** and Ricardo **Piglia** in Argentina; Felisberto **Hernández** and Juan Carlos **Onetti** in Uruguay; Augusto **Roa Bastos** in Paraguay; Augusto **D'Halmar**, María Luisa **Bombal**, Francisco **Coloane** and José **Donoso** in Chile; Julio Ramón **Ribeyro** in Peru; Gabriel **García Márquez** in Colombia; **Salarrué** in El Salvador; Sergio **Ramírez** in Nicaragua; Elena **Garro**, Rosario **Castellanos** and Juan **Rulfo** in Mexico; Virgilio **Piñera** in Cuba; José Luis **González**, Rosario **Ferré** and Ana Lydia **Vega** in Puerto Rico; and Juan **Bosch** in the Dominican Republic.

Short story anthologies from the region number in the thousands. Some are devoted to specific genres (the detective story, the fantastic story, science fiction), some to particular topics (the seven deadly sins, the Ten Commandments, Christmas, sex, revolution) military, bureaucracy, carnival, football/soccer), some to writers of particular kinds (women, blacks, Yugoslav-Chileans, policemen, writers working in advertising, actors, physicians). Argentina and Brazil are by far the largest producers of short story anthologies.

The short story came to prominence in twentieth-century Latin America with the growth of mass circulation newspapers and magazines. Borges, Quiroga, Onetti, **Arlt** and others published in the newspaper *Crítica*, Quiroga in *El Hogar* and

Borges in *La Nación*. The requirement that Poe set for the short story and the lyric poem – that they can be read during one sitting – has perhaps made possible the success of the genre in our busy world, as readers on noisy subways and buses confirm. Cortázar writes in a famous essay on the short story:

> A competent short-story writer can write stories that are valid in a literary way, but if someone has had the experience of trying to break loose from a story as if it were a vermin on the skin, one knows the difference between possession and literary recipes.... In a way that no technique could teach or provide for, the great short story condenses that obsession with vermin, it is a hallucinatory presence that imposes itself from the first sentences to fascinate the reader, to make him or her lose contact with the frayed reality around, to drag the reader to an intense, overpowering submersion.
>
> (*Ultimo round*, p. 38)

Further reading

Balderston, D. (1992) *The Latin American Short Story: An Annotated Guide to Anthologies and Criticism*, New York: Greenwood Press.

—— (1996) 'The Twentieth-Century Short Story in Spanish America', in R. González Echevarría and E. Pupo-Walker (eds), *Cambridge History of Latin American Literature*, Cambridge: Cambridge University Press, 2, 465–96.

Cortázar, J. (1969) 'Del cuento breve y sus alrededores', *Ultimo round*, Buenos Aires: Sudamericana.

Gotlib, N.B. (1990) *Teoria do Conto*, São Paulo: Editora Atica.

Jackson, K.D. (1996) 'The Brazilian Short Story', in R. González Echevarría and E. Pupo-Walker (eds), *Cambridge History of Latin American Literature*, Cambridge: Cambridge University Press, 3, 207–32.

Mora, G. (1985) *En torno al cuento: De la teoría general y de su práctica en Hispanoamérica*, Madrid: José Porrúa Turanzas.

Pacheco, C. and L. Barrera Linares (eds) (1993) *Del cuento y sus alrededores*, Caracas: Monte Avila.

Pupo-Walker, E. (ed.) (1973) *El cuento hispanoamericano ante la crítica*, Madrid: Editorial Castalia.

DANIEL BALDERSTON

Shrinivasi

b. 1926, Corony District, Suriname

Poet

Shrinivasi (Martinus Haridat Lutchman) published most of his poetry in Dutch, with a limited number in his native Hindi and Sarnami. Although at times quite critical of the social and political vicissitudes of his native Suriname, he is above all concerned with the wonders of the co-existence of various ethnic groups. Shrinivasi tends to emphasize the beauty, unity and grand moments of cultural diversity. Most of his work was privately published, but in 1984 a Dutch publishing house printed a wide selection of his work titled *Een weinig van het andere* (A Little of Something Else).

Further reading

Shrinivasi and T. Doelwijt (eds) (1981) *Rebirth in Words: Poetry and Prose from Suriname*, Paramaribo: Ministry of Culture, Youth and Sports.

Van Kempen, M. and M. Szulc-Krzyzanowski (1992) *Deep Rooted Words*, Amsterdam: Voetnoot, 173–97.

AART G. BROEK

Siete ensayos de interpretación de la realidad peruana

José Carlos **Mariátegui**'s *Siete ensayos* (Seven Interpretive Essays on Peruvian Reality), published in 1928, was described by its author as 'a contribution to the socialist critique of Peruvian history and its problems'. The framework was specifically Marxist – the product of the evolution of Mariátegui's own thinking through the previous decade. In its seven essays the work sets out to analyse the key contradictions in Peruvian society. The first essay considers the development of a Peruvian economy still locked in export-oriented production and dominated by the old land-holding class. Thus the key obstacle to social and economic transformation is 'The Problem of the Land' (the title of the third essay in the volume) – the forms of property that bind it to outmoded and backward forms of production. Peru's oppressed indigenous minorities are not only symbolic of the nature of those persisting relationships – they are also the key to the future development of Peruvian society in a socialist direction (as Mariátegui argues in the second essay, 'The Problem of the Indian'). He echoes his fellow *indigenista* (see ***indigenismo***) intellectuals in seeing in Indian communal organization (the *ayllu*) the basis of a co-operative and egalitarian society – in other words, a kind of 'historic socialism' that makes the contemporary socialist project realistic and feasible in a Peruvian context. In addressing the issues of religion and education in the fourth and fifth essays, Mariátegui acknowledges the impact of ideology on all social processes, and particularly where the Roman Catholic Church has colluded in maintaining the economic structures that he earlier analyses. In Peruvian 'regionalism' (the subject of the sixth essay) (see ***regionalismo***) Mariátegui sees the expression of local and sectoral interests that will inhibit progress towards national integration. The seventh essay is a masterly review of the history of Peruvian literature, set within the overall materialist interpretation of Peruvian reality. This seminal work of Latin American Marxism has been claimed by many political currents – Maoists, revolutionary nationalists, communists, Trotskyists.

Mariátegui died in 1930, having presented two lengthy articles to the Meeting of Latin American Communist Parties in Montevideo just months earlier, which suggested new developments in his thinking – one in the direction of a Latin American socialist programme on ethnicity, the other warning against any confusion between a populist anti-imperialism and a socialist perspective. The theses presented in the *Siete ensayos* could be seen as arguments for national liberation, for the kind of indigenous separatism advocated later by Sendero Luminoso or for a Trotskyist concept of 'permanent revolution' – acknowledging that the Peruvian bourgeoisie was incapable of carrying through the national project so that it would fall to indigenous and workers' organizations to carry through a revolutionary transformation. Mariátegui was, after all, vigorously engaged in the building of both throughout his brief political life. The polemic over the political practices that flow from the *Siete ensayos* will continue, but there can be no doubt of this work's integrated and epoch-making Marxist analysis of a Latin American society. The tragedy is that Mariátegui's early death, and the opportunist interpretations to which his work was subject in the years that followed, have served to obscure the importance of this foundational work.

Further reading

Romero, Emilio *et al.* (1979) *7 ensayos, 50 años de historia*, Lima: Biblioteca Amauta.

Falcon, J. (1978) *Anatomía de los 7 ensayos de Mariátegui*, Lima: Empresa Editores Amauta.

Mariátegui, J. (1971) *Seven Interpretative Essays on Peruvian Reality*, trans. J. Urquidi, Austin: University of Texas Press.

—— (1979) *7 ensayos de interpretación de la realidad peruana*, intro. A. Quijano, Caracas: Biblioteca Ayacucho.

MIKE GONZALEZ

Sieveking, Alejandro

b. 1934, Rengo, Chile

Playwright

Part of a new theatrical movement of the 1950s and 1960s, Sieveking's plays address reality through myth and a sophisticated awareness of psychology. His twenty-seven plays include *Mi hermano Cristián* (My Brother Cristian) (1957), *Animas de día claro* (Clear-Day Souls) (1962), which won the Laurel de Oro Prize, and *Tres tristes tigres* (Three Sad Tigers) (1967), whose cast of characters are lost and alienated beings in a consumer society that can offer them nothing.

Other works include *La mantis religiosa* (Praying Mantis) (1971), *La virgen de la manito cerrada* (The Virgin with the Little Closed Hand) (1973), which won the Critics' Prize, and *Pequeños animales abatidos* (Little Beaten Animals) (1975), which won the **Casa de las Américas** prize.

Further reading

Bravo Elizondo, P. (1979) 'Entrevista con Alejandro Sieveking', *Latin American Theatre Review* 12(2): 55–9.

—— (1991) 'Entrevista a Bélgica Castro y Alejandro Sieveking, teatristas chilenos (noviembre 25, 1989, San José, Costa Rica)', *Alba de America: Revista literaria* 9(16–17): 371–9.

Del Río, M. (1961) 'Alejandro Sieveking y el teatro en Chile', *Cuadernos de Bellas Artes* (Mexico City) 2(4): 31–6.

Sieveking, A. (1974) *Tres obras de teatro*, Santiago: Editorial Universitaria.

—— (1986) *The Praying Mantis and Other Plays*, Oshkosh, WI: G.M.W. Publications.

MARINA PIANCA

siglo de las luces, El

El siglo de las luces (Explosion in a Cathedral) is a novel by Alejo **Carpentier**, published in Mexico in 1962. It traces the influence of the French Revolution on late eighteenth-century Latin American independence movements. It embraces two decades (1789–1809) in the Caribbean, France and Spain, but specifically concerns Cuba at a time of economic change and growing anti-colonial ideas. The action focuses on the fate of an archetypal upper bourgeois Cuban family immersed in the social upheavals of the time. Its narrative experimentation corresponds to what its author called '*lo* ***real maravilloso***'. A film version, directed by Humberto Solás, appeared in 1991.

Further reading

Carpentier, A. (1963) *Explosion in a Cathedral*, trans. J. Sturrock, Boston: Little, Brown and London: Gollancz.

Castellanos, R. (1966) 'Incursión por *El siglo de las luces*', *Juicios Sumarios*, Xalapa: Universidad Veracruzana, 160–4.

García-Carranza, A. (1983) 'Bibliografía de *El siglo de las luces*', *Imán* 1: 261–80.

Márquez Rodríguez, A. (1970) '*El siglo de las luces* o la revolución trastornada', *La obra narrativa de Alejo Carpentier*, Caracas: Universidad Central de Venezuela, 97–154.

WILFREDO CANCIO ISLA

Silva, Aguinaldo

b. 1944, Pernambuco, Brazil

Screenwriter, novelist and journalist

Since 1964, Silva has written about the marginal population of Rio de Janeiro: drag queens, prostitutes, homosexuals, factory workers, murderers. He often explores the relationship between corrupt police and crime networks and chronicles the repressive tactics of the military dictatorship in works such as *Esquadrão da morte* (Death Squad) (1978), *A república dos assassinos* (The Assassins' Republic) (1979) and *O homem que comprou o Rio* (The Man Who Bought Rio) (1986). Silva has written many successful television screenplays and *telenovelas* for TV Globo in partnership with Doc Comparato and Dias Gomes. He was also one of the editors of Rio de Janeiro's gay newspaper, *Lampião*, during the 1970s.

Further reading

Antonio, J. (1986) 'Dois escritores brasileiros', *Minas Gerais, suplemento literario*, March, 21(1013): 10.

Foster, D.W. (1988) 'The Search for Text: Some Examples of Latin American Gay Writing', *Ibero Amerikanisches Archiv* 14(3): 329–56.

SUSAN CANTY QUINLAN

Simpson, Louis

b. 1923, Kingston, Jamaica

Poet, critic and academic

Joining his mother in New York upon his father's death in 1940, Simpson deliberately avoided Jamaica until 1991, when he returned at the invitation of the University of the West Indies. Best known as a poet and critic, Simpson has also written a novel and autobiography. Educated at Columbia University and the University of Paris, he has since 1967 taught English and Comparative Literature at Stony Brook (New York).

Further reading

Lazer, H. (ed.) (1988) *On Louis Simpson: Depths beyond Happiness*, Ann Arbor: University of Michigan Press.

Moran, R. (1996) 'Louis Simpson: An Interview', *Five-Points*, Fall, 1(1): 45–63.

Taylor, H. (1990) 'Great Experiments: The Poetry of Louis Simpson', *The Hollins Critic*, June, 27(3): 1–12.

PAT DUNN AND PAMELA MORDECAI

Sinán, Rogelio

b. 1904, Taboga Island, Panama; d. 1994, Panama City

Writer

Panama's leading writer, Sinán (Bernardo Domínguez Alba) was drawn early to experimental techniques. His inclusion in Seymour Menton's 1964 anthology *Antología del cuento hispanoamericano* (Anthology of Spanish American Short Stories) assured him of an international audience. Since then his stories, which explore the workings of the unconscious, have been widely anthologized; they include 'La boina roja' (The Red Beret), 'Hechizo' (Bewitchment) and 'A la orilla de las estatuas maduras' (On the Edge of Mature Statues). His first novel *Pelinunio* was acclaimed as the Best Latin American Novel of 1947 by the PEN Club of Santiago, Chile; his last novel, *La isla mágica* (The Magical Island) (1977), was re-issued in 1985 by **Casa de las Américas** to critical acclaim.

Further reading

García, I. (1989) 'Rogelio Sinán', in C.A. Solé and M.I. Abreu (eds), *Latin American Writers*, New York: Scribners, 2, 941–6.

Guardia, G. (1975) *Rogelio Sinán: Una revisión de la vanguardia en Panamá*, Panama City: Litho-Impresora Panamá.

Sinán, R. (1971) *Cuentos de Rogelio Sinán*, San José, Costa Rica.

NORMAN S. HOLLAND

Skármeta, Antonio

b. 1940, Antofagasta, Chile

Writer and media personality

One of Latin America's most important **post-Boom** writers, Skármeta has rejected much of the stylistic experimentation which characterized the work of many **Boom** writers, and has criticized these writers for their tendency to subvert reality at the expense of narrative unity and direct political engagement. Aside from his work as a writer and literary critic, he is also an accomplished filmmaker, winning awards in film festivals in both Europe and the Americas, most notably for the script for the Oscar-winning *Il Postino* (The Postman), which was based on his novel *Ardiente paciencia* (Burning Patience) (1985).

As a boy of 9, Skármeta left Chile for Buenos Aires where his parents were seeking work; he took a series of odd jobs to help his family, returning to Chile three years later. As a schoolboy, he began to read Pablo **Neruda**, who later became a major influence on him. His first short story 'El señor Avila' (Mr Avila) was published in 1959, while he was a student in Chile. After graduation, he studied at Columbia University in New York, completing an MA thesis on Julio **Cortázar**. During this period he translated the work of several US writers, among them Fitzgerald, Mailer and Kerouac. Returning to teach Latin American literature in Chile, he edited the literary magazine *Ercilla* and published his first collection of short stories, *El entusiasmo* (Enthusiasm) (1967). His second, *Desnudo en el tejado* (Naked on the Roof) (1969), won the **Casa de las Américas** prize.

Skármeta held various government positions under Salvador Allende's Popular Unity coalition and ran seminars and workshops for young writers. Subsequent collections of short stories, *El ciclista del San Cristóbal* (The Cyclist of San Cristobal) and *Tiro libre* (Free Shot), both appeared in 1973, the year the Allende government was toppled by Augusto

Pinochet (an English version of some of them, *Watch Where the Wolf is Going*, appeared in 1991). While in exile in Argentina, he published his first novel, *Soñé que la nieve ardía* (I Dreamt the Snow Was Burning) (1975), and began to write for the cinema and radio. Two novels followed: *No pasó nada* (Play On) (1980), which marked Skármeta's contribution to the Latin American novel of exile, and *La insurrección* (The Insurrection) (1982), set during the Nicaraguan Revolution days before the fall of Somoza. Skármeta returned to Santiago in 1988; *Match Ball* (1989) was his first novel to appear after his return. Since 1992 he has hosted a popular (and prize-winning) television programme *El show de los libros.*

Although his short stories and novels have been translated into twenty languages, his best-known work remains the novel *Ardiente paciencia*; set in Chile near the home of Neruda, the novel coincides with the rise and fall of the Allende government. The novel's adaptation as the screenplay for the film *Il Postino* brought Skármeta international popularity and renown.

Further reading

Lemaître, M. (1991) *Skármeta, una narrativa de la liberación*, Santiago: Pehuén.

Lira, C. (1985) *Skármeta: La inteligencia de los sentidos*, Santiago de Chile: Dante.

Pope, R.D. (2002) 'Antonio Skármeta', in C. Solé and K. Müller-Bergh (eds), *Latin American Writers: Supplement I*, New York: Scribners, 529–44.

Shaw, D.L. (1994) *Antonio Skármeta and the Post-Boom*, Hanover, NH: Ediciones del Norte.

—— (1997) 'Antonio Skármeta', in V. Smith (ed.), *Encyclopedia of Latin American Literature*, London: Fitzroy Dearborn, 765–7.

Silva Cáceres, R. (ed.) (1983) *Del cuerpo a las palabras: La narrativa de Antonio Skármeta*, Madrid: Literatura Americana Reunida.

Skármeta, A. (1983) *The Insurrection*, trans. P. Sharp, Hanover, NH: Ediciones del Norte.

—— (1988) *Burning Patience*, trans. K. Silver, New York: Pantheon.

LÁZARO LIMA

Slory, Michaël A.

b. 1935, Corony District, Suriname

Poet

In 1961 Slory published the first of his more than twenty poetry collections in Dutch and in Sranan Tongo. The social and political reality, both in Suriname and elsewhere, are the essential sources of inspiration for much of his writing. Thematically, his poetry is anti-colonial and politically leftist, while linguistically it shows a great command of the various registers of Sranan Tongo. In 1991 a large selection of his poetry was published in Dutch translation (*Een andere weg*), demonstrating his preoccupation with the beauty of Surinamese nature and black women.

Further reading

Egbers, H. (1991) 'Michaël Slory: Dichter van het onvervulde verlangen', *Ons Erfdeel* (Bekkem) 34(4): 482–91.

AART G. BROEK

Smith, Michael ('Mikey')

b. 1954, Kingston, Jamaica; d. 1983, Kingston

Poet and dub performer

Michael ('Mikey') Smith achieved great popularity as a dub poet (see **dub poetry**). In the two years prior to his death in 1983, he toured the Caribbean and Europe with tremendous success. A prophetic poem said he would die 'fighting': in fact, a stone hurled in a political incident killed him. An extraordinary performer, Smith used Jamaican creole and elements of popular culture to 'ground' his work; it appears recorded in *Mi Cyaan Believe It* (1982) and in the posthumous collection, *It a Come* (1986). In dub tradition, his poems inveigh against poverty, racism and dirty politics, the legacies of a greedy, culturally bankrupt society.

PAT DUNN AND PAMELA MORDECAI

Sna Jtz'ibajom

A non-profit writing collective of Tzotzil and Tzeltal Mayan speakers based in San Cristóbal de las Casas, in the south-eastern Mexican state of Chiapas, Sna Jtz'ibajom (The Writer's House) began as an oral history workshop, became a travelling puppet theatre and began performing live theatre under the name Lo'il Maxil ('Monkey Business') in 1985. Most of their plays are dramatized Mayan folktales conducted in Tzotzil but others address problems of family planning, domestic violence and immigration. Their production *De todos para todos* (From All, For All) (1994) portrays sympathetically the Mayan uprising that began barely a month before its premier. A feminist offshoot from this group started La Fomma theatre group.

Further reading

Frischmann, D.H. (1994) 'New Mayan Theatre in Chiapas: Anthropology, Literacy, and Social Drama', in D. Taylor and J. Villegas (ed.), *Negotiating Performance: Gender, Sexuality, and Theatricality in Latin/o America*, Durham, NC: Duke University Press, 213–38

Steele, C. (1994) ' "A Woman Fell into the River": Negotiating Female Subjects in Contemporary Mayan Theatre', in D. Taylor and J. Villegas (ed.), *Negotiating Performance: Gender, Sexuality, and Theatricality in Latin/o America*, Durham, NC: Duke University Press, 239–56.

CYNTHIA STEELE

Soca, Susana

b. 1906, Montevideo, Uruguay; d. 1959, Rio de Janeiro, Brazil

Writer and editor

Soca wrote several books of poetry – *En un país de la memoria* (In a Country of Memory) (1959) and *Noche cerrada* (Black Night) (1962) – but she is remembered chiefly for her activities as director of the journals *La Licorne* and *Cuadernos de la Licorne*, published in Paris. **Borges** wrote a beautiful sonnet about her after her death, and **Onetti** and **Real de Azúa** beautiful prose tributes. As a cultural figure she was somewhat comparable to Victoria **Ocampo**, but with a very different sphere of influence. She died tragically in a plane accident.

Further reading

Alvarez Márquez, J. (2001) *Susana Soca, esa desconocida*, Montevideo: Linardi y Risso.

DANIEL BALDERSTON

socialist realism

The term 'socialist realism' was coined by the Commissar for Soviet Culture, Andrei Zhdanov, during the All Russian Writers Congress held in 1934 in Moscow. In presenting the official line on literature of the Soviet Union under Stalin, Zhdanov argued that 'bourgeois literature was now in its final stage of collapse and decadence' and that Soviet writers must 'participate in socialist construction'. What this meant in reality was that the only acceptable writer was one who denied the reality of famine and poverty in Soviet Russia in 1934 and instead painted an optimistic and positive picture of the future. Literature, then, was to become an instrument of political education and mobilization.

Many writers, and particularly those who were influenced by the Communist Party, accepted the universalization of Zhdanov's fiat. It led to a didactic literary realism that exposed the brutality of Latin American reality in the most direct and photographic way, and to a form of 'proletarian literature' that idealized the struggles of workers and agitated for others to join them. The **Guayaquil Group** in Ecuador was exemplary of the movement. Demetrio **Aguilera Malta**, Enrique **Gil Gilbert** and Joaquín **Gallegos Lara**'s joint collection of stories, ***Los que se van*** (Those Who Go Away) (1931), narrated with brutal and often violent realism the exploited daily life of the *montuvios* of the Ecuadorean coast. Most representative of the genre, perhaps, was Jorge **Icaza**'s *Huasipungo* (1934), a novelized denunciation of the cruel exploitation of the Indians of the Andean regions. In Costa Rica, Carlos Luis **Fallas**'s *Mamita Yunai* (1941) documented the harsh treatment of banana workers by the United Fruit Company. Jorge **Amado**'s early novels, *Cacau* (1934) and *Suor* (Sweat) (1934), were both strictly documentary works.

Much *indigenista* writing of the 1930s and 1940s falls within this documentary realist mould (see ***indigenismo***); López y Fuentes's *El indio* (The Indian) (1936), López Albújar's *Nuevos cuentos andinos* (New Andean Stories) (1937) and Ciro **Alegría**'s *Los perros hambrientos* (The Dogs are Hungry) (1938) are some examples. Many poets penned anthems to the proletarian hero, although these rarely achieved any literary depth – they were rather proclamations or **manifestos**, like the Cuban Rubén Martínez Villena's long poem, *Manifiesto cívico-radical*, of 1930.

Socialist realism was not confined to literature; in art, the work of Diego Rivera and some of the products of the Mexican Muralist movement translated the types and caricatured figures of 'socialist realism' into the visual dimension, though graphic art lent itself more readily to the broad brushstrokes of this cultural didacticism.

Socialist realism's adherence to formulaic plots and stock character types rarely made for successful work – although at times the marriage of political purpose and art produced great and enduring works of art. But none of these were achieved within the political rather than aesthetic constraints imposed by the concept of socialist realism.

Further reading

Franco, J. (1967) *The Modern Culture of Latin America*, London: Pall Mall Press.

Martin, G. (1989) *Journeys through the Labyrinth*, London: Verso.

Rojas, A. (1948) *La novela ecuatoriana*, Mexico City and Buenos Aires: Fondo de Cultura Económica.

MIKE GONZALEZ

Soler Puig, José

b. 1916, Santiago de Cuba; d. 1996, Santiago de Cuba

Writer

Until the critical success of his novel *Bertillon 166*, which won Cuba's **Casa de las Américas** prize in 1960, Soler Puig was an industrial worker. He then devoted himself to writing professionally, becoming one of Cuba's most significant novelists. His *El pan dormido* (Sleeping Bread) (1976) is recognized by most critics as an outstanding work of contemporary Cuban fiction. Later works included *El caserón* (The Big House) (1976), *Un mundo de cosas* (A World of Things) (1982) and *Anima sola* (Lost Soul) (1986). In all his writings, he evokes the social and family environment of his native town.

Further reading

Benítez Rojo, A. (1979) '*El pan dormido*: Hacia una nueva preceptiva', *Casa de las Américas* 112: 150–61.

Camara, M. (1997) 'Soler Puig en la memoria', *Encuentro de la Cultura Cubana*, Spring–Summer, 4–5: 221–2.

De la Campa, R.V. (1982) '*El pan dormido*: Una aventura narrativa ante la farándula machadista', *Hispamérica*, April, 11(31): 85–92.

Repilado, R. (1990) 'La novelística de José Soler Puig', *Revista iberoamericana*, July–Dec., 56(152–3): 1001–7.

WILFREDO CANCIO ISLA

Sologuren, Javier

b. 1921, Lima, Peru

Poet and publisher

Sologuren has been a major promoter of poetic activity in Peru, publishing new talent in his prestigious La Rama Florida editions, editing anthologies and literary journals, and translating foreign poetry. He is also an important poet, author of a corpus spanning the period from 1938 to the present and characterized by its polished refinement. His early verse is that of a solitary contemplative engaged in the pursuit of timeless beauty. His later work, marked by a growing existential unease, is increasingly meditative in manner.

Further reading

Cabrera, M. (1988) *Milenaria luz: La poesía de Javier Sologuren*, Madrid: Ediciones del Tapir.
Ramírez, L.H. (1967) *Estilo y poesía de Javier Sologuren*, Lima: Biblioteca Universitaria.
Sologuren, J. (1999) *Vida continua: Nueva antología*, Madrid: Colecciøn Cruz del Sur.

JAMES HIGGINS

Solórzano, Carlos

b. 1922, Guatemala City

Critic and writer

Although he is best known for his plays, Solórzano also published two novels, *Los falsos demonios* (The False Demons) (1966) and *Las celdas* (The Jail Cells) (1971). The former is an existentialist novel which deals with the Estrada Cabrera and Ubico years, while the latter is Mexican in character. Among his most popular plays are three dramas from the 1950s: *Doña Beatriz*, *Las manos de Dios* (God's Hands) and *Los fantoches*, Solórzano has resided in Mexico since before the 1944 Revolution, and won the Miguel Angel Asturias prize in 1989. He has compiled anthologies of Mexican and Latin American theatre.

Further reading

Colecchia, F. (1997) 'Carlos Solórzano', in V. Smith (ed.), *Encyclopedia of Latin American Literature*, London: Fitzroy Dearborn, 768–70.
Dauster, F. (1975) 'Carlos Solórzano: La libertad sin límites. *Ensayos sobre el teatro latinoamericano*, Mexico City: Secretaría de Educación Pública.
Rivas, E. (1970) *Carlos Solórzano y el teatro hispanoamericano*, Mexico City: Ediciones de Andrea.
Solórzano, C. (ed.) (1964) *El teatro hispanoamericano contemporáneo*, Mexico City: Fondo de Cultura Económica, 2 vols.
—— (1972) *Teatro*, San José, Costa Rica: EDUCA.
—— (1993) *Crossroads and Other Plays*, trans. F. Colecchia, Rutherford, NJ: Fairleigh Dickinson University Press.

MARC ZIMMERMAN AND LINDA J. CRAFT

Somers, Armonía

b. 1920, Montevideo, Uruguay; d. 1990, Montevideo

Writer

Born Armonía Etchepare, under her pen name Somers created through her fiction a world that is unusual, uncanny, strange, disconcerting, repulsive and fascinating all at the same time. Her short stories have been collected in a two-volume edition and she has published five novels, among them her masterpiece *Sólo los elefantes encuentran mandrágora* (Only Elephants Find the Mandrake Root) (1986), which must be ranked among the outstanding literary works of the twentieth century. It awaits serious study and reflection.

Further reading

Biron, R. (2000) 'Fantasies of Erotic Domination: Armonía Somers "El despojo" ', in *Murder and Masculinity: Violent Fictions of Twentieth-Century Latin America*, Nashville: Vanderbilt University Press, 49–66.
Somers, A. (1967) *Todos los cuentos (1953–1967)*, Montevideo: Arca.

MAGDALENA GARCÍA PINTO

Soriano, Osvaldo

b. 1943, Mar del Plata, Argentina; d. 1997, Buenos Aires

Novelist

After an initial start in journalism, Soriano published his first novel, *Triste, solitario y final* (Sad, Lonely and Final) (1973), his homage to the hard-boiled detective novel, with Philip Marlowe as protagonist. In 1976 after the Argentine coup he moved to Paris where he lived until 1984, when he returned to Buenos Aires.

His novels *No habrá más penas ni olvido* (A Funny Dirty Little War) (1978) and *Cuarteles de invierno* (Winter Quarters) (1982) take place in the claustrophobic space of Colonia Vela, an imaginary town in Buenos Aires province. In both Soriano tries to recount the tragic history of the country in the decade of the 1970s. The rigor and concision of these novels (and his four later ones) have roots in his experience as a journalist.

Part of his journalistic production has been gathered in two volumes: *Artistas, locos y criminales* (Artists, Madmen and Criminals) (1983) collects the articles published between 1972 and 1974 in the newspaper *La Opinión* in Buenos Aires, while *Cuentos de los años felices* (Stories of the Happy Years) (1987) brings together his *crónicas* (see ***crónica***) that appeared in the newspaper *Página/12*, for which Soriano was a frequent collaborator after his return to Argentina.

Two of his novels have been adapted for the screen by the director Héctor Olivera.

Further reading

Canaparo, C. (1997) 'Osvaldo Soriano', in V. Smith (ed.), *Encyclopedia of Latin American Literature*, London: Fitzroy Dearborn, 770–1.

Soriano, O. (1986) *A Funny Dirty Little War*, trans. N. Caistor, New York: Readers International.

—— (1989) *Winter Quarters*, trans. N. Caistor, New York: Readers International.

JOSÉ J. MARISTANY

Sosa, Roberto

b. 1930, Tegucigalpa, Honduras

Poet

The most important Honduran poet of his generation, Sosa has published seven books of poetry. Since *Caligramas* (1959), Sosa's simple poetic style has highlighted both the drama of the Honduran people and universal human concerns. *Mar interior* (Interior Sea) (1967) is more personal and eschatological, while *Los pobres* (The Poor) (1967) and *Un mundo para todos dividido* (A World Divided for Everyone) (1971) addresses life under military dictatorship and social inequalities.

Further reading

Sosa, R. (1971) *Un mundo por todos dividido*, Tegucigalpa: Nuevo Continente and Havana: Casa de las Américas.

—— (2002) *The Return of the River: Selected Poems of Roberto Sosa*, trans. Jo Anne Engelbert, Willimantic, CT: Curbstone Press.

NICASIO URBINA

Soto, Pedro Juan

b. 1928, Cataño, Puerto Rico; d. 2002, San Juan, Puerto Rico

Writer

Soto's *Spiks* (1956) is a collection of short fiction about the experiences of Puerto Ricans who migrated to New York in the 1940s and 1950s. *Usmaíl* (1958) is a novel set in Vieques (a small island off the coast of Puerto Rico occupied by the US Navy since the 1940s) which deals with the relations between North Americans and Puerto Ricans, and the issue of racism. His other works of fiction include *Un oscuro pueblo sonriente* (A Dark, Smiling People), winner of the 1982 **Casa de las Américas** prize. In 1976 Soto's youngest son was ambushed and killed by the police in the political cover-up known as the killings of Cerro Maravilla.

Further reading

Casanova, O. (1985) *La novela puertorriqueña contemporánea: Los albores de un decir hasta 1975*, San Juan: Instituto de Cultura Puertorriqueña, 73–170.

Martín, J.L. (1972) 'La yuxtaposición tiempo-espacio en *El francotirador* de Pedro Juan Soto', *Nueva narrativa hispanoamericana* (New York) 2(2): 187–94.

MARÍA CRISTINA RODRÍGUEZ

Soto Aparicio, Fernando

b. 1933, Santa Rosa de Viterbo, Colombia

Writer and television scriptwriter

In his writings, Soto sets out to denounce and expose social injustice and the abuse of all forms of power (political, religious, military, civil). *La rebelión de las ratas* (The Rebellion of the Rats) (1962) is representative of Soto's work; it narrates the attempt of a group of miners to rebel against their oppressors in a fight that is predestined to fail when they are already so alienated by instances of disbelief, alcoholism or prostitution.

Further reading

Espinosa Ramírez, B. (1981) *Soto Aparicio, o, La filosofía en la novela*, Bogotá: Ediciones Hombre libre.

Williams, R.L. (1982) 'El tiempo en la novela: Observaciones en torno al tiempo en la novela colombiana contemporánea', *Explicación de textos literarios* 1982–1983, 11(2): 11–28.

MIGUEL A. CARDINALE

Soto Vélez, Clemente

b. 1905, Lares, Puerto Rico; d. 1993, San Juan, Puerto Rico

Poet

Soto Vélez's poetry is a key avant-garde text in Puerto Rican literature (see **avant-garde in Latin America**). He formulated the aesthetic propositions of one of the most vocal 1920s avant-garde movements, La Atalaya de los Dioses (Watchtower of the Gods) (1925–*c.*1935). He spent some time in jail for revolutionary activities linked to the nationalist movement of the 1950s. He then went into exile in New York. His works include *Escolios* (Reefs) (1937), *Abrazo interno* (An Inner Embrace) (1954), *Arboles* (Trees) (1955) and *Caballo de palo* (Wooden Horse) (1959).

JUAN CARLOS QUINTERO HERENCIA

Souza, Márcio (Gonçalves Bentes de)

b. 1956, Manaus, Brazil

Novelist

Amazonian novelist who studied sociology in São Paulo, where he also pursued his fascination with cinema through scriptwriting, Souza established a theatre company in Manaus in the 1960s which researched Amazonian history and indigenous culture. His depiction of the socio-historical reality of Amazonia in conjunction with his satirical humour has attracted international attention. Novels include *Galvez, imperador do Acre* (The Emperor of the Amazon) (1976), *A ordem do dia: Folhetim voador nao identificado* (The Order of the Day: An Unidentified Flying Opus) (1983) and *O fim do terceiro mundo* (The End of the Third World) (1990). Since 1995 he has been president of FUNARTE.

Further reading

Johnson, R. (1993) 'Literature, Film and Politics in Brazil: Reflections on the Generation of 1968', in *Tropical Paths: Essays on Modern Brazilian Literature*, New York: Garland, 183–98.

Maligo, P. (1993) 'Political Literature in Amazonia: Márcio Souza and His Predecessors', in *Tropical Paths: Essays on Modern Brazilian Literature*, New York: Garland. 53–75

PEGGY SHARPE

Spanish American modernism

Spanish American *modernismo* refers primarily to a late nineteenth- and early twentieth-century literary movement incorporating elements of French symbolism and decadence with highly elaborate language. As such, it is sharply differentiated from later Anglo-American and Brazilian modernisms (see **Brazilian modernism**). Nonetheless, its dynamism is based on a convergence of cultural and social factors which reshaped the role of the writer in Spanish America. The first generation of professional writers, many of them *modernistas*, such as José Martí, Rubén Darío, Julián del Casal and

Manuel Gutiérrez Nájera, were journalists, and many lacked aristocratic antecedents. Connected through an international network of periodicals and heightened cultural exchange, they helped to forge a new Spanish American literary unity. Often criticized for their exotic themes and highly wrought language, their openness to cosmopolitan trends reshaped the contours of writing in the continent, from Mexico to the Southern Cone, as well as influencing poetry in Spain. Particularly important were their contributions to newspapers and literary magazines, products of an expanded continental reading public. *Modernista* style includes both fiction and poetry, yet its most enduring legacy is associated with a certain style of poetry. *Modernismo*'s primary exponent, the Nicaraguan Rubén **Darío**, exemplifies the heterogeneous nature of the movement's impulses and achievements. Darío, while exalting the European (especially French) legacy in his poetry – *Azul* (Blue) (1888) and *Prosas profanas* (Profane Prose) (1896) – revitalized poetic language in Spanish by exploring musicality, archaic forms and formal innovation. His *Cantos de vida y esperanza* (Songs of Life and Hope) (1905) includes a focus on New World cultures, with a sharp critique of the emerging materialist culture of the USA (an echo of José Enrique Rodó's 1900 essay *Ariel*) (see ***Ariel* and *arielismo***).

Another direction of *modernismo* was initiated by the Cuban Jose **Martí**, whose *Ismaelillo* (1882) and *Versos sencillos* (Simple Verses) (1891) incorporated popular poetic forms into literary modernity. Independence hero and cultural leader, Martí combined the roles of statesman, orator, journalist, novelist and poet in his brief but prolific career. In contrast to many *modernistas*, Martí's spare poetic style has had an enduring resonance in Latin American letters.

As readership expanded dramatically due to public education, journalism became increasingly important. Periodicals offered employment to writers and a medium for their creative works. Especially important during this period was the ***crónica***, an essay form which included social and cultural commentary in an individualistic style, published in major newspapers and specialized magazines. Notable *cronistas* were Martí, Darío, Manuel Gutiérrez Nájera and José Asunción Silva. The two most important, though short-lived, *modernista* magazines were the *Revista azul* (Mexico) and *Revista de América* (Buenos Aires, founded by Darío and Jaimes Freyre).

Modernista prose fiction is more difficult to define, for its densely figured and ornate language was used in the service of novels and short stories of very different kinds. Inspiration drawn from symbolist and decadent movements can be seen in fictions ranging from regionalist emphasis (see ***regionalismo***) to **science fiction** to prose poems. It is in prose that *modernismo* and naturalism cross paths, for naturalism's emphasis on physicality merged with the luxuriance of *modernista* style. The short story (Martí, Darío, Silva, Leopoldo **Lugones**) was more important than the novel.

Modernismo is most remembered for its expansion and elaboration of poetic forms in Spanish. Here Spanish America led Spain in the revitalization of literature: Martí's inclusion of the popular octosyllable, Darío's renewal of alexandrine verse medieval forms as well as his adaptations of French poetics, and an almost religious attention to form in general display the innovative impulse of the *modernistas*. Yet their adherence to elaborate form was precisely the element that later generations, most famously González Martínez in Mexico and **Borges** in the 1920s, rejected as overwrought 'rubendarismo'. Even *modernista* contemporaries had their doubts about the preoccupation with baroque language, physicality and sometimes slavish attention to French culture. In particular, José Enrique Rodó was suspicious of Darío's early publications for their inattention to local concern and insistence on distant times and lands. Such criticisms were noted, especially by Darío, whose later poetry warns against the encroachment of the USA in Latin American territories and cultures. Later *modernista* poetry, particularly Leopoldo Lugones's *Lunario sentimental* (1909) and poetry by Uruguay's Julio **Herrera y Reissig**, carried *modernista* style to the breaking point through mockery and exaggeration, setting the stage for the rebellion of the following generation.

Overt eroticism is a major component of *modernismo*, particularly in its portrayal of the female through the evocation of the femme fatale, and this legacy has been as important as the renewal of poetic language. Because sexuality was centred on the female as object of the male gaze, the disruption of this axis created consternation. Uruguay's Delmira **Agustini** entered the poetic scene when *modernismo* was in full force. Her poetry, open in its expression of female sexuality, turns around *modernista* iconology and reverses the gaze, often with violent imagery.

Modernismo has been critically re-evaluated, after decades of dismissal, by figures such as Octavio **Paz** and Angel **Rama**. Viewing *modernismo* in the context of modernization in Latin America, they signal the complexities of its innovations and legacies. Paz, in particular, sees Darío as initiator of a movement to insert Latin American aesthetics into international dynamics; Rama studies the movement as an elaborate baroque edifice constructed against the onslaught of the popular which accompanies modernization. These views have made the study of *modernismo* an indispensable element for the debates on modernity within Latin American throughout the twentieth century.

Further reading

Aching, G. (1997) *The Politics of Spanish American Modernismo, By Exquisite Design*, Cambridge: Cambridge University Press.

Gonzalez, A. (1993) *Journalism and the Development of Spanish American Narrative*, Cambridge: Cambridge University Press.

—— (1996) 'Modernist Prose', in R. González Echevarría and E. Pupo-Walker (eds), *Cambridge History of Latin American Literature*, Cambridge: Cambridge University Press, 2, 69–113.

Jiménez, J.O. (1985) *Antología de la poesía modernista*, Madrid: Hiperión.

Jrade, C. (1983) *Rubén Darío and the Romantic Search for Unity. The Modernist Recourse to Esoteric Tradition*, Austin: University of Texas Press.

—— (1996) 'Modernist Poetry', in R. González Echevarría and E. Pupo-Walker (eds), *Cambridge History of Latin American Literature*, Cambridge: Cambridge University Press, 2, 7–67.

Kirkpatrick, G. (1989) *The Dissonant Legacy of Modernismo. Lugones, Herrera y Reissig and the Voices of Modern Spanish American Poetry*, Berkeley: University of California Press.

Montero, O. (1997) '*Modernismo* and Homophobia: Darío and Rodó', in D. Balderston and D.J. Guy (eds), *Sex and Sexuality in Latin America*, New York: New York University Press, 101–17.

Rama, A. (1985) *Las máscaras democráticas del modernismo*, Montevideo: Fundación Angel Rama.

GWEN KIRKPATRICK

Stewart, John

b. 1933, Trinidad and Tobago

Novelist, short story writer and anthropologist

Stewart studied in the USA and has lectured widely. His novel, *Last Cool Days* (1972), won the Winifred Holtby Prize. His *Drinkers, Drummers and Decent Folk* (1989) is an important work of fiction and anthropology which looks at the lives of canecutters in central Trinidad. Known for his anthropological work, Stewart has also made a film about ritual stick fighting in Trinidad, and is a professor of anthropology.

KEITH JARDIM

Stoep, De

The literary magazine *De Stoep* (The Steps) was founded by Chris J.H. **Engels** in Curaçao, Netherlands Antilles, in 1940 at the outbreak of the Second World War. With Frits J. van der Molen and Hendrik de Wit as co-editors, it continued until 1951. The magazine had a prize-winning layout and published prose and poetry by exiled Dutch writers. After the war, *De Stoep* drew various young Antillean poets to its pages, such as Tip **Marugg** and Oda **Blinder**. They too wrote in Dutch and cultivated an experimental style which produced poetry that required close reading, appealed to associative thinking, and was thematically centred around strictly personal sentiments.

AART G. BROEK

Storni, Alfonsina

b. 1892, Sala Capriasca, Switzerland; d. 1938, Mar del Plata, Argentina

Poet

Storni grew up in a happy provincial environment and began her professional career as a school teacher in Rosario, Argentina, at the age of 19. Having given birth to a son she had with her married lover, she left Rosario and established herself in Buenos Aires. Her efforts to make a living at a variety of jobs did not restrain her from writing poetry and gaining a strong although not undisputed literary reputation.

Storni's work is unmistakably marked by contemporary literary tendencies such as postmodernism – *Languidez* (Languidness) (1920) was dedicated to 'those who, like me, never realized even one of their dreams' – and the historical avant-garde – the 52 anti-sonnets in *Mascarilla y trébol* (Mask and Clover) (1938) (see **avant-garde in Latin America**). Her poetry has a passionate, uncompromising tone; its subject matter evolves from the confessional sentimentalism of *La inquietud del rosal* (The Rose Bush's Anxiety) (1916) to the complex expressionism of her last books. Given the very explicitly female perspective of her poetry, the epithet 'Latin America's first feminist poet' does not come as a surprise. Expressing the deeply suffered crisis of the feminine role with great honesty, Storni discloses the hypocrisy and injustice of a patriarchal culture which takes for granted the inferior position of women.

Storni's direct way of expressing her feelings and preoccupations met with the resistance of, for example, Jorge Luis **Borges**, who in 1925 scornfully characterized Storni's voice as shrill and vulgar. Indeed, Storni's poetry lacks the sophistication of the leading male writers of her times. It rebels against the oppressive stereotypes of patriarchal society but is not always capable of avoiding its clichés. Maybe this paradox is the grandeur and the misère of Storni's poetry in a nutshell. Suffering from cancer she committed suicide, drowning herself in the sea off Mar del Plata.

Further reading

Agostín, M. (1989) 'Alfonsina Storni', in C.A. Solé and M.I. Abreu (eds), *Latin American Writers*, New York: Scribners, 2, 739–43.

Andreola, C.A. (1976) *Alfonsina Storni*, Buenos Aires: Plus Ultra.

Delgado, J. (1990) *Alfonsina Storni*, Buenos Aires: Planeta.

Evans, J. (1997) 'Alfonsina Storni', in V. Smith (ed.), *Encyclopedia of Latin American Literature*, London: Fitzroy Dearborn, 773–4.

Jones, S. (1979) *Alfonsina Storni*, Boston: Twayne.

Kirkpatrick, G. (1995) 'Alfonsina Storni as "Tao Lao": Journalism's Roving Eye and Poetry's Confessional "I" ', in D. Meyer (ed.), *Reinterpreting the Spanish American Essay: Women Writers of the 19th and 20th Centuries*, Austin: University of Texas Press, 135–47.

—— (1990) 'The Journalism of Alfonsina Storni: A New Approach to Women's History in Argentina', in *Women, Culture and Politics in Latin America*, Berkeley: University of California Press, 105–29.

Phillips, R. (1975) *Alfonsina Storni: From Poetess to Poet*, London: Támesis.

Storni, A. (1980) *Antología poética*, ed. S. Zanetti, Buenos Aires: Losada.

—— (1987) *Selected Poems*, trans. M. Crow *et al.*, Fredonia, NY: White Pine Press.

—— (1998) *Nosotras ... y la piel: Selección de ensayos*, ed. M. Méndez, G. Queirolo and A. Salomone, Madrid: Alfaguara.

MAARTEN STEENMEIJER

Suárez, Clementina

b. 1902, Juticalpa, Honduras; d. 1991, Tegucigalpa, Honduras

Writer

Generation of 1935 Honduran poet, Clementina Suárez led a colourful and controversial life as an iconoclastic writer, political activist, feminist publisher and independent woman. A lover of the arts, Suárez promoted Central American painters and writers and travelled widely, associating with the leading intellectuals of her day. She counted Miguel

Angel **Asturias**, Pablo **Neruda**, **Salarrué**, Claudia Lars and members of the Salvadoran Generación Comprometida (Committed Generation) including Roque **Dalton** among her friends. In 1970 she received Honduras' top literary prize, the Premio Ramón Rosa. Her poems have been lauded for their tropical sensuality, voluptuousness, wisdom, vividness, and at times revolutionary commitment. She considered her 1957 novel *Creciendo con la hierba* (Growing with the Grass) as central to her self-definition. Suárez was brutally murdered by an unknown assailant in her Tegucigalpa home.

Further reading

Gold, J.N. (1995) *Clementina Suárez: Her Life and Poetry*, Gainesville: University Press of Florida.

LINDA J. CRAFT

Suassuna, Ariano

b. 1927, João Pessoa, Paraíba, Brazil

Writer

Suassuna has dedicated his career to the exploration and promotion of the popular culture of the rural interior of his native north-eastern Brazil. He established himself as a dramatist in the 1950s with his most successful play, *Auto da compadecida* (The Rogue's Trial) (1957), which draws on the narrative poetry of ***literatura de cordel*** and merges farce, satire and moral teaching. That set the pattern for subsequent plays, such as *O santo e a porca* (The Saint and the Sow) (1957) and *A Pena e a Lei* (The Sentence and the Law) (1959). Common to them all is the theme of Christian belief, the need to maintain faith in a world pervaded by anguish and strife, and the extensive use of the themes and language of north-east popular poetry.

In 1971, Suassuna published his first and highly acclaimed novel, *O romance d'a pedra do reino* (The Novel of the Stone Kingdom). The narrator and major protagonist, Quaderna, leads the reader into the world of the north-eastern *sertão* of the 1930s, with its rich folkloric traditions. Quaderna is himself a popular poet whose magical recreation of the north east gives the reader a colourful, folkloric vision of the region. Although Suassuna has constantly emphasized the closeness of his work to popular literature, he essentially uses folkloric material to explore the universal themes that concern him, above all humankind's eternal hope of redemption. What dominates the novel is Quaderna's search for a solution to his anguish in a world full of suffering, rather than the examination of north-eastern society and culture, which was the primary concern of the earlier social realist novelists of the region.

The guiding principle behind Suassuna's work has always been the belief that a truly national art can only be produced by assimilating the forms of popular culture central to the Brazilian population. With that objective in mind, he launched the **Movimento Armorial** in Recife in 1970, whose artists sought to create high art forms from popular and folkloric sources. Much original work was produced, but the movement was controversial. Accused of exploiting popular culture by some, and increasingly dissatisfied with the cultural policies of those in authority, Suassuna became disillusioned and in 1981 he announced his withdrawal from public life and a halt to his literary career. He finally resumed writing several years later, when Brazil's return to democracy after a long period of military dictatorship created new conditions for cultural activity. He became Secretary of Culture for Pernambuco in 1994, and launched a new project to promote popular regional art forms, with state support and funding. He has established himself as one of Brazil's best-known writers, although he remains a controversial figure.

Further reading

Barker, D. and P. Newman (1991) 'Redemption and Damnation in the *Auto da compadecida*', in M.A. Rees (ed.), *Leeds Papers on Hispanic Drama*, Leeds: Trinity and All Saints Colleges.

Dinneen, M. (1996) *Listening to the People's Voice*, London: Kegan Paul International.

Guidinari, M. (1992) *Os pícaros e os trapaceríos de Ariano Suassuna*, São Paulo: Ateniense.

Leal, M.T. (1989) 'Ariano Vilar Suassuna', in C.A. Solé and M.I. Abreu (eds), *Latin American Writers*, Scribners, 3: 1317–21.

Leal-McBride, M.O. (1989) *Narrativas e narradores em*

A Pedra do Reino: Estruturas e perspectivas cambiantes, New York: Peter Lang.
Rama, Angel (1975) 'Ariano Suassuna: El teatro y la narrativa popular y nacional', *La palabra y el hombre: Revista de la Universidad Veracruzana* 13: 7–13.

MARK DINNEEN

subaltern studies

Research into what is now called subaltern studies began in the early 1980s as an effort to rethink colonialism in India. Arguing against both liberal and Marxist traditions, historians working with Ranajit Guha attempted to reinvigorate popular anti-colonial struggles made independently of elite nationalism. Since the early 1990s, two groups have adapted this approach to Latin America, one in the field of history, the other in literary studies. Both are based in the USA, but they have pursued alternate methods and reached contrary conclusions.

Guha drew on the revisionist Marxism of Italian social theorist Antonio Gramsci. Gramsci's analysis of the failed national consolidation in Italy served as a broad template for rethinking nationalist legacies in India, and the term subaltern itself derives from Gramsci's prison writings, where it refers to the proletariat along with the peasantry and other subordinate social groups. For Gramsci, the failure to establish effective ties between these subalterns and radical segments of the elite accounted for the weakness of Italy's bourgeois revolution.

Historians, led by Florencia Mallon and Gilbert Joseph, have used this model to trace the convergence of elite and popular sectors that produced different possibilities for national consolidation in Latin America. Their group has focused on regionalism and rural insurgency in the nineteenth century. Literary scholars, led by John Beverley and Ileana Rodríguez, have worked more through theorists such as Gayatri Spivak, who insisted on the need to avoid the pitfalls of a residual humanism and historical positivism she found in Guha's group. For Spivak, colonial subordination generates heterogeneous systems of subordination that can only be addressed through a deconstructive procedure she calls 'strategic essentialism': a form of self-critical analysis focused not directly on the strategies of resistance employed by popular sectors, but rather on the 'subject effect' created by the subaltern within elite discourse.

For Beverley and Rodríguez, Spivak's methodology resolved a dilemma related to the social function of intellectuals. In his path-breaking study, *The Lettered City* (1984), Uruguayan literary critic Angel **Rama** had argued that the institutions of culture in Latin America are tied to the state in ways that are detrimental to forging relationships between intellectuals, popular culture and grass-roots social movements. Beverley and Rodríguez took Rama's critique as announcing an end to literature as a meaningful site for political contestation. In light of that conclusion, they initially turned to testimonial literature (see ***testimonio***) as a new genre that signalled a change in the relationships between **intellectuals** and popular culture as well as new techniques for articulating subaltern perspectives. Revolutionary movements in Central America, including the success of the Sandinistas, seemed to validate this proposal. However, by the early 1990s the waning of the revolutionary option and the end of the Cold War led to a reassessment of testimonial's ability to symbolize such fundamental social changes. A deconstructive subaltern studies then appeared as the next step to advance politically committed cultural criticism. In practice, however, this project has focused primarily on interrogating academic knowledge as an institutional practice that justifies and sustains structures of domination. A great deal of Latin American literary subaltern studies has been limited to a critique of the institutional and even epistemological barriers to creating linkages between elite and popular cultures.

With such a sharp critique of intellectuals as its centre, it is not surprising that the literary subaltern studies project has received a more mixed reception than the historical project, particularly among Latin American scholars. Moreover, the central concerns of subaltern studies have long been present in Latin American social and literary theory. As part of efforts to reassert national concerns into an international Marxist context dominated by Stalinism, extensive translations from Gramsci's writings were available in Latin America beginning in the late 1950s, decades before his work had been rediscovered outside of Italy. Particularly in political science and social history, Latin American intellectuals in the 1970s and 1980s engaged further with Gramsci as a tool to rethink the possibilities still open to the Left after military governments had dismantled civil society in many countries.

After the mid-1970s, the Left's self-critique had become widely diffused and many Gramscian-derived terms were common currency among Latin American intellectuals. However, this shared terminology centred not on subalternity, but on the question of hegemony and the social importance of intellectuals in forging alliances with and among popular sectors. While current efforts to create a Latin American literary subaltern studies propose a further revision of the leftist cultural agenda, it is not difficult to understand why many scholars feel uncomfortable with a project that seems to transform Gramsci from the philosopher of pragmatic cultural politics into the foundational figure of a vocabulary that often seems highly technical and at times even rarefied. The dense terminology that has developed around literary subaltern studies still awaits an effective translation into the Latin American academy, and its highly self-referential nature tends more towards exclusivity than to dissemination into new projects. Whether alternate projects for literary subaltern studies can be generated for the region remains to be seen.

Further reading

Aricó, José (1988) *La cola del diablo. Trayectoria de Gramsci en América Latina*, Caracas: Nueva Sociedad.

Beverley, John (1999) *Subalternity and Representation*, Durham, NC: Duke University Press.

Bustos, Guillermo (2002) 'Enfoque subalternista e historia latinoamericana: Nación, subalternidad y escritura de la historia en el debate Mallon-Beverley', in Alberto G. Flórez and Carmen Millan de Benavides (eds), *Desafíos de la transdiciplinaridad*, Bogotá: Instituto de Estudios Sociales y Culturales/Pontífica Universidad Javeriana, 59–80.

Chaturvedi, Vinayak (2000) *Mapping Subaltern Studies and the Post-Colonial*, London: Verso.

Joseph, Gilbert and Daniel Nugent (eds) (1994) *Everyday Forms of State Formation*, Durham, NC: Duke University Press.

Kokotovic, Misha (2000) 'Intellectuals and Their Others: What is to Be Done?', *Diaspora* 9(2): 287–308.

Latin American Subaltern Studies Group (1993) 'Founding Statement', *Boundary 2* 20(3): 110–21.

Mallon, Florencia (1994) 'The Promise and Dilemma of Subaltern Studies', *American Historical Review* 99(5): 1491–515.

—— (1995) *Peasant and Nation. The Making of Post-Colonial Mexico and Peru*, Berkeley: University of California Press.

Moraña, Mabel (1997) 'El "Boom" del subalterno', *Revista de crítica cultural* 14: 48–53.

Rodríguez, Ileana (ed.) (2001) *The Latin American Subaltern Studies Reader*, Durham, NC: Duke University Press.

Spivak, Gayatri and Ranajit Guha (eds) (1988) *Selected Subaltern Studies*, New York: Oxford University Press.

BRIAN GOLLNICK

Sucre, Guillermo

b. 1933, Bolívar province, Venezuela

Poet, essayist and literary critic

In 1957 Sucre founded the journal *Sardío* and its associated literary group, and began to teach in the School of Literature at the Universidad Central in Caracas. From 1968 to 1975 he taught literature at the University of Pittsburgh, and was a member of the University's Instituto Internacional de Literatura Iberoamericana. Returning to Venezuela he taught at the Simon Bolívar University in Caracas and became literary director of the publishing house, **Monte Avila**. Poetry and the essay have been the focus of his creative reflections, under the influence of the work and thought of Jorge Luis **Borges** and Octavio **Paz**.

Further reading

Chacon, A. (1994) 'Guillermo Sucre en la vastedad', *Cuadernos hispanoamericanos: Revista mensual de cultura hispánica*, June, 528: 111–14.
Sucre, G. (1967) *Borges, el poeta*, Mexico City: Universidad Nacional Autónoma de México.
——(1975) *La máscara, la transparencia: Ensayos sobre poesía hispanoamericana*, Caracas: Monte Avila.
—— (1991) 'Octavio Paz: La otra voz', *Vuelta*, June, 15(175): 24–8.

JORGE ROMERO LEÓN

Sudamericana, Editorial

Independent publishing house started in 1939 by a group of Argentine intellectuals including Victoria **Ocampo** and Oliverio **Girondo** to publish local and international contemporary writing. It began publishing youth literature, including Argentine writer Leopoldo **Marechal** and artists Antonio Berni and Horacio Butler. Its children and youth books are still a strong part of its business, but successes such as Gabriel **García Márquez**'s ***Cien años de soledad*** in 1967, as well as his subsequent books, have kept the house financially strong. Other leading Latin American writers on its list include **Roa Bastos**, **Onetti**, Antonio **Skármeta** and Isabel **Allende**. The business is currently managed by Gloria Rodrigué and her family. In 1998 it was taken over by the German publishing group Bertelsmann.

Further information

http://www.edsudamericana.com.ar/

ANDREW GRAHAM-YOOLL

Supervielle, Jules

b. 1884, Montevideo, Uruguay; d. 1960, Paris, France

Poet and writer

Although he wrote in French, Supervielle belonged as much to the River Plate as to France. He belonged to a group of French writers, including Valéry Larbaud, whose work he translated and introduced to the avant-garde of Uruguay and Argentina during the 1920s (see **avant-garde in Latin America**). Lautréamont, Jules Laforgue and Supervielle constitute the trio of writers 'that Uruguay gave to France'. His writing, in a minor key, is among the most original of his time, combining a decadent aesthetics with the avant-garde; thus his work provides a viewpoint from which to consider the relations between hegemonic and peripheral cultures. Twice exiled, he published in 1923 his *L'Homme de la pampa* (Man of the *Pampa*), a hybrid and disturbing text which examines with an ironic eye the culture of Europe and the River Plate.

Further reading

Hiddleston, J.A. (1965) *L'univers de Jules Supervielle*, Paris: Corti.
Roy, C. (1964) *Jules Supervielle*, Paris: Pierre Seghers.

GRACIELA MONTALDO

Sur

A cultural magazine, *Sur* was founded in 1930 by Victoria **Ocampo**, following a suggestion from the US writer Waldo Frank who proposed that the intellectual class of South America become involved in the exchange of ideas (somewhat analagous to two-way commerce) with the North, and that a magazine serve as a forum for that exchange. Frank's pan-Americanism, which was composed of a mystic or idealist communism, had a great impact on some Latin American intellectuals during his lecture tour in Central and South America in 1929–30; in Ocampo's case, it inspired her to bring together a number of her friends and acquaintances to found *Sur*. The logo of the new magazine (and eventually of its publishing house also) was a small arrow pointing downward, no doubt an inversion of the arrow on the compass pointing north; there was an interesting coincidence between this symbol and the 'upside-down' map of the Americas that Joaquín Torres-García used about the same time in his Escuela del Sur (Southern School) in Montevideo.

The magazine published its first issue in 1931; this was large format, on good paper, with twenty-four pages of illustrations by artists from Picasso to Spilimbergo, Basaldúa and Pettoruti, plus photographs of **Güiraldes** and of Brazilian and Argentine landscapes (**Borges** commented ironically on the 'travelogue' nature of these illustrations, which disappeared after issue 5). During the journal's first years, when it appeared as a quarterly, it published essays by Alfonso **Reyes**, Waldo Frank, Drieu La Rochelle, José Ortega y Gasset and Jules **Supervielle**, among others. Fascinated with modernization, it also included articles on the new architecture of Le Corbusier by Ocampo and Alberto Prebisch, as well as articles on new music, new currents in art and so forth. After 1935 the format was reduced and the frequency of publication increased to a monthly; it would maintain this new format for several decades.

José **Bianco** began his association with *Sur* in 1935, and was named editor in 1938; he would continue in this post until 1961, when his trip to Cuba at the invitation of **Casa de las Américas** became the occasion of two sour notes in the journal by Victoria Ocampo making clear that Bianco had gone to Cuba on his own account, not as a representative of *Sur*; he resigned upon his return to Buenos Aires. Bianco's period at *Sur* was notable for the changes brought to the journal, both in terms of its more consistent and careful style and a much greater hospitality to creative writing. For instance, Borges had written film and book reviews, and occasional short essays and notes, that had appeared toward the back of the magazine through the 1930s; it was only with his famous 1939 story 'Pierre Menard, autor del Quijote' (Pierre Menard, Author of *Don Quixote*) that his work would appear prominently – and boldly, considering the difficulties that that story was to cause its first and subsequent readers – at the beginning of an issue. In the following years, *Sur* would publish fiction and poetry by Adolfo **Bioy Casares**, Silvina **Ocampo**, Bianco himself, Juan Carlos **Onetti**, Ezequiel **Martínez Estrada**, Octavio **Paz**, Alberto **Girri**, Juan Rodolfo **Wilcock** and many others, both in the journal and in its small publishing house. Though never really forming a '*Sur* group', as is sometimes alleged, the writers who were close to Bianco — particularly Borges, Bioy Casares and Silvina Ocampo — did use the journal in the 1940s to promote their ideas on **fantastic literature** and **crime fiction**.

Sur was very fond of anthologies – of Brazilian literature, of contemporary French letters, of post-war British writing – and of surveys of opinion (on censorship and other topics of the day), of anniversaries and of obituaries. The somewhat ritual nature of some of these issues was grating to Bianco but part of Victoria Ocampo's mission to use the journal to showcase her enthusiasms and discoveries. Among the anthology issues, one of particular note was the September 1942 issue prepared by María Rosa **Oliver** on Brazil, which formed part of the attempts to forge pan-American unity during the war years.

The journal's fascination with French culture passed through several stages, with Drieu La Rochelle becoming an embarrassment due to his fascist beliefs, but a more steadfast attitude towards Malraux, Maritain and Bernanos. After the war, the journal was open to **existentialism**, although it eventually preferred Camus to Sartre; the latter, with his belief in 'engaged' literature, was the hero of the rival journal of the 1950s, ***Contorno***. During this period one of the dominant essayists in the journal was H.A. **Murena**, the successor to Martínez Estrada in his pessimistic analyses of Argentine and Latin American culture.

After Bianco was forced to resign in 1961, the journal entered into a crisis from which it never fully recovered. Editors in the 1960s included María Luisa Bastos and Enrique **Pezzoni**; the latter was instrumental in bringing new writers like Severo **Sarduy** to the pages of *Sur*, but in some sense the impetus had been lost to other international magazines published in Spanish such as ***Mundo nuevo***, published first in Paris by Emir **Rodríguez Monegal** and later continued in Buenos Aires. After 1970, when Pezzoni finished his period as editor, *Sur* was reduced almost entirely to a shadow of itself, publishing anthologies of its prior publications and compilations of articles by and about its favoured writers. And this crisis deepened with the death of Victoria Ocampo in 1978.

Sur was the dominant liberal organ in Argentina for forty years. Ocampo's strong opposition to Perón and his movement marked the journal from 1944 onwards; in 1955, with the fall of Perón, it published celebratory notes by Ocampo and others. More importantly, though, the model of liberalism that operated in *Sur* was one of a cosmopolitan intellectual community interested in the free exchange of ideas; internationalism was part of its mission. Ocampo and her journal were roundly criticized by Peronist intellectuals and by the younger intellectuals writing in *Contorno* and later in *Primera Plana*; these criticisms were no doubt inevitable given the sea changes that had taken place in Argentina between the 1930s and the 1950s and 1960s. In any case, a cultural history of twentieth-century Argentina is unthinkable without a consideration of *Sur*.

Further reading

King, J. (1986) *Sur: A Study of the Argentine Literary Journal and its Role in the Development of a Culture, 1931–1970*, Cambridge: Cambridge University Press.

Paz Leston, E. (ed.) (1981) *Sur: Selección*, Buenos Aires: Centro Editor de América Latina.

Sarlo, B. *et al.* (1983) 'Dossier "La revista Sur" ', *Punto de vista* 9(28).

Villordo, O.H. (1993) *El grupo Sur: Una biografía colectiva*, Buenos Aires: Planeta.

DANIEL BALDERSTON

surrealism

Surrealism began in France in 1924, and became known throughout the Western world by the publications of its **manifestos**, mostly authored by André Breton (1896–1966). Surrealist writing was known for the wild sequence of images, for automatic and collective writing and for its vociferous stands on the place of artistic creation in a complete remaking of the world. There were strong echoes of the movement across Latin America and the Caribbean from the 1920s through the 1940s, and Breton and other European surrealists spent time in Mexico and elsewhere in Latin America, countries which appealed to the surrealists because of the supposedly primitive and oneiric qualities of the cultures. Painters who were identified as surrealist include Frida Kahlo, Leonora Carrington and Remedios Varo. The Latin American poet who was most directly involved in the surrealist movement was César **Moro** of Peru, who organized the International Surrealist Exhibition in Mexico City in 1940 and wrote a considerable amount of surrealist poetry, much of it in French; others in the orbit of surrealism included Aldo **Pellegrini**, Oliverio **Girondo** and Enrique **Molina** in Argentina and Braulio Arenas in Chile, and novelists Alejo **Carpentier** (Cuba) and Miguel Angel **Asturias** (Guatemala). Octavio **Paz** was very interested in the movement and wrote numerous critical essays about it, as well as participating in the collective creation of a book of *rengas* (a sort of neo-surrealist project after the movement as such had died), and Julio **Cortázar** shows a profound interest in surrealism in his novel ***Rayuela*** (1963) and in many of his essays. Writers who were very much opposed to surrealism include César **Vallejo** and Jorge Luis **Borges**.

Further reading

Baciu, S. (1974) *Antología de la poesía surrealista latinoamericana*, Mexico City: Joaquín Mortiz.

—— (1979) *Surrealismo latinoamericano: Preguntas y respuestas*, Valparaíso, Chile: Universidad de Valparaíso.

Maturo, G. (1967) *Proyecciones del surrealismo en la literatura argentina*, Buenos Aires: Ediciones Culturales Argentinas.

Schneider, L.M. (1978) *México y el surrealismo (1925–1950)*, Mexico City: Arte y Libros.

Schwartz, J. (2002) 'Surrealismo', in *Las vanguardias latinoamericanas*, Mexico City: Fondo de Cultura Económica, 2nd edn, 445–76.

Wilson, J. (1997) 'Surrealism', in V. Smith (ed.), *Encyclopedia of Latin American Literature*, London: Fitzroy Dearborn, 775–6.

DANIEL BALDERSTON

Süssekind, Flora

b. 1955, Rio de Janeiro, Brazil

Literary historian and critic

One of the most productive and wide-ranging literary historians and essayists of the post-**Candido** generation, Süssekind's *Tal Brasil, qual romance* (Like Brazil, Like Novel) (1984) is a critical account of the naturalist tradition in Brazil, from the late nineteenth century to documentary fiction after 1964. *Literatura e vida literária* (Literature and Literary Life) (1985) examines the variety of literary responses to the authoritarianism, censorship and torture of the latter period. *O Brasil não é longe daqui* (Brazil is Not Far From Here) (1986) examines the vision of Brazil constructed by the writings of the nineteenth-century European travellers, while *Cinematógrafo de letras* (Literary Camera) (1987) explores the relationship between modernization and literary technique during the First Republic.

Further reading

Süssekind, Flora (1986) *As revistas de ano e a invenção do Rio de Janeiro*, Rio de Janeiro: Editora Nova Fronteira: Fundação Casa de Rui Barbosa.

—— (1987) *Cinematógrafo de letras: Literatura, técnica e modernização no Brasil*, São Paulo: Companhia das Letras.

—— (1990) *O Brasil não é longe daqui: O narrador, a viagem*, São Paulo: Cia. das Letras.

—— (1997) *Cinematograph of Words: Literature, Technique, and Modernization in Brazil (Writing Science)*, Stanford, CA: Stanford University Press.

—— (1998) *A voz e a série*, Rio de Janeiro: Sette Letras and Belo Horizonte, Minas Gerais: Editora UFMG.

DAVID TREECE

Sutherland, Juan Pablo

b. 1967, Santiago, Chile

Short story writer

Sutherland is a significant openly gay writer in Chile, although he is not as well known outside that country as Pedro **Lemebel**. He has published two books of short stories, *Angeles negros* (Black Angels) (1994) and *Santo roto* (Broken Saint) (1999). His stories are often narrated by gay individuals, and tell of nocturnal and marginal spaces in Santiago, as well as giving a sustained reflection on the place of gays in Chilean families. In 2001 he edited the first anthology of gay and lesbian writing in Chile, *A corazón abierto: Geografía literaria de la homosexualidad en Chile* (Open Heart: A Literary Geography of Homosexuality in Chile), which includes texts by Joaquín **Edwards Bello**, Augusto **D'Halmar**, José **Donoso**, Mauricio **Wacquez**, **Alone**, Enrique **Lihn**, Marta **Brunet**, Carlos Iturra, René Arcos Levi, Francisco Casas and others. As Sutherland explains in the extensive introduction to the anthology, he also wanted to include texts by Gabriela **Mistral** but was prevented from doing so by her estate.

Further reading

Sutherland, J.P. (2000) 'Movimiento homosexual en Chile', *Revista de crítica cultural* 21: 36–9.

—— (2001) *A corazón abierto*, Santiago: Editorial Sudamericana.

DANIEL BALDERSTON

T

Tablada, José Juan

b. 1871, Mexico City; d. 1945, New York City, USA

Poet

Tablada, who started writing during the long reign of Porfirio Díaz in Mexico (and was highly influenced by the French *belle époque*) was among the initiators of the avant-garde in Mexico (see **avant-garde in Latin America**). He was known particularly for his calligrams and haikus: poems in the shape of windows, singing birds, frogs, the moon. Some of his poems which follow the Chinese and Japanese models are adaptations of English translations. He also wrote sonnets and other more conventional poems, both before and after the calligrams of *Li Po y otros poemas ideográficos* (Li Po and Other Ideogrammatic Poems) (1920). He published a novel, written extensively on the visual arts and translated from the French, Portuguese and Japanese.

Further reading

Keeth, W.P. (1997) 'José Juan Tablada', in V. Smith (ed.), *Encyclopedia of Latin American Literature*, London: Fitzroy Dearborn, 777–9.

Lara Velázquez, E. (1988) *La iniciación poética de José Juan Tablada*, Mexico City: UNAM.

Tablada, J.J. (1971–81) *Obras*, ed. H. Valdés, Mexico City: UNAM, 2 vols.

Tanabe, A. (1981) *El japonismo de José Juan Tablada*, Mexico City: UNAM.

DANIEL BALDERSTON

Taibo II, Paco Ignacio

b. 1949, Asturias, Spain

Writer

Mexico's most popular and prolific writer of **crime fiction**. Beginning with *Días de combate* (Battle Days) (1974), Taibo's more than thirty novels feature the adventures of the Mexico City detective Héctor Belascoaran, a hard-boiled contemporary hero of the oppressed and fighter against corruption. Taibo has recently introduced two new protagonists: the contemplative detective writer Daniel Fierro in *La vida misma* (Life Itself) (1987), and the independent, foul-mouthed woman journalist Olga Lavanderos in *Que todo es posible* (Everything is Possible) (1995). He has twice won the Hammett International Prize for detective fiction, and has written biographies, most recently of Che Guevara.

Further reading

Braham, P. (1997) 'Violence and Patriotism: La Novela Negra from Chester Himes to Paco Ignacio Taibo II', *Journal of American and Comparative Cultures*, Summer, 20(2): 159–69.

Nichols, W.J. (1998) 'A quemarropa con Manuel

Vázquez Montalbán y Paco Ignacio Taibo II', *Arizona Journal of Hispanic Cultural Studies* 2: 197–231.

CYNTHIA STEELE

Taller

The journal *Taller*, published in Mexico City in twelve issues from 1938 to 1941, under the editorship of Rafael Solana (first four issues) and Octavio **Paz** (remaining eight issues), presented a strong and incisive critique of Mexican culture. The journal developed ideas earlier presented by Alfonso **Reyes** and the **Contemporáneos** group, in search of diversification and renovation in writing and cultural and aesthetic pursuits in Mexico. Contributors included the Mexican poets Efraín **Huerta**, Rafael Vega Albela, Alberto Quintero Alvarez and Neftalí Beltrán, as well as a number of Spanish writers living in exile in Mexico, among them Juan Rejano, María Zambrano, Antonio Sánchez Barbudo, José Bergamín and Francisco Giner de los Ríos.

Further reading

Cobo Borda, J.G. (1982) 'Paz's Workshop', *World Literature Today: A Literary Quarterly of the University of Oklahoma*, Autumn, 56(4): 619–25.

EDUARDO GUÍZAR-ALVAREZ

Tallet, José Zacarías

b. 1893, Matanzas, Cuba; d. 1989, Havana, Cuba

Poet and journalist

Tallet is probably best remembered as a journalist for *El País* (1943–60) and *El Mundo*, and in particular for his weekly columns in the journal *Bohemia*, advocating a correct use of the Spanish language – columns later collected in *Evitemos gazapos y gazapitos* (Let's Avoid Errors Big and Small) (1985). As a young man he was a leading figure in the student protests against the governments of Alfredo Zayas and Gerardo Machado. He was also a member of the **Grupo Minorista** and of the editorial board of the ***Revista de Avance***. He is also regarded as one of the founders of the school of social poetry rooted in black experience, together with **Guillén** and Regino Pedroso. His volumes of poetry include *La semilla estéril* (The Sterile Seed) (1951) and *Vivo aún* (Still Living) (1978). He won the National Literature Prize in 1984.

Further reading

Rodríguez Rivera, G. (1983) 'La poesía de José Z. Tallet', *Nuevos críticos cubanos*, ed. J. Prats Sariol, Havana: Editorial Letras Cubanas, 378–95.

Tallet, J.Z. (1979) *Poesía y prosa*, ed. Guillermo Rodríguez Rivera, Havana: Editorial Letras Cubanas.

WILFREDO CANCIO ISLA

Tamayo, Franz

b. 1879, La Paz, Bolivia; d. 1956, La Paz

Educator, writer and politician

Tamayo played a key role in the development of Bolivian education, insisting that it should have a specific national character. His attitude towards the Indian population was fundamentally paternalistic; he claimed direct descent from the Inca nobility, but argued that the contemporary Indian should be 'educated with love and patience'. He had less sympathy for the mestizo, towards whom his attitude was overtly racist and disparaging. In 1911 he founded the Liberal Party, was their Presidential candidate in 1919 and later became an important figure in the Bolivian parliament.

Further reading

Fernández, D. (1968) *La poesía lírica de Franz Tamayo*, La Paz: Los Amigos del Libro.

Rivera Rodas, O. (1991) 'Dialogismo y deconsturc-ción: Escritura vanguardista de Franz Tamayo', *Bolivian Studies* 2(1): 77–100.

Salmon, J. (1989) 'Naturaleza e historia en la ideología nacionalista de Franz Tamayo y

Alcides Arguedas', in G. Paolini (ed.), *La Chispa '89: Selected Proceedings*, New Orleans: Tulane University.

Tamayo, F. (1979) *Obra escogida*, ed. M. Baptista Gumucio, Caracas: Biblioteca Ayacucho.

MARÍA DORA VILLA GÓMEZ

Techo de la Ballena, El

El Techo de la Ballena was formed in Venezuela in 1960 after a split in the Sardio group over the issue of committed art. Their characteristic expressions were informality in art and in literature a kind of belligerent and challenging expressionism. Its most combative members (Caupolicán Ovalles, Carlos Contramaestre, Edmundo Aray and Adriano González León) provoked fierce controversies with their paintings, installations and poems. Their most famous expressions – books such as Ovalles's *¿Duerme usted señor Presidente?* (Are You Sleeping, Mr President?) (1962) and installations like *Homenaje a la necrofilia* (Homage to Necrophilia) (1962) – challenged a conflictive social reality marked by the initiation of armed struggle during the presidency of Rómulo Betancourt.

Further reading

Liscano, J. (1973) *Panorama de la literatura venezolana*, Caracas: Publicaciones Españolas, 249–75.

Rama, A. (ed.) (1987) *Antología del Techo de la Ballena*, Caracas: Fundarte.

RAFAEL CASTILLO ZAPATA

Teillier, Jorge

b. 1935, Lautaro, Chile; d. 1996, Santiago, Chile

Poet

Teillier was an exponent of *lárica* (from *lar*, home) poetry, a neo-romantic current in Chilean literature inspired by a desire to recuperate a sense of place, of rootedness. Teillier's narrative voice is sometimes evocative of a lost paradise represented by childhood and the daily life of southern Chilean villages, their landscapes and characters. Time passing and remembrance are leitmotifs of his poetry. His published volumes include *Muertes y maravillas* (Deaths and Marvels) (1971) and *Poemas del país de nunca jamás* (Poems from Never-Never Land) (1963).

Further reading

Giordano, J. (1966) 'La poesía de Jorge Teillier', *Poesía chilena (1960–1965)*, Santiago de Chile: Trilce, 114–26.

Teillier, J. (1979) *Para hablar con los muertos (antología)*, Mexico City: El Oso Hormiguero.

FERNANDO J. ROSENBERG

Teitelboim, Volodia

b. 1913, Chillán, Chile

Writer and politician

Leader of the Chilean Communist Party, and a deputy and senator during the Unidad Popular government in Chile, the military *coup* of 1973 found Teitelboim outside Chile. The military junta under Augusto Pinochet then stripped him of his Chilean citizenship.

Teitelboim belonged to the literary generation of 1938, responsible for a new direction in Chilean regionalist writing, taking it from a rural to an urban context. Associated with the aesthetics of **socialist realism**, the urban worker often figured centrally in his work. But he also extended *criollismo* (as Chilean regionalism was called) into new landscapes, in particular the north of the country dominated by the production of nitrates. Teitelboim's *Los hijos del salitre* (The Children of Nitrate) (1952) and *La semilla en la arena* (The Seed in the Sand) (1957) are set in that world. *Los hijos del salitre* is a biographical novel about the communist leader Elías Laferte. One scene in the book describes the strike and the ultimate slaughter of a group of nitrate workers and their families at Santa María de Iquiqe in 1906. This crucial page of Chilean history became the basis of one of the fundamental texts of the new Chilean song *La cantata de Santa María de Iquique*, written and performed by the group Quilapayún

Founder of the cultural magazine, *Aurora*, Teitelboim was a journalist and literary critic, whose other works included biographies of the poets Pablo **Neruda**, Jorge Luis **Borges**, Vicente **Huidobro** and Gabriela **Mistral**.

While still in exile in Madrid, Teitelboim was director of *Araucaria de Chile*, a cultural magazine of fundamental importance, which provided a meeting point and enduring link for the Chilean diaspora after the military *coup*. In 1987 Teitelboim secretly re-entered Chile and as a result of the trip wrote *En el país prohibido: Sin el permiso de Pinochet* (In the Forbidden Country: Without Pinochet's Permission) in which he described the experience of his return to his country, where the crushing presence of the dictator co-existed with the people's hope of an end to the nightmare imposed by the military government.

Teitelboim's political writing and fiction has a deep sense of social responsibility forged in those times and yet still has resonance in contemporary reality. In 2002 he was awarded Chile's National Prize for Literature.

Further reading

Otero, M. (1980) '*La guerra interna* de Volodia Teitelboim', *Casa de las Américas* 122: 116–20.

LUIS E. CÁRCAMO-HUECHANTE

Tejada Holguín, Ramón

b. 1961, San Francisco de Macorís, Dominican Republic

Writer

Although a trained sociologist, Tejada Holguín is best known for his short stories. In 1987, his short story 'La verdadera historia de la mujer que era incapaz de amar' (The True Story of the Woman Who Could Not Love) won first prize at the Casa de Teatro literary contest. Since then he has combined sociological research with his short stories. Two of his books, *Probablemente es virgen, todavía* (She is Still a Virgin, Probably) (1993) and *Blasfemia angelical* (Angelic Blasphemy) (1995), were written with René Rodríguez Soriano.

FERNANDO VALERIO-HOLGUÍN

Telemaque, Harold Milton

b. 1909, Plymouth, Tobago; d. 1982, Trinidad

Teacher and poet

First and foremost a teacher, in 1967 Telemaque was awarded the National Golden Award for service to education and community by the Trinidad and Tobago Teachers' Union. In addition to teaching and poetry, he was an active lay reader and preacher, becoming an ordained Anglican minister in 1980. His creative output is very slight but has always been highly regarded. His poems appeared in several journals and anthologies, including ***Kyk-Over-Al***, *Now* and *Caribbean Voices: An Anthology of West Indian Poetry*, and Henry Swanzy broadcast some of his work on the BBC's *Caribbean Voices* programme.

FUNSO AIYEJINA

Telles, Lygia Fagundes

b. 1923, São Paulo, Brazil

Writer

A master of the short story, Telles's first mature and fully developed work was a novel, *Ciranda de pedra* (The Marble Dance) (1954), which displays many of the elements characteristic of her prose: psychological introspection, an existentialist view of reality, the use of colloquialisms and of language as a reflection of the characters' psychological and social condition, and elements of the fantastic (see **fantastic literature**) and the gothic. Telles, who joined the Brazilian Academy of Letters in 1985, prefers female protagonists, portraying reality through their perspective, and has focused on issues concerning the condition of women in Brazilian society.

Further reading

Lisboa, M.M. (1997) 'Lygia Fagundes Telles', in V. Smith (ed.), *Encyclopedia of Latin American Literature*, London: Fitzroy Dearborn, 782–3.
Lucas, F. (1989) 'Lygia Fagundes Telles', in C.A. Solé and M.I. Abreu (eds), *Latin American Writers*, New York: Scribners, 3, 1271–5.
Pinto, C.F. (1990) *O Bildungsroman femenino: Quatro exemplos brasileiros*, São Paulo: Perspectiva, 109–46.
Silva, V.M.T. (1985) *A metamorfose nos contos de Lygia Fagundes Telles*, Rio de Janeiro: Editora Presença.
—— (1992) *A ficção intertextual de Lygia Fagundes Telles*, Goiânia: Cegraf/UFG.
Telles, L.F. (1986) *Tigrela and Other Stories*, trans. M.A. Neves, New York: Avon.
Tolman, J.H. (1970) 'New Fiction: Lygia Fagundes Telles', *Review* 30: 65–70.

CRISTINA FERREIRA-PINTO

Terán, Ana Enriqueta

b. 1918, Valera, Trujillo, Venezuela

Poet

Together with Enriqueta **Arvelo Larriva**, Ida **Gramcko** and Elizabeth Schon, Terán is considered one of Venezuela's outstanding women poets. Her writing, influenced particularly by the great poets of the Spanish Golden Age, Garcilaso and San Juan de la Cruz, is an exploration of home, nature, an almost mystical search for the essential rhythms of everyday life. Since 1946, when her first volume of poems – *Al norte de la sangre* (North of the Blood) – was published, she has continued to write and publish. She won the National Literature Prize in 1990.

Further reading

Bravo, V. (1997) Las figuraciones de luz de la utopía *Albatros*, de Ana Enriqueta Terán', *Cifra nueva: Revista de cultura*, Nov., 5–6: 35–40.
Cuartin, P. (1997) 'Exordio a tres textos de Ana Enriqueta Terán', *Cifra nueva: Revista de cultura*, Nov., 5–6: 63–72.
Terán, A.E. (2003) *The Poetess Counts to 100 and Bows Out*, Princeton: Princeton University Press.

JORGE ROMERO LEÓN

testimonio

Testimonio is a distinct form of documentary narrative, told in the first person by the actual witness of socio-historical events and edited by a professional writer, journalist or social scientist. The genre includes a wide range of works. However, the most striking difference between *testimonio* and other texts that qualify as non-fiction – such as documentary novels, autobiographies (see **autobiography**), life stories, memories, diaries and journalistic accounts – is the mediated character of the former: the witness is both subject and object of the narrative, with the editor as mediator between an authentic oral story and its discursive transcription.

Critics classify testimonial texts according to the degree of editorial intervention on a spectrum that ranges from 'raw' testimonies – Domitila Barrios de Chungara's *Si me permiten hablar* (Let Me Speak) (1976), edited by Moema Viezzer – to novels – Elena **Poniatowska**'s *Hasta no verte Jesús mío* (Here's To You, Jesus) (1969); Miguel **Barnet**'s *Canción de Rachel* (Rachel's Song) (1969); Manlio **Argueta**'s *Un día en la vida* (One Day of Life) (1980). Despite the explicit disavowal of literary intentions by some of the editors, the texts considered as representative of the genre – Rodolfo **Walsh**'s *Operación masacre* (Operation Massacre) (1957), Barnet's/Montejo's *Biografía de un cimarrón* (Autobiography of a Runaway Slave) (1966), Poniatowska's *La noche de Tlatelolco* (Massacre in Mexico) (1971), Elisabeth Burgos/Rigoberta Menchú's *Me llamo Rigoberta Menchú y así me nació la conciencia* (I . . . Rigoberta Menchú) (1983) – offer aesthetically enhanced transcriptions of original accounts.

Testimonio's legitimation in the 1970s coincided with the simultaneous waning of the experimentation of the 'new novel'. This process of canonization resulted from a constellation of factors: the critics' effort to bring to centre stage texts previously considered marginal or non-literary was reinforced by the authors/editors themselves

(Barnet, Poniatowska) as they highlighted the innovative character of their testimonial projects. In 1970 the prestigious Cuban cultural institution **Casa de las Américas** added the category of testimonial narrative to its literary competition. With Havana established as a centre for the dissemination of *testimonio*, the role of the new genre as a counterpoint to self-centred novels of the **Boom** became more evident than ever. *Testimonio* was hailed as a uniquely Latin American literary form, one that represented the creative vitality of Latin American culture and its power not only to alter the paradigm of subaltern representation but to effect socio-political change as well.

While the 1970s and 1980s saw eye-witness narratives – both individual and collective – emerge from the margins of literature, even a cursory historical overview will remind us that testimonial writing has been the most enduring tradition in Latin American letters. What these lengthy lists of texts have in common are discursive patterns deployed to produce the testimonial effect. *Testimonio* conflates and puts into play four deep-rooted orders of Western discourse: the religious, the anthropological, the psychoanalytic and the legal.

This formal cross-fertilization certainly invites transdisciplinary close readings, but some of the most compelling studies view *testimonio* primarily as a political device. Critics such as Beverley, Jara, Prada Oropeza, Randall, Vidal, Yúdice and Zimmerman focus on *testimonio*'s allegiance to the political Left and its mission to redress socio-political grievances, contest official history, raise consciousness and effect change within the post-colonial context. Without abandoning some of these extra-literary concerns, other critics (**Achugar**, Craft, Feal, Foster, Kerr, Moreiras, Sklodowska, Sommer, Steele, Vera León, Gareth Williams) describe *testimonio* in terms of its discursive characteristics. Despite their considerable differences in tone and focus, all critics recognize *testimonio*'s premise to recover the experience of the oppressed and the unspoken world of the disenfranchised that would otherwise be muted or forgotten.

The canonization of *testimonio* has set the stage for two trends in Latin American writing: since the 1980s outright parodies of testimonial conventions have become as common as self-conscious re-examinations of the genre's premises (as in Ruth Behar's *Translated Woman: Crossing the Border with Esperanza's Story* (1993)). While we may lament the demise of 'the dialogue essential to testimonial discourse' due, in part, 'to the retrenchment of the left' (Sanjinés, in Gugelberger 1996: 254), we should bear in mind that the loss of *testimonio*'s critical potential is likely to open spaces for previously unheard voices and for alternative venues of representation.

Further reading

Barnet, M. (1994) *Autobiography of a Runaway Slave*, trans. W.N. Hill, Willimantic, CT: Curbstone Press.

Craft, L.J. (1997) *Novels of Testimony and Resistance from Central America*, Gainesville, FL: University Press of Florida.

Foster, D.W. (1984) 'Latin American Documentary Narrative', *PMLA* 99(1): 41–55.

Gugelberger, G.M. (ed.) (1996) *The Real Thing: Testimonial Discourse in Latin America*, Durham, NC: Duke University Press.

Jara, R. and A. Vidal (eds) (1986) *Testimonio y literatura*, Minneapolis, MN: Institute of Ideologies and Literature.

Menchú, R. (1984) *I … Rigoberta Menchú: An Indian Woman in Guatemala*, ed. E. Burgos-Debray, trans. A. Wright, London: Verso.

Sklodowska, E. (1991) *Testimonio hispanoamericano: Historia, teoría, poética*, New York: Peter Lang.

Volek, E. (1997) 'Testimonial Writing', in V. Smith (ed.), *Encyclopedia of Latin American Literature*, London: Fitzroy Dearborn, 783–5.

ELZBIETA SKLODOWSKA

Texto crítico

The journal *Texto crítico* was founded in 1975 by exiled Uruguayan critic Jorge Ruffinelli at the Universidad Veracruzana (Xalapa, Mexico). Its avowed purpose was to form a body of critical work on Latin American literature with particular emphasis on Mexico. Cognizant of its historical moment – bloody dictatorships in the Southern Cone and repressive regimes in Central America –

the journal privileged studies on literary expressions in their socio-political context and published special issues on **Onetti** and **Cortázar**. Ruffinelli directed *Texto crítico* until 1986; from double issue 36–7 (1987), and appearing twice yearly thereafter, it continued to be devoted to similar expressed goals under the direction of Sixto Rodríguez Hernández.

See also: Nuevo texto crítico

SAÚL SOSNOWSKI

theatre

The term Latin American theatre is, in a certain sense, a misnomer. Theatre always arises out of a specific cultural context and Latin America as a region spans huge geographical and cultural regions stretching from the north of Mexico to the southern tip of Tierra del Fuego. The historical progressions of the countries involved have been diverse. Generally speaking the countries of the region can be divided into three main groups: those that share a history of great indigenous civilizations such as the Aztec, the Maya, and the Inca prior to the conquest whose cultural forms continue to shape those countries today; those – largely in South America – where there was a scarcity of indigenous presence or where such presence was wiped out, and, consequently, the cultural forms of those countries have been significantly shaped by the influence of European immigrants; and, finally, those countries such as Brazil and in the Caribbean where active trading in black African slaves existed during the colonial period leading to cultural forms heavily influenced by African aesthetics and philosophical orientation. Such a panoramic view of the region illustrates the broad outlines that distinguish individual countries from one another and militates against the notion of a monolithic Latin American theatre. What these countries do share, however, and what allows us to conceive of a particular Latin American sensibility in the theatre, is a history of ideological, artistic and economic marginalization. Located on the outskirts of European and North American consciousness, treated as the 'countryside' from which the dominant 'metropolis' extracts raw materials and human labour, Latin America has frequently been perceived as the hinterland to the power centres of the world. That perception has in turn all too frequently been incorporated into Latin Americans' perceptions of themselves, creating not only economic, but cultural dependency as well. While political independence from colonial rule was achieved in the late nineteenth century, cultural dependence upon colonial mentality lasted a great deal longer.

In the theatre the effort to break such cultural dependency began in 1925 when a series of university-affiliated and independent theatre groups sprang up throughout the region. These groups were organized in a variety of ways and adopted diverse methods of production, but the essential impetus behind their organization was the creation of a specifically Latin American theatre movement capable of speaking to and for the various countries in the region still struggling to find their own identity. The theatre groups founded in the 1920s formed part of a continuum that began with the *gaucho* (South American cowboy) play *Juan Moreira* (1884/86) performed in an Argentine circus ring and continues throughout the twentieth century. This search for a 'national soul' in the theatre comes to fruition in the socially engaged theatre of the 1960s and 1970s. The notion of theatre as a catalyst for social change is anticipated by the *teatro de masas* ('mass theatre') movement following the Mexican Revolution. Using thousands of actors in open-air theatres in a performance style reminiscent of indigenous ritual, this celebrated the blending of Spanish and indigenous bloodlines that formed the mixture of various classes necessary to create the new Mexican society. Such a socially conscious theatre can also be found in Elena Alvarez's *Dos dramas revolucionarias* (Two Revolutionary Dramas) (1926) and in the plays of Emilio **Carballido** such as *La zona intermedia* (The Intermediate Zone) (1950) and *El día que soltaron los leones* (The Day They Let the Lions Loose) (1963).

The search for a 'national soul' was by no means confined to the theatre. Perhaps the best example is Violeta Parra's radio recitals in Chile that rescued popular forms of expression in poetry and music from becoming merely artefacts for touristic consumption and, in turn, greatly influenced the Chilean 'new song' movement of the 1960s and

1970s. In the Chilean theatre, Egon **Wolff**, in plays such as *Los invasores* (The Invaders) (1963) and *er* *Flores de papel* (Paper Flowers) (1970), creates a world that represents the consciousness of those who seek to maintain the status quo and force all those around them to conform to it. This is the sector of Chilean society that was outraged by Salvador Allende's ascension to power and that, until the 1990s, supported the Pinochet regime.

There is a general tendency throughout the region in the mid-twentieth century towards a reinterpretation of the past, with a universalization of theatrical technique that can be seen in the work of playwrights such as the Argentinians Agustín **Cuzzani** and Osvaldo **Dragún**, the Cuban Virgilio **Piñera** and the Puerto Rican René **Marqués**. All of these playwrights employ a radical restructuring of history, ritual and mythology to treat Latin American political and sociological themes. Perhaps the best example of this incorporation of historical and mythological elements characteristic of mid-twentieth century Latin American theatre can be found in the plays of Guatemalan author Miguel Angel **Asturias**. His play *Soluna* (Sun/Moon) (1955) utilizes a combination of popular characters, folklore, Guatemalan social customs and mysticism to create a magical, cosmic vision of a battle between moon people and sun people. Peace between the two forces is achieved by a Church-sanctified wedding melding indigenous ritual to Christian doctrine and creating new methods of proceeding that show themselves in the forms created by theological and theatrical circles in the latter half of the twentieth century.

As any traveller in Latin America has observed, at the centre of any village or city is a plaza or central square. On one side of the plaza stands the church or cathedral, on the other side the municipal or national government building. Religious and temporal powers face each other across the space in which the community's daily life, its markets, its festivals, its strolls, take place. Funeral cortèges, wedding processions, children in white on their way to first communion, all cross this space. It provides a stage for the daily life and death of the community, as well as the actual stage for festive celebrations and theatre performances. While Church and State face one another from opposite sides of the plaza, Latin American history is, in fact, to a large extent, a history of mutual support between the two institutions.

It is precisely the conditions created by such an historical symbiotic relationship between Church and State, namely the immense disparity between rich and poor, that gave birth to new theological and theatrical approaches that attempt to comprehend Latin American reality with compassion for all, not just a handful, of Latin Americans. Based on the consciousness-raising techniques of the great Brazilian educator Paulo Freire, liberation theology and liberation theatre both began with an investigation of the history and concerns of a given community itself rather than approaching that community with a preconceived notion of its needs or what it will be interested in.

Liberation theatre is a method of theatrical creation that enables the audience to speak *for* itself through theatrical forms rather than using the theatre as a means of speaking *to* the people in the audience in a patronizing way that mirrors centuries of colonial oppression. The theatre, in other words, should become a force for liberation from certain inherited structures, whether societal, political or aesthetic, that have been externally imposed. Some of the best-known practitioners of liberation theatre are the Brazilian Augusto **Boal**, the Colombian Enrique **Buenaventura** and the Nicaraguan Alan Bolt. While Boal's work has become the best known internationally, all three men have worked to create theatre that speaks to their own particular cultural context. Buenaventura, along with Santiago García, was a prime mover in Colombia's New Theatre (*nuevo teatro*) movement. Bolt's work, arising directly out of his role as a Sandinista militant in the Nicaraguan Revolution of 1979, links the artistic work of the groups in the Communitarian Theatre Movement firmly to their primary role as agrarian collectives. While each of these men has worked within his own country, they share (as do many others) a central perception that the Latin American theatre has historically been an art form solely reflecting the concerns of the region's colonial and neo-colonial oppressors. Each man approaches the task of liberating the theatre from those inherited structures in a different way, but the wished-for result is the same: to put the means of producing theatre into the hands of the Latin American people themselves. Such a theatre is frequently the result of an investigation of a given community's concerns coupled with the theatre company's collective response to such concerns. What, potentially, is created is a highly dynamic relationship between the theatre and its audience.

Political upheavals throughout the region beginning with the Cuban Revolution in 1958–59, including a series of military *coup d'états* in South America in the 1970s and 1980s, as well as brutal civil wars in Central America during the same period, all served to transform the dynamic of the interaction between theatre and society. From the formation of Cuba's Teatro Escambray in 1968 with its explicit motto 'Theatre, an effective weapon in service of the Revolution', to the Argentinian Teatro Abierto's challenge to the military junta's repression between 1981 and 1983, Latin American theatre entered a period of political engagement that frequently created governmental backlash, censorship, imprisonment and exile. Figures such as Boal in Brazil and Mauricio **Rosencof** in Uruguay were imprisoned and tortured. Companies such as Chile's El Aleph and Uruguay's El Galpón were forced into exile as were important individuals such as the Argentine playwright Griselda **Gambaro**. Faced with such conditions the theatrical community fought back in a number of ways, creating productions that with simplicity and aesthetic beauty were metaphorical representations of contemporary events. Forms of encoded speech or images mutually understood by actor and audience were increasingly used, and classical texts were reinvigorated in such a way as to comment upon a totalitarian regime. Representative of these strategies is the work of the Chilean playwrights Isidora Aguirre and Juan **Radrigán** and the Argentinian Eduardo **Pavlovsky**.

With the demise of dictatorship throughout the region in the late 1980s and early 1990s, the kinds of themes, forms and theatrical techniques that had filled the stage under such regimes were no longer appropriate to the new context. No longer an essential site of resistance to dictatorship, Latin American theatre in general produced a profusion of forms and performance styles reflecting an initial disorientation on the part of theatre practitioners themselves. While the liberation theatre of the 1960s and 1970s was by no means abandoned, it became decidedly less doctrinaire. The liberation theatre of the 1980s and 1990s admits the possibility of magic, of sacrament, and of a sense of diversion in the theatre. Having firmly established its own identity it borrows from global theatrical forms in order to enhance its own practice. This can be seen in examples as diverse as Teatro Escambray's sophisticated theatre of images in *La paloma negra* (The Black Dove) (1974), the Mexican Grupo Espiral's *Nahui ollin* (The Fifth Sun) (1977), with its utilization of a combination of indigenous codexes and Southeast Asian shadow puppetry, or the Colombian Barco Ebrio's production *Crápula mácula* (1990) exploring contemporary Colombian society by means of a performance style that draws upon Japanese Noh and Bunraku. There is an increasing tendency towards investigation of historical figures and popular forms such as the tango in Argentina, the *murga* in Uruguay or African influences in Brazil and Cuba. From Venezuela to Mexico more and more attention is being paid to the cultural representation of the indigenous civilizations of the region. The trends most prevalent in Latin American theatre today are an increasing incorporation of an anthropological awareness of Latin American culture with twentieth-century theatrical practice and an emphasis upon experimentation with scenic space. While such trends have points of intersection with the 'metropolitan' centres of Europe and North America, the Latin American 'countryside' has finally found its own voice.

See also: Brechtian theatre

Further reading:

Albuquerque, S. (1991) *Violent Acts: A Study of Contemporary Latin American Theatre*, Detroit: Wayne State University Press.

—— (1996) 'The Brazilian Theatre in the Twentieth Century', in R. González Echevarría and E. Pupo-Walker (eds), *Cambridge History of Latin American Literature*, Cambridge: Cambridge University Press, 3: 269–313.

Albuquerque, S., E. de Costa, C. Boyle and W. Neate (1997) 'Theatre', in V. Smith (ed.), *Encyclopedia of Latin American Literature*, London: Fitzroy Dearborn, 785–97.

Cypess, S.M. (1996) 'Spanish American Theatre in the Twentieth Century', in R. González Echevarría and E. Pupo-Walker (eds), *Cambridge History of Latin American Literature*, Cambridge: Cambridge University Press, 2: 297–525.

Harris, M. (1993) *The Dialogical Theatre*, New York: St Martin's Press.

Solórzano, C. (ed.) (1994) *The World Encyclopedia of Contemporary Theatre*, vol. 2, London: Routledge.

Taylor, D. (1991) *Theatre of Crisis: Drama and Politics in Latin America*, Lexington: University of Kentucky Press.

Taylor, D. and J. Villegas (eds) (1994) *Negotiating Performance: Gender, Sexuality, and Theatricality in Latin/o America*, Durham, NC: Duke University Press.

Versényi, A. (1993) *Theatre in Latin America: Religion, Politics, and Culture from Cortés to the 1980s*, Cambridge: Cambridge University Press.

Weiss, Judith *et al.* (1993) *Latin American Popular Theatre*, Albuquerque: University of New Mexico Press.

ADAM VERSÉNYI

Thelwell, Michael

b. 1939, Kingston, Jamaica

Writer and academic

Thelwell's book *The Harder They Come* (1980) is unusual in being written *after* the film of that name, scripted by Perry Henzel and Trevor **Rhone**. The story of legendary ghetto gunman Rhygin, it exemplifies the realism which Thelwell considers the best technique for conveying black experience. Some critics accuse Thelwell of romanticizing the Jamaican experience, avoiding serious socio-political questions and glorifying *machismo*, but most reviews were enthusiastic. Thelwell studied English at Howard University, then did a Masters in Fine Arts at the University of Massachusetts, where he has taught since 1969.

Further reading

Thelwell, M. (1991) '*The Harder They Come*: from film to book', *Grand Street* 37.

PAT DUNN AND PAMELA MORDECAI

Thompson, Ralph

b. 1928, Poughkeepsie, New York, USA

Poet and painter

A sort of literary impresario, Thompson brought Caribbean writers to the USA, and musical theatre (including **Walcott**'s *Ti-Jean and His Brothers*) to Jamaica. He has published two collections of poetry: *The Denting of a Wave* (1992) and *Moving On* (1998). Like several other Caribbean poets – **Goodison**, Walcott, **Escoffery** – Thompson is also a painter. A businessman and art collector, he lives in Kingston.

PAT DUNN AND PAMELA MORDECAI

Torres, Ana Teresa

b. 1945, Caracas, Venezuela

Writer

A psychoanalyst who came late to literature, Torres's first novel *El exilio del tiempo* (Exile from Time) (1990) caused some surprise among readers and critics by returning to the provincial world of rural Venezuela which had disappeared from national literature with the demise of the Gómez dictatorship. Taking a lead from Teresa **de la Parra** and Antonia **Palacios**, Torres explicitly set out to recuperate that historical moment, as her 1992 novel *Doña Inés contra el olvido* (Doña Inés Against Forgetfulness) confirmed.

Further reading

Franco, F. (1997) 'Mujer, historia e identidad en Hispanoamérica: *Doña Inés contra el olvido*, de Ana Teresa Torres', *Inti: Revista de literatura hispánica*, July–Dec., 35: 63–73.

Rivas de Wesolowski, L.M. (1997) 'Metaficción e historia en la escritura de Ana Teresa Torres', *Cifra nueva: Revista de cultura*, Nov., 5–6: 163–82.

VERONICA JAFFÉ

Torres Bodet, Jaime

b. 1902, Mexico City; d. 1974, Mexico City

Writer and diplomat

One of the original members of the **Contemporáneos** group, Torres Bodet was co-editor for the first numbers of *Contemporáneos* (1928–31), the journal that gave the group its name. In 1929 he entered the Mexican foreign service and held important posts as Minister of Education and of Foreign Affairs in Mexico and Secretary General of UNESCO (1948–52). His voluminous literary production includes some fifteen poetry collections, among them *Destierro* (Exile) (1930) and *Cripta* (Crypt) (1937), several experimental novels written during the 1920s and 1930s, and a considerable number of critical and biographical works.

Further reading

Dauster, F. (1963) 'La poesía de Jaime Torres Bodet', *Revista iberoamericana* 49: 73–94.

Karsen, S.P. (1989) 'Jaime Torres Bodet', in C.A. Solé and M.I. Abreu (eds), *Latin American Writers*, New York: Scribners, 2: 933–9.

Torres Bodet, J. (1986) *La cinta de plata*, ed. L.M. Schneider, Mexico City: UNAM.

MERLIN H. FORSTER

Torres-Ríoseco, Arturo

b. 1897, Talca, Chile; d. 1971, Oakland, California, USA

Literary critic

Torres-Ríoseco was one of the first to write **literary histories** (and to compile anthologies) encompassing the whole of Latin America. He emigrated from Chile to the USA in 1918 and taught at Berkeley and elsewhere. Instrumental in the founding of the **Instituto Internacional de Literatura Iberoamericana**, he served several times as its president and as editor of the *Revista iberoamericana*. A friend of Gabriela **Mistral** (who called him 'the universal Chilean') and Cecília **Meireles**, the letters he received from them and others were published as *Literary and Cultural Journeys* (1995). Besides his literary studies, he published several books of poetry.

Further reading

Roggiano, A.A. (1972) 'Homenaje a Arturo Torres-Ríoseco', *Revista iberoamericana* 38: 15–29.

Zapata, M.A. (1997) 'Silueatas literarias de Arturo Torres-Ríoseco', *Anales de la literatura española contemporánea* 22(2): 299–326.

DANIEL BALDERSTON

Torri, Julio

b. 1889, Saltillo, Mexico; d. 1970, Mexico City

Poet and writer

A poet, essayist and short story writer, Torri's scant but innovative writings defied traditional literary genres. A member of the Ateneo de la Juventud (1909–10), he went on to work closely with José **Vasconcelos** in the first post-revolutionary period on his project to produce cheap editions of literary classics. His own writings lie somewhere between poetry and prose, the short **essay** and the **short story**, and deploy a highly concentrated language. The core of his writings, which began with *Ensayos y poemas* (Essays and Poems) (1917), was collected in the compilation *Tres libros* (Three Books) (1964).

Further reading

Torri, J. (1964) *Tres libros (Ensayos y poemas, De fusilamientos, Prosas disperas)*, Mexico City: Fondo de Cultura Económica.

Zaitzeff, S. (1983) *El arte de Julio Torri*, Mexico: Editorial Oasis.

RAFAEL OLEA FRANCO

Traba, Marta

b. 1930, Buenos Aires, Argentina;
d. 1983, Madrid, Spain

Writer

One of the most dynamic figures in the Latin American culture of the 1970s and 1980s, Traba was an influential art historian and prolific writer of fiction who advocated the dissemination of culture and fought against measures undermining creative work. Trained as an art historian, in 1954 she and her then husband, journalist Alberto Zalamea, moved to Bogotá, Colombia, where she lived until 1966 and had an outstanding teaching career as professor of art history. An advocate of disseminating cultural products to large audiences, she presented a television series on art history. Her initiative to found a museum of modern art in the capital city came to fruition in 1955 when the Colombian Congress passed a law to this effect, although the museum was not opened to the public until 1962; Traba was its first director.

In 1966 she won the prestigious **Casa de las Américas** prize for her first novel *Ceremonias del verano* (Summer Ceremonies). In 1969 she married the Uruguayan critic Angel **Rama**, and together they lectured throughout the region. They lived in Puerto Rico, teaching at the Universidad de Puerto Rico for a year. Between 1974 and 1979 they settled in Venezuela, where Traba taught at the Instituto Pedagógico de Caracas and at the Universidad Central. The couple hoped to settle in the USA, but she and Rama were accused of communist activity by the US State Department. Denied residency, they moved to Paris in 1982. The couple died tragically in a plane crash near Madrid Airport, when travelling to a conference in Bogotá.

Of combative spirit, Traba fought with ideas against arbitrary and unjust measures designed to undermine intellectual work. Among her most influential writings are *El museo vacío* (The Empty Museum) (1958), *La pintura nueva en Latinoamérica* (New Painting in Latin América) (1961), *Los cuatro monstruos cardinales* (The Four Cardinal Monsters) (1965) and *Dos décadas vulnerables en las artes plásticas latinoamericanas 1950/70* (Two Vulnerable Decades in Latin American Plastic Arts, 1950–70) (1973). Equally prolific in her fiction, she wrote one book of poems, two collections of short stories and seven novels, three of which appeared posthumously.

Further reading

Agosín, M. (1984) 'Marta Traba', *Sin nombre*, April–June, 14(3): 97–100.

Bautista Gutiérrez, G. (1995) 'Marta Traba: A Life of Images and Words', in M. Agosín (ed.), N. Abraham Hall (trans.), *A Dream of Light and Shadow: Portraits of Latin American Women Writers*, Albuquerque: University of New Mexico Press.

García Pinto, M. (1991) 'Marta Traba', in *Women Writers of Latin America. Intimate Histories*, trans. Trudy Balch and M. García Pinto, Austin: University of Texas Press, 183–93.

Glora, Z. (ed.) (1984) *Marta Traba*, Bogotá: Museo de Arte Moderno de Bogotá.

Picon Garfield, E. (1985) *Women's Voices from Latin America: Interviews with Six Contemporary Authors*, Detroit: Wayne State Univesity Press.

Poniatowska, E. (1985) 'Marta Traba o el salto al vacio', *Revista iberoamericana* 51(132–3): 883–97.

MAGDALENA GARCÍA PINTO

Tráfico

This group of six Venezuelan poets (Yolanda **Pantin**, Armando **Rojas Guardia**, Miguel and Alberto Márquez, Igor Barreto and Rafael Castillo Zapata) erupted onto the sleepy literary scene of the early eighties. The group's slogan – 'We came from the night and we are making for the street' – ironically referred to Vicente **Gerbasi**'s famous line, and announced the group's dedication to 'conversational poetry'. It published various poetry collections, but its most important contribution was to take poetry to the streets in frequent recitals which could take place anywhere. When the group dispersed, each member took a different and very personal direction.

Further reading

Castillo Zapata, Rafael (1993) 'Palabras recuperadas, la poesía venezolana de los ochenta: Rescate y transformación de las palabras de la tribu. El caso “Trafico” ’, *Inti: Revista de literatura hispánica* 37–8: 197–205.

VERONICA JAFFÉ

translation in Latin America

Translation has long been of central cultural importance in Latin America, and many Latin American intellectuals have worked as translators for important periods of their lives, making translation a part of their intellectual practice, and reflection on it a central part of their systems of thought. The names of **Borges**, **Cortázar**, **Paz**, **Girri** and Haroldo de **Campos**, for instance, are inseparably bound up with their work as translators, their overseeing of the translations of their own works, and their theorizing of translation as an integral part of communication and the intellectual life.

Alfonso **Reyes**, the Mexican essayist, wrote extensively about translation in the 1930s, as did his friend Jorge Luis Borges (whose classic essay on translations of Homer dates from 1932). Borges later wrote essays on the translators of the Arabian Nights (1936) and on Beckford's *Vathek* (1943), an essay in which he sums up his privileging of the translated text (in this case, the English translation of Beckford's French original, a translation with which the author was involved) over the original with his ironic comment: ‘El original es infiel a la traducción’ (The original is unfaithful to the translation). Borges also refers frequently to one of the classic nineteenth-century debates on translation, that between Newman and Arnold. Translation was a profession for various other writers. José **Bianco** was known for his translations of Henry James and for the theatre, while Julio **Cortázar** translated the works of Poe, but also worked for years at UNESCO in Paris translating dreary official documents, a job which he parodies in ***Rayuela*** (Hopscotch) (1963), and reflections on their experience had a strong impact on their literary work (the protagonists of several Cortázar stories are translators). Two other extraordinary translators were the literary critic Enrique **Pezzoni**, known for his versions of *Moby Dick* and *Lolita*, and Alberto Girri, a significant part of whose poetic work consists of translations. The journal ***Sur*** was known for its emphasis on literary translation.

In the last decades of the twentieth century, the dominant voices in translation studies in Latin America have been Octavio Paz, with his interest in ‘translating’ the experience of the avant-garde (see **avant-garde in Latin America**) across languages (a concern much earlier of the Chilean poet Vicente **Huidobro**, who declared his intention of writing poetry that would be translatable), and Haroldo de Campos, who has written extensively, though not always comprehensibly, on translation as re-creation. Campos's ideas have influenced a variety of scholars working in Brazil, with centres of literary studies at the University of Minas Gerais and at the Pontifícia Universidade Catolica de São Paulo, largely devoted to explicating his ideas. Two other centres of translation studies are the Universidade Federal de Santa Catarina in Florianópolis, Brazil, and the Universidad de Mar del Plata in Argentina.

Further reading

Aparicio, F.R. (1991) *Versiones, interpretaciones y creaciones: Instancias de la traducción literaria en Hispanoamérica en el siglo veinte*, Gaithersburg: Ediciones Hispamérica.

Balderston, D. and M. Schwartz (ed.) (2002) *Voice Overs: Latin American Literature and Translation*, Albany: SUNY Press.

Barbosa, H.G. and D. Gerdes (1997) ‘Translation’, in V. Smith (ed.), *Encyclopedia of Latin American Literature*, London: Fitzroy Dearborn, 798–802.

Bradford, L. (ed.) (1997) *Traducción como cultura*, Rosario, Argentina: Beatriz Viterbo.

DANIEL BALDERSTON AND MARCY E. SCHWARTZ

translations of Latin American literature

Before the **Boom** of the 1960s, Latin American literature was *terra incognita* for the common reader. The first systematic publishing attempt to introduce Latin American literature to a reading public outside the Spanish-speaking world was *La Croix* *du Sud*, a series dedicated exclusively to Ibero-American literature, started in 1951 by Roger Caillois and published by Gallimard in Paris. In the 1950s, translations of 'novels of the land' (*novelas de la tierra*) by Ciro **Alegría**, Ricardo **Güiraldes** and Martín Luis **Guzmán** and others took the lion's share in this collection, but the French translations of Jorge Luis **Borges**, Alejo **Carpentier**, Juan **Rulfo** and Ernesto **Sábato** showed its true pioneer spirit.

As it was the first country to embrace the new Latin American novel (*la nueva novela*), France served as an important model for other Western countries. Contrary to what has generally been assumed, the mediating role of the USA during the boom in translations was rather modest. In fact, it was, generally speaking, slower to introduce the *nueva novela* than Italy and, probably, Germany. At the bottom of the ranking we find the countries with a relatively small book market and language area (Sweden, Denmark, the Netherlands etc.). In all of these cases, the most prominent literature of three decades (the 1940s, 1950s and 1960s) was translated during only one decade (the 1960s).

Amongst the authors translated most often during the Boom period we find Jorge Luis Borges, Alejo Carpentier, Julio **Cortázar**, Carlos **Fuentes**, Gabriel **García Márquez**, Pablo **Neruda**, Manuel **Puig**, Octavio **Paz** and Mario **Vargas Llosa**. They were to give Latin American literature the strong identity it still has today in the Western world and win for it the status of a world literature. So far, not one writer of the **post-Boom** generations has had an impact similar to that of any single member of this group. Isabel **Allende**, for example, is a best-selling author without precedent, but her literary status is not unchallenged. That does not alter the fact that, from a commercial point of view, Allende has set a very important trend, because the market for fictionalized family chronicles told from a female perspective and spiced with ready-made **magic realism** is still booming.

Further reading

Balderston, D. and M. Schwartz (ed.) (2002) *Voice Overs: Latin American Literature and Translation*, Albany: SUNY Press.

Keenoy, R., D. Treece and P. Hyland (1999) *The Babel Guide to the Fiction of Portugal, Brazil and Africa in Translation*, London: Boulevard Books.

Keenoy, R. *et al.* (2000) *The Babel Guide to Latin American Fiction in Translation*, London: Boulevard Books.

Molloy, S. (1972) *La diffusion de la littérature hispano-américaine en France au XXe siècle*, Paris: Presses Universitaires de France.

Wiese, C. (1992) *Die hispanoamerikanischen Boom-Romane in Deutschland. Literaturvermittlung, Buchmarkt und Rezeption*, Frankfurt am Main: Vervuert.

Wilson, J. (1989) *An A to Z of Modern Latin American Literature in English Translation*, London: The Institute of Latin American Studies.

MAARTEN STEENMEIJER

travel writing

Travel writing by Latin American and Caribbean authors has been undervalued as a serious object of study even though, since the earliest period of their colonization, Latin America and the Caribbean have provided the raw material for exotic accounts by travellers from the Old World. These accounts, in their turn, have influenced the form of modern novels such as Gabriel **García Márquez**'s ***Cien años de soledad*** (One Hundred Years of Solitude) (1967) and Wilson **Harris**'s *The Guyana Quartet* (1985).

Such neglect is surprising, since the travel chronicle, often a journalistic commission, was a preferred form for nineteenth-century or early twentieth-century nationalists such as José **Martí** (1853–95), Eugenio María de Hostos (1839–1903) and José Enrique **Rodó** (1871–1917). In their *crónicas* (see ***crónica***) these writers, whose frequent and extended periods of exile drew them to this literary form, used their travels throughout Latin America, the USA and Europe as a pretext to discuss broader questions of identity, ethics, philosophy, politics and aesthetics. A preoccupation with all of these areas fed their search for a meaningful post-colonial nationality for their respective home countries.

An earlier generation of writers travelled *into* Latin America as part of a journey of national self-discovery; Horacio **Quiroga** both wrote and photographed the Misiones region, as unfamiliar to inhabitants of the Plate region as to Europeans in the 1920s. The *indigenistas* too travelled upwards into the Andes as part of their project of cultural renewal. Alejo **Carpentier**'s *Los* ***pasos perdidos*** (The Lost Steps) (1949) may stand as emblematic of that inward journey. In a sense, this was a 'naming' or a renaming of a hitherto alien landscape.

Meanwhile, while the *crónica* survived into the twentieth century as a legitimate form employed by major writers such as the Peruvian poet César **Vallejo**, travel intensified a politicized sense of pan-Americanism and, problematically, diasporic pan-Caribbeanism, not only in the early *cronistas* but also in at least two of their spiritual and intellectual successors. The revolutionary leader, Ernesto 'Che' Guevara, recorded his youthful travels throughout Latin America in his *Motorcycle Diaries* and the Jamaican writer, Andrew **Salkey**, retold his travels in *Georgetown Journal: A Caribbean Writer's Journey from London via Port-of-Spain to Georgetown, Guyana* (1972).

The professionalization and internationalization of the writer's vocation since the **Boom** has further afforded the often already privileged figure of the Latin American writer, such as Carlos **Fuentes**, the luxury to roam the world as a flamboyantly cosmopolitan intellectual. But, by following the distinct tradition of travel writing established by the (inter)nationalists mentioned earlier, contemporary writers are also able to take advantage of the detachment afforded by travel to reflect on questions closer to home and to search for fruitful – devalued or perhaps elusive – personal, national and cultural origins on which to build a pan-American future.

More recently, Europe and North America have reacquainted themselves with Latin America – empathizing lyrically with it, as in Bruce Chatwin's *In Patagonia* (1988); traversing it with less sympathy, like Paul Theroux in his *The Old Patagonian Express* (1979); or travelling as a witness to the north's continuing depredations, like Joan Didion in *Salvador* (1982). Those who travel the other way are still, however, markedly fewer in number.

Further reading

Greenblatt, S. (1991) *Marvelous Possessions: The Wonder of the New World*, Oxford: Oxford University Press.

Nuñez, E. (ed.) (1985) *España vista por viajeros hispanoamericanos*, Madrid: Ediciones Cultura Hispánica/Instituto de Cooperación Iberoamericana.

Pratt, M.L. (1992) *Imperial Eyes: Travel Writing and Transculturation*, London: Routledge.

Wilson, J. (1993) *Traveller's Literary Companion to South and Central America*, Brighton: In Print.

—— (1997) 'Travel Literature', in V. Smith (ed.), *Encyclopedia of Latin American Literature*, London: Fitzroy Dearborn, 803.

JOHN D. PERIVOLARIS

Traven, B.

b. 1882, Schwiebus, Pomerania, Germany; d. 1969, Mexico City

Writer

A German socialist/anarchist who emigrated to Mexico after the collapse of the 1919 Bavarian Republic, Traven (known as Ret Marut in his youth) became a Mexican citizen and kept his identity a mystery for forty-five years while writing a series of best-selling social protest novels. His five 'Jungle Novels', especially *Der Marsch ins Reich der Caoba* (March to the Montería) (1971) and *La rebelión de los colgados* (Rebellion of the Hanged) (1936), were impassioned critiques of the colonial exploitation of Mayan debt peons on the mahogany plantations of the Lacandón rainforest. Several of Traven's novels were made into well-known films, including *Treasure of the Sierra Madre* (1948) (directed by John Huston), and *La Rosa Blanca* (The White Rose) (1961) (directed by Roberto Gavaldón), a critique of the abuses committed by multinational oil companies in Mexico.

Further reading

Baumann, M. (1976) *B. Traven*, Albuquerque: University of New Mexico Press.

Chankin, D.O. (1975) *Anonymity and Death: The Fiction of B. Traven*, University Park: Pennsylvania State University Press.

Raskin, J. (1980) *My Search for B. Traven*, New York: Methuen.

Wyatt, W. (1980) *The Man Who Was B. Traven*, London: Cape.

CYNTHIA STEELE

Trefossa

b. 1916, Suriname; d. 1975, the Netherlands

Poet

An ardent defender of the use of the native creole Sranan Tongo in literature, Trefossa (Henny F. de Ziel) published his first poetry in **Koenders**'s magazine *Foetoeboi* (Messenger Boy). Trefossa showed himself a master of cultivating the literary use of his native tongue and was an example to his own and younger generations. His poetry is characterized by reflection and reverie, which more often than not is concerned with the beauty of Suriname and what threatens it. His collected poetry appeared in 1977 in Suriname.

Further reading

Rutgers, W. (1986) *Dubbeltje lezen, stuivertje schrijven*, Oranjestad/Den Haag: Charuba/Leopold, 44–57.

Trefossa (1990) *Trefossa: na wan njoen kari*, special monographic issue, *Mutyama* (Amsterdam) 1(1).

AART G. BROEK

Trejo, Oswaldo

b. 1928, Mérida, Venezuela; d. 1996, Caracas, Venezuela

Writer and diplomat

Trejo's first published work appeared in the journal *Contrapunto* in the 1940s; from then on he gained a reputation as one of the pioneers of experimental fiction writing in Venezuela, with works like his novel *También los hombres son ciudades* (Men are Cities Too) (1962) and his short stories, some of which are collected in *Horas escondido en las palabras* (Hours Hidden in Words) (1994). He was a diplomat and director of a number of cultural institutions such as the Museo de Bellas Artes and the publishing house **Monte Avila**. Together with Angel **Rama** and José Ramón Medina, he set up the **Biblioteca Ayacucho** collection and remained as its literary director until his death. He was awarded the National Prize for Literature in 1988.

Further reading

Antillano, L. (1972) 'Oswaldo Trejo al encuentro de la palabra', *Revista nacional de cultura* 205: 21–37.

Macht de Vera, E. (1982) *Indagaciones en el universo narrativo de Oswaldo Trejo*, Caracas: Fundarte.

Trejo, O. (1980) *Al trajo, trejo, troja, trujo, treja, traje, trejo*, Caracas: Monte Avila.

JORGE ROMERO LEÓN

Trevisan, Dalton

b. 1925, Curitiba, Paraná, Brazil

Writer

Associated with hyperrealism and pop art, Trevisan's realism fits best into the sceptical tradition of Machado de Assis. Beginning with economical short stories, the author constructed a vast body of work (some twenty-four titles) which, paradoxically, points increasingly towards silence, exemplified in his most recent work with haiku. He uses this form to attest to the increasing disconnection between people and the collapse of the short story as a genre. Repetition is the most characteristic feature of Trevisan's writing; characters and situations doubled on themselves indicate emptiness and the absence of communication in the prison of a Curitiba that is uterus, prison and grave. The film by Joaquim Pedro de Andrade, *Guerra conjugal* (Conjugal War) (1975), captures very well the atmosphere and the dramatic quality of Trevisan's work.

Further reading

Trevisan, D. (1972) *The Vampire of Curitiba and Other Stories*, trans. G. Rabassa, New York: Knopf.
Vieira, N. (1986) 'João e Maria: Dalton Trevisan's Eponymous Heroes', *Hispania* 69(1): 45–52.
—— (1997) 'Dalton Trevisan', in V. Smith (ed.), *Encyclopedia of Latin American Literature*, London: Fitzroy Dearborn, 804–5.
Villaça, N. (1984) *Cemitério de mitos: Uma leitura de Dalton Trevisan*, Rio de Janeiro: Achiamé.
Waldman, B. (1982) *Do vampiro ao cafajeste: Uma leitura da obra de Dalton Trevisan*, São Paulo: Hucitec.

BERTA WALDMAN

Trevisan, João Silvério

b. 1944, Ribeirão Bonito, Brazil

Writer and activist

In 1986 João Silvério Trevisan published *Devassos no paraíso* (Perverts in Paradise), a partly autobiographical, partly historical account of emerging gay and lesbian movements during the *abertura*. The work includes an historically provocative analysis of homosexuality in Brazil and identifies homosexuals as a repressed minority in Brazilian society. Trevisan also has written novels and collections of short stories including *Testamento de Jônatas deixado a David* (Jonathan's Last Testament to David) (1976) and *O livro do avesso: Romance* (The Backward Book: A Novel) (1994).

Further reading

Trevisan, J.S. (1986) *Perverts in Paradise*, trans. M. Foreman, London: Gay Men's Press.
—— (1992) *O livro do avesso: Romance; O avesso do livro*, São Paulo: Ars Poetica.
—— (1994) *Ana em Veneza*, São Paulo: Editora Best Seller: Círculo do Livro.
—— (1997) *Troços & destroços: Contos*, Rio de Janeiro: Editora Record.

SUSAN CANTY QUINLAN

Triana, José

b. 1931, Bayamo, Cuba

Playwright

Triana's 1965 play *La* ***noche de los asesinos*** (The Night of the Assassins) made him Cuba's best-known playwright internationally, yet much of his work after 1966 remains unpublished due to his complex relationship with the Cuban Revolution and his exile in 1980. Triana's interest in drama was stimulated while studying in Spain from 1955 until 1959, where he was exposed to the latest avant-garde drama. Upon the defeat of the Batista regime, Triana returned to Cuba to support the Revolution. He served as a literary adviser to several government institutions and began to produce his plays.

Triana's works contain elements from the theatre of cruelty, ritual theatre and the theatre of the absurd. His early plays such as *Medea en el espejo* (Medea in the Mirror) (1960) and *La muerte del ñeque* (The Death of the Strong Man) (1964) place Greek tragic figures in an urban tenement environment characterized by African culture, popular types and criminality. Román de la Campa suggests that Triana's plays enact a ritualization in which the oppressed attempt to overcome authoritarian forces. The masses are unsuccessful, however, for collective fear condemns them to repeating behaviours such as superstition, gossip and game-playing that evade real action.

The frustrated ritual process is most evident in *La noche de los asesinos*. In this metatheatrical play, three siblings of indeterminate age repeatedly rehearse the murder of their parents in a squalid attic or basement. Set in the 1950s, the play can be seen as critical of the Batista dictatorship, but it has also been interpreted as critical of the revolutionary process, which imposed a new authoritarianism. The play's ambiguous message led Cuban critics to question Triana's ideological stance and he was accused of privileging individual artistic commitment over political responsibility to the Revolution.

Triana's later plays are historical and more realist than his earlier works. *Palabras comunes* (Worlds Apart) (1979), for example, examines the problem of female honour at the turn of the century. By focusing on a transitional period, that of the emergence of the Cuban Republic, Triana returns to a constant question posed by his plays: can historical change ever break with a repetitive cycle of oppression?

Further reading

Dauster, F.N. (1976) 'The Game of Chance: The Theater of José Triana', in L.F. Lyday and G.W. Woodyard (eds), *Dramatists in Revolt: The New Latin American Theater*, Austin: University of Texas Press.

—— (1989) 'José Triana', in C.A. Solé and M.I. Abreu (eds), *Latin American Writers*, New York: Scribners, 3, 1415–19.

De la Campa, R. (1979) *José Triana: Ritualización de la sociedad cubana*, Minneapolis, MN: Institute for the Study of Ideologies and Literature.

Fernández Fernández, R. (1995) *El teatro del absurdo de José Triana: Ensayo de narratología greimasiana*, Boulder, CO: Society of Spanish and Spanish-American Studies.

Hoeg, J. (1997) 'José Triana', in V. Smith (ed.), *Encyclopedia of Latin American Literature*, London: Fitzroy Dearborn, 806–8.

Nigro, K.F. (ed.) (1994) *Palabras más que comunes: Ensayos sobre el teatro de José Triana*, Boulder, CO: Society of Spanish and Spanish-American Studies.

Triana, J. (1971) 'The Criminals', in G. Woodyard (ed.), *The Modern Stage in Latin America: Six Plays*, New York: Dutton.

CAMILLA STEVENS

Trinidade, Solano

b. 1908, Recife, Brazil; d. 1974, Rio de Janeiro, Brazil

Poet

Hailed as the 'People's Poet', Francisco Solano Trinidade wrote poetry for and about exploited and oppressed Brazilians, particularly those of African descent. His 1944 *Poemas de uma vida simple* (Poems of a Simple Life) addressed poverty, hunger, racism and workers' rights. The authoritarian regime of Getúlio Vargas seized several hundred copies of the book and jailed Trinidade for a short period. His work from that period evidenced a strong identification with orthodox Marxism, which emphasized the primacy of class over race in the struggle for social equality. During the 1950s Trinidade was influenced by the Paris-based Afro-Antillean ***négritude*** literary movement.

CHRISTOPHER DUNN

Triviño, Consuelo

b. 1956, Bogotá, Colombia

Writer and literary critic

Triviño belongs to a group of female writers whose prose reveals interesting characteristics and features of contemporary Colombian literature, which leaves canonic male authors and repetitive models behind. Her style evokes childhood memories and the description of a diverse landscape in which the city and urban settings figure greatly. Triviño has written short stories, published research studies on Colombian novelist José María **Vargas Vila**'s *Diario secreto* (Secret Diary), and in 1998 published her fine but never recognized novel *Prohibido salir a la calle* (Forbidden to Go Out to the Street). In this novel, a young, sensitive voice takes the reader to places and times of a Bogotá that grows and transforms rapidly alongside its inhabitants.

Further reading

Triviño, Consuelo (1998) *Prohibido salir a la calle*, Bogotá: Editorial Planeta.

ALVARO BERNAL

U

Ubidia, Abdón

b. 1944, Quito, Ecuador

Writer

Ubidia's early publications appeared in the iconoclastic review ***Pucuna***, where the questioning of social norms in decay was the rule. Ubidia, together with Iván **Egüez**, Raúl **Pérez Torres**, Ulises Estrella, Fernando Tinajero, Agustín Cuevas and others, is among the most distinguished cultural promoters and creative voices from Quito. He has excellent command of technique and great capacity as a storyteller. Among his works are the stories *Bajo un mismo extraño cielo* (Under the Same Strange Sky) (1979) and the novel *Sueño de lobos* (Wolves' Dream) (1986).

Further reading

Handelsman, Michael (1990) 'Entre el desencanto y la posmodernidad: Un análisis de *Sueño de lobos*', *RLA: Romance Languages Annual*, 2: 445–9.

Jaramillo, María Dolores (2002) 'Abdón Ubidia: Rostros y rastros de la ciudad', *Revista iberoamericana*, Jan.–March, 68(198): 123–36.

HUMBERTO E. ROBLES

Ugarte, Manuel

b. 1878, Buenos Aires, Argentina; d. 1951, Nice, France

Writer and diplomat

A passionate pan-Hispanicist and anti-imperialist, Ugarte's beliefs led him from a youthful association with the Socialist Party to numerous diplomatic posts under President Juan Perón. Active in literary and journalistic movements in Buenos Aires, Ugarte endeavoured to defend Latin American traditions and culture from foreign influence. He founded the daily *La Patria* and the magazine *Vida de Hoy*, and published essays, travel books and short stories. As a diplomat from 1946 until his death, he promoted pan-Hispanicism as an alternative to US-led pan-Americanism.

Further reading

Maíz, C. (2001) 'Nuevas cartografias simbólicas: Espacio, identidad y crísis en la ensayística de Manuel Ugarte', *Ciberletras*, Aug., 5.

Matilla, M.S. (1990) 'La poética de Manuel Ugarte: Emergencia de un campo intelectual', *Hispanic Journal*, Spring, 11(1): 121–31.

Pinillos, N. (1987) 'Manuel Ugarte, un hombre para este tiempo', *Cuadernos americanos* 1(5): 164–217.

Ugarte, M. (1978) *La nación latinoamericana*, ed. and intro. N. Galasso, Caracas: Biblioteca Ayacucho.

THOMAS EDSALL

ultraísmo

An avant-garde movement that began in Spain in 1918 and was brought to Argentina by **Borges**, one of its most fervent adherents, in the period from 1921 to 1923. The Spanish movement published the magazine *Ultra* and included Guillermo de Torre, who would later be an important historian of the avant-garde (see **avant-grade in Latin America**) and (after marrying Norah Borges, a painter) Borges's brother-in-law. The Argentine group published the two issues of a 'revista mural' *Prisma* (a literary magazine in the form of a poster that was pasted on the walls of Buenos Aires) and the first issues of *Proa*. By the time Borges published his first books in 1923 and 1925 he was no longer a true believer in *ultraísmo*. *Ultraísta* poems often consisted of disconnected series of images, eliminating logical connections, punctuation and 'poetic' language; there were pronounced similarities with the *creacionismo* of Vicente **Huidobro**, although the two movements were often virulently at odds.

Further reading

Videla, G. (1963) *El ultraísmo*, Madrid: Gredos.

DANIEL BALDERSTON

Umpierre, Luz María

b. 1947, Santurce, Puerto Rico

Poet

Umpierre's bilingual poetry is direct and striking in its intensity. Also a scholar, she grew up in Puerto Rico and has lived for many years in the USA, as a *Latina* writer, teacher and advocate of gays and lesbians in educational institutions and elsewhere. Her publications include several volumes of poetry as well as literary criticism, among them *Ideología y novela en Puerto Rico* (Ideology and the Novel in Puerto Rico) (1983), *... Y otras desgracias/And Other Misfortunes* (1985) and *The Margarita Poems* (1987).

Further reading

Martinez, E.M. (1996) 'Lesbian Themes in Luz María Umpierre's *The Margarita Poems ... Y otras desgracias. And Other Misfortunes...*', *Confluencia: Revista hispánica de cultura y literatura*, Fall, 12(1): 66–82.

Perez, Janet (2000) 'Biculturalismo, resistencia y asimilacion en la poesia y dialogo intertextual de tres poetas puertorriquenas transterradas', in F. Burgos (ed.), *Studies in Honor of Myron Lichtblau*, Newark, DE: Juan de la Cuesta, 275–88.

CATHERINE DEN TANDT

UNEAC

Founded in 1961 at a Writers and Artists Congress presided over by Nicolás **Guillén**, UNEAC (Unión de Artistas y Escritores de Cuba /Union of Artists and Writers of Cuba) was organized into sections corresponding to artistic fields: literature, plastic arts, cinema, radio and television, music and theatre arts. Guillén was its president until 1988, when he was replaced by Abel Prieto, who later became Minister of Culture.

One of its more important activities is its annual literary competition, founded in 1965, which has been an important means of promoting new Cuban writers. In 1968 the prizewinners were Antón **Arrufat**, for his play *Los siete contra Tebas* (Seven Against Thebes) and Heberto **Padilla**, for his book of poetry *Fuera del juego* (Outside the Game); both writers were then censured, setting in motion what came to be called the 'Padilla affair'. UNEAC also offers the David Prize for unpublished writers, which has brought to public attention writers such as Luis Rogelio **Nogueras**, Eduardo Heras León and Senel **Paz**.

UNEAC publishes the journals *Unión* and *La Gaceta de Cuba*. Its publishing house publishes only Cuban writers. Among the most significant works to appear under its imprint were José **Lezama Lima**'s *Paradiso* (1966) and volumes by poets Eliseo **Diego** and Nicolás Guillén. UNEAC has sponsored other festivals including the Caracol Festival of Film, Radio and Television, the Boleros de Oro International Festival and the International Festival of Contemporary Music for Symphonic and

Chamber Compositions. From 1995 it began to produce a television programme called *Hurón Azul*, and a year later founded its own documentary unit. Its headquarters, in a mansion in Havana's Vedado quarter, also houses the Nicolás Guillén Foundation.

UNEAC has faithfully followed the ebb and flow of Cuban artistic life since the Cuban Revolution. Although independent, its role has been mediated by state policies on art and culture, and its autonomy limited by them. Its constitution reflects the desire of the revolutionary leadership to centralize and unify the activities of all Cuban writers and artists, following the model of similar organizations in eastern Europe before 1989.

In the 1960s, UNEAC was an important promoter of Cuban culture, but after 1971 the decisions of the so-called Education and Culture Congress, the bureaucratic structures and the imposition of censorship combined to affect its work. The changes in Cuban life beginning in the second half of the 1980s have revitalized its work to some extent, reopening possibilities for cultural debate and a widening distribution of its publications.

Further information

http://www.uneac.com/

WILFREDO CANCIO ISLA

Urondo, Francisco

b. 1930, Santa Fe, Argentina; d. 1976, Buenos Aires, Argentina

Writer

Francisco Urondo was a writer in every genre – poet, novelist, playwright, journalist, scriptwriter (one of his best works was the script for *Pajarito Gómez* (1965), a ground-breaking film) and literary critic with *Veinte años de poesía argentina* (Twenty Years of Argentine Poetry) (1968). A member of the Montoneros movement, he died in action. Of all his literary activities, his poetry was most important; coherent, with a well-defined line of development, it was inseparable from his political commitment. The complete *Poemas* (1984) includes his published work and poems unpublished (1970–72) at the time of his death.

Further reading

Gelman, J. (1983) 'Urondo, Walsh, Conti: La clara dignidad', *Quimera: Revista de literatura*, Nov., 33: 23–8.

Orgambide, P. (1977) 'Francisco Urondo: Poesía y combate', *Casa de las Américas* 101: 28–33.

Urondo, F. (1984) *Poemas*, Havana: Casa de las Américas.

ENRIQUE FOFFANI

Uruguay

Despite its small size and population, Uruguay has an important place in Latin American literature and literary studies, having to its name major writers (José Enrique **Rodó**, Julio **Herrera y Reissig**, Delmira **Agustini**, Juan Carlos **Onetti**, Felisberto **Hernández**, Mario **Benedetti** and Cristina **Peri Rossi**) and literary scholars (Alberto **Zum Felde**, Emir **Rodríguez Monegal**, Angel **Rama** and Hugo **Achugar**). With an important university and national library, active theatres, and a vibrant cultural life in its cafes, museums and media, Montevideo (the home of a large percentage of the country's population) has been an important centre of cultural production for a century.

The national poem, *Tabaré*, published in 1888 by Juan **Zorrilla de San Martín**, is an improbable verse melodrama based on an indigenous legend that Zorrilla picked up in Chile; it defines the national culture as born of the struggle – and the hopeless love – between Spaniards and Charrúa Indians (long since disappeared when Zorrilla wrote). In contrast, José Enrique Rodó defines in his *Ariel* (1900) an urban space in which educated young people form part of a liberal intelligentsia; not in vain is Montevideo's most beautiful park called the Parque Rodó. During the period of **Spanish American modernism**, Uruguay was the home of Rodó and of the brilliant poets Julio Herrera y Reissig and Delmira Agustini, as well as of eminent intellectuals Carlos **Vaz Ferreira** and

Alberto Zum Felde. (Juana de **Ibarbourou** was the most famous poet of the period after *modernismo.*) The period of liberal ascendancy associated with the presidency of José Batlle y Ordóñez (1856–1929, president 1903–7 and 1911–15) included strong investments in education, libraries and cultural institutions. Curiously, at the same time that the cultural scene was dominated by the capital city, its themes were strongly rural, particularly in the area of prose fiction, marked by what was called 'nativismo'. Juan Carlos Onetti broke with this dominant mode, writing an urban literature of alienation as early as in his first novels, *El pozo* (The Well) (1939) and *Tierra de nadie* (No Man's Land) (1941). In 1939 Carlos Quijano founded the cultural magazine *Marcha* in Montevideo, and this vital cultural organ was the centre of Left-liberal discourse in the country up until the time of the military coup of 1974. In the 1950s a group of younger writers and critics, including for a time Emir Rodríguez Monegal, Idea **Vilariño** and Angel Rama, collaborated on the magazine *Número*, another important intellectual organ, although eventually there would be a break between Rodríguez Monegal and Rama that would last until their deaths in the 1980s. After the return to democracy *Brecha* was the successor to *Marcha.* Important publishing houses include Arca (founded by Angel and Carlos Rama), Banda Oriental and Trilce.

Uruguayan narrative is dominated by Onetti and Felisberto Hernández, contemporaries both of whom portrayed marginal people in urban settings though using very different tones and techniques. Onetti's fiction, focused on the imaginary city of Santa María, has memorable characters who struggle to realize their dreams in impossible situations. Felisberto Hernández's most memorable and grotesque situations revolve not around characters but around objects: dolls, floating candles, delicate glass figures, a balcony, the feet of a piano. Other well-known twentieth-century Uruguayan fiction writers include Francisco **Espínola**, Enrique **Amorim**, Mario Benedetti, Armonía **Somers**, Cristina Peri Rossi and Eduardo **Galeano**.

Major names in Uruguayan poetry after Zorrilla, Agustini, Herrera y Reissig and Ibarbourou include Benedetti (certainly the most widely read, with many of his poems turned into songs), Sara de **Ibáñez**, Cristina Peri Rossi, Idea Vilariño, Enrique **Fierro** and Ida **Vitale**. Important playwrights include Florencio **Sánchez** (the dominant figure in Argentine and Uruguayan theatre of the early part of the twentieth century), Carlos **Maggi**, Carlos Denis Molina, Mauricio **Rosencof** and Alvaro Ahunchaín, while Atahualpa del Cioppo (founder of the Teatro El Galpón) was the dominant director.

In literary studies, Uruguay was the place of origin of a number of leading critics, including Fernando **Ainsía**, Angel Rama, Emir Rodríguez Monegal, Jorge Ruffinelli, Hugo Verani, Roberto Echavarren, Hugo Achugar and Mabel Moraña, though most of them have produced their important work while living elsewhere, many having been forced into exile during the decade of military rule. Rama, who died in a plane accident in 1983, is widely considered one of the leading intellectuals of Latin America of the second half of the twentieth century; his legacy includes a solid group of critical works, publishing enterprises including Arca and the Biblioteca Ayacucho (the latter in Venezuela, where he lived for a time), and provocative critical ideas that continue to be actively debated in the field.

Further reading

Achugar, H. (1993) *La balsa de la Medusa: Ensayos sobre identidad, cultura y fin de siglo en Uruguay*, Montevideo: Trilce.

Benedetti, M. (1960) *El país de la cola de paja*, Montevideo: Arca.

Moraña, M. and H. Achugar (eds) (2000) *Uruguay: Imaginarios culturales*, Pittsburgh: Instituto Internacional de Literatura Iberoamericana and Montevideo: Ediciones Trilce.

Moraña, M. and H. Machaín (eds) (2003) *Marcha y América Latina*, Pittsburgh: Instituto Internacional de Literatura Iberoamericana.

Rodríguez Monegal, E. (1966) *Literatura uruguaya del medio siglo*, Montevideo: Alfa.

Sosnowski, S. (ed.) (1987) *Represión, exilio y democracia: La cultura uruguaya*, Montevideo: Ediciones de la Banda Oriental.

Zum Felde, A. (1930). *El proceso intelectual del Uruguay:*

Crítica de su literatura, Montevideo: Imprenta Nacional Colorada.

DANIEL BALDERSTON

Urzagasti, Jesús

b. 1941, Gran Chaco, Bolivia

Writer

Urzagasti is part of the 1950s generation alongside poets such as Pedro **Shimose** and Roberto Echazu. Key features of his writings are his attempt to reveal and depict his native region through a kind of landscape poetry, and his exploration of an internal universe. This can be clearly seen in his poetic novel *Tirinea* (1969), his volume of poetry *Yerubia* (1978) and his highly lyrical fiction *De la ventana al parque* (From the Window to the Park) (1992).

Further reading

Mitre, E. (1986) 'Jesús Urzagasti', in *Poetas contemporáneos de Bolivia*, Caracas: Monte Avila, 95–100.
Rivera-Rodas, O. (1972) 'Antinovela', in *La nueva narrativa boliviana*, La Paz: Editorial Camarlinghi, 185–218.

JUAN CARLOS ORIHUELA

Usigli, Rodolfo

b. 1905, Mexico City; d. 1979, Mexico City

Playwright

Born of an Italian father and a Polish mother, Usigli is considered the 'father' of modern Mexican playwrights, following the first generation of post-revolutionary playwrights. Usigli was professor of drama at the UNAM, a theatre critic, theoretician and director; he also translated Chekhov, O'Neill and Shaw. He joined Mexico's diplomatic service in 1944 and, during the 1960s, served in several European countries as well as in Lebanon.

Usigli is best known for his 'piece for demagogues', *El gesticulador* (The Gesticulator), written in 1938 and staged for the first time in 1947. It is a realistic drama criticizing Mexico's political system, the manipulation of official history, corruption and hypocrisy. The main character, César Rubio, is a failed history professor who returns to his home town in northern Mexico and meets a Harvard professor seeking information about the supposedly murdered César Rubio, hero of the Mexican Revolution. Rubio poses as his famous namesake and is swept into tragic history. The play was adapted for the screen by Emilio **Fernández** as *El Impostor* (The Imposter) (1956). The drama's critique of the Institutional Revolutionary Party's legacy of political murders has brought it to the stage again in post-1994 Mexico. His 'anti-historical' trilogy *Corona de sombra* (Crown of Shadow) (1943), *Corona de fuego* (Crown of Fire) (1943) and *Corona de luz* (Crown of Light) (1963) deals with the Habsburg emperors of Mexico, Hernán Cortés and the Indian Juan Diego (to whom the Virgin of Guadalupe appeared). Other important works are *Jano es una muchacha* (Jano is a Girl) (1952) and *Las madres* (The Mothers) (1949–60). Usigli's work consistently explores the psychology of the Mexican middle class, showing how social and political corruption leads to the disintegration of individuals and their families. He is also a master at revising official versions of Mexican history.

In 1932 he published *México en el teatro*, a historical account of Mexico's theatre beginning in the sixteenth century, and a critique of contemporary theatre, dance and cinema. Between 1939 and 1940 he directed several theatre groups, notably Teatro de Media Noche (Midnight Theatre), which produced 'clandestine' midnight stagings of national and international dramas, and published his main theoretical work, *Itinerario del autor dramático* (Itinerary of a Drama Author). His short novel *Ensayo de un crimen* (Rehearsal for a Crime) (1994) was adapted for the cinema by Luis Buñuel in 1955.

Further reading

Bearsell, P. (1989) 'Usigli's Political Drama in Perspective', *Bulletin of Hispanic Studies*, July, 66(3): 251–61.

—— (1992) *A Theatre for Cannibals: Rodolfo Usigli and the Mexican Stage*, Rutherford, NJ: Fairleigh Dickinson University Press.

Cohen, D. (2001) 'Usigli's Medio Tono and the Transition to Modern Mexican Theatre', *Latin American Theatre Review*, Fall, 35(1): 63–74.

Keightley, R. (1997) 'Rodolfo Usigli', in *Encyclopedia of Latin American Literature*, ed. V. Smith, London: Fitzroy Dearborn, 813–14.

Nigro, K. (1988) 'Light and Darkness in Usigli's *Corona de sombra*', *Chasqui: Revista de literatura latinoamericana*, Nov., 17(2): 27–34.

Scott, W.P. (1970) 'Rodolfo Usigli and Contemporary Dramatic Theory', *Romance Notes* 11: 526–30.

Usigli, R. (1963–79) *Teatro completo*, Mexico City: Fondo de Cultura Económica, 3 vols.

—— (1971) *Two Plays: Crown of Light, One of These Days*, Carbondale, IL: Southern Illinois University Press.

ANTONIO PRIETO-STAMBAUGH

Uslar Pietri, Arturo

b. 1906, Caracas, Venezuela; d. 2001, Caracas

Writer

Uslar Pietri was one of Venezuela's most eminent men of letters, known for his historical novels, his short stories and his weekly newspaper columns. His first historical novel *Las lanzas coloradas* (The Red Lances) (1931) was his most successful: dealing with battles in early 1814 between Bolívar's forces and the royalists, it makes bold use of experimental narrative techniques, including a cinematic perspective. The short stories of *Barrabás y otros relatos* (Barrabas and Other Stories) (1928) broke with ***criollismo*** and pioneered the modern short story in Venezuela. Some of the stories in the following volume, *Red* (The Net) (1936), partake of what would later be called **magical realism**. Uslar is also the author of *Letras y hombres de Venezuela* (Literature and Men in Venezuela) (1948), a history of the Spanish American novel (1954), and essays on the Venezuelan oil boom and on the idea of the New World (1969 and 1991 respectively). Politically active, he was Minister of Education in the early 1940s and senator after the fall of Pérez Jiménez, whose dictatorship he actively opposed. He founded the programme in Venezuelan literature at the Universidad Central de Venezuela in 1949. His newspaper column was published weekly almost without interruption since 1947 in various newspapers around the Spanish-speaking world and he was director of the Caracas daily *El Nacional* from 1969 to 1974.

Further reading:

Avendaño Vera, A. *et al.* (1989) *Contribución a la biblio-hemerografía de Arturo Uslar Pietri*, Caracas: Fundación Polar.

Eskenazi, M. (1988) *Uslar Pietri: Muchos hombres en un solo hombre*, Caracas: Caralex.

Marbán, J. (1997) 'Arturo Uslar Pietri', in *Encyclopedia of Latin American Literature*, ed. V. Smith, London: Fitzroy Dearborn, 815–17.

Miliani, D. (1969) *Uslar Pietri, renovador del cuento venezolano*, Caracas: Monte Avila.

Stabb, M. (1989) 'Arturo Uslar Pietri', in *Latin American Writers*, ed. C.A. Solé and M.I. Abreu, New York: Scribners, 3: 1057–62.

Uslar Pietri, A. (1963) *The Red Lances*, trans. H. de Onís, New York: Knopf.

Vivas Maldonado, J.L. (1963) *La cuentística de Arturo Uslar Pietri*, Caracas: Universidad Central de Venezuela.

DANIEL BALDERSTON

V

Vacarezza, Alberto

b. 1886, Buenos Aires, Argentina;
d. 1959, Buenos Aires

Playwright

Alberto Vacarezza was one of Argentina's most popular dramatists, outstanding among his one hundred or more works are *sainetes* (see ***sainete***) (multi-sketch dramatic genre developed in the River Plate region). *El conventillo de La Paloma* (The Slum Where La Paloma Lived) (1929) was presented both in the Teatro Colón and in travelling circus tents, as well as adapted for radio, television and cinema. *Tu cuna fue un conventillo* (Born in the Slums) (1921) stood out for its self-conscious language born out of lunfardo and cocoliche. Vacarezza was notable for his dramatic skill, his versification and his ability to invent new words.

Further reading

Castro, D.S. (1999) 'Villa Crespo: A Porteño Neighborhood: Alberto Vacarezza'a Theatric View and Reality', in G. Paolini and C.J. Paolini (eds), *La Chispa '99: Selected Proceedings*, New Orleans: Tulane University.

Mogliani, L. (2000) 'El teatro nativista de Alberto Vacarezza', in O. Pellettieri (ed.), *Indagaciones sobre el fin de siglo (Teatro iberoamericana y argentino)*, Buenos Aires: Galerna, Fundación Roberto Arlt.

NORA MAZZIOTTI

Valdés, Adriana

b. 1943, Santiago, Chile

Writer

An outstanding critic and intellectual, Valdés's work in the field of cultural criticism has won recognition at home and abroad. She has taught Latin American literature, art and culture in universities in Chile and elsewhere and is a member of the Chilean Academy and of the 'Imaginary Academy', a cultural foundation bringing together Chilean **intellectuals**, writers, filmmakers, critics, artists and philosophers to reflect upon the cultural implications of the millennium. Her *Composición de lugar: Escritos sobre cultura* (Composition of Place: Writings on Culture) was published in 1995.

Further reading

Valdes, A. (1992) 'Un ojo que falta: Reflexión sobre las culturas y los quinientos años', *Acta Literaria* 17: 45–57.

—— (1994) 'Identidades trasfugas: Lectura de *Tala*', *Revista iberoamericana* 60(168–9): 685–93.

ELIANA ORTEGA

Valdez, Diógenes

b. 1941, San Cristóbal, Dominican Republic

Writer

Valdez is a well-published critic who, like others of his generation, has won several awards. His 1978 short story book *El silencio del caracol* (The Silence of the Snail) (1978) shows his personal obsession with the overlapping of fantasy and reality. He has published three novels exploring everyday city life. His literary criticism in *Del imperio del caos al reino de la palabra* (From the Empire of Chaos to the Kingdom of the Word) (1986) analysed pluralismo, the **avant-garde** movement founded by Manuel **Rueda**.

FERNANDO VALERIO-HOLGUÍN

Valencia, Guillermo

b. 1873, Popayán, Colombia; d. 1943, Popayán

Writer

Valencia, together with José Asunción Silva, is one of the most conspicuous representatives of *modernismo* (see **Spanish American modernism**) in Colombia. His most representative poetry was published in *Ritos* (Rites) (1899); its heroes and images refer back to the ancient world and the Renaissance as revealed by titles such as 'Job', 'Pigmaleón' (Pygmalion) and 'El triunfo de Nerón' (Nero's Triumph). Some critics have accused him of an excessive concern with form. A member of an aristocratic family, Valencia was twice a presidential candidate (1918 and 1936). Between 1889 and 1901 he lived in Paris, where he encountered Oscar Wilde and Rubén Darío as well as the Symbolist poets.

Further reading

Espinosa, G. (1989) *Guillermo Valencia*, Bogotá: Procultura.

Karsen, S. (1951) *Guillermo Valencia, Colombian Poet*, New York: Hispanic Institute.

—— (1989) 'Guillermo Valencia', in C.A. Solé and M.I. Abreu (eds), *Latin American Writers*, New York: Scribners, 2, 477–82.

Nugent, R. (1962) 'Guillermo Valencia and French Poetic Theory', *Hispania* 45.

Valencia, G. (1952) *Obras poéticas completas*, ed. B. Sanín Cano, Madrid: Aguilar.

MIGUEL A. CARDINALE

Valente, Ignacio

b. 1936, Santiago, Chile

Literary critic and poet

For nearly thirty years (1966–94), Valente (born José Miguel Ibañez Langlois) wrote book reviews for the cultural pages of Chile's *El Mercurio* newspaper, and during the Pinochet military government (1973–90) he was the country's most influential critic of Chilean literature. Also an ordained priest, he has published twenty-three books, including nine works of poetry and fourteen scholarly works. Valente has argued that his disproportionate prominence as a critic was a product of the exile of most of Chile's important literary specialists, and that Chilean culture will not quickly recover from the silence that befell critical practices during so many years.

Further reading

Hernandez Galilea, Ana Francisca (1997) *Ibanez Langlois como Valente: 27 anos de critica literaria periodistica en Chile* (Ibanez Langlois as Ignacio Valente: Twenty-Seven Years of Journalistic Literary Criticism in Chile), Dissertation Abstracts International, Section C: Worldwide, (DAIC), 58(2): Item 1178 Degree Granting Institution: Universidad de Navarra.

AMALIA PEREIRA

Valenzuela, Luisa

b. 1938, Buenos Aires, Argentina

Writer

Valenzuela is one of the few Latin American women authors whose work has been translated almost in its totality and who has received considerable attention. A journalist for the Buenos Aires newspaper *La Nación*, after her first novel *Clara: Hay que sonreír* (Clara: You Have to Smile) (1966), she moved towards more linguistic experimentation in a traditional narrative with *Aquí pasan cosas raras* (Strange Things Happen Here) (1975) and *Como en la guerra* (As in War) (1977). During the military regime of the late 1970s, she moved to New York City. Her most recent writings deal with violence against women and violence by the State.

Further reading

Craig, L. (1997) 'Luisa Valenzuela', in V. Smith (ed.), *Encyclopedia of Latin American Literature*, London: Fitzroy Dearborn, 819–21.

Díaz, G. (2002) *Luisa Valenzuela sin máscara*, Buenos Aires: Feminaria Editora.

García Pinto, M. (1991) 'Luisa Valenzuela', in *Women Writers of Latin America. Intimate Histories*, trans. Trudy Balch and M. García Pinto, Austin: University of Texas Press, 195–221.

Magnarelli, S. (1988) *Reflections/Refractions: Reading Luisa Valenzuela*, New York: Peter Lang.

Picon Garfield, E. (1989) 'Luisa Valenzuela', in C.A. Solé and M.I. Abreu (eds), *Latin American Writers*, New York: Scribners, 3: 1445–9.

Valenzuela, L. (1987) *The Lizard's Tail*, trans. G. Rabassa, London: Serpent's Tail.

—— (1992) *Black Novel with Argentines*, trans. T. Talbot, New York: Simon & Schuster.

Valenzuela, L. *et al.* (2002) *Luisa Valenzuela: Simetrías/ Cambio de armas: Luisa Valenzuela y la crítica*, Caracas: eXcultura.

MAGDALENA GARCÍA PINTO

Valle, Rafael Heliodoro

b. 1891, Tegucigalpa, Honduras; d. 1959, Mexico City

Writer

Valle began as a *modernista* (see **Spanish American modernism**) poet with the publication in 1911 of his first book, *El rosal del ermitaño* (The Hermit's Rose Garden), followed by several other books of poetry that were similarly influenced by Rubén **Darío**. He served for decades in the diplomatic service of Honduras, although late in his life he expressed support for the Guatemalan reformist Arévalo, and for greater democracy in his own country, leading to his being removed from his diplomatic post. His most significant writings were in the field of Central American history; he earned his doctorate in that field in 1948. His *Historia de las ideas contemporáneas en Centroamérica* (History of Contemporary Ideas in Central America) (1960) is considered his most important work.

Further reading

Dorn, G.M. (1989) 'Rafael Heliodoro Valle', in C.A. Solé and M.I. Abreu (eds), *Latin American Writers*, New York: Scribners, 2, 721–5.

Romero de Valle, E. (1965) 'Los seudónimos de Rafael Heliodoro Valle', *Thesaurus: Boletín del Instituto Caro y Cuervo* 20: 297–324.

DANIEL BALDERSTON

Vallejo, César

b. 1892, Santiago de Chuco, Peru; d. 1938, Paris, France

Poet

Vallejo, particularly since his death, has come to be regarded as one of the major poets of the twentieth century, although his writing also includes short stories, novels, theatre, political essays and journalism. His 1918 volume *Los heraldos negros* (The Black Heralds) is a transitional work still heavily influenced by modernism, but he went on to revolutionize Spanish language poetry through a discourse based on defamiliarizing techniques, first in *Trilce* (1922), and then in his later work, published posthumously under the title *Poemas humanos* (Human Poems) (1938).

Of mixed Spanish and Indian descent, Vallejo inherited a tension between two cultural traditions that was central to his life and work. Brought up in the isolated Andean village of Santiago de Chuco, he followed the provincial's traditional route to self-improvement by moving to Lima via Trujillo. In 1922 he left Peru to settle in Paris. That journey from the periphery to the centre points to the ambition to be more than a local writer, but Vallejo was always concerned to speak with a Latin American voice and distanced himself from the Spanish American avant-garde (see **avant-garde in Latin America**), which he perceived as perpetuating cultural dependency by aping European modernity. His own distinctive style assimilated new developments in world literature but was largely forged on the margins of the avant-garde, and aimed above all to cast off imposed discourses and their accompanying ideological baggage.

Vallejo's poetry consciously inserts itself into the mainstream of Western literature as it is informed by the major intellectual currents of the age and deals with the major experiences of twentieth-century Western society. The collapse of traditional certainties is reflected in *Los heraldos negros* in the existential crisis of a young man who has lost faith in religious beliefs. That crisis intensified under the influence of evolutionist theory: *Trilce* evokes a world in which life ceaselessly reproduces itself for no other purpose than its own perpetuation, while the later poems insist obsessively on the extent to which life is lived at an elemental animal level. Vallejo's existential unease is not merely intellectual, but also takes the form of an acute personal sense of insecurity which expresses itself in his recurrent use of the persona of a child abandoned in a menacing world.

Vallejo's later poetry also registers his response to the political and economic crisis of Western capitalist society in the 1920s and 1930s, evoking the misery of mass unemployment in a world increasingly out of control. His European experience politicized him, leading him to join the Communist Party and to engage in political activism, which included the writing of prose works of a political nature. The Spanish Civil War inspired a collection of poems entitled *España, aparta de mí este cáliz* (Spain, Take This Cup From Me) (1939), which is identified with the cause of the Spanish people but uses historical events as a metaphor for the broader struggle to build a socialist society. The book also addresses the apparent collapse of the socialist ideal, for it was written with the knowledge that the Republican cause was lost; yet it reaffirms Vallejo's faith in a socialist future and bequeaths to coming generations the task of creating a society based on collective values.

Despite his incorporation into the Western mainstream, Vallejo continually questions Western civilization from the perspective of the Andean cultural tradition in which he was reared. The poems reflecting his urban experience portray him as an outsider in an alien environment, while nostalgic recollections of his provincial childhood privilege selfless maternal love and the shared family meal as emblems of a community culture absent in the West. Hence, his politicization was in part a reaffirmation of his roots as he saw in socialism an attempt to universalize Andean values.

Further reading

Ferrari, A. (1972) *El universo poético de César Vallejo*, Caracas: Monte Avila.

Franco, J. (1976) *César Vallejo: The Dialectics of Poetry and Silence*, Cambridge: Cambridge University Press.

Hart, S.M. (1997) 'César Vallejo', in V. Smith (ed.), *Encyclopedia of Latin American Literature*, London: Fitzroy Dearborn, 821–6.

Higgins, J. (1982) *The Poet in Peru*, Liverpool: Francis Cairns.

—— (1989) *Vallejo en su poesía*, Lima: Seglusa.

Ortega, J. (1989) 'César Vallejo', in C.A. Solé and M.I. Abreu (eds), *Latin American Writers*, New York: Scribners, 2, 727–38.

Vallejo, C. (1978) *The Complete Posthumous Poetry*, trans. C. Eshleman, Berkeley: University of California Press.

—— (1987) *César Vallejo: A Selection of His Poetry*, ed. and trans. J. Higgins, Liverpool: Francis Cairns.

—— (1988) *Obra poética*, ed. A. Ferrari, Paris: Archivos.

JAMES HIGGINS

Vallejo, Fernando

b. 1942, Medellín, Colombia

Writer and filmmaker

Fernando Vallejo has emerged in the last five years as Colombia's most controversial writer, known as much for his diatribes against the Catholic Church, Octavio **Paz**, the Colombian and Mexican political establishments, pregnant women, the poor and José Luis Cuevas as for his luminous prose and the extraordinary evocative quality of his autobiographical fiction. He began his career as a filmmaker, studying cinema in Rome before making several films about Colombia's 'La Violencia' in Mexico, where he has lived since 1971. He has written important biographies of the Colombian poets Porfirio **Barba-Jacob** and José Asunción Silva, published in 1991 and 1995 respectively, and began publishing his series of autobiographical novels, *El río del tiempo* (The River of Time), in 1985; the series was collected in a 700-page single volume in 1999. *El río del tiempo* traces his early life in Medellín and Bogotá, his studies in Rome and the beginnings of his subsequent career; it is frank and shocking in its portrayal of family conflict, homosexuality and violence.

Vallejo's best-known work internationally is *La virgen de los sicarios* (Our Lady of the Assassins), a 1994 novel that was adapted for the screen in 2000 by Barbet Schroeder. *La virgen de los sicarios* is the first person account of a return to Medellín by a Colombian writer who lives in Mexico City (a figure very similar to Vallejo himself), his falling in love with a young *sicario* (hired assassin in the employ of the Medellín cartels) named Alexis, his observation of (and sympathy with) a series of murders by Alexis, the murder of Alexis by another *sicario*, the narrator's falling in love with another young man, Wílmar, and the final revelation that the new lover is the murderer of Alexis. Narrated in an often cold and dispassionate way, the novel is shocking in its violence and troubling in its portrayal of the narrator's complicity in that violence. At the same time, it is lyrical in its evocation of gay love, particularly 'man–boy love'. This love involves not only a sharp difference in age but also in class and education, with the consequence that the exploration of the world of the *sicarios* involves 'slumming', a vicarious fascination with the world of drug trafficking, vendettas and sudden violence. One of the most important novels of the last decade, *La virgen de los sicarios* is striking for its exploration of homosexual relations in a violent, marginal setting.

Since the publication of *La virgen de los sicarios* and the launching of the Alfaguara edition of the complete series of *El río del tiempo*, Vallejo has published two more autobiographical fictions: *El desbarrancadero* (The Gorge) (2001), about the death from AIDS of his brother Darío, and *La Rambla paralela* (The Parallel Avenue) (2002), about his own death. At the same time, he published a book-length study of Darwinian thought, *La tautología darwinista y otros ensayos de biología* (The Darwinist Tautology and Other Essays on Biology), in 1998, with an expanded edition in 1999. He has said that after the completion of the work about his own death, *La Rambla paralela*, he intends to abandon fiction and devote himself to essays on scientific themes. Whether this declaration is more than a grandiloquent gesture remains to be seen.

Further reading

DuPouy, Steven M. (1994) 'Fernando Vallejo', in David William Foster (ed.), *Latin American Writers on Gay and Lesbian Themes*, Westport, CT: Greenwood Press, 439–3.

Fernández L'Hoeste, Héctor D. (2000) '*La virgen de los sicarios* o las visiones dantescas de Fernando Vallejo', *Hispania* 83 (4): 757–67.

Jaramillo, María Mercedes (2000) 'Fernando Vallejo: Desacralización y memoria', in María Mercedes Jaramillo, Betty Osorio and Angela I. Robledo (eds), *Literatura y cultura: Narrativa colombiana del siglo XX*, Bogotá: Ministerio de Cultura, 2, 407–39.

Ospina, William (2000) 'No quieren morir, pero matan', *Número* 26: 18–20.

Vallejo, Fernando (1994) *La virgen de los sicarios*, Bogotá: Alfaguara; trans. Paul Hammond, *Our*

Lady of the Assassins, London: Serpent's Tail, 2001.
—— (1999) *El río del tiempo*, Madrid: Alfaguara.

DANIEL BALDERSTON

Vallejos, Roque

b. 1943, Asunción, Paraguay

Writer

A medical doctor by profession, Vallejos has also published five books of poetry, including *Los arcángeles ebrios* (The Inebriated Archangels) (1964), *Los labios del silencio* (The Lips of Silence) (1986) and *Tiempo baldío* (Idle Time) (1988). He also compiled two literary anthologies: *Antología crítica de la poesía paraguaya contemporánea* (Critical Anthology of Contemporary Paraguayan Poetry) (1968) and *Antología de la prosa Paraguaya* (Anthology of Paraguayan Prose) (1973), volume I. His critical writings include *La literatura paraguaya como expresión de la realidad nacional* (Paraguayan Literature as an Expression of the National Reality) (1967) and *Josefina Plá: Crítica y antología* (Josefina Plá: Criticism and Anthology) (1995).

TERESA MÉNDEZ-FAITH

Varela, Blanca

b. 1926, Lima, Peru

Poet

Peru's foremost female poet, Varela is the author of four books published between 1959 and 1978. Her work expresses her experience as a woman and her love–hate relationship with her native city of Lima, but centres above all on the human condition. Its dominant notes are a rebellious dissatisfaction and a lucid awareness of life's ultimate absurdity, allied to a belief that living is an art form involving the creation of personal fictions to maintain the pretence that life is meaningful.

Further reading

Bados Ciria, Concepción (1995) 'La poética del espacio en la obra de Blanca Varela', *Lucero: A Journal of Iberian and Latin American Studies*, Spring, 6: 37–43.

Gazzolo, A.M. (1989) 'Blanca Varela y la batalla poética', *Cuadernos hispanoamericanos* 466.

Rebaza-Soraluz, L. (1997) 'Blanca Varela', in V. Smith (ed.), *Encyclopedia of Latin American Literature*, London: Fitzroy Dearborn, 826–8.

Rodriguez Nunez, Victor (1997) 'Blanca Varela: La poesía ya no es una dama burguesa', *Inti: Revista de literatura hispánica* 46–7: 285–92.

Varela, B. (1986) *Canto villano: Poesía reunida 1949–1983*, Mexico City: Fondo de Cultura Económica.

JAMES HIGGINS

Vargas Llosa, Mario

b. 1936, Arequipa, Peru

Writer

Modern Peruvian literature began in 1962 with the publication of one of Vargas Llosa's best known novels, ***La ciudad y los perros*** (The Time of the Hero). Before then, only José María **Arguedas**'s *Los* ***ríos profundos*** (Deep Rivers) (1958) matched the quality of Vargas Llosa's extraordinary fictional production. (Vargas Llosa would later be unsparing in his criticism of Arguedas.) The author of *La casa verde* (The Green House) (1966) is as prolific and disciplined as the great nineteenth-century French writers, not only in creating remarkable stories but also in vocalizing his compositional methods and techniques. Voicing his critical ideas is precisely what Vargas Llosa does best, even when he is not writing fiction, as his newspaper articles and cultural and political essays show. In the early 1990s, during a short-lived political career in Peru, the novelist articulated his political views in speeches and debates during his presidential campaign against Peru's president, Alberto Fujimori. The history of his apotheosizing political ascent, defeat and departure is fully documented in *El pez en el agua* (A Fish in the Water: A Memoir) (1993).

Vargas Llosa's career as a writer began in the mid-1950s when he started contributing to popular Peruvian periodicals. In 1959, after spending a year in Spain working toward a doctoral degree in literature, he returned to Peru for a short visit and won the Leopoldo Alas book prize for his collection of short stories, *Los jefes* (The Leaders) (1959).

Back in Europe, this time in France, the financially straitened author was forced to live an ascetic lifestyle distant from the tempting Parisian cafés. He worked to a rigorous schedule, divided between the writing of his first novel, *La ciudad y los perros*, and odd jobs. In 1962, Vargas Llosa finished the novel and received the prestigious Biblioteca Breve Prize, and the Critic's Prize, from Spain. Four years later his second novel, *La casa verde*, was a success. In 1967 he received the Rómulo Gallegos Prize, then Latin America's most distinguished book award. It was now quite clear that as a novelist, he had matured. By embracing a Flaubertian method of writing – a combination of archival research with a realistic and serious mode of representation – Vargas Llosa had defined himself as a writer. Coupled with this method was his passion for all things Peruvian, especially for the country's heterogeneous culture, and its troubled and repressive politics, as represented in his third novel, *Conversación en la Catedral* (Conversation in the Cathedral) (1969).

The year 1973 was an important landmark in Vargas Llosa's oeuvre, with the publication of *Pantaleón y las visitadoras* (Captain Pantoja and the Special Service). In his next novel, *La tía Julia y el escribidor* (Aunt Julia and the Scriptwriter) (1977), he introduced a new element into his writing: humour. He quickly realized that a more sardonic treatment of his fictional realities had a positive effect on his career. Not only did his books become best-sellers, but the shift in tone provoked a re-evaluation of all his past literature. Despite the great success of these two books, that reappraisal also revealed to him that his best option as a writer was the more serious register in which his early books had been written. Consequently, the author began writing his most ambitious novel, *La guerra del fin del mundo* (The War of the End of the World) (1981), whose central theme – apparently alien to Peru's history – is the Brazilian War of Canudos. Even though the story takes place in late nineteenth-century Brazil, the main cause of the war is identical to that breakdown of communication illustrated by the 1983 massacre involving Indians and journalists in the Peruvian Andes, to which Vargas Llosa has repeatedly referred.

Political violence permeated Vargas Llosa's works, and it continued to play a major role in his next book, *Historia de Mayta* (The Real Life of Alejandro Mayta) (1984), which exemplifies the conflicting political life that dominated Peru from approximately 1980 to 1992. The same theme was recast in *Lituma en los Andes* (Death in the Andes) (1993), after an interregnum marked by another novel dealing with the indigenous culture in the Peruvian Amazon, *El hablador* (The Storyteller) (1987). *Los cuadernos de don Rigoberto* (The Stories of Don Rigoberto) (1997) was followed in 2000 by his gripping novel about Dominican dictator Trujillo, *La fiesta del chivo* (The Goats' Party).

Further reading

Bernucci, L.M. (1989) *La historia de un malentendido*, New York: Peter Lang.

Castro-Klaren, S. (1990) *Understanding Mario Vargas Llosa*, Columbia: University of South Carolina Press.

—— (2002) 'Mario Vargas Llosa', in C. Solé and K. Müller-Bergh (eds), *Latin American Writers: Supplement I*, New York: Scribners, 545–65.

Kristal, E. (1999) *Temptation of the Word: The Novels of Mario Vargas Llosa*, Nashville, TN: Vanderbilt University Press.

Larsen, N. (2001) 'Mario Vargas Llosa: The Realist as Neo-Liberal', in *Determinations*, London: Verso, 143–68.

Oviedo, J.M. (1982) *Mario Vargas Llosa: La invención de una realidad*, Barcelona: Seix Barral.

—— (1997) 'Mario Vargas Llosa', in V. Smith (ed.), *Encyclopedia of Latin American Literature*, London: Fitzroy Dearborn, 828–31.

Rossman, C. and W.A. Friedman (eds) (1978) *Mario Vargas Llosa: A Selection of Critical Essays*, Austin: University of Texas Press.

LEOPOLDO M. BERNUCCI

Vargas Vila, José María

b. 1860, Bogotá, Colombia; d. 1933, Barcelona, Spain

Writer

Latin America's first best-selling author for fifty

years, Vargas Vila churned out potboilers that sold extraordinarily well in Spain and Latin America. Directly influenced by the decadentists, Vargas Vila's writing explores the seamy sides of human nature. Himself a misanthrope, he was continually the centre of stormy controversies, sparked by his personal attacks on others. His novels are turgid in language, the paragon of purple prose writing, and clumsy in plot, but the rhetorically trenchant way in which he depicted what the bourgeoisie considered unspeakable made him popular among readers. There is a current publishing project, Biblioteca Vargas Vila in Bogotá, which is reproducing many of his volumes in attractive cheap editions.

Further reading

Escobar Uribe, A. (1968) *El divino Vargas Vila*, Bogotá: Ediciones Tercer Mundo.

Triviño Anzola, C. (1988) *El sentido trágico de la vida en la obra de Vargas Vila*, Madrid: Ediciones de la Universidad Complutense.

Vargas Vila, J.M. (1973) *Obras completas*, Medellín: Editorial Beta.

—— (1988) *Diario secreto*, ed. C. Triviño, Bogotá: Arango Editores.

DAVID WILLIAM FOSTER

Vasconcelos, José

b. 1882, Oaxaca, Mexico; d. 1959, Mexico City

Writer, philosopher and educator

A key figure in the construction of the post-revolutionary Mexican state, Vasconcelos took up the battle of ideas against the positivism of the Díaz regime from the Ateneo de la Juventud, which he helped to found in 1909. Although he participated in the Mexican Revolution led by Francisco Madero in 1910, he declined a post in government; when Madero was overthrown, Vasconcelos joined the struggle against his successor, Huerta. With the victory of the Revolution, and its ending in 1917, he joined the Obregón government, first as Rector of the National University (1920–21) and later as Secretary of State for Education (1921–24). It was in this latter post that he set in motion the most ambitious educational and cultural programme ever undertaken by a post-revolutionary government in Mexico. He ordered the printing of cheap editions of universal literary classics in huge numbers, organized a public library system, launched an extensive literacy campaign and promoted the education of rural teachers. He edited journals such as *El maestro* and *La antorcha*, whose purpose was to raise the academic level of teachers, invited important Latin American cultural figures, like Gabriela **Mistral** and Pedro **Henríquez Ureña**, to Mexico, and encouraged and supported the development of the Mexican Muralist movement. This veritable educational 'crusade' was veiled by the 'official' character it was given.

Disagreement with the repressive methods employed by the Obregón government led Vasconcelos to resign from his post and leave the country. He returned in 1928 and one year later presented his candidacy for the presidency of Mexico. Defeated in fraudulent elections, he left the country again and returned only in 1940, when he took up the Directorship of the National Library, a post he held until his death. His electoral defeat in 1929 initiated an ideological turn that led him into increasingly conservative and often extreme right-wing positions.

In addition to his work as an educator, his writings are also important documents. In *La raza cósmica* (The Cosmic Race) (1925) and *Indología* (1926), he developed his Latin Americanist philosophical ideas, as distant from ***indigenismo*** as from Anglo-Saxon thinking. It is his four volumes of autobiography, however, for which he is best known – *Ulises criollo* (Latin American Ulysses) (1935), *La tormenta* (The Storm) (1936), *El desastre* (The Disaster) (1938) and *El proconsulado* (The Proconsulate) (1939). With his unique skill in the genre, he recounts his childhood and youth, his amorous adventures and his political experiences. His narrative of the events that led to the overthrow and assassination of Madero are a key historical document as well as fine literature.

Further reading

Bar-Lewaw Mulstock, I. (1966) *José Vasconcelos: Vida*

y obra, Mexico City: Clásica Selecta Editora Librera.
De Beer, G. (1966) *José Vasconcelos and His World*, New York: Las Américas.
—— (1989) 'José Vasconcelos', in C.A. Solé and M.I. Abreu (eds), *Latin American Writers*, New York: Scribners, 2, 575–84.
Earle, P.G. (1997) 'José Vasconcelos', in V. Smith (ed.), *Encyclopedia of Latin American Literature*, London: Fitzroy Dearborn, 834–6.
Fell, C. (1989) *José Vasconcelos: Los años del aguila 1920–25*, Mexico City: UNAM.
Robles, M. (1989) *Entre el poder y las letras. Vasconcelos en sus memorias*, Mexico City: Empresas Editoriales.
Vasconcelos, J. (1957–61) *Obras completas*, Mexico City: Libros Mexicanos Unidos.
—— (1979) *The Cosmic Race*, trans. D. Jaén, Los Angeles: California State University.

RAFAEL OLEA FRANCO

Vaz Ferreira, María Eugenia

b. 1875, Montevideo, Uruguay; d. 1924, Montevideo

Poet

M.E. Vaz Ferreira's first poems appeared in Uruguayan periodicals in 1894 alongside Uruguay's illustrious 'Generation of 1900' which included intellectuals and writers such as **Rodó**, **Quiroga**, J. **Herreira y Reissig**, her brother Carlos Vaz Ferreira and her younger compatriot and poet Delmira **Agustini**. Known for her personal eccentricity and literary talent, Vaz Ferreira also taught literature at the Women's University of Montevideo from 1915 until 1922. She is one of the initiators of a brilliant generation of female poets – Agustini, **Mistral**, **Storni**, **Ibarbourou** – who established a place for the female voice in literature. Her work, often described as nocturnal and idealistic, is collected in two posthumous volumes, *Fuego y mármol* (1922) and *La isla de los cánticos* (1924).

Further reading

Vaz Ferreira, M.E. (1986) *Poesías completas*, ed. and intro. H. Verani, Montevideo: Ediciones La Plaza.
Zum Felde, A. (1930) 'María Eugenia Vaz Ferreira', in *Proceso intelectual del Uruguay: Crítica de su literatura*, Montevideo: Imprenta Nacional Colorada, vol. 2, 239–58.

GWEN KIRKPATRICK

Vega, Ana Lydia

b. 1946, San Juan, Puerto Rico

Writer

Ana Lydia Vega's work is constantly preoccupied with the problem of writing in a literary and intellectual (see **intellectuals**) culture that has traditionally excluded the voices of women and other marginal groups. Like much contemporary Puerto Rican literature, her stories are written in a pointedly comic, or at least parodic, vein. For example, in *Encancaranublado y otros cuentos de naufragio* (Encancaranublado and Other Tales of Shipwrecks) (1982) and *Falsas crónicas del sur* (True and False Romances) (1991), she satirizes the gendered and racially specific stereotypes of national identity portrayed by canonical writers such as René **Marqués**. This satire is achieved by rewriting established literary genres, from the sensationalist pot-boiler, the nationalist essay and the melodrama, to the nineteenth-century romantic novel, or even medieval European classics. Furthermore, like Luis Rafael **Sánchez**, she looks beyond Puerto Rico's traditionally supposed isolation to a broader Caribbean culture where, this time, high and popular culture are appropriated from a woman's perspective.

A critical stance towards her intellectual heritage is also evident in her essays. Traditionally an authoritarian and conservative literary form exercised by patrician male intellectuals, her version of the Puerto Rican **essay** attempts to disown the solemn voice of authority and objectivity in favour of a humorous dialogue between literary erudition and the employment of a vernacular Puerto Rican Spanish. Thus, her vacillation between the ivory tower and popular culture allows her, following a strong tendency in contemporary Puerto Rican literature, to give up the conventional mantle of Spokesman (sic) of the Nation in favour of the critical inscription of a full range of Puerto Rican voices and participation in collaborative projects both in her fiction and her essays, as in the 1989 collection of essays *El tramo ancla* (The Home Stretch), jointly conceived by nine writers including Vega. Ultimately, Vega not only forgoes the bombastic rhetoric of past essay writing, but also its grand themes, in favour of a concern, also shown by her fiction, with everyday life as experienced in the kitchen, laundry, garage, street and other popular spaces.

Further reading

Boling, B. (1991) 'The Reproduction of Ideology in Ana Lydia Vega's "Pasión de historia" and "Caso omiso" ', *Letras femeninas* 17(1–2).

Fernández-Olmos, M. (1983) 'From a Woman's Perspective: The Short Stories of Rosario Ferré and Ana Lydia Vega', in D. Meyer (ed.), *Contemporary Women Authors of Latin America*, Brooklyn: Brooklyn College.

González, A. (1993) 'Ana Lydia Plurivega: Unidad y multiplicidad caribeñas en la obra de Ana Lydia Vega', *Revista iberoamericana* 161–2.

Rodríguez, L.M. (1997) 'Ana Lydia Vega', in V. Smith (ed.), *Encyclopedia of Latin American Literature*, London: Fitzroy Dearborn, 836–8.

Vega, A.L. (1994) *True and False Romances*, trans. A. Hurley, London: Serpent's Tail.

Vélez, D.L. (1985) ' "Pollito Chicken": Split Subjectivity, National Identity and the Articulation of Female Sexuality', *The Americas Review* 14(2).

JOHN D. PERIVOLARIS

Velasco Mackenzie, Jorge

b. 1949, Guayaquil, Ecuador

Writer

Velasco is the most accomplished and powerful writer of the 'Generation of Guayaquil' of the 1980s. His major works, *El rincón de los justos* (Refuge of the Righteous) (1983), *Tambores para una canción perdida* (Drums for a Lost Song) (1985), *El ladrón de la levita* (The Thief with the Jacket) (1990) and *En nombre de un amor imaginario* (In the Name of an Imaginary Love) (1996), show an excellent command of narrative technique and a profound knowledge of the multiple social textures of his native city: the world of the marginal and the excluded, of the delinquent, of the poor.

Further reading

Handelsman, Michael (1990) 'Lo popular en el vanguardismo transculturador de Jorge Velasco Mackenzie: Un analisis de *El rincón de los justos*', *Chasqui*, May, 19(1): 24–31.

Medina, Manuel F. (1994) 'En busca del Otro: La búsqueda de identidad social y sexual en *El ladrón de levita*', *Cuadernos de Guayas*, June, 57: 173–82.

HUMBERTO E. ROBLES

Veloz Maggiolo, Marcio

b. 1936, Santo Domingo, Dominican Republic

Novelist

A multi-faceted writer, Veloz Maggiolo won the 1980 National Literature Prize for his novel *La biografía difusa de Sombra Castañeda* (The Diffuse Biography of Sombra Castañeda). His most critically acclaimed work, *De abril en adelante* (From April Onwards) (1975), narrates the historical events of the last years of the Trujillo dictatorship, the April Revolution of 1965 and the post-revolutionary period, through the discontents of a group of **intellectuals** and bohemians. *Ritos de cabaret* (Cabaret Rituals) (1992) proposes a political reading of history through the bolero and gender conflicts. More recent works include *El jefe iba descalzo* (The Chief Went Barefoot) (1993).

Further reading

Sommer, Doris (1980) 'Good-Bye to Revolution and the Rest: Aspects of Dominican Narrative

since 1965', *Latin American Literary Review*, Spring–Summer, 8(16): 223–8.
Ugalde, Sharon Keefe (1988) 'Veloz Maggiolo y la narrativa de dictador/dictadura: Perspectivas dominicanas e innovaciones', *Revista iberoamericana*, Jan.–March, 54(142): 129–50.

FERNANDO VALERIO-HOLGUÍN

Venezuela

In the early twentieth century, positivist historians argued that geography and ethnic inheritance explained the violent and 'barbarous' nature of the Venezuelan people, and declared that only authoritarian leaders or 'necessary gendarmes' could restrain it. Scientific positivism also bore upon the dominance of realism, of landscape painting and of historicism in Venezuelan literature, the plastic arts and the architecture of the first half of the century. Its equivalent in the novel was the exemplary ***criollismo*** of Luis Manuel Urbaneja Achelpohl in *En este país* (In this Country) (1920) and the rural epics ***Doña Bárbara*** (1929), *Cantaclaro* (1934) and *Canaima* (1935) by Rómulo **Gallegos**. Social comment and an acerbic urban realism defined the novels of Rufino **Blanco Fombona** and José Rafael **Pocaterra** in his *Cuentos grotescos* (1922) and in the *Memorias de un venezolano de la decadencia* (Memoirs of a Venezuelan in the Time of Decadence) (1936), in which Pocaterra presented his implacable denunciation of the political oppression practised by the dictators. Positivist agnosticism and empiricism had an indirect influence also on a *modernista* literature characterized by sensuality and aestheticism, exemplified in Manuel Díaz Rodríguez's *Peregrina* (Pilgrim) (1922) and *Idolos rotos* (Broken Idols) (1901), in the stories of Pedro Emilio Coll (1872–1947) and in the early historical novels of Arturo **Uslar Pietri**, *Las lanzas coloradas* (The Coloured Lances) (1931) and *El camino de El Dorado* (The Road to Eldorado) (1947). In her *Ifigenia* (1924) and *Memorias de Mamá Blanca* (Memoirs of White Mamma) (1929), Teresa **de la Parra** explored the intimate experience of women, while Enrique Bernardo **Núñez**'s *Cubagua* (1931) took a historical theme as the starting point for a dense experimental novel. José Antonio **Ramos Sucre** also broke with naturalist and positivist models with his prose poems set in a world of visions overwhelmed by decadence and death, as too did the humorous fantasies of Julio **Garmendia**.

The beginning of oil exploitation in 1924 gave impetus to industrialization and urban growth; the death of dictator Juan Vicente Gómez in 1935 made it possible for the new urban masses to participate in political life through radical and populist parties. Writers expressed these realities by using the realism imposed by the positivists to a different purpose – namely, the rescue of a national tradition and a current of social criticism. Thus Miguel **Otero Silva**, in *Oficina No. 1* (Office Number One) (1961), painted a narrative fresco which described with great intensity the transition from a rural society to one dominated by oil. Uslar Pietri and Mariano **Picón Salas** explored the cultural roots of the country in a series of essays, while the poet Juan **Liscano** gave new impetus to the study of national folklore. The poetry of Andrés Eloy **Blanco** was graceful and flexible, and populist in tone.

Between 1948 and 1958 two military dictatorships (dominated by Marcos Pérez Jiménez), dubbed neo-positivist, interrupted the democratic process and launched a modernization policy which found expression particularly in the new architecture of the capital city. In poetry, the writing of Vicente **Gerbasi**, Juan **Sánchez Peláez** and Elizabeth Schon broke with modernist and romantic models to create a metaphorical language very close to symbolism. The starting point for Guillermo **Meneses**'s prose was the *criollismo* of *La Balandra Isabel llegó esta tarde* (The Isabel Arrives this Afternoon) (1934), but he later moved towards a more complex narrative structure in *La mano junto al muro* (The Hand by the Wall) (1952) and *La misa de Arlequín* (Harlequin's Mass) (1962). In the same spirit of rupture, Oswaldo **Trejo** pressed against the very frontiers of the narrative text.

The year 1958 ushered in a period of social democratic governments of a populist character. The sixties began with a radical guerrilla war which had repercussions in the cultural arena. Artistic groups such as El **Techo de la Ballena** rediscovered the procedures of surrealism and Dadaism and applied them in a bitter socio-political critique. The prose writing of Salvador **Garmendia**, Argenis Rodríguez, Adriano **González León**, Luis **Britto García**, Carlos Noguera and José **Balza** evolved within the same framework of provocation, formal experimentation and bitter criticism; they started from commitment and denunciation and gradually moved towards the absurd, complex form, personal exploration and atmospheres so rarified as to be almost unbreathable.

The same path can be traced in the drama of Isaac **Chocrón**, José Ignacio **Cabrujas**, Edilio Peña and Román Chalbaud, who also wrote screenplays and, in Chalbaud's case, directed films characterized by kitsch, sentimentality and an exaggerated lyricism. In the mid-sixties, cultural patronage was centralized in the Instituto de Cultura y Bellas Artes, later replaced by the Consejo Nacional de Cultura (National Council for Culture). Other important cultural institutions were the publishing houses **Biblioteca Ayacucho** and **Monte Avila** and the CELARG, the Centro de Estudios Literarios Rómulo Gallegos.

By 1970 the radical insurrection had been pacified; the remaining decades of the twentieth century, politically dominated by Carlos Andrés Pérez and later by Hugo Chávez, were a period of uncertainty. No new collective project arose to offer new certainties, and in their absence, there was a general return to the past on the one hand, and an exploration of the unknown terrain of the imagination and the empty spaces of postmodernity (see **postmodernism**) on the other.

Alfredo **Armas Alfonzo**, in *El osario de Dios* (God's Ossuary) (1969), Orlando Araujo in *Compañero de viaje* (Travelling Companion) (1970) and César Chirinos in *Buchiplumas* (1975), represented a literature of return to the roots, which began in the seventies, but avoided *criollismo* and the discourse of positivism – rather, their work was characterized by an existential narrative and a highly personal search for origins. The fiction of the historian and essayist Guillermo Morón traced a similar path; and the same themes and nostalgic tones permeated the poetry of Ramón **Palomares**, Efraín Hurtado and Luis Alberto **Crespo** as well as the work of the great contemporary humorous poet Aquiles **Nazoa**. Rafael **Cadenas**'s poetry, by contrast, is intimate and rigorous in its simplicity. Francisco **Herrera Luque**, José León Tapia, Denzil **Romero** and Ana Teresa **Torres** have generated a new historical novel based on the revision of myth and the recuperation of identity.

The most recent narrative includes Armando José Sequera, Igor Delgado, Earle Herrera, Luis Barrera Linares, Gabriel Jiménez Emán, Eduardo Liendo, Laura **Antillano**, Antonieta Madrid, Lourdes Sifontes, Milagros **Mata Gil**, Estefanía Mosca, Orlando Chirinos and Angel Gustavo Infante, and is developing in a resolutely experimental mode and with a shared concern for concision as well as a fascination with the fantastic, the absurd and the extraordinary – which does not exclude social criticism.

The contemporary crisis in Venezuela (political, economic and social) has affected the cultural institutions which for so long were generously supported by the Venezuelan state (thanks to abundant oil revenues), and the outlook for literature and for other cultural forms currently is very uncertain.

Further reading

Belrose, M. (1996) *La época del modernismo en Venezuela: 1988–1925*, Caracas: Monte Avila.

Diccionario general de la literatura venezolana (1987) Mérida: Editorial Venezolana: Consejo de Fomento: Consejo de Publicidad.

Kohut, K. (ed.) (1991) *Literatura venezolana hoy: Historia nacional y presente urbano*, Madrid: Iberoamericana and Frankfurt am Main: Vervuert.

Lewis, M.A. (1992) *Ethnicity and Identity in Contemporary Afro-Venezuelan Literature*, Columbia: University of Missouri Press.

Liscano, J. (1995) *Panorama de la literatura venezolana actual*, Caracas: Ediciones Alfadil.

López Álvarez, L. (1991) *Literatura e identidad en Venezuela*, Barcelona: PPU.

López Ortega, A. (1995) *El camino a la alteridad*, Caracas: Fundarte.

Márquez Rodríguez, A. (1991) *Relecturas: Ensayos de crítica literaria venezolana*, Caracas: Contexto Audiovisual 3: Pomaire.

Medina, R. (1993) *Noventa anos de literatura venezolana*, Caracas: Monte Avila.

Rama, A. (1985) *Ensayos de literatura venezolana*, Caracas: Monte Avila.

Ratcliff, D.F. *Venezuelan Prose Fiction*, New York: Instituto de España en los Estados Unidos.
Uslar Pietri, A. (1948) *Letras y hombres de Venezuela*, Mexico City: Fondo de Cultura Económica.

LUIS BRITTO GARCIA

Vera, Helio

b. 1946, Villarrica, Paraguay

Writer

A lawyer by profession, Vera is a journalist and frequently anthologized short story writer; some of his short fiction was collected in *Angola y otros cuentos* (Angola and Other Stories) (1984). His other writings include *En busca del hueso perdido: Tratado de paraguayología* (In Search of the Lost Bone: Treatise on Paraguayology) (1990), a kind of novelistic essay which earned him, in 1988, the Premio V Centenario of the Embassy of Spain and the Instituto de Cooperación Iberoamericana. He is also co-author (with Julio César Frutos) of *Pacto político* (Political Pact) (1993), and sole author of a book of humour, *Diccionario Contrera* (1994).

TERESA MÉNDEZ-FAITH

Vera, Pedro Jorge

b. 1914, Guayaquil, Ecuador

Writer

The patriarch of contemporary Ecuadorean letters, Vera's works range from **social realism** to subjective analysis. His major works offer interpretations of the social, political and literary life of Ecuador, and the dilemmas faced by committed intellectuals in an ambience not propitious to a contestary posture. His novels, *Los animales puros* (The Pure Animals) (1946), *Tiempo de muñecos* (A Time for Puppets) (1971), *El pueblo soy yo* (I the People) (1976) and *La familia y los años* (The Family and Years) (1983), speak to that effect. His personal and literary trajectory is recorded in his *Gracias a la vida: Memorias* (Memoirs) (1993).

Further reading

Calderón Chico, C. (1985) *Pedro Jorge Vera se confiesa*, Quito: Fondo Editorial de la Unión Nacional de Periodistas.
Carrión, B. (1981) 'Novela intelectualizada: Pedro Jorge Vera', in *Obras*, Quito: Casa de la Cultura.

HUMBERTO E. ROBLES

verdeamarelismo

Verdeamarelismo is a theory and movement of xenophobic cultural nationalism (its name derived from the colours of the Brazilian flag), founded in 1925 in explicit opposition to the forward-looking modernism and cosmopolitanism of Oswald de **Andrade**'s *Manifesto da Poesia Pau-brasil* (Brazil-Wood Poetry Manifesto). The *verdeamarelistas* harked back to a mythologized colonial history of pioneering heroism. The *Nhengaçu Verde Amarelo* Manifesto of 1929 celebrated the annihilation of the coastal Tupi tribes as the cornerstone of a mystical ethos of national identity, symbolized by the Tupis' totem animal, the Anta (tapir), which they adopted. The ideological implications of the movement were expressed as political practice in the 1930s in Brazil's fascist movement, Integralismo.

See also: Brazilian modernism

DAVID TREECE

Vergés, Pedro

b. 1945, Santo Domingo, Dominican Republic

Writer

Vergés is among the most important contemporary writers in the Dominican Republic because of his use of the bolero and popular culture to depict life during the political chaos that followed the murder of dictator Rafael Leónidas Trujillo in 1961. His early books of poetry are *Juegos reunidos* (Collected Games) (1971) and *Durante los inviernos* (During Winters) (1977). His well-known novel, *Sólo cenizas hallarás* (What You Will Find are Only Ashes)

(1980), also won two awards in Spain; it is concerned with Trujillo's dictatorship.

Further reading

Cruz Malavé, A. (1988) 'La historia y el bolero en *Sólo cenizas hallarás*', *Revista iberoamericano*, 54(142): 63–72.

Otero Garabis, J. (2000) *Naciones ritmicas: 'Descargas' desde el Caribe*, San Juan: Ediciones Callejon, 234–57.

FERNANDO VALERIO-HOLGUÍN

Veríssimo, Erico

b. 1905, Cruz Alta, Rio Grande do Sul, Brazil; d. 1975, Porto Alegre, Rio Grande do Sul

Writer

Veríssimo was a Brazilian novelist known for his panoramic historical novels, mostly focusing on the history of Rio Grande do Sul, the southern-most state in Brazil (bordering on Uruguay and Argentina). His trilogy, *O tempo e o vento* (Time and the Wind) (1949–62), deals with the history of Rio Grande from 1745 to 1945. Earlier novels focus on urban youth, while his wide-ranging later works include *O Senhor Embaixador* (Mr Ambassador) (1967) and *Incidente em Antares* (Incident in Antares) (1971), and deal with issues as varied as the Cuban Revolution, the Vietnam War and race relations. A teacher and diplomat, Veríssimo's long residence abroad led to accusations that he was distanced from Brazilian reality.

Further reading

Chaves, F.L. (1976) *Erico Veríssimo: Realismo e sociedade*, Porto Alegre: Globo.

Gonzaga, S. (1984) *Erico Veríssimo*, Porto Alegre: IEL.

Hulet, C. (1989) 'Erico Veríssimo', in C.A. Solé and M.I. Abreu (eds), *Latin American Writers*, New York: Scribners, 3, 1043–8.

Silva, T.V.Z. da (1997) 'Erico Veríssimo', in V. Smith (ed.), *Encyclopedia of Latin American Literature*, London: Fitzroy Dearborn, 841–2.

Veríssimo, E. (1951) *Time and the Wind*, trans. L. Barrett, New York: Macmillan.

—— (1966–67) *Ficção completa*, Rio de Janeiro: Aguilar, 5 vols.

DANIEL BALDERSTON

Vianen, Bea

b. 1935, Paramaribo, Suriname

Writer

Author of five novels and of poetry in Dutch, Vianen's novels, including *Sarnami, hai* (Suriname, I Am) (1969), *Strafhok* (House of Correction) (1971) and *Geen onderdelen* (No Spare Parts) (1979), are first of all concerned with the restrictions Suriname society imposes on its inhabitants. Vianen is quite critical of ethnic and religious diversity and its concomitant strict codes and prejudices. In her novel *Het paradijs van Oranje* (The Paradise of Royal Orange) (1973), she is equally critical of Surinamese migrants to the Netherlands.

Further reading

Walrecht, A. (1973) 'Gedomineerd worden in de West', *Ons Erfdeel: Algemeen Nederlands Tweemaandelijks Cultureel Tijdschrift* (Rekkem, Belgium) 16(5): 103.

AART G. BROEK

Vianna Filho, Oduvaldo ('Vianinha')

b. 1936, Rio de Janeiro, Brazil; d. 1974, Rio de Janeiro

Playwright, screenwriter and actor

An author and actor in theatre, cinema and television, Vianinha – as he was popularly called – was also an astute theoretician whose plays and critical writings offer a complex and immediate dialogue between theory and practice. His history as a playwright and leftist activist is inextricably bound with that of politically oriented theatre groups of the 1950s and 1960s (São Paulo's Arena Theatre Group; a founder of the Centro Popular de Cultura/Popular Culture Centre theatre groups; Grupo Opinião/Opinion Group after the 1964 *coup*). Vianinha's theatrical experimentation responded to his reading of the political moment and his valuation of Brazilian theatrical traditions, ranging from agitprop to realist drama. His major work, the play *Rasga coração* (Heart Torn Asunder) (1974), is a collage of historical fact and historical interpretation created by stage realism intercut by flashbacks, Brechtian estrangement techniques (see **Brechtian theatre**) and Brazilian musical revue conventions. Written in 'homage to the anonymous political activists', *Rasga coração* stages the political and interpersonal conflicts and doubts of three generations of activists – grandfather, father and son – from the 1920s to the 1970s.

Further reading

Damasceno, L.H. (1996) *Cultural Space and Theatrical Conventions in the Works of Oduvaldo Vianna Filho*, Detroit: Wayne State University Press.

—— (1985) 'Oduvaldo Vianna Filho: "Pessedismo" and the Creation of the Anonymous Revolutionary Hero', *Literature and Contemporary Revolutionary Culture, 1984–1985* 1: 229–46.

LESLIE H. DAMASCENO

vida breve, La

La vida breve (Brief Life) is the title of a novel by Uruguayan writer Juan Carlos **Onetti**, published in 1950, which inaugurates a series of novels and short stories set in an imaginary town in the River Plate area called Santa María. The novel opens when the narrator, Brausen, having separated from his wife after she underwent an operation for cancer, moves into an apartment next to a prostitute, Queca. He lives vicariously through two fantasies: one, the film script he is writing about a corrupt doctor, Díaz Grey, who is extorted into prescribing morphine to members of a criminal ring in Santa María; the other, to enter the life of Queca as a pimp named Arce. Later, after Queca is murdered, Brausen decides to flee to Santa María, at the very moment that Díaz Grey has to flee from that town's police.

In a brilliant chapter, later expanded into a scene of the novel *Juntacadáveres* (Body Snatcher) (1964), Brausen, sitting on the second floor of a restaurant, looks down on Díaz Grey and his co-conspirators and overhears their conversation, but does not recognize his own character.

Informed by the taste for metafiction brought into fashion by Jorge Luis **Borges** in the years prior to its publication, but more raffish in style and content, *La vida breve* established Onetti as the greatest novelist of urban spaces in the River Plate, whether on the Argentine or the Uruguayan side of the estuary. Intensely sardonic, the novel even includes a Borges-like moment when Brausen, frustrated writer of film scripts, shares an office in the southern part of Buenos Aires with a failed writer of advertising copy, Juan Carlos Onetti. The later texts in the Santa María cycle will reveal that the statue in the centre of the plaza in Santa María is a statue of 'Brausen-Founder' and that in their despair they call not on God but on Brausen, but the founder or creator in this novel is no more in control of his creation than he is of his own life, so often cast adrift.

Although metafictional in technique and fascinated with the interplay of experience and fantasy, *La vida breve* does not partake of the then current fashion for **fantastic literature**, strong in the region after the publication of ***Antología de la literatura fantástica*** by Borges, Adolfo **Bioy Casares** and Silvina **Ocampo**. Instead, Onetti establishes a new kind of literature of fantasy, the fantasy born of frustrated desire, but never free of gritty realism. In later masterpieces such as *Los adioses* (Goodbyes) (1954), *Para una tumba sin nombre* (Toward a Nameless Grave) (1959) and *El astillero* (The Shipyard) (1961), the reader will be as implicated in this desire as are the characters. Echoes of this novel can be felt not only in the rest of Onetti's work but also in **Cortázar**'s ***Rayuela*** (Hopscotch) (1963) and the work of Ricardo **Piglia**, who has worked on film scripts based on other Onetti novels.

Further reading

Kadir, D. (1977) *Juan Carlos Onetti*, Boston: Twayne.
Ludmer, J. (1977) *Onetti: Teoría de construcción del relato*, Buenos Aires: Editorial Sudamericana.
Millington, M. (1985) *Reading Onetti: Language, Narrative and the Subject*, Liverpool: Francis Cairns.
Onetti, Juan Carlos (1950) *La vida breve*, Buenos Aires: Editorial Sudamericana; English translation by Hortense Carpentier, Grossman: New York and Serpent's Tail: London, 1976.

DANIEL BALDERSTON

Vientós Gastón, Nilita

b. 1908, San Sebastián, Puerto Rico; d. 1989, San Juan, Puerto Rico

Lawyer and writer

Vientós Gastón founded and edited the most important literary review in Puerto Rican history, *Asomante* (1945–71), later known as *Sin nombre* (1971–84), which placed Puerto Rican letters in a Latin American context and introduced readers to major foreign authors. *El mundo de la infancia* (The World of Childhood), her memoirs, is her most important text. Her defence of Spanish as the legal language of Puerto Rico and her fight against large foreign land-owning corporations shaped her very successful career as a lawyer.

Further reading

Albornoz, A. de (1976) 'Nilita Vientós, puertorriqueña universal', *Insula* 31(356–7).
Gullón, R. (1976) 'Nilita, en Puerto Rico', *Insula* 31(356–7): 1–27.
Vientós Gastón, N. (1962–84) *Indice cultural*, Río Piedras, PR: Ediciones de la Universidad de Puerto Rico.
—— (1984) *El mundo de la infancia*, Río Piedras, PR: Editorial Cultural.

EFRAÍN BARRADAS

Vigil, Carlos

b. 1925, Mexico City

Publisher

Beginning his career in the comic book industry as a cartoonist's assistant, Vigil launched his own strips under the pseudonym Car Vig. Later, as director of Publicaciones Herrerías, he published the popular comic books *Chanoc* and *Alma Grande* (Big Soul), and Mexico's first *fotonovela* – *Novelas de amor* (Love Novels). After founding Editora Senda in 1966, Vigil published Mexico's first colour *fotonovela*, *Linda* (Pretty Girl), for which he won the prestigious Tlacuilo de Oro (1972). His other publications include the popular Western comic book *El Payo*, and the socio-political comic *Torbellino* (Whirlwind). In 1977 Vigil was named the most influential editor in *fotonovela* by the Mexican Association of Comic Book Artists and Creators.

Further reading

Silva, J.L. (1986) 'Carlos Vigil on Mexican Comic Books and Photonovels', *Studies in Latin American Popular Culture* 5: 196–210.

MARCIE D. RINKA

Vilariño, Idea

b. 1920, Montevideo, Uruguay

Poet

Vilariño's poetic voice is laconic; her poems are usually brief and always economical, with rhythmic patterns that create the effect of evocative silences. They address a number of themes ranging from the prosaic to the metaphysical and the amorous, in a tone that is consistently bleak; one celebrated poem, 'Ya no' (No More) marks the end of her relationship with Juan Carlos **Onetti**. She has published articles and essays on some Latin American writers, and Spanish translations of English and French literature. As a cultural journalist, Vilariño has taken an active role in the development of a pluralistic society in Uruguay.

Further reading

Berry Bravo, J. (1990) 'Idea Vilariño's Negation of Poetry', *Monographic Review/Revista monografica* 6: 282–92.

San Román, G. (1993) 'Expression and Silence in the Poetry of Juana de Ibarbourou and Idea Vilarino', in C. Davies and M. Ordóñez (ed. and intro.), *Women Writers in Twentieth-Century Spain and Spanish America*, Lewiston, NY: Mellen, 157–75.

Vilariño, I. (1997) *Poesía (1945–1990)*, Montevideo: Cal y Canto.

FERNANDO J. ROSENBERG

Villaurrutia, Xavier

b. 1903, Mexico City; d. 1950, Mexico City

Writer

One of Mexico's finest modern writers, Villaurrutia is known above all for his oneiric poetry, particularly the sequence of nocturnes from the collection *Nostalgias de la muerte* (Nostalgia for Death), published by ***Sur*** in Buenos Aires in 1938. One of the most famous of these, 'Nocturno de los ángeles' (Nocturne of the Angels/Los Angeles Nocturne), first published in 1936, is one of the monuments of gay writing in Latin America, playful, sexy and profound. But Villaurrutia's entire poetic production occupies less than a hundred pages in a collected work that runs to more than a thousand, as Villarrutia was also one of Mexico's major film and art critics, a playwright, short story writer and essayist.

Villaurrutia's career as a writer was bound up from high school onwards with that of his close friend Salvador **Novo**, as is recounted in Novo's posthumous (but only recently published) autobiography *La estatua de sal* (The Pillar of Salt) (1998), which recounts with glee the capers that Villaurrutia and Novo shared in their wild youth. The two eventually became the centre of a group of writers and artists that came to be known by the name of one of their journals, ***Contemporáneos*** (1928–31). Other members of the circle included the painter Agustín Lazo, one of Villaurrutia's closest friends and the subject of some of his art criticism, the poets Jaime **Torres Bodet**, José **Gorostiza**, Bernardo Ortiz de Montellano, Elías Nandino and Carlos **Pellicer**, among others. The Contemporáneos were an unusual result of the cultural scene in post-revolutionary Mexico, protected for a time by José **Vasconcelos** but attacked violently by Diego Rivera and the Estridentistas (see **Estridentismo**). Villaurrutia's defiantly homoerotic poems, and some of his essays, stand out in contrast to the witch-hunt atmosphere in which they were written. The influence of the group is felt in later works such as the anthology ***Laurel*** (edited by Villaurrutia and Octavio **Paz** alongside two exiled Spanish poets) and in Paz's *El laberinto de la soledad* (The Labyrinth of Solitude) (1950), many of whose themes were anticipated by Villaurrutia (as Paz rather grudgingly admits in several late essays).

Villaurrutia's perceptive criticism includes essays on **Borges** (among them one of the most intelligent early reviews of ***Ficciones***), Valéry, Rilke, the photographer Manuel Alvarez Bravo, and painters Rivera, Orozco, Siqueiros, Tamayo, Lazo, María Izquierdo and Alfredo Zalce; he was considered the premier art critic of his day. His film criticism includes reviews of *Citizen Kane*, *The Lady Vanishes*, *The Ziegfeld Follies* and *How Green Was My Valley*, among hundreds of others. His best-known work of fiction is 'Dama de corazones' (Queen of Hearts) (1928). His plays include an adaptation of Hamlet entitled *Invitación a la muerte* (Invitation to Death) (1944) and *La hiedra* (Ivy) (1941), as well as two versions of *La mulata de Córdoba* (The Mulatta of Cordoba), one a film script for Julio Bracho (1945), the other (written with Agustín Lazo) the libretto for an opera by Juan Pablo Moncayo (1948).

But Villaurrutia's reputation will largely rest on twenty or thirty pages of poetry, including 'Nocturno de la estatua' (Nocturne of the Statue), 'Nocturno en que nada se oye' (Nocturne in which Nothing Can be Heard), the astonishing 'Nocturno de los ángeles' mentioned earlier, and 'Décima muerte' (Tenth Death/Death in Décimas), all from *Nostalgias de la muerte*, and 'Nuestro amor' (Our Love) and 'Inventar la verdad' (Inventing the Truth) from *Canto a la primavera y otros poemas* (Song to Spring and Other Poems) (1948). Dense, suggestive, musical, these poems establish Villaurrutia as one of the major Latin American poets of the twentieth century.

Further reading

Balderston, D. (1998) 'Poetry, Revolution, Homophobia: Polemics from the Mexican Revolution', in S. Molloy and R. Irwin, (eds), *Hispanic Homosexualities*, Durham, NC: Duke University Press, 57–75.

Biriotti, M. (1997) 'Xavier Villaurrutia', in V. Smith (ed.), *Encyclopedia of Latin American Literature*, London: Fitzroy Dearborn, 843–4.

Dauster, F. (1971) *Xavier Villaurrutia*, Boston: Twayne.

Forster, M. (1964) *Fire and Ice: The Poetry of Xavier Villaurrutia*, Chapel Hill, NC: University of North Carolina Press.

—— (1989) 'Xavier Villaurrutia', in C.A. Solé and M.I. Abreu (eds), *Latin American Writers*, New York: Scribners, 3: 975–80.

Paz, O. (1978) *Xavier Villaurrutia en persona y en obra*, Mexico City: Fondo de Cultura Económica.

Quiroga, J. (2000) 'Nostalgia for Sex: Xavier Villaurrutia', in *Tropics of Desire: Interventions from Queer Latino America*, New York: New York University Press, 50–75.

Villaurrutia, X. (1966) *Obras completas*, Mexico City: Fondo de Cultura Económica.

—— (1993) *Nostalgia for Death*, trans. Eliot Weinberger, Port Townsend, WA: Copper Canyon Press.

DANIEL BALDERSTON

Villegas, Oscar

b. 1943, Ciudad del Maiz, San Luis Potosí, Mexico

Playwright and potter

A stylized representation of reality and a successful fragmentation of the dramatic material are the characteristics of Villegas's work. Often his characters are anonymous beings, represented in the text by a number or a hyphen, who move through a chaotic and superficial social world where appearances alone determine everything. His works include *La paz de la buena gente* (The Peace of the Good) (1966), *Santa Catarina* (1969), *La Atlántida* (Atlantis) (1973), *El reino animal* (The Animal World) (1996) and *La fama fuma* (Celebrity Smokes) (1998).

Further reading

Woodyard, G. (1978) 'El teatro de Oscar Villegas: Experimentación con la forma', *Texto crítico* 10: 32–41.

TITO VASCONCELOS

Villordo, Oscar Hermes

b. 1928, Machagal, El Chaco Province, Argentina; d. 1995, Buenos Aires, Argentina

Writer

Long a literary journalist, late in life Villordo became assistant editor of the literary supplement of *La Nación*, distinguished for its recognition of marginal, subaltern and dissident writers. He then began publishing novels; *La brasa en la mano* (The Burning Coal in the Hand) (1983), with its homoerotic theme, was one of the first novels to take advantage of the 1983 suspension of censorship. In three subsequent novels, Villordo described the closeted gay exposed to predatory violence. He was one of the first prominent Argentine writers to die of AIDS. His sexual autobiography, *Ser gay no es pecado* (It's No Crime to Be Gay) (1993), is an important entry in Argentina's struggle against homophobia.

Further reading

Foster, D.W. (1988) 'The Search for Text: Some Examples of Latin American Gay Writing', *Ibero Amerikanisches Archiv* 14(3): 329–56.

DAVID WILLIAM FOSTER

Viñas, David

b. 1929, Buenos Aires, Argentina

Writer and essayist

Viñas's intellectual activity began as co-editor (with his brother Ismael) of the magazine, ***Contorno***, published in the 1950s during the government of Perón. It was there that he began his revision of Argentine history through national literature, which culminated in 1963 in *Literatura argentina y realidad política* (Argentine Literature and Political Reality), a history of Argentina culture 'from the other side of the tracks'; the text has since gone through several editions and numerous rewritings. Viñas's strongly polemical style forged a new critical literature in Argentina, introducing politics as a constitutive element of all cultural practice and criticism. His erudition allowed him to trace multiple discursive and institutional relationships between periods, subjects and texts in Argentine culture, which make of his books a complex network in which literature and the formation and function of intellectuals havc privileged place.

Intellectually formed during the 1960s, Viñas has been linked too often to the **existentialism** of Sartre; although Sartre did contribute to his thought, it was to his fiction rather than his essays. Viñas's writing is strongly influenced by Argentine politico-cultural tradition, enabling him to cast a penetrating and critical eye over the relations between intellectuals, politicians and military men in his native country.

His novels rework the realist tradition through the colloquial discourse of his characters and the construction of subjectivities articulated with cultural and political referents. He has written within the historical and political genres, both of them essential to his critical re-evaluation of history. The intellectual concerns of the 1950s (definition of the national project, recuperation of history etc.) brought him closer to his literary 'enemies' like Leopoldo **Marechal**, Eduardo **Mallea** and Ernesto **Sábato**, but his critical responses place him at the beginning of a new reflection on culture.

Viñas has read Argentine culture, from literary production, as a process of a constant discrimination against the subjectivities and practices of the oppressed. His aesthetic project is another chapter of that history, written against the hegemonic culture and aesthetics. Thus in the 1990s his work has come to be seen as a precursor of the new critical perspectives of the end of the century.

Further reading

Schvartzmann, J. (1999) 'David Viñas: La crítica como epopeya', in S. Cella (ed.), *La irrupción de la crítica*, vol. 10 of *Historia crítica de la literatura argentina*, Buenos Aires: Emecé, 147–80.

Sims, R.L. (1997) 'David Viñas', in V. Smith (ed.), *Encyclopedia of Latin American Literature*, London: Fitzroy Dearborn, 848–50.

Terán, O. (1991) *Nuestros años sesenta*, Buenos Aires: Puntosur.

Valverde, E. (1989) *David Viñas: En busca de una síntesis de la historia argentina*, Buenos Aires: Plus Ultra.

GRACIELA MONTALDO

Virtue, Vivian

b. 1911, Kingston, Jamaica

Poet

Although critical opinion on Virtue's poetry varies widely, there is no doubt that, like fellow poets George Campbell, Ken **Ingram**, Una Marson and Basil **McFarlane**, he helped to indigenize Jamaican poetry. Educated in Kingston, Virtue emigrated to England in 1960, the year he received the Institute of Jamaica's Silver Musgrave Medal for Poetry. He wrote a commissioned poem celebrating Jamaican national hero Marcus Garvey for the first Commonwealth Festival of Arts in 1965. Although represented in journals, anthologies and the collection *Wings of the Morning* (1938), Virtue's work remains largely unpublished.

Further reading

McLeod, Marian B. (1991) 'The Poetry of Vivian Virtue', *Literary Half Yearly* (Mysore India), Jan., 32(1): 56–71.

PAT DUNN AND PAMELA MORDECAI

visual arts and literature

The interweaving of word and image seems at first sight to coincide with the *modernista* movement, for which the intertextual was an affirmation of the world of the imagined and a rejection of divisions which often seemed more commercial than aesthetic. Brazil's Modern Art Week (1922) brought together musicians, artists and writers; the collaboration between writer Oswald de **Andrade** and artist Tarsila do Amaral was extraordinarily creative, for example, and the work of Emiliano di Cavalcanti moved easily between all the genres. Similarly, there was a coincidence of method and vision in the recovery of Mexican history by the Muralist movement beginning in the early 1920s and echoed in the **novel of the Mexican Revolution**, in particular in the work of Gregorio López y Fuentes and Nellie **Campobello** with its intensely visual imagery and broad historical sweep. In the context of the **social realism** of the 1920s and 1930s, the collaboration was often much more immediate. In Mexico, the newspaper of the art workers union, *El Machete*, was designed by radical graphic artists such as Leopoldo Méndez while much of it was written by artists and writers linked to the Muralists. They echoed, often very consciously, the work of the illustrator and journalist José Guadalupe Posada, whose famous *calaveras* (skeletons) of the pre-revolutionary period were accompanied by verses in the popular tradition. Still in Mexico, the poets of the Estridentista group (see **Estridentismo**) were also, in many cases, designers and graphic artists whose drawings and etchings often illustrated their published work – Manuel **Maples Arce** was one example.

The connection between word and image in the surrealist movement (see **surrealism**) was more direct – it was a feature of the movement, for example, that the printed or written word often appeared in the visual vocabulary of the painters of the movement. The dialogue between art and literature was conducted with great intensity in literary circles which invariably embraced both literary and visual aesthetics. Thus José María **Eguren**, the Peruvian poet, was also a visual artist, and Oliverio **Girondo**, the noted Argentine avant-garde poet, was also known for his watercolours while Chilean painter Matta's early interest in literature is reflected in the puns and allusions that often give his work their titles. Wifredo Lam's explorations of the black cultural traditions of his native Cuba certainly owed much to his close friendship with Aimé **Césaire** of Guadeloupe. In the same period, new generations of writers were also contributing art criticism and commentary to the literary journals of the time, for example ***Sur*** and ***Amauta***. Thus the poets Xavier **Villaurrutia** and Octavio **Paz** in Mexico, and the prominent Guatemalan poet and historian Luis **Cardoza y Aragón** were prominent art critics in their own right.

The *indigenista* writers of the 1920s and 1930s constructed a new national myth around a critique of the oppression of indigenous peoples. The recuperation of their lived reality found its direct echo in the work of artists such as José Sabogal in Peru. **Concrete poetry** and its leading exponents, particularly Haroldo de **Campos**, created the conditions for a direct encounter between word and image, echoing perhaps the earlier 'calligrammes' of Apollinaire and the Mexican José Juan **Tablada**. In many ways, the word in concrete poetry moved from metaphor to sound and thence to design and drawing: for some a loss of the word, for others an exploration of its multiple possibilities.

Active collaboration between artists of different genres was a feature of the Cuban cultural milieu in the decade after the Revolution of 1959. The important journal ***Casa de las Américas***, based in the institution of the same name in Havana, was a forum for new Latin American writing and criticism of the period, but also a sponsor of the highly innovative poster art of the period and the avant-garde design that immediately identified the journal. Just as was the case after the Russian Revolution of 1917, artists co-operated precisely to contest the arbitrary divisions between artistic practices that seemed to rest on the separation between art and life. Under the guiding hand of Ernesto **Cardenal**'s Ministry of Culture, the Nicaraguan Revolution of 1979 embraced a workshop movement in both poetry and painting whose most powerful expression is in the Solentiname Gospels and poetry volumes produced at Cardenal's island Christian community.

Peruvian poet Jorge **Eielson** is also a visual artist, and the Argentine novelist and essayist Ernesto **Sábato**, having already combined professional science with literature, devoted himself increasingly to painting as he grew older. Latin America has produced a powerful photographic tradition exemplified by Manuel and Lola Alvarez Bravo in Mexico, Martin Chambi in Peru and Sebastião Salgado in Brazil. There have also been some remarkable collaborations between writers and photographers – between Juan **Rulfo** and José Emilio **Pacheco** in Mexico, for example, or Paz Errázuriz and Diamela **Eltit** in Chile. And artists have provided the subjects for a number of fictional portraits – Elena Poniatowska's unflattering portrayal of Diego Rivera in *Querido Diego* (1978) is one example, her novel about the life of photographer Tina Modotti, *Tinísima* (1992), another.

Further reading

Ades, Dawn (1989) *Art in Latin America: The Modern Era, 1820–1980*, London: South Bank Centre.

Baddeley, Oriana and Valerie Fraser (1989) *Drawing the Line: Art and Cultural Identity in Contemporary Latin America*, London: Verso.

Day, H. and H. Sturgess (1987) *The Art of the Fantastic: Latin America 1920–1987*, Indianapolis: Indianapolis Museum of Art.

Feal, Rosemary (1995) *Painting on the Page: Interartistic Approaches to Modern Hispanic Texts*, Albany: SUNY Press.

Fraser, Valerie (2000) *Building the New World: Studies in the Modern Architecture of Latin America, 1930–1960*, London: Verso.

Grau, Cristina (1995) *Borges y la arquitectura*, Madrid: Cátedra.

Méndez-Ramírez, Hugo (1999) *Neruda's Ekphrastic Experience: Mural Art and the Canto General*, Lewisburg, PA: Bucknell University Press.

Paz, Octavio (1987) *Convergences: Essays on Art and Literature*, London: Bloomsbury.

Rowe, William and Vivian Schelling (1991) *Memory and Modernity: Popular Culture in Latin America*, London: Verso.

Watriss, W. and L. Parkinson Zamora (eds) (1998) *Image and Memory: Photography from Latin America 1886–1994*, Austin: University of Texas Press.

MIKE GONZALEZ

Vitale, Ida

b. 1926, Montevideo, Uruguay

Poet and critic

Vitale, whose poetry is marked by concision and the haunting exploration of experience and poetic language, is known as one of the major poets of her generation in Latin America. Her books include *La luz de esta memoria* (The Light of this Memory) (1949), *Palabra dada* (A Pledge Given) (1953), *Oidor andante* (Walking Listener) (1972), *Jardín de sílice* (Silica Garden) (1980), *Léxico de afinidades* (Dictionary of Affinities) (1994), *Procura de lo imposible* (Attempting the Impossible) (1998), and anthologies including *Sueños de la constancia* (Dreams of Constancy) (1988). Resident in Mexico during the Uruguayan dictatorship (1973–89), her poetry and essays have been published in *Crisis*, *Eco*, *Plural*, ***Vuelta*** and *Sin nombre*, among other journals. She has also translated from the Italian, English, Portuguese and French.

Further reading

García Pinto, M. (1991) 'Ida Vitale', in *Women Writers of Latin America. Intimate Histories*, trans. Trudy Balch and M. García Pinto, Austin: University of Texas Press, 223–46.

Verani, H.J. (2002) 'Ida Vitale', in C. Solé and K. Müller-Bergh (eds), *Latin American Writers: Supplement I*, New York: Scribners, 567–9.

Vitale, I. (1988) *Sueños de la constancia*, Mexico City: Fondo de Cultura Económica.

—— (1994) *Léxico de afinidades*, Mexico City: Vuelta.

GWEN KIRKPATRICK

Viteri, Eugenia

b. 1932, Guayaquil, Ecuador

Writer

A writer of considerable suggestive power, Viteri's work addresses social issues, particularly those affecting women in *machista* society. Her works centre particularly on the psychological problems affecting the common people. A lyrical note of tenderness runs throughout her fiction. Her works include: *El anillo y otros cuentos* (The Ring and Other Stories) (1955), *Doce cuentos* (Twelve Stories) (1963), *A noventa millas solamente* (Only Ninety Miles Away) (1968), *Los zapatos y los sueños* (Shoes and Dreams) (1978) and *Las alcobas negras* (Dark Bedrooms) (1984).

Further reading

Espinoza, H. (1995) 'Voces y espacios femeninos en *Las alcobas negras* de Eugenia Viteri', *Letras femeninas*, Spring–Fall, 21(1–2): 47–56.

MERCEDES M. ROBLES

Vitier, Cintio

b. 1921, Key West, Florida, USA

Writer

Already well-known before the 1959 Cuban Revolution, Vitier has been an important link between pre-revolutionary and revolutionary periods. He came of age poetically in the late 1930s and 1940s, under the influence of exiled Spanish poet Juan Ramón Jiménez, and within the intellectual orbit of Cuban author José **Lezama Lima**. One of the key members of the group around ***Orígenes***, a journal edited by Lezama Lima and José, Rodríguez Feo, like many members of Orígenes Vitier was Catholic, albeit a convert. His poetry of this period is lucid yet somewhat abstract, hesitating between a philosophical search for essences and a certain nostalgic indulgence. He was also one of the ablest theoreticians of the group, developing a complex poetics gathered together in *Poética* (1961). At the end of this period he published his most influential essay collection, *Lo cubano en la poesía* (The Cuban Element in Poetry) (1958), a lengthy history of Cuban poetry which identifies essences of Cuban-ness at key moments in the island's poetic tradition.

After Batista's overthrow, Vitier and his wife, the fine poet and critic Fina **García Marruz**, remained on the island and became devoted supporters of the communist regime, although they did not hide their equally fervent Catholicism. Again demonstrating the zeal of the converted, Vitier's poetry sometimes revealed a sense of guilt for his somewhat patrician background and lack of heroism, while affirming his desire to belong to the larger revolutionary community; a stance typical of many Cuban **intellectuals** of this period. His novel *De peña pobre* (1978) and various essays form a part of this spirited defence against those who accused him and the Orígenes group of evading the social realities of the Batista period. He justified their devotion to literature by emphasizing the group's avid, imaginative pursuit of a more essential, Utopian Cuba. More recently, Vitier and García Marruz have extensively researched the work of José **Martí**. Despite a tendency to assimilate Martí with the values of the Cuban Revolution, Vitier's work has made an invaluable contribution to our understanding of this central Cuban figure.

Further reading

Bejel, E. (1991) 'Cintio Vitier', in *Escribir en Cuba: Entrevistas con escritores cubanos, 1979–1989*, Río Piedras, PR: Editorial de la Universidad de Puerto Rico.

Díaz Quiñones, A. (1987) *Cintio Vitier: La memoria integradora*, San Juan: Sin Nombre.

Garganigo, J.F. (1980) 'De la conciencia de la poesía a la poesía de la conciencia', *Revista de estudios hispánicos* 14(1): 93–100.

Santí, E.M. (1975) 'Lezama, Vitier y la crítica de la razón reminiscente', *Revista iberoamericana* 92–3: 536–46.

BEN A. HELLER

Vodanovic, Sergio

b. 1926, Gupice, Yugoslavia; d. 2001, Chile

Playwright

After the overthrow of the Allende government in Chile in 1973, Vodanovic – who had grown up and studied in Chile – worked closely with the ICTUS group, whose testimonial theatre was one of the few cultural activities permitted under the Pinochet dictatorship. His work for ICTUS included *Cuántos años tiene un día* (How Many Years in a Day) (1978), *La mar estaba serena* (The Sea was Calm) (1981) and *El mal espíritu* (The Bad Spirit) (1990). His earlier work included *Nos tomamos la universidad* (We Took the University) (1969), a critique of the university reforms presented as a collective creation by the Catholic University's Taller de Creación Teatral (Theatre Workshop).

Further reading

Layera, R. (1978) 'After the Coup: Four Dramatic Versions of Allende's Chile', *Latin American Theatre Review* 12(1): 39–42.

Pina, J.A. (1994) 'Ética y moral social en la obra dramática de Sergio Vodanovic', *Revista iberoamericana*, July–Dec., 60(168–9): 1091–6.

Smith, P.C. (1986) 'Speech Acts and Irony in Two Plays of Social Protest by Sergio Vodanovic', in E.L. Rivers (ed.), *Things Done with Words: Speech Acts in Hispanic Drama*, Newark, DE: Juan de la Cuesta.

MARINA PIANCA

vorágine, La

A novel by the Colombian José Eustacio **Rivera**, *La vorágine* (The Vortex) was published in 1924 and is usually classified in the genre of the novels of the land (*novela de la tierra*). The narrative presents Arturo Cova, an urban intellectual, moved by a romantic impetus to escape to the jungle. American nature is depicted as undomesticated and evil, driving human behaviour to its very limits of barbarism. Civilization is replaced there by the law of the survival of the fittest; and even Cova's ideals and personality are swayed by the forces of brutality. The novel combines the preciousness of *modernismo* with naturalist ugliness.

See also: civilization and barbarism

Further reading

Ordóñez, M. (1987) *La vorágine: Textos críticos*, Bogotá: Alianza Editorial.

Pérez Silva, V. (1988) *Raíces históricas de La vorágine*, Bogotá: Ed. Príncipe Apichaque.

Rivera, J.E. (1935) *The Vortex*, trans. E.K. James, New York: Putnam.

FERNANDO J. ROSENBERG

Vuelta

Vuelta was a Mexican monthly journal devoted to contemporary writings on philosophy, art, literature and politics. A group of Mexican and Latin American intellectuals led by Octavio **Paz** founded the magazine (whose title in English means Return) in 1976. The project was modelled after *Plural*, a magazine directed by newspaper publisher Julio Scherer García, which had had a similar agenda but which closed in 1976 after only five years. *Plural* released fifty-eight issues before Paz and most of his collaborators resigned in protest against the government of Luis Echeverría Alvarez, which had forced Scherer to step down as publisher of the newspaper *Excélsior* because of his political views.

With the help of donations from over 700 supporters and loyal readers, *Vuelta* launched its first issue only three months after *Plural*'s demise. The new magazine retained the same editorial board and team of contributors, but made significant changes to its design and appearance. Unlike *Plural*, which received government subsidies and had the backing of a major newspaper, the publishers of *Vuelta* depended exclusively on advertisements and subscriptions for the magazine's survival; it reached an estimated circulation of approximately 18,000.

At its founding, *Vuelta*'s publishers released a mission statement describing the magazine's goals as an open forum for all types of creative thought and critical analysis. Philosophy, art, literature and political critique remained the publication's major themes. It spotlighted poetry, short stories, historical narratives, reflective works, essays and commentaries written by some of Latin America's greatest authors, including Jorge Luis **Borges**, Octavio Paz, Julio **Cortázar** and Mario **Vargas Llosa**. In addition, however, the magazine featured writings by contributors from all over the world, including such international figures as Italo Calvino, Kostas Papaioannou and Roman Jakobson.

Far from being a purely literary magazine, *Vuelta* devoted a good deal of space to political analysis. Themes relating to ideology, bureaucracy, the State and revolutionary movements were discussed from the liberal democratic viewpoint that characterized the magazine's contributors. This political orientation distinguished *Vuelta* from Mexico's other main intellectual forum, *Nexos*, which approached political and cultural topics from a centre-left perspective.

The publishers of *Vuelta* attempted to balance the magazine's coverage of different genres and subjects with contributions by writers of many different nationalities. A cursory glance at the publication, however, confirms that Latin American, and especially Mexican, themes took pride of place in its pages. *Vuelta* ceased publication in August 1998, after the death of Octavio Paz; a new magazine called ***Letras libres***, founded by its former editor Enrique Krauze, is its continuation.

Further reading

Stavans, I. (1995) '*Vuelta*: A Succinct Appraisal', *Salmagundi* 108 (Fall): 208–18.

Van Delden, M. (2001) 'Mexico and the United States: The View from *Vuelta*', *Discourse: Journal for Theoretical Studies in Media and Culture*, Spring, 23(2): 62–80.

JUAN CARLOS GAMBOA

W

Wacquez, Mauricio

b. 1939, Cunaco, Colchagua, Chile; d. 2000, Calaceite, Spain

Novelist

Wacquez was trained as a philosopher and taught at universities in Santiago, Paris and Havana before settling permanently in Spain and devoting himself to his writing. His early works include *Cinco y una ficciones* (Five and One Fictions) (1963), *Toda la luz del mediodía* (All the Light of Noon) (1965) and *Excesos* (Excesses) (1971), all narratives of alienation, melancholy and desire, with evocations of a Chilean childhood. *Paréntesis* (Parenthesis) (1975), a single sentence eighty pages long, is woven from a series of monologues by the four characters. Wacquez's complex historical novel *Frente a un hombre armado (Cacerías de 1848)* (Facing an Armed Man (Hunting Scenes of 1848)) (1981) explores relations of subjection across time, with intense scenes of homosexual obsession. *Ella o el sueño de nadie* (She or the Dream of Nobody) (1983) tells of an erotic triangle set in an unreal and shifting landscape. Wacquez's final work *Epifanía de una sombra* (Epiphany of a Shadow) (2000) was to have been the first part of a trilogy entitled *La oscuridad* (The Darkness), which proposed to recreate scenes from Wacquez's childhood; sadly it is the only part that was written by the time of his death.

Further reading

Balderston, D. (1999) 'Las revoluciones sexuales de 1848: deseo, lucha de clases e historia imaginaria en *Frente a un hombre armado*', in *El deseo, enorme cicatriz luminosa*, Caracas: eXcultura, 83–90.

Dendle, B. (ed.) (2001) Special issue of *Romance Quarterly* 48 (3) devoted to Wacquez.

Marco, J. (1987) 'Mauricio Wacquez', in *Literatura hispanoamericana del modernismo a nuestros días*, Madrid: Espasa-Calpe, 469–73.

DANIEL BALDERSTON

Walcott, Derek

b. 1930, Castries, St Lucia

Writer

Nobel laureate Walcott is best known in the Carribean as a dramatist and in the outside world as a poet. Much of his dramatic work is poetic, particularly his early plays such as *The Sea at Dauphin*, *Malcochon*, and his masterpiece *Dream on Monkey Mountain* (in *Dream on Monkey Mountain and Other Plays* (1970)). *Tijean and his Brothers* (1970) is an absorbing retelling of a familiar folk tale as 'total theatre', using music and highly theatrical forms of masking. These early plays create heroes who have great poetic expression, out-of-the-ordinary Caribbean folk – woodcutters, charcoal burners, fishermen. Walcott deals with themes related to the collective Caribbean search for renewal and rehabilitation of identity after colonialism. After co-founding the Little Carib Theatre Workshop in 1959 (which later became the Trinidad Theatre Workshop), he produced his plays there until 1976, including the musicals *The Joker of Seville* (1978), *O Babylon!* (1978), the witty comedy on post-colonial black–white identities *Pantomime* (1980), and the domestic drama on post-colonial middle-class self-questioning, *Remembrance* (1980). *Three plays: The Last Carnival; Beef No Chicken; A Branch of the Blue Nile* (1986) are less impressive although still polished pieces. *A Branch of the Blue Nile*, reminiscent of Walcott's own life, depicts actors trying to come to terms with a complex cultural inheritance and to cope with the conditions of theatre in the Caribbean.

Walcott's poetic achievement has been great. His early mature volumes, *In a Green Night* (1962), *The Castaway* (1965) and *The Gulf* (1969), established a supple lyricism as much at home in European as in Caribbean rhythms. His poetic autobiography, ***Another Life*** (1973), in length and fluency presages the marvellous ***Omeros*** (1990). Other important works include *Sea Grapes* (1976), *The Star-Apple Kingdom* (1980), *The Fortunate Traveller* (1982), *Midsummer* (1984) and *The Arkansas Testament* (1987), in which Walcott demonstrated his remarkable ability to be both local and personal, international and everyman.

Further reading

Baugh, E. (1978) *Derek Walcott: Memory as Vision: Another Life*, Harlow, Essex: Longmans.

Brown, S. (ed.) (1991) *The Art of Derek Walcott*, Bridgend, Mid Glamorgan: Seren Books.

Goldstraw, I.E. (1984) *Derek Walcott: An Annotated Bibliography of His Works*, New York: Garland.

Hamner, R. (1981) *Derek Walcott*, Boston: Twayne.

—— (ed.) (1993) *Critical Perspectives on Derek Walcott*, Washington, DC: Three Continents Press.

King, B. (1995) *Derek Walcott and West Indian Drama*, Oxford, Clarendon Press.

ELAINE SAVORY

Walrond, Eric

b. 1898, Georgetown, British Guiana; d. 1966, London, England

Writer

Like Claude **McKay**, Eric Walrond emigrated early to the USA, where he became prominent in the Harlem Renaissance, attacking American racism through forthright essays in periodicals such as *Negro World*. In 1926 he published *Tropic Death*, a collection of ten short stories relating to the Caribbean common folk, and linked by the theme of untimely death from causes ranging from drought and starvation to the occult power of Obeah. Outwardly ironic, inwardly compassionate and vividly realistic, Walrond's powerful stories introduced Caribbean themes into US black literature.

Further reading

Parascandola, L.J. (ed. and intro.) (1998) *'Winds Can Wake Up the Dead': An Eric Walrond Reader*, Detroit, MI: Wayne State University Press.

Wade, Carl A. (1999) 'African-American Aesthetics and the Short Fiction of Eric Walrond: Tropic Death and the Harlem Renaissance', *CLA Journal*, June, 42(4): 403–29.

LOUIS JAMES

Walsh, Maria Elena

b. 1930, Buenos Aires, Argentina

Writer

'My ambition is to be Lewis Carroll's granddaughter', Walsh confessed on one occasion. Called the queen of children's writing, singer-songwriter, short story writer and poet, Walsh's tender and imaginative writing has captivated successive generations. She was 15 when she began to write for the literary supplement of *La Nación* and the magazine *El Hogar*. In 1947, age 17, she published privately her first book of poems, *Otoño imperdonable* (Unforgiveable Autumn), which won her immediate recognition and the praise of great writers such as **Borges**, **Neruda** and Rafael Alberti. In 1952, she published *Baladas con Angel* (Ballads with Angel) and met Leda Valladares, with whom she went on to form a folk duo. They travelled to Paris, where they worked for several years, and there she began her work for children, 'a way of reconciling myself to paradise lost and at the same time a search for roots, a journey through time'.

Returning to Argentina, the two artists began a long project to rediscover the traditional anonymous folk repertoire, travelling through the country and gathering information. By 1959, Walsh had set some of her poems to music and included them in a musical called *Los sueños del rey Bombo* (The Dreams of King Drum). In the same year Maria Herminia Avelleneda contracted her to write a series of television programmes for children – they would later go on to write and produce the film *Juguemos en el mundo* (Let's Play in the World) (1970). In 1968, she presented a concert of her own protest songs entitled *Juguemos en el mundo: show para ejecutivos* (The Executive Show) which won her critical acclaim and an adoring public. She continues to sing in concert and on television, to write in various genres and to work for children. *Canciones para mirar* (Songs for Looking) (1977) confirmed her success, and when her play *Doña Disparate y Bambuco* was put on at the Teatro San Martín the following year, the seats were filled with children and adults alike singing along with the actors on stage. In the 1990s she produced a children's encyclopedia, published in instalments by a local newspaper, and an autobiography.

Further reading

Bach, C. (1995) 'A Child's Wisdom in a Poet's Heart', *Americas*, May–June, 47(3): 12–17.

Foster, D.W. (1984) 'Playful Ecphrasis: María Elena Walsh and Children's Literature in Argentina', *Mester*, May, 13(1): 40–51.

Luraschi, I.A. and K. Sibbald (1993) *María Elena Walsh, o, el desafío de la limitación*, Buenos Aires: Editorial Sudamericana.

Pujol, S.A. (1993) *Como la cigarra: Biografía de María Elena Walsh*, Buenos Aires: Beas Ediciones.

Sibbald, K.M. (1997) 'María Elena Walsh', in *Encyclopedia of Latin American Literature*, ed. V. Smith, London: Fitzroy Dearborn, 851–3.

—— (1998) 'Tradición y transgresión en la poética de María Elena Walsh', in L. Rojas Trempe and C. Vallejo (eds), *Poética de escritoras hispanoamericanas al alba del próximo milenio*, Miami: Universal.

Walsh, M.E. (1996) *Poemas y canciones*, ed. M. Benedetti, Buenos Aires: Espasa Calpe.

RODRIGO PEIRETTI

Walsh, Rodolfo

b. 1927, Choele-Choel, Rio Negro, Argentina; d. 1977, unknown

Writer

A journalist and fiction writer who in 1977 joined the growing list of the disappeared in Argentina, Walsh began his career as a journalist in 1951. In 1959 he was one of the founders of the Prensa Latina news agency, and in 1968 established the weekly *CGT*, one of the most innovative contemporary trade union journals. In 1976, stemming from his active involvement in the resistance to the military, he founded the Agencia Clandestina de Noticias (Underground News Agency) and later the Cadena Informativa agency. His early writings were in the crime genre; *Variaciones en rojo* (Variations in Red) won the Municipal Prize for Literature in 1953. The stories of *Un kilo de oro* (A Kilo of Gold) (1967) and *Los oficios terrestres* (Earthly Professions) (1965) are path-breaking in Latin American short story fiction. *Operación masacre* was a work of investigative journalism first published in 1957 and then rewritten several times over the years in an attempt to find the best form for what became his most famous project. As testimonial writing (see ***testimonio***), *Operación masacre* anticipated by many years later documentary and non-fiction writing.

At first a supporter of Perón, Walsh's journalistic investigations enabled him to explore more deeply the theory and practice of the Left; this led him in the 1960s to join the Montoneros, in which he remained active until the group's collapse. The integration of politics and literature in his work has come to be seen as representative of a whole era. Concerned with artistic experimentation, he always also considered the political efficacy of what he produced. His work does not have a single style; each of his prose and journalistic writings lead towards a Utopian prose which balances writing and experience, politics and art.

His investigative works *Caso Sotanowsky* (1973) and *¿Quién mató a Rosendo?* (Who Killed Rosendo?) (1969) complete a trilogy exemplary of the 'new journalism', also demonstrated in his columns in the journal *Primera plana*. Walsh also wrote two plays, *La granada* (The Grenade) (1965) and *La batalla* (The Battle) (1981), in which allegory is employed to denounce and expose the military.

Further reading

Amar Sánchez, A.M. (1992) *El relato de los hechos. Rodolfo Walsh: Testimonio y escritura*, Rosario: Beatriz Viterbo

Ferro, R. (1999) 'La literatura en el banquillo: Walsh y la fuerza del testimonio', in S. Cella (ed.), *La irrupción de la crítica*, vol. 10 of the *Historia crítica de la literatura argentina*, Buenos Aires: Emecé, 125–45.

Lafforgue, J. (ed.) (1994) *Rodolfo Walsh*, special issue of *Nuevo texto crítico*, VI,12/13.

Walsh, R. (1981) *Obra literaria completa*, Mexico: Siglo XXI.

DANIEL LINK

Warner-Vieyra, Myriam

b. 1939, Pointe-à-Pitre, Guadeloupe

Writer

Although she has lived most of her life in Senegal, Warner-Vieyra's first novel, *Le quimboiseur l'avait dit* (As the Sorcerer Said) (1980), is set in Guadeloupe and Paris, her second, *Juletane* (1982) mostly in West Africa. Written simply in the form of a diary, *Juletane* deals with the subjects of insanity, dislocation, polygamy and disenchantment, Warner-Vieyra's main fictional preoccupations. She is considered both a Caribbean and African writer and accurately portrays the plight of women caught in the cross-cultural complications of West Africa and the Caribbean.

Further reading

Lionnet, F. (1993) 'Geographies of Pain: Captive Bodies and Violent Acts in the Fictions of Myriam Warner-Vieyra, Gayl Jones, and Bessie Head', *Callaloo: A Journal of African American and African Arts and Letters* (Callaloo, Baltimore, MD), Winter, 16(1): 132–52.

KEITH JARDIM

Wast, Hugo

b. 1883, Córdoba, Argentina; d. 1962, Buenos Aires, Argentina

Writer

Publishing as Hugo Wast (real name Gustavo Martínez Zuviría), his novels, realist with *costumbrista* elements (see ***costumbrismo***) and laced with Catholic militancy, were commercial successes. Two works, *Valle Negro* (Black Valley) (1918) and *Desierto de Piedra* (Stone Desert) (1925), won honours from the Spanish Royal Academy and the Argentine National Book Prize. Although known mainly for his novels, Wast also wrote short stories, poetry, biographies and plays. He was also director of the National Library, headed the National Commission of Culture and was minister of Public Justice and Instruction.

Further reading

Rapalo, M.E. and M.T. Gramuglio (2002) 'Pedagogías para la nación católica: *Criterio* y Hugo Wast', in M.T. Gramuglio (ed.), *El imperio realista*, vol. 6 of the *Historia crítica de la literatura argentina*, Buenos Aires: Emecé, 447–75.

FERNANDA A. ZULLO

Watunna

A cycle of creation myths from the So'to or Ye'cuana tribe of the upper Orinoco River, collected by ethnographer Marc de Civrieux and published in Spanish in 1970; *Watunna* has been translated into English and made into an animated film. One of the most complete indigenous South American creation cycles, it is aesthetically comparable to creation cycles such as Genesis and the *Popol Vuh*. It narrates the adventures of the creator god Wanadi and other ancestors; these myths refer to a timeless era when all things were created, yet also register the So'to's perspective on their first traumatic contacts with Europeans during the mid-eighteenth century.

Further reading

Bucher, H.B. (2001) *The Act of Storytelling and Gender Dynamics in 'Kaweshawa': A Study of the Watunna, the Makiritare Creation Myth*, in Elizabeth-Hoffman Nelson (ed. and preface), *Telling the Stories: Essays on American Indian Literatures and Cultures*, New York: Peter Lang, 29–38.

Civricux, M. dc (1997) *Watunna: An Orinoco Creation Cycle*, Austin: University of Texas Press.

BEN A. HELLER

Westphalen, Emilio Adolfo

b. 1911, Lima, Peru

Poet

A hermetic and withdrawn surrealist poet (see **surrealism**), Westphalen published two books of poems, *Las ínsulas extrañas* (Strange Islands) (1933) and, two years later, *Abolición de la muerte* (Abolition of Death), which were compiled in 1980 under a new title, *Otra imagen deleznable* (Another Despicable Image). Westphalen met César **Moro** in 1934, when he returned from Paris after joining Breton's surrealist movement. Through his friendship with Moro, he joined an incipient surrealist movement in Lima. Although he did not publish new poems after the 1930s, he remains an important literary figure in Latin American poetry.

Further reading

Bary, L. (1988) 'El surrealismo en Hispanoamérica y el yo de Westphalen', *Revista de crítica literaria latinoamericana* 27: 97–110.

Creación y Crítica (1977) special issue on Westphalen, no. 20.

Fernández Cozman, C. (1990) *Las ínsulas extrañas de Emilio Adolfo Westphalen*, Lima: Maylamp Editores.

Keeth, W.P. (1997) 'Emilio Adolfo Westphalen', in *Encyclopedia of Latin American Literature*, ed. V. Smith, London: Fitzroy Dearborn, 853–5.

MAGDALENA GARCÍA PINTO

Wickham, John

b. 1923, Barbados

Writer

One of the most important writer-editors of the English-speaking Caribbean, for years Wickham edited *Bim*, the Barbados literary magazine. In 1979 he became literary editor of *The Nation* newspaper, also in Barbados. His first two books, collections of short stories and essays, are *Casuarina Row* (1974) and *World without End* (1982). A third book, *Discoveries* (short stories), was published in 1993. He has been awarded several prizes and honours, among them the BBC World Service competition in 1967 for the short story 'Meeting in Milkmarket'.

Further reading

Pointer, F. (1977) 'Interview with John Wickham', *Ba Shiru: A Journal of African Languages and Literature*, Madison, WI, 8(2): 71–6.

KEITH JARDIM

Wide Sargasso Sea

Wide Sargasso Sea is Jean **Rhys**'s masterpiece and a brilliant evocation of the post-emancipation West Indies. Published in 1966, the novel refers to the creole madwoman locked in the attic in Charlotte Brontë's *Jane Eyre*, which became a trope for women writers in Gilbert and Gubar's feminist study *The Madwoman in the Attic* (1979). In the Rhys novel, the creole woman's history is told through a complex narrative shared with her unnamed husband, suggesting a revisionist reading of Brontë's novel in relation to the imperial English socio-political context. The critical responses of Caribbean critics such as Kamau **Brathwaite** and Kenneth **Ramchand** opened a dialogue on the place of the white creole subsequently extended by Caribbean feminist critics.

Further reading

Frickey, P.M. (ed.) (1990) *Critical Perspectives on Jean Rhys*, Washington: Three Continents Press.

Gilbert, Sandra M. and Sandra Mortola (1979) *The Madwoman in the Attic. The Woman Writer and the Nineteenth-century Literary Imagination*, New Haven and London: Yale University Press.

Mateo Palmer, M. (1990) 'Antoinette a través del espejo: Mito e identidad en *The Wide Sargasso Sea*', *Anales del Caribe* 10:131–43.

O'Connor, T. (1986) *Jean Rhys: The West Indian Novels*, New York: New York University Press.

ELAINE SAVORY

Wie eegie sanie

In the early 1950s Surinamese nationalism expressed itself in the movement 'Wie eegie sanie' (Our own things), founded in the Netherlands by Surinamese students, who remained the core members in their native country. The attempt to reassess the Surinamese cultural heritage was primarily an Afro-Surinamese affair, despite its aim, in ethnic terms, to create a unified country. The group focused on the creole language Sranan Tongo, which was then understood by *c*.85 per cent of the population. By doing so the members, among them Eddy **Bruma**, contributed greatly to the growing status of literature written in Sranan.

AART G. BROEK

Wilcock, Juan Rodolfo

b. 1919, Buenos Aires, Argentina;
d. 1978, Viterbo, Italy

Writer

An extraordinary, eccentric figure in the world of Argentine literature, Wilcock was known for his rather precious neo-romantic poetry of the 1940s. He left Argentina for the UK and then Italy in the 1950s, and ended up writing most of his work in Italian. His most important prose work in Spanish consists of his startling, cruel short stories, collected in 1974 as *El caos* (Chaos). With Silvina **Ocampo** he also wrote a verse drama set in ancient Rome, *Los traidores* (The Traitors) (1956). His six books of poetry are marked by a rejection of the avant-garde (see **avant-garde in Latin America**); in ***Sur*** in 1949, he wrote a long essay on the composition of one of his own sonnets. In Italy he was friendly with Moravia and Pasolini, and appeared in the latter's film of the Gospel. His Italian work includes several pieces reminiscent of **Borges**, while his extraordinary epistolary novel *L'ingegnere* (The Engineer) (1974), about a young Argentine engineer working on the trans-Andean railroad, is an ironic comment on the notion of Argentine culture being divided between 'civilization' and 'barbarism' (see **civilization and barbarism**).

Further reading:

Balderston, D. (1983) 'Los cuentos crueles de Silvina Ocampo y Juan Rodolfo Wilcock', *Revista iberoamericana* 125: 743–52.

Laddaga, R. (2002) *Literaturas indigentes y placeres bajos: Felisberto Hernández, Virgilio Piñera, Juan Rodolfo Wilcock*, Rosario: Beatriz Viterbo.

Wilcock, J.R. (2000) *The Temple of Iconoclasts*, trans. Lawrence Venuti, San Francisco: Mercury House.

DANIEL BALDERSTON

Williams, Denis

b. 1923, Georgetown, British Guiana;
d. 1990, Georgetown

Novelist and painter

On graduation from London's Camberwell School of Art, Williams stayed on in London to work as a painter and lecturer. After ten years in Britain, he left for Africa where he spent the next ten years divided equally between the Sudan and Nigeria. In both countries, Williams studied African classical antiquity and developed a strong interest in archeology, ancestry, and the notion of personal and group identities. He is the author of two novels,

Other Leopards (1963) and *The Third Temptation* (1968), some short stories and two books of art criticism, including *Image and Idea in the Arts of Guyana* (1970).

Further reading

James, L. (1999) 'Schrodinger's Cat versus Melville's Jaguar: Science and the Imagination in the Work of Three Guayanese Writers', in Jean-Pierre Durix (ed. and intro.), *Theory and Literary Creation/Theorie et creation litteraire*, Dijon, France: Editions Universitaires de Dijon, 121–7.

Lawrence, L.S. (1979) 'From Cultural Ambivalence to the Celebration of the African Heritage in British West Indian Literature', *College Language Association Journal* 23: 220–33.

FUNSO AIYEJINA

Williams, N.D.

b. 1942, Georgetown, British Guiana

Novelist, short story writer and teacher

Williams won the prestigious **Casa de las Américas** Prize for his first novel, *Ikael Torass*, in 1976. His collection of short stories, *The Crying of Rainbirds*, appeared in 1992. It was shortlisted for the Guyana Prize that year. Another novel, *The Silence of Islands*, appeared in 1994.

His fiction frequently looks at the difficult experiences people endure as they move into adulthood. 'Cats in the Eyes of a Pig', a short story in *The Penguin Book of Caribbean Short Stories* (1996), is a particularly interesting example.

Williams now lives in Canada. He was educated at the University of the West Indies, Mona, Jamaica, where he completed research in African literature. He has taught in St Lucia. His short stories have won Gold Medals in the Jamaican Festival Competition and have appeared in the journals *Savacou* and *Images*.

KEITH JARDIM

Wolff, Egon

b. 1926, Santiago, Chile

Playwright

Wolff's plays explore issues ranging from the euphoria that comes with the abandonment of traditional values to the realization that conformity ends in a loss of hope. The two moments coincide with the ascendancy of Unidad Popular (1970–3) and the 1973 military *coup*.

His first group of plays begins with *Mansión de lechuzas* (Mansion of Owls) (1958). In this play, the idealized world of the home of a young widow and her two sons is threatened by some Italian neighbours who challenge the lifestyle of the bourgeois family and represent alternative values. This period, identified with revolutionary changes, culminates with *Flores de papel* (Paper Flowers) (1970).

The threat persists in *Los invasores* (The Intruders) (1963), a circular drama that consists of a dream whose images are repeated later in reality. The invasion of the bourgeois house is an act of revenge by the socially marginalized classes, whose irruption represents the possibility of a new way of life. The atmosphere is marked by frustration and disappointment. The poor are incorporated in Wolff's work as a memory aid for the bourgeois and they act as activators of the conscience of the upper classes.

In the later group of plays the atmosphere is more bitter and sceptical. Although the aesthetic resources are the same, the invasion of the private world by a threatening exterior force means that the conflict becomes individual, the class perspective disappears and with it the possibility of any kind of change. The most notable among these works are *El signo de Caín* (The Sign of Cain) (1969), *Kindergarten* (1977), *Espejismo* (Delusion) (1978), *José* (1980) and *Alamos en la azotea* (Poplars on the Terrace) (1981).

In spite of the pessimism of Wolff's later work, his plays do offer moments of warmth and tenderness to prove that something could be saved from the horror and social impact caused by the dictatorship of Augusto Pinochet. Wolff's incorporation of elements from the epic theatre of the absurd and neo-realism contributed to a new theatrical aesthetics.

Further reading

Castedo-Ellerman, E. (1989) 'Egon Wolff', in *Latin American Writers*, ed. C.A. Solé and M.I. Abreu, New York: Scribner's, 3: 1311–15.

Piña, J.A. (1978) 'Evolución e involución en las obras de Egon Wolff', *Mensaje* 269.

Portl, K. (1979) 'Wolff's Theater der Angst', *Revista iberoamericana* 3.

Queline Eyring (Bixler) (1989) 'Language in/as Action in Egon Wolff's *Háblame de Laura*', *Latin American Theatre Review*, Fall, 23: 49–62.

Wolff, E. (1990) *Teatro completo*, Boulder: Society of Spanish and Spanish American Studies.

SANDRA GARABANO

women's writing

Latin American women's writing achieved significant recognition only at the end of the twentieth century. Driven by a predominantly male-dominated culture, the literary canon and literary history obliterated women's production in previous centuries (see **literary histories**). In contrast, feminist scholarship has promoted the study of texts written by women since the seventeenth century. In confessional texts through which nuns such as María de Jesús and María of Saint Joseph depicted their lives, we find some magnificent, exemplary writing by women. Another nun, Sor Juana Inés de la Cruz (Mexico, 1650–94), the most prominent female literary figure of the colonial period, entered the convent to escape marriage and wrote poetry, plays and theological essays (*Carta atenagórica* and *Primer sueño* (First Dream)).

Due to the exclusion of women's work from literary reviews and anthologies, the study of women's writing in Latin America focuses now on the limited corpus of available texts. Turn-of-the-century texts are most difficult to find and only very recent studies have allowed some of them to circulate. In spite of their exclusion and invisibility, a few women have received public recognition because of their literary work, among them the poet Delmira **Agustini** whose work displays a unique baroque representation of eroticism. The popularity of Gabriela **Mistral**, the only Latin American woman writer ever to win the Nobel Prize, was mostly because she was an advocate for children and her poems and songs were used in schools all over Latin America during the 1950s. A number of her most significant writings became available only during the last decade as a result of feminist analyses highlighting its substantial complexity. Mistral's writing addresses the question of identity through a witty vision of a mixed-blood, culturally mixed Latin America: distinctive voices – the native, the Spanish, the emigrant, the mestizo – create a democratic image of a culture strongly connected with God and the Earth.

During the 1940s and 1950s María Luisa **Bombal** and Elena **Garro** exposed the burden that the institution of marriage imposed upon Latin American middle-class women. Their fiction explores the eroticism of the female body and names women's sexual pleasure for the first time. Literary subterfuges borrowed from the surrealists made it possible for erotic texts by women to be published without disturbing the extremely rigid cultural scene.

During the 1960s and 1970s the writings of Rosario **Castellanos** and Clarice **Lispector** increasingly questioned the establishment and challenged hegemonic culture. Theirs and others' fiction is self-reflexive and committed to social justice, identifying with the cause of the oppressed and the underclasses. By the 1980s, Elena **Poniatowska** would make explicit that 'women's writing is part of the voices of the oppressed in Latin America'. In the last two decades of the twentieth century women's writing has become the most significant cultural phenomenon in Latin America: complex narratives, sophisticated poetry and incisive essays have opened up the canon to the incorporation of unconventional narratives, such as the ***testimonio***; examples include the work of Rigoberta Menchú and Hebe de Bonafini, whose texts inscribe the voices of the victims and survivors of political repression under dictatorship.

Influenced by cultural changes triggered by the strength of women's movements in the 1980s, the intersection of the political and the sexual is probably the most striking and powerful feature of current women's writing. The most recognized contemporary writers, such as Luisa **Valenzuela**, Cristina **Peri Rossi**, Rosario **Ferré**, Luisa **Futoransky**, Isabel **Allende**, Pía **Barros** and Diamela **Eltit**, have all produced sophisticated and distinctive works that explore pressing cultural subjects using unconventional literary strategies. Produced by women from diverse nationalities, classes and races, Latin American women's writing is also a consistent cultural phenomenon that challenges the ideological rigidity of the public sphere.

Further reading

Bergmann, E. *et al.* (1990) *Women, Culture, and Politics in Latin America*, Berkeley: University of California Press.

Castro-Klarén, S., S. Molloy and B. Sarlo (eds) (1991) *Women's Writing in Latin America*, Boulder: Westview.

Franco, J. (1989) *Plotting Women. Gender and Representation in Mexico*, New York: Columbia University Press.

García Pinto, M. (1991) *Women Writers of Latin America: Intimate Histories*, Austin: University of Texas Press.

González, P. and E. Ortega (1984) *La sartén por el mango. Encuentro de escritoras latinoamericanas*, Puerto Rico: Ediciones Huracán.

Marting, D. (ed.) (1986) *Women Writers of Spanish America: An Annotated Bio-Bibliographical Guide*, Westport, CT: Greenwood Press.

—— (ed.) (1990) *Spanish American Women Writers: A Bio-Bibliographical Sourcebook*, Westport: Greenwood Press.

Picon Garfield, E. (ed.) (1988) *Women's Fiction from Latin America*, Detroit: Wayne State University Press.

Rodríguez, I. (1994) *House/Garden/Nation: Space, Gender and Ethnicity in Post-Colonial Latin American Literatures by Women*, Durham, NC: Duke University Press.

LILIANA TREVIZÁN

workshop poetry

The Sandinista regime which came to power in Nicaragua in 1979 created a Culture Ministry under Ernesto **Cardenal**; its aim was to actively encourage the country's most uneducated and isolated citizens to be not just consumers, but also the creators of cultural works. Inspired by his experience at Solentiname, the Ministry under Cardenal created some seventy poetry workshops, or Talleres de Poesía, throughout the country, where people of every background could both write and gain access to the best of world poetry. The resulting poems were of very uneven quality; some were criticized as facile works of collage, pallid imitations of Cardenal's own work. Economic hardship reduced the number of centres to thirty by 1983 at the height of contra activity.

Further reading

Costa, E. de (1997) 'Workshops', in *Encyclopedia of Latin American Literature*, ed. V. Smith, London: Fitzroy Dearborn, 858–9.

Johnson, K. (ed. and trans.) (1985) *A Nation of Poets: Writings from the Poetry Workshops of Nicaragua*, Los Angeles: West End Press.

Kendig, Diane (1990) *Poetocracy: The Poetry Workshop Movement in Nicaragua*, in Leonard M. Trawick (ed.), *World, Self, Poem: Essays on Contemporary Poetry from the 'Jubilation of Poets'*, Kent: Kent State University Press, 59–71.

Pring-Mill, R. (1984) 'The Workshop Poetry of Sandinista Nicaragua', *Antilia* 1–2.

DEREK PETREY AND ILEANA RODRÍGUEZ

Wynter, Sylvia

b. 1928, Holguín, Cuba

Writer

Born in Cuba of Jamaican parents, Wynter grew up in Jamaica and won a scholarship to the University of London, where she read Spanish and advocated indigenous West Indian drama. Her play, *Under the Sun* (1962), written in London, was developed into the novel *The Hills of Hebron* (1962), vividly portraying religious conflict in rural Jamaica. In 1963 she returned to the University of the West Indies, Jamaica, to lecture in Hispanic Studies. From 1969 onwards her incisive articles attacked colonial influence in the Caribbean, championing an African-based local culture. In 1977 she emigrated to the USA, where she taught for many years at Stanford University.

LOUIS JAMES

Y

Yáñez, Agustín

b. 1904, Guadalajara, Jalisco; d. 1980, Mexico City

Writer and diplomat

Yáñez was a novelist and ambassador, Governor of Jalisco and Secretary of Public Education. His masterpiece, *Al filo del agua* (The Edge of the Storm) (1947), experimented with narrative techniques, paving the way for the work of Juan **Rulfo** and Carlos **Fuentes**. Set in rural Jalisco, his other novels were conceived within an overarching plan, based on the stages of an individual's life, and aspiring to trace the major contours of twentieth-century Mexican history. His fundamentally optimistic view of history saw Mexico moving away from religious obscurantism and provincialism towards modernity and progress.

Further reading

Canaparo, C. (1997) 'Agustín Yáñez', in *Encyclopedia of Latin American Literature*, ed. V. Smith, London: Fitzroy Dearborn, 861–2.

Clark, S.T. (1989) 'Agustín Yáñez', in *Latin American Writers*, ed. C.A. Solé and M.I. Abreu, New York: Scribners, 3: 991–4.

Flasher, J. (1969) *México contemporáneo en las novelas de Agustín Yáñez*, Mexico City: Porrúa.

Franco, J. (1988). *Lectura sociocrítica de la obra narrativa de Agustín Yáñez*, Guadalajara: Unidad Editorial.

Yáñez, A. (1963) *The Edge of the Storm*, trans. Ethel Brinton, Austin: University of Texas Press.

—— (1968) *Obras escogidas*, ed. José Luis Martínez, Mexico City: Ediciones Aguilar.

—— (1992) *Al filo del agua*, ed. Arturo Azuela, Paris: Colección Archivos.

CYNTHIA STEELE

Yáñez Cossío, Alicia

b. 1928, Quito, Ecuador

Writer

Ecuador's foremost woman author, her characters are strong women caught up in adverse circumstances. The world they face is governed by loneliness, a lack of private and personal space, the silence of others, a lack of communication, social prejudices, the absence of love and an alienating consumer society. Creativity and passion are the means of achieving dignity and transcending solitude in such circumstances. She has received several national and international prizes. Her works include: *Yo vendo unos ojos negros* (I am Selling a Pair of Dark Eyes) (1980), *La virgen pipona* (The Paunchy Virgin) (1985) and *El Cristo feo* (The Ugly Christ) (1995).

Further reading

Gerdes, D. (1990) 'An Embattled Society: Morality versus Writing in Alicia Yáñez Cossío's *La cofradía del mullo del vestido de la Virgen Pipona*', *Latin American Literary Review* 18 (36): 50–8.

Handelsmann, M. (1988) 'En busca de una mujer

nueva: Rebelión y resistencia en *Yo vendo unos ojos negros* de Alicia Yáñez Cossío', *Revista iberoamericana* 144–5: 893–901.
—— (1997) 'Alicia Yáñez Cossío', *Encyclopedia of Latin American Literature*, ed. V. Smith, London: Fitzroy Dearborn, 863–4.
Scott, N.M. (1987) 'Alicia Yáñez Cossío, una perspectiva femenina sobre el pasado del Ecuador', *Discurso literario* 4 (2).

MERCEDES M. ROBLES

Yo el supremo

Augusto **Roa Bastos**'s *Yo el supremo* (I the Supreme) was published in Buenos Aires in 1974. It is marked by a context of the rise of militant left Peronism and a crisis of military dictatorship in Argentina. The key mobilizing ideas of the moment were anti-imperialism and 'national liberation'. Roa Bastos shared the general political optimism about the conjuncture, writing the novel between 1968 and 1973, before having to leave the country for exile in France after the military *coup* of 1976.

The novel tells the story of the emergence of a modern nation-state, Paraguay, out of colonialism. El Supremo, modelled on the dictator, Dr José Gaspar Rodríguez de Francia, dictates in a number of ways: in the political sense – he runs and controls the totality of the State apparatus; in the discursive sense – he dictates the history of independence to his secretary, Patiño; and in the pedagogic sense – the history he dictates has a purpose, which is to educate the State bureaucracy and all Paraguayans into citizenship, to create a 'people'. But in representing the 'people', the dictator appropriates sovereignty for himself and becomes the mythified central character of his own story, the lone subject of national independence and nation-building.

El Supremo reads his way through the post-colonial archive in which Dr Francia was demonized, conversing with and evoking many of the key historical figures of the age, from Belgrano and Bolívar to Carlyle and de Sade. This intertextual richness is not only political but literary too. And Roa Bastos takes El Supremo's critique further, for the 'people' he represents – the *voquibles* – leave no traces of their history in writing and are thus absent from the historiographical archive. *Yo el supremo*, therefore, also contains a critique of writing as a medium; for this reason El Supremo's voice – his dictation – is also supposed to represent and restore the 'people's' history, and this is why he constantly attacks his secretary, Patiño, the transcriber of his voice, insanely monitoring the lost representativity of his script and thus generating more dictation. The other key character is the Compiler of the novel, who not only mimics the dictator in the process of composition, but also interrupts his discourse/dictation, provoking a battle between the literary practice of the Compiler and the political practice of the dictator.

Further reading

Aceves, R. *et al.* (1990) *Acercamientos críticos a 'Yo el Supremo'*, Guadalajara, Mexico: Universidad de Guadalajara.
Roa Bastos, A. (1983) *Yo el Supremo*, ed. and intro. M. Esquerro, Madrid: Cátedra.
—— (1986) *Yo el Supremo*, ed. and intro. C. Pacheco, Caracas: Biblioteca Ayacucho.
—— (1986) *I the Supreme*, trans. H. Lane. New York: Knopf.
Weldt-Basson, H.C. (1993) *Augusto Roa Bastos's 'Yo el Supremo': A Dialogic Perspective*, Columbia: University of Missouri Press.

JOHN KRANIAUSKAS

Yurkievich, Saúl

b. 1931, La Plata, Argentina

Poet and literary critic

Yurkievich moved to Paris in the early 1960s and taught there for many years. His literary and teaching activities meet in his poetry; the writer and the critic come together in the figure of one who elected to live outside Argentina yet within the territory of its language. The title of his first volume of poetry *Volanda linde lumbre* (untranslatable title) (1961) reveals his interest in linguistic experimentation, which gradually took over his critical work also. Among his many critical works, his *Fundadores de la nueva poesía latinoamericana* (Founders of New Latin American Poetry) (1971) is the best known.

Further reading

Krawietz, A. and F. Leon (1999) 'Entrevista con Saúl Yurkievich', *Cuadernos hispanoamericanos*, Jan. 583: 125–31.

Yurkievich, S. (1971) *Fundadores de la nueva poesía latinoamericana: Vallejo, Huidobro, Borges, Neruda, Paz*, Barcelona: Barral Editores

—— (1996) *La movediza modernidad*, Madrid: Taurus.

—— (1997) *Suma crítica*, Mexico City: Fondo de Cultura Económica.

ENRIQUE FOFFANI

Z

Zalamea, Jorge

b. 1905, Bogotá, Colombia; d. 1969, Bogotá

Writer

In 1925 Zalamea was a member of *Los Nuevos* (The New), a group seeking cultural and political renovation. His work, which includes poems, essays and fiction, reflects a profound social commitment. During the Rojas Pinilla dictatorship, with the closing of *Crítica* (Critique), his biweekly publication, Zalamea left for Buenos Aires. His two main texts are *El gran Burundún-Burundá ha muerto* (The Great Burundún-Burundá is Dead), published in exile in 1952, and the 1964 *El sueño de las escalinatas* (The Dream of the Steps). An avid traveller, Zalamea is also well known for his masterly translations of Saint-John **Perse** and served as ambassador to Mexico and Italy.

Further reading

Iriarte, A. (1989) 'De Gregorio Samsa al Gran Burundún, pasando por su Excelencia', prologue to *El gran Burundún-Burundá ha muerto. La metamorfosis de su excelencia*, Bogotá: Arango Editor, 9–37.

HÉCTOR D. FERNÁNDEZ L'HOESTE

Zamora, Daisy

b. 1950, Managua, Nicaragua

Writer

Although she can give the impression of frailty, Daisy Zamora is a woman of strong will. In 1977 she won the Mariano Fiallos Gil Poetry Prize. Her domestic, intimate poetry grew more political as the insurrection unfolded and she became more involved in the Sandinistas' work. Zamora, active supporter of the FSLN, was programme director and the known voice for the clandestine Radio Sandino. The group who took over the Palacio Nacional in Operation Pigpen, a landmark in the struggle against the regime, was sheltered in her elegant house in Managua. She was Vice-Minister of Culture and worked with Ernesto **Cardenal**. Zamora's poetry and political role points to the controversial dialogue between feminism and socialism.

Further reading

Jimenez, Luis A. (1999) 'Una mirada al cuerpo en los textos poeticos de Daisy Zamora', in O. Preble-Niemi, *Afrodita en el trópico: Erotismo y construcción del sujeto femenino en obras de autoras centroamericanas*, Potomac, MD: Scripta Humanistica, 123–32.

Randall, M. (1994) *Sandino's Daughters Revisited:*

Feminism in Nicaragua, New Brunswick: Rutgers University Press.
Zamora, D. (1993) *Clean Slate*, Willimantic, CT: Curbstone Press.

SILVIA CHAVES AND ILEANA RODRÍGUEZ

Zapata, Luis

b. 1951, Chilpancingo, Mexico

Writer

Zapata is best known for his groundbreaking novel *Las aventuras, desventuras y sueños de Adonis García, el vampiro de la colonia Roma* (Adonis García) (1979), published the year of the emergence of Mexico's homosexual liberation movement. This text combines narrative tropes from the picaresque novel and the counter-cultural stylistics introduced by the 1960s urban literary movement of La **Onda**. Written as a transcribed series of recorded interviews, Zapata's effusive fictional documentary narrative on the life of Adonis García, a notorious homosexual hustler in Mexico City, marks the era of sexual euphoria before the advent of AIDS. The novel's unapologetic celebration of same-sex desire was the target of vituperation in the press but was also hailed by influential contemporary critic-novelist José Joaquín **Blanco** as the best novel of his generation.

The immediate impact of Zapata's novel on Mexican **gay male literature** is indexed in the writings of social activist Luis **González de Alba**, who pays tribute to Adonis García in his 1981 short story 'Posdata que podría enviar el Vampiro de la Colonia Roma' (Postscript that the Vampire from Colonia Roma Might Have Sent). Zapata continues his formal experimentation in his subsequent novels. *Melodrama* (1983), a hybrid genre screenplay, is a camp rendition which self-consciously underscores how popular culture, especially the Mexican film industry, informs the identity and subjectivity of his characters. In the parodic *La hermana secreta de Angélica María* (Angelica Maria's Secret Sister) (1989), a hermaphrodite models her singing career along the lines of the popular 1960s singer-actress referenced in the novel's title. His short autobiography *De cuerpo entero* (Full Body) (1990) focuses on the formative role Mexican cinema played in shaping his identity during adolescence. In *En jirones* (In Shreds) (1985) the diary genre is a strategic vehicle for exploring how the act of writing parallels the frustrated, obsessive romance between a gay man and his sexually confused partner. Zapata also translated into Spanish Adolfo Caminha's nineteenth-century Brazilian novel, *Bom-Crioulo* (1987).

Further reading

Bautista, J.C. (1993) 'Pasión y muerte de la literatura gay: Luis Zapata', *Vice Versa* (Mexico) 4(May–June): 63–5.
Blanco, J.J. (1996) 'Luis Zapata: El salto de la muerte', in *Crónica literaria: Un siglo de escritores mexicanos*, Mexico City: Cal y Arena.
González de Alba, L. (1981) *El vino de los bravos*, Mexico City: Katún.

SERGIO DE LA MORA

Zapata Olivella, Manuel

b. 1920, Lorica, Colombia

Novelist and journalist

Zapata alternates his career as a physician with his work as a writer, journalist and scholar of Colombian folklore. His novels are usually concerned with exposing social injustice, particularly among Colombia's black community. In *Tierra mojada* (Wet Land) (1947), Zapata's first novel, he portrays the conflict between a landlord and a group of dispossessed people fighting for their land, an archetypal topic in Latin American history. *La calle 10* (10th Street) (1960) is set in the period of La Violencia, when the uprising following Jorge Eliecer Gaitán's assassination at first brings hope to a segment of marginalized people, which later turns to disappointment when the political elite announce that they have recovered control of the rebellion. *En Chimá nace un santo* (A Saint is Born in Chimá) (1964) narrates the confrontation between two types of fanatic: the orthodox Catholics of Lorica versus the superstitious people of a neighbouring small village who attribute miraculous powers to a boy who is crippled. In *Chambacú, corral de negros* (Chambacú, Black Slum) (1967), as in some of his earlier novels, there is the implicit thesis that poverty may drive individuals to a criminal marginality. *Un extraño bajo mi piel* (A Stranger under My Skin) (1963) and *Changó el gran putas* (Shango, the Holy Motherfucker) (1983) are Zapata's most representative novels about the experience of Afro-Colombians.

Further reading

Captain-Hidalgo, Y. (1993) *The Culture of Fiction in the Works of Manuel Zapata Olivella*, Columbia: University of Missouri Press.

Lewis, M.A. (1987) *Treading the Ebony Path: Ideology and Violence in Contemporary Afro-Colombian Prose Fiction*, Columbia: University of Missouri Press.

MIGUEL A. CARDINALE

Zig Zag

One of Chile's main publishing houses, Zig Zag was founded in 1934. For many years it was known for its editions of Vicente **Huidobro**, Francisco **Coloane**, Carlos Droguett, José **Donoso**, Marta **Brunet**, Manuel **Rojas** and many other Chilean authors, as well as for translations of foreign authors such as Somerset Maugham. In recent years it has concentrated on the high-school and college market, with cheap editions featuring didactic prefaces or epilogues and study questions. In 1970, the publishing house was taken over by the Unidad Popular government of Allende and became the State publishing house, Editorial **Quimantú**. After the military *coup* of 1973, Quimantú was closed down and most of its stock destroyed. The premises were later reopened as the Editora Nacional Gabriela Mistral and sold into private ownership in 1982.

Further information

http://www.zigzag.cl/

DANIEL BALDERSTON

Zobel, Joseph

b. 1915, Petit Bourg, Martinique

Writer

Zebel is best known for his 1950 novel ***La rue cases-nègres*** (Black Shack Alley) (1950), a semi-autobiographical tale of growing up in Martinique during the early twentieth century. The novel is a fierce indictment of the plantation system and French assimiliation policy. Set on a sugar plantation and filled with ethnographic details, it traces the initiation of José Hassam into the alienating world of colonial Martinique. A strongly didactic work, it exposes the injustice and hypocrisy of Martinican society and encourages the readers to be true to their African roots. The influence of the ***négritude*** movement is evident in the novel's celebration of black resistance, local culture, a racially based identity and the values espoused by its bohemian male characters. Even though the novel deals with establishing a strong sense of local identity, it would be wrong to confuse it with the novels of contemporary Martinican writers who use creole more effortlessly in their works, in contrast to an earlier generation that accepted the need to use French to express the experiences of colonized Martinicans.

The strength of Zobel's writing lies in its consistent and passionate defence of the working class and the peasantry. This is evident even in a very early peasant novel such as *Diab-la* (The Devil), written during the war but published in 1946, set in a fishing village in Diamant. However, Zobel, like many other Caribbean writers, did not remain in the region. *La rue cases-nègres* was written in France where he went to continue his education. He later published a sequel entitled *Fête à Paris* (Festivities in Paris) (1953) and some short stories, *Le soleil partagé* (The Shared Sun) (1964). In 1957 Zobel left for Senegal, where he spent much of his later life, first as a teacher and subsequently in the Senegalese media. His later work is limited to collections of short stories such as *Quand la neige aura fondu* (When the Snows Have Melted) (1978). Upon his retirement in 1976, he returned to France, where he has lived ever since.

Further reading

César, S. (1994) *La rue cases-nègres: Du roman au film: Etude comparative*, Paris: L'Harmattan.
Dunwoodie, P. (1975) 'Commitment and Confinement: Two West Indian Visions', *Caribbean Quarterly* (Kingston) 21(3): 15–27.

J. MICHAEL DASH

Zona de carga y descarga

Zona de carga y descarga was a literary review published in San Juan, Puerto Rico, between 1972 and 1975. Founded by writers Rosario **Ferré** and Olga Nolla, and edited by Ferré, it represents an innovative new direction in the island's literary history. In sympathy with the proposals of the European and Latin American avant-garde (see **avant-garde in Latin America**), as well as some of the writers of the Latin American literary '**Boom**', it opened an important space for young writers including Manuel **Ramos Otero**, and provided a point of encounter between different texts at a crucial moment in the development of Puerto Rican intellectual life.

Further reading

Ibáñez, J. (1992) 'Índice de autores publicados en *Zona de Carga y Descarga*', *La Torre: Revista de la Universidad de Puerto Rico*, July–Sept., 6(23): 333–47.

JUAN CARLOS QUINTERO HERENCIA

Zona franca

Zona franca was a Venezuelan literary journal edited by poet Juan **Liscano** and published in three phases between 1964 and 1983. The first phase (1964–69) coincided with a period of guerrilla war in Venezuela to which the editors were overtly opposed; nonetheless, the journal did not become, as the guerrilla leaders feared, a vehicle of government propaganda – instead it eschewed political debate and concentrated on artistic and philosophical questions. The journal's Latin American distribution was reflected in the range of its contributors. The years 1970–73 marked the second period, during which time the journal became more monographic and sociological, with issues on ecology, feminism and the burgeoning drug culture among other topics. In the third phase, from 1977 to 1983, the journal confined itself to literary topics.

MIKE GONZALEZ

Zorrilla de San Martín, Juan

b. 1855, Montevideo, Uruguay; d. 1931 Montevideo

Poet and essayist

Zorrilla is best known as the author of Uruguay's national poem, *Tabaré* (1888), a verse melodrama on contacts between early Spanish invaders and the native Charrúa Indians (who had disappeared long before Uruguay became a nation). A bizarre fantasy that masquerades as invented history, *Tabaré* has given Uruguay a series of common indigenous names such as Yamandú, but was actually based on a Chilean, not a Uruguayan, legend. A late work of Spanish American romanticism, *Tabaré* has been studied in conjunction with nineteenth-century novels of nation-building.

Zorrilla's other works include *La Leyenda Patria* (1879) and *La epopeya de Artigas* (1910). The first work resulted in his appointment as national poet (even before the publication of *Tabaré*) and was devoted to the struggle for Uruguay's independence, led by José Gervasio Artigas; the latter was written on the occasion of the building of a monument in Montevideo to that hero.

Further reading

Bordoli, D.L. (1961) *Vida de Juan Zorrilla de San Martín*, Montevideo: Imprenta Rex.
San Román, G. (1997) 'Juan Zorrilla de San Martín', *Encyclopedia of Latin American Literature*, ed. V. Smith, London: Fitzroy Dearborn, 865–6.
Sommer, D. (1991) *Foundational Fictions: The National Romances of Latin America*, Berkeley: University of California Press, 240–6.
Zorrilla de San Martín, J. (1984) *Tabaré*, critical

edition by Antonio Seluja Cecín, Montevideo: Universidad de la República.

DANIEL BALDERSTON

Zuleta, Estanislao

b. 1935, Medellín, Colombia; d. 1990, Cali, Colombia

Philosopher, literary critic and professor

One of the most distinguished and well-known philosophers and critics in Colombia, Zuleta was passionately interested in history, moral and political philosophy, civil society, Marxism, German literature and sociology. He was self-educated and his outstanding talents took him to work in different Colombian universities and academic institutions. Unfortunately, he was not a disciplined writer and much of his work was ignored and forgotten. His few essays vary from literary papers on Thomas Mann and Sigmund Freud to informal talks and surveys of general and daily issues. He was the founder of many magazines and journals. Zuleta will be remembered among his students and pupils as a marvellous and fervent lecturer and speaker. He participated in the government of President Belisario Betancur in several educational projects as both adviser and counsellor.

Further reading

Zuleta, Estanislao (1997) *Conversaciones con Estanislao Zuleta*, Cali: Fundación Estanislao Zuleta.

ALVARO BERNAL

Zuluaga Osorio, Conrado

b. Medellín, Colombia

Literary critic

Zuluaga is considered one of the best critics of Gabriel **García Márquez**; he has published multiple articles and essays in a variety of academic magazines and journals. Zuluaga taught literature at both Universidad de los Andes and the Universidad Javeriana in Bogotá. He has occupied many important and prestigious cultural positions in his native country Colombia. Zuluaga was also director of the National Library (1985–88) and participated in several projects for cultural promotion. He now resides in Spain, where he works for the Colombian Embassy in areas of cultural development.

Further reading

Zuluaga, C. (2001) *Puerta abierta a Gabriel García Márquez: aproximación a la obra del Nobel colombiano*, Barcelona: Editorial Casiopea.

ALVARO BERNAL

Zum Felde, Alberto

b. 1889, Bahía Blanca, Argentina; d. 1976, Montevideo, Uruguay

Literary critic

A work of 'militant' national criticism, the three volumes of his *El proceso intelectual del Uruguay: Crítica de su literatura* (The Intellectual Process of Uruguay and Criticism of its Literature) (1930) cover intellectual life from the colonial period to the turn of the twentieth century. His *Indice crítico de la literatura hispanoamericana* (Critical Index of Spanish American Literature) won the National Literature Prize. He also edited *Pluma*, an arts and science journal, and was director of the National Library in Montevideo (1940–44), testimony to the key role he played in Uruguayan intellectual history.

Further reading

Cortazzo, U. (1987) 'Alberto Zum Felde, teórico del nativismo', *Rio de la Plata: Culturas* 4–6: 409–17.

—— (1983) 'Crítica literaria, colonialismo e identidad en Alberto Zum Felde', *Revue Romane* 18(2): 228–39.

Zum Felde, A. (1941) *Proceso intelectual del Uruguay: Crítica de su literatura*, Montevideo: Ediciones del Nuevo Mundo.

—— (1954) *Indice crítico de la literatura hispanoamericana*, Mexico City: Editorial Guaranía.

—— (1959) *Cristo y nosotros; el problema religioso y la*

cultura contemporánea, Montevideo: Galería Libertad.
—— (1963) *Proceso histórico del Uruguay*, Montevideo: Universidad de la República, Departamento de Publicaciones.

VICTORIA RUÉTALO

Zurita, Raúl

b. 1950, Santiago, Chile

Poet

Zurita is one of contemporary Chile's boldest and most controversial writers. He came to prominence in the 1970s as part of the CADA collective that staged what were termed *escenas de avanzada* – avant-garde public events that were meant to disconcert and raise questions. With his then-partner Diamela **Eltit**, the photographer Lotty Rosenfeld and others, Zurita staged various dramatic events, including one more private drama when he disfigured his face by throwing acid on it. He wrote about this incident in a poem:

> Destrocé mi cara tremenda
> frente al espejo
> te amo – me dije – te amo
> Te amo a más que nada en el mundo
>
> (I destroyed my tremendous face
> while looking at the mirror
> I love you, I told myself, I love you
> I love you more than anything in the world)
>
> *Purgatorio* (Purgatory) (1979)

His great ambitions were indicated by the title of this volume, *Purgatorio*, which of course refers to Dante (as well as to Pinochet's Chile), as do the titles of the two volumes that followed: *Anteparaíso* (Anteparadise) (1982) and *La vida nueva* (The New Life) (1993).

Zurita's ambition to write himself into the world around him was realized in a series of poems that were written by a skywriter above New York City: photographs of these are included in *Anteparaíso*. *La vida nueva* includes an aerial photograph of a one-line poem written by bulldozer in the Atacama desert, that reads (in what must be enormous letters): 'ni pena ni miedo' (neither sorrow nor fear). The latter inscription on the earth, reminiscent of the Nazca lines in the coastal desert of southern Peru, in the book version bears the date August 1993, making clear that it is some sort of comment (although exactly what has been the subject of some argument) on the continuing legacy of dictatorship in post-Pinochet Chile.

Zurita's poetic voice, at once messianic and oddly fractured, is of great interest. The sequence in *Purgatorio* that has to do with the disfiguring of the face (and which includes a photograph showing him with a bandage on his cheek) opens with a brief poem that says:

> mis amigos creen que
> estoy muy mala
> porque quemé mi mejilla
>
> (my friends think that I
> am very sick
> because I burned my cheek)

Here, the feminine form of the adjective is oddly disconnected from the image on the following page and the name on the cover of the book. Zurita's poetry owes a great deal to **concrete poetry**, with a few words or shapes arranged very carefully on the white of the page; indeed, the sky- and desert-writing already mentioned could be considered a continuation of the concrete tradition.

Zurita refers frequently in his poetry to Chile's extravagant geography: its great deserts, volcanoes and mountain ranges, and its swift rivers. Perhaps the finest section of *La vida nueva* has as its theme the rivers of southern Chile. In it, the most startling section is a series of dreams and accounts of the life-experiences of pioneers in the valleys of southern Chile, focusing on the expert boatmen of the Yelcho River. Reminiscent of the section of **Neruda**'s ***Canto general*** called 'La tierra se llama Juan' (The Earth is Named Juan), in which miners and other working people tell of their lives in forceful, laconic verse, Zurita gives a vivid, almost surreal picture of the dream-life of a series of brave individuals. Their bravery is not only with regard to the rivers and the natural hardships they have faced: they have also had to face up to the local bosses and the representatives of the military regime. Another section of *La vida nueva* includes a series of grave inscriptions, little prose poems arranged as squares, in which the dead – and here they are not just the Chilean dead but also victims of repression in the USA and elsewhere in the Americas – speak of pain, of torture, of hunger and of exile.

Zurita is a poet of excess. Without doubt, his work could be pruned and trimmed. But the impulse that blasts out of control in his poetry – his rage, his cosmic love, his messianic delusions – make his production highly unusual and quite special.

Further reading

Carrasco, I. (1989) 'El proyecto poético de Raul Zurita', *Estudios Filológicos*, 24: 67–74.

Epple, J.A. (1994) 'Transcribir el río de los sueños. Entrevista a Raúl Zurita', *Revista iberoamericana* 55(168–9): 873–83.

Rowe, W. (1993) 'Raúl Zurita: Language, Madness and the Social Wound', *Travesia: Journal of Latin American Cultural Studies* 2(2): 183–218.

Zurita, R. (1986) *Purgatory*, trans. J. Jacobson, Pittsburgh: Latin American Literary Review Press.

—— (1986) *Anteparadise*, trans. J. Schmitt, Berkeley: University of California Press.

—— (1993) *La vida nueva*, Santiago: Editorial Universitaria.

DANIEL BALDERSTON

Bibliography

Agosin, Marjorie (ed.) (1995) *A Dream of Light & Shadow: Portraits of Latin American Women Writers*, Albuquerque: University of New Mexico Press.

Aira, César (2001) *Diccionário de autores latinoamericanos*, Buenos Aires: Emecé.

Alegría, Fernando (1986) *Nueva historia de la novela hispanoamericana*, Hanover, NH: Ediciones del Norte.

Alonso, Carlos J. (1990) *The Spanish American Regional Novel: Modernity and Autochthony*, Cambridge: Cambridge University Press.

Anderson Imbert, Enrique and E. Florit (eds) (1970) *Literatura hispanoamericana*, New York: Holt, Rinehart & Winston, 2 vols.

Arciniegas, Germán (ed.) (1944) *The Green Continent*, New York: A.A. Knopf.

Arnold, A. James (ed.) (1994–2001) *A History of Literature in the Caribbean*, Amsterdam and Philadelphia: J. Benjamins, 3 vols.

Avelar, Idelber (1999) *The Untimely Present: Postdictatorial Latin American Fiction and the Task of Mourning*, Durham, NC: Duke University Press.

Bacarisse, Salvador (ed.) (1980) *Contemporary Latin American Fiction*, Edinburgh: Scottish Academic Press.

Balderston, Daniel (1993) *The Latin American Short Story: An Annotated Guide*, Westport, CN: Greenwood Press.

—— (1999) *El deseo, enorme cicatriz luminosa*, Caracas: eXcultura.

—— (ed.) (2000) *Sexualidad y nación*, Pittsburgh: Instituto Internacional de Literatura Iberoamericana.

Balderston, Daniel and Marcy E. Schwartz (eds) (2002) *Voice Overs: Latin American Literature and Translation*, Albany: State University of New York Press.

Balderston, Daniel, Mike González and Ana M. López (eds) (2000) *Encyclopedia of Contemporary Latin American and Caribbean Cultures*, London: Routledge, 3 vols.

Bellini, Giuseppe (1985) *Historia de la literatura hispanoamericana*, Madrid: Castalia.

Benson, Eugene and L.W. Conolly (eds) (1994) *Encyclopedia of Post Colonial Literatures in English*, London and New York: Routledge, 2 vols.

Bergmann, Emilie, *et al.* (1992) *Women, Culture, and Politics in Latin America: Seminar on Feminism and Culture in Latin America*, Berkeley: University of California Press.

Berrian, Brenda F. and Aart Broek (eds) (1989) *Bibliography of Women Writers from the Caribbean*, Boulder, CO: Lynn Rienner.

Bethell, Leslie (ed.) (1998) *A Cultural History of Latin America: Literature, Music, and the Visual Arts in the 19th and 20th Centuries*, Cambridge and New York: Cambridge University Press.

Beverley, John and Marc Zimmerman (1990) *Literature and Politics in Central America*, Austin: University of Texas Press.

Bilbija, Ksenija (2001) *Cuerpos textuales: Metáforas del génesis narrativo en la literatura latinoamericana del siglo XX*, Lima: Latinoamericana Editores.

Brotherston, Gordon (1979) *The Emergence of the Latin American Novel*, Cambridge: Cambridge University Press.

Brown, Stewart (ed.) (1986) *Caribbean Poetry Now*, London: Hodder & Stoughton.

Brushwood, John (1984) *La novela hispanoamericana del siglo XX*, Mexico City: Fondo de Cultura Económica.

Burnett, Paula (ed.) (1986) *The Penguin Book of Caribbean Verse*, Harmondsworth, Middlesex, England; New York: Penguin Books.

Castro-Klaren, Sara, Sylvia Molloy and Beatriz Sarlo (eds) (1991) *Women's Writing in Latin America*, Boulder, CO: Lynn Rienner.

Colás, Santiago (1994) *Postmodernity in Latin America: The Argentine Paradigm*, Durham, NC: Duke University Press.

Coutinho, Afrânio (1969) *Concise History of Brazilian Literature*, New York: Columbia University Press.

Coutinho, Afrânio and J. Galante de Sousa (eds) (2001) *Enciclopédia de literatura brasileira*, São Paulo: Global Editora.

Crawford, William R. (1961) *A Century of Latin American Thought*, Cambridge: Harvard University Press.

D'Allemand, P. (2001) *Hacia una crítica cultural latinoamericana*, Lima: Latinoamericana Editores.

Dash, J.M. (1998) *The Other America: Caribbean Literature in a New World Context*, Charlottesville: University Press of Virginia.

Davies, C. (ed.) (2002) *The Companion to Hispanic Studies*, London: Arnold.

Davies, C.B. and Savory, E. (1990) *Out of the Kumbla: Caribbean Women and Literatures*, Trenton, NJ: Africa World Press.

de la Campa, Román (1999) *Latin Americanism*, Minneapolis: University of Minnesota Press.

Debrot, Cola (1964) *Literature of the Netherlands Antilles*, Willemstad: Department van Cultuur en Opvoedling.

deCosta-Willis, Miriam (ed.) (2002) *Daughters of the Diaspora: Afra-Hispanic Writers*, Kingston: Ian Randle Publishers.

Earle, Peter G. and Robert G. Mead (1965) *Historia del ensayo hispanoamericano*, Mexico City: Ediciones de Andrea.

Ellis, Robert Richmond (2002) *They Dream Not of Angels but of Men: Homoeroticism, Gender and Race in Latin American Autobiography*, Gainesville: University Press of Florida.

Elmore, Peter (1997) *La fábrica de la memoria: La crisis de la representación en la novela histórica latinoamericana*, Lima: Fondo de Cultura Económica.

Englekirk, John E., I.A. Leonard, J.T. Reid and J.A. Crow (eds) (1965) *An Outline History of Spanish American Literature*, New York: Appleton Century Crofts.

—— (1968) *An Anthology of Spanish American Literature*, Englewood Cliffs, NJ: Prentice-Hall, 2 vols.

Fernández, Teodosio (1990) *Los géneros ensayísticos hispanoamericanos*, Madrid: Taurus.

Fernández Moreno, César (ed.) (1990) *América Latina en su literatura*, Mexico City: Siglo XXI.

Figueroa, John (1973) *Caribbean Voices*, Washington: R.B. Luce.

Fitts, Dudley (ed.) (1976) *Anthology of Contemporary Latin American Poetry*, Westport, CT: Greenwood Press.

Fitz, Earl E. (1991) *Rediscovering the New World: Inter-American Literature in a Comparative Context*, Iowa City: University of Iowa Press.

Flores, Angel (ed.) (1981) *Narrativa hispanoamericana*, Mexico City: Siglo XXI, 8 vols.

Forster, M.H. and K. David Jackson (1990) *Vanguardism in Latin American Literature: An Annotated Bibliographical Guide*, Westport, CN: Greenwood Press.

Forster, Merlin H. (ed.) (1975) *Tradition and Renewal: Essays on Twentieth-Century Latin American Literature and Culture*, Urbana: University of Illinois Press.

Foster, David William (ed.) (1975) *A Dictionary of Contemporary Latin American Authors*, Tempe: Center for Latin American Studies, Arizona State University.

—— (1975) *Modern Latin American literature*, New York: Ungar.

—— (1991) *Gay and Lesbian Themes in Latin American Writing*, Austin: University of Texas Press.

—— (1992) *Handbook of Latin American Literature*, New York: Garland.

—— (1994) *Cultural Diversity in Latin American Literature*, Albuquerque: University of New Mexico Press.

—— (ed.) (1994) *Latin American Writers on Gay and Lesbian Themes: A Bio-critical Sourcebook*, Westport, CT: Greenwood Press.

—— (1997) *Twentieth-century Spanish American Literature to 1960*, New York: Garland.

—— (ed.) (1997) *Twentieth-century Spanish American Literature Since 1960*, New York: Garland.

Franco, Jean (1967) *The Modern Culture of Latin America: Society and the Artist*, New York: F.A. Praeger.

—— (1994) *An Introduction to Spanish-American Literature*, Cambridge and New York: Cambridge University Press.

—— (2002) *The Decline and Fall of the Lettered City*, Cambridge, MA: Harvard University Press.

Fuentes, Carlos (1969) *La nueva novela hispanoamérica*, Mexico City: Joaquín Mortiz.

García Pinto, Magdalena (1988) *Historias íntimas: Conversaciones con diez escritores latinoamericanas*, Hanover, NH: Ediciones del Norte.

Goic, Cedomil (1968) *La novela chilena: Los mitos degradados*, Santiago de Chile: Editorial Universitaria.

—— (1972) *Historia de la novela hispanoamericana*, Valparaíso, Chile: Ediciones Universitaria de Valparaíso.

—— (ed.) (1988) *Historia y crítica de la literatura hispanoamericana*, Barcelona: Editorial Crítica, 3 vols.

—— (1992) *Los mitos degradados: Ensayos de comprensión de la literature hispanoamericana*, Atlanta: Rodopi.

Gomes, Miguel (1999) *Los géneros literarios en Hispanoamérica: teoría e historia*, Berriozar: Universidad de Navarra.

Gonzalez, Ann and William Luis (eds) (1994) *Modern Latin-American Fiction Writers. Second Series*, Detroit: Gale Research.

Gonzalez, Mike and David Treece (1992) *The Gathering of Voices: The Twentieth-century Poetry of Latin America*, London and New York: Verso.

González Echevarría, Roberto (1988) *The Voice of the Masters: Writing and Authority in Modern Latin American Literature*, Austin: University of Texas Press.

—— (1990) *Myth and Archive: A Theory of Latin American Narrative*, Cambridge and New York: Cambridge University Press.

González Echevarría, Roberto, and Enrique Pupo-Walker (eds) (1996) *The Cambridge History of Latin American Literature*, Cambridge: Cambridge University Press, 3 vols.

Grünfeld, M. (1995) *Antología de la poesía latinoamericana de vanguardia*, Madrid: Hiperión.

Gugelberger, Georg (ed.) (1996) *The Real Thing: Testimonial Discourse and Latin America*, Durham, NC: Duke University Press.

Harss, Luis (1967) *Into the Mainstream: Conversations with Latin American writers*, New York: Harper & Row.

—— (1975) *Los nuestros*, Buenos Aires: Editorial Sudamericana.

Hart, Stephen (1993) *White Ink: Essays on Twentieth Century Feminine Fiction in Spain and Latin America*, London: Támesis.

—— (ed.) (1999) *A Companion to Spanish-American Literature*, London: Támesis.

Henríquez Ureña, Max (1978) *Breve historia del modernismo*, Mexico City: Fondo de Cultura Económica.

Henríquez Ureña, Pedro (1964) *Las corrientes literarias en la América Hispánica*, Mexico City: Fondo de Cultura Económica.

—— (1977) *Observaciones sobre el español en América y otros estudios filológicos*, Buenos Aires: Academia Argentina de Letras.

Iñigo Madrigal, Luis (1982–87) *Historia de la literatura hispanoamericana*, Madrid Cátedra, 3 vols.

Jackson, Richard L. (ed.) (1976) *The Black Image in Latin American Literature*, Albuquerque: University of New Mexico Press.

Johnson, Myriam Yvonne (1996) *Latin American Women Writers: Class, Race and Gender*, Albany: State University of New York Press.

Jrade, Cathy (1998) *Modernismo, Modernity and the Development of Spanish American Literature*, Austin: University of Texas Press.

Kadir, Djelal (1986) *Questing Fictions: Latin America's Family Romance*, Minneapolis: University of Minnesota Press.

Kaminsky, Amy (1993) *Reading the Body Politic: Feminist Criticism and Latin American Writers*, Minneapolis: University of Minnesota Press.

—— (1999) *After Exile: Writing the Latin American Diaspora*, Minneapolis: University of Minnesota Press.

Kerr, Lucille (1992) *Reclaiming the Author: Figures and Fictions from Spanish America*, Durham, NC: Duke University Press.

King, John (ed.) (1987) *Modern Latin American Fiction: A Survey*, London: Faber & Faber.

Kirkpatrick, Gwen (1989) *The Dissident Legacy of Modernismo: Lugones, Herrera y Reissig, and the Voices of Modern Spanish American Poetry*, Berkeley: University of California Press.

Klahn, N. and W.H. Corral (eds) (1991) *Los novelistas como críticos*, Mexico City: Fondo de Cultura Económica, 2 vols.

Lafforgue, Jorge (ed.) (1969–72) *Nueva narrativa latinoamericana*, Buenos Aires: Editorial Paidós, 2 vols.

Larsen, Neil (1995) *Reading North by South: On Latin American Literature, Culture and Politics*, Minneapolis: University of Minnesota Press.

—— (2001) *Determinations: Essays on Theory, Narrative and Nation in the Americas*, London: Verso.

Larson, Catherine and Margarita Vargas (eds) (1998) *Latin American Women Dramatists*, Bloomington: Indiana University Press.

Lasarte, J.V. (ed.) (2001) *Territorios intelectuales: Pensamiento y cultura en América Latina*, Caracas: Fondo Editorial La Nave Va.

Leal, Luis (1966) *Historia del cuento hispanoamericano*, Mexico City: Ediciones de Andrea.

Lindstrom, Naomi (1983) *Women's Voice in Latin American Literature*, Washington: Three Continents Press.

—— (1994) *Twentieth Century Spanish American Fiction*, Austin: University of Texas Press.

—— (1998) *The Social Conscience of Latin American Writing*, Austin: University of Texas Press.

Lindstrom, Naomi and Carmelo Virgilio (eds) (1985) *Woman as Myth and Metaphor in Latin American Literature*, Columbia: University of Missouri Press.

Lyday, Leon F. and George Woodyard (eds) (1976) *Dramatists in Revolt: The New Latin American Theater*, Austin: University of Texas Press.

Martin, Gerald (1989) *Journeys through the Labyrinth: Latin American Fiction in the Twentieth Century*, London and New York: Verso.

Martínez, Elena M. (1996) *Lesbian Voices from Latin America: Breaking Ground*, New York: Garland.

Masiello, Francine (2001) *The Art of Transition: Latin American Culture and Neoliberal Crisis*, Durham, NC and London: Duke University Press.

McGuirk, Bernard (1997) *Latin American Literature: Symptoms, Risks & Strategies of Post-structuralist Criticism*, London: Routledge.

Menton, Seymour (ed.) (1964) *El cuento hispanoamericano: Antología crítico-histórica*, Mexico City: Fondo de Cultura Económica.

—— (1993) *Latin America's New Historical Novel*, Austin: University of Texas Press.

—— (1998) *Historia verdadera de realismo mágico*, Mexico City: Fondo de Cultura Económica.

Meyer, Doris (ed.) (1995) *Reinterpreting the Spanish American Essay: Women Writers of the 19th and 20th Centuries*, Austin: University of Texas Press.

—— (ed.) (1995) *Rereading the Spanish American Essay: Translations of 19th and 20th Century Women's Essays*, Austin: University of Texas Press.

Meyer, Doris (ed.) (1988) *Lives on the Line: The Testimony of Contemporary Latin American Authors*, Berkeley: University of California Press.

Molloy, Sylvia (1991) *At Face Value: Autobiographical Writing in Spanish America*, Cambridge and New York: Cambridge University Press.

Molloy, Sylvia and Robert McKee Irwin (eds) (1998) *Hispanisms and Homosexualities*, Durham, NC: Duke University Press.

Montaldo, Graciela (1999) *Ficciones culturales y fábulas de identidad en América Latina*, Rosario: Beatriz Viterbo.

Moreiras, Alberto (1999) *Tercer espacio: Literatura y duelo en América Latina*, Santiago: Lom Ediciones.

—— (2001) *The Exhaustion of Difference: The Politics of Latin American Cultural Studies*, Durham, NC: Duke University Press.

Ormerod, Beverley (1985) *An Introduction to the French Caribbean Novel*, London: Heinemann.

Osorio, N. (1988) *Manifiestos, proclamas y polémicas de las vanguardia literaria hispanoamericana*, Caracas: Ayacucho.

Osorio, Nelson (ed.) (1995) *Diccionario enciclopédico de las letras de América Latina*, Caracas: Monte Avila and Biblioteca Ayacucho, 3 vols.

Oviedo, José Miguel (ed.) (1989) *Antología crítica del cuento hispanoamericano (1830–1920)*, Madrid: Alianza.

—— (ed.) (1992) *Antología crítica del cuento hispanoamericano del siglo XX (1920–1980)*, Madrid: Alianza Editorial, 2 vols.

—— (1995–2001) *Historia de la literatura hispanoamericana*, Madrid: Alianza Editorial, 4 vols.

Pacheco, Carlos and Luis Barrera Linares (eds) (1993) *Del cuento y sus alrededores: Aproximaciones a una teoría del cuento*, Caracas: Monte Avila.

Picon Garfield, Evelyn (1985) *Women's Voices from Latin America*, Detroit: Wayne State University Press.

Pons, María Cristina (1996) *Memorias del olvido: La novela histórica de fines del siglo XX*, Mexico City: Siglo XXI.

Pupo-Walker, Enrique (1995) *El cuento hispanoamericano ante la crítica*, Madrid: Castalia.

Quiroga, José (2000) *Tropics of Desire: Interventions from Queer Latino America*, New York: New York University Press.

Rama, Angel (1996) *The Lettered City*, Durham, NC: Duke University Press.

Ramchand, Kenneth (1970) *The West Indian Novel and its Background*, New York: Barnes & Noble.

Rey de Guido, Clara (1985) *Contribución al estudio del ensayo en Hispanoamérica*, Caracas: Biblioteca Nacional de la Historia.

Rodríguez, Ileana (1994) *HouseGardenNation: Space, Gender and Ethnicity in Post-colonial Literatures by Women*, Durham, NC: Duke University Press.

—— (ed.) (2001) *The Latin American Subaltern Studies Reader*, Durham, NC: Duke University Press.

Rodríguez Monegal, Emir (1968) *El arte de narrar: Diálogos*, Caracas: Monte Avila.

—— (1969, 1977) *Narradores de esta América*, Montevideo: Alfa, 2 vols.

—— (ed.) (1977) *The Borzoi Anthology of Latin American Literature*, New York: Alfred A. Knopf, 2 vols.

Rotker, Susana (ed.) (1994) *Ensayistas de nuestra América*, Buenos Aires: Losada, 2 vols.

Rowe, William and Vivian Schelling (1991) *Memory and Modernity in Latin America*, London: Verso.

Rubin, Don (ed.) (1999) *The World Encyclopedia of Contemporary Theatre, Vol. 2: Americas*, London and New York: Routledge.

Santí, Enrico Mario (1988) *Escritura y tradición: Texto, crítica y poética en la literatura hispanoamericana*, Barcelona: Laia.

Schwartz, Jorge (1991) *Las vanguardias latinoamericanas: Textos programáticos*, Madrid: Cátedra; 2nd edn, Mexico City: Fondo de Cultura Económica, 2002.

Schwartz, Kessel (1983) *Studies on Twentieth-century Spanish and Spanish American Literature*, Lanham, MD: University Press of America.

Schwarz, Roberto (1992) *Misplaced Ideas: Essays on Brazilian Culture*, trans. John Gledson, London: Verso.

Shaw, Donald (1998) *The Post-Boom in Spanish American Fiction*, Albany: State University of New York Press.

Sifuentes-Jáuregui, Ben (2002) *Transvestism, Masculinity and Latin American Literature*, New York: Palgrave.

Skirius, John (ed.) (1981) *El ensayo hispanoamericano del Siglo XX*, Mexico City: Fondo de Cultura Económica.

Sklodowska, Elzbieta (1992) *Testimonio hispanoamericano: Historia, teoría, poética*, New York: Peter Lang.

Smith, Verity (ed.) (1997) *Encyclopedia of Latin American Literature*, London and Chicago: Fitzroy Dearborn.

Solé, Carlos A. and M.I. Abreu (eds) (1989) *Latin American Writers*, New York: Scribners, 3 vols.

Solé, Carlos A. and K. Müller-Bergh (eds) (2002) *Latin American Writers: Supplement I*, New York: Scribners.

Sommer, Doris (1991) *Foundational Fictions: The National Romances of Latin America*, Berkeley: University of California Press.

—— (1999) *Proceed with Caution, When Engaged by Minority Writing in the Americas*, Cambridge, MA: Harvard University Press.

Sosnowski, Saúl (ed.) (1997) *Lectura crítica de la literatura americana*, Caracas: Biblioteca Ayacucho, 4 vols.

Stabb, Martin (1967) *In Quest of Identity*, Chapel Hill: University of North Carolina Press.

—— (1994) *The Dissenting Voice: The New Essay in Spanish America, 1960–1985*, Austin: University of Texas Press.

Standish, Peter (ed.) (1995) *Hispanic Culture of South America*, Detroit: Gale Research.

—— (ed.) (1996) *Hispanic Culture of Mexico, Central America, and the Caribbean*, Detroit: Gale Research.

Sucre, Guillermo (1985) *La máscara, la transparencia*, Mexico City: Fondo de Cultura Económica.

—— (ed.) (1993) *Antología de la poesía hispanoamericana moderna*, Caracas: Monte Avila, 2 vols.

Swanson, Philip (ed.) (1990) *Landmarks in Modern Latin American Fiction*, London and New York: Routledge.

—— (1995) *The New Novel in Latin America: Politics and Popular Culture after the Boom*, Manchester: Manchester University Press.

—— (ed.) (2003) *The Companion to Latin American Studies*, London: Arnold.

Tenenbaum, Barbara A. (ed.) (1996) *Encyclopedia of Latin American History and Culture*, New York: Charles Scribner's Sons and London: Simon & Schuster, 5 vols.

Torres Ríoseco, Arturo (1967) *Nueva historia de la gran literatura iberoamericana*, Buenos Aires: Emecé.

Unruh, Vicky (1994) *Latin American Vanguards: The Art of Contentious Encounters*, Berkeley: University of California Press.

Valcárcel, Eva (ed.) (1997) *El cuento hispanoamericano*

del siglo XX: Teoría y práctica, La Coruña: Universidad de La Coruña.

Verani, Hugo (1986) *Las vanguardias literarias en Hispanoamérica (Manifiestos, proclamas y otros escritos)*, Mexico City: Fondo de Cultura Económica.

—— (1996) *Narrativa vanguardista hispanoamericana*, Mexico City: UNAM.

Versenyi, Adam (1993) *Theatre in Latin America: Religion, Politics, and Culture from Cortes to the 1980s*, Cambridge and New York: Cambridge University Press.

Videla, Gloria (1994) *Direcciones del vanguardismo hispanoamericano*, Pittsburgh: Instituto Internacional de Literatura Iberoamericana.

Williams, Gareth (2002) *The Other Side of the Popular: Neoliberalism and Subalternity in Latin America*, Durham, NC: Duke University Press.

Williams, Raymond L. (1995) *The Postmodern Novel in Latin America: Politics, Culture, and the Crisis of Truth*, New York: St Martin's Press.

Young, Richard A. (ed.) (1997) *Latin American Postmodernisms*, Amsterdam: Rodopi.

Yúdice, George (2002) *El recurso de la cultura*, Mexico City: Editorial Gedisa.

Yúdice, George, Jean Franco and Juan Flores (eds) (1992) *On Edge: The Crisis of Contemporary Latin American Culture*, Minneapolis: University of Minnesota Press.

Yurkievich, Saúl (1978) *Fundadores de la nueva poesía latinoamericana*, Barcelona: Barral.

Index

Note: Page numbers in **bold** refer to main subject entries.